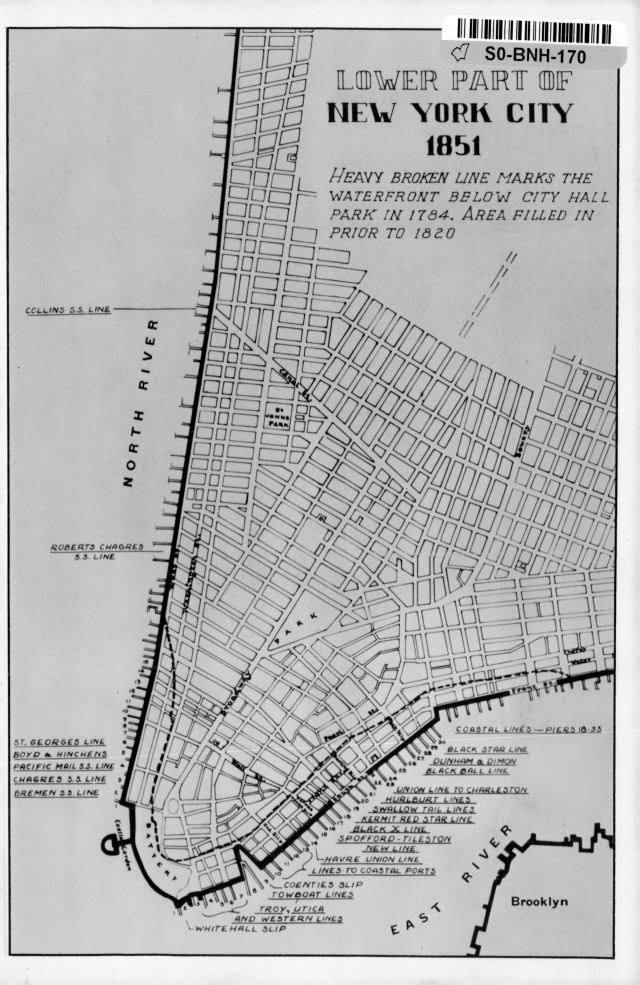

LOWER PART OF
NEW YORK CITY
1851

HEAVY BROKEN LINE MARKS THE
WATERFRONT BELOW CITY HALL
PARK IN 1784. AREA FILLED IN
PRIOR TO 1820

S0-BNH-170

COLLINS S.S. LINE

NORTH RIVER

Canal St.

St JOHNS
PARK

Bowery

ROBERTS CHAGRES
S.S. LINE

Washington St.

PARK

BROADWAY

Cherry St.

Front St.

COASTAL LINES — PIERS 18-33

ST. GEORGES LINE
BOYD & HINCHENS
PACIFIC MAIL S.S. LINE
CHAGRES S.S. LINE
BREMEN S.S. LINE

Pearl

WALL ST.

OLD SLIP

BLACK STAR LINE
DUNHAM & DIMON
BLACK BALL LINE

UNION LINE TO CHARLESTON
HURLBURT LINES
SWALLOW TAIL LINES
KERMIT RED STAR LINE
BLACK X LINE
SPOFFORD-TILESTON
NEW LINE
HAVRE UNION LINE
LINES TO COASTAL PORTS
COENTIES SLIP
TOWBOAT LINES
TROY, UTICA
AND WESTERN LINES
WHITEHALL SLIP

Castle Garden

BATTERY

EAST RIVER

Brooklyn

387.50973 C97q
Cutler, Carl C 1878-   000
Queens of the western ocean.   040101
HE745 .C8

0 1977 0033402 6

Carl A. Rudisill Library

387.50973
C97q   42,162

QUEENS OF THE WESTERN OCEAN

THE STORY OF
AMERICA'S MAIL AND PASSENGER SAILING LINES

WITHDRAWN

Courtesy, The Marine Historical Association, Inc.

Black Ball liner *Neptune* running through the fishing fleet on the Grand Banks. Of 1406 tons, she was built in 1855 by William Webb and commanded by H. W. Peabody.

QUEENS OF THE WESTERN OCEAN

THE STORY OF
AMERICA'S MAIL AND PASSENGER SAILING LINES

BY CARL C. CUTLER

WITH A FOREWORD BY

CHESTER W. NIMITZ
FLEET ADMIRAL, U.S. NAVY

CARL A. RUDISILL LIBRARY
LENOIR RHYNE COLLEGE

ANNAPOLIS · MARYLAND

UNITED STATES NAVAL INSTITUTE

387.50973
C 97g

COPYRIGHT © 1961 BY THE UNITED STATES NAVAL INSTITUTE
Annapolis, Maryland

Library of Congress Catalogue Card Number 61-11247

42,162
November, 1961

PRINTED IN THE UNITED STATES OF AMERICA

In Memoriam

G<small>ILBERT</small> B<small>ANCROFT</small> C<small>UTLER</small>
1848–1934

.   .   .

P<small>ACKET</small> S<small>HIP</small> S<small>AILOR</small>
S<small>OMETIME</small> C<small>HAPLAIN</small> <small>OF</small>
<small>THE</small> A<small>MERICAN</small> S<small>EAMAN</small>'<small>S</small> F<small>RIEND</small> S<small>OCIETY</small>
<small>AND</small>
<small>THE</small> B<small>OSTON</small> S<small>EAMAN</small>'<small>S</small> F<small>RIEND</small> S<small>OCIETY</small>

Foreword

THE title of this prodigious work—*Queens of the Western Ocean*—is only partially indicative of the tremendous task undertaken by the author in describing the origin and growth of the American merchant marine and its influence on the economic growth and welfare of our country. This book is actually a history of Colonial America from the earliest days of the thirteen original colonies down to the peace treaty that ended the War of the Revolution. It then continues the story of a rapidly growing America to the start of the Civil War.

Throughout this fascinating narrative runs an unbroken thread of understanding of the vital part played by our maritime strength and activity on the destiny of our country. By maritime strength is meant not only the armed vessels of our Navy, but also our merchant marine which contributed so much wealth for the rapid development of America.

More importantly, our merchant marine brought forth a host of sturdy, rugged men who not only understood the sea, but were equally at home in the creation and management of great business enterprises ashore. To these men, danger and risk were commonplace. The sea—a hard taskmaster —had done its job well and had produced a breed of men equal to all the dangers that confronted our country in its youth.

President Washington, in addressing both Houses of the Congress of the United States on December 7, 1796, took it for granted that a strong and efficient merchant marine was a vital necessity for our country. Our experience during the War of the Revolution was too fresh in the public mind. Everyone knew how much our merchant marine had done in supplying Washington with munitions, uniforms, and food. In his message he stated, "to an active external commerce the protection of a naval force is indispensable." He urged the Congress "to set about the gradual creation of a Navy" and added that "it is in our own experience that the most sincere neutrality is not a sufficient guard against the depredations of nations at war. To secure respect to a neutral flag requires a naval force organized and ready to vindicate it from insult or aggression." Thus spoke the man upon whom rested the responsibility of organizing the slender resources of the revolting colonies and leading their armed forces to victory.

The "Queens" of the Western Ocean, from which this book derives its title, were those beautiful ships designed by such marine architects as Donald McKay, with the advice of the master mariners who had gained their seagoing experience on earlier models of similar vessels. That the

"Queens" competed so vigorously and effectively with the early steamers is a tribute to the men who designed and built them, and to the skilled mariners who drove them so fearlessly and relentlessly across the Western Ocean, as the Atlantic once was almost universally called by seamen. Not until boilers, machinery, and propellers became reasonably efficient did the sailing vessels lose the race.

In the light of the rapidly approaching war years of 1861-1865, it is a significant fact that nearly all shipbuilding, sail and steam, was carried out in the northeastern, non-slaveholding areas of the country. Few large ships were built south of Philadelphia. It is interesting to speculate on whether the southern leaders who favored secession gave thought to this fact before they precipitated the country into civil war. They were soon to experience the bitter fact that their lack of maritime strength—or "sea-power"—would be the major factor in the defeat of the Confederacy.

Another factor which was of great importance in prewar consideration was that the major part of the massive tide of immigrants from Europe in the first half of the nineteenth century, after coming to this country, very likely in one of the "Queens," moved into the non-slaveholding areas of the nation. These sturdy settlers, whose love of liberty had impelled them to emigrate, gave great strength to the Union armies when they flocked to the Colors on Lincoln's call for volunteers. Did the southern leaders take this factor into account when they pressed for secession?

What does the future hold for the American merchant marine? Certainly it will have its ups and downs as it has had in the past—particularly after each World War. To be remembered is the fact that a healthy and efficient merchant marine is essential to adequate maritime strength. To be healthy our ships should carry at least half of our foreign trade. Will the nuclear *Savannah* and her successors become the "Queens" of the oceans they traverse? Will the future witness a long struggle between the nuclear-powered ships and those equipped with diesels or boilers fired by coal or oil? The correct answers to these questions will make the difference between profit and loss, and between adequacy and weakness.

Not the least of the author's contribution to students of the growth of the American merchant marine is the vast amount of interesting information contained in the several appendices and chapter notes. This book should be read by all who love the sea or earn their livelihood thereon, as well as by those who would like to know more about the men of Colonial America and the first four-score years of our independence.

C. W. NIMITZ
Fleet Admiral, U. S. Navy

Berkeley, California
March 1961

Preface

At the close of the War of 1812 America was still essentially sea minded, as she had been from the time of the first English settlements. The language, traditions, and ways of the sea bulked large in her culture. Quaint seafaring terms, the origins of which were lost in the mists of the ages, were everywhere in familiar daily use and imparted vigor, if not charm, to her songs and poetry. Even the newspapers abounded in salty nautical phrases. They veered and hauled to the tune of "roundhouses, spanker vangs, taut bowlines" and the like, and mystified no one. Madeira and the Canaries were still the "wine islands" of the colonists, and the stormy North Atlantic was still the "Western Ocean," as it had been since the days of good Queen Bess, and as it still is to all deep-water sailor men.

These and other age-old habits were to persist long after the spirit had departed. This writer well remembers the inestimable privilege accorded him, as an urchin of 10 or 12, of "riding horse" to plough an old sea captain's corn field. The ancient mariner between the stilts knew and used the only relevant commands he had learned in 40 years ploughing deep-sea furrows—"Stabbord a leetle! Labbord a leetle!" And horse and boy "steered small" and "gee'd" and "haw'd" without benefit of lubberly interpretation. But even then horse and man and boy were exceptions, rapidly becoming rarer.

In retrospect, the year 1818 would seem to mark the dawn of a new era, in so far as a continuous process may be said to have beginnings and endings. It saw the launching of an experiment that was to play a most important role in setting America, and measurably through her, the world, well on the road toward a strange new civilization. This was the establishment in January of the finest and most dependable mail and passenger service that had yet been developed—the Black Ball Line, first of the regularly scheduled ocean sailing lines.

Theretofore the entire seaborne commerce of civilization, aside from a trifling fraction carried in America by a few small steamboats and inland-water sailing packets, was transported in vessels few of which measured 300 tons and the majority of which registered less than 150 tons. All sailed irregularly and with only token regard for the comfort and convenience of passengers and prompt delivery of the mails. Few averaged more than three miles an hour throughout long voyages.

Attempts to improve those conditions had been stepped up somewhat during the Federalist period, but like promotion in the army, progress had been "dreadful slow." A few large ships with extra staterooms were built and highly optimistic, albeit misleading, advertisements of sailings became the rule. With rare exceptions, shipowners announced that their ships would "Sail In All This Week" or "With Immediate Dispatch." In like manner, every packet offered prospective passengers "Superior Accommodations" that sometimes included beds and bedding.

Ashore, comfortable "Exchanges" and "Reading Rooms" had been established in every large port, to which masters and merchants might resort to get the latest shipping news and deposit their letters in one of the numerous ships' letter bags there to be found. Anxious travellers, also, could obtain refreshments there and comforting, if not always reliable, assurances from mine host as to the probable departure of their long-delayed ships. But advertisements and assurances notwithstanding, the packets normally continued to take in cargo for weeks and sometimes months after the appearance of their first urgent sailing notices. Worse still, when topsails were finally sheeted home, disgruntled patrons usually found themselves in a damp, ill-ventilated 'tween decks scarcely five feet in the clear.

All this was shortly to be changed and in the main by the Black Ball Line and her competitors and imitators. By the time that most famous of all "reading room" hosts, rubicund Sam Gilpin, began to keep at No. 40, New York Merchants Exchange, shortly after the panic of 1837, packet ship advertisements had acquired a reputation for dependability, exigencies of wind and weather alone excepted.

The occasional small, cramped uncomfortable packet, sailing erratically at owner's convenience, had been replaced by a dozen substantial lines, each comprising four or five of the finest mail and passenger ships afloat, tripled in size and sailing every four days. Dark, stuffy cabins had made way for spacious, airy, well-lighted saloons and staterooms, rich in gilt and costly panelling; "the Queen's yacht boasted no finer." The sleazy, straw-filled sack—the time-honored "donkey's breakfast"—had been supplanted by soft, luxurious hair mattresses. Even the humble ship's letter bag had gained in stature. It had spawned a cartload of capacious mail sacks. A similar transformation had taken place in the coastal lines.

Something of the quality of the new packets and the impression they created both at home and abroad may be gathered from the encomiums of the contemporary press. "Grand and Majestic" they were, one and all, accorded royal honors: "Queens of the Western Ocean!"—"Palaces of the Railroad Route!"

This transformation from conditions that, in respect to comfort and convenience had changed but little since the first crossing of the *Mayflower*, had been accomplished wholly within the previous 20 years. In a world still for the most part bent on maintaining the status quo, it was an all-but-incredible performance. And it was only the beginning. The next decade would bring great three-deckers, carrying a thousand souls and stowing the freights of an entire line of earlier ships. At the same time comparable improvements and enlargements on an unprecedented scale were taking place in the humbler, but vastly important, coastal traffic.

Sam Gilpin would live to see this; would live, indeed, to see his merchant marine, paced by the passenger liners, climax two centuries of unparalleled progress with a prodigious burst of speed, to overtake and bypass the greatest sea powers in history. What Sam thought of it, how he accounted for it, or whether he thought of it at all, we have no means of knowing. On the whole, it is probable that he accepted it with stodgy complacence as the natural result of superior ability and energy. The American of today, however, who has small reason for complacency and none at all for accepting explanations based on national or racial superiority, may find it worthwhile to probe deeper into the matter. It is possible that an achievement ranking as one of the most noteworthy of all time involved moral and intellectual forces nations can ill afford to neglect.

Collection of the material here presented in part was begun shortly after the First World War. Members of the older generation will recall that the Western Allies had been brought to the verge of defeat in that conflict for want of ships. Nevertheless, hostilities had scarcely ended when the call went out for American withdrawal from sea trade and for the dispersal of the vast fleet constructed during the previous three years at a fabulous cost. "America," we were told, "was not a maritime nation, nor did sea pursuits accord with the American genius."

As one reared in the seafaring traditions of an earlier day, fortified by a trifle of square-rig experience, this compiler of data found that dictum extremely unpalatable. He believed it was not only based on false premises, but that it involved the abandonment of indispensable safeguards, both material and moral. The oft-repeated stories of ancestral seafarers and shipbuilders and their associates; memories of the ships themselves, and of the stalwart figures of ancient master mariners whose very presence told of great-hearted qualities tried and proved in many a hard sea test;

the dismal fate of vanished maritime powers—all rose in protest against a policy that had repeatedly brought disaster in its wake. The matter seemed of sufficient importance to warrant an attempt to state the case for the defense.

That task quickly proved a more difficult matter than anticipated. It soon developed (this, it will be remembered, was 40 years ago) that there was no convenient, readily accessible reservoir of facts to document the proposed thesis. In a word, there were no books. Special articles aplenty—biographical sketches, printed journals and letters, accounts of curious incidents, and several excellent monographs treating limited areas of activity—but no general histories. As for school texts, they contained hardly a reference to the enterprise that had played a major part in building the nation, an omission that presaged the loss of an entire body of inspiring tradition and the neglect and eventual abandonment of one of the country's stoutest and most indispensable bulwarks.

The source material that alone could tell the story and prove it—official customhouse records, log books, shipping lists and the marine columns of the contemporary press, amounting to hundreds of thousands of pages, undisturbed for the most part since ante bellum days—was scattered from Fundy Bay to Galveston Bar. Foreign shipping lists and prices current also contained much indispensable information. Obviously a vast amount of time and labor would be required to mine the relevant data buried in such widely distributed deposits. Nevertheless, the situation seemed challenging rather than insurmountable, and a start was made.

It soon became evident that there should be no stopping until the field had been explored as thoroughly as circumstances permitted. The labor, much of which would have been sheer drudgery but for its rewarding revelations, was paying off in scores of unanticipated ways. New heroes, long-forgotten exploits, records surpassing many of the greatest that had been handed down to the present generation, were coming to light. And with it all, old traditions were taking on an added depth, richness, and human warmth.

As the work proceeded, however, unforeseen difficulties cropped up. There were many gaps in the official records, making it necessary to dig through reams of faded, barely legible manuscript or search the files of a dozen newspapers to complete the identification of a single ship or master mariner. Each step, moreover, opened new and enticing vistas to be explored, with the result that research ran into years instead of the originally allotted months. The effect was to prolong that phase of the work to such an extent that the plan of producing a comprehensive account of American maritime activities finally had to be abandoned.

This text, accordingly, is confined to the rise and decline of the organized sailing lines. Although falling far short of aims originally contemplated, it has one potential advantage—it permits the presentation in briefer, and to that extent sharper, outline, of the record and traditions of the men who spearheaded the final spectacular advance in sailing design, construction, and operation which crowned two centuries of unprecedented progress in that most important field. If, therefore, it fails to contribute to a better appreciation of the character of the American merchant-mariner and his workaday associates and the significance and value of their contribution, it is the fault of the presentation rather than the subject matter.

American sailing lines, roughly nine-tenths of which appeared and vanished during the 40 years between 1820 and 1860, fall into two main classes, transatlantic and coastal. There were more than 60 of the former and 500 of the latter, in addition to a number of South and Central American, West Indian, Australian, and West Coast concerns.

All the transatlantic lines and approximately half the coastal lines, together with their vessels, masters, and operators, are listed in the appendices which constitute the backbone of this work.

Considerations of space have made it advisable to limit the account of the coastal lines to those operating between the eight principal East Coast and Gulf ports, viz. the northern ports of Boston, New York, Philadelphia, and Baltimore, and the southern ports of Charleston, Savannah, Mobile, and New Orleans. Reference, however, has been made to the packet activities of other coastal ports, which may serve to indicate the general scope of the traffic. Altogether, upwards of 5000 coastal packets are listed. In general, only the names of the first commanders are given, since nearly all packets had several masters and the inclusion of all would enlarge the roll beyond practicable limits. It is believed, however, that most readers whose American roots go back to the eighteenth century will find in it mention of some members of their families or remembered family associates. If so, the labor of identifying men usually mentioned in the records by last names only will have been justified. The best custodians of worthy traditions are the descendants of the men who established them.

A brief but fairly comprehensive account of the development of steam transportation has been included. It is impossible, on the one hand, to account for the remarkable rapidity with which the sailing ship developed during the period without reference to the influence of steam competition. One the other hand, it is equally impossible to explain the speed with which steam attained its decisive victory without reference both to the competition and cooperation of men of the sail. All the early steamship lines and many of the inland water steamboats owed their existence to sailing shipowners, and their increasingly successful operation to sailing ship masters. In retrospect, it is reasonable to assume that without the help of the "canvas-backs" the progress of steam transportation would have been greatly retarded.

Finally, it is a matter of regret that it has been impossible to treat in greater detail this subject, the importance of which can hardly be overestimated. There are many packet and emigrant lines to which entire volumes might well be devoted. There are scores of men—merchants, commanders, and builders—who deserve extended biographies, notwithstanding the criticisms that, with some justification, have been directed against them. By and large, they were not especially great and good men, after the commonly accepted standards of greatness and goodness. Most of them had in ample measure the faults and weaknesses of humanity, but they left a record of achievement that has never been excelled, if, indeed, it has ever been equalled.

If the writer were to attempt to explain that paradox in a word, he would say that, for reasons to be set forth, it was because in any conflict of interest, it was instinctive with them to put service above profit. In a most trenchant aspect, the story of the first two American centuries is the story of what a small leaven of such men can mean to a land and a people.

CARL C. CUTLER

West Mystic, Conn.
November 14, 1960

Acknowledgements

ASIDE from a few items of general historical significance, all the facts here presented were gathered personally from official custom-house records, early town records, shipping lists and prices current, and American and British newspapers. My chief indebtedness, therefore, is to the various public institutions, now the custodians of the greater part of such material, and to the individuals in charge thereof.

It is, accordingly, my pleasant privilege to record my sense of special obligation to the following:

The British Museum, London, for information from their files of Lloyds' Lists and for microfilm of files of Liverpool papers from 1817 to 1860, especially *Myers's Weekly Advertiser* and its successor, the *Liverpool Mercantile Gazette*.

The Congressional Library, Washington, for use of its early American papers, particularly its very comprehensive files of newspapers of the southern ports.

The American Antiquarian Society, Worcester, Massachusetts, for use of its incomparable files of early New England newspapers and its virtually complete file of the indispensable New York Shipping List and Prices Current, a use which has been immeasurably facilitated by the unstinted cooperation of the Society's Director, Dr. Clarence S. Brigham, through the years 1918 to 1959, inclusive.

The National Archives, Washington, with special acknowledgements to Mr. and Mrs. Forrest W. Holdcamper, in their respective marine departments, for long and helpful assistance.

The New-York Historical Society and its library staff, who have been helpful beyond call of duty in making available their extensive and carefully preserved files of New York papers.

The Peabody Museum of Salem, for prints and use of maritime records, and for the helpful assistance of its staff, especially Ernest S. Dodge, Charles H. P. Copeland, and Marion V. Brewington.

The Boston Athenaeum and its Director, Dr. Walter M. Whitehill.

The Rhode Island Historical Society, Providence, for use of its early Providence newspapers.

The library of the Marine Historical Association, Inc., Mystic, Connecticut.

The Maryland Historical Society, Baltimore, for use of its files of Baltimore newspapers.

The Mariners Museum, Warwick, Virginia, for prints of early packet ships.

The Smithsonian Institution, Washington, and Curator of Transportation Howard I. Chapelle, for lines and sail plans of packet ships.

The Penobscot Marine Museum of Searsport, Maine.

The Franklin Institute, Philadelphia.

The Whaling Museum and Old Dartmouth Historical Society, Dartmouth, Massachusetts.

The Liverpool Public Library, Liverpool, England.

The Seamen's Bank for Savings of the City of New York, for photographs of numerous New York sea captains and merchants and packet ships.

Dr. Vernon D. Tate, Librarian, U. S. Naval Academy, for many years of helpful cooperation.

My thanks are also due to the following public libraries, whose newspaper files I have had occasion to use repeatedly, viz. the public libraries of Boston, Providence, New York, Philadelphia, and Baltimore, and also the libraries of Brown and Yale Universities.

Finally, I wish to make an acknowledgement, now long overdue. Without the understanding sympathy and always dependable encouragement of my wife through the long years, this work would never have been completed.

CARL C. CUTLER

Contents

Illustrations

xix

Ship and Sail Plans

QUEENS OF THE WESTERN OCEAN

THE STORY OF

AMERICA'S MAIL AND PASSENGER SAILING LINES

CHAPTER I

∾ *1607-1725* ∾

Colonial Maritime Policy

"To Marchantes as a Patterne He Might Stand
Adventring Dangers New by Sea and Land"

THESE words, engraved on the tomb of Captain Richard Lord, late merchant-mariner of Hartford, in the colony of Connecticut, who departed this life in the year 1662, might serve as the common epitaph of his innumerable successors—the sea traders of the New World.

They may serve also to call attention to a fact we will do well to keep in mind—that in colonial America the terms merchant and master mariner were all but synonymous. Born of necessity, a long sea apprenticeship, which involved sharing with the humblest foremast hand the perils and privations of a harsh and dangerous calling, came to be regarded as an indispensable part of the merchant's training. In the afterlight of his record we are probably justified in assuming the practice was measurably responsible for the success of a venture that would need all, if not more than all, the help it could get.

It would be difficult to imagine an enterprise less promising at the outset. Seventeenth-century colonial theory was summed up in the word "exploitation," which involved among other things the rigid control of trade to ensure its profits to the Mother Country. If the colonist sought to mitigate the harsh effects of this policy—and he could do so only by building and operating his own ships—he would find himself confronted with the relentless competition of all the great powers of Europe. Nothing but harsh necessity could have warranted him in engaging in foreign commerce on his own account, or in anticipating from that trade more than a weak and precarious survival. Nevertheless he took the plunge and thereby prospered to an extent and with a rapidity unprecedented perhaps in human experience.

Captain Lord had seen and participated in the first uncertain steps of the new venture. Even before his comparatively early death, the infant commerce of New England had gained enormously in volume and efficiency. And so rapid was its development that he had occupied his allotted space in "Ye Antientest Burial Ground" less than a decade when its encroachments on the profits of the English merchants had reached such proportions that they were anxiously concerting measures for its restraint. It is, perhaps, a sufficient commentary on its growth and on the severity of repressive measures adopted to note that New England was "talking independence" as early as 1671—a thing hardly conceivable save on the assumption that a certain superior effectiveness in sea trade had convinced many of her colonists that she could stand alone.[1]

That superiority, however slight or relatively insignificant in a field already pre-empted by the four great maritime powers—England, France, Spain, and Holland—was a fact, and was to remain a fact of crucial importance during the first two centuries of English settlement. Indeed, the story of America, to an extent rarely appreciated is, or—more accurately, perhaps—should be the story of her merchant marine. It would be difficult to point to an outstanding achievement of the Western world prior to 1850 that was not sparked or, in any event, vastly accelerated by that enterprise.

History has much to say, and justly so, of the hardy pioneer, but it was the merchant marine that turned his produce into the cash, the tools, and the supplies which made pioneering on a scale never before attempted both possible and practical. And this was but the beginning. It provided the financial resources which founded our first great banks and insurance companies. Its profits built our first great foundries, factories, railroads, and canals, and developed our steamboats, and opened our mines. It paid the duties which made the purchase of Louisiana and other territories possible, thereby becoming primarily responsible for the fact that the present area of the United States is under one government. The importance of its role in all our wars from the first expedition against Louisburg, and in forestalling aggression thereafter, can hardly be over-estimated. It capped two centuries of fabulous achievement with the construction of the grandest and most efficient fleet of ships of the sail ever launched.

But however remarkable its material contributions, it is possible that they were dwarfed by intangible developments which accompanied them —developments which revolutionized the very character of Western civilization and, in particular, completely reversed its attitude toward change, the condition of all progress. All in all, we are probably justified in asserting that during the brief career of the American merchant-mariner more and vaster changes took place than in the preceding five thousand years. Certainly, the process had been accelerated to an almost incredible degree, and much of it could be counted for progress. The fact suggests a causal connection.

To those desirous of understanding one of the great chapters of American history and profiting by its lessons, it becomes important, therefore, to determine whether such a connection existed and, if so, where and how and why it worked.

As to the first, we take our departure from the assumption that it started in New England. There had been earlier instances of shipbuilding in the Western world, but they were invariably isolated events, leading nowhere. They served and were intended to serve special occasions or limited, private purpose. It is difficult to see any of them as the response to an awareness of the need for a colonial maritime establishment, much less the inception of a policy.

In New England there are definite indications from the beginning of a clear perception that colonial prosperity and colonial shipping were synonymous terms. Plymouth began building its own coasting vessels as early as 1624. Of Salem's little company in 1629, six were carpenters and with them came the rigging and sails for the colony's first vessels. Winthrop also made a special point of including skilled shipwrights the following year in his first group of colonists.

The very name of the Massachusetts Bay Colony's first substantial vessel—the 30-ton *Blessing of the Bay*—was at once a recognition of a common need and a declaration of a policy soon regarded as basic. It was as though Winthrop enjoined his hard-worked and ill-fed band to "Trust God and build ships." Whether the launching of the *Blessing* on the 4th of July, 1631, was prophetic or not, it is reasonable to assume that if that or an equivalent event had never taken place, the day would never have become celebrated for any other reason.

In like manner New Haven's first important craft was named *Fellowship*, a title also suggestive of community interest and enterprise. This vessel, the "Phantom Ship" of Longfellow's poem, probably measured 100 tons or more, and in any case was a weighty undertaking which could hardly have been carried out by the infant colony without the general cooperation of its members.

The identity of the pioneer ship of the American merchant marine is, however, of small importance. It matters little whether we find it in the *Blessing of the Bay* or an earlier pinnace or shallop of Virginia, Plymouth, or Sagadahock, or seek a closer connection in the greater vessels soon to be laid down in Boston, Salem, Marblehead, and New Haven for the express purpose of engaging in foreign trade on a broad scale. Our concern is to find the line that extends unbroken from early colonial times to the magnificent liners of the nineteenth century, and we find that in New England. The Virginia line is faint and broken in the seventeenth century. New York and Philadelphia did not start until long after New England had become a sea power to be reckoned with, and the rest of the colonies were not in it at all.

Virginia, indeed, manifested virtually no interest in providing her own shipping during the seventeenth century. Her first settlers, for the most part, proved incapable of eking out a bare existence, to say nothing of engaging in work requiring exceptional skill and endurance. They soon disappeared, victims of disease and exposure. The more efficient and industrious immigrants who replaced them turned their attention almost exclusively to the production of tobacco, the demand for which brought a glut of large English ships to their shores. That condition was later intensified and prolonged by the slave trade which originated in 1619 and in which London vessels predominated until the Liverpool slavers took over in 1730. They flocked by the score to the Chesapeake, and later to the Carolinas and Georgia, to discharge cargoes of "africoes" and then pick up a freight for the home port. Even if corn and tobacco planting had proved far less profitable there would still have been little incentive for the Virginian to build large ships.

Nevertheless, there was some construction in that colony even before the settlement of the Bay Colony, but the fragmentary information now available indicates that it consisted largely—and probably exclusively— of small pinnaces and shallops, ranging from 5 to 15 or 20 tons, suitable only for short coasting or fishing trips. Aside from those built primarily for plantation use, they were constructed by and for immigrants who were trained seamen—men unfitted by habit and inclination for planting or other land pursuits. Nowhere was there any indication of a top level policy to encourage or promote the construction of large vessels suitable for foreign trade, such as characterized the attitude of the New England leaders. On the contrary, the southern colonies, as opposed to proprietary New England, were originally, or soon became, Crown colonies. (Virginia had a royal governor by 1624.) It followed as an inevitable consequence that the efforts of representatives of the Crown—the most influential men in those colonies—would be exerted, if and when occasion arose, to discourage the building of great ships, as tending to reduce the dependence of the colony on the Mother Country. For these and other reasons, the

construction of ships continued to engage a relatively insignificant proportion of the energies of the South long after it became New England's
leading manufacture.

New England's situation, therefore, was not only different in the beginning but became increasingly so as time went on. Plymouth and the Bay
Colony, in turn, suffered not merely from lack of shipping, but from the
ill-advised use of such tonnage as visited their ports. In spite of a food
shortage that, in healthful variety at least, was all but chronic in the early
years, ship after ship came in crowded with lusty eaters but with little to
eat. Passage money being more profitable than freight, it was inevitable
that in the conflict of interest the English merchant considered his pocket
rather than the needs of a colony 3000 miles away. As a result there was
much unnecessary hardship and a correspondingly high death rate.

Other factors tended to stress New England's need for ships that she
could control. Among these was the discovery that her chief exports would
necessarily be fish and lumber, in spite of a valiant effort to develop a
remunerative fur trade. This put her in a most unfavorable situation, for
England produced, as a rule, all the fish she could consume, and was able
to get the cheap lumber she required from Norway and the nearby Baltic.
Nevertheless, pursuant to the policy of colonial exploitation then universal, she insisted that the products be shipped to English ports, where
they tended to bring the lowest going prices. The colonist, in turn, was
forced to use his meagre proceeds to buy English goods and all other goods
of foreign origin from the English merchant at the highest prices the
traffic would bear. To cap all, he paid a spanking freight rate both out and
home.

The full effect of these handicaps was postponed, as will be seen, for
several years. So long as immigration continued at a high rate, bringing
each year fresh supplies of money, manufactures, and new customers for
the settlers already established, the condition of the colony would be
endurable, even though far from satisfactory. If, however, anything should
happen to cut off this flow, the situation of the colony might well become
desperate.

The blow fell, as will be more particularly noted elsewhere, when the
Bay Colony had been established a little more than ten years. When it
did it required no great intelligence on the part of the New Englander to
reach the conclusion that his only hope of avoiding complete ruin lay in
building and operating his own ships; sending them, if need be, to more
profitable markets.

More, however, than the averting of disaster hung on the matter, and that more was a prosperity and growth unprecedented in colonial history. With his own ships, the freight money which had gone to the English shipowners would remain in the colony. With his own mariner agents and supercargoes—men whose interests marched with his own—he could buy and sell to the best possible advantage. The English factor, on the other hand, was always under the strong temptation to dump his colonial cargoes on the market for what they would bring, with no other concern than to see that they paid his charges. Not all factors followed this practice, but it became sufficiently general to bring many southern planters into serious straits during the eighteenth century.

Another result of vast importance was the part shipping played in the development of American character. New England had two colleges in 1638, Harvard and the quarter-deck. The first turned out specialists, clergymen, lawyers, and teachers; the latter, whole men, thinking men of action. The former produced many worthy, useful citizens, but it also produced the leaders of that intolerance which is still cited as characteristic of the workaday colonial Puritan. The latter were men of many faults, but if one may judge from the letters and journals they have left and many of their church records of kindly philanthropy, it is probable that they were on the whole more tolerant than accorded with the general standards of their day. It is doubtful whether it would have occurred to them to hang a Quaker or chase a Baptist through the woods, without the prodding of a few leaders, including some of the clergy.

Through the years thousands of boys, most of them from overcrowded farms and whose formal education ended with the "Three R's," acquired on shipboard far more than the rudiments of seamanship regarded as sufficient for the European sailor. By and large, the majority of any given crew were neighbors, members of the same little community from birth. For that reason more than wages were involved. Their reputation both for ability and right-minded attitude was at stake. It was a situation that made for a generally more kindly and helpful atmosphere than one encountered in Old Country ships, and goes far to explain why colonial seamen by the thousand quickly acquired not only an adequate knowledge of seamanship and the principles of trade and finance, but a broad understanding of the principles of healthy human relationships with alien races and peoples. They were America's first diplomats, and as ambassadors of good will they were unsurpassed. They produced the great majority of the colonial merchants.

Shipbuilding entailed a further advantage, that of providing employment for a large number of workers, both skilled and unskilled. Besides the men and boys whose chief qualifications were the ability to "throw an axe" or drive a team 12 or 14 hours a day, the industry involved the labor of a variety of skilled craftsmen in addition to shipwrights. There were sail makers, caulkers, rope makers, shipsmiths, pump, block and trunnel makers, mast and spar makers, and joiners. There was work, also, for tin and coppersmiths, painters, bakers, ship chandlers, ironmongers, and the like. Even in 1630, a full decade before her hour of greatest need, it was obvious that shipbuilding alone could enable New England to take care of a large and steady increase of population. And that is the way it turned out.

One might say with perhaps pardonable exaggeration that within a few years the first task of the newly arrived Puritan was to build a home and his next to build a ship. In the South, tobacco was King until displaced by cotton. In New England, King Log, in guise of houses, hogsheads and ships, ruled for two centuries. Which dynasty would develop the greater prosperity for the greatest possible number was still anyone's guess in the seventeenth century.

Although the foregoing indicates where and, in measure, why American sea trade started, it does not explain its success. The more obvious facts point, rather, to mediocrity of performance. The New England Puritan not only lacked material resources such as would account for notably superior achievement, but he was no braver or stronger than his contemporaries. Nor was he endowed with greater skill, experience, or education.

On the score of positive disadvantages, he was accused with some justice of inexperience, of ignorance, of being unduly contentious, and of wasting much time and energy in disputes over absurdly trivial doctrinal matters. Above all, he seemed hopelessly divided into a great variety of petty sects.

Nevertheless, it is doubtful if any people of any age were more firmly united in the bonds of a common belief. Certainly no people accepted more generally and wholeheartedly the fundamental principle of Protestantism: the sanctity of the individual and his duty to prove himself worthy of God's favor by striving his utmost to rise to ever-higher levels. This principle with its corollaries of personal responsibility and the obligation, transcending all human authority, of working out and directing his own destinies under divine rather than human guidance, was basic with every Puritan, however he might differ otherwise. In a world in which, for a thousand years, change had been anathema and the humble acceptance of one's lot the price of peaceful existence, its implications were so revolutionary that other things mattered little in comparison.

Among other things, it made the unending improvement of the individual the first concern of society. Such a principle might even prove the seed of all change and all progress.

We are not here concerned with the validity of beliefs but rather with their effects. It is our immediate task to account for the fact that a small, weak, and apparently commonplace people threw overboard accepted standards and traditions, repudiated established authority and, while doing so, somehow transformed a forbidding wilderness into a great nation with unmatched speed and efficiency. Did the Puritan concept stand for force? Did it in fact release energies that made for superior achievement? Was it, in short, a dynamic philosophy, or did it belong to the field of mere speculation?

These questions were answered in part long before the Puritan arrived in New England.

The essential principle, however vaguely or imperfectly conceived, had already figured mightily in the rise of the Dutch Republic. It was building a new and more prosperous France until halted by the massacre of the Huguenots. Although in the minority in England, its adherents there were bringing about vast changes.

In New England the situation was different. There the Puritan, for the first time in history, was in the driver's seat, virtually unopposed, for in the home country the government was in the hands of Puritans, led by the "Great Protector," Oliver Cromwell. For a long generation he was permitted to work out his destiny without interference. Until the restoration of the monarchy under Charles the Second, the colony subsisted as a virtually independent commonwealth. Whatever the outcome, therefore, it was clear that a trial of the new theory of personal rights and responsibilities would be relatively unhampered there.

The thing was soon tested. Pilgrim and Puritan alike landed on a bleak, infertile coast. They had claimed the God-given right to work out their own destinies and now for the first time they had unlimited scope for self-reliance. Their "Howling Wilderness" still bears witness to the years of harsh, unremitting toil required to clear rocks and forest from a fraction of its area. The New England workday, for generations to come, was to start at dawn and continue to early candlelight. Even so, the leisurely, Old World pace would not suffice. The days were all too short to accomplish what had to be done. The relentless pressure of need kept the colonist in a chronic state of hurry. He tended more and more to drive himself at top speed.

This speed is something to keep in mind. It was to become a notable, distinguishing characteristic of the American way long before it became an outstanding feature of modern civilization.

Another important factor in the situation was the relative uniformity of living and working conditions in New England, a condition which has been obscured by the tendency to assign undue importance to an "upper class" that was all but nonexistent in the seventeenth century. Most of the population, including those bred in England to special trades, lived on farms or followed the sea. Less than ten per cent lived in towns and many of those owned and worked outlying farms. They soon attained varying degrees of prosperity but, by and large, they lived and worked alike. Magistrate, selectman, deacon, all the small authority, milked cows, planted crops, and in all respects duplicated the labors of Goodman Hodge, who hadn't even qualified for church membership. For many years the comparatively well-to-do merchant and landowner who might, and sometimes did, assume an air of authority, constituted less than one per cent of the population. His contribution to the development of the colony, however creditable, was but a trifling fraction of the whole. Compared with the Puritan's conviction that his paramount duty was to direct his own life in accordance with God's law and his own best judgment, his influence was slight. If the other 99 per cent gave him a thought, it could be summed up in the phrase, "Strut and be hanged." Their pride and interest was fully occupied in turning out a sound, 75-hour workweek.

Other circumstances which tended to preserve this situation longer in New England than elsewhere included the almost complete homogeneity of the colony; the impossibility in the beginning of rapid accumulation of wealth; and the inability, due to a general lack of cash and credit, to develop a class of large landowners.

It came to this, that where Virginia, the only other contemporary English colony, was under a royal governor with his numerous train of officials, and was establishing a large and well-to-do planter class, New England soil was especially favorable to the growth of a common standard —and that standard was personal efficiency. The New England aristocrat of the seventeenth century was the man who could do the most, the best, and the fastest.

For a small, inexperienced group, about to cope, barehanded, with the entrenched competition of the world, it was, perhaps, the best practical philosophy.

We find therefore in New England, in a measure that obtained nowhere else in quite the same degree in the early seventeenth century, two prime requisites of a successful merchant marine: the spur of urgent necessity and the indomitable will to surmount all obstacles. There were other factors, and they will come to light in due course.

Detailed information is scanty, but general references, especially the frequent mention of local traders and trading vessels and the construction of numerous wharves, indicate that the building of small vessels was continuous in the colony after 1630. It is hardly necessary to point out that the inhabitants had to provide their own coasters and fishing craft. The large English ships were not suitable for such purposes, even if they could have been chartered. One of the first activities of each new settlement as it came into existence, therefore, was the construction of shallops and pinnaces for those purposes.

Salem had a pinnace in 1631. In the same year a Plymouth "bark" was trading to the Kennebec. During the Indian wars, which shortly broke out, the colony transported large numbers of troops in vessels which, though small, could carry 40 or more men and their supplies. Roger Williams wrote in 1637 of three pinnaces and two shallops riding at anchor near his home in Rhode Island.

Most of the vessels ranged from 5 to 20 tons in size, but one at least was much larger. That was the ship *Desire* of 100 tons, built in Marblehead. Winthrop reported that in 1639 she made the passage from Boston to Gravesend, England, in 23 days. It was the first Yankee sailing record and a run that would still be regarded as exceptionally fast.

The need for a substantial number of large vessels did not become pressing immediately. Up to 1640 immigration on a large scale in English ships was continuous, and although their trade tended to siphon off the colony's specie, its bad effects were measurably offset by the cash brought by the newcomers. In 1640, however, the colony was faced with the prospect that the flow of cash and immigrants would be cut off, for Charles the First had found it desirable to show a better countenance to the Puritans in England. The effect of this temporary and, as it proved, intentionally deceptive policy on the New England economy was thus described by Governor Winthrop:

> The general fear of want of foreign commodities, now our money was gone, and that things were likely to go well in England, set us on work to provide shipping of our own. . . . The work was hard to accomplish for want of money, etc., but our shipwrights were content to take such pay as the country could make.[2]

Two large ships were laid down at once and launched in the spring of 1641, sailing on their maiden voyages the ensuing summer. One, a ship of 300 tons, was built at Salem by Richard Hollingsworth. The other, the ship *Trial* of about 160 tons, was built at Boston by Nehemiah Bourne, who subsequently became an admiral in Cromwell's Parliamentary navy.

Disillusionment as to Charles' intentions soon followed, but with no improvement in the colony's prospects. On the contrary, the civil war which broke out in 1641 not only cut off immigration completely, but with it the Old Country ships on which the colony had depended to transport its produce to England. In addition, it soon appeared that unsettled conditions in England had greatly reduced the demand for such supplies as the colonists were able to send over in their own new ships.

A new factor—the imperative need for other markets—was thus injected into the situation, which was to set the Puritan a long day's journey down the road to independence. In the words of Winthrop:

> This year (1641) the Parliament of England setting upon a general reformation . . . this caused all men to stay in England in expectation of a new world, so as few coming to us, all foreign commodities grew scarce, and our own of no price. Corn would buy nothing: a cow which cost last year £20 might now be bought for £4 or £5. These straits set our people on work to provide fish, clapboards, plank, etc., and to sow hemp and flax (which prospered very well) and to look out to the West Indies for a trade in cotton.[3]

The new trade proved far more advantageous than trade with the Mother Country had ever been. It is altogether probable that the colonists regarded the venture as a temporary makeshift, but unsettled conditions in England were destined to continue another ten years, during which the West Indian trade increased tremendously in volume. Moreover, it was so profitable that when peace was restored in England, a substantial portion of the colony's trade remained with the West Indies and continued to increase in relative importance throughout the colonial period.

One other consequence of the decision to engage in the new trade was the impetus given to construction of large ships. Coasting vessels, of which the colony had a fair supply, were not well calculated for long foreign voyages, and the New Englander knew better than to suppose he could charter the needed tonnage from English merchants. Accordingly, the two large ships launched in 1641 were speedily followed by others. We learn, for instance, that in 1642 ships arrived in Boston from England with only five or six passengers "and but few goods, except rigging for the ships that we were building here."[4]

No references have come to light identifying the ships under construction, but there is evidence of a substantial increase in tonnage during the next three years. Winthrop mentions the return in 1645 of one colony ship from the Canaries, by way of Barbados, to which place she transported a number of "africoes"—apparently New England's first venture in the slave trade. The same year another colony ship of 260 tons was attacked near the Canaries by an Irish man-of-war, but fought her off—indicating that some colony ships were heavily manned and armed.

The largest vessel built about this time of which we have a record was the *Seafort*. She was a ship of about 400 tons and was launched at Boston in 1645 for Captain Hawkins. But it was not only in Boston that large ships were built. Salem, Marblehead, Newport, Hartford, New Haven— all the small seaports as they came into existence—began to lay down substantial craft and even to develop foreign trades of their own.

Thus, New London, which was settled in 1646, was sending vessels to Virginia and the Barbados within five years, although her male population did not exceed 50. By 1660, with an adult male population of less than 100, which, however, included three master builders, she was steadily engaged in the construction of vessels. During the remainder of the seventeenth century she turned out many a goodly craft ranging up to 70 tons or more, several of which were built for English merchants.

The early records of most of the coastal settlements from Connecticut to the District of Maine indicate a similar condition.

Most of the vessels built during this period were small. A few registered from 150 to 250 tons. Larger vessels were extremely rare, while the great majority even of those for the long trade routes were well under 100 tons. All, however, were larger, that is, were of greater carrying capacity than the rated tonnage would indicate—a statement which holds good for ships of the sail in general, until a few extreme clippers were built in the nineteenth century.

In the seventeenth century the practice in computing tonnage varied slightly, without greatly affecting the result. Some took the length of keel, or the length of the rabbet of the keel, instead of the length between perpendiculars or between the after side of the stem and after side of the stern post, as later. The early method led to the design of vessels with a tremendous forward swoop of the stem and more or less rake aft; resulting in an appreciable increase in carrying capacity without increasing the rated tonnage, on which port and tonnage dues were computed. Thus, the seventeenth-century colonial vessel with a 40-foot keel, might, and often did, have a 15-foot rake of stem or more, and a substantial rake of stern post, with the result that the length of hold was extended well beyond the 40 feet charged to the vessel.

The practice had another result which may not have been intentional at first, but which was to work to the advantage of the colonial mariner in an important way. By lengthening and fining out the lines, the builder obtained a faster ship. He was using, in fact, the basic principle of speed design later embodied in improved form in the Baltimore clipper; a principle, by the way, still used in the modern racing yacht.

In 1773 the method of using the length between stem and stern posts, or between perpendiculars, was adopted in computing tonnage. However, as that rule gradually became effective the ingenious shipwright soon found a way to defeat its purpose. He shortened the nominal length by setting the stem and stern posts upright—a fact which explains why later ships had virtually straight stems instead of the overhanging colonial bow, except when it was considered desirable to sacrifice carrying capacity for speed.

When the "Great Migration" ended in 1640, the English in America did not fall far short of the 50,000 estimate of 1641. The precise figure is less important than the distribution. Of the total, nearly four-fifths lived in New England. The great majority of the remainder were in Virginia, which was credited with a population of 5119 in 1635 and 15,000 in 1648. It was probably not far from 8000 in 1641. Maryland, then the only other English colony, had about 600. Aside from this, there were a few scattered English in the Jerseys and on the banks of the Delaware, where Swedes, Dutch, and Germans constituted the bulk of a population relatively insignificant in numbers.[5]

The drift in Virginia and Maryland toward the establishment of relatively large and isolated plantations prevented for many years the establishment of large towns. Early population figures for the South are almost wholly confined to county totals, but from these and other indications it seems probable that neither Virginia nor Maryland had a seaport in 1641 with a population of 300 whites. Boston then had upwards of 1200 and was growing rapidly. By 1650 its inhabitants numbered about 2000. Salem, Marblehead, and Newport were much smaller but they greatly exceeded any southern settlements in size. There were, indeed, a number of other New England towns which surpassed by liberal margins the largest places in Virginia.

One reason for the tendency to develop large towns in New England has already been indicated: shipbuilding. No great concentration of people was needed to conduct trade on a large scale, whereas shipbuilding, like any other manufacture, employed a relatively large number of workers, both skilled and unskilled. Nor did the matter rest there. The presence of numerous workers stimulated and facilitated the growth of other manufactures. In the long run this fact was to develop a distinct type of society in the North; a society which tended more and more to concentrate in huge industrial centers.

Boston, with its excellent harbor and central location, was the natural distributing center of New England. Thanks to these factors and its early start, plus whatever credit may be assigned to its dynamic philosophy, it ranked from the first as America's leading port, and was destined to maintain that position for more than a century. The profits derived through its relatively large West Indian trade enabled it to supply other towns, and even other colonies with English and European goods on more favorable terms than they could secure through direct trade. In the course of time even the great and growing towns of Philadelphia and New York were to depend for many years on Boston for a considerable part of their English merchandise.

It could be a mistake, however, to interpret the circumstance as indicating the servile dependence of other areas on Boston. The statement to the effect that "Boston engrossed the trade of New England" gives, unless duly qualified, a distorted picture, not only of the conditions but of the spirit of New England. The truth would appear to be that, in proportion to size, the smallest port was as actively engaged in trade and ship construction as Boston. Nothing else could explain the tremendous growth of New England's merchant fleet.

By 1676, Massachusetts alone was reported to have 430 vessels ranging from 30 to 250 tons.[6] There were, in addition, some 300 Massachusetts-owned craft of from five to ten tons engaged in the traffic between Boston and nearby ports. Besides these, New Hampshire, Rhode Island, and Connecticut had built and were operating substantial fleets of their own. Boston owned but a small part of this great merchant marine, and her English and European imports formed but a fraction of its cargoes.

Vessels did not go empty from the smaller ports to Boston and leave with holds stuffed with the riches of Europe. The matter was an arrangement of convenience. Small ports had no adequate distribution for entire shiploads of manufactured goods and luxury items, but they could and did send to Boston the sound equivalent of what they carried away.

In general, all ports, regardless of size, imported their own staples directly—sugar, molasses, salt, naval stores, and wines, with a few hogsheads of rum and tobacco for makeweight. By the same token, they exported lumber, fish, livestock, and various foodstuffs in cargo lots. There were few seaports that did not send one or more vessels to the West Indies each year, and with fair frequency to Lisbon or the "wine islands," Madeira and the Canaries. The vessel might be a sloop of only 20 or 30 tons, but it added its mite to the wealth and experience of the little settlement and opened the road to the construction of an ever-growing number of larger craft. Enterprising common sense, rather than a spirit of dependence, dictated the course of trade.

The redoubtable Captain Lord, of Hartford, was no rare exception in his day. Any New England port could have produced his double. But there was more to it than that.

Long before the close of the seventeenth century the Keepers of His Majesty's Conscience were beginning to take note that something unusual, if not deplorable, was going on in the American colonies. In particular, the New England merchant-mariners were outwitting and outsailing the royal cruisers to the detriment of the royal treasury and the outraged anguish of the British merchant. Their little sloops and brigantines, holds jammed with forbidden merchandise, were running the haughty British Bruisewater out of sight with profitable regularity, plus a scandalous indifference to protocol.

English merchants of Restoration Days did not complain of Boston alone, they made their moan of all New England. The entire area was prospering at their expense. Eventually, it proved that many of the ports were prospering at the expense of Boston; which is another way of saying that the colony as a whole was putting on a superior maritime show. Throughout the colonial period, the untutored but supremely self-reliant man from some newly cleared Connecticut River bank or lonely "Down East" cove was quite as likely to astonish the nautical world as the man from Boston or any other relatively rich and populous center.

While New England was thus working out its destiny with less regard for the law than for its own sweet will, other colonies were coming along.

In 1637 a few Swedes emigrated to the present Wilmington area of Delaware. Shortly thereafter a mixture of Swedes, Dutch, and Germans, with a sprinkling of English, settled in New Jersey and on the west bank of the Delaware in the vicinity of the Schuylkill River. They were interested almost exclusively in farming. Although they probably provided themselves with a few shallops and canoes, there is no record of their engaging in shipbuilding or sea trade. For purposes of maritime history, therefore, the area may be disregarded until after the settlement of Philadelphia, more than 40 years later.

North Carolina had a permanent settlement at Cape Fear as early as 1663, but the growth of the colony was slow and vacillating for many years. Like Virginia, and for similar reasons, it depended on English shipping to a much greater extent than New England did. The bulk of its early commerce was with England and the West Indies, in which the slave ships of Bristol and London and, after 1730, those of Liverpool, played an increasingly important role. Its coasting trade, although larger in the early period than that of South Carolina, was small, and was handled principally by New England vessels, an arrangement which was facilitated by the influx of a number of northern merchants.

Charles Town (later Charleston), South Carolina, was established in 1670. About 200 settlers came during that and the following year. They were mainly English and Irish adherents of the Church of England. By 1685 the population of the town had increased to approximately 900 and included a small group of Quakers, a number of Huguenots, skilled in the manufacture of silks, wines, and oil, and a few northern merchants, which several elements were to exert a commercial influence out of proportion to their numbers.

New York (late New Amsterdam) was taken over by the British in 1664, though the English influence did not become very effective for another ten years. By that time the colony, which included considerably more territory than the present state, contained an estimated 6000 to 7000 Dutch and about half that number of English and other whites.

On the basis of taxables reported in 1676 and other figures cited about that time, the population of the town could hardly have exceeded 2500 at the time of occupation, although several writers credit it with 4000. At that time the shipping belonging to the port totalled 11 vessels, mostly small.

Commercial development was retarded at the outset by the patroon system and the later, but similar, land-grabbing tactics of a small clique, both Dutch and English under the royal governors. The situation thus created tended to discourage initiative on the part of people of small means, and at the same time channelled potentially useful energies into unproductive activities.

On the other hand, the same interests created a monopoly which did increase the town's trade. In 1678, the port was given the exclusive privilege of bolting flour and packing breadstuffs for export to the West Indies. This monopoly lasted until 1694. Under it, the shipping of the port increased to 85 sail and population doubled. In 1700 it amounted to 5000, about equally divided between Dutch and English, with a few Swedes, Huguenots, and Jews. For many years, however, the progress of the port proceeded more slowly than in Philadelphia, where class lines were less sharply drawn.

Pennsylvania, the last English colony to be established in the seventeenth century, was founded in 1681. Its first inhabitants numbered about 500, but included some who had already settled there while the Dutch and Swedes were debating the question of proprietary rights. Growth was rapid, but early figures include the population of considerable areas outside the city of Philadelphia and give, therefore, a somewhat uncertain picture of the rise of the port. It is probable, however, that the town had about 2500 souls in 1685 and that it passed the 5000 mark in 1700. There are higher estimates but it is possible, if not probable, that they include the Liberties and other suburban areas.

Philadelphia was less cosmopolitan in character than either New York or Charleston, but much more so than New England, which remained quite homogeneous until the eighteenth century was well advanced. Yet the dominant influence in the city was similar to that which prevailed in New England. The Quaker element which was in control for many years accepted to the full the Puritan principle of individual rights and responsibilities. The chief and perhaps the only difference of importance was that one would fight for his principle; the other would not. This fact, qualify it as one may, left untouched the Quaker's predisposition to industry and his dogged determination to do his utmost best.

By 1685, or thereabouts—the precise year is unimportant—the American stage was set. The charter of Massachusetts had been forfeited in 1684 and that colony, together with the rest of New England, except Connecticut and Rhode Island, placed under a royal governor, without, however, effecting a corresponding change in the character of their inhabitants. All the English colonies with the exception of Georgia (still 50 years in the future) were now firmly established and their respective lines of future development somewhat definitely foreshadowed. Total white population was about 190,000, roughly 75,000 of whom were in New England.

New England had settled her local Indian problems temporarily in 1675 with no help from the Mother Country, but at a heavy cost, both in lives and money. Her growth was to be relatively free and unimpeded for the next 20 years, or until England started the long series of wars which brought the French and Indians down on her borders from the north.

There had been a heavy increase in the number of slaves and free blacks. People in the North, especially in Boston and New York, had many household slaves, imported because of the scarcity of whites willing to serve in menial capacities when land and independence could be had for the asking. The great majority of slaves, however, were in the South; Virginia and Maryland having the largest number. One reason for this early difference was the refusal of northern workmen to tolerate slave competition, although climatic conditions and plantation needs were mainly responsible.

New England's major interest was, and obviously would continue to be, shipping. The point was emphasized unmistakably when John Usher, of Boston, imported 874 books for the trade in 1685. Fifty of the volumes were works on navigation. Aside from a few histories, all of the rest were school books, religious works and Bibles, with fewer Bibles than nautical texts.

Nevertheless, her growing commitments in the manufacturing field, especially iron, leather and leather goods, cordage, hats, rum, and the like pointed to a future commercial-industrial commonwealth. The greater part of this manufacturing was in conflict with the spirit, if not the letter of the English law. Much of her trade, on the other hand, was legitimate, although smuggling—assertions to the contrary notwithstanding—accounted for a substantial and very profitable proportion.[7] She had also embarked on the slave trade, and although her slavers constituted but a fraction of her fleet, their enormous profits sped the growth of her merchant marine, besides tightening her hold on the southern coastal trade.

In the middle colonies, farm lands, much richer in general than those of New England, had come into production and foodstuffs were rolling down the North River and bumping over the primitive cart paths of eastern Pennsylvania to the ports of New York and Philadelphia. Already, mills in both colonies were grinding the "Superfine Flour" that was to constitute the chief exportable product of the two cities and play an important role in the development of a vast American merchant marine.

Another item destined to bulk large in their cargoes to Europe for the next century and a half were potash and pearl ash, by-products of the hardwood forests, which were relentlessly slashed and burned to clear the land. All colonies, north and south, contributed staves, clapboards, and plank for the export trade, but New York was most strongly entrenched in the extremely profitable fur trade. Pennsylvania and the colonies to the south exported a few furs but did a more substantial business in deer skins.

Neither New York nor Pennsylvania were under quite the same degree of economic pressure that pushed New England from the beginning into the field of small manufacturing, where men's industry could offset their lack of capital. In those colonies the land was richer, the mouths to be fed fewer, and in the early years they had a larger proportion of the well-to-do, including gentry of inherited wealth, men who were able, as opportunity offered, to find the capital required to establish heavy industries.

The differences were not great, but they effected in the course of time the establishment of a vast number of small enterprises in New England, as against a relatively small number of much greater industries in the middle colonies. The thing had certain intangible as well as material consequences.

There had been no place in the colonies at first for the specialist: the half man, or less. The man who, if he had remained in England, would have been bred to a single occupation and lived his life out in the narrow groove of a humdrum daily routine, found himself pitchforked into half a score of unfamiliar trades. His value to himself and his community depended upon his becoming a whole man—one able to make a shift in half a dozen trades besides the varied activities of farming or navigating a ship, and one who, in consequence, saw things clearly and saw them whole.

The small manufactory tended to preserve this condition, and through it to prolong the influence of the Puritan concept, whereas the greater industries tended to undermine it. The proprietor of the tiny shop or crossroads forge worked side by side with his men. Both he and they could, and did, do everything. Admitting imperfections and exceptions, the situation made strongly for a feeling of equality, mutual respect, and self-respect. It made for clear vision and a self-reliance that would admit no failure.

And, in truth, the colonist of 1685 had need of all the vision and self-reliance he could muster. He was a long way from being out of the woods.

Ever since the Restoration, English merchants had been trying, with small success, to recapture the lost trade of New England. Now, in the early 1680's, with that trade swelling to undreamed proportions and even threatening their colonial monopoly, they redoubled their efforts to plug the leak. One of their first measures—for they, rather than King William or George the First, Second, or Third, were responsible for the business and all it entailed, including the Revolution—was to procure the closing of the "Pine Tree Shilling" mint, established by Boston in 1652 because the colony had been drained of its cash. This was a more serious matter than it sounds. It was not merely that the shilling was then worth several dollars in present-day purchasing value, but the ensuing reduction of the colony's supply of sound money inevitably brought about a rise in prices that bore heavily on the inhabitants. Less immediately, it was to play a part a few years later in bringing about the colony's issuance of paper money to pay the costs of the Indian wars.

The next move was to step up the enforcement of the long-neglected Navigation Acts of 1651, 1663, and 1672. The first of these acts, though aimed ostensibly—or, if one prefers, primarily—at the Dutch, forbade the export of goods from England in any but English ships. Since, by common construction, colonial vessels were not entitled to rating as English ships within the meaning of the act, it was obvious to the New Englander that it could and would be so interpreted as to restrict his trade and deplete his cash in precise proportion to its effective endorsement.

By the act of 1663, the operation of the first act was extended to imports, and the act of 1672 laid an additional burden on American commerce by establishing imposts on all inter-colonial trade.

To complete the tale—since later measures throw light on the existing English attitude—in 1696-7, an act for preventing frauds and regulating abuses in the plantation trade was passed. In 1699 the export of colonial wool, whether raw or in the manufactured state, was forbidden. In 1719, Parliament declared its opposition to all colonial manufactures; thus putting royal governors under notice to use their admittedly powerful influence to discourage such activities. In 1732, the export of hats, manufacture of which had grown to substantial proportions, was outlawed. The following year a duty was placed on all sugar, rum, and molasses imported into America, except that from British West Indies. Rice exports from the Carolinas became important in 1707 and were subjected to a heavy discriminatory tax in favor of the Honorable John Company monopoly. That sacrosanct organization, better known as the East India Company, had a complete monopoly of Britain's East India and China trade, which, of course, included rice imports. The whaling industry, in turn, became the ungrateful recipient of a similar blessing. In 1750, all rolling and slitting mills, power forges, furnaces and smelters in America were outlawed, and in 1765 the "odious" Stamp Act was passed.

We are probably justified in concluding that the effect of these measures was precisely the opposite of that intended. There was no thought of acquiescence among a people whose very presence in the wilderness spelled protest. And in simple fact there couldn't be. They were up against a condition, not a theory. The balance of English trade was always heavily against them—sometimes as much as five to one—and they had to find a way to meet the payments or see their children reduced to beggary. The only way open to them was through trade which showed a profit, and in view of England's restrictions, illicit trade was the only thing which met the specifications. As it turned out, they prosecuted it with a vigor that more than filled the bill. It added to the wealth of the colonies with a rapidity rarely if ever equalled.

Immigration was also renewed on a large scale after the Restoration with its revival of persecution and discriminatory regulations in England. It was to fluctuate with war, famines, and recurrent epidemics, but after the Peace of Ryswick in 1713 ended the long wars with France and Spain which had ravaged colonial shipping for more than ten years, it increased year by year. As time passed, it brought a larger proportion of undesirables, but a majority still came from nonconformist ranks and for much the same reasons as the early settlers.

Population growth was exceptionally rapid after 1700. In that year the population of the 12 colonies was approximately 250,000, as against 160,000, or thereabouts, in 1660. The quarter million included some 45,000 blacks, of whom 35,000 were in Maryland, Virginia, and the Carolinas.[8] At the same time colonial trade was being enlarged by a similar increase in the population of England and Europe.

The field of colonial commerce was further extended in 1707 by the union of England and Scotland, which opened the way to direct trade between the colonies and Scotland. This traffic, although slight at first, was to grow to substantial proportions by the middle of the century. Quite as important, perhaps, was the fact that it shared with the Jacobite plots and wars the responsibility of stimulating Scottish emigration to the colonies. Few of the emigrants had any great love for the British government, and the result was the addition of a notably volatile element to a mixture which already had a low boiling point.

Natural increase had been and would continue to be chiefly responsible for the growth of colonial white populations, but the stepped-up immigration was to account for an increasing percentage. A large proportion of the new immigrants consisted of Scotch-Irish Presbyterians, driven out of Ireland by the persecutions of the Church of England. The balance was made up of Protestant Palatinates and Huguenots, with a liberal sprinkling of Welsh and Jews. After 1717 a majority of the Scotch-Irish went to Boston, fanning out from there, while the Palatinates settled mostly in Pennsylvania. Previously, a good many of both elements had emigrated to New York and Charleston, South Carolina. The Huguenots went everywhere and, in point of prosperity, were usually to be found among the upper half.

If one makes due mental reservation for the fact that one era always blends imperceptibly into the following, the end of the first quarter century might be taken as marking the coming of age of America. By 1725 the day of "every man a pioneer" had passed. The early state of flux, when families by the dozen and sometimes entire communities pulled stakes and headed for greener pastures, had given place to relatively stabilized conditions. The westbound pioneers of the future were to come mainly from the ranks of new arrivals and the surplus of oversize families. In the older towns, a social order of sorts was modifying almost imperceptibly the community spirit which had characterized pre-Restoration days. There, a new standard—new at least to the older natives of New England—the criterion of wealth—was being added to the test of personal worth. What it might lead to, time alone could show.

The period closed with New England still far in the lead. Boston, with its 12,000, or thereabouts, in 1725 was the largest town and most active seaport and manufacturing center in America. It had 14 shipyards which launched annually a majority of the larger vessels built in America, many of them for English account. A list of its prominent families included the Huguenots, Andrew and Peter Faneuil and Andrew Sigourney. There were many others: all merchants, among them Andrew Cunningham, Stephen Minot, Thomas Amory, Edward Bromfield, and Andrew Belcher. Some of their descendants were still active in the packet era of the nineteenth century.

Boston, however, was but a small part of New England, as her merchants were to learn during the next quarter century. Busy seaports and inland trading towns had sprung up by the dozen. Plymouth colony had established more than a score of towns, of which shipbuilding Scituate was the largest. Salem had a population of 4000 and her ships were sailing most of the seven seas. Marblehead was a substantial shipbuilding center. Competition was springing up in the villages of New Hampshire and the District of Maine. Nantucket and Sag Harbor were building a fleet of whalers. Newport was a thriving place about the size of Salem with excellent wharves, one of them 2000 feet in length, and more than a dozen master shipwrights.

Connecticut, with half the population of the Bay colony, had almost as many shipbuilding communities. New London, with its 600 inhabitants, broke the American record by launching "Jeffrey's Great Ship" in 1725. Built by John Jeffrey, she was a three-decker of 700 tons, and the largest merchant vessel laid down anywhere in the colonies prior to the construction in New York of the 1000-tonner, *Maria Wilhelmina*, half a century or so later.[9] Some conception of her size may be gathered from the fact that two men were killed by falling into her hold before her completion. Jeffrey followed this ship with the *Don Carlos*, of 500 tons. Both vessels were launched in the presence of a "vast concourse of people" who had gathered from miles around. Thereafter he continued to build large vessels for a number of years. Boston, at this time, had built no ships which exceeded the 400-tonners, *Seafort* and *Lese Frigot*, the latter launched in 1693.[10]

Every cove along the Connecticut shore and, far inland, many a convenient river bank, echoed to the sound of maul and axe and saw. There was hardly a community on tidewater that did not launch one or more craft a year. Few measured above 75 tons but the aggregate tonnage was impressive. By comparison, that amount for which the few wealthy merchants were responsible was almost insignificant.

The majority of ships were essentially cooperative ventures, built, freighted, and manned by neighbors, and commanded by a merchant-captain who often owned his own warehouse and wharf and "kept store" between voyages. Even the wealthiest merchants rarely owned their ships outright. Ownership as a rule was split up among several persons, sometimes as many as 20 or 30.

The character of Connecticut did not differ from that of the rest of New England. Even the smallest ports pushed their ventures to distant foreign ports with no thought of limiting their activities to humdrum coasting. They rarely failed to send one or more vessels each year to the "wine islands" or to the West Indies, deep loaded with local produce and a deck load of livestock—principally horses.

Many a "horse jockey" stowed 40 or more horses under a temporary "horse awning" of plank, in addition to pigs and poultry. The extent of the trade and the number of vessels it employed is indicated by the fact that the colony shipped out several thousand horses a year through the greater part of the eighteenth century. It was, moreover, a profitable trade —so much so that it brought about a serious impairment of local morals. If the American horse thief did not originate in Connecticut, he at least attained there a maturity of sorts.

Meanwhile New York was getting away to a slower start. Its 5000 inhabitants in 1700 became 7500 in 1725, a rate of increase less than half that of New England and several other colonies during the same period. Population, however, counted for less in the long run on the island of Manhattan than in most other centers. The port was the only outlet for the vast hinterland tributary to the Hudson and Mohawk Valleys, and half the inhabitants of the entire province were concentrated in the nearby counties of Queens, Kings, Richmond, Westchester, and Suffolk. Queens alone had nearly as many as New York County. Across the North River and along the western shore of the bay lay the most populous and active trading centers of New Jersey. All in all, it was obvious that most of the commerce of New Jersey, as well as New York, would, of necessity be handled through the port of New York.

In spite of this, the town continued to lag behind New England for many years. Probably there were others but aside from the Dutch ship-builders of the seventeenth century, the first builder of the new regime of whom we have a record was John Latham who established a yard near the foot of Dover Street, East River, in 1701. By 1725 there were six yards along the East River, five of which ranged northward from the foot of Beekman Street. Like all yards of the period, they were merely waterfront tracts of land where keels were laid in the open and men worked without the protection of buildings.

Facilities for handling freight were almost completely lacking. The few wharves were of the most primitive sort and could accommodate only the smaller craft. Most cargoes had to be lightered, a slow and expensive proc-ess at best and doubly so in the swift currents of the East and North Rivers. Arrivals and departures ran well below those of Philadelphia and con-tinued to do so down to the outbreak of the Revolution, despite the fact that the latter port was usually icebound one or two months every winter.

As previously noted, New York's situation was due in large measure to social conditions. The patroon system had tied up hundreds of thousands of acres of the best and most accessible land of the province; the later English grants on a princely scale, such as Robert Livingston's 150,000 acres, extended the evil. It had the effect not only of concentrating an undue proportion of wealth in the hands of two or three dozen men, but of prolonging that concentration indefinitely. Concentration of wealth in the hands of a few, however, quite aside from its tendency to discourage initiative, means a certain deficiency in the purchasing power of the many, even though the difference may not be great, and this, in turn, means a reduction in volume of commerce.

Nevertheless, it was only a question of time before the port's strategic position would make itself felt. The old order would pass. In spite of every obstacle, land would be developed; production and exportable sur-pluses would increase and commerce rather than land speculation would seize the center of the stage. The process would be stepped up by the in-flux of new blood from New England, where commerce had long been the principal interest, as well as by immigrants from abroad, Scotch-Irish, Huguenots, and others, whose chief reason for emigrating was that they felt they were as good as the next man, and, what is more, were determined to prove it.

By the end of the first quarter century, the port's notable families included the Alexanders, Beekmans, Bayards, Nichols, Livingstons, van Courtlands, De Peysters, Smiths, and Willets. Most of these, and others who might be named, were substantial landowners, but as commerce increased and grew more profitable, we find them among the ranks of the merchants and shipowners. One might add that their first ventures were much more modest than generally represented. For many a year it was much more common for a Roosevelt or a Schermerhorn to sell a gallon of Madeira, a few fathoms of rope, or a yard or two of Calcutta goods over the counter than to auction off a shipload of imported merchandise.

Philadelphia's early freedom from Indian troubles was a factor in the rapid development of her excellent farm lands, and with large exportable surpluses, trade boomed. Because of her late start, her population was slightly under that of New York in 1700, but it included very few blacks. By 1725 it had increased to upwards of 10,000, only a couple of thousand or so less than that of Boston.

From the first, great attention was paid to manufactures as well as trade. The town had shipyards and a ropewalk less than ten years after settlement, but in the meantime it had built sawmills, flour mills, established brickyards, made provision for a glass works and a paper mill, and was exporting flour, bread, grain, and lumber to the West Indies. Tobacco was an important item from the first. Fourteen cargoes were reported shipped to England in 1689.

The port had four shipyards in 1700 and was reported to have launched a total of 300 vessels besides small craft by 1710, although it seems probable that this achievement should be credited to the entire area, rather than to Philadelphia alone. However that may be, shipbuilding and shipyards increased until in 1724 the port launched 19 vessels aggregating nearly a thousand tons, and the Penrose and West families had established shipbuilding dynasties that were to last well into the nineteenth century.

By that time a system of wharves had been constructed second only to that of Boston, whose Long Wharf had been the wonder of the Western world. Philadelphia merchants could handle and store cargoes as safely and economically as any in America. The Quakers were meeting the promise of future greatness a trifle better than halfway. Aside from Quakers, the town contained a larger proportion of Swedes, Germans, and

Huguenots than any other colonial town. There were also a few Jews, Irish, and Welsh. It was a mixture that ensured vigorous competition, whatever form its activities might take.

Early prominent families included those of the Quaker shipmaster Richard Norris, who was one of Penn's trusted friends, Nicholas Waln, Thomas Wharton, Isaac Norris, Nathan Stanbury, and Levi Hollingsworth. There were also the Mifflins, Hills, Millers, Powells, Prices, Chandlers, Eldridges, Pembertons, Dickensons, and Fishbournes. The Biddles, Reads, and Chevaliers were non-Quakers. The wealthy Edward Shippen had been a Boston Congregationalist, but when he became a Quaker he also became an ex-Bostonian by request.

Hard in the wake of these came a score of future notables; skippers, craftsmen, shopkeepers, indentured servants, men who were to found some of the colony's leading families during the next quarter century. Many of them were plain working men. Thomas Fisher was a cordwainer, Paul Morris a sailmaker, Thomas Shoemaker a carter, George Coates a saddler, Jonathan Palmer a bricklayer, Evan Thomas a stable keeper, George Mifflin a bolter, George Emlen an innkeeper, Richard Clymer a mariner. One might extend the list indefinitely with the certainty that every name would stand out in Philadelphia's record for a century to come, and not a few to the present day. Men like Alexander Woodrop, John Cadwallader, Thomas Lawrence, John Price, George Claypole, and Andrew Sims left descendants who were helping with notable success to make Philadelphia the first city of the land when the Revolution broke.

Farther south the picture changed. One stepped across the borders of Pennsylvania and Delaware into a different—an almost feudal—atmosphere. The original permanent settlers of Virginia had been principally adherents of the Church of England, and in Maryland, Roman Catholics. To a greater extent than in New England they were possessed of substantial means, or failing that, were socially influential. Many of them were younger sons, cadets of the landed gentry of England, and their interest centered on the establishment of large, manorial plantations, on the order of those in the West Indies, a method of development favored by conditions. The soil, in general, was more productive than the thin, stony soil of New England. One early northern visitor described it as "champion land."

Aside from Virginia's briefly troubled period leading to the Indian massacre of 1622, there had been no external pressure to form compact settlements for defensive purposes, and the terrain, with its great tidal rivers and deeply indented bays, made large trading centers superfluous. Ships could moor at a hundred points convenient to several plantations, discharge and load, and save the cost of extra handling and transportation. The attractions of plantation life, its satisfying profits, and the problems incident to combining slave and skilled white labor, were among the factors which combined to retard the development of large manufacturing centers.

As a result neither Maryland nor Virginia developed ports with populations comparable to those of the North until the British army drove a parcel of Philadelphia merchants out to the thriving village of Baltimore. Socially and economically, the chief distinguishing characteristics of the two colonies were the little crossroads trading centers and the huge plantations with neighbors living several miles apart. Larger towns served mainly the purposes of local government and the trading convenience of the poorer whites. There were comparatively few shipyards and those were employed chiefly in repairs and the construction of small craft for use on Chesapeake Bay. A few large vessels were built and owned locally but foreign trade was conducted principally in English ships. A number of English merchants maintained branch houses in the two provinces.

The only large southern port in this period was Charles Town, South Carolina; hereafter referred to by its present designation, Charleston, adopted in 1783. Its early development was conditioned in some degree by the fact that the Carolina terrain made a central trading point highly desirable, and partly by apprehension of trouble with the Spanish in Florida. The first settlers lived in a huge fortification fronting the Ashley River.

Estimates for the eighteenth century vary greatly but in 1725 the town's white inhabitants could hardly have exceeded 2500 and probably numbered considerably less. The principal merchants included the Amorys, who traded principally to Boston, the Clapps, Manigaults, Colonel William Rhett, and Thomas Pinckney. Foreign trade, conducted almost exclusively in English vessels, was especially heavy with the West Indies. Coastal traffic, which was relatively small, was handled mostly by New England vessels and merchants trained in New England counting houses, several of whom had settled in Charleston at an early date.

By 1682 considerable quantities of naval stores—tar, pitch, turpentine and resin—were being exported to the Barbados, Jamaica, and the Caribbee Islands. Cultivation of rice began toward the end of the seventeenth century and came into heavy production shortly thereafter. It was reported as forming part of 17 foreign-bound cargoes in 1707. Indigo, destined to become one of the colony's most profitable crops, was not grown until 1744. Other exports consisted chiefly of tobacco, timber, and timber by-products, none of which involved skilled labor.

By the close of 1725 the pattern of development of the original colonies (aside from Georgia which was not officially settled until 1733) was established as it was to stand until new and incredibly vast sources of power were tapped a century later.

Population, now increasing with ever-accelerating rapidity, had passed the half million mark. One estimate placed it at 600,000 in 1727. New England, with approximately 180,000, less than 5000 of whom were slaves, had a larger white population than either the middle or southern group of colonies. The population of Maryland, Virginia, and the Carolinas was slightly greater than that of New England, but it included 50,000 blacks. That of the middle colonies was about 150,000. It was evident by this time, therefore, that in spite of her remarkable increase, New England was being overhauled slowly and surely by the other colonies.

On the other hand, New England's shipping still constituted more than two-thirds of the colonial merchant marine. Boston, with 12,000 inhabitants, as compared with New York's 7500 and Philadelphia's 10,000, was still the most productive shipbuilding center. Construction in the latter ports was increasing with somewhat greater relative rapidity, but the same was true of the smaller New England ports. Since their yards greatly exceeded in the aggregate the yards of the middle and southern colonies, it was altogether probable that the maritime leadership of the area would not be seriously challenged for years to come.

Nevertheless, New England's disadvantages in the matter of natural resources were serious; so serious, in fact, that by this time they were playing an important part in shaping her future and indeed the destinies of America.

She had already utilized her timber to the utmost in shipbuilding and the export of lumber, and had developed her fisheries to their practical limits. With her relatively small area of tillable land she had turned more and more to manufacturing as a means of supporting her large and growing population. It was not enough. It fell short of supplying the needs of families which produced offspring by the dozen, and in addition were handicapped by the necessity of feeding yearly swarms of hungry immigrants.

Only one resource remained. That was the export of surplus youth itself to greener fields and richer pastures. As it turns out, it not only helped solve the immediate problem, but proved one of New England's most important contributions to the building of America.

Migration was one of the striking phenomena of eighteenth-century colonial life—farm boys heading west for more fertile lands; young mariners "fetching up" in the newer ports to the south'ard where their services might be in greater demand; ambitious clerks just "out of their time," looking for "shoestring opportunities" where conditions were still fluid; planters' sons lured by tales of the fabulously productive soil beyond the hills.

This migration was going on everywhere, but nowhere on a greater scale than in long-settled New England, where even marginal lands were occupied and profitable trade largely pre-empted by long-established houses. All through the years the youth of New England went in droves. They went everywhere; not only to New York and Pennsylvania, but to a greater extent, possibly, than is generally realized, to the deep South. And where they went, they carried the New England way and philosophy and exercised an influence out of proportion to numbers.

More than a century later, De Tocqueville noted the fact in his familiar statement to the effect that although the State of Connecticut was entitled to but six Representatives and two Senators in Congress, he had ascertained that more than four times the number then serving had been born in that state. "You may laugh, Gentlemen," he continued, "but Connecticut, that little yellow spot on the map, is one great miracle to me."

The explanation, apparently, did not lie in any natural superiority of the New Englander, but in the training and experience already noted, plus a philosophy that equipped him to meet more effectively the demands of colonial life. Broadly speaking, he was of the same stock as the settlers of the middle and southern colonies, but for the most part he faced more difficult conditions than they did. On land, it was the difference between the sterile hillsides of New England and the broad farms of the middle and the rich plantations of the southern colonies. Afloat, the difference was even more pronounced.

Sea life—whatever else might be said of it—was superior to other occupations in the development of stamina, self-reliance, and the habit of decisive split-second action. The colonial forecastle preceded the one-room schoolhouse, and its first lesson was that marked resourcefulness and iron-clawed determination and hard-driving energy were essential to mere survival. Second graders learned that further steps, leading to the achievement of a modest competence, involved the exercise of those qualities beyond the generally accepted limits of human endurance and capacities;

plus a tolerant, if not always sympathetic, understanding of other ways and other people.

Men possessing such characteristics are the stuff of leaders. Their standards become the standards of the community, however observed in the breach. Their opinions shape public opinion. With a sound leaven of such men, whatever values New England might assign to other things in the early eighteenth century when the lightest work was still hard, and the longest days all too short to complete the indispensable tasks, and danger was everywhere, it was all but inevitable that resourcefulness and speed should come first, with speed—an objective as yet almost unnoted by the Old World—well out in front.

In whatever light we view the matter, it was evident that by 1725 a margin of superiority in speed, however slight and whatever its cost in lives and human suffering, had played some part in setting the northern colonies on the road to economic independence. Whether the trend would last; whether it would weaken or strengthen; whether, if maintained, it would prove sufficient to carry the colonists through the trial of wars and intensification of repressive measures that the next half century would bring, remained to be seen.

CHAPTER II

∽ *1726-1774* ∽

The Policy Pays Off

"Some futyre day shall crown us, the masters of the main."

OUR colonial merchant sailor had need to recall the old prophecy quoted above as the eighteenth century slowly revealed its perils.

Although the pattern of colonial maritime development, as noted, was established by 1725, that statement conveys but a faint conception of the realities involved: the remarkable acceleration of that development; its significance; its impact on civilization. It holds no hint of its cost in lives and suffering; in toll of ships and cargoes and wreckage of fortunes. It presents no picture of that unending procession of men and boys who sailed away through the long years to lie in plague-ridden forecastles; to endure undreamed privations and dangers; to ride the hurricane; and to return sea-changed—strong, great-hearted men, tempered to meet the threat, in whatever guise, of sudden, swift destruction with that calm assurance which outranges the most stubborn determination.

Change, for better or worse, had been and was to continue the distinguishing characteristic of the colonial contribution to a relatively static world. And it involved more than new, unforeseen emergencies; more than new enterprise; more than the adoption of improved methods or invention of new means. Intangible values were being affected. It is perhaps too much to say that ethical standards were being undermined, but they were certainly undergoing an almost imperceptible transformation; a transformation, moreover, which tended to divide the colonists into more and more sharply defined classes, although the extent to which it proceeded during the eighteenth century, in New England, has sometimes been overstressed.

In the North, indeed, and especially in rural New England which still included nearly nine-tenths of the inhabitants, the early vision of a land of modest homesteads, of families living in frugal comfort, of a competence for old age slowly acquired by hardy, personal industry, still

33

beckoned the great majority. Shipbuilding, manufacturing, and merchandising were still generally regarded as modes of subsistence rather than sources of wealth.

On the other hand, the proportion of those who had acquired wealth in excess of personal needs, as needs were then understood, continued to increase in slowly enlarging ratio. Their example was not lost. The lure of wealth, with its emancipation from grinding toil, grew more potent and spread in ever-widening circles through the years. Its pursuit led some into real estate speculation or the more useful manufacturing field. For others, it pointed to the slave trade or privateering—occupations which sometimes led to activities not readily distinguishable from even less reputable ventures; activities backed, moreover, here and there by ostensibly respectable individuals.

It has been a somewhat general practice to dismiss such matters, and especially the slave trade, with the comforting reflection that the standards of the day regarded them as permissible and even praiseworthy. As a matter of fact, those standards were far from universal in the eighteenth century. A great many, both North and South, and especially in Virginia, were strongly opposed to the slave trade, regarding it as a harmful institution foisted on the colonies by England for the profit of her merchants. Influential colonists petitioned the British government repeatedly to forbid the merchants of Bristol and London to send slaves to America. Even as late as 1774, Virginia asked that the Liverpool slave trade be abolished.

Moreover, the practice represented the reversal of earlier opinion, brought about by that growing urge to get wealth by any means, which resulted in the "South Sea Bubble" stock swindle of 1720, and the almost incredible corruption which characterized the British government of the eighteenth century. Elizabeth of England had been outraged long before by the suggestion that the ships of free England should engage in the slave trade. New England had slipped a long way from tough-minded Elizabeth, to say nothing of the "Kingdom of God in the Wilderness," when she encouraged her merchants to send their ships to the Gold Coast, and her clergy were advertising slaves for sale. Even the old diarist, Sam Sewall, turned an "honest" penny by it when more engrossing occupations, such as the pursuit of rich widows, permitted, and the "Cradle of Liberty" itself, Faneuil Hall, was built in part at least with the proceeds of Peter Faneuil's slave trade.

After 1725 it is possible to get a more detailed, though far from complete picture of the provincial merchant marine. America's first newspaper, the *Boston News Letter,* established in 1704, carried a considerable part of the shipping news which has survived from that period. James Franklin's *Boston Gazette* entered the field in 1719. Andrew Bradford's *Weekly Mercury,* founded in Philadelphia the same year, and William Bradford's *New York Gazette,* first published in 1725, enlarged the service. Following these, the number of newspapers increased fairly rapidly.

For many years their marine reports were fragmentary. With rare exceptions, only foreign arrivals and departures were noted. The ports of the other colonies were considered to be foreign. Coasters, that is vessels trading between the ports of any given colony as distinguished from those trading between colonies, were not reported. Nevertheless, the over-all result was to shed considerable light on the volume and character of the eighteenth-century trade and the men who conducted it.

Thus, the *Boston Gazette* reported the arrival of 81 vessels during the four weeks ending Sunday, May 22, 1726, a period of the year when trade normally was brisk. The same papers were much concerned with the life and adventures of the pirate, Captain Fly, whose body, neatly preserved in tar, was hung in irons on Nick's Mate, a small island in the outer harbor of Boston, the following July as a warning to all good sailormen frequenting the port of Boston.

Of the 81 arrivals above mentioned, only one was from England. Nearly half were sloops, among them the New York regular traders commanded by Arnout Schermerhorn and John and William Beekman, names destined to draw plenty of water later on. Eight of the sloops were from the Carolinas, and one from Maryland. The latter was commanded by Job Prince, later merchant and founder of a line of merchants from Boston.

A partial list of Boston's master mariners of the day reads like a nineteenth-century roll call of her merchants and industrialists: Captains Andrew Sigourney, Timothy Cunningham, Jacob Boardman, Isaac Woodbury, Benjamin Easterbrook, John Cheesebrough, Thomas Hatch, John Sampson, Jabez Gorham, and many another. Skipper Sam Adams had already made his contribution. He had a son born in 1722 who was to achieve a more enduring reputation as Sam Adams, the Patriot.

Most of Boston's leading seventeenth-century merchants were gone— William Tailler, Anthony Stoddard, Andrew Belcher, Thomas Clarke, Major Robert Keayne—but their places were filled. Among the newcomers Daniel Johonnot, a Huguenot, was a prominent distiller and slave trader, and Jacob Wendell, a Dutchman from Albany, was one of the wealthiest men of the town. He was one of the chief sufferers in the great fire of 1760 which swept away all his numerous warehouses with their contents. Messrs.

Palmer & Balston and George Bethune were very active; the former in ship chandlery and dry goods and the latter in dry goods. Edward Gray was the largest manufacturer of cordage in the New World.

By 1726, Boston, New York, and Philadelphia vessels were frequenting most of the important Western Ocean ports—among them Amsterdam, Rotterdam, Hamburg, Bordeaux, Belfast, Bristol, London, Lisbon, Gibraltar, and several Mediterranean cities; Guiana, most of the British, French, and Danish islands of the West Indies; and all the principal provincial ports, including those of Newfoundland. It followed as a matter of course that much of the traffic was illegal.

The trade of the southern ports was much less diversified, and a much larger portion went to England and the British West Indies. North Carolina accounted for most of the traffic with the northern colonies.

Even on the long deep-water routes nearly half the vessels were sloop rigged. A few were schooners and the rest square-rigged, brigs, snows, brigantines, and ships. The bark rig was rarely mentioned, and then usually to describe any of a variety of small craft without reference to rig. However, many of the vessels then listed as ships would be described as barks today. The prevalence of the sloop was dictated by considerations of economy rather than by the character of the trade for which it was intended. Roughly speaking, they cost one-third as much to rig and required one-third the crew of a ship of equal tonnage. Many of them, indeed, were as large as small ships and were sent on long foreign voyages.

Joshua Hempstead of New London, for example, noted quite incidentally in his diary about this time that he used a 65-foot spar with a diameter of $17\frac{1}{2}$ inches for a sloop of ordinary coasting size that he built for one of his sons.

After 1725 the commerce of New York and Philadelphia shows a steadily increasing tendency to creep up on that of Boston, although for a considerable time their trade was relatively small in proportion to population. For approximately the same period in 1726 as noted above for Boston (late April-early May), New York reported 13 arrivals, or less than one-sixth the number of Boston arrivals. Philadelphia's record for the same interval was 22 arrivals. Even with a generous allowance for omissions in the returns of the latter port, the discrepancy remains substantial. However, by 1735 it was clear that the gap was closing, with Philadelphia occasionally reporting eight to ten or more arrivals in a week.

Dutch sea captains still commanded many of the New York vessels. In addition to those already noted, Samuel Ten Eyck, Johannus (or John) Van Pelt and Jacob Kiersted skippered sloops in the coastal trade. John

Aspinwall, Gabriel Ludlow (son of the regicide judge, Edmund Ludlow), and John Neilson, the Irishman, were among the early commanders whose descendants were to figure in New York's future.

Merchants who attained a status of more than normal importance early in the period included John Alsop, who died in 1761, Samuel Bayard, a Huguenot, Sam and John Broome, whose family name survives in one of the city's streets, John Cannon, the Goelets, James Desbrosses, John Lawrence, Philip Livingston and Cornelius Kortwright. Just behind them came the Franklins, Walter and Sam; Peter Remsen, a Dutchman; the Welshman, Francis Lewis; and Robert Murray, the Scottish Quaker, who was credited with being the largest shipowner in New York in 1769. To these names one might add a score of others, still inconspicuous, but destined to surpass in post-Revolutionary days the wealth and sheer business magnitude of all who had preceded them.

In Philadelphia, the principal master mariners during the second quarter century and later, were Henry Wells, John Price, Joseph Bird, John and Richard Sims, John Norris, John Howell, Joseph Scattergood, Stephen Piper, Richard Evans, and John Parker. A majority of them were descendants of earlier mariners and merchants. The merchants included John Bartram, Samuel Bowne, Joseph Wharton, Evan Morgan, Richard Clymer, George Calvert, John Cadwallader, William Fishbourne, Samuel Cooper, and Reese Meredith.

Here, as elsewhere, it is to be remembered that the distinction between merchant and mariner frequently means little. Many merchants were sea captains who ran their own retail and wholesale stores and warehouses between voyages. There is substantial evidence pointing to the conclusion that a large proportion of merchants made one long or a couple of short voyages a year and "kept store" the rest of the time, at least during the early part of their career. A sound sea training, indeed, was considered an essential part of the experience to be acquired by one who aspired to become a merchant. Many of the Revolutionary patriots, including Benedict Arnold, were merchants who had sailed in their own vessels as masters and supercargoes.

Marine columns were not only incomplete, but they rarely went into the details that would be of special interest today. Exceptions to the rule of barren brevity occurred in cases of piracy, when long accounts were printed under the heading "Horrible Outrage," or in stories of shipwrecks, to which attention was usually directed by the arresting caption "Melancholy Incident." Occasionally, however, the port had a gala day and the printer threw off all restraint, at least to the extent of a couple of sticks of fine type. September 11, 1726, was a day of notable activity for New York, and the next *Gazette* reported:

> Yesterday Four Vessels arrived here, Viz. Two ships from Rotterdam with about 300 Palatinates. A brig and a sloop from Jamaica and Bermuda. Two more ships were to sail from Rotterdam in four or five days after these came away, with Palatines, one of them for New York, the other for Pennsylvania.

The death of a noted merchant or sea captain furnished another excuse for breaking the unwritten rule. When the news came to Boston that Samuel Appleton had died of smallpox at his lodgings in London during the preceding December, the *New England Weekly Journal* for March 10, 1729, published a long obituary, of which the following extract indicates the substance:

> A gentleman of ample fortune, great merit and rare and uncommon abilities . . . taken off in the prime of life at a time when he was carrying on the New England trade beyond what any man of his country had done before him.

Nearly a century later a Boston Appleton was still one of the city's great merchants and one of the principal promoters of the port's first two transatlantic packet lines.

Activity was increasing in other New England ports. Salem was listing two or three "foreign" arrivals weekly, Marblehead about the same, and Portsmouth one or two. Newport, with Captains James Brown, Dan Nicholson, Joe Rhodes and Henry Stanton, was second only to Boston, with New London not far behind, thanks to the "horse jockey" traffic, stimulated by the thirst of the natives. Every little settlement from the District of Maine to Greenwich, Connecticut, was by now making a weekly, fortnightly, or monthly contribution to the swelling tide of trade, besides launching its own vessels or branching out into such small manufacturing ventures as weaving and distilling; the making of shoes, hats or pig iron; the packing of beef, pork, and other provisions—all things formerly left largely to Boston.

All in all, it was evident by 1726 or thereabouts that decentralization was under way, and since Boston was the center, she would, of necessity, be the chief sufferer.

Commerce and shipbuilding, however, continued for some years to grow so rapidly that the port continued to expand, although relatively it was losing ground. By 1735, it was building from 30 to 40 large vessels annually, measuring, in the aggregate, 5000 to 6000 tons. The output included a generous proportion of those built in the colonies for British account. That this was no small matter is indicated by the fact that as early as 1725 the master builders of the River Thames had memorialized

Whitehall, complaining that their business was in a declining way and their workmen were emigrating because the colonies were furnishing England with ships.

The memorial, apparently, was "filed for future reference," for even Boston, the chief offender, continued to grow. By 1735 the town's population had risen to 16,000. It increased only slowly to 17,000 in 1740; remained at approximately that level for several years; and then began a long decline. By 1765 it had dropped to 15,500, although the population of the province continued to double every 25 years.

Such a reversal of trend appears the more remarkable in view of the fact that no other coastal town of importance showed a decrease during the period, save temporarily due to fire, pestilence or the exigencies of war. Marblehead had become a thriving seaport of nearly 5000. Salem had upwards of 4000; Dartmouth, Massachusetts, 4500; Portsmouth, New Hampshire, about the same; Newport above 9000; and New London, Connecticut, 4000. Nantucket, Newbury and York, in the District of Maine, were on the move. It has been said that the commerce of Newport exceeded that of New York during the year 1769-1770, but if the marine columns furnish a trustworthy guide, the ports were never very far apart at any time in the third quarter of the century.

Bostonians attributed their loss of trade and population principally to inequitable taxation. They pointed out that the town had been charged with payment of one-sixth to one-fifth of the taxes of the entire colony, when it had a virtual monopoly of trade and manufactures, and that this proportion continued to be exacted after business had ceased to be profitable. As a result, nearly half the town's taxables, *i.e.*, the group comprising the most prosperous and energetic citizens, had moved to other towns and engaged in direct competition with Boston, whose merchants were handicapped by the necessity of paying much greater taxes, amounting in many cases to 500 pounds and more per annum. Moreover, those who remained were additionally burdened by a great increase of paupers, the direct result of loss of business. As a result, where the town formerly spent a thousand to fifteen hundred pounds annually for the care of the poor, it was now compelled to spend from ten to twelve thousand pounds.[1]

Petitions to the General Court for relief appear to have been disregarded. It is possible—even probable—that the facts were exaggerated, but that serious discrimination existed, which brought bankruptcy and suffering in its wake, is proven by the record. The growing ability of the smaller ports to engage more extensively in trade and manufactures in some measure explains Boston's failure to retain her original commercial and industrial standing, but it does not explain her loss of population when all other towns were gaining. Whether this result was intended by representatives of the Crown acting at the behest of British merchants is another matter. Many of the citizens of Boston thought it was, and were convinced that it was part and parcel of a deliberate plan to weaken the town.

Bostonians, indeed, were a truculent lot when it came to dealing with a governing class their grandfathers had left England to escape, and which, after a century, they found once more snugly saddled on their backs. Nothing illustrates the fact better than the instructions drawn up for the guidance of their representatives to the General Court in 1744, with particular reference to the proposed taxation of the town. The original draft as submitted by Sam Adams, James Allen, Sam Wells, and others of the committee, included the following:

> We cannot Suppose, because in some extraordinary times, when a Party Spirit has run high, there have been some Abuses of Our Liberties and Privileges that therefore We should in a Servile manner give them all up. And have Our Bread and Water measured out to us by those who Riot in Luxury and Wantonness on Our Sweat & Toil and be told perhaps by them that We are too Happy because We are not reduced to Eat Grass with the Cattle.[2]

The paragraph was eliminated in the final draft, but possibly for diplomatic reasons rather than because it conflicted with the sentiments of the voters.

However that may be, there can be no doubt but that the period was one of growing strain, caused on the one hand by increased smuggling on the part of New England, and on the other by more determined efforts to repress it, instigated by the English merchant. A feature of the illicit traffic which greatly exasperated the English merchant was the practice of the northern colonies of sending their ships directly to Marseilles and Toulon:

> Laden with pitch, tar, train oil, timber trees and planks for building ships, spars, staves, logwood, beaver, martin, deer and elk skins, furs and naval stores, and have returned back again, without ever touching in Great Britain, with goods of the growth and manufacture of France and other foreign nations.[3]

New England was the chief and, aside from New York and Pennsylvania, the only important offender, as the following figures tend to indicate. In 1769, 49 vessels sufficed to handle the exports to Great Britain from the entire area which now constitutes New England. During the same period, 330 ships were required to carry the exports of Virginia and Maryland alone to the same destination. Even South Carolina required 140 ships. It is perhaps obvious that the figures do not prove that New England's illicit trade amounted to ten times that of the South, but they do suggest a wide divergence in the practices followed by the two areas.[4]

Another grievance was that the New Englander demanded cash of the British planter in the West Indies, and then went to the French and Danish islands to purchase their return cargoes of rum, sugar, and molasses.[5]

The New Englander might have answered that it was the only way in which he could meet the huge debit balance of his trade with England, but as a matter of fact his smuggling went a trifle farther than that. Regardless of right and wrong, there can be no doubt but that the northern colonies were prospering greatly, and to a substantial degree through defiance of the law. Southern colonies continued to prosper chiefly because their products, especially tobacco and naval stores, were still in short supply.

Perhaps nothing furnishes more striking evidence of the growing power of New England than the Louisburg affair of 1745. This fortress, the strongest French post in America, had long troubled the colony. Though there was nominal peace between France and England for 30 years after Utrecht, the Indians, stirred up by the French emissaries, continued their depredations, especially in the District of Maine. The conviction spread gradually that the colony would never be free from the threat of raids featured by indiscriminate massacre while the French had a foothold anywhere on the continent.

When open warfare again broke out between France and England in 1743, New England tried to unite all the colonies in an expedition to destroy Louisburg. Failing in that, and also virtually failing in her attempt to get assistance from the British government, she determined to go it alone. It was one of the critical decisions in American history. Back of it lay a sense of power and growing exasperation which were to play a part in shaping the future. In 1745 she sent to seize the great strong point an expedition of some 4000 militiamen and several squadrons of colonial ships, upwards of 70 large vessels in all. Contrary to general expectations in England and the non-cooperating colonies, the fortress was captured by quite unorthodox methods with little delay or loss of life, save from disease. The assistance afforded by England seems to have had little effect on the result. Four small British warships were sent after the main part of the expedition had arrived at Louisburg, and later several others came and went. They captured two or three small French vessels, but acted mainly as blockaders; a service which, as it turned out, the colonial armed ships could have rendered without their help. It was essentially a New England victory and one that every schoolboy in the colony would recall when confronted later with a similar problem. They would also remember that

England restored the fortress to France after the lapse of only three years, placing their outer settlements once more at the mercy of French-led scalping parties. As one disgruntled veteran put it: "Old England got the glory and New England the broken bones."

A rising tide of immigration was also having its effect, not merely in numbers, but in character. The terrible famine in Ireland in 1740 and its repetition the following year started a flood of Scotch-Irish immigrants which lasted without intermission until 1773. For several years at the outset some 12,000 sailed annually from Belfast alone, bound for American colonies and the West Indies. After a few years most of them went to New England.

Jacobite uprisings were responsible for the migration, especially after 1715, of large numbers of Scots, principally Highlanders, most of the latter going to the southern colonies, from whence in time they worked back into the mountains of Kentucky and Tennessee. At the same time, the wars and threats of wars in Europe kept up a constant flow of emigrants from Germany and France. Holland, Switzerland, and Sweden contributed a good many, and a few Jews from various countries added another element to the melting pot. The Jews tended to congregate in New York, probably because a considerable number of their people were there already, and possibly also because the fur trade was more active there than elsewhere.

All along the line there had been advances, some of which may be reckoned as improvements. Throughout the period, and especially during the last French War, provincial ships from New England and New York had engaged in privateering on a considerable scale. Even pacific Philadelphia had a fling at it, despite her Quaker principles. The governor of the province, disregarding the wishes of the local authorities, commissioned the small privateer *George* in 1739 to offset Spanish depredations during the War of Jenkins' Ear. After France entered the war in 1743, several others were commissioned. All were successful in capturing valuable prizes. By and large, the privateers everywhere made a lot of money, but local shipowners also lost a good many ships, with the result that the net gain to the provinces was comparatively slight, although it founded a number of new family fortunes. The moral effect on the colonist, who suddenly acquired undreamed of wealth or noted its acquisition by a neighbor, through force and violence, was another matter.

Nevertheless, there was progress in every direction. A vast amount of road building had been accomplished. Long-distance travel on land was still mainly on horseback, but wagon transportation and coach travel between coastal and inland towns was increasing daily.

First transatlantic packet ship to sail from America on fixed schedule, the Black Baller *James Monroe,* 424 tons, under Captain James Watkinson, sailed from New York for Liverpool on January 5, 1818.

Ship *Hercules* of the Byrnes, Trimble New Line, New York to Liverpool; a typical Liverpool packet of 1821.

Courtesy, The Peabody Museum of Salem

Courtesy, The Marine Historical Association, Inc.

Scale model of a Hudson River sloop. This is an accurate representation of the type of vessel that composed the first American packet line to sail on fixed schedule.

Courtesy, New-York Historical Society

First notice published in America of a packet line pledged to sail on a fixed schedule. Notice dated at Albany, N.Y., March 4, 1814, and published in *The New York Gazette* and *General Advertiser,* March 14, 1814.

For NEW YORK,
To sail on the 1st of January,
The COURIER,
WILLIAM BOWNE, Master;
Burthen 380 tons.

To sail on the 1st of February,
The PACIFIC,
JOHN WILLIAMS, Master;
Burthen 370 tons.

In order to furnish more certain Conveyance for Goods and Passengers, between Liverpool and New York, the owners of the American Ships, COURIER, PACIFIC, JAMES MUNROE, and AMITY, have undertaken to establish between the two Ports, a regular succession of Vessels, which will *positively sail, full or not full,* from Liverpool on the 1st, and from New York on the 5th of every month, throughout the year.

These Ships were all built in New York, of the best materials, and are coppered and copper-fastened; they are all remarkably fast sailers; their accommodations for passengers are uncommonly extensive and commodious, and their commanders are men of great experience and activity. These recommendations, and the dependance which may be placed upon the periods of their departure, afford to these conveyances advantages of so much importance to the Manufacturing Houses, and to the Shippers of Goods generally as it is hoped will secure to them general support.

The Courier now lies at the east side of the King's Dock.—For further particulars, apply to Capt. Bowne, on board, or to

CROPPER, BENSON, & CO. and
RATHBONE, HODGSON, & CO.

(*One property*)

New Line For Albany.

The Subscribers being duly aware of the advantages that would arise to shippers of Goods and Produce between Albany and New-York, by having a Line of Sloops formed to ply between the two places, to sail on set days, have therefore purchased three of the first rate Sloops, viz. the *Gold Hunter,* to be sailed by Capt. Martin, the *George,* Capt. Ostrander, and the *Hardware,* Capt. Weller. One to sail from Albany every Saturday, and one to sail from New York every Saturday, and one of which will be in New York ready to receive freight at all times, as she will arrive before the other leaves.

We solicit the patronage of our friends and a generous public, requesting them to call on James Keeler & Co. at their Store, no. 46, on the Dock at Albany, and on board the Sloops, at Lent's Basin, New York.

We pledge ourselves that nothing shall be wanting on our part to carry the foregoing into effect with the strictest punctuality and attention.

James Keeler & Co. have a fire proof Store on the Dock, in Albany, no. 46, Adams & Rathbone, No. 13, Hudson street, and John Clifford, no. 8 Hudson street, for the reception of Goods or Produce for all those who wish to store and have forwarded—and will transact all kinds of Commission Business.

J. & A. Townsend, Adams & Rathbone, John Clifford, James Keeler, Horace Lockwood, and Jasper S. Keeler.

N B. The *Gold Hunter* will sail for Albany, as soon as it is ascertained that the River is open.

Albany, March 4, 1814. m14

First notice published abroad of the establishment of the Black Ball Line between New York and Liverpool; the first transatlantic packet line warranted to sail on schedule. Published in the *Liverpool Mercury,* December 5, 1817.

Courtesy, Seamen's Bank for Savings

Packet ship *Orpheus,* showing her in winter rig with short fore and mizzen topgallant masts.

Packet ship and pilot boats.

Courtesy, Seamen's Bank for Savings

A regular overland mail service between Boston and Williamsburg, Virginia, had been instituted in 1738, the carrier making the trip in four weeks. Stage coaches were running out of Boston to Newport and other towns. New York had established a stage line to Philadelphia. The character of its service can be judged by the fact that some 25 years later, shortly before the outbreak of the Revolution, when a new line of light coaches made the run between New York and Philadelphia in two days, they were advertised as "flying machines."

Rough though the roads were, and almost impassable at times, they were better than most English roads of the same period. The service they accomplished in opening backwoods areas, enabling pioneers to get their produce to the seaports, and booming commerce generally, can hardly be overestimated. In Pennsylvania alone, by mid-century, thousands of wagons were jolting over the roads that led to Philadelphia, many of them coming from points a hundred miles away.

By this time the foreign commerce of Philadelphia had overtaken and passed that of New York. During 1750 the reported arrivals at Philadelphia totalled 320, as compared with 302 for New York. Boston arrivals for the same period were 562, with two weeks missing, showing that although her relative position was weaker, she still maintained her lead by a substantial margin. Her relative volume of coastal trade, including as it did the District of Maine, was probably even greater.

Manufacturing was making tremendous strides. Despite British prohibition, great forges, ironworks, and flour mills were springing up in every direction. Large quantities of hats and shoes were being produced. Production of cloth of all sorts had been stepped up. Home weaving was still the rule, but it had been organized by small capitalists who supplied thread and yarn, and collected and marketed the finished product. As an instance of the efficacy of the method, it was noted that Lancaster, Pennsylvania, had produced 27,739 yards of cloth in the year ending May 1, 1770,[6] quite a bit more than might have been produced by women weaving simply for their own homes.

In New England, optimistic inventors were turning out improved tools, Yankee notions, and labor-saving devices by the score. This meant that trade was not only increasing in volume, but it was changing in character, becoming more sophisticated. The brief list of early staples had been augmented by dozens of luxury items, a few of which were made by local craftsmen, but most of which were imported. About the time of the great fire in Boston, which broke out March 17, 1760, and destroyed 349 buildings and several ships, John and Jonathan Amory were advertising an itemized list of merchandise amounting to half a column of fine print.

Thomas Handasyd Peck had just received by the latest arrivals from London and Bristol a glittering array of hatters' trimmings. Five houses were importing books. Samuel Hewes, Isaac Hawes, Moses Deshon, Caleb Blanchard, Lewis Deblois, John Hancock, and Benjamin Church were constant importers of a great variety of merchandise. John Cunningham, in Cornhill, in the second house north of School Street, specialized in dry goods. John Cutler, at the sign of the Golden Cock, in Marlborough Street, carried a superior line of fusees, muskets, and bayonets, as well as a general line of cutlery. Nathanial Loring, ship chandler, whose descendants were to participate in founding the greatest cordage factory in America, did a large business in Russian duck and imported cordage.

As the period drew to a close, more and more familiar names appeared among the advertising merchants of Boston. John Gerrish & Company had a large stock of dry goods at the Auction Hall, near the Town House. Samuel Eliot returned from London with a great shipment of raven's-duck, pistol powder, wool and cotton cards, *etc.,* for his shop at the head of Dock Square. John Rowe notified the public that the ship *Hannah,* at Rowe's Wharf, about to sail for London, could accommodate a few passengers. Ward Nichols Boylston, in King Street, sold dry goods, glass, powder, shot, and nails, "a Great Pennyworth." Samuel Adams & Company specialized in English and India goods. John Gore and Samuel Gray were well-known merchants in the years preceding the Revolution. John Adams and Company filled their store "nearly opposite the Old South Church" with a peculiar assortment, in which tea, sugar, and spices mingled with logwood, redwood, and various oddments.[7]

Few merchants, even those who frequently sold large quantities in a single transaction, disdained the pettiest sort of retail business. Samuel Abbott, whose descendants became wealthy, was quite willing to talk to any prospective three-shilling buyer about the merits of his English and India dry goods. And, in truth, he had enough to talk about. English broadcloths, plushes of several sorts, jockeloys, grandurels, durants, starretts, montees, dorseteens, cotton velvet shapes, birdseye, camlets, pink, crimson, and cloth colored tammies, silk knee-straps, yellow and white none-so-pretties, stay strapping and galloons, figured messinetts, lutestrings, blue, black, crimson, and pink figured modes, drab, claret, and black qualities, made but a beginning on his London importations. He still had an imposing array of curiously named and long-forgotten India fabrics in reserve for lovely shoppers in their none-so-pretties.

Many of the merchants still were retired sea captains. We would not go far wrong in assuming that all were descendants of shipmasters and had made at least one or two voyages as supercargo, to learn the ropes. The conviction that a firsthand knowledge of foreign ports and customs was an indispensable part of a merchant's equipment was still universal, and it was still widely held down to the close of the nineteenth century. Many, like Captain Richard Tripp, whose store was near the drawbridge, and Captain Benjamin Waldo, who was located on Long Wharf, continued to combine the two professions.

New York's census of 1771 gave the city a population of 21,863, putting it well ahead of Boston and indicating that it had more than doubled in the preceding quarter century, while the New England metropolis had been losing ground. Progress in commerce and shipbuilding in New York was only slightly less pronounced.

The port, in 1774, had ten shipyards and a number of master shipwrights competent to build first-class vessels of the largest size. Totten & Crossfield were building superior ships, ranging from 200 to 300 tons and upward for the European trade, some of them for English account. The port also launched several of the English "Post Office Packets"; fine armed brigs which had to conform to the highest standards of naval construction. Thomas Cheeseman was perhaps the most noted builder of the period. His *Maria Wilhelmina,* of approximately 1000 tons, a three-decker launched in 1774, was the largest merchant ship launched in America at that time and for many years to come.

In manufactures also, the city was forging ahead. It had an iron furnace, turning out large quantities of ironmongery of various sorts, sugar refineries, ropewalks, and brass foundries, and had even ventured to build a steam engine. It constructed the first engine made in America for its infant waterworks in 1774 and maintained it in successful operation until after the occupation of the city by the British in 1776. Richard Deane's great distillery was in Murray's Street between the college and the North River, and there were several other distilleries in the town. James Webb was manufacturing grindstones at the end of little Queen Street on the North River, a humble occupation, but so essential that without it no genuine pioneer could have ventured far from the waterfront.

By the time the first Revolutionary committees were organized and the more radical of the Saturday night bathers were beginning to think of themselves as "Patriots," a good many new figures had appeared in the front ranks of the port's merchants and shipmasters. Many of them, however, came from old land-holding New York families, who had in comparatively recent years become impressed with the advantages of commerce as a means for the more rapid accumulation of wealth.

Among them the Rhinelanders were starting a new career destined to become outstanding among half a score of notable careers then getting under way. Their store was located at the corner of Burling's Slip where Sam Burling also had a shop. Jay & Barclay had a store on Roosevelt's Wharf. In 1774 they added a new store at the Albany pier. John Schuyler was in business at Great Dock Street. Mercer & Schenck's dry goods establishment was in Hanover Square, then and for fifty years to come, the business center of the city.

One might mention another hundred names without exhausting the list of merchants then regarded as important, and several times as many who were regarded by themselves as important. Henry Cuyler & Company were "heavy" merchants in the Virginia trade. David Van Horne had new rice for sale. At the "Horse & Cart," in Horse & Cart Street, David Phillips offered rum "by the wholesale and retail."

Most families active half a century earlier were still represented in business and shipping circles. Dennis Hicks was trading to New Bern, North Carolina, in the schooner *Polly*. Peter Schermerhorn was navigating the brigantine *Betsy* as a regular trader to Charleston, South Carolina, descending thereafter by slow degrees to the status of banker. Sam Wright had the brig *Charleston Packet* in the same trade. He, too, was getting ready to found a dynasty. One might mention Captains Thomas Randall, John Watkins, John Waddell, and 300 more, most of them among the founders of the New York Marine Society.

The important place held by master mariners in the community at this time is strikingly exemplified by the record of that organization. Founded in 1770, with active membership restricted to sea captains, its membership at the outbreak of the Revolution consisted of 326 captains and 255 merchants and public officials, the latter being considered as associate members. The list, both of captains and merchants, includes a remarkable proportion of the most prominent families of present-day New York.

Among the merchants, Anthony L. Bleecker had a vendue store where he sold wet and dry goods. The Van Zandts & Ketelas "kept" near the Coffee House. They dealt in Mount Hope pig iron, Honduras mahogany, old Madeira, gunpowder, port, and dry goods. Sam Bayard, Jr., on one day had 300 barrels of Canada pease on his hands. William McDougall wished to dispose of a general assortment of merchandise at the corner of the Fly Market, in Maiden Lane. Further south in Queen (now Pearl)

Street, Robert Hyslop's store stood next to the residence of Robert G. Livingston, Esq. The Lawrence, Goelet, Franklin, and Lennox families, hard by, were still heavily engaged in commercial activities. It would be a long time before they began to think of zoning laws.

Jews also were moving into the upper circles. The growing list included the native New Yorker, Benjamin Hendricks, who married the daughter of Hayman Levy, fur trader. Theophilacht Bache was a very prominent and wealthy merchant. Isaac Moses was also very wealthy and an ardent patriot. His contributions to the Continental cause during the Revolution were equalled by few.

Most of the business houses and a large proportion of the inhabitants were still huddled below Wall Street, an area then barely half its present size. The North River flowed along the edge of Greenwich Street on the west, while on the east the water came within a few yards of the present Pearl Street. Toward the south, the land extended only a few feet beyond the present Customhouse. The best residences were along lower Broadway and on Broad and Whitehall. Several were little short of palatial in size and quality. A majority of the well-to-do, however, lived over their stores in the simple but substantial Dutch houses: brick buildings with high-peaked gable ends to the street. Most of them vanished in the great fire of 1835.

All in all, New York had come a long way in the quarter century preceding the Revolution. It was estimated that the port was handling one-tenth of the foreign trade of all the colonies combined, although it rarely sent more than 40 vessels a year direct to England with local produce.

Nevertheless, as 1774 passed into history, Philadelphia still maintained a lead over New York in foreign commerce by a slight but narrowing margin. Their precise relative positions are difficult to determine, since reports vary and original official records have disappeared. Franklin, in his famous examination before the House of Commons, stated that in 1766 the province exported goods to England of the value of 40,000 pounds, while her imports from England during the same period amounted to 500,000 pounds sterling. As against this, we are informed by the *New York Gazette* that in 1769 Pennsylvania's exports to Great Britain amounted to 705,500 pounds, while New York's totalled 526,000 pounds. During the same year Boston sent more ships to Great Britain but the value of the goods they carried was only 370,000 pounds.[8]

The striking discrepancy in the above figures indicates the difficulty of determining the exact situation, although we are probably justified in assuming that the *Gazette's* figures were supplied by customs officials and are substantially correct. Nevertheless, one wonders whether in 1769 specie and bills of credit did not form a substantial part of the town's exports.

Arrivals at Philadelphia from 1771 to 1773 averaged slightly less than 400 a year, or about three times as many as in 1726. The later vessels, moreover, were much larger, aggregating 46,000 tons as against 6600 tons for the earlier year. Square-rigged craft made up nearly half the fleet, and the proportion of sloops had been greatly reduced. All things considered, we are probably justified in assuming an increase of not less than 500 per cent in the city's foreign trade during the half century, and this without allowance for unreported smuggling, which undoubtedly was of substantial proportions.

In shipbuilding Philadelphia was second only to Boston. During the latter part of the period her shipyards were launching 25 large vessels and upwards each year, many of which were built for foreign account. The province afforded a vast supply of superior ship timber and her shipwrights quickly established a reputation for superior workmanship. The number of vessels owned in whole or in part in Philadelphia—roughly 2500 during the 25-year period—did not greatly exceed, if indeed it equalled the number owned in New York, but Philadelphia vessels averaged somewhat larger in size. According to Governor Tryon, 709 vessels belonged to the port of New York in 1772.

A list of the prominent merchants of Philadelphia just prior to the Revolution would include George Bartram, Joseph Dean, William Miller, Robert Wilson, Alexander Tod, Caleb and Amos Foulke, and Joseph Carson. John Cadwallader was reputed to be the wealthiest, with Archibald McCall not far behind. He was a heavy importer of East India goods. There was Edward Shippen, whose beautiful daughter Margaret was to marry a dashing young general named Benedict Arnold. A few, like Captain Isaac Cox and Captain Sam Mifflin, still retained their seagoing titles. Levi Hollingsworth kept a store on Stamper's Wharf. Anthony Morris had a store and wharf near the drawbridge.

Descendants of most of the old families were still active—the Morgans, Prices, Edgars, Fishers, and Pembertons. Thomas Willing was one of the notables who drove about town in a coach, but there were 84 others, including Joseph ("Duke") Wharton, Tench Francis, Henry Kepple, Henry Hill, Samuel Shoemaker, William West, Jacob Lewis, and George Emlen, Jr. Williams & Eldridge and John & Clement Biddle were prosperous firms. Daniel Benezet was one of the more prominent Huguenot merchants, and had been for a quarter century.

Of the other ports, Salem was steadily increasing its trade, sparked by Bowditch, the Crowninshields, and "King" Derby, plus the growth of population in its general area. Newport had passed its peak, for it had no large tributary area which could not be served by the growing commerce of Providence and Bristol. New London and, indeed, most other New England seaports were booming, especially following the peace of 1763.

The volume of commerce in the Chesapeake area was increasing, but owing to tremendous advances elsewhere, it was declining in relative importance. On the other hand, ports farther south were on the upswing. Wilmington, the largest town in North Carolina, maintained a considerable and rapidly expanding trade with all the principal northern cities, surpassing Charleston, South Carolina, in this respect.

Nevertheless, Charleston, by reason of its huge foreign trade, was by far the most important commercial center of the South. It was the third port of America in 1774, being surpassed only by Boston and Philadelphia. White population was probably somewhat less than 5000, with approximately 6000 blacks. Josiah Quincy, who visited it in 1773, noted in his diary:

> The number of shipping far surpassed all I had seen in Boston. I was told there were then not so many as common at this season, though about 350 sail lay off the town. . . . The town is beautiful and in many respects magnificent . . . far surpassing anything I ever saw or expected to see in America.

Among the merchants most active at the time of Quincy's visit, the following were especially prominent: Mackenzie & Tunno, Dupont, Brewton & Company, Samuel Prioleau, Jr., Roger Smith, Bonneau & Slann, Hall & Smith, Jamieson, Simons & Company, William Donaldson, William Glenn & Son, Ledger & Greenwood and Israel Joseph. Some of these were still active when trade was resumed after the Revolution.

Henry Laurens, one of Charleston's most successful merchants and one of its most respected citizens, had already retired when Quincy visited the town. He went to London in 1771 and was one of the 38 colonists who advised Parliament against passing the Boston Port Bill. He was later President of the Continental Congress, succeeding John Hancock in November, 1777. In 1779 he was captured while on his way to Holland as American Minister and was later exchanged for Cornwallis.

Rice and indigo became extremely important crops after 1750, adding tremendously to the value of Charleston's exports. Cotton was first exported to England about 1754, the exact date being disputed. The amount, however, was insignificant and although shipments to the northern colonies were made from time to time, it did not become an important item until after the invention of the cotton gin in 1793, when it rapidly replaced tobacco as the principal crop.

Imports covered a wide range and in both character and quality indicated a degree of luxury unsurpassed, if not unequalled, elsewhere in the colonies. Direct trade with Great Britain and Europe was carried on chiefly through London, Amsterdam, and Bordeaux. That with Liverpool, then a rising city of 35,000, was small in comparison with its eventual importance. It was handled largely, if not exclusively, by the Liverpool slavers. Coastal trade was especially heavy with Philadelphia and New York because of the prominence of those ports in the flour industry. Elsewhere, Madeira and the West Indies accounted for a large part of Charleston's pre-Revolutionary shipping activities. The town does not appear to have engaged to any extent in Mediterranean trade.

Savannah, Georgia, had not as yet come into its own. The colony was officially settled in 1733 when 152 immigrants arrived, although a few English squatters had drifted into the area during the previous year. Development had been very slow and erratic. Fire, pestilence, and the ever-present menace of Spanish invasion had, at times, greatly reduced its population and even threatened it with extinction. On the eve of the Revolution the number of inhabitants, including slaves, probably did not exceed 1500, and of these less than a fifth remained when peace was declared. It was to become the first cotton port of America, but in 1774 that day seemed far distant. Trade with northern ports was light, rarely employing more than a ship or two a month.

When "the embattled farmers fired the shot heard round the world," a century and a half had elapsed since that memorable 4th of July when Winthrop and his little band watched the *Blessing of the Bay* slip down her ways into the waters of the Mystic River. The intervening years had witnessed almost incredible material changes in the English colonies of America, but the preceding 25 had eclipsed all previous records.

There had been numerous ingenious improvements in the design and rig of American vessels, due to the constant pressure for ever-greater speed and economy of operation. Many special types, especially of the smaller sort of coasting and fishing craft, had also been developed all along the coast. Nevertheless, it was left to Great Britain and Europe to introduce two innovations which were to prove of incalculable value to the shipping world.

One was the steering wheel, the precise origin of which is in doubt, but which may have appeared first in France. However that may be, its use on English ships dates from 1705, or thereabouts. Thereafter, it gradually supplanted the ancient tiller and whipstaff on large vessels.

The other was copper sheathing, which effectually checked the ravages of the dreaded teredo, the cause of the loss of many a stout ship. It was first used on the British frigate *Alarm* in 1758. Because of its cost, its use spread slowly and was confined for many years almost exclusively to warships. Throughout the first third of the nineteenth century, indeed, its use on American merchantmen was so exceptional that the fact a ship was coppered was advertised as a special inducement to shippers and prospective passengers.

Population had more than doubled since 1750, and now stood at two million whites and half a million blacks or thereabouts. Most of the white increase was the result of natural growth, although immigration had been heavy for many years and was still on the upswing. Despite a tendency toward cosmopolitanism, the colonies were still essentially homogenous. In Pennsylvania, indeed, the influx of German settlers had given some concern. Since the early 1740's nearly every year of peace had brought from one to three thousand Palatines, and occasionally more. Once six thousand came. Franklin and others were of the opinion that they were good farmers, but unaccustomed to liberty, and might make a troublesome use of it. As it turned out, the Franklinites made most of the trouble.

Growth would have been more rapid but for a death rate that would now be regarded as appalling. Repeated epidemics of smallpox, yellow fever, putrid sore throat, otherwise known as diphtheria, ship, or palatine fever, and the bloody flux decimated the inhabitants of the larger towns from time to time, and sometimes almost wiped out smaller settlements which had neither physicians nor medicines. Ravages of war accounted for other thousands, with Indian massacres and camp diseases claiming most of the victims. Hardship, overwork, and exposure took their toll. Comparatively few attained the Biblical span of three-score years and ten. In general, persons of 50 were regarded as aged.

The area of settlement had vastly increased. Where a few widely scattered groups had clung almost desperately to the shore, thousands of pioneers had now penetrated far inland and were moving westward, beyond the divide—heading into the great mid-continent expanse that was to become "the breadbasket of the world." In their wake they left chains of villages, loosely strung on crude but adequate highways. Comfortable homes with broad, cultivated acres had replaced lonely cabins in tiny stump-blackened clearings. Pioneer and permanent settler worked as few men had ever worked. Their produce rolled eastward in an ever-swelling tide to fill the holds of a thousand ships. Even so, the overland trail was too slow and expensive for the ramping, sea-conditioned New Englander who knew that his ships could carry supplies at a trifling fraction of the cost of oxcart transportation. He charted an all-water route which would open the entire Mississippi Valley at a single stroke. Companies were formed for that purpose, not unlike the later organizations which rounded the Horn in the gold rush of '49. General Lyman's band of "Connecticut Military Adventurers" arrived back in New York early in August, 1773, in the sloop *Mississippi* after an absence of six months. They had explored the Natchez country on the east bank of the Mississippi, found it to their liking, and laid out 23 town sites.[9] As a result of this and other less pretentious explorations, an important and commanding section of the South was in process of settlement by Yankees while the southern planter was still slowly pushing through mountain forests hundreds of miles away. Long before New Orleans was fully open to American trade, northern ships were running regularly and in substantial numbers to Natchez and nearby ports, advancing by years the development of the middle west.

In spite of Britain's blanket disapproval and specific prohibitions, the northern colonies were manufacturing virtually everything produced by the craftsmen and industrialists of Europe. Many of the items required a high degree of technical skill and knowledge, such as glass and pottery, tools, paper, lamps, watches, clocks, pots and pans, all sorts of clothing from hats to leather breeches and from silk stockings to shoes and splatterdashes, candles, oils, powder and shot, tin, brass and copper ware, furniture, coaches, saddles, and carts and wagons by the thousand.

As yet the plants were small, rarely employing more than a dozen or twenty men and boys, and usually only a journeyman worker or two and a couple of apprentices. The day of huge steam power plants was still in the distant future. Quantities produced were also small in relation to the country's needs, but the shops were everywhere, and increasing in number. Organization was on the march. Men were learning the art of management and the science of production. The thing was sparked and stimulated by a lively desire for economic independence. All in all, from the standpoint of 1774, it seemed only a question of time until domestic manufactures would overtake demand and exportable surpluses would become available.

Nor were America's industries confined to small articles. Substantial quantities of iron were being manufactured. Taunton, in Plymouth colony, which had been smelting iron since 1653, was now turning bog iron into the massive try-pots used by whalemen, and something like mass production of harpoons and other whaling gear was under way. Several establishments were casting cannon and forging anchors. Superior iron ores were being mined and smelted from the Catskills to Virginia. John Jane was making a fine grade of steel in West Jersey. Large mills all through the middle provinces were turning out hundreds of barrels of flour each week and booming the export trade of New York, Philadelphia, and the Chesapeake ports. The ironworks and flour mills around Baltimore were transforming that village into a city. Hemp canvas and linseed and flax-seed oils were manufactured in considerable quantities.

In the South, the production of turpentine and other naval stores was conducted on a broad scale. Aside from the universal gristmill, lumber and woodenware production, and shipbuilding, it was the South's only venture of importance into the manufacturing field. The establishment of every new enterprise, on however small a scale, raised problems which had to be solved by resourceful ingenuity. Each, as it came into being, stimulated the founding of others, suggested new lines of endeavor, or led to inventions that sometimes revolutionized an industry.

In nothing, however, had the colonists manifested greater interest or efficiency than in the construction and operation of ships. Precise figures are wanting, owing to the loss or removal of official records. Nevertheless, such fragmentary information as we have enables us to estimate the size of the colonial merchant marine at the close of the period with sufficient accuracy for practical purposes.

Thus, notwithstanding England's tax on colonial oil, designed to destroy her competition, New England led the world in whaling. By 1774 her fleet consisted of 360 vessels, averaging 90 tons.[10] Nantucket had 150, the rest being divided between several ports, with Sag Harbor, Long Island, with its predominantly New England population, in second place. Her fishing fleet consisted of about 600 staunch vessels.

Reports from various sources throw added light on the matter. Governor Tryon's estimate of New York shipping in 1772 has already been noted. We are informed that 11 of the original colonies employed 309,534 tons of shipping in 1770.[11] *Lloyd's Register,* in the year 1775, listed 2311 craft, aggregating 373,618 tons, which had been built in America during the preceding three years.[12] This was considerably more than half the number (3908) built in Great Britain during the same period, and with due allowance for the limited construction then under way in Canada, it indicates an almost incredible degree of activity.

As a further check we have an occasional official customs report. For example, the collector for New London, Connecticut, one of the minor ports, credited the town in 1774 with 92 vessels which employed 495 sea-

men. Salem, with a population of 5000 had 200 seagoing craft and upwards. We also learn from newspaper items published from time to time
that from 100 to 300 or more seagoing vessels were occasionally assembled
in the larger ports.

It is, however, to the port of Philadelphia that we are indebted for the
material that constitutes our most complete and convincing check on
pre-Revolutionary maritime conditions in America. In general, aside
from a few registers and enrollments, principally from the smaller New
England ports, the entire body of colonial customs records has disappeared. Philadelphia is the only exception. An apparently complete, and
certainly substantially complete, list of her shipping during the important
half century from November 7, 1726, to April, 1776, has been preserved
and reprinted in the *Pennsylvania Magazine of History and Biography,*
volumes 23 to 28, inclusive. It comprises a total of 2515 vessels, only a few
of which are duplicates.

From it we learn that only 100 vessels were registered in the first four
years of the period. Their aggregate tonnage was 3114, or a trifle over 31
tons per vessel. The largest was a ship of 300 tons, and the smallest a
shallop of four tons. The great majority registered less than 30 tons, and
a considerable proportion of the larger vessels were owned abroad, wholly
or in part.

In striking contrast, the last 100 vessels of the list were registered in the
14 months ending March 7, 1776, as compared with the first period of four
years. Moreover, they aggregated 7559 tons, or an average of 75 tons per
vessel, indicating that in half a century the rate of Philadelphia's maritime
growth had accelerated nearly 1000 per cent.

Nevertheless, the proportion of large ships continued to be almost
insignificant. The entire list contains only one of 400 tons, and only
two of 300 tons, and one of those was a captured Frenchman. Only 23, or
less than one per cent, exceeded 100 tons. It is further to be noted that of
the last 100 vessels in the list, 43 were built in New England; and finally,
that by far the greatest increase in rate of growth came after the Peace of
Paris, in 1763.

From such evidence as is now available, it seems probable that with the
exception of Boston, which differed chiefly in volume rather than in
kind, the foregoing indicated with reasonable fidelity the shipping conditions which prevailed throughout the northern colonies during the greater
part of the eighteenth century, prior to the Revolution. Boston differed in
that she built and operated a much greater proportion of craft of the
larger size. Also, for historic reasons, her fastest growth, relatively greater

prosperity, and greatest relative importance came before the middle of the century. After 1750, the maritime growth of New York and Philadelphia and many of the smaller ports outpaced that of Boston. After 1763, the differential was even more pronounced.

All things considered, we are probably justified in estimating the colonial merchant marine in 1774 as comprising upwards of 4000 seagoing vessels, aggregating not less than 300,000, and possibly exceeding 350,000 tons, in addition to a large fleet of small craft ranging from 5 to 20 tons. It included a modest proportion of ships of 200 and a few measuring 300 tons and upwards.

However conservatively one may estimate the material achievements of colonial America, it is difficult to escape the conclusion that on the whole, and with due recognition of England's tremendous industrial expansion of the eighteenth century, New England and the middle colonies had developed, and in 1774 were continuing to develop, more rapidly than any land in Christendom. In this connection, moreover, it is well to keep in mind two facts: first, that it was a balanced, well-rounded growth, extending to every important known field of endeavor; second, that in the main it was made possible by maritime activities which provided, roughly, nine-tenths of the all-essential cash and credit.

The South, too, was developing with remarkable rapidity, but in her case growth was one-sided. It was made possible in the first instance by profitable crops, and naturally—perhaps inevitably, under existing conditions—the southerner plumped for more and greater plantations. Shipping and manufacturing were left more and more largely to the North with the passing years, and because of their influence on future developments, rather than by way of invidious comparison, it is to be noted that they were occupations calling for more highly developed skills as well as greater initiative and resourcefulness. Incidentally, they provided insurance of a sort in the event of agricultural depressions, a fact to be impressed unpleasantly on the South 50 years later.

Whether the moral and intellectual progress of the colonist was keeping pace with his material achievements is less clear. Undoubtedly, in respect to the basic values of self-reliance and the acceptance of full individual responsibility, there is evidence of a certain falling away. More men were accumulating large fortunes; large, that is, for the day, and more and more men were yielding to the urge to accept the employment of the new capitalists with its promise of greater ease, comfort, and security. It was a step the logical end of which was a certain subordination of the individual to the control and direction of another, a return, however disguised or justified, to the chief of the evils responsible for the first great migrations.

As the last statement implies, there was nothing new in this. Both trends, as moral forces, one placing the highest value on self-reliance, and the other favoring conformity, had been operative since the dawn of civilization. Even in hardheaded, hard-working New England, they had been present from the start. That was understood. What was still undecided was which, in the end, would dominate public thought. On the answer to that question hung the future of America.

Without attempting at this juncture to supply the answer, on which there would be little agreement in any case, we have to note that the trend toward conformity was less marked in New England than elsewhere. One reason, the fact that men of wealth and position had been relatively more numerous in the middle and southern colonies from the start, has already been indicated. As against this, wealth had increased mightily in New England in the eighteenth century, but as yet it was more evenly distributed than elsewhere, and possessed more largely by men who had come up from poverty by the exercise of hardy self-reliance, the very bedrock of the Puritan philosophy.

Fine, even magnificent, mansions had multiplied. Comforts had increased all along the line. The grandson of the man who had brewed his own kettle of beer on his cabin hearthstone now had casks of brandy and Madeira in the cellar of a home that in our time would still be regarded as attractive. For Sunday wear he had substituted a pair of fetching plush inexpressibles, or their equivalent, for granddad's leather breeches. Nevertheless, the great majority of New Englanders lived on a common plane. Aside from an insignificant number—the governor, the clergy, and a few of the exceptionally wealthy, and their opposites in the social scale, the drones and criminals—everyone worked, and worked hard and long.

This work business is something to consider. It was the crucial fact in preserving the essential Puritan principle, whatever else may have gone into its shaping.

For the men who worked habitually 12 or 14 hours a day at the hard, physical toil without which the America we know could never have been built, personal achievement was the highest test of worth. Compared with that, the two-hour sermon on Sunday, or the occasional glimpse of a bewigged great man bumping along in his lumbering coach weighed but a trifle. Your workaday merchant-manufacturer, farmer-seaman reserved his greatest respect for the man who swung the heaviest hammer, cut the widest swath, or stowed the most cargo. Whatever encroachments time and the desire for ease or wealth or power had made on it, the thing was still a mighty force in 1774. It goes far to explain why a farmer decided, without benefit of high-level instructions, to cock his old flintlock at Lexington and found the same warrant sufficient for the Concord episode.

That there was then a "Brahmin class" is indisputable, but it is easy to overestimate its numbers, wealth, and influence. It is to be remembered that its members wrote the books. Naturally, they wrote about themselves. Before the Revolution the northern colonist who controlled a few hundred pounds "quick assets" was considered well-to-do. The five-thousand pounder was wealthy. Even his betters had little ready cash. Most of their property consisted of real estate, stock in trade, a few bills of exchange (some doubtful) and a share in two or three vessels. Their transactions were normally on the basis of long-term credits—6, 12, 18 months, and sometimes longer. A single broken voyage or a bad fire could, and frequently did, put them into bankruptcy. The seizure of one of his little smuggling sloops made even wealthy John Hancock wince.

One cannot ignore and should not belittle their contribution to the building of America. What they did was essential. Some of it, perhaps, could not have been accomplished by men of lesser means. This should not be permitted to obscure the fact that for every great capitalist of New York, Boston, and Philadelphia, there were scores in those ports and a hundred smaller centers, possessed of slender means, whose contribution in the aggregate was vastly greater. Much the same can be said of shipbuilding. Boston, America's greatest shipbuilding center prior to the Revolution, had 14 yards. New London County, in Connecticut, had 20, and a similar condition prevailed along the coast from the District of Maine to Pennsylvania. Moreover, the smallest towns turned out as large ships as any of the greater ports. Nor was that all. They played a part in proportion to their numbers in developing faster, more efficient craft, vessels which could do more than merely meet the competition of foreign ships. It was a vital factor in the commercial development of the colonies.

Speed had been a matter of grave concern to the Puritan from the beginning. His weakness had made him the natural prey of the warships and privateers of Europe, whose vessels in general were larger, more heavily armed and carried more men than he could afford. Piracy was another risk. Also, on occasion, he found it advisable to avoid the ships of his own navy. To cap all, his prosperity depended on his ability to make faster voyages than his competitors. Speed was the only answer. How he got it has been variously explained.

The remark is sometimes made that the lines of America's early fast vessels were derived from the Bermuda sloop. Admitting the similarity, it would be more accurate to say that both harked back to a common parent, a parent lost, moreover, in the shadows of antiquity. The truth is that the principles of fast sailing design had been the common property of shipwrights for centuries before the settlement of America. Bermuda's contribution consisted merely in minor refinements calculated to obtain a slight increase in speed.

New England's case was no different. Her shipwrights made slight experimental changes in angles and proportions, but they invented no new principle. Reference has already been made to the striking similarity between their seventeenth-century fast vessels and the nineteenth-century "Baltimore clipper," as indicated by specifications in their earliest building contracts.[13] New England built more ships of that type than other localities, but her chief contribution was "hustle."

Of the few colonial logs which have survived, a surprising proportion record speeds well in excess of the average speed of early nineteenth-century merchantmen. Instances of small, heavily loaded craft making 8, 9, and 10 knots hour after hour are common.[14] The log of the ship *Duke of Cumberland* shows that while on a privateering cruise out of New York in 1759, she made from 9 to 9½ knots on several occasions, and on the 15th of May she ran 201 miles, making from 8 to 9½ knots throughout the 24 hours.[15] Nor were such runs confined to isolated cases of single vessels. Hempstead, for instance, noted in 1712 that an entire fleet of colonial transports made the passage from Boston to New London, Connecticut, a distance of 200 nautical miles, in about 30 hours, a performance that would still be creditable for modern sailing yachts in racing trim.[16]

All in all, the old Puritan philosophy, long accepted by saint and sinner alike, and perhaps in somewhat less diluted form in New England than elsewhere, had paid off, and that for five generations. Now, in 1774, in the face of a common peril, its influence had never appeared stronger or more widespread. How it would stand the test of a great war; whether it could meet the changed conditions that war would inevitably bring about; or whether it would itself be changed beyond recognition, only time would show.

CHAPTER III

∾ *1775-1814* ∾

The Test of War

"Without a king, we trace the unbounded sea,
And traffic round the globe, through each degree."

AN ANSWER of sorts, whatever it might hold of truth or permanence, was not long delayed.

If the colonial merchant marine did not win the Revolution, it did the next best thing—it saved it. One can hardly overestimate the part played by the privateers and letters-of-marque built and equipped by the merchants and fought by merchant sailors. Even the Continental Navy was merchant marine almost to the last ship and man. Quite aside from the mariners' material contribution—the military stores they captured, powder, shot, guns, clothing and provisions, single cargoes often aggregating hundreds of thousands of dollars in value—the moral effect of their spectacular achievements was little short of decisive.

Through the long, dreary stalemate on land, the privateersman's hammer strokes, a thousand times repeated, not only held the wavering patriot line, but did more than anything else to spread the disaffection among British merchants that ultimately forced their government to make peace. Maclay, an able and conservative writer in the field of American naval history, voiced the opinion of several informed students when he said:

So far as the British were concerned it was our maritime forces, rather than our armies, that played the dominating part in both the war for our independence and the war of 1812.[1]

The British public had little to say about our armies ashore, but they complained long and bitterly of the havoc worked by our ships. Whether the circumstance that our soldiers were soon regimented after the continental fashion had anything to do with the matter, the fact remains that our privateersmen were not; on the contrary, they met and solved their individual problems without help of tradition or regard for accepted practice.

American warships and privateers have been credited officially with taking upwards of 800 British prizes during the war. The figure is probably grossly inadequate. Salem privateers alone took 445 prizes, and there are many instances of single privateers capturing from a dozen to twenty or more vessels. Captain Harraden did even better. With a 14-gun ship, he captured vessels mounting altogether over a thousand guns in his eight years of service. The success of the Yankee privateers is indicated by the fact that there were 449 in commission in 1782, the last year of general activity.

Nor does this tell the entire story. A great many prizes were released after being relieved of the more valuable portions of their cargoes, usually because the captor lacked men to take them into port, or because they were required for use as cartels. The privateers also cut off the flow of a substantial part of England's raw materials. Her navy, in particular, was greatly handicapped before the end of the war by lack of suitable mast timbers from the colonies.

In another respect, privateering success undoubtedly had much to do with bringing about the French alliance, with its Yorktown finish. The French were an eminently practical people, but they also loved a dashing fighter. One can hardly visualize the diplomatic success of Franklin and his associates if they had been unable to point to fairly satisfactory proof that, man for man and gun for gun, the colonials could turn British bunting upside down with gratifying regularity.

We are not concerned here to trace the course of that conflict, but rather with its bearing on the future of the American merchant marine. From that standpoint its most important effect was speeding up three trends which had been observable almost from the beginning and which had been slowly accelerating for several generations. These were the improvement of shipping, the centralization of ownership and management, and the development of manufactures.

Increased risks and the lure of huge profits in the event of a successful voyage redoubled the efforts of merchants, shipbuilders, and masters to improve the design and rig of vessels. Lines were fined out; royals set over high t'gallants; extra stuns'ls blocked in, and the "Old Man," although sometimes in the sere and yellow thirties, proceeded to give ten thousand farm boys sailing lessons that put them forever out of conceit with time-honored land speeds. We would not go far wrong, probably, in assuming that the Revolution produced American ships that added another full knot to the average speed of pre-Revolutionary fast vessels. Aside from that, it did much to confirm America in her already unique tendency to place speed at the top of the order—a tendency even then beginning to attract attention abroad, and which was to infect the entire world eventually.

An equally important result in its ultimate effect was the acceleration of concentration of ownership of vessels. Nothing, perhaps, illustrates the remarkable development of that trend more than the fact that between the close of the Revolution and the end of 1800 some 40 huge ships were built in the new Republic. They ranged from 400 to upwards of 1000 tons in size, with 18 well in excess of 500 tons, and that in a day when 300 tons was still reckoned a great ship. Most of them were owned by not more than two or three individuals, and several by single merchants.

The trend, as indicated, was not new. It had been operative from the first, quickened now and then by a series of lucky voyages in unsettled conditions (or by remunerative privateering and slaving ventures) but on the whole developing almost imperceptibly. The Revolution, however, which turned hundreds of privateers loose to prey for years on the richest commerce of the world, had enabled a few merchants to pile up large fortunes. Much the same thing happened on land, frequently under less creditable circumstances, what with war profiteering and trading with the enemy. As a result the number of those able to build and operate large ships and even entire fleets singlehanded was increased, while at the same time a large proportion of merchants and masters had become badly crippled or completely impoverished. The great whaling fleet, for instance, was virtually wiped out.

Accordingly, it is not surprising that after the Revolution the proportion of those registered as sole owners of several great ships should increase. Nor is it surprising that a far larger number were compelled to start afresh in humble colonial fashion; cooperating with friends and neighbors in the construction and operation of little sloops and schooners, the cheapest of all craft to rig and operate but the least suitable for long voyages, and for that reason foredoomed to the cheapest and least profitable trades.

Such a situation could not fail to stimulate the growth of class distinctions. It also had other results. The merchant of great wealth could establish his own branch house abroad or make favorable connections which freed him from the necessity of relying on the business judgment of his shipmasters. It was no longer necessary for him to man his vessels with friends and neighbors. He was, in short, no longer bound by practices which had gone far to ensure a fair division of profits; to check brutality and ensure conditions most favorable to the encouragement of young seamen and the production of officers of the highest type.

When, in the course of time, his estate passed to his heirs, it frequently happened that they were men who knew nothing of the problems and hardships of sea life, and whose only interest in the operation of ships was to secure the largest possible profit from every venture. Such a situation paved the way to something not unlike absentee landlordism in its ultimate effects. The transition was very slow, so slow as to be virtually imperceptible from year to year. It took another two or three generations to turn the native-born American completely away from the sea, and even then other important factors accelerated the process.

There can be little doubt but that the thing would have come to pass eventually, in any case. All that can be said with certainty is that the Revolution, and the other wars in which the country was involved from time to time, hastened the process by successively increasing the concentration of wealth in the hands of a few.

A third important effect of the Revolution was to stimulate the development of manufactures. This came about in part because of the necessity of replacing goods, importation of which was cut off or greatly reduced by the British blockade. It was also fostered by the tremendous increase in war prices, which made it possible to establish industries and conduct experiments that would have been impractical under normal conditions.

The trend was especially marked all along the coast from the Merrimack to Baltimore, with the exception of New York Town which was occupied in 1776 by the British and continued to be held by them until after the close of the war.

Growth of manufactures in Massachusetts was so rapid and varied that in 1787, in spite of a heavy increase in population, she imported less than half the amount of manufactured goods that she had imported 20 years earlier.[2] It is true that importations were reduced that year by a mild reaction to the post-war boom, but with due allowance for that fact, the discrepancy was highly significant. In Connecticut, a "flourishing manufactory" at Hartford was turning out a superior quality of woolen goods in such quantities that by the latter part of 1788 they were being distributed over a considerable area of the Republic. The output included fine "Hartford serges and Hartford greys" and a popular line of bottle greens and browns, as well as other colors.

Philadelphia and Baltimore and adjacent areas had made tremendous strides. Both had established a large number of flour mills and a variety of ironworks: forges, slitting mills, foundries, and nail and wire factories. They also engaged in other manufactures, including steel, glass, pottery, and paper. Immediately after the war it was noted that America was producing all her needs of paper and half her steel, while the export of flour had become an important factor in the development of her commerce.

The definitive treaty of peace was not signed until the 3rd of September, 1783, but resumption of trade did not await that event. It even anticipated the signing of the preliminary articles at Paris on the 30th of the preceding November. American shipmasters in European ports, confident that the step was imminent, began to sail for America in the fall of 1782.

It was a bad winter on the Western Ocean and long passages were the rule. The first to arrive of which I have found a record was the brig *Thetis,* Captain Wattles, which reached New London on the 4th of January. Wattles had sailed from Amsterdam in company with the sloop *Success,* commanded by John B. Hopkins, Esq., which entered Providence on the 26th of January, after a passage of 90 days. The following day the brig *Friendship* arrived at Boston, 60 days from Gothenburg, Sweden. All were deep loaded with a pleasing variety of much wanted merchandise; assorted dry goods, chinaware, case knives and forks, looking glasses, Russian and raven's-duck, all sorts of spices; everything, in short, but gunpowder. A few weeks later the Boston house of Eaton & Benson were advertising goods imported from Nantes in the ship *Union,* "at Peace Prices."

The first arrival in England from America was Captain Mooers, who entered London on the 6th of February with a cargo of oil from Nantucket. He was bound for a French port, but learned of the cessation of hostilities and changed his destination for a market which he considered more promising. The *London Times* for February 7, 1783, noted that he was the first to fly the Stars and Stripes on the River Thames. Shortly after, the brig *Firebrand,* Captain Frazier, from Amsterdam, reported that he had been forced into Dover by stress of weather, where he lay unmolested for several days with the 13 Stripes flying, although two 74's were anchored nearby.

In New York the prison ships discharged their pitiful cargoes of diseased and emaciated prisoners on the 11th of April. Many died before reaching home and many more soon after. Rumors were flying everywhere: New York was to be evacuated immediately, or all the terms of peace had been agreed upon and the final articles signed. Every new rumor was the signal for new and more ambitious trading ventures.

Anything like a complete and accurate account of the course of American trade during the next few years is impossible. Under the Confederation each state retained exclusive supervision of its own shipping, and the official records of the period have disappeared almost completely. The newspapers, however, give a picture of activity, both in trade and shipbuilding, that apparently exceeded anything that ever had gone before. All despite the fact that a considerable proportion of the commerce was handled by foreign shipping, especially British vessels.

As late as 1790, the first full year for which we have an official record, 41.4 per cent of our foreign trade was carried in foreign vessels.[3] It is probable that earlier percentages had been somewhat larger. After 1790 the proportion of foreign shipping diminished to a temporary low of 6.9 per cent in 1796. For several years thereafter it ranged between 11 and 15 per cent, dropping in 1811 to an all-time low of 3.4 per cent.

The course of participation of foreign vessels in American trade was in some degree the result of discriminatory policies adopted by the several foreign powers, and continued until conditions created by the French Revolution forced both England and France and indeed, to a lesser extent, all Europe, to rely more extensively on American shipping. In general, prior to 1795, American vessels were forbidden to enter British colonial ports in the West Indies, South Africa, and elsewhere. Other countries permitted trade with their colonies as a rule only when they were in serious need of foodstuffs or other essential supplies. Fortunately for the States, this condition was almost chronic among some of the West Indian and South American colonies.

There were at first two outstanding exceptions to the discriminatory policies of the other nations. Lord Cornwallis, who had been defeated at Yorktown in 1781, was appointed governor-general of India in 1786. When the question arose as to admission of American ships to the ports of India, this officer, who from the first had disapproved the policies which brought on the American Revolution, said he saw no objection to their admission. His policy, however, was reversed by his successor several years later. Thereafter, of all the great fields of trade, only one, that of China, was left open and unrestricted, and the erstwhile colonists lost no time in preparing to take advantage of it.

America's first ship in the China trade was the *Empress of China,* a new vessel designed expressly for that trade by the celebrated Dr. John Peck, which sailed from New York on Washington's birthday, 1784, under the command of John Green, with Major Samuel Shaw, one of Washington's former aides, as supercargo. What is less well known is that she was built in Massachusetts, not Baltimore, as commonly reported. As her original register, like most such papers of the period, has disappeared, her tonnage has also been in doubt. However, she was stranded on the Irish coast in 1789, and to preserve her reputation came off as the ship *Clara*.[4] From the *Clara's* register we learn that the ex-*Empress* measured 368¼ tons, was 104 feet, 2 inches in length, 28 feet, 4 inches in breadth, and was equipped with quarter galleries and a woman figurehead. Oddly enough she was totally lost on the Irish coast near Dublin, February 22, 1791, exactly seven years to a day from the time she sailed from New York for China, ending the career of one of the most notable ships of the new Republic. She was commanded at the time by Mark Collins, also notable as the progenitor of still more notable Cape Cod mariners.

Both New York and Philadelphia claimed the credit for initiating the China trade; Philadelphia because Robert Morris sponsored it, and New York because the ship sailed from that port. As a matter of fact merchants of both ports were heavily interested in the ship and it is difficult to see it in any other light than a joint venture, in which equal credit accrues to both parties. However that may be, it set an example which merchants of all the principal northern ports lost no time in following, and started a traffic which contributed all but critically to the prosperity of the nation during the Federalist period. It might even be said that Boston, which quickly resorted to the fur business of the Northwest Coast as a means of carrying on the tea trade, was in some measure responsible for the acquisition of the Oregon Territory. There is no doubt whatever that the China trade in general paid a lion's share of the Federal income which alone enabled the government to make the Louisiana Purchase. That, in turn, paved the way for the settlement of the West Coast and its incorporation into the Union.

It is doubtful whether any foreign trade was prosecuted in the critical early years of the Republic with greater vigor or more uniform success. Salem sent her first vessel to Canton in 1786. Before the end of 1788 she had sent out a total of seven ships. Boston's ship *Columbia*, Robert Gray, master, returned to that port in August, 1787, the first American vessel to sail around the world. In 1789, American vessels at Canton totalled 14, and in 1796 Salem had 40 vessels engaged in the East Indian trade. The smaller ports were also active. Providence and Hartford sent ships of the largest size to Canton. New Haven sealers picked up cargoes of sealskins in the Cape Horn area and made a number of extremely profitable voyages to China.

Before these things came to pass, however, the young Republic had to travel a long, weary road. The post-war boom was soon over. A commercial depression of unwonted severity followed. Shipbuilding was at a standstill and many a faint-hearted patriot was asking himself whether independence had not been a mistake after all. Nevertheless, conditions slowly returned to normal, thanks in a measure to the adoption of the Constitution which in 1789 replaced the weak and ineffective Articles of Confederation. The prosperity that ensued was to last for 20 years, interrupted only by the ill-advised embargo of 1808. Moreover, it was a prosperity that extended to every seaport in America, small and large. Some conception of its range may be gathered from the fact that in 1789 the little port of New London had 150 vessels engaged in the "horse jockey" trade alone. A total of 6688 horses and cattle in addition to huge amounts of provisions, staves and other local products were shipped to the West Indies during the year, and this represented only a part of Connecticut's share in the trade, some of which was quite as illicit as any of the pre-Revolutionary smuggling.

In spite of those and other regrettable peccadilloes, Connecticut was to contribute to the development of the merchant marine to an extent second to none, size and population considered. For many years she was to build a notably large proportion of New York ships. What was even more important, she supplied the merchants to operate and the mariners to sail them. New York, indeed, owed much the same debt to Connecticut that Boston did to Cape Cod, and in the matter of ships it was much greater.

In the first two years under the Constitution the total Federal income amounted to slightly more than four million dollars. All but ten thousand was derived from customs duties. It increased slowly to slightly under twelve million for the fiscal year of 1801 and reached a high of seventeen million in 1808, after which the embargo caused a sharp reduction. During all this period and for many years thereafter the customs never provided less than four-fifths of the national income, and the proportion was usually nine-tenths and sometimes more, indicating the tremendous growth of America's foreign trade in the early years of the Republic.

Nor was this all. Commerce not only was increasing in value but it was changing in character with almost inconceivable rapidity. It is true that the great majority of merchants were men of small means. Most of them were still in the financial class of that energetic Boston youth, Peter Chardon Brooks, who in 1789 became the proud possessor of a modest share in a little coasting schooner. During the next five years he slowly acquired an interest in five more, the largest of which was the 88-ton

Abigail. Thereafter, his progress was little short of miraculous. He was able to retire with a large fortune in 1803 and when he died in 1849 his estate of two million dollars was regarded as the largest in New England. His record was closely paralleled by many of his contemporaries. Even before his early retirement there were scores of northern men who owned and operated from three to a dozen or more great ships.

One such merchant of the Federalist period was Theodore Lyman. He was a resident of Wells, District of Maine, just after the Revolution, but removed to Boston early in 1790. During the next ten years he had 18 vessels, 13 of which he owned outright. The ship *George,* 262 tons, was the largest. Most of his fleet consisted of brigs, brigantines, and snows of considerable size. One of his captains was the well-known Dixey Wildes.

Thomas Handasyd Perkins was another large Boston owner, contemporary with Lyman. He owned 16 vessels engaged in foreign trade prior to 1802, most of them in conjunction with James Perkins. His earlier vessels were all of medium size, the *Charlotte,* of 204 tons, being the largest. Most of his later vessels were bigger than that, however, and in 1799 he was registered with Thomas Amory, Ebenezer Preble, and others as one of the owners of the ship *Massachusetts,* then reported as measuring 616 tons, but elsewhere rated 791 tons. Russell Sturgis, a felt-maker, was associated with him in the ownership of a couple of vessels. Sturgis also owned shares in ships built for James and Thomas Lamb, and eventually became one of Boston's most prominent merchants.

Other Bostonians with extensive shipping interests during this period and later included William Bordman, John Codman, Nathaniel Fellowes, Stephen Higginson, William and Eben Parsons, and George Lane. Before 1802, Bordman had eight vessels, five of which were ships of substantial size. Fellowes had 12 and was sole owner of seven, including the 455-ton *Monticello.* Ephraim Wales was one of his captains. Higginson and William Parsons owned nine, the largest of which was the ship *Barbara,* of 238 tons. Higginson also owned three others jointly with Samuel G. Perkins. Eben Parsons was sole owner of ten vessels. John Eldridge from "down on the Cape" commanded his schooner *Mary* in 1789.

In terms of tonnage the foregoing figures are not impressive, but it will be remembered that they represent the achievements of a few years—years, moreover, when the country was rebuilding its commerce from the bottom. William Gray, whose period of greatest activity fell in the larger days which followed the War of 1812, has often been mentioned as Boston's largest shipowner. Stone credits him with 60 ships.[5] He was undoubtedly one of the port's greatest merchants, but it is doubtful whether he ever owned more than 20 vessels at any one time, and most of them ranged from small to medium in size.

Ownership in vessels was not the sole criterion of a merchant's importance. Many Boston merchants of the Federalist period owned fewer ships but nonetheless vied with the others in importance. John T. and George H. Apthorp were outstanding in their day. So were Francis and John Amory and Elisha Bangs, who bestowed his name on the renowned Bangs Pepper, and chose for his commodore the equally well-known mariner, Comfort Bird. The Coolidges were active, William, Joseph, Daniel, and others. Sam Cabot had several vessels. Thomas Dickinson had three ships, including the *Charles,* of 348 tons.

John and Ebenezer Dorr were extensive operators. Ebenezer owned eight craft of various sorts. Samuel Eliot had two, one the *Minerva,* a ship of 317 tons. The Goddards were coming along, but as yet their interests were confined to three or four small schooners. John Hancock (not the patriot) owned one ship as late as 1798. The Hunnewells, John and Richard, were founding a dynasty with the help of the schooner *President.*

There were several Lorings, Caleb being the most substantial member during the closing years of the century. Along with other activities, he operated a large distillery in partnership with Thomas Curtis. Mungo Mackay, Captain Jonathan Merry, Asa Payson, Captain James Prince, Charles, Andrew, Elisha, and Daniel Sigourney, David Sears, Daniel Sargent, Captain William G. Weld, Ezra Weston, "trader" Abiel Winship, John Winthrop, and William Wetmore, all were laying or assisting in laying the foundations of substantial enterprises. Samuel Shaw, who in company with Thomas Randall owned the great ship *Massachusetts* in 1790, was one of the first of the noted Shaw family to become prominent.

In addition to those mentioned above, a number of other members of Boston's mercantile families were still sailing as shipmasters. The Appleton family was represented by Captains Sam and Oliver. John Atkins had the ship *Thomas,* of 248 tons. Josiah Bacon owned shares in several vessels and at the same time commanded the schooner *Mermaid.* John Collins, Ephraim Delano, Moses Grinnell, Robert Emery, and a score of young, ambitious master mariners from "down on the Cape" skippered craft ranging from coasting sloops to wall-sided East Indiamen. There were even a few ex-whalemen from Nantucket and the Vineyard.

New York had suffered more severely during the Revolution than any other large port. British occupation began in September, 1776, and lasted until "Evacuation Day," November 25, 1783. The occupation not only lasted longer than in any other large port, but it was at least partly responsible for two great fires which wiped out huge sections of the town. In addition, a vast amount of private property was destroyed or badly damaged.

Most of the prominent merchants left town when the British entered, but a few remained. Some of the latter, rather surprisingly, managed to escape the solicitous post-war attentions of the patriot group, and eventually ranked among the town's leading merchants. Many of the old merchants and a good many new ones came flocking in from Connecticut, New Jersey, and upstate New York during 1783 and the years immediately following.

The most active during the early Federal period included the Aspinwalls, Alsops, Buchanans, Bownes, Isaac Clason, the Coits, Champlins, Costers, Constables, Franklins, Archibald Gracie, John Jubel, Peter Kemble, who owned a number of vessels jointly with the Gouverneurs, Leffert Lefferts, Nicholas Low, Daniel Ludlow, Robert Lennox, the LeRoys, Livingstons, Murrays, Minturns, McVickars, William Neilson, Charles L. Ogden, and the Rhinelanders. All had extensive interests in shipping.

John and Gilbert Aspinwall were sons of old Captain John, one of New York's most respected shipmasters before the Revolution and a vestryman of Trinity in 1756. Their descendants were to establish the Pacific Mail Steamship Company and to play a most prominent role in the nineteenth-century development of America. John and Richard Alsop were also descendants of an earlier John, of Dutch extraction. They were among the patriots who left town and went "up-river" when the British appeared. Thomas Buchanan came over from Scotland before the war, with another Scot, Archibald Gracie. Both ranked among New York's first merchants. Robert Bowne was a Quaker and a very large owner of shipping. He was frequently associated in ownership with the ship chandler, Peter Schermerhorn, and also with Benjamin G. Minturn and John T. Champlin.

During the 1780's Isaac Clason owned a number of large ships, including the 400-ton *Ocean*. He employed the well-known master mariners Samuel Armour, Nathan Haley, and John Ferrier. Alexander McComb and William Edgar owned the new ship *America* in 1788, a fine vessel of 700 tons and upward, launched in September at New York. Jacob Sarley, one of the outstanding mariners of the day, commanded her. Her builder Ebenezer Young is today remembered chiefly as the builder in 1791 of the *Vigilant,* one of the first revenue cutters of the United States, a forerunner of the present Coast Guard fleet.

Henry A. and John G. Coster had four large ships prior to 1800. Captain Henry Kermit, whose descendants were active in the later packet service, was master and part owner of the ship *Patriot*. He was also associated with the great Dominick Lynch in ownership of the *Lydia* and was interested in several other vessels.

It would require a volume to trace the activities of the various Quaker Franklin firms. John, Thomas, and Abraham were exceptionally large shipowners. Their best known vessel was the *Ontario*, of 612 tons.

John M. and Ralph B. Forbes had a number of vessels but only one large one, the snow *Neversink*, of 221 tons. She is of special interest, for she was commanded in 1797 by John Stanton, who nearly a quarter of a century later was to be known as the "Commodore" of the Black Ball Line. He also commanded the *Warren*, a large William Minturn ship, in 1795. Miles R. Burke, another of the packet masters, commanded Forbes' little brigantine *Union* about the same time. If they had not served as powder monkeys in the Revolution, they undoubtedly took their seafaring traditions directly from the boys who had.

Archibald Gracie was registered as sole owner of five large ships before 1802, the *Sarah*, 327 tons, being the largest. Toward the end of the Federal period, however, he had the *Canton* and the *Braganza*, measuring 409 and 470 tons, respectively.

Theophilacht Bache was one of the port's most important merchants by the time the Constitution was adopted. He was especially interested in the Liverpool trade. About the same time, Ludlow & Goold, located at 47 Wall Street, became prominent in the Irish linen trade.

Few New York families were more active in shipping than the Murrays. Robert Murray, a Quaker who owned a flour mill in Lancaster, Pennsylvania, came to New York about 1753 and before the Revolution was reputed to own more vessels than anyone else in this colony. His brother John had the foresight to acquire the farm subsequently known as Murray Hill. Robert's farm was nearby, fronting on the East River. It was his wife who was credited with detaining Lord Howe when in pursuit of Washington's army, until the Continentals made their escape. His son Lindley achieved a less enviable reputation with thousands of schoolboys by taking up his residence in England and writing grammars.

Both the Minturns—William and Benjamin G.—owned substantial shares in ten vessels during the 1790's, and acquired still larger interests. Benjamin formed a partnership with John T. Champlin and his descendants were active in the great firm of Grinnell, Minturn & Company, one of the largest and most important shipping houses of the nineteenth century.

An Irishman, John McVickar, established himself as an importer of linens shortly after the close of the Revolution. He had seven sons, one of whom was the father of Bishop William McVickar, of Rhode Island, noted as the tallest bishop of the Anglican Church in the closing years of the nineteenth century. John was heavily engaged in the China trade prior to 1800, and thereafter was a director in the United Insurance Company and other financial organizations. John Miller of 16 Wall Street was also heavily engaged in both the Amsterdam and Irish trade, sending a number of ships to Newry and Londonderry. The list of Irish merchants in the 1790's included John Stewart and Shedden, Patrick & Company.

Philip and Frederick Rhinelander owned a number of large ships; the *Manhattan*, of 667 tons, being the largest. She was commanded by John Armour. Richard Black was another of their captains. He had the *Robust* and the *Niagara*, both ships measuring slightly less than 340 tons.

All large vessels of the period engaged in foreign or long coastal voyages were as heavily armed as circumstances permitted, a fact which explains why comparatively few of the larger size were molested by European cruisers. The *Manhattan*, a 667-ton ship, was pierced for 22 guns. Ratings of 10 to 14 guns or more were common.

Parenthetically, the first voyage of the *Manhattan* to London in 1801 throws a sharp light on trade conditions in those unsettled times, when a single successful voyage often paid for the ship in full, with enough over to satisfy all but the most rapacious. The following letter from a well-known and reputable New York merchant, which appeared in the *Herald* on February 26, 1847, tells the story:

To the Editors of the *Herald:*

In your paper this morning you stated that freights were higher here now than ever known before. Facts: I have been concerned in loading two ships for Liverpool, and have received freight of seven shillings sterling per barrel for flour. Now in the year 1801, I have seen paid twenty-one shillings per barrel for freight for flour to Liverpool and London.

Isaac Bell, No. 22 Broad Street.

P.S. The ship that received the freight for London was the ship *Manhattan*, belonging to Mr. F. Rhinelander.

The *Manhattan's* rate, then roughly 1000 per cent above normal peacetime levels, was cited as an extreme instance. The average, however, which prevailed for 20 years preceding the outbreak of the War of 1812, together with the concurrent high prices, was sufficient to enable America to found a notable crop of new family dynasties and build a vast new fleet. What was quite as important, it was enough to confirm the opinion, then slowly gaining ground, that it was her destiny to become the leading maritime nation of the world.

For each of the above-named New York merchants, there were several others, masters, tradesmen and merchants, of only slightly less importance in the early Federal period, some of whom would eventually rank among the city's great. John D. Aymar was a blockmaker whose interests in 1797 did not extend beyond the ownership of a 41-ton schooner, but he founded a very substantial shipping concern. John Jacob Astor's first large vessel was the 279-ton ship *Severn,* but in 1800 his share in the craft was subsidiary to that of his co-owners, William and Charles Laight.

James Bulkley, of Fairfield, Connecticut, a town which later achieved a position of some importance in the coastal packet service, was master of the 45-ton sloop *May Flower.* Ebenezer Bartram of the same place commanded the 60-ton schooner *Lucretia* in 1797. Theophilus Brower had three medium-sized vessels. Gasherie Brasher had a couple of small vessels about the same time, one of which, the schooner *Fabula,* was described as "sharp-built," a term then usually associated with slaving or privateering. William and James Constable, together with Nicholas and Martin Hoffman, were joint owners of the ship *Atlanta.* Charles Clarkson and John Vanderbilt, "Gent.," of Flatbush, had the *Minerva,* a ship of 259 tons, commanded in 1794 by Sam Armour. Still other Clarksons had the *Cheeseman,* a blunt-ended craft, noted as one of the dullest sailers out of New York.

Another famous mariner, Preserved Fish, late of New Bedford, was also on his way to riches in 1801. He owned, in company with John Howland, of New Bedford, the great ship *Penman,* rating 447 tons. John Earl, however, was one up, with the still greater three-decker *Grand Turk,* a vessel of 564 tons. The Griswold brothers, George and Nathaniel, had come down from Lyme, Connecticut, shortly before 1800, seeking a wider field of usefulness, but for some time they operated very modestly as "in-and-out" ship brokers, rather than as owners. Nevertheless, they ended as owners of some of the noblest of the great clippers more than half a century later.

Goold Hoyt, Dominick Lynch, Sam and Walter Howell, Elias Hicks, and Stephen Jumel each owned one or two vessels. Richard S. Hallett was sole owner of two ships in 1800, including the 429-ton *Mary.* Garet Keteltas was associated with Robert, Victory, and Prosper Wetmore in the ownership of the brigantine *Letitia* and the ship *Eleven Sons.* Herman, Jacob, and Robert LeRoy owned in several vessels, usually in connection with the Bayards. The DeForests and several of the Livingstons all owned a ship or two, as did Gilbert and Anthony Pell and Nathaniel Prime.

Among those struggling for a foothold at the close of the century, Samuel Russell, a native of Middletown, Connecticut, appears as owning a small interest in a couple of brigantines. He had a share in the *Thomas Pinckney,* of 117 tons. Other owners in the same vessel included John Motley, Leffert Lefferts, and Philetus Havens, the latter being a resident of Savannah. Isaac Roget owned three medium-sized vessels, two of which were commanded by John R. Skiddy and Richard Ward.

Several master mariners, who later became prominent merchants or noted New Yorkers in other respects, appeared during the late 1780's and the 1790's. They include Andrew Foster, later a successful specialist in the New Orleans trade, who commanded the schooner *Peggy's* in 1798; Thomas Butler, of the *Olive Branch;* Hubbard Skidmore, master of the schooner *Samuel & Margaret;* William Pell, ship *Columbus;* William A. Cannon, master of the "hermaphrodite-rigged brigantine" *Industry;* David Sherry, who commanded the ship *President,* 369 tons, owned by Alexander Dunlap, and also the ship *American,* owned by John Tom; Pierre De Peyster with James Arden's *Belvidere,* a fine new ship in '93; Moses Taylor of the schooner *Betsy,* and James Goelet, master of the ship *Friends,* in the London trade. William Whitlock, whose son was to be prominent in packet circles down to Civil War days, commanded the schooner *Union* in the Liverpool trade in 1789.

As with Boston and New York, the principal Philadelphia merchants of the early Federalist period were also large shipowners. Abraham Piesch, Philadelphia's most active shipbuilder, as well as merchant, led with 19 vessels, most of which were ships of 300 tons and upwards. The largest was the *Rose* of 560 tons and next in order were the *Swift* of 391 tons and the *Union,* of 380 tons. Only four of the 19 measured less than 250 tons, and Piesch was the sole owner of 13, including all the largest. Few merchants in America matched his record in that day.

Stephen Girard, who came to Philadelphia in 1777, had only one vessel in 1790, the little brigantine *Kitty,* of less than a hundred tons. His first large ship was the *Good Friend* which registered 247 tons and was built in Philadelphia in 1793. Most of the craft he owned prior to 1800 were small. The *Voltaire* of 305 tons, built in 1795, was the first to exceed 300 tons. In 1801 he had the *Rousseau* built. She was almost identical with the *Voltaire* in size and design. She outlasted all the other Girard ships, ending her days as a New Bedford whaler. One hot summer day in 1893 I sat on the stringpiece of a New Bedford wharf and watched the ship-breakers taking her to pieces. At noon one of them came up and sat down beside me to eat his lunch. He said that it was the slowest job of the kind he had ever tackled—that her live oak timbers were as sound as the day the Philadelphia ship carpenters drift-bolted them together, more than 90 years before.

Altogether, Girard owned 14 ships. He was registered as sole owner of all but two, in which the masters owned small interests. His largest vessels were the *North America* of 388 tons, built in 1810, and the *Superb* of 537 tons, built in 1817. His best known captains were Ezra Bowen of Rehoboth, Rhode Island, and Myles McLeven of Philadelphia.

William Cramond was another shipowning merchant of the first rank. He was listed as sole owner of five ships prior to 1800, including the 409-tonner *Kingston* and the *Hindostan* of 563 tons. Joseph Sims owned ten ships, either outright or in connection with Woodrop Sims. The largest was the *Woodrop Sims* of 524 tons, which was credited with exceptional speed. Other important owners included Moore Wharton with six ships; Peter Blight with six; John Wilcocks, five; John Ross, five, and Henry Pratt, five, the largest of which was the *Minerva* of 365 tons, complete with roundhouse, quarter galleries, and a female bust.

In addition to these, there were many who owned two or three vessels at this time, and eventually owned substantial fleets. Among them were Thomas Ketland, Thomas Mifflin, Jr., John Brown, Robert Waln, Jacob Shoemaker, Thomas P. Cope, William West, James Yard, William Keith, Gideon Hill Wells, Thomas and Samuel Penrose, who were primarily shipbuilders but usually owned several vessels, James and Thomas Willing, Benjamin Morgan, E. Dutilh & Company, Jacob Gerald Koch, Willing, Morris & Swanwick, John Hollingsworth, James Gamble, Philip Nicklin, and David Maffit. Some of the above had equally well-known merchants associated with them. John Hollingsworth generally owned vessels in company with John Shallcross. Pattison Hartshorne and Jesse Waln held shares in several of the Robert Waln ships. William Parker was usually associated with Moore Wharton.

Samuel and William P. Meeker had the fine ship *Mount Vernon,* of 432 tons. Other prominent operators included John and Bohl Bohlen, John and Thomas Clifford, Samuel Eyre, William Massey, and Thomas Britton, John and William Newbold, George Bartram, Samuel and Philip S. Bunting, Anthony and Israel Morris, Samuel Howell, and two score more. Many were to disappear during the Napoleonic era, ruined by the depredations of the French and British, seconded by the privateers of every maritime nation. Others voluntarily abandoned commercial shipping for banking, manufacturing, or other enterprises.

David Grim, co-founder of Grim's New York-Philadelphia "D" Line. Established in 1817, it was one of the earliest coastal lines.

Courtesy, New-York Historical Society

Courtesy, New-York Historical Society

Preserved Fish, master mariner and merchant. Co-founder of the Swallowtail packet lines.

Captain John Rathbone, lost overboard January 13, 1846, from Black
Ball packet ship *Columbia*.

Courtesy, Mrs. Walter M. Oates

Packet shipmaster, Captain John
Pearce Penhallow, of Portsmouth,
N. H.

Courtesy, G. W. Patch

Courtesy, Maryland Historical Society

Packet brig *Harriet* of Baltimore.

Packet ship *Birmingham* of the Byrnes, Trimble Red Star Line, New York to Liverpool.

Courtesy, Peabody Museum of Salem

Courtesy, Seamen's Bank for Savings

Packet ship *Rambler*.

Packet brig *American* of New York.

Courtesy, The Marine Historical Association, Inc.

It has been stated that after the Revolution Philadelphia held first place in American maritime pursuits for many years, building not only the greatest number, but the finest and largest vessels produced by any port. The claim calls for notice only because it tends to convey the impression that the progressiveness of a community was somehow dependent on size—which certainly was not true in post-Revolutionary America.

The fact is that Philadelphia's leadership was extremely brief and due primarily to the circumstance that she had suffered less through British occupation than other important ports. Relatively, she reached her shipbuilding zenith in 1783 and 1784. In those two years she launched 84 vessels, aggregating 9780 tons. Obviously, a great proportion of the number were small vessels. In 1786, a year of mild depression, her construction dropped to a trifle over 900 tons, and it never again equalled that of New York.[6] Philadelphia undoubtedly built as fine ships as were built anywhere in the States, but any claim for general superiority conflicts with a record of achievement unbroken for nearly two centuries, when the performance of the smallest communities was on a par with the largest, volume alone excepted. In this connection it is to be noted that of the 40 great ships of the early Federalist period previously referred to, 20 were built in the smaller ports of New England, places like Exeter, Amesbury, and Braintree in Massachusetts, and Guilford, Chatham, and Glastonbury in Connecticut, and other towns not much larger. Philadelphia produced seven, but Providence, with barely a fifth of her population, accounted for four, including the *General Washington* of nearly a thousand tons.

Just when New York's commerce bypassed that of Philadelphia is somewhat uncertain, owing in part to the disappearance of official records under the Confederation, and in part to the fact that the mere number of arrivals and departures is not a completely reliable index of the value of trade. However, it was certainly not later than 1791, and may have been during the preceding year.

Total arrivals of "sea vessels" at New York during the calendar year of 1788 were reported as amounting to 952, while arrivals at Philadelphia during the same period were given as 1058 vessels.[7] During the next two years the respective arrivals were much closer, with Philadelphia slightly in the lead in the matter of numbers, but with no information as to tonnage involved. In 1791, however, New York was credited with 1819 arrivals, 718 of which were from foreign ports. For the same period Philadelphia reported 1261 arrivals, 567 of which were from foreign ports.[8]

From that time onward, New York continued to draw farther and farther ahead.

At this time Charleston was the third port of the new Republic, and crowding Philadelphia closely. Baltimore was fourth with "sea arrivals" ranging between 600 and 700 a year, and was running far ahead of Boston, whose trade was slow in reviving after the war. As late as 1793 her foreign arrivals were only 456.[9]

Aside from one or two of the smaller privateering ports, Baltimore was the only American town which benefited by the Revolution to any noteworthy extent. About the middle of the century it was a village of 200 inhabitants. In 1775 it was credited with a population of slightly under 6000, including blacks, and was producing and shipping flour in substantial amounts, as well as tobacco and foodstuffs. Its growth was stepped up during the war by the rapid development of manufactures and by the removal of many Philadelphia merchants to the town after the former port was occupied and the Delaware effectively blockaded by the British in 1777.

By 1790 Baltimore had become the fourth town in America, with a population slightly in excess of 13,000, including some 1300 slaves. It then had 102 registered vessels in addition to a very large number of coasters and Bay craft, and its trade was increasing almost visibly. In the year 1795, the principal arrivals amounted to 612, in addition to upwards of 5000 Bay craft.

Important shipowners during the Federalist period included James Biays, Acquila Brown, Jr., John Hollins, James A. Buchanan, William Patterson, Robert and Alexander McKim, Jeremiah Yellot, James Clark, John McFadon, David Stewart, and Samuel Hollingsworth.

Biays appeared on the scene in 1794 with the little brig *Fells Point*. By 1800 he had accumulated a fleet of 13 vessels, the largest of which was the ship *Defiance,* of 302 tons. David Stewart had the schooner *Fly* and ship *Union* in 1790, the latter a 214-ton vessel. Before 1800, he had owned 15 vessels, mostly ranging from small to medium size. The largest was the ship *George* of 298 tons. Buchanan owned 14 vessels before 1800, ranging from a 98-ton schooner to the ship *Elizabeth* of 305 tons.

Yellot's nine vessels were mostly big, sharp schooners, of which the 170-ton *Ariel* topped the list. Only one of his fleet was a ship—the 348-ton *Montezuma*. William Patterson had 19 vessels, only one of which was ship rigged. All, except the 271-ton *London Packet*, were brigs or schooners. William Wilson, who became one of the port's most prominent merchants, had only one vessel in 1790, the brig *Juliana,* registered for foreign trade. It was not until 1799 that he acquired a large ship, but in that and the following year he added five in rapid succession. The largest of the five was the 348-ton *Sally.*

James Clark owned four ships, two brigs and a schooner by 1795. His largest vessel was the *Birmingham,* of 285 tons. John McFadon had a large number of vessels, the best known of which was the *Clothier.* She registered 376 tons and in 1799 was one of the largest ships sailing out of Baltimore. Acquila Brown, Jr., had eight vessels, five of which were medium-sized ships, the largest being the *Hampton,* of 247 tons.

Other prominent Baltimore merchants of the Federalist period included Thomas Tennant, William and James Barclay, Robert Dorsey, Mark Pringle, Henry Courtenay, Richard Curzon, May & Payson, Von Kapff & Brune, Andrew Buchanan, James Williams, Thomas Sheppard, Messrs. G. & P. Wirgman, John Carriere, and R. Hewes & Company. Altogether, Baltimore had upwards of 100 merchants who were substantial shipowners in the Federalist years.

Charleston, whose commerce had been handled largely by English and northern vessels before the Revolution, resumed business in 1783 with local talent in the main. Her rice, tobacco, and naval stores were badly needed everywhere. An era of notable prosperity seemed assured.

Her situation was reflected in the fact that although the city's white population was still hovering around the 5000 mark, by early 1784 upwards of 50 merchants were advertising extensively in the local paper, the *South Carolina Gazette.* The figure does not include mere tradesmen, but only merchants in the strict sense of the term, exporters, importers, factors, and ship operators. A few maintained large retail stores where they offered a bewildering variety of merchandise, ranging from negro cloth and pigtail tobacco to London-built chariots and silver-mounted saddles. A vast amount of business, however, was conducted on the wholesale plan, either by private sale or public vendue.

Aside from the material advantage which Charleston possessed, for the moment at least, there was another factor destined to play a part in shaping her future. This was the character of her population. In this respect her situation, though less marked, was not unlike that of New York. All the other ports of the North were much more homogeneous: a circumstance which made for greater stability; sometimes, it must be admitted, at the expense of material progress.

All through the first half of the eighteenth century Charleston's original stock of English and Irish Protestants and French Huguenots had been supplemented by large numbers of Scots; victims of repeated uprisings in behalf of the old and young "Pretenders." To these were added a sprinkling of Dutch, Germans, Acadian French, and Jews. Later on a few Quakers and a large number of traders and mariners from the northern colonies, who had decided for one reason or another to settle in the South, completed the diversification.

Pioneers always live and act as individuals, but the Scottish and Huguenot elements of Charleston's population were more highly individualistic than the average. Extremely tenacious of their rights, they were always ready to fight any real or fancied encroachment on their liberties. It was a factor which had not a little to do with the subsequent history of the town, and indeed of the South as a whole, for they spread rapidly over the entire area.

Nothing indicates with greater clarity the cosmopolitan character of the port than a list of Charleston merchants in 1784. It includes in part the following: M. Defraye, at No. 30, on the Bay, importer of French wines; Scarbrough & Cook, London importers; the Smiths, Desaussure & Darrell, heavy in both the West Indian and English trades; one of the Darrells, master of the fast-sailing Bermuda-built ship *Sally;* Winthrop, Tod & Winthrop, of New England origin, in the London and Amsterdam trades, with a store and warehouse at 89 Broad Street; Ballentine & Wareham, 3 Tradd Street, and Thomas Morris & Company, 50 Bay, traders principally to Philadelphia and Amsterdam; Colcock & Gibbons, with a vendue store on Scott's Wharf.

James and Edward Penman, 15 Bay, were large importers of coffee, old London particular, Madeira, and spermaceti candles. W. Cunningham, 6 Bedon's Alley, was in the general importing business. He sold "Genuine Old Jamaica Rum" by the hogshead at the boom price of a dollar a gallon and also carried an extensive line of fine saddlery. Daniel Bordeaux was in the French trade. Robert Norris, next door to Cunningham on Bedon's Alley, acted as agent for Liverpool slave ships and sold slaves by the cargo, as did Fisher, Hughes and Edwards, at Prioleau's Wharf. John Kirk specialized in the Philadelphia trade. He owned the good ship *Delaware* jointly with Jacob Shoemaker, of that town.

The Scots were represented by William McLeod, Alexander Bethune, George Knox, Stewart, Hayes & Company, and half a dozen more. Jacob Jacobs and Israel Joseph added another element to the list. Adam Tunno and a few others had survived the Revolution. North & Blake, S. Midwood, and Roger and Peter Smith were among the more active merchants of the period.

Aside from naval stores, rice and indigo, tobacco was the chief export. In 1791, it was reported that 8000 hogsheads had been received in the town. This was sufficient to load 30 ships of the size then generally used in foreign trade. Two factors, however, contributed to change this condition. One was the invention of the cotton gin, already mentioned, coupled with the development in 1790 of the long-staple, sea-island cotton. The other was the rapid establishment of great power-driven cotton factories in England after the turn of the century, and somewhat later in New England. As a result, the Carolina and Georgia planters turned more and more to cotton, and tobacco ceased within a few years to be an important export.

Meanwhile the effect of peace on southern prosperity is indicated by the fact that through 1784 upwards of 20 vessels entered the port each week, not counting sloops, which seem to have been somewhat neglected in reports which were fragmentary at best. Sometimes the number was much larger. Thus, in two days, the 3rd and 4th of November, the arrivals included one ship, seven brigs, five schooners and an unstated number of sloops. Many of them brought one or more cabin passengers besides steerage. The ship *Hunter*, from London, reported Miss Bisset, Messrs. Ward, Maitland, Farquahar, Tillet, Captain Bray, and a few in the steerage, not otherwise identified. The brig *Peggy*, also from London, landed John McNair and Henry Maxwell, merchants, and Messrs. Smith, Crab, Duff, Rea, Bulgin, Watson, and Williamson.

This, then, was the position of Charleston in the closing years of the eighteenth century. It held a sound competitive place in the tobacco trade. It shared with Savannah a virtual monopoly of the American rice, indigo, and naval stores traffic, a situation soon extended to include cotton.

Several causes combined to extend these advantages for many years. Chief among them were the rapid growth of world population, the tremendous increase in shipbuilding which entailed an unprecedented use of naval stores, and the disturbances incident to and following the French Revolution, which put a premium on all American exports and gave profitable employment to hundreds of American ships. True, the trade involved grave risk of seizure and condemnation. Upwards of a thousand ships and cargoes were thus lost, and hundreds of owners ruined, but, roughly speaking, every ship that got through safely paid for two that were lost. For Charleston, as well as for many other ports, it was a period of exceptional prosperity.

Savannah was subject in general to the same conditions which determined the direction and rate of Charleston's development, but her situation at the close of the Revolution was much less favorable. The town had suffered heavily and was almost deserted. Contemporary estimates credit her with a population of 300 in 1785. While her trade was of the same character as Charleston's, it was at the outset correspondingly smaller.

Customhouse records of the port are fragmentary, but enough remain to enable us to make a rough reconstruction of her commerce in the closing years of the century.

In 1794, the first year in which the records are substantially complete, 32 vessels, mostly small, were registered, though the possibility exists that a register or two are missing. Of this small number, only half were owned in Savannah. In view of the fact that the commerce of the port had grown to very considerable proportions by that time, the circumstance indicates that most of her trade was handled by ships belonging to other ports.

The same apparently was true of Charleston. The customhouse records of that town for the early Federalist period have disappeared, but the occasional references to Charleston vessels and contemporary comments on her trade, as well as the evidence of her official records a few years later, indicate that only a small number of vessels were owned locally. Reported arrivals at both ports include a very large number of English, as well as a few French and Dutch ships.

Foreign trade accounted for the bulk of Savannah's commerce, but the number and character of her merchants engaged in coastal trade furnishes evidence of the remarkable growth of the port. Philetus Havens, of the New London and Sag Harbor Havens, was one of the more prominent Savannah merchants and continued to be for many years. He was principally engaged in the New York trade. William Vanderlocht shipped to Charles Sigourney of Boston. William Belcher developed a heavy trade with Joseph Ripley of Boston. Joseph Arnold and George D. Sweet flourished around the turn of the century. William Scarborough and William Taylor were especially active in the northern trade after a cheap and plentiful supply of cotton was assured. Richard F. Williams did a large business with Post & Russell, of New York. William Ewing's New York trade was handled by Anthony Pell. Other Savannah merchants who specialized in northern trade included Robert and John Bolton and Richard Dennis and Thomas F. Williams, all of whom were linked with merchants of Hudson, New York, around the turn of the century.

One of America's few barks, the *Nixon*, of Savannah, was owned by the Boltons. She measured 156 tons. Aside from the *Nixon,* it is doubtful whether there were more than half a dozen bark-rigged vessels in the United States at that time. Very few, indeed, were built before 1830, after which the rig became fairly common, thanks in part to the widespread fad for re-rigging large brigs as barks.

The Scots, James Robertson and Matthew and James Johnston, Jr., had become substantial Savannah merchants before 1800. They owned the *Cleopatra,* a fine Baltimore-built craft of 271 tons, and the 198-ton brig *Independent.* William Hunter and Isaac Minis had the brig *General Warren.* John Coit, sometime of Norwich, Connecticut, owned the schooner *Laurel,* of 115 tons. Edward Loring, of Boston, was another New Englander who had come down to try his luck. With Peter Seaver of Savannah, and Sam Sargent and Josiah Adams of Boston, he put his savings into the brig *Minerva.*

All in all, it is doubtful whether the commerce of any American port showed a greater relative increase during the last decade of the eighteenth century than Savannah's. In 1800 there were 164 clearances of large vessels for foreign ports, and 33 coastwise clearances. Most of the latter were bound for New York and Boston. It was a remarkable record for a town which 15 years earlier had only 300 inhabitants, a large proportion of whom were slaves. In the matter of foreign trade, it exceeded that of New York and Philadelphia in 1725, when those towns were, roughly, three or four times its size.

In the closing years of the eighteenth century, the conditions which affected the character and rate of growth of the American merchant marine were similar in two important respects to those which had prevailed during the Revolution. The wars which followed the outbreak of the French Revolution and which lasted with few and brief intermissions until the downfall of Napoleon at Waterloo, twenty-odd years later, increased the risks of foreign trade, but offered almost fabulous profits to those successful in running cargoes through hostile fleets of vigilant cruisers and hungry privateers. Inevitably, the supply of foreign manufactures was greatly reduced and an era of generally high prices prevailed in America, favorable to the further development of home manufactures on an enlarged scale.

It was a period of great material progress and even greater projects for the Republic in every field of endeavor. The first permanent American bank, the Bank of North America, in Philadelphia, which began business in 1781, was followed by the establishment of the Bank of Massachusetts in Boston in 1784. Thereafter bank after bank was founded in rapid succession in all the larger towns and the movement spread quickly to the smaller places. A similar development was taking place in the field of insurance, which, before the Revolution, was limited to the insurance of ships, cargoes, and freight money by private contract.

Broadly speaking, all the first American banks and insurance companies were established by merchants and with capital derived from seaborne commerce. It would be difficult to point to an officer or promoter of any of the early institutions who was not a merchant or the immediate descendant of merchants, or whose fortune did not originate in shipping and seafaring activities.

It was a time of great improvement in the general condition of people. Something like a leisure class was being established. Literature and authors, art and artists began to flourish. More and better schools sprang up everywhere. America, and especially New England, had had them from the first, but now their value was being recognized generally, and for cultural as well as utilitarian uses.

Most of the spade work which cleared the way for the Louisiana Purchase in 1803 had been accomplished during this period. One John Ledyard, a boy from Groton, Connecticut, had accompanied Captain James Cook on his last exploring voyage during the 1770's, and had been favorably impressed by the Oregon country. Later he made other voyages to the Northwest Coast and still later made a personal report to President Jefferson, who became interested in the advantages of that area. His report was confirmed and elaborated by the Boston and New York China traders who resorted to the West Coast for furs. The merchant marine capped the matter by piling up the Federal revenue which made the purchase of the Louisiana territory financially feasible. This income amounted to nearly $15,000,000 in 1802, a gain of nearly 400 per cent since 1792. This was exactly the sum we paid Napoleon for that vast expanse of land. With the Louisiana territory under the Stars and Stripes, the annexation of Oregon became practical.

Despite European depredations on a massive scale—the seizure of ships and impressment of seamen by England, the ruthless condemnations by the French, the piratical activities of the Barbary States, and the legalized buccaneering of the Dutch and Swedes—the late 13 colonies were on the move as never before.[10]

Immigration and emigration were breaking all records. As early as 1786 thousands of settlers were streaming westward over the mountains and along the Mohawk Trail. From August, 1786, to May, 1789, nearly 20,000 emigrants were listed as passing Muskingum, Virginia, bound for Kentucky, and the tally was far from complete. Farther north, the Mohawk Valley rush was so great that large numbers were reported on the verge of starvation in western New York in the early summer of 1790. Within ten years Kentucky would be producing for export bourbon and burley and little Abe Lincolns, and great ships would be built along the banks of the Ohio.

For some years canals and roads had been advocated everywhere from the Merrimack to Georgia, and a few short canals around rapids and waterfalls actually were built. A canal across Cape Cod was proposed in 1796, but its estimated cost, 70,707 pounds, 10 shillings, was considered prohibitive.

Practical men, including most scientists, were being mildly amused by the efforts of a few harebrained enthusiasts to apply steam to navigation.

Nothing, it seemed, could beat America's sailing merchant marine. By 1793 it amounted to 889,804 tons, having more than doubled since 1790, the first year in which approximately complete records became available. As the century turned the corner, tonnage passed the million mark. Construction, indeed, was fast closing up on that of Great Britain.

Exports in 1795 exceeded $50,000,000, and the *Columbian Centinel* complacently remarked: "The exports of Great Britain in 1791 were not more." And within five years they amounted to $67,000,000; New York leading with $14,000,000, followed by Maryland, Pennsylvania, Massachusetts, and South Carolina, in that order.

Each year saw new "unbeatable" records of achievement established. Each successive year saw these records left in the ruck and competitive enterprise stimulated to new heights. Hardly a crossroads in the North was without its eager-eyed promoter-inventor. Fitch, Oliver Evans, and others, handicapped by the lack of a few hundred dollars, were building crude steamboats. The Gould brothers patented a revolving log. Another genius developed a patent, geared steering wheel. Down in Baltimore, Leonard Harboh brought out a version of the dredge, for which he was probably substantially indebted to some unknown French inventor. He celebrated the adoption of the Constitution by patenting a horse-powered threshing machine, with which three or four men could do the work of 40, and a mowing machine with which one man could cut five acres of grain a day.

Gadgets came in endless profusion; new shoestring enterprises sprang up everywhere; Yankee notions flooded the markets. Already the Connecticut tin peddler was abroad with the horse and cart that was to run a hundred years, picking up and salting away pennies and new ideas for getting rich as he ambled through strange, interesting communities from York State to Georgia.

All civilization was falling for the early Puritan idea of the right of man to change and improve his condition, with increasing stress on the physical aspects of the matter.

As yet only in the new Republic was the trend unopposed. In England traditional conservatism did not yield without a struggle that stretched through another half century. There were riots and bloodshed over the introduction of the labor-saving inventions of Arkwright and Hargreaves, but on the whole there was progress. Even the iron ship, about which fools had been prophesying for centuries, had become a reality.[11]

Whatever might be said of the situation of the individual in America, the opening years of the nineteenth century brought no improvement in world conditions. On the contrary, if anything, they became worse. France, flushed with victory on land, decided to take control of the sea. In the ensuing struggle with England, the merchant fleets of Europe were decimated and the remainder bottled up. As a result America fell heir to a large part of the profitable carrying trade of the world, though at a heavy cost to herself in ships and men. Meanwhile the factors of price, scarcity, and the ever-widening range of demands, all of which favored the growth of domestic manufactures, continued in full and even increasing force and effect.

Five things, in particular, happened during the first decade which affected the future of the American merchant marine and with it the character of world civilization: the Louisiana Purchase; the British Orders in Council and Napoleon's retaliatory Berlin and Milan Decrees; Jefferson's embargo; the prohibition of the importation of slaves into the United States; and the development of the first commercially successful steamboat.

First in importance from a national standpoint was the purchase of the Louisiana territory in 1803, which included a vast, indefinite expanse vaguely described as the Oregon country. Its effect was for all time. It doubled the area of the nation and in the long run raised the American prospect from that of just another country to that of a world power. Its more immediate result was to hasten the development of the Ohio and Mississippi Valleys, and, incidentally, the merchant marine, by opening the commanding and convenient port of New Orleans to the unrestricted use of American ships.

The British Orders in Council and Napoleon's Decrees in 1806 and 1807 successively extended actual and paper blockades to Great Britain and all the important ports of Europe. Their ruthless and arbitrary enforcement led eventually to the War of 1812 and more immediately to Jefferson's embargo.

That embargo, proclaimed December 22, 1807, was important mainly for its harmful, though temporary, effect on northern shipping, and the compensating stimulus it imparted to the industrial development of that area. It was repealed, save as to England and France, March 15, 1809, but in the meantime a considerable amount of idle shipping capital had been diverted to the establishment of mills and plants of various sorts.

Fulton's development of the steamboat, with Robert Livingston's financial backing, was revolutionary in its effect. The significance of that particular event, however, is lessened by the fact that it would have come to pass within a few months in any event. John Stevens of Hoboken was engaged in building a vessel which possessed points of superiority over the Fulton craft, and which, less than two years later, became the first steamer to make a sea voyage.[12] It must also be noted that the monopoly insisted upon by Fulton and Livingston actually retarded the development of steam transportation until declared unconstitutional in 1824.

Nevertheless, the steamboat was destined to figure almost immediately in several important respects in advancing the development of the country. In particular, it made possible more rapid and comfortable travel between New York and Philadelphia, and by 1812 had demonstrated its value in the swift currents of the Ohio and Mississippi. It seems reasonable to assume, moreover, that it played a part, at least by way of suggestion, in the revolutionary decision to run sailing packets on fixed schedules.

Prohibition of the slave trade, effective January 1, 1808, had several consequences, one of which was to stimulate further improvements in the design of fast sailing vessels, which maintained the traffic, although illegally and on a reduced scale, for another 50 years. It was estimated later that more than 50 merchants of the principal American ports owned and operated slavers in the 1850's and down to the time of the Civil War. Oddly enough, although much of Liverpool's wealth had come from the trade and her merchants prophesied ruin would follow its loss, that event coincided with the start of that port's greatest growth, and, incidentally, with a remarkable expansion of her American commerce. Her foreign trade in 1809 increased one-third over that of the previous year and for this America was largely responsible. It marked the beginning of a development which eventually made Liverpool the greatest of the transatlantic packet ports.

Most of the merchants and masters of the early Federal period carried over into the Napoleonic era, although some transferred their activities to the fields of banking, insurance, and manufacturing. Many had increased mightily in wealth and had added to their several fleets. Still others appeared for the first time and quickly attained a standing of importance, which can be explained only by inheritance or a long and profitable apprenticeship in a place or position of obscurity.

Among the latter, Cornelius Coolidge emerged in 1806 in Boston as a substantial owner of ships. During the next five or six years he acquired eight square-riggers, the largest of which was the *Roxana,* of 331 tons. Israel Thorndike and Francis J. Oliver were associated with him in the ownership of an occasional vessel.

Another newcomer, Nathaniel Goddard, was registered as owner of four large vessels in the same period, one of which, the *Ariadne,* measured only slightly less than 400 tons. Oliver Keating and David Hinckley each acquired three or four ships after 1804, Hinckley's 398-ton *Milo* being the largest, as well as one of the best known, of Boston craft.

One of William R. Gray's early Boston ships was the *Rising States,* of 299 tons, which he bought in the summer of 1806. His own rise thereafter was rapid. Before the war he had four other vessels and had also established a branch office in Charleston where he continued for many years, doing both a shipping and banking business, especially in English bills.

Benjamin Rich was another product of the times. He had two stout ships before the embargo. Paschal P. Pope had three by 1812, including the first *Topaz,* of 385 tons. Andrew Cabot had the *Dromo* built. She measured 493 tons—the largest ship out of Boston in 1806. Thomas B. Wales took off in 1805 with the little brig *Traveller,* which proved a healthy nest egg.

Philip Ammidon, Daniel Hastings, Lot Wheelwright, John Bacon, Atkins Adams, and William Appleton had served their clerkships during the period and after postgraduate courses afloat, were starting hopefully up the ladder. There were many others: Amasa Delano, Ebenezer Nickerson, Jesse Sumner, John Dodge, John Holland, Moses and Benjamin Wheeler, Samuel Parkman, Stephen Codman, Daniel Tuttle, George Blanchard, John Couthouy, John and Samuel Swett, William Brooks, Jr., and some whose names have been long forgotten. A few carried on the family interests, but many, as always in America, started from scratch. These men, like Robert Bennett Forbes, of a later day, did much to carry on and prolong the kindlier traditions of the early days of sail in New England.

The Napoleonic period saw many additions to the commercial community of New York from the neighboring states, especially Connecticut, whose ambitious farm boys had contributed a stout quota ever since the Revolution. Thaddeus Phelps, John and Peter Crary, Gurdon Mumford and Henry Coit belong to this generation. Joseph W. Alsop was master of a ship in 1802, the little Connecticut-built *Hunter.* Of more immediate importance, however, was the remarkable progress of merchants who had started out with little or nothing in or about the early 1790's. Among these, John Jacob Astor and Samuel Russell, Sylvanus Jenkins, Jacob Barker, Henry Post, and Samuel Hicks were becoming marked men. Charles King, John Pierpont, John Flack, and Isaac Iselin—the latter usually in association with the LeRoys and Bayards—were playing an increasingly active part in the development of the port.

A few of the captains of the future packet service were already walking their own quarter-decks. John R. Skiddy, who lived to command great ships and to bestow his name on others, had the little schooner *Fanny* in 1799, rating less than 80 tons. Pierre De Peyster, Denison Wood, Reuben Brumley, Park Benjamin, John Stanton, and William Whitlock were farther advanced, but they would live to see, and some of them to take an active part in, the establishment of the packet service. Captain Rowland R. Crocker, of New Bedford, who commanded the fine ship *Tontine* before the war, was destined to live to cross the Atlantic more than 150 times, and that in a period when four crossings a year were rarely exceeded.

Philadelphia's maritime community was characterized at this period by growth in wealth rather than in numbers. There was no lack of activity to attract new blood to the port, but conditions were more crystallized there than in other large northern ports, and wealthy merchants more deeply entrenched in the more profitable lines of trade. However, there were a few newcomers, among them John H. and William Brown, sons of Alexander Brown of Baltimore. They appeared in 1807 and two years later owned the *Atlanta,* a fine ship of 380 tons.

Other merchants who were exceptionally active in the years preceding the war included Lewis Clapier, who had the *Asia,* a ship of nearly 500 tons. Abraham Kintzing, Alexander Balch, Thomas H. and Henry Pratt, and the Hollingsworth brothers, all of whom had been established in modest fashion for some years, rose to positions of considerable prominence during this period.

Jacob Clarkson, Quaker, was sole owner of the *Harmony,* a fine 359-tonner, in 1810. Samuel Allen, Robert Imlay, Joseph Clark, and Bankson Taylor, all prominent merchants, owned the slightly larger *Gleaner* in 1811, and had interests in other vessels. Charles Ross and Robert Waln were joint owners of the splendid 445-ton *Caledonia* during the same period, and John Strawbridge was the sole owner of the good ship *Hope.* Among others, William Maris, Joshua Lippincott, Samuel Veacock, John R. Evans, William Coates, Edward Thompson, and Samuel Keith were all attaining increasing prominence in the years immediately preceding the war. Lewis Clapier and George Emlen shared ownership of the *George Washington,* of 627 tons, with five others in 1803.

Baltimore was growing with tremendous rapidity all through the Napoleonic era. Perhaps no more striking indication of the fact could be mentioned than the appearance in rapid succession of more than 50 house flags, indicating the establishment of an equivalent number of private fleets, where in the beginning few merchants owned more than a share in a single vessel. The list includes Isaac McKim, Alexander Brown, Falls & Brown, Richard Curzon, R. & J. Oliver, Thomas Tennant, Hollins & Mc-Blair, P. A. Karthause, Isaiah Mankin, Henry Payson, Hugh Thompson, George W. Blackiston, Ely Balderson, N. Saltonstall & Company, Henry Messioner, John Carriere, Alexander Mactier, McFadden & Harris, N. Levering, and William Wilson & Sons. Many of these, or their descendants, were to play a worthy part in building the city in the future. The names of many others, of equal prominence at the time, soon disappeared from the registers.

Charleston's mercantile fraternity was undergoing rapid changes. Joseph Winthrop replaced the old Winthrop firm. He was active in the London trade. Tait, Wilson & Company's large establishment was located at the corner of the market, 110 East Bay Street. A. & T. Napier became Napier, Smith & Company in Charleston and Thomas Napier & Company in New York. John Gadsen, Charles Edmonston, and John Black all appeared on the scene. They will be heard from later, as will James Missroon, master mariner.

John F. Schmidt was heavy in the Amsterdam trade. All Scotland, a good part of Ireland, and the various ports of France manned Charleston's stores and warehouses and operated her ships: McLures, Macauleys, Mulligans, McKenzies, O'Haras, Muirs, Verrees, Freneaus, Depaus, and always a few names reminiscent of New England, New York, and Philadelphia—Pearce & Tillinghast, J. R. Mauran, Josiah Sturgis, Thomas Flemming.

Of Savannah and New Orleans, it is sufficient for the moment to note their commerce continued to increase rather more rapidly than that of other southern ports. Trade with the North was very active and on the uptrend, due in part to the North's growing industrialization, and in part to the risks incident to foreign trade.

It was a remarkable period in the world, pregnant with promise and despair—a time of fortune and failure; of progress and retrocession; of vision and blindness; all multiplied and intensified to a degree surpassing anything in human experience, and all blurred and obscured by a feverish, darting, seemingly purposeless activity. In France, privilege was on the scaffold; all the rest of Europe and Great Britain were fighting to put her back on the throne. America, the not always innocent bystander, was reaping the rewards, both good and evil, usually associated with that character. She was losing ships and men almost daily, snapped up by hostile cruisers and privateers or seized in supposedly friendly ports under arbitrary edicts, enforced without notice. Her losses as a result of that struggle have never been computed with any degree of accuracy. New England merchants— pro-British as a rule—were inclined to minimize that nation's encroachments, while pro-French sentiment, strong in other sections, performed the same service for the French. That the losses were enormous, however, cannot be disputed.

In the brief space of time from August, 1796, to June, 1797, the French alone seized 308 American vessels. By 1800, the number amounted to more than 600, and it will be remembered that at the same time the British and several of the nations of Europe, especially Denmark, were engaged in the same activities. The situation, moreover, continued for many a long year, until the downfall of Napoleon. Eventually, 1011 petitioners filed spoilation claims against the French alone. It would seem reasonable to conclude that American losses aggregated not less than 1500 vessels of an average value, with cargoes, of $16,000, and may have exceeded that figure.[13]

Whatever the number, the losses had to be made up by increased shipbuilding. The shipyards of America, however, did more than make up the losses. For the first time since Britannia ruled the waves, another nation surpassed her in the construction of merchant shipping, and that nation was America. In 1804 her output exceeded that of Great Britain by a small but decisive margin and continued to do so until the outbreak of war eight years later. During that time merchant vessels built in America aggregated 971,405 tons, as against 872,365 tons built in Great Britain.[14]

In 1810 American-registered tonnage reached a temporary high of 1,424,783 tons.[15] New York led all other ports with 243,638 tons. Boston was second with 133,257 tons; Philadelphia trailed with 121,443; and Baltimore was last of the major northern ports with 102,434 tons. The remainder, more than half the total, was widely scattered. In general, the tonnage actually owned in the largest southern ports was exceeded by that of the secondary New England ports.

Between 1800 and 1810 almost 2,000,000 persons had been added to the population, and the trading ports were growing out of proportion to the rest of the country. In round figures, New York had 96,000 inhabitants; Philadelphia 54,000; Boston and Baltimore were about even with 46,000 each. Charleston had 25,000; Savannah 5000 and New Orleans 17,000. New York, Baltimore, and Charleston had grown more rapidly than other towns but, as it happened, Charleston had reached a saturation point of sorts. Her population remained almost stationary during the next decade, while that of Savannah increased approximately 50 per cent.

Among the many indications of America's growing wealth and sophistication, there was one destined to do more than any other thing to set the stamp of greatness on her future merchant marine. As yet, it was so slight and obscure as to pass unremarked by the annalists of the day.

Supplementing the scanty and inadequate service of the British Post Office Packets, America had operated both transatlantic and coastal packets throughout the eighteenth century; individual, private vessels, that is, plying with fair regularity over the same routes, carrying the mails and providing somewhat better and more extensive passenger facilities than those available in the ordinary transients. Passenger quarters, indeed, were crude. The steerage was merely a space fitted with rough bunks in a 'tween-decks rarely more than 5 feet high, and usually less. Permanent staterooms were sometimes provided for cabin passengers, but usually they had to be satisfied with temporary rooms hastily knocked together when, as frequently happened, the main cabin could not accommodate all the applicants.[16] The great majority of these packets were sloops, schooners, and brigs, with an occasional small ship.

With the increase of travel after 1800, and the growth of a travelling public habituated on land to every comfort, there was a slow but definite improvement in the service. The improvement had become quite marked before the outbreak of "Madison's War" and was especially marked in the service between the northern ports and Charleston and New Orleans, then the most important southern ports from the standpoint of passenger traffic. There was even a tendency to develop a few packet lines.

In New Orleans, John C. Wederstrandt was operating two new packet ships on the Baltimore run, the *Clifton* and the *Balize*. In Philadelphia Messrs. Hand & Downing had been operating the smart new ships *Pennsylvania* and *South Carolina Packet* two years earlier in the Charleston service.

A number of other ships were specially built for the traffic about the same time. Chandler Price of Philadelphia, who became one of the leading coastal packet operators after the war, had the *Ohio* constructed and equipped for the New Orleans trade. Megrath & Jones of New York built the ship *Belle* in 1812 for the Charleston run.

As yet, however, there were no packet lines or, indeed, lines of any sort. Even those who operated more than one vessel with some degree of regularity between two given ports never undertook to maintain a service beyond the voyage in immediate prospect, and it is doubtful if any of them thought in terms of line operation. It was not until the conditions of war indicated in no uncertain manner the need for cooperation that steps were taken which led to the establishment of the first American sailing lines. In order to evade the British blockade, coastal cargoes were carried over alternating stretches of land and water. Owners pooled their ships and their wagons, merchants combined their shipments, in order to get the goods through with dispatch.

None of the new packets were large vessels, judged by post-war standards. They ranged from the 240-ton *General Wade Hampton* to the *Ohio* of 284 tons, and from 90 to slightly under 100 feet in length. They were, however, comfortably equipped for their day, and able, good ships for any day. One, the 280-ton *Caroline,* of Philadelphia, was credited with a 62-hour run from the Delaware Capes to Charleston in October, 1810, a record which has rarely been beaten in all the years since. Her time from city to city—sailing distance roughly 625 nautical miles—was 73 hours, itself a notable run.

The three-year struggle which followed the declaration of war in June, 1812, merely intensified, so far as American merchants and mariners were concerned, the conditions they had encountered for two decades. For the one, the financial, and for the other, the physical risks and rewards were multiplied, with the result—as in previous contests of the sort—that the survivors were better equipped to take advantage of post-war opportunities. What form those opportunities would assume, their range and extent, few attempted and none were qualified to predict.

In the meantime, the merchant was to reinforce his resources by the use of a few well-served six-pounders, rather than the reluctant expenditure of cash money, while masters and men were to gain interesting but less negotiable experience serving the aforesaid six-pounders, and ducking in and out of blockaded harbors in the dark of the moon. Whatever else might come of it, bigger and faster ships and harder drivers were inevitable. The men about "to sail through bloody seas" would see to it.

CHAPTER IV

❧ *1815-1821* ❧

The First Western Ocean Queens

"To Sail on their Appointed Days, full or not full."

ALTHOUGH peace was assured by the Treaty of Ghent, signed December 24, 1814, the news did not reach New York until February 13, 1815, when the British sloop-of-war *Favourite* arrived off Sandy Hook with the King's Messenger and "Commissioner" Carroll, messenger for the American delegation. Meanwhile, on January 8, the battle of New Orleans was fought. As at Bunker Hill 40 years before, it was raw pioneer versus disciplined regular, and the debate was brief. In less than an hour the British army was in retreat, leaving its commander, Sir Edward Pakenham, and 2600 killed, wounded, and prisoners on the field. The American loss was seven killed and six wounded.

Before the British sailed away the news of peace was received and the former enemies mingled as though there had never been a war between them.

On one occasion Vice Admiral Alexander Cochrane of the Royal Navy, conversing with a gentleman named Laverty, expressed surprise that even the merchants of New Orleans fought in the ranks against the British who came to bring them the benefits of British trade. He remarked, "We expected, when we came, to find balls and suppers given." Mr. Laverty replied, "We have given you balls: you must look out for suppers." The Admiral, turning to one of his officers, said, "Take that out of your wig."

The victory, nevertheless, was needed to strike a balance, for with the exception of two or three minor engagements, such as Lundy's Lane, the American record on land was a series of defeats, some of them of a disgraceful description.

At sea it was otherwise. Both sides had captured or destroyed about the same number of enemy merchant vessels—roughly 1700 each—but the British ships were larger than the American and their cargoes much more valuable on the average. The American Navy record was quite as impressive as that of the privateers, as indicated by the various attempts of the British to account for it. The typical explanation, however, was offered by Admiral Warren, while his squadron was blockading the Chesapeake, to the American Captain Smith who had been sent to arrange an exchange of prisoners. As reported in the *Columbian Centinel:*

> The news had just arrived of the capture of the *Java* by the *Constitution,* and the Admiral, speaking of the event, asked Captain Smith how it was that our frigates were so successful in taking theirs. Captain Smith answered that he knew no reason for it unless we fought better. "No," said the Admiral, "that cannot be; but the reason is that two-thirds of your crews are British seamen." "Then" replied Captain Smith, "the other third being Americans, makes the whole difference." It closed the game. The Admiral had not another move.[1]

At all events, in view of the superiority of both the British Navy and her armed merchantmen in numbers and tonnage, the Yankee sailorman was satisfied he had won a victory. Perhaps he had. In any case, he crowed a lot louder than his brother across the water, and for similar reasons he didn't think much of the treaty.

In Federalist Boston, which had been against the war from the start, they were saying it had settled nothing. "What about the 6257 seamen we went to war about? What of the ships captured under Orders in Council? What about the Canadian boundary?"

Still, people cheered, though with no great enthusiasm. One old Revolutionary veteran expressed the general attitude when he said, "Huzza for Peace, anyway! Free trade and Sailor's Rights—and up goes my old beaver (not quite so high, however, as in '83)."

It was time for peace. Twenty-five years of almost continuous warfare, interrupted only by an occasional quasi-truce, during which economic reprisals, Berlin decrees, Orders in Council, spur-of-the-moment proclamations, and suchlike, continued to restrict trade to a minimum, had swept Europe's cupboard bare, as repeated "bread riots" testified. Her inventories of essential raw materials, moreover, had been reduced to the danger point.

England was in better shape, on the whole, than the Continent, but her situation is perhaps sufficiently indicated by the fact that her own merchants had resorted to trading with the enemy on a substantial scale.[2] In defiance of the blockade proclaimed by their own government, they sent ship after ship to America, especially to southern ports for cotton. Many were seized and confiscated with their cargoes, but considerable contraband cotton found its way to the Midland mills to ease, briefly, the miseries of hungry workmen.

Conditions in the States were much better. The country had managed to maintain a small but helpful coastwise trade and some traffic with the West Indies. Nevertheless, during three years of war, she had built an embarrassing surplus of exportable staples. She had also accumulated a huge backlog of pressing demands for a great variety of manufactured goods, from workaday tools to "elegant" coaches.

To the merchant at home and abroad, it was clear that his problem in 1815 would be ships, not cargoes. All foresaw that restoration of normal conditions would involve the annual shuttling of hundreds of thousands of tons across the Western Ocean for months to come. Few saw the extent of the demand for increased and better passenger accommodations; the scurry of merchants back and forth to make new, or revive old business connections; the latent urge of the well-to-do to travel for culture or amusement; or the spread of emigration fever among the masses of Europe, who could only view the future as a dreary, unending struggle for a bare subsistence, punctuated by devastating wars.

America was unprepared to meet this demand. In spite of recent sporadic attempts at improvement, which had resulted in several new ships capable of carrying 25 or 30 first-class passengers with a modest degree of comfort and privacy, there still were comparatively few vessels offering such accommodations to more than six or eight passengers. Even then, rough, dark, unventilated compartments and cabins with a scant six feet of headroom were the rule. Such things had sufficed for a generation enured to hardship and discomfort. They presented no attractions to one that had become accustomed to a fair degree of ease, and even luxury.

For the moment, however, anything that would float was badly needed. Thanks to their quaint interest in collecting souvenirs of their profession, Yankee sailors had almost as many ships—such as they were—when the war ended as when it began. They lost no time getting them in commission.[3]

Gangs of catlike riggers went through the idle fleet in record time. They boarded a ship, stripped to a gantline, and in a few days had her yards across, sails bent, running rigging rove off and shrouds set up, ready to sail. A few more days of feverish loading, and she was off to the eastward or headed for a southern port to discharge and load again: cotton, tobacco, naval stores, and foodstuffs for Europe.[4]

In the meantime foreign ships by the score flocked to American ports, with the British greatly in the majority. For a time they threatened to outnumber American vessels in the transatlantic trade.

Swift privateers heard the news of peace, raced home, dumped their carronades and double fortified sixes and settled down as peaceful coasters, or kept their guns and headed for China, the West Indies, or South America. Some vanished mysteriously, and it was whispered not without warrant that they might be found in the "black ivory" trade. The slave traffic had long been outlawed, but captains of captured slavers continued to grace the gallows occasionally, down to Civil War times. It would have been a more effective deterrent if they had hung a few of the respectable merchants of Bristol, New York, and other ports, who owned the ships and sent them out.

A man in a hurry was Captain Sam Glover of the "fast sailing ship" *Milo,* of Boston. He purchased his anchor on March 12 and dropped it 18 days later in Liverpool. Still hustling, he was loaded and ready to sail 35 days after leaving Boston, "the first American master to enter Liverpool and the first to return after the war." Others, however, were hard on his track, and if he did not meet a score of stout British ships, westward bound, it was not because they were not there to be met.

A tremendous upsurge of shipbuilding soon reduced the competition of foreign bottoms to normal proportions. All the old yards and many new ones from Maine to the Gulf were busy. By 1822 the old balance had been restored. Of 1172 vessels which arrived that year in New York from foreign ports, 1054 were American.[5] Only 76 were British. It is significant to note that in that same year 24 ships, averaging 402 tons, were launched in New York alone. This was in addition to small coasters and steamboats. Before the war it would have been difficult to pick a year when half that number were built there, or when more than three or four exceeded 300 tons. A similar increase all along the coast, but especially in New England, was in progress. This upward trend was to continue for 40 years after the war, subject only to temporary recessions during the frequently recurring depressions. By mid-century, single districts were exceeding the annual pre-Revolutionary output of all the colonies.

It was of inestimable benefit to the nation in the long run. For a time, however, in the immediate post-Napoleonic period, it created a competition of the domestic variety that brought many a merchant to bankruptcy.

Two years of trade such as the world had never witnessed sufficed to stock the shelves and fill the warehouses of Europe and America. Demand, which had been conditioned by the need for complete replacement of stocks of merchandise and produce, shrank, in 1817, to routine replacement levels. By mid-summer the signs of hard times ahead were unmistakable. The situation was later reflected by the fact that import duties fell off approximately $10,000,000 during the year, and dropped another

$9,000,000 the following year.[6] At the same time, merchants were confronted with the problem of finding profitable employment for a greatly enlarged fleet.[7]

Transatlantic ship operators, scanning the commercial horizon, could see only two possible sources of increased revenues; neither of them had a particularly impressive past, but both, a great future.

One was travel. First-class passenger traffic, apparently, was on the upswing and destined to expand, while immigration promised to break all records for years to come.[8]

The other was the increase of small individual shipments, usually of considerable value, which paid premium rates—the sort, in fact, which constituted the principal source of business of the later express companies.

Neither of the above sources of revenue had heretofore figured appreciably in the calculations of the general run of ship operators. They did not despise passenger and parcel money but regarded it, rather, as an extra something, a pleasing finish on the stout fabric of bulk freighting profits. The question of developing it into a substantial and permanent part of their operations, however, was a completely novel one. The necessary factors, indeed, were simple and familiar enough: speed and dependability. America had long relied on them to gain her share of the bulk freights of the world. It was common knowledge, moreover, that a few of her ships had won so outstanding a reputation for efficiency that they were preferred by shippers everywhere.

The question now was whether an entire fleet could be operated on a basis of superior efficiency, and if so, whether it could effect the desirable result of building a presently small, highly profitable business into a big one.

It was left to a group of New York Quakers to come up with the answer. The circumstance might be passed without comment, were it not to the present purpose to explain as well as record an American achievement.

Many of us, perhaps, have been inclined to think of the Quaker as a rather retiring individual, much preoccupied with odd notions about peace and the taking of oaths. Few think of him as a Puritan first of all. Yet he was as much a Puritan as any man in the world. He held, if anything, more strongly to the one essential, distinguishing concept of the Puritan—the concept of personal responsibility, with all its corollary rights and duties—than most Massachusetts Puritans of 1630. True, he was always at odds with the Massachusetts Puritans, but it was because he insisted on carrying their common principle to its logical end. He would, for instance, have no man standing between himself and God, not even the minister. He was, in short, more Puritan than the Puritan.

It followed that the same forces which operated to develop self-reliance and kindred qualities to new heights in the New England Puritan, operated with equal, if not greater, force on the Quaker. Far from being the slow, ultra-conservative, timid creature of caricature, he was bold, quick to size up a situation, and resolute to act. Nothing else can explain the fact that he took and held, despite the disparity of numbers, the lead in the great whaling industry, and became a figure of power in the mercantile circles of New York and Philadelphia. It explains, possibly, why the Western Ocean packet service that was to mark a step for America and the world started when and as it did.

The first notice of the establishment of a regularly scheduled transatlantic packet line appeared in the *Commercial Advertiser* and other New York papers on Friday, October 24, 1817. It was signed by Isaac Wright & Son and Francis Thompson, only. This was the earliest intimation to the world that, beginning on the 1st of the following January, prospective transatlantic travellers could depend upon "an uncommonly extensive and commodious" mode of conveyance, sailing on a certain day, "full or not full," the latter guarantee referring to the ship and not the passenger. Thus began the Black Ball line.

It will be recalled that although the above was the first transatlantic packet line which proposed to observe fixed sailing dates, it was not the first transatlantic line. Isaac Wright & Son and Francis Thompson had already tried the experiment of operating a line of three packets in regular succession between New York and Liverpool, but not on a pre-arranged schedule, and the venture had worked satisfactorily for several months. The fact is important as indicating that their decision was not the leap in the dark it might otherwise appear to be, but was preceded by a series of tests conforming as nearly as circumstances permitted to practical conditions to be expected.

Four days later, on October 28, the names of Benjamin Marshall and Jeremiah Thompson were added to the advertisements as joint proprietors. Why their names were omitted from the original notices does not appear. It is possible they first planned to charter their ships to the line for a fixed sum, and later decided to become full participants.

On the other side of the Atlantic the earliest advertisement appeared in the *Liverpool Mercury* on November 26. A facsimile of this advertisement, slightly enlarged, is included among the illustrations in this book.

It will be remarked that the New York and Liverpool notices differed in certain particulars. The Liverpool agents fixed the price of cabin passage at 45 guineas and included with it beds, bedding, stores and wines. New York advertisements mentioned no price and stated only that beds and bedding were furnished by the ship. These omissions suggest the possibility that the proprietors adhered at first to the American practice of dickering, with a view to getting all the traffic would bear while reducing the risk of losing a customer. Their reticence in matters culinary and ambrosial may have been dictated by previous experience with the American appetite.

However that may be, the fare for the eastbound passage was fixed at 40 guineas early the following year, and included food and wines. It remained at that figure until Byrnes, Trimble & Company started their opposition line early in 1822, when it was reduced to 30 guineas. It soon rallied, however, to 35 guineas, where it continued to stand for many years.

As opposed to—or more correctly, perhaps—in addition to the considerations already cited as leading to the establishment of the line, two ingenious suggestions have been put forward to explain in part its founding.

One was that the coming of the steam towboat was an important factor in the decision. The other was that British initiative exercised a strong influence.

It is doubtful whether either suggestion possesses any appreciable merit.

The development of the towboat will be considered in detail in another place. For the moment it is sufficient to observe that when our New York Quakers were coming to a decision, there were no towboats, either in New York or Liverpool, capable of towing their ships under weather conditions which would have rendered such a service necessary. They probably were aware that a steamboat (the *Nautilus,* later to be skippered by a youth named Vanderbilt) was being built in New York for the Staten Island ferry which was intended to render towing services occasionally, as opportunity offered. But even if they had been open to influence by a project still in the experimental stage, which is most unlikely, they knew from practical experience that at New York the same heavy, southeasterly weather, which might render towing down the bay necessary, would also make it impossible for the ship to go to sea without grave risk of piling up on a New Jersey or Long Island beach. It is highly improbable that owners reared to put their trust in sail, or masters who prided themselves on the ability to do anything with their canvas-backs, would place their reliance on any double-duty ferryboat then in being or in prospect. It is true, the Black Ballers eventually resorted to towing, but I have found no recorded instance in 1818 and only one in the following year, when the *Courier* towed out of Liverpool on the 1st of January, 1819.[9] Several more years were to elapse before the practice became common.

There is even less to indicate that British initiative played a part in founding the line. For one thing, weeks after notice of the establishment of the line had been published in New York papers, Liverpool agents were still advertising the "proposed" sailing of the *Courier* (one of the ships involved) as an independent vessel and not as a "line ship." For another, not a penny of British capital was involved. No British citizen ever owned a ropeyarn in any American packet, although, as will appear, several British lines of the emigrant type eventually were started. And hardheaded New York Quakers were unlikely to be influenced materially by initiative which consisted of conversation only.

It is difficult to escape the conclusion that the founders of the line were influenced almost exclusively by the two prosaic and eminently practical considerations already indicated. Through superior speed and dependable sailings they hoped to capture a large share of the remunerative passenger and express shipment traffic. They also hoped that a reputation for short passages would enable them to charge higher freight rates.

The *James Monroe*, registering 424 tons, was the largest of the four ships which constituted the line. Only the *Monroe* and the *Courier*, of 381 tons, were new. The *Amity*, 382 tons, and the *Pacific*, 384 tons, were, respectively, one and ten years old. The latter, however, had the reputation of being one of the fastest vessels afloat. Her reported passage of 17 days from New York to Liverpool earlier in the year stood as the accepted record for several years. On that occasion she was credited with making the Irish coast in 12½ days—a remarkable run for that or any other period.[10]

Cropper, Benson & Company and Rathbone, Hodgson & Company, the firms chosen to act as Liverpool agents (each being responsible for two ships) were old firms of the first rank, a fact which was to play no small part in the success of the line. William Rathbone, the founder of the latter firm, was already a prominent Liverpool merchant in 1754 when he imported a shipment of cotton from Savannah, said to have been the first cotton shipped from America to an overseas market.[11] He was of the same family as the Connecticut Rathbones, formerly prominent in New York shipping circles, whose exodus from England is traceable to a difference of opinion on the subject of Charles the First.

On the New York side the venture got under way promptly, as scheduled. The *James Monroe*, James Watkinson, master, sailed Monday morning, January 5th, 1818, in snowy, blustery weather.

America was sea minded those days, even the West, where the shipbuilders and seamen of New York and New England flocked by the hundreds to build and man the river and lake steamboats and sailing craft. Plenty of them were fresh from serving the guns of privateers. They knew that, as long as they could remember, America's answer to the world had been speed. From the moment they read the first Black Ball advertisement, every merchant and shipmaster knew the thing would stand or fall on speed.

Every man-jack on the *James Monroe,* as she slipped out by Sandy Hook into the gathering gloom of the winter night, knew it, from Captain Watkinson, vigilantly pacing the quarter-deck, to Snowball, the cook, tailing onto the mainsheet while his neglected slumgullion slopped in the boiler.

The captain knew it, for his salary of $30 a month meant nothing unless he could "up it" at least a thousand per cent through his cut of the passage money and his five per cent primage, both of which hung on the performance of his ship.[12]

The crew knew it, for they got seven cents a day extra to drive the ship as ships had never been driven before. They also knew that if they showed signs of undervaluing this unparalleled generosity, there were a couple of mates skilled in imparting a thorough college education in ship driving, complete in one lesson, with Jack on the absorbing end.

The passengers knew it, as they went shivering down to their low quarters and tall bottles, for they had paid a $40 premium to get to Liverpool "by the short route."

Most of all, the four Quakers knew it, as they mentally booted their packet across the Western Ocean, for they were out to make records or lose face and money.

There, knowledge stopped. Not one of the four proprietors, not one of the 30-odd souls on that little pioneer packet dreamed he was witnessing the start of a far-reaching competition, between sail and steam, between man power and mechanical power. It was destined to play a notable role in spurring a world on and into a strange new road, and would not end until 500-foot steamships were ploughing the sea at 18 knots and men on land were travelling a mile a minute.[13] The pilot, on his return to the city, reported that the ship got to sea at four o'clock. She made a good run to Liverpool, arriving February 2nd, in a passage of 28 days. Most of the other arrivals about the same time took 40 days or more for the crossing. Her passenger list of eight gentlemen of sufficient importance to be listed by name, together with some others less fortunate, must be considered large for a winter crossing at that time.[14]

Her cargo consisted of 1141 barrels of apples, 860 barrels of flour, 400 barrels of ashes, 71 bales of cotton, and small quantities of cranberries, hops and wool. Since the normal capacity of a ship of her tonnage was 3500 barrels and upwards, she was little more than three-quarters loaded —evidence, for what it is worth, that her owners were determined to send their ships out on schedule, "full or not full."

Over in Liverpool the *Courier* was less fortunate. Captain William Bowne did not get away until the 4th of January, four days after his scheduled date. It must have tried his Quaker soul, although there is no record that he let on. The Liverpool papers assigned no reason for the delay, but it was probably due to the chronic Liverpool complaint, a stiff nor'wester. The prevailing winter wind at that port was and is from the northwest, and when it blew strongly from that quarter no ship could get to sea under sail. As a matter of fact, few packets sailed from Liverpool on their appointed days until towing became general.

Liverpool, nevertheless, had certain advantages over London as a port for American trade. It was a day's sail nearer in point of distance, and usually several days' sail nearer in time, owing to delays commonly incident to working up and down the English Channel. Its central location with regard to Great Britain and Ireland made it a convenient point of embarkation for emigrants, which was to stand it in good stead when larger packets were built, which were more commodious and comfortable than the transient ships and regular traders which called at Scottish and Irish ports for steerage passengers. The Black Ball line eventually had "Old Established Emigrant Passage Offices" in Glasgow, Dublin, Cork, Belfast, and Londonderry.

The situation of Liverpool with respect to the mines and heavy industries, then developing with tremendous rapidity, was of still greater importance. With few exceptions, all the nation's coal, salt, lead, and iron mines were concentrated within a hundred miles of the city's docks. The same was true of all the heavy manufactures: machinery, tools, ironmongery, pottery, cottons, and woolens. She had the further advantage of being served by an extensive system of canals.

London, on the other hand, was as far removed from all those things as Liverpool was near. This alone, when the cost of hauling heavy freight over bad roads was staggering, automatically eliminated her from the bulk of American nineteenth-century trade.

The result is indicated by the marine reports of 1818. During the six days from March 26 to March 31, 26 ships sailed from Liverpool for American ports.[15] In any comparable period about that time not more than two or three sailed from London for the States. The figures afford

CARL A. RUDISILL LIBRARY
LENOIR RHYNE COLLEGE

a rough but substantially accurate picture of the situation as it then existed, and which was to become more marked as time went on. Within a few years the preponderance of American shipping in Liverpool was so striking that it was usual to refer to it as an "American port."

The first year passed with but one serious interruption of the service. On his return trip, Watkinson set out from Liverpool on the 3rd of March. He had slipped a bit on his schedule, but it was nothing to what was coming. He took a dusting in the Irish Channel and a few days later limped ruefully back to Liverpool in company with five other similarly depressed mariners.

Having refitted, he sailed again on March 26th and made New York in 34 days, a good winter run but one which gave him barely a week to discharge and reload for his next scheduled departure. Whether for this or some other reason, his sailing date was changed to May 10th. This arrangement was made permanent and continued in effect until the Black Ball added a second line in February, 1822, when all future sailings from both ports were fixed for the 1st and 16th of each month.

Captain William Bowne, the lone Quaker commander in the line, figured in the only other noteworthy incident of the year. On the 7th of May, a few days out of Liverpool, he ran the *Courier* into a breeze of wind which relieved him of his main- and mizzen-topmasts, fore-topgallant mast, main yard, and fore-topsail yard. To add to his injuries, he was insulted by an offer of assistance from a passing ship. Saving what he could of the wreckage, he got a jury rig aloft and made New York 45 days out from Liverpool.

It was a bad year for westbounders, a fact which must be borne in mind in estimating the performance of the Black Ballers. Few passages were made in less than 40 days, and 50- to 60-day crossings were more common. A 90-day passage was the longest, and Seth Macy's 27 days, in the *Hercules,* the shortest, although in most years a ship had to make the run in from 20 to 25 days to hold the year's record.

General economic conditions, which had shown unmistakable signs of deterioration in 1817, grew steadily worse. By the spring of 1818 every merchant knew he was in another depression. Glutted markets, due to post-war overtrading, contributed, but overspeculation and a highly discreditable banking situation were mainly responsible. The recently chartered United States Bank was the most conspicuous offender. The Baltimore branch, alone, lost $3,000,000 in a short time through transactions which had many of the aspects and all the results of criminal malfeasance

The full impact of these and a mass of minor factors produced a nation-wide situation little short of panic proportions in 1819, the effects of which were still felt in 1821.

This, perhaps, explains in part the fact that the Black Ball line—far from being an outstanding success from the start, as sometimes reported—generally sailed from New York during its first year with very light freights. The lightest of all was probably that of the *James Monroe.* She left New York on September 10th, 1818, with 212 bales of cotton, 1265 quintals of corn, and a few odds and ends.[16] Even allowing for the fact that she was sharper built than the majority of the ships of her day, this was barely a fourth of her capacity. The following month, when ships were usually carrying the new crops, the *Amity* stowed less than 150 tons, although she could carry 500 tons with ease.[17]

Cabin and steerage patronage was also light. The packets usually sailed with less than half their staterooms occupied and frequently reported lists of only four or five first-class passengers. Steerage traffic was even less satisfactory. Any of the ships could have accommodated upwards of 200 emigrants, in easy accordance with prevailing standards. Yet the largest list noted, 51, was that of the *Courier,* sailing from Liverpool on September 1st. The largest number of cabin passengers carried by any packet during the first year, 20, arrived in New York on the 15th of July, in the *Pacific.* Many of the crossings were made with half a dozen or less of each class.

Fortunately for the experiment, return freights from Liverpool showed to better advantage. Westbound packets were reported several times with full cargoes, and, what was more important, the cargoes consisted principally of dry goods and other fine manufactures in individual consignments ranging from 70 to 90 in number, and comprising in the aggregate a thousand or more separate packages. Since shipments of that character paid much higher rates than the usual bulk cargo, it followed that a packet lightly loaded with fifty, sixty, or a hundred thousand dollars worth of valuable merchandise made a profit, whereas a ship deeply loaded with three or four thousand dollars worth of coal or salt barely paid expenses, and if delayed by heavy weather, with or without damage to spars and sails, might even show a substantial loss.

Nevertheless, the over-all situation, which did not improve materially for three years, and sometimes showed signs of becoming far worse, could hardly have failed to give the proprietors a few anxious moments. The temptation to scamp their schedule must have been strong, at times. However, they hung to it, whatever of grim determination may have been involved. Not only that, but they proceeded to improve the service.

Before the year ended, Sidney Wright had built the *Albion*. She registered 434 tons, ten tons more than the *Monroe,* largest of the pioneer ships. She replaced the old *Pacific* and sailed on her maiden voyage March 10th, 1819. Although only three and one-half feet longer than the *Pacific,* she was beamier and had a roomier 'tween decks and more "elegant" cabin accommodations. Her staterooms, however, retained the old dimensions, a trifle over six feet square. In materials, workmanship and appointments, she was hailed as the equal of any ship of her size then afloat. Notwithstanding her staunch construction and the undoubted ability of John Williams, her commander, she was the first vessel of the line to be lost.[18]

Although 1818 had proved a year of small beginnings, the Black Ball proprietors, as the event showed, were justified in concluding that there were no basic errors in their calculations. It was possible, indeed, to interpret the results in a more favorable light than mere volume of business would seem to suggest.

For one thing, they were doing better than most shipowners engaged in transatlantic trade. They had secured from the first more than a normal share of the profitable cabin passenger traffic, light though it was, and had some reason for hoping that they could maintain and improve the advantage. They had grounds for confidence, based on long experience and superior connections, that they could attain a similar advantage in the emigrant traffic, and when the full tide of emigration set in, it would be a most profitable business.

Barring a small reward to his captors (the emigration agents scattered through Scotland and Ireland) the emigrant's five pounds was almost clear profit. He had to furnish and cook his own grub, supply his own bedding, and shift his own freight. If he didn't that was his hard luck. The ship even got a little work out of him now and then. In emergency, or if the sailors got tired, he was permitted to renew his health and vigor by a spell at the pumps. If his presence did not add particularly to the comfort of the cabin passengers, especially when the wind was ahead, that, too, was not serious. In a day when there was a three-letter indispensable under every bed, even lovely women possessed olefactory organs that could take it or leave it.

Another favorable prospect was the outlook for monopolizing the extremely profitable package trade, already showing indications of a rapid increase in volume. It was the growing demand for service of this sort that led to the establishment in America of the highly successful express companies, of which Harnden's and Adams' were the outstanding examples.

Even sailing on schedule with half a cargo in dull times had its compensations. If it involved small profits, or none at all, it meant at least that the ships were not lying idle at a dock for months while cut-rate shipments slowly dribbled into their holds. Meanwhile the packets were building a "good will" that would be invaluable when times improved.

Circumstantial evidence of their growing popularity was not lacking. Other ship operators began to advertise their vessels as "The Next Regular Packet," with the rather obvious intention of conveying the impression to the unwary that the ship in question belonged to an "established line" and would sail on a fixed schedule. It is possible, if not probable, that two or three merchants were considering the establishment of a line on the Black Ball pattern, but for several years none of them indicated any intention of sending their ships out, "full or not full." Byrnes, Trimble & Company eventually succeeded in doing so, but it took them four years to round the buoy. Other transatlantic houses continued to advertise "Regular Traders" and "Constant Traders" for many years, until ships were sailing with such regularity and frequency that the terms lost all significance.

Judged by performance alone, the Black Ball record for the first year would not impress a jet-plane generation. The average time for the 24 crossings (12 in each direction) was slightly under 25 days, eastbound, and 43 days, westbound, the latter performance unfavorably affected by an abnormal amount of heavy westerly weather. The eastbound average of 25 days, however, constituted an unprecedented performance for a fleet of ships sailing in regular succession throughout the year, entirely aside from the fact that it included two 18-day crossings.[19]

On the other hand, none of the individual passages established new, or equalled the old records. The crux of the matter, however, lies in the phrase "average time." On this score the achievement of the line was definitely encouraging.

This is not to assert that it was superior to that of all competitors. Regular trading masters such as William Sketchley, James Rogers, and Benjamin L. Waite, to mention but three, not only had fine ships, but were drivers, to boot. Generally speaking, aside from the fact that they might be delayed several weeks in sailing, there was little to choose between their records and those of the packets. They, however, represented but a fraction of the competing fleet, the greater part of which took much longer than the packets to make the crossing. The 54-day trip of the *James Monroe* in the latter part of 1818 was the longest packet passage of the year. Yet the same day she arrived in New York, the good ship

Savannah, Captain Morgan, arrived 70 days out from the same port, and the brig *Hope,* Captain Pillsbury, passed the Hook 80 days from Leith. On the 15th of the following month (January, 1819) the *Amity* arrived after a hard passage of 44 days. Two other vessels arrived with her—the fine ship *Sterling,* 90 days from Havre, and the brig *Melanie,* 100 days from Nantes.

For the merchant, anxiously awaiting his goods and knowing that the market, depleted today, might be glutted tomorrow by a rival's shipments, the margin of a single day often made the difference between a swinging profit and a sacrifice sale. He had learned by hard experience the necessity of "playing percentage," and to do this successfully, where ships and shipments were concerned, meant superior average performance. To be first three times out of five was success. Anything less was failure.

Their fixed schedule was important, but the question whether the packets, as a fleet, could set up and maintain a new and higher standard of speed was even more so. The fact that they did goes far to explain their ultimate success. That reward didn't come in a day, impressions to the contrary notwithstanding. It came slowly, and at a price; the price was an all but superhuman endurance doggedly centered on a policy of relentless, ruthless drive. All the calculations of the ablest packet proprietors would have gone for naught but for the cooperation, however stimulated, of masters and men, far beyond any latter-day conception of the line of duty.

It has been said that the packet was a hard school. It had to be, or fail. By and large, it was probably as hard a school as ambitious youth ever attended. It had but one motto, which served each successive class for 50 years—"Drive her! You gentlemen's sons! Drive her! You dukes in disguise! You can't live forever!"

Their lives indeed were short, but in the brief time allotted them, they did more than their part to speed the building of the kindly refuge that serves our ends—its inscription now obliterated and all but forgotten.

CHAPTER V

∽ *1815-1821* ∽

The First Coastal Queens

"Speed the plough, the ship and the loom."

ALTHOUGH Isaac Wright and associates were the first to put ocean transportation on its present-day basis—regular "liner" sailings on schedule—they did not originate the idea. That had been tested on inland coastal waters several years earlier.

A few months' experience in 1812 with British blockaders and privateers had convinced American merchants that coastal trade by sea was no longer practical. They had suffered severe losses almost from the beginning, and the blockade became more effective month by month. Confronted with this situation, they decided to combine forces and form lines of inland packets and wagons, "Land and Water Packets," to supply the more pressing needs of North and South.

The first of these lines began operations in March, 1813, between southern New England and Baltimore, by way of New Haven, New York, and Philadelphia. It was called the "Mercantile Line of Wagons and Packets," and ran three times a week.[1] Agents were appointed in the principal towns and cities along the route. Southbound freight went by wagon train from Boston and Providence to New Haven; thence by sailing packets to the Jersey shore; thence by wagon to Trenton; thence alternately by water and land to Philadelphia and Baltimore. For northbound freight and passengers the process was reversed. Farther south, traffic depended on an irregular service maintained by individuals on inland water routes, using wagons where necessary.

Additional lines were soon established between New York and Philadelphia, where traffic was especially heavy.[2] They included the "Exchange," "Commercial," "Union," "Pilot," and "New Pilot" lines and one oddly named "Crosswick's Drawbridge Line."[3]

The latter was owned by the then well-known New York merchants, L. L'Hommedieu and John W. Brown. Their Philadelphia agent was the equally well-known George Bird. Like many of his name, George was a bird of passage, and we find him domiciled now in Philadelphia, now in New York. He must have been a striking character, for long after he passed from the scene some of the Philadelphia concerns were still referred to as the "Bird Lines."

None of the above mongrel outfits ran on a set schedule, other than undertaking to make one or more trips weekly, but the fact was unimportant. Schedules would have served little purpose where packets and wagons were passing and repassing in virtually continuous procession. What was important was that it was the first large-scale attempt of highly individualistic merchants, who regarded secrecy as their chief stock in trade, to effect economies, which had become essential to survival, through cooperative combinations.

These lines accounted for the bulk of coastwise traffic during the rest of the war, but the fact did not prevent a few hardy individuals from handling their own business. One such horse-marine venture is described in the *Providence* (R. I.) *Patriot* of May 24, 1814:

> Yesterday arrived at this port a fleet of four and five horse wagons, laden with sea-island cotton, 110 days from Savannah, belonging to Mr. Eben Jenckes. The fleet consisted of 25 sail when it left port, 18 of which reached here, the other seven were laid up about 20 miles distant, and the horses put to pasture. The bare expense of the voyage, we are told, amounted to $6000, and the proprietor has lost six of his horses since it commenced.[4]

Although the "union lines" provided the element of orderly succession in loading and departure, they failed to bridge completely the gap between the old regular trader and the later "line packets." There was no hard and fast adherence to a fixed sailing schedule, nor was there any assurance that certain packets or even a certain number of packets would be maintained in the lines. That step, however, was not long delayed.

On the 4th of March, 1814, the *New York Gazette* and other local papers carried an advertisement which, so far as ascertained, was the first published notice of the establishment of a line of packets in America, pledged to sail on a set schedule. It read in part as follows:

> NEW LINE FOR ALBANY. The subscribers being duly aware of the advantages that would arise to shippers of goods and produce between Albany and New York, by having a line of sloops formed to ply between the two places on set days, have therefore purchased 3 of the first class sloops, viz, the *Gold Hunter,* Captain Martin, the *George,* Captain Ostrander, and the *Hardware,* Captain Weller. . . .

The notice went on to state that the sloops would leave Albany and New York every Saturday, starting as soon as the river was open, and that there would be a third sloop loading at Lent's dock in New York at all times. Modest though the experiment was, it embodied every essential of the later Liverpool packet practice. The New York proprietors were Adams & Rathbone, with offices at 13 Hudson Street, and John Clifford and I. & J. Townsend. Horace Lockwood and James and Jasper Keeler, who had a "fireproof warehouse" on the Albany dock, made up the northern contingent.

Nothing was said about passenger service, but there was no need. We know from other evidence that the Hudson River sloops carried passengers as a matter of course, and had handled, and continued to handle a substantial part of that traffic, regardless of steam competition. Some were elaborately fitted out for the purpose, even to ancient quarter galleries.

Success attended the enterprise from the start. The convenience to merchants and travellers of a fixed sailing date was so great that competing packets soon found it advisable to adopt the same course.

Within three months a second Albany line was formed, called the "Trotter & Douglass Thursday Line." It used the same terminals as the first line and consisted of the sloops *Morgan, Columbia* and *Perseverance,* commanded in that order by Henry Green, William W. Brower, and B. Whipple.[5]

These lines proved so profitable that in the following March a third and larger line was established, to sail twice each week on Wednesday and Saturday. It consisted of five sloops, and nine New York and Albany firms participated as owners and agents.[6]

Space is lacking to follow the fortunes of the Albany lines in detail. They continued to multiply and grow in size until single lines were furnishing a daily service. They remained a factor of considerable importance in western trade well down toward the close of the century, despite the competition of steam and canal boats.

Ugly and clumsy though these latter craft were, they were rendering essential service long before the Erie and Northern (the passageway between the upper Hudson and Lakes George and Champlain) canals were completed, as one section after another was finished. When the entire project was completed and formally opened with elaborate ceremonies on November 5th, 1825, they had the added advantage that they could embark entire families with all their goods in New York and deposit them, without change or transfer, alongside a Lake Erie steamboat. All through the second quarter of the century, Connecticut emigrants loaded their possessions, including livestock and wagons, on these miniature Noah's arks and started the month-long journey to the "Far West."

Where river traffic alone was involved, the sloops could hold their own.

They were a highly specialized and efficient craft, designed to carry enormous deckloads, which made for cheap and rapid stowage. Although extremely broad and shallow, they had easy lines and lofty spars designed to catch the light airs that drifted high over the steep, canyon-like banks of the Hudson. Pivoting on a deep centerboard and steering with a long tiller, they could turn on a dime—a maneuver they might be called upon to perform a dozen times on a single trip, as swift steamers or unwieldy tows swung suddenly around the sharp, narrow river bends ahead.

As a class they were remarkably good sailers. One early passage from Troy to New York was made in 14 hours, at a time when the fastest steamboat on the river, the 494-ton *Chancellor Livingston,* required 20 hours to make the trip from the nearer port of Albany.[7] Most of them measured 50 to 80 tons, but many were larger. There is a record of one of 155 tons, sporting a mast 102 feet in length, and having a carrying capacity of 2000 barrels and upwards.[8]

Although the "Land and Water Packets" served a useful, and even indispensable purpose, they were slow and expensive, warranted, so far as freights were concerned, only as a wartime emergency measure. After the war, they survived only as passenger routes in the remarkable expansion of stagecoach and steamboat service which started almost immediately. Steamboats were substituted for the sailing packets and fast passenger coaches for the wagons, with the result that travelling time between Boston and Baltimore was greatly reduced. Aside from this, the all-water routes were resumed for both freight and passengers, and, with minor exceptions, the traditional hit-or-miss, all-out competition again prevailed.

There was, indeed, no reason why it should be otherwise for the moment. Trade in the summer of 1815 was booming as never before. Every shipowner knew he could secure all the business he could handle without the cooperation of others, and without assuming risks incident to the delegation of responsibilities. Moreover, he knew that for the time being, at least, larger profits were to be made by sending his ships to ports most in need of merchandise than by confining them to a single trade. It was not until the boom was over and his vessels lay for weeks and even months in port, competing for freights which dribbled slowly down to the docks, that he would have occasion to reconsider his position.

Signs were not lacking in the summer of 1816. Word came drifting back from every quarter of glutted markets and shipments sold at a loss. By the next year every shipowner knew a depression was on. What he did not know was that it would last four long years and become devastatingly acute in the near-panic year of 1819, and that during all that time his concern would be less for profits than for mere survival.

Shippers were in no better case. Many an enterprising and competent exporter was to view with helpless dismay his mounting insurance and interest charges, while his goods lay month after month in the bottom of a half-loaded ship. Not a few were to go to the wall because payment for their long delayed shipments failed to arrive in time to meet maturing obligations.

As with David Harum's dog and his fleas, a reasonable amount of competition is good for trade, but when it becomes overly sharp it may be ruinous to all concerned. When it became obvious in 1817 that such a condition existed and that it was more than a passing phase, it was inevitable that merchants should recall the lesson in cooperation of the wartime "union lines," the more so because several of those lines, together with two or three more added since, continued to operate with notable success. They could hardly fail to be impressed, moreover, by the fact that with one exception all the small post-war lines were established by men who had been active in the cooperative wartime lines.

Thus, Davis & Center, of Albany, who were agents for one of the sloop lines between New York and Albany, founded Boston's first line. In May, 1815, they announced that a line of packets would be operated between Boston and Troy and Albany during the coming season.[9] It consisted of the sloops *George Washington,* Daniel Atwood, and *Favourite,* William Ingraham, masters. There were no fixed sailing dates; nothing but the fact that shippers could depend upon two vessels loading and departing in regular succession. All in all, it was a very modest affair. Its interest lies chiefly in the fact that it was established by men who had already had experience with the fixed-schedule Hudson River packet lines.

The second coastal packet line was organized the following November by Cornelius R. Duffie, 87 Wall Street, New York City, to ply between Richmond, Virginia, and New York. It comprised the schooners *Indian Hunter, Logan, Lycurgus,* and *Jane,* commanded in that order by Isaac Seaman, Samuel Holmes, Isaac I. Seaman, and William I. Nichols.[10] Although it had no set schedule, the early record of the line showed that it approximated a regular weekly succession so closely that it was a decided improvement over the earlier and still general practice.

A third coastal packet line was established about three months later by the New York firm of L'Hommedieu & Brown, who had already tested the general idea as agents of the old "Mercantile Line." It ran between

New York and Philadelphia and was called the "Union Line." (No connection with the wartime "Union Line.") Incidentally, it was the first line of packets out of Philadelphia if we except such activities as the "Union Steamboat Line," and its competitor, the steamboat "Dispatch Line." These continued, in conjunction with stagecoaches, the operation of passenger service begun by the wartime land and water packets. We will have occasion to notice them later.

The stated purpose of the New York-Philadelphia Union Line was:

To obviate delays owing to two packets loading at the same place at the same time.

Operations started in March, 1816, with six schooners and, as the sequel showed, the tacit ambition to provide a weekly service. The redoubtable George Bird, with headquarters at the counting house of Emlen & Howell, 17 South Wharves, was the Philadelphia agent.[11]

A month later another Boston line was established by Stanton & Spelman, 30 India Wharf. It ran between Boston and New York, and consisted of the sloops *Ceres, Boston,* and *Astrea,* commanded respectively by E. Cary, A. Rogers, and E. Ripley. It had no fixed sailing schedule but proposed merely "to expedite and remove the evil so much complained of by shippers of vessels stopping in ports on their passage."[12]

Although no other coastal packet lines definitely committed to the maintenance of a schedule were established during the next two years, the fact is probably due to the progress of the depression, which reduced the movement of merchandise to such an extent that shipowners could not guarantee to sail with any degree of regularity without risk of serious loss. This, however, did not prevent merchants operating between all the larger ports from representing their vessels as constituting regularly established lines. It is clear, whatever of timidity or sound caution was involved, that at all times after the peace there was a growing sentiment favoring the formation of lines, as opposed to the old pre-war preference for the operation of casual ships by individuals.

What is more to the present purpose is the fact that the success of such coastal lines as found it possible to sail on schedule was outstanding and continuous. It is difficult to escape the conclusion that their example must have entered, to some extent, into the calculations of Isaac Wright and his associates.

America's coastwise trade in the post-war period, however, was destined for greater things than the chance presentation of a laudable precedent. It had been growing in relative importance for years, following the industrial development of the northern states, which enabled them to supply the

South with an increasing variety of manufactures formerly imported from abroad. This, in turn, stepped up the North's requirements for southern staples. Now, as the commercial boom slowly subsided in 1816, the process of industrialization was accelerated.

Depressions are rarely an unmixed evil. With a hardy, energetic people, indeed, they often prove a blessing in the long run. Such was America's post-war depression. It shook the nation, but it shook it up. The active redoubled their efforts. The lazy found themselves face to face with the unpalatable alternatives of their colonial forebears, who prescribed the simple barnyard remedy, "Root, hog, or die!" as the answer to all temporal ills.

Fortunately or otherwise, at this juncture New England rum, aged in the wood, sank to 37, and Kentucky whiskey to 23 cents a gallon. Few, even of the lazy, wanted to die. They rooted, even though it took rum or whiskey to get some started. In retrospect, the period stands out as one of great fundamental development of the shirtsleeves variety when the foundations of undreamed prosperity were being laid, broad and deep.

Everyone suffered but, all things considered, the times bore hardest on maritime interests, due in large measure to overproduction of ships. In the three years 1815 through 1817, an average of 1282 vessels had been added annually to the American merchant marine.[13] Once the pressing needs of the post-war world had been supplied, it would be impossible to employ all that tonnage profitably until demand should have caught up with production, and that was largely a matter of population.

Fortunately, that factor was favorable. Population growth continued, notwithstanding the depression, at a constantly accelerating rate. It had increased two and one-half millions in the decade following 1810. It would show a further increase of three and a quarter millions during the next ten years. Few people, however, are in a position to await the slow workings of economic laws. They have to eat now. As it happened, they solved their immediate problem by speeding up two processes, migration and industrial development.

These were no new things, save in the sense that they suddenly took on added stature and importance. Through the Napoleonic era they had gone almost unheeded, while commerce ruled the roost and merchants everywhere laid ship and cargo on the barrel head and gambled for fortune on a single throw. With the depression, the situation was all but reversed. Migration to new lands and the establishment of new industries stepped up overnight to a point where they threatened to supplant trade as the major American interest.

The center of population—almost motionless since the Revolution—began to move westward with ever-increasing speed. Stalwart young farmers from stony ancestral acres; merchants who had lost ships and credit; sea captains, still in the prime of life, whose ships lay rotting at the docks; shipbuilders; jobless workers of all sorts, joined the rolling wagon trains, now lengthened by a rising tide of emigration from Europe. They went in droves, to the amazement of conservative stay-at-homes.

As early as the fall of 1817, the *Albany Argus* reported an estimated 500 a week crossing the Hudson at that point alone, bound for western New York and the Ohio.[14]

That same fall, 3000 passed through Easton, Pennsylvania, in seven weeks.[15] The local editor thought the world was going crazy, but concluded, "We fear it will not stop until the disease is cured by its own exhaustion."

It did not stop. On the contrary, it grew in volume from Maine to Georgia as in 1819, and later, more and more southern planters began to cross the Mississippi to assure the admission of Missouri as a slave state, and still others headed for the fabulously rich "black lands" of Texas.

What it might portend was made clear within a few years, as cheap western produce began to pour eastward through the Erie Canal and southward down the Mississippi to the markets of the world. Paradoxically, the flight from trade was destined to play a major role in building a new and vaster commercial empire.

Meanwhile, northern merchants everywhere, unable to employ their capital profitably in commerce, seized the opportunity afforded by cheap labor and materials offering at bankruptcy prices, to build manufacturing plants.

Throughout New England cotton and woolen mills, foundries, slitting mills, machine shops, dye works, shoe factories, tin, copper, and other metal-working plants sprang up as if by magic on every brook that could turn a wheel. Stockings, laces, hats, bonnets, clocks, lamps, glass, crockery, jewelry, and all kinds of Yankee notions came into mass production.

The rapidity with which manufacturing developed in the North is indicated by the fact that as early as 1817 Boston had a warehouse on Cornhill Square devoted exclusively to domestic fabrics.[16] They ranged from superfine broadcloths and satinets to ginghams and hats. Samuel Davis & Company, the proprietors, proclaimed:

> They will be sold much less than cloths of equal quality can be imported, and are now selling for. Gentlemen are requested to examine them, as they are worthy the attention of those who love their country and wish to promote its independence.

By 1821, cotton mills in the vicinity of Providence, Rhode Island (even then the jewelry manufacturing center of America) were using 31,000 bales a year.[17]

Another mill, established in 1814 at Waltham, Massachusetts, was the first factory to use power looms, and reputedly the first to combine all processes of manufacture under one roof. In 1822 it employed 500 workers and turned out 35,000 yards of cloth a week.[18]

Long before this, President Monroe, intrigued by what he had heard, made a "Progress" through New England in 1817, visiting the more important plants, including the vast new ironworks at Vergennes, Vermont. Everywhere he was met by welcoming delegations, loaded and half-cocked with long-winded addresses—it being then the quaint custom for the people to do the talking and Presidents the listening.

A similar, but less varied program was under way in the other North Atlantic states, with notable additions. Philadelphia, Alexandria, Georgetown, Petersburg, Richmond, and Baltimore had built huge flour and feed mills, and Philadelphia and Albany were also turning out quantities of newfangled cookstoves to supplant the ancient wasteful fireplace.

Baltimore was the largest producer of flour in America during this early period. Her capacity was well above half a million barrels a year. For the three months ending December 31, 1819, the flour inspected there amounted to 191,283 barrels.[19] Aside from supplying the northern states, she exported direct to Great Britain, Europe, and South America. By the summer of 1822 there were, in the immediate vicinity of Baltimore, 13 cotton and 2 woolen mills, 1 copper rolling mill, 3 iron rolling mills, and 30 flour mills.[20] The exportable manufactures of all the other ports of the Chesapeake did not equal those of Baltimore.

New England, which had been devoted almost exclusively to farming, lumbering, fishing, and seafaring pursuits, no longer raised enough grain for her population, now enlarged by thousands of factory workers who produced no food. She became of necessity a flour-importing area. After the war Boston alone had a dozen vessels plying regularly to the flour ports. Brands like Philadelphia "Superfine," Baltimore "Dexter Street," and Richmond "Gallego" became household words throughout New England.

In New York, Pennsylvania, and farther west, coal, iron, copper, lead, and salt—once obtainable only at the cost of long foreign voyages—were beginning to be mined on a large scale. In Baltimore, Wilmington, Patterson, and Salem, a few reckless individuals had embarked on the manufacture of cotton canvas, which was much superior to the dingy, baggy flax sails of Europe. The venture proved an expensive one for the pioneers. It used a lot of cotton from the start and eventually accounted for thousands of bales annually.

These and similar developments reacted adversely on foreign trade, retarding its growth while fostering a proportionately rapid expansion of domestic commerce. Granted a continuance of the industrial trend, it was clear that America's coastal trade would far outweigh her foreign business in any conceivable future. The fact was obvious, even before 1820.

In that year her shipping engaged in coasting amounted to 588,025 tons, as against 583,657 tons in foreign commerce. Five years earlier her foreign trade employed 894,295 tons, as against 475,666 coastal tons.[21] The shift in relative amounts of freight handled becomes more striking when we reflect that coasting vessels landed a full cargo every few weeks, while deep-water craft required from several months to a year to make a single round trip. Disturbances abroad, wars, crop failures, or the superior efficiency of American ships occasionally boomed her foreign commerce for brief periods. On the whole, however, the trade never again ranked better than a poor second to the humble coasting activities. Some conception of its volume may be gained from the fact that as early as 1817 it was estimated that between 4000 and 5000 vessels passed Cape Cod annually, heading north or south.[22] That a similar condition prevailed all along the coast is indicated by the marine columns of the daily papers.

No one despised the prosaic coaster. Boston, whose merchants often have been described as dwelling in a rarified upper realm, inaccessible to ordinary mortals, men who might have been expected to blackball anything less than a China packet, devoted a greater part of her shipping to the trade than any other port. In 1816 her coastal arrivals amounted to 1684, almost as much as New York's 1832, although New York's foreign tonnage was then almost equal to that of Boston and Philadelphia combined.[23] Indeed, Boston, which had fallen for a time to fourth place, had risen again as a result of New England's industrialization to become the second American port, both in foreign and coastal trade.

The character of the coastal trade had also changed. Where formerly it consisted of bulk cargoes of relatively cheap, and consequently less profitable, raw materials, it now included a large and rapidly increasing volume of expensive manufactured goods. The very profitable first-class passenger traffic was also showing a similar increase. Few Boston merchants remained aloof.

As soon as peace with England was assured, Cornelius Coolidge, who "kept" at 53 Long Wharf, laid the ship *Marcellus* on for Norfolk. Thomas Amory & Company, a few doors away at number 58, put the *Latona,*

William Low, master, up for New Orleans. Edward Cruft loaded the brig *Edward Foster* for Charleston and Joseph Ripley advertised an 80-ton schooner for the same port. All these, and more, three days after the news of peace. By coincidence, all had "extensive and commodious" accommodations for passengers.

Within a few weeks the list had grown to a score of packets bound for southern ports. Lemuel Pope, Jr., was one of the most energetic of the Boston operators. For years he usually had several vessels up for domestic and foreign ports. E. Silsby, 9 Bray's Wharf, put up the brig *Angelina* as the first packet for Savannah. Edward & William Reynolds, another very active firm, had the well-known ship *Mentor* loading for Charleston, and T. K. Jones & Company, the *Factor*, for Savannah. Josiah Bradlee and David Hinckley were both heavily engaged in southern trade from the start. Stevens & Athearn, Hill & Mills, John Richards, and John W. Holland sent packet sloops and schooners to ports ranging from the Chesapeake to the Gulf. The great majority of vessels in the immediate post-war trade were sloops and schooners; the latter measuring from 100 to 150 tons for the most part, while the sloops were generally smaller.

The foregoing by no means exhausts the list of Boston's early coastwise packet operators. One might name 50 concerns regularly engaged in the business at the time of Monroe's visitation. Among the more active, aside from those already mentioned, were the substantial firms of Thomas & Edward Motley, Baker & Sargent, and Joseph Peabody & Company. Lincoln & Wheelwright, on Fort Hill Wharf, and John Pratt & Son, 19 India Wharf, were running brigs and ships to New Orleans. Calvin Bailey specialized in packet schooners to Philadelphia. William Goddard, T. Battelle & Company, and Henry Hall traded mostly to Savannah. Munson & Barnard, Stephen Brigham, and Henry Sigourney were all over the lot. William F. Weld, who later became one of Boston's largest shipowners, ran sloops and schooners to Wilmington, North Carolina, and occasionally to Chesapeake ports. John Hovey had a couple of schooner packets operating between Boston and Robbinston and Lubec, District of Maine, bringing back principally plaster and grindstones from the Canadian provinces. Richard D. Tucker & Company, in conjunction with Lemuel Pope, Jr., was one of the first Boston merchants, if not the first, to send a packet to Mobile. This was in September, 1817.

Many of the above were also prominent in foreign trade, as well as active in a variety of other enterprises—banking, insurance and manufacturing. Some conducted retail emporiums on State Street or Cornhill Square. The heaviest concentration of warehouses and counting rooms was to be found on Long, Central, and India Wharves, although a considerable number of firms were scattered among the smaller docks that lined the waterfront. Calvin Spear & Company's Charleston packets sailed from Spear's Wharf.

New York not only had more merchants in the coastal packet trade, but they established eventually a large majority of the noted coastal lines and an even greater majority of the Western Ocean lines. We will not go far wrong if we assume that for the years 1815 to 1821, inclusive, there were a dozen or more New York houses competing for the packet business of each of the more active ports between, and including, Boston and New Orleans. Among them we find the names of such well-known firms as Fish & Grinnell, Goodhue & Ward, John & Charles C. Griswold (Griswolds & Coates, in 1817), Peter Remsen & Company, Lockwood & W. DeForest, John Aspinwall, and H. Cary & Company. For most of these the coastal trade occupied only a portion of their attention. Within a few years they were sending only an occasional vessel to southern ports as feeders for their foreign trade.

Considerations of space make it advisable to omit for the present any comprehensive consideration of New York's packet service to the nearby ports of the Delaware and Chesapeake. J. & C. Seguine and John M. Lowry & Company were, however, specially important traders to the Chesapeake from the beginning, and played a part in significant later developments. The "D" line (Dispatch) operated by D. & Peter Grim was giving regular and dependable service to Philadelphia. Other concerns will be noticed from time to time as occasion arises.

In the Charleston trade, Anson G. Phelps was one of the more prominent early figures. Phelps started as a Connecticut tinsmith. After he had served his apprenticeship he decided to travel and peddle his wares. When he got to Charleston, South Carolina, he traded his horse and cart for a bale of cotton, figuratively speaking. When he had learned the cotton business he returned to New York and became one of her largest cotton merchants. George Sutton, who later managed one of the noted Charleston lines, was one of his packet masters. Years later, after Anson Phelps had become wealthy, he returned to Connecticut and his first love. He built the largest tin-smithy in America and a town to go with it, modestly naming the result Ansonia.

Henry Cowing had the well-known ship *Telegraph* on the New York-Charleston run. Titus and Van Zandt operated a line of schooners for some years. The fast-sailing *Ambuscade*, Captain Skidmore, was one of their vessels. G. Gibbs had the schooner *Bright Phoebus,* among others. Edward Gamage had a branch packet office in Charleston. He operated, among others, the fine ship *Corsair,* long a familiar sight on the New York waterfront. John Bulkley, 190 Pearl Street, was running the ship *South Carolina* to Charleston as a regular packet as early as November, 1815. The firm, however, which figured most conspicuously in the early years on the New York-Charleston run was the above-mentioned J. & C. C. Griswold and its successors. They were running packets to Charleston and also to Havre, which was hungry for southern cotton, by the summer of 1815. Occasionally they ran one to Savannah. Eventually, the senior member, John Griswold, founded the famous London line, which carried the "Black X" (X for express) Griswold flag for many a long year. Boyd & Suydam, Saul Alley, Pott & McKinne, Falconer, Jackson & Company, and several others ran packet brigs and ships to Charleston immediately after the peace and, with the exception of Alley, continued to do so for several years.

Thaddeus Phelps, who like his competitor, Anson, was a Connecticut boy, but no kith nor kin, was a prominent operator of packets between New York and Savannah for several years after the peace. Thomas C. Butler, Jr., at 74 South Street, was another. He had the brig *Tybee* as a regular packet in the "Brig" line. He also sent packets to Mobile and New Orleans, and ran the *Minerva* and the new ship *Martha* as regular traders to Liverpool. William Sketchley, later a popular Liverpool packet master, was one of his commanders.

Other packet operators between the two ports included Albert Ogden & Company, 119 Pearl Street, who operated the packet brigs *Eliza* and *Savannah Packet;* Griswolds and Coates, already mentioned in connection with the Charleston trade, and Thomas Carpenter, who, in association with S. Bell, ran both sloops and brigs as packets. The brig *Speedy Peace,* a fast sailing craft of 186 tons built at New York in 1813, was their best known vessel and her commander was equally well known. He was Reuben Fosdick, one of the Fosdicks later active for many years on the run between New York and New Orleans. Strong & Havens were also among the earlier and more active of the Savannah packet houses. They had the brig *Sea Island,* William Jocelin, master, on the run in the fall of 1815.

Thaddeus Phelps' best known ship was the *Cotton Plant* and Michael Fash, her commander, was for many years a favorite packet master with the travelling public. The Griswolds & Coates ships included the *Venus, Adonis, Ellen,* and *Mary Augusta,* the latter commanded by the old reliable, Daniel L. Porter. They were all small—the *Mary Augusta* being the only one to measure 300 tons—but there were few larger vessels in the coastwise trade at the time. The firm also operated brigs and schooners and for a time traded all over the place, occasionally sending vessels to New Orleans. Bogert & Kneeland, 70 South Street, were also irregularly active in the Savannah packet trade.

New barks were launching out on New York's turbulent waters. On June 28, 1819, young William Whitlock, Jr., son of the stout old eighteenth-century shipmaster, started his long career by advertising the little schooner *Undaunted* for Savannah. He went on to found a line of Savannah packets and later, in company with J. & C. Sequine, the Havre line that bore his name down to Civil War days. His offices at 71 South Street are still occupied by members of his family, as well they might be, for one could and can yet see a cross section of the world's commerce from their windows.

Whitlock himself saw a strange sight from those windows a few months later. Looking out on South Street about noon on the 22nd of October, he noted a vast, turbulent crowd, such as the city had never witnessed, pouring into the street. It overflowed the docks and blackened the rigging of scores of ships—an estimated 25,000, all gazing out on the East River where a lone, dingy, two-topsail schooner lay anchored in mid-stream.

Soon a procession slowly made its way down Fulton Street—U. S. marshals and U. S. Marines with fixed bayonets. In its midst, there was a rough, horsedrawn cart bearing a coffin on which was seated a young man clothed in white; beside him, two clergymen singing hymns, surely a cruel and unusual punishment. They entered a boat and rowed with measured beat to the schooner, where for a few moments they eddied and huddled, a dark cluster of figures, amidships. A brief pause—then a smaller huddle running swiftly along the deck. In a twinkling, a convulsed, jerking bundle of ropebound white swayed aloft to the main yardarm. George Brown, late first mate of the schooner *Retrieve,* had paid the penalty for the murder of his captain on a voyage from Cadiz to Havana.[24]

Several months later another "Junior" turned up who was destined to be one of the outstanding figures in New Orleans packet circles and who was still active more than 60 years afterwards. This was Charles Morgan, Jr., who was the "Company" in Charles Morgan & Company. The firm was located at 37 Peck Slip and it cleared its first Charleston packet in February, 1820, the ship *Franklin,* commanded by S. Hoyt.

Packets and regular traders were running to Mobile in 1817, but the following year Peters & Herrick, a young and enterprising firm at 29 Coenties Slip, started the "First Line" with the new schooner *Thomas*

Shields. She was advertised on the 1st of January, 1818, "with dispatch." The venture paid so well that they soon had an imposing succession of schooners, brigs, and ships on the run, and even sent an occasional packet to New Orleans. Competition was not long in developing. Within the year Tom Butler, Jr., had a string of packet sloops, and Beekman Brothers & Company and E. M. Southwick had several brigs competing for the business which was doubling and trebling year by year as the rich Alabama cotton plantations came into production.

Three New York firms, all with branch houses in New Orleans, stood out above all others in the rapidly developing post-war packet service between the two cities: Foster & Giraud, John W. Russell & Company, and N. & D. Talcott, known as Talcott & Bowers in New Orleans. The Russell concern proved to be the most important and longest lived, although Andrew Foster used to claim the credit of originating the New Orleans packet service. There is no doubt but that he became wealthy through the trade. He was credited with clearing $50,000 year after year at a time when few of the greatest merchants of the country did as well. However, the firm discontinued its New Orleans activities, as did N. & D. Talcott and Talcott & Bowers, at a comparatively early period, while the Russell outfit and its successors endured as long as sailing packets ran.

By 1817 the Talcotts had a line of packet brigs and ships, sailing in regular succession during the busy season. One of their brigs was the *Thames,* commanded by William S. Sebor, whom we will have occasion to notice from time to time. Another of their vessels was the "fine, fast-sailing ship" *Caravan,* commanded by young John Rathbone, sometime blockade-runner out of Stonington, Connecticut. Captain Rathbone had the girlish appearance of a Hollywood hero, which sometimes proved painfully deceptive to slow-moving sailormen. The firm also had the brigs *Fredonia,* B. A. Muzzy, master; *Superb,* Captain James Meek; and the *Day,* Alexander Don, all packets, and operated a number of other brigs and ships. It was extremely active for a time but ceased its packet operations during the depression of 1819.

John W. Russell was operating a line composed principally of brigs as early as 1818. One of his captains was Silas Holmes, another Stonington blockade-runner, who eventually founded the Holmes Line.

There were a number of other New York men and firms active in the New Orleans packet service in 1816 and for several years thereafter. They include Bogert & Kneeland, whose brig *Tom Hazard* was a familiar sight for many years to strollers along the levee; N. G. Minturn & Company, Henry Coit and Henry Cowing, Ripley, Center & Company, and Laidlaw & Gerault. These and others were frequently to be found dispatching packets to other southern ports as well as to New Orleans. It was several years before the coastal packet traffic settled into regular grooves.

One of the most colorful of the early packet operators was the noted—or notorious, as one prefers—Jacob Barker, of the Nantucket Barkers. He was located at 84 South Street, and was heavily engaged in both the Savannah and New Orleans trade. One of his ships, the 260-ton *Loan,* commanded by John Barstow, figured, in the latter part of 1816, in an attempt to kidnap free New York Negroes and take them to New Orleans to be sold into slavery. This, unfortunately, was an all-too-common practice at the time. What it meant to the free Negro is indicated by the fact that during this period New Orleans papers contain many notices of Negroes taken up and held in jail, who were wearing iron collars and iron bands about the waist, with chains to the ankles. The Quakers, who had fairly clear-cut notions about human rights, petitioned Congress repeatedly to put an end to the kidnapping traffic.

In Philadelphia, on the 15th of February, 1815, 40 Philadelphia merchants fired 40 simultaneous broadsides to announce through the local papers the news of peace and the still more important news that their packets would have "immediate dispatch" to London, Liverpool, and Havre, and every coastal port from Boston to New Orleans. Said "immediate dispatch" was conditioned on the opening of the Delaware for navigation and certain other contingencies, concerning which the advertisers maintained a discreet silence.

Gustavus & Hugh Colhoun laid their brig *Dromo,* David Brown, master, on for New Orleans. Wm. Montgomery & Son advertised the ship *Caroline* "with accommodations for 30 passengers" as "a constant packet" for Charleston. Messrs. Perry & Gaston—the latter one of Savannah's most prominent merchants—had the brig *Olynthus* up for Savannah "without delay." Jacob S. Waln began running packet schooners and brigs to Boston and other northern ports. John J. Downing put the fine pre-war packet ship *Pennsylvania* back on the Charleston run. Robert Fleming followed suit with the *General Wade Hampton,* and Sam Brooks entered the *Georgia Packet* in the same trade.

The firms of Patton & Manly, Allen & Taylor, and Tunis & Way were very active, sending brigs and schooners in considerable numbers to various ports along the coast. One of Patton & Manly's commanders for a time was young John Rathbone who, as already noted, had the ship *Caravan* in the New Orleans trade. The fact indicates the unsettled conditions which prevailed for several years after the close of the war, when one frequently found the same men operating the same ships on several different packet routes in quick succession.

Daniel C. Ellis specialized in Charleston and Savannah packets. Another firm heavily interested in the Charleston trade was Wiggin & Whitney. They had, among others in 1820, the old fast-sailing ship *Telegraph,* one of the best known vessels in the coastal trade and usually reported as "one of the line ships."

New names and old names in new combinations were constantly appearing. Chandler Price, one of Philadelphia's energetic pre-war merchants, took a partner and Messrs. C. Price & Morgan began trading to New Orleans in 1819. The following year they were running the ship *Tennessee* as a regular packet to that port and soon had something on the order of a line in operation. After Tom Morgan's death, Price continued for several years, dispatching ships and brigs with considerable regularity. The line survived many years under successive changes in management as one of the more important coastal operations.

In common with others, Philadelphia developed a number of packet lines to the various towns on the Chesapeake as well as to New York.

Baltimore's extensive foreign trade, together with her intensive development of manufactures, made her the principal distributing center for the entire Chesapeake area. For this reason her post-war packet activities included an abnormally large proportion of inland water traffic. By the summer of 1815 a dozen or more of her merchants were clearing packet sloops and schooners by the score to every port on the Bay. Among these, the three most important, from the standpoint of their influence on the development of lines which adhered to a fixed sailing schedule, were Reuben Ross, Wm. McDonald & Son, and Benjamin Ferguson, whose activities will be considered later in this chapter.

Among the early coastal packet operators, N. W. & C. H. Appleton and Henry Thompson were engaged in the Charleston trade. James Creighton & Company, Charles & Peter Wirgman, and Charles W. Karthaus & Company sent most of their vessels to New Orleans. Bucklin & Olyphant and Isaiah Mankin specialized in New York packets. Ballard & Hall, Henry Payson & Company, Thomas Marean, and Hammond & Newman, together with Brundige, Vose & Company, maintained services to Boston. R. H. & Wm. Douglass were active in the Savannah trade.

If one were to take in the old firms which occasionally laid one of their ships on as a packet, although usually confining themselves to foreign commerce, we would have to include such concerns as Wm. Wilson & Sons, Hugh Boyle & Company, James Corner, Wm. Parrish and Alexander

Brown & Sons. These, and others, had occasion from time to time to send their vessels to southern ports to load for Europe or Great Britain, and when this happened they frequently sailed as "the next packet."

Charleston's population in 1815 was slightly under 25,000, approximately that of New Orleans. Her coastwise traffic on the resumption of trade, however, was more than four times that of the latter port, and even exceeded that of Baltimore by a substantial margin. Only New York, Philadelphia, and Boston surpassed her in domestic commerce. In foreign trade she ranked fifth among American cities.

It would serve no worthwhile purpose to trace in detail the early development of Charleston's post-war packet trade. For several years business was in a state of flux; its changes of little importance except to the individuals involved. Firm succeeded firm and ship followed ship in rapid succession. Packets sent to New York by one agency on Monday were dispatched to Philadelphia or New Orleans on Tuesday by another. Houses appeared and disappeared in short order.

The earlier and more active packet operators on the New York run included T. & H. Tupper; E. Gamage & Company (later Gamage & Moore); Henry Cowing & Company; and Phelps & Olmstead. The Tuppers had a fine ship *Rising States*. Gamage operated first the *Telegraph* and then the very handsome new *Corsair*. Phelps & Olmstead had the *Telegraph* for a time, and also ran a large number of schooners and brigs. Megrath & Jones and Bours & Bascome also ran packet schooners to New York as early as 1816.

In the summer of 1819 yellow fever was added to the pressure of hard times to reduce Charleston's commerce to a mere trickle, but even before that, old firms had been dropping out one by one, or had curtailed their operations almost to the vanishing point. Instead of ships and brigs in quick succession, they now sent out an occasional small sloop or schooner, leaving the larger risks to the later arrivals.

One such newcomer was Timothy Street & Company, who appeared on the scene in 1818 with the ship *Favourite*. Another was D. W. Hall & Company, who took over the *Telegraph*. Hall soon disappeared, but Street had come to stay. By 1821 he had secured the agency for the best of the New York ship packets—the *President, Commodore Perry,* and others. The line was to stretch on for another generation as Charleston's most celebrated and important packet line, "The Ship Line."

Local operators of Boston packets included Daniel Perkins and Jerome Loring & Company, both of whom ran schooners for the most part. D. Crocker & Company became agents for a line of brigs in 1818 and J. Leland & Bros. began operating schooners about the same time. Many years later the Lelands were running a brig line to Boston.

Early agents and proprietors for Charleston-Philadelphia packets included Brooks & Potter, who had the ship *Georgia Packet,* commanded by the well-known Jared Bunce. Robinson & Patton operated the famous schooner *Calypso* for a time. She was the largest of the early schooner packets, measuring 326 tons. Most schooners in the packet service measured from 100 to 150 tons. Josiah Wheeler also ran schooners to Philadelphia. By 1818 the firm of W. E. Snowden & Company handled a substantial part of the Philadelphia packet business. They were agents for the fine ships *Pennsylvania* and *General Wade Hampton.*

Another firm which was to hold an important place in Charleston commerce was Adger & Black. This house was running vessels to Baltimore in 1818, among them the old ship *Congress.* It eventually became one of Charleston's largest shipping firms.

In addition to the strictly coasting firms, there were a number of very substantial Charleston houses engaged in foreign trade, usually operating their ships as regular trading packets. Among them Robert Maxwell, Broadfoot & McNeel, Buchanan, Wood & Company, Higham & Fife were active in the Liverpool and Greenock trades. Gibson, Falconer & Company had several ships running to Greenock, and Andrew Low & Company was one of the heaviest traders to Liverpool. The firm, indeed, was a branch of a great Liverpool house. Francis Depau & Company not only traded to Havre but operated packets to New York.

For some years the Charleston packet service was superior to that of other American ports. Savannah and New Orleans, indeed, had a few ships that were little, if any, inferior to the best Charleston vessels, but the Charleston fleet, as a whole, was superior in size and in the quality of accommodations until 1822, after which New Orleans began to come into its own.

All southern packets were designed for speed with special reference to light weather conditions and those of Charleston were no exception, as the noted run of the *Caroline* in 1810 would indicate. Many were built on the old "cod head and mackerel tail" lines with the long, fine run that tended to make a fast ship in moderate weather. Consequently, a good many creditable passages were made through the years. The best early run found from New York to Charleston was a 77-hour passage of the *Franklin,* Captain Munro, in December, 1820. The all-time record, according to the *Charleston Courier* of November 23, 1833, was established by the ship *Henry Allen,* under the command of Henry Wilson, which arrived in Charleston harbor the previous day in the remarkable time of 67 hours from New York. Through the years there were a few 84-hour records, and four-day passages were fairly common, with 14 days even more common, plus an extra week occasionally thrown in for good measure.

Few ports in America exceeded Savannah in enterprise in 1815. Before the year ended the brothers, Samuel and Charles Howard, fortified by a grant of the exclusive right to navigate vessels by steam in State waters, had built the hull of the 90-foot steamboat *Enterprise*—the first towboat to be launched in America, aside from the rather insignificant craft of John L. Sullivan. She was completed early in 1816, with power "equal to the united force of 22 horses."

Savannah also possessed her full quota of able and energetic merchants. Barnabas McKinne, who represented the New York firm of Messrs. Pott & McKinne, was active in the Bordeaux trade as well as in the coastwise packet field. He managed the packet ship *Woodbine* and packet brigs *Casket* and *Sea Island* on the New York run, and the ships, *Juno, Sagadahock, Ellen* and *Exporter* and brig *Eliza* in foreign trade.

Charles Perry of Philadelphia, late of Gaston & Perry, formed a partnership with Thomas Wright, with offices at Smith's Stores. Within a short time we find them running the packet brig *Hero,* William Coit, to New York, and the packet brig *Olynthus,* John Bailey, to Philadelphia. They also loaded Philadelphia ships for Liverpool.

Jonathan Battelle was especially prominent in New York packet circles, as well as active in the Bordeaux and Amsterdam trades. He handled, among others, the fine New York packet ship *Oneida,* commanded by the able and popular Captain Nathaniel Green Hilliard.

Other early packet operators of Savannah included M. Herbert & Company, in the Philadelphia trade; Meigs & Reid, who ran schooner packets to New York; Calvin Baker, who came out with the new ship *Cotton Plant,* Captain Michael Fash, in December, 1815; Whitney & Parkman, who ran the packet brig *Eliza Lord* to New York, and *Adeline* and *Almira* to Boston; P. Schenck & Company on Rice's Wharf, who had the brig *Savannah Packet* in the New York trade; Pelot & Merrick; Ballard & Spencer; Edes & Potter, on Knox's Wharf, whose sloops traded regularly to Providence; Morris Ketchum and P. Stanton, both of whom ran brigs and schooners to New York; W. T. Williams, who loaded the packet brig *Sally,* Captain Myrick, for Philadelphia, and many others who appeared briefly in the years immediately succeeding the peace.

They were soon followed by several firms who were destined to wield considerable influence for years to come.

One of the greatest of these was the firm of Hall & Hoyt who first began to attract notice in 1817, when they ran the schooner *Mary,* Dick Laha, master, to Baltimore. Soon they were handling a number of packet brigs and ships in the New York trade, as well as acting as agents for the new local steamboats. Among the best known of their early packets were the brig *Levant,* commanded by the veteran, Denison Wood; ships *Rubicon,* Nathan H. Holdredge, and *General Carrington,* Thomas Wood, and the schooners *John Dorcas* and *Undaunted.*

Few Savannah merchants ranked higher in public esteem than William Gaston. For some years after the war he was agent for a number of fine Philadelphia ships that loaded at Savannah for Liverpool on the "triangle route," returning to their home port from Liverpool. One of the best known of these was the *William Penn,* a live oak ship of 400 tons, long commanded by James Hamilton. He also sent packet brigs to New York occasionally.

George Gordon, on James' Wharf, had been running packet brigs to New York for several seasons. In June, 1820, he came out with the smart brig *Othello* which he could specially recommend, "Her births (sic) are prepared with sacking bottoms."

A few days earlier Perry & Wright had advertised that the brig *Fox* was "Particularly fitted up for 100 steerage to New York, fare $7.00; passengers to find all but wood and water."

In addition to firms which were quite consistently engaged in the coastal packet service, there were, as in the case of Charleston, a number of substantial houses trading for the most part to Great Britain and the Continent which usually operated their vessels as packets.

Among these, the branch house of the great Liverpool firm of Andrew Low & Company was outstanding. John Speakman & Company, on Fraser's Wharf, William Taylor and Johnston & Ellis were active in both Liverpool and Greenock trades and R. Richardson & Company cleared ships for Havre as well as Liverpool. Isaac Cohen & Company—a name destined to become prominently identified with Savannah shipping interests throughout the packet era—loaded most of the Philadelphia ships engaged in the Bordeaux trade.

Sturges & Burroughs was another enterprising concern. Their best known vessels were the *Crisis* and *Fair Trader,* the former employed on the Havre run under John Skiddy. Most of their ships, however, went to Liverpool.

Long before 1822, both Savannah and Charleston had adopted the practice of referring to their coastwise packets as "line ships" or brigs or schooners, as the case might be. At that time, however, most of the "lines" might be more precisely described as "composite lines." With few exceptions, none were under a single management but consisted of vessels owned and managed by several firms whose only relationship consisted of a working arrangement to dispatch their respective ships in regular succession. The arrangement did not extend to a schedule of fixed sailing dates, nor did it include any commitment to maintain any particular vessel or any definite number of vessels in service.

The coastal trade of New Orleans, which had continued relatively light since the Louisiana Purchase, increased slowly but with growing momentum after the war. Its early volume is indicated by the fact that from November 1st to December 24th, 1815, a period when post-war trade was at its booming height, it was reported as a noteworthy circumstance that 76 ships and brigs, two schooners, and one sloop had entered the Mississippi.[25] Since some of these vessels were bound to Natchez and other river ports, and many others were engaged in foreign trade, it is evident that New Orleans' coastwise business must have ranked far below that of Charleston or Savannah.[26] The fact was that the city still maintained a heavy trade with France, and her commerce with Liverpool was mounting year by year.

After the war, however, as it became more and more obvious that much of the traffic of the great Mississippi Valley would pass through the port, young northern merchants flocked to the city in considerable numbers. In a comparatively brief time they changed completely the character of its commercial activities. By 1816, several firms were sending substantial ships and brigs as regular packets to and from northern ports, but by 1818 two firms stand out as especially active and successful.

Gilbert E. Russell & Company represented the Russell line to New York. They had the ships *William, Remittance, Edward,* and brigs *Nancy* and *Planter,* and occasionally loaded other vessels at the height of the season. Their early masters included Captains Purrington, Holmes, Downs, Packard, and Hart.

Morgan, Dorsey & Company were local proprietor-agents for the C. Price & Morgan Philadelphia line. Their ships included the *Balize,* Hezekiah Harding, master; *Orleans,* John Grover; *Ohio,* S. Tobey; and the brig *Feliciana,* Nathaniel Franklin.

Both these lines maintained a steady and quite regular service for many years but it was not until 1826 that New Orleans lines began to advertise and observe fixed sailing schedules, being, so far as I have been able to ascertain, the last of the important packet ports to do so.

There were many other packet operators, dating from the early post-war months. Samuel T. Colt was in the New York trade and frequently loaded the packet ship *Telegraph,* owned principally by Henry Colt of that city. Thomas L. Servoss and Dunlap & Wooster cleared a good many packets for New York. Judah Touro, another ex-Bostonian, ran packets to Boston.

He was for years one of the most active of the New Orleans merchants. Amory, Callender & Company also sent packets regularly to Boston, as well as engaging in other coastwise and foreign commerce.

Richards, Spicer & Company traded to Philadelphia, Ward & Goodale ran line schooners to Baltimore and R. D. Shepherd & Company, another extremely active concern, traded to Baltimore and Boston and handled a large amount of foreign traffic as well.

Other houses which figured more or less prominently in local packet circles about this time included H. Munro, Milne & Company; Gordon, Grant & Company; Gardiner & Center; Vincent, Nolte & Company; William Boyd & Son; Curell, Ure, Donald & Company; John Minturn; Zacherie & Turner; Palmer, Hall & Company; Harrod & Ogdens; Rogers & Collins; Henry Marston; T. & D. Urquart; McLanahan & Bogart; and Dennistoun, Hill & Company. Although the above list includes several of the most ably managed and important of the New Orleans houses, the majority of them disappeared within a few years, but while they lasted they contributed heavily to the development of the city and the nation. What they accomplished may, perhaps, be gathered from the statement of Captain Grover of the packet ship *Orleans*. When he arrived in the Delaware River below Philadelphia the latter part of February, 1818, he reported that he had left 200 sail at New Orleans and had passed 50 more in the Mississippi, bound up.[27] This, it will be remembered, was when the depression was well under way.

The early packet history of Mobile and Blakeley (which may, for present purposes, be treated as one port) followed closely the pattern set by New Orleans, although on a much smaller scale. In both instances the packet service was developed by newcomers from the North. When the first northern packets arrived in 1817, Blakeley had but one permanent building. Mobile, which was reported to have a population of 500, including Negroes, when captured by General Wilkenson in 1813, probably did not greatly exceed that number when the aforesaid invasion began; which invasion, it should be noted, included more brickmakers, bricklayers, and carpenters than merchants.[28]

By 1820 the population of Mobile was estimated at 1500. River steamboats had been running cotton to the port for two years. The town was incorporated; a bank had been established and the volume of trade was climbing rapidly. Its relations with New Orleans were close from the start. William H. Robertson, Mobile's leading merchant in the early years, who had vessels up for every port along the coast, ran packet brigs and schooners to that city with considerable regularity. Thomas L. Hallett, C. Heartt, Judson & Banks, Lee & White, and the ubiquitous Winthrop &

Company were all there and all busy. Most of them, by 1820, had taken turns at loading Hurlbut packets for New York.

With one exception, none of the Mobile packets down to 1822 were operated in groups or lines. John D. Hurlbut, however, gathered several vessels together by degrees and by 1820 was advertising them as the "Regular Line to New York." All his early ships and brigs were built on the Connecticut River and were owned and commanded by Connecticut men. Service was quite irregular during the early years, and it was not until 1825, under the management of E. D. Hurlbut & Company that it began to give a dependable service. Eventually it became one of the greatest of all the coastwise lines.

A second line to New York was established in 1821. John Hunter was the local agent. It consisted of a combination of ships and brigs, and maintained approximately weekly sailings during the active season.

As with New Orleans, none of the Mobile packet operators adopted a set schedule of sailings until 1826, but they did, nevertheless, sail at fairly regular intervals.

Despite the fact there was no heavier American traffic than that between the North and South, not a single ship operator in that trade adopted a schedule of sailings before the great packet year of 1822. The principal reason undoubtedly was that southern traffic was intermittent in character. From March to early July and again during the late fall and early winter months, it was exceptionally heavy. At other times the managing owner of half a dozen ships found it difficult to secure a cargo for a single sloop or schooner, and at such times usually sent them on foreign voyages or laid them up for an overhaul. It was also subject to wide fluctuations even during the peak months. A sudden drop in the price of cotton or in freight rates might bring it to a standstill. Recurrent yellow fever and smallpox epidemics, which were more frequent than indicated by general report, had much the same effect. These were conditions that made it hazardous for a shipowner to commit his vessels to a series of voyages at regular intervals, especially where long, expensive trips were involved.

The first packet line sailing on schedule to be established after the Hudson River lines mentioned early in this chapter was founded by Reuben Rose, of Baltimore, who operated "The Line Alexandria Packets." On the 14th of July, 1817, he advised the public that in the future his packets would sail every Saturday.[29] He maintained this service for many years, increasing it from time to time as the port grew.

The first coastal—as opposed to inland tidewater—line to operate on what may be termed an approximately fixed schedule out of Baltimore, was the "Regular Line—New York Packets." Isaiah Mankin was the local proprietor-agent and Wm. W. & Jas. H. Todd, corner of Old Slip and Front Street, the New York representatives. They had maintained irregular sailings for several years. In November, 1818, they established a line of four schooners and one sloop "to sail in regular succession every ten days, at most." In May, 1821, another schooner was added to the line and the sailings fixed for every Saturday.[30]

Two other Baltimore concerns which began operations immediately after the war quickly established combination steamboat and sailing packet service, in which the steamboats were run on schedule.

Wm. McDonald & Son continued the wartime "Pilot Line" between Baltimore and Philadelphia. At first they used sailing packets and stages exclusively, but in the summer of 1816 they put the steamboat *Eagle,* commanded by Moses Rogers, on the run. The next year they had two steamboats giving a daily service, in addition to their irregularly sailing packets. The Baltimore steamer ran to Elkton, Maryland. From there a stage ran to Newcastle, Delaware, and met the steamer to Philadelphia.[31] Briscoe & Partridge started the "New Daily Line of Steamboats" in opposition, but their competition was short lived. They folded up in 1819, but the McDonalds continued until long after the completion of the Chesapeake & Delaware Canal, in the fall of 1829, enabled them to run their steam and sail packets direct to Philadelphia.

Benjamin Ferguson, who began by running sloop packets between Baltimore and Norfolk after the war, started a similar combination line in 1817 with the addition of the Baltimore-built steamboat *Virginia,* John Ferguson, master. She sailed on her first trip to Norfolk the 30th day of July, the pioneer steamer of the great Bay Lines.[32] She remained on the route for several years, making one round trip a week. Her average running time was about 24 hours. The Fergusons continued to manage the line for a number of years, during which other steamboats and many sailing packets were added.

One other regularly scheduled Baltimore line was established during this period. Ely Balderston, the local manager of the Baltimore-Philadelphia line, was also agent for a sailing line between Baltimore and Richmond. In May, 1820, when "hard times" was the principal topic of conversation and ladies' morocco shoes were selling for 50 cents a pair, he announced that his Richmond packets would sail every Saturday, "loaded or not loaded."[33]

By the close of 1821, therefore, the two concepts—cooperative management and regularly scheduled service—had been tested and proved in both coastal and transatlantic packet fields. It still remained to be seen whether the experiments presaged a general reformation of the time-honored practice of multiple competition and hit-or-miss sailings.

CHAPTER VI

ᔥ *1815-1821* ᔥ

Start of Steam Competition

"Then ships of uncouth form shall stem the tide."

W HILE men of the sail were taking the available measures to speed up travel and supplying, at the same time, the means to step up manufactures, a few visionary amateurs continued their efforts to perfect a new mode of transportation, that, strange to relate, was to prove of more immediate importance to the human race than all the labors of the greatest scientists of the day. Incidentally, they contributed mightily, both to the rise of the packet and to its ultimate downfall.

Within two years after the peace, steamboats were under construction from Lake Champlain to the Gulf of Mexico, and the Mississippi steamboat experiment had been extended to the Great Lakes and the St. Lawrence. Construction, confined largely to New York waters before the war, was proceeding vigorously in half a dozen other areas. The effect was not merely to increase steam tonnage rapidly, but to put scores of practical, ingenious men to work studying the possibilities of changing and improving both boats and engines. One of the most striking facts in connection with the steamboat is the remarkable swiftness of its transformation from a crude, clumsy, crawling monster to a thing of beauty, unexcelled in speed for some years on land or sea by any of man's creations.

All things considered, it was probably on the swift waters of the Mississippi and Ohio that it demonstrated its value most spectacularly. Before its appearance, traffic on those rivers was dependent on flatboats and keelboats which rarely made more than a single trip, owing to the impracticability of taking them back against the powerful current. They were manned by four or five men whose principal function was to keep them in mid-stream by means of long sweeps, and who, when their voyage ended at New Orleans, usually made their way back overland. Depending on their starting point, the round trip consumed from several weeks to several months, plus the weeks spent in constructing craft which were fit, as a rule, only for scrap after delivering a single cargo.

The steamboat changed all this. Nicholas J. Roosevelt's clumsy, Pittsburgh-built craft of 1811 pioneered a mighty fleet of ever larger, faster, and more powerful vessels. Blunt, deep-draft hulls like those of the *New Orleans* and other early boats, were soon being replaced with broader, shallower craft which slipped easily over, rather than through, the swift currents. Heavy, complicated engines were giving way to lighter, simpler, and more powerful equipment, the result of the shrewd thinking of river skippers who understood that their job was to put their boat alongside a waiting pile of freight before a competitor got there.

Within a few years they had doubled the power and speed of their vessels. What this meant was demonstrated by the performance of the *James Ross.* In June, 1819, she ran from New Orleans to Louisville, Kentucky, a distance of nearly 1500 miles against the current, in 14 days, in spite of numerous stops to refuel and take on and discharge freight and passengers. At this time the only other fast craft attempting the passage upstream— the light, fast-sailing, two- and three-masted barges, ranging from 70 to 90 feet in length and upwards—took from six weeks to two months to make the trip. Many years later the record of the *Ross* was reduced to a trifle over three days by such fliers as the *Eclipse* and *Robert E. Lee,* but in 1819 the wondering editor could only exclaim: "What a progress is this against the currents of the mighty rivers of the West!"[1]

Other uses were being found for steamboats. One was in the ferry service, where their superior speed and reliability quickly made them indispensable.

Fulton's catamaran *Jersey* was the first steam ferry to be put in service in America. It began running between New York and Jersey City early in 1812. It was a substantial affair of 118 tons, and met with sufficient success to encourage Fulton to build two more of similar type and size, the *York,* in 1813, and the *Nassau,* in 1814.

The superiority of steam over sail and rowing ferries stimulated the growth around New York of nearby Long Island and New Jersey communities, and their rapidly increasing population in turn stimulated further improvement in ferry service. As a result, the steam ferry attained very early a degree of efficiency that was all but final. In July, 1820, for example, the *Williamsburg* established a record of 52 trips across the East River in a single day; her average time for the run of a mile and a half from Corlear's Hook to Long Island being seven minutes.[2] During the next century ferryboats became larger and accommodated more passengers, but their service was little, if any, faster or more dependable.

Philadelphia's ferry problems were much simpler. She brought out a little craft called the *Camden,* a 37-tonner, which was in operation back and forth across the Delaware by May 30th, 1812, and possibly a short time earlier.[3] The city fathers, however, were so skeptical that they ordered the old ferry to be kept in readiness for service in event of the *Camden's* failure.

The reign of the steam ferry was challenged but once. In April, 1814, New York papers noted that a new ferryboat, propelled by six horses on a treadmill, the invention of Moses Rogers, Esq. (the merchant, not the master of the *Savannah*) was plying between New York and Brooklyn. It crossed in seven minutes in "slack water" and carried upwards of 300 passengers.[4]

Rogers' invention, however, proved inadequate to New York needs, partly because the East River failed to provide enough "slack water," partly because it appeared that six horses produced somewhat less than 100 horsepower; and partly, perhaps, because the Corporation of the City decided to begin running two steam ferries from Beekman Slip to Brooklyn in the spring of 1814. Nevertheless, "teamboats" continued in use for some years in areas where water and traffic conditions were more favorable. The *Blazing Star* teamboat was still plying the Narrows between Staten Island and the Jersey shore in 1824, and possibly later.

A third use for steamboats, and one fraught with far-reaching consequences, was for towing.

William Symington, of Scotland, had built a small steamer called the *Charlotte Dundas* in 1802 and had demonstrated the practicability of towing canal boats. He was not permitted to continue the use of the invention, but his example was not lost. Fulton, among others, saw and studied the *Dundas.*

America's first towboat came 12 years later. *Niles' Register* for June 14, 1814, recorded:

John L. Sullivan, of Boston, has obtained a patent for the use of steam engine power in towing luggage boats, being a new and useful application of steam engines, and put in practice by him on the Merrimack River.

Sullivan's description of his invention was destroyed in a fire which swept the patent office several years later, but the fact that he was issued a patent for a "Steam Tow Boat and Warping Windlass" indicates that it included one of the first versions of the steam winch, which eventually did so much to speed waterborne traffic. As for the boat itself, it was undoubtedly a small and crude affair; its chief, if not its only importance, lying in the fact that it directed attention to the problem of towing. Sullivan continued his efforts, patenting another towboat in 1816 and building a larger craft in 1819; but such fragmentary information as is now available indicates that he devoted his attention in the main to developing small steam craft suitable for use on canals rather than for heavy-duty towing.

That, oddly enough in view of her traditional conservatism, was left for the South to accomplish, although her first steps in that direction were postponed for several years by the War of 1812. The *Boston Gazette* for May 17, 1813, noted:

> Three companies have been formed in South Carolina for the purpose of navigating its waters with steamboats. One of these associations is to run boats between Pasquotank and Blackwater and Newbern; another between Beaufort and Portage; the third between Wilmington and Charleston. The capitals employed amount to $85,000. There are also to be steam ferry boats between Edenton and Salmon's Creek.

The tightening of the British blockade halted these activities and three years elapsed before South Carolina merchants again turned their attention to the matter. Meantime, people in the great and sovereign State of Georgia decided to take a hand.

Toward the end of 1815 a group of Savannah merchants built the steamboat *Enterprise*. Her engines were installed and she was put in service early in 1816. She was a shallow-draft vessel whose tonnage has been variously stated as 118 and 152 tons. In view of her performance, her tonnage is of little importance. She was the first American steamboat to demonstrate beyond reasonable doubt the practicability of steam towboats. Although she was built primarily to haul cotton barges or "pole boats," as they were called, between Savannah and Augusta, she proved early in her career that she was capable of greater things.

On the 11th of May she towed the ship *Georgia* down the river to Five Fathom from her Savannah dock "with the greatest of ease, at the rate of five miles an hour."[5] Two months later she was in a neighboring port. The *Charleston Courier* noted that on July 12th she towed the brig *Arethusa*, bound from Charleston for New York, down to the outer buoy in an hour and a half, and added: "This is the first vessel that has been towed down by steam."[6]

The *Enterprise* was no less successful with the "pole boats." For many years those craft, which ranged from 70 to 90 feet or more in length and carried from 400 to 700 bales of cotton, had been poled slowly, laboriously and expensively up and down the rivers and in and out of tidal inlets by large crews of slaves. The *Enterprise* handled two boats of the largest size more expeditiously than the slaves could, and at a vast saving in labor. She had the further advantage that her costs of operation were largely met by increased passenger revenues.

It was no mere chance that made Savannah the pioneer in transatlantic steam navigation.

Charleston promptly met the challenge of her sister city by organizing the Charleston Steamboat Company in June, 1816.[7] There were 500 shares, half of which were reported subscribed in Philadelphia where Daniel Large was building the 20-horsepower engine. The hull of the pioneer craft, which was 90 feet in length on deck, was built in Charleston by "that ingenious mechanist" John O'Neale. She was launched as the *Charleston,* 160 tons, on the 4th of March, 1817, and put in service on or about the 24th of June, as a "packet" to Sullivan's Island; fare, $31\frac{1}{4}$ cents; children and Negroes, 25 cents. She lacked the power, however, to compete successfully with the other local steamers which soon appeared and, after engaging in various activities, including excursions with brass bands and sundry trips to Savannah, she was put up for sale in March, 1820.

A second Charleston steamer, the *Georgia,* of 138 tons, built locally in 1817, was a much abler craft and continued to run until 1831. Savannah's second steamboat, the *Carolina,* 170 tons register, was also built in 1817 and, like the *Georgia,* was in active service down to 1831. Although built primarily for freight and passenger service, all the early steamers did considerable towing, especially of pole boats.

The interest of Charleston and Savannah in steam was undoubtedly stimulated by the success of the steamboat lines on the Delaware and Chesapeake during the war years. As early as 1813 there were five steamers in operation which, in conjunction with the post chaise and stage lines, enabled a passenger to travel from New York to Baltimore in a theoretical two days, but which "unusual" road conditions generally prolonged to nearly double the advertised time. Such delays, however, were rarely chargeable to steamboat failure but to the fact that in wet weather the best horses could not haul the stages at the average rate of two miles an hour.

Under the leadership of Captains Moses Rogers and James Lefevre, the steamboats on the New York-Baltimore route soon increased to eight, grouped in two competing lines, each of which did its best to out-steam and out-maneuver the other. For several years, racing at the imminent risk of collisions and boiler explosions was the order of the day, to the gratification of excited passengers and the indignation of "Vox Populi" and "Pro Bono Publico," who then, as now, wrote long, wrathful, protesting letters to their favorite papers.

Several of these early craft, indeed, were remarkably fast. The *Boston Gazette* for June 26th, 1817, quoted a Philadelphia paper as stating:

On Tuesday last, were made the shortest passages between Burlington and Philadelphia since the Delaware has been navigated by steamboats. The *Philadelphia,* Jenkins, ran the distance, 46 miles, in 1 hour, 46 minutes. The *Bristol,* Myers, in 1 hour, 48 minutes.

Making due allowance for a favoring current and exaggerated mileage, it is evident that the rate of the vessels through the water could not have fallen much short of 15 statute miles an hour. At the same time it was noted that the fine new 500-ton steamer *Chancellor Livingston* required an average of 20 hours to make the 144-mile trip between Albany and New York.

With the above demonstrations of speed on their northern borders a matter of common experience, the early interest of North Carolina and Virginia in steam navigation was not long in reviving after the return of peace in 1815. Between 1817 and 1821 they financed a series of vessels, mostly small, shallow-draft craft, which did much to step up local transportation of packet freights, as well as passengers.

The list included the *Norfolk,* designed to run between Norfolk and Edenton, North Carolina, built at Norfolk in 1817; the *Richmond,* built at the same place in 1818; the *Albermarle,* built in New York in 1818 and owned in Edenton; the *Petersburg,* owned in Petersburg, and built in New York in 1819; and the *North Carolina,* built in Fayetteville in 1819. They ranged in size from the 80-ton *Albermarle* to the 162-ton *Richmond.*

Another early steamer, the *Virginia,* of Norfolk, a 289-ton craft, built in Baltimore in 1817, had the distinction of being the first vessel to tow an American man-of-war. She was credited with taking the frigate *Congress* from Reedy Island to Hampton Roads in December, 1817, "at the rate of 4 miles an hour against a strong wind and tide."[8] The *Virginia,* in fact, was rather more of a craft than most of her contemporaries. Later, lengthened and enlarged to 340 tons, as the *Temple of the Muses,* she had a long and useful career on the Hudson, and was still going when steamboats nearly three times her length and five times her tonnage were plying those waters at a good 21 statute miles an hour.

As opposed to intriguing visions of steamboat flyers, the towing idea spread comparatively slowly. Probably ingrained considerations of economy were mainly responsible, but pride and confidence in one's sailing ability played a part. Certainly, a good many master mariners felt it would be an admission of incompetence to "take a line" except in serious emergencies.

Accordingly, when the *Nautilus* was built in New York, late in 1817, she was designed and intended to serve, primarily, as a steam ferry to Staten Island. Her owners were aware, however, that during the winter months she could not profitably make more than two or three trips a day, and they equipped her with towing bitts to enable her to fill out a day's work with whatever towing offered, knowing that her best, if not her only chance of securing such work was when winter storms and floating ice prevented ships from making their docks under sail. As already noted, it was under just such conditions that she took her first tow, the packet *Corsair,* on the 26th of January, 1818. Thereafter, all her towing of which we have any record was done in the winter months. During the rest of the year her time was quite fully occupied making eight or more round trips to Staten Island every day.

Aside from the Sullivan craft, above mentioned, New England's first towboat was the steamer *Enterprise,* built at Hartford, Connecticut, in 1818. She was launched early in November and was expressly designed for use in towing vessels between Hartford and the mouth of the Connecticut River.[9]

It is strange, in view of the fact that ships of sail had to make their way 100 miles up-river against a strong current to reach New Orleans, that the use of towboats in that area was delayed. One cannot rule out the possibility that some early towing occasionally took place, but it was not until the summer of 1822 that a regular towboat was provided for this service.[10] This was the steamboat *Post Boy,* and it is to be noted that she was constructed in response to complaints of long delays in the river, made by passengers of the fast-growing packet fleet.

Over in Liverpool, where, owing to tidal and weather conditions the towboat was badly needed, progress was even slower. It is possible, and perhaps probable, that small steamboats were used to a considerable extent to move ships about the port and haul them in and out of the wet docks. On the other hand, aside from the small privateer *Harlequin* and the *James Monroe,* an extensive search has disclosed no other record of towing large vessels to sea prior to 1822. On the 8th of November in that year, just as Boston was loading the *Topaz,* her first packet liner, for her maiden voyage, the Philadelphia packet *Lancaster* was towed down the Mersey by two steamers.[11] Whether there were other instances or not, the fact that two boats were required to tow a 380-ton ship indicates, perhaps, the state of towboat development at that time and place.

It is, indeed, one of the anomalies of history that England, after developing the steam engine, lagged behind America in applying it to naviga-

Courtesy, New London County Historical Society

Courtesy, Mrs. Clifford Day Mallory

Captain Francis Allyn who commanded the *Cadmus*, which brought Lafayette to New York in 1824.

Charles H. Mallory, master of coastal packets and founder of Mallory Steamship Lines.

Bark *Lexington* of Boston, built in 1833. She was typical of the little barks of about 200 tons employed in the coastal trade in considerable numbers from 1830 to 1850.

Courtesy, The Peabody Museum of Salem

Courtesy, The Mariners Museum

Brig *Mail*, formerly of the Union Regular Line, Boston to Philadelphia. A typical coastal packet brig of the eighteen-forties.

Captain John E. Williams, master in coastal packet lines during eighteen-forties and later master of clipper ships.

Courtesy, Dr. Roger N. Ryley

Captain Addison Richardson master of New York to Havre Union Line packet ship *Duchesse d'Orleans* in 1838 and later years.

Courtesy, The Peabody Museum of Salem

Courtesy, The Marine Historical Association, Inc.

Packet ship *Marengo*.

Packet ship *Duchesse d'Orleans* of the Union Line, New York to Havre.

Courtesy, Whaling Museum

Courtesy, Seamen's Bank for Savings

James Brown

Courtesy, Seamen's Bank for Savings

Captain Moses H. Grinnell

Courtesy, Seamen's Bank for Savings

Captain Silas Holmes

Courtesy, Seamen's Bank for Savings

William Whitlock, Jr.

tion. Her seeming indifference was probably due in a measure to the discouraging reception of the *Charlotte Dundas,* but possibly even more to the widespread opposition to innovations in general, which motivated that reception. There is also the fact that her navigational problems were different. The great inland waterways of America provided an ideal spawning ground for steamboat fry.

Whatever the reason, ten years were to elapse before she produced a practical successor to the *Charlotte Dundas,* the tiny, 42-foot *Comet,* built on the Thames in 1812. Notwithstanding her diminutive size, the *Comet* amazed thousands of Londoners by her performance on the swiftly flowing river, and did much to arouse a more active interest in the subject. Tales and sketches brought back by English travellers of "floating palaces" on the Hudson—the 330-ton *Paragon, Car of Neptune* and others—incomparable for size, luxurious appointments, and the swift, dependable accomplishments of their rounds, also had their effect. They afforded indisputable evidence of a serviceable and, above all, a highly profitable achievement.

Nevertheless, another four years drifted slowly by before the *Eliza,* the first British steamer to cross the narrow English Channel, arrived at the port of Havre in March, 1816. Her passage of 20 hours from London indicates an average speed of ten nautical miles an hour, but her actual steaming speed was probably less, since her crossing would be timed to get the benefit of the tides. She steamed up the Seine from Havre to Paris, "where she arrived to the astonishment of thousands, who had assembled to witness the novel sight."[12]

At this time Great Britain had few steamboats, and most of them were small. Her largest, as late as 1821, was the 128-foot *Tourist,* launched at Perth in the spring of that year.[13] America, on the other hand, had built in the neighborhood of 50 by the close of 1816, and several exceeded 150 feet in length. The exact number is unascertainable, owing to the failure of some early owners to enroll their vessels. Of those which can be identified beyond question at the close of the year, 28 were built for coastal waters, 12 were Ohio and Mississippi River craft, and the rest scattered. The precise number, however, is of less importance than the wide distribution of construction, which forecast a rapid acceleration of production.

Even before the close of 1817 the "steamboat fever" had affected the entire nation. In addition to localities previously mentioned, Vermont had already contributed three side-wheelers to speed communication with Canada by way of Lake Champlain. Sackett's Harbor had built the *On-*

tario, the first steamer to navigate the Great Lakes, nosing out by a narrow margin the Canadian *Frontenac,* launched earlier but delayed in completion. Down in the District of Maine, groups were enthusiastically planning the construction of several river steamers. From the deep South came the report that a steamboat was being built at St. Stephens, Alabama, on the Mobile River, although that territory was not yet legally in the possession of the United States.[14] Louisiana chartered the Atlantic Steam Coasting Company with the exclusive privilege of entering the Mississippi from the sea "with vessels impelled by fire or steam" for 20 years; the objective being the establishment of steamship service between New Orleans and New York.[15] On the Mississippi itself, the demand for steamers was so great that New York and Philadelphia were building vessels up to 500 tons, to supplement the output of the numerous Ohio River yards.

Massachusetts had shown relatively little interest in steam, but in 1817 a Salem group had the steamboat *Massachusetts* built in Kensington. After some tinkering with her machinery, she was given a trial trip the latter part of June, and was credited with making between six and seven knots. Her advertisers were able to improve this rate somewhat, as shown by the following, used to drum up trade:

> Shawmut's Sons! with teeth sharp set,
> As Bodkin's sheers for cabbage whet:
> Come lounge no more; the city flee;
> And glut on dainties of the sea.
>   With fire and steam; eight knots at least,
> I'll speed your way—to Squantum Feast.

As forerunner of the singing commercial it fell somewhat short of the cultural triumphs of that notable achievement, but it seems to have appealed to the Proper Bostonian in the year of the great Nahant Sea Serpent.

Massachusetts acquired two more steamboats the following year, both built at Norwich, Connecticut, and both originally named the *Eagle.* The smaller, an 80-ton craft, became Nantucket's first steamer in 1818, having been re-christened the *Hancock.* The other, which measured 104 tons, had a long career in Boston waters. None of the three were particularly successful, all being small and insufficiently powered.

There were, indeed, a good many failures and near-failures in the years before the great ocean-going steam packets of the next generation.

The Boulton & Watts-type engines, still the general favorite, were crude, clumsy, inefficient, enormously heavy, and space consuming. They were also difficult to operate. It was frequently necessary to start them with handspikes, as they had a trick of stopping on dead center. A thousand problems awaited the ingenious mechanics of England, Scotland, and America, and if the Scot led the way, the Yankee was never far behind.

Boilers were quite as bad as engines. They devoured vast quantities of fuel in proportion to horsepower developed, and required long, laborious cleaning every few days. They blew up on the slightest provocation and sometimes with none at all. When all else failed, they set the ship afire. Many an unsung river pilot was destined through the years to "hold her nozzle against the bank 'til the last galoot's ashore." The need for stronger and lighter metals, more complete utilization of prodigally wasted steam, better combustion and more effective insulation and packing, was obvious. Even the vessels themselves called for far-reaching changes in lines, proportions, and construction.

Books could not help, for there were no books. Lacking books, the great authoritative scientists of the day devoted no little time to proving that the untutored practical mechanics were concerning themselves with impossibilities.

There were exceptions, it is true, but visionary men in scientific circles, walled in on every side by the accepted dicta of learned ignoramuses, found all too often that departure from the beaten track meant long years of heartbreaking frustration, if not loss of reputation and relegation to obscurity.

Thus, the one man in America who visualized most accurately the true line of development of the modern high-pressure engine spent years in unsuccessful efforts to get a practical test of his theories. This was Jacob Perkins of Newburyport, Massachusetts, who in the period following the Peace of Ghent invented an engine which he claimed could utilize pressures up to 1500 pounds with almost fabulous savings in weight, space, and fuel, and actually built one that operated at 900 pounds. Eventually he went to London where, according to report, he sold his invention, after which he turned his attention to the invention of a steam cannon later taken over by the French government.[16]

A still more revolutionary invention of a contemporary Frenchman was also rejected by his contemporaries. Professor Meincke, of Paris, must have been a remarkable man, for in 1819 he invented fluorescent lighting—60 years before a youth named Edison found a way to make an inferior electric lamp after long research and experiment.[17] What happened to his discovery is still unexplained. Possibly it would have met the same fate even in America where there were fewer monopolies and influential scientists to block the roads of the future, for the American genius was of the practical, workaday sort, which advanced slowly, cautiously, step by step. Instances of intuitive leaps from hopeful but bumbling inefficiency to approximate perfection were rare indeed. In general, any such short-cut suggestions were frowned on as wildly visionary.

It was so with the steamship. Even the great and, in his proper field, extremely able Professor Benjamin Silliman of Yale was numbered among those who regarded the transatlantic steamer as an impractical pipe dream. Such conclusions cut no ice with grimy apprentices, too ignorant to realize the "insuperable difficulties." In retrospect, it would seem that the scientific sceptics of the day failed, in similar degree, to impress the mechanically minded Scots.

Whatever the explanation, early improvement of the steamship engine and steamship lines came in the main through obscure men, born to manual labor, and a few amateurs—men like John Stevens of Hoboken, Oliver Evans of Philadelphia, and Captain Henry Shreve on the Mississippi. It should be noted, too, that aside from stimulating inquiry in other fields, it was largely experimentation with the steamboat engine that made possible the early successful application of steam to land transportation. Without the long, preliminary work of marine engineers—sooty men, for the most part, with dirty hands—the advent of the locomotive might well have been postponed to an unpredictable future.

Early official statistics of steamer construction are incomplete. The summary, "Merchant Marine Statistics," for example, issued by the U. S. Department of Commerce in 1928, lists only 23 new steam vessels enrolled in 1819. Actually 37 were built and enrolled that year, and others were built for which no enrollments have, as yet, been discovered. It was the biggest year yet in the history of steam, and by far the biggest for the river boats. Twenty-eight new steamers were built on the Ohio, and if there was an *Esau Sludge* or two among them for Martin Chuzzlewit to travel upon, there was also a promise of future *Robert E. Lees*.

The year is notable, moreover, as the first in which steamships were laid down: vessels constructed for ocean steam navigation. The story of the *Savannah,* Moses Rogers, master, is too familiar to warrant repetition. It is to the purpose, however, to note—statements to the contrary notwithstanding—that she was as much an ocean steamship as any of the early craft to which the title has been accorded. As the first, she was understandably smaller, cruder and less efficient, but the difference was in degree, not in kind.

All the early steamships were precisely what she has been derisively termed, "auxiliary sailing ships." There were few afloat 50 years later, in fact, which were not rigged to make port under canvas alone, in the event of power failure, and most of them used their canvas habitually when conditions permitted.

In connection with the *Savannah*, it has been incorrectly claimed that the *Royal William*, a 700-ton steamship which crossed from Pictou, Nova Scotia, to London, England, in 1833, was the first to use steam all the way, and is therefore entitled to the credit of being the first transatlantic steamship. She was undoubtedly better powered than her earlier rival, for her designers had the benefit of an added 12 years of engine improvement, but her steaming record was little better, if any, than the *Savannah's*. Instead of making the voyage under steam alone, as has sometimes been stated, she used her sails almost continuously, and for a substantial part of the trip, exclusively. Her engines were repeatedly out of commission in dangerously stormy weather. Once they were unusable for about a week. Fortunately, she carried the substantial rig of a three-masted, topsail schooner, with spars as long and heavy as was usual in a 300-ton vessel of that rig. But for that fact—on the evidence of Captain McDougal himself—she would almost certainly have been lost.[18]

Her crossing—less than two-thirds the distance traversed by the *Savannah* but made under less favorable conditions of wind and weather—occupied 19 days, as against the 26-day passage of the *Savannah*, a fact sufficient in itself to indicate there was little difference between the vessels, from a steamship standpoint.

By one of those coincidences in which history abounds, the world's second ocean steamship was laid down in New York the same year as the *Savannah*, although she was not completed until early the following year.

The *Robert Fulton*, more than twice the size of the *Savannah*, registering 702 tons, was in every way superior to her rival, as a steamship. Her length of 158 feet exceeded that of any merchant steamer then afloat. She was owned by David Dunham & Company, a wealthy mercantile firm at 144 Pearl Street, in New York, but shortly after located at 45 Broadway, which still is the center of that city's steamship offices.

David Dunham, who was familiar with the New Orleans trade, having had the ship *Orient* on that run for some years, planned to use the *Fulton* as a New Orleans passenger packet, exclusively, touching at Charleston and Havana. The only freight accepted was specie. He also proposed to rely chiefly on engine power, and she was originally very lightly rigged with lug sails. Later this was changed to full ship rig. An early cut of the vessel shows her with two smokestacks side by side, and a walking beam between the fore and mainmasts.

She sailed on her maiden voyage to New Orleans April 25, 1820, under command of Captain Richard Inott, stopping only at Havana.[19] She arrived at New Orleans on May 15. Deducting the two days' stopover at Havana, her running time was slightly under 18 days.[20] On her return trip she stopped at Charleston, and her local agents, Buchanan, Wood & Company, reported that her actual steaming time from Havana was 90 hours, and her time from New Orleans a trifle over seven days.[21] This was an excellent performance with a new ship and stiff engines. Her passenger list of about 70 persons was encouraging, since the peak of northbound travel was still several weeks in the future.

Charles Edmonston, a prominent merchant of Charleston and owner of Edmonston's Wharf, where the *Fulton* docked, was soon appointed as the Charleston agent for the ship. He continued to act for her during the rest of her career, and later was most active and influential in coastwise steamship circles.

Dunham continued to operate the *Fulton* until his death three years later, when he was lost overboard in March, 1823, while on a trip to Albany in a packet sloop. After his death, his heirs continued to run her for two more seasons. She was laid up very late in 1824 and eventually sold to the Peruvian government, who, in 1827, converted her to a sailing corvette. In that capacity she established a reputation for exceptional speed, indicating that she was a sharp-built vessel.

It has been said that her withdrawal was due to lack of patronage. Since she continued to run for five years, during which time traffic was increasing, it would seem that this is not the full explanation. It is quite possible that Dunham's heirs did not consider her profitable, and it is perhaps equally possible that her sale was necessary to settle the estate. But the fact remains that no ocean steamship for 50 years to come could show a satisfactory profit on passenger traffic alone. They had to carry a fair amount of freight.

Coastal passenger traffic, as already noted, was seasonal. It was heavy when southerners were flitting northward in the late spring and early summer, and again from mid-September to late November when they were returning home. At such times the *Fulton* was usually reported with large passenger lists, the largest noted being 150, and in that trade "passenger" meant a first-class passenger.[22] Servants were not passengers, although they were always present in force, to the enlargement of the ship's revenues.

In the matter of speed, after a shaking down and adjustments of machinery, the *Fulton* logged an average of eight knots, or thereabouts, at sea. In quiet water she was capable of a trifle over nine knots. On one occasion she ran from the Battery, in New York, to a point outside Sandy Hook, a distance, probably, of 20 statute miles, without the aid of sail in one hour and fifty minutes.[23]

From the standpoint of a theorist who is not called upon to put up the cash, it is regrettable that Dunham did not try the *Fulton* on the transatlantic run. Her record between New York and New Orleans—no mean test, what with "line gales," Gulf hurricanes, and Hatteras hard athwart the course—proved she was better, faster and more dependable than either the *Savannah* or the *Royal William*. It suggests that she could have crossed to the eastward in 15 or 16 days with some degree of regularity. Such an achievement, even though a losing speculation, might easily have led to the early construction of larger steamships and advanced transatlantic steam navigation many years.

Two other steamers designed for ocean navigation were built in New York shortly after the *Robert Fulton*.

One was the steam brig *Mexican*. She was sent to Havana and put on the run between that port and Vera Cruz. The other was the steam schooner *Fidelity,* commanded by Captain Richard Leach, intended for a packet between New York and Norfolk. She left New York on her first trip, the 7th day of May, 1821, and arrived at Norfolk on the 10th. Her performance was not encouraging. Under the best conditions, she required two days to make the trip and many of the sailing packets could do as well or better under similar conditions. Moreover, she was too small for comfort and could not stow a paying cargo. A single season was enough to convince her owners of the advisability of cutting their losses.

By the close of 1821, the pattern of steam and sail development for the next decade was definitely indicated. No one then living, unless it was John Pintard, of New York, could or did forecast its volume or rate of acceleration. Brother Jonathan was no shrinking violet when it came to describing what he could or would do, but his noisiest boastings, in the light of what came to pass, bore the same relation to reality that a sand barge bears to a clipper. Perhaps John Jacob Astor, possessor of several ships in the fur and China trades, estimated more accurately than any other. At any rate, he gathered in New York's choicest real estate with all the assurance of a bank clerk with a straight tip on the third race. Even so, he took few chances, for most of his holdings came by way of foreclosure at bankruptcy levels.

Prosperity had returned to America in the dear old year of one thousand, eight hundred and twenty-one. Ten-cent cotton was again edging toward the twenties. Freights had jumped to two cents a pound. Ten-dollar Baltimore flour was on its way back from the three thirty-seven depression low, with a few shiploads headed for the twenty-dollar markets of South America. Thanks in part to the stimulus of European discriminatory measures, the infant industry of the North was enjoying tariff protection of a sort, and planning "The Tariff of Abominations," which in 1828 was to serve as the entering wedge to split the North and South. Langdon Cheeves had chased the looters out of the Bank of the United States. Scores of other "Rag Banks," unburdened by assets, had swindled themselves and their depositors out of existence, to make room for the builders of the future. Only an informal extension of the 1812 war—privateering and piracy along the southern coast and in the West Indies—remained to pose a threat to relatively stabilized conditions.

Population was increasing faster than in other countries; faster, indeed, than in any country in history. It had jumped more than two and a quarter million in the decade since 1810, and passed the ten million mark by the close of 1821.

Since we are interested in the fortunes of the passenger packets, it is worth noting that more of the increase was due to immigration than meets the eye. Thus, official United States statistics report a total of 8385 immigrants in 1820, while New York ship reporters set the figure at approximately 13,000 for New York alone.[24] Since nearly 30 other American ports, to say nothing of an always-heavy seepage across the Canadian border, contributed to the total, it would seem that one or the other of the above authorities was roughly 300 per cent wrong. Possibly the truth lies somewhere between the two extremes. There are, however, other things which tend to throw doubt on the official figures.

All through this period London papers were reporting an extraordinary wave of emigration to America. For example, there were 11,300 from Glasgow in 1818; upwards of 30 ships were loading emigrants in London and Glasgow alone in the spring of 1819, and this at a time when ships often carried between three and four hundred steerage.[25] With due allowance for error and even intentional exaggeration, it is difficult to assume that conservative London papers would multiply actual figures several times, even to point a moral.

It is, indeed, possible that official British figures fall short of the correct total. British laws provided that ships could carry only one passenger for every two tons register. Nevertheless, ships were occasionally seized in

British ports with nearly double the legal quota of emigrants.[26] How many got away with the connivance of underpaid customs officials is anybody's guess but, human nature being what it is, or rather, was, there is reason to assume the number was substantial. Ship masters would be unlikely to report more passengers in American ports than they reported to British authorities, regardless of the effect on statistics. Nor, at this early period, was there any provision on the part of America for obtaining an accurate count. Her hard-worked customs officials were interested primarily in smuggling, not in immigrants. Anyone who could totter down a gang plank was welcome to step ashore and no questions asked.

It was not until 1819 that the Federal government, in belated response to criticism of conditions on the emigrant ships, conditions which sometimes resulted in the death of ten per cent and more of the steerage passengers, took steps destined to lead by degrees to a closer check on immigration. It passed a measure which granted the humble occupant of the steerage a trifle greater deck space than his shrunken corpse would require.

Fortunately or otherwise, the Act did nothing to reduce the flow of cheap labor, the supply of which was threatened by the westward push of population in an ever-increasing stream, and included not only recent arrivals, but thousands of New England farm boys and youths from all along the coast. On the whole, Europe was doing rather more than plugging the gaps in the cotton mills, iron foundries, and elsewhere.

Thousands of Irishmen and a few others—among whom might be found a stout York State boy named George Law—were digging a ditch along the Mohawk. Both the ditch and George will be heard from again, especially George. His experience with the pick and shovel was such that he soon found his greatest pleasure in assembling wielders by the hundred, and watching them perform. He became one of the nation's first large contractors, building canals, locks, bridges, and aqueducts. Eventually he turned to steam, and established a mighty line of steamships in the gold rush days. Before that came to pass, however, he served a long and highly remunerative apprenticeship moving dirt.

It was a time of many eras in America, all going at once. The canal era was only one. In the early eighteen-twenties, 50,000 more immigrants would have been needed to dig half the canals that were planned, as navigation tried to follow the pioneer over the hill. The story of the canal as a prop and support to the packet service would justify a volume by itself. For the moment, the country was "canal crazy," as 20 years later it was to be "railroad crazy," and for precisely the same reason: cheap, fast transportation. One enterprising newspaper publisher took advantage of the mania by naming his paper the *Norwich Canal of Intelligence*.[27]

Steam, anticipating Horace Greeley, started for the Rockies. The first steamboat "that ever attempted the current of the Missouri," the *Independence*, Captain Nelson, arrived at Chariton, Missouri, on the 31st day of May, 1819.[28] Within a short time steamers were running far up the Missouri and the Platte (then known as the Nebraska), carrying supplies a few hundred miles farther westward, in the wake of the pioneer, and bringing his produce back to New Orleans and the world.

Seven steamboats were navigating the St. Lawrence in the summer of 1820, but as early as 1816 a Quebec steamboat was connecting with the Champlain boats to complete the longest (699 miles) and fastest continuous passenger route in the world. With or without the advice of a Philadelphia lawyer, a man in a hurry could leave that city and reach Quebec by a varied land and water passage in a trifle over four days.[29] It was Boston's quickest route to Canada, although it involved coaching all the way to Burlington, Vermont. French Canadians later used it to get to the factories of New England, where their eight-year olds could earn a dollar a week to stretch the family budget.

Steamboats had multiplied everywhere. Charleston and Savannah had half a dozen for their own special needs. They had increased mightily on the Delaware, the Chesapeake, and the Great Lakes. In 1821 Maine was building two on the Kennebec. St. Stephens, Alabama, had built two, and was building another. There were 72 on the Mississippi and building was reported going on in 1821 at the rate of 30 or more a year. It was asserted that a thousand New Orleans steamboatmen were doing the work of twenty thousand flatboatmen.[30]

As 1821 passed into history, the stage was set. The canals were dug or a-digging. The steamboats were ready. The brave, new ships—nearly seven thousand since the war—were ready. Hard-bitten, skeptical merchants and master mariners, convinced at last that their future lay with the union line sailing on schedule, were ready.

King Cotton was ready: half a million bales a year. A million little pigs, self-fattened in pig family tradition, were ready. Beef cattle in proportion were ready. A vast new corn and wheat belt was ready, and everywhere the sound of grinding was high. Even the publicity man was ready, and the remote corners of Europe were echoing his tales of rich manorial farms to be had for the taking, plus five pounds passage money.

CHAPTER VII

◦ *1822-1826* ◦

The Greater Queens Move in Check

"And floating palaces—winged symbols of a brave new world."

THE CURTAIN rose on New Year's Day, 1822, to disclose a scene in a drab little shipping office at 159 South Street, New York City. Two young men, Tom Byrnes and George Trimble, were busily concocting an advertisement. They were specialists of sorts in the Liverpool trade. All through the depression they had run their ships to that port with considerable regularity, and through 1821, indeed, had operated four ships, the *Panthea, Manhattan, Meteor* and *Hercules,* in regular succession but on no prearranged schedule. Now, with business clearly on the upturn, they had decided to take the latter step.

When their joint composition appeared a few days later in the local papers, the maritime world learned that "A New Line of Liverpool Packets" had been established by the enterprising firm of Messrs. Byrnes, Trimble & Company.[1] Although actually the second Liverpool line in point of time, it was generally referred to as the "Third Line" for the reason that the second Black Ball line was started almost immediately; had, in fact, been under construction for several months past.

The new line was popularly known as the "Red Star Line"—a red star being the chief distinguishing mark of the Byrnes, Trimble house flag. Its ships were small, much smaller than the new Black Ballers. They ranged from the 325-ton *Meteor,* commanded by Nathan Cobb, one of the outstanding packet masters of the day, to the *Manhattan,* of 390 tons. The latter was to have been commanded by Captain F. W. Marshall, but he dropped out for unexplained reasons, and the ship was taken over by Rowland R. Crocker, who even then had a record of 132 Western Ocean crossings. Jonathan Eldridge had the *Panthea,* a new ship of 370 tons, built by Fickett & Crockett. The fourth ship was to have been the old *Hercules,* but she was replaced temporarily by the 360-ton *John Wells,* a small but excellent vessel commanded by Isaac Harris.

The new line was to sail from New York the 25th, and from Liverpool the 2nd of each month, starting with January. Cropper, Benson & Company were the Liverpool agents.

It was the Black Ball's first real competition and, as it happened, Wright and his associates were ready. Their arrangements, indeed, for starting a second Liverpool line were already well advanced. The original line had been greatly improved. Only one of the pioneer ships, the *Amity,* remained. The substituted packets included the *Albion, Nestor* and *James Cropper;* the latter named for one of the Liverpool agents. All three measured well over 400 tons, the largest being the 485-ton *Cropper.*

In addition to these they had four new Black Ballers, two of which, the *Columbia* and *William Thompson,* had been completed, while the *New York* and *Liverpool* were in an advanced stage of construction. The two former measured nearly 500 tons and the others rated approximately 516 tons. They were the largest, most commodious, and most luxuriously equipped packets built in America up to that time. As such, they attracted the same attention of marvelling throngs and evoked the same newspaper encomiums as the *Queens* of a later date. In the phrase of the day, they were "Floating Palaces," the first of scores to come. From the moment of their appearance all their competitors were outdistanced, from the crack Post Office Packets to the stoutest "regular trader."

Six of the first seven ships especially designed for the Black Ball line were built by Sidney Wright in his yard near the foot of Clinton Street, on the East River, New York City. With the exception of the first, the little *Courier,* they were the largest and finest packets of their day, and they established Wright's reputation as one of the port's leading naval architects.

The seventh ship, the *New York,* was launched in 1822 by Brown & Bell, a firm later responsible for the construction of many of New York's famous packets. They built the record-breaking *Canada* the following year and most of the new Black Ballers thereafter until the line changed hands in 1834.

Any list of the prominent New York shipbuilders of the period would also include Noah Brown, Isaac Webb, Henry Eckford, Blossom, Smith & Dimon, Scott & Francis Fickett, Henry Morgan, Fickett & Crockett, and Christian Bergh & Company. Such a list, however, fails to give a realistic impression of the extent of interest in ship construction. All the above-named builders had associates—merchants and well-to-do sea captains, both active and retired—who could be depended upon to take substantial shares in the vessels they constructed. Many had little-known silent partners, to whose financial support, skill, experience, and vision much of the port's maritime development was due.

Such a man, for example, was Robert Carnley, master builder, shipowner, and with Jacob Westervelt, silent partner of Christian Bergh & Company, and holding after 1835 a similar position in the firm of Jacob Westervelt & Company. During the 40 years following the War of 1812, he owned or participated in the construction of 98 vessels, most of them first-class ships and steamers. The list included a notable percentage of transatlantic and coastal packets, ranging from stout New Orleans liners to the great *Constellation,* which arrived in New York repeatedly during the early fifties with upwards of 900 passengers. First and last, there were scores of the Carnley stamp, not only in New York but in all shipbuilding centers.

With such reinforcements as the above-listed ships available, the Black Ball proprietors wasted no time. On the 14th of February they announced the formation of their second Liverpool line, with sailings from each port on the 1st and 16th of each month.[2] If they noted that their Liverpool departure on the 1st might prove a source of embarrassment to the Byrnes, Trimble packet of the 2nd, the fact probably gave them less concern than did their decision to shave the fare to 30 guineas.

Captain John Stanton, who had commanded Isaac Wright's ships long before the war—had, in fact, stood his watch in the days of the French Revolution—was now retired, but all the ships, new and old, were commanded by master mariners of the first rank, ex-privateersmen and blockade-runners who knew carriage guns and boarding pikes as they knew their own topsail halliards. If they were hard men, they were fair, even kindly when circumstances permitted. John Williams was the first American shipmaster to put a library on board his ship, the *Albion,* for his crew. Robert Marshall, William Bowne, Seth G. Macy, and William Lee, Jr., were men of outstanding ability and character, men who won and held the sincere regard of their passengers and the loyal respect of their crews. George Maxwell was destined to embroider a similar reputation by breaking the record from New York to Liverpool. Last, but not least, came Sam Reid, whose defense of the brig *General Armstrong* in the neutral harbor of Fayal against odds of five to one, was still fresh in patriot memories.

With 90 men he fought the boats of a British squadron of 2000 veterans on the way to reinforce the impending attack on New Orleans, killing and wounding nearly 300, with a loss of two killed and seven wounded. It was commonly reported, with perhaps pardonable exaggeration, that the damage he inflicted delayed that battle long enough to enable Jackson to prepare a suitable reception for Pakenham's "visiting firemen."

Later, he redesigned the American flag to its present form; reorganized the New York pilot service; moved the establishment of a lightship off Sandy Hook, and invented a signal telegraph. He was that kind of a man, and he had plenty of congenial company among the packet masters. We are probably justified in concluding that without such men all the best laid plans of the ablest merchants of America would have fallen far short of the success they attained. The pity was, their day was fast passing.

The above Black Ball announcement contained what proved to be the last notice of an *Albion* sailing. She left New York, as scheduled, on the 1st of April with nearly a full complement of cabin passengers, and made the Irish Channel in a fine run of 21 days. Working up-channel in a heavy gale on the 21st of April, Captain Williams had just announced to his anxious passengers that the worst was over and they could expect to arrive safely at their destination within a couple of days, when disaster struck.

We are indebted to Mr. Camman, the first mate and only surviving officer of the ship, for an account of what happened.[3] He reported that the ship was hove-to on April 21st, under close-reefed main topsail and fore and main trysails. About 8:30 P.M., she was swept by a tremendous sea which put her on her beam ends; carried away the mainmast; partly filled the cabin with water, and washed overboard five men who had been stationed with axes to cut away the masts, together with one cabin passenger, Mr. Converse, of Troy. The loss of the axes left the ship with no means to clear the wreckage and, although Captain Williams did everything in his power to accomplish this, she continued to drift helplessly toward the Irish coast. At midnight the light on the Old Head of Kinsale was sighted dead to leeward, and Williams knew that nothing could save the ship. She struck shortly before daybreak about three miles west of Kinsale in Courtmashery Bay where steep cliffs, 150 feet in height, came down to the water's edge. In a few moments it was all over, though the quickly silenced shrieks of the women and children were to ring in the dreams of the survivors for many a long year. Only one of the 23 cabin passengers and one in the steerage gained the shore in safety. Captain Williams and all his crew but the mate and six men were lost.

William Everhart, of Chester County, Pennsylvania, the surviving cabin passenger, left the only picture we have of those last hours in the crowded after cabin, knee-deep in swirling water. Men, women, and children, English, French, and American, some badly injured when the ship was knocked down, thrust in an instant from assured safety to the certainty of mortal danger. There was stouthearted Colonel Provost, who gained a foothold on the crags, only to be washed to his death as his strength failed. There, too, was Major Gough, of the British Army, who remarked, as they worked the pumps: "Death, come as he would, was an unwelcome messenger, but we must meet him as we could."

One of the passengers was Professor Alexander Metcalf Fisher, a gifted young scientist from Yale College, who was engaged to Catherine Beecher. He assisted Captain Williams to the last in his efforts to work the ship, hampered as she was by a dragging tangle of spars and rigging. Taking his station at the foot of the cabin companionway with the one remaining compass, he continued to call the bearings until warned by Williams that the ship was about to strike. When last seen he was standing inside his stateroom door, the upper half of which was open. "His face was bloody, his head bowed, in deep and anxious meditation."

The loss cast a gloom over shipping circles and many a home. Unfortunately, it was quickly followed by the loss of another Black Ball liner. The new *Liverpool*, commanded by William Lee, Jr., sailed from New York on her maiden voyage the 16th of the following July. Nine days out she hit an iceberg in a dense fog and went down in less than two hours. The 22 members of the crew and 14 passengers reached St. John's, Newfoundland, in the boats. Unlike the series of steamship losses a few years later, however, these disasters did not halt or even retard the formation of packet lines or the expansion of those already in operation. Their advantages were now so obvious that men began to announce the establishment of others while still quite unprepared to maintain the scheduled service.

Thus, the notice of the "Fourth Line of Liverpool Packets" appeared on the 1st of the following August, when the hopeful proprietors had only two ships available. It was November before their arrangements were complete with the ships *Robert Fulton* and *Cortes* in sailing order and the *Leeds* and *Corinthian* under construction. Henry Holdredge, a native of Mystic, Connecticut, and later a substantial New York merchant and shipowner, had the *Fulton*. Nash DeCost, a New Bedford boy, had the *Cortes*. The *Leeds* was to be commanded by William Stoddard and the *Corinthian* by stout old George Washington Davis. While waiting for the new ships, William Sketchly, Jr., was called upon to make the November crossing with his good ship *Martha*. Eventually he joined the regular packet service and became one of its popular commanders.

The proprietors, Messrs. Fish & Grinnell and Thaddeus Phelps & Company, 70 South Street, fixed on the 8th of the month as their sailing date from New York and the 24th from Liverpool, an arrangement which gave a weekly packet service between the two ports. As with Byrnes, Trimble & Company, the ships were inferior in size to those of the Black Ball, the larger vessels of the line measuring about 400 tons. Their accommodations were also necessarily slightly inferior, but the line was well managed. New York boasted no cannier merchants than its proprietors, and in Liverpool their agents, William and James Brown, were front rankers. William, the son, as previously noted, of the famous merchant-banker of Baltimore, Alexander Brown, possessed much of his father's ability. He ended as Sir William, one of the wealthier merchants of Liverpool. With such a start the line prospered. Later, as the Grinnell, Minturn "Swallow-tail Line," it ranked as one of the most substantial and colorful of all the Western Ocean lines.

Four scheduled packet lines to Liverpool meant not only that weekly service had replaced the original monthly sailing, they also spelled competition, which in turn made for improvement in the quality of that service. To that end, the Black Ball added in rapid succession during the years 1824 to 1826 the new *Pacific,* whose 587 tons made her, temporarily, the largest packet afloat; the *Florida,* of 523 tons; the *Manchester,* rating 561 tons; capping the performance in 1826 with the *Britannia* of 630 tons, the first packet to exceed 600 tons.

Byrnes, Trimble & Company countered with the *William Byrnes,* of 518 tons, and the *Birmingham,* 571 tons; the latter added in 1826 and the biggest ship of the line until the slightly larger *Sheffield* was built in 1831.

Messrs. Fish & Grinnell, who became Fish, Grinnell & Company in 1825, dropping partners who had been active for more than a quarter century, were content to replace the *Robert Fulton* and *Martha,* both ships well under 400 tons, with the *York* and *Silas Richards,* of 433 and 450 tons, respectively.

Passenger quarters of all the new liners, regardless of size, presented so many striking improvements as to excite the admiration of the most critical. When, for instance, the *Silas Richards* arrived in Liverpool after a 22-day crossing on her maiden voyage, the staid—not to say, stodgy—*Liverpool Courier* printed on the 5th of January, 1825, a long and enthusiastic description, declaring her "the equal in beauty and equipment, to any of the other packet ships." It noted that her magnificent cabin, "seven feet in height," was entered from a house on deck, doing away with the old-fashioned companionway, the cause of so many cabins flooding. The main cabin, 36 feet by 14 feet, gave access to 11 staterooms, each 6 feet 4 inches by 6 feet 3 inches instead of the usual six-foot square boxes. The ladies' cabin was 13 feet by 14 feet with four staterooms of similar size. Lifelike busts of the late Silas Richards ornamented both bow and stern of the ship.

Although few ships equalled the new packets in finish and design, they were not the largest merchant ships of their day. Jeremiah Thompson built two that exceeded the tonnage of the *Britannia,* the *Great Britain,* of 725 tons, and the *United States,* 678 tons register, while Charles Hall topped the last with the 742-ton *Washington.* All were built in 1825-6, as were several others ranging from 550 to 630 tons, in response to the increasing immigration and the cotton boom.

While these developments were taking place in the Liverpool trade, another group was trying to establish a New York-London packet service. Compared with Liverpool, the London traffic with America had shrunk to insignificant proportions, but it could use and furnish a few cargoes a year and it had certain definite advantages from the passenger standpoint.

It appealed to John Griswold and Samuel W. Coates, who had been running packets to Savannah for several years, and for the past two years and more had been sending others to London. They sometimes referred to their London vessels as a "line" but the ships were little more than regular traders. However, by 1822 they had the *Packet* and *Cincinnatus* on the London run, with the *Comet* filling in as needed, and were building a stout little ship, later launched as the *Hudson.* Coates also built the fine 400-ton *London,* so that they might be said to have a potential packet line. They had not, as yet, obligated themselves to maintain the above or any other vessels in the service, nor did they meet specifications in the matter of sailings. They frequently advertised that a ship would "positively" sail on a given date. The date came and with it a disarmingly worded notice that the vessel had been "unavoidably detained."

The venture ended, so far as Coates was concerned, by the dissolution of partnership at the close of the year. This was probably due to the ill health of Coates rather than to any disagreement, as he died early in 1823. Griswold, however, did not give up, as will appear.

Other attempts to develop New York-Liverpool packet lines continued through 1822. The ships of Hicks, Lawrence & Company, and John Flack, especially, were dispatched at frequent but irregular intervals as "line ships" but after the establishment of the "Fourth Line" all such efforts gradually lapsed into tacit acceptance of the "regular trader" status. It was not until 1824 that New York had another line of packets running to British ports; that year she had not one, but two new lines. The first in chronological order was a regularly scheduled packet line to London, and the second was also the second of all the so-called "emigrant lines" which were destined to play a most important part in the development of America during the next half century.

The regular packet line was another union venture. Following the dissolution of Griswold & Coates, John Griswold had attempted to maintain a packet service between New York and London, but with indifferent success. In the spring of 1824, however, he concluded to throw in his lot with the decidedly strong and active firm of Fish & Grinnell. Their joint announcement of the establishment of the first London line appeared on May 11th in the New York papers.[4]

The line started with four ships, the *Brighton, Hudson, Acasta* and *Crisis.* A fifth ship was to be added later, since the run was normally several days longer than the Liverpool passage, and in accordance with this plan the new 433-ton *York* was built. The sailing date from each port was fixed for the 1st of the month, with the ships touching at Cowes going and coming. Operations began with the departure of the *Brighton* for London on the 1st day of July, 1824, under the command of William S. Sebor, who for the previous ten years and more had been engaged in the coastal trade as master of the brig *Diamond* and other small craft.

The proprietors referred to their packets as ships "of about 400 tons," an assertion which subjected the verities to considerable strain. Actually, two of the ships measured 340 tons or less, and the two largest only 369 tons. Their captains, however, put up a sound 400-ton performance, and that, perhaps, was what the advertisements were intended to convey.

Fish & Grinnell, as a matter of fact, were able to command the services of superior men. All their captains were exceptionally able, but Henry L. Champlin was a master of unusual ability and attainments. He acquired, eventually, a substantial interest in the line as well as in coastal packets, especially the Hurlbut liners. After he retired from active service afloat he was instrumental in founding the first bank of Deep River, Connecticut, his native town, serving as president during the first ten years of its existence. Not that his case was unique. A good many packet masters, first and last, ended as successful bankers, manufacturers, or insurance executives.

The second Western Ocean line to be established by New York merchants during 1824 was the Greenock-New York emigrant service founded by Messrs. Stewart, Lee & Company, Abraham Bell & Company and Jeremiah Thompson. Notice of the proposed undertaking appeared in the local papers early in May, and stated that the line would consist of the ships *Camillus, Robert Fulton* and *Minerva,* all rating 340 tons, and the *Friends* and *Mentor,* of 403 and 459 tons, respectively. They were to sail from Greenock on the 10th of every month, starting with the *Camillus,* Norman Peck, master, on the 10th of October. There were no fixed dates for sailing from New York.

About the same time other New York firms began to manifest a special interest in the steerage traffic. Among them, Masters & Markoe, 113 Front Street, and Messrs. Gray & Harden, 70 Pine Street, sent many emigrant ships, both British and American, to Liverpool, Belfast, and Londonderry, during 1825 and thereafter. The new firm, Francis Thompson & Nephews, 97 Beekman Street, which by 1824 was handling much of the Black Ball business, became quite active in 1825 and 1826, sending vessels to Belfast and otherwise arranging for passage of Irish emigrants. Abraham Bell, later a very heavy emigrant operator, owned shares in some of their ships. All their Belfast ships, the *Frances Henrietta, Louisa, Atlantic* and *Meteor,* were packet-built, and their commanders, J. J. Dickenson, P. G. Fosdick, Robert L. Taylor, and Henry Huttleson, respectively, were also of sound packet-grade stuff. Taylor later became one of New York's important steamship operators.

It was not, however, until the booming year of 1828, when immigration had expanded from the official low of 6000 in 1823 to a high of 27,000, that the firm actually operated on a definite schedule. In the interval the number of immigrant firms and "Old Established Passage Offices" continued to increase mightily. Most of them operated at first in the simplest and most economical ways possible, merely collecting passage money and arranging with owners and agents of ships to transport their assembled groups. Among them, there were some, it must be admitted, who collected passage money but neglected to arrange for the passage, a circumstance which led to the establishment of societies for the protection of immigrants. Most of the passage agents, on the other hand, were reliable and some eventually became important owners and operators of their own lines. Tapscott's, Dunham's, and Samuel Thompson & Nephews were examples of the more successful of such enterprises, continuing to prosper long after most of their early competitors had disappeared.

Due, measurably, to the establishment of the packet lines, the slight but effective superiority the American merchant marine had long demonstrated was speedily transformed into a competitive force of tremendous power. The all-round efficiency of the "Palace Ships" was so marked and their patronage so advantageous to merchant and traveller alike that by the close of 1826 they were all but monopolizing the first-class passenger and merchandise traffic on the Western Ocean.

Nor was this all. The merchants of every trade where competition was to be met were taking note of their triumphs and profiting thereby. The part played by the sailing liners in the struggle that was to end a generation later in something resembling Yankee supremacy on the high seas, can hardly be overestimated. What their influence, however temporary, would be, was already becoming clear.

Among the more obvious indications, the fact that America was once more carrying roughly 88 per cent of her foreign trade, both export and import, looms large. Liverpool docks already held more American vessels than those of all other foreign nations combined, and a similar situation was developing at Havre. A minor but significant development was the almost complete withdrawal of patronage from the century-old British Post Office Packet service between Falmouth and New York, which led in 1827 to its abandonment.

Success in the early transatlantic packet field, however, involved more than the ability to assemble a palatial fleet or open a passage office. High-class representation abroad, as has been noted, was necessary, but a close tie-up with the southern trade was equally essential. Cotton, rice, tobacco, and naval stores constituted an indispensable prop of the eastbound service. This was especially true of the French trade where those staples were in greater demand than northern beef, flour and grain.

Following the war, direct trade between the southern ports and France had been very heavy. France was badly in need of foodstuffs and, as time went on, required more and more cotton for her factories. Nevertheless, it was not long before huge quantities of southern produce were being shipped abroad out of northern ports, especially to Havre. The bulk of this trade centered in New York, since her merchants were not only the heaviest buyers of southern staples for distribution to northern industrial centers, but also were able, through personal representatives located in strategic southern centers, to buy on terms which permitted them to re-ship to European markets on a sound competitive basis.

In 1822 and before there were three New York groups with well-established southern connections, that were especially active in the Havre trade.

William Whitlock, Jr., represented one group so thoroughly, indeed, that one rarely heard his associates mentioned. His father, old Captain Whitlock, had started him in the grocery business in New York at an early age. His next venture took the form of an extended residence in Georgia, where he learned the cotton business. In 1819 and later he was agent and part owner of a number of vessels trading between New York and Charleston, Savannah and New Orleans.

Another group was represented by Dias & Crassous, soon replaced by Crassous & Boyd, and still more speedily replaced, to all active intents, by the honorable "J. J." Young John J. Boyd, in fact, was a human dynamo, and possessed the further qualification of being closely allied to Jacob LeRoy and the Bayards with their highly influential French connections.

A third group was composed of the former Charleston merchant Francis Depau and two master mariners, Isaac Bell and Miles R. Burke, both dating from eighteenth-century quarter-decks. Depau had married Silvie, the daughter of Count de Grasse, victor of the Chesapeake Capes in 1781. As a young girl, she had fled from France to Charleston during the "terror." Their four daughters, in turn, had married merchants prominent in New York shipping circles, two of whom, Samuel M. Fox and Mortimer Livingston, were later noted operators of Havre packets. It was Depau's firm that founded the first New York-Havre packet line. Its establishment was announced in July, 1822. The line consisted of three ships, the *Montano,* 365 tons, commanded by Burke, the *Stephania,* 315 tons, John P. Smith, and the *Lewis,* registering 412 tons, then under construction in Noah Brown's yard for the well-known master mariner, John R. Skiddy. As it happened, Smith withdrew at the last moment and Skiddy assumed temporary command of the *Stephania.* The ships were to sail the 10th of every other month from each port, beginning the 10th of November. Cabin passage was fixed at $140.[5]

The line had been in operation only two months when John Boyd, agent, announced the formation of a second Havre line.[6] It consisted of the ships *Niagara,* commanded by William Beebe; *Marmion,* Elnathan Hawkins; *Bayard,* Daniel Van Dyke, and the *Cadmus,* Sidney B. Wheelock. All four men were graduates of the coastal packet service. Another ship, the *Paris,* to be commanded by Henry Robinson, was under construction in New York to complete the line. Operations started with the sailing of the *Niagara* on the 1st of February, 1823, with regular departures to be maintained thereafter on the 1st of the month from each port.

Crassous & Boyd began to act as agent for some of the ships in March, and William Whitlock, Jr., indicated his interest in the venture by advertising sailings from time to time, although his southern packets continued to demand most of his attention for several years.

All the ships were small; all, with the exception of the *Paris,* having been built for the coasting trade. They ranged from the 253-ton *Niagara* to the *Paris* and *Bayard,* 339 tons register. Three, the *Niagara, Cadmus,* and *Marmion,* were less than 100 feet in length and were old ships to boot. Everything about the enterprise, from barely adequate equipment to minutely divided ownership, suggests its tentative nature. More than most of the other transatlantic enterprises, its stands out as a trial balloon, where no one assumed any appreciable risk. It proved a notable success, however, and in its original divided ownership we have a useful clue to the origins of the great Havre Union Line.

Through the remainder of 1823 there was no important change in either of the Havre lines. The *Paris* was reported wrecked near Cherbourg on October 21st, but got off. Crassous & Boyd continued to act as general agent for the line, with Whitlock attending to the sailing of the *Cadmus,* and LeRoy, Bayard & Company indicating a special interest in loading the *Bayard, Marmion* and *Paris.*

The first intimation of impending change came in May, 1824, when Crassous & Boyd advertised a new schedule of monthly sailings under the suggestive title, "First Line."[7]

What this portended was made clear by their notice less than two months later of the establishment of a new Havre "Second Line."[8] It was composed of the ships *Queen Mab, Don Quixote, Howard,* and a new ship, the *Desdemona,* then under construction at Middletown, Connecticut. They were commanded in that order by Henry Richards, James Clark, Nathan Holdredge, and Francis Naghel, all of whom had served in the brigs and schooners of the coastal trade. The ships of this line were to sail on the 1st, and the ships of the "First Line" on the 15th of each month, from each port. The composition of the "First Line" remained as before, except that the new 388-ton ship *Edward Quesnel* had been substituted for the *Paris,* and Francis Allyn, a native of Groton, Connecticut, now commanded the *Cadmus.*

For a young man, Whitlock, Jr., was by this time a substantial shipowner. His only connection with the Havre lines, however, was through his controlling interest in the *Cadmus.* Yet that little 95-foot hooker was destined to bring him greater and more lasting fame than all his later huge, three-decker packets combined.

Lafayette had expressed, early in 1824, a desire to revisit America. On learning this, the government offered to send a frigate for him, but he refused, saying that he preferred to come as a private citizen. Moved by an impulse that seems to have been decidedly at variance with a lifelong practice, Whitlock directed Captain Allyn to send his freight and passengers by another ship, and place the *Cadmus* at the disposal of the General.

When the *Cadmus* arrived in New York the morning of August 15th with Lafayette and his suite, she was greeted by the greatest demonstration the city had ever beheld. Down the harbor, as far as the eye could see, the waters were covered with craft of every description, freighted with cheering thousands. Ships were dressed; bells clanged; fog horns blared; and cannon boomed. Even the brand-new ferryboat *Thistle* was on hand, with her skipper, a youth named Vanderbilt, peering curiously out of the pilothouse. Six of the largest steamboats of the port, crowded to capacity, went down to meet the ship and escort the General to the Battery, where other thousands waited to see him step ashore after an absence of more than 30 years. As owner of the *Cadmus,* Whitlock basked for a brief hour in the outer fringes of reflected glory and then went thoughtfully back to the office.

Lafayette remained in America a year, visiting every section of the country, receiving everywhere honors and adulation such as had been accorded only to Washington in the hour of his greatest popularity. When he set out for home, the people would not hear of his leaving as a private citizen. A new frigate, named the *Brandywine* in his honor (said to have been the first ship ever built with the elliptical stern)[9] was placed at his disposal under the command of Charles Morris. She sailed from Norfolk the morning of September 9th, 1825, with a young lieutenant, David Glasgow Farragut, busily passing the orders, and a much younger midshipman, Matthew Fontaine Maury, twice as busy. Long before nightfall she had dropped the land.

Several weeks before this event the first of the three Havre lines was revived by Francis Depau and his associates, Captains Bell and Burke, of 29 South Street. Depau had ceased to operate his ships on schedule after the establishment of the third Havre line, possibly because he felt there was too much Crassous & Boyd in the set-up, but more probably because he believed the traffic would not support so many lines. Now, with the cotton trade booming as never before, he announced his return as proprietor-manager of the "Old Line of Packets to Havre:"

> The proprietors of this line at the solicitation of many of their friends, have resumed the regular departure of their ships both from here and from Havre.[10]

It was arranged that the vessels should sail from New York on the 5th and from Havre on the 25th of each month. They included the earlier ships of the line, *Stephania, Montano,* and *Lewis,* and a fourth, the *Henry,* a new vessel measuring only 258 tons. Save for the *Niagara* she was the smallest of the regular Western Ocean liners.

Nevertheless, she was destined to bring one of the heaviest cargoes of culture that had yet arrived in America. Part of the culture was debarked in the person of Captain Hadlock when the ship reached New York at the end of her second voyage, the 8th of June, 1826. The culture the worthy captain embodied, however, was largely the reflected light of the dioramas he brought with him—the recent curious invention of M. Daguerre and associate. They speedily became the sensation of the day. Every New Yorker who could scrape together four bits went to see them, coming away with the conviction, still an important by-product of culture, that he had shown himself up to snuff and abreast, if not ahead, of the times. Fortunately for his ego, he was spared the knowledge that what he had witnessed was but a crude beginning; the seed of far greater marvels, the daguerreotype, photograph, television, and a thousand other discoveries.

There were other developments in the Depau line. Skiddy had left the *Lewis* but Robert Macy filled his place, shipshape and Bristol fashion, as the following incident indicates:

NEW YORK—On Saturday afternoon, immediately after the safety barge *Lady Clinton* left the wharf, a small boat was proceeding on board with several passengers, among whom were some ladies and children. By accident the boat was upset and the passengers precipitated into the water. Captain Robert Macy of the packet ship *Lewis*, in the Havre Line, lying at some distance below, happened to be on the quarter deck of his vessel and beheld the accident. He immediately plunged into the river and swam to the aid of the unfortunate sufferers—and by his magnanimous conduct greatly assisted them, and saved the life of at least one poor little innocent, who must otherwise have perished. We take great pleasure in recording the generous act of this amiable and promising young commander.[11]

With the return of Depau and associates the New York-Havre packet situation was reconstituted about as it was to stand for another decade, subject to minor shifts and changes in management and ownership and such operational agreements as changing conditions made advisable from time to time.

Meanwhile, in 1822 three other ports developed packet ambitions.

Baltimore was the first to make public her plans. The *National Gazette* of Philadelphia for Saturday, March 16, 1822, noted:

We rejoice to hear from good authority that a line of packets is in contemplation to be established between Baltimore and Liverpool.

Niles' Register also reported the matter as virtually settled. At the very moment, however, when Baltimore ardor had reached the boiling point, certain Philadelphia interests decided to contribute a neighborly dash of cold water. Within a week after the Baltimore cat was out of the bag, the Quaker firm of Thomas P. Cope & Sons announced the establishment of the first line between the City of Brotherly Love and Liverpool. The announcement indicated at once the modest character of the venture and the caution with which even wealthy concerns then approached new undertakings. It read in part:

LINE OF PACKETS TO LIVERPOOL: Ship *Tobacco Plant,* to sail the 10th of the 4th month (April). Ship *Lancaster,* to sail the 10th of the 5th month (May).

The subscribers have agreed in conjunction with their friends, to establish a line of packets from Philadelphia to Liverpool; one to sail from Liverpool the 8th of each month, except December, and from Philadelphia the 20th of each month, except the 1st month (January).

The line will commence at Liverpool on the 8th of the 6th month (June) and at Philadelphia the 20th of the 8th month (August).

Until which time their departure will be as near that date as practicable, of which notice will be regularly given.

Two new ships are building expressly for the line.[12]

Neither of the above ships was new and both were decidedly on the small side. The *Tobacco Plant* measured only 278 tons, or considerably less than 250 tons by present computation.

Probably the mere establishment of a Philadelphia line would not have deterred the Baltimore merchants. Cope's ships were not only old and small, but the Copes, although substantial, were no wealthier or more influential than several Baltimore houses. What really mattered was the fact that Alexander Brown & Sons, of Baltimore, had thrown their weight to the Cope line. They owned the *Alexander,* the largest of the new ships under construction for the line, and it was understood that they would act as the Baltimore agents for the concern. The firm was not only the wealthiest house in Baltimore, but it had strong branches in Philadelphia and New York. Moreover, William, the oldest son of Alexander Brown and even then one of the more influential merchants in Liverpool, was to act as agent for the line in that city.

Baltimore, indeed, might view the Cope competition without serious apprehension but the "conjunction with their friends" was quite another matter. To further complicate the situation, William Brown was already well entrenched in the Liverpool-Baltimore trade. His establishment of "spring and fall ships," usually three or more substantial vessels each season, served Baltimore's more pressing needs and continued to do so under successive changes of management for another quarter century. After the Cope announcement nothing further was heard of Baltimore-Liverpool packet lines for many a year.

This did not mean that the Cope line had no competition. Several Philadelphia operators, among whom Eyre & Massey and perhaps John Welsh were most prominent, continued to operate "line ships" to Liverpool for several years. Their packets, such as Welsh's *Philadelphia, Manchester,* and *Mary Ann,* were inferior to those that soon made up the Cope line, but their nuisance value for a time was considerable.

The Philadelphia line got under way as scheduled and continued to prosper throughout the packet era. Thomas Cope delivered more than he promised. By May, 1823, he had thoroughly revamped the line. The little *Tobacco Plant* was out and the 379-ton *Tuscarora,* under James Serrill, took her place. The new ships *Alexander,* Stephen Baldwin, master, and *Montezuma* commanded by Thomas Potts, both rising 400 tons, had been added, leaving only the *Lancaster* of the original fleet. She was commanded by Charles Dixey, a popular shipmaster with a long and varied experience. The new ships were smaller than the Black Ball replacements, but they were as well built and as handsomely equipped as any ships afloat. All in all, the Cope line of 1824 was second only to the Black Ball in size and quality of ships.

Philadelphia's second transatlantic line, incidentally, the first of the impressive roster of American immigrant lines, was established in February, 1824. Spackman & Wilson, 21 Church Alley, were the Philadelphia agents, and Rathbone Brothers & Company, who had succeeded Rathbone, Hodgson & Company a few weeks before, acted as the Liverpool agents. The line consisted of five ships: the *Florida,* 522 tons; *Julius Caesar,* 346 tons; *Colossus,* 399 tons; *Delaware,* 412 tons; and *Courier,* 388 tons; commanded in that order by James L. Wilson, Francis M. French, Richard Urann, John Hamilton, and Robert Marshall.[13]

It was announced that operations would begin with the sailing of the *Florida* from Liverpool on the 20th of March; sailings from that port to continue throughout the year on that day of the month. Eastbound departures were to be at the convenience of operators with the ships proceeding by way of Savannah. In general, this practice, with slight variations, was followed by most of the later immigrant lines, although some of the New York lines announced fixed schedules for eastbound packets and usually sailed direct instead of proceeding to a southern port. Cabin passengers were carried at rates substantially below those of the regular packet lines. It soon appeared that the arrangement served a widespread need, with the result that immigrant lines eventually outnumbered their haughty competitors.

Boston was the third American port to establish a transatlantic packet line in 1822. Under the leadership of William Appleton, worthy descendant of an eminent eighteenth-century merchant, the "Boston & Liverpool Packet Company" was incorporated to operate four packets between the two ports.[14]

The generally reported version of the establishment of this line is inaccurate, a fact of importance mainly because it gives a picture quite at variance with the meagre beginnings of this and most other early packet companies. Captain Clark's statement, for example, that the line started with four new ships, the *Amethyst, Emerald, Sapphire* and *Topaz,* all built by Joshua Magoun, suggests well-matured plans soundly backed by ample funds.[15]

Actually, when the line was reported organized it had but one ship ready for service, the *Herald,* built in Newburyport in 1818 and commanded by Hector Coffin, late of the Philadelphia coastal packet *Telegraph.* The second ship, the *Emerald,* was still in the Magoun yard and when she sailed in October she cleared for Charleston instead of Liverpool.[16] The *Topaz,* Joseph Callender, master, was built by John Wade in Boston. She was completed barely in time to clear for Liverpool the 15th of October. The *Amethyst* was built in Boston in 1823 by John Robertson and the *Sapphire* was Medford-built in 1825 by Messrs. H. & H. Rogers. Her first trip to Liverpool was not made until long after the agents had abandoned all pretense of maintaining a regular schedule.

So far as schedules were concerned, indeed, the performance of the line was no better than that of the immigrant ships and inferior to several of those lines. From the first the Boston vessels sailed from Liverpool in close succession as "spring and fall ships" and not as regular monthly packets. Boston sailings were equally irregular. In short, the record of the line closely resembled that of several independent traders of the day whose only concern was to dispatch their ships in succession as rapidly as possible.

All the ships were small. The fact that they were all approximately the same size as the pioneer *Herald* (359 tons) suggests that they may have been built on her lines. If so, there was sound reason for it, for she was a remarkably fast vessel. She missed by a matter of hours making the best passage of all time from Liverpool to Boston in 1819. Coming on the coast in December, only 13 days out of Liverpool with but a few more miles to go, she was headed off by a vicious westerly gale and driven down toward Cape Cod. It took her three days to beat back to Boston. Even so, her 17-day passage from port to port had been equalled but once before, and then by her own skipper, Philip Fox, of Cohasset.[17]

The Boston agents were S. Austen, Jr. and J. W. Lewis, with offices at the end of India Wharf. Both were master mariners and further qualified by extensive experience in the Liverpool and southern coasting trades. Four Liverpool agents were selected, a fact which probably reflected the divided ownership of the vessels. They were Maury, Latham & Company;

A. & F. Lodge; Curwen & Haggerty; and Thomas & John D. Thornley. This division of responsibility has been suggested as one of the causes of the failure of the venture. It is possible the practice entailed certain disadvantages, but its effect was probably slight in comparison with the disadvantages which affected the entire port of Boston. At all events, when the four agents dropped out and a single agent took over early in 1826, the line was discontinued after the briefest of trials. That the original arrangement was approved by several of the leading merchants of the town is indicated by the fact that when the second Boston-Liverpool line was started a few years later, four more Liverpool agents were appointed, two of whom had acted as agents of the first line.[18]

The line suffered from the start from a lack of passenger patronage. Many of New England's first-class travellers probably would have succumbed to the lure of New York's bigger and more luxurious packets in any case, especially since swift palatial steamboats made the journey to that port an experience to be recalled with pleasure. However, all but a handful of the faithful minority, who would have supported the Boston liners as a home enterprise, were deterred by the prospect of a long and tedious voyage to Liverpool by way of Charleston, coupled with the knowledge that even that service would probably be extremely irregular.

It was evident almost from the beginning that the controlling factor in the Boston packet situation would be the inability of the port to provide paying eastbound cargoes. One after another, as sailing day arrived, the ships were compelled to head southward with barely enough cargo for ballast, and this at a time when the Erie Canal, although still incomplete, was providing ample freights for a New York fleet which now included a large and rapidly increasing number of "spring and fall ships" carrying passengers of all classes. The fact did not pass unnoted by Boston merchants, who eventually made several determined attempts to siphon a share of the canal traffic overland to their own port, but without success as will be seen.

Philadelphia labored under the same disadvantages as Boston but in less pronounced fashion. The Cope passenger traffic suffered from the lure of the big New York packets, but to a lesser extent and, principally, because the latter sailed weekly instead of monthly. Boston ships frequently cleared with not more than two or three and rarely more than half a dozen cabin passengers. Cope's patronage, roughly stated, doubled those figures, while the New York packets, in turn, doubled Cope's figures.

The freight situation of the Quaker City was also better than that of Boston. The port provided sufficient eastbound cargoes for the Cope line, but when other Liverpool lines were added it was found necessary to send their ships south to fill. Nor was there any reason to believe the condition would improve as regards either Boston or Philadelphia. On the contrary, there were indications that it would grow relatively worse, as may be judged from the fact that in 1826, the first year of full operation of the Erie Canal, nearly 7000 canal boats sent their cargoes down the Hudson for reshipment at New York.[19]

From the foregoing resume it will be seen that the Western Ocean liner situation, which had remained almost unchanged for four years, suddenly sprang into such activity in 1822 that within three years the number of transatlantic lines had increased from one to twelve.

Change in the character of the service was quite as marked. The occasional, pennypinching cabin passenger of a few years before, who had viewed the ordeal of his crossing with apprehension, if not downright dread, and who had been regarded by shipmaster and owner alike as the cash equivalent of a hogshead of tobacco, had been replaced by scores of seasoned, well-to-do travellers accustomed to all the comforts and many of the luxuries of the day. They were willing to pay liberally for the best and would be satisfied with nothing less. To secure their patronage and that active goodwill which is the most effective of all advertising, owner and master went all out.

The owner's task ended when he provided what might be termed without too obvious exaggeration "the finest packet afloat, replete with every modern improvement." The captain's work was never done. He might be, and usually was, a New England or York State farm boy who had hammered himself into a master mariner of consummate skill and endurance, but unless he was something more, he was a failure as a packet master. He had to be a past master of diplomacy and the social graces. His passengers included generals and ambassadors, talented actors, temperamental prima donnas, haughty, narrow-minded provincials—all sorts and varieties. He had to possess the ability to meet each on his or her own level, to give each his expected due, to weld for a time all the inharmonious elements into a harmonious, carefree group. It was for the most part a matter of little things; small attentions, suggestions for diverting activities, passing on interesting information—anything to make time pass pleasantly without once descending from his position as monarch of the realm or neglecting equally important points of seamanship, such as observing the condition of the buntline stops or noticing a spot of tar where no tar should be.

There were many such captains. Young Charles H. Marshall was one, as the following occurrence on his first Black Ball command may indicate. The *Cornwall* (England) *Gazette* for November 20, 1824, reported that a bottle had been picked up a few days earlier on the neighboring coast, contained the following message:

> This bottle was thrown overboard from the *James Cropper,* Captain Marshall, now on her voyage from Liverpool to New York, in lat. 48.20 N., lon. 38.5 W., all well, out 25 days, and experienced a succession of southerly gales and bad weather. The purport of this being cast into the sea, is to try the current of the Ocean, and therefore should it reach land the persons who find it are requested to make known when and where it was found.
>
> C. H. Marshall, Captain.
>
> Passengers—S. T. Corrie, Liverpool; Wm. Abraham of Miramichi, N. B.; J. Robertson, of St. Johns, N. B.; O. Satchell, of Quebec; Werner, of Hamburgh; E. Canning, of Birmingham; Nolfe, of Germany; and J. Dewy, of New York. ALL JOLLY FELLOWS AND THIRSTY DOGS.
> 10th January, 1824.

A trifling thing, but of the sort that Messrs S. T. Corrie, *et al.,* would remember to the credit of young Marshall and his ship long after more important events of the voyage had been forgotten, and would incline them to wait a month, if necessary, to make their next crossing in the same packet.

The last of the above-mentioned transatlantic lines had hardly been organized when rumors began to drift across the sea of developments abroad that were destined to exercise a profound effect on their fortunes for several years to come.

In January, 1825, James Rogers brought the smart Black Baller *Canada* across from Liverpool in a fast 25-day passage. He had a special reason for making time, for he brought the very hush-hush news of an extraordinary rise in the price of cotton. He reached New York on the 31st of January.

Six days later a New York pilot boat with a board nailed over her name hove-to off Tybee Island, Georgia; put a passenger on board a Savannah pilot boat and stood off again to the south'ard. The next day, cotton to the amount of $2,000,000 changed hands in Savannah. Two days later the price jumped four cents a pound. The following week a very similar thing happened in New Orleans. Early in March the fast-sailing pilot boat *Grand Canal* slipped in by Sandy Hook after an absence of 36 days on a mission that brought fabulous profits to a small group of New York merchants. And another boom was on.

For the next six months speculation in cotton rivalled that of the "South Sea Bubble." By May, New Orleans cotton, a common grade, sold at 31 cents, or more than double the normal price, while sea-island was no longer available at any price. The rise carried with it substantial advances in other staples: rice, flour, beef, and naval stores. Everyone was coining money. Huge amounts of cotton changed hands repeatedly without once leaving the warehouse. Great ships were rushed to completion to take advantage of rising freight rates. An April letter from Liverpool reported the sale of 101,500 bales in the preceding six days.[20] Later it transpired that American exports for the year ending September 30th, 1825, exceeded the average for the preceding three years by the then enormous total of $17,000,000.[21]

In September the tone of Liverpool dispatches changed. The *Amethyst,* Captain John Bussey, brought word of the failure in August of two large Liverpool houses. Soon other particulars drifted in: failure of more commercial and industrial concerns and banks; manufactured cloth selling for less than the price of raw cotton; and then the complete cessation of demand for cotton at any price. It was further reported that British importation of cotton for the preceding year amounted to 551,500 bales, as again 396,000 for 1824.[22] A similar overshipment characterized the Havre trade, though on a smaller scale.

It soon became evident that, stimulated by several years of good business, both industry and finance had embarked on a course of overexpansion and speculation. This was equally true in Great Britain and America. Tremendous amounts of capital had been put into canals, turnpikes, and steamboats, as well as into banks, insurance companies and industrial plants of all kinds. By 1825 the number of canals in England had increased from none at all in 1753 and very few in 1784 to 103, with a total length of 2682 miles.[23] In the United States, the Erie Canal was credited with a length of only 363 miles, but travellers on it reported meeting as many as 500 boats in the course of 100 miles or thereabouts, including handsomely fitted passenger packets which provided food and quarters for 30 or more passengers "equal to the best hotels." All of this involved a very heavy investment in boats, stagecoaches, horses, and accessories.

The investment in manufacturing plants was even more remarkable. Manchester, England, which did not have a single power loom in 1814, had upwards of 30,000 in 1824.[24] In the United States, construction of steam cotton and woolen mills had spread through New York State and was spilling out into the Ohio Valley. Mills within a radius of 20 miles of Boston were producing, among other products, nearly 2,000,000 yards of flannel a year, and the *Boston Gazette* for February 24th, 1825, remarked:

> Not a vessel now leaves the port of Baltimore (and we presume this is true of other ports) for South American ports, which does not carry, as part of her cargo, American Manufactures of Cotton to the value of ten to twenty thousand dollars.

Steam flour mills were springing up in every direction. In 1822 Isaac McKim built one near Baltimore at the then enormous cost of $80,000, with a capacity of 1200 barrels and upwards weekly. Before the year ended, the activity had extended to the Mississippi Valley, with two large mills under construction in St. Louis.

The amount of capital frozen in the many hundreds of new enterprises and—in America—real estate speculation produced a shortage of ready cash which could hardly fail to have serious consequences when a real need for cash arose. Such a need developed when the price of cotton and other commodities began to drop and speculators found it necessary to cover their commitments. As one firm after another came into the market for money, it was not to be had. In England, banks and stock companies, as well as cotton houses, began to fail; every failure toppling still others into the pit.

Thirty-six days out of Liverpool, the *Canada* again drove in by Sandy Hook, docking on the 7th of June, 1826. On board was an old Boston boy who had made good, Admiral Sir Isaac Coffin, of the British Navy. He had come, gouty leg and all, to pay a final visit to the land of his birth and, incidentally, to found at Nantucket the Coffin School, in memory of his parents. The *Canada,* however, brought a less welcome visitor, news of appalling conditions throughout Great Britain, Ireland, and France. Mills were closed everywhere. Cotton cloth sold, when it sold at all, for less than the cost of the raw staple. Thousands, especially in the crowded manufacturing districts of England, were reported as starving, and other thousands on the verge of starvation. Rioting, arson, pillaging, and murder went almost unchecked in the Midlands, where the situation had passed completely out of control.[25]

There were no such scenes in America, where mutton, in ample supply, cost two and one-half, and the best beef, four cents a pound, but several of the largest cotton houses of New Orleans and other southern ports had already failed, and many more were in serious difficulties. In

Courtesy, The Peabody Museum of Salem

Packet ship *Orpheus* of the Black Ball Line. Of 573 tons, she was built in New York in 1832. Nathan Cobb was the master. She was one of the few ships of the regular packet lines to make the passage from New York to Liverpool in less than 15 days. She was very lofty, carrying skysails on long gunter poles.

Packet ship *Chancellor*.

Courtesy, The Peabody Museum of Salem

Captain Daniel Marcy

Courtesy, G. W. Patch

Captain Charles H. Salter,
master of packet *Typhoon*.

Courtesy, G. W. Patch

Thomas Whitridge, merchant and operator of packet lines between Baltimore and New York and Boston from 1830 to 1850; later owner and operator of the *Mary Whitridge* and other clipper ships.

Courtesy, Maryland Historical Society

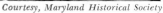

George Raynes, shipbuilder.

Courtesy, G. W. Patch

Courtesy, The Peabody Museum of Salem

Packet ship *Europe*.

Packet ship *Corinthian*.

Courtesy, The Mariner's Museum

New York, Jeremiah Thompson of the Black Ball line, and reputedly the heaviest cotton trader in America, was putting up the fight of his life. He managed to survive for another year, a sadly diminished figure. The great Liverpool house of Andrew Low & Company crashed, carrying down with it the Savannah branch and several smaller concerns. The situation, in short, exhibited all the aspects of what financial writers are wont to characterize as a minor depression.

Slight it undoubtedly was, measured by the great events of history, but serious enough for those involved. Next to the cotton speculators, it bore hard on owners and operators of ships, whose very survival would depend on the intelligence and determination with which they tackled their problems.

To add to their troubles, a larger number of vessels than usual were lost or badly damaged in 1826. The smart packet schooner *Tell Tale* was run down and sunk in the Chesapeake in April. The fine ship *Ajax* foundered at sea the same month. On May 5th the ship *Orleans* was lost on Carysfort Reef while bound from Santiago de Cuba for Philadelphia. The ship *Ellen,* from Havana for Philadelphia, was lost on Florida Reef, and the three-masted schooner *Roanoke,* from Philadelphia for Norfolk, was lost on Smith's Island Beach the 6th of December.

In addition to these disasters, fortunately attended with no loss of life, the line ship *Algonquin* arrived at Philadelphia April 6th, reporting the loss of her captain and two men, washed overboard. The ship *George Clinton* also had a bad time. In a gale on September 26th, she lost nearly all her sails, all three topgallant masts, jibboom and rudder, and shipped a sea which swept the deck clean—house over the cabin gangway, round-house, caboose house, binnacle, boats, and spare spars—everything went, and three of the crew wound up with broken legs. In the same gale two whaling brigs were capsized, their crews being rescued by the British brig *Sir Charles McCarthy.*

In New York and Philadelphia the situation was aggravated by a long-standing overexpansion of the tea trade. For several years Thomas H. Smith, of the former, and Edward Thompson, of the latter city, both of whom were reputed to be among the wealthiest men in America, had been importing far more tea than the market could absorb. Both had accumulations in bonded warehouses on which duties of several millions would become payable on withdrawal.

Late in 1825 it was discovered that Thompson, with the connivance of customs officials, had withdrawn, without the formality of payment, teas on which more than a million dollars were due. Investigation showed that a similar situation existed in New York, with Smith as chief culprit. Banks and merchants went to the wall and numerous prosecutions were started. Thompson spent a few months in jail in company with a few underlings, and died in obscurity some 20 years later. Smith went out of business, apparently penniless, but it was noted that an associate of his had somehow acquired a large fortune. As in the case of the Greek frigates —the other great scandal of the period—it was soon forgotten by the American public, although the latter affair, especially, should have aroused the retributive indignation of any liberty-loving people. The sordid business involved two of New York's most prominent mercantile houses, two of her leading shipbuilders, and three "eminently respectable merchants" who had been brought in as "arbitrators." In the end the Greek patriots, then fighting desperately to throw off the Turkish yoke, received one frigate after successive costly delays running to more than a year beyond the agreed delivery date. For this they were mulcted in the sum of $775,000 instead of the $247,500 which they had been assured would be the cost of each vessel, and which in fact represented the cost of similar vessels built about the same time. The other frigate was ordered sold by the compliant "arbitrators" to pay the scandalous overcharges of the two houses in charge of construction, and she eventually wound up in the American Navy. Treated like the unwanted thing she was, she spent most of her life in idleness until broken up in 1844.

CHAPTER VIII

～ *1822-1826* ～

High Tide of the Coastal Lines

"In willing partnership, they trace their native shore."

WHILE the Western Ocean packet service was being expanded and improved, coastal operators were by no means idle. The pioneer "Dispatch Line" between Boston and New York increased its fleet in February, 1822, to six sloops in order to give extra sailings "on Wednesdays when necessary," in addition to the regular Saturday service it had maintained through the previous year.

Even this failed to meet the demand. Almost immediately thereafter a second Boston-New York service called the "Union Line" was established with sailings to begin in March. It proposed to sail twice weekly during the season, with a reduced schedule for the winter months. The Boston agents were J. D. & M. Williams and Everitt, Childs & Company. In New York the first agents were T. N. Wood, 62 Wall Street, and S. S. Newman, of Burling Slip. They were soon supplanted by the energetic tinman, Anson G. Phelps, who, in turn, gave place in the fall to a couple of ambitious youngsters destined to achieve a reputation of sorts as Messrs. Spofford & Tileston, pioneer steamship operators and one of New York's great shipping firms of the fifties. As in the case of the "Dispatch Line," the "Union Line" was composed of six sloops. The vessels of both concerns ranged from 80 to a trifle less than 100 tons.

A second line between Boston and Philadelphia, also called the "Union Line," was started about the same time. It began with five schooners, soon increased to six, and instituted regular weekly sailings. The well-known firm of Stanton, Fiske & Nichols and Calvin Bailey were the Boston agents. Fiske, regarded as one of Boston's most promising young merchants, was the son of an eminent clergyman. In Philadelphia, the firm of Moody, Wyman & Company and Messrs. Grants & Stone handled the business.

Albany, which had pioneered the thing, decided it was on the right track and the firm of Davis & Center started a line of three sloops on the Boston run early in the spring of 1822, with Joseph Attwood acting as the first Boston agent. All the sloops were large, smartly equipped vessels of more than 100 tons register. In 1824 the *General Brown,* 146 tons, was added, and the line continued to prosper for many years, although after 1825 the sloops were replaced by schooners.

Short and relatively insignificant though these and many other of the coastal lines were, they rendered a greatly improved service and handled in the aggregate an enormous amount of freight and for many years a substantial number of passengers. In the process they turned hundreds of raw farm boys into competent master mariners. The need they supplied is indicated by the fact that similar lines continued to be added everywhere in rapid succession, until five or six were operating regularly between the principal ports, some of which sailed every other day.

It may be noted in this connection that early sloop and schooner packets furnished passenger accommodations little, if any, inferior to those of contemporary ship and brig lines. The chief difference in capacity between the fore-and-afters and the square-riggers lay in depth of hold. Where the sloops ranged from six to seven, and the schooners rarely exceeded nine, ships and brigs ran from 8 to 15 feet in depth. In other dimensions the difference was comparatively slight. The larger sloops, for instance, had a length on deck of 75 feet and upwards, and a breadth of 27, giving them a deck space equal to that of square-riggers of double their tonnage. Such vessels could, and frequently did, carry 30 to 50 or more passengers in the busy season.

The establishment of regular lines between Boston and Baltimore and Boston and Charleston was delayed several years, although numerous individual packets plied between the ports.

On the longer run between Boston and Savannah, Josiah Whitney established the famous "Brig Line" in 1822. The Savannah representative was S. B. Parkman, whose large and commodious warehouse was located on Hunter's Wharf.

Boston's early attempts to found lines to Mobile and New Orleans met with little success. Adams & Amory, Hall & Williams, and John Pratt & Son had been sending packets to those ports since shortly after the war, and as early as 1822 announced the establishment of regular lines to New Orleans. Their performance, however, was hardly up to liner standards. Of the three, Hall & Williams' brigs maintained the most frequent and reliable service. William Fitz, Jr., acted as their New Orleans agent, and in 1825 Parker & Stevens of Boston were associated with them in the dispatch of several vessels. All four firms discontinued sailings with the collapse of the cotton boom later in the year.

John A. Bacon started Boston's first line to Cuba in 1823 with a couple of smart little brigs sailing monthly to Matanzas. In later years the line was composed of handsome, clipper-like barks. Its earlier masters included Ephraim Harding and Caleb U. Grozier, both prominent in Boston packet circles during the colorful thirties and forties. Harding, indeed, survived to command the beautiful clipper *John Milton* and to die with all his crew in the wreck of that ship near Montauk Point on the night of February 20th, 1858. Aside from Bacon's line, the only other regular packet line communication between the United States and Cuba at the time consisted of four small schooners operated between New Orleans and Havana by J. W. Zacherie, 111 Royalist Street, New Orleans.

A line of considerable importance was established in 1824 to run between Boston and Eastport, Maine, by Messrs. Crackbon & Howe of Boston and Pillsbury & Noyes, of Eastport. It sailed from T Wharf and was the first of an eventually long list of "Down East" lines to sail on schedule. Three schooners ranging from 85 to 140 tons composed the line and sailed from Boston every Saturday and from Eastport every Wednesday. It supplied the States with plaster, grindstones and immigrants from the provinces, and continued to run as long as coastal packets sailed, although other substantial lines to the same port were soon started, one from New York being the most important. Meanwhile, Boston continued to found other lines to all the principal Maine ports.

Aside from those ventures, Boston established but one other noteworthy line during the period. This was the old reliable "Scudder" or "New Line," a Boston-New York service founded by a typical Cape Cod boy, Horace Scudder. It was not Scudder's first bid for fame. He had already established one record that stood, and will doubtless continue to stand unique in the annals of Yankee seafaring. The following extract from the *American Sentinel and Mercantile Advertiser,* of Philadelphia, tells the story:

Some dozen or fourteen years ago a brig arrived at Liverpool from Boston. When her papers were presented to the collector of the port, he learned that her name was the *Mary Scudder,* and that she was owned by Horace Scudder & Company of Boston. Her captain was Isaiah Scudder, first mate George W. Scudder, second mate Enoch Scudder, seamen Zerrubabel Scudder, Jonathan Scudder, Josiah, Samuel and Ezra Scudder. Her cook was Hannibal Scudder and steward Cato Scudder and Isaiah Scudder, Jr., boy. Mrs. Elizabeth Scudder and two little infant Scudders were passengers.

"For mercy's sake," exclaimed the astonished collector throwing down the papers, "are there any more Scudders left in New England or have you brought them all with you?"[1]

The Scudder line started operations March 24, 1825, sailing from Boston and New York on Wednesday and Saturday of each week. Aside from Horace Scudder, John H. Smith acted as Boston agent. In New York, Samuel S. Conant and M. & J. Brett were the principal agents for several years. A majority of the masters in the line were from Cape Cod, a statement which applies equally to all the Boston coastal packets except those running to the eastward, which were mostly commanded by lanky, hard-laid "down-Easters."

Two important lines between New York and points south were founded in 1822. One, like Scudder's Boston-New York service, called the "New Line," was started in September to provide weekly sailings between New York and Charleston. It was composed of five brigs, from roughly 175 to 200 tons in size. Saul Alley, 74 South Street, and J. & C. Williams, 171 Water Street, were the New York, and Drake Mills, the Charleston, representatives.

The second line ran to Mobile and was started by DeForest & Son. It continued to run for many years, but its service was irregular and occasionally suspended altogether for considerable periods. Another line to Mobile, which soon disappeared, was established about the same time by L. M. H. Butler.

Aside from the foregoing, the enlargement of "Grim's Philadelphia Line" to include four schooners and one sloop to provide a reliable weekly service, and the establishment of two others, J. M. Lowry's and J. & C. Seguine's lines to the Chesapeake, summed up the year's coastwise achievements. The Grim line was now managed in New York by David Grim and John W. Brown, 34 Old Slip, while David G. Meyer, 1 Chestnut Street, was the Philadelphia representative. Lowry's line figured later in one of the earliest attempts to start a coastwise steam service.

A line destined to become one of the most important of all the coastal lines was established the following year. This was Foster & Hutton's "New Line" (another one) between New York and New Orleans, which began operations in the spring of 1823 with the ships *Venus* and *Superior,* both well under 300 tons. In a way the line was the successor of the earlier one established by Andrew Foster and Jacob P. Giraud in 1816, which ceased operations during the depression of 1819; Foster later going into the Rio de Janeiro trade, where his smart little clipper packets eventually made some famous runs.

The new proprietors, who succeeded to the southern connections of the earlier firm, were James Foster, an old New York merchant, and his partner, Timothy Hutton. By 1825 they had five ships in the regular line, the largest of which was the 415-ton *Illinois,* commanded by young John Rathbone, a graduate with honors of the Connecticut blockade-busting school.

Meanwhile, New York's first permanent New Orleans line, the "Russell Line," was forging ahead with the help of the noted firm of Fish & Grinnell, which was associated with the line for a time. With the return of prosperity John Russell began to substitute ships for the original brigs, starting with the *William* and *American* in 1822, followed by the "new and elegant" *Florian* in 1823. Colby Chew, of New London, whose family was also associated with the early history of Virginia, had the *American,* and Henry Packard the *Florian.* William Fosdick and James Wibray were also numbered among the better known Russell commanders, but Silas Holmes, late of Stonington, Connecticut, outclassed them all in one respect. He packed the marlinspike of a proprietor-agent in his sea chest.

Conditions continued to improve and two more New York-New Orleans lines got under way in 1824. John Laidlaw, 78 South Street, put the little brig *Edwin* on the run and quickly built up a line of six ships, although it did not get into full operation and on a definite schedule until 1827. Two of his captains were Allen Miner and the ultimately wealthy "steamerite" Robert L. Taylor. The other line was the "Holmes Line."

Silas Holmes "swallowed the anchor" in 1824, but did not get further from salt water than New York's 62 South Street. The maiden voyage of his "line" was performed by one of Cape Cod's ablest sons, Sherburne S. Sears, in the 310-ton ship *Lavina.* As with many of the new lines, the names of the first ships of Holmes' line meant little. Often the same vessel was advertised by several different agents, and this was the case with Holmes in the beginning. However, the ability to secure freight and passengers was what counted and our ex-captain from Stonington possessed that to a remarkable degree. By the spring of 1826 he had four good ships under his exclusive management and had secured the services of several of the ablest masters in the trade; namely, John Rathbone, Robert Waterman, and Gideon Parker. By the following fall he had six ships and was sailing on a fixed schedule, the 1st and 15th of each month during the season, being the first on the New Orleans run to take the step.[2]

A second New York-Mobile line was started in 1824 by Ripley, Center & Company of New York; Messrs. Center & Company, of Mobile, acting as the southern agents. It ran haphazardly but continued through the greater part of the packet era, the well-known firm of Eagle & Hazard taking the New York agency in 1848. Its luster was doubtless dimmed by the "Hurlbut Line" that was established in October of the following year (1825) by Elisha D. Hurlbut & Company. That company, composed of men from the vicinity of New London, Essex and Deep River, Connecticut, started operations with four ships, the *Extio, Jane Blossom, Indiana,* and *Henry Hill.* They were all small, their average measurement being 260 tons, but they were commanded by able men, most of whom had been in the New Orleans and Mobile trades for several years in ships and brigs managed by John D. Hurlbut. It had no fixed sailing dates at first but was advertised to "sail each month in regular succession." Throughout its long career its ships were managed and almost, if not quite, exclusively commanded by Connecticut men—a statement, indeed, which applies equally to an impressive number of New York packet lines.

Several Connecticut mariners who later commanded noted clipper ships acquired their early experience in the Hurlbut line. The list included Captain Jack Williams, sometime of the medium clipper *Andrew Jackson* which performed notably on the Western Ocean and Cape Horn routes; Joseph W. Spencer, of the *David Crockett,* which rounded Cape Horn more times than any other clipper; Gurdon Gates of the *Electric* and *Twilight;* and half a dozen more.

There are indications of intensified competition by 1824 among the coastal packet lines. Improvement and expansion of service began to play almost as important a part as the establishment of new lines. On the 5th day of January, William Whitlock, Jr., and J. & C. Seguine discovered that they were operating the "Established Line" to Savannah and "at the urgent request of their customers" determined to dispatch a packet each week from each place, throughout the season.

The following day, by a coincidence of quite modern flavour, Thaddeus Phelps, John Griswold, and John Green Pearson, of 47, 68, and 67 South Street, respectively, became aware of the fact that they had been operating the "First Established Line" between the said ports, and advertised the first fixed sailing schedule on that run. In the future their three ships would sail on the 1st, 10th, and 21st of each month.

A similar improvement in the Charleston service was instituted early in 1826. Anson G. Phelps and Elisha Peck, doing business as Phelps & Peck, were interested in the New York-Charleston "Ship Line" with Oroondates Mauran, an old Providence boy. On the 7th of February they announced that provision had been made for adding four fine ships to the line and that, beginning with the "tenth inst.," they would dispatch two ships each week, sailing every Wednesday and Saturday.

In the fall of the same year one of their captains, George Sutton, a master mariner of long experience, took over the New York agency of the line and announced that the line would provide sailings every four days, starting September 25th. The same firm which had been associated with the Phelps group, Messrs. Timothy Street & Company, continued to act as Charleston agents.

In some respects the Charleston run ranked first among the various coastal lines. The fact that it was a comparatively short run, coupled with the general character of its patronage, made its ships especially desirable commands. Charleston's wealth enabled her citizens to travel at will. Entire families came north in droves to avoid the summer heat, and returned in late October and early November to avoid the cold. At such periods the packets, ships, brigs and schooners alike, were crowded with the chivalry and beauty of the South, often to double the normal capacity of the vessels. Thus, on the 1st of June, 1825, when cotton was at the all-time post-war high, the packets *Calhoun* and *President* arrived in New York, one with 63 and the other with 60 cabin passengers.

Boston, Providence, and Philadelphia packets reported similar conditions. By this time, however, Charleston had eight steamboats running up the Savannah River to Augusta, Georgia; Hamburg, South Carolina; and other nearby ports, which contributed substantially to the passenger traffic of the packets, as well as to her cotton shipments.

In the fall of 1825, J. M. Catlin, 90 South Street, put the "Union Line" of five schooners on a regular schedule, sailing every Wednesday from New York and Charleston. T. J. Wyman was the Charleston agent. In this connection, it is to be remembered that with rare and temporary exceptions, none of the southern lines maintained such schedules beyond the busy or "regular" season. At all other periods of the year they sailed in regular succession but on no fixed dates. The service was further liable to reduction or complete interruption when epidemics, such as yellow fever and smallpox, were raging in either southern or northern ports.

Another line of some importance, the New York-Savannah "Schooner Line," was started in 1826. It consisted of six schooners sailing twice weekly, although brigs and even ships were added after several years. The first New York agents were Howland & Cornwall, 136 Front Street. Cohen & Miller were the Savannah representatives. One of the best known masters in the line was Joseph Bartram, of Fairfield, Connecticut. A typical coastal packet master of his day, he served many a long year and eventually retired to live to a ripe age as one of the numerous well-to-do shipowners of his little New England village.

One other New York line established that year deserves mention. Baldwin & Spooner, 96 Coffee House Slip, had begun running brigs to Cartagena in 1825, one of their brigs being commanded by young Nat Palmer, who had already discovered Antarctica in 1820 at the age of 19, and who would later become one of the outstanding packet and clipper commanders. In August, 1826, they announced the formation of a line of three brigs to provide monthly sailings. Two years later the management of the line was taken over by Silas E. Burrows, a neighbor and contemporary of Palmer. His subsequent career was quite as remarkable as Palmer's, but for very different reasons.

Like a good many other Connecticut Yankees, Silas was better at establishing precedents than following them. A brief turn at seafaring convinced him that managing others was preferable to being managed, with the result that he qualified as a small-scale New York merchant in the early twenties, varying this activity with the construction of a couple of tiny pioneer steamboats for the South American market. Management of the Cartagena line led to the formation of a line to Panama, connecting with a line in the Pacific serving the principal ports on the west coast of South America. This, in turn, led to the transpacific trade, in which he built up a large and profitable business. His establishment in Hong Kong in the eighteen-fifties was a veritable palace, and he had substantial branches in Valparaiso and other South American ports.

He was on intimate terms with many of the notables of the day, including presidents and other high officials. One of his ships was christened the *Lady Pierce* in honor of President Pierce's wife, and it was in this vessel that he sailed for Japan immediately after the return of Perry's expedition and became, reputedly, the first American merchant to trade with that country. His interest in exploration led him to take an active part in organizing the unsuccessful Henry Grinnell expeditions for the rescue of Sir John Franklin. And when one of his ships rescued upwards of 200 officers and men from the wreck of a Russian man-of-war, he did not let the resulting broken voyage and the loss of thousands of dollars deter him from spending additional thousands to return the men to their homeland. Years later, he decided to go to Russia to appeal to the Czar personally for repayment of the expense incurred. He sailed from New York on the 30th of June, 1848, in his yacht *Patapsco,* carrying dispatches for the American Minister to Russia. Bennett of the *New York Herald* noted: "It was the first trip across the Atlantic by an American gentleman in a pleasure yacht."

Most of the coastal lines started by Philadelphia down to and through

1826 were of a secondary order. In 1823, Messrs. Bevan & Porter followed the example of merchants in several other ports by cooperating with Providence merchants in the establishment of a line to that port, in response to the increasing industrialization of Rhode Island. It consisted of four schooners.

The following year Bailey & Willis, 37 South Wharves, and Baldwin & Spooner of New York increased the "Regular" New York line to three schooners and three sloops. Andrew C. Barclay, Philadelphia agent of the "Union Line" to Boston, now had six schooners and was giving a weekly service, sailing from Philadelphia on Wednesday and from Boston on Saturday.

In 1825, Smith & Stewardson, on Girard's Wharf, began to run a line of ships to Charleston, the firm of Fleming & Ross acting as agents in Charleston. Their fleet included the ships *Carolinian* and the *Georgia Packet* and for a time Benjamin R. Smith acted as the Charleston agent.

By far the most important Philadelphia line established during the period was the C. Price & Morgan line to New Orleans. Chandler Price, who had been active in that trade before the war, had run packets sporadically through the years following the peace. In 1825, however, he took Tom Morgan into partnership and put two ships and two brigs on the run. One of the ships was the handsome new *Ohio*—a 350-tonner, and therefore larger than most coastal packets of the period. She was also one of the first American packets to abandon the flush deck in favor of the comparatively light and airy poop cabin, a practice which later became universal. Morgan, Dorsey & Company were the New Orleans agents. The line lasted many years and we are probably justified in regarding it as Philadelphia's most important coastal line.

In Baltimore a line of five sloops running to New York was started in 1824 by Rogers & Symington, who occupied a warehouse on Bowly's Wharf, the city's principal packet terminal. Andronicus Cheesebrough, a native of Stonington, Connecticut, commanded the *Connecticut,* one of their sloops. Connections between Baltimore and Stonington were always close. Later, Robert Cheesebrough and other Stonington men were masters of Baltimore clippers.

The line, called the "Dispatch Line," was reorganized in March, 1825, with five schooners and one sloop, sailing weekly. In the following September it increased its service by adding Wednesday sailings "when necessary." Anderson & Adams, 100 Coffee House Slip, and later David Anderson, acted as New York agents. Eventually, the line was operated by Thomas Whitridge, who became one of Baltimore's noted merchants, with the famous house of Sturges & Clearman as New York representatives.

Another Baltimore venture, the "Union Line" to Boston, also improved its service in 1825 by adopting a fixed schedule. It began trimonthly sailings on the 20th of February, leaving each port on the 10th, 20th and last days of the month, wind and weather permitting.

Aside from the foregoing, only one important Baltimore line was established during the period, a line composed of the brigs *Talent, Arctic* and *Trafalgar,* running to New Orleans, started in 1826. Messrs. Hammond & Newman, with offices at 82 Bowly's Wharf, were the local managers. They dispatched their vessels in regular succession but did not adhere to a schedule.

Conditions in America became somewhat stabilized toward the end of summer in 1826 and improved steadily thereafter as news from abroad became more favorable. Cotton, which had dropped to a low of 8 to 10 cents from a high of 28 to 31 cents, for upland grades, was in good demand at steadily increasing prices.

Although many large and substantial houses had been ruined and important projects delayed, the period had been, on the whole, one of notable achievement. A vast amount of wealth had changed hands, but it had not been destroyed. Commerce had increased beyond precedent. Trade had been good from 1822 to 1825. In the latter year American exports had reached the record figure of $99,535,388, and it is to be noted that less than 12 per cent of the total had been carried in foreign bottoms.[3] There was a substantial drop in the value of exports for the next five years, it is true, but the reduction was due in great measure to lower prices rather than to a falling off in volume.

Steam was playing an increasing role in progress. Most packets and a good many general freighters were being towed in and out of port as a routine practice, especially where arrivals and departures were normally subject to delay, as was invariably the case at New Orleans and usually also at Liverpool. At the latter place the number of steamboats had increased to more than 50 by 1826. By this time every northern packet bound for New Orleans advertised that steam would be taken up and down the river, and the business had become so profitable that regular towboat companies were being organized in that city.[4]

In New York waters, steam development had been greatly retarded by the unpopular North River Steamboat Company (Robert R. Livingston) monopoly. The decision of the United States Supreme Court in the case of Gibbons vs. Ogden in 1824 changed all that. One of its more immediate effects was a tremendous boom in local steamboat construction. In the year ending March 31, 1825, 30 steamboats, ranging to 500 tons and upwards, were laid down in the city of New York alone.[5] Nor did this include the new engineless "safety barges" *Lady Clinton* and others launched in the spring of 1825 for the use of timid travellers. Towed by the new "Independent" boats, they frequently carried 200 to 300 passengers in addition to the hardy souls who dared to patronize the more explosive craft.

The former monopoly's competition, however, did not wait on new construction. The first independent steamboat which began running between New York and Albany in the latter part of June, 1824, was an old vessel, having been built in 1816. She bore the ingratiating name of *Olive Branch,* but she was poison ivy to the old North River Steamboat Company. When she left New York for Albany on Sunday morning, July 11th, 1824, it was reported that she carried nearly 600 passengers.[6]

Aside from steamers for towing the safety barges, new construction included a number of powerful general-purpose towboats, with the result that canal boat traffic on the Hudson soon showed a very substantial increase. According to one contemporary account, the number leaving Albany during the 90 days ending July 17, 1826, was 3019.[7] Meanwhile, Hudson River sloop tonnage was steadily moving upward.

In the same year four steamboats were running out of Boston to Maine ports, connecting with others from the maritime provinces. Philadelphia put on a line of steamers to Norfolk, with the intention—sometimes realized—of cutting the passage to 36 hours. The running time between New York and Providence had been slashed to 18½ hours by the *Connecticut* in March, 1825. On the 21st of the following April, the *Chief Justice Marshall* arrived at New York in 14 hours, 15 minutes, "the best time yet," and the old Livingston monopoly boats, completely outclassed, were put up for sale.

On the Mississippi the *Pioneer* ran from New Orleans to Louisville in 9 days, 22 hours, "the shortest passage ever made," arriving at the latter city March 12, 1825. It is difficult today to appreciate the impression made on the travelling public by these and similar modest feats; the extent to which they quickened the speed mania and instilled impatience with the old modes of transportation. Everywhere steamboat travel was on the rise at the expense of sail, with passenger lists ranging from 300 to 600 and upwards, and, in the South, two cotton bales for every passenger. By 1826 every substantial port had one or more steamers. A total of 14 were credited to Charleston and Savannah, and the Chesapeake was alive with them.

Across the Atlantic, after a strangely slow start, England was building coasting steamers by the score, and was reaching out into new fields. Among others, she built a little steamer in 1825 for use on the Hooghly River, which successfully negotiated the passage around the Cape of Good Hope. In July, 1826, the ship *New England,* newly arrived at Philadelphia from Calcutta, reported passing the steamboat *Enterprise* in the Hooghly on the 4th of March. She was soon followed by the *Experiment,* reputedly equipped with one of Perkins' high-pressure engines. Also in England men were talking of a steamship line to India by way of the Mediterranean and Suez. The talk resulted in a line still operating as the Peninsula & Oriental Steamship Company, and which, from the beginning, cut weeks off the run to the Orient for passengers, mail, and light, costly merchandise.

Inventions and innovations had multiplied. An "ingenious mechanic of Baltimore" conceived the feathering paddle wheel. Sam Nichols of Plymouth, Massachusetts, invented a capstan by which one man could do the work of three with a windlass. The great ship *Washington,* built by Brown & Bell, was the first American ship to adopt iron chain for lower shrouds, paving the way for the eventual use of wire rope for that purpose. A Boston man devised a ropemaking machine so efficient that, with minor improvements, it is still used on occasion to supplement the present-day automatic machines. The number of those experimenting with high-pressure steam multiplied, and the day of the practical locomotive drew nearer. Dr. Buchanan, of Louisville, Kentucky, had a steam wagon in operation, propelled by "a small capillary engine which succeeded beyond the most sanguine hopes of its ingenious inventor."[8]

America had also produced her first iron steamboat, the *Codurus,* an extremely light, shallow-draft craft for navigating the upper reaches of the Susquehanna. It was built at York, Pennsylvania, in 1825, and was 80 feet in length, with a beam of 9 feet; drawing only 6½ inches with its engine on board.[9]

Nevertheless, in 1826 canvas-backers still held the center of the stage. Aside from James P. Allaire and one or two other engine builders, and a handful of young enthusiasts like Charles Morgan and Silas E. Burrows, no one risked any substantial amount of capital in the construction of ocean-going steamers. Morgan's interest is largely explained by the iron-works which he acquired about that time, while Burrows' commitments never represented more than a fraction of his shipping investments. A dozen ships of the sail were being launched for every steamboat, and hundreds for every steamship, so-called. Whatever of interest the latter might hold, they failed to arouse the enthusiasm created by the huge new packets, of which the *Britannia* was chief, or the stately emigrant liners, now ranging well above 700 tons.

Such developments undoubtedly did much to keep potential steamerite enthusiasm within bounds. As the brave new ships took the water one by one, they attracted much the same attention as the latest present-day super-liner. The size and finish of their cabins, number of staterooms and style of furnishings were described meticulously in laudatory terms justified only by the new and ingenious features embodied in each successive packet. They were, indeed, notable achievements in naval architecture, and recognized as such both at home and abroad.

Nor were they the largest vessels built in America about that time. Other canvas-backers were being launched which served to convince forward-looking men that the passenger liner of the sail was only in its infancy. There were several warships registering 1700 to 1800 tons and more, including one for South America and two frigates for the Greeks, then fighting desperately for independence.

The Greek incident (or swindle, to call it by its right name) was discussed briefly in the previous chapter. It is referred to here only as warrant for the assertion that it evidenced a certain step-up of the always-present trend toward unhealthy social practices. In New England, in particular, the mill owners had already gone as far as it was possible to go, short of slavery. They had fixed the weekly wage of their women operatives in the majority of cases at $1.00, when room and board were not to be had for less than $1.17. As to the fate of the little children they employed, the less said, the better.

Aside from such general practices, there were innumerable isolated instances to show that the old Puritan concern for the welfare and dignity of the individual was giving place to an overriding concern for property. In the *Louisiana State Gazette* for September 11, 1826, for example, we note that:

Noah Buzzell, aged about 70, who fought at Bunker Hill, died in a debtor's prison August 13, at Haverhill, Mass. He lived at Alexandria, Mass., and was in debt 10-12 dollars.

It was a far cry from the days—not so long before the Revolution—

when every church in New England took up frequent voluntary collections for the poor and unfortunate, and profit was so little regarded that the assize of bread was still strictly enforced.

There were other things besides Greek frigates and children in bondage to indicate that America was becoming sophisticated. Beautiful Georgian mansions and Greek-revival homes were rising everywhere, even in the smaller seaports, where they are still to be seen. Schools and academies were multiplying. Interest in art and literature was growing. Scott's latest novel was eagerly awaited and as eagerly devoured. America even had a novelist or two of her own, chief of whom was Cooper, namesake of the old Philadelphia merchant, James Fenimore. Among others, a recent Bowdoin graduate named Longfellow and a youth named Emerson joined the windjammer caravan to Europe, with a view to absorbing still larger doses of culture. One Washington Irving went along, to gain fame and a trifle of cash in the fields of serious and humorous history. The tragedian Booth and Messrs. McCready and Kean were rolling westward, responsive to the promise of huge, enthusiastic audiences.

American taste was embracing a wider, if not always a more creditable variety of objects of art, and articles of personal adornment and household furnishings, although years were to elapse before "the only shower bath in New York" was included in the list of offerings. Shopping centers of a magnitude and richness undreamed before the war had sprung up in all the principal cities, that of New York being the most extensive. Her Pearl Street with its solid mile of stores crammed with merchandise from every quarter of the globe was the wonder of all visitors, as communications, of which the following is a sample, testified from time to time:

I have with delight witnessed the hustle along the wharves, the loading and unloading of ships, the busy carman and untiring laborer. I have traversed that long avenue of business known as Pearl Street and have been astonished at beholding the uninterrupted range of stores, the insides of which exhibit the richest treasures from abroad, neatly arranged, and under the management of persons who carry business in their very countenances.

(Signed) Marylander.[10]

An international incident of curiously modern flavour, one of the first of its kind, was in the making when the wealthy and slightly shopworn New York merchant and shipowner, Mr. E. Malibran, married the beautiful and accomplished Spanish songbird, Lucia Garcia. Within a matter of months his warehouses and fleets—including the fine ex-packet, *James Monroe*—were gone, and with them Madame Malibran. Not that the lady was altogether to blame. She happened to be there, however, when strict attention to business in the debacle of 1825 and 1826 was a matter of crucial importance to Mr. Malibran.

Here and there relics of an older and cruder day still lingered. Piracy was still prevalent and apparently becoming more so, especially in the West Indies and the Gulf. Every vessel engaged in foreign trade and all southbound coastwise packets were still heavily armed and still found occasional use for their guns, despite the rather recently announced discovery that tales of murder constituted a libel on a rather harmless class of men who engaged in robbery, it is true, but rarely committed acts of cruelty and almost never killed. If that verdict is correct, a remarkable number of newspaper accounts through the eighteen-twenties and later are false, and the findings of courts which hung a substantial number of pirates executed a lot of innocent men; innocent, at least, of the more revolting crimes with which they were charged.

One turns with relief from the long series of newspaper stories of murder, rape, and torture by pirates to the following account of one of the rare instances in which great bravery, coupled with ingenuity, turned the tables. It appeared in the *Weekly Louisiana Gazette,* a paper noted for its veracity, on the 28th of May, 1825, under the heading: "Pirates. A Yankee Trick."

The following anecdote is strictly true. It is contained in a letter from a young gentleman who lately went out in a vessel from this port (Norfolk, Va.) for St. Thomas —"We were chased by a pirate off King's channel on Sunday morning, last. (18 March) The Villain was close in under the land in a small sloop with about 25 men, when he discovered us. We were nearly becalmed. He gave chase and came down on us very fast. I thought there was no chance of escape but by strategem, and having a man on board whom I could metamorphose into anything, I observed to Capt. . . . that he had better make a gun of Billy Luly and give chase in our turn.

We accordingly went to work; put a black cap on Billy's head, stretched him fore and aft on the keel of the boat with a rope made fast to his heels, so we could slew him on the centre of Gravity freely, pointing his head into the enemy. The next thing to do was to fire it, and this we did by discharging a pistol in a barrel and raising a smoke by throwing ashes into the air. The trick was successful; the sloop tacked and made off; we hauled on a wind and pursued her close under the land, then tacked ship and stood into St. Thomas.—Thus were 25 men driven by four.

The United States Government sent many expeditions against the pirates, but another 20 years elapsed before their activities in southern waters were halted.

The period was further marked by the acceleration of two trends destined to play no small part in shaping the future course of America. One was the tendency—heretofore referred to and especially noticeable after the Revolution—of American youth to seek their fortunes on land rather than at sea. The other was the reduction of seagoing tonnage built and owned throughout the South, Virginia alone excepted.

By the end of the first quarter of the nineteenth century, comparatively few boys of outstanding ability were interested in a sea career, a complete reversal of the situation which had prevailed throughout the seventeenth and the greater part of the eighteenth centuries. One reason lay in the changing conditions afloat as ownership became concentrated more and more in the hands of a few, and long-distance management and control increased, and the most competent masters became relegated to the status of mere order takers.

Denial of the right to independent thinking and the restriction of personal responsibility, however justified by practical considerations, has the result, among others, of making room for men of inferior ability, as well as discouraging interest, enthusiasm, and initiative. That such denial was rapidly spreading to the shipping interests in 1826 is indicated by the slogan coined about that time for the benefit of sea captains: "Obey orders if you break owners." The resulting dry rot spread from captain to cabin boy. It did not become a serious matter from a material standpoint until a generation later, when a new and far more effective competition was developed abroad, while at home the shipping men, both afloat and ashore, who possessed the enthusiastic determination and informed resourcefulness of an earlier day, which alone might have countered it, had almost disappeared from the active stage.

The other and probably more compelling reason the ablest sought careers ashore rather than afloat stemmed from the new and greater opportunities ashore. The tremendous growth in manufacturing; the development of mines; huge new construction projects; the recent availability of uncounted millions of rich new acres; the multiplication of great banking, insurance, and mercantile concerns—all beckoned the eager, ambitious youngster down golden vistas, away from the hard, uphill route through the hawsepipe and over the quarter-deck. Nor was the parental push lacking.

As the years passed, these factors were to become more potent. In the end America had to choose between maintaining the world's first merchant navy and the greater task of developing a continent. It was that, rather than the destruction of war, which was responsible for her downfall as a maritime power.

The drift away from maritime pursuits had—at least for the South—

more immediate and serious effects. Its results were becoming apparent by 1826, even in the richest centers of that area.

The experience of Charleston may be taken as typical. The town had prospered greatly and, in general, continuously throughout colonial times. Her advantageous position in the profitable tobacco, rice, and indigo trades toward the close of the eighteenth century will be recalled. The growing competition of other southern ports, especially Savannah, following the Revolution, failed, apparently, to lessen her prosperity. Her business continued to increase year by year. Her position as fourth port of the nation seemed unassailable.

Several factors combined to prolong her prosperity for some years. Chief among them were the rapid growth of population and the unprecedented industrial development of the northern states and Great Britain. To these must be added the disturbances and wars incident to and following the French Revolution, which put a premium on American exports. For Charleston and the South as a whole, the long, slow-moving years from 1783 to the outbreak of the War of 1812 were years of great prosperity. A generation was born and grew to manhood which knew no other condition, and which regarded southern prosperity as permanent and unassailable.

Nevertheless, peace, assured to the United States by the Treaty of Ghent in December, 1814, and to Europe by the defeat of Napoleon at Waterloo the following June, presaged the end of Charleston's golden era. The simple fact was that a potentially ruinous competition had been in the making for some years. Its impact had been cushioned by abnormal trade conditions, and its full effect further postponed by the usual postwar boom. By the latter part of 1818, however, the merchants of Charleston were confronted by the almost incredible fact that the world was unable or unwilling to pay a profitable price for southern products, and that those who escaped crippling losses might consider themselves fortunate.

Several causes contributed temporarily to this condition. One was the depression at home and abroad, brought about by overexpansion and overspeculation; another was the banking scandals which involved even the new United States Bank, and which had undermined public confidence. But for the long pull, the all-important fact was competition, for it was to become permanent. The men of Charleston who, in the opening months of 1818, had looked forward confidently to a carefree, prosperous future, were destined, although they long failed to realize it, to pass most of their remaining years in the shadow of sharp, worrying competition. For the moment it sprang from one major source, but it was shortly to be enlarged and intensified by two other factors.

With the Louisiana Purchase in 1803, the vast resources of the Mississippi Valley were tapped, and a swelling flood of exportable produce began to make its way through New Orleans to the markets of the world.

A few years later the fortunes of war made it obvious that Spain would have to relinquish her Florida and Alabama territory to the United States, as she did, formally, in 1819. Even before that, however, spurred by reports such as that of the traveller who asserted that Florida was the most fertile land he had ever seen—"it produced 40 bushels of frogs to the acre, with alligators enough to fence them"—Mobile and the Florida ports were exporting large and rapidly increasing quantities of cotton and lumber.

At the same time a thin trickle—which would presently become a deluge—of mid-western produce was beginning to seep through the unfinished Erie Canal to New York. Some of this produce was not directly competitive, but cheap western beef, wheat, and corn could and did cut the demand for the more expensive southern rice and other foodstuffs. For the most part, however, Charleston's new competition was fostered by the South itself, southern made and southern grown.

It has since become recognized (as, indeed, it was then by a few far-sighted southerners) that the South's only remedy in the long run lay through diversification of industry; but, despite efforts here and there, the South proved incapable of coping with the situation. There was, for instance, the early attempt to establish cotton mills in Georgia:

> A memorial has been presented to the legislature of Georgia by a Mr. (John) Schly (*sic*) praying for the establishment of manufactories for coarse cotton and woolen goods to determine whether slave labor can be profitably employed.[11]

The outcome of this and similar efforts is indicated by the fact that after the lapse of more than 20 years the cotton mills of the entire South hardly equalled in value those of a single large manufacturing center of the North. The greater part of their product consisted of coarse yarns, for many of the mills engaged in spinning only, and those which engaged in weaving had comparatively few looms. The state of South Carolina was by far the most active in the industry, but her total investment in 1849 was a scant million dollars. Few of the other southern states had engaged in the enterprise to an extent much in excess of a hundred thousand dollars, and several had no mills at all.[12]

It is impossible to escape the conclusion that the South as then constituted was incapable of solving her most pressing economic problem, and for this, the institution of slavery was chiefly to blame. It was, in its very nature, unchanging and unchangeable. It was the same in 1818 and in 1860 that it was in Greece and Rome and all the other great civilizations of the past for whose downfall it had been measurably responsible. It was incapable of adjustment to meet new conditions. In particular, it was incapable of meeting the growing skill, initiative, and resourceful inventiveness of the machine age already well under way in 1826.

If proof of this assertion is required, we have only to look to the South's maritime industry. Although never comparable with that of the North, it had been conducted for generations on a scale which guaranteed the South a substantial share in her more profitable carrying trade, and in ship construction. With the nineteenth-century demand for huge, lavishly equipped, and magnificently finished vessels, slave labor proved incapable of meeting northern competition. Construction fell off and, with it, southern ownership dropped.

The trend was further accelerated by the failure of the South to develop, at least in adequate supply, a highly trained and thoroughly competent merchant class of her own. Her commerce was not only increasing in volume at a tremendous rate, but was reaching out to new fields. Every year more and more merchants were required to handle the business. Quite as important was the fact that trade was becoming more sharply competitive, calling for operators of the soundest judgment and broadest possible experience.

That the South could and did produce many such men is beyond question. Some of New York's ablest merchants were born and bred in the South. That she failed to produce enough of them for her material good is equally beyond question, and for this the institution of slavery must accept a substantial measure of the blame. It required a long and arduous apprenticeship, involving much labor regarded as menial, supplemented by years spent in ill-paid subordinate positions, to produce a sound merchant. In the light of such information as has come down to us, it would seem that comparatively few southern boys looked forward with enthusiasm to a career that started with sweeping out a dingy, waterfront office and entailed years of confinement at a desk, goosequilling endless copies of dull letters and duller documents.

One immediate consequence of the shortage of local talent was that northern merchants were under a compulsion of sorts to send more and more of their clerks south to act as their agents. This meant a certain reduction in the income of the South. To be sure, it amounted to little in the course of a year, but, like the mortgage on the old homestead, it went on and on, to the increasing discontent of Charleston merchants and tributary planters.

Customhouse records tell the story in part.

In the years just after the war, Charleston, then the largest exporting center of the South, still issued from 75 to 110 ship registers annually. During the next 15 years, while northern ports were everywhere showing substantial increases, her new issues dropped to a low of 23, and an average of approximately 30 annually, a majority of which were small coasters, and more than half of which were owned wholly or in large part by northern merchants. At the same time, the numbers of vessels registered in the larger northern ports ranged from 300 to 600, annually, and were increasing. Moreover, roughly 90 per cent of the tonnage represented was owned in the port of registration.

During the depression years of the eighteen-thirties, mass meetings were held in Charleston and Savannah to concert means of regaining control of their traffic. Newspapers also carried from time to time strongly worded appeals for direct trade with Europe. One of these, published in the *Savannah Daily Georgian* for August 29, 1837, called attention to the fact that 890 vessels were built in the United States during 1836, and of these only six (less than seven-tenths of one per cent) were built in South Carolina and Georgia, although they were the third and fourth exporting states of the Union.

Admitting that the figures alone do not afford a completely accurate picture, they do point beyond a reasonable doubt to a situation extremely unfavorable to southern merchant and planter alike.

The fact was that the South was drifting back toward a status similar to that in which the northern colonies found themselves in the early seventeenth century when they learned in the school of hard knocks that permanent prosperity came the hard way—by conducting their own trade in their own ships and through their own merchants. It was no fault of the individual southerner. Change from within was impossible. He was caught in the vicious round of an orbit, powered by 6,000,000 slaves, from whose slowly descending spiral there was no escape short of a cataclysm which would blow it to flinders.

Such was the situation of Charleston in 1826. Aside from the fact that she, in common with Savannah and several other large ports, was charged with the support of planters accustomed to most of the luxuries and some of the extravagancies of the age, it was the situation of every southern port. The fact is essential to an understanding of the coastal packet era then starting, which was to contribute mightily to the progress of civilization, and perhaps to its "growing pains" as well.

As the period closed, vociferous America left no doubt that her outstanding trend (or "mania," as one prefers) was rapidly gathering volume and momentum. Nevertheless, with all due allowance for boastful national pride, her merchant marine had long since demonstrated a certain superiority in speed, economy, and all-round efficiency. With the establishment of the packet lines and the aid of notable advances in steam navigation, its efficiency was not only stepped up in marked degree, but was extended so far afield that it must be credited with a major contribution to the development of the vast empire of the West. By the same token it was playing an increasingly important role in breaking down the ancient and still powerful European prejudice against change.

CHAPTER IX

∼ *1827-1837* ∼

Steam Competition Gains Headway

"Faint portents of impending doom."

LACK of assurance had never been a particularly obtrusive American trait, an observation which applied with special force to her men of the sail. With the return of prosperity late in 1826, and their ships handling, roughly, nine-tenths of the nation's foreign commerce—not to mention their carrying of a large and growing share of the trade of other countries—their confidence was unbounded. Nothing could or ever would surpass their ships.

Yet, almost unnoted, the period from 1827 to the panic of 1837 was marked by the slow marshalling and multiplication of forces that would eventually drive their finest and fastest craft from the sea.

During those years more and more operators, no longer restrained by the threat of monopolies, attacked the problem of ocean steamship service, and undismayed by successive failures, rallied to the attack again and again. In the coastal field huge, swift, river and sound steamboats were built by the score; more canals dug; turnpikes laid out; and railroads stretched from seaport to seaport, gobbling up huge chunks of the re-munerative passenger traffic. Here and there "crackpot" inventors: Ericsson searching for a practical version of the Archimedian screw; Morse employed on the hopeless task of harnessing Ben Franklin's mys-terious "galvanic fluid"; a thousand bemused mechanics obsessed by quaint problems of valves, packings, metals, fuels, compounds, and the like; imperceptibly smoothed the paths for still unforeseeable advances that would end in making canvas-powered ships forever obsolete.

Despite the improvement in business at home and abroad, there was no marked increase in the number of new packet lines for several years. Probably the fact that business was neither good enough to attract that venturesome element which always appears in boom times, nor bad enough to force elimination of competition, was largely responsible.

There was also the fact that merchants everywhere had been "scared out of a year's growth." Although the recent collapse was to go down in history as a "slight recession," it was the end of the world for many great houses, while others which had somehow managed to survive were known to be shaky. For some time the apprehension persisted that one or more of them might go under and start a chain reaction that would topple others. As a matter of fact something of the sort actually came to pass, with results that might have been catastrophic but for the fact that speculation had not been resumed on a large scale.

Jeremiah Thompson, one of the proprietors of the Black Ball line, and regarded as the largest shipowner in America since the death in 1825 of William Gray, failed in November, 1827. He had been deeply involved in cotton speculation. It was estimated that he shipped half the cotton exported from New York in the three preceding years, and he was certainly by far the largest exporter of the staple in the city.

Other considerations undoubtedly operated to restrain the formation of new lines. Chief among them was the growing tendency of merchants to sink their surplus funds in unfamiliar investments—banks, factories, canals, railroads, and land—a process which ended for many in sending their credit after their cash.

We may take the case of land speculation as typical of what was going on during the latter part of the period. For many years the public had been purchasing government lands at the rate of one or two million dollars a year. In 1834 there was a remarkable jump. Then in 1835 purchases amounted to fifteen millions, in round figures, and in the following year to twenty-five millions.[1]

This and similar developments, which steadily converted huge amounts of liquid into frozen assets, were fostered in the first instance by good business. As always, however, in eras of modest prosperity, the evil effects of the process were intensified by other contributing factors, chief among which was extravagance, both individual and national.

The government, confronted with an embarrassing surplus arising from the protective tariff of 1828, and unwilling to risk modification of that instrument, embarked on a policy of aiding the construction of canals, turnpikes, and railroads, some of which soon slipped into bankruptcy, and most of which were many a long year repaying their original cost. Thus, on the 4th of July, 1828, the President turned the first sod for the great Chesapeake & Ohio Canal, and about the same time the Blackstone Canal between Providence and Worcester opened its first section. Both tied up huge amounts of capital, and few of the original stockholders realized more than a small fraction of their investment.

The individual spent lavishly, especially in the purchase of costly imported goods, including vast quantities of ephemeral luxury items, of which the cargo of the Havre liner *France* was an example. She arrived at New York in March, 1828, with a manifest reported to amount to $5,000,000, principally silks. All in all, in the ten years prior to 1837, a debit trade balance of nearly $150,000,000 was built up, most of which remained in America in the form of investments. In addition, another $45,000,000 in specie was sent over, principally from England, to swell the flood of "easy money."

One result was to speed the development of vast new farming areas, both North and South, which in turn caused the repeated overproduction of many staple commodities. This was especially true of the principal southern crops. As early as 1826 cotton alone amounted to 950,000 bales; nearly a quarter more than in 1825, and by 1834 such increases had become the rule. In general, they made temporarily for greater prosperity, but in time of depression, with its accompanying drop in consumer demand, could only serve to intensify distress. Such a situation developed toward the end of 1833, and as the markets weakened a few farsighted bankers and merchants began to take in sail. Loans were called, and as speculators were squeezed, they redoubled their speculative ventures in the effort to recoup or forestall losses.

The shipping situation at that time is indicated by the fact that customs duties, which amounted to $29,000,000 in 1833, dropped in 1834 to a trifle over $16,000,000.[2] The matter is particularly relevant to our inquiry, for it indicated a huge reduction in freight offerings, and merchants once more began to form new packet lines on an increasing scale, in order to secure a profitable share of the dwindling traffic.

Boston, meanwhile, had not been idle. Her second "Boston & Liverpool Line" was organized in 1827, and started operations on November 1 with the old ships *Amethyst* and *New England*. These were supplanted in the following year by the new ships *Boston, Dover, Liverpool,* and *Trenton,* ranging from 428 to 431 tons register. They were ably commanded by the ill-fated Ira Bursley and Jabez Howes, William Homan and Henry C. Mackay, under the competent management of George C. Jones, 51 India Wharf. Their sailing record was excellent. It included one 16-day crossing in 1828 by the *Amethyst* under the command of Charles Hunt.

Nevertheless, it was evident from the first that the promoters realized that the success of the line depended on their success in overcoming some of the disadvantages of the port. Even before the line was established, a substantial number of Boston's leading merchants, including such men as Abbott Lawrence and William Appleton, were agitating the subject of a horse-drawn railroad between Boston and Albany, to secure a share of the canal traffic. Surveys and plans were made and estimates prepared. It was reported that a road over which one horse could draw eight tons on the steepest grades could be built for $20,000 a mile, approximately the cost of the Erie Canal. A bill for the construction of such a road was submitted to the legislature but failed to pass, owing to opposition of the coastal packet interests, stage line proprietors, and the general public, who saw in it merely a benefit to a few shipowners at the expense of the people.

As the promoters had feared, the packet venture was doomed when the railroad bill failed to pass; an ominous instance of the growing indifference to the nation's maritime interests. The ships were compelled to resort once more to the triangle route. The *Boston* burned at sea while on a voyage from Charleston for Liverpool, having been struck by lightning the 25th of May, 1830. The crew and six cabin passengers, including Sir Isaac Coffin, were rescued by the brig *Idas* of Liverpool after two days in the boats, during which time one lady died of exposure.

Chief among the new lines of 1827 from the standpoint of length and volume of service, was Fish, Grinnell & Company's New York and London line, the second of the famous "Swallowtail" lines. This company, which had been, as noted, one of the operators of the Griswold line, decided the time was ripe for a second service. Accordingly, in the summer of that year they parted company with John Griswold and started an independent line with five ships, sailing from each port on the 1st of each month.

All their ships were small, the largest being the *Columbia*, of 492 tons, but management and masters atoned for material deficiencies. William S. Sebor, Daniel Chadwick, Joseph S. Delano, and Judah Baker were among the first of a long line of captains which eventually included such outstanding mariners as Elisha E. Morgan, Henry L. Champlin, George Moore, Thomas Britton, Edward G. Tinker, and a dozen more of similar calibre, who helped to make the line notable among the great Western Ocean services.

A third line established in 1827 gave such intermittent and irregular service that it is doubtful whether it is entitled to a place in our list. This was the Hurlbut line between New York and New Orleans. Although sailings in this so-called line continued to be advertised for many years, it appears to have been operated only when business was especially active. A fairly comprehensive, although incomplete check of clearances indicates that it rarely adhered to a schedule.

Several minor ventures were started this year, including a Davis & Brooks line to Gibraltar, but for the most part they soon disappeared. A new line between New York and Vera Cruz, however, deserves mention for the part it played in developing one of the most noted of all the packet operators. This was the "Line of Mexican Packets" established by Israel G. Collins & Son, who hailed originally from Cape Cod. The son was Edward Knight Collins, who later took over the Foster & Hutton "New Line" between New York and New Orleans; founded the "Dramatic Line" which set a new standard of comfort, speed, and efficiency in the Western Ocean service; and played a prominent part in the establishment of the famous Collins line of steamships.

Aside from short coastal lines, only one permanent New York packet line was founded in 1828. This was the "Union Line of Brigs," usually referred to as "The Brig Line," operating between New York and Charleston. George Bulkley, 39 Burling Slip, was the local manager, and W. Jones, a commission merchant with other substantial shipping interests, the Charleston representative, with offices at 15 Vendue Range. Both were exceptionally able men, but George Bulkley possessed one other asset which lightened his task if it did not account in some measure for the notable success of the line.

He had, in his native town of Fairfield, Connecticut, five brothers, all well to do, who contributed the major part of the capital required from time to time by the line. With a management thus fortified against the officious and sometimes harmful interference of small shareholders, a fleet of five brigs, ranging from 150 to 200 tons, was quickly built up, and increased to eight in 1837, sailing twice weekly.

Another British emigrant line appeared this year, indicating an increasing volume of emigration to America. This was "The British Packet Line" running between Hull and New York. It consisted of two brigs and a bark "to sail on the day appointed, full or not full." John Hollingsworth was the Hull operator, and Masters & Markoe represented the line in New York.[3]

About this time several New York firms were running casual immigrant ships with considerable regularity and success. Among them A. (Abraham) Bell & Company, who had followed the business for a number of years, were now exceptionally active. Their ships sailed principally from Belfast and Londonderry, and frequently brought from 150 to 175 steerage.

After 1826 there was also a heavy increase in German immigration, and the firm of Peterson & Mensch, 118 Hanover Square, New York, was the first to take advantage of it. In January, 1827, they announced the establishment of a packet line, which was to all intents and purposes an immigrant line between Hamburg and New York. It was to start with the sailing of the ship *Europa,* Edward Nicoll, master, from Hamburg on the 15th of February. Cabin rates were fixed at $100.[4]

Baltimore's first venture in the Western Ocean packet field came in 1829 with the establishment of a line of three ships, the *Benjamin Rush, Dumfries* and *Ulysses,* which sailed irregularly from Belfast and other Irish ports. It continued in operation for a number of years, always one of the looser organizations of the sort. William & Thomas Adair, 1 South Charles Street, were the Baltimore agents, with branches in Pittsburgh and St. Louis. They were essentially emigrant agents on the order of Samuel Thompson, of New York, the first to specialize in that field.

Thompson's early activities are not well documented, but in later years he claimed that his business was established in 1817. In any case, he undoubtedly worked in close cooperation with the Black Ball from a very early date, and possibly from its founding. By 1825 he was doing a substantial business at 273 Pearl Street and advertising regularly in the local papers the establishment of his "Emigrant Offices":

Where persons wishing to send for their friends from Great Britain and Ireland, Can secure their passage on the most moderate terms, in vessels of the first class, sailing from Liverpool every week.

By the time the Baltimore concern was founded, several other houses had engaged in the business, most of them in New York City. All followed closely the Thompson pattern. Their success led to the opening of a long series of "Passenger Agencies" of which Tapscott's is perhaps the best remembered. Thompson's, however, had the longer career, continuing long after the Civil War as Samuel Thompson's Nephew.

American passenger agents, however, could hardly be expected to monopolize a business that originated 3000 miles away. With the renewal of emigration on a large scale it was not long before English and, to a lesser extent, German merchants began to engage in the traffic on their own initiative. One of the first ventures of the sort was the "Union Line of Packets for New York" organized in March, 1829, by Fitzhugh and Caleb Grimshaw, of 11 Brooks Square, Liverpool. The line consisted of 12 American ships, none of which were attached to any of the American lines, and the service started with the sailing of the ship *Bowditch* from Liverpool for New York on the 5th of April. Thereafter the line was scheduled to sail from Liverpool the 5th and 20th, and from New York the 12th and 28th of each month.[5]

Although essentially an emigrant service, the Grimshaws advised the public that "a few respectable passengers can be accommodated in the first and second cabins" and that "no salt would be taken," this as a special inducement to prospective first-class patrons, salt having a strong tendency to make a ship damp and uncomfortable. With the exception of one small vessel, the ships ranged around 400 tons, and the records show that they frequently carried from 150 to 200 steerage and several cabin passengers. The experiment was so far successful that by 1831 the firm was sending a ship every week or ten days. It was the forerunner of a number of similar lines, of which the famous "Black Star" was the most important.

The "Union Line" and its imitators represented only a part of the competition encountered by the American firms. The old, established institution of "spring and fall ships," formerly sent out singly by British merchants, was expanded until several firms were sending three or more each season, and finally dispatching a regular succession of ships throughout the year.

Fortunately, the transatlantic lines had several years of comparative freedom from serious disasters while this competition was shaping up. However, 1830 was marked by the loss of several fine coastal packets. The ship *Charles & Henry* was wrecked near Beaufort in the gale of August 16th, Captain Kelly and crew drifting ashore on the quarter-deck. The same gale caused the dismasting and stranding of the Sutton packet *Othello,* Captain Mike Berry, bound from New York for Charleston with 30 passengers. Other packets badly damaged about that time included the *Statira,* for Savannah, and the *Empress,* for Charleston. A day or two earlier the Collins packet schooner *Neuse,* from New York for Vera Cruz, was lost on the Abaco, Captain Peter Barnard, two seamen, the cook, and eight passengers being drowned.

The following year was not particularly hard, but an even greater number of packets were lost in 1832. The fine ship *George Canning* went ashore near Egg Harbor, New Jersey, the night of January 7th. The *De Witt Clinton,* Henry Packard, bound from New York for New Orleans, was totally lost on the Abaco in the gale of January 30th, only the crew being saved. Another Collins packet, the ship *Lavina,* from Vera Cruz, was lost the 16th of February on Colorados Reef. On March 31st the Havre packet *De Rham* was lost on Rockaway Beach. The packet brig *Edwina* capsized off Hatteras on the 3rd of June, drowning five passengers. In November the wreck of the brig *Patrician,* of Baltimore, was sighted with nothing standing but the foremast and two dead men lashed in the foretop. The good ship *Kentucky,* of the Holmes line, was lost October 29th on Florida Reef, while bound from New Orleans for New York. Captain E. S. Dennis, an old and popular mariner, was drowned; the cook and two other men being lost at the same time. Other packet losses for the year included the old *Pennsylvania,* of Philadelphia, and the former Black Baller *James Cropper,* the latter being lost at the entrance of Delaware Bay on the 15th of December.

From 1830 to 1833, inclusive, Boston accounted for the great majority of the new coastal lines, a fact for which the growing industrial needs of Massachusetts was primarily responsible. The most important among these were Ammi C. Lombard's "Regular Line" to Charleston, of which the well-known firm of Joseph Leland & Bros. were the southern representatives; John H. Pearson's "Regular Line" to Baltimore; John Fairfield's "Regular Line" to New Orleans; R. Lincoln & Company's "Commercial Line" to Philadelphia, and the "Cunningham Line" to Mobile, the latter operated by N. F. Cunningham & Company, 38 India Wharf. At the same time Lombard began running packet brigs and barks to Savannah at frequent intervals, although he did not establish a line to that port until the fall of 1840.

A mere enumeration of the lines, however, gives only a faint conception of the volume and value of their business. Boston, for instance, had three lines to New York composed of six vessels each, during the greater part of the early packet era. It was estimated in 1831 that the three lines carried $6,000,000 worth of merchandise annually between New York and Boston, in addition to which the steamers and other transient vessels carried approximately another $6,000,000.

Compared with Boston, New York and Baltimore did very little during this period toward developing new coastal lines. New York's only permanent contribution was in assisting Boston to establish the Boston-New York "Commercial Line" in 1830; Hart, Herrick & Company, 19 South Street, being the New York agents. In the same year Baltimore started a schooner line to Savannah, Sorrell & Anderson acting as Savannah agents. In the following year one of Baltimore's noted merchants of a later day, young Thomas Whitridge, a boy from Tiverton, Rhode Island, who had removed to Baltimore and engaged in the oil and candle business about 1827, began running a couple of schooner packets to Providence, in opposition to Henry Payson's line.

Philadelphia was the only northern port which approached Boston's record in the matter of new coastal lines at this time. Joseph Hand, 7 North Wharves, started the "Hand Line" to New Orleans in 1831, Thomas Toby acting as New Orleans agent. Hand, a native of New Jersey, was a prodigiously active man who already had several Chesapeake operations under way. Another New Orleans line was established by Sam Comley and Robert Fleming in 1833, with a member of the Comley family in charge of the southern office. It was known as the "Louisiana & Philadelphia" or "Regular Line." Messrs. Sloan & Morris and Francis & Company joined forces in the same year to establish the "Regular Line" to Charleston; the well-known and energetic firm of Smith, Mowry & Company acting as Charleston agents. The latter firm was also active in the Providence trade.

The year 1833 also saw the first important permanent line established between Charleston and New Orleans, although a fleet of schooners usually referred to as liners had been in operation several years. It began with five good brigs and continued until the panic of 1857. W. Jones and M. C. Mordecai, both prominent merchants, were the Charleston agents, and J. A. Barelli, 65 Common Street, was the New Orleans manager.

Another Liverpool line was founded in 1833 by James Brander & Company of Petersburg, Virginia, and James Ferguson of Spear's Wharf, Baltimore. Ferguson was an experienced packet man, having operated a line between Baltimore and Norfolk for some years with outstanding success. The new line was popularly referred to as the "James River Line," and consisted of four ships which sailed from Hampton Roads on the 15th, and from Liverpool the 1st of each month. It proved to be Virginia's only venture in the transatlantic packet field. It failed to survive the depressed conditions of the following year.[6]

Although no other transatlantic lines were started in the years between 1826 and the close of 1833, packet progress was by no means at a standstill. All through the period the old lines were adding to the number of their ships, increasing their size, and bending every effort to increase their speed.

The Black Ball line, indeed, lagged for several years, seemingly content to rest on its laurels after launching the 630-ton *Britannia* in 1826. Nevertheless, by 1834 it had added five more ships of about the same size, and several others only slightly smaller. It was not until 1836 that the line built its first 700-tonner, the *England,* of 730 tons register, but she was quickly followed by the slightly larger *Oxford* and, in 1837, by the *Cambridge,* measuring 800 tons.

Courtesy, The Marine Historical Association, Inc.

Schooner *Mary and Francis,* built at Baltimore in 1832. A typical Baltimore coasting schooner of this period.

Packet ship *Baltimore* of the Union Line, New York to Havre.

Ship *Poland* of the Union Line, New York to Havre, Captain Caleb Anthony, burning at sea May 16, 1839.

Brig *Globe* of Baltimore.

Courtesy, Maryland Historical Society

Courtesy, J. Welles Henderson

Packet ship *Berlin* of Pleasant's Philadelphia to Liverpool Line.

Schooner *May* of the Central Wharf Line, Boston to Baltimore, in 1834.

Courtesy, The Peabody Museum of Salem

Painted by S. Walters

Packet ship *Roscius* of the New York to Liverpool Dramatic Line.

Packet ship *Charlemagne* of the Havre Union Line dismasted in a hurricane, January 28, 1838.

Courtesy, The Peabody Museum of Salem

To Fish, Grinnell & Company's Liverpool line belongs the distinction of putting the first 700-ton packet afloat. This was the noted *Independence* of 733 tons, launched in 1834 and commanded first by Ira Bursley, followed by Ezra Nye in 1836. Ezra, who, like Ira, was a Cape Cod boy, had commanded the Boston packet *Amethyst* in 1826, and had earned a reputation of sorts as a driver—a reputation he did not allow to lapse in the *Independence*. The line also beat the Black Ball to the 800-ton mark, with the ill-fated *Pennsylvania*, of 808 tons, launched in 1836, and the largest packet built until the Dramatic liners appeared the following year.

Byrnes, Trimble & Company did not build a 600-tonner until 1832, when they launched the *Virginian*. Their largest ship was the *Adirondack*, of 699 tons, which was not completed until early in 1838 and therefore did not take her place in the line during the period now under consideration.

Aside from the "Kermit Line" to Liverpool, which was not founded until 1834, none of the other packet lines produced ships which approached the tonnage of the larger vessels mentioned above, although several independent operators of single packets built an occasional ship which compared favorably with them, both in size and quality. All the new packets, indeed, were the marvels of their day, both at home and abroad, and as much for elegance of appointments as for size. It would be difficult, even today, to surpass the rich and beautiful joiner work of their cabins which were finished with the finest and most costly woods obtainable.

They were, moreover, very heavily sparred and somewhat faster than their predecessors; not a great deal faster, but they did bring down the average passage a day or two. They were also responsible for instituting the series of eastbound runs, called "fourteen-day passages," although they usually exceeded the 14 days by a few hours, and in many instances would have been more accurately described as "fifteen-day passages."

The westbound passage, as is well known, was quite another matter, but here, too, the period set one remarkable record. It was in April, 1830, that the port of New York was treated to a sight that had never happened before and was never to happen again in packet annals.

For a century Yankee captains in Liverpool had prayed for easterly weather, while their brother mariners in New York prayed with equal fervor for a brave west wind. And for a century the mariner of New York —whether he was more righteous at home than in foreign ports, or for some other reason—had prevailed.

There must have been an unusually godly set of captains gathered in Liverpool the latter part of March, since, for the first and last time in history, they raised the wind. For three weeks, as a disgruntled shipmaster in New York remarked, "It blew from the east like a bat out of hell." From the 9th to the 17th of April, no less than 13 ships arrived from Great Britain and France, almost all of which had been only 13 days from land to land. Four were a few hours more or less than 16 days from port to port. The rest made the crossing from port to port in from 17 to 20 days.[7]

The passages, which are listed in Appendix V, indicate that the ships *De Rham, Josephine, Caledonia,* and *Columbia* made the best time. The *Josephine's* crossing in 15 days, 12 hours, was the shortest, but it was made from Belfast, which due to prevailing winds was normally a slightly shorter run than from Liverpool. The *Caledonia,* commanded by James Rogers, left Liverpool at half-past five on the afternoon of April 1st and made the Highlands at 4 P.M. on the 17th, in a passage of 16 days, $3\frac{1}{2}$ hours, mean time. The *Columbia* from Portsmouth, with Joseph C. Delano in command, sailed and arrived on the same day in a run which differed little from that of the *Caledonia,* distance considered. She left Portsmouth at noon on the 1st and reached Sandy Hook on the night of the 16th, where she was becalmed. She passed the lighthouse at 6 A.M. Saturday, the 17th, having crossed in 15 days, 18 hours. Her time to Sandy Hook was slightly longer than that of the *Josephine.*[8]

The dearth of 14-day passages, even on the faster eastbound course, was not due to lack of effort. The packets were not faster than many of the transient ships, but their record tells a story of hard driving that was rarely equalled and never surpassed. Through the years not a packet sailed whose commander failed to do the utmost humanly possible to set a new mark, in spite of which 30-day crossings were far more common than shorter ones, and 15- or 16-day runs were extremely rare. This was true even in the great days of the clippers, most of which took 25 or 30 days to cross, although they eventually set a majority of the 13- and 14-day records.

It is no matter for wonder, therefore, that no true 14-day passages were made by the packets until the huge, powerful ships of the eighteen-forties appeared. In the period now under consideration the best runs were made by the *Independence* and *Pennsylvania,* and both exceeded 14 days by a substantial margin. Ezra Nye reported that the *Independence* was $14\frac{1}{2}$ days from pilot to pilot on her voyage from New York to Liverpool in the spring of 1836, and John P. Smith drove the *Pennsylvania* from pilot to pilot in 14 days, 14 hours over the same course in November of the following year, making the port to port run in 14 days, 17 hours.

A very fine run was made in 1833 by the little Philadelphia packet *Pocahontas,* while commanded by James West. She sailed from the Delaware Capes on the 20th of November and arrived at Liverpool on the 7th of December, making a 17-day port to port passage. Her land to land time, however, was 14 days.

America's commercial and industrial juggernaut ground slowly to a halt in 1833. Cotton was quoted as low as eight and one-half cents by the summer of 1832. It was to fluctuate sharply thereafter, but the general up-trend of the previous six years was at an end. In 1834 the uptrend began to go in reverse, although there was a temporary spurt owing to a heavy demand for cotton in the fall. Imports dropped off nearly one-half. A long decline started which was to culminate in 1837 in the most devastating panic the country had ever experienced, the effects of which were to be felt for another seven years. Although shipping had not increased in proportion to the industrial establishment and farm production, the scarcity of freights soon became a serious matter to shipowners. It was undoubtedly in some measure due to this condition that they once more turned their attention to the formation of packet lines.

In 1834 there were 14 fairly substantial new lines started, in addition to a number of minor ones, and others which had short shrift. In other words, the first year of depression saw four times as many new lines started as the average for the preceding four years. That this was no mere coincidence is indicated by the fact that nine more lines were established in 1835, 10 in 1836, and 15 in the panic year of 1837. Even so, the effect in many instances was to reduce losses rather than to increase profits.

This was equally true of both the transatlantic and coastal packets. Liverpool packets in the 600- to 700-ton range, for instance, cost from $45,000 to $60,000 to build, and the operating expense for each trip was from $4,000 to $4,500, with no allowance for depreciation or interest on investment. In view of this, figures compiled for the voyages of 11 Liverpool packets from December, 1833, to July, 1834, are of interest. They show that the average freights carried amounted to considerably less than $2,000 a trip, or less than half the actual out-of-pocket operating expense.[9]

The debit balance obviously had to be offset by passenger and postal traffic, or not at all. Here New York had a decided advantage. Her mammoth packets attracted the cream of the patronage. Where Boston and Philadelphia ships usually sailed with not more than three or four cabin passengers, and sometimes none at all, and with few in the steerage, the New Yorker generally carried a minimum of 12 or 15 in the cabin, and a sizeable steerage quota. Boston and Philadelphia packets usually were compelled to go south for a cotton cargo to make up the deficiency.

Under the circumstances, it would seem normal and logical to adopt a policy of rigorous retrenchment, but this was not what happened. All through the thirties we find a constant trend toward the construction of bigger and better ships, coupled with efforts to provide better and more dependable service. There was no yielding to discouragement—no public indication, indeed, of apprehension—but merchants and owners alike concentrated more and more on the development of ships and combinations which might ensure a profit through increased patronage and the resulting economies.

One great combination, it is true, gave up the struggle, but that was due to the ravages of time rather than want of resolution. Francis Thompson was the first of the old Black Ballers to go. He died on the 10th of July, 1832, aged 56. Isaac Wright passed away the following August at the advanced age of 72. Benjamin Marshall died August 15th, 1833, at age 61. Jeremiah Thompson outlived all the original founders, dying on the 10th of November, 1835, aged 53. He had, however, relinquished all interest in the Black Ball line nearly ten years before.

The line changed hands in January, 1834, the old and well-known firm of Goodhue & Company being agents for the new owners. Only the *Britannia, Caledonia, North America, Europe* and *Hibernia* were included in the sale, the reported price being $36,000 each. The oldest ships of the fleet, the *Pacific* and *New York,* were regarded as too small for the purpose of the new owners, who had the mammoth *Columbus,* of 663 tons, nearing completion, and even then were contemplating 700-ton packets. With the change in ownership, a change in Liverpool agents also took place, the great firm of Baring Brothers now serving in that capacity. The following fall Captain Charles H. Marshall was added as a New York agent, and this arrangement continued until C. H. Marshall & Company became the sole New York agent in 1851. With the great captains Robert H. Waterman, Nathan Cobb, Benjamin L. Waite, Ira Bursley, A. C. Marshall, and other notable mariners added from time to time, it was an unbeatable combination.

Shortly after the sale of the Black Ball, New Yorkers learned that a fifth Liverpool line was contemplated, and in March the "Kermit Line" was established, sponsored by Robert Kermit, Stephen Whitney and the noted firm of Gracie, Prime & Company. The Liverpool agents were T. & J. Sands & Company, and the increasing importance of the immigration business was recognized by the appointment of Wm. & Thomas Adair as Baltimore agents, who, it will be recalled, already had an extensive clientele among the new settlers of the West.

Oddly, in view of the fact that the line continued until the panic year of 1857 and numbered some of the finest three-decker packets among its later fleet, it has been stated that the line was unsuccessful and soon disappeared, with the intimation that Kermit, the active manager, had more enthusiasm than experience. Kermit, however, was not only an able, but an experienced operator. He had been running immigrant ships to Liverpool since 1824 and, indeed, might be credited with operating a profitable line of sorts as early as 1830.

Meanwhile, new coastal lines were coming thick and fast. Sam Allen, of 110 Milk Street, who had commanded several of John H. Pearson's packets, founded one of Boston's great New Orleans lines, which ran until interrupted by the Civil War. It was latterly the "Allen & Weltch Line."

Joshua Sears and Benjamin Conant, 12 Central Wharf, established the "Central Wharf Line" between Boston and Baltimore, with Thomas Whitridge as Baltimore representative through 1834, after which he was succeeded by Garland & Elwell. They also started the "Merchants' Line" to New York with eight schooners, ranging from 115 to 157 tons. Charles Seguine and A. & T. F. Cornell were the New York agents.

Due in part to New York's more frequent and dependable transatlantic service, traffic between that port and Philadelphia continued its rapid increase. It was the only coastal trade route that seemed to be completely unaffected by the spreading depression in 1834. James Hand, of 58½ South Wharves, who operated several short lines, had established a new line of sloops and schooners on the New York run. His New York agents were J. Briggs and William J. McKee of 34 Old Slip. A. B. Cooley, 52 South Wharves, had also put 11 schooners on the sea route. Both lines sailed twice a week and oftener "when necessary." In the fall of 1834 both concerns began to send daily packets by way of the Delaware & Raritan Canal, in addition to their sea service.

Down in Baltimore, Thomas Whitridge, 13 Bowly's Wharf, began running the "Dispatch Line" to New York. Charles Gwinn, 7 Spear's Wharf, Baltimore, established the substantial "Gwinn Line" to Charleston and another to Savannah, both composed of brigs and schooners. Another Baltimore-New Orleans line was founded in 1834 by Clark & Kellogg. It consisted of brigs and the New Orleans agent was George Bedford. All in all, it was a fairly active year for Baltimore, with still other lines being started to New Orleans, Mobile, Salem, New Bedford, and Havana. Most of them were short-lived, wiped out in the panic of 1837, or abandoned in the ensuing depression.

Notwithstanding the high casualty rate, the renewed interest in coastal packet lines continued with little abatement for several years, and each year marked an increase in the number of lines and size of vessels. One of the more important of those established in 1835 was the Connecticut-owned Hurlbut Line between New York and Apalachicola, Florida, then coming into prominence as a cotton port. In this connection, it will be recalled that we have had occasion to refer to the migration of New Englanders to the seaports of the South from colonial days onward.

What this might and sometimes did involve may be gathered from a letter dated Apalachicola, November 28, 1837, and sent by a young merchant, William H. Starr of that place, to Latham Fitch, a sea captain then living at Key West. Both were natives of Mystic, Connecticut. In his letter Starr mentioned by name 14 Mystic men then living in Apalachicola—"a queer sort of place"—and noted that several other Mystic men, not named, were there. At that time Mystic had less than a thousand inhabitants, and since it is a matter of record that other Mystic natives were scattered from Baltimore to Texas in considerable numbers, the situation suggests, perhaps, something of the extent of the influx of energetic, ambitious northern boys, and its impact on the southern economy.

One of the more significant packet developments of 1835 was the entry of E. K. Collins into the cotton trade. In that year he became the New York agent of the former Foster & Hutton "New Line," later the "Louisiana & New York Line," one of the more important New Orleans lines. His southern representatives were J. D. Bien and Aaron Cohen. The fleet consisted of five fine ships which sailed twice monthly in season. Four ranged in size from the *Huntsville,* of 523 tons, commanded by Nat Palmer, to the *Yazoo,* of 678 tons, and Collins added the *Shakespeare,* a fast new 748-ton ship.

Palmer, by now, was not only a man of broad experience, but one of the ablest master mariners of all time. He had started life in the sloops of Stonington: small, very broad, and very flat-bottomed craft that had outsailed the King's cutters in the War of 1812, although the latter had been designed especially for speed. He was now to learn that the relatively flat-floored cotton packets—so constructed to cross the shoal-water bars of southern ports as well as to afford more cargo space—were also remarkably fast although their design violated one of the generally accepted rules for the production of speedy vessels. The lesson proved of value later, when he was called upon to assist in designing the ships of Collins' famous "Dramatic Line."

Before those ships were laid down nearly all transatlantic packets, with the exception of a few designed by Henry Eckford, followed closely the lines of the American frigates of the period. They were "sharp-bottomed." That is, they had considerable dead rise and some afterdrag. They represented, in fact, a conservative application of the theories carried to greater length in the type generally called the Baltimore clipper. In common with that type they suffered the disadvantage of a decided reduction in carrying capacity, a disadvantage believed to be offset by increased speed. Palmer's experience, however, proved to his satisfaction that the flatter floored cotton packets not only carried more cargo, but made as fast passages as much sharper bottomed vessels. Accordingly, the ships of the Dramatic line were given much less than the customary dead rise, notwithstanding which they proved superior to the old line packets in both speed and carrying capacity.

Boston's new ventures for 1836 included the "New Line" to Albany which started with four schooners and soon increased to eight, most of which registered about 100 tons. David Snow & Company, 9 City Wharf, were the Boston agents. J. K. Wing and William Chapman handled the Albany interests. There were also new lines to Philadelphia and Baltimore and a short-lived venture in the Apalachicola trade, called the "Merchants' Line," managed by G. M. Fowle, 1 Granite Wharf.

The new line to Philadelphia was called the "Dispatch Line." Seth E. Hardy & Company and Palmer & Hale were, respectively, the Boston and Philadelphia agents. The line survived the depression of 1857 and during that period was represented by several of the more substantial firms of the two cities. They included Alpheus Hardy and Hardy, Baker & Morrill, of Boston, and Andrew C. Barclay & Company and John M. Kennedy & Company, of Philadelphia.

Garland & Elwell, 86 Bowly's Wharf, represented the new Boston-Baltimore "Manufacturers' Line" in Baltimore and Adolphus Davis, Ezra Whiton, Jr., and others were the Boston agents. The line consisted of five brigs and a schooner and started out bravely to provide regular weekly sailings, but it actually sailed rather irregularly during the depression years of its early career.

New York had a couple of new lines that year, of which the "Commercial Line" to Charleston was the most ambitious. Dunham & Dimon, 61 South Street, were the New York, and Wm. A. Caldwell & Son, the Charleston agents, the line usually being referred to in Charleston as the "Caldwell Line." It consisted at first of brigs sailing weekly, but eventually included a number of ships and barks.

A complete summary of the new lines of 1836, many of which failed to survive the panic of the following year, is hardly worthwhile. Some of the more important, however, should be noted.

The James Hand lines of Philadelphia included a new line to New Orleans. In Baltimore, Matthew & Hopkins, 10 Bowly's Wharf, started a new schooner line to Charleston and John K. Randall & Company, 105 Smith's Wharf, established a brig line to Savannah. Claghorn & Wood, of Savannah, followed the lead of Charleston with a line to New Orleans.

There were several others of some importance, but the attempt of Charleston to develop a Liverpool line deserves special mention. The Charleston agent was J. C. Chamberlin and the line consisted of five ships intended to provide monthly sailings. It got under way in September with the ships *Byron* and *North America*. Whatever chances of success it had were quashed by the panic of 1837, the following spring, and the ensuing depression.

Boston, more conservative than most of the large seaports, was less affected by the panic. In the matter of new packet ventures, indeed, 1837 was a banner year for that port. Twelve coastal lines were established by or with the cooperation of Boston interests, and nine were of exceptional importance. Among them were two lines to New Orleans, three to Charleston, two to Savannah, and two to Mobile.

The "New Line" to New Orleans owed its existence to Ammi C. Lombard, and the "Dispatch Line" to Daniel Deshon, of 3 Long Wharf. Both were ship lines and both had long and active careers under the successive managements of well-known Boston and New Orleans firms.

Samuel R. Allen and R. Lincoln & Company, who had been engaged for several years in packet operations, were responsible for two new Boston-Charleston lines, and John Fairfield, a newcomer who was destined to play an important role in the field, accounted for a third. Allen also started one of the Savannah lines and another to Mobile. In addition, he ran a line to Havana and sent a considerable number of packets to Natchez. He must have been, for some years, one of the busiest men in Boston. Fairfield also started a line to Mobile that year which eventually became one of Boston's important carriers. One of his captains was the young "State of Mainer" Charles E. Ranlett, who later commanded some of the finest clippers.

The most noted of the lines established in 1837 was the New York-Liverpool Dramatic line already mentioned. Its first three new ships, the *Garrick, Siddons* and *Sheridan,* were not only larger (they registered 895 tons) but as a fleet they made faster average passages than those of any other line, although occasionally beaten on individual crossings by a competitor. The line was completed in 1838 by the addition of the *Roscius,* of 1031 tons, the first packet to pass the 1000-ton mark. Collins chose for his Liverpool agents the firm of William & James Brown & Company.

One other line started in 1837 deserves notice for the reason that it was planned as a British emigrant line on a much more ambitious scale than any other previous undertaking of that character, indicating the importance that the steerage traffic was beginning to assume. This was the "Robinson Line" which proposed to run from the provinces of Leinster, Ulster, Munster, and Connaught (via Liverpool), beginning February 1st and sailing regularly every five or six days thereafter. The agents were Douglas Robinson & Company, 334 Pearl Street, New York; Robinson & Brothers, Liverpool; and Robinson & Company, Dublin. Unfortunately for the promoters, the panic, with its aftermath of depression, forced them to postpone their ambitious plans, although they were able to continue as one of the more important emigration agencies.

By the close of 1837, accordingly, there were 13 transatlantic lines and upwards of 90 coastal lines operating between the eight principal coastal cities, plus another dozen running to foreign Gulf and West Indian ports. Aside from these there were scores of other lines, such as those between Boston and New England towns, the New York Hudson River and Sound packets, the inland Chesapeake lines and those serving the smaller southern ports, such as Wilmington, Georgetown, and the larger Florida shipping centers. Most of these lines were composed of superior craft, efficiently operated. Roughly, they would more than double the above coastal figure, and although individually less important, they handled immense quantities of merchandise and played an indispensable part in the development of the packet service. Their role in developing superior shipmasters and outstanding merchants was possibly even more important.

It is to be remembered also that through the years almost as many lines were established that went out of existence after relatively brief careers, varying from one or two sailings to a single spring or fall season, as survived long enough to justify their inclusion in the above summary. They, too, contributed heavily in the aggregate to the volume of packet traffic and to the growth and prosperity of America. One might, indeed, be justified in asserting that the nation owes no small part of its rise to the merchants who failed. Possibly it owes relatively more to them than to those who succeeded, for in the long run less than ten per cent survived the vicissitudes of alternating boom and depression.

As with the men, so with the ships—long before the close of 1837 all the early packets were gone. A few won reprieves for a brief day of glory in the China trade, for they were stout, nimble craft; but many more slipped into the dull, inglorious whaling industry, to leave their bones eventually on far-off coral reefs or in the crushing grip of polar ice. Others had succumbed while still shuttling back and forth across the Western Ocean or up and down the coast.

Every year took its toll, but the storms of 1827 were especially bad and the packet losses of that year broke all records. Altogether, ten ships, seven brigs, and seven schooners foundered or stranded to become total losses, in addition to those dismasted and otherwise badly damaged.

The Byrnes, Trimble liner *Panthea,* commanded by William Hathaway, became a total wreck near Holyhead on the 14th of January, in a gale which put the *Amethyst* of Boston and the *Globe* of Philadelphia ashore, to be salvaged later in a badly damaged condition. Other packets driven ashore or otherwise badly mauled included the ships *Brighton, Montano, Stephania, Niagara, Manhattan,* and *Lavinia.* Kermit's immigrant ship *Aurora* foundered at sea and the old *Liverpool Packet* was burned in the harbor of Cork early in the year.

Coastal packets suffered quite as severely. The ships *Samuel Robertson, Jane Blossom, Caroline Ann, Louisa Matilda,* and *Commodore Chauncey* became total losses at various times during the year. The small but smart ship *Lewis* was wrecked on Hatteras early in March.

Among the brigs lost were the *Emeline,* one of the Crassous & Boyd Vera Cruz liners; the *Greek,* another Vera Cruz packet, and the *Burrows,* of the New York-Cartagena line. The brig *Rambler* of Boston, Solomon Corey, master, was fallen in with, abandoned and full of water, with three dead in the cabin. The brig *Jew,* also of Boston, capsized in the gale of August 17th, drowning the captain and three passengers.

Coastal schooner packets lost included, in addition to those mentioned elsewhere, the *Caroline, Experiment,* and *General Pike.*

Losses among the regular freighters were correspondingly heavy, especially in the West Indies and Gulf areas. Altogether, it was a costly year for both operators and underwriters.

On the credit side of the ledger, it was left to the stout little *Henry IV* to set the rescue record of the decade. She arrived in New York on the 15th of June, eight days out of Charleston. It had been a busy eight days for old "J. B." (Captain John B. Pell) and his crew. During that brief period they had taken off, under conditions of extreme danger, the crews and passengers of three sinking coastal packets—the schooner *Coral,* Captain Jocelyn, with 21 members of the Charleston theatrical company; the schooner *Grampus,* Egen, master, from Charleston for Philadelphia; and the schooner *Catherine,* Captain Waring, from New Orleans for New York—50-odd souls in all.

A rescue of a different sort took place when a modern Jonah was credited with saving the Sutton line packet ship *President,* commanded by that old favorite of the travelling public, Captain E. L. Halsey. The incident was related in the *New England Palladium* of February 10th 1829:

> A curious and melancholy instance of aberration of intellect occurred on board the ship *President* on her outward bound passage from New York to Charleston. She encountered very heavy weather and a sailor named "Sam" told his shipmates that it was owing to his wicked course of life and that the offended majesty of heaven could be appeased only by his immediately precipitating himself into the sea. Officers and men tried to dissuade him but one evening he went up into the main rigging and threw himself into the sea, after which the storm ceased.
>
> Then, when returning to New York, a storm arose and the sailors cried that the ship would be lost unless Sam's chest were sacrificed. They threw it over and the storm at once ceased. Shortly after, another storm arose and they found an old shoe of Sam's and threw that over and the storm at once ceased.

While coastal packet men were stoutly improving their service under conditions already highly adverse, the steamboat, which in the beginning had operated only in helpful capacities, occasionally performing tasks impossible to sailing vessels, or going where they could go only with difficulty, began to add to their problems. Long before 1830, it was demonstrating all along the coast a decided ability to take over some of their most profitable business. Slowly, but none the less surely, it was cutting into their first-class passenger traffic in the most unexpected fields.

Early in 1827, the small steamer *Columbia,* with a capacity of 50 cabin passengers, was sent from New York to Mobile, to carry mail and passengers to New Orleans three times a week. She made the Mobile-New Orleans run in a day, whereas the Payson sloops often consumed several days on the passage. A few weeks later the new steamboat *Marco Bozzaris* started another passenger service between New York and Boston. She ran to Dighton, connecting there with a relay of fast stages to Boston. Although slow and generally inadequate, she pointed the way to a Fall River line that eventually carried hundreds of travellers daily.

The impact of steam on the Hudson is indicated by the fact that on the 26th of August, in the same year, six steamboats arrived at Albany in the space of an hour, three of which towed two safety barges each. It was estimated that they landed between 1400 and 1600 passengers. On the 1st of the following October, 45 steamboats were counted in New York harbor.

By the spring of 1829, four steamers, the *Benjamin Franklin, Washing-*

ton, Fulton, and *Chancellor Livingston,* were running between New York
and Providence daily, Sundays excepted. They ranged up to 495 tons in
size, and, in addition, the *President,* of 550 tons and almost 160 feet in
length, was being built for the run. She had 135 berths in first-class staterooms besides a more extensive accommodation for ordinary cabin passengers. Her engines, the largest yet designed, were being built at the great
works of James P. Allaire, in New York, who employed the unprecedented
number of 200 men. The steamboat *Connecticut,* which had been in the
Providence line since 1822, was transferred to Boston, where she ran twice
a week to Portland. She connected there with the 98-ton steamer *Patent,*
which continued to Augusta, the through fare from Boston to Augusta
being $7.50.

A majority of these early ventures in steam encountered difficulties of
their own. Many a steamboat, after losing money on the service for which
she was built, was shifted to other routes in quick succession, in the attempt to save the investment. A few were converted to sailing craft. Nevertheless, progress continued. One after another paying steamboat routes
were developed, with the result that by the close of the period under
consideration, steam lines were in constant and regular operation on the
shorter runs everywhere from Eastport, Maine, to the Gulf of Mexico.
And wherever they ran, they took over the bulk of the first-class passenger
business.

Two important canals were completed late in 1829. One was the Wel-
land around Niagara Falls; the other was the Chesapeake & Delaware Canal.
The completion of the latter made possible direct steamboat communication between Philadelphia and Baltimore, and the following spring saw
two steam lines in operation, the "Citizens Canal Line" with the *Carroll
of Carrollton,* and the "Union Canal Line" with the *Washington.* Both
these lines maintained a daily schedule, Sundays excepted. This proved to
be a greater service than the traffic warranted, and the following year only
one line remained in operation, the "Citizens Union Canal Line."

With the opening of this canal, the old sailing packet service between
Baltimore and Philadelphia was also greatly facilitated. Not only that, but
its sheltered course provided the easiest and most comfortable—not to say,
lethargic—run in the history of the packets. Packet masters in general
were a lean and sinewy race, but an enterprising Philadelphia reporter
made an investigation several years later and ascertained that the 11 sailing packet captains on the canal run between Baltimore and Philadelphia

averaged 265 pounds in weight, the lightest being 225 and the heaviest 350 pounds.

Local passenger traffic between Charleston, Savannah, Augusta, and nearby points, an area of great activity, was by this time largely handled by steamboats. Ever since the withdrawal of the steamship *Robert Fulton* from the New York-New Orleans run, however, there had been considerable agitation for a direct steamship service between the Charleston-Savannah area and the ports of New York, Philadelphia, and Baltimore. The first attempt to provide such a service, which promised even a fair degree of regularity, was instituted in 1833 by the 190-ton *David Brown,* commanded and managed by James Pennoyer.

Pennoyer advertised the *Brown* to sail for Charleston from Pier 32, New York, on the 22nd of December, 1832, but her departure was delayed until the 5th of the following January. It was not until the ensuing April that she began to sail on a regular fortnightly schedule. John J. Boyd assumed the management the latter part of the month, but both he and Pennoyer soon had had enough. The ship was not only far too small for such a run but was insufficiently powered. On the 23rd of August she put into Norfolk on the tail end of a hurricane, under command of Captain Coffey, with the loss of her rudder and other extensive damage to ship and good will as represented by 50 disgruntled paying guests.

After the vessel reached New York, Boyd was satisfied to relinquish her to Charles Morgan, who soon found that he would have to supplement his enthusiasm with plenty of hard cash. He took over the 1st of October. After extensive repairs, he hopefully cleared the ship for Charleston on the 14th of December, but she was forced to return to New York on the 18th, after which she was laid up while Morgan set about raising the money for a new set of more powerful boilers.

Undeterred by this unpromising beginning, he bought a managing interest in the new steamer *William Gibbons* which was built at New York the latter part of the year. She registered 295 tons and her engines were built by James P. Allaire, who was associated with Morgan in her ownership, together with John Q. and Benjamin Aymar, John Haggerty, and Thomas Andrews. With the *Gibbons* and the rejuvenated *David Brown,* Morgan began a weekly service to Charleston on the 1st of March, 1834, which continued without special incident during the remainder of the year. First-class fare was fixed at $30 and the Charleston representative of the line was the very able and well-known William

Patton, with offices at Fitzsimmons Wharf. During the busy season the vessels carried about 60 cabin passengers as a rule, which, with servants and steerage, amounted to reasonable encouragement. Moreover, patronage increased substantially during the next two years; partly due to the completion of the Charleston-Augusta railroad, which was in successful daily operation by the end of April, 1834.

In the following year Morgan further improved the service by substituting the new 423-ton steamer *Columbia* for the *Brown*, which was then held in reserve. The *Columbia*, commanded by Coffey, sailed for Charleston on her maiden voyage the 21st of March, and thereafter with the *Gibbons* maintained a weekly service. Morgan advertised that they carried the U. S. Mails and made their passage in 70 to 80 hours, sailing every Saturday from Pier 3, North River, New York, and from Mey's Wharf in Charleston. This schedule was observed with reasonable fidelity until the loss on the 10th of October, 1836, of the *Gibbons,* then commanded by E. L. Halsey, formerly master of the Charleston liner *President*. Fortunately, the stranding of the vessel on Boddy's Island was attended with no loss of life, all 160 passengers and crew being landed safely. After this loss the *Columbia* continued to sail twice monthly from each port.

Meanwhile, the *David Brown* had been dispatched to the Gulf the latter part of 1835, where she ran for a time between Havana and New Orleans. She sailed from Havana the 10th of November, just a month after the loss of the *Gibbons,* and was never reported. Her disappearance with all hands was the first of a long series of coastal steamship tragedies which did much to retard development of that service through the ensuing decade.

Baltimore failed to get a steamer on the Charleston run until the latter part of the season of 1835, when the connecting steam packet *South Carolina* arrived from Norfolk with the respectable number of 96 cabin passengers, which compared not badly with the 139 brought four days earlier from New York by the *William Gibbons*. Patton attempted to supplement this service by putting the new steam packet *Dolphin* on the run between Charleston and Norfolk in the summer of 1835, stopping at Beaufort, North Carolina. The *Dolphin* was even smaller than the *David Brown* and proved quite inadequate for the purpose. She was soon withdrawn and sent south, only to be destroyed with a loss of 15 lives in a boiler explosion on the coast of Florida the following year. Her record is of value only as indicating the consistency with which the minimum requirements for an efficient coastal steamship were underestimated then and for several years thereafter.

Eighteen hundred and thirty-six—Alamo year for America; Pickwick Paper year for England and the world—was a busy one for "Texans," as Davy Crockett proved. When he was found in an angle made by two buildings of the Alamo, "he was lying on his back, a frown on his brow, a smile of scorn on his lips—his knife in his hand, a dead Mexican across his body, and twenty-two more lying pell mell before him in the angle." As a result the Texan emigration associations throve, but it was quite otherwise with merchants and shipowners. Business was almost at a standstill. Among other things, it was the end of Charles Morgan's first coastal steam packet line. He was numbered among the bankrupts in 1837; but, like many other victims of that panic, came back to greater things, among others to build the noted Morgan line whose fine steamships were still running between New York and New Orleans a century later.

In spite of depressed conditions in 1836 there were important new developments, many of them the result of undertakings previously started. Two new railroads began to handle the passenger traffic between New York and Philadelphia, both starting at Amboy, New Jersey, and running to Camden and Bordentown, respectively. Steamboats ran between Amboy and New York, and between Philadelphia and the railroad termini on the Delaware River to complete the trip, which was now reduced to a short day's journey.

Steam on the Western Ocean, meanwhile, was making heavy weather of it. An ambitious British attempt in 1825 to establish a steamship service between Valentia on the west coast of Ireland and Halifax had resulted in the construction of a large hotel in the Irish port and the announced intention of building four steamships of 1000 tons each. Whatever its chances for success, they were effectively squelched by the depression of the following year.

The next important moves came from America. In or about 1832 (the precise time is uncertain, since the first steps were veiled in secrecy) two men advanced independent proposals for steamship lines between New York and England. One was the well-known packet master William C. Thompson; the other was Junius Smith, a Connecticut Yankee and an admiralty lawyer who had resided in England for some years representing American shipping interests.

Thompson made no progress with his proposals and Smith's reception was so unfavorable that, in despair, he went to England to secure the needed capital, where his struggle was so prolonged that the story of his eventual success and ultimate failure belongs to a later chapter.

Meanwhile, in 1836, another American attempt to promote a transatlantic steamship line got under way. Stout old Captain Nathan Cobb, late of the Black Baller *Columbus,* got a New York group to back a venture to be called "The Atlantic Steam Company." It was reported in June that they had contracted with Brown & Bell, of New York, for a large steamship and were about to incorporate with a capital of $2,000,000. Whatever the truth, the panic of 1837 put an end to the scheme quite as effectively as the depression of 1826 had wrecked the British plan for a Valentia line.

The cataclysmic affair, which threatened for a time to engulf the greatest firms of America's seaports, was touched off in March by the failure of a New Orleans house with liabilities of $7,000,000. That failure brought others in its wake to the amount of $5,000,000.[10] By April the debacle had reached enormous proportions, far exceeding anything of the kind within the memory of men then living.

Oddly enough, the panic had no comparable effect on coastwise steamship plans, possibly because the contracts had been made and construction too far advanced to permit withdrawal; possibly because it was felt that all the important factors of risk were now understood and that success was assured. If this latter consideration was involved, the coastal operators were due for a sad disillusionment. By April, 1837, while New York concerns were going to the wall right and left—the complete list was to include 239, exclusive of banks, many of which failed and all of which suspended[11]—Allaire and associates had Lawrence & Sneeden lay the keel in their East River yard of the *Home,* as the first of three new steamships intended for a line of steam packets between New York and Charleston. They were to be slightly larger than the Morgan liners which, in retrospect, seems a move in the right direction, but far too conservatively executed. Morgan's steamers were undoubtedly too small for economical operation under prevailing conditions, and the new ones were no great improvement. Coastal steamers of 500 tons could carry a paying load of freight and passengers combined, but they could not carry freight alone in paying volume, which is equivalent to saying they could not meet the rates of the sailing packets during the long "off season."

The seasonal character of coastal, as compared with transatlantic traffic, has already been noted. It ranged from light to heavy with almost clocklike regularity. The passenger business, in particular, was very slack during two-thirds of the year, and steamers which could not stow a paying cargo of heavy freight necessarily ran at a loss much of the time, a fact which goes far to explain the bewildering rapidity with which steamers of the period were switched back and forth from northern coastal to Gulf runs. It was not, indeed, until steamships of approximately 800 tons and upwards were built and equipped with lighter, more compact and efficient engines that anything like permanent prosperity came to the coastal steam packet service. Meanwhile, however, they cut more and more heavily into the passenger business of the coastal sailing packets.

As the effect of the sharp impact of the panic of April, 1837, wore off, the optimism which was characteristic of America, both North and South, reasserted itself. New England's second railroad of major importance was completed and on the 10th of November a large and enthusiastic crowd assembled at Stonington, Connecticut, the western terminus, to see the first train come in from Providence. A special excursion was run from New York on the steamboat *Narragansett,* which made the trip in the remarkable time of seven and one-half hours, averaging slightly in excess of 16 statute miles an hour.[12] Few noted or cared that the Stonington steamboat line thus initiated would lop off another fat slice of sailing packet profits.

As the year closed a cheerful spirit replaced the gloom that for months had overlain every community. The following quotation from a New Orleans paper might, with appropriate minor changes, have emanated from any of the larger American seaports:

Our levee begins to exhibit evidence of the approaching business season. A file of nearly forty steamboats are moored along its edge, busily engaged in taking out and putting in freight. This keeps a multitude of boat hands, sailors and laborers, in constant motion, and their merry songs and loud outcries, mingled with the rattling drays and the noise of steamers arriving and departing, raises quite a din and uproar on the landing.

The large piles of produce, too, that may be seen strewn in every direction, is another sign of better times. Here may be discerned an accumulation of barrels, rising in regular tiers above each other to the height of many feet; then a heap of boxes, bales and trunks, tossed and thrown together in most inextricable confusion; and, perhaps, not far off from these, a mountain of cotton bags swells up its head to give variety to the landscape.

Add to these features a forest of masts, springing up on the margin of the harbor, and stretching a mile down the crescent—a broad sheet of water, covered with fleets of steamers, and ships, and small craft, lying at anchor, or passing and repassing up and down the stream—a shore thronged with a busy crowd, moving and jostling, and agitated with an infinite variety of pursuits and avocations—and there will be presented a picture bearing some resemblance to the present aspect of the levee at New Orleans.[13]

Unfortunately for the cause of steam transportation, as the foregoing was being written the new steamship *Home,* 537 tons, of the New York-Charleston line, was about to set out on her last voyage. The *Home* was typical of the coastwise steamships of the period—an excessively long and slender craft, so designed to attain the greatest possible speed with the inefficient engines then available. One need only refer to her proportions —220 feet by 22 feet by 12 feet—to realize the impossibility of making such a vessel seaworthy save by use of exceptionally strong construction, reinforced by heavy iron cross-strapping, which was a precaution quite neglected.

Starting on the Charleston run early in 1837, she was fortunate in meeting with mild weather on her first passages. On her second trip she set a new record, 64 hours from New York to Charleston. It was not until she left New York on the 6th of October that she ran into moderately heavy weather, in consequence of which she quickly developed a bad leak off the Virginia coast. Captain John Salter, a passenger and a very able master mariner from Portsmouth, New Hampshire, earnestly advised Carleton White, her commander, to make for the shelter of the land, or, in the alternative, put the steamer on the beach.

This, Captain White, who was a veteran commander of sailing packets, including such smart ships as the *Frances Henrietta* and the *Henry Kneeland,* refused to do, insisting on pushing ahead with women and children from the first families of Charleston and Savannah bailing the cabin. When, finally, he was forced to adopt Captain Salter's advice it was too late. The ship was so full of water and so deep that instead of stranding in the relatively quiet waters near shore, she struck in the terrible outer breakers, disintegrating in a matter of moments.

Approximately 95 perished; among them the promising young engineer, James P. Allaire, of New York, the popular and talented young merchant William H. Tileston, and a youth, Philip S. Cohen, who had survived the wreck of the *William Gibbons* a few months earlier.[14]

There were, it is true, equally serious disasters in the sailing fleet, but they proceeded from familiar causes, operative throughout the history of sail. Moreover, they were comparatively rare in proportion to the number of vessels involved, whereas a very large percentage of the steamships speedily became total losses or were the victims of serious accidents involving great suffering and heavy financial loss.

Thus, the wreck of the immigrant bark *Mexico,* Captain C. Winslow, was attended with a greater loss of life than resulted from any steamship disaster during the period, but it was due to stress of wind and weather in the main, and caused no apprehension of a series of similar tragedies.

This vessel, with 104 immigrants, mostly women and children, arrived off Sandy Hook on the night of January 1st, 1837, from Liverpool. Her lanterns were displayed for a pilot, but it so happened that all the pilots were ashore celebrating the day. Early Tuesday morning, January 3rd, she went ashore off Hempstead, Long Island, about 26 miles east of the Hook. A boat from shore took off Captain Winslow and seven of the crew who went to summon help. The rest of the crew and all the passengers froze to death; but the disaster, terrible though it was, made little impression on a public who were well aware that for every such loss, hundreds of brave ships came safely to port.

In any event, the destruction of the steamships *Home* and *Gibbons*, followed shortly by the disappearance of the *David Brown* with all her crew and passengers, and the loss by fire and explosion of several other coastal steamers in quick succession, put a damper on similar enterprises, which was prolonged, as will appear, by other catastrophes of the sort in 1838 and thereafter. It was several years before coastal steamship construction was resumed on a scale equalling that planned in 1837, and it is to be noted that the new craft were better designed, more strongly constructed, and averaged roughly 50 per cent larger than the earlier coastal steamers.

CHAPTER X

~ *1838-1847* ~

New Queens Meet the Challenge

"Ceaseless the order changeth, the old giving place to the new."

THE ten years from 1838 to 1847, inclusive, are of exceptional interest to the student of maritime history. They were marked by a notable advance in the size of ships of the sail, and by inventions, improvements and developments in the field of mechanical engineering that were to effect more and greater changes in the character of the merchant marine, not only of America, but of the world, than in any similar period in history. On land, the telegraph had become a fact, and a locomotive credited with a speed of 90 miles an hour had been produced. At sea, they were the years in which the steamship came of age, the years in which the course of its future development was plainly mapped, and its potential effect on sail clearly indicated. Ocean liners of 1000 horsepower and more had been built, and still greater monsters were on the drafting boards.

These things would have come to pass in time, in any case. As it happened, they were vastly accelerated by a tremendous increase in emigration to America.

It will be recalled that at the outset of the period emigration was at a new low. Due to aftereffects of the panic, it dropped in 1838 to less than 39,000. Thereafter it rose fairly steadily to nearly 105,000 in 1842. In 1843 it tumbled to 52,000, owing to severe financial troubles in Europe and Great Britain, and especially in London and Glasgow, where there were numerous failures. Few prospective emigrants could raise the five pounds necessary to land them in New York. Besides, there was depression in America, too. It was back in full swing by 1845 and in 1847, stimulated by the famine in Ireland which sent 105,000 Irishmen scurrying to the land of plenty that summer, it reached a temporary high of 235,000.[1] Moreover, other factors—among them the rising tide of discontent in Europe that culminated in the revolutionary movements of 1848,

222

and the Mexican War, which would obviously throw vast new areas of rich farm lands open for settlement—strongly indicated that immigration was headed for even higher levels. These, and a renewed prosperity for America exceeding anything experienced for some years, produced a demand for more and greater passenger ships that reached unprecedented proportions in the years from 1845 to 1847, inclusive.

Under existing rules, which, in general, since 1819 had permitted but two passengers for every five tons register, few ships in 1838 were entitled to carry more than 250 to 300 passengers.[2] Even if such vessels could have handled the traffic, the prospect of the huge profits awaiting those equipped to carry several times the number would not have permitted the situation to continue.

By the close of 1847 a score or more liners had been launched which could carry from 400 to 500; several could accommodate 600, and one had a legal capacity in excess of 700, with others of similar size and capacity on the stocks.[3]

The net increase in sailing tonnage was even more impressive. It amounted in the ten years to nearly 1,000,000 tons. On December 31st, 1847, the grand total of the merchant marine, steam included, was a trifle under 3,000,000 tons.[4]

Progress in steam had been less spectacular than in sail from the standpoint of volume, but was fraught with greater significance by reason of innovations and improvements achieved, and social and cultural changes involved.

Before 1838 there were slightly over 700 steam vessels in America, with approximately 750 in Great Britain, and the number was increasing at a tremendous rate. By the close of 1839 it was estimated that Great Britain had 950, all but one of which—a tiny Ericsson craft—were sidewheelers. Much the same situation existed in America, where by far the greater number were steamers of 300 tons and less for use on the rivers and sounds. There were several coastal vessels, called "steamships" by courtesy, the largest of which measured a little over 700 tons. Few of these were capable of ten knots under favorable circumstances. All faster craft were river and sound steamers. These, with the help of the railroads, had already cut heavily into the coastal passenger traffic—had, indeed, all but monopolized it between Boston and Baltimore and intermediate points.

Seagoing steamers, and especially those plying the longer routes between northern and southern ports, had been less successful, owing to the previously noted shortcomings, which not only reduced their patronage, but had the further effect of discouraging construction sufficient to accommodate more than a small proportion of the travellers in the busy season.

Great Britain, on the other hand, partly because of her insular position, had devoted relatively more attention from the first to ocean steam transportation. Even the short channel trips to France, Ireland, and Scotland required steamers capable of encountering the storms and stresses incident to long deep-water voyages. As a consequence, she constructed small, but seaworthy ocean-going steamers in comparatively large numbers. Her favorable experience with these was destined, during the period now under consideration, to lead to a program of far-flung steamship expansion which greatly surpassed the modest ventures of America.

Revival of confidence in America, signs of which were not wanting as early as the summer and fall of 1837, was further accelerated by the discovery that many firms and individuals were in better condition than had been supposed. Many who undoubtedly were bankrupt were able to make compositions with their creditors and start anew. Others, forced to suspend, proved to be reasonably sound, financially, and were able to resume operations within a few weeks. By the spring of 1838 there was a general atmosphere of robust—if unjustified—optimism observable in every port. Nevertheless, as New Orleans was to discover, in spite of its crowded levee, it was easier to pile up produce on the docks than it was to find a profitable market for it. For the shipping industry in particular, seven lean years remained; anxious years of cutthroat competition for survival, relieved only by occasional hopeful, but misleading, bursts of activity.

Various factors conspired to delay recovery, not the least of which was the fear that had been instilled into the hearts of even the wealthiest capital holders of Europe and America, and which was partly responsible for a long and stringent curtailment of credit. It cannot be said that business went on a cash basis, but the effect was much the same. Those who could choose accepted none but bills so sound as to be equivalent to cash. The less fortunate found it necessary to discount their paper at rates which reduced their profits to a minimum when, indeed, it did not involve them in a loss. In the phrase of the day, it was almost as common "to gain a loss" as to gain a profit.

As an inevitable consequence, the volume of trade was rigidly restricted in spite of the fact that the country continued to grow rapidly. Immigration, as already noted, was on the rise and headed for unprecedented heights. Population increased, roughly, 5,000,000 during the ten years following the panic. Both industrial and agricultural production were expanding at a tremendous rate, facts clearly involving a huge potential increase in freight offerings. Nevertheless, with the exception of a slight temporary betterment in 1839 and again in 1842, shipments and rates continued through 1843 at levels which made it impossible to employ all the ships, or to secure a normal profit for those so fortunate as to be engaged.

The proximate cause—lack of purchasing power at home and abroad, due to credit conditions—is reflected in the fact that foreign trade which amounted to $318,000,000 in the depression year of 1836, shrank to $229,000,000 in 1843, despite population growth.[5] The shrinkage, it is true, was due to lower prices rather than to a reduction in the volume of merchandise. Cotton, for example, which brought 13½ cents for the cheaper grades in 1836, was quoted at 4½ cents in 1843. On the other hand, the lack of paying freights sufficient to employ available shipping is explained in large part by the fact that the tonnage of the merchant marine had almost doubled in the previous ten years. In 1830 it amounted to 1,191,776 tons. By the end of 1840 it had gained another million tons; enough, considering the increase in fast steamers and the improved quality of ships, to handle twice the 1830 volume of freights.[6]

The very energy of America tended to prolong stagnation. In the absence of other employment, native-born and recent immigrant alike, their ranks swelled by a host of newly made bankrupts, joined in opening vast tracts of virgin land to provide a larger surplus of unwanted produce. Those with capital, lacking incentive to engage in trade, took advantage of greatly reduced costs to build more factories, plants, and railroads to produce more unwanted goods. Shipbuilders continued in desperation to lay down more keels to join the idle fleets, as the only alternative to short rations for their communities. Everything, in brief, made for the tightest of tight money for shipowners and operators.

For several years steam packet progress in the coastal field was almost imperceptible, in spite of valiant but ill-planned attempts to increase and improve the service. Wetmore & Cryder put the little *Charleston* and the big *Neptune* on the New York-Charleston run in 1838, but the experiment was soon abandoned. Our old steamerite, Charles Morgan, showed his metal by coming back with the new 366-ton packet *New York* early the same season, but after a short trial on the Charleston route, he sent her to the Gulf where early in 1839 she joined the *Neptune* and *Columbia* in the trade between New Orleans and Galveston.

James Ferguson, of Baltimore, who had been running the *South Caro-*

lina between Charleston and Norfolk, added the steamer *Georgia,* 551 tons, in March, 1838, to give a weekly service. In the fall he added the *Neptune* to give a direct service between Charleston and Baltimore every four days, but this arrangement lasted only through the short busy season. After this, the *Neptune,* as intimated, was sent to the Gulf, the last refuge of the inadequate coastal steamers, most of which were plagued with mechanical troubles involving costly repairs and exasperating delays, in addition to the risks incident to flimsy construction.

Just how serious those deficiencies were may be judged from the rate of total losses of new and nearly new steamers in 1838 and 1839. Among others, they included the *Motto* which was struck by a heavy sea off the coast of Texas, with the result that one of her boilers blew up and the other went through her bottom. She sank in three minutes with a loss of five lives. The *Wilmington,* commanded by Captain John Gallagher, from Philadelphia for Mobile, was lost on the 10th of November about 60 miles north of Cape Florida. The worst disaster of the year was the destruction of the *Pulaski* by boiler explosion at sea on the 14th of June, with a loss of life variously reported as 141 and 145. The toll would undoubtedly have been heavier but for the efforts of Eli Davis, master of the little Philadelphia packet schooner *Henry Camerdon,* who rescued 30 from the detached wreckage of the bow which remained afloat for a time.

A slightly smaller steamer, the *Cuba,* of 562 tons, built at Baltimore in 1837, which went on the Galveston-New Orleans run in the summer of 1838, foundered off Galveston the following June. Losses continued at an abnormal rate for several years. Moreover, few of those which survived were in much better case from the investment standpoint. Delays, broken voyages, costly repairs which sometimes involved an expensive trip from a Gulf port to New York, long periods of idleness and frequent changes in management and ownership, tell the story.

All in all, it is less surprising that the public were reluctant to invest in coastwise steamships than that men of broad experience, with reputations for sound judgment, continued to risk their capital, notwithstanding the almost unbroken record of past failure.

One such man was the banker George Brown, of Baltimore. In 1838 he had the steamer *Natchez* of 793 tons register built at Baltimore. She was put on the route between New York and Natchez that fall, with John Laidlaw & Company acting as New York agents. From a practical standpoint the project appeared to be logical and promising, but the vessel encountered various delays in the Mississippi, once going aground and remaining hard and fast on a mud bank for several weeks, which, with the inevitable costly repairs, soon disillusioned the stockholders of the Natchez Steam Packet Company. The venture was discontinued in 1840 and the vessel was lost two years later.

Nevertheless business continued to improve slowly and the steamerites persisted in their efforts, with special credit going to the merchants and capital holders of Charleston and Savannah, who furnished most of the funds for the construction of the steamers trading to those ports. Charles Morgan was another stubborn customer. He had the *Galveston* of 545 tons built in 1845 and sent her to New Orleans to go on the Galveston run in competition with the *Neptune*. Together they provided a weekly service to the Lone Star Republic, loaded to the guards with bowie-toting gentlemen, who would shortly be voting loyally for the annexation of the United States to Texas.

Broadly speaking, not one of the above vessels, or any other built for the steam coastal service theretofore, was capable of giving a dependable performance. All were lacking in reliability of engines, or in sound construction, or both. Breakdowns were frequent and often there were far more serious consequences.

This situation changed with almost startling suddenness in 1846. In that year the *Palmetto* was built to operate between New York and Charleston. She sailed in May on her maiden voyage and made the run in the then record time of 55 hours, reducing the previous average time by more than half a day, and at the same time reducing the fare to $20. She was strongly built, and her engine and machinery gave every promise of reliable performance. Her size, however, 533 tons, was hardly sufficient to meet the demands of the Charleston passenger trade.

It remained for the new steamer *Southerner* to meet this deficiency. The *Southerner* was a stoutly constructed craft of 785 tons, built in New York but owned chiefly in Charleston and Savannah. She was managed by Henry Missroon of the former city, and Spofford, Tileston & Company, of New York. Her speed not only equalled that of the *Palmetto,* but in safety, comfort, and all-round dependability she exceeded any coastal steamer afloat when she cleared for her first voyage in September, 1846.

She sailed on the 13th of the month with an old Charleston resident, the genial and popular Mike Berry, in command; a recent graduate, *summa cum laude,* of the old Sutton line packet *Amelia.* Her first voyage presaged the dawn of a new era in coastal travel. What it portended for the sailing liner was not long in doubt. From 125 to 150 first-class passengers and upwards crowded her cabins on every trip during the season, while their servants jammed the steerage and even pre-empted at night the sofas and tables of the saloon. The following year the still larger steamer *Northerner* was added, clearing at New York for her maiden voyage on the 2nd of October, to provide a dependable weekly service. Before the end of 1847, first-class travel on Charleston and Savannah canvas-back liners was very light indeed, and by that time a somewhat similar condition was to be noted in the very important and heavy traffic in and out of New Orleans.

Whether these developments had anything to do with breaking down the traditional southern opposition to Federal support of steamship lines through mail contracts is perhaps impossible to state with certainty at this late date. There can, however, be no doubt that they led almost immediately to the construction of a number of other coastal steamers of superior seagoing qualities, most of which exceeded the *Southerner* and her contemporaries in size, and, in some instances, in speed.

All through the period emigration to Texas continued to boom, despite the opposition of the anti-slavery element and the mysterious "Man in the White Hat" who was ag'in' Texas and all its works. These and similar efforts were latterly countered with some success by the "Captain from Vermont" who advertised for "14,000 coon hunters to go to Texas." Charles Morgan decided that his little steamer was too small to accommodate an army of that size, and placed an order for another to be named the *New Orleans*. She registered a moderate 762 tons, but had a deck length of 220 feet, and by this time Morgan knew just what to do with deck space in the passenger trade. William H. Brown, of New York, built the hull, and Morgan's own ironworks provided the engine. She was completed late in 1846 and the farm boy from Killingworth, Connecticut, was on his way. From that time forth Morgan was never headed until he had established a mighty railway-steamship empire in the South.

During the same years, steam was writing a parallel chapter in Western Ocean history, but with far from comparable success.

It was perhaps fortunate for the nerves of the shipping fraternity that the tensions of 1838 were temporarily relaxed by an event then without precedent in history, and which today we can only compare with the memory of a lone aircraft winging into the sunrise of a May morning, nearly 90 years later.

For months a somewhat skeptical Western world had been hearing rumors of great steamships building in England for the transatlantic service, and had been reading also the prophecies of scientists that they were doomed to failure. On the morning of April 23, 1838, all New York was electrified by shouting newsboys announcing the arrival of a steamer from England. They rushed to the waterfront and presently the Battery was thronged with excited, cheering thousands. There at anchor, a short distance from Castle Garden, she lay—the first transatlantic steam packet, the *Sirius*—a long, low, black paddle-wheel steamer of 700 tons, already surrounded by hundreds of boats of all sorts. She had made Sandy Hook the night before and had come up in the early morning, after a 17-day passage from Cork.

That afternoon, while the crowds still milled about the Battery, a second and more massive steamship was observed coming up through the Narrows. It was the *Great Western*, variously reported as registering 1340 and 1390 tons, 15 days out of Bristol.

An editor of one of the older New York papers has thus described the scene:

THE STEAM PACKETS.—The arrival yesterday of the steam packets *Sirius* and *Great Western*, caused in this city that stir of eager curiosity and speculation which every new enterprise of any magnitude awakens in this excitable community. The Battery was thronged yesterday with thousands of persons of both sexes, assembled to look on the *Sirius*, the vessel which had crossed the Atlantic by the power of steam, as she lay anchored near at hand, gracefully shaped, painted black all over, the water around her covered with boats, filled with people were passing and repassing, some conveying and some bringing back those who desired to go aboard. An American seventy-four in one of the ports of the Mediterranean, or of South America, would hardly be surrounded with a greater throng of natives.

When the *Great Western*, at a later hour, was seen ploughing her way through the waters toward the city, a prodigious mass, blacker, if possible, than her predecessor, the crowd became more numerous, and the whole bay, to a great distance dotted with boats, as if everything that could be moved by oars had left its place at the wharves. It seemed, in fact, a kind of triumphant entry.

The problem of the practicability of establishing a regular intercourse by steam between Europe and America is considered to be solved by the arrival of these vessels, notwithstanding the calculations of certain ingenious men in England, at the head of whom is Dr. Lardner, who have proved by figures that the thing is impossible.[7]

Possibly there were those in our complacent and patronizing editor's "excitable community" who sensed better than he the "magnitude" of the occasion. He, at least, seems to have been completely unaware that the steamships were freighted with a new civilization. In that respect he possessed no great advantage over the learned gentlemen who, for years, had counselled Junius Smith, the Connecticut Yankee promoter of the *Sirius*, "to build a railroad to the moon."

However that may be, the event not only put a definite, though temporary end to the unpopularity which the recent tragic loss of several coastal steamships in quick succession had created, but it made 1838 the

"Steamship Year." For the moment, steam took almost undisputed precedence over sail. The waterfront abounded with prophecies of the impending doom of the packet lines, and if the event did not increase coastal steamship activity, it at least confirmed the confidence of operators in that field.

Meanwhile the newly aroused enthusiasm was building up competition for Junius Smith and his rival, the Great Western Steamship Company. On the 24th of July a third steam packet arrived from Liverpool. She proved to be the *Royal William,* the second steamer of that name, and one which might more appropriately have been christened the *Little Willie.* She rated only 617 tons, a fact which in itself reflects the unthinking enthusiasm aroused by the success of the *Sirius* and *Great Western.* Her New York representative was the old immigration agent, Abraham Bell. She reported making 12 knots on one occasion, but her passage of 19 days would seem to put her in the seagoing 7-knot class at best.

She was, however, only a makeshift substitute for the *Liverpool* which had been delayed in completion, but which arrived in New York before the year ended. The *Liverpool* registered 1150 tons and developed 463 horsepower. New Yorkers were impressed by her great length and the lightness of her standing rigging which was of a new type: iron rods bound together with thrums, one of the experiments which led to wire rigging. However, although well patronized at first, she proved inadequate as a Western Ocean packet, especially in speed and stability. Her time from Cork was 16 days.

It was not until the summer of 1839 that the permanent ships of Smith's British and American Steam Navigation Company arrived, but they were worth waiting for. The *British Queen* came first. Her length of 275 feet and 2016 tons register made her the largest ocean steamer New Yorkers had ever seen. She was followed closely by the still larger *President,* whose 2366 tons made her for the moment the largest steamship afloat.

In the midst of these spectacular events one arrival passed almost unnoted by the general public, although in the sequel its importance far outweighed any other maritime achievement of the year, a fact which seems to have been dimly appreciated only by the editor of the "scurrilous little *Herald,*" who gave the event more space in his paper than all the other New York papers combined.

EXTRAORDINARY ARRIVAL. New Era in Steam Navigation. Yesterday morning the people at the Battery were astonished to see a long, low, piratical, rakish, black-looking schooner stealing her way up through the Buttermilk channel towards the East

River. Some imagined her one thing—and some another, and scarcely one thought correctly. They had not the slightest idea of her being the little iron steamer *Robert F. Stockton,* from England. But it was her, and she did present the most singular and nondescript appearance. She is commanded by John R. Crane, Esq., long and favorably known as a sea captain out of this port. The *Robert F. Stockton* sailed from London early in April and has been forty-five days in crossing the Atlantic. She is but 35 tons burthen, 71 feet long and 10 feet beam—is schooner rigged and came all the way under sail. Annexed are some extracts from her log book.

Apr. 7.—Left City Canal Dock, London, with John R. Crane, commander; Richard Cannay, chief officer, and 6 men. Experienced fair winds and weather until the 17th.

Apr. 17.—Fresh breezes and heavy squalls with rain—wind SW to NW.

Apr. 18.—Strong breezes and squally. 6 A.M. tacked ship to the westward. 6.15, the ship gave a heavy lurch which threw one of the crew, named Diamond, over the quarter; he was drowned. From the 18th to the 26th experienced continually strong westerly breezes, with squalls.

May 27.—Light winds—calm—sounded 30 fathoms with mud. Daylight, light airs and calm, foggy; wind N, SE and E. 12 M. sounded at 17 fathoms. Passed Sandy Hook at 12 o'clock, midnight, and arrived up at the dock, foot of Delancy Street, at 9 A.M. yesterday.

Although Captain Crane experienced head winds nearly all the way and passed through several terrific gales, he did not lose a sail or even a rope yarn. When the wind was fair she easily performed eight miles per hour, and she behaved the entire passage remarkably well.

We visited her yesterday afternoon and inspected her throughout. When in Liverpool we saw her several times and attended one of the experiments of her power and capabilities. The principle on which she is constructed is entirely new, and the success of her trials on the Mersey and Thames have fully and satisfactorily proved to us as well as to the scientific of England, the immense advantages the screw paddle will have in Ocean Steam Navigation. The *Robert F. Stockton,* although but 35 tons, large, towed the packet *Toronto* on the Thames against a strong tide at the rate of 6 miles an hour. Alone, she performs eleven knots with ease. She has been so successful in every instance, we should not be surprised to see a larger vessel of two hundred and fifty tons out here before the summer is over. While in England we visited a ship on the stocks of three hundred tons burthen, which was building with the screw paddle for the American trade. So convinced were the builders of the incalculable advantages of Capt. Ericsson's invention that they were about laying the keel of another, to be of 2000 tons, and capable of performing from 12 to 14 miles per hour.

The fact is, as the years slip by, there will not be a steamer ploughing the Atlantic on the old jarring and racking principle. Every steam packet will be constructed on Captain Ericsson's plan, and they will move through the waters, the passengers scarce knowing how. But this is not all. The vessels are more compact; they have much more space for cargo and passengers, and there is such a material saving in fuel. They sail faster, and there is not that disagreeable jar and noise that we suffer in steamers on the old principle.

People will be surprised when they see the *Stockton:* the machinery is all packed away so snugly abaft the amidships that no one would imagine that she had any boilers, wheels or cogs in her. Her hull is divided into three compartments, and there is a neatness and symmetry of form about her that we seldom see in vessels of her description.

Captain Crane was, while he was in England, considered insane. The English had no idea that he could cross the Atlantic in such a craft—only 10 feet wide and seventy-one long, but he has done it and can do more. The crowd on the piers in London was immense, to witness her departure, and singular were the remarks among them. One Johnny Bull, after hearing that she was bound to America, jammed his hat down on his head and exclaimed—"To America! What, that cockleshell? What damned fool is going in her?" We will answer. Captain Crane, familiarly known as "Mad Jack," and a better and truer sailor never trod a deck. He has immortalized himself, and deserves more honor than any navigator extant. Never before has man crossed the broad Atlantic in a small iron steamer, like the *Stockton,* with a screw in her stern. What are we coming to? Will the Corporation present the freedom of the city to Captain Crane? They should do something to immortalize themselves.

She is intended for the Delaware and Raritan Canal and will commence running in about two weeks.[8]

Admitted to American registry as the steam propeller *New Jersey,* the ex-*Stockton* started a towing career that lasted for 30 years, a fact which indicates how completely Ericsson had solved the screw propeller problems in his first full-size towboat. Her success was immediate and complete. Indeed her influence was such that she may be said to have started a train of events that revolutionized the steamship; incidentally, bringing about the downfall of sail far more swiftly than the clumsy and inefficient paddle steamer could have accomplished it.

Ericsson followed the *Stockton* to New York in November, 1839. By the close of 1841 he had built six more propellers. The next year he launched nine and in the following year sent 26 down the ways. His contractors were the young and enterprising firm of Hogg & Delamater, who took over Cunningham's old Phoenix Foundry in New York soon after he came to America. Aside from the sloop-of-war *Princeton,* a couple of foreign warships, the merchant bark *Clarion,* and several others, most of the propellers were used for towing.

One of the most immediate results of his activities was the establishment in April, 1840, of the Swiftsure Steam Transportation Line, which operated a line of barges between New York and Philadelphia, via the Delaware & Raritan Canal. The agents were J. & N. Briggs, 34 Old Slip, New York, and Armer Patton, 46 & 47 South Wharves, Philadelphia. The pronounced success of the venture exercised an influence on steam transportation quite out of proportion to the magnitude of the enterprise.

Iron steamship construction on a substantial scale was started. There had been some experimentation in this direction. A small concern, "The Iron Steamboat Company" of Charleston, managed by Messrs. Holcombe & Peck, had been in operation for several years, running between that city and Augusta by way of Savannah. Their steamers were built on the Clyde, and shipped over and assembled on this side. Now, in 1842, four iron propellers designed by Ericsson were laid down in New York for the purpose of carrying coal on the Delaware & Raritan Canal. They rated about 230 tons. Two years later, Richard Loper began the construction of iron propellers in Philadelphia for the Philadelphia-New York run over the same canal. His subsequent operations in steamship construction were on a scale then unequalled in the City of Brotherly Love.

In 1847 it was estimated that America had approximately 50 propellers while as yet England had only one, the steamship *Great Britain*. They included the auxiliary steamship *Massachusetts* and the iron twin-screw *Alleghany*, the latter a naval vessel built at Pittsburgh in 1847, while down in Boston the Tuft's Foundry was building the first twin-screw iron tug, the *R. B. Forbes*.

Compared with paddle steamers, the early propellers were at some disadvantage in the matter of speed, and their adoption was further hampered by the fact that few of the large foundries wanted to build an engine with which they were not familiar and in which they had little faith. On the other hand, the propeller offered certain very substantial advantages, which summed up to more space for passengers and cargo and lower operating costs. Also, as time went on it became increasingly apparent that speed presented no insurmountable difficulties, but seven years were to elapse before the screw was given a thorough trial on the Western Ocean, and nearly double that time before its eventual substitution for the paddle became assured.

Boston's transatlantic steam service was delayed until the summer of 1840 and when it came it was of a quality that gave New Yorkers little concern. The pioneer Cunarder *Britannia* followed hard in the wake of the little general utility steamer *Unicorn,* arriving in Boston on the 18th of July with 60 passengers in a trifle under 15 days. Her tonnage was reported as 1200 by British computation (1154 by the American rule) and her engines turned up "the power of 400 horses" (750 h.p., nominal, by American computation) to give her an average rate of eight and one-half knots at sea. Passage to either Halifax or Boston was 38 guineas without wines or liquors, with an additional steward's fee of one guinea. Dogs fared somewhat better. They paid only one pound.

The Cunarders, therefore, were little more than half the tonnage of a couple of New York steamships, and they were relatively slow and uncomfortable, their accommodations for 115 cabin passengers being decidedly cramped. Their running time averaged slightly over 15 days for the westbound and a trifle under 13 for the eastbound passage, and this over a route a full day shorter than the New York crossing. Judged solely from the standpoint of equipment and efficiency of passenger and freight service (cargo being limited to 225 tons), the outlook for the line's survival was not impressive. However, the company had two things that together more than made up for all deficiencies, a thumping big mail contract ($385,000) and a canny Scotch management.

The real Cunard Company was the firm of Burns & McIver, late of Glasgow. Burns was a merchant and McIver an old sea captain. Together they had built up a prosperous line of sailing packets between Glasgow and Halifax, with some help from Judge Thomas Chandler Haliburton (author of the once celebrated "Sam Slick" stories about a Yankee clock peddler) and when they conceived the idea of getting a mail contract for a steamship line, the Judge recommended his relative, Sam Cunard, as possessing exceptional qualifications for "conducting the negotiations." Sam, who had been actively interested in the first *Royal William* and was undoubtedly qualified to that extent, was so far successful that he acquired the contract in his own name. After that it was a question of management, and there Burns & McIver proved they had little to learn in any branch of the business, and nothing at all in the matter of conservatism, which was to carry the company through the early difficult years, although at times it seemed more likely to prove an insurmountable handicap.

More than 30 years later, when the Cunard was the world's leading steamship concern, this characteristic attracted the attention of an obscure individual who wrote under the pen name of "Mark Twain." Mark had noted that the company still served the same prunes and rice that had doubled for "plum duff" on its first bill of fare in the little *Britannia,* and commented on the fact in a letter that Horace Greeley printed in the *New York Tribune* under the heading, "Queer Old Ways of a Pioneer Steamship Company," the first paragraph of which ran, in part, as follows:

Old fashioned is the word. When a thing is established by the Cunarders, it is there for good and all, almost. Before adopting a new thing the chiefs cogitate and cogitate: then they lay it before their head merchant, their head builder, their head engineer, and all the captains in the service, and *they* go off and cogitate about a year: then if the new wrinkle is approved it is adopted and put in the regulations.[9]

The pioneer steamers of the line, aside from the little 700-ton *Unicorn* which served a feeder route between Pictou, Nova Scotia, and Quebec at times, and occasionally brought the mail and passengers on to Boston from Halifax when the regular steamship service was interrupted, carried crews of 70 to 75. They had no steerage or second-class accommodation. As with all the early Western Ocean steamships, they experienced con-

Courtesy, J. Welles Henderson

Deck scene (looking forward) on board the packet ship *Margaret Evans* of the Griswold New York to London line. This and other scenes from the Henderson collection were painted by John A. Rolph (1833-82) in 1851.

Stateroom scene on packet ship *Margaret Evans,* showing another ship in distance through transom window.

Courtesy, J. Welles Henderson

Stateroom on packet ship *Margaret Evans.*

Courtesy, J. Welles Henderson

Courtesy, J. Welles Henderson

Deck scene on board packet ship *Cornelius Grinnell* of the Grinnell, Minturn Swallowtail Line.

Packet ship *Margaret Evans* of the New York to London Black X Line.

Courtesy, The Peabody Museum of Salem

Courtesy, J. Welles Henderson

Stateroom scene on the packet ship *Margaret Evans* of the Griswold New York to London Line.

siderable engine trouble but, on the whole, less than the larger craft.

The lead thus acquired by the British enterprises—whatever it may owe to the prodding of a Connecticut Yankee—was never relinquished. Britain's steamship development thereafter is too familiar to warrant more than the briefest recapitulation here. The famous Peninsula & Oriental Line instituted its Mediterranean service the year the Cunard began operations. It was not until late in 1847 that the second permanent British transatlantic line, the Cunard to New York, got under way, but in the interval England had put a dozen lines in operation over long sea routes. They covered all the principal ports of Europe and the West Indies. All the steamships, with the exception of the *Great Britain,* were side-wheelers. In that respect only may America be said to have maintained a lead of sorts, with her 50-odd propellers. However, even that slight advantage was soon allowed to pass by default.

In spite of the foregoing developments, the predicted embarrassment of the canvas-backs was strangely delayed. James Gordon Bennett, who is said to have pawned most of his possessions, his paper excepted, for a return ticket on the pioneer steamer *Sirius,* came back with a vocabulary enriched by a dozen or so French idioms, but otherwise a sadder, if not a wiser man. He told his readers, and proved it with the aid of his newly acquired Gallicisms, that the steamships were dirty and highly uncomfortable "modes of travel" and, moreover, it was a question whether they were safe. He predicted that travellers would never use them for a second crossing. However, consistency was never one of his strong points.

When the *Liverpool* made an extremely long passage on her second trip from England, there was great anxiety in New York and many a resolution formed to stick to sail. The always helpful Bennett, with one of the flops for which he was famous, allayed the fears of friends and quenched the hopes of relatives with the following sound prediction:

THE LIVERPOOL NOT HEARD OF YET. She is, however, perfectly safe—reasons hereafter. We now give those reasons. We have always felt a solemn conviction that John Van Buren or any Van Buren, could never be drowned. They may get hanged— but nothing can drown them.[10]

His prediction proved correct, in part at least. The *Liverpool* and John Van Buren arrived safely and the steamers went on for a time, skimming the cream of the first-class patronage.

It did not last. Initial enthusiasm quickly cooled—the process hastened by the steamship patrons themselves, who were not long in confirming Bennett's criticism. Even the Royal Mail Steam Packets of the Cunard line brought no improvement if the blistering comments of Dickens, who crossed to America in the *Britannia* in 1842, are to be taken at face value. Grime, smut, and smoke were everywhere, plus an interminable racket. It was bad enough when passengers found their fancy duds pock-marked with cinder burns, but it added insult to injury when the selfsame cinders parked themselves in one's eye. One disillusioned victim reported that the Cunarders resembled nothing so much as a block of Nova Scotia coal. Even their motion was far more uncomfortable than that of the sailing packets, especially when the wind was ahead and the vessel was no longer steadied by her sails.

Nor were the Cunarders the only offenders. All the early steamships came in for a share of criticism that was all but unanimous. Many of the complaints seem to have stemmed from a combination of inexperience and inadequate financing, but some of them reflected conditions that can be attributed only to callous indifference. Certainly the informed and meticulous concern of the canvas-back mariner for the comfort of his charges was conspicuous by its absence on many a steamship crossing.

The neglect of the most elementary precautions to safeguard the health and well-being of the passenger was vividly described in a long, bitterly worded letter signed by 67 cabin passengers of the S.S. *British Queen* on her arrival at New York late in November, 1839. Briefly, a mob of passengers, greatly exceeding in numbers the first-class accommodations available, were herded in miserably cold, rainy weather on board an officerless and completely unheated ship, and left for hours without food or warm drink, and without the means of obtaining any. The food, when it became available, was wretched; the vessel filthy, noisy, and overcrowded, with servants bedded down on saloon sofas and even on the saloon decks. Requests and complaints were treated with indifference. In short, "the line as now conducted, was unworthy of patronage."[11]

Small wonder the old line packet operators and masters, who were fully informed as to such conditions, regarded the steamship with a tolerant complacency—the outcome never in doubt. Their passengers published "cards" of appreciation and praise and their gratitude frequently took the form of suitably engraved silver pitchers, extolling the indefatigable care and sailorly virtues of their "urbane and gentlemanly commander."

Optimism of the steamerites, still tinctured by lingering memories of earlier sea tragedies, was almost obliterated when the grandest of the new fleet disappeared without a trace.

The steamship *President,* regarded as the last word in safety afloat, arrived in New York on the 4th of March, 1841, as President William

Henry Harrison was being inaugurated in Washington. She sailed again for Liverpool on the 12th of March with a crew and passenger list of 136, including the popular American comedian, Tyrone Power. President Harrison died the 4th of the following month, just as it began to be rumored in Liverpool that the magnificent craft named in honor of his office was overdue. Months passed, during which rumor succeeded rumor, of wreckage sighted, or huge, abandoned steamship hulks glimpsed briefly in storm-wracked waters; but of the *President* and all her people, no word ever came back.

It broke Smith's company. The *British Queen* was withdrawn and sold the following August to the Belgian government which restored her to the New York run. However, the enterprise did not pay and soon was abandoned.

The impression made on the public by the loss of the *President* was reflected in sharply curtailed passenger lists for many months. In September of the following year it was announced that the *Great Western* would be sold for lack of patronage. The sale did not materialize and in 1845 she was joined by her consort which had been under construction for nearly six years. This was Isambard Kingdom Brunel's masterpiece, the *Great Britain,* the first large iron seagoing propeller, which broke all records for size and number of decks and masts. She measured 3443 tons, had three decks and originally had six masts. What was more important, her speed was nearly, if not quite, equal to that of the fastest paddle steamers and superior to that of the Cunarders.

She sailed on her maiden voyage July 26, 1845, and crossed to New York in 12 days, 21 hours. Her coal consumption was only 65 tons daily, approximately the same as that of Cunarders one-third her tonnage. On her return trip her best day was 287 nautical miles. Her crew of 350 and cabin capacity of 360 constituted two more records. From the standpoint of the sailing liner, however, her greatest significance lay in the fact that she strengthened America's determination to build a fleet of superior steamships.

Thus reinforced and further encouraged by improved conditions accompanied by a marked increase in travel, the Great Western Company continued to operate with fair success until the stranding, September 22nd, 1846, of the *Great Britain* on the Irish coast, a disaster due to compass troubles which plagued all early iron ships. It was August of the following year before she was refloated, and by that time the company had decided to go into liquidation. The *Great Britain* was sold to the Royal Mail Steam Packet Company in 1847. In 1850 she was turned over to the

Liverpool & London Steam Navigation Company and eventually put on the Australian run.

Three other attempts to establish transatlantic steam services were made during the period. All were of relatively minor importance, but two are of interest as examples of the early efforts to solve one of the most serious steamship problems—how to ensure fast, dependable service without the excessive noise, vibration, violent motion, and general discomfort of the orthodox, heavily engined craft..

The first was the full ship-rigged, auxiliary propeller *Massachusetts.* She was built in 1845, and the old China merchant and master mariner, Robert Bennett Forbes, who was having the famous and very successful iron tug *R. B. Forbes* built the same year, was largely responsible for her general specifications. She was launched during the middle watch, the night of July 22-23, a circumstance which doubtless inspired the following effusion which appeared in the *Boston Post* a few hours later:

> The beautiful packet ship *Massachusetts,* was launched from the yard of Mr. Samuel Hall, at East Boston, between one and two o'clock on Tuesday morning. Few were present except the workmen, to witness the beautiful sight. The moon herself, "pale regent of the night," was oft obscured by passing clouds, and shed at best, a dull and broken light. But the sheet lightning seemed with one continuous blaze to light the vaulted firmament. When all was ready and the "tide brim full," the last connecting plank was cut in twain, and, smooth and swiftly down the inclined ways, the noble ship descended to the main, and ploughing through it, cut the swelling foam, and floated lightly on her destined home.

"And this," commented a New York editor under the heading, LAUNCH BY LIGHTNING, "is the pioneer of the new steamship line to run between New York and Liverpool. It certainly begins with brilliant prospects."

The editor was evidently more concerned with his wit than with the practical aspects of the case. Even if the auxiliary steamer could have solved the problem, the *Massachusetts* was foredoomed to failure by her size. She measured a scant 751 tons. She had fair accommodations for 30 first-class passengers in a long poop cabin, but her second-class and steerage quarters were below in a 'tween decks barely six feet in height between deck beams. Her engine (rated 175 horsepower, nominal) was expected to drive her at nine knots, an achievement that proved well beyond its capabilities, although she was an excellent sea boat and a good sailer. Other features of her equipment included a telescoping "smoke pipe" and an Ericsson propeller nine and one-half feet in diameter, ingeniously rigged abaft the rudder in a manner that permitted its unshipment quickly and easily. It was estimated that her eastbound crossings would average 13 and her westbound 16 days, with the possibility that the latter might run to 20 days in excessively bad weather. If the enterprise "met with encouragement" her sponsors planned to build three more sister ships to maintain a regular weekly service.

She cleared at New York December 11th on her first and only Liverpool voyage, and arrived on the 31st in the disappointing time of 20 days. On her return she sailed from Liverpool the 21st of January, 1846, and arrived in New York the 4th of March after a stormy passage of 42 days, Captain Wood reporting that her engine was of little help in bad weather. Much better passages would not have been good enough. And to stress her shortcomings, the little packet *Toronto,* Captain Edward Tinker, followed her up the bay 24 days out of Portsmouth, England. Although capably represented in New York and Liverpool by the pioneer express agency, Harnden & Company, the public would have none of her. When she next cleared, it was for Washington City and eventually, a long career in the United States Navy.

A similar but more promising attempt was made the following year by a couple of Liverpool merchants. Thomas and Joseph Sands, who represented the Kermit line in Liverpool, had the *Sarah Sands* built in 1846. She was a four-masted auxiliary iron propeller of 1000 tons, and much more of a ship than the *Massachusetts.* Her engine developed 200 horsepower as computed by the British rule (roughly, a third more than that of the *Massachusetts*) and she stowed 620 tons of cargo, 400 more than the Cunarders. Her bunker capacity was 300 tons and her fuel consumption was less than half that of the paddle liners, although her crossings averaged several days longer.

On her first voyage she arrived in New York on the 10th of February, after a passage of 21 days. She sailed for a couple of years in connection with the Kermit line under the able command of William C. Thompson, a highly respected veteran master of packets, but a brief experience indicated that the orthodox steamship and even the large new sailing liners would have little to fear from her competition. It was the old story, inferior accommodations and slow passages. Nevertheless, while with the Kermit line, she was for the most part fairly well patronized. On her second trip to New York she brought 43 first- and 123 second-class passengers, and thereafter usually brought about the same number. However, her patronage depended less on her merits than on the fact that all the other steamers had been taken off the New York run. When the big Collins, Bremen, and Cunard liners came along two or three years later she was hopelessly outclassed and was sold to go into less exacting trades.

The third venture was the first French attempt to maintain a trans-atlantic steamship service. This was the short-lived "Union Line" between Bremen and New York. It was started in the summer of 1847 with four small, converted French warships and lasted barely six months. The steamers were not only completely inadequate in both speed and accommodations, but were so badly managed that even patriotic Frenchmen would not travel on them.

While steamship enterprise on the Western Ocean—the Cunarders excepted—was meeting the common fate of pioneer ventures, America was slowly becoming more and more steamship-minded. By 1845 two new developments joined forces to speed the process. One was the lively prospect of war with Mexico; the other, anticipation of trouble with England over the Oregon question. With the slogans, "Remember the Alamo" and "54.40 or fight," resounding through the land, an apprehensive but reluctant Congress passed its first bill looking to the establishment of an auxiliary steam navy.

It took the form of an act authorizing a ten-year mail contract with a line to be composed of four steamships of 1750 tons, readily convertible to sloops-of-war, to run between New York and Bremen, touching at a British channel port. The bill was introduced and passed largely through the efforts of Junius Smith, who hoped to arrange for a line to Liverpool. To his disappointment, it was changed at the last moment, substituting Bremen for Liverpool and giving the contract to another group.

Unfortunately, America's pioneer mail steam packet, the 1642-ton *Washington,* did little to improve the actual situation, whatever promise she may have held for the future. She was launched by Westervelt & Mackay on the 30th of January, 1847, to the booming of great guns, the tolling of innumerable bells, and the cheers of assembled thousands. To unaccustomed New York eyes, she was an impressive sight as her sleek 260-foot hull, painted man-of-war fashion, took the water. Predictions were freely made that she would excel any seagoing craft afloat or planned, including the four 1600-ton Cunarders then under construction for the New York run. Her performance, however, left much to be desired.

She sailed the 2nd of June and reported 13 days, 20 hours to Southampton, which barely equalled the speed of the old slow-coach Cunarders. What was quite as bad was the fact she proved crank and uncomfortable. As one nautical cynic remarked, "They had built a city on her deck." On her return to New York the "city" was removed. But in spite of that and other expensive tinkering there was no improvement in her performance and the unpalatable truth gradually emerged that 1847 had not produced the American answer to British steam competition or even to the liner of the sail. Whether it would be provided by the as yet untried independent steamships, of which the Black Ball's *United States,* an 1800-tonner, was the largest, or by the 3000-ton monsters of the Collins fleet, on which construction was just starting, remained to be seen. In any case the answer would be deferred to 1848 and possibly much later.

Of all the original ventures, therefore, only one survived at the close of 1847. The Cunard alone plodded on, equally indifferent to criticism and the public comfort, apparently content so long as its mail contract held. The mails, indeed, had been a critical factor from the start. As early as January, 1842, the *Unicorn* brought upwards of 40,000 letters from Halifax to Boston, on which postage in excess of $4,000 had been paid.[12] This was in addition to several cartloads of newspapers reckoned by the bushel, and which represented the grist of a single crossing. As this state of affairs not only persisted but continued to improve year after year, it was evident that the subsidy was safe.

From the standpoint of statistics, therefore, on December 31st, 1847, the victory of sail over steam was all but complete. Of the 18 original steamships only five continued to run, six if we include the recently added wretched little *Sarah Sands* with the five almost equally wretched little Cunarders, none of which could have survived without strong outside support. All other companies had gone on the rocks with losses running into the millions.

In sharp contrast with that situation, the Western Ocean sailing liners were never more numerous, grander, or more prosperous. Their record proved they were undoubtedly safer, and the travelling public in general agreed that they were more comfortable than the steamships. Until they went emigrantish in a big way, they were both quieter and cleaner. On occasion they equalled and even beat the eastbound steamships, as when the little *President,* an old vessel of only 469 tons register, beat the S.S. *Great Western.* The two vessels sailed from New York in company early in 1839, the former passing Cape Clear well ahead of the latter.[13] Later, when it developed that the smart new packet *Louis Phillipe,* that had also sailed at the same time, had actually arrived at the more distant port of Havre before the steamer reached Bristol, the old canvas-backs held a special celebration in which they took pains to stress the point that one of the celebrated "tea kettles" had been beaten by a windjammer barely a third her tonnage. Nevertheless, in spite of occasional 14- and 15-day crossings, there was no disguising the fact that the steamers beat their rivals nine times out of ten, and that by margins usually ranging from one to three weeks.

Aside from immediate superiority of performance, the steamship had one thing that would have ensured its survival if every criticism levelled against it had been justified twice over. That was the promise of ever-increasing speed—the objective that, above all others, summed up America's most insistent material aspirations of two centuries' standing. At the very moment when the battle seemed lost, powerful interests were working and, as it proved, successfully, for government support of a comprehensive system of mail steam packets, readily convertible at need into swift, heavily armed sloops-of-war. Leading men of the sail, indeed, had been pressing the matter actively for several years. The list included such outstanding sailing packet operators as Charles H. Marshall, Edward K. Collins, and John Ogden. Their efforts were ably reinforced by Junius Smith. As time went on, they were greatly aided not only, as we have seen, by the growing realization that Great Britain was acquiring a superior naval arm, but by the practical lessons of the Mexican War which had demonstrated that even third-rate steamers like the *Massachusetts* possessed certain decisive advantages over sail in a wide variety of operations.

It was not, however, until the 4th of March, 1847, that an adequately comprehensive mail subsidy measure was adopted, and the fact it was adopted at all indicates the diversity of the forces and interests that had combined to overcome America's distrust of everything in the nature of government support of private enterprise, a distrust especially marked throughout the South.

As it happened, the measure of necessity called for a vast increase in the volume, as well as a marked improvement in the quality, of steamship service to southern ports. This was a fact which could hardly fail to affect favorably the attitude of a people who had recently experienced the unprecedented comfort and convenience of travel in the new steamers, of which the *Southerner* was first in importance. At all events, the bill received the hearty support of a majority of southern representatives; among them the able and influential T. Butler King, of Georgia, a state which more than once had taken the lead in steamship matters.

Our highly vocal James Gordon Bennett evaluated his contribution in the following manner:

AMERICAN STEAM MARINE.—

We seldom see a man or an association of men so completely devoid of all right and proper feeling, that have not at some time or other done an act, that entitled them to praise and admiration to a certain extent: some act, that like a meteor, illumines the dark night of their existence.

No unprejudiced person can persuade himself that the Congress which had just adjourned has not been the most unprofitable one that ever assembled at the Capitol. They wasted their time in discussing absurdities and fallacies until the last day of the session; but at the eleventh hour they certainly transacted a little business of importance. If they did nothing else, they are certainly entitled to some praise for passing the bill introduced by Mr. King of Georgia, in relation to the government employing ocean steamships in the foreign mail service of the country.

This bill provides for the construction of four steam vessels of war—a line of five steamers from New York to Liverpool, of 2,000 tons burthen—a line of five from New York to New Orleans, touching at Savannah and Havana, with a branch from Havana to Chagres, of 1,500 tons burthen—a line from Panama in the Pacific, to Oregon, touching at intermediate ports—comprising in the aggregate, sixteen or more steamships of the first class.

We congratulate the country on the passage of this bill. The United States is at last about to take her proper position in ocean steam navigation, and will, before a very long time, have an extensive steam marine that will answer for commercial as well as naval purposes. We understand that E. K. Collins, Esq., well known throughout the United States as one of our most experienced and extensive ship owners, has received the contract for the Liverpool line. A better man could not get it. Mr. Collins has conferred much honor on his country and made for himself a reputation for enterprise, skill and perseverance from his connection with the packet ship business, which he may well be proud of. His reputation is a guaranty that if he should get the contract, he will fulfill it in a way satisfactory to the Government, and honorable to himself.

It is presumed that Charles H. Marshall, Esq., another extensive and well known ship owner, will contract for the New Orleans, Havana and Panama lines. He is now building several steamships, which he designed for the Liverpool trade, but he can easily construct them so they will answer for any of the others."[14]

For convenience, therefore, the passage of this Act may be taken as marking, roughly, the close of a preliminary, experimental period, and the beginning of full-scale competition between steamship and sailing liner. At all events, the large ocean-going steamer had been tested and shown to possess certain valuable advantages, and there were many who were now persuaded that it held vastly greater possibilities. Nothing else will account for the fact that several of the more energetic and successful sailing packet operators had decided to add steamships to their lines, or the intense enthusiasm which greeted every new announcement of developments in both steam and sailing liner circles.

In spite of the poor showing of the transatlantic steamer, we are probably justified in rating the decade (1838-1847) as the most remarkable America had yet witnessed in respect to advances in the speed-up of communication and transportation.

The most revolutionary of the new inventions, Morse's "Electric Magnetic Telegraph," had gone into successful operation between Baltimore and Washington in June, 1844. On the 17th of July, 1846, news from abroad was first telegraphed from Boston to New York on the arrival of the Cunarder *Cambria* from Liverpool, and the papers printed exultant "Flashes from Boston" and hailed the completion of "Another Link in the Lightning Line."

Paced by Baldwin, Rogers, Norris, Winans, and others, the locomotive had raised the rate of land travel in breath-taking fashion to 50 miles an hour and upwards, setting off an orgy of railroad construction that would quadruple the nation's trackage in the next ten years, raising it to nearly 25,000 miles and contributing, incidentally, to the severity of the panic of 1857.

Steamboat improvement had been no less striking. From Long Island Sound to the "Big Muddy," reports of new records rolled in endlessly, year after year. Racing was the order of the day. One of the classics of the period was the contest between George Law's *Oregon* and the *Cornelius Vanderbilt*. Both were new vessels of about the same size, slightly over 1000 tons and about 340 feet in length. They were matched for a race from the Battery in New York to Sing Sing and return (distance reported 78, but actually about 68 miles) for a purse of $1,000 a side.

The race started at 10:56 A.M., June 1st, 1847, just as Charleston's crack steamship *Southerner* came steaming up the bay with the great Daniel Webster and party. It ended in a pandemonium of sound 3 hours and 15 minutes later when the *Oregon* crossed the finish line 400 yards ahead of the *Vanderbilt*. Allowing for time consumed in getting under way and in rounding the stake boat at Sing Sing, the boats had averaged not far from 21 statute miles an hour. To make sure that Vanderbilt got the point, Law offered to race the still bigger *Hendrick Hudson* with one wheel. And to round out their day of thrills, the passengers of winner and loser alike were disembarked in time to rush to the next spectacle, the sailing of the steamship *Washington* for Bremen to set—it was confidently asserted—a new mark for the Cunarders. Cheering thousands, milling around the steamship dock provided a fitting finish to an exciting day.

Next morning a complacent editor delivered the popular verdict, "All things yesterday were done, well done, and done quickly." As usual, with Brother Jonathan, "quickly" was the punch word.

It, and similar phrases, were to be accorded special prominence in the story of the years of sail which lay between the panic of 1837 and the discovery of gold in California.

CHAPTER XI

~ *1838-1847* ~

The Queens Triumph

"Brave ships, with more than cargoes in their holds."

ALTHOUGH the travelling public might back and fill, now tendering its loyalty to steam and now to canvas, there was no such vacillation among men of the sail. They left a straight wake; now organizing additional lines, now building new, larger, and more costly packets; acting on the whole as though there were no such things as steamships. There is much to indicate that few of them took steam seriously for the long pull. On the other hand, by 1839 they were quite aware that their new competitors were getting an undue share of first-class patronage and, regardless of their views as to the permanency of the situation, they took special measures to meet it.

In that year, accordingly, all the older Liverpool, London, and Havre lines out of New York closed ranks; reduced fares from $140 to $100, and for the first time issued joint advertisements advising the public of their action and setting forth a new joint sailing schedule. Only the Dramatic line held aloof; possibly for the reason that its magnificent new ships were generally well patronized, while the smaller and less luxurious vessels of the older lines usually sailed with less—and frequently many less—than a quarter of their staterooms occupied.

No new Western Ocean sailing lines were established during the three years following the founding of the Dramatic line. That, however, was due less to steamship competition than to the sharp drop in immigration noted in the previous chapter. That, and other economic factors, conditioned the course and volume of sailing ship activity far more than the several hundred shipping disasters which occurred each year and ranged from damaged spars and sails to the total loss of the vessel, sometimes accompanied by a heavy loss of life. Steamship losses might dismay the steamerites for a time, but the tough old canvas-backs took their losses as a part of the day's work. What they might mean to the individuals in-

245

volved was another matter. For many, it meant beginning life over again after long years of toil and hardship.

The loss of the New York-Norfolk packet schooner *Portsmouth* was but one of scores of such incidents, the yearly grist of personal tragedies through the centuries. She was a smart Fairfield-built craft of 190 tons. She sailed from New York the 29th of October, 1838, and struck on Hog Island off the coast of Virginia on the 31st, where she remained, burst open and masts gone, a complete wreck. Her commander, Captain Hart, whose life savings were invested in the vessel and cargo—the hard-won earnings of 153 successful voyages, lost everything but his life.

Two of the coastal packets lost about the same time were large ships. The *Kentucky* of the Holmes line, John Bunker, master, was wrecked on one of the Bahamas in the gale of September 7th, while bound from New York for New Orleans. On the 17th of November the Hurlbut liner *Russell Baldwin* stranded on the Abaco, on her passage from New York for Mobile under the command of Joseph N. Magna. Passengers and crew drifted safely ashore on the upper deck of the ship and were taken to Nassau.

Yellow fever added its might to prolong and accentuate the depression. In 1839 it ravaged the coastal cities from New York to New Orleans and brought southern trade to an all-but-complete standstill. So many seamen died that it was difficult to man such ships as did sail, and wages rocketed to $15 a month. Ships' officers were no more immune than foremast hands. Sutton's Charleston line lost three of its oldest commanders within a few days, including the Besher brothers of the packets *Catherine* and *Niagara*. The pestilence also was responsible for a serious crop shortage in the south which was reflected in reduced freight offerings for months to come.

To make matters worse, it was an exceptionally bad year on the North Atlantic and the loss of life in American sailing ships was heavy. In February word was received that three large packets had been wrecked near Liverpool on the 6th of January, the *St. Andrew, Oxford* and *Pennsylvania,* in addition to other American ships wrecked on the English coast. It later developed that the *Oxford* had been saved by the resourceful seamanship of her commander, John Rathbone, who put her ashore in a sheltered spot where she received little damage. The *St. Andrew* was also salvaged later and returned to the line after extensive repairs, but the *Pennsylvania* was gone and with her John P. Smith, one of the most capable and popular of the packet masters.

The year ended as it began, in disaster. Three hurricanes swept the New England coast in quick succession between December 15th and 27th, wrecking scores of vessels, including coastal packets, and leaving nearly 200 known dead, in addition to unreported missing vessels and individuals. The storm of the 15th was the worst. It was especially violent in the vicinity of Gloucester, where a large number of bodies came ashore opposite the reef of Norman's Woe—among them the body of a girl lashed to the windlass bitts of a schooner. The same storm had damaged, among others, a schooner named the *Hesperus* in Boston harbor. Henry Wadsworth Longfellow, then a rising young Harvard professor, wove the incidents into a ballad—"The Wreck of the Hesperus."

If 1839 had been a bad year at sea, 1840-41 showed little improvement. One reviewer stated that "never in the annals of shipwreck have so many vessels been abandoned at sea in one year." In the 14 months ending December 31st, 1841, a total of 557 vessels were reported lost, most of them along the Atlantic coast, in addition to 28 missing. The known loss of life was 650. About 500 more were lost in British waters. All shipping suffered heavily during this period except the Western Ocean packets. They not only escaped serious damage, but added to their prestige by making an unusual number of rescues from sinking ships. Their record in that respect for the stormy 30 days beginning November 21, 1840, is unique. During that time six packets saved the crews of six British vessels —64 men in all—under conditions of extreme peril.

The liners involved were the *Sheridan,* commanded by Frederick Depeyster; the *Rhone,* under James A. Wotton; *Columbus,* Thomas B. Cropper; *Stephen Whitney,* William C. Thompson; *Garrick,* Alexander S. Palmer, and the *Ville de Lyon,* under Charles Stoddard. In due course all six captains received gold medals suitably engraved and embossed with a likeness of Queen Victoria, and presented by the British Minister at Washington on behalf of the British government.

Steamship loss of patronage, especially after the mysterious disappearance of the *President,* is strikingly indicated by the passenger lists of the sailing packets. All of them benefited, but the new *Hendrick Hudson,* with genial and popular Elisha E. Morgan in charge of the quarter-deck, set the record. His tally of cabin passengers when he backed his topsail off Sandy Hook the 8th of October, 1841, was 72, "the largest number ever arrived here in a wind packet."

A succession of terrific gales early in 1842 did nothing to restore the confidence of faint-hearted steamerites. The stout packet *Independence* arrived in New York in March without losing a rope yarn, after encountering for 20 days running a series of the worst hurricanes in the memory of her veteran master, Ezra Nye. It was later ascertained that the Cunarder *Caledonia* had been forced to turn back to Liverpool during the earlier and less violent of the storms.

This and similar incidents confirmed many in the determination to travel in sail, and were measurably responsible for the fact that for the next two years the old line packets continued to clear with well-filled cabins, while the steamships sailed with quotas usually well under half their capacity. Month after month New York papers continued to record items similar to that of the 28th of April, 1842, which noted that the packets *Siddons* and *Ville de Lyon* put to sea with crowded cabins and "a cracking west wind," while the fine steamship *Great Western* went out on the same tide "with plenty of empty berths." Even Charles Dickens, who had arrived in America the preceding January in the Cunarder *Britannia,* decided to return in sail; a fact to which we are indebted for the following literary gem which appeared in the *New York Herald* a few weeks later:

Boz at Niagara.—Letters have been received from Dickens. He has been at Niagara and lost his senses. Samuel Weller has also lost his. On the first returning symptoms of sanity, Boz immediately took berths for himself, lady and Samuel Weller, (Sam disguises himself as a Mr. Putnam) in the crack ship *George Washington,* which sails for London on the 7th of June. Ho! for England.

But valuable as the first-class patronage undoubtedly was to the wind packets, another source of revenue was already showing indications of surpassing it in importance. This was the steerage traffic, the sudden remarkable increase of which in 1840 was mentioned in the previous chapter. On the 16th and 17th of June, 1842, more than 3000 immigrants were landed at the New York quarantine. It was an all-time record, but it stood for less than two weeks. On the 30th of June 2600 prospective citizens were disembarked in the port in a single day. Again it was enthusiastically hailed as an all-time record, but for another 12 years it was to be surpassed repeatedly by ever-increasing margins. It was to go on until, as will be more particularly noted in a later chapter, New York ships landed in 1854 the largest number of passengers that have ever been landed from abroad in any American port in a single day—recent claims on behalf of the super-liners of our time to the contrary, notwithstanding.

Records, however, are of small importance compared with the changes the new migration was working. One of its more immediate effects was to boost the activities of the "old established passage offices" to that feverish pitch responsible for the mid-century formation of those great, loosely organized emigrant lines of which the "Black Star" was chief.

In 1840 the New York firms of Glover & McMurray (later Joseph Mc-

Murray), Samuel Thompson, Douglas Robinson & Company, Wotherspoon & Company, Herdman & Keenan, Roche Brothers & Company, and Harnden & Company expanded their organizations to handle the unprecedented volume of business. The same upturn brought other new houses in 1841 to share in the prosperity, among them the energetic Tapscotts of New York and Liverpool. It would require a volume to trace the ensuing activities of such firms in the port of New York alone during the next 12 years, most of whom were soon advertising the sailing every few days of "first-class" packets and transient ships in "New," "United," or "Union" lines and the like. It will, however, contribute to a readier understanding of what was happening if we assume that a considerable proportion of the emigrant ships normally sailed in two or three such lines at one and the same time. The simple fact was that any passage office which expected to put a baker's dozen of ragamuffins on a given ship, seized the opportunity to advertise that ship as belonging to its own particular private line. It made no difference whether the vessel was a haughty, old line packet or a run-of-the-mill transient. Even that was a passing phase, for eventually, Tapscott, Thompson, and others operated very substantial lines of ships which they owned or controlled.

Progress in the early forties was by no means confined to the great sea routes. Scores of men and firms who, a few years before, had operated two or three little brigs and schooners on short coastal runs, were now managing as many lines, each comprising several large square-riggers. Skippers of tiny coasters, veterans of hundreds of short, prosaic trips between neighboring ports, were now proud commanders of the greatest liners ever seen—ships ranging up to 1000 tons, with sumptuous, airy cabins excelling in richness and comfort anything afloat.

There was Robert L. Taylor, late master of the little brig *Sarah Herrick,* now managing owner of half a dozen ships and barks, the *Lancashire, Liverpool, Superior,* and the like, besides manifesting more than a passing interest in steam. Old Jed Frye, who had slowly accumulated a small fleet of brigs and schooners of 100 tons or so, was now picking up 300- and 400-tonners. Captain Augustus Zerega, Peter Hargous, Moses Taylor, and many more were branching out in similar fashion.

Many of the older shipmasters, Robert H. Waterman, Nathaniel B. Palmer, Frederick Hewitt, William T. Glidden, most of the masters of the Western Ocean packets, the bigger coastal liners, and a few of the China traders, had already passed on to more glamorous heights, but a new and more numerous group was coming along. Kimball R. Smith,

Charles E. Ranlett, Archibald G. Hamilton, Gurdon Gates, Joseph W. Spencer, John A. Burgess, Levi F. Doty, and scores more were still driving their little coasters. They would live to command some of the noblest packets and fastest clippers afloat. Down in Boston, Rodney Baxter, Oliver Eldridge, and others of similar stamp were emerging from the ruck of Cape Cod packeteers—the Bassets, Lewises, Bacons, Mayos, Delanos, and Nickersons—headed for notable commands and a hatful of records.

The first new transatlantic line of the period did not come until 1841, and even the stepped-up activities of that year resulted in but one line of importance. That was the Woodhull & Minturn "New Line" between New York and Liverpool. Herdman & Keenan started an immigrant line between Hamburg and New York which they dubbed "A Succession of Fine Packets." It sailed twice monthly but had no regular days. E. D. Hurlbut & Company advertised new packet sailings to Cadiz, Bremen, and Marseilles, all of which soon lapsed with the exception of the Bremen line, and for some years that gave very irregular service.

In the following year, however, a trend started that was to continue for another ten years and was to result in the establishment of new lines on a scale that surpassed all previous records, not only in number but in size and quality of ships.

That year seven new transatlantic lines were started by New York firms. In Boston, Colonel Enoch Train made what proved to be a highly optimistic claim to the founding of the port's third Liverpool line. It was not taken very seriously in Boston and until 1845 it was regarded in Liverpool merely as an irregular succession of ships, and not particularly outstanding ships at that.

During the six years from 1842 to 1847, inclusive, 29 new Western Ocean lines were formed. Of this impressive total a majority were immigrant lines, but some were true packet lines—at least for several years—and some of the immigrant lines attracted a considerable number of cabin passengers and adhered closely to regular schedules. In the establishment of these lines New York led by a wide margin, accounting for 23, as against one, two, and three, respectively, for Boston, Baltimore, and Philadelphia.

Twelve of New York's new lines ran to Liverpool, and one each to Belfast and Glasgow. The remainder served continental areas, two each going to Hamburg, Antwerp, and Marseilles, and the balance to Havre, Bremen, and Cadiz. The Cadiz venture was soon abandoned. Its mention here is not justified by any practical importance which attached to it as a line, but because it indicates the optimism with which packet men were once more trying the ports.

New York also maintained a substantial lead in size and elegance of new liners, although several of the later Philadelphia additions were reported as equal in finish, though not in tonnage, to any ships afloat.

In 1838 the largest line ship in service was the 1031-ton *Roscius,* added in November as the fourth and final ship of the Dramatic line. Aside from her three consorts, and the *Pennsylvania,* soon to sail on her last voyage, no other packet registered 800 tons, though the Black Baller *Cambridge* fell short of the mark by a single ton only. The importance of the new flat-floored packets, however, lies in their design rather than their size. With the advent of the *Roscius,* the contest between the old and new theories of sailing design was on in earnest.

It will be recalled that in Captain Clark's *Clipper Ship Era* he gives an account of the first pre-arranged "race" between packet ships. The story is referred to here as suggesting, possibly, the extent of the rivalry between exponents of the two theories of design, as evidenced by "slightly apocryphal" accounts of contests offered in substantiation of their claims.

Captain Clark related that a wager of $10,000 was made between the little 597-ton *Columbus* of the Black Ball line and the great new 895-ton *Sheridan* of the Dramatic line, both ships sailing from New York the 2nd day of February, 1837, the *Columbus* winning the race to Liverpool by two days in the excellent time of 16 days.

Aside from the fact that the *Columbus* did undoubtedly beat the *Sheridan* on that occasion by a margin that may have ranged anywhere from a trifle over one day to two days (hours of departure and arrival not being given) there are strong reasons for believing the rest of the story is pure fabrication; not, be it understood, by Captain Clark but by his informant. For one thing, it is all but incredible that a wager of $10,000 (equivalent to more than $100,000 today) could be made on an event of such public interest without any mention whatever in the contemporary press, as undoubtedly was the case. For another, Captain Russell cleared the *Sheridan* two days before Depeyster cleared the *Columbus,* and that he intended to sail two days before her is indicated by the advertised closing date for his letter bags at Hudson's. That he did not sail as intended is accounted for by the fact that all local shipping was held up for two days by river ice and bad weather. Then there are minor errors which indicate that the originator of the story was unfamiliar with pertinent facts well known in New York shipping circles at the time, such as the passage of the *Columbus,* which was 18 and not 16 days, and her size, which was 663 and not 597 tons.

Still, she did make the better passage, although the *Sheridan* was not long in taking her revenge. Both ships sailed for New York the same day on the return trip, normally a much more difficult test of sailing ability, the *Sheridan* winning by a margin of two days.

Single passages prove little, however, for defeat or victory may be explained by such valid excuses as overloading, relatively adverse winds, or foul bottoms. It is average performance over an extended period which determines the superiority of a vessel, and here the Dramatic line was not long in presenting conclusive evidence. During the first full year of operation of the completed line, from November, 1838, to October, 1839, inclusive, the average of its 12 eastbound crossings was approximately 21 days, while the corresponding 12 westbound passages averaged 32 days.

During the same period the Black Ball made the best average of the competing lines, taking the 12 passages made by the packets clearing nearest the Dramatic sailing dates. The Black Ball average was 23 and 35 days, respectively.

If further evidence of the superiority of the new design is needed, it is to be found in the reaction of the travelling public. Before many months the Dramatic ships frequently sailed with full or nearly full cabins, while three-quarters of the staterooms of the other packets were empty. The fact undoubtedly played some part in stimulating the construction of ships of unprecedented size, finish, and efficiency. Before the close of 1847, great three-deckers had been launched that exceeded the *Roscius* by 400 tons and were more than double the average size of the largest liners of the previous decade, and more than double their passenger capacity.

The first of these, and the first three-deck liner to be built, was the *Liverpool,* laid down by Brown & Bell in New York and launched early in 1843. Her measurement as first recorded was 1077 tons, a gross underestimate due to the complete omission by the surveyor of the third deck from his calculations. Whether the omission was caused by uncertainty as to application of measurement rules to three-deckers or was superinduced by the well-known aversion of shipowners to large tonnage dues is, perhaps, uncertain. Whatever the case, her correct rating under the existing rule was 1364. Under the present, and more accurate, method of calculation the figure would be very substantially increased. Since many of the improvements she embodied (and even her distinctive position as the first three-decker packet) have been credited to other and later vessels, one of the several descriptions printed about the time of her launching is here given in full.

ANOTHER LINE OF LIVERPOOL PACKETS.—WHAT NEXT?

When the little *Sirius* came over the Atlantic and went ashore on the point of the Hook in the spring of 1838, it was said that our famous packet ships would soon become so many "obsolete ideas." It appears, however, that they have become absolute and not obsolete ideas, for the number is increasing almost daily. There are now no less than three on the stocks, and the keel of another is to be laid immediately.

One of these is the longest, broadest and deepest vessel ever built in America, and in point of beauty is not to be surpassed in any part of the inhabitable globe. Indeed none but New York shipwrights can turn out such a packet ship. Her builders are the well known Brown & Bell, who have never been guilty of launching any but first class vessels, such as the *Roscius,* the Spanish war steamers, the *Garrick,* the Mexican schooners of war, the *Siddons,* the *Sheridan,* and hundreds of others.

The beautiful vessel of which we have now to speak is called the *Liverpool.* She has three decks, and is eleven hundred tons burthen. The length of her upper deck, which is almost flush from stem to stern is one hundred and eighty-three feet, and has a small cabin for smokers and for the men at the helm. This will be exclusive for the use of the cabin passengers, who are to be kept entirely separate from the steerage passengers. No other ship has such a clear uninterrupted promenade as this deck gives. The main deck is one hundred and seventy-six feet long, and upon it are built the cabins, bathing houses, apartments for the cuisine, houses for cows, sheep, swine and poultry. We never saw such perfect arrangements as are presented on this deck.

The main saloon is constructed on the most improved idea. It is large enough for forty cabin passengers and is high enough for any man under eight feet in his boots. The state rooms are fitted up somewhat like those of the *Ashburton* and *Stephen Whitney,* and connect so that families can have a suite of rooms as at the Astor House. But more anon about the saloon. Forward of it is the first and second mate's cabin. Then comes another cabin for the second class passengers, in which there is a large dining room, where they can live and be comfortable by themselves if they like. Next to this is the bathing room with shower baths and other conveniences for refreshing one's self with pure salt water dipped from the ocean. But it should be recollected that this dipping does not make it fresh water. This bathing room is a new idea and it is as capital as it is new. It has heretofore been a desideratum in packet ships. Forward of all are the pantries for making pastry, and two excellent cabooses, one for the cabin and the other for the steerage passengers. These are divided by an iron partition. And then in the bows are the most ample and comfortable accommodations for the sailors we ever beheld. In their "cabins," for they have two, each thirty feet in length, they have stores, twenty or thirty berths, and plenty of light from above and through the sides. In these they can read, sleep, and mend their clothes, without being cramped for room, as they too often are on board merchant ships. And for the benefit of steerage passengers and sailors, and indeed all on board, there are vent holes between each timber head. These, however, can be closely stopped in bad weather. On either side of the mates' cabins, cabooses, etc., there is a promenade for second class passengers.

Beneath these two decks, is still another, which is clear fore and aft. This is one hundred and seventy-five feet long, thirty-six feet broad and seven and a half feet in height. It will hold fifteen hundred bales of cotton, and carry five hundred steerage passengers. Here we see the strength of the vessel. The sides look like large steam boilers, such as are made at the Novelty works, the planks are so riveted together. There are no less than six thousand iron bolts running through them, and we must here mention that there are ninety tons of iron, and twelve tons of copper fastenings, used in building the *Liverpool.* On the lower deck are the coal and bread houses, and under them the water tanks, capable of holding four thousand gallons of water from the Croton. Between decks are six stern windows, besides six glass ports on each side, throwing plenty of light throughout the whole.

Everyone who has seen this ship, pronounce her a "none such." Her appearance is striking in the highest degree. She looms up immensely, with a full length figure of Lord Liverpool beautifully carved by Dodge on her bows, and the cotte d'armes of the City of Liverpool on her stern. She is complete and beautiful.

She is to be launched about the 15th inst., and the keel of another packet of 1250 tons is to be laid the same day. Both are for the new line of packets to run between New York and Liverpool. This line is to be composed of the following ships:

Ships	Captains	Size	Departure
Rochester	Philip Woodhouse	800 tons	Feb. 16
Hottinguer	Ira Bursley	1050 tons	Mar. 16
Liverpool	John Eldridge	1150 tons	Apr. 16
Great Western	P. Woodhouse	1250 tons	May 16

It is seen that Captain John Eldridge is to command the *Liverpool*. It is unnecessary for us to speak of him. He is too well known to need any praise from our hands. It is sufficient to say that he commanded the *Huntsville* for many years out of this port. This is proof enough that the *Liverpool* will be under a very popular commander.[1]

The language of the foregoing, however fulsome by twentieth-century standards, conveys no exaggerated conception of the impression created by the *Liverpool,* or her influence on subsequent packet construction. The decision to build a three-decker packet was, indeed, little short of revolutionary. From a practical standpoint, it was visionary in the extreme to conclude that packets which could carry from 600 to 700 passengers would pay, when as yet packets with a capacity of half the number were rarely filled; and it took courage to continue to back that belief when immigration showed signs of dropping to a new low in 1843.

Woodhull & Minturn never faltered, however. They went on to launch a second and larger packet later in the year, the *Queen of the West.* Under John Eldridge and Philip Woodhouse, also a New Orleans packet graduate, the two made better than average passages in a day when every packet was driven to the utmost. On her second voyage the *Queen of the West,* which replaced the *Rochester,* slipped into Liverpool the 9th of February, 1844, to report a 15-day crossing. It was actually 15½ days.

Other lines were not backward in meeting the challenge. Black Ball laid the keel of the *Yorkshire,* a magnificent two-decker which later was greatly exceeded in size, but never in performance until the day of the huge clipper packets of the fifties and then only by a trifling margin. She was launched late in 1843. A few weeks later Bennett described the ceremonies which marked the beginning of her active service, a service destined to be outstanding in one of the most exacting of all enterprises:

ATLANTIC PACKET SHIP YORKSHIRE.—This magnificent packet was thrown open last Saturday to the public. Between eleven and three she was visited by the elite of the city. At two o'clock she was presented with a splendid set of flags, signals and cabin cutlery, by the Yorkshire gentlemen of this city, in return for the compliment paid them in naming her after their birthplace.

This exhibition of ship, gifts and company, cannot be passed without remark. In the *Yorkshire* there is most everything that is splendid. In the flags, cutlery, etc., the gentlemen of Yorkshire have thrown in a portion of the beauty of the ship. Nothing is now wanting to make her parfait but a few views of the "Eye of England," as the shire is called. We understand that these views are to be given her by the leading men on the other side of the Atlantic. We are glad of this.

The presentation of the flags, etc., on Saturday, was a splendid affair throughout. There was assembled in the cabin at the time, about two hundred of our first merchants and shipmasters. Before them was a capital dinner with the new cabin cutlery; above them gently floated the flags and signals; and in their midst was the immortal Tom Thumb, walking around the plates as easily as those who have signed the pledge walk through our streets. Mr. Henry Jessup, on behalf of his fellow-countrymen presented the flags, etc., wrapped up in a neat speech, to Captain Marshall, part owner and agent of the ship. Captain Marshall replied in a very handsome manner. He stated that the packets were first started in 1817, and since then the most astonishing improvements have been made in shipbuilding. Then packets were looked upon as so many floating chimeras on the Atlantic; now they are looked upon as so many floating palaces, as useful as they are splendid, floating off from our shores to those of old England.

After this presentation, which was so apropos, Tom Thumb, who has engaged five staterooms for himself and his friends, hopped upon a piece of excellent a la mode beef and sung the "Deep, deep sea!" He then resumed his seat on a cut glass tumbler, and the utmost conviviality prevailed till late in the afternoon.

When Captain Bailey, the gentlemanly commander of the *Yorkshire* was toasted, he made a capital speech, in which he explained to the satisfaction of everyone, that fourteen days was time enough to take in running across the Atlantic, wind and weather permitting, and that icebergs were only so many big boulders from the north. It is the common remark among the sharks when Captain B. goes to sea, that "it is useless to attempt to follow that ship, for Bailey is on board of her." Such is his reputation for speed even among the inhabitants of the deep.

Among those on board were Captains Cobb, Rogers, Barstow, Marshall, etc., old packet commanders, all of whom except Captain Barstow, have retired from active service, but who have invested a large part of their riches in building such ships as the *Yorkshire, Ashburton, Queen of the West,* etc., etc. And it is a fact that at least one third of the shipping belonging to this port is owned by shipmasters in and out of service.

Many of our finest packets are almost wholly owned by these enterprising men, and it is to them that our country is indebted for the superiority of our ships over those of every other nation in the world. Within the last ten years, a dozen or more of our packet captains, namely, Maxwell, Cobb, the Marshalls, the Palmers, Waite, etc., etc., have left their big wooden ploughs on the Atlantic, and gone to small iron ploughs on land. It is said that Captain Maxwell is the largest farmer in Pennsylvania, and Captain Waite owns a lovely place in Connecticut, called "Waite Manor" and at last accounts he was up for Town Clerk, the highest office in the gift of the people in his part of the country. When on the Atlantic, these sailor-farmers reaped dollars and silver pitchers; now they reap oats, wheat, rye, etc. With their cattle it is "starboard," instead of "gee-bright," and "larboard," instead of "haw-buck." There are no such words as "gee-up—gee-ho," in their language.

But in the midst of the gaiety and conviviality on board the *Yorkshire,* intelligence reached town that the much esteemed Burrows, of the *George Washington,* was no more! Instantly everything turned from gay to grave; flags and streamers that had floated so joyously over the splendid *Yorkshire,* were lowered half-mast, and all looked sad and gloomy. Captain Bailey, who was so happy, was now the most sorrowful, for he had lost one of his dearest friends. Never was change so sudden or so great as this change from pleasure to sadness. Throughout that night and throughout yesterday, the flags of all the shipping, as well as the *Yorkshire,* were displayed at half-mast in token of respect to the departed captain.[2]

One may excuse the sentimentality of the *Herald's* reporter, for the friendship of Captains Bailey and Burrows was based on an exceptionally stout foundation of character and common experience and achievement. Neither had reached the prime of life, but both stood at the top of one of the most arduous of all professions. Ambrose Hilliard Burrows was only 30, but he had made two long voyages to Canton and had crossed the Western Ocean 66 times, and that when six crossings a year were rarely exceeded save by steamship masters. He had capped this record by the distinguished command of one of the crack Western Ocean packets. He was buried in the little family burying ground, now overgrown and deserted, on a Connecticut hillside looking out over the waters on which half his life had been passed. The inscription on his stone reads, in part:

> The pride of all our hopes lies here,
>
> * * *
>
> His sails now furled, his anchor cast
> Ne'er to be weighed again,
> No more he feels the wintry blast
> Nor dreads the raging main.

Whatever forces may have operated to transform raw New England farm boys like Ambrose Burrows, whose schooling ended with the "Three R's," into the cultured and gentlemanly commanders of noted passenger packets, they did not lack for precedents, and those of a sort which go far to explain the development of the American Merchant Marine. Ambrose was perhaps as fortunate as most in that respect, but he also had a somewhat special family tradition to maintain.

His father—also Ambrose H. Burrows—as a youth had commanded the little sloop *Hero* (the same in which Captain Nat Palmer discovered the Antarctic continent) in an expedition which cut the British armed sloop *Fox* out from under the guns of the blockading fleet off Stonington, Connecticut, in the War of 1812. Later he gave a still more striking demonstration of his quality while in command of the ex-sealing brig *Frederick.*

He had taken a cargo of provisions and Yankee notions a hard winter's passage around the Horn to Callao in 1823, and while trading on the coast was captured by pirates on the 27th of December. After plundering his vessel, Captain Mataleana of the piratical brig put a crew of ten men on board; removing all the original crew except Captain Burrows and his 16-year-old son Brutus, who were left to navigate the vessel to Chiloe, the hideout of the gang.

In spite of the odds, Burrows, who had previously secreted his pistols when he saw that his brig was about to be taken, determined to recapture her or die in the attempt. Seizing a favorable opportunity, he placed a pistol in his belt and took one in each hand, and told his son Brutus to take the others and follow him on deck, "saying to him at the same time, if I discovered in him the least sign of fear, I would forever disown him as a son." Reaching the deck, they cowed the helmsman and drove the watch forward into the forecastle "like a flock of sheep over a stone wall," where they were secured and eventually set adrift in the longboat under circumstances which ensured their reaching land safely.

Packets of the size and finish of the *Yorkshire, Queen of the West,* and *Liverpool* cost $100,000 and upwards; nearly double the cost of the average packet of the thirties. They were also about 40 feet longer and with nearly or quite two feet more headroom than the earlier "floating palaces." The enterprise reflected in such commitments was the more creditable in view of the fact that business conditions were at a low ebb and the outlook uncertain when they were ordered.

Construction of a few monster packets, however, by no means told the story. The demand for medium-sized ships, vessels equal to the greatest of the previous decade, was even more insistent. Less than two weeks after the festivities of the *Yorkshire,* the editor of the *New York Herald* noted the circumstance in his issue of January 22nd:

There seems to be a perfect mania in this city for new ships. One scarcely rounds off the Hook before another is ready to try her speed. Three are now on the stocks. One is for the London Line to take the place of the *Montreal;* the other will be launched this noon from the yard of William H. Webb, at the foot of Seventh street.

This new packet, to be dipped today, is named the *Zurich,* after the "fair Zurich waters" of Switzerland, and her model will astonish the cottagers living on the borders of that beautiful lake, and the brave mountaineers of Glavis and Schweitz, should they chance to see her. She is eight or nine hundred tons in size, and built like the *Montezuma* and *Yorkshire,* with all the late improvements. Her commander is to be Captain J. Johnston, formerly of the *Albany* and lately of the *Rhone,* and favorably known wherever the Gospel is read.

The *Zurich* is to take her place in the Union Line of Havre Packets, and will be the favorite of the "brave Swiss boys." All who can ought to see her launched, for she will be sent off completely rigged, "all a-taunto," as the sailors say.

The "mania" was not noticeably abated by news brought a few days later by the *Roscius,* "Express over the Atlantic." Business was beginning to boom in Europe. Prices were rising. The tide had turned and the normal needs of a growing world, supplemented by famine abroad and the gold of California and Australia, were to keep it at flood for ten long years.

Other fine two-deckers were soon afloat, but it was not until 1845 that the construction of three-deckers was resumed. In that year Brown & Bell launched the *Henry Clay* for Grinnell, Minturn & Company's Liverpool line. Her depth of hold was 29 feet, 8 inches and her registered tonnage was given as 1207 tons, although it was actually somewhat in excess of 1400 tons. The *New York Herald* for March 26, 1845, gives the following account of her launching:

> The new packet ship *Henry Clay* was launched yesterday morning from the yard of Brown & Bell, on the East River. She is 189 feet and 6 inches in length, 38 feet and 6 inches in breadth, 30 feet in depth, and 1402 tons in bulk. She is, probably, the longest, broadest and deepest merchant ship now floating on the ocean. In a word, she is a monster of the deep.
>
> The launch was a beautiful and highly successful one. It was witnessed by nearly ten thousand persons. Notwithstanding the crowds all around the ship—swarming on her decks and rigging—covering the sheds, fences and masts of other vessels near by—filling up every nook and corner with the carriages of the rich, the cabs of the moderate (in pocket) people, and the carts of laborers—not an accident happened.
>
> All went off smoothly as the ship glided into the Atlantic. Nothing marred the splendor of the day, the beauty of the thousand women present, the music of the band on board the packet, or the magnificence of the launch itself. Even the sailor who ascended to the bows of the ship to embrace the full length figure of Henry Clay, went off with eclat, although efforts were made to dislodge him.
>
> This new packet ship, so beautifully launched, is to be one of the best ever finished in this city. No money is to be spared to make her complete in every respect. She is the largest, and her owners, Messrs. Grinnell, Minturn & Co., and Capt. Ezra Nye, are determined to make her the handsomest. Her cabins are to be fitted up differently from those of other packet ships; they will be more costly and showy. . . . The rapid progress our shipwrights made in shipbuilding is to be seen from one launch to another. It is truly astonishing.

The next three-decker also went to the same line. She was the *New World,* built by Donald McKay in 1846. Her measurement was given as 1407 tons, although both her length and depth of hold were approximately two feet less than the dimensions of the *Henry Clay.* She was two feet wider than that vessel, but even with due allowance for that fact, it is evident that the tonnage rule was differently computed in the case of the two ships.

Three other three-deckers followed in quick succession: the *Constitution* of 1327 tons, built in 1846 by Brown & Bell for Woodhull & Minturn's line; the *Columbus,* of 1307 tons, a Portsmouth, New Hampshire, production by Fernald & Pettigrew for D. & A. Kingsland's line; and the *Ocean Monarch,* built by McKay in 1847 for Train's line. Interspersed among them were a number of noble two-deckers, ranging from 1000 to 1200 tons and upwards; ships like the *Columbia, Jamestown,* and *America,* the latter a 1200-tonner for the Kingsland line.

The seven New York firms who started transatlantic lines in 1842 included Boyd & Hincken, who, in association with Chamberlain & Phelps, put four small ships on the Marseilles run, while the Hurlbut line turned its attention to the Havre trade. All the others—Williams & Guion, Woodhull & Minturn, John Herdman, Samuel Thompson, and the Taylor & Merrill and Taylor & Ritch combinations—started lines to Liverpool. Williams & Guion were reported to be acting in cooperation with the Cunard Steamship Company, which did not carry steerage passengers. Both Herdman and Thompson were essentially passenger agents who had formerly acted in conjunction with the several established packet lines, and now concluded to control their own sailings, or, in the alternative, arrange for the exclusive use of certain ships of other lines for the transportation of their immigrants. It proved to be an arrangement which prospered mightily in the years ahead, and was soon adopted by a majority of the larger passenger offices, including the great Tapscott organization. What it portended may be gathered from the fact that as early as the spring of 1846 J. Herdman & Company, 61 South Street, and Herdman, Keenan & Company, 86 Waterloo Road, were advertising regular packet sailings every five days, in addition to transients guaranteed "to sail positively on their appointed days." The following spring Sam Thompson listed 16 ships of the "Thompson" or "Star" line scheduled to sail every six days.

Foreign trade dropped sharply in 1843, with the result that only three new transatlantic lines were started in that and the following year. One was a line to Antwerp, established in 1843 by Gerding & Kunkelman, a New York firm with offices at 15 Broad Street. David Ogden brought out the famous "St. George Line," popularly known as the "Red Cross," operating between New York and Liverpool, and Schmidt & Balchen, 83 Wall Street, founded a trimonthly service between Hamburg and New York.

There was a decided improvement in business in 1844 that carried through 1845, owing to a partial crop failure in Europe, and in 1846-47 developed into the greatest shipping boom in American history, stimulated by the Irish famine and short crop conditions everywhere in Europe and the need for vessels in the Mexican War; the only restraining influence, apparently, being a timidity in certain circles caused by a fear of war with England over the Oregon boundary. Freight charges tripled in some instances and rates everywhere were the highest known since the blockade-running days of the Napoleonic wars. Exports of foodstuffs jumped from $28,000,000 in 1846 to $69,000,000 the following year.[3]

The three years from 1845 to 1847, inclusive, witnessed the establishment of seven more lines between New York and Great Britain and Ireland. In 1845 Stanton & Frost added a Liverpool line to their other ventures, and Woodhull & Minturn put a Glasgow line, the second to that port, in operation. A line to Belfast was started by Richardson & Watson the following year, and the substantial firm of D. & A. Kingsland organized another to Liverpool which soon developed into one of the most important of the new lines. In 1847 three more Liverpool lines were established by the firms of Chamberlain & Phelps, Sturges & Clearman, and Messrs. Slate, Gardner & Howell, the latter being composed of comparatively recent arrivals from the old whaling port of Sag Harbor. About this time, also, Chamberlain & Phelps began to participate in the active management of the Boyd & Hincken line to Marseilles.

In marked contrast to New York, neither Philadelphia nor Baltimore showed any great interest in transatlantic lines. Both ports were to some extent handicapped in the matter of projects which involved regular year-round sailings by reason of the fact that they were often closed by ice for weeks at a time. A more important consideration, however, was the fact that by this time they had become so heavily involved in manufacturing and railroading and in certain aspects of the coastal trade, especially the rapidly expanding coal traffic, as to preclude extensive commitments in other fields. The coastal trade alone was becoming a major enterprise in which substantial fortunes were being realized. Its expansion is indicated by the frequency with which Philadelphia and Baltimore merchants were advertising as early as 1839-40 for vessels to carry coal to northern ports. The vision, dogged persistence, or crackpot enthusiasm of the individual who peddled the unpopular "hard-to-burn" Lehigh coal by the bushel from house to house in the Quaker City 20 years earlier, was paying off.

In this connection it is to be noted that a striking expansion of Maine's shipbuilding industry coincided closely with the growth of the coal trade in the early eighteen-forties. The point is of interest because of the impression in certain quarters that Maine functioned from time immemorial as the chief source of American ships. Many older persons will recall the saying "Maine built the ships and New York sailed them," still current in the closing years of the nineteenth century. Still more misleading are such specific claims as that published in 1904 to the effect that "Bath was the chief shipbuilding centre of the United States for over 100 years," and that "fully half the ocean vessels of the nation, up to 1900, were made in Maine."[4]

Such claims not only give a distorted picture of the entire maritime industry but of Maine's own record, in which the districts of Portland and Waldoboro once played quite as important a part as that of Bath. A more accurate impression may be gained from a comparison of official shipbuilding statistics for any year embraced in this study. The year 1834, for example, may be taken as fairly typical. In that year the entire state of Maine, which embraced several dozen shipbuilding centers, produced 174 vessels, totalling 28,503 tons of which Bath accounted for 6470 tons. In the same year the three states of Massachusetts, New York, and Maryland built 434 vessels, aggregating 53,552 tons.[5] The record, indeed, indicates that from 1800 to 1840—to go no further—New York City alone usually built from two to four times the tonnage produced by Bath each year.

It is also to be noted that very few large ships were built in Maine for ports south of Boston before 1842, that being the first year in which as many as three such vessels were sold to New York in a single year. The great majority of the craft which found their way to the New York market before that time and, indeed, for some years thereafter, were schooners and brigs ranging from 100 to 250 tons.

Maine's shipping record is sufficiently great and grand without the interpolation of claims that reflect on the progressiveness of other districts. It is doubtful whether any other state produced as great a tonnage in proportion to population. Certainly, man for man, the drive and energy displayed by the "Down Easters" was nowhere surpassed and rarely equalled. On the other hand, a large proportion of the Maine ship timber was inferior to that of other sections. Her vast pine and spruce forests produced comparatively little that equalled the oak which ranged from New Hampshire to Virginia. Her pine was less durable than the hard pine of the Carolinas and Georgia, while no other section produced timber equal to the live oak of the Gulf states. The fact explains why so many Maine vessels were described as "soft wood" ships and given inferior ratings by Lloyds. It may also be in a small measure responsible for the fact that New York looked mainly to Connecticut and Rhode Island, and occasionally to Portsmouth and Newburyport, to supply her lack of big vessels, until the growth of the coal trade, closely followed by the Irish famine of 1847 and the gold rush two years later, forced her to go farther afield for needed tonnage. However, it was long before Maine showed any marked tendency to monopolize the business. It was not, indeed, until 1847 that Bath showed any marked superiority over Portland in ship construction.

Save that most of Philadelphia's earlier vessels were built on the Delaware and in the Jerseys, and those of Baltimore were constructed in Maryland and Virginia, the above remarks may be taken as applying to those ports as well.

Philadelphia's only new Western Ocean lines came in the years 1845 to 1847, inclusive. In 1845 the firm of Mecke, Plate & Company started an emigrant line sailing out of Bremen. Richardson, Watson & Company, who already had a line between New York and Liverpool, founded a Philadelphia-Liverpool line in 1846. Sam Pleasants, of the old Quaker family of that name, started another Liverpool line in 1847.

Baltimore, as noted, established only one transatlantic line during the period; its second, by liberal interpretation. It was organized by the substantial Corner firm—James Corner & Sons—in 1849. Like the great majority of Western Ocean lines founded after 1837, it was an immigrant line, although it was equipped to carry first- and second-class cabin passengers, and frequently did, at rates well below those of the old, regular packets, especially on the eastbound passages.

While American merchants were establishing new and enlarging old lines to take advantage of the immigration boom, British and German merchants were by no means idle. From 1842 onward they engaged in the traffic in constantly increasing numbers, not only as agents of American lines but also as independent operators, sometimes combining the two functions. During the early part of the period under consideration by far the most active of such concerns was Caleb Grimshaw & Company, successor of the Messrs. Grimshaw who were specializing in emigration traffic as early as the late eighteen-twenties. When Sam Thompson decided to start his New York-Liverpool line in 1842, the Grimshaws became his Liverpool representatives but their activities did not end there. They secured passengers and freight not only for the Thompson packets but for many others, ranging from ships of other lines to run-of-the-mill transients, looking for what business they might pick up. Regardless of size, age, or origin, all proved to have "magnificent cabin accommodations" and "lofty and spacious second-class and steerage quarters" when they sailed under the Grimshaw "New Line" flag.

By 1845 the line was advertising a dozen or more ships at a time and dispatching them every five to seven days. In addition to the Thompson vessels they handled ships of several other lines, notably Herdman's,

Kingsland's and Kermit's, besides helping out an occasional Black Baller for good measure. So much business was coming their way, in fact, that they could not take care of it properly. Accordingly, in 1845 they delegated the steerage traffic to William Tapscott and George Rippard & Son, both of Liverpool. It was all the dynamic Tapscott needed to start the great firm of W. & J. Tapscott on its long and prosperous career. Before the year ended he had established branch agencies all over Great Britain and Ireland and had opened an office in New York. It was also a profitable arrangement for the Grimshaws for they continued to collect their commissions all along the line, in addition to retaining exclusive control of the lucrative freight and cabin traffic.

Their first-class cabin rate was 16 guineas as compared with the 39 guineas of the steamships and the 25 pounds and upwards of the old line packets; the saving it represented was equivalent to several hundred dollars in present-day purchasing power, and it attracted large numbers of "those who wished to go at an easy rate." That patronage explains in part the success of the Grimshaw and other similar lines soon to be established, although the unprecedented rise in emigration was by far the most potent factor. Grimshaw's progress, indeed, was so rapid that the proprietors decided a more imposing title was in order. Accordingly, in January, 1845, the name was changed from "New Line" to "Black Star" and it may be noted here that during the boom decade then under way more American emigrant ships cleared under the Black Star flag than under any other.

Grimshaw, however, was not the first to establish what may be termed "the one-way line" destined to play so important a part in the emigrant service. That distinction is to be credited to the dynamic P. W. Byrnes, who was active in the Liverpool steerage traffic in 1841 and for several years thereafter. Byrnes was a high-pressure character who did not permit the natural modesty of his race to restrain him from appropriating any credit that he found lying around loose. Although he was a shipless emigrant agent and nothing more, he began to advertise the vessels for which he supplied passengers as ships of the "Byrnes Lines," thus creating the impression that he arranged and controlled their sailing. This ingenious bit of "window dressing" failed to appeal to the old line operators, and when, in March, 1841, he advertised the Black Baller *Oxford* as one of his ships, it aroused the ire of Captain John Rathbone who decided to take immediate and appropriate action. He countered by inserting an advertisement in the same paper (*Liverpool Mercantile Gazette*) that after the usual "whereases" and "therefores" stated unequivocally that said "P. W. Byrnes has no authority." Nevertheless, as the traffic grew, competition increased, and in the end even the old-timers saw no reason to object to a practice that might mean a batch of 500 emigrants for one of their ships.

There were several British firms in 1841, or who appeared during the next five or six years, who eventually operated lines of this character. One of the greatest was Ingleby & Browne, who always operated in association with George Brown & Harrison. These firms and their successors, James Browne & Company and Brown & Harrison, etc., were responsible for dispatching hundreds of fine American ships in their various emigrant lines. Focke & Boult was another substantial house, as was Pilkington & Wilson, who ran "White Star" lines to Boston and New Orleans, and briefly to other American ports. Jacot, Taylor & Tipper also developed several one-way lines, including a short-lived line to Charleston in the early fifties. Among the individuals, the most important, as well as the most active, was John Taylor Crook, who handled the second division of the "Black Star" until his eclipse in 1851 by Guion & Company.

Some of the one-way firms had a foot on both shores, among them the Tapscotts and Messrs. Harnden & Company whose Liverpool office was an 1844 offshoot of the famous pioneer express company. Harnden, it appeared, was charged with a special mission. By this time another figure had entered the lists—the swindler and confidence man—whose operations among the ignorant steerage passengers were becoming notorious. Something of their extent may be judged from the fact that Harnden advertised that his company "was under the patronage of various benevolent societies established in New York for the purpose of protecting emigrants from fraud and imposition."[6]

Development of the coastal sailing packets closely paralleled the course of the ocean liners. Comparatively few new ventures were started in 1838, but the following year saw the beginning of an expansion that continued with few and minor interruptions for many years, and that dwarfed everything that had gone before. Altogether, roughly 125 coastal packet lines were established between the eight principal ports during the ten-year period. Nor does this include scores of short feeder lines, or a number of ventures soon abandoned, or lines between southern ports, including several between New Orleans and Charleston and Savannah.[7]

Boston accounted for two new coastal lines in 1838, one to New Orleans and another to Savannah. Both were established by Cabot & Frazer, of 94 State Street, who, however, did not continue long in the field. Their "Dispatch Line" to Savannah, indeed, was taken over the following year by Nathaniel Winsor, Jr., and Benjamin Bruce, of 103 State Street.

In New York, a new firm, Sturges & Clearman, destined to become one of the city's leading houses in the coastal trade, began operations the same year with the establishment of a Mobile line. O'Connor & Ryan were their agents until 1848, when they were succeeded by the Mobile firm of Fosdick & Charlock. Another newcomer in the packet field, Moses Taylor, an old New Yorker who was said to have started his long business career as rent collector for John Jacob Astor, organized a line of fast barks to Havana that year, the little *Rapid* being his pioneer packet. Still another firm, Post & Phillips, mentioned at this juncture because of the future importance of Ralph Post, its senior member, entered the growing Florida trade with a line of brigs and barks to Apalachicola.

Philadelphia's contribution for 1838 consisted of a couple of schooner lines started by James Hand, who was already heavily engaged in trade to various Chesapeake Bay points. The new ventures extended his operations to Savannah and Mobile. James is believed to have been a brother of the irrepressible Joseph Hand, another of Philadelphia's extremely active packet men. Both were natives of New Jersey, as many of the city's coastal shipping men were. For many years, in fact, the port depended largely on that state, for both coasting vessels and their commanders and operators. The James Hand lines were taken over in 1845 by Levi Eldridge, then and later an exceptionally successful operator.

A feeling of greater optimism characterized the shipping industry in 1839. General business was better, although the southern trade, as previously noted, was slowed down for a time by the yellow fever. More important new coastal lines were started than in any year since the war.

Boston's principal new venture was the Winsor & Bruce "Dispatch Line" to Charleston, which became the "Winsor Line" in 1844, when the partners broke up. Aside from this there was a second line of five schooners running to Hartford and an unusual development in the shape of a voluntary association of eight independent masters of packet schooners plying between Boston and Portsmouth, New Hampshire. Wainwright & Tappan, 25 Central Wharf, started a ship line to Savannah, which seems to have operated briefly and irregularly, and Edmund Wright, Sr., founded a line of schooners to Mobile.

New York acquired a couple of substantial lines. Dunham & Dimon, 67 South Street, and L. Baldwin, Esq., were the New York and Savannah agents, respectively, of the "Georgia Line," which seems to have operated much of the time in close association with the "Old Established Line," often loading the same vessels. Peter Laidlaw also got back into the New

Orleans business with the "New Line." Johnson & Lowden, 86 Wall Street, were associated with him in the venture for some time. John Laidlaw & Company put the rejuvenated steamer *Natchez* on the New York-New Orleans run, fare in the main cabin $100.

It remained for Philadelphia to break the coastal packet record. In 1839 her merchants established 14 lines of considerable importance. Seven of them were founded by Armer Patton, whose lines ran to New York and all the important southern ports and the smaller cities of Wilmington and Washington, North Carolina. Three lines, to Charleston, Savannah, and New Orleans, respectively, were started by the firm of Barclay and Bernabeu, of 9 North Wharves. The firm of Missroon & Milliken represented their line in Charleston; White & Bartel, in Savannah; and Messrs. Moss & Harris, in New Orleans. The latter firm was succeeded by Aaron Cohen in 1842.

Another of Philadelphia's many notable men climbed into greater prominence that year. Richard F. Loper, who had come up through the hawsepipe of a Stonington sealer, thereby becoming an adept in the art and mystery of skinning, took a post-graduate course in packet sloops and schooners between Philadelphia and Hartford during the twenties. He now decided to start a line of his own on a new principle and put three schooners and a brig on the Hartford run, sending them through the Delaware & Raritan Canal. The schooners belonged to a highly specialized type which came to be known as "canal schooners." They were extremely long and narrow, shallow-draft vessels, ranging about 100 feet in length with a beam of 17 feet, or thereabouts—roughly eight feet narrower than the ordinary schooner of the same length. Palmer & Hale, of Market Street Wharf, were associated with Loper in the venture for a time.

The difficulty of operating brigs and schooners over a canal route which began and ended in long swift rivers was, perhaps, sufficiently obvious, especially after Ericsson came along with his tug. At all events, Loper soon shifted to steam, with the result that his subsequent career as a steamship man was noteworthy in a day when remarkable careers were commonplace. A secondary consequence of the increased employment of steam on the canals was the tremendous step-up in the construction of canal boats and tow barges of the larger size all through the forties.

Interest in the coastal packets, which had resulted, in 1839, in the establishment of 29 substantial lines in the four principal northern ports, continued unabated through 1847. It manifested itself not only in organization of new lines but in far-reaching improvement of old lines. To cite a typical instance, the firm of Johnson & Lowden, of New York, had been operating the "Old Regular Line" between New York and Baltimore with a lot of old, well-worn schooners, ranging from 125 to 175 tons, several of them with a waterline length of less than 75 feet, with cabin accommodations in proportion. In the space of a single year (1845) they added four smart new schooners of 200 tons and upwards. They had a waterline length of 90 and a beam of 26 feet and upwards, and their large and handsomely decorated cabins set new standards of comfort and privacy in the shorter coastal lines.[8]

The great majority of Boston's new lines ran to Philadelphia, Savannah, Mobile, and New Orleans; the number in each case ranging from five to seven, reflecting New England's growing demand for flour and cotton. Only one new line was started to New York, indicating that six were sufficient to handle that traffic. Four were established to Baltimore and Charleston; two to each port.

Among the new Boston operators, the following may be noted in order of appearance: Nathaniel Winsor, Jr., who developed strong lines to Savannah and New Orleans; John H. Pearson, a tremendously energetic man, whose line to New Orleans was outstanding, and who established several others of first importance so far as volume of business was concerned; Alfred C. Hersey and Messrs. Bigelow & Cunningham, who had excellently managed lines to Philadelphia and New York, and R. Lincoln & Company. Charles T. Savage, William and Henry Lincoln, J. Silloway & Company, and J. H. Rivers were also active toward the close of the period and for some years thereafter. Several of the foregoing acquired existing concerns in addition to the new lines which they organized.

New York's interest in new coastal lines centered chiefly on New Orleans. In all, twelve strong lines were established between the two ports during the ten-year period. Baltimore came next in New York's interest with six lines, while only four sailing lines were started to Philadelphia. This, however, was not because of any disproportionate increase in trade with Baltimore, but because, as previously noted, two large steamboat lines were put on the run between New York and Philadelphia.

Among the New Yorkers who engaged heavily in coastal sailing packet enterprises, the following are especially worthy of mention.

In 1840, John Ogden put a new line in operation to Galveston, and soon added a Wilmington line. In 1841 he founded a line of brigs to Savannah. Another 1840 venture destined to become of more than passing importance was Spofford & Tileston's Havana line. John Elwell, 57 South Street, established a very substantial line to New Orleans in 1841, and another to Charleston in 1845.

Robert L. Taylor and Nathaniel W. Merrill, doing business as Taylor & Merrill, were responsible for another very active line to New Orleans in 1842. Hargous Brothers & Company, 33 South Street, put on a line to Vera Cruz the same year, which may have been a continuation of the old Cadillac line. In the same year, also, J. O. Ward, who had been running brigs to the West Indies for some years, announced the start of a line to Matanzas.

I. B. Gager, 88 Wall Street, formerly of Baltimore, had a line to Baltimore in 1844. He was soon metamorphosed into Gager & Mailler, with lines to Philadelphia and New Orleans, the firm becoming in turn Mailler & Lord and then Mailler, Lord & Quereau, an important house of the fifties. N. L. McCready & Company, of 7 Coenties Slip, also had a new line to Baltimore, started about the same time. In 1844, also, Nesmith & Walsh, formerly Nesmith & Leeds, put on two new lines, one to Savannah and one to New Orleans.

In 1845, Brower & Neilson engaged in the cotton trade with a line to Galveston, which was continued in 1847 by John H. Brower, later one of the prominent clipper ship operators of New York.

Not all the new coastal lines were started by the above newcomers. A number were founded by old New York firms who were engaged in operating one or more lines prior to 1838, some of which, indeed, continued to expand their operations until the depression which ended in the panic of 1857.

In Philadelphia the establishment of coastal lines was carried on in 1842 by Stilwell S. Bishop, a newcomer who eventually became one of the port's largest ship operators. He was especially active in the California clipper trade. Prior to that, he organized a line to Mobile, and his success in that venture enabled him to take over the management of the Barclay & Bernabeu lines to New Orleans, Savannah, and Charleston in 1843.

Another New Orleans line of considerable magnitude was established in 1843 by the firm of Penrose & Burton. In 1845 Alexander Heron & Company put on a service to Charleston, following up with one to New Orleans in 1846, and another to Savannah in 1847. Other Philadelphia coastal ventures during the period included lines to New Orleans and Savannah, for which A. J. Harper & Company were agents; a line to New Orleans represented by B. Lincoln & Company, and one to Charleston managed by A. J. Culin & Company. All three got under way in 1846.

Very few lines to southern ports were started by Baltimore from 1838 to 1847, inclusive, partly for the reason that the port was engaging more and more in the lucrative South American and West Indian trades. On the other hand, her merchants took part—and sometimes the leading part —in the establishment of lines already referred to, running to other northern ports. Thomas Whitridge was one. He traded principally to northern cities during this period and was responsible for starting several large and well-managed lines.

Other Baltimore operators included the old master mariner, Thomas Hooper, who organized a line to Mobile in 1841; Charles Pendergast & Son, a Charleston line; John Henderson & Company, 77 Pratt Street, trading to New Orleans; and William Mason, 88 Spear's Wharf, who put on a smart schooner service to Wilmington, North Carolina.

Increase in size and quality of vessels was quite as important as the number of lines added. This improvement was less marked in the brig and schooner than in the ship lines, partly for the reason that the former existed primarily to supply the need for small craft, which was quite as urgent as the need for big two-deckers. Consequently, improvement of the schooners and brigs was mainly in the direction of speed and cabin appointments, although by 1842 or thereabouts there was a definite tendency to increase their size as well.

Another development of the period was a much greater use of the economical bark rig. This rig had been growing in popularity all through the 1830's. By the 1840's its use was threatening the ancient reign of the brig and ship for it was increasing in size quite as rapidly as in numbers. During the 1830's the rig was confined almost exclusively to vessels ranging from 175 to 200 tons. By 1847 barks of 400 tons and upwards were common.

Most of the coastal packets of the 1820's had been single-decked craft with a depth of hold ranging up to 10 feet for brigs and schooners, and 15 feet for ships. Even in the New Orleans lines where the packets averaged larger than elsewhere, few measured more than 300 tons. The 416-ton *Kentucky*, built in 1827 by Scott & Fickett for the Holmes line, held the coastal record for size for several years.

In the 1830's the limit had been raised; at first by such fine, speedy craft as the 523-ton *Huntsville* and the slightly larger *Creole;* and then in 1833 by several which exceeded 600 tons, to which class the 678-ton *Yazoo* and the 647-ton *Mississippi* belonged. Aside from the old Dramatic liner *Shakespeare,* transferred to the New Orleans run in 1838, it was not until

1841 that the 700-mark was passed by the *Memphis* of the Collins line, a ship of 798 tons with cabins superior in size and finish to the smartest of the earlier vessels.

Coastal packets on the longer routes had also been improved in another respect, an improvement so advantageous that eventually it was adopted by the Western Ocean lines. Besides being single-deckers, nearly all the early packets were flush-decked, or virtually so. All cabins were below and as they were little more than six feet in height, the sun beat down on them with blistering heat in summer, while in winter they were excessively damp, cold and uncomfortable. The new two-deckers were built with a high, raised poop on the spar deck, which made it possible to raise the height of the cabins without invading the cargo space, and also secured maximum ventilation for the staterooms. Another innovation was the construction of one or more large deck houses that could be used for steerage accommodations.

It cannot be said that these "improvements" met with universal acceptance. On the contrary, some of them were anathema to a stout minority of the older shipmasters, who had few good words for the newfangled ideas of ship operators who put financial considerations too near the top of the list. Most of them, indeed, had few words for anything, but old Captain John Codman of Boston—the Captain Ringbolt of *A Sailor's Life and a Sailor's Yarns*—was articulate enough. When word came in the summer of 1847 that Warren Delano's new immigrant ship *Mameluke* was lost on her first voyage, boarded while lying to in a hurricane the night of August 15th by a tremendous sea which swept away her deck house with 38 steerage passengers who would have been saved if they had been sleeping below in a flush-deck ship, he dipped his pen in caustic:

> We must be allowed to express an opinion that there is no improvement in the fast sailing and real beauty of former times. Instead of the former beautiful symmetry of spars and hull, so gratifying to the seaman's eye, barks (ugly, half formed things) are the order of the day: the sticks of a three hundred ton ship are stuck into one of five hundred; and the decks, instead of exhibiting the clear and flush appearance of former days, so convenient for working ship, are now cluttered up with so many houses and blocks of buildings, that one can scarcely find his way fore and aft without a directory. These sort of vessels are real eyesores . . .[9]

Nevertheless, deck houses, poop decks, and the bark rig were here to stay. Coastal operators faced—or thought they faced—the constant necessity of securing additional paying space and effecting new economies. This, as yet, was less a matter of steam competition than of the multiplication of sailing lines with their new and bigger ships. Steam, indeed, had cut deeply into the revenues of the shorter lines between the northern ports but had made no very serious inroads elsewhere. On the lines to Charleston and points south, the key to profitable operations still lay in larger and more luxurious sailing craft, even after the steamship *Southerner* began her fortnightly rounds.

Cabin fares to Charleston and Savannah in the crack packets of 1847 still held their original levels, $25 to $30 depending on location of staterooms. Comparable liners to the Gulf ports charged $100 with, and $80 without, wines. Inferior packets and transients had to be content with cuts ranging to 25 per cent and upwards; no small consideration in a day when Delmonico's best steak dinner cost ten cents and the weekly rate for board and room in the best New York boarding houses averaged $2.50, with reductions for permanent patrons.

In 1847 the ascendancy of steam still lay in an undreamed future. Men were still saying that it might do on short hauls but could never replace sail on the long runs, just as they were saying 50 years later that sail would always be needed on the great circle routes to the Orient and on the hard Cape Horn passage. In spite of the ominous preparation of the steamerites for the construction of a dozen liners of unprecedented power, the canvas-backers were supremely confident of their ability to meet any conceivable competition. And so they were. It was the inconceivable that put them out of business.

Their attitude was reflected—albeit somewhat humorously—by a paragraph that adorned the pages of the *New York Herald* on Wednesday morning, January 13th, 1847:

> The packet ship *Yorkshire,* Captain Bailey, takes the place of the steamer of the 16th inst. This packet, under the command of Capt. B., is equal to the speed of any steamer, and the stoppage of the mail boat for that day will never be noticed. It will be recollected that Capt. B. brought over the charming little Viennoises in 16 days and a pirouette—Those beautiful children were so delighted with him and his ship that they danced the splendid Pas des Fleurs on his quarter deck in coming up the harbor, and on Saturday presented him with a magnificent silver pitcher, with their hearts engraved all over it—all of which was very beautiful and touching.

In spite of the long depression, the ravages of pestilence, and the inroads of steam, the years from 1838 to 1847 were the great years of the coastal sailing packet. Not that the contest ended then. The coming years were to see their competitive efforts redoubled; see larger and more efficient vessels; see them clustered still more thickly along waterfronts resounding with an ever-louder clamor of feverish activity; see more beautiful craft —the swift, rakish clipper brigs and barks and the smart four, five, and six hundred-ton schooners of the fifties—but so far as the travelling public was concerned, their day had passed. They came and went unnoted. Their captains, once the toast of the itinerant aristocracy, no longer collected golden harvests from letter bags at John Gilpin's, or played genial host to crowded cabins. They sailed with empty staterooms, their glory vanished, their status reduced to mere navigators of cargo droghers. The steamships carried the passengers and the mails. They monopolized the transportation of fine merchandise. Their commands were sought by ever-increasing numbers of the ablest master mariners, while others flocked to the brave new clipper ships.

During the ten-year period, sailing packet losses, both deep-water and coastwise, had been rather more serious than usual. In addition to those mentioned earlier in the chapter, the *President,* bound for London from New York, got on the Nore Sands and was so badly wracked that she was sold at auction, fetching only 850 pounds. This was in 1841.

Shipwrecks with loss of life were commonly marked by agonizing scenes, but the annals of the sea hold no more harrowing tale than that of the loss of the emigrant ship *William Brown.* She foundered in June, 1841, shortly after striking an iceberg. Part of her complement pulled away in the boats, leaving of necessity upwards of 30, mostly passengers, to go down with the ship. The longboat had 33 persons, including a large proportion of the crew. Shortly after leaving the ship the mate in charge had 16 of the passengers thrown overboard.

After the lapse of more than a century, one cannot read the account of the scenes enacted on that little craft as one by one the victims—young girls as well as men—were forced over the side, without a feeling of indescribable horror.

In the same year Sidney B. Whitlock's *Poland* was struck by lightning and burned on the 16th of May. The following year the old *Britannia* was lost. Two grand old packets went missing in December, 1845, the *England,* Captain Samuel Bartlett, and the *United States,* commanded by Thomas Britton, a brother of John Britton who then had the *Rochester* which was lost on the Blackwater in April, 1847, under the command of Philip Woodhouse. The following month Train's *Anglo Saxon* stranded on Cape Sable and became a total loss.

The latter year, indeed, was exceptionally hard on Western Ocean packet masters but it enabled one of them to make a notable contribution to scientific and geographical knowledge, as the following extract from a New York paper attests:

THE USE OF THE BAROMETER AND THE DISCOVERY OF SYMMES'S HOLE.—The precise position of the mysterious place known to navigators by the name of Symmes's Hole, has at length been discovered, a fact which seriously interests our packet and ship masters.

To Captain Dunn, of the ship *Philadelphia,* is due the credit of having first, solely through his faith in the barometer, learned its whereabouts. It may now be set down on the charts, and as the latitude and longitude is given in the annexed letter from Captain Dunn, it is very easily found. We hope some of our indefatigable "chart makers" will cause a survey of the entrance to be made immediately:—

Ship *Philadelphia* at sea. Mr. Editor—Permit me to make a remark that may be beneficial to shipping generally. It may not be amiss, as many of my brother chips put no faith in the barometer. On the morning of the 7th of March it was blowing strong from the S.E., ship under closereefed topsails, courses furled; the wind moderated and the weather continued fine for two hours. Now if I had been without a barometer, with a fair wind and high freights in prospect, I would have made sail and been totally dismasted, but the mercury was down to 28.10. Thinking a new closereefed topsail would stand anything, I employed the time during the lull to put extra gaskets on the furled sails. At 10:30 A.M. it came out butt end first, burst the foretopsail like a cannon shot, the main one stood a few minutes longer and followed suit—Fore topmast staysail, a new sail, patent banded, every square foot of canvas a double seam, blew to tatters; foresail and main spencer were torn away from under the gaskets. When I find the barometer down to 28.10 again, I'll put the ship under bare poles, batten down the hatches, and lay alongside the keelson until the frolic is over. Gentle skippers, I recommend you to pay attention to the barometer: it is one of the best friends you have.

I have frequently experienced extra heavy gales about this lat. 45, and long. 40. Last September I was dismasted within 20 leagues of the same spot. I am sure here must be the northern entrance to Symmes's Hole. All the gales that have blown about the Atlantic for six months, congregate here at the equinoxes, and enter Symmes's Hole with a perfect rush. The reason ships don't get into it, is because the water makes a counter current to the wind. (We always experience a southerly current hereabouts.) And this accounts for ships escaping the mouth of the hole. You may rest assured Mr. Editor, if you ever have any news from Symmes's Hole, you will find the meeting houses down there are shingled with old sails.[10]

Among the coastal packets, the 685-ton *Fairfield,* of Johnson & Lowden's New York-New Orleans line was lost on the Bahamas in September, 1844, and the slightly smaller *Yazoo* of the Collins line was wrecked in the spring of 1847. Other losses included the ship *Trenton,* bark *Gazelle,* and brig *Charles P. Williams.*

A sad chapter in coastal history was written in February, 1846. On the night of the 14th the ship *John Minturn,* from New Orleans for New York, went ashore on Barnegat in a heavy snow storm. Captain Dudley Stark, his wife and two children, and all the passengers and crew took refuge in the rigging, where all 41 slowly froze to death. Meanwhile the crowds assembled on the nearby beach, looting the wreckage as it drifted ashore, made not the slightest attempt to rescue them.

The period, notwithstanding its many promising developments, was destined to end on this note. Early in December, 1847, word came back to New York that the fine packet *Stephen Whitney* of the Kermit line, had been lost with Captain C. W. Popham and over 90 of his passengers and crew. The *Whitney* had sailed from New York for Liverpool on October 17th with a crew and passenger list of 110. At 10 P.M., the night of November 10th, she struck on the West Calf, a rock near Cape Clear, and went to pieces in a few minutes. Only 18 were saved.

It was recalled at the time that four years earlier, almost to an hour, Captain Popham had narrowly escaped a similar fate in the old packet *Sheffield*. He had been dismasted off Sandy Hook and had drifted on to the Romer Shoals the night of November 11th, where the ship filled. With four feet of water in the cabin, Captain Popham, with many a joke and exhortation to "hold on tight," back-packed his lady passengers to the dubious safety of the quarter-deck. All were rescued eventually, but the ship was so badly wracked that she was sold out of the line.

CHAPTER XII

∽ *1848-1857* ∽

Steam Brings Up the Reserves

"New-fashioned, in a mould of vaster powers."

ALTHOUGH the outlook for steam packet service on the Western Ocean in 1847, viewed from the standpoint of material achievement, was far from promising, powerful invisible forces—some of which have been indicated—were already in motion that within the year would so far change the situation as to make victory seem inevitable. They appeared in various guises, but their sum was the enticing prospect of greater and more dependable speed.

Whether the Cunard line, then the only survivor of the original companies, would of its own volition have improved its service to the point where it would pose a serious threat to the sailing liner, is at best doubtful. The fact was that in nearly eight years it had made no appreciable advance either in speed, comfort, or frequency of sailings. The only steamers it had added in that time, the *Hibernia* and *Cambria,* were to replace the lost *Columbia* and to enable it to maintain its original schedule, rather than to effect positive improvements. Both were inferior in several respects to earlier vessels, rating less than half the tonnage of the *Great Britain,* and barely half a knot faster than the first Cunarder, a nine-knot ship. Possibly Messrs. Burns & McIver were "cogitating" changes for the better, but if so their mental processes must have been somewhat accelerated by the passage of the Act of 1845, followed, as it was, by rumors of big Yankee liners planned and a-building and still more comprehensive acts on the congressional agenda.

During the previous ten years, the marine engineers of America—to say nothing of Scotland—had acquired an education of sorts; at an enormous cost, it is true, but the results, though spotty, had been reasonably commensurate, as demonstrated by the huge 19-knot river boats and the efficiency attained by recent coastal steamships both in America and Great Britain.

275

Self-taught engineers—John Ericsson, Robert L. Stevens, Richard F. Loper, and a few more—and scores of bright young men in a dozen great plants, even then employing hundreds of mechanics on engines that towered from bed to massive walking-beam the height of a four-story building, were feverishly transmuting visions into lighter, more compact, more powerful, and more efficient machinery. They still had a long way to go, but there was no gainsaying the fact that they had already outstripped the wildest prophecies of 1819 and the little *Savannah.* Moreover, they were supremely confident in their ability to match the talents of Europe. It was a confidence that seemed to be justified by recent successes, and was certainly so regarded by the travelling public, who were both willing and able to pay a premium for speedier transportation.

Naval architects also had acquired invaluable experience. In particular, they had learned at the price of a heavy toll of life and property that the steam engine, far from making lighter hull construction everywhere permissible, as in the case of the flimsy river boats, demanded stronger than standard construction for ocean-going steamships. Their earlier vessels had demonstrated an alarming tendency to founder in fairly moderate weather; their latest examples rode the hurricane.

These and other previously noted considerations conspired to develop interest in steamships to an unprecedented degree in 1847 among practical operators, and to push it to new heights in the following year. If 1838 had been Britain's steamship year, 1848 was America's beyond a shadow of a doubt. Every effort was made to set afloat an imposing array of the greatest and finest craft skill and scientific attainments had yet produced, and it is to be noted that efforts were not confined to the government-supported mail lines. Several large, independent steamers were completed early in 1848 and others started throughout the year, a statement which conveys a quite inadequate conception of the boldness with which vast sums were being risked in a venture that had almost invariably proved a losing one.

One of the first of the new independents, the steamship *United States,* had already made her first trip to England. Her trials were held in February, 1847, with the result that she was credited with an average speed of 13 knots, a rate which might be reduced to eight or nine knots in rough weather at sea. Some 30 New York merchants and shipmasters contributed toward her construction. She registered 1858 tons, as compared with the 1600 tons of the new Cunarders.

She sailed for Liverpool under Black Ball management on the 8th of April with 46 passengers. It was later reported that Sam Cunard had made suitable arrangements for her reception, including an extremely liberal but quite temporary reduction in freight and passenger rates. However that may be, Charles H. Marshall concluded to change her destination for Havre in the future. That arrangement was cut short a few months later by a new development which caused her to be taken up for the New York-Chagres run.

Other independent steamships of the larger sort included the *Isabel,* 1215 tons, built in Baltimore, and the 900-ton *Philadelphia,* built in Philadelphia. Both were completed in 1848 and both proved exceptionally fast. Vanderbilt was later so favorably impressed with the speed of the *Isabel* that he bought her for his Nicaragua line. She was credited with 15 knots under favorable conditions.

The *Hermann,* second steamer of the Bremen line, made 13 knots on her trial trip, the 8th of March, a rate suggesting, roughly, a nine-knot average performance at sea. Her engines by Stillman & Allen rated 1600 horsepower, far in excess of the stated, though probably not greatly in excess of the actual power of the new Cunarders.

Owing to disagreement among the subscribers to the first American mail company, some of whom wished to make Havre, rather than Bremen, the European terminus, it was decided to form a second company to be known as the New York & Havre Steam Navigation Company, to build and operate the two remaining vessels, originally intended for the Ocean Steam Navigation Company. Under the energetic leadership of Mortimer Livingston, proprietor of the "First Line" of Havre sailing packets, the *Franklin,* a 2200-tonner with a length of 263 feet, was ready in the summer of 1850. She proved to be faster and more efficient than either the *Washington* or *Hermann,* her best time being 11 days, 8 hours from New York to the Needles, indicating that in the matter of speed she was in the class of the new Cunarders.

The second steamship of the line, the *Humboldt,* was slightly larger but not so fast as the *Franklin.* Both were short-lived. The *Humboldt* was lost December 5th, 1853, while attempting to enter Halifax to refuel. The *Franklin* went ashore near Montauk Point, Long Island, July 17th, 1854. In neither case was there any loss of life.

Thereafter, the line employed the coastal steamships *Union, St. Louis,* and *Nashville* until the completion of its new ships, the *Arago* and *Fulton,* in 1855 and 1856, respectively. They measured 2300 tons; were 280 feet in length and proved to be the most economical and generally efficient of the early American transatlantic paddle steamers. Under the able management of Livingston the company survived the panic of 1857 and the

Civil War, notwithstanding the loss of its mail contract. When it ceased operation in 1867, it was the only American steamship company in the Western Ocean service.

Although the two lines cut heavily into the first-class traffic of the sailing liners, the Bremen concern was markedly inferior to the Cunarders in performance. We would not go far wrong, indeed, in terming it, as several contemporary critics did, a complete failure. At all events, something of its quality is indicated by the fact that it was found necessary to lay up both steamers for the entire winter of 1849-50 in order to make indispensable changes and repairs.

The first vessels of the Havre line were better, but it is doubtful whether they were equal to the new Cunarders.

On all counts, therefore, it was left to the new Collins liners to prove that America could equal, if not surpass, her European competitors in the design, construction, and operation of ocean steamships. The first two, the *Atlantic* and *Pacific,* were launched about midday, the 1st of February, 1849, roughly 11 months from the laying of their keels. Another year was to elapse before they were ready to sail. Both registered approximately 2850 tons, but were actually larger than their official figures indicate. In size they greatly exceeded all steamships afloat with the exception of the *Great Britain*. In quality of accommodations and luxurious appointments they were superior to all others of their year, with the possible exception of the *Cresent City,* which was finished on a notably lavish scale. In due course it appeared that they were somewhat faster than the new Cunarders. Whether they would demonstrate a similar superiority in the critical point of efficient and economical operation, time alone would show.

Long before that question could be decided, the big steamers of the other authorized American mail lines had established several new records for fast and safe performance.

The *Crescent City,* first of the new U. S. Mail Line between New York and New Orleans, made 16 knots on her trial trip, May 30th, 1848. On her first voyage to New Orleans she was credited with reducing the running time to six days, which seems probable in view of the fact that she made the round trip in 20 days, including stopovers, arriving back in New York with 180 passengers. On her second trip she brought 463 passengers (245 cabin and 218 steerage), a rather convincing demonstration of what was in store for the coastal sailing packets. Running up the Florida coast on her third round, she reported making 376 miles on the 20th of August —with the unacknowledged assistance of the Gulf Stream.[1]

Other fine steamers were coming thick and fast.

Howland & Aspinwall's *California,* 1100 tons, the first of their Panama-Oregon U. S. Mail Line (later the Pacific Mail) was launched by Webb on May 19th, just as Dame Fortune was completing special arrangements for her reception on the banks of the Sacramento.

Down in Savannah several merchants, including Joseph S. Fay, Robert Habersham, and the ex-Bostonian, ex-Philadelphian, Edward Padelford, had decided to out-do Charleston. As a result, the 1350-ton *Cherokee* was launched in New York on June 12th. She was put under the management of Sam Mitchell, who had been running small sailing craft between New York and Savannah for several years, but who speedily proved that he was capable of greater things.

In October his second steamer, the *Tennessee,* was afloat to round out a weekly service between the two ports, until she was snapped up by Howland & Aspinwall to meet an unexpected situation in California.

Several days later another new steamship firm, Messrs. J. Howard & Son, 73 South Street, New York City, put their pioneer steamship *Galveston,* built in 1845 for the New Orleans-Galveston trade, on the run between New York and New Orleans. An insignificant craft from the standpoint of progress, she was adequately skippered by John R. Crane.

Still another New York-New Orleans packet steamer, the smart 1000-ton *Falcon,* was put under the joint management of Marshall O. Roberts and Wetmore & Cryder, also of 73 South Street. Wetmore & Cryder soon withdrew, but Roberts will be heard from again.

Aside from the Collins liners, the largest of the new steamers were designed for the Chagres line of an ex-farm boy, "Hell Fire" (alias "Live Oak") George Law. The 2500-ton *Ohio* was launched August 12th and the 2800-ton *Georgia* followed on the 6th of September. The deck length of the latter was 275 feet.

Meanwhile, news had been arriving from the West Coast which was to exercise a profounder effect on the future of steam and sail—and indeed on the course of history in general—than the activities of all the monarchs of civilization.

In August of the ever-memorable year of 1848, as the echoes of abortive revolutions were dying away in Europe, a letter came telling of a remarkable gold discovery in California. Few, apparently, gave it a second thought. It was followed a month later by another which Bennett printed in the *New York Herald* on the 17th of September under the stereotyped heading, "Interesting from California." It was one of the rare occasions when the wild Scot missed the boat. How interesting it was, he discovered three days later when Midshipman Beale arrived in Washington "express from California" with full, official confirmation of the richest gold strike of modern times.

America went to bed on the 20th of September, 1848, enveloped in general with a soothing alcoholic aroma but otherwise sound in mind and body. It awoke on the 21st with a temperature. Experts were not long in diagnosing a serious case of "yellow fever."

Weeks before this, Howland & Aspinwall, already a prosperous clipper ship firm, but atop of that, destined shortly to rate the luck of the century, had been advertising their new steamship *California* "positively" for San Francisco—then a village of 500 shack dwellers—on September 25th, with the *Panama* to follow in December. The news of the 21st changed their modest calculations. It was only through the greatest exertions that they were able to get the *California* off on October 2nd, crowded with gold seekers and their hastily assembled picks and pans. Even then, their wildest imaginings fell far short of the fortune in store for them, and the same was true of every shipowner in America.

As late as the 10th of November only three vessels in New York were "up for California" by way of the Horn. On the 10th of December there were 43.[2] By then thousands were clamoring for transportation, and it was evident that all the ships available, sail and steam alike, would not be enough.

With the fare to Chagres, on the Caribbean shore of the mosquito-plagued Isthmus of Panama, fixed at the bonanza price of $150, and cabin passengers competing for six feet of deck space, Law was in a position to induce Sam Mitchell to pull his new Savannah steamer *Falcon* out of the line, to sail December 1st. He promised that other fast steamships would follow, pending the completion of the *Ohio* and *Georgia*. On the day before Christmas he cleared the steamships *Crescent City* and *Isthmus,* and they sailed for Chagres to the cheers of thousands assembled to see them off. At Chagres the gold-hungry passengers debarked. They walked to the Pacific side through 50 miles of swamps, mountains, and jungles. Those who survived then had to catch a ship north to California. It was seven years before a railroad was put through from one side of the isthmus to the other.

The rush was on. Other prominent steamship men were studying the situation, among them Vanderbilt and Charles Morgan. By then it required no special clairvoyance to foresee that whatever California gold might do for the world, it would accelerate American steamship development to a notable degree.

Nor was progress confined to the big craft. The short haul operators were busy. Hogg & Delamater and the ironworks of H. R. Dunham & Company, both located on the North River, New York City, were turning out small iron propellers of the Ericsson pattern. One of the Dunham craft was a 360-ton revenue cutter, the *Legare,* said to be the first of five similar vessels, all to be powered by Ericsson engines built by the Phoenix Foundry.

In Philadelphia, Loper had a large steamer or two under construction, but he was launching small iron propellers in rapid succession, boats of 125 tons for towing and lightering, and others ranging up to 600 tons for the shorter coastal runs, especially to the ports between Boston and Wilmington, North Carolina. Wilmington, Delaware, and Baltimore were also turning out small steamers in profusion, with an occasional sizeable craft for makeweight.

Boston was expanding its steamship service eastward as far as Nova Scotia with craft ranging up to 500 tons or thereabouts, and New York was steadily forging ahead in sound and river, as well as ocean steam navigation. Among others, the port laid down the steamboat *New World.* Her 367 feet made her the longest vessel in the world when she was launched, surpassing even the 318-foot *Oregon.* Her iron paddle wheels, 46 feet in diameter, constituted another record and helped her set new speed records of upwards of 22 statute miles an hour. For the first time New York's steam tonnage, launched and building in 1848, exceeded her sailing tonnage.

In 1849, however, the situation was sharply reversed. California's needs and promises were too pressing. Sailing ships of the largest size could be launched ready for sea in four months, while it took nearly two years to get a large ocean steamer ready for her trial trips, to say nothing of the fact that one cost several times as much as the other. Consequently, comparatively few large steamships were started in 1849, although several laid down in the previous year were launched.

Law's steamers, being smaller, were ready for service before the Collins vessels. His *Ohio* sailed on her maiden trip to Chagres with a full passenger list on the 20th of September. She was superbly appointed after the standards of the day. Two sets of washtroughs, instead of the usual one, were provided for first-class passengers. Equally lavish bathroom facilities were furnished on request, by a bucket brigade.

Howland & Aspinwall found all their planning had been on a far too modest scale, and they were compelled to go into the open market and pay premium prices to operators whose needs were less pressing. In addition to Sam Mitchell's *Tennessee,* they eventually bought Spofford & Tileston's *Northerner* and several other steamers. Meanwhile, the latter firm found themselves in a position to supplement their sailing service to Havana by putting the new 1125-ton S.S. *Isabel* on the run.

Though the great sailing ships—packets, immigrant liners, Cape Horners, and China traders—of 1849 greatly exceeded the new steamships in numbers, it was on the whole a year of progress for the latter. In particular, the reports of their financial success, their fast and regular passages, and even the spectacular appeal of their sailings broke down the resistance of many a skeptical canvas-backer. Hard-bitten old merchants might turn a deaf ear to the cheering mobs that assembled to see the monsters steam out to sea, but the sight of decks and rigging swarming with passengers who had paid premium rates for crowded cabin space was something to be considered seriously.

So great, indeed, was the demand for accommodations that Howland & Aspinwall could not resist the temptation to invade Law's preserves, and they put opposition steamers on the New York-Chagres run, as well as on the Pacific side which was the proper sphere for their Pacific Mail Line. In return, Law sent steamships to the West Coast to compete with the Pacific Mail, with results far from satisfactory to both parties.

The thing reached a very temporary climax the 14th of December when the *New York Herald* exulted: "A day long to be remembered in the annals of our shipping." At 3 P.M. on that day four large steamships cast off their lines along West Street and proceeded to sea in stately procession, the *Cherokee, Crescent City,* and *Ohio* for Chagres and the *Great Western* for Bermuda.

For a second time Bennett's prophetic powers were unequal to the occasion. The incident was forgotten overnight. Too much was happening, most of it connected with salt water. For the first time since the landing of the Pilgrims, news from Europe was relegated to second place. All through '49 California held the center of the stage. Even Vanderbilt, whose steamers on the sound were making money "hand over first," was not proof against the siren call. Much to "Hell Fire" George's disgust, he organized "The American, Atlantic and Pacific Ship Canal Company's Line of Nicaraguan Steamers." It was fortunate the Commodore's geographical knowledge was limited, or the title would have been longer.

Steamships were again in heavy demand in 1850, with a record-breaking 60,000 tons launched during the year. What was equally important from the standpoint of their future, they began to break a few records themselves.

James West, late of the Philadelphia packet *Shenandoah,* was given command of the *Atlantic,* pioneer steamship of the Collins line. Occasionally one of the family had fallen from grace by going into picture painting and that sort of thing, but James was the sound product of a century of Philadelphia seafaring. He sailed on April 27th. On his return passage, he broke the Cunard record for the westbound crossing. On his second voyage he broke it again, running from Liverpool to New York, dock to dock, in 10 days, 15 hours, the first such passage to be made in less than 11 days.[3] Continuing, the *Atlantic* arrived at New York on the 1st of September with 145 cabin passengers, claimed to be the largest number ever brought over by a transatlantic steamship. It may have been, for P. T. Barnum and Jenny Lind were among the number, either of them equivalent to a round dozen of the ordinary run.

These were not the only steamship records of 1850; records, incidentally, which did much to popularize steam travel. Much earlier in the year—January 13th, to be precise—the smaller *Philadelphia,* commanded by John ("Let 'er go") Gallagher, arrived at Savannah from Havana, distance 698 statute miles, in 48 hours, 45 minutes.[4]

It remained for the *Pacific,* not the big Collins liner but the new 1000-tonner of that name, to set the record of the year. She sailed for New Orleans on the 12th of October. On her arrival, Captain Jarvis reported that she ran from the foot of Warren Street, New York, to Morro Castle, Havana, in 3 days, 22 hours, and that on October 14th she logged 360 miles, which was 27 miles better than the best day's run of her big namesake.

Another record—in reverse—was established by the little screw steamer *Hartford.* She arrived at San Francisco on January 5th, 320 days out of New York, a passage still unmatched for length by any steamer. She was, however, completely unsuitable for such a voyage, having been built by Loper at Philadelphia for the Hartford trade. She measured only 251 tons, had very little freeboard and was fitted inadequately, but, as it proved, indispensably, with a light schooner rig. The fact she arrived at all was due to the grit and ability of her master, Captain Lefevre, who was rewarded in due time by a more seaworthy Vanderbilt command.

A somewhat similar attempt to reach the land of promise was made in 1850 by the *Rhode Island,* an ordinary sound-steamer. She set out in February and promptly disintegrated. A few of her passengers and crew were picked up in boats, but there was a heavy loss of life. The news of the rescue of the last boat reached New York the 26th of February, the day Bennett first ran the ominous headline: "The Union Must and Shall be Preserved."

Although the enthusiasm excited by the beautiful new clippers and the reports of their record-smashing achievements mounted month by month, the steamship continued to hold the center of the stage throughout the year. It is difficult to find terms which will now convey an adequate impression of the prideful amazement which greeted each new "improved" monster in turn. One can only recall that the same throngs that witnessed their launchings; viewed their "razor-sharp lines"; wandered down the long, graceful sheer of their richly decorated saloons, flanked by a hundred staterooms; and inspected with awe their massive machinery; had thrilled but yesterday at the sight of apple-bowed, "floating palaces" less than a fifth their tonnage.

Their performance was equally impressive. Passenger lists of the larger steamers on the 2000-mile run to Chagres usually ranged from 600 to 900, and upwards, the names filling at times a long column of newsprint.

The California situation was still fluid in 1850. J. Howard & Son, who acted for a time as one of the early New York agents for the Pacific Mail, sent the S.S. *Northerner* to San Francisco under Robert H. Waterman, late of the clipper *Sea Witch* and the lovely but unfortunate *Challenge*. Another Howland & Aspinwall steamer, the propeller *Carolina,* James Marks, master, late of sundry Gulf steamers, made a record run to Panama to reinforce the Pacific Mail fleet, which by August comprised four good steamships of medium size. By that time, Marshall O. Roberts, with offices at Warren and West Streets, New York, was selling through tickets between New York and San Francisco as passenger agent for the line.

In the summer of 1850 Charles Morgan and J. Howard & Son, possibly with the secret blessing of Vanderbilt, put the 2000-ton steamer *Empire City* on the New York-Chagres route. She was the first American steamer to have a deck house from stem to stern, which enabled her to "carry enough passengers to break her back." She sailed July 17th, 1850, at which time it was reported that 22 steamers had been launched or laid down at New York alone in the previous six months, as against 16 sailing craft.

Vanderbilt's first steamship for his jaw-breaking Nicaraguan line, the *Prometheus,* was launched the 3rd of August. She measured 1203 tons. Her engines were built by Charles Morgan at the Morgan Iron Works, and for several years thereafter Morgan was closely associated with Vanderbilt in his California venture. Three weeks after the launching of the *Prometheus,* Vanderbilt sailed for the isthmus on the smaller S.S. *Pacific,* with a commission to investigate the Nicaragua canal possibilities. It later developed that he had other important steamship plans in a state of forwardness, but for the moment all the public knew was that he decided to start the *Pacific* around Cape Horn.

Less than a month later, on September 21st, the big *Pacific* of the Collins line arrived at New York from Liverpool in the record passage of 10 days, 4 hours, and 45 minutes, dock to dock.

About the same time two other steamers were launched, the *Humboldt* for the New York-Havre line, and the *Louisiana* for Messrs. Morgan & Harris, of New Orleans. The latter was a 1000-ton vessel intended for trade between New Orleans and the Gulf ports. A few weeks later another steamer of about 1200 tons, the *Mexico*, also destined for Morgan & Harris, was launched by William Collyer. The engines of both these vessels were built at the Morgan Iron Works, and it is possible, if not probable, that Charles Morgan was heavily interested in their ownership under cover of the above firm.

Among other steamships of the year, the 1161-ton *Florida* was being readied for Sam Mitchell's Savannah line, with her sister ship, the *Alabama*, not far behind.

All in all, 1850 was a good year for the steamerites. There were few serious losses. The little Charleston steamer, the *Southerner*—not the Spofford, Tileston liner—was sunk early in October by the packet bark *Isaac Mead*, with a loss of 24 lives, only Captain R. T. Brown, six seamen and two passengers being saved.

A more serious disaster from the standpoint of steamship development, although attended with a smaller loss of life, was the foundering of the new propeller *Helena Sloman* on the 29th of November. She was an auxiliary ship of 1200 tons, built "without regard to expense" as the first of a proposed Hamburg-New York line. On her maiden voyage she sailed from New York for Hamburg on the 5th of July, sponsored by the firm of Schmidt & Balchen, 105-107 Wall Street. Her first crossings were without special incident, but leaving Hamburg the 26th of October she ran into a series of terrific gales off the Nova Scotia coast from the 19th to the 23rd of November, during which her propeller tore out her stern post and carried away her rudder, leaving the vessel unmanageable and leaking badly.

It required the utmost exertions of passengers and crew to keep the ship afloat until the 29th, when the packet *Devonshire*, Captain Henry Hovey, rescued her passengers and crew under conditions of grave peril. All were saved except five passengers who were drowned when one of the *Devonshire's* boats was smashed against the side of the *Sloman*, the third mate and three men of the *Devonshire* being lost at the same time. The incident did much to increase the unpopularity of the propeller and was instrumental in retarding, for a time, its more general use.

Steamship construction dropped in 1851, relatively speaking, although it still remained at a high level.

Philadelphia, in particular, which for years had been loudly proclaiming her desire for a transatlantic steamship line, was beginning to get results, Philadelphia fashion, with a minimum risk of local capital. On the 15th of March, 1851, a new iron propeller built and owned by Tod & McGregor of Glasgow, the *City of Glasgow,* sailed from Philadelphia to inaugurate a service between that city and Glasgow. She rated about 1600 tons and her length on deck was 237 feet. She was fitted with five watertight bulkheads and turned a wheel 13 feet in diameter. She quickly demonstrated an efficiency of operation which made every paddle steamship afloat obsolete. Her coal consumption was 20 tons a day, as compared with the 75 tons and upwards consumed by Cunarders of approximately the same size, and she carried 1200 tons of cargo, where 500 tons represented their utmost capacity.[5]

A less promising venture was initiated the following month when the new steamer *Lafayette,* built in New York for J. G. Williams and others, and commanded by Charles Stoddard, late of the Havre packet *Ville de Lyon,* sailed from New York for Philadelphia on April 22nd, to load for Liverpool. The *Lafayette* proved too slow and too small to compete with the New York steamers and the project was soon abandoned, Stoddard going to the fine new S.S. *Brother Jonathan* on the New York-Chagres run.

Fortunately for Philadelphians, a third project, conceived on a more ambitious scale, was getting under way about the same time. Messrs. Richardson, Watson & Company, with offices in both New York and Philadelphia, were cooperating with a group of Liverpool associates in organizing the Liverpool & Philadelphia Steam Ship Company, the line to be composed of a steamer built in New York and another built on the Clyde. The *City of Pittsburg,* a wooden steamer of 1875 tons, was built in New York pursuant to the plan, while an iron steamer of about the same size, the *City of Manchester,* was built in Scotland. Both were propellers, the line being the first transatlantic service to be composed exclusively of vessels of that description.

A short trial convinced the management that the *City of Pittsburg* was too slow to maintain a sound competitive schedule and she was withdrawn, going to the Pacific in the following year. The *City of Glasgow* was purchased to fill the vacancy thus left in the line, to the great joy of Philadelphians who feared that the project would be abandoned, as shown by the fact that when the *City of Glasgow* arrived on the 2nd of January,

1852, on her first crossing in the new line, Captain Matthews was tendered a banquet by 800 of the port's most distinguished citizens. Richardson, Watson & Company, whose financial interest in the line ceased with the withdrawal of the *City of Pittsburg,* continued to act as New York and Philadelphia agents of the line for some years.

Within a short time the Inman Line, as it was called later, under the management of William Inman, carried not only a majority of the port's first-class passengers, but a substantial number of steerage, being the first Western Ocean steamship line to engage in that traffic. The *City of Glasgow,* in fact, was originally equipped to carry 400 emigrants in addition to first- and second-class passengers.

Philadelphia was about 38 hours farther from Liverpool than New York in the average steaming time for the faster ships of the day, and as the new Philadelphia liners were slower than the Collins steamships, they were usually a trifle more than 16 days on the run. To compete with the New York steamers their rates ranged from $55 to $90, depending on location of staterooms. Steerage rates were fixed at $20, eastbound, and $30, westbound, including cooked provisions, the line being the first of the transatlantic services to introduce that desirable improvement in its steerage accommodations.

On the Isthmus route to California, George Law and Howland & Aspinwall reached an agreement in February, 1850, to become effective in April. Thereafter, Law was to operate only on the Atlantic side and the Pacific Mail only on the Pacific. Law and his associates retained or purchased the *Georgia, Ohio, Empire City, Cherokee, Crescent City,* and *Philadelphia* for exclusive operation on the New York-Chagres run. The Pacific Mail kept the *Oregon, California, Panama, Tennessee, Northerner, Republic, Columbia,* and the little 600-ton *Columbus* and five others of about the same size, the small craft being utilized to maintain connecting services on the Pacific coast.[6]

Everyone was happy until June when Vanderbilt started his Nicaraguan line, with the new *Prometheus* theoretically operating in conjunction with the *Pacific* on the West Coast. Vanderbilt had a special knack for making competitors unhappy, but on this occasion he surpassed himself, for his own clientele were the unhappiest of all. When his first steamer arrived in San Francisco several hundred passengers paraded with banners advertising "Vanderbilt's Death Line" and complaining loudly of broken promises, misrepresentations, delays, and insufficient and unwholesome food, all of which had cost the lives of scores of passengers.

As a matter of fact, none of the lines were blameless in this respect. The rush was too heavy and the urge to profit by it too great. Even the old transatlantic lines were losing steerage passengers at a terrific rate, as will be seen. Nevertheless, Vanderbilt's line got a large share of the criticism, with, probably, some justification. The temptation to promise a service not yet in being, and which could be provided only by a series of achievements that dovetailed with almost miraculous precision, is hard to resist when huge profits are at stake. Eventually Vanderbilt put the *Daniel Webster* and other good steamers on the run and the complaints ceased.

Vanderbilt's activity, however, did not. He conceived the idea of running a steamship from New York to Liverpool to furnish a direct, continuous service between San Francisco and Europe, with a view to reaping the profits that would accrue from through shipments of gold, which at that time the British West India steamers were monopolizing. With this in mind he had his first large steamship, the *Northern Light,* 1767 tons, laid down.

Meanwhile, Spofford, Tileston & Company concluded to expand their steamship activities. They too decided to have a fling at the transatlantic trade, and the propeller *Pioneer,* rating 1875 tons, was built to go under their management. She sailed for Liverpool late in October, 1851, under the command of Asa Eldridge, but a single round was enough to demonstrate that, like the *City of Pittsburg,* she lacked the speed to compete with the Cunard and Collins ships. Three other steamers completed for them during the year were more successful. Two were built by William H. Webb at New York: the *Union,* 1200 tons, and the *Winfield Scott,* 1291 tons, both for a new line between New York and New Orleans. Messrs. Brooks, Davis & Company advertised the latter vessel for a time and may have managed her temporarily. The third vessel, the fine 900-ton steamer *Marion,* was also built in New York for the firm's Charleston line.

The Pacific Mail acquired one of their most famous steamers in July, 1851. This was the *Golden Gate.* She was built by Webb, and her oscillating engines by Stillman & Allen were the largest of the type that had ever been built. She registered 2067 tons, and although not particularly notable for size, was regarded at the last word in finish and design. William H. Aspinwall, president of the company, was so proud of her that he sent her to Washington on one of her trial trips, where she was visited by President Fillmore, Daniel Webster, and most of the cabinet members.

Law continued to add to his Chagres line with, as the event proved, a reckless disregard of the law of averages. He put the *Brother Jonathan* on the run in March. She was a new 1359-ton steamship commanded by Charles Stoddard, who by this time had compiled quite a record of steamship commands. Stoddard sailed on her maiden voyage three days after the trial of another Law steamer, the *El Dorado,* which was held the 12th of March. Another steamer, the *Independence,* rising 1300 tons, under construction for Lauchlan McKay, the very able and versatile brother of the more famous Donald, was acquired by Law later in the year. These three were in addition to the big 2123-ton *Illinois,* originally intended to complete the line, which sailed August 28th on her first trip to Chagres, and was shortly proclaimed "The Fastest Steamer in the World."

Boston, which had never been wholly satisfied with the Cunard service, developed patriotic Liverpool steamship aspirations, and Loper built the propeller *Lewis* at Philadelphia.

Intended as the first of four to comprise a Boston-Liverpool line, she was owned principally by Loper, E. Lincoln, and Sam Reynolds, of Philadelphia. She was, however, under the management of R. Lincoln of Boston. The *Lewis* registered only 1104 tons, which was on the small side for a Western Ocean boat, and to complete the education of her owners, she lost her propeller on her first trip in the gale of October 15th, 1851. On her return to Boston she was promptly put up for sale. Eventually, she found her way into the Pacific to prolong for a few years the hardships of the hardy forty-niners.

The city had better luck with her coastal steamers. Loper also built the 613-ton propellers *William Penn* and *Benjamin Franklin* that year for the Boston-Philadelphia line of R. Lincoln & Company, which proved able and successful vessels, although withdrawn early the following year to go on the Chagres route. Loper, indeed, was extremely active at this time and all through the decade, turning out propellers of assorted sizes in rapid succession. All were equipped with a screw of his design, afterwards adopted and used extensively by the U. S. Navy.

New York also got another short coastal line that year, when the firm of Ludlam & Pleasants began running the 1071-ton steamer *Roanoke* to Norfolk. It was one of the minor ventures of the year, but the firm prospered, added another vessel or two, and eventually cut deeply into the sailing packet business.

Although the reckless enthusiasm of the preceding year had abated somewhat, 50 steamers were built at New York in 1851, as compared with 55 sailing vessels. Other ports had produced from one or two to a dozen or more, with Philadelphia, Baltimore, and Wilmington, Delaware, especially active, in that order.

A belated recognition of the new navigational problems created by the ocean steamship came in February, when all American steamers were ordered to carry a white light at the masthead, with red and green lights to port and starboard, a practice which had already been adopted by progressive operators.

All in all, the steamships of 1851 cut heavily into the potential first-class passenger traffic of the sailing liners, both transatlantic and coastal. Their impact on the latter, however, was more pronounced, partly for the reason that all the great New Orleans, Chagres, Nicaraguan, and Havana steamers called at one or more intermediate ports, thus providing a frequent and increasingly popular service for former patrons of the wind packets. In the transatlantic field, however, the loss of cabin passengers was hardly felt by the sailing liners. Immigration from Europe continued to increase so rapidly that the problem for the moment was to find ships to transport it. What the outcome would be in the event travel should be seriously curtailed was something few shipping men stopped to consider. Even the rush to California was on the rise, supplemented as it now was by the return of hundreds of forty-niners to lead their families into the promised land. At the very end of the year the S.S. *Northerner* cleared at San Francisco with 600 eastbound passengers and $1,700,000 in gold. All the westbound steamers sailed with capacity lists, topped in the spring of 1852 by Vanderbilt's *Northern Light,* which left New York with 900 prospective citizens of California, one of five large ocean steamers to leave the port in the space of three hours, all crowded with passengers.

At this time one of the more important results of American steamship activities, so far as their bearing on efforts to improve the service was concerned, was the disappointing performance of the three big propellers already noted. Now, as if to clinch the matter, the shortcomings of the type were further stressed by Charleston's unfortunate experience. The merchants of that city had built the 1301-ton propeller *South Carolina* at a cost of approximately $200,000 as the first of a proposed Charleston-Liverpool line. She sailed on her maiden voyage the 7th of April, 1852, and promptly wrecked her propeller on the Charleston Bar. She eventually turned up in New York for a long and expensive repair job, after which she was converted to sail the following year. Nautical experts estimated that the total loss to the owners was not far from $400,000.

At the very moment the *South Carolina* was limping toward New York and the Fiddlers' Green of all the big American propellers, the paddle liner *Pacific* was breaking the record for fast Western Ocean crossings. She arrived in New York on the 19th of April, 9 days, 20 hours and 15 minutes from Liverpool, thereby becoming the first vessel to cross in less than 10 days.[7] It was only natural that the steamship fraternity should draw conclusions highly unfavorable to the propeller, and those conclusions were undoubtedly largely responsible for the fact that for several critical years American engineers continued to devote their efforts almost exclusively to the improvement of paddle steamers.

In the end, only Vanderbilt profited. He bought the propellers *Pioneer* and *Lewis* at bargain counter prices and sent them round the Horn, where anything that floated and moved was being requisitioned for the California travel. He also sent the *Brother Jonathan* to the Pacific after an extensive overhaul. This gave him three steamers on the West Coast until G. W. Kitteridge piled up the *Pioneer* in October, to the great gain of Robert H. Waterman, late of the clipper ship *Challenge*. Waterman bought the wreck for a trifle; got her off with little trouble and converted her into a huge sailing ship. Vanderbilt also had three steamers on the Atlantic side running to San Juan, Nicaragua, and was building two more of the tonnage of the *Northern Light,* the largest of his vessels.

By this time the "independents" had a number of actual contenders on the Isthmus route, with others in prospect. R. Lincoln & Company's Boston-Philadelphia line steamers, the *Benjamin Franklin* and *William Penn,* were withdrawn to go on the more profitable Chagres run. E. Mills, of New York, had the 1433-ton side-wheeler *Uncle Sam* under construction for the same purpose. The new Morgan liner *Sierra Nevada,* 1247 tons, started to run to Chagres in March, 1852, connecting with the *Monumental City* on the Pacific side.

Davis, Brooks & Company, of New York, had been running the *Winfield Scott* as an independent, with another steamship under construction. She was launched by Westervelt & Mackay on March 29 as the *Cortes,* registering 1117 tons. The extent to which the old canvas-backs were being metamorphosed into steamerites was indicated by the fact that her construction was supervised by Captain William B. Skiddy and she was commanded by Thomas B. Cropper. Before the *Cortes* was ready, Davis, Brooks found it necessary to add the *United States* to their line.

So great indeed was the pressure for a time that even the smallest sea-going steamers were withdrawn from the shorter routes to form new opposition lines. Mailler & Lord, a firm that will be heard from again, had the little steamship *City of New York,* registering 574 tons, ready to put into their Boston-Richmond line to supplement their sailing service when it was decided to send her to Chagres instead.

Notwithstanding the numerous withdrawals, coastal steamship activity continued heavy through 1852. Mobile got her first line in that year; William Collyer of New York building the 1556-ton S.S. *Black Warrior* for the New York & Alabama S.S. Company, of which Herman T. Livingston was secretary.

After getting rid of their white elephant, the *Pioneer,* Spofford, Tileston acquired an interest in the fine new steamer *James Adger,* 1151 tons, and put her in their New Orleans line. She was named after a prominent Charleston merchant, and owned principally in Charleston.

Another famous coastal operator appeared on the scene early in July when Thomas Clyde participated in the establishment of the "Independent Daily Line" (later Sanford's) between Philadelphia and New York with three small steamers, the largest of which was the 616-ton *Delaware,* a Loper propeller of a class usually rigged as three-masted schooners.

Coastal lines were also started between Baltimore and Charleston with the steamer *Palmetto,* between Philadelphia and Savannah with the new 1204-ton *State of Georgia,* and between Philadelphia and Boston with Loper propellers rating about 580 tons.

Other developments of the year included the 1900-ton "caloric steamer" *Ericsson,* which proved a failure through inability to generate sufficient speed; the return to the New York run on May 15th of the monster iron propeller *Great Britain;* the complete destruction by fire at Valparaiso of the California-bound *City of Pittsburg,* late relic of Philadelphia's transatlantic experiment; and the slowly spreading realization that steamship operation was a business by itself. James Gordon Bennett, fired by stories of the huge, new clippers that were making records wherever they went and were returning their costs in a single voyage, raucously proclaimed that "steam was too expensive, if not too slow."

His verdict failed to impress the old Cunarders, D. & C. McIver, of 14 Water Street, Liverpool, who proceeded to establish another line consisting of the steamships *Andes, Alps, Aetna* and *Jura,* to begin monthly sailings in the fall of 1852 to New York and also to Chagres, via Jamaica. In December the *Taurus* and *Teneriffe* were added to permit bimonthly sailings. The line was intended to attract the cheaper class of cabin passengers, and first- and second-cabin rates were fixed at 20 and 15 pounds, respectively. The remunerative gold shipments awaiting transportation at Chagres also entered into the McIver calculations. Edward Cunard was the New York agent.

On land, to speed the immigrant westward and make room for more, the first locomotive west of the Mississippi made its initial trip on the 2nd day of December, at St. Louis.

There was little change in the steamship situation in 1853. The little *City of New York* was taken off the Chagres run to sail between Boston and Philadelphia in conjunction with a similar vessel, the *City of Boston*. Phineas Sprague was the Boston agent and he assured the public that the steamers would leave T Wharf every Saturday, "full or not full."

The Collins line was apparently prospering in spite of a more than liberal share of engine troubles. The *Atlantic's* cargo in February was valued at $1,500,000, "the most valuable ever brought from Liverpool." It must have paid a thumping profit, for the westbound freight rate of the line was six pounds per ton, as against the average 25 or 30 shillings of the sailing packets.

In performance, the record of the line was substantially better than that of her competitors. On the basis of 23 eastbound passages of the Collins steamers and 24 of the New York Cunarders in 1852, the average time of the former was reported as 11 days, 1 hour and 47 minutes, and of the latter, 11 days, 6 hours and 38 minutes. Westbound, the difference was greater, the Collins' time being 11 days, 5 hours and 24 minutes, while that of the Cunarders was 12 days, 11 hours and 42 minutes. The best passage of the year was the February run of the *Arctic*—9 days, 23 hours and 15 minutes—to the eastward[8]

It is to be noted, however, that the compiler of the above statistics made no allowance for longitude in his computations. The true—or mean —times, therefore, must be ascertained by subtracting five hours from the eastbound figures and adding five hours for the westbound.

In patronage also, the Collins line maintained a substantial advantage. In 45 crossings during the year it carried 4213 passengers, compared with 3024 carried by the New York Cunarders in 48 crossings.[9]

Vanderbilt's famous yacht, the *North Star*, 1867 tons register, was launched by Simonson at the foot of East 19th Street, New York, on March 10th, and her command was given to Asa Eldridge, an old Cape Cod boy. A few other fine steamers were completed. Among them were the 1310-ton *Augusta*, for Sam Mitchell's New York-Savannah line; the 960-ton *Star of the South*, at Philadelphia; and the ill-fated *San Francisco;* but the construction of large ocean steamers hardly replaced those lost during the year.

On the 16th of February the S.S. *Independence,* under the old packet master F. L. Sampson, was burned off the coast of Lower California.

Although she was beached, about 15 of the crew and 110 passengers were lost. The *South Carolina* went into the Liverpool-Melbourne emigrant business as a sailing ship. The *Monumental City* was wrecked on the coast of Australia May 15th, with a loss of 32 of the passengers and crew; 54 being saved. The Havre liner *Humboldt,* commanded by the ex-packet master, David Lines, was lost on the 6th of December, going ashore in a fog a few miles from Halifax. On Christmas Day the *San Francisco* was disabled, and on January 6th, 1854, she foundered with a loss of more than 200 lives. Upwards of 500 were saved, principally by the splendid work of the ships *Three Bells,* of Glasgow, and Zerega's *Antarctic,* with the bark *Kilby* rescuing 108 or thereabouts.

Walt Whitman thus described the sinking with special reference to the part played by the Scottish skipper of the *Three Bells,* who, in seven long, storm-wracked days and nights, took off more than 200 of the survivors:

> I understand the large hearts of heroes,
> The courage of present times and all times,
> How the skipper saw the crowded and rudderless wreck of
>   the steam-ship, and Death chasing it up and down the storm,
> How he knuckled tight and gave not an inch, and was
>   faithful of days and faithful of nights,
> And he chalked in large letters on a board, BE OF GOOD CHEER,
>   WE WILL NOT DESERT YOU;
> How he follow'd with them and tack'd with them three days
>   and would not give it up,
> How he saved the drifting company at last,
> How the lank loose-gown'd women looked when boated
>   from the side of their prepared graves
> How the silent old-faced infants and the lifted sick, and
>   the sharp-lipped unshaven men:
> All this I swallow, it tastes good, I like it well,
>   it becomes mine,
> I am the man, I suffered, I was there.

Steamship construction was off in 1854, while ships of the sail registered a heavy increase. The few large steamers completed or launched during the year included the Fall River Line steamboat *Metropolis,* the largest sound-steamer yet built. She was 350 feet in length and registered 2108 tons.

Two other steamboats of similar type were completed during the year, both named *Plymouth Rock.* One was the 1752-ton boat built at New York for the Long Island Sound traffic. The other was a Great Lakes craft measuring 1991 tons, built at Buffalo.

Another transatlantic service was established in January. One of the most ambitious railway projects yet undertaken, that between Portland, Maine, and Montreal, was completed late in 1853, whereupon the Canadian Steamship Company announced that its Montreal service would be routed by way of Portland during the winter months. Bimonthly sailings were scheduled, to start with the departure of the steamship *Charity* from Birkenhead Docks on the 12th of January, and the fares, ranging from 7 guineas steerage to 20 guineas first cabin, included the railway fare from Portland to Montreal. The line was composed of three steamers of 1500 tons and three under construction of 1750 tons.

The new steamship *Golden Age,* a 2281-tonner, was put on the New York-Liverpool run under David B. Porter. However, Porter had an opportunity to make an advantageous charter, and took her to Melbourne in 51 days, running time. This was said to be 11 days better than the best British steamship time. At any rate, the broad-minded Melbournites were enthused to the point of tendering Porter a banquet costing $2,000.

One of the largest coastal steamers to be completed during the year was the side-wheeler *Quaker City,* a vessel later made famous as the conveyance of Mark Twain's *Innocents Abroad.* She measured 1429 tons and was put on the New York-Mobile run. Another steamer to engage in the rapidly growing Mobile trade about the same time was the "six-day" steamship *William Norris,* which had been taken over by new owners and completed on a less pretentious plan, after which she was launched as the *Ocean Bird.*

Vanderbilt continued building large steamers but none were completed during the year. Charles Morgan was still in charge of his Nicaraguan line, now dubbed "The Accessory Transit Company." Why "accessory," was not explained, but it probably sounded like a good word to the Commodore.

On the other side of the Isthmus, the Pacific Mail added the fine steamers *Sonora* and *Saint Louis,* vessels registering a trifle over 1600 tons.

Several fast coastal steamships made their trial trips toward the end of the year and were turned over to various New York firms, most of them to sail on their maiden voyages in January, 1855. They included the *Knoxville,* 1240 tons, which went into Sam Mitchell's Savannah line; the 1220-ton *Nashville* (later a Confederate cruiser), which joined the *Marion* in Spofford, Tileston & Company's Charleston line; and the *Cahawba,* 1600 tons, destined for Livingston, Crocheron & Company's New Orleans line. The *Nashville* proceeded to break the record between New York and Charleston, making the run early in March to the Charleston Bar in

45 hours, "A Glorious Triumph over Old Father Time," proclaimed the *Charleston Courier*.

Three serious steamship disasters occurred during 1854 to curb steamerite enthusiasm. On May 19th the New York papers announced that the Inman liner *City of Glasgow* had been missing 70 days. She was never reported, her disappearance involving a loss of 480 lives. Another vessel of the same line, the *City of Philadelphia*, was wrecked the night of September 14th at Chance Cove, Newfoundland, fortunately without loss of life. On the 27th of September the Collins liner *Arctic* was sunk on the Grand Banks by the French steamer *Vesta,* with a loss variously estimated at from 300 to 400 lives. Among those lost were the wife, son, and daughter of Mr. Collins and eight members of the family of James Brown, senior partner of the New York firm of Brown Brothers & Company.

According to third mate Dorian, the great loss of life was due largely to the wholesale desertion of the ship by officers and men, and accounts of survivors who stayed by the ship until she went down, as well as the list of those who escaped in the boats, seem to bear out his assertion, although some of the responsibility must be attributed to a grave misapprehension of the situation at the outset. It was thought at first that the *Arctic* was not seriously damaged, with the result that Captain Luce not only sent his chief mate with a boat to the assistance of the *Vesta,* but lost valuable time in preparing to abandon ship. The sea was fairly smooth and the steamer remained afloat for nearly four hours: ample time for the crew to construct a huge raft out of the masts and yards. Instead, considerable time elapsed before anything was done, and when it was finally realized that the *Arctic* was sinking there was a frenzied rush for the boats, one of which was swamped, drowning the occupants. The others pulled away with only a part of their quotas, the occupants consisting principally of members of the crew and a few male passengers. Out of the 80 survivors, more than 50 were crew members. Most of the women and children were lost. Whatever may be urged in explanation or palliation, there can be no doubt that the ancient law of the sea, "Women and children first," was quite generally disregarded. All in all, the conduct of the crew suggested a certain deterioration in the quality of seamen since colonial days. And the *Vesta,* which might have rescued everyone, steamed off, concerned only to save herself.

There were bright spots. Francis Dorian remained by the ship doing his utmost to assist Captain Luce to restore order and forward the work of making a raft, until ordered to take charge of the last boat. Young Stewart Holland, an engineer who went down with the ship, volunteered for duty and was assigned to the signal gun, which he continued to load and fire methodically and with seeming indifference until warned by the water lapping about his feet that the ship was soon to take its final plunge. Captain Luce, holding his small son in his arms, went down with his command in the old tradition of the sea. He came to the surface and managed to get on one of the old paddle boxes that had become detached, but his son had been killed by a surging timber. He and several others were picked up two days later by the ship *Cambria,* but in the meantime most of those who had gained a temporary refuge on bits of wreckage had perished, the temperature of the water being about 45 degrees.[10]

Today, after the lapse of more than a century, one cannot read unmoved the story of those last moments on the deck of the sinking vessel—the sullen boom of the signal gun; amidships, a few men working feverishly, trying to get another spar over the side in a belated effort to make a raft; most of the passengers huddled on the after deck, instinctively massed for human companionship. Little groups were here and there, quietly awaiting the end. Mrs. Collins, her arms about her son, refused to take any precautions for safety that her children could not share. William Brown, his wife and child and two young sisters, about to go down, were locked in an embrace death itself could not break. The deck sloped more and more steeply as the water began to wash across the after end of the ship— warning shouts—the slow plunge—the death cry of drowning hundreds. It was a scene played before and destined to be replayed many times through the years.

Captain James A. Wotton, sometime master of the crack Union line packet *Admiral,* but now commanding Mortimer Livingston's Havre steamer *Franklin,* was more fortunate. He went ashore near Montauk Point, Long Island, in thick weather and the steamer broke up in a July storm, but he put all his passengers ashore safely.

By coincidence rather than intention, the first British line between New York and Havre was established just as the *Franklin* began to go to pieces, the *Indiana,* pioneer of the line, sailing from Southampton for Havre on the 8th of July. Her New York agent, C. H. Sand, a prominent steamship man, cleared her on the 9th of August for her maiden passage to Havre.

It was a bad year at sea and a large number of stout ships were lost, among them Train's Boston packet *Winchester,* commanded by Frederick Moore, which foundered May 3rd, but not before the steamship *Washington* had taken off her 420 passengers, who had been on the totally dismasted hulk for 16 days. The only persons lost were three seamen who were on the fore-topgallant yard when the mast went overboard.

Immigration, as noted elsewhere, reached its high mark in 1854. It was especially heavy from Ireland and Havre, where steerage rates were raised to five pounds, ten shillings. The fact was undoubtedly responsible for the continuation of construction of sailing vessels on an unprecedented scale. It was estimated that 40,000 to 50,000 tons were under construction in New York during September, and that about 250,000 tons were being built in Maine. A similar condition was said to exist in Boston where a single builder, Donald McKay, had laid down four ships of approximately 2000 tons each for a McKay Boston-Liverpool line of emigrant ships.[11]

At the very moment construction was at its most feverish high, the tide turned. Even in September ships were accumulating at the docks; 777 in New York alone, while similar conditions prevailed all along the coast. Freights suddenly seemed headed for a record low. Still more ominous, on the 2nd of October, 1854, the packet *Manhattan* sailed for Liverpool with 300 second-class and steerage passengers, most of them recent arrivals. A whisper began to go the rounds—"Depression!"—to be met with optimistic scoffing. By December there was no scoffing. A widespread depression of no common sort was on, and it found the merchants of America carrying several million tons of new and nearly new ships.

For shipbuilders and operators alike, depression and gloom, unparalleled for years, characterized New Year's Day, 1855. Not a clipper was being built and in the great shipbuilding center of New York less than 6500 tons were laid down during the first quarter of the year, as compared with a normal 25,000 tons and upwards. Maine was doing a little better, but it was an unprofitable business. Prices were down 30 per cent. Shipping people, forgetting all other factors, blamed conditions on high wages and the refusal of carpenters to work more than two or three days a week, a practice which often caused builders to forfeit large sums, and in some instances entailed bankruptcy.

Travel everywhere dropped sharply, but especially in California. It did not worry George Law, for he had disposed of his interests in the Chagres line in 1854. His defection did not appear to cause the remaining trustees any vain regrets, for they immediately rechristened his favorite steamer, the *George Law,* naming her the *Central America.* Notwithstanding this precaution, ill-luck pursued her. She foundered at sea the 12th of September, 1857, with a loss of 423 lives, one of the worst tragedies of the California trade.

On the whole, the steamship fared better during the depression than the sailing liners, which had lost more than 50 per cent of their steerage traffic. The steamers, in contrast to ships of the sail, depended largely on

Courtesy, The Marine Historical Association, Inc.

Packet ship *Commodore Perry*.

Packet ship *American Eagle* of the Griswold Black X Line.

Ship *Joshua Bates* of Train's White Diamond Line, Boston to Liverpool.

Packet ship *Huguenot* of Thompson's Black Star Line, New York to Liverpool, being struck by lightning.

Courtesy, The Peabody Museum of Salem

Courtesy, The Marine Historical Association, Inc.

Medium clipper packet *David Crockett* of Everett & Brown's Washington Line of New York to Liverpool packets. Built in 1853 at Mystic, Conn., by George Greenman & Co., the *Crockett* originally carried a single topsail on the mizzen, later changed to a double topsail.

Packet ship *Queen Victoria* of the Union Line of New York to Havre packets, in a gale off the Azores, 1847.

Courtesy, The Marine Historical Association, Inc.

Packet ship *Emerald* of Baltimore, in Corner's Line of Liverpool packets in 1847.

Packet ship *Edwina* of Hurlbut's Line, New York to Mobile.

Courtesy, The Mariner's Museum

first- and second-class passengers, and by 1855 they had gained control of the greater part of that trade. Accordingly, there was a somewhat reassuring activity among them.

In March of 1855 Vanderbilt announced that he would start a new line between New York and Havre immediately. For this purpose he advertised the steamship *North Star,* lately under charter to the Law line, to sail the 21st of April. The S.S. *Ariel,* a 1300-tonner launched the 3rd of March, was to follow, and the line was to be completed by the *Vanderbilt,* then under construction by Simonson at Greenpoint, New York. She was launched on the 11th of December. Her 3360 tons register, together with her over-all length of 335 feet and 42-foot paddle wheels, made her the most imposing steamship in America until the Collins liner *Adriatic* went down the ways the following year. The *Vanderbilt* engines were built by Secor & Braisted, who had succeeded to the Allaire works, and she proved one of the fastest steamships of her day.

Mortimer Livingston's Havre line, meanwhile, was meeting the depression with plans for more efficient and economical steamers. After the loss of the two original steamers, he continued operations with chartered vessels while the 2307-ton *Fulton* and the 2240-ton *Arago* were under construction. He proposed, on the one hand, to save expense by running them at a slightly reduced speed, and on the other, to make them the most comfortable and even luxurious vessels afloat. The *Arago* cleared for her maiden voyage on the 2nd of June, with the well-known and popular David Lines in command. She was followed the last of the month by her new competitor, Vanderbilt's *Ariel,* under Captain Peter E. Lefevre, late of the San Francisco record-breaker *Hartford.* The line was called the "Vanderbilt European Steamship Line." Its New York offices at 5 Bowling Green were under the management of D. Torrance.

The picture of further steamship development on the Western Ocean between 1854 and 1857 is somewhat confused by transfers and requisitions of the British liners occasioned by the Crimean War, followed in 1857 by the Indian Mutiny.

Thus, the *Clyde,* the only steamship possessed by the Clyde Screw Steam Packet Company at the time of its establishment in 1854, was taken over for the Crimean transport service almost immediately. She was an iron vessel of 1150 tons and designed to carry both first-class and steerage passengers between New York and Glasgow. Service of the line was interrupted until the return of the steamer in January, 1857, after which she made a couple of voyages before abandoning the venture.

A similar fate awaited the second French line, the Compagnie Franco-

Americaine, which started operations in 1855 with three new iron side-wheelers of 1600 tons. It ran between Havre and New York, but its vessels were slow and unpopular. It ceased operations at the close of 1856, partly because of the depression and partly because of the tragic sinking of its new steamer *La Lyonnais,* off Nantucket, the night of November 2nd, 1856, with a loss of 120 lives, only 16 being saved out of the entire ship's company.

Belgium also made a second attempt to establish a line between Antwerp and New York in 1856, with two iron ships of 2150 tons, the *Belgique* and *Constitution.* A third, the *Leopold I,* was added in 1857, but the project was abandoned almost immediately thereafter, operations ceasing in the summer.

All three of the above lines carried steerage passengers, but their combined service was too brief and irregular to have any perceptible effect on the sailing liners.

Whatever problems confronted steamship men and however apprehensive they may have been in 1855, there was no doubt as to the enthusiasm of the public for the "new and desirable mode of conveyance." The following description of the sailing of the *Pacific* on the 2nd of May is typical of the scenes at the departure of all the larger steamers.

As the hour approached for the departure of the vessel, crowds wended their way to the pier at the foot of Canal Street, where West Street was completely jammed with carriages, and other vehicles engaged in conveying passengers and their friends on board the steamer. All was confusion, bustle and excitement. Hacks were driven down to the pier at a fearful rate, the drivers being entirely regardless of the inconvenience they caused ladies and gentlemen there assembled.

As the hour of 12 was fast approaching, the scene was really interesting and exciting; the promenade deck was literally crammed with passengers, whose eyes were anxiously directed to the thousands assembled on the pier. Hurried messages were sent from the gangway to those on the dock, all varying alike in their purport and mode of delivery. "Five minutes to twelve o'clock, and the mails not here yet."

"Good gracious, we shall have to sail without them!" said a sallow complectioned passenger, evidently suffering from nervousness. "Oh, no, we shan't" rejoined a more sanguine friend, "for here they come." As he spoke two capacious wagons came dashing down the pier, at no ordinary rate. Quick as lightning, the immense loads were discharged, fastened to the hoisting tackle, and safely deposited on the steamship.

Then came one or two of the "better late than never" class of passengers, who, with the assistance of about a dozen porters, managed to ensconce themselves safely on board, just as the order to "cast off" was given by the commander. A grand rush then took place for the end of the pier. Fifth Avenue ladies and gents were by no means behind hand in the race, and as over two thousand persons were extremely anxious to occupy a position at the end of the dock that could not conveniently accommodate more than five hundred, the squeezing and crushing was terrible to the ladies but they seemed to care little about the annoyance, if a good situation for witnessing the departure of the steamship could only be obtained.

At twelve o'clock, the *Pacific* majestically moved from her berth, and as her stern glided gracefully along the wharf, clouds of handkerchiefs fluttered in the breeze, hasty adieus were bade and until the second gun was fired the touching word "Good-bye" might be heard in the distance. The steamship now having gotten under full headway, the handkerchiefs were waved for the last time, the crowds commenced to disperse. A few lingered behind until the forms of those on board could no longer be distinguished and then with saddened hearts turned their faces homeward.[12]

As an aftermath to the above, it was reported that the *Pacific* sailed with a capacity crowd of 226 and that a number of applicants were turned away.

In spite of such enlivening scenes, 1855 was a year of deepening gloom which, before its close, had spread far beyond the confines of shipping circles. The new year showed no improvement. On the contrary, 1856 brought an almost unprecedented flood of rumors of ruin and impending failures, and, in addition, proved one of the stormiest in history, causing the loss of an exceptional number of fine ships and hundreds of lives, among others the entire complement of the great *Pacific*. She sailed from Liverpool in February under command of Asa Eldridge with a crew of 140 and a passenger list of 145, and disappeared without a trace, the eighth transatlantic steamship to be lost.

With the depression in full swing, there were fewer new developments in the transatlantic steamship world than in any of the previous five years, and most of those were the result of commitments made during the great migration of 1854.

The first was a new line of 1300-ton steamers which started operations between Cork and New York in February. On the 1st of March a new Cunarder, the *Persia*, arrived at the latter port. She was the first iron steamship of the line and marked a great increase in size, being 390 feet in length and registering 3600 tons. She was also the first Cunarder to beat consistently the performance of the Collins steamers, her crossings as a rule being made in nine and one-half days.

Another new British line was started in October. This was the stout little Anchor Line established by Wm. Laird & Company, 23 Castle Street, to run between Glasgow and New York. It was composed of the steamships *United Kingdom,* 2000 tons; the *John Bell,* 1800 tons; and the *Tempest,* 1500 tons.

America's steamship achievement of the year was the launching of two important vessels.

One was the *Fulton,* built by Smith & Dimon for the New York and

Havre Steam Ship Company. She was a wooden side-wheeler of 2308 tons, a brig-rigged four-decker, equipped to carry 300 cabin passengers. Her chief significance lies in the fact that she was the first American Western Ocean steamship capable of maintaining a creditable service without the support of a mail contract.

The other was the *Adriatic*, which had been laid down early in the previous year. She went down the ways on the 8th of April in the presence of a crowd estimated at 60,000. Registering 4145 tons, her dimensions, 351′ × 53′ 2″, made her the largest wooden steamship in the world, until exceeded by a couple of post-war monsters of the Pacific Mail fleet. She was longer and broader than the clipper ship *Great Republic* as originally built, although the 38-foot depth of the sailing vessel gave her a greater tonnage.

Like the *Vanderbilt*, the *Adriatic* was not completed until 1857, the delay in both instances being due to the necessity of making extensive changes in their machinery. Both vessels claimed the speed title of the Atlantic, but it seems probable that the record of the *Persia* was somewhat better than either. The *Vanderbilt* ran on a different course and the *Adriatic* made but two trips to Liverpool in the Collins line, so that it is difficult to forecast the result if the three ships had sailed over the same course under similar conditions of wind and weather. Later, under British ownership, the *Adriatic* averaged slightly under 16 knots in four successive runs over a measured mile.

Two new European services were established in 1857, known respectively as the Hamburg-American line and the Compagnie Transatlantique Belge.

The S.S. *Borussa*, registering approximately 2000 tons, arrived at New York on June 17th, to start a monthly service between that port and Hamburg. She sailed under the Hamburg flag and was advertised to leave New York the 1st of each month.

The Belgian line initiated a similar service between New York and Antwerp with the new iron steamer *Belgique*. August—better known as "Fats"—Belmont, represented the latter vessel in New York. The service was discontinued after a few months, but the Hamburg-American survived to become one of the major lines of the twentieth century.

Although few large vessels were built, the year, nevertheless, marked one important step in steamship progress. That was a rather general reversal of the earlier attitude toward the propeller, which for some time had been demonstrating its superiority over the paddle in economy, if not in speed and safety. Much credit for this development is due to the persistence of the Scots. By 1854 the screw had taken first place in the British Mediterranean trade, and in February, 1856, it was noted that of the 42 steamers running regularly across the Western Ocean, 20 were propellers, one of which, at least, had equalled the average time of the Cunarders. From that time, there was never a doubt but that the screw would eventually displace the side-wheel on ocean-going craft.

Nevertheless, before the close of the year the new paddle steamer *Persia* was claiming the Western Ocean title, with the first crossing in less than nine days. According to the abstract of her log which appeared in several papers at the time, she dropped her pilot off Sandy Hook at 12:45 P.M., August 6th, and arrived at the bar of the Mersey at 5:15 P.M., August 15th, making the passage in 8 days, 23 hours and 30 minutes, mean time. Her best day's run, 393 miles, also constituted a new steamship record, although it had been surpassed several times by both American- and Canadian-built clippers.

If 1856 had been a bad year at sea, 1857 was no better. On one count, indeed, there was general agreement—it was the coldest winter of the century. January found harbors, rivers, bays, and sounds as far south as the Chesapeake full of ice, while one gale after another roared across the Atlantic. Less obtrusive, but more deadly in its effects, was the increasing pressure of hard times.

The Pacific Mail Steamship Company laid down the 2700-ton *Ocean Queen,* but aside from that, few large steamers were started during the year. Several, however, were completed, in addition to those already noted; among them Spofford & Tileston's new Charleston liner, the *Columbia,* 1348 tons, which was finished in time for the June rush northward. Like all steamers of that line she was owned principally by Charleston residents, including the merchants James Adger and George E. West, and stout old Captain Mike Berry.

A few smaller craft were constructed, the most important of which was Vanderbilt's *Galveston,* a 945-tonner. And, by way of variety, the first large steamer for Chinese waters was built by Thomas Collyer. This was the *Yang Tsze,* a sharp, topsail schooner-rigged vessel of 875 tons. Her first owners were the tea importers, Russell & Company.

As the year wore on, tension increased, to be brought to a fever pitch in steamship circles by the action of President Buchanan, one of whose first decisions was to cancel the mail contracts of the Havre, Bremen, and Liverpool companies. This measure was regarded by many as morally indefensible in view of the fact that investors had been induced to contribute

millions of dollars toward the construction of vessels on the assurance of
Federal support comparable to that enjoyed by the Cunard and other
foreign competitors. It broke the Collins line and forced the withdrawal of
the Bremen company. The Collins steamers were sold at sheriff's sale, the
entire fleet bringing but a fraction of the cost of the new *Adriatic*.

On this note our ten-year period of steamship development ended. For
practical purposes, indeed, there is little to be gained by further pursuit of
the subject. Even the panic just ahead, by far the worst America had yet
experienced, was anticlimactic. Compared with the Buchanan monkey
wrench, its effect on the American steamship in foreign trade was brief
and trifling. Its effect on the coastal steamers was negligible. During the
next half century capable and experienced operators were to make repeated attempts to secure a share of the transatlantic cabin traffic, but
always without that degree of success which warranted long continuance
in the venture.

By the close of 1857 steamship designers and engineers had completed
the essentials of their task, and completed them so well that steamers built
in the late fifties were still giving satisfactory service a long generation
later. There would be larger ships, faster ships with more powerful engines. There would be better materials—more trustworthy alloys, more
efficient lubricating oils, more durable packings—but as far as steam was
concerned, all the fundamental principles were known and tested.

Even the effect of steam on sail, both actual and potential, had been
clearly indicated. In the foreign field, sail had been all but eliminated so
far as the cabin passenger was involved, and steamships had begun their
inroads on the steerage traffic. The early steamers catered to the first-class
trade, exclusively. As they became larger and more numerous, it became
evident that there were not enough first-class cabin passengers to go
around, and the second saloon came into being. About the same time, one
or two of the independents offered inducements to the humble steerage
passenger. The *Sarah Sands,* for example, an experimental venture of the
Kermit line, was fitted to carry upwards of 200 steerage, in addition to
first- and second-class passengers.

It will be remembered that the line later popularly known as Inman's
began to accept steerage passengers in the summer of 1852. Then, as steam
ships continued to increase in size and numbers and the depression of the
mid-fifties became more acute, it was discovered that one of the decks of
the big three- and four-deckers was admirably suited for steerage quarters.
By 1855, vessels like the new *Ocean Bird* were being equipped to carry

approximately 200 first, second, and sometimes third class, plus 400 or 500 steerage.

This did not mean the speedy elimination of immigrant ships of the sail, many of which continued to operate long after the Civil War. It did, however, cut more and more deeply into the traffic, putting the less efficiently managed lines and transients out of business one by one, as immigration dropped year by year.

On the other hand, coastal travel between the principal ports had been taken over almost completely by the steamers and railroads. By 1857 a man could "take the cars" in Boston and arrive in New York in eight hours, if, as sometimes happened, his train was on time. Or he could board an afternoon "accommodation" for Providence, Fall River, Stonington, or Norwich; transfer to a fast, comfortable steamer; and arrive at his destination by seven o'clock the following morning.

From New York he could pursue his course southward by several combination steamboat and railroad routes, and go through to Baltimore by daylight.

New Orleans merchants also had a wide choice. They could take a fast boat to Cincinnati and proceed by train to New York. They could take a packet to Memphis and transfer within a few hours to a series of connecting railroads, and bump their way—as Pat pulled on the mainsheet, "steady, by jerks"—to New York in a trifle over three days. Or they could take an ocean steamer and reach their destination in six or seven days, with comparable savings of time for intermediate ports. As early as 1855 few except steerage passengers travelled in sail between the larger coastal ports. After 1857 many of the packet lines serving southern ports ceased to advertise for passengers. Operators of lines between northern ports had discontinued the practice several years earlier.

CHAPTER XIII

∾ *1848-1857* ∾

Armageddon

"Far, far away thy children leave the land."

EVEN though the outcome seems, in retrospect, inevitable, the victory of steam was not attained without a debate epic in proportions and quality; a debate, moreover, in which a tremendous rise in immigration was to play an important part. The Yankee canvasbacker of 1848 was the equal of any man on earth in resourcefulness, daring, and that all-round efficiency which is the product of complete self-reliance. Nevertheless, it was largely through his monopoly of the steerage traffic (which the steamship was not equipped to handle) that he was able to counter the competition from steam so successfully that for several years the issue was regarded as doubtful.

The confident determination with which men of the sail fought the encroachments of steam is indicated by the tonnage of new liners they built to accommodate a traffic they proposed to hold—a tonnage that not only exceeded in volume, but surpassed in costly magnificence anything afloat in previous years. It is true that fewer new lines were started during the current ten-year period, but the difference was more than offset by the size of the new ships, as well as by the enlargement of old lines. Altogether, 23 new transatlantic and 48 coastal lines were established in the four principal northern ports. In addition, several lines to the West Indies and approximately a dozen more between the principal southern ports were put in operation.

Boston accounted for 12 coastal and two Havana and Matanzas lines and, subject to a qualification to be noted hereafter, one Liverpool line. The port also had plans and preparations well advanced for McKay's "Nebraska Line," designed as one of the greatest of American immigration lines, but abandoned when that traffic slowed to a mere trickle toward the close of 1854.

In the coastal field Pierce & Kendall, located at 3½ Commercial Street, founded schooner services to Charleston and New Orleans, known as the "Excelsior Lines." Their Charleston associates were Messrs. Trout & Delange. In New Orleans they were represented by Charles Beake & Company.

Silloway, Calef & Company, 5 Commercial Street, instituted services to Mobile and Charleston in 1855. They were represented in Mobile by H. O. Brewer & Company, while N. W. Webb acted as their Charleston agent. The following year they engaged in the Texas trade with packets to Matagorda and Galveston, a traffic in which Pierce & Bacon, 61 Broad Street, were already heavily engaged.

Other prominent Boston concerns included Messrs. Wheeler & Peck, 16 Long Wharf, who established lines to New Orleans and Charleston in 1854. Their New Orleans associate was the active and prosperous George Hynson & Company. Two years later Henry Lincoln, 57 Commercial Street, developed a line of barks and ships to New Orleans that was represented by George Hynson, individually.

Boston coastal lines—with due acknowledgements to Cape Cod—had always produced a sound proportion of exceptionally able commanders, but the crop of 1848, to go no farther, included two men who were not only mariners of the first rank, but were destined to play the leading roles in two of America's great sea tragedies. In 1848 Nicholas Holberton had the packet ship *Noemie* in Pearson's "Regular" line between Boston and Charleston. Later he commanded Ogden's clipper packet *Driver* which sailed from Liverpool in February, 1856, with a complement of 372, and was never reported. The other, Captain Josiah Richardson, was master in 1848 of the little packet ship *Townsend* in Allen & Weltch's Boston-New Orleans line. As related elsewhere, he was to go down with 180 more in the great clipper packet *Staffordshire*.

The only new Western Ocean line serving Boston, and it is possible to regard it as a continuation rather than a new line, was the Warren & Thayer Liverpool-Boston line that succeeded Train's "White Diamond" outfit.

Train, with the vast increase in immigration during the early fifties, had overextended his operations to such an extent that he became one of the first depression victims. It has been stated that his firm failed in 1857, the panic year. However that may be, the known facts would seem to indicate that it was in serious financial straits at a much earlier date. In August, 1854, Train was advertising a line of 13 ships scheduled to sail from Liverpool that fall, all but two of which ranged from 1500 to 2000 tons—a situation that suggests the firm had made commitments it was unable to honor when emigration came to a virtual halt the following month. Whatever the explanation, the line ceased operations as a line in December, 1854.

Immediately thereafter—that is, in January, 1855—Warren & Thayer, of Boston, took the field with a fleet of 14 medium-sized ships and advertised that they would sail twice monthly out of Liverpool on the original Train dates. Train did not appear as a participant in the management, although he may have held some undisclosed interest. He did, however, continue to advertise regular bimonthly sailings out of Boston, a service that he failed completely to maintain. He cleared a scant half dozen packets during the entire year and none that sailed on schedule. In 1856 even his advertisements ceased, and his ships were scattered, some going into the despised guano trade. On the other hand, it is to be noted that Warren & Thayer continued the use of the Train name for a time, probably because it was well known in the emigrant trade.

As usual New York led all competitors by a wide margin. In the transatlantic field she founded 16 new lines. New coastal activities included eight Charleston, three Savannah, nine Mobile, and nine New Orleans lines. In addition, 26 other substantial coastal lines were established to such ports as Philadelphia, Baltimore, Wilmington, North Carolina, and several Florida and Texas ports.

A majority of the new Western Ocean ventures were Liverpool emigrant lines, most of them established by operators who had been active in the general field for several years. Such founders included the eventually noted house of Williams & Guion, as well as Augustus Zerega & Company, who started the "Red Z" line to Liverpool in 1848, a line of the same name to Antwerp in 1851, and a third to Glasgow two years later. Another important firm was Stanton & Frost whose great three-decker packets frequently carried upwards of 900 passengers at a time. Messrs. Everitt & Brown started a similar Liverpool line in 1849 largely composed of huge three-decker clipper ships, including the *Governor Morton, David Crockett, Ocean Herald,* and *Monarch of the Sea,* all exceptionally fast, able ships, and one of which, the *Crockett,* set several notable Cape Horn records in her later career.

Lane & West was another prominent firm. They had a London line in 1852 and in spite of the fact that several fine steamships were then running to Havre, established their "Union" line to that port in 1856. They also maintained regular services to Mobile and New Orleans. Their Mobile associate was the vociferous and energetic James G. Whitaker, whose memory was embalmed for a time in the late eighteen-hundreds in the small boy "cuss word," "Gee! Whitaker!"

Other important new transatlantic operators were Messrs. Dunham & Dimon, who put their "New Line" to London in operation in 1854; Schuchard & Gebhard, in the Amsterdam trade; Spofford, Tileston & Company, who began their "Patriotic Line" to Liverpool in 1852, and William F. Schmidt & Company, who succeeded to the Antwerp line of Schmidt & Balchen after the *Helena Sloman* disaster.

The firm of E. D. Hurlbut & Company, who had been operating the fine New York-Mobile line and other lesser southern lines since 1825, expanded their operations in 1848 by establishing a line to Rotterdam. By the fall of 1850 they had seven lines in full operation, serving Havre, Antwerp, Rotterdam, New Orleans, Mobile, Apalachicola, and a line to St. Marks and Newport, Florida, that touched at Key West. For a time they were one of the most active firms in New York. By 1855, however, they were in financial straits and some of their southern and transatlantic enterprises were taken over in that year by Post, Smith & Company, who continued to operate the Antwerp line until the outbreak of war.

The flood of immigration noted in 1847 subsided slightly in 1848, but the following year witnessed the start of a spectacular six-year rise that was to culminate in the deluge of 1854, when more than 425,000 entered the States between the 1st of January and the 30th of September. To assemble and care for this mass of humanity in foreign ports, and especially in Liverpool, in the early manner, that is, with special representatives for each new line, would have been impractical, since it would have involved the duplication in a score of instances of complicated organizations with passage offices in communities scattered throughout Great Britain and Ireland. As a result there was a small increase in the number but a very decided increase in the size of loose organizations on the order of the "Black Star" line; loose, that is, in the sense that they represented several regular American lines and also supplied emigrants and cargoes indiscriminately to numerous transients.

As it happened, one of the first lines so affected was the "Black Star." In 1848 a new figure, John Taylor Crook, turned up in Liverpool as the second agent of that line. For a time he had some sort of working arrangement with Caleb Grimshaw & Company, but soon both concerns were advertising separate lists of "Black Star" ships to sail for New York at intervals varying from five to ten days. Something of the pressure of traffic confronting them is indicated by the fact that in February Crook's section of the line consisted of eight vessels. In July it comprised 24 and was clearing ships every four or five days and sometimes oftener, while Grimshaw's section was almost as active. Williams & Guion were the New York agents for the Crook ships, with offices at 40 Fulton Street. In 1851 the Liverpool agents were J. T. Crook & Guion, a fact that boded no good for Crook. He was dropped in 1852—Guion & Company becoming sole agents—and shortly thereafter he committed suicide.

Tapscott's line was a somewhat similar venture. It began operations in 1852 and soon became one of the more important immigrant lines. With Samuel Thompson's Nephew's line, it continued long after the Civil War. It is to be noted that the title of Thompson's line changed from time to time. At one time it was S. Thompson & Nephew's line and at another S. Thompson's Nephews', and at still another S. Thompson's Nephew's.

Another organization of the sort was the "Blue Ball" line started by Jacot, Taylor & Tipper, of Molyneaux Place, in 1851, usually advertising eight or ten ships at first, but increasing to 25 in the banner year of 1854. The line cleared most of its vessels for New York but first and last sent a good many to Philadelphia and New Orleans. In 1852 the firm figured in one of the long series of attempts to found a Liverpool-Charleston line, but its services were irregular and soon discontinued.

Messrs. Pilkington & Wilson and James Baines & Company—later specialists in the Australian emigrant trade, where their great three-deckers, mostly built in the United States and Canada, set records for speed and length of passenger lists never since equalled by sailing ships—also engaged for a time in the American traffic. Pilkington & Wilson established the "White Star Line of Boston Packets" in 1849 and a similar line to New Orleans somewhat later. In 1851 James Baines started a line to New York. Both firms sent large numbers of transient emigrant ships to other American ports, a practice followed by a number of British houses, among them James Browne & Company and Messrs. English & Brandon, both of which maintained a couple of regular "one-way" lines at the same time. In the busy early fifties this transient business assumed almost incredible proportions.

Broadly speaking, the activities of the above English firms and others listed in Appendix I, constituted the only important British competition that American passenger lines were called upon to meet, and, at that, it was heavily diluted competition. Virtually all the ships engaged on both sides were American built and for the most part American owned. There is also reason to believe that many of the operations were promoted, as undoubtedly they were supported, by American merchants. However, they did take a certain amount of business from exclusively American owned and operated lines, and while the latter profited, without question the lion's share of the earnings in many cases remained in England.

In the coastal trade New York's new firms included Eagle & Hazard, who went into the Mobile and New Orleans trades in 1848 with the famous "Eagle" lines. Their New Orleans representative was Levi H. Gale, while H. O. Brewer & Company represented them in Mobile. Other prominent New York houses were N. L. McCready & Company, 36 South Street; Alfred Ladd, 69 South Street, who had, among others, the "Empire" line to Mobile; Sturges & Clearman, who added an Havana line to their already long list in 1851, and D. Colden Murray, 62 South Street, who had been active for years in the Galveston trade in the firm of Hussey & Murray, and who in 1853 began to establish other coastal lines.

There were many others, among them Scranton & Tallman, of 19 Old Slip, and J. H. Brower & Company, 45 South Street, whose handsome medium clipper *Harvey Birch* (capacity, 700 steerage) was the first victim of the Confederate raider *Nashville,* formerly the pride of the New York-Charleston steamship line. Other active concerns included J. R. Gilmore, Van Brunt & Slaght, James W. Elwell, I. S. Gager, and Smallwood, Anderson & Company, some of whom not only maintained their old, but started new lines during the period.

It should be noted, also, that there were many important southern firms in addition to those mentioned heretofore. Among them Hunter & Gammell of Savannah, Fowler & Stannard and Edward J. Rivers of Mobile, and Messrs. Holmes & Storey of Charleston, were well-known representatives of coastal lines.

A somewhat disproportionate share of Philadelphia's new line activities during the period was devoted to the immigrant traffic. Three transatlantic lines were started as against only nine new coastal lines to the four principal southern ports. However, several other quite important services were installed, including four to the fast-growing port of Galveston, but as compared with Boston and New York the port manifested relatively little interest in new coastal ventures.

Stephen Baldwin & Company, a rising Philadelphia house, established a regular packet line to Liverpool in January, 1851. It consisted of four good ships ranging up to 1000 tons and was scheduled to sail from the home port the 1st, and from Liverpool the 18th of each month. At the same time Robert Taylor & Company started a substantial emigrant line between Londonderry and Philadelphia, sailing from the former port on the 1st, 10th, and 20th of each month. The following year the well-known house of Dawson & Hancock put their relatively short-lived Liverpool line in operation with the medium clipper packets *Sirocco* and *Euroclydon.*

Another Philadelphia firm, Messrs. Penrose & Burton, announced their intention of establishing a Liverpool line in 1854, but postponed the project when it became evident that a shipping slump of unusual severity was impending. However, they got under way early in 1856 with the fine ships *Lancaster* and *Westmoreland,* and developed a small but efficient service that John R. Penrose continued through and after the Civil War.

It is also to be noted that throughout the period James Browne & Company operated one of the larger and more substantial emigrant lines to Philadelphia with a high degree of regularity.

Most of the new Philadelphia coastal lines sailed to New Orleans and Mobile. A. J. Culin started a line to each of those ports, both called "Culin & Company's Regular Line," in 1848, following with a similarly named line to Charleston in 1851. The latter line, however, was sponsored by Messrs. Bolton & Culin. Fosdick & Charlock were the Culin associates in Mobile and R. M. Harrison & Company in New Orleans. H. F. Baker was the Charleston agent.

Another important figure in the coastal trade was Alexander Heron, Jr., who established the firm of Heron & Martin. He founded lines to New Orleans and Wilmington in 1849, and a third to Mobile in 1851. In 1856 the firm established a smart schooner line to Galveston.

Levi Eldridge took over the old "Hand Line" to New Orleans in 1848, and in 1851 extended his operations to Galveston and other Texas ports. Baker & Stetson, 43 North Wharves, got under way in 1852 with their "Merchant" lines to New Orleans and Wilmington, North Carolina. Their New Orleans associate was G. C. Bogert, 70 Camp Street. In 1856 they began the operation of a third line to Charleston.

Only one Western Ocean line was started by Baltimore during the period, although it is perhaps more in accord with the facts to regard it as the enlarged successor of the "spring and fall ships" that had been operated by the Liverpool Browns for many years, and that more recently had sailed as a "regular line of packets" under the management of Brown, Shipley & Co., of Liverpool, and James Corner & Sons, of Baltimore. This was the "Regular" line established in 1851 by Henry Mankin, of Baltimore, and James Browne & Company and Brown & Harrison of Liverpool. Mankin was succeeded in 1856 by Messrs. Foard & Rogers and the line continued down to the outbreak of war. Its operations always included a number of "one-way" emigrant packets in addition to those regularly scheduled out of both ports.

Virtually all of Baltimore's new coastal ventures came early in the period, only two important lines being established after 1852. "The Baltimore & Louisiana Regular Line" to New Orleans was founded in 1849 by Messrs. B. Buck & Sons, 93 Smith's Wharf. The same year James Hooper (soon succeeded by Messrs. Hooper & Graff) started the "Hooper Union Line" to the same port. Another New Orleans service was started in 1851 by William Sterling.

James W. Brown, 81 Smith's Wharf, put on a line of schooners to Charleston in 1850, and in 1852 had a line to Mobile in operation. James Girvin, 93 Smith's Wharf, started a mixed line of schooners and brigs to Savannah early in 1850. The enterprising firm of Brigham, Kelly & Company acted as the Savannah representatives. Another old Baltimore firm, W. Rhoades & Son, expanded its business in 1850 to include new lines to Savannah and Mobile. Still another Baltimore house, Kelsey & Gray, entered the packet field in 1851 with their "Southern Lines" to Charleston and Savannah. Their Savannah agents were Ogden & Bunker.

Aside from the foregoing, there were several miscellaneous lines to Wilmington, North Carolina, and other ports. Perhaps the most important, and certainly the most significant of these as indicating the growing industrial importance of Rhode Island, was the "New Dispatch Line" to Providence, founded in 1852 by Sam Phillips, 91 Bowly's Wharf. It comprised seven fine schooners and was still going in 1861. Its Providence office was on the "Packet Wharf" at Hughes Quay. About the same time other Providence lines were established to Philadelphia and several of the southern ports.

The southern ports, in fact, founded a number of lines during the period, which deserve more than passing notice. Included among these were lines between New Orleans and Charleston and Savannah, and also between New Orleans and Liverpool and Havre. One of the coastal services, the "Sumpter" line, was founded in 1850 by R. H. Harrison, of 14 Gravier Street, New Orleans. It ran to Charleston, and consisted of barks and schooners. The firm extended its operations to Savannah in 1852. Another important New Orleans firm was S. L. & E. L. Levy. They were running a line of brigs and barks to Charleston in 1852 and continued to do so through 1860.

A substantial emigrant line between Liverpool and New Orleans was started in 1850. It was called the "Crescent City Line" and operated seven or eight ships on a bimonthly schedule. The Liverpool agents were Webster & Company, 19 Dale Street. Fosdick & Company, 57 Camp Street, were the New Orleans agents. The line was represented in New York by Foster & Nickerson, 25 South Street. As with other emigrant lines the ships had no scheduled sailing dates from New Orleans, but were advertised to sail from Liverpool the 1st and 20th of each month, "or others in their places."

Another New Orleans-Liverpool line was founded in 1856. It was called the "Regular Line" and the Liverpool agents were Messrs. English & Brandon. J. P. Whitney & Company acted as the New Orleans agents. It was advertised to sail from Liverpool the 1st and 15th of each month. The venture was quite successful. In 1860 the line was operating nine ships, at which time its Liverpool representatives were Boult, English & Brandon, the New Orleans agents then being Cammack & Converse.

Charleston and Savannah both attempted to establish lines to Liverpool, and Charleston had a Havre line in operation briefly during the period. None of the attempts were attended with any great degree of success, probably for the reason that the ports failed to attract immigrants in sufficient numbers, although there were many individual transatlantic clearances advertised as packet line sailings through the years. New Orleans was more successful with its lone Havre venture. In 1854 Captain Sagory, an old New Orleans packet master, established a line consisting of three and, eventually, four ships which continued to sail throughout the decade in regular succession.

The year 1855 marked the end of the period of expansion of sailing lines. Thereafter a number of important operations were started but the abandonment of old services, especially from 1857 onward, brought about a steady reduction in both number of lines and net tonnage. In point of volume and numbers, the zenith of the canvas-back liner falls within the years 1853-55. Its zenith in relative importance and value of service was probably attained during the first half of 1854, the peak year of both coastal and immigration activity. Steam competition was still being contested vigorously in the Western Ocean passenger traffic and the coastal liners of the longer routes were still fighting a desperate but slowly retreating rear guard action.

By 1855, 24 of the early transatlantic lines had been discontinued but the number of those still active stood at 50, an all-time high. And it is to be remembered that the ships were more than triple the average tonnage of the first Black Ballers, with an impressive number ranging to five times their size. Of the 50 lines, 3 ran to Boston, 36 to New York, 5 to Philadelphia, 1 to Baltimore, 1 to Charleston, and 4 to New Orleans. In addition to these there were several French and German emigrant lines running more or less regularly to various American ports, especially to Philadelphia, Baltimore, and New Orleans, from 1848 onward. Although individually they were relatively unimportant, they handled in the aggregate a substantial number of emigrants.

In the same year there were 124 well-equipped coastal lines operating between the eight principal ports under consideration. Of these, 36 sailed from Boston, 47 from New York, 24 from Philadelphia, 11 from Baltimore, and 6 from New Orleans, 4 of the latter to Charleston and 2 to Savannah. A majority consisted of from four to six vessels, but many lines had more, ranging up to a dozen "regulars."

In this connection, however, it is to be noted that many operators ran "extras" during the busy season. Thus, an outfit like the Pearson concern of Boston frequently ran from one to three extra ships a week when freights were good.

The foregoing summary, confined as it is to a few of the principal ports, gives a quite inadequate picture of coastal packet activities as a whole. All eight ports had numerous lines running to the smaller ports outside the purview of this study. Boston, for instance, had a dozen substantial lines trading to the smaller New England ports, with still others ranging from Albany to Galveston. The same in varying degree may be said of New York and the other six.

As early as 1851, indeed, the New York directory listed 85 sailing packet lines and 17 towing lines handling barges and canal boats, including passenger packet boats, none of which are included in the foregoing summary. All the towing lines and many of the sailing packet lines sailed daily, serving the smaller coastal towns from Maine to Texas and from the Jerseys to the Great Lakes. From this it will be seen that New York alone is to be credited with a total of 119 coastal lines in 1851, most of which were still operating in 1855.

In addition to these, all the larger seaports from Eastport to Galveston maintained from two to eight or ten lines. Wilmington, North Carolina, had eight lines to northern ports alone. Galveston had ten. Georgetown, Darien, Norfolk, St. Marks, Apalachicola, to mention but a fraction of the packet ports, were served by several lines each. Salem had several coastal lines, including one to Charleston. Providence had six southern lines. Chesapeake Bay was not only alive with local packet lines, but Norfolk, Portsmouth, and Alexandria in Virginia, and Georgetown, D.C., had extensive packet connections with both northern and southern ports.

Still other packet lines, similar in character but distinct from the coastal lines, were those trading to the Canadian Maritime Provinces and the West Indies, principally to Nova Scotian ports and to Havana, Matanzas, Vera Cruz, Cartagena, and St. Thomas. They usually consisted of smart-sailing little barks or topsail schooners, but in the aggregate they handled a large volume of freight. The character of the West Indian trade had changed little through the years since colonial days. The provincial lines of the period supplied most of the grindstones and plaster for the eastern states, besides conveying large numbers of recent immigrants to the land of their second choice.

Even the addition of the foregoing facts and figures fails to give a comprehensive picture of the American merchant marine as a whole. We must still sketch in other highly significant details. In the five years from 1851 to 1855, inclusive, the country had launched nearly 2,500,000 tons of the finest craft afloat, a scant 500,000 tons less than its entire fleet in 1850. The line ships, impressive as they had become for size and numbers, accounted for only a fraction of this growth.

It will be remembered, moreover, that this expansion had been accomplished in spite of an enormous and growing diversion of manpower and capital to other activities. Thousands of miles of railway and telegraph; scores of huge coal, iron, lead, and copper mines; great foundries and factories by the dozen; hundreds of new towns and cities—all the vast and varied elements of a new, machine civilization had been and continued to be developed with unparalleled rapidity.

It is well to keep these facts in mind, for they explain in large measure that ruthless competition for both freights and capital (including the capital earnings of the ships themselves) which confronted the sailing liners of 1855 and which was largely responsible for their eventual disappearance. In addition, they had a distinct bearing on the depression culminating in the panic of 1857 and the hard times which followed it. In another aspect, the explanation of the remarkable and prolonged increase in ship construction is essential to an intelligent understanding of maritime history and—it may be—American history in general.

Why was it that a merchant marine which had required more than two centuries to reach the 3,000,000-ton mark, added little short of another 2,500,000 in the space of five years, to reach a high of 5,212,000 tons in 1855, a volume that exceeded for a time that of Great Britain, the "Mistress of the Seas"? Many factors were involved, only the more important of which can be noted here.

It will be recalled that construction was stepped up sharply by the extraordinary demand for foodstuffs abroad in 1846-47. Although the return of that traffic to normal in 1848 produced for a time widespread unemployment of ships of the general freighter sort, the need for superior ships of the largest size was prolonged by a huge prospective increase in immigration, induced by want and the social unrest that resulted, among other things, in the Second French Republic. This demand assumed unprecedented proportions in September, when the announcement of discovery of gold in California created a new and greater need for tonnage, which, with the help of successive lesser stimuli, was to continue unabated for another five years.

There was, for instance, the factor of Britain's repeal of her navigation laws in June, 1849, which made it possible for American vessels to compete on equal terms in her foreign trade, thus giving immediate and profitable employment to scores of large ships. Australian gold discoveries in 1850-1851 further stimulated construction which, incidentally, was responsible for some of the noblest clippers that ever sailed the seas. The Crimean War which broke out in 1854 took up more of the slack.

However, for our purpose, which is concerned primarily with line ships of the sail, the most important single factor was immigration. Before 1847 it had exceeded 100,000 a year on only three occasions. Usually it ran well below that figure. In both 1847 and 1848 it ranged above 225,000 for the first time. The following year it jumped to nearly 300,000 and in 1850 fell only a trifle short of 270,000. The upward trend continued, however, through 1854, in which year the influx exceeded 425,000, a record which was to stand for 20 years.

Another record, which still stands, was established on the 19th of May in the same year, when 35 ships entered New York harbor in a single day, bringing 12,741 immigrants.[1]

More than a century later New York papers acclaimed the arrival of several super-liners on September 3rd, 1957, with 9358 passengers as constituting the all-time record for arrivals in a single day at any American port.[2]

In 1855 the eight-year trend was sharply reversed, barely 200,000 arriving. Thereafter the traffic dropped year by year during the remainder of the decade, until in 1861 less than 92,000 entered the country. During the record-breaking eight years, however, the enormous total of nearly 2,500,000 immigrants had arrived (the official figure being 2,441,078), the vast majority of whom came in sailing ships, since ocean steamers of that period, with few exceptions, did not carry steerage passengers.

One can appreciate now only with difficulty the impact of this vast, unheralded increase of traffic on American shipping circles, supplemented as it was by the new California and Australia requirements. It may be useful, however, to recall that despite the earlier construction of a few large vessels, the average capacity of the transatlantic liner before 1847 was, roughly, 300 steerage. Transportation of the immigrants of 1850 would have required more than a thousand round trips of such vessels. Even when due allowance is made for British, French, and German ships engaged in the traffic—and the number, though substantial, was relatively small—it is sufficiently evident from the standpoint of today that the situation would soon call for a huge increase in size and number of passenger vessels. It is perhaps equally obvious that coastal shipping would be affected in somewhat similar fashion, both in the transshipment of immigrants to their ultimate destinations and in assembling the cargoes of the Western Ocean liners themselves, as well as in meeting the needs of the industrial North, then increasing at a rate that threatened to outstrip the remarkable expansion of British industry.

The shipping fraternity of 1848 did not have the advantage of present-day hindsight, but it had what served quite as well, a dynamic mixture of vision and nerve. As word of the throngs flocking to the principal ports of Europe slowly filtered through in 1847 and 1848, they began to lay down keels of craft that made pigmies of the great three-deckers already afloat. Liners were built, such as the *Great Western, Constellation,* and *Washington,* which could and did accommodate nearly a thousand steerage in addition to crews of 40 or more. And for every one of these there were half a dozen with capacities ranging from 500 to 700 and more passengers, ships in the *Universe-, Andrew Foster-,* and *Isaac Webb-*class, all hailed in turn as marvels of the shipbuilder's art, and all embodying some new improvements for comfort or safety.

It is not strange that the new sailing liners excited admiration and wonder second only to that of the larger and longer steamships, the first of which were even then on the stocks. Men who had spent most of their lives building and navigating craft of 90 or 100 feet in length, single-deckers with eight- or ten-foot holds, could hardly look unmoved on the huge three-deckers towering 40 feet above them and stretching 225 feet and more from knightheads to taffrail, the whole massive fabric embodying the inspired craftsmanship of workmen who had no superiors. As one by one the new liners took the water the press described them in terms of unmeasured praise. Each of the thousand details of construction was recounted, and every new feature designed for the greater comfort or safety of passengers and crew indicated at length.

The greatest of the new sailing liners, laid down in 1848 and launched in the spring of 1849, was the *Constellation*. She rated 1602 tons, register, although actually, as was the case with all three-deckers of her day, she was a ship of much greater capacity. She also rated nearly a column of praise, much of it devoted to a meticulous account of the huge size of her timbers, knees, hooks, pointers, planking, and so on, together with the manner of their fastening; the fact that such technical details were regarded as of general interest suggesting, perhaps, the extent to which seaboard America was still nautically minded. The part devoted to the passenger quarters indicates the new and special interest in the comfort and health of passengers, which was undoubtedly due in part to the prospect of a new and lively competition. It read as follows:

> The spar deck contains a magnificent cabin of 45 feet in length with rosewood and mahogany finishings. The entrance to this is effected through a semicircular passage and folding doors at the "break" of the poop. The interior, in addition to large and capacious mess and sleeping apartments for the officers, bath room, closets, pantries, etc., is fitted up with six elegantly lighted staterooms for passengers. Throughout, the greatest taste is displayed; and though lacking the flimsy and gingerbread air of saloons in general, there is a richness and beauty in the fittings which does great credit to Messrs. Cutter & Youngs, to whom this part of the equipment has been confided.
>
> At the entrance of the cabin, and forming the passage to which we have referred, is situated a circular apartment, containing the dispensary and the main deck cabin staircase, by means of which latter, communication can be had with the passengers below, without exposure to the spar deck. Further forward, and between the fore and main hatchways, a large and capacious house is fitted up for the accommodation of second class passengers, range, galley, etc.; while the crew are comfortably provided with quarters under the forecastle deck.
>
> On the main deck (which contains six cargo ports four feet square) the lower cabin is situated. This, though not yet complete, is upwards of fifty feet in length, and is designed to contain ten or twelve double staterooms, together with pantries, storerooms, closets, etc. As with the other cabin, it is extremely well lighted, and so high between decks, that nothing can preclude that great desideratum to passengers, a free circulation of air throughout.
>
> The lower deck is thus left clear for freight or cargo, although the smoothness and finish of the knees and beams would rather lead one to conclude the contrary.[3]

As a matter of fact, it soon developed that the lower deck was also needed for passengers, so great was the increase in immigration during the next two or three years. Before long, the *Constellation* and her sister ships were bringing 800 and 900 and more passengers at a crossing. As time passed and the steamships cut more and more deeply into the first-class trade of the sailing liners, the operators of the sailing packets redoubled their efforts to attract and retain that desirable patronage. Not a new sailing liner was launched that did not have some new feature, and sometimes several, designed to promote the comfort or appeal to the pocketbook of prospective travellers. One move in particular proved helpful for a time, the provision for an extra class "for passengers who desired to go at an easy rate" but did not wish to mix with the steerage.

The *Joseph Walker,* a two-decker of 1325 tons, launched for Samuel Thompson & Nephew's Black Star line by Webb on the 22nd of August, 1850, was an instance in point. Her bid for patronage was described in the following manner:

> The *Joseph Walker* is built in the strongest manner and furnished with all the modern improvements and conveniences which make a journey to Liverpool in these packets so agreeable.
>
> The arrangements for the first, second and third cabins and steerage passengers are very comfortable. There are 3 skylights to the second and third cabins, and 3 skylights to the steerage, and 4 gangways to the steerage, which is well ventilated from the deck side lights below. The cooking arrangements are very complete, and are acknowledged by most shipmasters out of the port, to be the best in use. On the fore deck is an engine manufactured of sufficient power to throw the water over the main topgallant yard, to which is attached 120 feet of hose. There are likewise introduced through the sides of the ship, patent valves which will flood the hold of the ship with water in a short time, in case of fire or for cleansing purposes, which is one of the most useful improvements got up for ships.[4]

Magnificent as were the packets of 1849, grander and more lavishly equipped canvas-back liners were yet to come. Ships only slightly smaller were even more numerous. Among others, the *George Washington,* registering 1534 tons, was built for the Williams & Guion emigrant line in 1851, and the same year the *John Stuart,* of 1654 tons, was launched in Portsmouth, New Hampshire, for the short-lived venture of J. & J. Stuart & Company. In 1852 Spofford & Tileston sold the Dramatic line and started their new Patriotic line. They retained the old *Henry Clay* and added the new *Orient* built by George Raynes, of Portsmouth, New Hampshire. The *Orient* was a three-decker, 201 feet in length and measuring 1560 tons by the existing rule. Under the rule adopted in 1865 she registered 1833 tons.

After 1852 the big ships came thick and fast. Tapscott in 1853 got the *Emerald Isle,* called a clipper but actually a rather full-built vessel. She rated 1736 tons and was 215 feet in length. The same year Spofford & Tileston added two of the largest packets yet built to their Patriotic line, the *Calhoun* and *Webster.* The *Calhoun* was 1749 tons (1865 by the new rule) and the *Webster* was a trifle smaller with a length for measurement of 205 feet as against 207 for the *Calhoun.* As Westervelt & Mackay were preparing to launch the latter on the 6th of July, New York papers noted that she was the largest ship of packet mould ever built. However, she did not retain the distinction long.

With one exception, the three largest ships of orthodox packet design ever built in America were launched in 1854. They were the *City of New York* for the D. & A. Kingsland line; the *Jeremiah Thompson,* for S. Thompson & Nephew's line; and the *Aurora,* for Grinnell, Minturn & Company's line, all plying between New York and Liverpool. Of these, the *Thompson* was the largest, registering 1811 tons on a length of 216 feet. Her tonnage was the same as that of the *New York* under the old rule, but under the new it was 1904 tons. The *Aurora's* tonnage, originally 1639, was raised later to 1858 tons, indicating that she was quite full-built.

It remained for the old southern packet firm of Stanton & Frost to attest their faith in the sailing liner by putting the largest ship of clipper packet type ever built in commission in 1856. She was the *Ocean Monarch,* the second of that name; a Webb production registering 2145 tons, with a measurement length of 240 feet, which would indicate an over-all length exceeding 250 feet. Her depth was slightly more than 30 feet. Two years later, when Stanton & Frost sent her to New Orleans, it was stated that she was the largest ship that had ever moored along the levee, and she also stowed the largest cargo in that port, 6900 bales of cotton.

However, the *Ocean Monarch* was neither the first nor the only one of her kind. As competition between sail and steam tightened, it was inevitable that the clipper ship should be given a thorough trial. Aside from the *Universe,* called a clipper but actually a rather full-built vessel, one of the first of these was the extreme clipper *Typhoon,* a 1600-tonner and the longest packet afloat when she was launched in 1851 for D. & A. Kingsland's Empire line of Liverpool packets. She proved as fast as she was sharp. On her first crossing in March, she ran from Portsmouth, New Hampshire, to Cape Clear, Ireland, in 11½ days and was off Holyhead, Wales, befogged, in less than 13 days.[5]

About the same time David Ogden and associates in the "St. George" line had the *Racer* built at Newburyport by Currier & Townsend. She rated 1669 tons. She also proved exceptionally fast, reporting a day's run of 394 nautical miles in 1852. Later Ogden added three more clippers, the *Highflyer, Driver,* and *Dreadnought,* the latter of which survived for many years and made many fast passages. Incidentally, her commander, Samuel Samuels, instituted a new feature to attract the first-class trade. The *Dreadnought* carried a brass band.

Boyd & Hincken, who had maintained for a quarter of a century a reputation for trying anything once, had the medium clipper *Mercury* built by Westervelt & Mackay. She was launched the 3rd of September, 1851, and took her place in the Havre line that fall. Although she set no records, her passages were usually shorter than average.

The clippers of Everitt & Brown's Liverpool line have already been mentioned. Their *Ocean Herald,* a noble ship of 2135 tons, was the second largest clipper that ever sailed in an American line. Her official measurement length was 235 feet. Her over-all length was a trifle short of 260 feet.

Philadelphia had three clipper liners. Richardson, Watson & Company operated the *Nonpareil,* a vessel so sharp that her rated tonnage was reduced under the later rule from 1437 tons to less than 1100 tons. She was credited with a remarkable run of 13 days from the Delaware Capes to Liverpool in 1855.[6] The Hancock & Dawson line acquired the *Sirocco* and *Euroclydon,* medium clippers built in Baltimore in 1852 and 1853, respectively.

Down in Boston, Train added three medium clippers to the White Diamond line as early as 1853, the ill-fated *Staffordshire,* 1817 tons, and the *Chariot of Fame* and *Star of Empire,* sister ships of 2050 tons. All were built in Donald McKay's yard.

Other sharp ships were put on the Western Ocean run by various operators from time to time. In general, they made rather better passages than the full-built packets, but it is doubtful whether they did much to retard the gradual elimination of sail from the first-class passenger traffic. Few remained in the service long, and almost none after 1855; the *Dreadnought* and *Nonpareil* being notable exceptions. Most of the others were soon diverted to the longer trade routes, especially the Californian, Indian, and Australian trades. Several were lost.

Nevertheless, the victorious course of steam was by no means smooth or altogether continuous. Down to 1853, it was retarded and even reversed from time to time by the grimly determined efforts of masters of the cotton-powered craft who made a number of well-advertised passages of 14 or 15 days—fair steamship time—and by the tragic loss of several fine steamships; the two circumstances combining to revive, temporarily, the popularity of sail.

In addition, there were a few master mariners whose qualities assured them of a substantial personal following which continued to fill their cabins long after the majority were sailing with a scant half dozen to monopolize their spacious saloons. Down to the closing days of sail, indeed, there were always some who for reasons of health, curiosity, economy, or downright preference, continued to travel in the wind ships.

But in spite of all that man and the elements could accomplish, cabin passenger lists of the Western Ocean sailing liners continued to shrink in comparison with those of the steamships to such an extent that by the summer of 1853, the practice of giving them to the newspapers for publication was discontinued. This did not necessarily mean that their owners and operators had lost confidence. There is much to indicate that they continued to look for a revival of first-class traffic until the sharp curtailment of travel after 1857 finally put the matter beyond all doubt. At all events, they continued to build ships with magnificent, spacious, and airy cabins capable of accommodating upwards of a hundred first- and second-class passengers long after the average number carried amounted to less than ten per cent of capacity.

Of the several factors which combined to speed the process of separating the great sailing liners from their cabin patronage, two deserve special mention. One was the very thing that had affected adversely the fortunes of the steamship at the outset, the loss of ships supposedly possessing a superior margin of safety, accompanied by terrible suffering and heavy loss of life. The other, paradoxically, was the very success of the sailing liners, which led to overcrowding to such an extent that emigrants died by the score in conditions of indescribable squalor, with the result that many first-class passengers ceased to patronize such ships.

As one after another of the stout windjammers foundered, burned, or beat their lives out on rocky coasts, the sailing liner's strongest argument went with them. The emigrant ship *Omega* from Liverpool with 315 steerage foundered in March, 1848, with a loss of 170 lives, the remainder being saved by the ship *Aurora* and bark *Barbara*. On February 28, 1849, Hurlbut's Antwerp packet *Floridan,* commanded by E. D. Whitmore, was lost with 200 German emigrants, only one passenger and three seamen being saved. The fine, new *Caleb Grimshaw* was burned at sea the 12th of the following November. Although the bark *Sarah,* of Yarmouth, Nova Scotia, Captain David Cook, master, rescued 399, at least 60 were lost and all the survivors suffered terrible hardships.

By a curious coincidence the skipper of the little Baltimore brig *Francis Travers* was more fortunate. Bound for the West Indies in the month of May, 1848, he lost his mate and three men overboard in a squall. The following day as he was debating the question of abandoning his venture and making for the nearest port, he picked up a ship's boat with four men. Thus reinforced, he was enabled to proceed on his voyage.[6]

Whether because the decade then beginning was exceptionally stormy or because the number of ships had increased, the loss of fine packets and liners during that period was unprecedented. Word came to New York in January, 1850, of the total loss of the *Oneida* near the island of Guernsey. The new packet *L. Z.* of Zerega's "Red Z" line, foundered the 17th of the month. Shortly after, the Havre liner *Argo* went ashore 25 miles east of

Fire Island Light, where she remained for a year. Late in March the packet *John R. Skiddy* was lost on the English coast, and on April 2nd the old *Champlain* was wrecked on the Bahama Banks. In July the ship *Elizabeth*, from Italy, went ashore on the eastern end of Long Island. Among others, Horace Sumner, a brother of Charles Sumner, and Margaret Fuller (Marchioness Ossoli) perished in the wreck. Henry Thoreau came down from Concord to salvage her manuscripts but found only a few shreds of clothing.

However regrettable such losses were, the vessels themselves were replaced in general by larger and finer ships, a development further facilitated by the transfer of a number of packets, some of which were only five or six years old, to the California run. During 1849 the list of transferred ships included the *Silvie de Gasse, Sheridan, St. Patrick, Saratoga, Victoria, Versailles, Francis Depau, Hibernia, Natchez, Utica,* and *Virginian.* Most of them ranged from 525 to 600 tons and upwards. All were replaced with ships ranging from 800 to 1400 tons.

The old captains were harder to replace, and in general their successors lacked the same generous measure of certain qualities of heart and soul many of the older generation possessed; qualities perfected in the greater independence and greater hardships incident to navigation of the little craft of an earlier day. Such, at least, was the contemporary verdict, if obituaries are to be believed, on such men as the old Black Baller Hugh Graham, Captain Charles C. Berry, and Robert Waterman, late master of New Orleans packets, all of whom had the good fortune to die in their beds.

Others were less fortunate. Stout old Captain S. C. Knight, late of the packet *Nicholas Biddle,* was swept off the poop deck of Taylor & Merrill's *Ivanhoe* by a tremendous sea in the early morning of November 29th, 1850, while hauling on the main-topsail brace. Four months later the ship herself was lost off Montauk. There was also the master of one of Dunham & Dimon's packets, whose loss was reported in the New York papers of June 30, 1852.

Capt. John D. Hasty of the packet bark *Jasper,* from Charleston was lost overboard Saturday evening, June 19, in spite of superhuman exertions by the crew to save him. In the sight of a crew who loved him as a father, and friends whose agonized hearts were breaking, the mighty waters closed over one of the noblest spirits and bravest sailors that ever trod a vessel's deck. 'Til the sea give up its dead, rest in peace.

In January, 1852, it was reported that D. & A. Kingsland's fine packet *Columbus,* Captain Robert McCerren, was totally lost on the Irish coast, 12 of the passengers and crew perishing. The *St. George* was burned December 24th with a loss of 51 lives, the remainder being rescued by the ship *Orlando,* Captain White. One of the worst disasters in packet history was the sinking of the great clipper packet *Staffordshire* on December 29th, 1853, near Sable Island, with a loss of 180—a disaster made doubly tragic by the death of her master, Josiah Richardson, a seaman of exceptional ability and a beloved and respected Christian gentleman. There were other losses during the year where all hands were saved, but the fact that "the safest ships in the world" were disappearing faster than the "dangerous steamship" was duly noted.

For the social or political historian all years are alike. It is much as though their great men control even the forces of nature and smooth the seasons to an even pattern. For men concerned with the fundamental businesses of life and its material supports, it is quite otherwise. For them each year is marked by, and remembered for, some outstanding characteristic. Here is what one of their spokesmen, the editor of the *New York Shipping and Commercial List,* had to say of 1854:

It may be said without any exaggeration, that the year just closed will be long remembered for the number and variety of its convulsions—its collapses and general embarrassments in business, not only in our own country, but in and about all other lands coming within the sphere, or subject to the influence of commerce and finance.[7]

It was, among other things, a bad yellow fever year, and as such had caused a partial crop shortage through its curtailment of southern planting. It was the year in which the nation began to reap the reward of long-continued, reckless speculation. The last six months, indeed, brought ruin for many, and staggering losses for all shipping houses. It was, in short, the beginning of seven years of acute depression which culminated in the panic of 1857 and continued to the outbreak of civil war.

Those who sailed and travelled in the ships had still another story. For them the year was the beginning of four years of almost unparalleled violence—four years when the "Wild Atlantic" seemed to take special pains to deserve its title—when gale followed gale in endless succession—when more stout, A-1 line ships were lost than in any other period of equal length in the nineteenth century.

First to go were the packets *Waterloo* and *Leviathan.* They were reported missing early in 1854, and with the *Leviathan* that fine master mariner, Captain Knapp, of Fairfield, long a popular commander of southern packets. The packet *Prince Albert* foundered early in January, Captain Bradish and crew, with 16 passengers, being rescued and landed in Queenstown. On March 15th the Boston packet ship *Russell Sturges* foundered.

Her passengers were taken off by the packet *Isaac Webb,* of New York; Captain Hamlin of the bark *Rainbow* taking the crew. Shortly thereafter the emigrant ship *Powhatan,* of Baltimore, piled up 12 miles below Barnegat with the loss of every soul on board, about 250 in all. The loss of the Boston packet *Winchester* is described elsewhere. The *Argo,* an ex-Havre packet, then running in Samuel Thompson & Nephew's line, foundered on or about April 15th, her crew being rescued by the British ship *Mohongo.* About the same time word was received that the *Sea Nymph* had foundered in March, her passengers and crew being taken off by the ship *Pride of the Ocean* and carried to London. On the 17th of May the Black Baller *Montezuma* went ashore opposite South Hempstead, Long Island. Fortunately, her 400 passengers were landed without the loss of a single life. The same papers that reported her loss reported the foundering of the new packet *Black Hawk,* a Sturges, Clearman & Company emigrant liner. Captain Bunker, crew, and 356 passengers were rescued by the ship *Currituck,* Foster, master, and brought to New York.

The toll of coastal packets was also greater than usual. Among them were the ships *Columbiana, Camillus, Niagara,* and *Delia Maria,* and the barks *Loretto Fish* and *Quinebaug.* The old packet *Great Britain* which had been in the coastal trade for a time was lost in the St. Lawrence River. The foregoing losses were without loss of life, except in the case of the *Quinebaug* which went missing with all hands. They were accompanied, however, with severe, and in some instances, terrible hardship.

Captain Fletcher of the packet ship *Cornelius Grinnell,* who rescued the crew of the *Columbiana,* said when he arrived in New York February 24th that they had encountered the worst weather he had ever experienced. When he fell in with the *Columbiana* on January 26th, her decks were swept, all the masts gone and the crew were lashed to the pumps. Their rescue was performed under conditions of great danger, not to mention the hardship of the men who had to be hauled through the water to the boats of the *Grinnell.*

The year ended with the total loss of the Grinnell, Minturn Liverpool packet *Queen of the West,* Pennell, master. She went ashore the 16th of December on Longharne Sands, Carmathem Bay, and broke up, fortunately without loss of life.

Almost as bad in their effect on the travelling public were the stories of extraordinary hardship and suffering entailed, not merely in the numerous wrecks, but in the regular passages of the stoutest sailing craft afloat. All through the stormy fifties the tales came drifting back. There was the first-class packet ship *Jacob A. Westervelt* which sailed from Liverpool the 5th of October, 1853, with 700 passengers. She encountered one head gale after another and when she finally arrived weeks later on the Banks of Newfoundland, stripped of sails and partly dismasted, her pump-weary crew mutinied and forced the captain to return to Liverpool, the passengers siding with the crew. The suffering of those on the ship *Continent* about the same time was even worse. She eventually reached port, but when her passengers were taken off by the ship *Philanthropist* she had nine feet of water in the hold and for days they had labored to free their quarters of four feet of water that had poured below through smashed hatchways.

The largest and strongest ships afloat were not exempt. In the winter of 1854, McKay's great *Chariot of Fame* and the first-class packet *Parliament* encountered a hurricane that forced them into Provincetown on the 24th of February. The *Chariot* was a 2000-tonner, one of McKay's staunchest productions and a virtually new vessel to boot. She had lost every sail she had bent when she left Liverpool, most of them blown out of the gaskets. Her main yard, mizzen-topgallant mast, boats, and figurehead were gone and her cabin filled. Her crew of 40-odd were frostbitten and completely "beat out." The *Parliament* was in little better condition.

Winter after winter such passages were reported with depressing regularity, until early in 1856 when a temporary climax was reached. Usually they were accepted—however ruefully—as part of the day's work. Captain Dunn, the famed discoverer of Symmes's Hole, however, considered that he had a special grievance. In the smart clipper packet *Nonpareil* he limped in by the Delaware Breakwater the 12th day of February, 1856, 72 days out of Liverpool. His passage was nothing unusual for length, for most packets were taking from 60 to 80 days for the crossing about that time. His plaint was that for a second time he had been a reluctant contributor of shingles for the subterranean "meeting houses," this time to the extent of two full suits of heavy sails. At that, he was more fortunate than many another, as the lengthening list of missing ships attested.

Few packet logs recorded more serious accidents mingled with hardships than that of the *Underwriter* of the Kermit line, while under the command of Thomas Shipley, late master of the Dramatic liner *Garrick*. Shipley sailed from Liverpool the 23rd of January, 1856. He took his pilot off Sandy Hook 76 days later. His log noted that on the 31st of January, while reefing topsails, a man fell from the fore-topsail yard and was seriously injured. A hurricane on February 12th blew away every sail set, and two men fell from aloft and were badly hurt. On the 3rd of March a man fell from the main-topsail yard. The 80-foot drop cost him only a sprained wrist, for he had the good fortune to bounce off a couple of stays on the way down. A bad leak developed on the 12th of March and thereafter the passengers and crew exercised the pumps and threw cargo overboard. The same day one man was swept overboard and another fell from aloft and was killed. On the 27th of the month the decks were swept clear of everything movable by an enormous wave that carried a passenger to his death.

Loss of ships attended with great loss of life was another matter. Something of what might be and frequently was involved may be gathered from the story of the *John Rutledge,* a Howland & Ridgeway immigrant ship of 1060 tons, commanded by Alexander Kelly. She hit an iceberg the night of February 19, 1856, and Captain Kelly and crew of 24, and as many of the 120 passengers as could find space, took to the boats, leaving the first mate and about a third of the steerage to go down with the ship. The rest is told in the journal of young Charles H. Townshend of New Haven, Connecticut, then chief officer of the *Germania,* one of Whitlock's Havre packets:

February 29th fine breeze from the NNW, ship under reefed sails, standing to northward. It had been blowing hard the night before and a tremendous sea was heaving up from the NW. At meridian I was relieved by the second mate after dinner. I went to my room to write the log book up. About 2 p.m. the 2nd mate came and said he was forward with some men rebending the outer jib, and thought he saw a boat ahead with a signal of distress flying. I took my glass, went on deck and went into the weather fore rigging, and made out a ship's boat with a man sitting in it, and to all appearance frozen stiff. I ordered the other watch to be called up, the lee quarter boat to be cleared away, ready to be lowered, main sail to be hauled up, and went and called Captain Wood, who was asleep having been up the greater part of the night before. He came on deck. We got ready to lower the boat and stood toward him until when about a mile from him the wind veered to the NNW, and as we could not fetch him on the other tack we hauled the main topsail to the mast—lowered the starboard quarter boat, and four men and myself went to his relief. After leaving the ship we could not get sight of the boat, the seas being so high, but was directed on our course by Captain Wood standing on the veranda deck pointing with his telescope towards the object of our search. When we were midway between the ship and the boat and in the trough of the seas the skysail truck of the *Germania* was out of sight, and another thing which was not agreeable, the intense cold. Every drop of spray which touched the boat seemed to turn to ice. I think I never suffered so much with cold.

From the time we first saw the boat until we were within three rods of her the man in her did not move, and I made up my mind that he was dead, but it proved to the contrary. Previous to our reaching the boat I had an opportunity to judge for myself the condition that I would find her frozen crew as every roll of the sea added horror to the scene. There sat a man in the stern with his pea jacket buttoned tight to his chin and on his head was his southwester slouched over his eyes, with both legs in water up to his knees, bare footed and frozen white. In the bow was an oar lashed to the stem—blade up, and to that a stick about four feet long, with the back of a shirt lashed to it, and a spring stay running from the top of the oar blade to the boat's stern, on which hung two shirts a red and a white one. He had raised them that morning hoping some passing ship might be attracted and rescue him from the jaws of death.

In the bow lay a man with his hat off, eyes wide open staring you in the face, and from the expression of his countenance showed he must have died a dreadful death. In the stern lay another stiff and cold in death, and about midship lay two women with their long hair washing from side to side with every roll of the boat, eyes and mouths wide open, firmly clasped in each others arms so firm that it was with difficulty that they were separated.

Upon the stern lay the ship log book, compass, chief officer's quadrant and epitomie, and floating around in the water was a number of belaying pins, bottles, blankets, shawls and wearing apparel of both sexes, also a coil of rope, a bolt of canvas, twine, etc. In the bottom a hammer, knife, ship's bell, binnacle, lamp and many other things showing discouragement and suffering.

When we had approached within four rods of the boat, I called to him, he looked up and showed his care worn face and crawled on his knees to the bow of the boat. I called to him, telling him that I could not board him bow on, but to give me a rope so that we could tow the boat. He caught hold of the boat rope or painter and tried to clear it. It being foul in the middle of the boat (the women that lay in the midship of the boat lay on it). He gave it a feeble jerk and made the following expression which was the first words I heard him utter—"God damn the rope, I can't clear it, for Christ sake let me get into that boat." By the time he had finished what he had to say our boats came together, he sprang head first into the boat (striking his head) and said, "O damn the boat let her go she is good for nothing."

As soon as he got into the boat he commenced to tell me his name which was Thomas W. Nye of Fairhaven, Mass. He said he belonged to the ship *John Rutledge,* which was lost in the ice on the evening of the 19th of February. Five boats left the ship and about forty or fifty passengers went down with the ship, the mate and carpenter being among the number. Said the dead bodies in the boat (there being four) were Mrs. Atkinson, the first mate's wife, a woman passenger and two men, one of them a passenger and the other a sailor. Said there were 13 in the boat when she left the ship, and all had starved to death excepting himself. Eight he had buried with his own hands and the others he had not the strength to do so. It was a horrid sight all laying with their mouths and eyes open, frozen stiff. He had no boots on. He said when they froze they pained him so much he cut them off and put them in one of the passengers coats. Said he expected to lose the use of them. After he had been in the boat ten minutes a stupor came over him and he became insensible. Got to the ship about 5 p.m. Passed a rope about Nye and took him aboard and put him in one of the cabin staterooms. Captain and Mrs. Wood commenced staying with him and with the greatest difficulty brought him to. The dead were consigned to the deep. Hoisted boat on board and filled away, stood on the starboard tack until 6 p.m. when we hove to, set lights in the rigging and kept a good lookout in case any of the boats should be near we might render them assistance.

Morning came. Sent men aloft at daylight but saw nothing, filled away. Set all sail with a fresh breeze from the NE.[8]

It was later ascertained that Nye was the sole survivor. Thanks to the care of Captain Wood and his wife, "who knew how to save legs but not how to amputate them," his frostbitten legs healed, although they seemed to be mortifying after Captain Wood had applied poultices to draw out the frost. It was four months before he was able to walk, but a short time thereafter he turned up in New York and asked to ship on the *Germania.*

The suffering at sea that terrible year of 1856 can never be told. The *Rutledge* was only one of an inordinate number of ships lost. Of that number the packets and immigrant liners were only a fraction, but a fraction that exceeded the loss suffered by the industry in any year before or since.

In quick succession during the early part of the year the London packet *Ocean Queen* with 90 passengers and the Liverpool packet *Driver* with 372, were posted as missing, closely followed by the old *Independence*. The Antwerp packet *Robert Carnley,* James D. Whitmore, master, sailed from New York the 2nd of January and was never reported. Two days later the new packet *Leah,* Captain Jonathan Latham, sailed from the same port and vanished without a trace. Early in May the fast clipper packet *Racer* was lost on Arklow Bank, off the Irish coast.

Captain Nathaniel Webber, who had commanded the little Baltimore brig *Triton* nearly 30 years before and who had hankered all his life for a big, fast ship, had taken charge of the huge three-decker *Trade Wind.* With 3400 tons of measured cargo—the largest that had ever been loaded in New York—and 46 first-class passengers in a hurry, he drove her around the Horn in 1852 to San Francisco in 103 days. When he lost her in collision in 1854, he went back into the coasting trade as master of the ship *Diadem,* one of William Frost's line of New Orleans packets. He sailed from New York for New Orleans in her on the 22nd of August, 1856, and a few days later the *Diadem* foundered in a hurricane.

There was little improvement as the year advanced. On the 12th of November the packets *Silas Wright, Samuel M. Fox,* and *Louisiana* were all lost in a terrific gale near Liverpool. The new "Red Z" packet *Adriatic* struck a sunken wreck and went ashore on the 5th of December, near Dunvargan; the second ship of the line to be lost on her maiden voyage. About the same time the *New York,* with 300 passengers, was wrecked on the Jersey coast and Captain Alexander McKinnon was nearly killed in the endeavor to protect his passengers from the brutalities of his crew. The old *Garrick* went ashore near Cardiff the same month and became a total loss. Other line ships which had been diverted to other trades went down or went missing in distant seas.

There is, perhaps, a temptation to exaggerate the part played by suffering and death in the sailing liners, in promoting steamship travel. Steamers also were sinking or going missing. Several were lost on the California run with tragic results, foundering in hurricanes or put ashore by convivial officers. The story of the Collins liner *Arctic* needs no further tell-

Old woodcut of loss of coastal steamboat *Home* showing the vessel at the moment she broke in two. Her loss with many prominent people retarded efforts to develop the coastal steamship service for several years.

Courtesy, Seamen's Bank for Savings

Courtesy, Seamen's Bank for Savings

Captain Elisha E. Morgan

Captain Ambrose Snow

Courtesy, The Marine Historical Association, Inc.

Scale model of Black Ball packet ship *Isaac Webb*. She was a three-decker built by William Webb in 1850. This model shows the typical deck arrangements of the great packets of the eighteen-fifties.

Packet ship *James Foster*.

Courtesy, Seamen's Bank for Savings

Courtesy, Maryland Historical Society

Contemporary scale model of Havre packet *Duchesse d'Orleans*. Model shows simplicity of deck arrangements and passenger conveniences in 1838 as compared with those of 1850, shown in model of *Isaac Webb*.

Courtesy, Seamen's Bank for Savings   *Courtesy, Seamen's Bank for Savings*

Elias Hicks   Joseph W. Alsop, Jr.

Courtesy, Seamen's Bank for Savings

Anson G. Phelps

Courtesy, Seamen's Bank for Savings

Paul Spofford

Clipper ship *Typhoon* of Portsmouth. One of the packets of the Emigrant Lines.

Courtesy, G. W. Patch

ing, nor that of the *San Francisco.* The great *Pacific,* of the Collins line, and the iron propeller *City of Glasgow,* both with heavy passenger lists, disappeared without a trace, and there were other distressing losses. The effect of such unfortunate occurrences was temporary at most. Looking backward, it seemed probable that the net result in the long run was merely to strike a balance of sorts between wind ship and steamship—but a balance in which the idea of the superior safety of the former went by the board, along with whatever influence it exerted on the travelling public.

The other factor, the overcrowding of both packet and immigrant ships, had, possibly, a greater influence. We have previously noted that it was legal for sailing ships to carry, broadly speaking, as many passengers as could be allotted a space of two by seven feet. It worked well enough during the years when they rarely carried much more than half their legal capacity, but when the great rush came in 1851 and succeeding years, it soon appeared that those responsible for the regulation had been hopelessly unrealistic.

All through 1851 and 1852 both large and medium-sized packets had been reporting near capacity passenger lists. On May 20th, 1851, the *Isaac Webb* arrived in New York with 760 steerage besides a handful of cabin passengers, and the *New World* followed the same day with 761. On the 29th of May the *Constellation* discharged 912, a record at the time. One can imagine conditions on such vessels, especially in bad weather with hatches closed. Even before the overcrowding had become so marked, the press was commenting on the heavy losses by ship's fever and the terrible conditions on arriving emigrant ships. Although nothing was more obvious than the fact that the conditions would continue to deteriorate so long as the ships continued to carry such swarming masses of humanity with only the most primitive notions of sanitation, while those responsible for operating the ships used quite as primitive measures for disinfecting the vessels between trips, nothing was done to correct the situation.

By 1853, however, conditions became so bad that public feeling was aroused. In October the *Winchester* arrived at New York from Liverpool, having lost 79 of her steerage, and the *Sagadahock* reported 70 deaths on reaching Boston a few days later. On the 15th of November the packets *American Union* and *Calhoun* arrived at New York, the former reporting 80 deaths, and the latter 54, of whom eight were members of the crew. A few days later the *Antarctic,* of the "Z" line, passed Sandy Hook with her flag half-masted for 65 passengers, and the Havre packet *Empire* lost 75 out of a total of 675 emigrants. On the 27th of November another Havre packet reported 75 deaths. By December it was noted that the packets were losing nearly ten per cent of their passengers, the observation having been evoked by the arrival of the *Constellation* after having buried 100 of her 922 passengers, and this in spite of her having 11 less than the law permitted. Her 922 passengers constituted a near record, but it was surpassed several times, the record being held by the *Washington* which landed 956 immigrants in New York on the 30th of March, 1852.[9]

In time there were the usual belated investigations, followed, after the usual dignified interval, by the usual inadequate recommendations, but the damage had been done. Thereafter, few who could afford steamship rates travelled in vessels carrying steerage passengers. In the course of time a few operators in the coastal trade considered it to their advantage to advertise that they carried no steerage, but the practice came too late to save their cabin traffic.

Although by 1854 the handwriting was on the wall—plain, in the light of after years—the Western Ocean contest was by no means ended. Men of the old packet breed were not built that way. They continued to lay down fine packets for several years, in lessening numbers, it is true, but the fact, as above noted, that they still equipped them with full-sized, expensively decorated cabins, indicated that they had not given up the fight for the first-class traffic. It was not until the terrible year of 1857 that anything like complete disillusionment came.

That year also started badly for the canvas-backers. A great gale swept the coast on the 20th of January, accompanied by a blinding snow storm. Many vessels went down with all on board, and more were wrecked with considerable loss of life. The day after the gale the fast clipper packet *Typhoon* limped in past Sandy Hook, 47 days from Liverpool, a mass of ice. Captain Salter had lost seven close-reefed topsails during the previous fortnight and had only 10 men out of a crew of 40 able to stand watch.

Abnormally bad weather continued on both sides of the Atlantic. Several days later, on January 23, Nesmith & Sons' fine ship *Confederation* went to pieces near Liverpool. Captain Corning, his first mate, and a boy who had stayed by the ship in the hope of getting her off, were drowned. In February the *Cathedral,* of Train's old line, foundered off Cape Horn, and in the latter part of April his *Star of Empire* was lost near Currituck, North Carolina.

Everywhere business was at a standstill. On the 30th of January New York papers listed 13 big American ships unchartered in the port of Havre alone, most of them nearly new vessels. Many packets and immigrant liners of the largest size were withdrawn for lack of passengers and sent to San Francisco, the guano islands, or the East Indies, among them the clipper *David Crockett,* which ultimately made more passages around Cape Horn than any other sailing ship in history—24 voyages to San Francisco and 24 return voyages, 48 in all.

Still, the new packets continued to come. Whitlock had the *Logan,* 1541 tons, built for his Havre line. William H. Webb launched the 1100-ton *Roger A. Heirn* on April 9th for Post, Smith & Company's line of Antwerp packets. In March David Ogden put the new *Victory* in his Red Cross line, a move which nearly offset the loss in May of the *Andrew Foster,* sunk in the English Channel by the *Tuscarora.* Williams & Guion commissioned Webb to build a 1400-tonner, launched the following September as the *Resolute.* In October the *Marianne Nottebohm,* 1202 tons, went down the ways and into Laytin & Company's Antwerp line.

For a time such optimism seemed justified. Immigration showed indications of reviving in the early spring. Several ships, including Spofford & Tileston's *Orient* and Taylor & Merrill's *Guy Mannering,* arrived in New York on April 10th with from 200 to 400 steerage apiece. On the 14th the *Jacob A. Westervelt* landed 590, followed on the 15th by the *John J. Boyd* with 675 immigrants consigned to William Tyson. A month later William T. Frost's *Ocean Monarch* brought several cabin passengers and 954 in the steerage. She was commanded by Pitkin Page, late of the little bark *Orbit* owned by Josiah Macy. The rush reached its peak on the 1st of July, when 15 ships arrived in New York on a single day, each bringing from 200 to 800 immigrants.

It did not last—could not last, in fact—in view of the tremendous overconstruction and overexpansion of all kinds during the preceding ten years, accompanied as it was by the reckless speculations and peculations of men who had learned nothing from 1837. On the 24th of August, as the first Atlantic cable was being laid, the country's second great financial panic started, touched off by the news that the great Ohio Life Insurance & Trust Company had closed its doors. Delauncy, Iselin & Clark and several other bankers suspended on the 26th and thereafter failures came thick and fast. On September 25th there was a "run" on every bank in Philadelphia. On the 13th of October, 18 New York banks closed and the remaining 33 suspended specie payments. The situation was quite as serious in Great Britain and Europe, with failures involving huge amounts. In England the great firm of J. & A. Dennistoun, Cross & Company, which had a branch in New York, eventually went under with liabilities exceeding $10,000,000.

A condition little short of complete paralysis affected business everywhere, but shipping with its enormous new tonnage was especially hard hit. All over the world, ports were jammed with vessels of the finest quality, waiting for cargoes that never came, finally to sail in ballast to repeat the experience in some distant harbor. In packet circles, the effect of the panic was to establish beyond all doubt the monopoly of steam in the first-class passenger traffic.

In the coastal service the contest between sail and steam was shorter and the results even more conclusive. One reason was that critical steamship problems were simplified or completely eliminated by the comparative shortness of coastal runs. Far less space was required for fuel, which made it possible to provide more adequately for passenger comfort, in addition to ensuring greater cargo space. The same circumstance also made for greater regularity in the performance of voyages. The transatlantic steamers, because of enormous fuel requirements, always sailed with paddles buried so deeply that their speed was materially reduced at the beginning of a crossing, while toward its end the ship rode so high as to affect its speed adversely again. The coastal steamer, with its smaller consumption and frequent opportunities for replenishing its bunkers, was able to maintain a fairly even rate throughout its passage.

It was, in last analysis, dependable speed that cast the deciding vote in the coastal passenger contest. As the fact was established that it was no mere fluke, but had come to stay, its appeal to the travelling public was irresistible. By 1850, moreover, it had largely offset the disadvantage the steamship was under in the matter of freight capacity. The S. S. *James Adger,* of Charleston, was fairly typical of the coastal steamships throughout the eighteen-fifties. Reference to her lines, reproduced in the appendix, indicates that science and experience could go little farther in the direction of speed design. There was, in fact, no appreciable improvement until the big iron propeller and more efficient engines replaced the wooden side-wheeler.

Such steamers made the run between New York and Charleston with almost perfect regularity in approximately two days, and covered the New York-New Orleans route in six to seven days, including stops. Despite tremendous efforts on the part of the sailing packets, which resulted in an occasional three-day run to Charleston or a near-record ten days to the Balize, below New Orleans, their average was nearer four or five times longer.

Nevertheless, they made an able and determined fight. Their first and most obvious move, larger ships and more attractive accommodations, failed because of the rapid multiplication of still larger and more attractive steamers. The time-honored weapon of fare reduction failed because the short passages—which greatly reduced steamship expenses in the matter of food, wages, and upkeep—enabled them to meet any cuts the sailing packets could make.

As sometimes happens, however, the competition led to one unanticipated gain which proved to be of inestimable value to sail for many years to come. This was the development—or, more accurately—the popularization of the tern, or three-masted schooner, which pointed the way to the great multiple-masted schooner of the latter part of the century, the most economical carriers of their day.

It came about in the following manner. The increase in size of the coastal packets, which was especially marked in 1845 and thereafter, affected the schooner as well as other rigs. As time went on, the schooner packet which had rarely exceeded 150 tons became the 200-tonner of 1846-47, while by 1848 smart 250-tonners were becoming popular. In the early eighteen-fifties, two-stickers of 300 and 400 tons and upwards began to appear. Their huge, heavy lower sails soon made it clear that the practical limits of the rig had been reached.

One of the first of the oversize two-masters was the *Cataract,* 319 tons, built in the summer of 1851 for Nathaniel L. McCready. She was followed closely by the *Norfolk Packet,* of 350 tons register, launched at East Haddam, Connecticut, by the Goodspeeds. She went into the Hunter Brothers' line between New York and Norfolk. Another two-sticker launched about the same time was the 305-ton *Wake,* built at Belleville, New Jersey, by Cornelius C. Jeroleman, who eventually built some of the largest schooners of the fifties.

Evidently McCready, or rather, Mott & McCready, were satisfied with the *Cataract* for they had a still larger two-sticker laid down before the end of the year. She was launched as the *North State* very early in 1852, her 431 tons making her the largest craft of the rig ever built up to that time. However, Nehemiah Hayden, of Saybrook, Connecticut, soon eclipsed her by launching the *Harriet Stephenson* the following October, a monster of 466 tons, and one of the few two-decker two-masters built before the Civil War.

By this time the big two-masters were going down the ways in rapid succession, a dozen or more before the year ended. Altogether, at least 16— the number is probably greater—were built in 1852 and it is to be noted that most of them provided cabin accommodation for 50 or more first-class

passengers, in addition to steerage. Even the *Julia M. Hallock* built at
Brookhaven, Long Island, early in 1851, was equipped to carry 50 passengers, although measuring only 280 tons. Her main cabin was 50 feet in
length, which would seem to indicate that her owners were not seriously
disturbed by the prospect of keener steamship competition.

Large two-masters continued to be built all through the eighteen-
fifties. By 1856 several were launched with a tonnage approaching the
500 mark. One of the first was the *Walter Raleigh,* 472 tons, built by
Cornelius Jeroleman at Belleville early in 1856. Jeroleman quickly followed with the *Langdon Gilmore* of 497 tons and the *Robert Caldwell*
which registered 447 tons, the latter intended for Mott & McCready's
New York-Charleston line. All two-sticker records were broken, however, when the schooner *Cordelia* was launched in Brooklyn in 1856 for
Thomas Dunham's New York-Savannah line. She was 145 feet in length
and registered 659 tons. After two or three years service, she was re-rigged
as a tern.

The three-masted schooner was nothing new. The rig, which usually
included a square fore-topsail, dates from the eighteenth century. Several
were built in America around 1800 and occasionally thereafter. It was
not, however, until the tightening of coastal competition in mid-century
that the type showed indications of becoming popular, although it had
become fairly common on the long seagoing steamships.

Even before the big *Stephenson* was launched in the fall of 1852, the
new terns were sliding down the ways. The largest of the year was the
clipper schooner *Indianola,* 523 tons, which soon went into the foreign
trade. Her length for measurement was 139 feet and 4 inches, indicating
that her over-all length probably exceeded 150 feet. Close in her wake
came the *Kate Brigham,* a fine yacht-like craft of 470 tons, which began to
sail in Dunham's New York-Savannah line in the fall of 1852. She was
named for a member of the family of Henry Brigham, a well-known Savannah merchant who represented the line. Evidently Dunham regarded
her as a success for he had the famous *Eckford Webb,* measuring 495 tons,
built in 1855. The *Webb* was followed in the fall of the same year by the
Fleet Wing, a tern of 497 tons, also built by Eckford Webb.

Following the *Kate Brigham,* the three-masters came in a never-ending
procession. They were launched from yards located all the way from
Maine to Maryland. At least 44 were built in the ten years from 1851 to
1860, with the probability that the list was much longer. They included
the 355-ton *Moses Taylor,* built in Milton, Delaware, in 1852; the *Mobile,*

a 399-tonner built by Francis West at Old Saybrook, Connecticut, late in 1853; the 412-ton *Mary Lucretia,* a product of the Zepheniah Hallock yard in Derby, Connecticut; the *Augusta G. Brewer,* a 399-ton tern built at Millbridge, Maine; the *Ralph Post,* 426 tons, of Port Jefferson, New York, all launched in 1854, and another Eckford Webb vessel, the *William L. Burroughs* of 497 tons, built for the Dunham lines in 1855. Philadelphia built very few terns during the period, the best known being the 360-ton *Andrew Manderson.*

A substantial majority of the big schooners of the period were produced by New York and the New Jersey area now included in the present port of New York. Several were built up the Hudson and in the smaller Long Island ports, with Brookhaven especially active. Connecticut ranked second in production of the type.

Hard-driven though they were, and notwithstanding the fact many of them were of out-and-out clipper mould, it does not appear that they set new records to any significant extent, although a number of their successors made some remarkable passages in later years. However, they were able to sail closer to the wind than the square-riggers, an advantage which enabled them to make slightly better average time. Unfortunately, the margin of superiority was slight in comparison with the improvement of steamship speed.

They were also more comfortable than the earlier sailing packets. With decks ranging up to 130 or 140 feet in length, and a breadth of from 30 to 32 feet, they surpassed many a 600-ton ship in deck space for passenger recreation and relaxation. But here also, the steamships provided deck accommodation on an even more liberal scale.

In final analysis, the big schooner claims to superiority were reduced to a single category. They were the most efficient and economical coastal freighters that had yet been produced. So far as passenger traffic was concerned, the most that could be said of them was that they prolonged somewhat the struggle between sail and steam. On the other hand, their superiority as carriers of bulk freight—coal, lumber, cotton, and the like—was so marked that they rapidly displaced the square-rigger almost completely in the coastal trade. Something of what was in store for the rig may be gathered from the fact that as early as 1860 it was reported that 5935 schooners had passed the Cross Rip lightship in Nantucket Shoals during the three months ending September 30th of that year.[10] Impressive as this figure is, it obviously gives an inadequate picture of the traffic, since a substantial proportion of the total went by way of Vineyard

Sound, and it fails to include any of the thousands engaged in the southern trade originating in southern New England, New York, Philadelphia, and Baltimore.

In the coal trade, especially, now expanding with tremendous rapidity, the three-master soon became the overwhelming favorite. One of the first coal schooners of this rig was the *Young America,* 370 tons, built at Elizabeth Port, New Jersey, in the summer of 1853 for the Cumberland Coal & Iron Company of Maryland. After the Civil War vessels of this type ranging up to 700 tons and more were laid down, not by the score, but by the hundreds. The part they played in supplying cheap coal did much to accelerate the industrial development of the northeastern states, and, indirectly, the entire nation.

Long before that came to pass, however, the last of the coastal packet lines had been transformed into freighting lines, exclusively.

CHAPTER XIV

∼ *1858-1860* ∼

Triumph of Steam

"Great in victory and in defeat, unconquered."

THE SHIPPING graph that had been climbing for 30 years—during the past ten of which it had resembled the course of a rocket rather than the curve of normal, healthy growth—had levelled off abruptly in the latter part of 1854. Sixty years were to elapse before it again resumed an upward trend, stimulated by the demands of a great war. Not that efforts ceased or that hopeful indications were altogether lacking at times. The stout determination with which men of the sail pitted bone and muscle against steel and steam set the stage for a final struggle that even in defeat was to add luster to their record. They never wavered.

It will be recalled that there was a brief upturn in business in 1856, followed by a sharp increase in immigration during the late spring and summer, developments which convinced many that the worst was over. New lines were started and orders for ships rolled in once more. Unfortunately the same optimism affected the entire business world, with the result that there was a sizeable addition to the already dangerous volume of rash speculative ventures. It was the old story of the thirties repeated, with enlargements. By the time of the panic of 1857, America's frozen assets had reached an all-time high. Largely because of this, in the years between the 1857 debacle and the greater cataclysm of the Civil War, depression became, for the great majority, the American way of life.

Nothing, it had seemed, could surpass the gloom that had prevailed in January, 1856, but January of 1858 was the darkest within the memory of the oldest merchants, both at home and abroad. From England word came back that British shipping was facing its worst depression in history. There and in America hundreds of the finest craft afloat were accumulating in their home ports. New York reported 800 and more, all of the larger sort, many of which were laid up for periods ranging from six months to two years. Immigration dropped to 123,126, approximately one-half the annual average 10 or 12 years earlier.[1] The next year was even worse.

Nominal wages of ship carpenters fell from $3.50 a day to $1.25, with little work to be had at that or any other rate. Master mariners who had commanded great three-decker packets and the noblest clippers afloat returned to the humble coasters that had given them their start in life, or went to farming or opened a tavern or engaged in some other small business venture. Others, who had carefully salted away their dollars, were able to view falling prices with equanimity, and even take advantage of opportunities to acquire desirable properties at bankruptcy prices. For the majority, however, the period was one of unrelieved anxiety.

Something of the situation in which merchants and mariners found themselves may be gathered imperfectly from the tally of customs receipts. In 1854 they had reached a record high of $64,224,000. In 1855 they dropped more than eleven millions to $53,025,000. The slight upturn in 1856-57, above referred to, followed, but in 1858 there was another drop and this time to a new low of $41,789,000. From there they climbed by degrees to slightly more than fifty-three millions in 1860, only to fall again in the first war year to less than forty millions.[2] This, it will be remembered, occurred in spite of the fact that tonnage had nearly doubled during the previous ten years and population had increased approximately eight million, or roughly 35 per cent, during the same period.

It was the hardest of hard times. Plants, factories, and shipyards were closed everywhere, many of them not to reopen until war contracts were forthcoming. For the first time mobs paraded the streets of New York with banners inscribed: "Give Us Work." There was, however, virtually no violence, such as rocked the industrial districts of Europe, and indeed few overt indications that the situation was anywhere regarded as critical. Harried and crippled merchants kept their mouths shut and gave an excellent and all but convincing demonstration of "business as usual." Christy's Minstrels and their imitators worked overtime to make the American public laugh, and *Uncle Tom's Cabin* duplicated their labors to make it cry, and so preserve a healthful balance. A froth of social and cultural activities gave an illusory picture of prosperity.

To take up the remaining slack, youngsters who a generation or two earlier would have been quite sufficiently exercised at tops'l halliards and lee braces, invented a new and strenuous game called "baseball." "It was played by nine men, including a pitcher and a behind man."

In the seaports it was only by going to the docks that one could get a reasonably faithful impression of conditions. There, instead of the innumerable clattering carts and hurrying crowds—all the noise and bustle of ships feverishly loading, discharging, and coming and going in rapid succession—one saw the same vessels week after week, the majority idle and deserted, topgallant masts housed and upper yards on deck; all but a favored few of the remainder loading so slowly that one could scarcely discern a difference in their draft from one week's end to another.

Sailings told a similar story, indicating that many operators who had cleared one or more ships a week for years now rarely sent a vessel to sea in the course of a month, and then with freights that barely paid expenses. Fortunately this condition was not universal. A number of the old, solidly entrenched lines were able to control a substantial part of such business as offered. Consequently they continued to observe at least a semblance of a schedule, although in many instances on scales successively reduced, until in the end sailings ceased altogether. This is not to be taken as indicating any general or precipitate abandonment of the contest, but as reductions enforced by the conditions of the moment and regarded as routine and temporary. That they were so regarded is further indicated by the fact that the establishment of new lines continued down to the outbreak of war.

Some of the stronger firms, indeed, continued to make money and, as will be seen, several built new ships, finished and equipped for the passenger trade in the most costly manner. For this, the old captains were measurably responsible. They were the last to be convinced that the day of the sailing passenger ship was over, and for some years they continued to furnish much of the money required to maintain the various services. Many—perhaps most—of the great packets were largely owned by them. They were responsible, also, for many of the expedients devised to attract patronage, which ranged from privately negotiated "excursion rates" to the interpolation of additional low-rate classes between the first cabin and steerage grades. Nevertheless, in spite of determined and shrewdly planned efforts which often entailed heavy losses, the period was characterized by a gradual deterioration in the sailing liner's position.

In this process the steamship continued to play the role that ultimately proved decisive, regardless of financial conditions. Those conditions could and did improve and the same was true of the steamship. The wind ship could not be improved, or, more accurately, could not be improved as a passenger and express carrier. In respect to those critical functions it had reached its peak in the years preceding 1857, while the steamship was still on the threshold of developments that were to astonish its most ardent protagonists.

Nevertheless, the progress of steam was by no means rapid or continuous, facts that justified in some degree the stubborn optimism of the sailing fraternity. The withdrawal of the Cunarders and the New York-Philadelphia-Liverpool steamers from the New York and Philadelphia runs during the Crimean War (1854-56) had eased the pressure on the canvas-backs to some extent. Other fine coastal and transatlantic steamers were laid up or their sailings curtailed during the same years for lack of paying business. The failure of the Collins' line and the voluntary withdrawal of the Ocean Steam Navigation Company from the Bremen route in 1857 had promised a further measure of relief. Two other minor steamship ventures, the little Clyde line and the British line between Havre and New York were soon abandoned. The effect of all these developments on the outcome of the contest was relatively slight. Possibly their most important result was to stress the fact that only the more advanced, efficient, and best managed steamships could compete with the sailing liners without the aid of a subsidy.

Both the Vanderbilt and Livingston vessels were in this class. They continued to furnish a superior service throughout the rest of the decade.

It will be remembered that the Cunard had restored its service early in 1856 with three wooden paddlers smaller than the Collins' vessels, but little, if any, inferior to them in speed, and a fourth, the *Persia,* the first iron steamship of the line and nearly 100 feet longer than the original Collins' quartet.

About the same time the Liverpool & Philadelphia Steam Ship Company (Inman Line) resumed operations with alternate sailings to New York and Philadelphia. Its three iron propellers ranged 2000 to 2500 tons register. They were somewhat slower than the side-wheelers, averaging 16 days on the westbound run to Philadelphia, but they were far more economical, a fact that enabled the company to operate without a subsidy.

In addition to the four old lines that had survived, five more were started during the years from 1858 to 1860 which were of sufficient importance to be regarded as effective competitors of the sailing packets. They included the Hamburg-American, the Norddeutscher Lloyd, and the Glasgow & New York Steamship Companies. A fourth, the Anchor Line, ran to New York only during the winter, its destination during the remainder of the year being Montreal. All the vessels of these lines were superior Scottish-built propellers ranging up to 2500 tons. They averaged ten knots or slightly more, and were capable of carrying nearly double the cargoes stowed by the side-wheelers of the same tonnage on approximately a third of their fuel consumption. Of greater relevance from the competitive standpoint was the fact that all were equipped to carry 300 or more steerage, in addition to first- and second-cabin passengers. It was this innovation that was to spell the final and complete elimination of the passenger sailing ship during the next 20 years.

A fifth line of considerable importance was established in 1859. This was the Atlantic Royal Mail Steam Navigation Company organized to maintain a service between Galway and the ports of Boston and New York. Its first steamship, the *Connaught,* an iron side-wheeler, launched April 21, 1860, on the River Tyne, was 378 feet in length and therefore somewhat longer than the *Adriatic,* which it was said to resemble. Its official 800 horsepower was about equivalent to 2000 horsepower according to the American computation then in use. The first five vessels of the line were 4400 tons register, all paddlers. The next four were propellers ranging from 3000 to 4100 tons.

It was reported that the first steamship of the line brought over upwards of 600 passengers and that 700 were already booked for the next one.[3] With due allowance for the customary exaggeration, it was evident that the line's policy of tapping Irish emigration at the source had an excellent chance of paying dividends, and largely at the expense of the Liverpool canvas-backers. In any case, it led to the immediate formation of another line by John Orrell Lever and other wealthy merchants of Manchester, which eventually took over several of the screw steamers of the Galway line.

These ten lines—only two of which were American, operating only four steamships, all told—appropriated a steadily increasing share of the old sailing ship business as the years passed.

Even the gloom of 1858 failed to depress the steamerites seriously. Their coastal lines multiplied quite as rapidly as the Western Ocean ventures. Vanderbilt ordered the largest iron steamship yet laid down in America, the three-decker *Champion.* She was built by Harlan & Hollingsworth and launched on the 28th of May, 1859. Her length was 235 feet and she registered 1419 tons. Another large iron steamer was under construction in New York at the same time. Her length of keel was 200 feet, and she was the first American iron steamship to be built to Lloyd's A-1 specifications. Launched by Delamater as the propeller *Matanzas* on the 1st of December, 1859, she proved both fast and economical.

All in all, it would have been remarkable if the steamship had not conquered in the end. The wonder is that the contest was so prolonged. Broadly speaking, from the standpoint of the canvas-backer, the period was one of slow contraction—consolidation of position from time to time— rather than continuous retreat. Several transatlantic lines were discontinued but they were newcomers for the most part, established when the immigration boom was approaching its zenith. The remaining lines merely curtailed operations during the worst periods of depression. The five oldest—Black Ball, Black X, the two Swallowtail lines of New York, and the Cope line of Philadelphia—continued to sail on schedule as before, with little change beyond the elimination of "extra" or "intermediate" sailings.

At times, indeed, as conditions improved temporarily, the men of the sail showed a disposition to counterattack. With the brief revival of immigration in 1858 Boston established two substantial new immigrant lines, the Page, Richardson & Company's "Merchant Line" to Liverpool, and Glidden & Williams' London line. Both houses were old, well-established concerns. Glidden & Williams had conducted a line for some years on the longest coastal run in the world, that between Boston and San Francisco, with conspicuous success. Their London ships ranged from 1100 to 1200 tons, only one of which, the *Franklin Haven,* was new. Most of the Page, Richardson vessels were smaller but the venture proved so profitable that two new ships were built in 1860, the *Liverpool Packet,* 993 tons, and the *City of Boston,* registering 908 tons. Neither line observed a fixed schedule, and in fact the older Warren & Thayer line had been forced to abandon its schedule in the summer of 1858. Nevertheless, the three firms combined to maintain a frequent and reasonably dependable service despite the added competition of the big Galway steamers.

Neither New York nor Philadelphia established any new transatlantic lines, owing to the great increase in the frequency and efficiency of steamship service, as well as to marked reductions in their rates. The remaining sailing lines, however, continued to be maintained in good order by the frequent substitution of superior A-1 ships for badly worn packets, and the addition of an occasional new ship. Howland & Frothingham had the fine ship *Richard S. Ely* built, and chartered the *Pomona* and *Harvey Birch* for their Dramatic line. The tragic loss of the *Pomona* has been noted elsewhere, and the *Harvey Birch* did not long survive her, being the first victim (of only two) of the Confederate commerce-raider *Nashville.* A smart new ship, the *Alexander Marshall,* was added to the Black Ball line. Other lines made similar additions to their fleets and it is to be noted that all were still provided with ample first-class quarters equal in all respects to the best steamship accommodations.

On the whole, it would appear that down to and through the Civil War the remaining sailing liners did not fare too badly. They had, it is true, lost the greater part of their first-class trade, and the fraction retained confined their patronage mainly to the "down-hill" eastbound run. They had also lost the greater part of the profitable express and odd-lot shipments, otherwise referred to as measurement goods. On the other hand, they retained most of the steerage and much of the bulk cargo business of the better sort, and continued to do so for years to come. Down to 1860, indeed, it was comparatively rare for a steamer, aside from an occasional Galway liner, to arrive with more than a hundred or so in the steerage, or, as sometimes designated, the "third-class" quarters, while the canvas-backers frequently brought three or four hundred, and much larger lists were by no means rare. In May, 1860, as the rumbles of secession were becoming louder with every passing day, Samuels brought the *Dreadnought* into New York with 600 prospective citizens. Three weeks later, 736 arrived in the Mystic-built three-decker *Harvey Birch*. A similar condition on a narrower scale prevailed in Philadelphia, and in neither port was it seriously affected by the war. Several times during that four-year struggle, Cope ships arrived with from 500 to 700 steerage and upwards, and they generally carried a substantial number.[4]

It was not until the early eighteen-seventies, when 400-foot steamships had entered the lists and 500-footers were on the drafting boards that sailing ship operators began to admit the possibility of defeat. By that time most of the packets were worn and leaky and their owners had failed to maintain them in first-class order otherwise, especially in the matter of sails and rigging. The writer well remembers the account of an old sailor of his last crossing from London to New York in the packet ship *American Congress* in 1871. Among other particulars, he said the ship had only one of her original studding-sail booms left, and the men became so disgusted with the heavy labor of shifting it from one yardarm to the other as the wind changed, that one dark night they cut it adrift and let it go to loo'ard. The condition of the ship in other respects is possibly indicated by the fact that she went missing a year or two later while still under the command of Captain Ghiselin. Nevertheless, a number of years were to elapse before the sailing of the last Western Ocean packet.[5]

Elimination of the sailing liner in the coastal service proceeded much more rapidly than in the transatlantic field, with one exception. The process was retarded in the Boston traffic, particularly that with the more distant southern ports, largely because of the delay in establishing direct steamship communication with those centers. It was not until 1860 that her first steam lines to Charleston and Savannah began operations, and it was not until after the war that she had steam service to the Gulf ports.

A change in the Merchants & Miners line between Boston and Baltimore was responsible for the Savannah line. The company, following the custom of those times, owned only a very small interest in its ships, which belonged, for the most part, to people outside the firm. When the northern terminal of that concern was removed from Boston to Providence in February, 1860, new iron steamers were substituted for the old wooden vessels; whereupon the owners of the supplanted craft decided to employ them in a "New Line" between Boston and Savannah. That service was accordingly inaugurated in June by the old Merchants & Miners paddler *Joseph Whitney*, 1003 tons, commanded by Winslow Loveland. Erastus Sampson, who had been the Merchants & Miners Boston agent, continued as agent for both lines, a position for which he had qualified by a long and successful career as master of some of the smartest New Orleans packets, among them the well-known *Constantine* and *Palmyra*. Messrs. Crane & Graybill were the Savannah agents.

The Charleston line was a more pretentious affair. It was started at the same time as the Savannah line by the recently incorporated Boston & Southern Steamship Company with the fine new iron steamships *South Carolina* and *Massachusetts*, sister ships of 1150 tons. Phineas Sprague & Company were the Boston agents and John Caldwell & Son, the Charleston representatives. The vessels sailed every nine days, their running time averaging 90 hours or thereabouts. They were equipped with three ostensibly watertight compartments, a separate ladies' cabin and staterooms eight feet in height, and were commanded by men who had worked their way aft in the old-fashioned style.

Rodney Baxter, who skippered the *South Carolina*, was from "down on the Cape," a Barnstable boy. His qualifications were sound but by no means exceptional. For years he had chaperoned the little schooner packets *May* and *American Belle* on innumerable trips between Boston and New York, without losing a passenger or even a plum duff. Seeking a broader scope for his talents, he turned to the clippers and in the winter of 1855-56 drove the magnificent Maine-built *Flying Scud* from New York to Marseilles in the record time of 19 days and 20 hours, and followed this exploit by taking her from New York to Bombay in 81 days.

The establishment of these lines had the effect of giving Boston virtually direct steamship connection with all the principal southern ports, since passengers could transfer at Charleston and Savannah to any of the numerous steamers bound farther south. As a result, they cut heavily into what was left of the coastal passenger traffic of the canvas-backers. It is reasonable to assume that they would have put at least a part of the remaining sailing lines out of business if all the southern packet activities had not been interrupted shortly by war.

Something of what was in store for coastal packets everywhere was indicated by the experience of the Boston-New York and Boston-Philadelphia operators. As previously noted, very efficient steamship service between those ports had been established long before 1857. Thereafter, the services were further expanded and improved until large and powerful vessels were sailing four times a week between each port, and oftener on occasion, with the result that one after another the old sailing lines were abandoned. By 1860 only three of the original six serving each port remained. Quite as important was the fact that their sailings were greatly reduced and became more and more irregular as time passed.

The Boston-Baltimore sailing packets were less affected, four of the lines surviving through 1860 and beyond, a circumstance reflecting in some degree the inadequacy of the competing steamship service. However, the quality of their traffic suffered. The Baltimore, and indeed the Philadelphia packets, were frequently compelled to load full cargoes of coal in order to sail at all.

Farther south the number of lines remained about the same. Three continued to run between Boston and each of the three ports of Charleston, Savannah, and Mobile, and five to New Orleans. None, however, maintained a dependable schedule with the exception of Joseph Silloway & Company, then the most active, if not the most important of Boston's coastal operators. The firm had taken over the agencies of H. G. K. Calef for the Savannah and Charleston lines in 1857, and these, in addition to their Mobile and New Orleans lines and others to Galveston and ports of the Chesapeake, amounted to six lines consisting of some 30 assorted first-class vessels, including several of the big tern schooners. Only Henry Lincoln's clipper barks on the Mobile run maintained a service of comparative regularity, although the advertising claims of several others were calculated to create a different impression.

In passing, it is to be noted that Wm. G. Weld & Company, whose fleets of magnificent ships were ranging the world, still continued the trade with Wilmington, North Carolina, that William Weld had started at the close of the War of 1812 with a line of little sloops and schooners.

Of the coastal sailing lines out of New York, the first to start, those to Philadelphia and Baltimore, were the first to go. By 1860 all but two lines to each port had been supplanted by steamers maintaining daily sailings.

Four Charleston lines continued through 1860, but three of those were newcomers. Of the old lines, McCready, Mott & Company alone survived.

Of the other old lines, only George Bulkley and Dunham & Dimon remained after 1857, and Bulkley sent very few vessels after that year. Both withdrew completely in 1859.

Only one of the six New York-Savannah lines was in existence at the close of 1860, that of W. B. Scranton, which continued weekly sailings until the outbreak of war.

Other firms, notably D. Colden Murray and Sturges, Clearman & Company, continued to send vessels at rare intervals, but for all practical purposes their Savannah lines ceased to operate as lines after 1859.

Five New York-Mobile lines continued through 1860, but only one—Sturges, Clearman & Company—observed a regular schedule. Most of the others reduced their sailings to six or seven a year or less. McCready, Mott & Company cleared 21 in 1860, but in order to do this they combined with Messrs. Oakley & Keating in loading the same vessels. Robson & Fosdick suspended operations in 1857 and Post, Smith & Company retired from the field early in 1860, although they continued their very efficient service to Antwerp with a fleet of seven good ships.

Eight of the lines between New York and New Orleans had survived the panic year, but by 1860 half of those were gone, victims of the competition set up by three fine steamship lines with powerful vessels ranging from 1200 to 2000 tons and upwards. The firm of Laytin, Ryerson & Hurlbut, successor to the old firm of E. D. Hurlbut & Company, dispatched a last ship or two in 1858, but their operation as a line had virtually ended in the previous year. Thomas P. Stanton pulled out in 1858, and the following year Post, Smith & Company and Eagle & Hazard gave up the struggle. Of the remaining four, only William T. Frost and William Nelson & Company continued regular weekly sailings to the end. The other two, Robson & Fosdick and N. H. Brigham, observed no schedules but dispatched a number of good ships each year.

All of Philadelphia's regular Western Ocean lines had disappeared by 1860 except the Cope line, Robert Taylor's Irish emigrant line (now operating out of Liverpool), and the John R. Penrose line, formerly Penrose & Burton. However, James Browne & Company and associates continued their very substantial "one-way" emigrant service from Liverpool, and a similar service was established in 1859 by Boult, English & Brandon.

The port still maintained one line to each of the ports of Charleston and Savannah, two lines to Mobile, and three to New Orleans. Of all the sailing lines out of Philadelphia, only the Copes continued their service virtually unimpaired.

Baltimore still had the old Mankin line to Liverpool, under the management, after 1857, of Messrs. Foard & Rogers. It also maintained a single line of sorts to each of the ports of Charleston, Savannah, and New Orleans, but the recently established lines from Baltimore and Philadelphia to Providence sailed with greater frequency and regularity.

All through the period the individual liners were going fast; some to seek more profitable employment, others to founder in lonely seas or leave their bones on far-off uncharted reefs.

Two of the newest and best of the Dramatic line, the *Pomona* and *Plutarch,* were lost in 1859. The *Pomona* went to pieces on the dreaded Blackwater Bank a few hours after leaving Liverpool for New York. It was one of the worst tragedies in the history of the immigrant traffic. Captain Charles Merrihew, his first and second officers, and 421 of the passengers and crew perished.

Down in the Gulf of Mexico, the *Heidelberg* of the New Orleans-Liverpool line foundered just two weeks after the *Plutarch* stranded off Flushing. The old Train packet, *Chatsworth,* one of several which had gone into the guano trade, was wrecked in the summer of 1860 on the coast of Chile. Earlier in the year the line ships *John J. Boyd, Endymion,* and *Jacob A. Westervelt* were destroyed by fire, and the Baltimore-Liverpool immigrant ship *Jane Henderson* piled up 25 miles south of Cape Henry. Her crew and passengers were saved under conditions of extreme danger only by the skill and bravery of Captain Gault and his officers.

A number of the smaller coastal packets also disappeared, among them the smart little bark *Exact,* long a familiar sight to strollers on the New York and Savannah waterfronts. She was lost on Frying Pan Shoals the morning of February 5th, 1859, several days after leaving New York for Savannah. One of the New York-Galveston liners, the 300-ton brig *South,* went to pieces on Sheep Cay Shoal in June the following year. A few weeks earlier Captain Smith, his wife, and several of the crew of the ship *Cicero,* from Boston for New Orleans, were lost when she struck on the island of Abaco, going to pieces in 30 minutes. The steward made the land safely after a series of misadventures. "He got on a hatch but could not hold on; then got an oar but lost that, and then got hold of something which proved to be the leg of a live pig and was towed ashore insensible, but soon recovered."

Ships, however, could be replaced. Men of the breed that had piloted the American merchant marine to greatness—the merchants and master mariners whose metal had been tempered in the fierce heats of post-revolutionary and Napoleonic conflicts, and whose traditions stemmed from a still earlier day when gruelling toil and the casual acceptance of life and death risks constituted the all but universal sea routine—could not. The conditions which favored their development no longer existed, and for years their number had been rapidly decreasing, a fact even then the subject of frequent newspaper comment. What manner of men they were is indicated imperfectly by the following notice from 1860, one of many similar items recorded during the mid-century years:

Captain Robert Waterman, one of the oldest shipmasters in the country, died at New Orleans on the 29th of April. He was one of the last survivors of that race of seafaring men now rapidly disappearing, whose daring and enterprise established the high character of the American merchant marine. He was a native of Nantucket, Mass., born about 1785, and like most of those hardy islanders, followed the sea from boyhood, commencing at the age of eleven years. In 1804, he came to New York, and was in the employ of Jacob Barker, as a shipmaster, sailing from that port. During the war between England and France he sailed from Bordeaux under French colors in the merchant marine, running the risk of capture by English cruisers, and with many a hair breadth escape, succeeded in getting his cargoes into port, where the war prices enabled him to sell at a handsome profit.

In the war of 1812-15 he sailed under a letter-of-marque, and was captured by a British frigate, but succeeded in getting permission to remain on his vessel, which was put in charge of a prize crew and sent to the nearest English port. On the voyage, an American ship, also sailing under letters-of-marque, retook the vessel and Waterman escaped from his captors.

He afterwards, for many years, commanded one of the ships of the old line of Liverpool packets from this port. On his retirement from sea service he went to New Orleans to reside with his family, among whom he died in a good old age. Capt. Waterman was a fine specimen of the American shipmaster of the old school—courageous, courteous and inflexibly honest.[6]

In like manner, the eulogy pronounced on James Perkins, one of Boston's eminent merchants, could with justice be applied to the majority of the great merchants of his day, many of whom were skilled shipmasters in their own right:

His chosen object was the commerce of the world. He embraced in his extended view, the condition of the family of nations; and the involved problems of the wants and means of widely separated countries. . . .

Society has reason to rejoice in that success which has for its object honorable gains; and for its general result, the diffusion, through all regions, of the products peculiar to each. Nor is it wealth, merely, that follows commercial enterprise. The moral, social, political and religious attainments of favored communities, find their modes of diffusion through the paths of commerce. The liberal, enlightened merchant, need not fear comparison with any of the benefactors of the human race.[7]

Hardly a month went by that did not mark the passing of one or more such men. Nash DeCost, the stout old commander of early Fish & Grinnell packets, died on his farm in upstate New York in February, 1858. S. W. Rich, of the packet *Zurich,* succumbed in Havre a month later. In the following May, Richard D. Conn, of Conn & Tyson, and late master of the clipper packet *Mercury,* died at his home in New York City. He was quickly followed by Robert B. Boyd, James P. Allaire, and master mariner Henry Russell.

Later the same year yellow fever was raging in the south and word came to New York that Joseph Hamilton was numbered among its victims in Charleston. "A nobler sailor or truer hearted man never trod the deck." He had been a clipper master for the greater part of the previous decade, latterly commanding the *Adelaide,* an 1800-tonner, but had been forced by the depression to return to the southern packet service in which his sea career began.

Another well-known commander of southern packets, James Wibray, died the first of the following October on his farm in Illinois at an advanced age.

Three more of the ablest and most popular of the packet masters had gone down with their ships.

Ira Bursley, whose first packet command back in 1828 was the little Boston-Liverpool ship *Dover,* commanded the Liverpool liner *Hottinguer* in 1850. On one occasion, at the end of a hard winter passage, he had been presented by his cabin passengers with a letter expressing the respect and esteem in which they held him, accompanied by the gift of a handsome dressing case. In a pithy but heartfelt acknowledgement which, somehow, seems to bring the scene and the man vividly back, he thanked the little group, closing with the words: "The long passage—long nights— head winds—and cold watches on deck, will soon be forgotten, while I shall long retain the memory of such kind passengers, and such a happy termination of our voyage."

The memory was destined to be brief. He was lost in the same ship on the Irish coast, a few miles from the spot where the body of his brother Allen had washed ashore 15 years before.

Captain Alonzo Follansbee and 34 of his passengers and crew went down with the *St. Denis* when she foundered in a hurricane on the 6th of January, 1856, two days out of New York bound for Havre. Both mates and nine seamen were picked up in a boat.

On the 12th September, 1857, Captain William L.—"Hands hard to row and heart soft to feel"—Herndon was lost with 423 of his ship's complement when the steamer *Central America* foundered in a hurricane in the Gulf of Mexico.

All the older captains—those whose sea life had begun during or before the War of 1812—had retired long since. Nathan Cobb had a fine country estate up the Hudson. Robert H. Waterman, formerly of the Black Ball line, was settled on a big ranch in California. Nathaniel Brown Palmer, sometime of the Dramatic line, and his fellow townsman, Richard F. Loper, who had once commanded a "punkin seed" on the Hartford-Philadelphia packet run, were doing a little yachting out of Stonington by way of relaxation.

British-born Benjamin L. Waite had "swallowed the anchor" after crossing the Atlantic more than 160 times, and was living at Stamford, Connecticut. As early as 1841, while he was still master of the crack Black Baller *England,* it was said of him:

> Capt. Waite, by right and title, belongs to the Atlantic Ocean. He has made it his home, came within an ace of being born thereon, and crossed it when he was but nine months old. And since then he has crossed to Liverpool and back one hundred and forty-nine times without a disaster. He has been a commander of a packet ship longer than anyone now in the service, and is in fine, Admiral of the Fleet.[8]

Several of the Grinnells were still active, although all had left the sea many years before. As a family, they were remarkably long-lived. Joseph, the oldest, and the founder of Grinnell, Minturn & Company, died in 1885 in his 97th year. In his later life he was president of a New Bedford bank and the New Bedford-Taunton railroad. What manner of men the Grinnells were is suggested by the following remarks made at a meeting of shipmasters, pilots, stevedores, mates, and seamen, held in Franklin Square, New York City, the 28th of October, 1840, to nominate Moses H. Grinnell for Congress:

> Shipmates—Moses H. Grinnell is one of us, and from among us. He is one of our own make. He has not gone upward through the lubber hole, but he has gone up like a man. Shipmates ahoy! Turn out, turn out, for all is not well. A storm is brewing, and we start the Ship of State for a four years voyage. What master at the helm better than an old salt.[9]

With the passing of such men America was losing something that could no longer be replaced, but the fact went almost unnoted. Old standards were going by the board. Among other undermining influences, a new institution euphuistically termed "Ships' Cousins" was gaining ground. More and more men were coming up through the lubber hole—relatives and friends of merchants and shipowners, who bypassed much of the long, hard apprenticeship of the older generation through favoritism—promoted over the heads of more experienced and deserving men.

If any voices were raised in protest against such practices, they were quickly drowned out. Too many exciting things were happening. Railroads and telegraph companies were piling up mileage to speed Brother Jonathan's boastings. A Connecticut visionary named Whitney was even conducting a party of wealthy New Yorkers on a tour through the northwest to study the feasibility of a railroad to the Pacific.[10] Steamship records were being smashed as soon as made, but a few weeks before the death of James Wibray on a farm far from the Atlantic, the world was thrilled by an event which suggested that even the fastest steamers of the future would soon become matters of relatively small importance.

This was the completion of the first Atlantic cable. On the 9th of August, 1858, the first "regular" message from Newfoundland was received at Valentia, Ireland, "with perfect clarity." Excitement knew no bounds. Lager beer saloons put marriage certificates of the Old and New Worlds in their windows, and a clergyman "proved" the achievement was a fulfillment of prophecy. In the midst of these and a thousand other amazing events, an insistent and troublesome rumble was all but lost in the closing months of Buchanan's administration.

For what a date may be worth, America's great day of sail passed with 1860. Much of its glamor had long since departed. As already intimated, the master mariner had been deprived years before of his once complete responsibility, and the further eclipse of the coastal packet master has been noted in an earlier chapter. In the decade just closing, the steamship had deprived the commanders of the great Western Ocean sailing liners of their last treasured mark of leadership, their social prestige. The wealthy and occasionally cultured passengers who had once thronged their splendid cabins and showered them with adulation, and sometimes more substantial tokens of regard, had transferred their attentions, silver teapots included, to the lordly steamship captain, now host to hundreds of admiring notables. Even he had lost in relative stature. America, as a whole, had turned its serious attention almost exclusively to industry, finance, and the development of its vast new territories.

All in all, their day had been short. Little more than two centuries had elapsed since the first American mariner put to sea on the pioneer trading voyage of the New World, along a strange and dangerous coast, the only sign of habitation in a long day's sail the smoke of a solitary campfire or a lone canoe slipping stealthily around a distant headland. But brief though the time was—as nations reckon time—for the colonist and his immediate successors they were long, slow-moving years, when progress was hardly perceptible from one decade to another. It was in those years, however, that our mariners laid the foundations for a structure that was to tower above anything civilization had yet produced.

Boys grew to manhood and passed into old age, their lives spent in hard, unremitting toil and dangerous living, and saw no change. Endlessly in summer heat and winter frost, the dull routine of land and sea—the rasp of saw, thud of beetle, smack of broadaxe, clew-down, reef, shake-out, masthead, and drive again—never ceasing, each day a seeming replica of a thousand weary bygone days. Yet change there was and it was proceeding more rapidly than anywhere else. Ramshackle cabins and crude, hastily built cottages were replaced by homes that still speak of gracious living. The ships grew larger, lines fined out, spars lengthened, numbers and tonnage increased. Voyages speeded up, became more profitable, brought more comforts, and even a few luxuries. The cost in toll of lives and suffering was another matter.

One by one through the years the boys of the farm and village sailed away to face the strange new loneliness and perils of the sea, to learn that survival depended not only on the hard work and stubborn endurance to which they had already become enured, but on the exercise of instant, resourceful initiative a thousand times repeated. It was the lesson of all pioneering, but land pioneering soon passes, changing swiftly to settled safety and dull routine. For the sailor of the sail, the sea was a perpetual frontier. Those who followed it could never relax their vigilance or lose sight of their mutual dependence, knowing that the safety of the ship and all on board might sometime hang on the dependability of cook or cabin boy. Such a mode of livelihood pursued by a people already disposed to place the highest value on individual worth, made for moral and intellectual standards of association and achievement which—crude and roughhewn though they were—were then unequalled, and possibly may still be unsurpassed for practical purposes.

They sailed away as boys. They returned in shrunken numbers as men; men who had contended with the hurricane; matched wits with hostile cruisers and piratical craft; and learned the uses of tolerant, fair-minded diplomacy in dealing with alien races and peoples. They had survived deadly tropical plagues; nursed shipmates through cholera, yellow fever, smallpox, and black vomit. They came back quiet, assured, dependable men; knowing that life, though it should last another half century, would bring no sterner tests.

Long before the close of the seventeenth century there was a stout leaven of such men in every community along the coast, New England's mixture being of extra-special strength. Their influence can hardly be overestimated. By sheer force of example they raised the level of the whole. And therein lies a most important clue to America's material progress. The colonies could produce few to compare with the more gifted men of the Old World in scientific attainments. The crucial fact, however, was that their people, as a whole, stood—morally and intellectually—head and shoulders above the subservient peasantry which then composed the bulk of Europe's population, and that of the remaining New World colonies, as well. That, and that alone, explains why a people few in numbers and weak in resources swiftly overhauled and bypassed powerful nations with a head start of a thousand years.

It took two centuries to lay the foundation. It took but 30 years to rear the vast superstructure—swift, drama-packed years, when progress became visible. In that advance it was the sailing passenger liner that led the way; led it, moreover, so effectively that it must be credited in some degree with stimulating a general advance all along the line, both at home and abroad.

Until the first ships of the Black Ball and other contemporary lines were specially designed and equipped for passenger comfort, there had been little change in the cabin accommodations of commercial vessels from time immemorial. Naval architects had confined their attentions almost exclusively to speed and carrying qualities, with the result that in 1815 and for several years thereafter passenger quarters ranged from somewhat worse to slightly better than those of the *Mayflower.*

The new Western Ocean liners presaged the dawn of a new age, the age of travel for culture and pleasure. Small, plain, and crudely outfitted though they were, they constituted so great an improvement over the ships they replaced that, one after another, they evoked the most lavish praise, not only in their home ports but abroad. Here, for example, is what the *British Traveller* (London) had to say on May 7th, 1825, of the new packet *York:*

The convenience and beauty of this ship, and her various accommodations, are such as we have never seen in any vessel, calculated at once for the purposes of commerce, and for passengers.

High praise from the editor of a publication devoted to the travel interests of the "Mistress of the Seas." Yet the *York,* the first specially designed ship for Fish & Grinnell's London line, registered only 433 tons, and would register considerably less than 400 tons today. Her length was less than 119 feet. Her staterooms accommodated 24 adults, plus, presumably, whatever "small fry" could be stowed away in their narrow confines. She was, in fact, only slightly larger than the whaleship *Charles W. Morgan,* built 17 years later and now being preserved at Mystic, Connecticut. Her staterooms were undoubtedly more neatly finished than those of the *Morgan,* but they were no larger and it is doubtful whether they were more comfortable.

Whether they were or not is a matter of relatively small importance. The *York* was outclassed before she had returned from her first voyage. Other ships were going down the ways in quick succession, a stout proportion of them embodying some new feature of equipment, rig, ventilation, cabin layout, or stateroom convenience, or excelling in size, finish, speed, or seaworthy qualities. For 30 years it went on, with the packets always setting the pace for America and the world, until by 1854 scores of the largest, finest, and most efficient sailing liners ever to be set afloat were ploughing the Western Ocean and ranging up and down the coast. Many had accommodations for a hundred and more first- and second-class passengers, which, save in spaciousness, equalled those of the best hotels ashore. In addition they were equipped to carry nearly a thousand steerage in vast 'tween decks, eight feet or more in height.

And there, for the cotton-powered packets, it ended. Some of the grandest were ranging the seven seas in search of employment before their first set of sails were half worn. A few years more and old, retired seamen would be writing of them in stilted, nostalgic phrase, as one might write of vanished dream ships of long ago. Thus "Q. Q., in the country," in the year of our Lord, 1859:

Noticing a day or two since in your paper, the arrival of the ship *John Jay* (a twin ship of the *John Wells*—two good names, worthy good ships) from Shanghai with a cargo of tea to Mr. Hathaway, brought vividly to mind the excellent qualities and endurance of a well built New York ship. The *John Jay* is now 32 years old: "lang syne" she was a crack Liverpool packet, under those worthy commanders, Capt. Harris or Capt. Cobb, and was one of the favorite packet ships when flourished the *Rosalie,* Capt. Merry; the *Hercules,* Capt. Cobb; the *Pacific,* Williams; the *Ann,* Crocker; the *Martha,* Sketchley; the *Britannia,* Marshall; the *Anna Maria,* Waite; the *Criterion,* Avery; the *Dublin Packet,* Newcomb; the *Venus,* Candler; the *Importer,* Lee; the *James Monroe,* Rogers; the *Independence,* Nye; the *Panther,* Hathaway; the *Roscoe,* Delano; the *Hector,* Gillender; the *Erie,* Funck; the *Charlemagne,* Robinson—and others equally famous in the Liverpool, London and Havre trade—not to mention Capt. Stanton, the father of Liverpool packet men, and his good ship *Amity.* . . .

Old ships, old scenes, men of the old breed. They were fast passing—had passed, so far as their once dynamic influence went—although it would be years before they disappeared completely. There were many in 1860 to mourn their loss, actual and impending. There were few to note that

America was losing something of greater significance if not of greater importance.

Yet it was so. The wheel was nearing full cycle as the decade ended. The failure of the New England experiment, so hopefully begun more than two centuries before, was definitely foreshadowed. Its basic premise—that the first concern of society was the continuing self-improvement of its members—its most important product citizens of superior character—had been pruned and qualified little by little, until what was left bore a strange resemblance to the same Old World philosophy with its five millenniums of recorded failure that Pilgrim and Puritan alike had sought to escape.

For two centuries property, profit, and privilege had been calling the turn with slowly increasing frequency as imperative public needs were met and dangerous living gave place to stodgy routine. Steam and the telegraph had implemented a further concentration of power and responsibility. Inventions to render superfluous the skill, ingenuity, and even the labor of the individual were multiplying, and a few "crackpots" were fumbling for sources of still vaster and more revolutionary powers. What it might portend was not clear, but for some time northern factories had been in mass production, turning out human products grading far below their smart new fabrics—creatures who spent their lives in monotonous, robot-like repetition of simple, all but effortless operations. The specialist, whose preoccupation with a single, engrossing interest made him especially vulnerable to exploitation, was also on the increase.

Few, however, gave a thought to the possibility that the modern machine might do for America what the slave machine had done for Greece and Rome. "Bread and Circuses" was still an empty phrase. As yet the country had but a few harmless "Broadway Dudes" to ape the fops and voluptuaries who had comprised the bulk of decadent Rome's ruling class. Nevertheless, there was no gainsaying the fact that the concept of service was being supplanted more and more by the seductive vision of a life of perfect ease and unending pleasure. The possibility that the ultimate product might be a human jellyfish seems to have occurred to no one.

Whatever the outcome, the successor of the merchant-mariner of 1860 would not affect the result materially. He would be as skilled, as competent, and as courageous as his predecessor. His ships would be, if anything, greater and more magnificent. More than half a century would pass before they vanished from the sea. Twenty years would elapse before the last Western Ocean liner cleared for her last voyage. He would still contribute mightily to the nation's welfare. His stout sea traditions of devoted courage and service would stand to the end. But, as a factor in shaping public opinion and in the preservation of early Puritan principles, his work was done. For many years, indeed, his example had been noted and followed by slowly lessening numbers until it had come to exercise little more than a slight retarding effect on the return of the old materialistic rule.

They were not great men, the old canvas-back merchant-mariners. On the contrary, they were common men; common in the sense that they were of the class once pronounced ignorant and incapable by those who had assumed from time immemorial the right to think and act for them. They were so common that they did not even think of greatness. It was enough for them to achieve greatly.

Explain it as one will, the fact remains that for two centuries they led the world; two centuries in which the very shape of civilization was transformed. In that time they were responsible for initiating most of the improvements in transportation, the life stream of nations, which paved the way for the marvellous advances of recent years. They developed a majority of the later improvements in sailing craft and built the greatest, fastest, and most efficient fleet of their day. They are to be credited with most of the early steamship progress. Their success did much to stimulate the nineteenth century spirit of inquiry and desire for change, which resulted in a flood of inventions and notable improvements in methods and practices. Their vision, daring, and resourcefulness made possible the gains which advanced by many years the financial and industrial growth of the nation and, in addition, provided the funds to purchase the vast territories that now comprise two-thirds of its area.

Through it all they played a notable part; it may be, a more effective part than other groups; in protecting and preserving the colonists and their heirs. Their role in the American Revolution and the War of 1812 has been indicated. There is much to warrant the conclusion that they were primarily responsible for the preservation of the Union in the great civil conflict just ahead. One can only speculate now as to the outcome of that struggle if their incomparable fleet had not been available to challenge European intervention. There is no doubt, however, that England and France favored the secessionist cause and were, more than once, on the verge of adopting measures which would have gone far to ensure its success.

Notwithstanding these and other achievements, which in sheer physical bulk outranked anything that had gone before, other and greater forces had pronounced their doom. They did not pass wholly unnoted and unregretted. There were still many to echo the sentiments of the unknown New England villager:

In memory we see the ships that crept slowly up the river, that overshadowed the wharves, that in their unloading and refitting filled the valley with the hum of business, and then hastened away on their distant and hazardous errands. The river alive with boats, the docks crowded with casks and sailors, the lofts peopled with sail-makers and riggers, while the shops rang to the strokes of smiths and coopers. . . .

Old ships, old scenes, men of the old breed. Another generation would see the end. The traffic of the little ports would dwindle. One by one their last ships would be finished and go down the ways to the cheers of the assembled townspeople, all unaware that it was for the last time. One by one the master builders would cease to return to the shipyard offices where they had long awaited the once confidently expected orders. One by one the yards would stand, weed-grown and deserted, their sheds and docks crumbling away. One by one the young men would leave the drowsy villages once so alive with the clatter and bustle of business. One by one aged captains, once familiar figures in ports the world over, would take to dropping into the little general store to recall with other ancients half-forgotten tales of long ago. Master mariners who had once risked life itself for an extra knot of speed would be seen drifting leisurely down the river for a day's untroubled fishing. Now and again a shrunken old man hobbling down the village street would be pointed out to chance visitors as Captain Blank, who drove his magnificent clipper round the Horn for a world record, or, with his ship leaking and half dismasted, picked 300 soaked and shivering emigrants off a sinking liner.

The last have long since gone. And the number of those who hold to their outmoded ways and standards continues to diminish. Yet such is the vitality of great truths that they return, and return again, until they prevail. If, in some distant future, our old mariner-merchant, Captain Lord, should be permitted to revisit the scene of his labors, he would sometime, perhaps, find a nation once more united in the bond of a common purpose, a purpose not unlike that envisioned in his rugged Puritan philosophy, but shaped in kindlier fashion and dedicated to the uses of all men everywhere.

Notes

CHAPTER I

[1] See, e.g., Diary of John Evelyn, Colonial Commissioner, August 3, 1671, *et passim*.

[2] John Winthrop, *History of New England, 1630-1649,* Vol. II, p. 29.

[3] *Ibid.,* Vol. II, p. 37.

[4] *Ibid.,* Vol. II, p. 89.

[5] Authorities consulted on Colonial population include the following:

Greene & Harrington, *American Population before the Federal Census.*
Bridenbaugh, *Cities in the Wilderness.*
Sloan, *French War and the American Revolution.*
Bradford, *Narrative and Critical History.*
A Century of Population Growth.
Niles' Weekly Register (Baltimore).
Andrews, *Colonial Period of American History.*
Franklin B. Dexter, "Estimates of Population in the American Colonies," Published in *Proceedings* of the American Antiquarian Society, Vol. V, New Series, pp. 22-50.
General American histories, such as Johnston and Bancroft.
Local histories and articles in the *Americana* and other encyclopedias have been consulted with reference to population of towns.

In general, estimates are based on tax and militia rolls and number of houses.

All vary and none can be taken as exact.

[6] Report of Edward Randolph, Collector of the Port of Boston.

[7] The conclusion that smuggling was quite rare, drawn, possibly, from the circumstance that relatively few instances have been proven definitely, overlooks the fact that smuggling was an industry in which prosperity depended on failure to advertise.

[8] Maryland is here coupled with the southern colonies because of her large slave population—a factor which had an important bearing on the development of maritime activities.

[9] Joshua Hempstead, *Diary, 1712-1758,* p. 161.

[10] Two British naval vessels had been built at Newcastle, District of Maine, in Colonial times. One was the *Falkland,* a fourth-rate, launched in 1690, and the other the *Bedford Galley,* launched in 1696. At that time a fourth-rate measured approximately 700 tons.

CHAPTER II

[1] See petitions to the General Court. Boston Town Records, 1753 and 1756.

[2] Minutes of Town Meeting held in Boston, September 25, 1744.

[3] A Short View of the Smuggling Trade carried on by the British Northern Colonies, in violation of the Act of Navigation, and several other Acts of Parliament (London, 1732), p. 1.

[4] *New York Gazette,* January 8, 1770.

[5] A Short View of the Smuggling Trade, etc., p. 2.

[6] *Pennsylvania Gazette,* June 14, 1770.

[7] *Massachusetts Gazette,* October 31, 1771. Advertisements in general from 1770 to outbreak of hostilities indicate a sharp rise in variety and quality of imports.

[8] *New York Gazette,* January 8, 1770.

[9] *New York Mercury,* August 9, 1773.

[10] Alexander Starbuck, *History of the American Whale Fishery from its Earliest Inception to the Year 1879,* p. 57. See also statement in footnote, p. 59, to effect that as early as 1764 the fisheries employed 45,880 tons of shipping and 6002 men.

[11] J. L. Bishop, *History of American Manufactures,* Vol. I, p. 81.

[12] Admiral French Ensor Chadwick, *History of American Navy,* pp. 4, 5.

[13] New London (Conn.) Land Records, Vol. IV, Folio 22. Contract dated January 2, 1680, between Jos. Wells, shipwright, and Alexander Pygan, *et al.,* calls for construction of a ship of 41-foot keel "to have a 12-foot rake forward under her load marks" and "the sweep at the buttocks to be 9 feet and at the transom 12 feet." Other similar contracts in the land records.

[14] See, e.g., log of schooner *Eagle,* of Salem, for October 21, 1753. (Peabody Museum, Salem, Mass.)

[15] Log of ship *Duke of Cumberland* on a privateering cruise out of New York in 1759 shows that she made 9 to 9½ knots on several occasions, and on the 15th of May ran 201 miles in 24 hours, averaging from 8 to 9½ knots throughout the entire day. (From log in possession of the New-York Historical Society.)

[16] Joshua Hempstead, *Diary,* May 7, 1712.

CHAPTER III

[1] Edgar Stanton Maclay, *History of American Privateers,* p. xxiii.

[2] Davis Rich Dewey, *Financial History of the United States,* p. 77.

[3] On the general subject, see Reports of the Secretary of the U. S. Treasury, printed Washington, 1837. Vol. I, p. 240, *et passim.*

[4] *Daily Advertiser* (New York), May 20, 1788, reported ship *Empress of China* ashore near Waterford, Ireland. *New York Daily Gazette,* April 7, 1791, reported: "The ship *Clara,* formerly the *Empress of China,* was totally lost off Dublin Harbor, Feb. 22nd, last—all the hands were saved."

[5] Edwin A. Stone, *A Century of Boston Banking* (1894), p. 111.

[6] Pennsylvania Annual Report of Secretary of Internal Affairs, 1891, Official Documents, No. 10, C. 53.

[7] *New York Weekly Museum,* January 17, 1789. *Pennsylvania Packet & Daily Advertiser,* January 22, 1789.

[8] *New York Journal & Patriotic Register,* January 14, 1792.

[9] *Columbian Centinel* (Boston), January 6, 1796.

[10] *Aurora General Advertiser* (Philadelphia), April 7, 1801, listed by name 37 American vessels seized by the British and brought into the port of Nassau in the first two months of the year, besides others whose names could not be ascertained. This record was being duplicated in other ports and the activity was to continue for a number of years to come.

[11] *New York Journal,* September 10, 1789, quoted a letter from Colebrook Dale, England, dated March 9, 1789, which said: "A short time since was launched a fifty ton vessel, completely built of cast iron. She appeared when at anchor, the most compleat, light and elegant vessel ever seen on the Severn." From the *Merchant Marine Magazine,* June, 1865, pp. 188-9, we learn that the vessel was built by John Wilkinson at Willey, in Shropshire, and launched July 6, 1787.

[12] The steamboat *Phenix,* commanded by Moses Rogers, cleared at New York, June 8, 1809, for Philadelphia, and made the run without incident.

[13] See on the general subject: House of Representatives Report No. 16, December 29, 1841, on French Spoilation Claims.

[14] *Niles' Weekly Register* (Baltimore), July 19, 1817.

[15] Adam Seybert, *Statistical Annals of the United States* (1818), Vol. I, p. 317. Also, U. S. Department of Commerce, *Merchant Marine Statistics* (1928).

[16] The term "stateroom" was not derived from the practice of Mississippi River steamboat operators naming their rooms after the states of the Union, as has sometimes been asserted. The term was in general use before the American Revolution and possibly much earlier.

CHAPTER IV

[1] *Columbian Centinel* (Boston), September 3, 1828.

[2] *New York Gazette,* January 4, 1815, reported seven ships seized at Liverpool with cargoes of cotton and tobacco worth 140,000 pounds sterling, in spite of which the illicit trade was on the increase. It was estimated that it then amounted to a million pounds annually.

[3] See any New York newspaper for February 14, 1815, *et seq.* The *New York Gazette,* which for several years had carried only an occasional shipping advertisement, ran 35 the morning after confirmation of the news of peace. Within a fortnight the number exceeded 75.

[4] Extent of post-war boom is indicated by the fact that customs receipts jumped in 1816 from a wartime low of six million dollars to thirty-six, a figure which was not equalled again until 1850.

[5] *New York Evening Post,* January 7, 1823.

[6] Davis Rich Dewey, *Financial History of the United States,* Sec. 75.

[7] U. S. Department of Commerce, Bureau of Navigation, *Merchant Marine Statistics* (1928), No. 8, p. 30. In 1814 there were 490 vessels built and documented in the United States aggregating 29,751 tons. During the next three years 3847 were built, totalling 378,391 tons.

[8] Emigration from Great Britain and Ireland to the United States was on such a scale that it was said to have aroused apprehensions on the part of the British government as to its effect on the labor situation. It continued to increase for several years, a fact which undoubtedly entered into the calculations of Wright and his associates. In 1819 London papers advertised 15 ships to take emigrants to America and as many more were advertised in Belfast. (See *Norwalk* (Conn.) *Gazette,* June 2, 1819.) Official figures on United States immigration are, in general, incomplete during this period.

[9] *New York Gazette,* March 4, 1819. The next recorded towing of a packet was that of the *James Monroe,* which was towed to sea by the steamboat *Swift* on the 10th of January 1820, because of ice in New York harbor.

[10] *Niles' Weekly Register* (Baltimore), August 23, 1817. "Fast Sailing:—The ship *Pacific* reached the Irish Coast from New York in $12\frac{1}{2}$ days, at the rate of 216 miles per day, for an average."

[11] Charles C. Jones, *History of Savannah* (1890).

[12] Although practice varied, packet masters usually received 25 per cent of the cabin passage money, out of which they had to provide the food and wine for the cabin table. A long passage, therefore, meant short profits.

[13] As early as 1846, long before the question of sail versus steam was decided, James Gordon Bennett ran an express from Boston to New York, on which his train must have averaged approximately 45 miles an hour. The Cunarder *Cambria* (later wrecked with a loss of 170 lives) arrived in Boston with a *New York Herald* reporter on board. He leaped to the dock; galloped to the Worcester & Norwich station, where Bennett's special was waiting with safety valve popping; rocketed to Norwich full speed; thence crossing to Greenport by the fast steamer *Traveller,* and thence to New York by train —a printer feverishly setting type all the way. "250 miles in 7 hours and 5 minutes. The Fastest Express Ever Run in the Country." *New York Herald,* February 19, 1846.

[14] *New York Commercial Advertiser,* January 6, 1818: "Yesterday morning the packet ship *James Monroe,* Captain Watkinson, sailed for Liverpool. Among the passengers were the following gentlemen:—Messrs. Daniel Fisher, of Montreal; John Large and Lewis Waln, of Philadelphia; S. Sweeter, jun., of Baltimore; A. Spooner, of Boston; Hugh McNeill, of Kentucky; William Stanley and Hugh Graham, of New York."

[15] *Liverpool Mercury,* April 3, 1818.

[16] *Ibid.,* October 8, 1818.

[17] *Ibid.,* November 6, 1818.

[18] One can get a fairly accurate conception of the appearance of the first Black Ball

packets from the ship *Charles W. Morgan,* now at Mystic, Conn. She is similar in size, lines, and general design, being, in fact, slightly longer than the *Amity, Courier,* and *Pacific.* They were, however, somewhat loftier in rig and carried studding sails.

[19] The figures are compiled from contemporary newspaper reports of arrivals and departures, the ships' logs not being available, if, indeed, they have survived.

CHAPTER V

[1] *Federal Gazette* (Baltimore), March 25, 1813.

[2] *Boston Gazette,* December 6, 1813. Agents for the Mercantile Line at this time included George Burroughs, Jr., of Boston; Isaac Bowen, Jr., of Providence; Leman Dunning, New Haven; Muir & Merritt, New York; Scrueman & Perrin, New Brunswick; James and Samuel Lenox, Trenton; Emlen & Howell, Philadelphia; and James Levering, Baltimore.

[3] *New York Gazette,* April 7, 1814.

[4] The statement sometimes quoted that lines of freighting wagons maintained a 22-day service between Savannah and New England during the war is undoubtedly due to an oversight. Heavily loaded wagons could make 20 miles a day over existing roads only under exceptionally favorable conditions. The average rate rarely exceeded 10 miles a day and was often less.

[5] *New York Gazette,* June 14, 1814.

[6] *Ibid.,* March 18, 1815.

[7] *New York Commercial Advertiser,* December 11, 1819.

[8] *Ibid.,* April 21, 1823.

[9] *Boston Gazette,* May 18, 1815.

[10] *New York Gazette,* November 28, 1815.

[11] *Poulson's American Daily Gazette* (Philadelphia), February 28, 1816.

[12] *Boston Gazette,* April 15, 1816.

[13] U. S. Department of Commerce, *op. cit.,* p. 30.

[14] *Boston Gazette,* November 13, 1817.

[15] *Ibid.,* November 10, 1817.

[16] *Ibid.,* December 18, 1817.

[17] *Ibid.,* October 11, 1821.

[18] *Ibid.,* September 26, 1822.

[19] *Ibid.,* January 27, 1820.

[20] *Ibid.,* September 9, 1822.

[21] U. S. Department of Commerce, *op. cit.,* p. 22.

[22] *Boston Gazette,* December 11, 1817.

[23] *Niles' Weekly Register* (Baltimore), July 19, 1817.

[24] *New York Gazette,* October 23, 1819.

[25] *Poulson's American Daily Gazette* (Philadelphia), January 25, 1816.

[26] *Niles' Weekly Register* (Baltimore), July 19, 1817. For the calendar year of 1816 the total number of vessels entering New Orleans was 387, slightly more than half of which were from foreign ports.

[27] *Franklin Gazette* (Philadelphia), February 28, 1818.

[28] *Boston Gazette,* November 19, 1818. "One hundred brickmakers and fifty ship carpenters left New York a short time ago to work at Blakely."

[29] *Baltimore American,* July 14, 1817.

[30] *Ibid.,* May 14, 1821.

[31] *Ibid.,* March 21, 1817.

[32] *Ibid.,* July 29, 1817.

[33] *Ibid.,* May 27, 1820.

CHAPTER VI

[1] *Norwalk Gazette,* July 7, 1819.

[2] *Boston Gazette,* July 3, 1820.
[3] *Poulson's American Daily Gazette* (Philadelphia), May 30, 1812.
[4] *Niles' Weekly Register* (Baltimore), April 30, 1814.
[5] *Boston Gazette,* May 23, 1816.
[6] *Ibid.,* July 25, 1816.
[7] *Charleston Courier,* July 12, 1816.
[8] *Boston Gazette,* December 18, 1817.
[9] *Ibid.,* November 12, 1818.
[10] *Louisiana Courier,* August 26, 1822.
[11] *Poulson's American Daily Gazette* (Philadelphia), December 31, 1822.
[12] *New York Commercial Advertiser,* May 9, 1816.
[13] *Boston Gazette,* July 4, 1821.
[14] *Ibid.,* December 18, 1817.
[15] *New Orleans Gazette,* March 17, 1817.
[16] *Niles' Weekly Register* (Baltimore), May 10, 1823, and September 6, 1823. See also *New York Evening Post,* February 4, 1826.
[17] *Niles' Weekly Register* (Baltimore), October 16, 1819. "Paris, August 27: Professor Meincke has recently made a very important discovery. He has found the means of lighting by electricity, an artificial gas, in glass tubes, which diffuses a light without burning. The electric sparks spread and multiply to an infinite number. With one of these electrical machines a whole city can easily be lighted, and with a very trifling expense."
[18] Letter of Captain John McDougal to William King of Quebec, dated November 16, 1833. Printed in the *Transactions of the Literary and Historical Society of Quebec* (1878).
[19] *New York Commercial Advertiser,* April 26, 1820.
[20] *Orleans Gazette,* May 16, 1820.
[21] *Charleston Courier,* June 8, 1820.
[22] *New York Evening Post,* July 15, 1822.
[23] *Ibid.,* January 3, 1822.
[24] *Boston Gazette,* January 25, 1821.
[25] *Ibid.,* June 17, 1819.
[26] *Liverpool Mercury,* June 19, 1816. Ship *Iris* seized at London with 100 passengers above the legal limit.
[27] *Boston Gazette,* September 21, 1826.
[28] *Norwalk Gazette,* July 28, 1819.
[29] *Boston Gazette,* August 8, 1816.
[30] *Niles' Weekly Register* (Baltimore), January 4, 1823.

CHAPTER VII

[1] *New York Gazette,* January 3, 1822.
[2] *New York Commercial Advertiser,* February 14, 1822.
[3] *Baltimore American,* June 8, 1822.
[4] *New York Commercial Advertiser,* May 11, 1824.
[5] *New York Gazette,* July 23, 1822.
[6] *New York Evening Post,* January 13, 1823.
[7] *New York Commercial Advertiser,* May 11, 1824.
[8] *New York Gazette,* July 4, 1824.
[9] *Niles' Weekly Register* (Baltimore), November 19, 1825.
[10] *New York Gazette,* July 1, 1825.
[11] *Weekly Louisiana Gazette* (New Orleans), September 4, 1825.
[12] *National Gazette* (Philadelphia), March 23, 1822.
[13] *Liverpool Mercury,* March 12, 1824.
[14] *Boston Gazette,* September 23, 1822.

[15] Arthur H. Clark, *Clipper Ship Era*, p. 51.

[16] *Charleston Mercury*, October 28, 1822.

[17] *Boston Gazette*, December 27, 1819, and other Boston newspapers of December 24, *et seq.*

[18] *Myers's Weekly Advertiser* (Liverpool), March 30, 1829.

[19] *Louisiana State Gazette* (New Orleans), October 13, 1826, reported 4380 canal boats for the year to September 1, and estimated total for year would amount to nearly 7000, which seems justified as the busiest third of the year was still to come.

[20] *Boston Gazette*, May 19, 1825.

[21] U. S. Treasury Report for 1825.

[22] *Boston Gazette*, September 12, 1825. Same issue carried "ad" for sale of packet *Herald*.

[23] *Register of Arts and Sciences*, article on canals.

[24] *Boston Gazette*, April 25, 1825.

[25] All commercial New York and Boston newspapers for September 4, 1826, *et seq.*

Chapter VIII

[1] *American Sentinel* (Philadelphia), March 9, 1833.

[2] *New York Gazette*, October 25, 1826.

[3] U. S. Treasury Report for 1825. See also Reports of the Secretary of the U. S. Treasury (1851), Vol. IV, p. 285.

[4] *Boston Gazette*, September 25, 1826. Report that a Mississippi towboat company had been organized.

[5] *New York Evening Post*, April 1, 1825.

[6] *Boston Gazette*, July 15, 1824.

[7] *Boston Gazette*, July 27, 1826.

[8] *Ibid.*, June 1, 1826.

[9] *Niles' Weekly Register* (Baltimore), December 3, 1825.

[10] *New York Evening Post*, June 22, 1825.

[11] *Boston Gazette*, December 20, 1827.

[12] Report of the Secretary of the U. S. Treasury for 1849, Vol. VII, pp. 832-4.

Chapter IX

[1] Davis Rich Dewey, *op. cit.*, pp. 168 and 246.

[2] *Ibid.*

[3] *Baltimore Patriot*, September 5, 1829.

[4] New York Shipping and Commercial List, January 9, 1827.

[5] *New York Commercial Advertiser*, June 23, 1829.

[6] *Baltimore American*, March 18, 1834. Advertisement dated October 28, 1833, at Petersburg.

[7] *New York Evening Post*, April 22, 1830.

[8] *New York Commercial Advertiser*, April 19, 1830.

[9] *Ibid.*, August 13, 1834.

[10] *Baltimore Patriot*, March 16, 1837.

[11] *New York Herald*, May 10, 1837.

[12] *Boston Advertiser*, November 14, 1837.

[13] *New Orleans Commercial Bulletin*, November 2, 1837.

[14] *Daily Georgian* (Savannah), November 2, 1837. *New York Commercial Advertiser*, October 17, 1837.

Chapter X

[1] U. S. Department of Commerce, Bureau of Census, *Historical Statistics of the United States, 1789-1945* (1949).

[2] Passenger Act. Signed by President Monroe, March 2, 1819.

³ Following the appearance of the big two- and three-deckers of the forties with their height between decks raised to seven and one-half or eight feet, the rule was changed to allow each passenger (exclusive of infants) deck space varying with height between decks but which was, in general, about two by seven feet.

⁴ U. S. Department of Commerce, Bureau of Navigation, *Merchant Marine Statistics* (1928), p. 22.

⁵ Reports of the Secretary of the U. S. Treasury, Vol. VII, p. 687.

⁶ U. S. Department of Commerce, *op. cit.,* pp. 13 and 63.

⁷ *New York Evening Post,* April 24, 1838.

⁸ *New York Herald,* May 29, 1839.

⁹ *Mystic* (Conn.) *Press,* February 21, 1873. Item credited to *New York Tribune.*

¹⁰ *New York Herald,* November 24, 1839.

¹¹ *Ibid.,* November 25, 1839.

¹² *Ibid.,* March 14, 1842.

¹³ *New York Evening Post,* January 11, 1839.

¹⁴ *New York Herald,* March 6, 1847.

CHAPTER XI

¹ *New York Herald,* February 6, 1843.

² *Ibid.,* January 8, 1844. Capt. Burrows died of brain fever at sea on packet ship *George Washington,* December 23, 1843.

³ Reports of the Secretary of the U. S. Treasury, Vol. VII, p. 688.

⁴ *Encyclopedia Americana* (1904), Vol. IX, article on Maine.

⁵ Reports of the Secretary of the U. S. Treasury, *Shipbuilding in the United States,* Vol. VI, p. 442.

⁶ *Liverpool Mercantile Gazette,* May 13, 1844.

⁷ This and similar summaries relating to packet lines may be regarded as approximate only, as there are many borderline cases which may be included or omitted, according to criteria adopted.

⁸ *New York Herald,* January 10, 1846.

⁹ *Ibid.,* August 27, 1847.

¹⁰ *Ibid.,* April 7, 1847. "Symmes's Hole" was the popular designation of a mythical entrance located near the North Pole to an equally mythical inhabited region in the interior of the earth. It received the name from Captain Symmes, an officer of the War of 1812 who advocated the theory that the earth was composed of concentric hollow spheres which were inhabited.

CHAPTER XII

¹ *New York Herald,* August 24, 1848.

² *New York Commercial Advertiser,* December 10, 1848. See also *New York Evening Post* and *New York Herald* for same date.

³ *New York Evening Post,* July 21, 1850.

⁴ *New York Herald,* January 15, 1850.

⁵ C. Vernon Briggs, *Passenger Liners of the Western Ocean,* p. 93.

⁶ *New York Herald,* February 17, 1851.

⁷ *New York Commercial Advertiser,* April 20, 1852.

⁸ *New York Herald,* January 1, 1853.

⁹ *Ibid.*

¹⁰ *Providence Journal,* October 13 and 16, 1854. See also Boston and New York newspapers of same dates or thereabouts.

¹¹ *New York Herald,* September 23, 1854.

¹² *Ibid.,* May 3, 1855.

Chapter XIII

[1] *New York Herald,* May 20, 1854.

[2] *New York Herald Tribune,* September 4, 1957.

[3] *New York Herald,* March 12, 1849.

[4] *Ibid.,* August 21, 1850.

[5] *Ibid.,* April 11, 1851.

[6] *Myers's Weekly Advertiser* (Liverpool), March 16, 1855.

[7] New York Shipping and Commercial List, January 3, 1855.

[8] Quoted from Captain Townshend's Journal by permission of Mrs. Raynham Townshend.

[9] *New York Commercial Advertiser,* March 31, 1852, and other New York newspapers of the same date.

[10] *New York Herald,* October 5, 1860.

Chapter XIV

[1] U. S. Department of Commerce, Bureau of Census, *Historical Statistics of the United States, 1789-1945.*

[2] Davis Rich Dewey, *op. cit.,* p. 267.

[3] *Daily Picayune* (New Orleans), May 5, 1860.

[4] *Daily Evening Bulletin* (Philadelphia), April 20, 1864, reports arrival of packet *Tonawanda* with 731 passengers to Cope Bros.

[5] It is doubtful whether the last regularly scheduled sailing of a transatlantic packet can be determined with assurance. The last two lines to maintain a service were the Black Ball and Grinnell, Minturn & Company's London line. The operations of Black Ball ended with the voyage of the *Charles H. Marshall* from New York to Antwerp in the summer of 1881. The line had discontinued its Liverpool sailings in 1879, although it sent the *Hamilton Fish* to Liverpool in the early part of 1881. Grinnell, Minturn & Company discontinued its London service in 1879 and thereafter ran its vessels to various ports as transients. It went out of active business at the end of 1880, although it continued for years winding up its affairs. Its Liverpool line had been discontinued in 1873, or thereabouts. Of the immigrant houses, the last to go was Thomas Dunham's Nephew who discontinued operations with the arrival of the old *Hamilton Fish* at New York in December, 1894, from Bergen, Norway. The firm had discontinued the immigrant traffic years earlier.

[6] *Daily Picayune* (New Orleans), May 7, 1860.

[7] *Boston Gazette,* August 5, 1822.

[8] *New York Herald,* February 10, 1841.

[9] *Ibid.,* October 29, 1840.

[10] *Ibid.,* June 14, 1845.

Appendixes

Notes to Appendixes

Abbreviations used in these appendixes to describe the rig of vessels named:

Sp. Ship
Bk. Bark
Bg. Brig
Sch. Schooner
Sl. Sloop

The letters (Cl.) after a vessel's name indicate that she was clipper-built, *i.e.* had fine, rather than full lines.

The expression (tern) after a schooner's name indicates she was a three-masted vessel.

The names of many master mariners listed herein appear now for the first time in a printed narrative and, unlike more familiar names, have not been subjected to time's corrective processes. Accordingly, a greater percentage of error than usual may be anticipated in the spelling of these names. In part, this will be due to mistakes, variations, omissions and illegibilities in customhouse and other records, and in part to the impossibility of deciphering with complete certainty manuscript material carelessly written with quill pens. Many writers of the period, for example, made no distinction between the capital letters "I" and "J." Still other capitals, such as "R," "B," and "K" are frequently indistinguishable, while badly faded manuscripts furnish a grist of other problems. It sums up to a situation where the labor of supplying corrections and additions of this character must be left largely to the descendants of the old captains and to informed local historians.

As for the tonnages of the ships themselves, it is possible in many instances to cite "sound official authority" for wide variations.

Sailing Lines Between the United States and Foreign Ports

SECTION 1. BOSTON—LIVERPOOL

BOSTON & LIVERPOOL LINE

Boston & Liverpool Packet Co., Proprietors. S. Austin, Jr. and J. W. Lewis, India Wharf, Boston agents; A. and F. Lodge, Thomas and John D. Thornley, Curwen & Haggerty, and Maury, Latham & Co., Liverpool agents for *Herald*, *Amethyst*, *Emerald* and *Topaz*, in that order. Operation started with clearance of *Emerald* for Charleston, Oct., 1822. All line sailings ceased in 1826.

YEAR	VESSEL	TONS	MASTERS	REMARKS
1822	Sp. *Herald*	359	Hector Coffin	*Topaz* destroyed by pirates in 1828 with no
"	*Emerald*	359	Philip Fox	survivors. Line never sailed with any degree
"	*Topaz*	363	John Callender	of regularity and no attempt was made to
1823	Sp. *Lucilla* (Chartered)	360	John Candler	maintain monthly sailings from Liverpool,
"	*Amethyst*	359	John Bussey	the ships sailing in close succession as "spring
1825	Sp. *Sapphire*	366	Joseph Callender	and fall ships." All original Liverpool agents

had dropped out by spring of 1826, and Charles Humberston & Co. was sole Liverpool agent. The liner *Sapphire* made but one trip as a packet. Operations were affected by competition of numerous "spring and fall ships," especially those of Wm. & James Brown & Co. who always sent at least three such ships each season.

BOSTON & LIVERPOOL PACKETS

George G. Jones, 41 India Wharf, Boston agent. Thomas & J. D. Thornley, Maury, Latham & Co., Latham & Gair, and Charles Humberston & Co., Liverpool agents for *Amethyst*, *Dover*, *Boston* and *Liverpool*, in that order. Operations started Nov. 1, 1827. Discontinued in 1830.

YEAR	VESSEL	TONS	MASTERS	REMARKS
1827	Sp. *Amethyst*	359	Jabez Howes	Ships sailed from Boston the 1st and from
"	*New England*	375	Charles Hunt	Liverpool the 20th of each month.
1828	Sp. *Boston*	429	Henry C. Mackay	
"	*Dover*	431	Ira Bursley	
"	*Liverpool*	428	Jabez Howes	
"	*Trenton*	429	William Homan	

TRAIN'S LINE

Enoch Train, 37 Lewis Wharf, Boston agent. Baring Bros. & Co., Liverpool agents. Sailed from Boston the 8th and Liverpool the 24th of month, commencing with Liverpool sailing June 24, 1844. Sailings were quite irregular during the first year.

YEAR	VESSEL	TONS	MASTERS	REMARKS
1844	Sp. *Dorchester*	389	Daniel P. Upton	Foundered Dec. 15, 1844. Crew and passengers rescued by packet *Rochester*.
"	*Cairo*	556	James Murdoch	
"	*Governor Davis*	768	Daniel P. Upton	Henry Neef master in 1845.
"	*St. Petersburg*	814	Theodore Train	Abandoned at sea, 1858.
1845	Sp. *Washington Irving*	751	Ebenezer Caldwell	Began sailing from Liverpool 20th and from Boston 5th of month.
"	*Joshua Bates*	621	James Murdoch	T. S. Stoddard master in 1848.
"	*Concordia*	602	William J. Dorr	
"	*Ashburton*	449	J. D. White	
"	*Columbiana*	631	George M. Pollard	George Barker master in 1845–6.
1846	Sp. *Mary Ann*	497	Albert H. Brown	H. A. Patten master in 1848.
"	*Anglo-Saxon*	704	Joseph R. Gordon	Lost Sable I. May 3, 1847.
"	*New World*	1405	William Skiddy	Enoch Train & Co. became Boston agents.

TRAIN'S LINE (*continued*)

YEAR	VESSEL	TONS	MASTERS	REMARKS
1847	Sp. *Anglo-American*	704	Albert H. Brown	W. Chipman master in 1849.
	" *Sunbeam*	843	George Winsor	George W. Putnam master in 1851.
	" *Robert C. Winthrop*	781	Allen H. Knowles	Gaius Sampson master in 1850.
	" *Ocean Monarch*	1301	James Murdoch	Burned Aug. 21, 1847. 180 lost.
	" *Minstrel*	454	Justus Doane	Later master of clippers *R. B. Forbes* and *John Gilpin*.
	" *Milton*	598	Josiah Gorham	
1849	Sp. *Plymouth Rock*	973	Ebenezer Caldwell	Gaius Sampson master in 1850.
	" *Parliament*	1001	E. D. Thayer	Train & Co., 5 India Buildings, replaced Baring Bros. & Co. as Liverpool agent.
	" *Hope*	971	G. B. Weston	
	" *Townsend*	719	Josiah Richardson	Burned in Pacific in 1854, 12 lost.
1850	Sp. *Western Star*	820	Allen H. Knowles	E. D. Thayer master in 1852.
	" *Niobe*	686	Freeman Soule	
	" *Moses Wheeler*	872	James B. King	Cabin rate varied from 15 guineas to £20 but stood at latter figure most of the decade.
	" *Robert Hooper*	757	William Churchill	
	" *Revere*	734	Frederick Howes	
1851	Sp. *Eva*	800	W. J. Philcrook	Var. Philcook.
	" *President*	1021	Josiah S. Cummings	Var. Comings.
	" *Daniel Webster*	1188	William H. Howard	George W. Putnam master in 1856.
	" *Staffordshire*	1817	Albert H. Brown	*Staffordshire* lost off Cape Sable Dec. 30, 1854, with Capt. Josiah Richardson and about 180.
	" *John H. Jarvis*	740	N. S. Rich	Line began sailing 5th and 20th of month
	" *William Jarvis*	675	F. H. Jarvis	from Liverpool with many extra sailings.
	" *George Raynes*	999	Pierce W. Penhallow	
	" *William Wirt*	1100	Erastus Sampson	
	" *Cromwell*	748	George Barker	
	" *Old England*	917	A. Lowell	
	" *Mary Glover*	593	Isaiah Chase	
	" *Coquimbo*	671	Thacher Gorham	
1852	Sp. *Shirley*	911	Thomas G. Hiler	
	" *Levi Woodbury*	998	Joseph J. Nickerson	
	" *George Hallett*	425	Thomas P. Howes	
	" *Clarissa Currier*	1000	Samuel Knapp	
	" *North America* (Cl.)	1388	Albert Dunbar	William M. Dunbar master in 1854.
	" *North Atlantic*	799	Henry Cook	
	" *Bell Rock*	780	J. C. Penhallow	
	" *Milan*	700	Isaac F. Sturdivant	
	" *Faneuil Hall*	548	Joseph H. Sears	
	" *Rose Standish*	939	R. H. Pearson	
	" *Clara Wheeler*	996	Clark Delano	
	" *Tirrell*	943	G. N. Elliot	Thomas G. Hiler master in 1853.
1853	Sp. *Chariot of Fame*	2050	Allen H. Knowles	
	" *Star of Empire*	2050	Albert H. Brown	Wrecked 1857.
	" *Champion*	1024	William B. Drew	
	" *Anna Rich*	800	Albert A. Burwell	
	" *Agnes*	929	J. Edwards Scott	
	" *Windermere*	1108	J. W. Fairfield	
	" *Meridian*	1200	J. Manson	
	" *Frank Pierce*	1145	Daniel Marcy	J. Leach master in 1856.
	" *Shawmut*	1035	John C. Hubbard	J. C. Higgins master in 1856.
	" *Stephen Glover*	733	Samuel Baldrey	
	" *Neptune*	1000	Isaac Beauchamp	
	" *White Diamond*	1000	Allen H. Knowles	
	" *John Bunyan*	597	A. Nichols	
1854	Sp. *John Eliot Thayer*	1919	Gaius Sampson	Burned, Gulf of California, 1858.
	" *Cathedral* (Cl.)	1606	William H. Howard	Foundered, Cape Horn, Feb. 18, 1857.
	" *Winchester*	1474	Frederick Moore	Foundered May 3, 1854, crew and 420 passengers rescued by S. S. *Washington* and other vessels.
	" *Asterion*	1135	Moses Gay	During the summer of 1854 Train's Liverpool office advertised 14 ships of the largest
	" *Chatsworth*	1153	Josiah Gorham	size to sail for Boston during the fall. How-
	" *North America*	1461	William M. Dunbar	ever, by fall emigration had almost com-
	" *Mariner*	1282	George Barker	pletely ceased. Whether because of difficulties
	" *Reporter*	1474	Octavius Howe	created by that situation or for other reasons,
	" *George Washington*	1534	Josiah S. Cummings	

TRAIN'S LINE (*continued*)

YEAR	VESSEL	TONS	MASTERS
1854	Sp. *Wellfleet*	1353	Albert A. Burwell
"	*Young Brander*	1469	John Eldridge
"	*Russell Sturges*	1100	James H. Snow
"	*Wild Rover* (Cl.)	1100	C. W. Hamilton
"	*Victory*	670	Gaius Sampson
"	*Storm King* (Cl.)	1399	J. Harding, Jr.
"	*Hamlet*	760	Eben T. Sears
"	*Russell Sturges*	999	James H. Snow
1855	Sp. *George Peabody*	1402	J. Manson
"	*Zephyr*	1184	James B. King
"	*Mary E. Balch*	1199	J. T. Woodberry
"	*Neptune's Favorite*	1347	Oliver G. Lane
1856	Sp. *City of New York*	1811	J. G. Moses
"	*Santa Claus*	1256	Bailey Foster
"	*Jeremiah Thompson*	1818	C. H. Blake
"	*Bostonian*	1099	M. C. Maling
"	*James Nesmith*	991	J. K. Watts
"	*Enoch Train*	1618	H. S. Rich
"	*S. Curling*	1467	Sanders Curling
"	*William Wirt*	899	A. Wadsworth
"	*Arkwright*	1244	John Davis
"	*Dragoon*	1433	Gershom B. Weston, Jr.
"	*Messina*	1243	William B. Hatch

REMARKS

Enoch Train's active management of the line apparently ended in Dec. At all events in 1855 Warren & Thayer announced a new line that took over the Train Line's sailing dates and some of the ships. Sailings continued to be advertised under the Train name, but whether because it was thought advisable to retain the benefit of that name, or because Train still retained an interest is uncertain. This arrangement continued until Jan. 1857 when Warren & Thayer's name supplanted that of Train in Liverpool. Because of this, sailings advertised under the Train name during 1855–6 are listed as Train line sailings. Most of these represent Liverpool clearances. The line service out of Boston was greatly reduced and very irregular. Var. A.S. Rich.

WARREN & THAYER'S LINE OF LIVERPOOL AND BOSTON PACKETS

Warren & Thayer, 99 State Street, Boston agents. Baring Bros. & Co., Liverpool agents. Established Jan., 1855. Sailed 5th and 20th of each month from each port. Scheduled sailings discontinued in 1858.

YEAR	VESSEL	TONS	MASTERS	REMARKS
1855	Sp. *Cicero*	995	Bailey Loring	Lost on the Abaco, 1860.
"	*Western Star*	842	Allen H. Knowles	
"	*Alice Monroe*	1400	Josiah S. Cummings	Var. Comings.
"	*Agnes*	929	Edward Scott	William F. Jones master in 1857.
"	*Wilbur Fisk*	949	Albert A. Burwell	
"	*Meridian*	1453	F. Crowell, Jr.	
"	*S. Curling*	1467	S. Curling	
"	*Chatsworth*	1152	Josiah Gorham	N. Proctor master in 1857.
"	*George Washington*	1534	Josiah S. Cummings	B. Crowell master in 1857.
"	*Western Empire*	1398	Charles T. Winsor	Kimball Harlow master in 1857.
"	*Neptune*	1000	N. T. Snell	Cabins usually restricted to 10 or 12 first class
"	*Addie Snow*	990	Octavius Howe	in addition to second class.
"	*Sea Flower*	1024	H. W. Thornhill	
"	*William F. Storer*	1573	Charles Comery	
1857	Sp. *Sea King*	1160	George Barker	
"	*Coosawattee*	960	Thomas Paxton	Var. Paxon.
"	*Bridgewater*	1488	Edwin W. Barstow	
"	*Emerald*	1080	William Cook	
"	*Plutarch*	1322	A. R. Barker	
"	*Parliament*	1001	George M. Pollard	
"	*Arkwright*	1244	T. J. Davis	
"	*Dragoon*	1433	G. J. Weston, Jr.	Var. G. B. Weston, Jr.
"	*Messina*	1243	William B. Hatch	
"	*Mary E. Balch*	1199	J. T. Woodbury	Var. Woodberry.
"	*North American*	1402	S. Clarke	
"	*Daniel Webster*	1188	George W. Putnam	
"	*Canvas Back*	731	H. S. Clark	
"	*Endymion*	1360	F. Hallett	
"	*Alice Counce*	1156	W. J. Singer	Cabin $80. Steerage $18. Later $75, $24,
"	*Mary O'Brien*	1300	Peter Vesper	and $18.
"	*R. Jacobs*	1268	James Henderson	
"	*Rising Sun*	1375	Samuel Skolfield	
1858	Sp. *Hesperus*	1019	John Lewis	
"	*S. Emerson Smith*	1326	E. Creighton	
"	*Mary Hammond*	999	G. W. Colson	Var. Coulson.
"	*Anna Decatur*	1045	N. H. Parsons	

WARREN & THAYER'S LINE (*continued*)

YEAR		VESSEL	TONS	MASTERS	REMARKS
1858	Sp.	*Mary Washington*	934	G. W. Chapman	
	"	*Thornton*	1422	Charles Collins	
	"	*Oliver Putnam*	1020	Ammi Smith	
1859	Sp.	*International*	1003	M. Seavey	Var. Seavy.
	"	*Havelock*	1100	L. Snow	S. Young master in 1860.
	"	*Pocahontas*	995	B. Delano	
	"	*Sagamore*	1163	G. W. Gerrish	
	"	*Rockingham*	976	George Melcher	
	"	*Charter Oak*	860	Franklin Houdlette	
	"	*Weymouth*	1370	D. Elliott	
	"	*Delft Haven*	941	A. J. Freese	
	"	*Kate Prince*	995	T. Jones	
	"	*Atlantic*	895	S. B. Dinsmore	
	"	*Emily Gardner*	750	R. Limeburner	
	"	*Nauset*	1000	J. Westcott	A. C. Childs master in 1860.
	"	*Barnabas Webb*	1300	Alfred Watts	
	"	*Kentuckian*	1050	A. H. Merryman	
	"	*Samuel Lawrence*	1050	H. A. Patten	
	"	*Autocrat*	1100	Albert A. Burwell	
	"	*Eagle Speed*	1113	D. S. Fuller	
	"	*Charmer*	1055	Isaac S. Lucas	
	"	*Lady Blessington*	995	W. Bennett	
1860	Sp.	*Eagle*	1296	Sanders Curling	
	"	*Volant*	896	S. B. Bray	
	"	*Enoch Talbot*	992	A. H. Merryman	
	"	*Valentia*	799	Robert Jack	
	"	*Consignment*	1131	A. Purington	
	"	*Belle of the Sea*	1255	Dennis Janvrin	
	"	*Richard III*	900	J. E. Scott	
	"	*Lion*	828	Cyrus Cooper	
	"	*J. P. Wheeler*	675	H. Gadd	
	"	*Ironsides*	1319	F. Chase	
	"	*William H. Prescott*	1390	C. Batchelder	

MERCHANTS LINE

Page, Richardson & Co., (Samuel Page, Hy. L. Richardson & Preston A. Ames) Boston agents. Taylor, Tipper & Co., Liverpool agents. Established Feb., 1858.

YEAR		VESSEL	TONS	MASTERS	REMARKS
1858	Sp.	*Albatross*	746	Silas Weeks	
	"	*Commodore*	1097	Eli C. Bliss	
	"	*Junius*	562	David M. Erskine	
	"	*Otseonthe*	1138	William K. Maxwell	
	"	*Carlyle*	1181	Robert W. Simpson	
	"	*Rochambeau*	916	George W. Gillchrist	
	"	*Argo*	1078	Calvin Ballard	
	"	*Shawmut*	1035	J. C. Higgins	
	"	*M. R. Ludwig*	1049	Peter Miller	
	"	*Richard Morse*	873	N. B. Dinsmore	
	"	*Isabella*	1022	J. W. Coffin	
	"	*Calliope*	1163	S. R. Goodwin	
	"	*Martha*	1179	Samuel Baldrey	Var. Baldry.
	"	*Britannia*	1194	Charles E. Patten	
	"	*D. L. Choate*	920	George W. McManus	
1859	Sp.	*Leucothea*	949	Moses Gay	Taylor, Tipper & Richardson, Liverpool
	"	*William F. Storer*	1573	Charles Comery	agents.
	"	*Mongolia*	967	G. Melcher	
	"	*Walter Scott*	1196	William B. Hatch	
	"	*Tigress*	912	Horatio Stevens	
	"	*G. F. Chapman*	1035	J. F. Chapman	
	"	*Robert Treat*	694	Robert Treat, Jr.	
	"	*J. Morton*	1149	Lewis W. Gilley	
	"	*Susan Hicks*	783	F. P. Claussen	
	"	*De Soto*	799	S. B. Reed	
	"	*Morning Star*	1105	William L. Foster	

MERCHANTS LINE (*continued*)

YEAR		VESSEL	TONS	MASTERS	REMARKS
1859	Sp.	*Gleaner*	999	M. Lunt	Taylor, Tipper & Co., Liverpool agents in and after Dec., 1859.
1860	Sp.	*Exchange*	596	Lawrence	
	"	*Columbus*	707	Jefferson G. Hathorne	
	"	*Maritana*	990	George W. Williams	
	"	*Regulator*	908	Newcomb	
	"	*City of Boston*	908	Elisha F. Sears	
	"	*Liverpool Packet*	993	Freeman Crosby	
	"	*North America*	1388	David L. Lincoln	
	"	*Fear Not*	1117	T. G. Hiler	
	"	*Speedwell*	691	E. Radcliffe	
	"	*Birmingham*	1185	D. Elliott	
	"	*Benjamin Bangs*	886	George S. Bartlett	
	"	*Sebasticook*	549	E. Chase	
	"	*Thomas Jefferson*	989	Smith	

LIVERPOOL-BOSTON EMIGRANT LINES

REGULAR LINE

Harnden & Co., 6 Cook Street. Emigration Office, 60 Waterloo Rd., Liverpool agents. Established Mar., 1849, to sail from Liverpool the 5th, 15th and 25th of month. Line consisted of eight ships. Firm engaged in steerage traffic from 1844, and had offices in Boston, New York and Philadelphia, to all of which ports it began to operate lines in 1849.

YEAR		VESSEL	TONS	MASTERS	REMARKS
1849	Sp.	*Chasca*	675	George D. Wise	Although most of the emigrant lines engaged several ships regularly year after year, a majority of their vessels were transients which sailed in the line only once. As such ships ran in the aggregate to a very large number, no attempt will be made here to list more than enough to give a general idea of the extent to which they competed with the regular American lines. As a matter of fact Harnden and most of the other British emigrant lines supplied many emigrants for American lines, but there can be no doubt that at times they preempted a large share of the traffic.
	"	*Robert*	720	S. Beauchamp	
	"	*Living Age*	727	Jabez Snow	
	"	*Maine*	749	A. H. Littlefield	
	"	*Townsend*	719	Josiah Richardson	
1850	Sp.	*Fanchon*	968	E. Pike	
	"	*John Haven*	1038	S. Harding	
	"	*Middlesex*	496	L. Snow	
	"	*Bell Rock*	780	N. Pendleton	
	"	*Amelia*	573	George Agry	
	"	*Sylphide*	400	Z. Lowry	
	"	*South Carolina*	768	C. Owens	
	"	*Squantum*	647	David Crocker	
	"	*Caledonia*	780	D. McLean	In addition to Harnden and Pilkington & Wilson, the firms of Focke & Boult, Baring Bros. & Co., James Browne & Co. and Brown & Harrison were very active in competition with the American lines serving the larger American ports. Harnden's emigrant lines were discontinued the latter part of 1851, possibly because the growth of the express business demanded the entire attention of the company.
	"	*Saxony*	393	B. M. Melcher	
	"	*W. D. Sewall*	672	Robert Jack	
	"	*Sarah Louisa*	607	G. H. McLellan	
	"	*Blanchard*	394	P. G. Blanchard	
	"	*Cambridge*	799	Joseph L. White	
	"	*Fidelia*	895	F. W. Abeel	
1851	Sp.	*Forest State*	850	J. Polister	
	"	*Medomac*	632	E. Rich	Var. *Medomah*.
	"	*Edward*	674	Stephen P. Bray	
	"	*Ocean Queen*	824	Henry Shoof	

WHITE STAR LINE

Pilkington & Wilson, Commercial Bldgs., Water Street, Liverpool agents. Established May, 1849.

YEAR		VESSEL	TONS	MASTERS	REMARKS
1849	Sp.	*Amelia*	573	George Agry	Pilkington & Wilson associated with Harnden & Co. in dispatching emigrant ships to Boston in 1846–7. They continued the White Star Line through 1856, doing a very heavy business through 1854, but a comparatively light business thereafter.
	"	*Cromwell*	740	George Barker	
	"	*Mount Washington*	547	Jonathan Blaisdell	
	"	*Bay State*	502	I. B. Simmons	
	"	*Charlemagne*	742	D. Healey	
	"	*Jane H. Glidden*	700	Ambrose Child	
	"	*Olive Branch* (British)	950	Drake	
	"	*Equity*	550	T. Nason	

ENGLISH & BRANDON LINE

English & Brandon, 18 Water Street, Liverpool agents. Established 1855.

YEAR	VESSEL	TONS	MASTERS	REMARKS
1855	Sp. *Sentinel*	913	E. C. Soule	Firm continued its Boston line through 1858,
"	*Moonlight*	820	Benj. F. Pendleton	latterly as Boult, English & Brandon.
"	*Jane H. Glidden*	700	B. Lovett	
"	*Frank Pierce*	1143	Daniel Marcy	

SECTION 2. BOSTON—LONDON

WINSLOW LINE

Isaac Winslow & Sons, 13 Long Wharf, and Lombard & Whitmore, 19 Lewis Wharf, Boston agents. Maclean, Maris & Co., London agents. Established May, 1842, to sail from each port every six weeks, to begin with sailing of brig *Messenger* from Boston, May 25th, "full or not full." Discontinued in 1844.

YEAR	VESSEL	TONS	MASTERS	REMARKS
1842	Bg. *Messenger*	213	Ellis	
	Sp. *Leland*	350	James Miller	
	Bg. *Mars* (British)	322	Beckwith	
	Bk. *Owen Evans* (British)	305	Evans	
	" *Sharon* (British)	290	Lucas	
	Bg. *Vanguard*	225	Card	
1843	Bk. *Niagara*	232	Scudder	
	" *Natchez*	300	John B. Linsay	

BURRILL LINE

Charles Burrill & Co., 3 India St., Boston agents. Established May, 1857. Discontinued after sailing of *Thomas Killam* in December.

YEAR	VESSEL	TONS	MASTERS	REMARKS
1857	Bk. *Hesper*	640	Briard	
	" *Consigliere Jenny*		Ribigihini	
	Sp. *Timor*	670	J. C. Bixby	
	Bk. *Thomas Killam*	556	Crosby	

GLIDDEN & WILLIAMS LINE

Glidden & Williams (William T. Glidden and William H. Williams), 114 State St., Boston agents. Firm was heavily engaged in London trade in 1857, but did not announce establishment of regular line until Nov., 1858.

YEAR	VESSEL	TONS	MASTERS	REMARKS
1858	Bg. *R. B. Porter* (British)		Cowan	
	Sp. *Winfield Scott*	1128	George Crocker	
	" *Franklin Haven*	1106	Daniel Coxe	
	" *Queen of the Seas*	1286	Seth Crowell, Jr.	
1859	Bk. *Canada* (British)			
	Sp. *Mogul*	797	Nathaniel Spooner	
	" *Leaping Water*	1145	H. D. Gardner	
	" *King Philip*	1126	Elias D. Knight	

SECTION 3. NEW YORK—LIVERPOOL

BLACK BALL LINE

Line of three ships established April, 1817, sailing in succession, but not on fixed schedule. Isaac Wright & Son and Francis Thompson, Proprietors. A fourth ship added Oct. 24 and announcement made that ships would sail on schedule from New York the 5th and from Liverpool the 1st of month beginning Jan., 1818. On Oct. 28, 1817, Benjamin Marshall and Jeremiah Thompson were added as proprietors.

YEAR	VESSEL	TONS	MASTERS	REMARKS
1817	Sp. *Pacific*	384	John Williams	Cropper, Benson & Co. and Rathbone, Hodg-
	" *Courier*	381	William Bowne	son & Co. appointed Liverpool agents of line
	" *Amity*	382	John Stanton	about Dec., 1817.
	" *James Monroe*	424	James Watkinson	Added Oct. 24, 1817. Lost on Tasmania, 1850.
1819	Sp. *Albion*	434	John Williams	Replaced *Pacific*. Lost 1822.
1821	Sp. *Nestor*	481	Seth G. Macy	Replaced *Courier*. *Nestor* lost 1824.

BLACK BALL LINE (*continued*)

YEAR	VESSEL	TONS	MASTERS	REMARKS
1821	Sp. *James Cropper*	495	William Bowne	Chas. H. Marshall master in 1824; ship lost 1832, at mouth of Delaware.
				Rathbone, Hodgson & Co., dropped as Liverpool agents.
1822	Sp. *Columbia*	492	James Rogers	A second line of four ships added Feb. 1822.
	" *William Thompson*	495	William Thompson	Lines sailed 1st and 16th from each port.
	" *Liverpool*	496	William Lee, Jr.	
	" *New York*	518	William E. Hoxie	Thomas Bennett master in 1824.
	" *Orbit* (Temporary)	384	Josiah Macy	Lost near Squan Inlet, Jan. 1827.
1823	Sp. *Canada*	545	Seth G. Macy	Hugh Graham master in 1828.
1824	Sp. *Pacific* (New)	587	Solomon Maxwell	Rowland R. Crocker master in 1827.
1825	Sp. *Lafayette* (Temporary)	341	Thomas Fanning	Replaced by *Manchester*.
	" *Florida*	523	James Tinkham	Also reported and probably Jos. Tinkham.
	" *Manchester*	561	William Lee, Jr.	William Sketchley master in 1829.
1826	Sp. *Britannia*	630	Charles H. Marshall	N. P. Durfey master in 1835.
1828	Sp. *Caledonia*	648	James Rogers	
1830	Sp. *Hibernia*	551	George Maxwell	Maxwell was master of *Amity* in 1823.
1831	Sp. *North America*	610	Robert Macy	Alfred E. Lowber master in 1839.
1832	Sp. *South America*	616	Charles H. Marshall	Robert H. Waterman master in 1836.
	" *Orpheus*	573	Nathan Cobb	Ira Bursley master in 1834.
1833	Sp. *Europe*	618	Alexander C. Marshall	Sale of line announced Jan., 1834. Goodhue & Co., New York agents. Baring Bros. & Co. became Liverpool agents.
1834	Sp. *Columbus*	663	Nathan Cobb	
1835				Charles H. Marshall added as New York agent.
1836	Sp. *England*	730	Benjamin L. Waite	Went missing winter of 1844–5.
	" *Oxford*	752	John Rathbone	Samuel Yeaton master in 1842.
1837	Sp. *Cambridge*	799	Ira Bursley	
1839	Sp. *New York*	863	William C. Barstow	Thomas B. Cropper master in 1840.
1843	Sp. *Montezuma*	924	Alfred B. Lowber	
	" *Yorkshire*	997	David G. Bailey	Cabin capacity, 44 passengers. Edward G. Furber master in 1848; Jas. Bryant in 1857.
1845	Sp. *Fidelia*	895	William G. Hackstaff	Samuel Yeaton master in 1849; W. A. MacGill in 1856.
	" *Shenandoah* (Temporary)	738	James West	
1846	Sp. *Columbia*	1051	John Rathbone	Reputed first American sailing ship to have iron knees and straps. C. Hutchinson master in 1856.
1847	Sp. *Sardinia* (Temporary)	734	T. R. Crocker	
	" *Isaac Wright*	1161	Alexander C. Marshall	David G. Bailey master in 1848; E. Abeel master in 1853.
1849	Sp. *Manhattan*	1300	William G. Hackstaff	First three-decker of line.
1850	Sp. *Isaac Webb*	1360	Thomas B. Cropper	Edward G. Furber master in 1853; James M. Bryer master in 1855.
1851	Sp. *Great Western*	1443	David S. Sherman	C. H. Marshall & Co., in 1851 sole New York agents. In 1854 line consisted of *Manhattan*, *Harvest Queen*, *Great Western*, *Isaac Webb*, *Isaac Wright*, *Yorkshire*, *Columbia*, and *Fidelia*, sailing 1st & 16th. Line continued to 1881 but sailed irregularly towards last. The larger of above packets had a capacity of 800 to 900 passengers.
1854	Sp. *Harvest Queen*	1383	Edward Young	
	" *James Foster, Jr.*	1411	James M. Porter	
1855	Sp. *Neptune*	1406	E. W. Peabody	
1860	Sp. *Alexander Marshall*	1493	Alexander C. Marshall	

NEW LINE or RED STAR LINE

Byrnes, Trimble & Company, 159 South St., New York agents. Cropper, Benson & Co. and A. S. Richards & Co., Liverpool agents.

YEAR	VESSEL	TONS	MASTERS	REMARKS
1821	Sp. *Panthea*	370	Jonathan Eldridge	Wrecked off Holyhead, Jan., 1827.
	" *Manhattan*	391	David Tarr, Jr.	These ships sailed irregularly in 1821. They were established in Jan., 1822, as a regular line to sail from New York the 25th and from Liverpool the 12th of month.
	" *Meteor*	325	Nathan Cobb	
	" *Hercules*	335	T. W. Gardner	
1823	Sp. *William Byrnes*	517	William G. Hackstaff	Benjamin Sprague master in 1833.
				Began leaving New York the 24th and Liverpool the 8th.

NEW LINE OR RED STAR LINE (*continued*)

YEAR	VESSEL	TONS	MASTERS	REMARKS
1825	Sp. *John Wells*	366	Isaac Harris	Replaced *Hercules*.
1826	Sp. *Birmingham*	571	Nathan Cobb	Sold Chile, 1851.
				Samuel Hicks and Co. added as New York agents.
1827	Sp. *Hamilton* (Temporary)	455	Thomas G. Bunker	
	" *John Jay*	503	N. H. Holdredge	
	" *Silvanus Jenkins*	547	Francis P. Allen	Out of line in 1832.
1831	Sp. *Sheffield*	578	William G. Hackstaff	Wood and Trimble replaced Byrnes, Trimble
1832	Sp. *Virginian*	616	Isaac Harris	& Co. in association with Samuel Hicks &
1833	Sp. *Henry Clay* (Temporary)	436	Josiah Spaulding	Co.
	" *United States*	676	N. H. Holdredge	
1834	Sp. *England*	730	George Maxwell	
1835	Sp. *Scotland*	627	William G. Hackstaff	Lost on Arklow Bank, Ireland, Jan. 19, 1846. Ships *United States*, *Sheffield*, and *Virginian* went into Kermit Line at close of 1835. George Trimble continued a reduced service for some years with Isaac Hicks, as Hicks, Trimble & Co.

FOURTH or SWALLOWTAIL LINE

Fish & Grinnell and Thaddeus Phelps & Co., New York agents. A. & S. Richards & Co., Liverpool agents. Established July, 1822, to commence operations Aug. 8, sailing from New York the 8th and from Liverpool the 24th of each month.

YEAR	VESSEL	TONS	MASTERS	REMARKS
1822	Sp. *Robert Fulton*	340	Henry Holdredge	Dropped from line in 1824.
	" *Cortes*	382	Nash De Cost	
	" *Martha* (Temporary)	260	William Sketchley, Jr.	
	" *Corinthian*	401	George W. Davis	Daniel Chadwick master in 1827.
	" *Leeds*	408	William Stoddard	Frederick H. Hebard master in 1827.
	" *Indian Chief* (Temporary)	401	Jabez Humphreys	
1824	Sp. *Silas Richards*	450	Henry Holdredge	Ira Bursley master in 1832.
1825	Sp. *York*	433	William Baker	Fish, Grinnell & Co. replaced Fish & Grinnell.
1827	Sp. *Napoleon*	539	John P. Smith	Replaced *Corinthian* in Oct.
1828	Sp. *George Canning*	552	Francis Allyn	
1832	Sp. *Roscoe*	622	James Rogers	
	" *George Washington*	627	Henry Holdredge	Sold New London, 1845, for whaler.
	" *St. John*	398	T. Spencer	
1834	Sp. *Independence*	733	Ezra Nye	
1836	Sp. *Pennsylvania*	808	John P. Smith	Lost off Liverpool, Jan. 6, 1839.
1838				Wildes, Pickersgill & Co., Liverpool agents.
1839	Sp. *Patrick Henry*	882	Joseph C. Delano	William B. Moore master in 1860.
1842	Sp. *Ashburton*	1015	Henry Huttleson	William Howland master in 1848. Chapman, Bowman & Co., 9 Rumford Place, became Liverpool agents, Jan. 1842.
1843	Sp. *Queen of the West*	1161	Philip Woodhouse	Went ashore coast of Wales, Feb. 1855, and sold to Liverpool.
1844	Sp. *John R. Skiddy*	980	William Skiddy	Wrecked on English coast April, 1850. Liverpool sailing date changed to 21st of month. Cabin fare £25 without wine.
1845	Sp. *Henry Clay*	1207	Ezra Nye	Burned Sept. 5, 1849. Bought and rebuilt by Spofford, Tileston & Co.
1846	Sp. *New World*	1404	William Skiddy	Hale Knight master in 1856.
1847	Sp. *Constitution*	1327	John Britton	
	" *Izaak Walton* (Temporary)	437	J. Goodhue	
1848	Sp. *Sir Robert Peel*	941	T. J. Bird	Nathan F. Larrabee master in 1856.
	" *Channing*	535	Henry Huttleson	
	" *Memnon*	1068	Oliver Eldridge	
	" *Yorktown*	1150	William S. Sebor	
1849	Sp. *Albert Gallatin*	1435	John A. Delano	
	" *London*	1145	Frederick H. Hebard	
1850	Sp. *Constantine*	1162	Richard L. Bunting	Richard Duryee master in 1853 and Samuel Macoduck in 1855-7.

FOURTH OR SWALLOWTAIL LINE (*continued*)

YEAR	VESSEL	TONS	MASTERS	REMARKS
1850	Sp. *Liverpool*	1077	John Eldridge	Line enlarged in 1851 to eight regular packets sailing from Liverpool 6th and 21st of each month. New establishment consisted of ships *New World, Liverpool, Queen of the West, Constantine, Albert Gallatin, Constitution, Ashburton,* and a new ship building.
1852	Sp. *American Union*	1147	Justus S. Doane	Albert H. Caldwell master in 1855. Bowman, Grinnell & Co., Liverpool agents.
1853	Sp. *Arabia*	1274	J. R. Boutelle	
1854	Sp. *Aurora*	1639	Richard L. Bunting	In 1854 management divided between Cornelius Grinnell and Grinnell, Minturn & Co., the former taking four and latter five ships, sailings continued as before.
1855	Sp. *Ontario*	1501	William H. Wood	
	" *Cornelius Grinnell*	1118	Artemas T. Fletcher	
	" *John Currier*	697	Benjamin R. Butman	
	" *James L. Bogert*	1220	Joseph Conway	
1856	Sp. *Plymouth Rock*	973	Edmund Hammond	In 1856 Grinnell, Minturn & Co. again became sole New York agents until discontinuance of line.
1857	Sp. *Rachel*	818	S. Hamblin	
1859	Sp. *Star of the Union*	1057	F. A. Stall	Var. Stahl. Robert M. Grinnell, Commercial Bldgs., Water Street, became Liverpool agent.
1860	Sp. *Adelaide* (Cl.)	1831	Samuel Kennedy	

KERMIT LINE

Stephen Whitney, Gracie, Prime & Co., and Robert Kermit, New York agents. Wm. & Thos. Adair, Baltimore agents. Thomas & Joseph Sands & Co., Liverpool agents. Sailed from New York the 14th and from Liverpool the 24th of month.

YEAR	VESSEL	TONS	MASTERS	REMARKS
1834	Sp. *St. George*	408	William C. Thompson	
	" *St. Andrew*	660	John T. Taubman	Lost off Liverpool Jan. 6, 1839.
	" *Howard*	399	T. M. Harvey, Jr.	
	" *Ajax*	627	Charles A. Heirn	
1835	Sp. *Virginian*	616	Isaac Harris	Withdrawn 1847.
1836	Sp. *Sheffield*	579	Francis P. Allen	Sold for a whaler in 1843.
	" *United States*	650	N. H. Holdredge	
	" *Switzerland*	568	Charles Hunt	Formerly of Packet *Louvre.*
1840	Sp. *Stephen Whitney*	869	William C. Thompson	Lost Nov. 10, 1841, West Calf, Cape Clear, Ireland, with Capt. Popham and over 90 of passengers and crew. Sands, Turner, Fox & Co. added as New York agents.
1843	Sp. *Samuel Hicks*	780	Thomas G. Bunker	
1845	Sp. *Waterloo*	893	William H. Allen	*Waterloo,* Capt. Edmund Harvey and 25 officers and men reported missing Dec. 1853.
	" *Empire*	1049	Jos. G. Russell	
	" *John R. Skiddy*	980	William Skiddy	Thomas Shipley master in 1849. Firm chartered S. S. *Sarah Sands,* 1845.
1847	Sp. *West Point*	1046	William Henry Allen	Thomas Williams master in 1854 and William H. Harding in 1858.
	" *Louisiana*	747	S. E. Cole	
1848	Sp. *Richard Alsop*	836	Jeremiah G. Smith	Spooner, Sands & Co., Liverpool agents.
1849	Sp. *Constellation*	1568	James C. Luce	William H. Allen master in 1851; W. R. Mulliner master in 1857.
1850	Sp. *Underwriter*	1168	Thomas Shipley	J. P. Roberts master in 1857. Kermit & Carow, New York agents.
1853	Sp. *James Nesmith*	991	S. Wales	Var. S. Watts
	" *John Hancock*	746	J. Gilchrist	
1854	Sp. *Phoenix*	1458	John Hoxie	Burned at Melbourne, Feb. 28, 1860.
	" *Charles Buck*	1424	W. W. Smalley	
	" *William Hitchcock*	699	Joseph Cowman	Called Red Star Line in Liverpool. A. Taylor & Co., agents.
1855	Sp. *Wm. F. Schmidt*	775	B. W. Sears	Charles Carow, New York agent.

DRAMATIC LINE

Edward Knight Collins, 74 South St., New York agent. William & James Brown & Co., Liverpool agents. Notice of establishment of line published Sept. 19, 1836, to start with sailing of *Garrick*, Mar. 30, 1837. Sailing dates eventually fixed at 25th from New York and 12th from Liverpool.

YEAR	VESSEL	TONS	MASTERS	REMARKS
1837	Sp. *Garrick*	895	William Robinson	Wrecked near Cardiff, Jan. 1857.
"	*Shakespeare*	747	Alexander S. Palmer	Ship replaced by *Roscius* in 1838.
"	*Siddons*	895	Edward B. Cobb	Nathaniel B. Palmer master in 1838.
"	*Sheridan*	895	Joseph G. Russell	Frederick A. Depeyster master in 1842 and George B. Cornish in 1848.
1838	Sp. *Roscius*	1031	John Collins	Foundered at sea Aug. 26, 1860, from Liverpool for New York. Collins sold line to Spofford, Tileston & Co. in Sept. 1848.
1849	Sp. *James Drake*	483	Benjamin Smith	
1850	Sp. *Henry Clay*	1207	Francis M. French	D. Caulkins master, 1853–8. Spofford, Tileston & Co. sold four original ships in Nov., 1852, for $120,000, retaining *Henry Clay*. See Patriotic Line. J. H. Foster, Jr., 106 Wall St., New York agent. John Collins and Foster in 1853 became New York agents. Richard S. Ely, Liverpool agent.
1854	Sp. *Gazetteer*	1119	Benjamin Watlington	
"	*John Rutledge*	1061	W. A. Sands	Alexander Kelly master in 1855. Hit iceberg Feb. 19, 1856. Captain and 24 men and 120 passengers took to boats, leaving mate and about 50 passengers to go down with ship. Only one survivor. Picked up by ship *Germania*, Capt. Wood.
1855	Sp. *Caravan*	1362	W. A. Sands	Howland & Ridgeway, 106 Wall St., became New York agents.
"	*Emerald*	1080	William Cook	
1856	Sp. *Endymion*	1327	Franklin Hallet	Burned in Mersey Jan. 31, 1860.
"	*Plutarch*	1322	Alexander R. Barker	Stranded on Flemish coast and went to pieces Feb. 7, 1860.
"	*George Evans*	723	E. Cooper	
1857	Sp. *Marianne Nottebohm*	1169	George W. Lamb	Howland & Bartholemew became New York agents.
1858	Sp. *Richard S. Ely*	1207	Malcolm Livingston	
"	*Pomona*	1181	Charles Merrihew	Lost Apr. 28, 1859, on Blackwater Bank 60 miles west of Holyhead, with loss of Capt. Merrihew and 423 passengers and crew. T. & D. R. Sellar, became Liverpool agents.
1860	Sp. *Ann E. Hooper*	1146	J. Hooper	Register surrendered Aug. 2, 1863. Lost at sea.
"	*Harvey Birch*	1482	William H. Nelson	

NEW LINE

Woodhull & Minturn, 87 South St., New York agents. Fielden Brothers & Co., Liverpool agents. Established 1841.

YEAR	VESSEL	TONS	MASTERS	REMARKS
1841	Sp. *Southerner*	671	Alexander S. Palmer	Theodore D. Palmer master in 1845.
"	*Rochester*	715	Philip Woodhouse	Lost on Blackwater Bank, Apr. 18, 1847.
"	*Hibernia*	551	Nathaniel B. Palmer	Sold New London, 1844, for whaler.
1842	Sp. *Palmyra*	612	Erastus Sampson	
"	*Tarolinta*	549	Jeremiah G. Smith	
1843	Sp. *Hottinguer*	993	Ira Bursley	Lost Jan. 12, 1850, near Wexford, Ireland, with Bursley and 12 of crew.
"	*Liverpool*	1077	John Eldridge	J. H. Blethen master in 1848.
"	*Great Western*	1443	Philip Woodhouse	William G. Furber master in 1852.
1844	Sp. *Queen of the West*	1161	Philip Woodhouse	Stranded on Irish coast in 1856, got off, repaired, and sold British.
"	*Ashburton*	1015	Jeremiah D. White	
1847	Sp. *Constitution*	1327	John Britton	Woodhull & Minturn New York agents in 1845. Grinnell, Minturn & Co., took over operation of ships in 1847.
"	*Bavaria* (Temporary)	908	G. W. Howe	

REGULAR COMMERCIAL LINE

John Herdman, 61 South St., New York agent. Herdman, Keenan & Co., 86 Waterloo Rd., Liverpool agents.

YEAR		VESSEL	TONS	MASTERS	REMARKS
1842	Sp.	*Memphis*	799	Ebenezer Knight	Firms were merely emigration agents supply-
	"	*Samuel Hicks*	780	Thomas C. Bunker	ing passengers for ships of old established
	"	*Talbot*	624	John Storey	lines. They continued for several years ad-
	"	*Ondiaka*	749	William Childs	vertising their ships to sail on schedule every
					five days in addition to transients "to sail
					positively on their appointed days."

TAYLOR & MERRILL LINE

Robert L. Taylor & Nathaniel W. Merrill, as Taylor & Merrill, New York agents. Ships cleared from Liverpool in Black Star Line. C. Grimshaw & Co. agents. Established July, 1842.

YEAR		VESSEL	TONS	MASTERS	REMARKS
1842	Sp.	*Birmingham*	571	W. J. Robinson	
	"	*Helen*	424	Allen	
	"	*Atlantic*	699	John Mallet	Ex-packet *Winchester*. Sold for whaler at New London, 1845.
1844	Sp.	*Robert Isaac*	435	George Barrell	Ship condemned Apr. 1, 1846.
	Bk.	*Superior*	576	Allen	
	Sp.	*Huron*	515	John A. Paine	
	"	*Sea*	807	William Edwards	Reported lost near Liverpool early May 1857.
1845	Sp.	*Lancashire*	661	William L. Lyon	
	"	*Goodwin*	595	John Davis	Nathaniel G. Weeks master in 1851.
1846	Sp.	*Marmion*	903	William Edwards	Thomas F. Freeman master in 1850.
	"	*Nicholas Biddle*	784	S. C. Knight	William Evers master in 1858.
1847	Sp.	*Kate Hunter*	731	W. H. Parsons	W. P. Healey master in 1858.
	"	*Enterprise*	837	Edward Funck	
	"	*Atlas*	790	H. Coffin	
	"	*Chaos*	771	J. L. Wilson	
	"	*Alliance*	525	Robert H. Tucker	
	"	*Columbiana*	631	John Mallet	
	"	*Ivanhoe*	1157	William Edwards	S. C. Knight, master in 1848, lost overboard, Nov. 29, 1850. Ship lost off Montauk, Mar., 1851.
1848	Sp.	*De Witt Clinton*	1066	Edward Funck	
	"	*Carolina* (Temporary)	396	Daniel P. Caulkins	
1849	Sp.	*Guy Mannering*	1419	William Edwards	Thomas F. Freeman master in 1853.
	"	*Jacob A. Westervelt*	1418	William R. Hoodless	Thomas Austin master in 1854. H. L. Ritch & Co., 136 Front St., became New York agents, 1859.

SAMUEL THOMPSON'S LINE

Called "New Line" in Liverpool, and later, Black Star Line. Samuel Thompson, Old Established Packet Office, 273 Pearl St., New York agent. Caleb Grimshaw & Co., 12 Goree Piazzas, Liverpool agents. Established May, 1842. Thompson, who had operated approximately 25 years as passenger agent, began clearing ships on his own account in Dec., 1841, including British vessels.

YEAR		VESSEL	TONS	MASTERS	REMARKS
1842	Sp.	*General Parkhill*	554	John C. Hoyt	
	"	*Sarah & Arselia*	482	Thaddeus Smith	
	"	*Delaware*	662	D. Patton	Var. Patten
	"	*Europe*	557	Samuel Barker	
1843	Sp.	*Ohio*	768	Hezekiah Lyon	
1845	Sp.	*Kensington*	494	J. H. Shumway	Name changed to Black Star Jan., 1845. "Ap-
	"	*Sea*	807	William Edwards	pointed days of sailing strictly adhered to.
	"	*Liberty*	692	P. P. Norton	Passage 15 guineas without wine. Fine goods
	"	*Cornelia*	1040	Francis M. French	20 shillings a ton. Steerage find own provi-
	"	*Memphis*	798	C. H. Coffin	sions except bread stuffs." Ships *Ohio* and
	"	*Tarolinta*	604	J. G. Smith	*General Parkhill* retained in line. Richardson,
	"	*Republic*	676	James C. Luce	Watson & Co., associated in operation. W. & J. Tapscott handled steerage business in Liverpool.
1847	Sp.	*Samuel Hicks*	780	T. G. Bunker	On March 1st, Samuel Thompson & Nephew

SAMUEL THOMPSON'S LINE (*continued*)

YEAR	VESSEL	TONS	MASTERS	REMARKS
1847	Sp. *Empire*	1049	J. G. Russell	advertised as agents for the Black Star line of
"	*Panthea*	642	W. B. Lane	packets from Liverpool to New York. Vessels
"	*Indiana*	607	James D. Bennett	sailed every six days throughout year. Line
"	*Huguenot*	935	S. Goodhue	included *Sea, Liberty, Cornelia*, and *Ohio*, and
"	*Marmion*	903	William Edwards	the 14 ships listed for 1847. The correct
"	*Elizabeth Denison*	645	F. W. Spencer	official tonnage given here is in general sub-
"	*Devonshire*	778	W. T. Thompson	stantially lower than the advertised tonnage.
"	*Niagara*	730	Hy. Russell	The firm continued to use British ships, in
"	*Atlas*	790	H. Coffin	addition to those listed here.
"	*Chaos*	771	J. L. Wilson	
"	*Sardinia*	734	C. R. Crocker	
"	*America*	1137	S. Weare	
"	*Peter Hattrick*	554	J. D. Post	
1848	Sp. *Caleb Grimshaw*	987	William E. Hoxie	Burned Nov. 12, 1849, near Fayal.
"	*Milan*	700	E. D. Manson	Williams & Guion advertised Black Star Line
"	*Fanchon*	968	George Lunt, Jr.	of 12 ships, including most of the Thompson
"	*Toronto*	631	J. Pratt	vessels; Crook in Liverpool advertised a line
"	*Nathaniel Hooper*	427	J. Girdler	of 24 ships.
"	*Boston*	411	J. Pratt	
1849	Sp. *Elizabeth*	669	J. L. Lambert	
"	*Excelsior*	1000	C. R. Crocker	J. E. Hadley master in 1852.
1850	Sp. *Star of the West*	1122	Alfred M. Lowber	Eighteen ships in line; weekly sailings.
"	*Joseph Walker*	1326	William E. Hoxie	Burned Dec. 28, 1853, in the *Great Republic* fire.
1851	Sp. *Lady Franklin*	1283	Samuel Yeaton	
"	*Castilian*	999	Alexander Graves	
"	*Argo*	967	Samuel Macoduck	
1853	Sp. *Princeton*	1131	William H. Russell	
"	*Lucy Thompson*	1500	Charles B. Pendleton	
"	*Empire State*	1324	L. J. Briggs	
1854	Sp. *Jeremiah Thompson*	1819	Charles H. Blake	
1860	Sp. *Volant*	899	John Bray	Samuel Thompson's Nephews became New York agents.

EMPIRE LINE

D. & A. Kingsland & Co., 55 Broad St., New York agents. Sailed from Liverpool in Black Star Line, C. Grimshaw & Co., agents.

YEAR	VESSEL	TONS	MASTERS	REMARKS
1844	Sp. *Powhattan*	521	William L. Stone	W. B. Brown master in 1849.
1845	Sp. *Kalamazoo*	798	Robert McCerren	
"	*Empire*	1049	Joseph G. Russell	
1846	Sp. *America*	1137	Samuel Weare	J. J. Lawrence master in 1850.
1847	Sp. *Columbus*	1307	Robert McCerren	
"	*Empire State*	1324	Joseph G. Russell	Rescued 60 crew and passengers, ship *Eudocia* of St. John, N.B., Apr., 1856.
1850	Sp. *Western World*	1354	Samuel Weare	Wrecked Squan Beach, Oct. 22, 1853, with 600 passengers; all saved.
1851	Sp. *Typhoon* (Cl.)	1611	Charles H. Salter	Arrived New York Jan. 21, 1857, 49 days from Liverpool, a mass of ice, 30 of crew of 40 unable to do duty. Lost seven close-reefed topsails.
				D. & A. Kingsland & Sutton, 55 Broad St., became New York agents in 1853.
1854	Sp. *City of New York*	1811	J. G. Moses	James S. Salter master in 1856.

ST. GEORGE LINE

David Ogden, New York agent. A. Taylor & Co., Liverpool agents. Established Sept., 1844. Discontinued 1860.

YEAR	VESSEL	TONS	MASTERS	REMARKS
1844	Sp. *St. George*	845	Watson G. Ferris	Burned at sea Dec. 24, 1852, with loss of 51 lives.
	" *Pacific*	531	J. Hall	Var. J. Hale

ST. GEORGE LINE (*continued*)

YEAR	VESSEL	TONS	MASTERS	REMARKS
1844	Sp. *St. Patrick*	900	B. Seymour	Wrecked on Barnegat, Dec. 19, 1854, Capt. Stephen Whitman. 400 passengers, all saved.
1845	Sp. *Susan E. Howell*	730	Edwin Bailey	
	" *Haidee*	648	J. S. Soule	
1847	Sp. *Magnolia*	649	Edward Gray	
1848	Sp. *Republic*	972	A. Bliven	
	" *Andrew Foster*	1287	Jabez Howes, Jr.	Nicholas Holberton master in 1853. Sunk in English Channel, Apr. 28, 1857.
1849	Sp. *Gertrude*	783	David Sands Shearman	
1851	Sp. *Racer* (Cl.)	1669	Henry W. Steele	Lost, coast of Ireland, May 6, 1856.
1853	Sp. *Forest King*	992	H. M. Allen	
	" *Dreadnought*	1414	Samuel Samuels	
	" *Highflyer* (Cl.)	1195	Gurdon B. Waterman	Sailed from San Francisco for Hong Kong,
	" *Mongolia*	1000	W. L. Sprague	Oct. 25, 1855, and went missing. Supposed
	" *Charles Cooper*	977	B. F. Delano	lost on Formosa and crew massacred.
1854	Sp. *Escort*	1367	Stephen Whitman	E. A. Hussey master in 1859.
	" *Driver*	1594	Nicholas Holberton	Sailed from Liverpool Feb. 12, 1856, and went missing, with crew and passengers variously reported from 339 to 372.
1856	Sp. *Switzerland*	1139	J. G. W. Trask	Line called Dreadnought line in Liverpool.
1857	Sp. *Victory*	1314	James Ainsworth	
1858	Sp. *Gallego*	597	William Wolfe	

DUNHAM & DIMON'S LIVERPOOL LINE

Dunham & Dimon, 67 South St., New York agents. Ships consigned to various Liverpool agents. Line composed principally of ships chartered or on freight. The only vessel cleared by the firm more than once was the *Samuel Hicks*. Firm continued active during 1847–50 but discontinued shortly thereafter. It returned to the trade in 1856, with the re-establishment of a line called the New Line. Discontinued in 1857.

YEAR	VESSEL	TONS	MASTERS	REMARKS
1845	Sp. *Monticello*	392	T. D. Lambert	
	" *Isabella*	649	George Briggs	
	" *Shenandoah*	738	William H. West	
	" *Samuel Hicks*	780	Thomas G. Bunker	
	" *Colombo*	577	Albert A. Burwell	
	" *South Carolina*	581	Joseph Hamilton	
	" *John Baring*	529	J. Sherman	
1846	Bk. *Apthorp*	246	Philip Blake	
	Sp. *Metoka*	775	John H. McLaren	
	" *Rappahannock*	1133	William Drummond	
	" *Diadem*	657	H. M. Barstow	
	" *Mount Vernon*	446	S. V. Given	
	" *Far West*	598	William A. Briard	W. H. Mather master in 1853.
	" *Victoria*	602	R. J. Hartshorne	
	" *Ashland*	631	A. Hawley	
	Bk. *Alverton* (British)	409	E. Clerke	
1856	Sp. *Camden*	525	C. E. Bolles	
1857	Sp. *G. B. Lamar*	933	P. N. Mayhew	
	" *Robena*	778	George Martin	

SLATE'S LIVERPOOL LINE

Slate, Gardner & Howell, 114 South St., New York agents. Ships sailed from Liverpool in Black Star Line, C. Grimshaw & Co., agents. Established 1846; sailed irregularly after 1854; discontinued 1857.

YEAR	VESSEL	TONS	MASTERS	REMARKS
1846	Sp. *Atlas*	790	H. Coffin	William Homan master in 1848.
	" *Chaos*	771	J. L. Wilson	
1847	Sp. *Senator*	777	Rowland T. Coffin	
	" *Niantic*	452	Giles Isham	
	" *Nicholas Biddle*	784	S. C. Knight	
	" *Jamestown*	1151	John G. W. Trask	B. J. H. Trask also master same year.
1851	Sp. *Saratoga*	1200	B. J. H. Trask	Slate, Gardner & Co. became New York agents in 1850.

CHAMBERLAIN & PHELPS LINE

Chamberlain & Phelps, 103 Front St., New York agents. Ships cleared from Liverpool in Black Star Line, John Taylor Crook, agent. Established 1847.

YEAR	VESSEL	TONS	MASTERS	REMARKS
1847	Sp. *Arcole*	664	William R. Hoodless	S. P. Crafts master in 1858.
"	*Mortimer Livingston*	749	Edwin W. Barstow	G. W. Sampson master in 1853.
"	*Nebraska*	516	Joseph R. Brown	Lost near Galveston, Nov. 7, 1857.
"	*Prince de Joinville*	527	W. W. Lawrence	James Adams master in 1849.
1850	Sp. *Robert Kelly*	1131	Edward M. Barstow	Sailed from Liverpool, Jan. 26, 1860, M. E. Sherman, master, and went missing.
1853	Sp. *James Wright*	980	Samuel Clark	
1855	Sp. *Bridgewater*	1498	Edwin W. Barstow	
1858	Sp. *William Chamberlain*	950	B. Sherman	Chamberlain, Phelps & Co. became New York agents in 1860.

BLACK STAR LINE

John Taylor Crook, 2 Tower Chambers, Old Churchyard, Liverpool agent. Williams & Guion, New York agents.

YEAR	VESSEL	TONS	MASTERS	REMARKS
1847	Sp. *Ivanhoe*	1157	William Edwards	Crook parted company with Grimshaw in Dec., 1847, and became associated with the Liverpool firm of Bird, Gillian & Co., but seems to have played the most active part in dispatching ships. He listed at times as many as 25 ships with which he had made special arrangements. Most of the ships listed were dispatched once during the year but a few sailed twice. Both Grimshaw and Crook continued as separate divisions of the Black Star Line.
"	*Martha Washington*	473	J. Stewart	
1848	Bk. *Ann Welch*	381	William G. Furber	
	Sp. *Louisiana*	747	Nathaniel Barstow	
"	*Marmion*	903	Thomas F. Freeman	
"	*Jamestown*	1151	B. J. H. Trask	
"	*Senator*	777	H. Coffin	
"	*Sea*	807	T. H. C. Barstow	
"	*Chaos*	771	James L. Wilson	
"	*Atlas*	790	William Homan	
"	*Nicholas Biddle*	784	S. C. Knight	
"	*Republic*	972	A. Blivens	
"	*Pacific*	551	Joseph Ludlam	
"	*Columbiana*	631	John Mallet	
"	*Enterprise*	837	Stanbury Funk	Jacob N. Funk master in 1849.
"	*Samuel Hicks*	780	Samuel Goodhue	
"	*St. John*	562	S. Skolfield	
"	*E. Z.*	673	Richard T. Hartshorne	
"	*Forest King*	991	W. T. Thompson	C. A. Ranlett master in 1849
"	*Richard Cobden*	711	George Barrell	
"	*De Witt Clinton*	1066	Edward Funk	Var. Funck
"	*Peter Hattrick*	554	J. R. Rockwell	
"	*Aberdeen*	719	Asahel Hubbard	
"	*Liberty*	692	Pratt	
"	*J. Z.*	676	G. S. Porter	
"	*A. Z.*	675	John G. Moses	
"	*Nestorian*	698	Samuel Goodhue	
"	*Arcole*	663	Augustus Proal	
"	*Elsinore*	597	John Riley	
1849	Sp. *I. Z.*	673	John G. Moses	
"	*Kate Howe*	596	Josiah S. Comings	
"	*William Harbeck*	907	Robert Shinn	
"	*William Jarvis*	675	F. H. Jarvis	
"	*Emperor*	597	Richard Brown	
"	*Burlington*	534	J. Cook	
"	*Silas Greenman*	733	Joseph Spencer	
"	*Hibernia*	877	Charles E. Salter	
"	*Guy Mannering*	1419	William Edwards	

BLACK STAR LINE (*continued*)

YEAR	VESSEL	TONS	MASTERS	REMARKS
1849	Sp. *Richard Alsop*	836	Jeremiah G. Smith	
	" *Danube*	749	J. Chase	
	" *Ashland*	631	Edward G. Rice	
	" *Shannon*	808	Joseph Ludlam	
	" *Galena*	881	Thomas J. Leavitt	
	" *Jersey*	849	John Day	
	" *Minnesota*	800	William M. Allen	
	" *Philadelphia*	1102	William C. Stotesbury	
	" *Vandalia*	775	J. M. Norton	
	" *Ticonderoga*	1089	John S. Farren	
1850	Sp. *Jacob A. Westervelt*	1418	William R. Hoodless	
	" *William Rathbone*	917	William G. Spencer	
	" *Sandusky*	943	James Borland	
	" *Washington*	1655	Pitkin Page	
	" *Esmeralda*	908	Robert McManus	
	" *Universe*	1298	Thomas J. Bird	
	" *Princeton*	1131	William H. Russell	
	" *Helen McGaw*	598	William H. Lunt	
	" *Colombo*	577	C. H. Gerrish	
	" *Niagara*	730	Martin Smith	
	" *States Rights*	825	J. D. Warren	
1851	Sp. *Hemisphere*	1024	E. Whittlesey	
	" *Forest Queen*	856	Olney Lovett	
	" *Fairfield*	588	Samuel Loveland	
	" *Compromise*	745	James Riley	
	" *Leviathan*	1195	Rufus Knapp	Sailed from New York, Dec., 1854 and went missing.
	" *Trumbull*	855	W. D. Smith	In May, 1851, the firm of J. T. Crook & Guion replaced John Taylor Crook as Liverpool agents.
	" *Francis P. Sage*	1234	W. H. Robson	
	" *Colonel Cutts*	781	F. J. Chase	
	" *E. C. Scranton*	1186	Alfred G. Spencer	Crook left firm in Nov. 1851, and Guion & Co. became sole Liverpool agents and continued the line for many years, finally going into steam. During the fifties they often listed from 20 to 25 ships in the line, most of which are listed elsewhere in this appendix.
	" *Connecticut*	1081	James O. Williams	

STURGES & CLEARMAN LINE

Sturges, Clearman & Co., 88 Wall St., New York agents. Ships cleared from Liverpool in the Black Star Line, J. T. Crook, agent. Established 1847. Discontinued 1856.

YEAR	VESSEL	TONS	MASTERS	REMARKS
1847	Sp. *Aberdeen*	719	Samuel Nichols	Asahel Hubbard master in 1850.
	" *Ashland*	631	A. Hanley	
1850	Sp. *Sandusky*	943	John Borland	
1851	Sp. *Leviathan*	1207	Rufus Knapp	Went missing Dec., 1853, with Capt. Knapp and crew of 26.
	" *Advance*	1276	Arthur Child	Var. Childs.
1854	Sp. *Irene*	1187	Edward C. Williams	
	" *Black Hawk*	1579	D. M. Bunker	Foundered Apr. 24, 1854. Crew and passengers, 858 in all, were taken off by various vessels.

STANTON'S LINE

Stanton & Frost, New York agents. Ships sailed from Liverpool in Blue Ball Line, Jacot, Taylor & Tipper, agents. Establishment of line announced in 1845, but actual operation as a line did not begin until 1847. Discontinued 1857.

YEAR	VESSEL	TONS	MASTERS	REMARKS
1847	Sp. *Niagara*	730	William H. Russell	Firm operated *Niagara* in Liverpool trade during 1845–6.
	" *Palestine*	470	Oliver R. Mumford	
	" *Creole*	769	G. B. Rollins	
	" *Atlantic*	736	Samuel Rose	
1848	Sp. *Princeton*	1131	William H. Russell	Frost & Hicks became New York agents.
	" *Wisconsin*	943	Oliver R. Mumford	

STANTON'S LINE (*continued*)

YEAR	VESSEL	TONS	MASTERS	REMARKS
1849	Sp. *Washington*	1655	Pitkin Page	Arrived at New York June, 1853, with 965 passengers—largest number noted by any sailing liner.
1850	Sp. *Francis P. Sage*	1147	Nathan H. Robson	
1851	Sp. *Middlesex*	1413	Hosmer B. Parmelee	
1856	Sp. *Ocean Monarch*	2145	Pitkin Page	Abandoned at sea Mar. 10, 1862.

RICHARDSON'S LINE

Richardson, Watson & Co., New York agents. This firm also maintained a Philadelphia office. Richardson, Spence & Co., Liverpool agents. Line established 1848. Line discontinued 1851, probably to permit the firm members, Thomas Richardson and William Watson, to devote their energies to transatlantic steamship activities.

YEAR	VESSEL	TONS	MASTERS	REMARKS
1848	Sp. *Helen McGaw*	598	Albert A. Burwell	William H. Lunt master in 1850.
1849	Sp. *Hibernia*	877	Charles H. Salter	Daniel W. Maloney master 1849–50.
"	*Philadelphia*	1080	William C. Stotesbury	

NESMITH & WALSH LINE

Nesmith & Walsh, New York agents. Line established Sept. 1848.

YEAR	VESSEL	TONS	MASTERS	REMARKS
1848	Sp. *Onward*	791	J. Chase	
"	*Jane H. Glidden*	700	Ambrose Child	
"	*Virginia*	650	B. Salisbury	Abandoned at sea, Dec. 1851.
"	*Gondar*	645	George Barstow	
1849	Sp. *Ozark*	398	J. Davis	
"	*H. H. Boody*	665	J. Alexander	
"	*John Hancock*	760	A. Snow	
"	*Joseph Badger*	891	J. Skolfield	
1850	Sp. *Caroline Nesmith*	833	James Eaton	
"	*Ellen Maria*	769	A. Whitmore	Var. A. Whitman. Firm became Nesmith & Sons, New York agents.

TAYLOR & RITCH LINE

William C. Taylor and Henry L. Ritch, as Taylor & Ritch, New York agents. Cleared from Liverpool in Black Star Line, John Taylor Crook, agent. Line continued through 1860.

YEAR	VESSEL	TONS	MASTERS	REMARKS
1848	Sp. *Enterprise*	837	Stansbury Funk	Henry H. McLane master in 1857.
"	*De Witt Clinton*	1066	William C. Taylor	Edward Funk master 1848–59.
1849	Sp. *Jacob A. Westervelt*	1417	William R. Hoodless	T. Austin master 1856–7.

RED Z LINE

A. Zerega & Co., New York agents. Ships cleared from Liverpool in Black Star Line, John Taylor Crook, agent. Established 1848.

YEAR	VESSEL	TONS	MASTERS	REMARKS
1848	Sp. *J. Z.*	676	John Zerega	Burned at sea July, 1853.
"	*L. Z.*	897	John G. Moses	Foundered Jan. 17, 1850.
"	*A. Z.*	675	John G. Moses	Foundered Oct. 5, 1858.
"	*E. Z.*	673	Richard T. Hartshorne	J. B. Hodges master in 1856.
"	*James H. Shepherd*	635	James Ainsworth	
"	*Elsinore*	597	J. Riley	
"	*Roscoe*	622	Moses D. Ricker	
"	*New Hampshire*	593	Charles H. Chase	
1849	Sp. *Victoria*	602	Benjamin Watlington	
"	*Centurion*	745	Moses D. Ricker	Daniel P. Caulkins master of *Centurion* in 1859, saved crew of British ship *Dromahair*, Jan. 9, 1859.
1850	Sp. *Arctic*	1115	John A. Zerega	Theodore Zerega master in 1856.
"	*Antarctic*	1115	Moses D. Ricker	George E. Stouffer master in 1853–8, saved 197 from S.S. *San Francisco*, Dec. 1853.

RED Z LINE (*continued*)

YEAR	VESSEL	TONS	MASTERS	REMARKS
1850	Sp. *Compromise*	794	Augustus Zerega	Focke & Boult replaced Crook as Liverpool agent in 1851.
1853	Sp. *Robert Hooper*	757	William Churchill	
	" *Queen of Clippers*	2361	John A. Zerega	
1855	Sp. *Empire*	1272	John A. Zerega	Tapscott & Co. associated briefly with Zerega
	" *Cultivator*	1448	Thomas Austin	& Co. as New York agents.
1856	Sp. *Adriatic*	1327	Edward Coombs	Wrecked on first voyage.
	" *Baltic*	1320	Benjamin Babbidge	Boult, English & Brandon Liverpool agents, 1856. Tapscott & Co. left Zerega and continued own line, 1857. A. Taylor & Co. became Liverpool agents, 1859.

WASHINGTON LINE

Everitt & Brown, 68 South St., New York agents. Rathbone Bros. & Co., Liverpool agents. Established 1849. Sailed monthly as advertised.

YEAR	VESSEL	TONS	MASTERS	REMARKS
1849	Sp. *Silas Greenman*	733	Frederick W. Spencer	S. C. Magna master in 1853.
	" *William Rathbone*	917	Joseph W. Spencer	J. Livermore master in 1853 and J. C. Dowd in 1856.
1850	Sp. *Governor Morton*	1429	John A. Burgess	
1851	Sp. *E. C. Scranton*	1186	Joseph W. Spencer	Albert G. Spencer master in 1855.
1853	Sp. *Leviathan*	1195	Rufus Knapp	Reported missing after sailing from New York Dec. 23, 1854.
	" *Washington*	1655	Pitkin Page	J. G. White master in 1856.
	" *Shannon*	808	Joseph Thompson	
	" *Owego*	888	J. Borland	
	" *Irene*	1188	Edward C. Williams	
	" *Jersey*	849	John Day	
	" *David Crockett*	1679	Joseph W. Spencer	
	" *Rochambeau*	865	H. Stackpole	
	" *Niagara*	730	J. S. Bennett	
1854	Sp. *Ocean Herald*	2135	Edward G. Furber	J. Simmons master in 1854. Abandoned at sea Mar. 10, 1862, 37N–62W.
	" *Boston Light*	1150	J. Smith	
	" *Monarch of the Sea*	1975	W. R. Gardner	Pitkin Page master in 1858.
	" *Princeton*	1360	William H. Russell	W. R. Bell master in 1858.
	" *Tornado*	1802	Oliver R. Mumford	
	" *Pride of the Sea*	1661	E. Hooper	
1855	Sp. *Pioneer*	1841	James Montgomery	
1856	Sp. *Wisconsin*	943	H. E. Scott	George Balchen, 159 Front St., added as New
	" *Uncle Joe*	750	J. M. Boysen	York agent.
1857	Sp. *B. D. Metcalf*	1189	J. Stetson	
	" *Simoon*	1435	Martin Smith	
	" *Annie Size*	1031	C. F. Size	
1858	Sp. *Cornelia Lawrence*	1474	William Knapp	Lawrence, Giles & Co., New York agents.
1859	Sp. *Valentia*	880	Robert Jack	Line continued on substantial scale for several
	" *John Stuart*	1653	Henry Hanson	years.
	" *Delft Haven*	941	A. J. Freese	

BLUE BALL LINE

Jacot, Taylor & Tipper, Molyneux Place, 22 Water Street, Liverpool agents. Established 1851, firm acted as agents for individual American ships. No fixed sailing schedule.

YEAR	VESSEL	TONS	MASTERS	REMARKS
1851	Sp. *E. Bulkley*	735	Daniel Brown	
	" *Philadelphia*	1102	W. Taylor	Charles T. Poole master in 1854.
	" *American Union*	1147	Dodge Healey	
	" *Hibernia*	877	Daniel W. Maloney	T. Maloney master in 1852.
	" *Forest Queen*	856	B. Lovett	
	" *John Hancock*	760	Caleb Levansaler	
	Bk. *Tyringham*	608	Carleton Howes	
1852	Sp. *Middlesex*	1423	H. B. Parmalee	
	" *Meridian*	1300	John Manson	
	" *Java*	715	D. Jackson	

BLUE BALL LINE (*continued*)

YEAR	VESSEL	TONS	MASTERS	REMARKS
1852	Sp. *St. Charles*	798	Chester Hilliard	
"	*Hero*	760	Charles R. Griffiths	
"	*Esmeralda*	908	George W. McManus	
"	*Chace*	625	William White	
"	*Francis P. Sage*	1234	W. H. Robson	
1853	Sp. *Sandusky*	943	James Borland	Including earlier vessels and the five listed
"	*Julia Howard*	590	W. C. Bulkley	for 1853, the line comprised 15 ships in Jan.
"	*Owego*	888	J. D. Rice	1853, and 25 in Sept. 1854. Like the Black
"	*C. Jerome*	1000	Jun. Cone	Star lines it continued active beyond 1860,
"	*Fairfield*	588	Samuel Loveland	most of its ships being also listed in other lines at various times. Taylor, Tipper & Company became agents in 1858.

TAPSCOTT'S LINE

W. & J. T. Tapscott, New York agents. William Tapscott, Liverpool agent. Line established in 1851 but operations on a substantial scale did not get under way until 1853. However, firm had been an important factor in steerage traffic since 1841, becoming very heavy operators in 1846. During this early period they purported to maintain a Glasgow and a Liverpool "Union Line" but had no responsibility in the matter of sailings.

YEAR	VESSEL	TONS	MASTERS	REMARKS
1851	Sp. *Continent*	1033	Ezekiel B. Drummond	James L. Gibbs master in 1854.
1852	Sp. *William Tapscott*	1525	James B. Bell	George B. Cornish master later in 1852.
"	*Emma Fields*	949	S. Snow	*Tapscott* brought 896 passengers, June, 1853.
"	*Adriatic*	870	Robert Jack	
1853	Sp. *Benjamin Adams*	1170	John Drummond	
"	*Houghton*	787	Samuel B. Doane	
"	*Emerald Isle*	1736	George B. Cornish	Brought 924 passengers in July, 1854.
"	*Albion*	1320	R. C. William	Firm also cleared a number of British emi-
"	*Rappahannock*	1133	William Cushing	grant ships in 1853–4.
"	*Richard Morse*	930	S. B. Dinsmore	
"	*Golconda*	1224	A. Kerr	
"	*Cambria*	1188	E. Perry	
1854	Sp. *Shamrock*	1125	Samuel B. Doane	John Drummond master in 1856.
"	*Progress*	1398	Edwin Chase	
"	*Coosawattee*	960	Thomas Paxton	
1855	Sp. *Francis A. Palmer*	1425	Addison Richardson	
"	*Sea Lark*	973	Charles Adams	
"	*John J. Boyd*	1311	Thomas Austin	I. H. Thomas master in 1857.
"	*Marshall O. Roberts*	863	John Fulton	
1856	Sp. *William Nelson*	1039	Charles Cheever	
"	*George Hurlbut*	1047	Ezra D. Post	
"	*Carolus Magnus*	1449	George Coffin	
"	*Samuel M. Fox*	1062	Allen C. Ainsworth	*Fox* lost at Liverpool in gale of Nov. 12, 1856. Ships *Silas Wright* and *Louisiana* lost at same time.
"	*Rock Light*	1583	Ezekiel B. Drummond	
1857	Sp. *Middlesex*	1423	Hosmer B. Parmalee	
"	*J. Morton*	1196	G. L. Gilley	Var. Gillet.
"	*City of Brooklyn*	1514	T. A. Mitchell	
"	*Kossuth*	1100	T. Dawson	
"	*Samuel Willets*	1387	Elihu Spicer, Jr.	Stranded July 2, 1857, south of Squan Inlet.
1858	Sp. *Roger A. Hiern*	1089	James Stewart	Fish, Goldie & McFie, 30 Oldhall Street
"	*Marianne Nottebohm*	1202	George N. Lamb	were Liverpool agents; Tapscott, Fish & Co.
"	*St. Louis*	938	A. C. Hoyt	became agents in Aug. 1858.
"	*Margaret Tyson*	1183	T. M. Morrison	
"	*Frederick Gebhard*	1124	F. N. Hayden	
"	*Francis B. Cutting*	976	Ezra D. Post	
"	*Potomac*	1198	William Reed	Var. Read.
1859	Sp. *Thirty-One States*	930	C. C. Smart	Throughout the period the ships *William*
"	*Vandalia*	775	R. E. Patton (Patten)	*Tapscott, Emerald Isle, John J. Boyd,* and *Benja-*
"	*John H. Elliott*	1077	J. H. Tucker	*min Adams* were dispatched with great regu-
1860	Sp. *Kate Prince*	995	M. F. Pickering	larity and frequency. Line continued active throughout next decade.

PATRIOTIC LINE

Spofford, Tileston & Co., 30 Broadway, New York agents. Caleb Grimshaw, 10 Goree Piazzas, Liverpool agent. Established 1852. Line continued to 1872 but ran very irregularly in later years.

YEAR	VESSEL	TONS	MASTERS	REMARKS
1852	Sp. *Orient*	1560	Francis M. French	George S. Hill master in 1856.
	" *Henry Clay*	1207	David Caulkins	
1853	Sp. *Webster*	1727	Robert L. Bunting	J. J. Lawrence master in 1856.
	" *Calhoun*	1750	Daniel H. Freeman	Foundered off Newfoundland, Aug. 1872, George B. Crary, master.
1856	Sp. *Ellen Austin*	1699	William H. Garrick	
1857	Sp. *Resolute*	1513	T. W. Freeman	

BAINES LINE

James Baines & Co., American & Australian Emigration Office, 113 Waterloo Road, Liverpool agents. Established August, 1852, "to dispatch a succession of fine ships every week and oftener when required." Baines had been engaged in American emigration for several years before announcing establishment of a line. He was not given to understatement. His advertisements reported the tonnage of the *Great Western* as 3000 and all the others as 2000 tons. He continued his American operations irregularly through 1855.

YEAR	VESSEL	TONS	MASTERS	REMARKS
1852	Sp. *Great Western*	1434	William G. Furber	
	" *Hemisphere*	1024	John S. Pray	
	" *Isaac Webb*	1360	Edward G. Furber	
	" *William D. Sewall*	672	Small	
	" *Anna Kimball*	848	Joseph Webster	

EASTERN STAR LINE

Songey, Smith & Co., Fenwick Chambers, Liverpool agents. Established June, 1858. W. F. Songey & Co. became Liverpool agents in August. Operation discontinued end of year.

YEAR	VESSEL	TONS	MASTERS	REMARKS
1858	Sp. *Seaman's Bride*	669	A. B. Wyman	Sailed June 12.
	" *Moloka*	700	A. H. Hale	
	" *Arabia*	1274	Richard Harding	
	" *Byzantium*	1048	W. R. Hilton	
	" *S. R. Mallory*	1048	C. F. Bunker	
	" *Eastern Star*	1017	H. Jones	
	" *Belle of the Ocean*	966	William Reed	
	" *Juventa*	1187	Gideon Young	
	" *Marquette*	1363	James Watts	
	" *Martha Rideout*	780	J. T. Morse	
	" *Robert Treat*	694	J. Abbott	

SECTION 4. NEW YORK—LONDON

GRISWOLD & COATES LINE. Later BLACK X LINE.

Griswold & Coates, New York agents. Line established in Jan., 1822, but sailed irregularly and virtually abandoned after withdrawal of Coates at end of year. Re-established by John Griswold and Fish & Grinnell in May, 1824, sailing from the Fly Market Wharf in New York, 1st of each month, touching at Cowes, England. Also sailed on 1st from London.

YEAR	VESSEL	TONS	MASTERS	REMARKS
1822	Sp. *Comet*	304	George Moore	
	" *London*	408	Samuel Candler	Lost off Sandwich Islands, 1827.
	" *Hudson*	368	Henry L. Champlin	Elisha E. Morgan master in 1830.
1824	Sp. *Brighton*	354	William S. Sebor	
	" *Hudson*	368	Henry L. Champlin	
	" *Acasta*	330	Augustus H. Griswold	
	" *Crisis*	337	John McManus	
	" *York*	433	William Baker	
1825	Sp. *Europa*	253	Caleb Anthony	Took place of *Acasta*, Jan. 1825. Line sailed from New York the 20th and from London, the 1st of month.
1826	Sp. *Cortes*	381	Benjamin Sprague	Took place of *York*. From Feb. 1826 to Jan.
1827	Sp. *Cambria*	362	J. A. Warnack	1827, Fish, Grinnell & Co. cleared all ships.

GRISWOLD & COATES LINE (*continued*)

YEAR	VESSEL	TONS	MASTERS	REMARKS
1827	Sp. *Robert Edwards*	356	Samuel Sherburne	Griswold and Fish, Grinnell & Co. separated
	" *Acasta*	330	Daniel Chadwick	June, 1827, and established two separate
	" *Hudson*	368	Henry L. Champlin	London lines, Griswold continuing with the
1828	Sp. *Electra*	347	Jesse Baker	four ships listed opposite, sailing 15th of
	" *Chelsea*	396	Thomas Barnes	month.
	" *Henry*	258	George Moore	Sailed from New York the 16th, beginning
	" *Leeds*	408	Benjamin Sprague	Jan. and stopped at Portsmouth.
1829	Sp. *Helen*	424	Nathan Cobb	Ships *Amulet, Robert Fulton,* and *Helen* in line,
	" *Amulet*	253	Gresham Winsor	apparently chartered temporarily during
	" *Hannibal*	441	F. H. Hebard	1829 and part of 1830.
	" *Robert Fulton*	340	John Britton	
1830	Sp. *Cambria*	362	George Moore	Sailed from New York the 16th and from
	" *Brighton*	354	Henry Huttleson	London the 10th, beginning May, 1830. At
	" *Sovereign*	462	Henry L. Champlin	end of year line consisted of *Brighton, Cambria,*
	" *President*	469	C. H. Champlin	*Sovereign,* and *President.*
				(Note resumption of joint operations with Grinnell, Minturn & Co. in 1833 and continuing to 1852, as described in Fish, Grinnell & Co. London Line.)
1832	Sp. *Philadelphia*	543	Henry L. Champlin	Henry R. Hovey master in 1841.
1836	Sp. *Ocmulgee*	458	Thomas I. Leavitt	
1841	Sp. *Hendrick Hudson*	824	Elisha E. Morgan	Foundered in hurricane Mar. 12, 1855, Capt. William B. Smith and crew rescued by bark *Elk* of Boston, E. G. Atkins, master.
1843	Sp. *Victoria*	869	Elisha E. Morgan	
1844	Sp. *Northumberland*	893	Robert H. Griswold	Foundered Dec. 4, 1857. Crew and passengers saved by British brig *Jessie.*
1846	Sp. *Christiana*	666	Edmund Hammond	
	" *Margaret Evans*	900	Edward G. Tinker	E. G. Furber master in 1848.
	" *American Eagle*	900	J. M. Chadwick	
1848	Sp. *Devonshire*	1150	Elisha E. Morgan	
1849	Sp. *Southampton*	1299	Elisha E. Morgan	
1850	Sp. *Ocean Queen*	1182	Robert H. Griswold	Sailed from London Feb. 1856, and went missing; Capt. W. B. Smith, 33 crew and 90 passengers.
				Line consisted in 1852 of eight ships with commanders as follows: *Victoria,* Edmund Champion; *Devonshire,* H. R. Hovey; *Ocean Queen,* R. H. Griswold; *Northumberland,* Josiah M. Lord; *American Eagle,* J. S. Doane; *Margaret Evans,* Isaiah Pratt; *Hendrick Hudson,* J. C. Warner; and *Southampton,* Edward G. Tinker.
1853	Sp. *Wisconsin*	943	H. E. Scott	Griswold retired May, 1853. Morgan & Wiley became New York agents.
1854	Sp. *Amazon*	1771	Henry R. Hovey	Line in 1855 consisted of ten ships sailing
	" *Palestine*	1751	Edward G. Tinker	every 12 days.
1856	Sp. *Challenge* (Temporary)	2007	John Kenney	
1858	Sp. *Daniel Webster*	1188	Samuel L. Spencer	Ex-Train packet.
1860	Sp. *Nestorian*	698	T. Worth	Line continued through and after Civil War.
	" *James R. Keeler*	1292	C. Delano	
	" *Hero of the Nile*	377	Pavey	

SWALLOWTAIL LINE

Fish, Grinnell & Co., Pier 9, North River, New York agents. In 1833, Grinnell, Minturn & Co., 134 Front St., New York agents. Established June, 1827, to sail from each port 1st of month. Fish, Grinnell & Co. withdrew from previous connection with John Griswold in London Line.

YEAR	VESSEL	TONS	MASTERS	REMARKS
1827	Sp. *Hudson*	368	Henry L. Champlin	Elisha E. Morgan master in 1830.
	" *Cortes*	382	Benjamin Sprague	
	" *Brighton*	350	William S. Sebor	
	" *Columbia*	492	Joseph S. Delano	Sold 1836 for New London whaler.
	" *Electra*	347	Jesse Baker	

SWALLOWTAIL LINE (*continued*)

YEAR	VESSEL	TONS	MASTERS	REMARKS
1827	Sp. *Corinthian*	401	Daniel Chadwick	
"	*Leeds*	409	Frederick H. Hebard	Benjamin Sprague master in 1828.
1829	Sp. *Hannibal*	441	Frederick H. Hebard	Oliver R. Mumford master in 1848.
1830	Sp. *Ontario*	489	William S. Sebor	Henry Huttleson master in 1836.
1831	Sp. *Samson*	484	Daniel Chadwick	Lost off Nova Scotia, June, 1841.
"	*Andes* (Temporary)	364	James S. Tompkins	Firm resumed joint operations Oct., 1832,
1833	Sp. *Sovereign*	462	James Kearney	with John Griswold.
"	*Thames*	350	Robert H. Griswold	On Jan. 12, 1833, the two firms gave notice
"	*York*	433	S. G. Nye	of establishment of a line of 12 packets to sail
"	*Philadelphia*	543	C. H. Champlin	from New York the 1st, 10th and 20th, and
"	*President*	469	George Moore	from London the 7th, 17th, and 27th of
"	*Montreal*	543	Henry L. Champlin	month, starting with sailing of *Ontario*, Jan.
"	*Samuel Robertson*	422	Augustus H. Griswold	20, George Wildes & Co., London agents.
"	*Canada* (Temporary)	546	Thomas Britton	Joint arrangement halted Oct. 1833, by
				death of Preserved Fish, until renewed by
				Grinnell, Minturn & Co. latter part of 1834.
				Line consisted of seven ships opposite and
				Ontario, Hudson, Columbia, Hannibal, and
1835	Sp. *St. James*	641	William S. Sebor	*Samson.*
"	*Gladiator*	650	Thomas Britton	R. L. Bunting master in 1844.
"	*Toronto*	631	Robert H. Griswold	Lost, Mantanilla Reef, Jan. 2, 1850.
"	*Westminster*	631	George Moore	
1836	Sp. *Ocmulgee* (Temporary)	458	Thomas I. Leavitt	
"	*Mediator*	661	Henry L. Champlin	John M. Chadwick master in 1841–5.
"	*Quebec*	649	F. H. Hebard	George S. Brewster master in 1847–8.
"	*Wellington*	727	Daniel Chadwick	
1841	Sp. *Hendrick Hudson*	824	Elisha E. Morgan	Foundered Mar. 12, 1855. Crew rescued by
				bark *Elk*, of Boston.
1843	Sp. *Victoria*	869	Elisha E. Morgan	Edmund Champlin master in 1856.
"	*Prince Albert*	885	William S. Sebor	Abandoned at sea late Dec. 1853, Wm. K.
				Bradish, master.
1844	Sp. *Northumberland*	893	Robert H. Griswold	J. M. Lord master in 1850.
1846	Sp. *Christiana*	666	Edmund Hammond	P. A. Owens master in 1857.
"	*American Eagle*	900	John M. Chadwick	Line composed of 16 ships sailing 1st, 8th,
"	*Sir Robert Peel*	941	Daniel Chadwick	16th, and 24th from each port.
1847	Sp. *Yorktown*	1151	William S. Sebor	Frederick R. Myer master in 1855.
"	*Diana*	568	Pugh	Octavius Howe master in 1848.
1848	Sp. *London*	1145	Frederick H. Hebard	S. E. Hubbard master in 1854.
1850	Sp. *American Congress*	864	John H. Williams	Went missing 1873. Ghiselin master.
"	*Cornelius Grinnell*	1118	Artemas T. Fletcher	
1851	Sp. *Patrick Henry*	882	S. E. Hubbard	J. Hurlbut master in 1855.
1852	Sp. *Independence*	733	R. Gordon	Lines returned to separate operation in 1852,
				each line consisting of eight ships. Baring
				Bros., London agents for Swallowail Line.
1855	Sp. *Liverpool*	1077	James Kearney	F. M. Lambert master in 1869.
"	*Mary Bradford* (Temporary)	802	J. B. Thompson	
"	*Rhine*	1037	Cornelius R. Doane	G. Moses master in 1856.
1856	Sp. *Defiance* (Temporary)	1691	John Kendrick	Line continued operation until 1881, but
				very irregularly toward last.

CRASSOUS & BOYD LONDON LINE

Crassous & Boyd and Cheavens & Burdett, New York agents. Established Nov. 30, 1831, "To sail in regular succession," but discontinued after 1832.

YEAR	VESSEL	TONS	MASTERS	REMARKS
1831	Sp. *Samuel Robertson*	422	A. H. Griswold	
"	*William Byrnes*	518	Benjamin Sprague	
"	*Florida*	523	Robert H. Griswold	

UNION LINE OF LONDON PACKETS

Wadsworth & Smith, 34 Broad St., and George Sutton, 88 South St., New York agents. Junius Smith, New York Packet Office, Fenchurch St., and Charles Gumm, Broker, 1 Plough Court, Lombard St., London agents, and

UNION LINE (*continued*)

John Lindigree, Portsmouth, England, agent. Line established April, 1835, to consist of three British and two American ships, to sail punctually 25th of each month from both ports. Line abandoned schedule in 1836 but continued as regular trading line into 1839.

YEAR	VESSEL	TONS	MASTERS	REMARKS
1835	Sp. *Angelique*	420	E. L. Halsey	Other British vessels employed included ship
"	*Henry Allen*	373	H. Wilson	*Eleanor*, Samuel Turney, and *Egyptian*, Nevile
	Bk. *Gratitude* (British)	500	John Lidgett	R. Sayers.
"	*Union* (British)		Hendewell	
	Bg. *Resolution* (British)		Robson	

NEW LINE

Dunham & Dimon, 67 South St., New York agents. Charles Gumm, 4 King's Arms Bldg., Change Alley, London agent. Line comprised of seven ships sailing semi-monthly.

YEAR	VESSEL	TONS	MASTERS	REMARKS
1854	Sp. *Ocean Herald*	2135	Edward G. Furber	
	(Temporary)			
"	*Woodcock*	1091	Frederick M. Lambert	Wrecked on Dungeness, Mar., 1856.
"	*Quickstep*	823	E. C. Weeks	Stephen Wade master in 1858.
"	*G. B. Lamar*	933	P. N. Mayhew	R. P. Bradley master in 1857.
"	*President Fillmore*	872	P. Nelson	P. Conway master in 1859.
"	*Robena*	778	C. W. Bartlett	George Martin master in 1857.
"	*New England*	573	Peter Protteau	
"	*Richard Cobden*	710	William F. Black	
1855	Sp. *Medomack*	632	N. Livingston	Lost abroad late in 1856.
1857	Sp. *Jacob A. Stamler*	1101	I. T. Hiltz	Ran irregularly after 1857.
1860	Sp. *Sea Star*	668	J. Robertson	Var. Robinson.
"	*Byzantium*	1048	W. B. Hilton	
"	*Robin Hood*	1182	Richard Bearse	

SECTION 5. NEW YORK—MISCELLANEOUS BRITISH PORTS

New York—Greenock

NEW YORK—GREENOCK LINE

Stewart, Lee & Co., 111 Pearl St., and Abraham Bell & Co., 61 Pine St., and Jeremiah Thompson, 273 Pearl St., New York agents. Established May, 1824. First New York Immigrant Line. Sailed 10th of each month from Greenock. No fixed date from New York.

YEAR	VESSEL	TONS	MASTERS	REMARKS
1824	Sp. *Friends*	403	Thomas Choate	
"	*Mentor*	459	Josiah L. Wilson	New London whaleship in 1831.
"	*Minerva*	408	John C. Mayell	George W. Wallace master in 1827.
"	*Robert Fulton*	340	Hugh Graham	John Britton master in 1825.
"	*Camillus*	340	Norman Peck	Jeremiah Thompson withdrew in 1827.
1828	Sp. *Fabius*	432	William C. Thompson	Line continued irregularly for several years.

New York—Belfast

NEW YORK—BELFAST LINE

Francis Thompson & Nephews, New York agents. Established Jan., 1825.

YEAR	VESSEL	TONS	MASTERS	REMARKS
1825	Sp. *Frances Henrietta*	407	J. J. Dickenson	Carleton White master May 25, 1825.
"	*Louisa*	382	P. G. Fosdick	
"	*Atlantic*	323	Robert L. Taylor	Alexander Britton master in 1828.
"	*Meteor*		Henry Huttleson	Line ran irregularly for several years.

New York—Hull

NEW YORK—HULL LINE

British Emigrant Line. Masters & Markoe, 113 Front St., New York agents. John Hollingsworth, Hull agent. Notice of establishment of line in Dec., 1828—vessels sailed on day appointed, "full or not full."

YEAR	VESSEL	TONS	MASTERS	REMARKS
1828	Bk. *Diana* (British)		John Sugden	
	Bg. *Freak* (British)		James Bouch	
"	*Dapper* (British)		William Dickinson	

New York—Glasgow

OLD LINE

Woodhull & Minturn, 87 South St., New York agents. Reid & Murray, Glasgow agents. Established 1845. Sailed 1st and 15th of each month from each port.

YEAR	VESSEL	TONS	MASTERS	REMARKS
1845	Bk. *Alabama*	280	Charles E. Ranlett	
	Sp. *Saracen*	397	Nathaniel T. Hawkins	Lost November, 1847.
	Bk. *Adam Carr* (British)	350	Robert Scott	
	" *Ann Harley* (British)	450	Duncan Smith	
1846	Sp. *Brooksby* (British)	505	Hugh McEwen	Line consisted of four ships and five barks
	" *Monticello*	392	Frederick K. Lambert	sailing 1st and 15th from each port. Dunham
	" *Duncan*	278	Philander Daggett	& Dimon, 67 South St., added as New York
	Bk. *Mary Morris*	393	Philander Daggett	agents.
	" *Urania*	316	D. B. Swan	
	Sp. *Hudson*	335	Russell Doane	
1847	Sp. *Warren*	416	Job G. Lawton	Var. Job E. Lawton.
	Bk. *Elizabeth*	437	Robert Cowan	
1848	Sp. *Corra Linn*	618	Frederick K. Lambert	
	" *Harmonia*	610	H. Churchill	Went ashore Dec. 17, 1857. Condemned and
	Bk. *Elijah Swift*	391	Joseph Swift	sold.
1849	Sp. *Switzerland*	568	John H. Lowell	Woodhull & Minturn withdrew. Dunham &
	" *Sir. Wm. Molesworth* (British)	468	Lawrence	Dimon continued as New York agents.
1850	Sp. *Moro*	418	W. P. Larrabee	
	" *Sarah* (British)	536	Tims	
1851	Sp. *Robena*	778	James M. Kane	
	" *Dirigo*	497	Russell Doane	
	" *Martha's Vineyard*	499	Oliver J. Graffam	
1852	Sp. *Statira Morse*	551	Job G. Lawton	Went ashore Scotland Jan. 1855, and sold.
	Bk. *Gov. Hinckley*	399	William Loring	Pickersgill & Co. and John Fyfe & Co., Glasgow agents.
1853	Sp. *Java*	715	David Jackson	Line in 1853 consisted of ten ships sailing
	" *John Fyfe*	790	Oliver J. Graffam	semi-monthly.
	" *New England*	573	Peter Protteau	
	" *Warner*	416	Job G. Lawton	
1854	Sp. *Quickstep*	836	W. Cook	Philander Daggett became Glasgow agent.
1856	Sch. *Eckford Webb* (tern)	495	Oliver J. Graffam	
	Bk. *Clara*	664	Enoch Cook, Jr.	Foundered Oct. 28, 1858. Three lost.
	" *Mary Dunham*	595	Hollis R. Jencks	
	Sp. *Prince de Joinville*	527	William Chamberlin	Var. Chamberlain.
1858	Bk. *Jane Daggett*	865	Frederick M. Lambert	
	" *Jehu*	396	George Little	
	Sp. *Ivanhoe*	868	J. W. Pollard	
	" *Richard Alsop*	830	Benjamin Watlington	
1860	Sp. *Missouri*	824	Thomas Hughes	

RICHARDSON'S LINE

Richardson, Watson & Co., 43 Exchange Pl., New York agents. Established Dec. 1846, discontinued 1848.

YEAR	VESSEL	TONS	MASTERS	REMARKS
1846	Sp. *Glenmore*	467	Joseph Mitchell	
	" *Monterey*	449	Tully Crosby	
	Bk. *Thetis*	393	Wm. Collins	
	Sp. *Pontiac*	538		

NEW YORK & GLASGOW LINE OF PACKETS

A. Woodhull, 87 South St., New York agent. Reid & Murray, 62 Jamaica St., Glasgow agents. Founded 1852 by A. Woodhull after withdrawal of Woodhull & Minturn from the Glasgow Old Line. Line consisted of British vessels and sailed punctually as advertised.

YEAR	VESSEL	TONS	MASTERS	REMARKS
1852	Sp. *Sarah*	536		
	" *Brooksby*	505	Hugh McEwen	
	Bk. *Hyndeford*	510	Tims	
	" *Adam Carr*	383		
	" *Sir Wm. Molesworth*	463	Henderson	
	" *Ann Harley*	500	McDonald	

SECTION 6. NEW YORK—CONTINENTAL EUROPE

New York—Havre

OLD LINE, FIRST and SECOND LINES, and UNION LINES

During the first 30 years the Havre packet trade was dominated by three interests which sometimes acted separately but for the most part in close association. It is believed that the situation as it existed from time to time will be made more intelligible by treating the activities of those interests during that period in chronological order, rather than by tracing the activities of each interest separately.

YEAR	VESSEL	TONS	MASTERS	REMARKS
1822	Sp. *Montano*	365	Miles R. Burke	Line later known as the Old Line. Established 1822 by Francis Depau, Isaac Bell, and Miles R. Burke, to start with sailing of *Montano* Sept. 10th, and the 10th of every other month thereafter. Capt. Skiddy took the *Stephania* in place of Smith. Fare $140.
	" *Stephania*	315	John P. Smith	
	" *Lewis*	412	John R. Skiddy	
				First Line established by Crassous & Boyd, in association with Wm. Whitlock, Jr., to start with sailing of ship *Niagara*, Feb. 1, 1823 and to maintain sailings on 1st of each month from each port.
1823	Sp. *Niagara*	253	William Beebe	Second Line established by Crassous and Boyd in summer of 1824, to sail on 1st of month; the ships of the First Line to sail the 15th. After the establishment of this line the Depau line ceased operation, temporarily.
	" *Marmion*	278	Elnathan Hawkins	
	" *Bayard*	339	Francis Naghel	
	" *Cadmus*	307	Sidney Whitlock	
	" *Paris*	339	Henry Robinson	
1824	Sp. *Queen Mab*	270	Henry Richards	*Edward Quesnel* and *Desdemona* put in First Line in place of *Paris* and *Marmion* which were dropped. Whitlock interest in lines represented by ships *Cadmus* and *Howard*. *Edward Bonaffe* replaced *Desdemona* in Second Line. In summer of 1825 Depau and associates revived the Old Line, adding ship *Henry* to the original three and undertaking to sail from New York the 5th and from Havre the 25th of month.
	" *Don Quixote*	260	James Clark	
	" *Howard*	357	Nathan Holdredge	
	" *Desdemona*	297	Francis Naghel	
	" *Edward Bonaffe*	325	James Funk	
1825	Sp. *Edward Quesnel*	388	Elnathan Hawkins	First and Second Lines combined Jan. 1827, under management of Crassous & Boyd to sail 1st and 15th each month. Ship *France* added.
	" *Henry*	258	Aaron Kemp	
1827	Sp. *France*	411	Edward Funk	New ships *Henry IV* and *Sully* added to Old Line in 1827.
	" *Henry IV*	427	John B. Pell	
	" *Sully*	447	Robert J. Macy	
1828	Sp. *Charles Carroll*	412	James Clark	Added to First and Second Lines. *Francois I*, *De Rham*, and *Havre* added to Old Line in 1829. *Erie* and *Formosa* added to First and Second Lines in 1829.
1829	Sp. *Francois I*	496	William Skiddy	Agreement between the three lines effective Feb. 10th, 1829, to dispatch ships on 1st, 10th and 20th of month from each port. Ships affected referred to as the Union Line of Havre Packets.
	" *De Rham*	492	Frederick A. DePeyster	
	" *Havre*	481	E. L. Keene	
	" *Erie*	451	James Funk	
	" *Formosa*	451	William B. Orne	
	" *Charlemagne*	442	Henry Robinson	The Union Line as thus constituted consisted of 12 of the 13 ships last listed, the *Henry* being dropped. William Hathaway succeeded to command of the *Edward Bonaffe* and William H. Pell to the *Sully*. In 1830 Bolton, Fox & Livingston took over agency for Depau, etc., interests.
1832	Sp. *Albany*	469	Elnathan Hawkins	Charles D. Crawford master in 1844.
	" *Manchester* (Temporary)	561	L. Weiderholdt	
	" *Poland*	547	E. Richardson	Burned May 16, 1839, Caleb Anthony, master.
1833	Sp. *Francis Depau*	596	Henry Robinson	
	" *Utica*	525	Frederick DePeyster	Burned at San Francisco, July, 1850.

OLD LINE (*continued*)

YEAR		VESSEL	TONS	MASTERS	REMARKS
1834	Sp.	*Normandie*	500	Wm. W. Pell	Reported missing Dec. 1844.
	"	*Silvie de Grasse*	641	L. Weiderholt	Lost, mouth of Columbia River, about Sept. 1849.
1835	Sp.	*Emerald*	518	William B. Orne	
1836	Sp.	*Baltimore*	658	James Funk	R. D. Conn master in 1848.
	"	*Burgundy*	762	John Rockett	Lost Nov. 14, 1848, near Goodwin Sands. James Wotton master in 1844.
1837	Sp.	*Louis Phillipe*	794	John Castoff	Samuel Rich master in 1844.
	"	*Ville de Lyon*	791	Charles Stoddard	Lost near La Hogue Feb. 2, 1845.
1838	Sp.	*Duchesse d'Orleans*	799	Addison Richardson	In 1838 Boyd & Hincken became general New York agents for entire line.
1839	Sp.	*Iowa*	875	William W. Pell	
1841	Sp.	*Oneida*	792	James Funk	Lost Dec. 19, 1849, Guernsey.
	"	*Argo*	967	Caleb Anthony, Jr.	Went ashore Mar. 1850, at Fire Island. Salvaged a year later and sold to Samuel Thompson. Foundered about Apr. 17, 1857, Macoduck, master.
1842	Sp.	*St. Nicholas*	797	John B. Pell	Boyd & Hincken agents for four ships only, *Oneida, Baltimore, St. Nicholas,* and *Utica,* which they operated as the Second Line. Remaining ships operated by Bolton, Fox & Livingston and William Whitlock, Jr., but still in association as Union Line.
1844	Sp.	*Zurich*	817	William C. Thompson	Whitlock's line advertised in 1844.
1845	Sp.	*Havre*	871	Allen C. Ainsworth	
	"	*Versailles* (Temporary)	570	Charles Hunt	
1846	Sp.	*Metoka*	775	John H. McLarren	Line composed of 18 ships sailing 1st, 8th, 16th, and 24th, with Whitlock and Boyd & Hincken operating four each and Fox & Livingston the rest. Albert N. Chrystie was Whitlock's Havre agent.
	"	*Bavaria*	908	George W. Howe	
	"	*Excelsior* (Temporary)	444	William H. Williams	
	"	*Alliance* (Temporary)	525	Robert H. Tucker	
	"	*Eli Whitney* (Temporary)	552	Benjamin Dyer	
	"	*Tallahassee* (Temporary)	489	Charles Stoddard	
1847	Sp.	*Mortimer Livingston*	749	E. M. Barstow	Wrecked Jan. 25 near Carson's Inlet, N. J.
	"	*Admiral*	929	James A. Wotton	
	"	*Queen Victoria*	711	Charles A. Ranlett	
	"	*Splendid*	643	Charles D. Crawford	
	"	*New York*	991	David Lines	William C. Thompson master in 1853.
	"	*Severn* (Temporary)	575	Charles Cheever	
	"	*Exchange* (Temporary)	425	James Funk	
1848	Sp.	*St. Denis*	959	George W. Howe	Foundered Jan. 6, 1856. Loss of 35.
	"	*Noemie*	547	Nicholas Holberton	Built for a Charleston-Havre packet.
1849	Sp.	*Gallia*	1191	Addison Richardson	
1850	Sp.	*William Tell*	1154	John Willard	
	"	*Robert Kelly*	1165	Edwin M. Barstow	Reported missing from Liverpool Jan. 26, 1860, for New York, Capt. N. E. Sherman.
	"	*La Suisse*	917	B. F. Marsh	Boyd & Hincken's Second Line sailed from New York the 1st and from Havre the 16th.
	"	*Samuel M. Fox*	1062	Allen C. Ainsworth	Passage $100 without wines or liquors.
	"	*Helvetia*	1351	B. F. Marsh	
	"	*Germania*	997	D. H. Wood	
	"	*Mercury* (Cl.)	1351	Richard D. Conn	Charles H. Townshend master in 1858.
1851	Sp.	*Isaac Bell*	1072	John Johnston	
1853	Sp.	*Rattler*	1121	Richard Brown	
	"	*Carolus Magnus*	1449	William Chase	
	"	*Charles Hill*	699	David Lecraw	
	"	*Parthenia*	849	Henry Shoof	
	"	*Art Union*	750	J. S. Stubbs	
	"	*John N. Cushing*	632	J. W. Plumer	
	"	*John G. Coster*	714	H. Foster	
1854	Sp.	*William Nelson*	1039	Charles Cheever	Mortimer Livingston, 53 Broadway, & William Whitlock, Jr., 46 South St., established enlarged Union Line as of Jan. 1854, with 12 ships to give four monthly sailings. Boyd & Hincken, 161 Pearl St., advertised Second Line as "The Sole Regular Line," 1855.
	"	*Samoset*	725	G. W. Chapman	

OLD LINE (*continued*)

YEAR	VESSEL	TONS	MASTERS	REMARKS
1855	Sp. *Wisconsin*	943	H. E. Scott	
	" *John J. Boyd*	1310	Thomas Austin	
	" *China*	726	D. Keaser	
1856	Sp. *Logan*	1541	Eleazer A. Taylor	Union Line sailed 8th, 16th, and 24th from
	" *Orphan*	682	G. H. Kempton	New York and 1st, 8th, and 24th from Havre with sailings becoming somewhat irregular.
1857	Sp. *William Frothingham*	830	Thomas P. Stetson	Mortimer Livingston retired to devote his attention to his steamship line to Havre. W. S. Drayton, 7 Broadway, took charge of his interests in the Union Line.
1860	Sp. *Paragon*	900	Levi Drinkwater	S. M. Fox & Bro., New York agents, for old
	" *Mazeppa*	799	D. Weeks	Union Line vessels. Whitlock continued irregular sailings and Boyd & Hincken maintained a regular schedule with ships *William Frothingham*, *St. Nicholas*, *Mercury*, and *William Tell*.

HURLBUT LINE

E. D. Hurlbut & Co., New York agents. Hurlbut had been sending occasional ships to Havre since 1842 as the Hurlbut Line, but does not appear to have maintained a genuine line until 1845 and then only by diverting ships from his other lines.

YEAR	VESSEL	TONS	MASTERS	REMARKS
1845	Sp. *Hector*	557	Alfred G. Spencer	
	" *Cotton Planter*	502	Cornelius R. Doane	
	" *Tuskina*	421	S. O. Williams	
1849	Sp. *Connecticut*	1081	James O. Williams	Sailed from New York the 25th and from
	" *Seine*	785	Edward C. Williams	Havre the 15th of each month. Regular line consisted of six ships.
1850	Sp. *George Hurlbut*	1047	George West	
	" *Rhine*	1037	Cornelius R. Doane	
	" *Loire*		Cornelius R. Doane	
	" *Marathon*	890	H. S. Tyler	
	" *Elizabeth Denison*	644	Frederick W. Spencer	
	" *Robert Kelly*	1165	Edwin W. Barstow	Readmeasured, 1131 tons.
1853	Sp. *Edwin Forest*	1141	Braddock W. Crocker	
	" *Chesapeake*	647	R. H. Lambert	Var. R. T. Lambert
1854	Sp. *Granite State*	956	S. Billings	Lost 1858.
	" *Charles Hill*	699	Hale	
	" *Advance*	1276	William Lecraw	J. G. Barstow master in 1857.
	" *Francis A. Palmer*	1425	Addison Richardson	Post & Ryerson took over management of line in Jan. 1855. Discontinued 1857.

MARINE UNION LINE

Lane, West & Co., 77 South St., New York agents. V. Mazin & Co., Havre agents. Established Jan. 1854. Sailed from New York the 16th and from Havre the 1st of each month.

YEAR	VESSEL	TONS	MASTERS	REMARKS
1854	Sp. *Robert L. Lane*	1080	E. Cornell	
	" *Connecticut*	1081	G. E. Welch	
	" *Confederation*	1186	Asa A. Corning	Lost Jan. 7, 1857, near Liverpool.
	" *St. Bernard*	711	U. W. Mather	Lost Mar. 23, 1855, Berry Island.
	" *St. Paul*	620	Eleazer Crabtree	
	" *Metropolis*	964	J. T. Hay	
	" *Shannon* (Temporary)	808	J. T. Setzer	
	" *Rotunda* (Temporary)	1050	F. Houdlette	
	" *Russell* (Temporary)	796	N. B. Robbins	
1855	Sp. *Switzerland*	1139	John G. W. Trask	Regular line consisted in 1856 of the first six
	" *North Wind*	1042	H. Ripley	ships listed in 1854 and the *Switzerland*, and sailed from New York the 17th, and from Havre the 1st of month. Line discontinued in 1857.

New York—Antwerp

REGULAR LINE

George F. Gerding, 15 Broad St., New York agent. Bischop, Basteyns & N. J. DeCock, Antwerp agents. Established July, 1842. Sailed the 15th of each month.

YEAR	VESSEL	TONS	MASTERS	REMARKS
1842	Sp. *Georgiana*	554	Charles F. W. Behm	
	" *Sarah Sheafe*	401	William Gray	
	" *Florida*	523	Edwin J. Devries	
	Bk. *Zephir* (Belgian)	300	Wetteveen	
	" *Maria Louisa* (Belgian)	300	Vandersteen	
1843	Sp. *Emma* (Belgian)		Sheridan	Gerding & Kunkelmann, became New York
	" *Harriet* (Belgian)		Bunning	agents. Retained *Sarah Sheafe* and *Florida* and
	" *Amalia* (Belgian)		Knudson	added the three Belgian vessels. Other small
				vessels added during 1844–6.

HURLBUT LINE

E. D. Hurlbut & Co., 84 South St., New York agents. Schuchardt & Gebhard, Antwerp agents.

YEAR	VESSEL	TONS	MASTERS	REMARKS
1845	Sp. *Martha Washington*	473	J. S. Doane	
	Bk. *May Flower*	515	G. H. Hitchcock	Capsized Aug. 3, 1858, from New Orleans to Nantes. Capt. W. H. Platt and three men saved, 18 lost.
1846	Sp. *Edwina*	538	George West	
1849	Sp. *Seine*	785	Edward C. Williams	
1850	Sp. *Westminster*	631	E. D. Pratt	Var. Post.
	" *Elizabeth Denison*	645	M. L. Carpenter	Firm stated the five ships listed opposite
	" *Atlantic*	699	G. N. Lamb	would be kept in the trade and dispatched
	" *Emblem*	610	A. L. Dyer	once a month or as often as business demanded. A sixth ship, the *Louise*, was also
	" *Cotton Planter*	501	Jabez Pratt	dispatched during year.
1851	Sp. *J. Z.*	675	Augustus Zerega	In addition to the six vessels listed opposite,
	Bk. *Jane E. Williams*	397	T. L. Mason	the ships *Emblem* and *Atlantic* were also dispatched this year.
	Sp. *Peter Hattrick*	554	John E. Rockwell	
	" *South Carolina*	581	James Stewart	
	" *Richard Alsop*	835	Ezra D. Post	
	" *New Hampshire*	593	Charles M. Chase	
1853	Sp. *Shelter*	426	W. H. Robinson	
1854	Sp. *Rochambeau*	865	Stockwell	
	" *John W. White*	540	Reuben Snow	
	" *Wm. Layton*	961	L. M. Carpenter	Foundered Feb. 28.
	" *Catherine*	611	J. Edwards	Passengers this year sometimes consigned to
	" *J. H. Ryerson*	955	Paul H. Latham	Post & Ryerson, vessel to E. D. Hurlbut & Co.
	" *Francis B. Cutting*	976	John E. Rockwell	
	" *David Hoadley*	975	Joseph N. Magna	
	" *Hampton*	443	J. A. Brown	
	" *George Hurlbut*	1047	Ezra D. Post	
	" *Sarah G. Hyde*	890	Anthony Snow	
1855	Sp. *Vandalia*	775	R. J. Patten	Post & Ryerson, 84 South St., New York
	" *Ionian*	749	James Colley	agents as of Jan. 1st, but replaced Jan. 8th by
	" *Charlotte A. Stamler*	999	Robert E. Lyttle	Laytin, Ryerson & Hurlbut, who also were
	" *Leila*	614	W. W. Stafford	agents for the Mobile line.
	" *Sheridan*	895	Samuel Clark	Post, Smith & Co., became agents for remaining Hurlbut lines early in Jan.
	" *Fides* (German)		Cutter	
	" *Wabamo*	670	Levi F. Doty	Burned outside Sandy Hook Mar. 14, 1860, bound for Antwerp.
1856	Sp. *Charles Cooper*	977	G. N. Lamb	Ryerson retired Jan. 1, 1856, firm becoming
	" *Jacob A. Stamler*	1101	J. T. Hiltz	Laytin & Hurlbut composed of William
	" *Frederick Gebhard*	1125	John Edwards	Laytin and Edwin H. Hurlbut.
	" *Matilda*	660	Lee	
	" *Graham's Polly*	708	H. W. Hayden	
1857	Sp. *Marianne Nottebohm*	1202	G. N. Lamb	Var. G. W. Lamb.
	" *Troy*	712	J. W. Balch	
1859	Sp. *New World*	1404	Ebenezer Knight	
	" *National Guard*	1046	George W. Gates	

HURLBUT LINE (*continued*)

YEAR	VESSEL	TONS	MASTERS	REMARKS
1860	Sp. *Corinthian*	1098	J. W. Dyer	Post, Smith & Co. became New York agents in Nov. 1860. Line composed of the two ships listed, a new ship to be added, and the old ships *Elizabeth Denison, David Hoadley, Francis B. Cutting,* and *J. H. Ryerson*; sailed semi-monthly.
"	*Vulture*	604	G. L. Smith	

Z LINE

Zerega & Co. and Schmidt & Balchen, New York agents. Established Sept., 1847. No fixed sailing dates.

YEAR	VESSEL	TONS	MASTERS	REMARKS
1847	Sp. *Luconia*	481	George S. Porter	
"	*New Hampshire*	593	Charles H. Chase	
"	*E. Z.*	693	R. T. Hartshorne	
"	*James H. Shepherd*	635	James Ainsworth	
"	*Victoria*	602	Benjamin Watlington	
"	*Shakespeare*	749	George S. Porter	
"	*Hercules*	371	M. Madigan	
Bk.	*Harriet*	275	P. W. Beers	
"	*Epervier*	264	Nathan A. Farwell	
1848	Sp. *Roscoe*	622	Moses D. Ricker	
1850	Sp. *Helen Augusta*	448	R. Henderson	Sailings fell off in 1850, possibly due to loss of S.S. *Helena Sloman* operated by Schmidt & Balchen. All line sailings discontinued after 1851.
"	*Zenobia*	700	S. Barker	
Bk.	*Autoleon*	345	William C. Park	

S LINE

Schmidt & Balchen, New York agents. Established 1853.

YEAR	VESSEL	TONS	MASTERS	REMARKS
1853	Sp. *Sultana*	662	Theo. A. Barrett	
"	*Eliza Mallory*	649	John E. Williams	
1854	Sp. *Sea Lark* (Cl.)	974	Jacob T. Woodberry	Sunk by C.S.S. *Alabama*, May 3, 1863.
"	*Electric* (Cl.)	1274	Gurdon Gates	Sold Hamburg.
"	*Anna F. Schmidt*	784	M. T. Milliken	
"	*Lochinvar*	637	Lufkin	
"	*Tropic Bird*	413	Charles Foulkes	
"	*Robert M. Sloman*	759	A. Woodside	
1855	Sp. *Matilda*	690	Lee	
"	*Rochambeau*	865	George W. Gilchrist	Readmeasured, 916 tons.
"	*Wm. F. Schmidt*	775	B. Sears	
"	*Helen R. Cooper*	723	Reuben Colburn	
"	*Anna Kimball*	849	John Davis	
"	*Trumbull*	855	Jeremiah G. Smith	
1856	Sp. *Henry Reed*	850	George A. Dearborn	W. F. Schmidt & Co., 105-7 Wall St., became New York agents.
"	*Robert Parker* (British)	1052	Pritchard	
1858	Sp. *William Patten*	606	R. W. Parker	
"	*Hero*	765	G. E. Stafford	Var. J. C. Stafford.
1860	Sp. *Elizabeth Hamilton*	742	R. Harding	W. F. Schmidt became New York agent.

REGULAR LINE

Post, Smith & Co., 85 South St., New York agents. Sailed twice each month from each port.

YEAR	VESSEL	TONS	MASTERS	REMARKS
1856	Sp. *David Hoadley*	975	Joseph N. Magna	
"	*Elizabeth Denison*	645	E. Williams	
"	*Francis B. Cutting*	976	John E. Rockwell	
"	*Corinthian*	1098	J. W. Dyer	
"	*John H. Ryerson*	954	Paul W. Latham	
"	*Vulture*	604	G. L. Smith	
"	*John H. Elliott*	1077	J. H. Tucker	
"	*Leah*	1438	Jonathan Latham	Reported missing on first voyage
"	*Robert Carnley*	921	James N. Whitmore	
"	*Mary Matilda*	667	Munroe	

REGULAR LINE (*continued*)

YEAR	VESSEL	TONS	MASTERS	REMARKS
1857	Sp. *Roger A. Heirn*	1089	James Stewart	
"	" *Mary Ogden*	969	Samuel Loveland	
"	" *Isaac Bell*	1072	John Johnson	Var. Johnston.
1858	Sp. *Harvest*	646	D. C. Loring	
1860	Bk. *Alice Tainter* (*Taintor*)	667	W.S. Hatton	Post, Smith & Co. took over ships of Hurlbut Antwerp line in Nov., 1860, and continued sailings.

New York—Hamburg

PETERSON & MENSCH LINE

Peterson & Mensch, 118 Hanover Square, New York agents. Established Jan., 1828, "with a view to creating a more regular intercourse between New York and the North of Europe, have established a Line of Packets between this city and Hamburg. Cabin $100, for which beds and bedding and stores of the best kind will be furnished."

YEAR	VESSEL	TONS	MASTERS	REMARKS
1828	Sp. *Europa*	253	Edward Nicoll	Sailed irregularly through 1828 and gradu-
"	" *Howard*	337	Lewis Weiderholdt	ally faded out in 1829.
"	" *Indiana*	306	George Parker	

SCHMIDT & BALCHEN LINE

Schmidt & Balchen, 83 Wall St., New York agents. Established Feb., 1844, to maintain trimonthly sailings on 1st, 15th, and 25th of each month, commencing Mar. 1st, from New York, employing principally small vessels of German registry.

YEAR	VESSEL	TONS	MASTERS	REMARKS
1844	Sp. *Stephani*		O. H. Flor	
	Bk. *Washington*		F. D. Kruger	
	Sp. *Howard*		P. H. Paulson	
	Bk. *Franklin*		W. M. Sleeboom	
	" *Sir Isaac Newton*		J. C. Weinholtz	
	Sp. *Columbus*		O. H. Flor	
	Bk. *Diana*		P. Ehlers	
1845	Bk. *Miles*		P. Ehlers	Schedule of 17 sailings from Hamburg and 14
	" *Brarens*		O. H. Flor	from New York on fixed dates through 1845. Similar schedules continued through 1854 but gradually included large American ships.
1852	Sp. *Sir Robert Peel*	882	Jurgens	
1854	Sp. *Cheshire*	500	N. Rich	W. F. Schmidt & Co. became New York agents.

New York—Rotterdam

NEW YORK—ROTTERDAM LINE

E. D. Hurlbut & Co., 84 South St., New York agents. Established 1848. No fixed schedule. In general five of the Hurlbut vessels were devoted to the service each year, to maintain monthly sailings. Discontinued in 1857.

YEAR	VESSEL	TONS	MASTERS	REMARKS
1848	Bk. *Rose Standish*	427	Joseph W. Spencer	J. N. Magna master in 1851.
	Sp. *Louvre*	374	J. Weeks	F. A. Drinkwater master in 1850.
	" *Emblem*	610	W. Cammett	Schmidt & Balchen added as New York
	Bk. *Mayflower*	515	George H. Hitchcock	agents in July, 1848.
1850	Sp. *South Carolina*	581	James Stewart	
	" *Edwina*	538	H. G. Parmelee	
	" *Lorena*	527	W. Urquhart	
	" *Gertrude*	507	J. Weeks	I. R. Silsby master in 1852.
1851	Sp. *Leila*	614	W. W. Stafford	
	" *Elisha Denison*	359	William Morton	
	Bk. *Manchester*	570	H. Tyler	
1852	Sp. *Probus*	647	J. Weeks	
1854	Sp. *Shelter*	426	W. H. Robinson	
1855	Bk. *Jane E. Williams*	397	John Urquhart	Post, Smith & Co. became New York agents
1856	Sp. *Sheridan*	895	Joseph G. Russell	in February, 1855.

New York—Gibraltar

NEW YORK—GIBRALTAR LINE

Davis & Brooks and Baldwin & Spooner, New York agents. Davis and Brooks had run transient brigs to Gibraltar all through 1826 and 1827. In Nov. 1827, they joined Baldwin & Spooner in announcing establishment of a regular packet line to sail the 1st of each month. Fare $100.

YEAR	VESSEL	TONS	MASTERS	REMARKS
1827	Bg. *Mazzinghi*	142	James C. Delano	
"	*Bogota*	154	J. P. Sheffield	
"	*Spartan*	171	Israel Chapman	
"	*Mary Ann*	137	Whittemore	
"	*Globe*	215	Jacob Smith	
1828	Bg. *Thatcher*	145	I. Thatcher	Line ceased operation with sailing of *Orion* in
"	*Eliza*	181	Samuel Chew	Oct., 1828. Davis & Brooks continued in the
"	*Orion*	185	C. F. Bridges	trade on a transient basis for several years and Baldwin & Spooner dispatched an occasional vessel.

New York—Marseilles

BOYD & HINCKEN LINE

Boyd & Hincken, New York agents. Sailed 1st of month throughout year from New York and on 10th from Marseilles.

YEAR	VESSEL	TONS	MASTERS	REMARKS
1842	Bk. *Nashua*	301	Perry	Rinier Skaats master in 1843.
	Sp. *Spring*	283	Hamilton	
	Bk. *Everton*	230	H. D. Mayo	
	Sp. *Henry Thompson*	315	John Sylvester	
	Bg. *Isaac Mead*	384	Davis Studley	
	Sp. *Minerva*	308	Jos. M. Brown	S. Brown & Co., 103 Front St., added as
	" *Courier*	293	Michael Duggan	New York agent.
	" *Trescott*	342	Myrick	
	" *Hellespont*	345	James Adams	Sold to Mystic, 1845, for whaler.
	" *Coriolanus*	269	James Haile	Boyd & Hincken and Lawrence & Phelps were agents in Nov. 1843.
1844	Bk. *Marcella*	285	George Hagar	P. Ingham master in 1845.
	Sp. *Italy*	299	Stephen Coulter	
1845	Sp. *Gaston*	456	Stephen Coulter	Chamberlain & Phelps, proprietors. *Gaston* sold Bremen 1848.
	" *Missouri*	319	J. Sylvester	
	Bk. *Duc d'Orleans*	311	John Robertson	
	Sp. *Prince de Joinville*	527	W. M. Lawrence	
	" *Agnes* (Temporary)	430	G. W. Wethered	Var. Wetherill.
	" *Nebraska*	516	Jos. K. Brown	Also reported Joseph R. Brown.
	" *Huguenot*	935	James Haile	
	" *Arcole*	663	Nath'l. W. Everleigh	
1846	Sp. *Marianna*	379	John T. Phillips	Line composed of *Prince de Joinville*, *Arcole*, *Nebraska*, *Gaston*, and *Missouri*.
1848	Sp. *Sarah & Arselia*	482	B. Putnam	
	Bk. *Philena*	272	Ganford	
	Sp. *Minerva*	508	J. R. Brown	
1852	Bk. *Hungarian*	319	J. Mountford	H. Champlain master latter part of 1852.
1855	Bk. *Florence*	349	Mitchell	
1856	Sp. *Crescent*	853	David Forbes	Also reported 753 tons.
1857	Sp. *Sea Lion*	664	Reuben Colburn	
1858	Bk. *Voyager*	325	Freeman	

SECTION 7. NEW YORK—MEXICAN, CENTRAL AMERICAN, AND WEST INDIAN PORTS

As stated elsewhere, the principal objective of this study is to record the operations of all the American transatlantic sailing lines and the coastal lines between the eight largest East Coast and Gulf ports. In addition, however, it has been considered advisable to indicate generally the extent of the field of American line operations, and for that purpose the lines listed below have been included. It will be noted that in most cases only the first few years of the activities of such lines are covered—the exceptions being lines of outstanding importance or significance. In addition to those listed below, John P. Garcia ran packets to Havana; Everett & Battelle, to Cartagena; Andrew Foster & Son to Rio de Janeiro; Aymar & Co. and Charles Morgan to Kingston, Jamaica, and St. Croix; W. W. DeForest to Buenos Aires; all during the eighteen forties.

New York—Vera Cruz

LINE OF MEXICAN PACKETS. Later FIRST REGULAR PACKET LINE.

I(srael) G. Collins & Son, 88 South St., New York agents. William Howell & Son, Baltimore agents. Line sailed irregularly through 1826, but beginning Sept. 1, 1827, was scheduled to sail from New York the 1st and from Vera Cruz the 15th of every month. It is to be noted that Crassous & Boyd were also sending packets to Vera Cruz and at times thereafter were credited with operating a regular line. Zacherie & Co. also operated a packet line between New Orleans and Vera Cruz. Line discontinued 1837, after which much of the trade was handled by W. W. DeForest who had been heavily engaged in it for the previous two or three years.

YEAR	VESSEL	TONS	MASTERS	REMARKS
1826	Sch. *General Pike*	113	Joel T. Pike	Vessel lost March, 1827.
	Sp. *Gov. von Scholten*	322	Asa W. Whelden	
	" *Virginia*	356	Edward Knight Collins	John Collins master in 1827–8.
	" *Savannah*	248	Henry Austin	George Moore master in 1827. *Savannah* lost at Rio Grande, 1831.
	Bg. *Conveyance*	208	John Hipkins	
1828	Sp. *Lavinia*	310	Allen Miner	*Lavinia* readmeasured 1831, 263 tons. Lost on Colorado's Reef, Feb., 1832.
	" *Mobile*	285	Henry Austin	
	" *Leonidas*	231	George Bugnon	
1830	Sch. *Neuse*	121	Peter Barnard	Lost on the Abaco, Aug. 15, 1830, with master, cook, two seamen, and eight passengers.
1831	Sp. *Congress*	376	Allen Miner	E. K. Collins became New York agent in 1831. John Collins, New York agent in 1833.
1832	Sp. *St. Louis*	354	William W. Story	
1833	Sp. *Mexican* (Bk. in 1835)	226	Henry Davis	Benjamin J. H. Trask master in 1834.
1835	Sp. *Montezuma*	436	Henry Davis	

NEW YORK—VERA CRUZ LINE

Hargous Bros. & Co., 33 South St., New York agents. Established 1842.

YEAR	VESSEL	TONS	MASTERS	REMARKS
1842	Bk. *Anahuac*	308	Thomas W. Wilson	
	" *Eugenia*	356	James Biscoe	
	Bg. *Charles Carroll*	140	Vanstavoren	
	Bk. *Ann Louisa*	298	Clifford	John T. Marshalk master in 1843.
1843	Bg. *Petersburg*	183	Lorin Larkin	Edmund Cooper master in 1849.
1848	Bg. *Nenuphar*	192	Thomas W. Wilson	
1851	Bk. *Braziliero*	231	Charles Marsh	P. Hargous & Co., New York agents.
1852	Bk. *Flash* (Cl.)	344	Thomas W. Wilson	

New York—Cartagena

NEW YORK—CARTAGENA LINE

Baldwin & Spooner, 96 Coffee House Slip, New York agents. Established 1825. Sailed monthly. Cabin $75.

YEAR	VESSEL	TONS	MASTERS	REMARKS
1825	Bg. *Tampico*	125	Nathaniel B. Palmer	Alexander S. Palmer master in 1827.
	" *Bunker Hill*	144	T. S. Breed	Var. S. S. Breed.
1826	Bg. *Bogota*	154	J. P. Sheffield	
1827	Bg. *Athenian*	148	Thomas V. Sullivan	Crassous & Boyd became New York agents.
1828	Bg. *Medina*	169	C. P. Shipman	Silas E. Burrows became New York agent in June, 1828. Line called "New York & Cartagena Mail Packet Line."
1830	Bg. *Montilla*	161	Henry Beekman	In 1833 the regular line consisted of brigs *Athenian*, Wm. Chapman; *Montilla*, Hy. Beekman; and *Medina*, E. L. Haff; sailed from New York the 1st and from Cartagena the 10th of each month.
1833	Bg. *Hesper*	157	H. Butman	

New York—Havana

NEW YORK—HAVANA LINE

Burckle Brothers, 108 Pearl St., New York agents. Line established May, 1827, to provide bimonthly sailings. Line ceased operations in 1828.

YEAR	VESSEL	TONS	MASTERS	REMARKS
1827	Bg. *Dromo*	153	James Morgan	
	" *Claudio*	136	Philip S. Meyer	

MOSES TAYLOR LINE

Moses Taylor, 44 South St., New York agent. Established 1838 to sail monthly. Line continued through 1860.

YEAR	VESSEL	TONS	MASTERS	REMARKS
1838	Bk. *Rapid*	189	Richard L. Ward	Lost Orange Keys, Bahamas, May 26, 1851.
	Sp. *Norma*	292	D. B. Barton	
1843	Bg. *Factor*	141	William Handy	
1855	Bk. *Lyra*	217	Bemis	G. Wiggins master in 1858.
1858	Bk. *Albertina*	335	D. B. Barton	Moses Taylor & Co. became New York agents.

SPOFFORD & TILESTON LINE

Spofford & Tileston, 149 Water St., New York agents. Established 1840, sailed monthly. Firm had been heavily engaged in Cuban trade since 1826.

YEAR	VESSEL	TONS	MASTERS	REMARKS
1839	Sp. *Hellespont*	249	R. H. Ellis	
	" *Christoval Colon*	341	Benjamin Smith	
1843	Sch. *Adaline*	130	Isaac Linscott	
1846	Sp. *Adelaide*	373	Richard Adams	
1849	Sp. *James Drake*	483	Benjamin Smith	Spofford, Tileston & Co. continued line with steamships.

New York—Matanzas

NEW YORK—MATANZAS LINE

Spofford & Tileston, 149 Water St., New York agents.

YEAR	VESSEL	TONS	MASTERS	REMARKS
1839	Sp. *Caspar Hauser*	181	Richard Adams	
	" *Adelaide*	373	H. Mickell	J. A. Cobb master in 1852.
1845	Bk. *Pario*	300	Matthew Kinney	

NEW YORK—MATANZAS LINE

Moses Taylor, New York agent.

YEAR	VESSEL	TONS	MASTERS	REMARKS
1843	Bg. *Warsaw*	194	P. Koopman	
	" *Freeman*	147	D. Kilburn	Var. Kilbourn. Abandoned near Bermuda, Mar. 1844.

NEW YORK—MATANZAS LINE

J. C. Ward, New York agent.

YEAR	VESSEL	TONS	MASTERS	REMARKS
1843	Bg. *Levant*	137	Joseph Alexander	
	" *Borodino*	233	Thomas Trott	

NEW YORK—MATANZAS LINE

R. D. Read, 31 South St., New York agent.

YEAR	VESSEL	TONS	MASTERS	REMARKS
1851	Bk. *Panchita*	234	R. C. Reed	
	Bg. *Abeona*	120	S. C. Stallknicht	

New York—Jamaica

NEW YORK—JAMAICA LINE

B. Aymar & Co., 34 South Street, New York agents. Cater & Tyrrell, Kingston, Jamaica agents. Sailed from New York the 10th, and from Kingston the 15th of month. Cabin $75 from New York and $100 from Kingston. Established Jan., 1838.

YEAR	VESSEL	TONS	MASTERS	REMARKS
1838	Sp. *Orbit*	283	Waren Fox	
"	*John W. Cater*	217	John R. Crane	

SECTION 8. PHILADELPHIA—LIVERPOOL AND MISCELLANEOUS TRANSATLANTIC PORTS

COPE LINE

Thomas P. Cope & Son, Philadelphia agents. Alexander Brown & Son, Baltimore agents. William Brown, Liverpool agent. Established to begin operations June 10, 1822. Cabin fare £30, including stores of all kinds.

YEAR	VESSEL	TONS	MASTERS	REMARKS
1822	Sp. *Lancaster*	383	Thomas Potts	
"	*Alexander*	461	Stephen Baldwin	
"	*Tuscarora*	379	James M. Serrill	
"	*Montezuma*	424	Charles Dixey	William West, Jr., master in 1827.
"	*Tobacco Plant*	279	Stephen Baldwin	Took first sailing from Liverpool on June 10, arrived Philadelphia July 18. Commanded on second voyage by George Reed.
1824	Sp. *Algonquin*	482	Charles Dixey	Replaced *Lancaster*
1828	Sp. *Monongahela*	509	Charles Dixey	Enoch Turley master in 1842.
1833	Sp. *Pocahontas*	535	James West	
"	*Susquehanna*	582	Charles Dixey	Jona. W. Miercken master in 1842. Albert Turley master in 1845.
1839	Sp. *Thomas P. Cope*	727	James West	Henry F. Miercken master in 1846. *Cope* burned at sea. Passengers and crew rescued by British ship *Emigrant* on Dec. 5th and 6th, 1846.
"	*Shenandoah*	738	James West	William H. West master in 1849. Abandoned at sea Aug., 1854.
				John A. Brown & Co., and Henry and Alfred Cope became Philadelphia agents.
				In 1843 sailed 25th of month from Philadelphia and 8th from Liverpool.
1844	Sp. *Saranak*	816	Enoch Turley	R. R. Decan master of *Saranak* in 1852.
				Line consisted of *Saranak*, *Monongahela*, *Susquehanna*, and *Thomas P. Cope*.
				Brown, Shipley & Co. became Liverpool agents in 1845.
1845	Sp. *Wyoming*	891	Jona. W. Miercken	Theodore Julius master in 1851. Albert Turley master in 1855. William Burton master in 1858–68.
1848	Sp. *Tuscarora*	1232	Enoch Turley	Joseph A. Spedden (Spedder) master in 1855. Richard M. Dunlevy master in 1858.
"	*Tonawanda*	1241	Jona. W. Miercken	Theodore Julius master in 1868.
				Continued through and after Civil War with packets *Tonawanda*, *Tuscarora*, *Wyoming*, and *Saranak* under Capts. Theodore Julius, R. M. Dunlevy, William Burton, and James Rowland, respectively.

WELSH LINE

John Welsh, 51 South Wharf, Philadelphia agent. Line established to begin operations Apr. 5, 1823. Discontinued in 1824.

YEAR	VESSEL	TONS	MASTERS	REMARKS
1823	Sp. *Amanda*	222	Cash	In her only voyage in the line the *Amanda* was 70 days from Liverpool to Philadelphia.
"	*Dido*	343	T. Bliss	

WELSH LINE (*continued*)

YEAR	VESSEL	TONS	MASTERS	REMARKS
1823	Sp. *Manchester*	321	Charles Winslow	
"	*Plato*	240	William West	
"	*Woodbine*	260	Charles Avery	Replaced *Manchester*.
"	*Sarah Ralston*	334	Ezra Bowen	

NEW LINE OF LIVERPOOL AND PHILADELPHIA PACKETS

Spackman & Wilson, 21 Church Alley, Philadelphia agents. J. Willis, Latham & Gair, and Rathbone Bros. & Co., Liverpool agents. Established Feb. 1824, to sail from Liverpool the 20th of each month.

YEAR	VESSEL	TONS	MASTERS	REMARKS
1824	Sp. *Florida*	522	James L. Wilson	
"	*Julius Caesar*	346	Francis M. French	
"	*Colossus*	399	Richard Urann	Hasadiah Coffin master in 1831.
"	*Delaware*	412	John Hamilton	
"	*Courier*	388	Robert Marshall	G. H. Wallace master in 1824–5.
1825	Sp. *Globe*	479	James Hamilton	*Globe* replaced *Florida*.
	Bg. *Newcastle* (extra)	213	H. Wilkenson	Thomas E. Walker & Co. added as Philadelphia agents.
1826	Sp. *Minerva*	380	John C. Mayell	Samuel Spackman replaced Spackman & Wilson as Philadelphia agent.
"	*Bolivar*	480	Josiah L. Wilson	
1827	Sp. *Arab*	336	John Ball	Line reorganized in Feb. as a new line retaining only the *Delaware* and *Julius Caesar* of the old line.
"	*Ann*	299	Charles L. Bartleson	
"	*Lima*	298	John Wiley	
"	*Delaware*	412	John Hamilton	
"	*Julius Caesar*	346	William West	
1828	Sp. *John Wells*	366	Eli Curtis	Wm. & James Brown & Co. became Liverpool agents, 1831.
1832	Sp. *Benjamin Morgan*	396	Charles M. Bartleson	Charles M. Wotherspoon master in 1834. Thos. E. Walker & Co. were only Philadelphia agents.
1833	Sp. *Carroll of Carrollton*	696	Thomas J. Bird	Sailings were quite irregular and discontinued in 1837.
1834	Sp. *Kensington*	494	John Ball	

BLACK DIAMOND LINE

Richardson, Watson & Co., Philadelphia, and 40 Exchange Pl., New York, agents. Richardson Bros. & Co. and John Taylor Crook, Liverpool agents. Established 1846 to sail from Philadelphia the 12th and from Liverpool the 26th of month.

YEAR	VESSEL	TONS	MASTERS	REMARKS
1846	Sp. *Shenandoah*	738	William H. West	James West master in 1848.
"	*Adirondack*	699	Thomas Shipley	
"	*Kalamazoo*	798	Robert McCerren	Geo. W. Foulke (Faulk or Faulke) master in 1849.
"	*Franconia*	499	J. A. Smith	
1847	Sp. *Pennsylvania*	1000	Anthony Michael	
"	*William Penn*	811	Anthony Michael	T. P. Folger master in 1852.
"	*Glenmore*	467	A. B. Clarke	
1848	Sp. *Helen McGaw*	599	Albert A. Burwell	G. T. Tucker master in 1849.
1849	Sp. *Philadelphia*	1102	Wm. C. Stotesbury	Charles F. Poole master in 1855.
"	*Hibernia*	877	Charles H. Salter	
"	*George Thatcher*	599	J. Freeman	
"	*Thomas H. Perkins*	670	George Conn	
"	*North Star*	431	W. Bishop	
				Guest & Gilmore became Baltimore agents in 1850. Very little activity noted during next three years but stepped up in 1854.
1854	Sp. *Nonpareil*	1431	Edmund Dunn	Var. Edward Dunn. B. G. Green master in 1854.
"	*Isaac Jeanes*	843	William Chipman	Richardson, Spence & Co. became Liverpool agents. Packets sailed from Liverpool the 1st and from Philadelphia the 15th.
"	*Westmoreland*	999	Peter A. Decan	
1855	Sp. *Bridgewater*	1498	Edwin W. Barstow	
"	*Juventa*	1187	Alfred Watts	
"	*William Chamberlain*	950	Isaac Jennings	

BLACK DIAMOND LINE (*continued*)

YEAR	VESSEL	TONS	MASTERS	REMARKS
1855	Sp. *Stalwart*	1108	George W. Foulke	A. H. Lucas master in 1856.
"	*Levi Woodbury*	998	William Chipman	
1856	Sp. *Western Ocean*	1153	James Hamilton	
1857	Sp. *Evelyn*	1198	H. B. Ray	Line virtually abandoned in 1857.
1859	Sp. *St. Patrick*	1049	Washburn W. Fales	Went missing in 1860.
"	*Chicago*	1242	John Chase	Line comparatively inactive after 1857 and discontinued in 1859.

NEW LINE

Samuel Pleasants, 13 Walnut Street, Philadelphia agent. James McHenry and A. Taylor & Co., Liverpool agents. Established 1847, sailed from Philadelphia the 1st and from Liverpool the 10th of each month. Cabin, 15 guineas. Discontinued in 1855.

YEAR	VESSEL	TONS	MASTERS	REMARKS
1847	Sp. *Shenandoah*	738	James West	Richard R. Decan master in 1851.
"	*Arabella*	680	Samuel Rice	
1848	Sp. *Berlin*	613	Alfred F. Smith	
"	*Mary Pleasants*	681	J. Q. Bowne	Anthony M. Michaels master in 1850.
"	*Europe*	619	Henry F. Miercken	W. McDowell master in 1850.
"	*Finland*	549	H. Johnson	
1849	Sp. *Robert Burton*	398	Peter A. Decan	
1851	Sp. *Shackamaxon*	1090	William H. West	Sailed from Philadelphia on 15th and from
"	*Rip Van Winkle*	1095	Alfred F. Smith	Liverpool on 1st of month. Geo. McHenry & Co. became Philadelphia agents.
"	*Westmoreland*	999	Peter A. Decan	
"	*Thomas H. Perkins*	670	John Wylie	
"	*Hero*	760	Charles R. Griffith	Var. Griffiths.
1852	Sp. *Lizzie Harward*	868	L. Parker	
"	*Masconomo*	824	Augustus Proal	
"	*Buena Vista*	661	Simeon S. Howard	
"	*Caroline Nesmith*	832	B. Salisbury	
"	*Florida*	1039	George R. Nickerson	
1853	Sp. *Hope Goodwin*	1199	W. H. Parsons	
"	*Arcadia*	715	William Jordan	
"	*States Rights*	825	Thomas Paxton	
"	*Mary Carson*	700	J. Johnstone	
"	*Henry Grinnell*	944	T. O. Johnson	Var. T. C. Johnson.
1854	Sp. *B. L. Harriman*	642	John Arey	
"	*Philadelphia*	1102	George W. Foulke	

LINE OF LIVERPOOL PACKETS. Known in Liverpool as "Philadelphia Line of Packets."

Stephen Baldwin & Co., Philadelphia agents. James Browne & Co. and Brown & Harrisons, Liverpool agents. Established Nov. 1850, to sail from Philadelphia the 1st and from Liverpool the 18th of each month. One of several lines partaking of character of regularly scheduled and "one way" emigrant lines, many ships sailed on schedule only from Liverpool.

YEAR	VESSEL	TONS	MASTERS	REMARKS
1850	Sp. *Jane H. Glidden*	700	Ambrose Child	W. F. Howes master in 1852.
"	*James Browne*	997	Arthur Child	William Crabtree, Jr., master in 1857.
"	*Gondar*	645	J. G. Barstow	
"	*Atalanta*	700	Edwin G. Colby	
1851	Sp. *George Raynes*	999	Pierce W. Penhallow	
"	*Onward*	791	Jonathan Chase	
"	*Eva*	631	J. W. Philbrook	
"	*St. Louis*	630	C. M. Davis	
"	*Mary Annah*	500	R. S. Keating	
1852	Sp. *Java*	715	T. G. Monroe	Sailed from Liverpool the 20th.
"	*Rio Grande*	541	D. F. Ryan	
"	*John Henry*	549	James H. Oxnard	
"	*Forest State*	850	Joseph Pollister	
"	*John Spear*	629	A. K. Spear	
"	*Philadelphia*	1102	George W. Foulke	
"	*Florida*	1039	George R. Nickerson	
"	*Horizon*	963	A. C. Thompson	

LINE OF LIVERPOOL PACKETS (*continued*)

YEAR	VESSEL	TONS	MASTERS	REMARKS
1853	Sp. *Rockaway*	815	S. R. Goodwin	Mark H. Lufkin master in 1855.
	" *Switzerland*	571	F. W. Carter	
	" *Cerro Gordo*	877	J. Chandler, Jr.	J. L. Randall master in 1859.
	" *Westmoreland*	999	Robert R. Decan	Thomas & James Harrison replaced Brown
	" *Mermaid*	1222	C. S. Robinson	& Harrisons as Liverpool agents in July.
	" *John Merrick*	692	H. Stevens	
	" *Montgomery*	893	John Davis	
	" *Annapolis*	896	John C. Graham	
	" *General Dunlap*	946	W. S. Skolfield	
	" *Zenobia*	630	William Robinson	
1854	Sp. *Tempest*	861	Lincoln Patten	
	" *A. Cheesebrough*	615	J. Kelly	
	" *W. V. Kent*	676	J. O. Flitner	D. L. Wilcox master in 1856.
	" *Huguenot*	934	J. G. Storer	Var. Stover.
	" *Neptune's Favorite*	1347	Oliver G. Lane	
	" *Bosphorus*	1470	N. Pendleton	James G. Pendleton master in 1855.
	" *S. Gildersleeve*	848	Cicero Brown	
1855	Sp. *Fanny McHenry*	1237	Alfred F. Smith	
	" *Edwin Flye*	1298	George Hagar	
	" *Celestial Empire*	1390	J. G. Pierce	
	" *Thomas H. Perkins*	670	James S. Theobald	Thomas Wayne master in 1856.
	" *Old Dominion*	619	H. Q. Dampson	
	" *Crest of the Wave*	1014	William S. Colley	Ships *James Browne*, *Westmoreland*, *Fanny*
	" *Louisa Hatch*	853	O. S. Amsbury	*McHenry*, and *Rockaway* ran regularly in line.
	" *Kate Hunter*	731	John C. Bush	
	" *Charter Oak*	841	Franklin Houdlette	
	" *Napier*	1811	John L. Sanford	
	" *Tigress*	912	E. Lawrence	
	" *Northern Crown*	1380	C. W. Lane	
1856	Sp. *Muscongus*	669	F. W. Carter	Messrs. Burton & Penrose became Phila-
	" *Lancaster*	1195	Peter A. Decan	delphia agents for ships *Lancaster* and *West-*
	" *George West*	1071	Robert Couch	*moreland* and possibly others.
	" *Asia*	930	W. H. Duncan	
	" *Northland*	931	S. O. Flitner	
	" *Ionian*	749	J. Colley	Var. W. J. Colley.
	" *Confederation*	1186	Asa A. Corning	
	" *Lawson*	597	T. G. Harrison	
	" *Helen McGaw*	598	W. S. Tucker	
1857	Sp. *Fanny Fosdick*	729	William Crabtree	
	" *Emma Jane*	1096	F. C. Gordon	
	" *Otseonthe*	1138	John H. Young	
	" *William Cummings*	791	William G. Jones	Var. Johns.
	" *North American*	1402	Samuel Clarke	
	" *Arkwright*	1244	John Robertson	John Davis master in 1859.
1858	Sp. *Star of the West*	1122	C. G. McAlmond	Var. McCallum.
	" *J. G. Richardson*	857	H. Lewis	Var. B. Lewis.
	" *Thomas Jefferson*	989	W. Hill	
	" *North Carolina*	669	Seth Foster	
	" *Chimborazo*	937	R. G. Morse	
	" *Annie Size*	1031	C. F. Size	
	" *John Frazar*	882	Thomas R. Herbert	
	" *Yemassee*	767	D. C. Child	Var. Childs.
1859	Sp. *Lizzie Harward*	868	S. Lawrence	
	" *Bolton*	987	William M. Cotter	
	" *Richard Morse*	930	T. Oliver	Var. F. Oliver.
	" *Amelia*	623	J. McKenzie	
	" *Emily Augusta*	1150	S. Strickland	William Strickland master in 1860.
	" *Sir John Franklin*	999	H. Galt	
	" *Pleiades*	1172	Nathan Winslow	
	" *Calliope*	1163	S. R. Goodwin	
	" *Ann E. Hooper*	1146	W. B. Hooper	
1860	Sp. *R. S. Kimball*	1250	P. A. Hosmer	Var. Hosman.
	" *S. Baker*	830	William G. Allen	
	" *Gulf Stream*	900	R. G. Higgins	
	" *Southern Rights*	930	John T. Harward	

LINE OF LIVERPOOL PACKETS (*continued*)

YEAR	VESSEL	TONS	MASTERS	REMARKS
1860	Sp. *Sagamore*	1164	E. A. Gerrish	Var. Garrish.
"	*John Clark*	1161	P. G. Latourneau	Ships *Lancaster, Westmoreland, Arkwright,* and
"	*Hortensia*	702	John Atkin	*James Browne* ran regularly in line. John R.
"	*Mary Washington*	934	D. F. Tinkham	Penrose, Philadelphia agent. Continued
"	*Alexander McNeill*	657	William Somers	through Civil War.

PHILADELPHIA—LIVERPOOL LINE

Dawson & Hancock, Philadelphia agents, announced intention of establishing a line in Oct., 1852. Discontinued in 1854.

YEAR	VESSEL	TONS	MASTERS	REMARKS
1852	Sp. *Sirocco*	1130	J. L. Sanford	
1853	Sp. *Euroclydon*	1402	R. Bennett	

PHILADELPHIA—LONDONDERRY LINE

Robt. Taylor & Co., 32 Walnut St., Philadelphia agent. Established Jan., 1851, to sail from Londonderry, 1st, 10th, and 20th. Line consisted of British and American vessels.

YEAR	VESSEL	TONS	MASTERS	REMARKS
1851	Sp. *Helen Thompson*		Gray	
"	*Spartan*		Muirhead	
"	*Actaeon*		Benson	
"	*Vermont*	398	E. Perry	
"	*Creole*	767	Watt	
1859	Sp. *Elizabeth*	669	Gillespie	Robt. S. Taylor, agent.
1860	Sp. *Zered* (British)	821	McGonagal	Robt. Taylor & Co., advertised passage to and from Liverpool sailing 8th and 24th of month.

BOULT, ENGLISH & BRANDON LINE OF PHILADELPHIA PACKETS. Called REGULAR LINE in 1859.

Boult, English & Brandon, Richmond Bldgs., 26 Chapel Street, Liverpool agents. English & Brandon, followed by Boult, English & Brandon had been sending ships to Philadelphia for several years but did not advertise as a line until 1858. No fixed schedule but ships sailed as a rule twice monthly with good regularity from Liverpool.

YEAR	VESSEL	TONS	MASTERS	REMARKS
1858	Sp. *Ironsides*	1319	Joseph R. Curtis	
"	*Juniata*	812	A. H. Wilson	
"	*Josiah L. Hale*	1093	Jeremiah Lunt	
"	*Dashaway*	1012	J. Cooper	
"	*J. Wakefield*	1225	Anson Butler	
"	*Emily Gardner*	750	R. Limeburner	
"	*Pleiades*	1172	Nathan Winslow	
"	*Shamrock*	1125	Samuel B. Doane	
"	*Crown Point*	1098	Henry Cook	
"	*Frank Haynie*	1056	J. L. Randall	
"	*Delfthaven*	941	W. A. Cooper	
"	*Ionian*	749	G. A. Mitchell	
"	*Noemie*	548	John Johnson	
"	*Columbus*	706	Jefferson Hawthorne	
"	*American Union*	1000	Albert C. Otis	N. C. Lincoln master in 1859.
"	*Consignment*	1131	A. Purington	
"	*Barnabas Webb*	1300	Alfred Watts	
1859	Sp. *B. D. Metcalf*	1188	James Stetson	
"	*Juventa*	1187	William Young	
"	*R. H. Tucker*	898	Joseph Tucker	
"	*Eloise*	882	Collins	
"	*Jane Henderson*	670	Washington Galt	
"	*Ceres*	547	J. J. Humphries	
"	*Northampton*	799	Joseph S. Elwell	
"	*Governor Langdon*	1100	William P. Stone	
"	*Wallace*	977	A. T. Lane	
"	*Robert Cushman*	1181	J. T. Morse	
"	*Thomas Jefferson*	989	George Meacom	

BOULT, ENGLISH & BRANDON LINE (*continued*)

YEAR	VESSEL	TONS	MASTERS	REMARKS
1859	Sp. *Pam Flush*	1007	Thomas McGuire	
"	*Roswell Sprague*	616	John Drummond	
	Bk. *Betsey Williams*	399	B. T. Nickerson	
1860	Sp. *Sebastian Cabot*	1335	William H. Watts	
"	*Sarah E. Pettigrew*	1193	James H. Burdick	
"	*Joseph Fish*	1199	Gideon Young	
"	*Narragansett*	640	Thomas Saunders	
"	*R. Jacobs*	1122	James Henderson	
"	*Oliver Moses*	999	William M. Otis	
"	*Western Ocean*	1153	Simmons	J. A. Bowman master next voyage.
"	*Atalanta*	975	P. M. Whitmore	
"	*Lorenzo*	1095	L. T. Merrow	
"	*Montebello*	1100	Dunbar Henderson	
"	*Annie Kimball*	595	J. F. Stinson	
"	*John Trucks*	767	James P. Lindsay	

Philadelphia—Bremen

BREMEN PACKET LINE

Mecke, Plate & Co., 34 Front St., Philadelphia agents. Established 1845. Line consisted of six German brigs to sail 1st of each month from Mar. 1st to Sept. 1st, then Oct. 15th and Nov. 15th.

YEAR	VESSEL	TONS	MASTERS	REMARKS
1845	Bg. *Louisa* (Bremen)		C. Wenke	
"	*Bremen* (Bremen)		B. D. Koper	
	Bk. *Philadelphia*		H. W. Greve	

SECTION 9. BALTIMORE & HAMPTON ROADS—LIVERPOOL

Baltimore—Liverpool

CORNER LINE. Known in Liverpool as "Baltimore Line of Packets."

James Corner & Sons, Baltimore agents. Brown, Shipley & Co., James Browne & Co., and Brown & Harrisons, Liverpool agents. Established Mar., 1846. "A contemplated line of ships to sail monthly."

YEAR	VESSEL	TONS	MASTERS	REMARKS
1846	Sp. *Rhone*	471	Joseph Harvey	Brown, Shipley & Co. were apparently not active in management after 1846. The other agents continued to send many extra emigrant ships.
"	*Cincinnati*	457	F. Codman	
"	*Hargrave*	484	James Bailey	
"	*Powhattan*	521	J. F. Hayden	
1847	Sp. *Lydia*	543	E. Soule	Francis B. Soule master in 1852.
"	*Richard Anderson*	584	Richard Bennett	E. M. Fitch master in 1856.
"	*Manchester*	570	S. H. J. Prentice	
	Bg. *Colonel Howard*	333	J. Pickett	
	Sp. *Napier*	469	Jacob Higgins	
"	*Hermann*	419	Charles Welch	
"	*Emerald*	518	Charles W. Buck	
"	*Roanoke*	319	T. Kelly	
"	*Scotia*	559	Joseph Miskelly	H. M. Merrill master in 1852.
1848	Sp. *Harkaway*	545	Thomas Pescub	
"	*Alexandria*	492	H. D. Ordemann	
"	*Wakona*	430	G. Payne	
"	*Leila*	613	W. R. Benson	
"	*James Corner*	679	H. S. Walker	W. C. Corner master in 1849.
"	*Robert Fulton*	562	J. S. Wade	
"	*Republic*	644	Charles W. Buck	
"	*Andalusia*	772	Francis W. Williams	
"	*Monterey*	442	Tully Crosby	
1849	Sp. *Chesapeake*	647	R. T. Lambert	Var. R. H. Lambert.
"	*Patrick Henry*	442	A. A. Watts	
"	*American*	391	Thomas Saunders	
"	*Telasser*	473	G. H. Wood	
"	*General Washington*	677	J. C. Graham	C. A. Berry master in 1850.
"	*Zenobia*	699	J. T. Jackson	
"	*Macedonia*	415	J. E. Snow	Var. J. H. Snow

CORNER LINE (*continued*)

YEAR		VESSEL	TONS	MASTERS	REMARKS
1849	Sp.	*Franconia*	499	John A. Smith	
	"	*Augustus*	737	Tobias Lord	
	Bk.	*Stella*	338	Theodore Littlefield	
1850	Sp.	*Albus*	688	M. B. Gregory	Regular line composed of *Albus*, *Mary Hale*,
	"	*Mary Hale*	648	C. H. Rollins	*Annapolis*, and *F. W. Brune*.
	"	*Annapolis*	896	John C. Grahame	C. W. Buck master in 1855.
	"	*A. Cheesebrough*	615	John Kirby	Robert C. Cheesebrough master in 1852.
	"	*Alexander*	591	J. L. Sanford	
	"	*F. W. Brune*	871	D. C. Landis	
	"	*Henry Nesmith*	428	A. Butler	
	Bk.	*Sarah Bridge*	484	Jonathan Strout	
1851	Sp.	*Living Age*	727	J. H. Snow	Henry Mankin, 16 Bowly's Wharf, became
	"	*Jane Henderson*	670	James Stewart	Baltimore agent. Name changed to Mankin
	"	*Flora McDonald*	841	W. S. Wedge	Line. "Ships to sail about the first of month." In 1852 line sailed from Liverpool on the 20th.
1852	Sp.	*Pioneer*	640	D. C. Childs	
	"	*Art Union*	750	J. S. Stubbs	Var. J. J. Stubbs.
	"	*William Patten*	606	Charles Theobald	
	"	*Lucy W. Hale*	648	Charles H. Rollins	
	"	*Inca*	577	W. Wyle	
	"	*Mary Annah*	488	R. S. Keating	J. Wade master in 1853.
	"	*Sewall*	597	Lewis J. Manson	
1853	Sp.	*Lizzie Harward*	868	F. Lawrence	Thomas and James Harrison replaced Brown
	"	*Isabella*	649	W. F. Hayden	& Harrisons as Liverpool agents.
	"	*Narragansett*	640	Charles Faye	
	"	*Rockaway*	815	S. R. Goodwin	
	"	*Wabash*	398	W. H. Barnes	
	"	*Eastern Queen*	757	R. T. Emery	
1854	Bk.	*Paladin*	460	T. Murphy	
	Sp.	*Juniata*	812	H. J. Wilson	
	"	*Flora McDonald*	841	H. M. Merrill	T. B. Skinner master in 1856.
	"	*Susan E. Howell*	730	J. D. Raffles	Liverpool agents announced in December
	"	*Zone*	496	T. S. Ellis	that ships *Annapolis*, *Mary Hale*, *Muscongus*,
	"	*A. B. Thompson*	981	George F. Mustard	and *A. B. Thompson* would sail from Liver-
	"	*S. Gildersleeve*	848	Cicero Brown	pool 20th of each month.
	"	*Muscongus*	669	F. W. Carter	
	"	*Waltham*	549	C. Wheeler	
	"	*Sea Nymph*	732	Jarvis Patten	Abandoned at sea Mar. 14, 1854. Crew taken off by ship *Pride of the Ocean* of Providence.
1855	Sp.	*Minnesota*	799	William M. Allen	
	"	*Julia G. Tyler*	857	Z. Lowry	
	"	*William Witherle*	874	T. Atwood	
	"	*Emily St. Pierre*	883	E. L. Tessier	
	"	*Mackinaw*	1094	E. A. Robinson	L. Hammer master in 1858.
	"	*Ocean Traveller*	695	J. M. Boardman	
	"	*Harvest*	614	Josiah Fuller, Jr.	
	"	*Jane Henderson*	670	T. F. Knowles	
	Bk.	*Harriet Francis*	454	D. M. Reed	
1856	Sp.	*Ann E. Hooper*	1146	L. Rains	Var. T. S. Rains. N. C. Walker master in 1858
	"	*Glance*	850	J. W. Gillespie	Var. J. M. Gillespie.
	"	*Caroline*	722	J. Connor	J. F. Hayne master in 1859.
	"	*Fanny Fern*	594	F. C. Gordon	Var. Jordan.
	"	*Robert C. Winthrop*	781	W. Norville	
	"	*Northland*	931	S. A. Flitner	Foard & Rogers became Baltimore agents.
	"	*Avondale*	727	J. H. Fry	Var. Fay.
	"	*Macauley*	1130	J. G. Rogers	
	"	*John Clark*	1160	W. Hale	Philip M. Hale master in 1858.
	"	*William Penn*	1074	W. A. Meade	
	Bk.	*Linwood*	491	Orlando Martin	
1857	Sp.	*Casilda*	991	W. G. Stafford	
	"	*Gosport*	886	W. Strickland	
1858	Sp.	*Omar Pasha*	769	W. Torrey	
	"	*Ellen Stewart*	1118	E. C. Wambersie	C. E. Coffin master in 1859.
	"	*David Stewart*	674	S. H. G. Prentice	

CORNER LINE (*continued*)

YEAR	VESSEL	TONS	MASTERS	REMARKS
1859	Sp. *Susan G. Owens*	735	J. Norton	
"	*Alexander*	591	S. A. Bain	T. A. Bain master in 1860.
"	*John G. Richardson*	857	B. Lewis	
"	*John N. Cushing*	632	J. W. Plummer	
"	*Sir John Franklin*	999	H. Galt	
1860	Sp. *Juliet Trundy*	899	T. R. Pilsbury	
"	*Amelia*	572	J. McKenzie	
"	*Borneo*	610	Z. Flitner	
"	*Currituck*	650	T. D. Knowles	
"	*Medallion*	548	G. H. Theobald	
"	*Annapolis*	897	J. Pickett	

Hampton Roads—Liverpool

PETERSBURG LINE

James S. Brander & Co., Petersburg, Va., agents. James Ferguson, Spear's Wharf, Baltimore agent. Established Oct., 1833, to sail from Hampton Roads the 15th and from Liverpool the 1st of month. Operation as a line ceased in 1834.

YEAR	VESSEL	TONS	MASTERS	REMARKS
1833	Sp. *Harkaway*	545	Reuben Fisher	
"	*Jefferson*	434	H. B. Newcomb	
"	*Tally-Ho*	420	J. Nicholson	
"	*California Brander*	549	P. Dowson	Var. Dewson.

Charleston Transatlantic Lines

Several attempts were made to start a line between Charleston and Liverpool none of which played an important part in the commerce of the two ports. That of 1847–8 with the ship *Noemie* as the pioneer of the proposed line has been noted elsewhere. In 1852 the Liverpool firm of Jacot, Taylor & Tipper started a short-lived line as a "one way" emigrant service, but it was not until 1860 that a line was established on a basis that promised a fair degree of success.

LIVERPOOL—CHARLESTON LINE

"Regular Sailing Packets Between Liverpool & Charleston." James Browne & Co. and Thomas & James Harrison, Liverpool agents. Line started with sailing of the *Eliza Bonsall* the 5th of July. Discontinued early in 1861.

YEAR	VESSEL	TONS	MASTERS	REMARKS
1860	Sp. *Eliza Bonsall*	1274	B. Michaels	Name of line changed in August to Southern
"	*Gondar*	710	Gooding	Line of Packets.
"	*Emily St. Pierre*	934	E. L. Tessier	Sailed from Liverpool the 5th and 20th of
"	*John Frazar*	950	T. R. Herbest	month.
"	*Susan G. Owens*	784	D. H. Norton	Although all ships were American their ton-
"	*Amelia*	664	J. McKenzie	nage was stated in accordance with British
"	*Matilda*	840	William Cummings	computation and is larger than their American registered tonnage.

SECTION 10. NEW ORLEANS—LIVERPOOL AND HAMBURG

New Orleans—Liverpool

There is some uncertainty regarding the beginnings of regular service between these ports. It has been stated that the first line—the "Crescent City Line"—was established in Jan., 1850. On the evidence of available records that assumption would seem to be due to its confusion with the Crescent City Line between New York and New Orleans. (*q.v.*) The Liverpool Crescent City Line undoubtedly was developed as an extension of the activities of the New York line, but no evidence has come to light that the extension took place before the announcement of the establishment of a Liverpool-New Orleans Crescent City Line in Nov., 1851, by the Liverpool firm of Jacot, Taylor & Tipper. However, lack of evidence does not rule out the possibility that the firm was popularly credited with the operation of such a line at an earlier date.

In like manner, it is also possible that the very extensive early activities of Pilkington & Wilson in the New Orleans trade were popularly regarded as operations of the White Star Line, but here again no evidence has come to light that such was the case.

CRESCENT CITY LINE

Jacot, Taylor & Tipper and Anson, Hardy & Co., Liverpool agents. Fosdick & Co., 73 Magazine St., New Orleans agents. Foster & Nickerson, 25 South St., New York agents. Established Nov., 1851. No fixed schedule.

YEAR	VESSEL	TONS	MASTERS	REMARKS
1851	Sp. *Shirley*	911	Thomas G. Hiler	
	" *Glance*	515	J. Taylor	
	" *Pyramid*	740	R. Robson	
	" *Saxon*	734	Edmund Crosby	
1852	Sp. *Squantum*	647	David Crocker	Webster & Co., 19 Dale Street, became
	" *Inez*	699	Micajah Lunt	Liverpool agents.
	" *Crescent*	754	David Forbes	Jacot, Taylor & Tipper associated as agents
	" *Muscongus*	669	James H. Kelleran	for some of the ships.
	" *Tyringham*	608	Carleton Howes	
	" *Commonwealth*	636	E. N. Doane	
1853	Sp. *John Henry*	549	J. H. Oxnard	Line divided in August between Liverpool
	" *Clifton*	599	James B. Ingersoll	agents A. Hardy & Co. and Webster & Co.,
	" *Ashburton*	550	J. Taylor	Hardy dispatching eight ships and Webster
	" *Costello*	587	Horace A. Gray	seven, sailing 5th and 20th of month. Hardy
	" *James N. Cooper*	549	B. Lovett	retained name Crescent City Line and Web-
	" *Northampton*	983	W. Reed	ster called his line the Webster Line. Both
	" *General Taylor*	597	S. B. Mitchell	sailed the 5th and 20th as before.
	" *Dirigo*	608	C. Cooper	Crocker, Hardy & Co., 5 Tower Chambers,
	" *Sheffield*	590	Christopher Lewis	became Liverpool agents in Dec. 1853.
	" *Henry H. Boody*	665	J. Snow	
	" *Hamlet*	760	Eben Sears	
	" *Charles Cooper*	977	William A. Cutts	
	" *Sea Flower*	1024	Bailey Loring	
	" *Constellation*	587	Horace A. Gray	
	" *Volant*	457	H. B. Sears	
	" *Caroline & Mary Clark*	813	Richards	
1854	Sp. *John Hancock*	760	J. L. Carney	Jacot, Taylor & Tipper became Liverpool
	" *Franklin King*	1108	John Borland	agents.
1855	Sp. *Charles Buck*	1424	W. W. Smalley	Line irregular and under reduced schedule in
	" *Rockaway*	825	S. R. Goodwin	1855 although it continued to send an occa-
	" *Tirrell*	943	Thomas G. Hiler	sional ship; firm became Taylor, Tipper &
				Co. in 1858.
1856	Sp. *Carlyle*	1181	Robert W. Simpson	
	" *Chicora*	467	F. W. Sawyer	

WHITE STAR LINE

Pilkington & Wilson, Commercial Bldgs., Water Street, Liverpool agents.

YEAR	VESSEL	TONS	MASTERS	REMARKS
1852	Sp. *Ellen Maria*	775	A. Whitmore	
	" *Osborne*	596	Robert T. Nowell	
	" *Samuel Lawrence*	1035	H. A. Patten	
	" *International*	1003	David Brown, Jr.	
	" *Tantivy* (British)	840	J. Spencer	
	" *Otomco*	600	Abner Howes	
	" *Hartley*	496	Charles M. Morrill	
	" *Windermere*	1107	John W. Fairchild	
1853	Sp. *Lexington*	953	J. Murphy	
	" *Waban*	706	A. B. Day	
	" *Olympus*	744	Horace A. Wilson	
	" *May Flower*	807	E. Crabtree	
	" *Neva*	849	M. C. Maling	
	" *Holyoke*	459	J. P. Perkins	
	" *Fanny Giffney*	745	Henry Moody	
	" *H. M. Hayes*	1271	D. Elliott	
1854	Sp. *Horizon*	963	Charles Thompson	
	" *R. C. Johnson*	1300	J. H. Cousins	
	" *Ophelia*	597	W. B. Nason	Var. Mason.
	" *Mary Ward*	594	G. W. Nowell	
	" *Onward*	791	Jonathan Chase	
1855	Sp. *Levitt Storer*	880	F. Green	Var. *Levett Storer.*

WHITE STAR LINE (*continued*)

YEAR	VESSEL	TONS	MASTERS	REMARKS
1855	Sp. *William Nelson*	1039	Charles Cheever	Pilkington Bros., 17 Water Street, became
"	*Weymouth*	1370	D. Elliott, 2nd	Liverpool agents. No indication that ships
"	*Crimea*	900	G. W. Nowell	continued to sail under White Star flag. Line
"	*Scotland*	821	D. Burt	ended this year but Pilkington Bros. sent an
				occasional ship through 1857.

REGULAR LINE

English & Brandon, 2 Rumford Place, Liverpool agents. J. P. Whitney & Co., New Orleans agents. English & Brandon very active in New Orleans trade in 1853, but did not announce establishment of line until 1854. Established Feb., 1854.

YEAR	VESSEL	TONS	MASTERS	REMARKS
1854	Sp. *Shanghai*	650	Horace A. Gray	
"	*Josiah Bradlee*	648	J. M. Boysen	
"	*Marshfield*	999	Joseph Torrey	
"	*George Green*	868	Saint Croix Redman	Var. Rodman.
"	*Cromwell*	748	James Ball	
"	*Favorite*	777	John E. Thomas	
"	*Charles Sprague*	743	W. F. Pike	
"	*Germanicus*	1167	Arthur M. Fales	
"	*Meridian*	1300	James Simpson	
"	*Lizzie Harward*	868	W. Robinson	
"	*Windermere*	1107	Horace A. Wilson	
1855	Sp. *Jersey*	849	Tully Crosby	Line sailed from Liverpool the 1st and 15th
"	*Bell Rock*	780	Francis Pendleton	of month.
"	*Ann Washburn*	861	J. B. Minot	
"	*Pyramid*	798	Dunbar Henderson	
1856	Sp. *St. Charles*	798	Thomas Conway	Boult, English & Brandon became Liverpool
"	*Carnatic*	602	John Devereux	agents.
"	*John Cottle*	1745	R. S. Hallowell	
"	*Mongolia*	967	William Barnes	
"	*Western Chief*	997	John Dyer	
"	*Mary & Susan*	550	Thomas Scott	
"	*R. B. Sumner*	924	Elisha Dyer	
1857	Sp. *Addie Snow*	990	Octavius Howe	
"	*John H. Jarvis*	741	George W. Collier	
"	*Marcia Greenleaf*	1177	Richard Merryman	
"	*American Union*	999	Albert C. Otis	
"	*Charles S. Pennell*	975	George M. Melcher	
"	*Castine*	962	James Simpson	
"	*Golden Eagle*	1273	Edward P. Stone	
"	*R. Jacobs*	1122	James Henderson	
"	*St. James*	1175	James Coley (Colley)	
"	*Thomas Jefferson*	989	T. Hill	
"	*Susan Hicks*	783	F. F. Claussen	
1858	Sp. *Old England*	917	Frank Delano	
"	*Alice Tainter* (Bark)	667	W. M. Post	
"	*Knickerbocker*	875	J. E. Barstow	Lost on the Abaco, May 1858.
"	*Artisan*	924	George Pollard	
"	*Edward Hyman*	1056	Thomas M. Neill	Var. McNeill.
"	*Henrietta Marcy*	1098	George Nickerson	
"	*Dictator*	1293	Albert Zerega	
"	*Ariel*	1329	Frank Delano	H. W. Green master in 1859.
"	*Barnabas Webb*	1300	Alfred Watts	
"	*Ironsides*	1318	Joseph H. Curtis	
"	*B. S. Kimball*	1125	J. F. Hosmer	
"	*James F. Patten*	980	Seth P. Woodward	Var. Seth T. Woodward.
"	*Felicia*	1243	James Ball	Var. Balls.
1859	Sp. *Arno*	916	J. W. Deering	
"	*Wurtemburg*	840	S. B. McLellan	Var. *Wurtemberg*.
"	*New England*	922	George W. Edge	
"	*Arizona*	744	George M. Roberts	
"	*Regulus*	600	Joshua Thompson	
"	*Constitution*	999	John Higgins	
"	*Peter Marcy*	821		

REGULAR LINE (CONTINUED)

YEAR	VESSEL	TONS	MASTERS	REMARKS
1859	Sp. *Robert Harding*	760	John Dyer	
	" *John Merrick*	692	E. Crabtree	
	" *Assyria*	1363	John P. Delano	
	" *Sarah E. Pettigrew*	1192	James H. Burdick	
	" *Volant*	896	S. P. Bray	
	" *Carlyle*	1181	Robert W. Simpson	Var. Robert H. Simpson.
	" *Yorick*	1787	F. B. Soule	Cammack & Converse succeeded J. P.
	" *Emily A. Hall*	1015	Abel Sawyer	Whitney & Co. as New Orleans agents, Sept.,
	" *Compromise*	794	John H. Child	1859.
	" *Levi Woodbury*	998	S. Young	
	" *Joseph Clark*	1094	Walter Emerson	
	" *Potomac*	1198	William Reed	
1860	Sp. *Picayune*	960	J. H. Brooks	
	" *George West*	1071	Robert Couch	
	" *Georgiana*	1100	John Salter	
	" *J. F. Chapman*	1035	J. F. Chapman	
	" *Golden Cross*	1097	Davies	
	" *Vanguard*	1196	J. M. Norton	
	" *Frank Pierce*	1145	C. H. Brooks	
	" *Crimea*	900	T. Lord	
	" *Corinthian*	1098	S. H. Sweetzer	
	" *William Singer*	1142	Robert Marshall	
	" *Thomas Hammond*	975	W. F. Robinson	
	" *Endymion*	1327	William Williams	
	" *Conquest*	1064	Winthrop Sears	
	" *J. Webster Clark*	1318	H. Kopperholdt	
	" *Pocahontas*	995	B. F. Delano	

New Orleans—Hamburg

SAGORY'S LINE

Charles Sagory & Co., New Orleans agents. Established 1852. Line ran through 1860.

YEAR	VESSEL	TONS	MASTERS	REMARKS
1852	Sp. *Wurtemberg*	840	Charles Sagory	
	" *Heidelberg*	1053	Charles Sagory	Frederick G. Rodewald master in 1856–60.
1854	Sp. *Johannisberg*	1098	George Ulrick	
	" *Nuremberg*	1086	Schneider	
	" *Gottenberg*	1092	T. Weeks	

Coastal Lines

SECTION 1. BOSTON—NEW YORK

DISPATCH LINE

Stanton, Fiske & Nichols, 19 Central Wharf, and John Hallett, 10 India St. Wharf, Boston agents. S. H. Herrick & Co., and Van Nortwick & Miller, 23 Coenties Slip, New York agents. Line established Mar., 1821, to sail each Saturday.

YEAR		VESSEL	TONS	MASTERS	REMARKS
1821	Sl.	*Orion*	96	D. Godfrey, Jr.	
	"	*Glib*	75	George Lovell	
	"	*MacDonough*	76	Ezra Lewis	
	"	*Mechanic*	60	Benjamin Hallett	E. Nickerson master in 1822.
1822	Sl.	*Echo*	99	George Lovell	Beginning Mar. 1822, line consisted of six
	"	*Sabine*	76	Mulford Howes, Jr.	sloops sailing each Sat. and Wed. when necessary.
1824	Sch.	*Eclipse*	87	Ezra Lewis	Spofford & Tileston added as New York
	"	*Wave*	94	Mulford Howes, Jr.	agents. Sailed each Wed. and Sat.
	"	*Spy*	98	Joshua Nickerson	
1825	Sch.	*Greek*	119	Joseph Nickerson	
	"	*Mirror*	109	Zenas Bassett	
1827	Sch.	*Turk*	103	D. Godfrey, Jr.	
	"	*Sun*	128	Mulford Howes, Jr.	
	"	*Advance*	83	J. Lewis	
1830	Sch.	*Trio*	141	Joseph Nickerson	
	"	*Warrior*	117	George Lovell	
	"	*Tremont*	129	Isaiah Lewis	
1833	Sch.	*Renown*	140	George Lovell	E. & J. Herrick and Howes, Godfrey &
	"	*Page*	149	Zenas D. Bassett	Robinson became New York agents in 1833;
	"	*Jasper*	157	William Howes	Nichols & Whitney, Davis & Blake and Jas. S. Wilder & Co., Boston agents.
1841	Sch.	*Samuel H. Appleton*	177	Franklin Nickerson	
1845	Sch.	*Homer*	175	M. N. Kent	Howes & Godfrey replaced Howes, Godfrey & Robinson in 1845.
					C. Lovell and Adolphus Davis replaced Davis & Blake in 1846.
1847	Sch.	*Era*	188	J. M. Chamberlin	Alpheus Mayo master in 1860.
					E. & W. Herrick replaced E. & J. Herrick in 1860.
1849	Sch.	*Cabot*	199	Moses Taylor	E. W. Hamilton master in 1860.
1853	Sch.	*G. L.*	197	Warren Lovell	
1854	Sch.	*Glide*	110	Warren Lovell	
1856	Sch.	*Howard*	185	William O. Parker	
1859	Sch.	*American Belle*	198	Albert Chase	W. T. Herrick, 28 Coenties Slip, New York agent.
1860	Sch.	*Lottie*	237	Moses Taylor	Alfred C. Hersey & Cornelius Lovell became
	"	*Lacon*	178	Richard L. Bearse	Boston agents. Line consisted of five schooners. James W. McKee, New York agent.

UNION LINE OF SLOOPS

J. D. & M. Williams and Everitt, Childs & Co., Boston agents. T. N. Wood, 62 Wall St., and S. S. Newman, Burling Slip, New York agents. Line established Mar., 1822, comprising six sloops. Line continued active for many years gradually changing to schooners.

YEAR		VESSEL	TONS	MASTERS	REMARKS
1822	Sl.	*Hero*	85	W. Robenson	John Robenson, Jr., master in 1824; Robinson probably correct spelling.
	"	*Fulton*	78	Joseph W. Davis	

UNION LINE OF SLOOPS (*continued*)

YEAR	VESSEL	TONS	MASTERS	REMARKS
1822	Sl. *Delight*	84	Sturges Nichols	
	" *Express*	74	Abel Beers	Moses Bulkley master in 1826.
	" *William*	69	Jonathan Bangs	
	" *Laura*	57	Jonathan Bangs	Lot Bulkley master in 1827.
	" *Boston*	82	John Osborn, Jr.	All original vessels of line owned in Fairfield
	" *Manilla*	83	Walter Perry	district.
				Anson G. Phelps, 191 Front St., and David G. Hubbard became New York agents in May, 1822, and three new sloops substituted in the line. Spofford & Tileston became New York agents in October.
1825	Sl. *Comet*	76	Ebenezer Silliman	Walter Perry master in 1827.
	" *Globe*	95	Joseph W. Davis	Zalmon B. Wakeman master in 1829.

NEW LINE

Horace Scudder & Co., 14 Central Wharf, and John H. Smith, Boston agents. M. & J. Brett, 47 Front St., Samuel S. Conant, 27 South St., and S. Griggs, 17 South St., New York agents. Line, consisting of one schooner and four sloops, established in 1825, and started operations on Mar. 24th, sailing Wed. and Sat. from each port.

YEAR	VESSEL	TONS	MASTERS	REMARKS
1825	Sch. *Atlantic*	79	Alexander Baxter	
	Sl. *Eliza Ann*	41	Richard Gould, Jr.	
	" *Ocean*	81	Joseph Lewis	
	" *Dispatch*	105	Heman Smith	
	" *Mechanic*	60	Thomas Sparrow	
1826	Sl. *Globe*	95	Timothy Baker	Conant & Codman, 27 South St., became
	Sch. *Jew*	187	Richard Gould	New York agents in 1826.
	" *Gentile*	100	Heman Smith	Samuel H. Howes master in 1831.
	" *Chariot*	115	Alexander Baxter	
1827	Sch. *Mohican*	107	Thomas Sparrow	Four best schooners to run through winter.
1829	Sch. *Champion*	121	Seth Baker	
	" *Boston*	138	Richard Gould	
	" *General Stark*	120	Alexander Baxter	
1831	Sch. *Oscar*	145	Timothy Baker	Lewis & Jenkins, Coenties Slip, New York
	" *Pequot*	149	Joshua Baker	agents.
1832	Sch. *Splendid*	152	William Baker	Ryder & Lewis and Martin W. Brett, New York agents.
1835	Sch. *Compliance*	144	Thomas Sparrow, Jr.	Nelson Kelly master in 1844.
	" *Excel*	139	Timothy Baker	Frederick Lovell master in 1844.
1837	Sch. *Trio*	141	Thomas J. Nickerson	
	" *Page*	149	H. Hallett	
	" *Convoy*	81	Zadock Crowell	
1842	Sch. *Victor*	167	Jacob P. Hallet	Horace Scudder & Chas. Siders, Boston
	" *Fancy*	137	Herman Chase	agents. Ezra Lewis, Coenties Slip, New York agent. In 1844 line consisted of six schooners sailing every Wed. and Sat.
1845	Sch. *Howard*	185	Timothy Baker, Jr.	Foster & Nickerson, New York agents in 1845.
1847	Sch. *Andrew Brown*	127	David A. Allen	
1848	Sch. *Louisa*	185	Joshua A. Chase	
	" *Lewis*	195	Gorham Crowell	
	" *Enterprise*		Jeptha Sears	
1850	Sch. *Granite State*	199	Jacob P. Hallet	Ezra Lewis, 2 Coenties Slip, New York agent.
	" *Tom Kearney*		Frederick Lovell	
1853	Sch. *Copia*	165	M. Sears	Bearse master in 1860.
				Name changed to Scudder & Co.'s Line.
1854	Sch. *Roxbury*	118	D. Brown	Charles Siders & Co., Boston agents with H.
	" *L. H. Nickerson*	181	Anthony Chase, Jr.	Scudder & Co. in 1857.
1858	Sch. *Susan*	186	Loring	
1859	Sch. *Princess*	247	Frederick Lovell	
1860	Sch. *Millard Filmore*	240	J. A. Chase	S. W. Lewis & Co., New York agents. Chas.
	" *Samuel Gilman*	197	Abner T. Crowell	Siders & Co., Boston agents.

COMMERCIAL LINE

Wm. Parker & Co., 116 State St., Bigelow & Bangs, 15 Long Wharf, Ezra Whiton, Jr., and Bixby, Valentine & Co., Boston agents. Hart, Herrick & Co., 19 South St., New York agents. Sailed twice weekly.

YEAR	VESSEL	TONS	MASTERS	REMARKS
1830	Sch. *Henry*	121	Hezekiah Davis	
	" *Vesper*	98	Zalmon B. Wakeman	
	" *Banner*	97	Stiles Bulkley	
	Sl. *Express*	74	Stiles Bulkley	
	" *Hero*	85	P. Beers	
	" *Helen*	83	Jonathan Burr, Jr.	
	" *Manchester*	119	Henry Baker	
	" *New York*	72	Gideon Allen	Charles Allen master in 1831.
1831	Sch. *Orleans*	125	J. W. Davis	Stevens & Palmer, 39 Burling Slip, added as
	" *Rochester*	127	Ebenezer Silliman	New York agents.
	" *Hudson*	136	L. Wells	
	" *Mail*	149	Stiles Bulkley	
1834	Sch. *Reeside*	149	Seth Hallet	Stanley, Reed & Co. and John J. Valentine,
	" *Cambridge*	150	B. K. Hale	Boston agents.
1835	Sch. *Wm. Roscoe*	168	Joseph W. Davis	Stanley, Reed & Co., sole Boston agents.
1836	Sch. *Tasso*	100	Howes	Stanley, Reed & Co., and Ezra Whiton, John Stevens, Burling Slip, New York agents.
1838	Sch. *Abbott Lawrence*	179	Darius Meeker	
1840	Sch. *Wolcott*	181	Elijah L. Ryder	J. D. & M. Williams and Geo. Dimon, Boston agents.
1841	Sch. *Cornelia*	197	Henry Perry	John Stevens and E. D. Sprague, New York agents. Ezra Whiton, Jr., replaced George Dimon. Line composed of nine schooners.

MERCHANTS' LINE

Josiah Stickney, Joshua Sears and Benj. Conant, Boston agents. A. & T.F. Cornell & Charles Seguine, New York agents. Established Jan., 1834.

YEAR	VESSEL	TONS	MASTERS	REMARKS
1834	Sch. *Warrior*	117	Seth E. Hardy	
	" *Spy*	114	Joshua Chamberlin	
	" *New Jersey*	151	E. S. Hardy	
	" *Phoebe Baxter*	99	Obed Baxter	Also reported Hebe Baxter.
	" *William Wallace*	120	Freeman Baker, Jr.	
	" *Nile*	109	Josiah Baker	
	" *Jasper*	157	B. C. Howes	
	" *Empire*	119	Reuben Baker	
1835	Sch. *Mohican*	107	Abner Crowell	Seth E. Hardy & Co., Boston agent in Sept.
	" *Empire*	119	Reuben Baker	
	" *Glide*	151	Jonathan Godfrey, Jr.	
	" *Henry*	121	George Dimon	
1836	Sch. *Fairfield*	99	E. Chase	Ephraim Burr master in 1837.
	" *John Allyne*	104	W. Myrick	Reuben Collins, Jr., master in 1841.
	" *Union*	85	I. Chase	
1837	Sch. *Salem*	99	A. Eldridge	Alpheus Hardy, Boston agent.
	" *Friend*	149	Judah Baker	
	" *Wave*	118	Caleb Nickerson	James S. Higgins master in 1839.
	" *Convoy*	82	Howes Baker	
1838	Sch. *Torch*	123	Caleb Nickerson	Hardy & Baker, Boston agents.
	" *Grecian*	152	Austin Matson	J. Atkins & Co., 38 South St., New York
	" *Marietta*	118	Austin Matson	agents.
	" *Benjamin Bigelow*	154	Francis Wells	
	" *Edwin*	103	Peleg Howes	
1839	Sch. *Albert M. Hale*	135	E. Chase	
1842	Sch. *John Cooley & Co.*	184	Asa Eldridge	J. H. Rogers added as a Boston agent. H. Claflin, 29 Old Slip, New York agent. Hardy, Baker & Morrill, Boston agents.
1846	Sch. *Lacon*	178	Robert L. Bearse	
1848	Sch. *Cyrus Chamberlain*	135	Phineas S. Berry	
	" *American Belle*	198	Rodney Baxter	
	" *Richard Rush*	73	Elnathan Crowell	

MERCHANTS' LINE (*continued*)

YEAR	VESSEL	TONS	MASTERS	REMARKS
1850	Sch. *Emma*	196	Alexander Lovell	
1855	Sch. *Jane P. Glover*	87	Doane	Freeman Baker, Jr. & Son, Boston agents.
"	*Charles Henry*	118	C. Baker	Crowell & Hazard, 26 Coenties Slip, New
"	*Cora*	100	J. B. Nickerson	York agents.
"	*Gen. Clinch*	131	Jeptha Baker	
"	*E. T. Lewis*	133	Crowell	
"	*Albert Dexter*	138	Nickerson	
"	*Henry Gibbs*	95	F. Snow	
"	*Charm*	173	F. Nickerson	
"	*Corelli*		Eldridge	
"	*Chauncey St. John*	86	Wright	
1856	Sch. *Sarah Elizabeth*	101	Bearse	Samuel Crowell, New York agent.
"	*Pavilion*	129		
"	*Moses Waring*	98	Hallet	F. T. Crowell master in 1858.
"	*Knight*	164	Jeptha B. Sears	
"	*Fakir*	99	Joshua F. Dickens	

HARDY'S LINE

Seth E. Hardy, 9 Commercial Wharf, Boston agent. Ezra Lewis, New York agent. Hardy, who had been running packets to New York irregularly, gave notice of establishment of Hardy's Line in Apr., 1843. The line was not composed of definite vessels but of schooners chartered or otherwise contracted for as needed, but sailing in close and fairly regular succession three or four times a month. A partial list of vessels so dispatched follows.

YEAR	VESSEL	TONS	MASTERS	REMARKS
1843	Sch. *Mandarin*	95	Leander Hinckley	
"	*Victor*	48	J. Gould	
"	*Anaconda*	58	T. Hall	
"	*Henry*	121	John K. Nickerson	
"	*Telegraph*	85	Seth Nickerson	
"	*Utica*	136	Austin Bearse	
"	*Thomas Hooper*	99	Abijah B. Mayo	
"	*Deposit*	81	Josiah Kendrick, Jr.	
"	*Augusta*	99	L. W. Nickerson	
"	*Rubicon*	117	Doane	
"	*Clinton*	83	Harding	
"	*Phoebe Eliza*	178	William Osborn	
"	*Velocity*	85	A. Montgomery	
"	*Lexington*	96	H. Crowell	
"	*Harvest*	96	J. C. Kelley	
1844	Sch. *Pilgrim*	121	Thomas Dodge	Daniel S. Kendall, 1 Comey's Wharf, added
"	*Dodge*	196	Rufus Knapp	as Boston agent.
"	*Ganges*	95	Allen	
"	*Wankingo*	66	E. Crowell, Jr.	
"	*Henry Curtis*	99	Jonathan Hallet, Jr.	
"	*Chief*	145	S. Reeves	
"	*Frances Hallet*	79	Lewis	Freeman Crowell master in 1848.
"	*Constitution*	168	Joab Endicott	
"	*Aranzimanda*	89	Hatch	Var. *Arenzamendi*.
1845	Sch. *Perseverance*	83	Denight	Line called Lewis's Line. Ezra Lewis, New
"	*Orleans*	125	George W. Segee	York agent.
"	*Lady Clinton*	121	Joseph B. Kramer	
"	*Boston*	104	Jonathan Collins	
"	*Red Jacket*	156	Samuel Dearborn	

HERSEY'S LINE. Later NEW ENGLAND LINE.

A. C. Hersey, 67 Commercial Wharf, and Bigelow & Cunningham, Boston agents. Foster & Nickerson, New York agents.

YEAR	VESSEL	TONS	MASTERS	REMARKS
1846	Sch. *Cinderella*	91	Sylvester Crowell	
"	*Nimrod*	99	Hiram Baker	
"	*Mariner*	117	Nickerson	
"	*Mary C. Ames*	108	Eleazer P. Short	
"	*Ornament*	74	John W. Waitt	Var. Waite.

HERSEY'S LINE (*continued*)

YEAR		VESSEL	TONS	MASTERS	REMARKS
1846	Sch.	*Mankin*	198	Lucas B. Terry	
	Bg.	*Will*	156	George W. Collins	Var. Collings.
	Sch.	*Jerome*	105	Joseph H. Parker	
	"	*Charleston Packet*	99	Prentice Thatcher	
	"	*October*	114	Alpheus Baxter	
	"	*Two Marys*	116	Leonard Chase	
	"	*Isis*	167	J. Simmons	
	"	*Maria M. Klots*	148	Luke B. Chase	
1847	Sch.	*Croton*	148	Luke B. Chase	
	"	*Ellen*	166	Joseph H. Brown	
	"	*John Q. Adams*	161	John Morris	
	"	*Star*	96	James Smalley, Jr.	
	Bk.	*Carib*	205	Bacon	Albert Dunbar master in 1848.
	Sch.	*David Cox*	141	Samuel Nickerson	
	"	*John O. Ireland*	114	Luther Crowell	
	"	*Abby P. Chase*	150	Freeman Chase	
	"	*James Barbour*	76	Jonathan Baker	
1848	Sch.	*L. H. Nickerson*	181	Samuel Nickerson	A. C. Hersey & Samuel Bigelow became
	"	*Alabama*	140	Willard Gorham	Boston agents.
1853	Sch.	*Charter Oak*	139	E. C. Kelley	Samuel Bigelow, sole Boston agent.
	"	*Mercy Taylor*	143	Cyrus Nickerson	
	"	*Renown*	140	George Crowell	
1854	Sch.	*C. & N. Rogers*	98	T. S. Rogers	
	"	*Knight*	164	Jeptha B. Sears	
	Bk.	*Exact*	431	Thomas Grumley	
1855	Sch.	*Virginia Price*	175	L. Case	James W. McKee, 42 Front St., New York
	"	*T. O. Thompson*	131	Elnathan Baker	agent. Line called McKee's Line in New York.
1856	Sch.	*David Howes*		Wixon	
1857	Sch.	*John Knight*	96	Sawyer	William H. Law master in 1858.
	Bk.	*Storm Bird*	496	Henry C. Small	
1858	Sch.	*Ann S. Cannon*	196	A. P. Nowell	Var. Norwall.
	Sp.	*Meridian*	1453	Crowell	William Elliott, 115 Wall St., New York agent.
1859	Sch.	*Harrison E. Weston*	156	James L. Maloy	Alfred C. Hersey and C. Lovell, Boston agents, 1860.

SECTION 2. BOSTON—ALBANY & TROY

REGULAR LINE

Davis & Center, Albany agents. Joseph Attwood, Philadelphia Packet Wharf, Boston agent.

YEAR		VESSEL	TONS	MASTERS	REMARKS
1822	Sl.	*George Washington*	106	D. Attwood	
	"	*Visscher*	118	W. Ingraham	
	"	*Native*	83	Austin Matson	
1824	Sl.	*Gen. Brown*	146	Joseph Attwood	Robert Lyon became Boston agent.
	"	*Mary*	96	Austin Matson	
	"	*Albany*	76		
1825	Sch.	*Enterprise*	106	Philander Daggett	
1833	Sch.	*Victor*	167	Amaziah Atwood, 2nd	Bigelow & Bangs, Boston agents; L. Gay &
	"	*Benjamin Bigelow*	154	Francis Wells	N. Davis, Albany agents; and T. P. Bigelow,
	"	*Grecian*	153	Austin Matson	Troy agent.
	"	*Deborah*	114	D. A. Allen	Isaiah Bangs, 15 Long Wharf, Boston agent, 1835.
1837	Sch.	*Stranger*	87	Nelson Bearse	Bangs & Alcott, Boston agents.
	"	*Niagara*	88	Andrew Lovell	Gay & Willard, Albany and Troy agents.
	"	*Albany*	99	Edwin Scudder	
	"	*Henry Curtis*	98	Austin Bearse	
1838	Sch.	*Louisa*	108	Lot Hinckley	Called Bangs' Regular Line in 1841. Isaiah
	"	*Vintage*	98	Sylvester Bearse	Bangs sole Boston agent. Line continued to
	"	*Detroit*	100	John Cammett	run for some years.

NEW LINE

David R. Griggs, 12 Long Wharf, Boston agent. E. W. Whiting, 77 Quay St., Albany agent. Established June, 1828.

YEAR	VESSEL	TONS	MASTERS	REMARKS
1828	Sch. *Alert*	91	Sewell Fessenden	
	" *Ellen*		H. H. Stimson	
	Sl. *Ocean*	82	Joseph Lewis	
	" *Avon*	60	Philander Scudder	
	" *Diamond*	78	Wilson Crosby	
1836	Sch. *William Seymour*	127	George K. Miller	Davis, Snow & Co., 9 City Wharf, Boston
	" *Henry Franklin*	83	Ansel Matthews	agents.
	" *Florence*	84	Thomas L. Adams	William Chapman & J. K. Wing, Albany
	" *Clarion*	81	S. C. Ames	agents.
				Sailed once a week from north side of City Wharf.
1837	Sch. *Ornament*	74	H. Scudder	"All vessels register about 100 tons."
	" *Baltic*	86	I. Hinckley	Schs. *Henry Franklin* and *Clarion* retained and
	" *Oliver*	92	David Fuller	line provided biweekly sailings.
	" *Ganges*	95	W. Hinckley	David Snow, 2 City Wharf, became Boston
	" *Banner*	90	E. Lewis	agent.
	" *Balance*	75	Isaac Hodges	
	" *Henry Curtis*	99	Austin Bearse	
1839	Sch. *Condor*	100	Isaac Hodges	David Snow & Wing & Scudder, Boston
	" *Henrietta Matilda*		S. C. Ames	agents, C. W. Bentley, Albany agent, in 1841.
1846	Sch. *Daniel Webster*	122	Cornelius Lovell	Scudder, Chipman & Co., Boston agents.
	" *Saginaw*	95	Lot Hinckley	J. K. Wing of Albany retired from firm of
	" *William H. Turner*	120	Wright	Howes, Scudder & Co.
	" *Lavinia*	65	Isaiah Nickerson	

COMMERCIAL LINE

Chipman & Baker, 47 Commercial St., Boston agents. Charles T. Smyth, 40 Quay St., Albany agent.

YEAR	VESSEL	TONS	MASTERS	REMARKS
1840	Sch. *Nimrod*	99	D. Linnell, Jr.	
	" *Montano*	86	J. W. Crowell	
	" *Utica*	136	Austin Bearse	
	" *Eliza Matilda*	89	Joseph D. Crowell	
	" *Two Marys*	116	Cornelius Lovell	
	" *Balance*	75	H. Linnell	
	" *Talent*	87	J. Bates	
	" *Tigris*	75	E. Lewis	
1842	Sch. *Saginaw*	95	Cornelius Lovell	Horace Scudder & Co., and Charles Siders, Boston agents.
1845	Sch. *Convert*	96	Asa Coleman	
	" *Aeriel*		C. W. Boult	Var. *Aerial.*
	" *Amanda*		Nickerson	Foster & Doane, 18 City Wharf, Boston
	" *Elizabeth*	97	Baker	agents. Sailed weekly.
	" *Spy*	114	Hawkins	
	" *Camella*		George Faulklin	
	" *Juno*	107	J. Kelly	Var. *Seeley.*
	" *Isabella*	150	James Nickerson	
1847	Sch. *Wolcott*	182	Elisha L. Ryder	Dayton & Sprague, New York agents, 1849.
	" *New York*	187	Curtis B. Goodsell	
1851	Sch. *Plymouth Rock*	198	Brutus Lacey	T. J. Norris master in 1860.
1854	Sch. *Bay State*	199	Henry Sherwood	Curtis & Peabody and E. Whiton, Boston
	" *Mary Mankin*	232	William Beers	agents. E. D. Sprague, 107 Front St., New York agents.
1858	Sch. *James Lawrence*	195	Gershom B. Allen	Line consisted of eight schooners of about 200
	" *J. W.*	250	George Faulklin	tons, sailing each Wed. and Sat., full or not full.
1860	Sch. *Gazette*	149	C. W. Boult	Curtis & Peabody and H. Davis, Boston
	" *Oregon*	114	John Bates	agents in 1860.
	" *Galota*	145	H. S. Lovell	
	" *Daniel Webster*	122	Isaac Hodges	
	" *Empire*	119	C. A. Lovell	
	" *Glide*	110	Daniel Lovell	
	" *Ann T. Stipple*	148	Alexander Bacon	Var. *Sipple.*

PEARSON & CO.'S LINE

John H. Pearson & Co., 75 Long Wharf, Boston agent. Charles T. Smyth, Albany agent. Line established Apr., 1846. Bangs Harding added as Boston agent in Aug.

YEAR	VESSEL	TONS	MASTERS	REMARKS
1846	Sch. *Clarion*	81	Lovell	
"	*Oliver*	94	Hallet	
"	*Convert*	96	Asa Coleman	
"	*Benjamin H. Field*		S. L. Boult	
"	*Nimrod*	99	J. C. Parker	
"	*Aeriel*		C. W. Boult	
"	*Highlander*	94	S. Nickerson	

BENTLEY'S LINE

A. W. Bentley & Co., 83 Quay St., Albany agents. John J. Newcomb, 133 State St., Boston agent. Line established May, 1853, sailed semi-weekly.

YEAR	VESSEL	TONS	MASTERS	REMARKS
1853	Sch. *Montano*	86	James West	
"	*Mary*	96	Lewis Crosby	
"	*Oliver*	94	David Fuller	
"	*Banner*	97	Horace Lovell	
"	*Andrew Brown*	127	Austin Lowell	
"	*Albany*	99	Isaac Hodges	
"	*Glide*	110	Daniel Lovell	
"	*Susan*	101	Handy	

SECTION 3. BOSTON—PHILADELPHIA

UNION LINE. Later REGULAR LINE.

Grants & Stone, 43 N. Water St., and Moody, Wyman & Co., 10 S. Wharves, Philadelphia agents. A. C. Barclay & Co., also agent for some vessels for a time. Stanton, Fiske & Nichols, 19 Central Wharf, and Calvin Bailey, Boston agents. Established Feb., 1821, sailed each Sat. throughout season.

YEAR	VESSEL	TONS	MASTER	REMARKS
1821	Sch. *Mexican*	106	Moses Whiton, Jr.	Hawkes Loring master in 1824.
"	*Delaware*	98	Timothy House	Line in general consisted of five or six schoon-
"	*Pilot*	99	Thomas Cobb	ers sailing weekly.
"	*Eliza Jane*	109	Thomas Milton	
"	*Regulator*	74	Presbury Luce	
1822	Sch. *Echo*	99	Presbury Luce	
1823	Sch. *Hector*	99	Lot Gage	Wyman & Hazeltine replaced Moody, Wy-
"	*Benjamin Franklin*	98	Josiah Wing	man & Co. in 1823.
"	*William Penn*	99	Josiah Rogers	
1824	Sch. *Lovely Hope*	95	Barnabas Lincoln	Russell & Hinckling replaced Calvin Bailey
	Bg. *Emeline*	99	Reuben Horton	in 1824. Become Regular Line.
1825	Sch. *Brilliant*	98	John Amazeen	
1828	Bg. *Palm*	166	Barnabas Lincoln	
"	*Acorn*	126	Timothy House	
"	*Thorn*	132	Presbury Luce	
1830	Bg. *Georgiana*	134	J. Thatcher	Stanton, Nichols & Co. and Rice & Thaxter, Boston agents in 1830. Grants & Stone sole Philadelphia agents.
1832	Bg. *Swan*	148	Zenas Atkins	
"	*Ella*	164	Nathaniel Matthews	
1834	Bg. *Sylph*	195	Joshua Atkins	
1837	Bg. *Acorn*	198	Elijah S. Howes	*Acorn* replaced brig *Georgiana*.
"	*Oak*	178	George R. Ryder	Line consisted of five brigs sailing weekly.
"	*Eagle*	142	Pitts Howes	Nichols & Whitney replaced Stanton & Nichols.
1839	Bg. *Pearl*	195	Joshua Atkins, Jr.	
1841	Bg. *Sterling*	201	Jonathan Twining	R. F. Loper & J. Palmer & Co., Philadelphia agents.
1842	Bk. *Pilot*	200	Francis M. Boggs	Joseph Swift master in 1844.
"	*Delaware*	198	William B. Fisher	
"	*Anne Reynolds*	197	Heman Doane	

UNION LINE (*continued*)

YEAR		VESSEL	TONS	MASTERS	REMARKS
1842	Bg.	*Granite*	153	H. Eldridge	
	"	*Peru*	158	Clenrick Crosby	
1843	Bg.	*Home*	137	Baker Howes	
	"	*Eliot*	141	William Baker	
1845	Bk.	*Elk*	198	Moses Nickerson	J. Palmer & Co., sole Philadelphia agents.
	Bg.	*Sun*	184	Josiah N. Flinn	Rice & Thaxter and Richard Howes became
	"	*William Pitt*	175	Abraham Howes	Boston agents. Nichols & Whitney discon-
1847	Bk.	*Elm*	199	James S. Taylor	tinued.
1849	Bk.	*Zion*	199	S. Reynolds	
1852	Bk.	*Oak*	196	Enoch Ryder	Grants & Stone, Philadelphia agents.
1853	Bk.	*Gem*	199	Hezekiah Mayo	M. Nickerson replaced Richard Howes as one
	"	*Echo*	196	Enoch H. Howes	of Boston agents.
1854	Bk.	*Chester*	200	Elijah Crosby	In 1855 Grant & Twells, Philadelphia
	"	*Sarah L. Stevens*	175	Orin Studley	agents. Twells & Co., 5 & 7 S. Wharves, Philadelphia agents. H. Mayo added as Boston agent.
1856	Bk.	*Amy*	298	Stephen G. Hammond	
1858	Sch.	*Sarah A. Hammond*	294	Thomas J. Paine	
	"	*William A. Hammond*	259	John Cain	
	"	*H. W. Morse*	149	J. W. Phillips	Var. *H. S. Morse.*
	"	*Edwin Reed*	226	Barnabas H. Chipman	
	"	*Village Gem*	148	J. N. Hinckley	
1859	Sch.	*E. H. Atwood*	280	Elisha W. Smith	
	"	*Grace Girdler*	226	Lewis Paine	
1860	Sch.	*L. A. Danenhower*	283	Ansel Weeks, Jr.	Twells, Mellon & Co., Philadelphia agents.

UNION REGULAR LINE

A. C. Barclay & Co., Philadelphia agents. Edward & William Reynolds, Boston agents. Line established 1824, using some of the vessels of the original Union Line and sailing every Sat. Usually referred to as the Union Line.

YEAR		VESSEL	TONS	MASTERS	REMARKS
1824	Sch.	*Pilot*	99	Thomas Milton	
	"	*William Penn*	99	Josiah Rogers	
	"	*Benjamin Franklin*	98	Josiah Wing	
	"	*Eliza Jane*	109	Thomas Cobb	
	"	*Delaware*	98	Timothy House	
1826	Bg.	*Benjamin Franklin*	98	Josiah Wing	
	"	*Shawmut*	150	Thomas Cobb	
1832	Bg.	*Echo*	197	Nathan Clark	
	"	*Fairy*	185	Josiah Wing	Heman Doane master in 1837.
	"	*Mohawk*	176	Thomas Howes	Vessel lost Oct. 11, 1846.
	"	*Gem*	162	Nathan Foster	
	"	*Barclay*	167	Nathan Clark	
	"	*Pilot*	148	Thomas Milton	S. P. Snow master in 1834.
1834	Bg.	*Robert Waln*	178	Enoch Clark	Packets sailed from Boston Sat. and from Philadelphia middle of week.
1835	Bg.	*Oswego*	184	N. D. Kelly	
1837	Bg.	*Granite*	153	William B. Fisher	Name changed to Union Line in 1834. Wil-
	"	*Norfolk*		Francis M. Boggs	liam B. Reynolds & Co., and John Albree,
	"	*Pearl*	194	Joshua Atkins, Jr.	Boston agents. Palmer & Hale, Philadelphia
	"	*Peru*	158	Francis M. Boggs	agents, corner Market St. and So. Wharves.
	Sch.	*J. Palmer*	125	David Davidson, Jr.	
	"	*Home*	137	Howes Baker	
1839	Bk.	*Delaware*	198	William B. Fisher	
1840	Bg.	*J. Sears*	144	H. D. Booth	Var. *Joshua Sears*
1841	Bk.	*Anna Reynolds*	197	Heman Doane	
	"	*Mohawk*	198	Henry Eldridge	
1842	Bg.	*Eliot*	141	William Baker	J. Palmer & Co. succeeded Palmer & Hale. John Albree succeeded by Foster & Doane, 18 City Wharf.
1843	Bg.	*Sun*	184	Josiah N. Flinn	
	Sch.	*Fame*	96	Caleb S. Crowell	
	Bg.	*Ocean*	172	Jonathan Eldridge	
1844	Sch.	*Elizabeth*	117	William Baker	Grants & Stone, Philadelphia agents.

UNION REGULAR LINE (*continued*)

YEAR		VESSEL	TONS	MASTERS	REMARKS
1845	Bg.	*Acorn*	198	Elijah S. Howes	
1846	Bg.	*William Pitt*	175	Abraham Howes	
1847	Bg.	*Mail*	191	Edward Lewis	
	Bk.	*General Jesup*	189	William B. Fisher	
1848	Bk.	*Mary F. Slade*	199	Peleg Howes	J. Palmer & Co., returned as Philadelphia agents.
1851	Bk.	*Selah*	199	John Atkins	
	Bg.	*Empire*	197	Peter Crowell	Grant & Twells, Philadelphia agents, 1852.
1856	Bk.	*Elm*	199	J. S. Taylor	Twells & Co., Philadelphia agents.
	"	*Gem*	199	Stephen G. Hammond	Rice & Thaxter, Boston agents.
	"	*Amy*	298	Stephen G. Hammond	
	"	*Oak*	196	Enoch Ryder	
1858	Sch.	*Edwin Read*	226	Barnabas H. Chipman	John S. Twells, Philadelphia agent. Name
	"	*H. W. Morse*		Phillips	changed to Regular Line. David Hooper
	"	*S. A. Hammond*	294	Thomas J. Paine	loaded same vessels.
	"	*Wm. A. Hammond*	259	John Cain	
	"	*Village Gem*	148	J. N. Hinckley	
1859	Sch.	*Grace Girdler*	226	Lewis Paine	Twells, Mellon & Co. became Philadelphia
	"	*L. A. Danenhower*	283	Ansel Weeks, Jr.	agents in 1860.
	"	*E. H. Atwood*	281	Elisha W. Smith	

SCHUYLKILL LINE

John Albree, 34 Commercial Wharf, Boston agent. John Dalzell, Chestnut Street Wharf, Philadelphia agent. Discontinued 1835.

YEAR		VESSEL	TONS	MASTERS	REMARKS
1834	Sch.	*Mechanic*	111	J. Simmons	
	"	*Henry Franklin*	83	Isaiah Hatch	
	"	*Village*	99	Reuben Newcomb	
	"	*Mercy*	99	Obed Baxter	
	"	*Franklin*	91	E. Nickerson	
1835	Sch.	*Wave*	68	Jonathan Nickerson	

DISPATCH LINE

Seth E. Hardy & Co., 16 City Wharf, Boston agents. Palmer & Hale, Philadelphia agents. Established Mar., 1836, sailed every Sat.

YEAR		VESSEL	TONS	MASTERS	REMARKS
1836	Sch.	*Torch*	123	Edmund Flinn	
	"	*Thorn*	114	Joshua Taylor	
	"	*Franklin*	91	John Eldridge	
	"	*New York*	118	George Taylor	
	"	*Pocasset*	76	J. Atkins, Jr.	
	"	*Harriet*	98	George Taylor	
	"	*William Wilson*	97	E. H. Baker	
1837	Bg.	*Man*		Joshua Taylor	Alpheus Hardy, 13 City Wharf, Boston agent.
	"	*Swan*	147	John Eldridge	A(ndrew) C. Barclay & Co., Philadelphia agents, second wharf above Walnut St.
	"	*William Penn*	159	Joshua Taylor	
1838	Sch.	*Hope Howes*	100	Pitts Howes	Hardy & Baker, Boston agents.
1839	Bg.	*William M. Rogers*		George Taylor	Packets sailed every Sat. from head of Baltimore Pier, opposite 44 Commercial Street.
	"	*Benjamin Franklin*	98	Edmund Flinn	
	"	*Eagle*	142	Jonathan Eldridge	
	"	*William Pitt*	175	Howes Baker	Iohn Albree added as Boston agent.
	Sch.	*Home*	137	Howes Baker	
1842	Bk.	*Turk*	197	Jonathan Eldridge	John M. Kennedy & Co., 40 N. Wharves, Philadelphia agents, 1843.
1844	Sch.	*Isaac Franklin*	140	Harding	
	"	*Berry*	97	B. H. Sears	Called Express Line in August.
	"	*Zone*	116	Gideon Crowell	
	"	*Oregon*	94	Carson	
	"	*J. & W. Errickson*	173	David Smith	
1845	Bg.	*Vulture*	140	Benjamin Walker	Hardy, Baker & Morrill & L. T. Lynde became Boston agents.
	"	*Victorine*	239	J. Small	
	"	*Mary H.*	148	Atherton H. Baker	
	Sch.	*Fame*	96	Caleb S. Crowell	

DISPATCH LINE (*continued*)

YEAR	VESSEL	TONS	MASTERS	REMARKS
1845	Sch. *Denmark*	99	J. Crowell	
	Bg. *Emma*	196	Freeman Baker	
1846	Bg. *Paulina*	193	Edmund Flinn	
1848	Bk. *Selah*	199	Joshua Taylor	Alpheus Hardy and L. T. Lynde, Boston agents.
1852	Bg. *Sarah Vose*	153	Joseph Kelley	
1853	Sch. *Edna C.*	179	Joseph Kelley	
1854	Bg. *Rolerson*	196	R. H. Crowell	L. T. Lynde became sole Boston agent, continuing through 1856.
	Sch. *Lacon*	178	Robert L. Bearse	
	" *Cyrus Chamberlain*	135	Hallett	

COMMERCIAL LINE

R. Lincoln & Co., 56 Commercial St., Boston agents. Lincoln & Ryerss, 33 South Wharves, Philadelphia agents. Notice of establishment of line given in 1833, but operation on a substantial scale did not start until 1837.

YEAR	VESSEL	TONS	MASTERS	REMARKS
1837	Bg. *Robert Waln*	178	Oliver Matthews	Horace Scudder & Co. and Alfred C. Hersey, 1 Mercantile Wharf, added as Boston agents.
	" *Lodi*	145	Freeman J. Nickerson	
	" *Ella*	165	Nathaniel Matthews	
	" *Antares*	147	John T. Davis	Packets sailed every Wed.
	" *Impulse*	135	Nathaniel Matthews	
1838	Bg. *Sulla*	145	Nathaniel Matthews	
	Sch. *Osceola*	81	Eleazer Rich	
	" *Richmond*	105	Ellery	
1843	Sch. *Governor Arnold*	94	Smith Bacon	
1844	Bg. *Erie*	278	Baxter	Hersey dropped out in 1845.
1846	Bk. *Mary*	195	B. Whelden	Washburn Baker master in 1851.
	" *Governor Briggs*	198	J. H. Hallet	Lincoln and Scudder dissolved relations in 1847. The Lincolns continued as the Old Commercial Line and the Scudder interests continued as the Commercial Line: The Original and Old Established Line.

PEARSON & CO.'S LINE. Later EXPRESS LINE or PEARSON & CO.'S EXPRESS LINE.

John H. Pearson & Co., Foster's Wharf, Boston agent. Line established in Sept. 1841 by Pearson who had been sending packets to Philadelphia for several months.

YEAR	VESSEL	TONS	MASTERS	REMARKS
1841	Sch. *Lyon*	100	Obed Baxter	
	" *Wave*	118	Peter Crowell	James S. Higgins master in 1844.
	" *Palm*	127	Crowell	
	" *Governor Arnold*	94	Smith Bacon	
	Bg. *Victor*	125	Francis Gorham	
	Sch. *Home*	137	Pitts Howes	
1842	Bg. *Lincoln*	174	Foster Rogers	
	Sch. *Fame*	96	Caleb S. Crowell	
	" *Caroline*	83	Ensign Studley	Asa W. Nickerson master in 1847.
	" *Cinderella*	91	Sylvester Crowell	
1843	Sch. *Phoebe Baxter*	99	F. B. Crowell	
	Bg. *Baltimore*	167	Kimball Eldridge	
1844	Bg. *Esther*	135	Joseph Emery	Var. Emory.
	" *Metamora*		Edmund Flinn	
	Sch. *William Wilson*	97	Obed Baker	
1845	Bg. *Chicopee*	189	Jos. Emery	John H. Howes master in 1860.
1846	Bk. *Laconia*	190	Alfred Howes	
	Bg. *Sun*	184	Josiah N. Flinn	
1847	Sch. *Zone*	99	Elihu Kelley	John W. Baker, 9 No. Wharves, Philadelphia agent.
	Bk. *Nashua*	196	Benj. F. Clifford	
	" *Lowell*	181	Elijah Loveland	Bangs Harding added as Boston agent.
	" *Pioneer*	195	Kimball Eldridge, Jr.	Name changed to Express Line.
1848	Bk. *Vesta*	196	John Flinn	Harding replaced in July by John J. Sperry as Philadelphia agent. Sperry & Cooper, Philadelphia agents, 1851.
1853	Sch. *Frances*	161	Grafton Sears	David Cooper, Philadelphia agent. Israel Whitney Lamson and J. Walter added as Boston agents.

PEARSON & CO.'S LINE (*continued*)

YEAR	VESSEL	TONS	MASTERS	REMARKS
1854	Sch. *Copia*	164	M. Sears	
	Bk. *Mary F. Slade*	199	E. Baker	
	" *Chester*	200	Elijah Crosby	
1856	Bg. *M. & J. C. Gilmore*	185	Alfred Eldridge	
1857	Sch. *John W. Rumsey* (tern)	368	Lewis P. Taylor	
1858	Sch. *Wm. A. Hammond*	259	John Cain	The Regular Line appeared to act jointly
	" *Sarah A. Hammond*	294	Thomas J. Paine	with Express Line in loading some of the
	" *Helen Mar*	195	Jos. H. Tuthill	vessels from 1858 onward.
	" *Courier*	200	Loring	
	" *Frank Herbert* (Cl.)	255	Timothy L. Mayo	Cooper & Twells, Philadelphia agents.
1859	Sch. *Lizzie Maull* (Cl.)	281	Henderson	
	" *E. H. Atwood*	281	Elisha W. Smith	
	" *Grace Girdler*	226	Lewis Paine	
1860	Sch. *L. A. Danenhower*	283	Ansel Weeks, Jr.	

WELLS & CO.'S LINE

Thomas F. Wells & Co., 12 Lewis Wharf, and P. B. Burke & Co., 25 State St., Boston agents. Line established 1843 and consisted of schooners and brigs engaged as required. Operations suspended in summer of 1844.

YEAR	VESSEL	TONS	MASTERS	REMARKS
1843	Sch. *Patmos*	148	William Clark	
	" *Burlington*	96	James Wixon	
	" *Phoebe D.*	116	C. Smith	Burke & Co. ceased operations in Oct. 1843.
	" *H. C. King*		Bailey	
	" *Wellington*	80	Ezekiel Brown	
	" *Evelina*	98	W. C. Chase, Jr.	
	" *Mary*	99	Archelaus F. Trefethen	
	" *Fountain*	75	Samuel York	
	" *Squire & Brothers*	163	Hy. S. Steelman	
	Bg. *Packet*	100	Andrew Clark	
	Sch. *Melvina*	114	Burton	
	" *Talma*	100	Nathan A. Conklin	
	Bg. *Emerald*	169	David Hodgdon	
	" *Vandalier*	166	Nelson Pendleton	
1844	Sch. *Dusky Sally*	87	Davis Humphrey	
	" *Swan*	99	L. Webber	
	" *Brunswick*		Reed	
	" *Council*	99	William Baker	
	" *John*	100	Ephraim Eldridge	

HARDY'S LINE. Later EXPRESS LINE.

Seth E. Hardy, Boston agent. Established Feb., 1844.

YEAR	VESSEL	TONS	MASTERS	REMARKS
1844	Sch. *Isaac Franklin*	140	Harding	Zenas Crosby master in 1847.
	" *Oregon*	94	Carson	
	" *Berry*	97	B. H. Sears	
	" *Zone*	99	Gideon Crowell	
	" *Harriet*	116	Sears	Simeon S. Crowell master in 1850.
	" *Elizabeth*	97	Sears	
	" *A. Marshall*		Johnson	Name changed to Express Line.
	" *J. & W. Errickson*	173	David Smith	
1845	Sch. *Vulture*	140	Benjamin Walker	
	" *Denmark*	99	J. Crowell	
	" *Fame*	96	Caleb S. Crowell	
	Bg. *Victorine*	96	D. H. Small	
	" *Mary H.*	151	Atherton H. Baker	

A. C. HERSEY'S LINE

Alfred C. Hersey, 67 Commercial Wharf, and Bigelow & Cunningham, Packet Office, on said Wharf, Boston agents. John M. Kennedy & Co., 40 N. Wharves, Philadelphia agents. Line established Mar., 1846.

YEAR	VESSEL	TONS	MASTERS	REMARKS
1846	Bg. *Lewis Bruce*	113	C. Studley	
	" *Home*	137	T. Crowell	
	" *Mary H.*	151	Atherton H. Baker	

HERSEY'S LINE (*continued*)

YEAR	VESSEL	TONS	MASTERS	REMARKS
1846	Bg. *Canton*	148	Caleb S. Crowell	Elnathan Baker master in 1848.
	" *Myra*	129	L. Studley	Stephen Hall master in 1848.
	Bk. *Imogene*	179	Samuel Rogers	
	Sch. *Jacob Raymond*	109	Heverin	
	Bk. *True Man*	230	Truman Doane	
1847	Bg. *Sea Flower*	150	Edward Sears, Jr.	Samuel Bigelow replaced Bigelow & Cunningham as one of Boston agents.
	Sch. *Gwenemma*	141	Abiam Perry	
1848	Bg. *Abbott Lawrence*	197	Rowlin Baker	
	Sch. *Florence*		Leonard R. Chase	John Bowden master in 1850.
1853	Sch. *L. H. Nickerson*	181	Anthony Chase	Name changed to Merchants' Line. Samuel Bigelow, Boston agent. Baker & Stetson, Philadelphia agent.
	" *Florida*	157	E. Crowell	
1854	Sch. *Ann E. Cattell*		Williams	
	" *Charter Oak*	139	E. C. Kelley	
	" *John J. Mather*		Nickerson	
	" *W. H. Seymour*		Kelley	
1856	Sch. *Henry Payson*	151	Joseph Eldridge	Crowell & Collins, Philadelphia agents.
1859	Sch. *James S. Hewitt*		Rose	Samuel Bigelow located at 1 Central Wharf.

OLD COMMERCIAL LINE

E. Lincoln & Co., 25 Central Wharf, and N. Matthews, Boston agents. E. Lincoln & Co., Philadelphia agents. Sailed every Wed.

YEAR	VESSEL	TONS	MASTERS	REMARKS
1847	Bk. *Mary*	195	Zimri Whelden	Washburn Baker master in 1851.
	Bg. *Elizabeth Felton*	159	Alfred Eldridge	
	" *Isabella*	149	Oliver Matthews	
	" *Robert Waln*	178	E. Baker, Jr.	
	" *Sulla*	145	Bray	
1848	Bk. *Tremont*	188	Winthrop Sears	George Curtis replaced Matthews as Boston agent.
	" *Merrimac*	197	Henry Bangs	
	Bg. *Empire*	197	Robert Crowell	

COMMERCIAL LINE—THE ORIGINAL AND OLD ESTABLISHED LINE

Horace Scudder & Co., and Charles Siders, Boston agents. Bishop & Boggs, Philadelphia agents.

YEAR	VESSEL	TONS	MASTERS	REMARKS
1847	Bg. *Isabella Reed*	159	William Rogers	
	" *Foster* (Late Sch.)	146	Lincoln F. Baker	
	" *Myra*	130	Stephen Hall	
	Bk. *Gov. Briggs*	198	J. H. Hallet	
	Sch. *Edith*	144	G. Crowell	
1848	Bk. *Girard*	199	Remark Chase	Bishop & Watson, Philadelphia agents.
	Sch. *Richard Rush*	73	Samuel Robbins	
	Bg. *Empire*	197	Robert Crowell	
1850	Bk. *Oak*	178	George R. Ryder	

SECTION 4. BOSTON—BALTIMORE

UNION LINE

Stanton, Fiske & Nichols, and Worthington, Vose & Co., Boston agents. Brundige, Vose & Co., Baltimore agents. Established 1819.

YEAR	VESSEL	TONS	MASTERS	REMARKS
1819	Sch. *Helen*	146	Zenas D. Bassett	A. Hallet master in 1822.
	" *General Jackson*	88	Warren Hallet	
	" *Harriot*	122	Jesse Lewis	
	" *Caroline*	120	Walter Chipman	
1820	Sch. *Pacific*	130	Jesse Lewis	
1822	Sch. *Reaper*	131	Thomas Percival	Line composed of six vessels sailing every Sat. Geo. Hallet, 10 India St., replaced Worthington, Vose & Co. Hall & Marean added as Baltimore agents.
	" *Leander*	128	Freeman Nickerson	
	" *Fornax*	111	James Huckins	
	" *Algerine*	145	Warren Hallet	

UNION LINE (*continued*)

YEAR		VESSEL	TONS	MASTERS	REMARKS
1826	Bg.	*Calo*	155	Thomas Percival	James Brundige and Perkins & Saltonstall
	"	*Ida*	164	Allen Hallet	became Baltimore agents.
1827	Bg.	*Vesta*	155	James Huckins	Jonathan Tyson & Co. replaced Perkins & Saltonstall, 1827.

DISPATCH LINE

Ammi C. Lombard, 9 Wharf T, J. H. Pearson and E. W. Williams, Boston agents. Clark & Kellogg, Baltimore agents. Established 1827, sailed weekly. In 1825–6 A. C. Lombard sent packet brigs and schooners regularly to Baltimore. Line combined in 1828 with Union Line to form Union & Dispatch Line.

YEAR		VESSEL	TONS	MASTERS	REMARKS
1827	Sch.	*Fornax*	111	James Harding	
	"	*Spy*	114	Daniel Harding	
	"	*Bethiah*	125	Joshua Harding	
	"	*Leander*	128	J. Nickerson	
	"	*Chatham*	101	Samuel Small	
	"	*New Priscilla*	125	James Crowell	

UNION & DISPATCH LINE

A. C. Lombard, Stanton & Nichols, and Horace Scudder, Boston agents. Clark & Kellogg, Baltimore agents. Line continued through early 1861.

YEAR		VESSEL	TONS	MASTERS	REMARKS
1828	Bg.	*Cecilia*	152	Freeman Nickerson	Line consisted of six brigs sailing every Sat.
	"	*Pocket*	141	Warren Hallet	
1829	Bg.	*Calo*	155	Thomas Percival	
	"	*Ida*	164	Warren Hallet	
	"	*Marshall Ney*	193	James Crowell	
	"	*Vesta*	158	James Huckins	
1830	Bg.	*Choctaw*	193	Eli Nickerson	John C. Kendrick master in 1845.
1831	Bg.	*Chatham*	171	Elisha Small	Stanton & Nichols left the line.
1832	Bg.	*Chickasaw*	172	John Taylor	Joshua Taylor, Jr., master in 1833.
1836	Bg.	*Wankingo*	98	Elisha H. Ryder	
	Sch.	*Cordova*	93	Nathaniel Bacon	
1837	Bg.	*Sarah Abigail*	211	Nelson Scudder	
1838	Bg.	*Malaga*	183	Nelson Scudder	
	Sch.	*Eliza Hand*	112	G. Harden	
1839	Bg.	*Gem*	162	Calvin Howes	George M. Goodspeed master in 1840.
	"	*Dover*	167	Franklin Percival	
1841	Bk.	*Ida*	164	Samuel W. Hallet	
1842	Bk.	*Lawrence*	198	Samuel C. Howes	James W. Osborne, Baltimore agent.
	"	*James W. Paige*	198	Christopher Taylor	
1844	Bk.	*Elvira*	198	Chase	Osborne & Whitridge, Baltimore agents.
1845	Bk.	*Zulette*	198	Anthony Kelley, Jr.	A. C. Lombard & Co., retired from line.
	"	*Maryland*	195	Samuel Davis	
	"	*Anita*	195	Nathaniel Percival	
1847	Sch.	*Edith*	144	Rowlin Baker	James W. Osborne, sole Baltimore agent.
	"	*Foster*	146	Lincoln F. Baker	
	Bk.	*Helen Maria*	194	Taylor	
	"	*Union*	199	John C. Kendrick	
1848	Sch.	*Copia*	164	Sylvanus Sears	
1850	Bk.	*Edmund Dwight*	199	William A. Hallet	J. Nickerson master in 1860.
	Sch.	*Harriet*	116	Simeon S. Crowell	
1853	Bk.	*Mary F. Slade*	199	E. Baker	
	"	*John H. Duvall*	196	Smith	
1854	Sch.	*Wm. Tyson*	157	Nickerson	R. R. Whelden master in 1856.
1856	Bg.	*John R. Rhodes*	178		
	Sch.	*Joseph Lawrence*	165	Martin L. Rogers	
	Bg.	*Elisha Doane*	187	George H. Loring	
	"	*Element*		Harvey Jones, Jr.	
1858	Bk.	*Sylph*	199	Gershom Jones	
	"	*Justice Story*	199	Joshua Atkins	
1859	Sch.	*West Dennis*	299	Luther Studley	
	"	*Charm*	173	L. B. Baker	John Walter, 119 Smith's Wharf, Baltimore agent.

REGULAR LINE

John H. Pearson & Co., Commercial St., Boston agents. Matthew & Hopkins, 10 Bowly's Wharf, Baltimore agents. Packets sailed weekly.

YEAR		VESSEL	TONS	MASTERS	REMARKS
1831	Bg.	*Hamilton*	164	Jonathan Foster	
	"	*Victor*	125	S. Chaffee	Francis Gorham master in 1841.
	"	*Roxanna*	137	G. Bowly	
	Sch.	*Spy*	114	Elisha Small	Joshua Chamberlin master in 1834.
	"	*Henry Clay*	89	Tully Nickerson	
	"	*Classic*	110	Reuben C. Smith	
1833	Bg.	*Gambia*	155	Francis Chase	Francis Smith master in 1836.
	"	*Patapsco*	170	Thomas Kendrick	
	"	*Boston*	171	Reuben C. Smith	
	"	*Baltimore*	169	Tully Nickerson	
1834	Bg.	*Eagle*	142	Joseph Smith	
	"	*Cashier*	150	John Kenney	
1837	Sch.	*Chariot*	74	Wiley	Thomas R. Matthews became Baltimore agent in 1837.
1838	Sch.	*Franklin*	91	Elisha Crowell, Jr.	
	Bg.	*Cecilia*	152	David Kent	
1840	Sch.	*Eurotus*	101	Ezra Snow	
	Bg.	*Sun*	183	Ryder	Var. Rider.
	"	*Colombo*	156	John Atkins	
	"	*Token*	138	Elisha Loveland	John Loveland master in 1843.
	"	*Esther*	135	Joseph Emery	Var. Emory.
1841	Bg.	*Ocean*	165	Zeph. Eldridge	Hardy & Baker became Boston agents in
	"	*Almena*	175	S. C. Howes	1841. Pearson took the Manufacturers'
	"	*Vesta*	155	J. Hallet	Line.
	Sch.	*Columbia*	92	Jabez Berry	
	Bg.	*Rienzi*	108	J. E. Bowly	
1845	Bg.	*Phoebe Baxter*	99	F. B. Crowell	
1847	Bk.	*Wyman*	194	Elijah Crosby	Hardy, Baker & Morrill became Boston agents in 1847.
1848	Bk.	*Helen Maria*	194	Elijah Crosby	
	"	*Justice Story*	199	Howes Ryder	
1850	Bk.	*Sylph*	199	Gilman N. Rider	
	Sch.	*Samuel H. Appleton*	177	Frederick Nickerson	
	"	*Park*	311	J. K. Knapp	Vessel lost Nov. 21, 1850.
1852	Bk.	*Modena*	200	Zeph. Eldridge	Baker, Morrill & L. T. Lynde became Boston agents in 1852.
	"	*Bay State*	199	Samuel Dill	

PACKET LINE

Tyson & Littlefield, 79 Bowly's Wharf, Baltimore agents.

YEAR		VESSEL	TONS	MASTERS	REMARKS
1833	Sch.	*Pamela*	89	Erastus Allen	
	"	*Evalina*	98	F. Rogers	
	"	*Meridian*	85	Hiram Small	
	Bg.	*Omar*	124	Jonathan Twining	
	Sch.	*March*	85	Valentine Doane	
	"	*Spy*	114	Daniel Harding	

CENTRAL WHARF LINE

Benjamin Conant, Joshua Sears & Edward D. Peters, 12 Central Wharf, Boston agents. Thomas Whitridge, Baltimore agent.

YEAR		VESSEL	TONS	MASTERS	REMARKS
1833	Bg.	*Eagle*	142	Joseph Smith	Thos. Whitridge or Garland & Osborn,
	"	*Ranger*	164	Jonathan Eldridge	Baltimore agents.
	Sch.	*May* (tern)	126	Daniel B. Lovell	Mulford Patterson master in 1834.
	Bg.	*Junius*	121	Joshua Elwell	Henry B. Parker master in 1835.
1834	Sch.	*Rowena*	100	George Drew	

Garland & Elwell, 86 Bowly's Wharf, became Baltimore agents in 1835.
Whitridge took Tremont Line.

CENTRAL WHARF LINE (*continued*)

YEAR	VESSEL	TONS	MASTERS	REMARKS
1838	Bg. *Eagle*	142	Joseph Smith	
1856	Sch. *Cohasset*	87	Davis	Benj. Conant & Co., 18 Central Wharf, & B. Williams & Co., became Boston agents.

MANUFACTURERS' LINE

Adolphus Davis, Edward D. Peters & Ezra Whiton, Jr., Boston agents. Garland & Elwell, 86 Bowly's Wharf, Baltimore agents. Line composed of six brigs and schooners to provide weekly sailings, but actually sailed irregularly during first several depression years.

YEAR	VESSEL	TONS	MASTERS	REMARKS
1836	Bg. *Junius*	121	Henry B. Parker	
"	*Eagle*	142	Pitts Howes	
"	*May*	126	Mulford Patterson	Rodney Baxter master in 1839.
"	*Plutus*	128	Zenas D. Bassett	Asa Bearse, Jr., master in 1839.
"	*Baltimore*	167	M. S. Manduill	James Parker master in 1842.
	Sch. *China*	129	James Crowell	Benjamin Hallet master in 1839. Davis & Blake, 43 Central Wharf, and E. Whiton, Jr., Boston agents.
1837	Sch. *Samuel*		A. J. Lewis	
"	*March*	88	Valentine Doane	
	Bg. *Vesta*	155	J. Jenkins	
1838	Bg. *Luna*	181	Benjamin Hallet	
"	*Castel*	132	James Crowell	
1839	Bg. *Mohawk*	177	Allen B. Snow	Thomas Whitridge & Co. became Baltimore
"	*Martha*	169	James W. Davis	agents.
"	*Mary Stanton*	158	Oren Crowell	
1840	Sch. *Magnet*	110	Washburn Baker	
1841	Bg. *Joseph Balch*	153	James W. Davis	
	Bk. *Prompt*	197	John H. Hallet	Sumner Pierce master in 1844.
	Sch. *Augusta*	99	L. W. Nickerson	Nichols & Whitney added as Boston agents, 1843. John H. Pearson & Co. added as Boston agents, 1846.
1847	Bg. *Cotuit*	93	J. R. Nickerson	Pearson withdrew to establish Express Line.
	Bk. *Pioneer*	195	Kimball Eldridge, Jr.	Nichols & Whitney also withdrew and Bangs
	Sch. *George & Emily*	190	B. Oaks	Harding was added as Boston agent.
"	*Rio Grande*	150	J. Race	Name changed to Express Line. Adolphus
"	*Jerome*	108	Joseph H. Parker	Davis, R. Lincoln & Co., and Nathaniel Matthews started Merchants' Line.
1850	Bk. *Hadley*	198	David Kent	
"	*Zion*	199	Stephen Reynolds	
	Bg. *Metamora*	190	H. Kendrick	
1853	Bk. *Ella*	196	Edmund Flinn	Israel Whitney Lamson, J. Walter, and John H. Pearson & Co. became Boston agents.
1854	Bk. *Edward Everett*	199	Elijah Loveland	John H. Pearson & Co. became sole Boston
"	*Daniel Webster*	264	Richard Ryder	agents.
"	*Georgiana*	194	Stephen Reynolds	
	Bg. *M. & J. C. Gilmore*	185	Alfred Eldridge	

COMMERCIAL LINE

Alpheus Hardy, 13 City Wharf, Boston agent. Weld & Jencks, Bowly's Wharf, Baltimore agents. Line established late 1837, sailed every Sat.

YEAR	VESSEL	TONS	MASTERS	REMARKS
1837	Sch. *Village*	99	Eldridge	
"	*Edward Everett*	105	Seth Howes	
"	*James*	98	Peter Crowell	
"	*New Union*	115	Benjamin F. Chase	
"	*Richard*	94	Richard Baker	
	Bg. *Shield*		Chase	
	Sch. *Mazeppa*	98	Jairus Baker	
1838	Sch. *William Wilson*	97	William Baker	Hardy & Baker, 12 City Wharf, became Boston agents.

COMMERCIAL LINE (*continued*)

YEAR		VESSEL	TONS	MASTERS	REMARKS
1838	Sch.	*Hope Howes*	100	Pitts Howes	
	"	*Susan*	107	Atkins Taylor	
	"	*Argon*	113	Jeremiah Howes	
	"	*Jew*	85	Archelaus F. Trefethen	
1839	Bg.	*Ocean*	165	Zepheniah Eldridge	Hardy & Baker, 44 Commercial St., Boston
	"	*Vesta*	155	Elijah Loveland	agents.
	"	*Boston*	171	Reuben C. Smith	Josiah Nickerson master in 1848.
					Name changed to Regular Commercial Line.
1841	Bg.	*Almena*	175	S. C. Howes	
	"	*Token*	138	John Loveland	
	"	*Sun*	184	Mayo	
1843	Bg.	*Yucatan*	177	S. Baker	L. T. Lynde added as Boston agent.
	Sch.	*Shylock*	119	Isaac Matthews	
	"	*Berry*	97	Dean Sears	
1844	Sch.	*Lewis Bruce*	113	C. Studley	
	Bg.	*Medford*	108	Harding	
1845	Bk.	*Wyman*	193	Samuel Dill	
	Sch.	*Phoebe Baxter*	99	F. B. Crowell	
1846	Bk.	*Helen Maria*	194	Taylor	Elijah Crosby master in 1847.
	Sch.	*Foster*	146	Lincoln F. Baker	Hardy & Baker became Hardy, Baker & Morrill.
1847	Sch.	*Roxbury*	118	N. Sears	
	Bk.	*Justice Story*	199	Howes Ryder	
	"	*Sylph*	199	Gilman N. Ryder	David Eldridge, 2nd, master in 1848. Line consisted of four barks and two brigs sailing every Wed. Baker & Morrill and J. T. Lynde, Boston agents.
1850	Sch.	*Samuel H. Appleton*	177	Frederick Nickerson	
	Bk.	*Park*	311	J. K. Knapp	
1852	Bk.	*Modena*	200	Zepheniah Eldridge	
	"	*Bay State*		Samuel Dill	
1854	Sch.	*Charm*	173	Jabez Berry	
	Bg.	*Rolerson*	196	R. H. Crowell	
	Bk.	*Starlight*	298	Howes Ryder	L. T. Lynde, sole Boston agent, 1856.
1857	Sch.	*Abby Whitman*	225	William D. Clifford	T. R. Matthews & Son, Baltimore agents.
	Bk.	*Laconia*	190	Stephen Bearse	
1858	Sch.	*Luther Child*	168	Joseph Nickerson	F. H. Forbes and L. T. Lynde, Boston agents.
	"	*E. W. Pratt*	218	S. B. Whelden	
	"	*Highlander*	99	Mayo	
1860	Sch.	*Maria L. Davis*	195	Samuel M. Hallet	Baker & Morrill and L. T. Lynde, Boston agents. T. R. Matthews & Son, Baltimore agents. Line consisted of six barks sailing every Wed. from Baltimore Packet Pier.

WELLS & CO.'S LINE

Wells & Co., 11 and 12 Lewis Wharf, Boston agents. Elder, Gelston & Co., Baltimore agents. Line established in 1843. Abandoned in 1844.

YEAR		VESSEL	TONS	MASTERS	REMARKS
1843	Bg.	*Mary*	115	Lorenzo Baker	
	Sch.	*Caroline*	97	W. Curtis	
1844	Sch.	*John*	100	Ephraim Eldridge	
	"	*Helen Frazar*	90	Richard Leavitt	

HARDY'S LINE

Alpheus Hardy, City Wharf, Boston agent. Established Mar., 1844. Discontinued in 1846.

YEAR		VESSEL	TONS	MASTERS	REMARKS
1844	Sch.	*Blue Rock*	69	A. Bacon	
	"	*Cohasset*	87	S. Sears	
	"	*Porto Rico*	138	Rowland Smalley	
1845	Sch.	*Nassau*	108	Ezra Howes, 2nd	Name changed to New Line.
1846	Sch.	*Oneko*	111	Simeon Crowell	Clement Snow master in 1846-9.

MERCHANTS' LINE

Adolphus Davis, 13 Central Wharf, R. Lincoln & Co., 25 Central Wharf, and Nathaniel Matthews, Packet Office, Boston agents. Weld & Seaver, 8 Bowly's Wharf, Baltimore agents. Line established in Nov., 1847, when Manufacturers' Line broke up. Usually called Jencks' Line in Baltimore, after 1848.

YEAR		VESSEL	TONS	MASTERS	REMARKS
1847	Bg.	*David K. Aiken*	183	Jos. Baker	
	"	*Samuel Brown*	165	Anthony Thatcher	
	Bk.	*Lilius*	199	Amos Whorf	
	"	*Elvira*	198	George R. Nickerson	
	"	*Prompt*	197	Francis G. Wellman	Burned at sea, May 26, 1857.
1848	Bg.	*Elisha Doane*	187	John Loring	George Curtis replaced Matthews as a Boston
	"	*Massachusetts*	164	S. S. Burgess	agent.
	"	*J. Cohen*	223	Nathaniel Hathorn	Francis H. Jencks replaced Weld & Seaver
	"	*Susan Lord*	161	Michael Hodgkinson	at Baltimore.
1849	Bg.	*Lincoln*	174	William H. Averill	Charles Baker replaced Adolphus Davis
	"	*Susan*	147	Hiram Hall, 2nd	
	"	*Candace*	180	Isaac Matthews	
	"	*Foster*	146	Lincoln F. Baker	
	"	*Joseph Nickerson*	198	L. Nickerson	
	"	*Eutaw*	200	Samuel Matthews	
	"	*Titus*		V. R. Nickerson	
1850	Bg.	*Robert Wing*	197	Luther Crowell	
1851	Bg.	*China*	186	W. Haffard	
1853	Sch.	*Catherine*	138	Loring	Clap & Bros., 47 Commercial Wharf, and
	"	*Edith*	144	Rowlin Baker	Thomas Matthews became Boston agents.
	"	*Delaware*	170	Peter Harding	

EXPRESS LINE

J. H. Pearson & Co., 75 Long Wharf, and Bangs Harding, 37 Long Wharf, Boston agents. Thomas Whitridge & Co., Bowly's Wharf, Baltimore agents. Pearson established this line in 1847 after leaving Manufacturers' Line.

YEAR		VESSEL	TONS	MASTERS	REMARKS
1847	Sch.	*George & Emily*	130	B. Oaks	
	"	*Rio Grande*	91	J. Race	
	Bg.	*Cotuit*	93	J. R. Nickerson	
	Bk.	*Pioneer*	195	Kimball Eldridge, Jr.	
1852	Bk.	*Gov. Briggs*	198	J. H. Hallet	Israel Whitney Lamson and J. Walter became Boston agents in 1853 in place of Bangs Harding.
1856	Sch.	*Roxbury*	118	D. Brown	J. Walter and J. H. Pearson & Co. became
	"	*Monte Christo*	134	Jonathan Young	Boston agents.
1857	Bk.	*Selah*	199	David Gould, Jr.	
1859	Sch.	*Searsville*	261	B. R. Sears	
1860	Bg.	*Chicopee*	189	John H. Howes	
	"	*Elisha Doane*	187	George H. Loring	

SECTION 5. BOSTON—CHARLESTON

REGULAR LINE. Later LOMBARD'S LINE.

Ammi C. Lombard, Wharf T, Boston agent. Joseph Leland & Bros., Charleston agents. Established Jan., 1830, sailing on a prearranged schedule but at irregular intervals.

YEAR		VESSEL	TONS	MASTERS	REMARKS
1830	Bg.	*Colombo*	156	Nathaniel Weston, Jr.	
	"	*Baltimore*	130	Seth Ryder, Jr.	
	"	*Chatham*	172	John Tyler, Jr.	
	"	*Cashier*	150	James A. Stetson	
	"	*Leander*	150	Micah Humphrey	
	"	*Metamora*	164		George P. Marston master in 1838.
	Sch.	*Mary*	169	E. Weeks	
	Bg.	*Triumph*	166	David Eldridge	
	"	*Choctaw*	193	Joshua Harding	Pitts Howes master in 1833.
1832	Bg.	*Chief*	195	David Eldridge	Oliver W. Eldridge master in 1837.
1833	Bk.	*King Philip*	201	Micah Humphrey	Sailed every ten days. A. C. Lombard & Co.,
	Bg.	*Chicasaw*	172	Joshua Taylor, Jr.	Boston agents.
	"	*Cherokee*	232	James A. Stetson	

REGULAR LINE (*continued*)

YEAR		VESSEL	TONS	MASTERS	REMARKS
1833	Sp.	*Seaman*	241	Joshua Harding	
1835	Bg.	*Cervantes*	250	Edward Kendrick, Jr.	B. J. Tufts master in 1839.
1836	Sp.	*Carolina*	396	Joshua Harding	
"	"	*Charleston*	373	David Eldridge	
1837	Bg.	*Angola*	221	Benjamin I. Tufts	Leland Bros. & Co., Charleston agents.
	Sp.	*Admittance*	427	F. Soule	Line called Lombard's Line.
1838	Bg.	*Carrier*	199	Ephraim Atkins	
	"	*Almena*	175	Edward Kendrick	
	"	*Token*	138	Crowell	Elijah Loveland master in 1840.
	"	*Shield*		Chase	Abandoned at sea, Sept., 1838.
	"	*Arcturus*	254	Carter	
	"	*Mary Helen*	158	Charles W. Hamilton	
	Sch.	*Spy*	114	Justus Doane	
	Sp.	*Henry Eubank*	330	Leach	
	"	*Liverpool*	424	William C. Barstow	
	"	*Congaree*	321	Justus Doane	
	Bk.	*Arethusa*	320	Silvester Baxter	
	Bg.	*Columbia*	131	Joseph Dexter	
	"	*Wankingo*	98	Mayo	
	Sp.	*Hercules*	371	George Gregerson	
1839	Sp.	*Leland*	347	Edward Kendrick, Jr.	Nathaniel Kendrick master in Oct., 1839.
	"	*Switzerland*	567	Charles Hunt	Regular line composed of four ships sailing
	"	*Lucas*	350	C. W. Eldridge	every ten days.
	Bk.	*Mary Ballard*	267	Thales Curtis	
1840	Sch.	*Saratoga*	95	Ezra Taylor	
	Sp.	*Marathon*	382	Albert H. Brown	
	Bg.	*Souther*	197	David Eldridge	David E. Mayo master in 1847.
1841	Sch.	*Orleans*	125	Orlando Bassett	Parker H. Pierce, Jr., added as Boston agent
	"	*Zone*	99	J. C. Kelley	in July.
	"	*Michigan*	164	Lucas B. Perry	
	Bg.	*Franklin*	198	Richard Bearse	
	"	*Lincoln*	174	F. Ruggles	
	Bk.	*Hersilia*	309	Higgins Crowell	
	Sp.	*Medora*	479	S. C. Turner	
1843	Bk.	*Ida*	196	Alvin S. Hallet	Daniel Sharp, Jr., replaced Parker H. Pierce,
	Sch.	*Cotuit*	93	David B. Nickerson	Jr,. as Boston agent.
	Bg.	*Archelaus*	112	John Crowell	
	Bk.	*Carib*	200	Francis Nickerson	
	Bg.	*Boston*	171	C. W. Hamilton	
	Sp.	*Moselle*	398	Charles Hunt	
	Bk.	*Roman*	245	Lendol N. Doane	
	"	*Saxony*	346	Nelson Scudder	
	"	*Brewster*	215	Justus Doane	
	"	*Como*	225	C. W. Eldridge	
1844	Sch.	*Forest King*	99	N. D. Kelley	
	Bk.	*Catherine*	226	Benjamin F. Tufts	
	"	*Catalpa*	260	Justus Doane	
	"	*Valhalla*	275	Jonathan Thatcher	
1845	Bk.	*Convoy*	249	Micah Humphrey	Lombard & Hall became sole Boston agents
	"	*New World*	229	John Crowell	in May.
	"	*Jupiter*	317	James Carter	John W. Caldwell, Charleston agent.
	"	*Palmetto*	282	Nathaniel Kendrick	
	"	*Morgan Dix*	281	Charles Hamilton	
	Bg.	*Christiana*	226	J. D. Warren	
	Sp.	*Mary Ann*	497	Albert H. Brown	
	Bk.	*Saranac*	245	Daniel L. Carlton	
	"	*Brontes*	292	G. H. Curtis	
	"	*Hualco*	274	James H. McCrillis	
1846	Bg.	*Ruby*	126	W. McKenzie	Var. McKinnie
	"	*Clement*	197	Seth Ryder, Jr.	
	Bk.	*Zulette*	198	Horatio Howes	
	Sp.	*Versailles*	547	George Agry	
	"	*Geo. A. Hopley*	549	Charles F. W. Behm	
	Bk.	*Edward*	355	William C. Bulkley	
	"	*Verona*	238	John Bogardus	

REGULAR LINE (*continued*)

YEAR	VESSEL	TONS	MASTERS	REMARKS
1847	Sch. *Coquette*	85	J. Auld	
	Bk. *Wave*	197	John Bogardus	
	Bg. *Cyclops*	227	Benjamin I. Tufts	
	Bk. *Avola*	309	Nathaniel Kendrick	
	" *Cherokee*	232	Micah Humphrey	
	Bg. *J. C. Dow*		Stetson	
	Bk. *Souther*	197	David E. Mayo	
1848	Sch. *Gen. Clinch*	131	Rowland S. Hallet	
	" *Wm. Thompson*	151	Abner Crowell	
1849	Bk. *A. R. Taft*	318	John Bogardus	
1852	Bk. *Edisto*	366	E. H. Harding	Nathaniel Kendrick master in 1855.
1853	Bk. *Radiant*	287	Edmund Flinn	Var. Flynn.
				Lombard & Co., Boston agents.
1854	Bg. *Emily*	322	T. H. Davis	John W. and Andrew Caldwell became
	Bk. *Sumter* (*Sumpter*)	381	G. M. Humphrey	Charleston agents.
	" *Jeddo*	242	John Paine	Var. Payne
1858	Bk. *Moneynick*	368	Ephraim Smith	
1859	Bk. *Lyman*	369	Edward Humphrey	
	" *Modena*	200	Zephaniah Eldridge	

PACKET LINE

Samuel R. Allen, 110 Milk St., Boston agent.

YEAR	VESSEL	TONS	MASTERS	REMARKS
1837	Bg. *Josephine*	232	Smith	Cyrus Howes master in 1843.
1839	Sch. *Meredian*	74	I. Wait	
	" *Amanda Ophelia*	58	Ezra Taylor	
	Bk. *Henry Newell*	257	Charles T. Burnham	
	" *Valhalla*	275	Benjamin F. Berry	
1840	Sch. *Magnet*	80	Anthony Kelley	William B. Sawyer added as Boston agent.
	" *Black Warrior*	80	Kelley	Line called Allen's Line.
	" *Daty Chase*	100	William Thomas	Sawyer & Slater became agents in Dec.
	" *Marion*	111	Jeremiah Varnum	
1841	Sch. *Morea*		George W. Prime	
	" *Delta*	99	Baker	J. L. Davis master in 1843.
	" *Atlantic*	103	Joseph Nickerson	
	Bk. *Em*	235	John Procter	
	Sch. *John A. Lancaster*	160	Rogers	
	" *Alabama*	92	Henry Kingsbury	
	Bk. *Vernon*	307	William A. Robbins	
	" *Saxony*	346	Nelson Scudder	
	Sp. *Saxon*	344	Charles Mansfield	
1842	Bg. *Mary Jones*	120	Kelley	John O. B. Minot added as agent in Sept.
	Sch. *Wellington*	80	Ezekiel Brown	and line became Allen & Minot's Line.
	Bk. *Effort*	271	Samuel B. Hussey	
	Bg. *Odeon*	118	Cyrus Howes	
	Sch. *Rienzi*	108	Isaac Fessenden	
1843	Sch. *Eagle*	74	Samuel Gallagher	Samuel Weltch replaced Minot in May and
1847	Sch. *Henry Franklin*	83	Nickerson	line became Allen & Weltch's Line.
	" *Flavilla*	103	Gorham	
	" *Barton*	90	Nelson Waldron	
1848	Sch. *Brothers*	142	Ephraim W. Hosmer	
1856	Sch. *Franklin Nickerson*	258	Mather R. Gooding	
1859	Sch. *George Davis*	336	Samuel F. Phillips	

COMMERCIAL LINE

R. Lincoln & Co., 56 Commercial St., Alfred C. Hersey, 1 Mercantile Wharf, and Stanley, Reed & Co., 10 City Wharf, Boston agents. M. C. Mordecai, Charleston agent.

YEAR	VESSEL	TONS	MASTERS	REMARKS
1837	Bk. *Bevis*	214	William H. Brown	
	Bg. *Franklin*	198	Allen Baxter	
	" *Robert Waln*	178	Oliver Matthews	
	" *Russell*	183	Samuel Matthews	

COMMERCIAL LINE (*continued*)

YEAR		VESSEL	TONS	MASTERS	REMARKS
1838	Bg.	*Globe*	214	Joshua Foster	
	"	*Arabian*	169	Haws	
	Sp.	*Chilo*	413	Isaac S. Lucas	
1842	Bk.	*Yarmouth*	326	Nathaniel Matthews	
1846	Bk.	*Hualco*	274	James H. McCrillis	Parker H. Pierce, Jr., & Co., 16 Commercial Wharf, became Boston agents.
1851	Bk.	*Velocity*	247	Gustavus Ryder	John W. Caldwell became Charleston agent.
1855	Bg.	*Souther*	198	Nelson	P. Mayo master in 1856.
	Bk.	*Jeddo*	242	Kendrick	
1857	Bk.	*Betsina*	331	Arthur S. Phinney	

NEW LINE

John Fairfield, 26 Central Wharf, Boston agent.

YEAR		VESSEL	TONS	MASTERS	REMARKS
1837	Sp.	*Frances Ann*	446	Henchman S. Soule	
1841	Sp.	*Switzerland*	567	Frank Smith	Called Fairfield's Line.
1843	Bk.	*Barrington*	273	George Barton	M. C. Mordecai became Charleston agent.
	"	*Mary Kimball*	158	Francis Freeto	
	Sch.	*Baltic*	92	Christopher Godfrey	
	"	*Harriet*	116	Hewes	
	Bg.	*Alpine*	227	Freeman S. Nickerson	
	Sch.	*Forest King*	99	N. D. Kelley	
	"	*Hopewell*	96	David Lawrence	
	"	*Rodolph*	123	Simpson Pendleton	Josiah N. Flinn master in 1844–5.
1844	Bg.	*Caroline & Mary*	180	Rufus Cole	
	Sp.	*Nathaniel Hooper*	427	William Churchill	
	"	*Mary Ann*	497	Albert H. Brown	
	"	*St. Petersburg*	814	Richard Trask	
1845	Bk.	*Howland*	275	Joshua Harding	J. O. B. Minot and Reed, Hurd & Co. became Boston agents. N. G. Bourne became Charleston agent.

DISPATCH LINE

Nathaniel Winsor, Jr., and Benjamin Bruce, 103 State St., Boston agents.

YEAR		VESSEL	TONS	MASTERS	REMARKS
1839	Bk.	*Neptune*	231	William Long	Benjamin Fay master in 1841.
	Bg.	*Josephine*	232	Smith	Cyrus Howes master in 1843.
1840	Sp.	*Oceanus*	473	Silas J. Bourne	
	"	*Minerva*	291	Josiah Knowles	
	"	*Hercules*	371	George Gregerson	Madegan master in 1842.
1842	Bk.	*Daniel Webster*	264	Thomas L. Manson	
1844	Bg.	*William Davis*	173	Luther Handy	Became Winsor's Line. Nathaniel Winsor, Jr., 109 State St., Boston agent.

REGULAR LINE

John H. Pearson, 75 Long Wharf, and John O. B. Minot, Boston agents. N. G. Bourne, Charleston agent.

YEAR		VESSEL	TONS	MASTERS	REMARKS
1844	Bg.	*Caroline & Mary*	108	Rufus Cole	
1845	Bk.	*Brewster*	215	E. C. Taylor	
	"	*Howland*	275	Joshua Harding	
1846	Bk.	*Gen. Greene*	242	S. Clark	
	"	*Hamilton*	273	William L. Hallet	
	Sp.	*James Calder*	390	Joseph Hollister	
	"	*Sullivan*	437	Waite	
	"	*Amelia*	572	George Agry	
	"	*Switzerland*	570	J. S. Nichols	
1847	Sch.	*Edward Kent*	127	Nichols	
1848	Sch.	*Mary F. Lutterloch*	158	Somers Scull	
	Bg.	*Michigan*	130	Gideon G. Varney	
	Sp.	*Camera*	386	Albert Dunbar	
	"	*St. James*	641	Nathan Godfrey	

REGULAR LINE (*continued*)

YEAR		VESSEL	TONS	MASTERS	REMARKS
1848	Sp.	*Europa*		Charles Mercier	
	Bg.	*Diantha*	285	Brown	
	Sp.	*Noemie*	548	Nicholas Holberton	
1849	Sp.	*Charles Carroll*	388	Elihu Merchant	Foundered, Dec., 1849.
1850	Bk.	*Jupiter*	317	T. T. Bigley	
	Sch.	*J. A. Hobart*	149	John H. Luther	
1854	Sp.	*Emily St. Pierre*	883	E. L. Tessier	Lamson & Pearson became Boston agents.

DISPATCH LINE

Silloway, Calef & Co., Boston agents. M. W. Webb, Charleston agent.

YEAR		VESSEL	TONS	MASTERS	REMARKS
1853	Sch.	*Mohawk*	141	Woodbury	
	Bg.	*America*		Bray	
1854	Bk.	*Sarah Ann*	431	Drinkwater	
1855	Sch.	*Myrover*	356	Isaac F. Horton	Var. Isaac T. Horton.
1856	Sch.	*Eveline*	130	H. S. Ray	H. G. K. Calef, Boston agent.
	Bg.	*Julia* (Cl.)	263	Henry L. Sheffield	F. J. Ogden, Charleston agent.
1858	Bg.	*Minnie*	225	J. McLeish	J. Silloway & Co., Boston agents.
1859	Sch.	*Target*	388	Zachariah Howe	Holmes & Stoney, Charleston agents.
	"	*Wm. H. Gilliland*	348	J. Erickson	Var. G. Erickson.

SECTION 6. BOSTON—SAVANNAH

WHITNEY LINE

Josiah Whitney, Boston agent. S B. Parkman, Hunter's Wharf, Savannah agent. Established 1824.

YEAR		VESSEL	TONS	MASTERS	REMARKS
1822	Bg.	*Almira*	229	Isaac Atwood	Samuel Harding master in 1824.
1824	Bg.	*Sea Island*	213	Isaac Parker	Marcus Sidrick master in 1834 and S. B. Hobart master in 1839.
1826	Sch.	*Diana*	142	Elkanah Higgins	
1830	Bg.	*William*	166	Daniel Atwood	Josiah Whitney & Co., 43 Central Wharf, became Boston agent in 1834.
1837	Sp.	*Eli Whitney*	532	Benjamin Dyer	Josiah Whitney, 43 Central Wharf, Boston agent; he advertised sailings as regular packets but not as a line.

LOMBARD'S LINE

Ammi C. Lombard, Wharf T, Boston agent. Padelford & Fay, Savannah agents. Ammi C. Lombard—later A. C. Lombard & Co.—sent packets to Savannah all through the 1830's but did not establish a line until the fall of 1840.

YEAR		VESSEL	TONS	MASTERS	REMARKS
1832	Bg.	*Wm. & Henry*	134	Joseph Smith	
1833	Bg.	*Ranger*	164	Jonathan Twining	
1834	Bk.	*Chief*	196	Joshua Harding	
	Bg.	*Mary Helen*	158	Seth Ryder, Jr.	
1840	Sp.	*Susan Drew*	696	Winthrop S. Babbidge	Became Lombard's Line, A. C. Lombard &
	"	*Hercules*	371	George Gregerson	Co., 13 Lewis Wharf, Boston agent.
	Sch.	*Columbia*	92	Watson Baker	
1841	Bg.	*Michigan*	130	Perry S. Coleman	
	"	*Pandora*	261	Jos. R. Tillinghast	
	Bk.	*Don Juan*	123	Eben Harden	
	"	*Z. D.*	311	Zenas D. Basset	
	Sp.	*Majestic*	297	John C. Hardy	
	Sch.	*Deborah Ann Somers*	144	J. Tilby	
	Bg.	*Trio*	179	Edmund Doane	
	Bk.	*Apthorp*	246	Philip Blake	
	Sp.	*Colombo*	577	Asa Eldridge	
1843	Sch.	*Ceylon*	75	Webb	Daniel Sharp, Jr., added as Boston agent.
	"	*Atlantic*	97	Thomas E. Brewer	
	"	*Emperor*	88	Seth W. Ellis	
	"	*European*	82	Seth W. Ellis	
1844	Bk.	*Mohawk*	198	Remark Chace	Var. Chase
	Sp.	*Eli Whitney*	533	Ephraim Harding	Ammi C. Lombard ceased active operation of lines in 1845. Lombard & Hall continued to operate some of the lines for a time.

PACKET LINE

Samuel R. Allen, 110 Milk St., Boston agent. Edward Padelford, Savannah agent. First called a packet line in Dec., 1837. Allen ran packets to Natchez, and also had lines to New Orleans and Havana at the time.

YEAR		VESSEL	TONS	MASTERS	REMARKS
1837	Bg.	*Alexandria*	206	Covell	
	Sp.	*Elizabeth Bruce*	586	John L. Rogers	
	"	*New England*	549	Davis	
	"	*Timoleon*	422	Daniel L. Winsor	
	"	*Marathon*	382	E. A. Shaw	
	"	*Louisa*	324	Fisher A. Newell	
	Bg.	*Falco*	211	Kimball Harlow	
1838	Sp.	*Saladin*	356	John Simpson	
	Sch.	*September*	115	N. Burgess	
	Bg.	*Pauline*	150	Joel L. Manson	
	Sp.	*Argo*	450	Joseph K. Farley	
	"	*Plymouth*	425	A. Kendrick	David S. Fuller master in 1844.
	"	*Chatham*	424	Josiah Richardson	
	Bk.	*Burlington*	406	Richard Evans	
	Sch.	*Leontine*	82	Francis Kelley	
	Bk.	*Wolga*	285	S. H. Davis	
	Bg.	*Massasoit*	206	Thomas Trott	
	Sch.	*Albion*	107	E. Bray	
1839	Sch.	*Wm. Granger*		John Allen	
	Bg.	*Trenton*	227	William Pitman	
	Sch.	*Magnet*	80	Anthony Kelly	
	"	*Sea Drift*	90	B. Walker	
1840	Bg.	*Tybee*	329	Joseph Livermore	William B. Sawyer, 133 State St., added as
	Sch.	*Atlantic*	95	A. Stevens	Boston agent in June.
	"	*Eagle*	97	John Kinnear	Firm of Sawyer & Slater replaced William B.
	"	*Rienzi*	108	Elisha T. Cushman	Sawyer in Sept. Line called Allen's Line.
	"	*Elijah Chase*		Ellis	
	"	*Daty Chase*	100	William Thomas	
1840	Sch.	*Redondo*	118	John Pitcher	
	"	*La Grange*	87	Ebenezer Kelley	
	"	*Savannah*	88	Lawrence	
	Sp.	*Trenton*	429	Snow	Lost on Man-of-War Key, Jan. 2, 1843.
	Bg.	*Mary Ann*	138	Joseph R. Curtis	
	Bk.	*Hersilia*	309	Higgins Crowell	
	"	*William & James*	264	Joseph H. Shepard	Var. Shepherd.
1841	Bg.	*Charles Joseph*	314	Nathaniel Mauran	Lost at sea prior to May 27, 1850.
	Sch.	*Mechanic*		Litchfield	
	"	*Harvest*	96	Small	
	"	*Arenzamendi*	89	Benoni J. Chace	
	Bk.	*Adeline & Eliza*	249	William Drew	
	Bg.	*Nauvoo*	168	J. Burnham	
	Sch.	*Henry G. King*	141	E. B. Lynmire	
	Bk.	*New World*	229	Benjamin Young	
	Sp.	*Monsoon*	381	John A. Paine	
	Sch.	*Governor*	70	George M. Prime	
	"	*Charles Carroll*	65	Jenkins	
	Bg.	*Senator*	193	Bangs Pepper	
	Sp.	*Colombo*	577	Asa Eldridge	
1842	Sp.	*Charleston*	373	Kimball Harlow	S. R. Allen and William B. Sawyer became
	Sch.	*Charlotte*	100	Alexander Fuller	Boston agents in 1842.
	"	*Sarah Wales*	100	Daniel C. Joy	John O. B. Minot replaced Sawyer and line
	"	*Casket*	99	Doane Kelley, Jr.	became Allen & Minot's Line in Aug.
	"	*Bride*	94	Samuel Blunt	
	Bg.	*Romulus*	251	Samuel English	
	"	*Acton*	184	Philander Daggett	
	Sch.	*Wanderer*	142	Freeman B. Lewis	
	Sp.	*Aurelius*	388	Elisha Foster	
	Bg.	*Odeon*	118	James Nickerson, 2nd	
	"	*Havre*	291	Augustus A. Carpenter	
1843	Bg.	*Ceres*	290	S. Blanchard	Samuel Weltch replaced Minot May 1 and
	Sch.	*Sparta*	94	D. D. Carlton	line became Allen & Weltch's Line. Minot
	"	*Billingsgate*	61	James Swett	joined Fairfield, Lincoln & Co.'s lines.
	"	*November*	108	David Ellis	L. Baldwin & Co. became Savannah agents.
	"	*Brilliant*	99	Seth M. Cotton	

PACKET LINE (*continued*)

YEAR		VESSEL	TONS	MASTERS	REMARKS
1843	Sp.	*Franconia*	499	John P. Gannett	
	Sch.	*January*	64	Cahoon	
	"	*Pandora*	261	Joseph Tillinghast	
	"	*Oneko*	111	Seth Kelley	
1844	Bg.	*Loretto*	245	James Henderson	
	Sp.	*Eli Whitney*	532	Elisha Dyer	
	Bg.	*Philura*	198	Russell Doane	
	Bk.	*Carlos*	323	Augustus C. Mauran	
1845	Bk.	*Baltic*	395	Wheaton Allen	Abandoned at sea, 1852.
	Bg.	*Kimball*	182	S. L. Ingraham	
1846	Sp.	*Caledonian*	514	Nathaniel S. Mauran	
	"	*Herculean*	542	Isaiah Chase	
	Bk.	*Globe*	364	Charles Theobald	Register surrendered Feb. 23, 1857. Stranded and abandoned.
	Bg.	*Growler*	247	Henry Washburn	
1847	Bk.	*Exact*	431	Jacob Johnson	
	Sch.	*Southerner*	99	Benjamin Eldridge	
	"	*Edward*	84	Benoni Baker	
	Bk.	*New England*	238	John S. Curtis	
	"	*Isnardon*	247	T. G. Moulton	
1848	Bk.	*Backus*	195	Porter	Brigham & Kelley became Savannah agents at Telfair's Wharf.
	Sch.	*Boston*	171	Corson	
	"	*Empire*	250	Thomas Underhill	
	Sp.	*Southport*	500	Robert McCormick	William Wilson master in 1854.
	Bg.	*Frank*	160	Lorenzo Baker	
	Sch.	*Henry Payson*	151	Payson Crowell	
	Sp.	*Richmond*	475	John Ewer	
	Bk.	*Benj. Adams*	245	John Coombs	
	Bg.	*Robert Waln*	178	Nelson Brown	
	"	*William F. Stafford*	175	David W. Pierce	
1849	Bg.	*Candace*	181	A. Matthews	
	"	*Gen. Taylor*	151	W. Shute	
	Sch.	*Lamartine*	114	Smith	
	"	*T. P. Johnson*	119	Martin W. Cornell	
1850	Bg.	*Paulina*	272	Edmund Flinn	
1853	Bk.	*Charles William*	298	Reuben C. Hawes	Dashington master in 1858.
	Sch.	*Victory*	177	Rowlin Baker	
1854	Bg.	*Albion Cooper*	188	G. W. Nichols	
	Bk.	*Peter Demill*	294	Nicholas Hoey	
	Sp.	*Unicorn*	397	George Pollard	
1858	Bk.	*Radiant*	287	William W. Flinn	
1859	Sp.	*Nicholas Biddle*	784	William Ewer	Var. Evers.

DISPATCH LINE. Later REGULAR LINE.

Edmund Wright, Jr., 11 Wharf T, Boston agent.

YEAR		VESSEL	TONS	MASTERS	REMARKS
1837	Sch.	*Scotland*		R. Chase	
	"	*Odeon*	118	Cyrus Howes	
1838	Sch.	*James*	98	Joseph Crowell	Called Regular Line, 1838.
	"	*Richard*	94	Richard Baker	
	"	*Uncle Sam*	119	George Matthews	
	"	*Eurotas*	101	Ezra Snow	
	"	*William Tell*	86	Ezra Snow	
	"	*Rowena*	100	Oliver Arey	
	"	*Shamrock*	135	H. Carrol	Var. Henry Currell.
	Bg.	*Ben Franklin*	164	Edmund Flinn	
	Sch.	*Hitty Tom*	98	Rogers	Wright appeared to make no further attempt to maintain a line after 1839.
	"	*Frances*	71	Grafton Sears	
	"	*New England*	92	Seth Rogers	
	"	*Gen. Warren*	91	James Baker	

DISPATCH LINE

Cabot & Fraser, 79 State St., Boston agents. Line established fall of 1838.

YEAR		VESSEL	TONS	MASTERS	REMARKS
1838	Sp.	*Transit*	395	G. Windsor	
	Bk.	*Turbo*	294	Isaac Beauchamp	
	"	*Neptune*	231	Pickett	Benjamin Fay master in 1841.
	Sch.	*Harvest*	96	Hawkes Loring	
1839	Sch.	*Kanahwa*	98	Richard H. Cook	Continued by Bruce & Winsor.

DISPATCH LINE

Nathaniel Winsor, Jr., and Benjamin Bruce, 103 State St., Boston agents. Francis Sorrell & Co., Savannah agents.

YEAR		VESSEL	TONS	MASTERS	REMARKS
1839	Sp.	*Coromando*	636	Robert Pierce	
	"	*Medford*	545	Briggs Thomas	
	Sch.	*Eliot*	141	B. Morley	Var. Morey.
1840	Sp.	*Timoleon*	422	A. Winsor	Winsor & Bruce became Boston agents.
	"	*New Jersey*	636	J. G. Dickinson	
	Bk.	*Binney*	292	Reuben Paine	
	"	*Neptune*	231	William Long	
	Sp.	*Perdonnet*	478	David Foote	
	Bg.	*Emily*	124	C. Peter Kuhn	
1841	Bg.	*Tower* (Late Sch.)	120	D. Wilson	
	Sp.	*Oakland*	550	Charles E. Barry	
	Sch.	*John Allyn*	104	Reuben Collins, Jr.	
1842	Bk.	*William Ladd*	297	Thomas P. Wyman	
	Sp.	*Franconia*	499	Eleazer Crabtree	
1843	Sp.	*Monticello*	392	Job G. Lawton	Winsor & Bruce dissolved during summer
	"	*Olive Branch*	366	Samuel English	and Winsor continued the line. Bruce at-
	"	*Eli Whitney*	532	Samuel Harding	tempted to continue as Bruce's Line but
	Sch.	*Apprentice Boy*	117	J. Loring, Jr.	service was very irregular.
	Sp.	*Apollo*	413	Thomas Winsor	
1844	Sp.	*Delphos*	398	Thomas E. Curtis	Francis Sorrell & Co. dissolved and Sorrell
	Sch.	*Talma*	100	Nathan A. Conklin	continued as agent.
1845	Bg.	*Talleyrand*	145	William Seavey	
	Bk.	*Baring Brothers*	291	John Crocker	
	Sp.	*Thomas W. Sears*	500	Prince S. Crowell	
1846	Bk.	*Lagrange*	259	Daniel L. Porter	Lippett & Wright became Savannah agents.
1848	Bg.	*Cornelia*	127	Freeman Rogers	J. H. Rivers and J. Silloway became Boston
	"	*Sea Belle*	149	Royal Harriman, Jr.	agents.
	"	*Carolina*	166	Caleb Gilkey	Washburn, Wilder & Co. became Savannah
	Sch.	*Linnell*	144	E. Brown	agents.
1853	Bg.	*Tiberias*	250	J. Bramhall	Silloway, Calef & Co. became Boston agents
					and Bunker & Ogden, Savannah agents.
1854	Bg.	*James Wallace*	189	W. G. Foster	
1856	Bg.	*Robert M. Charlton*	148	J. H. Lightbourne	H. G. K. Calef, 61 Commercial St., became
					Boston agent and Ogden, Starr & Co., Savan-
					nah agents.
1858	Bg.	*M. & J. C. Gilmore*	185	Alfred Eldridge	
	"	*John Freeman*	299	John Loring, Jr.	

REGULAR LINE

Fairfield & Lincoln, 26 Central Wharf, Boston agents. Called Regular Line commencing in 1843.

YEAR		VESSEL	TONS	MASTERS	REMARKS
1840	Sp.	*Eli Whitney*	532	Samuel Harding	
1843	Sch.	*Salem*	99	George W. Prince	Fairfield, Lincoln & Co., and J. O. B. Minot,
	Sp.	*Milton*	598	J. B. Dickson	7 and 8 Lewis Wharf, became Boston agents.
	Sch.	*Savannah*	97	Lawrence	
	"	*Gen. William Washington*	69	L. Halberson	
	"	*Alpine*	227	William French	
1844	Sp.	*Merchant*	347	James C. Jordan	
	Bk.	*Ligonia*	286	John Hamilton	
	Bg.	*Osage*	179	Stephen Hall	
	"	*St. Simon*	187	Thomas Sloman	Var. Slowman.

BRIG LINE

Washburn, Lewis & Co., Boston agents. Shapter & Woodbridge, Savannah agents.

YEAR	VESSEL	TONS	MASTERS	REMARKS
1840	Bg. *Savannah*	396	J. R. Shapter	
	" *Excel*	375	Edwin Sherwood	
	" *William Taylor*	249	Nicholas Hoey	
1841	Bk. *Hersilia*	309	Higgins Crowell	
1850	Bk. *Vesta*	259	Edmund Flinn	Washburn, Wilder & Co. became Savannah agents.

FORBES & CO.'S LINE

F. H. Forbes & Co., 15 India St., Boston agents. S. W. Wight & Co., Savannah agents. Line established Mar., 1847.

YEAR	VESSEL	TONS	MASTERS	REMARKS
1847	Sch. *Wave*	118	James P. Lansill	
	" *Democrat*	110	N. N. Berry	
	" *Alhambra*	198	E. Blanchard	

NEW LINE. Later DISPATCH LINE.

J. Silloway & Co., 5 Commercial St., and J. H. Rivers, 15 Commercial St., Boston agents.

YEAR	VESSEL	TONS	MASTERS	REMARKS
1847	Bg. *Madison*	315	Watkins	
	" *Monterey*	200	J. S. Kellar	
	" *Judge Whitman*	174	Charles W. Peterson	
	" *Marsellois*	223	George Thorndike	
	" *Watson*	146	Smith Watson	
1848	Sch. *Arietis*	131	Robert M. Wheeler	J. Silloway, J. P. Farley and T. Davis be-
	" *Phoenix*	121	Levi Loring	came Boston agents; J. Silloway and J. H.
	Bg. *Lucy Atwood*	181	B. Atwood	Rivers, agents in Dec. Name changed to
	" *Sea Flower*	150	Studley	Dispatch Line.

REGULAR DISPATCH LINE

J. H. Rivers & Co., 14 Commercial St., Boston agents. Carleton & Parsons, Savannah agents.

YEAR	VESSEL	TONS	MASTERS	REMARKS
1856	Bk. *Fernandia*	238	Asa Wright	
1858	Sch. *Emma Amelia*	249	Archelaus E. Harding	
	Bk. *Nashua*	196	Augustus A. Lewis	
	" *Indiana*	255	W. W. Rivers	
	" *Col. Ledyard*	404	Leonard W. Merrill	
1859	Bk. *Laconia*	190	Howes	Charles Parsons became Savannah agent.

DISPATCH LINE

H. G. K. Calef, 61-2 Commercial St., Boston agent. Ogden, Starr & Co., Savannah agent.

YEAR	VESSEL	TONS	MASTERS	REMARKS
1856	Bg. *Robert M. Charlton*	147	J. H. Lightbourne	
1858	Bg. *M. & J. C. Gilmore*	185	Alfred Eldridge	J. Silloway became Boston agent in Jan.,
	" *John Freeman*	299	John Loring, Jr.	1858. Name changed to Silloway's Dispatch
	" *E. Doane*			Line. Continued into 1861.
	Sch *Walter Raleigh* (Cl.)	472	Isaac F. Horton	

SECTION 7. BOSTON—MOBILE

CUNNINGHAM LINE

N. F. Cunningham & Co., 27 and 38 Indian Wharf, Boston agents.

YEAR	VESSEL	TONS	MASTERS	REMARKS
1833	Bg. *Roderick Dhu*	200	Elbridge G. Wiswell	
1837	Bk. *Nashua*	301	George Pollard	
	Bg. *Silsbee*	105	Benjamin Harlow	
	" *Wellingsley*	210	Jabez Churchill	
	Sp. *Rajah*	531	E. C. Bliss	
	" *Emerald*	520	B. Prindle	

CUNNINGHAM LINE (*continued*)

YEAR		VESSEL	TONS	MASTERS	REMARKS
1838	Bk.	*Tartar*	321	Edward C. Nickels	Became regular packet line.
	Bg.	*Acton*	184	Albert Winsor	Lost at sea, Oct., 1847.
	Sch.	*Albert*	79	David K. Hamilton	
	Bg.	*Catherwood*	199	Remark Chase	
	Sp.	*Elizabeth Bruce*	586	William H. Russell	
	"	*Austerlitz*	407	William Hammond	
	Sch.	*Shylock*	120	Hopkins	Enoch Hall master in 1839.
	Bg.	*Peru*	158	Clenrick Crosby	
1839	Sp.	*James H. Shepherd*	635	St. Croix Redman	
	Sch.	*Rowena*	100	Isaiah Young	
	"	*Wave*	68	Jonathan Nickerson	James S. Higgins master in 1844.
	"	*Red Rover*	99	Charles Penfield	
1840	Sch.	*Cohannet*	99	George Brewster	Line continued through early 1841.
	"	*Combine*	48	Elkanah Winslow	

REGULAR LINE

John Fairfield, 26 Central Wharf, Boston agent. Child & Hooper, Mobile agents.

YEAR		VESSEL	TONS	MASTERS	REMARKS
1837	Bk.	*Venice*	354	Loring	Christopher Gill master in 1841.
1838	Bk.	*Zenobia*	280	Samuel T. Remington	E. Knowlton master in 1848.
1840	Sch.	*January*	115	G. M. Holmes	Fairfield & Lincoln became Boston agents.
1841	Bk.	*Alabama*	280	Charles E. Ranlett	Fairfield, Lincoln & Co., 18 India St., and
	"	*Southerner*	277	Leander Hallet	7 and 8 Lewis Wharf, became Boston agents.
	"	*New England*	239	R. W. Welch	
	"	*Northerner*	233		
	"	*Chester*	202	Peter Hanna	
	"	*Sophronia*	198	R. Newcomb	
	Bg.	*Esplata*	221	Robert Sproul	
	Sp.	*Tarquin*	516	Thomas G. Hiler	
1842	Bg.	*Miles Standish*	153	N. Gorham	James A. Hooper became Mobile agent.
	Bk.	*Ranger*	246	Alexander Milliken	
	Sch.	*Tallas*		Taylor	
1843	Bk.	*Nautilus*	216	Edmund Crosby	Fairfield, Lincoln & Co., and John O. B.
	Bk.	*Kosato*	246	James Cook	Minot, became Boston agents.
	Bg.	*Falco*	211	John C. Carter	Harrod & Darling became Mobile agents.
	Bk.	*Missouri*	319	Peter Hanna	
	"	*Arab*	354	Edmund Crosby	
	"	*Miquelon*	182	Ezra C. Smith	
	Sp.	*Glendover*	495	William H. Parsons	
1844	Sp.	*William Gray*	296	Edmund Crosby	
	Sch.	*H. A. Schroeder*	96	N. H. Deshon	
1845	Sp.	*Clarissa Andrews*	397	E. G. Colby	John Fairfield & Co., and J. O. B. Minot
	Bg.	*Boston*	171	Nathaniel Percival	became Boston agents in Apr.
	Bk.	*Lucretia*	314	William Rea	John H. Pearson & Co. replaced John Fair-
	Bg.	*R. W. Brown*	152	J. Spinney, Jr.	field & Co. in Sept.
	"	*Timoleon*	422	A. Blevin	Name changed to Pearson & Co.'s Line.
	"	*Lowder*	149	William Lowder	
	Sp.	*Michigan*	441	B. Mason	
	"	*Thracian*	375	Brown	
	"	*Pactolus*	494	Samuel Harding	
	Bg.	*Neptune*	196	Benjamin F. Basford	
	"	*Oak*	177	Daniel Pepper	
	Sp.	*Manco*	350	George W. Nickels	
1846	Bg.	*Talleyrand*	145	E. Knowlton	Whitaker & Sampson became Mobile agents
	"	*St. Simonds*	187	D. Eldridge	in Sept.
	Bk.	*Apphia Maria*	250	Samuel Billings	
	"	*Mallory*	300	Benjamin K. Babbidge	
	Bg.	*Quincy*	167	Zaccheus Kempton	
	Bk.	*Martha*	242	Ebenezer G. Adams	
	Sch.	*Neptune*	160	William H. Leland	
	Bg.	*Hector*	198	John Pendleton	
	"	*Token*	138	Hammond	
	Sch.	*Santee*	92	Robert Carle	

REGULAR LINE (*continued*)

YEAR		VESSEL	TONS	MASTERS	REMARKS
1847	Bg.	*Voltaire*	144	Walden	Name changed to Express Line. John H.
	"	*Venus*	195	Gray	Pearson & Co., Foster's Wharf, became
	"	*Fanny Coit*	208	Hy. B. Parker	Boston agents.
	"	*Curacao*	131	James S. Higgins	
	Bk.	*Harriet T. Bartlett*	197	Elisha Baker	
	Bg.	*Ottoman*	205	Hannum	
	"	*George F. Williams*	199	Myrus New	
	Bk.	*Mousam*	321	A. B. Day	
	Sp.	*Adrian*	570	J. Edward Scott	
	Bk.	*Walter*	257	John B. Thompson	
	Sp.	*Hannah Eddy*	414	John H. Pearson	
	Bk.	*New World*	229	John Crowell	
	Bg.	*Consuelo*	173	S. B. Ray	Var. Kay.
1848	Bg.	*Rollerson*	196	Kelly H. Crowell	Name changed to Pearson & Co.'s Express
	"	*Cleora*	262	T. G. Ward	Line.
	"	*Niagara*	232	James Jarvis	
	"	*Howland*	275	Clarington W. Eldridge	David E. Mayo master in 1852.
	"	*Osceola*	195	Hiram Baker	
	Bk.	*E. A. Kinsman*	269	E. A. Kinsman	
	"	*Alice Tarleton*	287	Levi R. Tobey	
	Bg.	*Henry Buck*	184	David Woodside	
	"	*Cornelia*	127	Freeman Rogers	
	Bk.	*Eureka*	276	Joseph Ryder	
	"	*Rowland*	411	Eldridge	

PACKET LINE

Samuel R. Allen, 110 Milk St., Boston agent.

YEAR		VESSEL	TONS	MASTERS	REMARKS
1837	Sp.	*Hercules*	371	L. Snow	
	"	*Rajah*	531	E. C. Bliss	
	"	*Merchant*	347	T. B. Cunningham	
	Bk.	*Tartar*	321	Edward C. Nickels	
1838	Sp.	*Louisa*	324	Fisher A. Newell	
	"	*William Goddard*	536	S. Potter	
	"	*Sterling*	360	H. Neef	
	Bg.	*Falco*	211	Kimball Harlow	
	"	*Cambrian*	197	Stanwood	
	Sp.	*Paragon*	359	Winslow H. Curtis	
1839	Bg.	*Otho*	132	Stephen Smith	
	"	*William & James*	160	J. Elwell	
	Sp.	*Charlotte*	390	N. Gorham	
	Sch.	*Delaware*	169	J. S. Brookfield	
	"	*Larkin*	115	Willis B. Churbuck	
	"	*Cape Fear*	103	Bearse	
	Bk.	*Triton*	267	W. Harris	
	"	*Beaver*	299	Seth M. Tripe	
1840	Bg.	*Champion*	209	Denison	S. R. Allen and W. B. Sawyer, 133 State St.,
	"	*Vesta*	155	J. B. Hallet	became Boston agents.
	"	*Miles Standish*	153	N. Gorham	Line called Allen's Packet Line.
	"	*Margaret*		Smith	
	"	*Senator*	193	Bangs Pepper	
	Sch.	*Henry*	92	John Fessenden	
	"	*Queen*	100	Oliver Arey	
	Bk.	*New World*	229	Benjamin Young, Jr.	
	Bg.	*Mary Jones*	120	J. Johnson	
1841	Sch.	*Jack*	75	Leavitt	S. R. Allen, 21 Commercial Wharf, and
	"	*Joseph Warren*	76	Isaac Fessenden	Sawyer & Slater, 133 State St., became Bos-
	"	*Cornelia*	97	Zadoc Kelley	ton agents.
	Bg.	*Gipsey*	164	Collin C. Baker	
	Bk.	*John Odlin*	257	William F. Hanover	
	"	*Adario*	268	William C. Rogers	
	Bg.	*Escalus*	195	Solomon Taylor	
	Bk.	*Hebron*	384	Daniel Hood	
	Sch.	*Patapsco*	90	Springer	
	Sp.	*Deucalion*	513	Howes	Oliver G. Lane master in 1849.

PACKET LINE *(continued)*

YEAR		VESSEL	TONS	MASTERS	REMARKS
1841	Sp.	*Corea*	366	George C. Gardner	
	Bg.	*China*	181	Joe Small	
	Sch.	*Two Marys*	116	Francis W. Miner	
1842	Sch.	*Edwin*	103	William Hinckley	
	"	*Joy*	100	Alexander Gage	
	Bg.	*Catherine*	239	Peter Vesper	
	Bk.	*Columbia*	289	Samuel Trussell	
	Sch.	*Chattahoochee*	116	Doane	
1843	Sch.	*Alabama*	92	Henry Kingsbury	S. R. Allen and John O. B. Minot became
	"	*August*	116	Joseph Holmes	Boston agents. Name changed to Allen &
	"	*Dover*	88	Asa Curtis	Minot's Line.
	"	*Bride*	95	Samuel Blunt	John Phillips became Mobile agent.
	Bg.	*Odeon*	118	James Nickerson, 2nd	In May, S. R. Allen and Samuel Weltch be-
	"	*Palestine*	249	Joseph L. Sturtevant	came agents; became Allen & Weltch's Line.
	"	*Ganza*	225	Robert T. Soule	Note: The following vessels were dispatched
	Sch.	*Tyro*	113	Henry M. Adams	repeatedly and appeared to form the nucleus
	Bk.	*Marine*	213	Matthew R. Vennard	of the regular line: Ship *William Goddard;*
	Bg.	*Susan Spofford*	199	William Spofford	brigs *Growler, Commerce, Ganza;* bark *Huma*
	"	*Growler*	247	Barnard Ulmer	and schooner *Alabama.*
	Bk.	*St. Cloud*	299	Francis Davis	
	Bg.	*Commerce*	281	J. G. Allen	
	"	*Hokomok*	228	Westcott Harris	
1844	Sp.	*Sweden*	646	William Homan	
	Bg.	*Souther*	197	John C. Hardy	
	Sp.	*Republic*	644	James C. Luce	
	Sch.	*Stranger*	98	Stevens	
	Bg.	*Sylph*	196	George Pollard	
	Bk.	*Baltic*	395	Wheaton Allen	Abandoned at sea, 1852.
	"	*Montpelier*	264	Samuel Stackpole	
	Sch.	*Saganaw*	95	Wright	
1845	Sch.	*Henry Clay*		Downes	
	Bk.	*Washington*	286	Joshua Bartlett, Jr.	
	"	*Huma*	380	Ingersoll	
	"	*Harriet T. Bartlett*	197	Elisha Baker	
	Sch.	*Emily Knight*	100	Ephraim Hosmer	
1846	Bg.	*Oscar*	145	C. H. Reed	Register surrendered Nov. 13, 1854. Vessel
	Sp.	*Thomas Wright*	623	W. P. Gardner	lost.
	Sch.	*Shetland*	98	J. Tobey	
	Bg.	*George Shattuck*	210	Daniel Bragdon	
	Sp.	*Gloucester*	338	George Pollard	
	Bk.	*Carlos*	322	Joseph H. Tillinghast	
	Sch.	*Andes*	114	C. A. Snow	
	Bk.	*Julia*	318	James G. Allen	
1847	Sch.	*Somerville*	128	Rudolphus Pendleton	O. W. Savage became Mobile agent in Dec.
	Bk.	*Gov. Briggs*	198	J. H. Hallet	
	Sch.	*Retrieve*	99	J. Ellis	
	Bg.	*Rebecca C. Fisher*	222	Hamilton D. Conklin	
	Sch.	*Barton*	90	Nelson Waldron	
	"	*Emblem*	82	H. Hatch	
1848	Bg.	*Samuel Brown*	165	Anthony Thatcher	Savage & Calef became Mobile agents in Mar.
	Bk.	*Ork*	244	Azariah Doane	Discontinued at end of 1848, but revived in
	Bg.	*Gen. Worth*	199	Samuel Walton	1854.
	"	*Globe*	239	Hiram Hall, 2nd	
	Bk.	*Isnardon*	246	T. G. Moulton	
	"	*Peri*	265	Simon H. Cotter	
	Sp.	*Adrian*	570	J. Edward Scott	
	Bk.	*J. H. Millay*	249	Benjamin Adams	
	Bg.	*Isabella*	149	Oliver Matthews	

ALLEN & WELTCH'S LINE

Savage, Calef & Co., Mobile agents. Allen & Weltch, Boston agents. Sailed very irregularly.

YEAR		VESSEL	TONS	MASTERS	REMARKS
1854	Bk.	*Ocilla*	368	Sidney Ashby	
1858	Bk.	*Sumter*	385	G. M. Humphrey	Var. *Sumpter.*
	"	*Leland*	347	Luther Eldridge	

DISPATCH LINE

Cabot & Frazar, 79 State St., Boston agents. Notice of establishment, Sept., 1838.

YEAR	VESSEL	TONS	MASTERS	REMARKS
1838	Sp. *Palmyra*	612	John Cushing	
1839	Sch. *Frazar*		Harding	Nathaniel Winsor and Benjamin Bruce, 103
	Bg. *Bogota*	154	Elkanah Rich	State St., became Boston agents.
	" *Nimrod*	197	Oakman	
1840	Sch. *Casket*	99	Doane Kelly, Jr.	Vessel lost in Dec., 1843.
	" *Rantoul*			
	Bg. *Casket*	155	Edmund Reed	
	" *Patriot*	164	Elkanah Rich	
	" *Palestine*	111	Fearing	
1841	Sch. *Delta*	99	Baker	
	" *Caroline*		Joseph Lamson	
	Bg. *Osceola*	158	Bennett Morgan	
	Bk. *Wyandot*	287	O. Farnham	
	" *Bostonian*	267	Levi B. Gilchrist	
	" *Adeline & Eliza*	249	Farley Hopkins	
	Bg. *Mozart*	129	Thomas Cunningham	
1842	Sch. *Crescent*		Babcock	
	Bg. *Hallowell*	203	Isaac Smith	
	Bk. *Cowper*	391	John C. Buffington	
	" *Strabo*	420	Henry Shoof	
	Sch. *Frances Hallet*	79	Rogers	
1843	Bg. *Growler*	247	Bernard Ulmer	
	Bk. *Julia*	318	Bennet	John A. Burgess master in 1844.
	Sch. *Shylock*	120	Isaac Matthews	In Sept. Winsor continued line alone; Bruce
	" *Navarro*	100	Damon	started Bruce's Line.
	" *Atlantic*	95	Hiram Baker	
	Bg. *Charlotte*	199	Charles Littlejohn	
1844	Sp. *Norman*	508	Robert Spavin	Name changed to Winsor's Line. J. H. Rivers
	Bg. *Philura*	198	Russell Doane	& Co. became Mobile agents.
	Bk. *Mauran*	348	George W. Williams	
	Bg. *Chastena*	170	V. Hamer	Var. Hamor.
	Sp. *Nile*	334	Joshua Harding	
	Bg. *Espalata*	221	Robert Sproul	
	Bk. *Craton*	334	Amos Towne	
	" *Empire*	248	David Keazer	
1845	Sch. *Gil Blas*	96	Joseph Lamson	
	" *Independence*	95	Jacob H. Dow	
1846	Bg. *Maria Spear*	199	Henry Prior	J. H. Rivers started Regular Line in Sept., 1846, and Winsor continued alone with very irregular sailings.

REGULAR LINE

N. F. Frothingham, 25 Long Wharf, Mobile agent. Line established May, 1841.

YEAR	VESSEL	TONS	MASTERS	REMARKS
1841	Sch. *Galaxy*	74	James R. Potter	
	" *Laurel*	99	Lewis Burgess	
	" *Ann*	80	Newman	
	" *Adelaide*	92	Hiram Sampson	
	Bk. *Avola*	309	G. Davis	Swanton Whitmore master in 1847.
1842	Sch. *Ellen*	103	S. Morse	
1843	Sch. *Nahant*	84	William Thomas	

BRUCE'S LINE

Benjamin Bruce, 110 State St., Boston agent. Line established Sept., 1843, after dissolution of Winsor & Bruce.

YEAR	VESSEL	TONS	MASTERS	REMARKS
1843	Bg. *John A. Lancaster*	175	J. Loveland	
	Sch. *Atlanta*	132	Cooper	
	" *Gleaner*	75	Warren Hamilton	
1844	Bg. *Washington*	260	Waldo Stevens	Name changed to Bruce & Cheney's Line. Benjamin Bruce and J. H. Cheney, 9 India St., became Boston agents; Thomas H. Cheever, Mobile agent.
1845	Bk. *W. T. Wheaton*	437	Silas P. Martin	
1847	Sch. *Patriot*			

REGULAR LINE

J. H. Rivers, 15 Commercial St., C. T. Savage, 8 Lewis Wharf, and William Lincoln, Boston agents. J. H. Rivers & Co., Mobile agents. Line established Sept., 1846, an offshoot of Winsor's Dispatch Line.

YEAR		VESSEL	TONS	MASTERS	REMARKS
1846	Bk.	*Apphia Maria*	250	Samuel Billings	
	"	*Epervier*	264	Nathan A. Farwell	
	Bg.	*Carter Braxton*	132	Morse	J. H. Rivers became sole Boston agent.
	"	*Attakapas*	149	William M. Sartelle	
	"	*St. Simons*	187	D. Eldridge	Var. *St. Symonds*.
	Sch.	*Extio*	149	William S. Emerson	
1847	Sp.	*Hebrew*	399	Badger	J. Silloway & Co., 5 Commercial St., and
	Bk.	*Weskeag*	248	Bartlett	J. H. Rivers became Boston agents.
	"	*Washington*	286	Joshua Bartlett, Jr.	
	"	*Zenobia*	280	E. Knowlton	
	Bg.	*Josephine*	232	Timothy N. Porter	
	"	*Marsellois*	223	George Thorndike	
	Sch.	*Gen. Wm. H. Washington*	69		
	Bk.	*Carlos*	323	James Brown	
	Bg.	*Irving*	236	Edward Robinson	
	Bk.	*Nahumkeag*	266	Henry Champlin	
1848	Bk.	*Robert Walsh*	282	William Singer	J. Silloway, J. P. Farley, and J. Davis be-
	Bg.	*Dr. Hitchcock*	143	J. B. Elwell	came Boston agents; J. H. Rivers & Co.,
	"	*Wellingsley*	210	John J. Davis	Mobile agents.
	"	*Ohio*	250	William Davis	J. Silloway and J. H. Rivers became Boston
	Bk.	*Helen*		Barnard Ulmer	agents in Aug.
	"	*Alabama*	280	Artemas W. Wall	
	Bg.	*Alphage*	173	John Brown, Jr.	
	"	*Globe*	239	Hiram Hall	
	"	*Frank*	159	L. Baker	
	"	*Tartar*	199	J. R. Paul	
	Sch.	*Kate Aubrey*		Wilson	
	Bg.	*Sea*	249	Robert Norton	
1849	Bk.	*Eagle*	142	Charles Davis	
1851	Bk.	*Montpelier*	264	J. Colby	Silloway, Calef & Co. became Boston agents.
1852	Bk.	*N. C. Buchanan*	276	Hans J. Hanson	E. C. Center & Co. became Mobile agents;
	Bg.	*Francis P. Beck*	247	J. E. Avery	J. H. Rivers, Boston agent.
1853	Bg.	*Annawan*		Murdock	E. H. Rivers became Mobile agent. Name
	Bk.	*Maine*	272	P. H. Perkins	changed to Regular Dispatch Line. Silloway,
	Sch.	*Republic*	250	Thomas Snow	Calef & Co. started Dispatch Line, *q.v.*
1854	Bk.	*John Carver*	298	D. Nichols	J. H. Pendleton master in 1858.
	Bg.	*Niagara*	268	W. Fitz	Var. Feltz.
					Register surrendered Sept. 12, 1856; vessel lost.
	"	*Central America*	246	Martin L. Chase	
	"	*Yuba*	228	Pepper	D. C. Hall master in 1856.
	Bk.	*Daniel Webster*	313	Jonathan B. Atkins	
1855	Bg.	*Selma*	205	Rogers	
	"	*Lydia Frances*	262	H. Daggett	
1856	Bk.	*Growler*	484	T. R. Pillsbury	J. H. Rivers & Co. became Boston agents.
	"	*Ninevah*	439	Harris Stackpole	
1858	Bk.	*Grampus*	240	Cunningham	J. Silloway & Co. started Silloway's Dispatch
	Sp.	*Ohio*	738	William B. Hutchings	Line. Hetty Green was part owner of *Ohio*.
1859	Bk.	*Chester*	200	Elijah Crosby	
	"	*Champion*	391	David E. Mayo	

FORBES LINE

F. H. Forbes & Co., 15 India St., Boston agents.

YEAR		VESSEL	TONS	MASTERS	REMARKS
1847	Bk.	*California*	187	Drew	
	Bg.	*Loretto*	244	Waln	D. Henderson master in Sept., 1847.
	Sp.	*Lancaster*	687	Lyon	
	Sch.	*Gypsum*	136	John Small	Var. *Gipsum*.
					M. H. Pike master in 1849.

DISPATCH LINE

Silloway, Calef & Co., 5 Commercial St., Boston agents. H. O. Brewer & Co., Mobile agents.

YEAR	VESSEL	TONS	MASTERS	REMARKS
1853	Sch. *Alida*	121	Chadwick	
1854	Bk. *Grampus*	241	J. Dyer	J. Silloway & Co. became Boston agents in 1858.
1859	Bk. *Sumter*	381	J. M. Humphrey	Var. *Sumpter*.
	Sch. *Langdon Gilmore*	497	Jonathan Chase	

Note: Henry Lincoln & Co., 43 Commercial St., Boston, attempted to establish Lincoln's Line in Jan., 1859, starting with cl. sch. *Grandilla*, 220, Capt. Baker, but the move came to nothing.

SECTION 8. BOSTON—NEW ORLEANS

REGULAR PACKET LINE

John Pratt & Son, 19 India Wharf, Boston agents. George Green, Conti St., New Orleans agent. Established Jan., 1822.

YEAR	VESSEL	TONS	MASTERS	REMARKS
1822	Bg. *George*	273	Richard King	
	" *Orleans*	283	Peter Pratt	
1823	Bg. *Buck*	89	P. Reed	
1824	Bg. *Louisiana*	202	Joseph Proctor, Jr.	
1825	Sp. *Pocahontas*	300	Henry Bancroft	Lincoln & Green, Bienville St., became New Orleans agents.

ESTABLISHED LINE

Hall & Williams, 38 Central Wharf, Boston agents. William Fritz, Jr., & Co., New Orleans agents. Established Sept., 1822. Sailed "positively at the time appointed. All the above vessels will be armed and furnished with beds and bedding." Discontinued, 1826.

YEAR	VESSEL	TONS	MASTERS	REMARKS
1822	Bg. *Massachusetts*	222	Samuel B. Hobart	
	" *Creole*	222	Richard King	
	" *Delta*	225	Braddock Loring	Bradford B. Williams master in 1823.
1823	Bg. *Envoy*	264	Charles Pearson	
1824	Sp. *Java*	295	Abraham Rich	
1825	Bg. *Virginia*	172	John Luce	Parker & Stevens added as Boston agents.
	" *America*	172	John Luce	Howard & Mercy became New Orleans
	" *Pilgrim*	137	Farnsworth	agents.

REGULAR LINE

John Fairfield, 27 Central Wharf, and Hartshorne Homer, 17 Central Wharf, Boston agents. John A. Merle & Co. and Stetson & Avery, New Orleans agents. Established Aug., 1830. Sailed 1st and 15th during season.

YEAR	VESSEL	TONS	MASTERS	REMARKS
1830	Bg. *William*	198	James A. Collins	
	" *Baltic*			
	" *Delta*	225	Isaac Parker	
	" *Margaret*	186	Scudder	
	" *Cygnet*		Fogg	
1831	Sp. *Henry Thompson*	316	Bradford B. Williams	
	" *Homer*	296	Bradford B. Williams	
1832	Sp. *Helen Mar*	307	Paraclete Holmes	
	" *Ohio*	297	Christopher Howes	
1834	Sp. *Ambassador*	452	John W. Upton	It was a common practice with Fairfield in
	" *Arab*	276	John Marshall	the business season to advertise fixed sailing
	Bg. *Rapid*	233	David R. Lecraw	for four or five vessels in advance, usually at
	Sp. *Margaret Forbes*	383	King	ten-day intervals. He would frequently load a
	" *Hobart*	306	John Sprague	substantial number of other vessels in addi-
	" *Allbree*	387	Bangs	tion to those he designated as the regular
	Sch. *May*	126	Mulford Patterson	packets. This practice was followed by a num-
	Sp. *Harold*	438	Christopher Hall	ber of operators.
	" *Hamilton*	398	Christopher Hall	
	" *Caravan*	330	Samuel Nichols	
	" *Morea*	331	Richard Girdler	

REGULAR LINE (*continued*)

YEAR	VESSEL	TONS	MASTERS	REMARKS
1835	Sp. *Eagle*	283	Saul	
	" *Heraclide*	348	Bradford B. Williams	
	Bk. *Cyrus Butler*	360	Suchet Mauran	
1836	Sp. *Apollo*	413	William W. Thompson	
	" *Calumet*	318	Samuel V. Shreve	
	" *Tiger*	399	John D. Blanchard	Richard Baker master in 1838.
	" *New Jersey*	636	W. C. Barstow	
	Bg. *Charles Joseph*	314	William Frost	
1837	Sp. *Tarquin*	516	Lyman Hunt	
	" *Emperor*	314	Abraham Hayward	
	" *Saxon*	345	Charles Mansfield	
	Bk. *Roman*	245	Ebenezer Davis	
	Sp. *Ohio*	297	George Barker	Stephen Cutter master in 1838.
	" *Robert Pulsford*	406	Benjamin F. Miner	
	" *Perdonnet*	478	Nathaniel Ingersoll	
	" *Deucalion*	513	A. Winsor	Oliver G. Lane master in 1849.
	" *Adrian*	570	John L. Rogers	
	" *Victoria*	394	Nicholas P. Snell	
	" *Medford*	545	Francis W. Welch	
	" *Rialto*	459	Edward Holmes	
	Bg. *Horace*	283	Albert G. Nason	
	" *Two Sisters*	122	M. H. Parkinson	
	Sp. *Liverpool*	428	William C. Barstow	
	Bk. *Cambridge*	215	Benjamin Tay	
1838	Sp. *Lagoda*	341	Benjamin Freeman	John Fairfield & Co. became Boston agents;
	" *Stieglitz*	349	Gibson	Hiler & Waterman, New Orleans agents.
	" *Emily Taylor*	388	Simon Gill	
	Bg. *Maria Theresa*	229	Cushing	
	Sp. *Clifton*	599	James B. Ingersoll	
	" *Columbus*	595	Isaac S. Coffin	
	Bk. *Nautilus*	216	Charles Lincoln	
	Bg. *Champion*	201	John D. Blanchard	
	" *Metamora*	164	George P. Marston	
	Sp. *Pharsalia*	617	Charles F. Winsor	
1839	Sp. *St. Louis*	459	Orice King	Fairfield & Lincoln became Boston agents.
	" *Kentucky*	629	Joseph Nickerson	Charles E. Ranlett master in 1846.
	" *St. Petersburg*	814	Richard Trask	
	" *Bashaw*	392	John Freeman, Jr.	
	" *James H. Shepard*	635	St. Croix Redmond	
1840	Sp. *Oswego*	647	David Wood	At this time and for several years, Fairfield
	" *Tennessee*	457	Enoch Eastman	ran packets to Natchez.
	" *Mary Frances*	326	C. D. Percival	
	" *Riga*	345	William Williams	
	" *Propontis*	426	Edward G. Wise	
	" *Herculean*	542	Benjamin Cook	
	Bk. *Natchez*	300	Albert A. Burwell	Vessel lost on the South Shore of Massa-
	Bg. *Frances*	191	Stetson	chusetts Bay, Feb., 1848.
	" *Chester*	202	Peter Hanna	
	" *L'Orient*	167	J. Jackson	
	" *Calvin*	216	D. Lawrence	
1841	Sp. *Memphis*	799	Ebenezer Knight	Fairfield, Lincoln & Co. became Boston
	" *Louisa*	496	A. B. Mulford	agents; Harrod & Darling, New Orleans
	" *Aurelius*	389	W. F. Hines	agents.
	Bk. *Sultan*	354	Henry Hodge	
1842	Sp. *Don Juan*	645	H. L. Soule	Stranded abroad, Nov., 1843.
	" *Hampden*	646	Nathaniel Spooner	
	" *Norman*	508	Alfred Kendrick	
	" *Walpole*	593	William Thomas	
	" *Glasgow*	424	James L. Lambert	
1843	Sp. *Diana*	568	John Freeman	Frederick Howes master in 1845.
	Bk. *Southerner*	277	Leander Hallet	
	" *Nancy W. Stevens*	340	J. J. Stevens	
	Sp. *Prentice*	442	Reuben Paine	
	" *Colombo*	577	Asa Eldridge	Dennis Janvrin master in 1846.
	" *Berlin*	613	Barker G. Baker	

REGULAR LINE (*continued*)

YEAR	VESSEL	TONS	MASTERS	REMARKS
1843	Sp. *Mary & Susan*	392	N. G. Weeks	Became Stonington whaler in 1850.
	" *Edward Everett*	622	Octavius Howes	
	" *Bengal*	650	Josiah Gorham	
	" *Astrachan*	536	Ebenezer H. Webster	
	" *Columbiana*	631	George Baker	Foundered, Jan. 27, 1854. Crew saved by packet ship *Cornelius Grinnell*.
	" *Granada*	593	Nathaniel Spooner	
	" *Coquimbo*	672	Allen H. Knowles	Octavius Howe master in 1844.
	" *Oceanus*	473	Horace S. Crocker	
	Bk. *Missouri*	319	Peter Hanna	
1844	Bk. *Iris*	245	Thomas Merryman	Regular Line consisted of five barks: *Ohio, Alabama, Southerner, Missouri,* and *E. H. Chapin.*
	" *Teazer*	249	Jonathan Crockett	
	" *Epervier*	264	N. A. Farwell	William A. Briard master in 1845.
	Sp. *Harriet Rockwell*	448	John A. Briard	
	" *Olive & Eliza*	386	C. Flanders	
	" *Sarah*	453	A. G. Cutter	
	" *Viola*	495	William Jameson	
	Bk. *Ranger*	246	Alexander Milliken	
	Bg. *Billow*	173	E. Lawrence	
	Sp. *William Gray*	296	Edmund Crosby	N. T. Thompson master in 1849.
	Bk. *Frances Burr*	298	George Foster	
	Bg. *Talleyrand*	145	Seth Tripe	William P. Swasey master in 1854.
	Bk. *Ohio*	373	Thomas Ellis	
	" *E. H. Chapin*	424	Robert W. Welch	G. W. Collier master in 1847.
	" *Alabama*	280	Charles E. Ranlett	
	" *Gazelle*	269	David Allen	
	Bg. *Taranto*	278	John T. White	
	Sp. *Nile*	334	Edward K. Smith	
	" *Oxnard*	595	William B. Hinckley	
	" *Isaac Newton*	600	Lyman D. Spaulding	
	Bk. *Caspian*	321	David Bartlett	
	Sp. *Neptune*	498	B. Peach	
	" *Hamlet*	494	Lyman Hunt	
	" *Ilzaide*	411	John C. Buffington	
	" *Ann*	334	James M. Hill	
	" *Arvum*	364	Wooster Smith	
	" *Mary Ann*	497	Albert H. Brown	
	" *Gov. Davis*	768	Henry Neef	
	" *Cygnet*	499	J. J. Heard	
1845	Bk. *Murillo*	309	William Woodside	Fairfield, Lincoln & Co., and John O. B. Minot became Boston agents; in Apr., John Fairfield & Co. and J. O. B. Minot, Boston agents. McGaw & Lincoln, Boston agents in June. McGaw retired in Dec. and William Lincoln and Charles T. Savage became agents.
	Sp. *Rowland*	412	F. G. Blanchard	
	" *Amazon*	570	Levi L. Batchelder	
	Bk. *Talisman*	347	George W. Somes	
	" *New England*	357	William Long	
	Sp. *Faneuil Hall*	548	James H. Sears	
	" *London*	637	Israel E. Lovett	
	Bk. *Thaetus*	286	Stephen Cutter	
	" *Santee*	192	George P. Marston	
	Sp. *Franklin*	301	Theodore Stanwood	
	" *Robert Patten*	376	Robert Patten	
	" *Antwerp*	414	George W. Robinson	
	Bg. *Perfect* (Cl.)	157	Stephen A. Gardner	
	" *Cleopatra* (Cl.)			
1848	Sp. *Marcellus*	660	Nathaniel Spooner	Hy. Lincoln & Co. and C. T. Savage became Boston agents.
1849	Sp. *Monsoon*	381	Alexander Scudder	
1850	Sp. *North Atlantic*	799	H. Cook	George W. Hynson became New Orleans agent.
	" *Adams*	597	Moses Gay	
1851	Sp. *Ophelia*	597	William B. Nason	Snow & Rich and C. & T. Savage became Boston agents; J. W. Stanton & Co., New Orleans agents.
	" *Sheffield*	590	Christopher Lewis	
	" *James Corner*	678	R. Bennett	
1852	Bk. *Georgia*	363	John B. Lindsey	A. C. Hersey and J. H. Rivers became Boston agents.
	Sp. *Muscongus*	669	James H. Kellerman	
	" *Bay State*	592	Alexander Baxter	

REGULAR LINE (*continued*)

YEAR	VESSEL	TONS	MASTERS	REMARKS
1853	Bk. *Boynton*	438	Smalley	J. H. Rivers and David Snow & Co. became
"	*John Bird*	275	H. G. Bird	Boston agents; William J. Dewey, New Or-
	Sp. *Reporter*	1474	Octavius Howe	leans agent.
1854	Sp. *Middlesex*	496	Henry Paine	George W. Hynson became New Orleans
				agent.
"	*Wellfleet*	1353	Bradford	Called Regular Dispatch Line.
"	*Neva*	842	Brown	
"	*Mariner*	1282	George Barker	
"	*John Spear*	629	A. K. Spear	
	Bk. *Saragossa*	348	Albert Turley	
	Sp. *Bennington*	513	James Young	
"	*Oregon*	649	Higgins	T. N. Porter master in 1855.
"	*Sheffield*	590	Christopher Lewis	J. W. Nelson master in 1856.
"	*Hamlet*	760	Eben Sears	
1855	Sp. *J. Montgomery*	893	J. D. Dennett	
"	*Golden Cross*	1100	J. T. Little	Var. Littell.
"	*Wilbur Fiske*	980	Albert A. Burwell	
1856	Sp. *Colchis*	422	John Douglas	J. H. Rivers & Co. became Boston agents;
"	*Geo. Hallet*	420	Henry Merritt	S. L. & E. L. Levy and G. W. Hynson & Co.,
				New Orleans agent.
1857	Sp. *Venice*	616	Whitman	
	Bk. *Julia Ford*	199	E. W. Griffin	
"	*Priscilla*	597	H. Newton	
"	*Saone*	292	G. A. Karstens	
"	*P. R. Hazeltine*	399	W. Gillis	
	Sp. *Luna*	625	Jos. L. Nason	
"	*Charles*	381	A. Ruark	John S. Vent also master in 1857.
"	*Champion*	564	Wilson	
1858	Sp. *Kate Howe*	596	Gorham Burket	
	Bk. *Harriet Hazeltine*	527	T. Drinkwater	
"	*Victorine*	540	I. Jones	
	Sch. *Augusta C. Brewer* (Cl.)	399	M. Cox	
1859	Bk. *Grace Hammond*	499	Harrison Mahoney	Line continued through 1860. William J.
"	*Our Union*	366	R. D. Kent	Dewey & Co. became New Orleans agents.
"	*Diana*	499	George Davis	
1860	Bk. *Ellen Stevens*	354	J. L. Howe	

PACKET LINE

Samuel R. Allen, 110 Milk St., Boston agent. Levi H Gale, New Orleans agent.

YEAR	VESSEL	TONS	MASTERS	REMARKS
1834	Bg. *Banner*	359	S. B. Robinson	
	Sp. *Hobart*	306	John Sprague	
"	*Trenton*	429	William Homer	Also reported W. Homan.
"	*Lucy Ann*	309	Asa Pratt	
"	*Lion*	378	Allen Bursley	
"	*Timoleon*	422	D. L. Winsor	
"	*Mattakeesit*	481	J. Drew	
	Bg. *Diamond*	150	George Chase	
1835	Bk. *Venice*	354	Dauphin King	
	Sp. *Corea*	367	Charles Prescott	
"	*Lowell*	414	J. L. Crocker	
"	*Molo*	495	A. Winsor	
"	*Frances Ann*	446	Henchman S. Soule	
1836	Sp. *Concord*	321	J. M. Miltimore	
"	*Arnold Wells*	372	Howes	
"	*Empire*	437	John O. Baker	
"	*Cowper*	391	George Henchman	
	Bg. *Aquila*	288	S. Eldridge	
1837	Bg. *William*	166	B. McNear	
	Bk. *Bashaw*	392	N. A. Tucker	
	Sp. *Timor*	289	Lovett	
"	*Vespasian*	318	Benjamin Winsor	Kimball Harlow master in 1844.
"	*Henry Clay*	435	David Elwell	
"	*Henry*	396	Benjamin Pierce	

PACKET LINE (*continued*)

YEAR	VESSEL	TONS	MASTERS	REMARKS
1837	Sp. *Nantasket*	435	William H. Wilson	
	" *Arno*	299	S. Poller	
	" *Norman*	508	E. Wood	Alfred Kendrick master in 1842.
1838	Sp. *Nonatum*	694	B. F. Miner	
	" *Constantine*	742	George Winsor, Jr.	Alexander Wadsworth master in 1842.
	" *Forum*	294	Ebenezer Caldwell	
	" *Hellespont*	347	Michael Parsons	
	" *Paugus*	321	H. Upton	
1838	Bg. *Forest*	158	Robert Hutchinson	
1839	Sp. *Clarissa Andrews*	397	Samuel Crowell	
	" *Oneco*	640	Joshua Drew	
	" *Damascus*	694	Eli C. Bliss	
	" *Rajah*	531	Eli C. Bliss	
	" *Trenton*	429	James S. Bennett	Ex-Boston to Liverpool packet.
	" *Plymouth*	425	Alfred Kendrick	
1840	Sp. *Massachusetts*	388	Life Wilson	S. R. Allen, 21 Commercial Wharf, and William B. Sawyer, 133 State St., became Boston agents; Sawyer & Slater agents in November. Line now called Allen's Line.
	Bg. *Emma*	131	Fernald	
	Bk. *Henry Newell*	258	Charles T. Burnham	
	" *Adario*	268	Calvin Adams	
	Sp. *Loo Choo*	639	William Whippen	William B. Hinckley master in 1843.
	" *Bowditch*	578	Samuel Crowell	
	" *Louvre*	374	Pierce W. Penhallow	
	" *Oceana*	623	William Hammond	
	" *Chaos*	771	Levi Pratt	
1841	Sp. *Susan Drew*	696	Charles E. Ranlett	Also reported Charles A. Ranlett.
	" *John Holland*	529	William Henderson	
	" *Claiborne*	663	Joseph S. Burgess	
	" *Tioga*	419	Joshua Harding	
	" *Birmingham*	571	William J. Robinson	
	" *Viola*	495	Edward Sprague	
	" *Taglioni*	798	George L. Rogers	
	" *Ontario*	606	John Holmes	
	" *Vermont*	477	Nathaniel Mayhew	
	" *Wm. Badger*	334	John E. Lane	
1842	Sp. *Desdemona*	630	William Clark	Sawyer & Slater discontinued as Boston agents in August and John O. B. Minot added as a Boston agent.
	" *Monsoon*	381	John C. Paine	
	Bg. *Lincoln*	174	Thomas Ellis	F. M. Weld & Co. became New Orleans agents.
	" *Fornax*	249	Joseph Wilson	
	" *Falco*	211	John C. Carter	
	Bk. *Ten Brothers*	273	George Crawford	
	" *Columbia*	289	Samuel Trussell	
	Sp. *Bengal*	650	Josiah Gorham	
	" *United States*	684	Samuel Swanton	
	" *Charlotte*	391	Richard Tripe	
	" *St. Cloud*	299	Walter Emerson	
	" *Columbus*	595	Isaac S. Coffin	George E. Balch master in 1848.
1843	Bk. *Charles Williams*	298	Richard Keating	Minot retired in May and Samuel Weltch was associated with S. R. Allen.
	Sp. *Atlas*	790	John Prince	
	" *William Goddard*	536	James Potter	Line called Allen & Weltch's Line.
	" *Walpole*	593	Briggs Thomas	Weltch also associated with Allen's Savannah, Charleston, Norfolk, City Point, Richmond, and Mobile Lines.
	" *Rubicon*	488	Joseph Thompson	
	" *Lochinvar*	635	Isaiah Westcott	
	Bk. *Kensington*	357	Ezekiel Gorham	
	" *Ellen*	373	Nathan Briggs	
	" *Nahant*	304	Albert Winsor	
1844	Sp. *Leonore*	370	Thomas Milton, Jr.	
	Bg. *Talleyrand*	145	E. Knowlton	
	Bk. *Adeline & Eliza*	249	Samuel Higgins	
	Sp. *Rockingham*	359	Pierce W. Penhallow	
	" *Thomas H. Perkins*	670	John W. Shaw	
	Bk. *Suwarrow*	292	George Snow	
	Sp. *Russell Glover*	795	Jonathan Bisson	
	" *Charlemagne*	442	William J. Fales	
	" *Thomas B. Wales*	600	David Crocker	

PACKET LINE (*continued*)

YEAR	VESSEL	TONS	MASTERS	REMARKS
1844	Sp. *Milton*	598	Josiah Gorham	
	" *Magnolia*	679	Edward Gray	
	" *Shanunga*	546	David Patten	
	" *Caledonia*	514	William Massicot	
1845	Sp. *Niobe*	347	David R. Lecraw	
	" *Martha*	534	Samuel Snow	
	" *Arragon*	741	Daniel Knight	
	Bk. *Dana*	299	Oliver Smith	
	Sp. *Lapland*	545	Samuel P. Poor	
	" *Cairo*	537	Alexander C. Childs	
	" *Adrian*	570	Elias Davis	
	" *Epaminondas*	549	James H. Chick	
	" *Louisa*	496	Benjamin Tay	
	" *Ashburton*	449	Jeremiah D. White	
	Bk. *Marcia*	343	Otis Harward	
	Sp. *Sunbeam*	844	George Winsor, Jr.	
	" *Emperor*	597	Richard Brown	
1846	Bk. *Adeline*	250	Edward Lincoln	George W. Hynson became New Orleans
	Sp. *Paris*	356	William Symmes	agent in Mar.
	Bk. *Luzon*	300	J. F. Goodrich	
	Sp. *Granada*	593	Nathaniel Spooner	
	Bk. *Brighton*	337	Reuben Snow	
	Sp. *Gloucester*	339	George Pollard	
	" *Rialto*	459	W. W. Chase	
	" *Berlin*	613	Barker G. Baker	
	Bk. *Lepanto*	299	George Hagar	
	Sp. *Martha*	534	Richard Rich	
	" *Boston*	639	George Barker	
	" *Judah Touro*	741	Jos. J. Nickerson	
	Bk. *Hebron*	384	Silas D. Gregg	
1847	Bk. *Bostonian*	267	George W. Main	
	" *Gulnare*	273	Robbins	Edward F. Byrne master in 1847.
	Sp. *Russell*	349	William Symmes	
	Bk. *Isnardon*	247	T. G. Moulton	
	Sp. *Merchant*	390	George M. Pollard	Sunk in collision, Apr., 1848.
	" *Coquimbo*	672	Abram Hedge	N. W. Town master in 1853.
	" *St. Lawrence*	356	P. B. Bowers	
	" *Harvard*	493	John F. Corliss	
	" *Marathon*	382	John Johnson	Martin Waterman master in 1850.
	" *Independence*	827	Elias D. Knight	
	" *Niagara*	458	David A. Nye	First ship built in East Boston, 1835. Foundered, Oct. 25, 1854.
	" *Kate Howe*	596	Josiah S. Cummings	Var. Comings.
	Bk. *Laura*	219	Phineas Leach	
	" *Tiberius*	299	Benjamin Taylor	
	" *Cactus*	260	Albert G. Nason	
	" *Riga*	345	Edward G. Wise	
	Sp. *Unicorn*	397	William Cushing	
	" *Mary*	268	Nathaniel Francis	
	" *Suffolk*	518	Obed Snow	
	" *Gov. Davis*	768	Daniel P. Upton	
	" *Parthenon*	560	Samuel T. Woodbury	
1848	Bk. *Gov. Hinckley*	399	William Loring	
	Sp. *New England*	549	Alfred T. Robinson	
	" *Kedron*	455	Eben Howes, Jr.	
	" *Abby Pratt*	669	Ebenezer A. Shaw	
	" *Mary Ann*	497	Horatio A. Patten	
	" *Austria*	645	Robert McManus	Register surrendered Nov. 11, 1853. Vessel lost.
	" *Gen. Veazie*	443	John W. Fairfield	
	" *Cordova*	333	Caleb R. Moore	
	" *Oxnard*	596	F. W. Welch	
	" *Peter Marcy*	821	Daniel Marcy	
	" *Townsend*	719	Josiah Richardson	
	" *Robert*	778	Isaac Beauchamp	

PACKET LINE (*continued*)

YEAR	VESSEL	TONS	MASTERS	REMARKS
1848	Sp. *Palmyra*	612	Edward F. Byrne	
1849	Bk. *Susan W. Lind*	263	C. V. Clark	
	Sp. *Uriel*	799	Simpson	Condemned and sold at St. Thomas prior to Apr., 1863. J. G. Foster master in 1852.
1850	Sp. *Oxenbridge*	527	Solomon Taylor	
	" *Arcadia*	715	C. S. Counce	Wrecked, Nov., 1854.
1851	Sp. *Huron*	515	John A. Paine	
	" *Frances*	595	Ellis	
	Bk. *Forest Prince*	355	Lewis Crowell	
1852	Sp. *Moses Wheeler*	872	James B. King	Fosdick & Co. became New Orleans agents.
	" *Trenton*	668	Snow	
	Bk. *Emma Lincoln*	299	J. R. Bartlett	
1853	Bk. *Ithona*	315	John Leckie	Charles A. Farwell associated with Fosdick
	" *Sarah Olney*	200	John H. Remick	& Co.
	Sp. *Serampore*	499	Phinley W. Reed	
1854	Bg. *Anglo-Saxon*	200	Sullivan	
	Bk. *James Briant*	518	E. Howe	
	Sp. *Ocean Traveller*	695	E. McGrath	J. M. Boardman master in 1856.
	" *Corsica*	429	George Melcher	
1855	Sp. *Callender*	428	William B. Nason	George A. Fosdick became New Orleans
	Bk. *Saxony*	346	Allen Howes	agent.
1856	Bk. *Delphos*	398	Soule	
	Sp. *Rubicon*	488	William T. Becket	
1857	Sp. *Helen*	976	J. Edwards Scott	
1858	Sch. *Wm. C. Mershon* (tern)	390	William C. Mershon	
	Sp. *Sea Belle*	785	J. Lanphear	Var. Lamphear.
1859	Sp. *Hartley*	469	Alfred Howes	
	Bk. *Scio* (Cl.)	429	John Ewer	
1860	Sp. *Valentia*	880	Robert Jack	Also reported 799 tons.

NEW LINE

Ammi C. Lombard & Co., 13 and 14 Lewis' Wharf, Boston agents. Jos. A. Barelli & Co., New Orleans agents. Line established Aug., 1837, to begin operations Sept. 1st, sailing on 1st and 15th of each month.

YEAR	VESSEL	TONS	MASTERS	REMARKS
1837	Sp. *Cherokee*	415	Edw. Kendrick, Jr.	Baily Loring master in 1838.
	" *Carolina*	400	Joshua Harding	
	" *Charleston*	373	David Eldridge	
	" *Columbiana*	630	David Elwell	George Barker master on first voyage.
	" *Brighton*	337	Sam C. Howes	
	" *Seaman*	241	Sam C. Howes	In place of unfinished *Carolina*.
1838	Sp. *Cincinnati*	457	Sam C. Howes	In place of unfinished *Columbiana*
	" *Concordia*	602	Joshua Harding	John A. Merrit became New Orleans agent.
	" *Bombay*	466	Micah Humphrey	Line now consisted of six ships and called
	" *Coromando*	635	Robert Pierce	Lombard's Line.
	" *Grand Turk*	369	Charles Thompson	
1840	Sp. *Prentice*	442	Reuben Hopkins	
	" *Clarendon*	536	Erastus Sampson	
	" *Nantasket*	435	Hosea Winsor	
	" *Woodside*	664	Francis W. Walsh	Var. Welch.
	" *Tyrone*	538	John A. Spear	
1841	Bk. *Z. D.*	311	Zenas D. Bassett, Jr.	
	Sp. *Brunette*	333	Oliver Robinson	
	Bk. *Hersilia*	310	Higgins Crowell, Jr.	
	" *Sherwood*	457	Jabez Churchill	
1842	Sp. *Walpole*	593	B. Thomas	Sampson & Tappan added as Boston agents.
	" *Nonantum*	694	James B. King	
	" *Espindola*	742	George Barstow	
1843	Bk. *Saxony*	346	Nelson Scudder	Daniel Sharp, Jr., added to Boston agents.
	Sp. *Flavio*	638	E. S. Coffin	
	Bg. *Vulture*	140	Benjamin Walker	
	Sch. *Roanoke*	99	Lemuel Webb	
1845	Bk. *Roman*	245	Lendol N. Doane	Sampson & Tappan retired and A. C. Lombard retired from active participation in his lines.

DISPATCH LINE

Daniel Deshon, 3 Long Wharf, Boston agent. William H. Fuller, New Orleans agent. Line established fall of 1837. Later known in New Orleans as the Crescent Line.

YEAR	VESSEL	TONS	MASTERS	REMARKS
1837	Sp. *Telumah*	346	George C. Barstow	
	" *Caravan*	330	Samuel Nichols	
	Bk. *Diantha*	285	C. Williams	
1838	Sp. *Niagara*	438	S. E. Cole	
1839	Sp. *Saxon*	344	Charles Mansfield	Nathaniel Winsor, Jr. and Benjamin Bruce,
	" *Oneco*	640	Joshua Drew	103 State St., became Boston agents.
1840	Bk. *Francis Stanton*	393	Amos Lafavour, Jr.	
	Bg. *Grand Turk*	175	Amos Nichols	
	Bk. *Fairfield*	198		Samuel Loveland master in 1847.
	Bg. *Hogan*	254	Stanwood	
	Bk. *Richmond*	313	Benedict Andros	
	Sp. *Mattakeesit*	481	Stephen Higgins	
	" *Ferax*	373	Dodge Healey	Solomon Taylor master in 1847.
	" *Pharsalia*	617	D. L. Winsor	
	" *Timoleon*	422	A. Winsor	
	" *Deucalion*	513	Howes	
1841	Bk. *Hull*	296	Albert Dunbar	Winsor & Bruce became Boston agents.
	" *Henry Newell*	257	Matthew Martin	
	Sp. *Tallyrand*	549	Dodge Healy	
	Bk. *Edinburg*	283	Franklin Houdlette	
	Sp. *Oceanus*	473	Silas J. Bourne	
	Bk. *Ranger*	246	Alexander Milliken	
	Sp. *Talbot*	624	John Story	
	" *Caspian*	529	O. Patten	
	" *Trenton*	429	R. P. Manson	Lost on Man-of-War Key, Jan. 2, 1843.
	" *Manchester*	570	Robert Bosworth	
	" *London*	637	John O. Baker	
	Bk. *Galileo*	268	John Lombard	
	Sp. *Hope*	870	Freeman Soule	
1842	Sp. *Lochinvar*	635	Isaiah Westcott	F. M. Weld & Co. became New Orleans
	" *Palmyra*	612	Erastus Sampson	agents; Wiggin & Davenport, New Orleans
	" *Hargrave*	600	James Bailey	agents in Aug.
	" *Wakona*	430	James Borland	
	" *Columbus*	595	Isaac S. Coffin	
	" *Franconia*	499	Eleazer Crabtree	
	" *Soldan*	648	Ebenezer A. Shaw	
	" *Perdonnet*	478	David L. Foote	
	Bk. *Florence*	349	William Decker, Jr.	
	" *Clarissa Perkins*	240	John H. Perkins	
1843	Bk. *Chusan*	240	Timothy O. Cushing	Winsor & Bruce, 120 State St., dissolved in
	Sp. *Essex*	698	Francis W. Welch	May, 1843. Winsor continued Dispatch Line
	Bg. *Commerce*	281	Washington Read	at 109 State St.
	Sp. *Antwerp*	413	Henry Smith	
	" *Shaw*	343	Alfred M. Lunt	
	" *Palmyra*	612	John J. Scobie	
	" *Rockall*	644	Stephen Higgins	
	" *Charleston*	373	David Eldridge	
	" *Constantine*	742	Erastus Sampson	
	" *Herculean*	542	Paraclete Holmes	
	" *North Bend*	365	Ferdinand A. Crocker	
	" *Dalmatia*	359	Laban Howes	
	" *Plato*	397	William L. Phinney	
1844	Bk. *Craton*	334	Amos Towne	Name changed to Winsor's Line.
	Sp. *Abby Pratt*	669	George Pratt	
	" *Arvum*	364	Harrison Robinson	
	" *John Hollana*	529	William Henderson	
	" *Birmingham*	571	William J. Robinson	
	" *Lady Arabella*	399	James Simpson	
	" *Levi H. Gale*	422	Charles Thompson	
	Bk. *Narragansett*	640	Peter Destebecho	
	Sp. *Walpole*	593	William Thomas	
	" *Brewster*	696	David Lincoln	

DISPATCH LINE (*continued*)

YEAR	VESSEL	TONS	MASTERS	REMARKS
1844	Sp. *Scotland*	548	J. Merryman	
1845	Sp. *Waldron*	550	Hy. A. Cheever	Andrews & Dewey became New Orleans
	" *European*	593	Leonard Gay	agents in Nov.
	" *Megunticook*	473	Shubael Mayo	
	" *Sartelle*	416	Solomon Taylor	
	" *Berwick*	472	Charles Flanders	
	" *Alkmaar*	399	Leonard Eustis	
	" *Judah Touro*	741	Daniel Marcy	
	" *South Carolina*	768	Charles Owen	
	" *Chaos*	771	James L. Wilson	
	" *Dalmatia*	358	Benjamin Smith, Jr.	
	Bk. *Maria*	324	Judah Baker	
	" *Oberlin*	331	William Balch	R. B. Gilbert master in 1848.
1846	Sp. *Ann*	334	James M. Hill	
	Bk. *Hannah Sprague*	409	William L. Hunt	
	Sp. *La Grange*	259	Benjamin L. Sandford	
	" *Serampore*	499	Richard Baker	
	Bk. *Lepanto*	299	William B. Hatch	
	Sp. *Robert G. Shaw*	402	George Dunbar	
	" *R. D. Shepard*	795	Daniel Marcy	
	" *Albanian*	448	Ambrose Crowell	
	" *Washington*	372	John Riley	John H. Burleigh master in 1847.
	" *New Jersey*	636	Albert Winsor	
1847	Bk. *Solomon Piper*	196	J. C. Merrithew	
	" *Jane Andrews*	275	Hartwell W. French	
	Sp. *Deucalion*	513	Baker	Oliver G. Lane master in 1849.
	" *Grotius*	299	James Smith	
	" *John Currier*	697	Samuel Knapp	
	" *Moselle*	398	Abraham Somerby	
	" *Cheshire*	499	Augustus Hitchcock	
	" *Carnatic*	602	John Devereux	
	" *Haidee*	396	Clement H. Soule	
	" *Newton*	410	Cyrus Howes	
	" *Uriel*	799	Dennis Janvrin	
	" *Monsoon*	381	John A. Paine	
	Bk. *Yarmouth*	326	Howes	
	" *Mousam*	321	Alden B. Day	
1848	Bk. *Tiberias*	299	Benjamin Taylor	
	Sp. *Jacob Perkins*	379	Albert Winsor	A. C. Hersey, 67 Commercial Wharf, added
	" *Timoleon*	422	Benjamin Freeman	in Sept. as Boston agent.
	" *Medford*	545	J. Dreyer	Condemned at Pernambuco, 1859.
	Bk. *John G. Colley*	389	W. Smith	
	Sp. *Persia*	332	Charles Babson	
	" *Ashland*	422	Harding	
	" *James Titcomb*	492	William P. Stone	
	" *Bertrand*	397	Laban Howes	Later master of clipper ship *Fleetwing*.
	" *Harriet Rockwell*	448	C. H. Gerrish	
	Bk. *Turbo*	294	James Young	
	Sp. *Herbert*	586	Bangs Hallet	
	" *Chasca*	659	George D. Wise	
	" *Sheffield*	590	Christopher Lewis	
	" *Huron*	515	John A. Paine	
1849	Sp. *Astracan*	536	Jefferson Ford	J. H. Rivers and J. Silloway, 5 Commercial
	" *William Badger*	334	Lewis Thomas	St., became Boston agents; J. W. Andrews &
	" *Ocean Queen*	824	Henry Shoof	Co., New Orleans agents.
	Bk. *Santee*	192	J. H. Parker	
	" *Desdemona*	298	S. G. Stinson	
	Sp. *Medallion*	548	Franklin Houdlette	
	" *Louisa*	496	William Bradford	
	Bg. *Russian*	222	W. G. Veazie	
1850	Sp. *Ionian*	749	Charles E. Ranlett	
	" *Emily Taylor*	388	Francis F. Claussen	
1851	Sp. *Statesman*	673	Anderson	
1852	Sp. *Delaware*	662	D. Patten	
	" *John W. White*	549	Baker McNear	

DISPATCH LINE (*continued*)

YEAR	VESSEL	TONS	MASTERS	REMARKS
1852	Sp. *Bennington*	513	James Young	
1853	Bk. *Marcia*	343	John Wilson	J. H. Bass, 89 Common, became New Or-
"	*Murillo*	309	Thomas B. Woodside	leans agent.
1854	Bk. *Mary Smith*	324	W. Fitz	Lost near Charleston, June, 1855.
"	*R. G. W. Dodge*	306	John W. Friend	
	Sch. *Kate Brigham*	470	John H. Luther	
	Sp. *Lorenzo*	1091	L. T. Merrow	
	Bk. *Crusoe*	343	Burgess	
1855	Sp. *Zephyr*	1184	John B. King	
	Bk. *Emma Cushing*	292		
1856	Sp. *Inca*	577	Isaac F. Goodrich	Silloway, Calef & Co., dissolved. J. Silloway
"	*Crimea*	900	Townsend	retained agency in New Orleans and Mobile
				Dispatch Lines.
1858	Sch. *Edward S. Janes* (Cl.)	231	J. P. Godfrey	Jones, Mackinder & Co., became New Or-
	Sp. *Maritana*	991	George W. Williams	leans agents.
"	*Egeria*	644	William A. Adams	H. G. K. Calef, 61 Commercial St., took
"	*Delhi*	608	Gustavus C. Lovell	Dispatch Lines to Savannah and Charleston
	Bk. *Grace Hammond*	499	Harrison Mahoney	
	Sp. *Ocean Romp*	862	Manson	
1859	Sp. *Luna*	626	Joseph T. Nason	
"	*Berkshire*	615	Josephus J. Williams	
	Bk. *Aurelia*	475	Lucius C. Beattie	

CABOT & FRAZAR'S LINE

Cabot & Frazar, 94 State St., Boston agents.

YEAR	VESSEL	TONS	MASTERS	REMARKS
1838	Sp. *Denmark*	512	George W. Frost	
"	*Medora*	314	Edmund Pike	Lost on Langley I., July 25, 1856.
	Bk. *Gulnare*	273	Richard Wheatland	
"	*Beaver*	299	John Edmonds	Vessel lost, Oct. 18, 1849.
	Sp. *Parthenon*	560	Samuel T. Woodbury	
"	*Propontis*	426	Nason	
"	*Rambler*	340	John A. Baxter	
1839	Sp. *Pickering Dodge*		W. A. Holbrook	

NEW LINE

John H. Pearson & Co., Foster's Wharf, Boston agents. John A. Merritt, New Orleans agent. Line established Sept., 1840. Sailed 1st and 15th of each month.

YEAR	VESSEL	TONS	MASTERS	REMARKS
1840	Sp. *Suffolk*	518	Freeman Crosby	
"	*Charles Carroll*	388	Freeman Crosby	George Dean master in 1843.
"	*Niagara*	458	Obed Snow	
	Bk. *Ganges*	226	Elliot	
	Bg. *Cameo*	222	James Jarvis	
	Sp. *Shaw*	343	James Murdock	
"	*Middlesex*	496	Caleb U. Grozier	David Elliot master in 1844. Seth Rogers
				master in 1844.
1841	Sp. *Norfolk*	548	Obed Snow	
"	*Peruvian*	388	John A. Spear	
"	*Tyrone*	538	John A. Spear	
1843	Sp. *Essex*	699	Francis W. Welch	
1844	Sp. *Vespasian*	318	Benjamin Winsor	John O. B. Minot added as Boston agent.
"	*Grotius*	299	Miller	
	Bk. *Nautilus*	216	Tewksbury	Bailey Loring master in 1847.
1845	Bk. *Attica*	349	Jacob McLellan	
"	*Marcia*	343	Otis Harwood	
"	*Barrington*	273	George Barton	
"	*Sylphide*	349	E. D. Choate	
1846	Sp. *Russell Glover*	795	Jonathan Bisson	Ricker & Pearson became New Orleans
				agents.
"	*Tyrian*	511	D. L. Jackson	Lost on coast of Scotland, 1847
"	*Rialto*	459		

NEW LINE (*continued*)

YEAR	VESSEL	TONS	MASTERS	REMARKS
1846	Bk. *Mauran*	348	George W. Williams	
	" *Santee*	192	George P. Marston	
	Sp. *Ontario*	606	John Holmes	Henry N. Cheever master in 1847.
	" *North Carolina*	669	James Drummond	
	" *James Calder*	390	Joseph Hollister	
	" *Colombo*	577	Albert A. Burwell	
	Bk. *Odd Fellow*	230	Lauchlin McKay	
	Sp. *Oneco*	640	Joshua Drew	
	" *Medora*	400	Henry Shoof	
	" *Epaminondas*	549	William Lambert	
	Bk. *Thaetus*	286	Charles Newell	
1847	Bk. *Mousam*	321	Alden B. Day	Henry R. Sampson became New Orleans
	" *Brazil*	250	James B. Homer	agent.
	Bg. *Saltillo*	162	Gilbert F. Crocker	
	Sp. *John Cumming*	721	W. L. Dwight	
	" *Damascus*	694	Philip M. Hale	
	" *Persia*	332	John Simpson	
	" *Megunticook*	473	Daniel Ilsley	
	" *Bengal*	650	Henry Cook	
	" *Lochinvar*	635	Isaiah Westcott	
	" *Danvers*	386	Joseph Grafton, Jr.	
1848	Bk. *Kanawha*	260	Aaron C. Higgins	George W. Hynson, 68 Camp St., became
	Sp. *Judah Touro*	741	Joseph J. Nickerson	New Orleans agent.
	Bk. *Lucy Elizabeth*	335	William Reed	
	Sp. *Robert C. Winthrop*	781	Allen H. Knowles	
	" *Leodes*	445	Moses A. Low	
	" *Euphrasia*	487	John Simpson	
	" *Essex*	699	Francis W. Welch	
	" *Frances Ann*	446	James E. Robinson	
	" *Delphos*	398	Crowell	
	" *Danvers*	386	David Elliot	
	" *Nestor*	397	John A. Russell	
	" *Alciope*	378	Henry Smith	
	" *Henry Ware*	540	Edward Nason	
	" *Granada*	593	Charles Batchelder	
	" *Clyde*	398	Jacob G. Homer	
	" *Soldan*	648	William Thomas	
	" *Oxenbridge*	526	Solomon Taylor	
	" *Equity*	494	James Mason, Jr.	
	" *Abaelino*	606	Caleb U. Grozier	
	" *Nathaniel Thompson*	546	Nathaniel Thompson	
	" *Desdemona*	624	Walter Emerson	
	" *Rockall*	644	Thomas G. Hiler	
	" *Amelia*	623	W. Henderson	
	Bk. *Isabella*	285	William S. Given	
	Sch. *Crescent City*	112	William H. Talbot	
1849	Bk. *Turbo*	294	Young	George H. Pearson became New Orleans
1850	Sp. *Beatrice*	777	George L. Rogers	agent.
	" *James Brown*	997	Arthur Childs	
1851	Bk. *Lucy*	397	William Davis	Lovett master in 1854.
	Sp. *Marathon*	485	Christian Van Dyke	
	" *Faneuil Hall*	548	Joseph H. Sears	
	Bk. *Attica*	349	Seth B. McLellan	
	Sp. *Ashburton*	449	George W. Williams	
1852	Sp. *Oregon*	649	Thomas Patterson	
1853	Bk. *Saone*	292	Aaron C. Sargent	J. H. Pearson & Co. and Israel W. Lamson
	Sp. *Bennington*	513	James Young	became Boston agents in 1853. Name
	" *Cairo*	536	Bailey Loring	changed to J. H. Pearson & Co.'s Line.
1854	Sp. *Richmond*	475	James Hamilton	George W. Hynson & Co. became New Or-
	" *Franconia*	499	George W. Pool	leans agents, 1857. Called Regular Line in New Orleans.
1858	Sp. *Milton*	598	W. E. Kingman	
1860	Sp. *Golden Cross*	1097	John Davis	
	" *Indian*	786	William H. Averill	
	Bk. *Arctic*	489	H. T. Walter	

NEW LINE (*continued*)

YEAR	VESSEL	TONS	MASTERS	REMARKS
1860	Bk. *Speedwell*	335	Enoch H. Howes	
	" *Undine*	532	Patten	
	" *Panama*	414	E. Graves	R. Merryman master in 1858.

BRUCE'S LINE

Benjamin Bruce, 110 State St., Boston agent.

YEAR	VESSEL	TONS	MASTERS	REMARKS
1843	Bk. *Tuskar*	248	Samuel S. Lovell	
	Sp. *Adams*	597	Moses Gay	
	" *Edmund Perkins*	617	Nathaniel Ingersoll	
	" *Elizabeth Bruce*	587	John Day	
	" *Mary Francis*	326	Albert Jewett	Var. *Mary Frances*
	" *Gen. Harrison*	410	Moore	
1844	Sp. *Euphrasia*	487	Charles Buntin	Bruce & Cheney became Boston agents.
	" *Morea*	331	Simon Gill	
	" *Oceanus*	473	Horace S. Crocker	
	" *Angelo*	417	James A. Clarkson	
	Bk. *Abbot Lord*	437	Acter P. Patterson	
	Sp. *Tyrian*	511	Daniel L. Jackson	
1846	Sp. *James Perkins*	385	William Hall	Thomas H. Cheever became New Orleans
	" *Gen. Veazie*	443	John W. Fairfield	agent. William A. Clark became New Or-
	" *California*	369	George Davis	leans agent in Dec.
	Bg. *Annah*	171	Charles B. Fowler	
	" *Vandalia*	133	W. R. Bunker	
1847	Sp. *James Calder*	390	Joseph Hollister	
	" *York*	341	Christian Van Dyke	Var. Christopher Vandyke.
	" *Burmah*	338	John Adams	
	Bg. *Sutton*	196	Oliver Perkins	
	" *Joseph Balch*	153	Asa Wright	
1848	Sp. *Excelsior*	444	Claudius Williams	Line characterized throughout by rather ir-
	" *Washington*	372	Snow	regular service.
	" *South Carolina*	580	Charles Owen	
	" *Arkansas*	627	William M. Otis	

MERCHANTS' LINE

William Eager and Robert Morss, 25 Central Wharf, Boston agents. Line established to begin sailings in fall of 1843.

YEAR	VESSEL	TONS	MASTERS	REMARKS
1843	Sp. *Tallyrand*	549	Dodge Healy	
	" *Parthenon*	560	Samuel T. Woodbury	
	" *Monsoon*	381	John A. Paine	
	" *Niobe*	347	William R. Lecraw	
	" *Denmark*	512	G. W. Frost	

NEW LINE

J. Silloway & Co., 5 Commercial St., and J. H. Rivers, Boston agents. Fosdick & Bros., New Orleans agents. Line established Aug., 1847.

YEAR	VESSEL	TONS	MASTERS	REMARKS
1847	Sp. *Avalanche*	396	William Whittlesey	
	" *John Holland*	529	William Henderson	
	Bk. *Aquila*	247	J. Murphy	
	" *Mandarin*	275	James Colby	
	" *Alice Tarleton*	309	Archelaus Trefethen	
	Bg. *Almira*	194	John M. Brown	
1848	Bk. *Onyx*	245	Joshua Harding	*Onyx* was cleared for Galveston by Leffert
	Sp. *California*	369	William Montgomery	Lefferts.
	" *Devonshire*	740	Charles E. Ranlett	Line called Dispatch Line.
	Bk. *Star*	298	Dennis Pilsbury	
	" *Loretto Fish*	247	Miles S. Gates	
	Sp. *Walter R. Jones*	400	J. Colley	
	Bk. *Robert Walsh*	282	William Singer	

NEW LINE (*continued*)

YEAR	VESSEL	TONS	MASTERS	REMARKS
1848	Sp. *St. Louis*	533	Charles W. Davis	
	Bk. *Louisiana*	249	William S. Emory	
	" *Delaware*	300	James Stetson	

REGULAR LINE

Charles T. Savage, 8 Lewis Wharf, and William Lincoln, Boston agents. Harrod, Darling & Co., New Orleans agents. Line established Jan., 1847.

YEAR	VESSEL	TONS	MASTERS	REMARKS
1847	Sp. *Kentucky*	491	Henry P. Rogers	
	" *Emily Taylor*	388	Octavius Howe	
	Bk. *Antelope*	335	William L. Phinney	Zenas Crosby master later in year.
	Sp. *Columbia*	708	Henry G. Bridges	
	" *Edward Everett*	623	Knowles	Lost at sea, Feb., 1862.
	" *Frances Ann*	446	James E. Robinson	Henry Lincoln succeeded William Lincoln in
	" *Diana*	568	Charles F. Winsor	Aug.
	" *Charlotte*	541	William Johnston	
	" *Colombo*	577	John S. Pray	
	" *Iowa*	479	Lorenzo Parker	
	Bk. *Sherwood*	447	Isaac Bursley	
	Sp. *A. Z.*	676	John G. Moses	
	" *Unicorn*	397	John C. Lincoln	George Pollard master in 1848.
	Bk. *Orion*	449	Octavius Howe	William F. Pray master in 1848.
	Sp. *Harrisburg*	493	Richard Matthews	
1848	Bk. *Rienzi*	422	Hiram B. Bangs	
	" *Murillo*	309	Thomas S. Minot	
	Sp. *Granada*	593	Nathaniel Spooner	
	" *Bay State*	592	Samuel B. Simmons	
	" *Jenny Lind*	533	Lauchlin McKay	
	Bk. *Thetis*	399	William M. Dunbar	
	Sp. *Zone*	365	Foster	
	" *Plato*	397	William T. Becket	
	" *Marcellus*	660	Nathaniel Spooner	
	" *Leodes*	445	Nathan B. Robbins	
	Bk. *Amos Patten*	250	Christopher E. McNear	

FORBES & CO.'S LINE

F. H. Forbes & Co., 15 India St., Boston agents. Notice of establishment of line made in Mar., 1847. Line apparently abandoned after the spring season.

YEAR	VESSEL	TONS	MASTERS	REMARKS
1847	Bk. *Cumberland*	386	Joseph Hiscock	
	Bg. *Forrest*	187	William C. Varina	
	" *Maria*	129	William Freeman	
	Bk. *Isnardon*	247	T. G. Moulton	
	Sp. *Louisa*	496	Benjamin Tay	

WHEELER & PECK'S LINE

Wheeler & Peck, 16 Long Wharf, Boston agents. George W. Hynson & Co., New Orleans agents. Discontinued in 1855.

YEAR	VESSEL	TONS	MASTERS	REMARKS
1854	Sp. *Judith*	993	Richard S. Brown	
	" *John W. White*	549	Reuben Snow	
	" *Stephen Glover*	733	Samuel Baldry	
	" *Harrisburg*	493	Elbridge G. Wiswell	
	" *Jonas Waern*	747	Charles P. Washburn	

LINCOLN'S LINE

Henry Lincoln, 57 Commercial St., Boston agent, "Wants good vessel to load in this line." George W. Hynson, New Orleans agent.

YEAR	VESSEL	TONS	MASTERS	REMARKS
1856	Sp. *Middlesex*	496	David R. Cook	
	" *Rockaway*	833	Mark H. Lufkin	

LINCOLN'S LINE (*continued*)

YEAR	VESSEL	TONS	MASTERS	REMARKS
1856	Sp. *Ariel*	1329	Frank Delano	
	Bk. *Gen. Taylor*	597	St. Croix Redman	
1857	Sp. *John M. Mayo*	656	Stephen Cutter	
1858	Sp. *Egeria*	644	W. A. Adams	George A. Fosdick became New Orleans
	" *Maritana*	991	George W. Williams	agent.
	" *E. F. Gabain*	1396	John F. Von Hagen	
	Bk. *Annie Kimball*	598	Leonard R. Merrill	
	Sp. *Isaac Newton*	600	Thomas M. Fulton	
1859	Bk. *Brilliant*	349	William P. Sigsbee	
1860	Bk. *Caroline Wells*			

SECTION 9. NEW YORK—ALBANY AND TROY
NEW YORK—CHESAPEAKE BAY

NEW YORK—ALBANY & TROY PACKETS

J. & J. Townsend, Adams & Rathbone, and John Clifford, New York agents. James and Jasper S. Keeler and Horace Lockwood, Albany agents. Established Mar., 1814, the first American sailing line to sail on schedule.

YEAR	VESSEL	TONS	MASTERS	REMARKS
1814	Sl. *Fashion*	93	Nathan Blydenburgh	Sailed from Lent's Dock, North River, New
	" *Sea Witch*	95	Charles Wells	York City, and from Albany Dock every Sat.
	" *Capitol*	100	William Barker	
	" *Chase*	95	Havens T. Aldrich	

THURSDAY LINE

John Trotter and James B. Douglass, as Trotter & Douglass, New York agents. Jasper S. and James Keeler, Albany agents. Established Apr., 1814.

YEAR	VESSEL	TONS	MASTERS	REMARKS
1814	Sl. *Morgan*	85	Henry Green	Sailed from above docks every Thurs.
	" *Columbia*	88	William W. Brower	
	" *Perseverance*	88	B. Whipple	

NEW LINE

S. P. Jermain, Pratt & Durant, Washburn & Knower, William Chapman, Henry W. Delavan & Co., Willard Walker, James & Flack, Charles Smith, and Fay & Jones, agents. Established Mar., 1815.

YEAR	VESSEL	TONS	MASTERS	REMARKS
1815	Sl. *Franklin*	100	Randall Bently	Sailed from above docks every Wed. and Sat.
	" *Merchant*	109	James B. Douglass	
	" *Henry*	95	Israel P. Hand	
	" *Lion*	73	Joseph Gillespie	

RICHMOND LINE OF PACKETS

Cornelius R. Duffie, 86 Wall St., at Coffee House Slip, New York agent. Established Nov., 1815.

YEAR	VESSEL	TONS	MASTERS	REMARKS
1815	Sch. *Indian Hunter*	131	Isaac I. Seaman	Sailed between New York and Richmond,
	" *Logan*	159	Samuel Holmes	Va., in regular succession but not on a fixed
	" *Lycurgus*	102	Isaac I. Seaman	schedule at outset.
	" *Jane*	127	William H. Nichols	

CHESAPEAKE LINE

J. M. Lowry & Co., 58 South St., New York agents. Established 1822, serving Norfolk, Petersburg, Alexandria, Richmond, Georgetown, D. C., and Washington City.

YEAR	VESSEL	TONS	MASTERS	REMARKS
1822	Sch. *Mark Time*	78	D. Post	This line was responsible for inaugurating the
	" *Tell Tale*	101	Richard Churchward	first steam service between New York and
	" *Maria Ann*	85	J. Cole	the Bay—the steam brig *New York*, Richard
	" *Bold Commander*	88	I. Bogart	Churchward, master.
	Sl. *Abeona*	71	William H. Nichols	
	Sch. *Superior*	84	J. Daniels	

SECTION 10. NEW YORK—PHILADELPHIA

UNION LINE

L'Hommedieu & Brown, 34 Old Slip, New York agents. George Bird, 17 South Wharves, Philadelphia agent. Established Feb., 1816. No fixed schedule. Firms had run regular packets since spring of 1815.

YEAR	VESSEL	TONS	MASTERS	REMARKS
1816	Sch. *Pocahontas*	136	William Seybert	S. H. Herrick & Co., 30 South St., added as New York agents, 1821.
	" *Maria*	124	James DeGroot	D. P. Noble master in 1820.
	" *Martha*	104	Samuel Thompson	Samuel Wiley master in 1822.
	" *True American*	115	John Kelley	Samuel Basset master in 1824.
	" *Jersey*	87	John Osborn	
	" *Express*	110	Benjamin Webb	
1822	Sch. *Logan*	159	J. C. Denison	
1823	Sch. *Two Brothers*	85	Thomas Marshall	James G. Stacey & Co. and Joseph Emlen,
	" *Knickerbocker*	92	Benjamin Webb	17 S. Wharves, added as Philadelphia agents.
	Sl. *William Henry*	85	Jeremiah Briggs	
1824	Sch. *Valiant*	114	Benjamin Webb	James G. Stacey & Co. and Bird & Goodwin became Philadelphia agents.
1826	Sch. *Diana*	142	Jeremiah Briggs	
1828	Sl. *Lady Adams*	91	Daniel Goldsmith	

"D" (DISPATCH) LINE

Philip Grim, 30 Old Slip, New York agent. James G. Stacey, 22 South Wharves, Philadelphia agent. Established 1817. Firms were running several sloops in 1816.

YEAR	VESSEL	TONS	MASTERS	REMARKS
1817	Sl. *Superior*	84	Samuel Storer	John B. Clements master in 1820.
	" *Scourge*	77	James DeGroot	
	" *Rover*	82	James Parks	A. J. Brittingham master in 1822.
	" *Nancy*	80	Eleazer Harding	George Gramsby master in 1818.
1818	Sl. *David*	97	Eleazer Harding	David & Philip Grim became New York
1822	Sch. *Mercator*	83	Henry Allen	agents. David Grim and John W. Brown, 34
	" *Martha*	104	Samuel Wiley	Old Slip, became New York agents, and David G. Meyer, 1 Chestnut St., Philadelphia agent.

REGULAR LINE

Simeon Baldwin and Francis J. Spooner, as Baldwin & Spooner, 98 Coffee House Slip, New York agents. Bailey & Willis, 37 South Wharves, Philadelphia agents. Established 1824.

YEAR	VESSEL	TONS	MASTERS	REMARKS
1824	Sch. *Herald*	90	Hiram Fox	
	" *Leaper*	64	Reuben Snow	
	" *Eliza Barker*	88	Lot Gage	
	Sl. *Boston Packet*	69	Levi Snow	T. C. Crowell master in 1826.
	" *Reaper*	74	Mark L. Crowell	
	" *Intrepid*	59	Nathaniel Snow	
1831	Bg. *Hope Retrieve*	129	Richard H. Tittle	Edmund Flinn master in July, 1831.

NEW LINE

Cornell, Cooper & Co., Coenties Slip, and Howes, Godfrey & Robertson, 28 South St., New York agents. Andrew C. Barclay, 38 South Wharves, and William Mann, Jr., Walnut St. Wharf, Philadelphia agents. Established Apr., 1831, to sail Wed. and Sat. from each port. Vessels sailed from Pier 9, East River.

YEAR	VESSEL	TONS	MASTERS	REMARKS
1831	Sch. *Tomboy*		H. Baker	
	" *Bethlehem*	94	R. Baker	
	" *Citizen*	77	J. Baker, Sr.	
	" *Boston Packet* (ex-sloop)	69	Freeman Baker	
	Sl. *Mechanic*	60	Zenas Nickerson	
	Sch. *Jew*	85	Freeman Baker	
	" *Hope & Hannah*	93	Zenas Nickerson	

EXTRA LINE

Later known as Dispatch or Cooley's Line. Miller & Bancker, 19 Coenties Slip, New York agents. Aaron B. Cooley, 52 South Wharves, Philadelphia agent. Established Jan., 1834.

YEAR		VESSEL	TONS	MASTERS	REMARKS
1834	Sch.	*Elizabeth & Rebecca*	109	S. Burroughs	James S. Lee master in 1835.
	"	*Mark*	74	J. Sparks	
	"	*Erie*	93	F. Smith	
	"	*Catherine & Amanda*	74	L. Teal	
	"	*William Francis*	60	J. Scull	
	"	*Star*		R. G. Somers	
	"	*Ajax*	137	J. T. Pearce	
	"	*Fifield*	107	Andrew Ketchum	
	"	*New York*	109	O. Smith	
	"	*Mediterranean*	139	Thomas Ireland	Isaac Henry master in 1839.
	"	*Christopher Columbus*	86		
1835	Sch.	*Rebecca Albright*		Bartlett	George O. Van Amringe, 70 Water St.,
	"	*Doctor Franklin*	74	F. Williams	became New York agent in June.
	"	*Pedestrian*	127	J. Collins	
1841	Sch.	*Two Pollies*	134	Matthew D. Fountain	A. B. Cooley, 9 Coenties Slip, became New York agent.
1844	Sch.	*Iodine*	97	D. Blew	N. L. McCready & Co., 7 Coenties Slip, became New York agents.
	"	*Joseph Brown*	130	George E. May	
1845	Sch.	*Althera Cornelius*	135	Hadden	
	"	*Lion*			
	"	*Elizabeth*			
	Sp.	*Edwina*	538	Francis West	
1846	Sch.	*Henry W. Safford*	108	George E. May	Cooley & Webb became Philadelphia agents.
	"	*James P. Lofland*	128	William T. Clark	Leander Hallet master in 1849.
	"	*Sage*	151	Henry W. Johnson	
	"	*Forest*			
	"	*Amphibious*			
1848	Sch.	*Anna Somers*		J. Somers	
	"	*Staunch*	91	Beever	

NEW LINE

Called James Hand's Schooner Line in 1836. J. Briggs and William J. McKee, 34 Old Slip, New York agents. James Hand, 58½ S. Wharves, Philadelphia agent. Vessels dispatched both by sea and by Delaware & Raritan Canal.

YEAR		VESSEL	TONS	MASTERS	REMARKS
1834	Sl.	*United States*		Derrickson	James Hand was engaged in several opera-
	"	*William Strickland*		John Leonard	tions, all of which seemed to be conducted at
	"	*Caledonia*		Rice	times on an extensive scale and then lapsed,
	"	*Charlotte & Sarah*	63	T. Hand	to be renewed several years later. Thus, after
	Sch.	*Amity*	98	W. Brown	several years' lapse, he re-established the
	"	*Traveller*		H. Pedrick	schooner line to Philadelphia in 1848, with
	"	*Mary Picken*		J. Smith	himself as the New York agent, and con-
	"	*Diana*	142	Samuel Baymore	tinued it through 1857.
	"	*Indiana*	63	M. Peal	
1835	Sch.	*Fair Trader*		Bennett	Line discontinued in 1837 and re-established in 1848.
1848	Sch.	*Kensington*	179	Enoch Stephenson	Armer Patton & Co., 30 South St., became
	"	*Exile*	82		New York agents.
	"	*Mary Ann Guest*	90		
	"	*James Barrett*	179	Henry May	
	"	*Joseph Rusling*	111	John W. Smith	
	"	*Virginia*	161	Fox	
1849	Sch.	*Julius Pringle*	94	Daniel Crocker	
	"	*Samuel R. Paynter*	109	John Neal	
	"	*Amazon*	71	P. Steelman	
	"	*Columbia*	112	Thomas P. Crowell	
	"	*James C. Fisher*		Anderson	
	"	*Charles Hawley*	94	Samuel W. Hough	
	"	*Benjamin Douglass*		Taylor	
	"	*Boreas*	129	Andrew Thompson	

NEW LINE (*continued*)

YEAR	VESSEL	TONS	MASTERS	REMARKS
1849	Sch. *Joseph R. Chandler*	100	John W. Smith	
1850	Sch. *Barton*	90	Barker	
	" *William H. DuBosc*		Winsmore	

PATTON'S LINE

Armer Patton, Philadelphia agent.

YEAR	VESSEL	TONS	MASTERS	REMARKS
1835	Sl. *Charlotte & Sarah*	63	Andrew Thompson	Benjamin Room master in 1837.
1837	Sch. *Extra*	88	John R. Somers	David String master in 1840.
1839	Sch. *Pennsylvania*	136	John J. Wood	James M. Patton master in 1843.
	" *Republican*	88	George Hoover	
1840	Sch. *American Eagle*	126	J. Hickman	James S. French master in 1845.
1841	Sch. *Brandywine*	96	John Townsend	A. B. Cooley became Philadelphia agent.
	" *Sarah Ann*	146	John W. Ireland	
	" *Columbia*	112	John Townsend	
1842	Sch. *A. B. Cooley*	95	Edward Camp	
	" *Ezra Wheeler*	136	Aaron Gandy	

UNION LINE

J. & N. Briggs, 40 South St., New York agents. R. F. Loper and William Baird, Philadelphia agents. Vessels dispatched via Delaware & Raritan Canal.

YEAR	VESSEL	TONS	MASTERS	REMARKS
1840	Bg. *Chatham*	171	Myers	
	Sch. *John Cooley & Co.*	184	William R. Derrickson	
	" *Excel*	139	William Wilcox	
	" *J. Palmer*	125	Ernest Ardley	
	" *H. Westcott*	122	D. Blew	Joseph Vance master in 1843.
	" *W. J. Watson*	152	Charles D. Marshman	John P. Levy master in 1841.
	" *Eri Stevens*		Caleb L. Briggs	
	" *Ann*	116	William R. Derrickson	
	" *Valiant*	114	Honeywell	
	" *Traffic*	105	John Rose	
	" *Augusta*	99	Williams	
	" *Lois*		A. L. Derrickson	
1841	Sch. *Direct*	135	Caleb L. Briggs	

McKEE'S LINE

Ackerman & McKee, New York agents. McKee & Pendexter and Ackerman & McKee, Philadelphia agents.

YEAR	VESSEL	TONS	MASTERS	REMARKS
1841	Sch. *Fortitude*	93	J. Cherry	
	" *Greenbury Holt*	110	Crammer	
1846	Sch. *Alabama*	96	Thomas H. Nickerson	McKee, Hand & Co., 42 Front St., became
	Bg. *Relief*	156	S. D. Sawyer	New York agents.
1848	Sch. *Arcade*	96	John Williams	Name changed to McKee's Daily Line.
	" *Princeton*	71	Baker	William J. McKee & Bro., became New York
	" *Rainbow*	247	Warren G. Raynor	agents.
	" *Commerce*	95	William Johnson	
	" *George Washington*	129	Edward Camp	
	" *Welcome*	140	Besse	
1849	Sch. *Alfred Barrett*		McCully	
	" *Samuel Castner*	143	Burton Robinson	James Cullen master in 1851.
	" *Louisa Gray*		Sharp	
	" *Mary A. Williams*		Rogers	
	" *New Haven*		Kelsey	
	" *Live Oak*	81	Rogers	
1850	Sch. *Jarvis Lyon*	169	Charles Burroughs	
	" *Mary Ann Guest*	90	Holmes	
1851	Sch. *Triumph*	95	John Mason	
	" *Nancy Mills*	85	Benjamin Tyler	
	" *Jerome*	108	Willard	

MCKEE'S LINE (*continued*)

YEAR	VESSEL	TONS	MASTERS	REMARKS
1851	Sch. *Lavinah Jane*		Ketcham	
	" *John W. Bell*	99	Amos N. Lowden	
1852	Sch. *Pennsylvania*	146	Bill	
	" *Joseph P. Ross*	129	Abel S. Parker	
	" *Hope W. Tandy (Gandy)*	141	Joab B. Jeffries	Var. Jeffrey.
1853	Sch. *Mary A. Howland*	109	Warren G. Raynor	
	" *Echo*	197	Amos N. Lowden	
	" *Asa Eldridge*	127	Thomas W. Rowland	William H. Lowden master in 1857.
	" *Corbulo*	123	Thomas W. Rowland	
	" *Robert P. King*	136	Joel Leeds	
1856	Sch. *Treasurer*	194	Joseph Waples	
	" *Evergreen*	156	E. G. Bliven	
	Bk. *Charles W. Poultney*	399	Benjamin W. Conant	Var. Benjamin N. Conant.
1857	Sch. *James G. Stille*	180	F. Corson	

SECTION 11. NEW YORK—BALTIMORE

REGULAR LINE

W. W. & James H. Todd, Corner Old Slip & Front St., New York agents. Isaiah Mankin, Gay & Pratt Sts., Baltimore agent. Line established May, 1816, but sailed irregularly until 1818.

YEAR	VESSEL	TONS	MASTERS	REMARKS
1816	Sl. *Constitution*	65	Henry Leforge	
	" *Hiram*	73	Wallis Evans	Var. Evins.
	Sch. *William & Mary*	95	Kirwan	
	" *Leonidas*	96	Samuel W. Turner	
	" *Resolve*	105	Harris Watrous	
1817	Sch. *Paragon*	122	Laban Thayer	R. L. Wood master in 1822.
1818	Sch. *Diana*	102	J. Bird	Sailed every Wed. and Sat.
	" *Mary Ann*	103	N. Chapman	
1820	Sch. *Ontario*	96	Samuel Griffing	
	" *Post Boy*	106	Zind Denison	John Osborn master in 1822.
1821	Sch. *Experiment*	100	Chaplin Conway	William W. Todd became New York agent
	" *Martha*	119	Daniel Griffing	in May
1822	Sch. *Logan*	159	J. C. Denison	
	" *Little William*	110	Luther Evans	
1826	Sch. *Vineyard*	77	B. P. Jones	
1827	Sch. *Control*	128	Samuel Griffing	
1828	Sch. *Pacific*	126	James Gould	Line consisted of one brig and seven schoon-
	Bg. *Solon*	135	J. Evans	ers.
	Sch. *Ocean*	112	William Dennett	
1829	Bg. *Sarah*	136	Gorham P. Holmes	
1830	Sch. *Orator*	127	A. C. Boyce	Isaiah Mankin & Son became Baltimore agents.
1831	Sch. *Celeste*	132	Abraham Cole	D. Johnson master in 1841.
1833	Bg. *Pavillion*	150	E. Case	Line consisted of six brigs and seven schoon-
	Sch. *La Bruce*	98	B. Bourne	ers.
	" *Mokena*	91	Simeon Hamlin	J. W. Brown, 65 Smith's Wharf, added as
	" *Mary Archer*	84	Abraham Cole, Jr.	Baltimore agent.
	" *Julia Martling*	121	Joseph Oakley	
	Bg. *America*	129	S. D. Gregg	
	" *Sarah*	136	John Bishop	
	" *North*	122	Michael Terrill	Var. Terral.
	Sch. *Armada*	95	Joseph Philbrook	
1834	Sch. *Potomac*	147	Thomas Jennings	
1835	Sch. *Maria*	171	David Latourette	L. Woglam master in 1837.
	" *Dorchester*	100	John Rose	
	" *Champion*	77	Abraham Cole	
	" *Eagle*		M. Tier	
	" *President Jackson*	126	D. Johnson	
	" *Lucinda*	175	Seth Chester	
	" *Daniel H. Smith*		Smith	
	" *Eliza Jane*	75	T. Dawson	
	Bg. *Empress*	180	J. Ward	
1836	Bg. *Patriot*	174	W. Rodbird	

REGULAR LINE (*continued*)

YEAR		VESSEL	TONS	MASTERS	REMARKS
1836	Bg.	*Orion*	159	Isaac Card	
	Sch.	*Wave*	74	Jabez Churchill	
	"	*Carolinian*	154	Jackson B. Bedell	Joseph Oakley master in 1841.
	"	*Helen*	149	David Latourette	
1837	Sch.	*Levins Return*	75	A. S. D. Evans	
	"	*Planet*	127	Isaac Cole	
	"	*Emma*	165	David Latourette	A. C. Woglam master same year.
	"	*Arrival*	119	Frederick Van Gilder	
1838	Sch.	*Tuscarora*	176	John Bell	
	"	*Delaware*	74	C. W. Waite	
1841	Sch.	*Barbara*	126	Stephen Squires	Robert Johnson and Stephen Lowden, as
	"	*Edwin A. Stevens*	144	Burton Briggs	Johnson & Lowden, 86 Wall St., became
	"	*Rochester*	127	Burton Briggs	New York agents.
	"	*Millicent*	136	Abraham Cole	
	"	*William Seymour*	127	Walter Carpenter	
	"	*Mexico*	81	Tomlin	
	Bg.	*Galveston*	178	Jonathan Burr, Jr.	
1842	Sch.	*Bergen*	227	David Latourette, Jr.	
	"	*Wanderer*	142	Freeman B. Lewis	
1843	Sch.	*Michigan*	163	Lucas B. Terry	
	"	*Roe*	163	Isaac S. Snedecor	
1845	Sch.	*Ellicott*	200	Abraham Cole	Mark Dissoway master in 1852.
	"	*Seguine*	200	Winant S. Cole	A. K. Swain master in 1850.
	"	*Mankin*	198	Lucas B. Terry	
	"	*Josephine*	212	David Latourette, Jr.	
1848	Sch.	*Baltimore*	187	James Haight	
1849	Sch.	*Mary Mankin*	232	David Latourette, Jr.	Sailed every four days "full or not full."
	"	*Emily Johnson*	192	James W. Johnson	Mark Dissoway master in 1853.
	Bk.	*Oregon*	348	J. P. Davis	James Corner & Son became Baltimore agents in 1851. Line consisted of six schooners.
1852	Sch.	*Fair*	218	C. Gillett	Hiss & Corner, 73 Smith's Wharf, became
	"	*Westover*	212	McGee	Baltimore agents in 1852. Seven schooners.
1855	Sch.	*Maria*	170	T. Wyckoff	Stevenson Hiss, 73 Smith's Wharf, became Baltimore agent in 1855. Rose & Lyon became Baltimore agents in 1856 and line was combined with New Line.

NEW LINE

J. M. Lowry & Co., 58 South St., New York agents. Rogers & Symington, Baltimore agents. Established 1824.

YEAR		VESSEL	TONS	MASTERS	REMARKS
1824	Sl.	*Express*	74	E. Baker	S. H. Herrick & Co., 23 South St., and John
	"	*Victory*	75	Oliver Ripley	J. Adams, 100 Coffee House Slip, became
	"	*Flora*		Hawes	New York agents in Sept.
	"	*Adelia*	78	Wakeman Thorp	
	Sch.	*Eclipse*	97	Ezra Lewis	
	"	*Barracoa*	131	John Reed	Var. *Baraco.*
	Sl.	*Connecticut*		Andronicus Cheesebrough	
	"	*Cadet*	65	Nehemiah Robbins	
	"	*Columbus*	96	Daniel Griffing	
1825	Sl.	*Intrepid*	74	Nathaniel Snow	Discontinued early in 1825, Lowry continu-
	Sch.	*Thrasher*	126	Pease	ing his Norfolk and other Chesapeake lines.

DISPATCH LINE

David Anderson, 88 Coffee House Slip, New York agent. Rogers & Symington, Baltimore agents. Established Mar., 1825. "To sail every Saturday and Wednesday when necessary."

YEAR		VESSEL	TONS	MASTERS	REMARKS
1825	Sch.	*China*	97	M. B. Perry	J. G. Nickerson master in 1828.
	"	*William*		William Anthony	Jonathan Rogers became sole Baltimore
	"	*Rolla*	97	Andronicus Cheesebrough	agent in Sept.
	"	*Advance*	83	Isaiah Lewis	Anderson & Adams became New York
	"	*Clarion*	81	E. Baker	agents in Oct.

DISPATCH LINE (*continued*)

YEAR		VESSEL	TONS	MASTERS	REMARKS
1825	Sl.	*Commodore Perry*	64	Kimball R. Smith	S. Snow master in 1828.
1826	Sch.	*Reaper*	131	M. Hinckley	W. Rhoads, 12 Bowly's Wharf, became Baltimore agent in 1827.
1828	Sch.	*Atlantic*	134	J. Kirby	M. B. Perry, 88 Coffee House Slip, became
	"	*Nancy & Maria*	80	Kimball R. Smith	New York agent. "To sail every Saturday through the year and oftener when necessary."
1831	Sch.	*Martha*	126	Andronicus Cheesebrough	
1833	Sch.	*Palestine*	99	D. Smith	
	"	*Olivia*	94	Ebenezer Smith	
	Bg.	*Henry*	98	Ebenezer Smith	
1834	Sch.	*Hope*		J. Bealy	Thomas Whitridge, 13 Bowly's Wharf, be-
	"	*Baltimore*	167	Andronicus Cheesebrough	came Baltimore agent.
	"	*Tionet*	89	Gibbs	
	"	*Othello*	137	Hamilton	
	"	*Citizen*	77	Nathaniel Baker	
	Bg.	*Victor*	125	J. Jarvis	
1835	Sch.	*Robert Gordon*	130	Andronicus Cheesebrough	Benjamin Atwell master in 1837.
	"	*Freedom*	131	Morris Osborn	
	"	*May* (tern)	126	Mulford Patterson	
	"	*Hyperion*	125	P. Baker	James Tyler master in 1836.
	"	*Thaddeus*	139	T. Bedell	
1836	Sch.	*Premier*	97	Morris Osborn	
	"	*Edward Vincent*	187	Elbert Latham	
	Bg.	*York*	150	F. Nichols	
1837	Sch.	*Sarah*	94	Epps Knowlton	
1838	Sch.	*Eliza Hand*	112	Gideon Harden	Sturges & Clearman became New York
	"	*Hornet*	132	Morris Osborn	agents. Sailed every Thursday.
	"	*Victory*	177	Charles Penfield	
	"	*Tom Wood*	135	Benjamin Atwell	Joseph Symonds master in 1840.
	"	*Potomac*	147	Rufus Knapp	
	"	*Washington*	146	Charles Penfield	
	"	*President*	143	J. B. Nock	
1839	Sch.	*Alexandria*	165	John P. Britton	Henry Lewis master in 1843.
	"	*Amanda*	154	Daniel Perry	
1843	Sch.	*Candace*		Brightman	

UNION LINE

J. & N. Briggs, 40 South St., New York agents. W. Rhoads, 61 Smith's Wharf, Baltimore agent. Established Oct., 1835.

YEAR		VESSEL	TONS	MASTERS	REMARKS
1835	Sch.	*Traffic*	105	Ethan C. Briggs	
1836	Sch.	*Eclipse*		Green	
	"	*Valiant*	114	Burton Briggs	
1837	Sch.	*Centreboard*		Wallace Smith	
	"	*Direct*	133	Caleb L. Briggs	
1838	Bg.	*Pavillion*	150	Walter Kelley	John W. Brown, Smith's Dock, became Balti-
	"	*Solon*	135	B. Bourne	more agent; J. & N. Briggs, 38 Old Slip, New
	Sch.	*Charles M. Smith*	132	E. T. Totten	York agents.
	"	*Henry Barger*	147	Ethan C. Briggs	
	"	*Laconic*	100	J. C. Denison	
	"	*Rochester*	127	Burton Briggs	
1839	Bg.	*Science*	147	David Harding	
	Sch.	*Edwin A. Stevens*	144	Burton Briggs	
1841	Sch.	*Gen. Call*	98	Ethan C. Briggs	
	"	*Two Pollies*	134	Matthew D. Fountain	
1842	Sch.	*Leader*	130	Joseph Somers	
	"	*Sarah*	130	Michael Wallace	
	"	*Denmark*	99	Vincent Davis	
1844	Sch.	*Cosmopolite*	107	Lorenzo D. Morgan	
	"	*Maria*	115	Benjamin Atwell	
1848	Sch.	*Joseph Brown*	130	Jeremiah Briggs	
1849	Sch.	*Gen. Worth*	122	Benjamin Atwell	

UNION LINE (*continued*)

YEAR	VESSEL	TONS	MASTERS	REMARKS
1850	Sch. *Francis A. Goodwin*	146	James Carlisle	
"	*Connecticut*	118	John B. Elwood	Var. Ellwood.
1851	Sch. *Aurora*		S. H. M. Burch	
1852	Sch. *Pacific*	164	Benjamin Atwell	

NEW LINE

I. B. Gager, 88 Wall St., New York agent. Rose, Merrill & Dodge, 71 Smith's Wharf, Baltimore agents. Estabtablished Apr., 1844.

YEAR	VESSEL	TONS	MASTERS	REMARKS
1844	Sch. *Chesapeake*	100	James Post	George C. Stewart master in 1846.
"	*Virginia*	134	George W. Hall	
1845	Sch. *Col. Hanson*	131	Amos Grant	Gager & Mailler became New York agents.
"	*Amelia*	126	Wilson J. Terry	Noah Smith master in 1847.
1846	Sch. *Vermillion*	122	Alanson Seaman	
"	*Ann Smith*	130	Charles Wheeler	
"	*Amanda Frances Myrick*	154	Isaac Cathcart	
"	*Margaret Ann*	108	Edmund Hammond	
"	*Brave*	128	Thomas G. Halleck	Agents reported four new schooners under
"	*John E. Smith*	119	William D. Cargill	construction.
"	*John D. Moran*		Voorhis	
"	*Alexandria*	165	Henry Lewis	
1847	Sch. *Lydia*	136	James Post	Mailler & Lord, 108 Wall St., became New
"	*Plato*	170	Edmund Hammond	York agents. Name changed to New & Regular Line.
"	*Sarah Ann Roe*	178	William P. Benjamin	
1848	Sch. *Sarah E. Merrill*	172	Charles T. Strong	Var. *Gebhard.*
"	*Hiram Gerard*	127	Alfred Price	Var. Albert Price.
				Rose, Merrill & Co. became Baltimore agents in 1848.
1849	Sch. *Bay State*	90	W. Yeaton	
"	*Alice*	184	Alanson Seaman	B. Wickes master in 1852.
"	*Ariadne*	98	B. F. Griffing	
1850	Sch. *Hamilton*	198	Albert Dayton	
"	*New Regulus*	120	Edward N. Smith	
"	*Fair*	218	James Post	C. F. Gillett master in 1853.
1851	Sch. *Samuel P. Lord*	227	Noah Smith	
"	*Charles Colgate*	243	Alanson Seaman	George B. Lowden master in 1858.
				John Rose, O'Donnel's Wharf, became Baltimore agent in 1852.
1853	Sch. *Charles T. Strong*	247	Charles T. Strong	Sailed every four days.
"	*William H. Mailler*	191	Alfred Price	Payson Crowell master in May, 1853.
"	*Memento*	228	Edmund Hammond	
1855	Sch. *Somerset*	200	C. J. Sterling	
"	*John Price*	249	Alfred Price	
"	*Neptune's Bride*	263	C. F. Gillett	
1856	Sch. *Seguine*	200	John Bell	Mailler, Lord & Quereau, 108 Wall St., became New York agents; John Rose, Baltimore agent. Sailed semi-weekly. Rose & Lyon became Baltimore agents latter part of year.
"	*Mist*	260	Mark Dissoway	
1857	Sch. *Baltimore*	187	James Sleicht	Var. James Slaght.
"	*Francis Elmore*	187	Jarvis Smith	
"	*Virginia*			
1858	Sch. *Ellicott*	199	Mark Dissoway	
1860	Sch. *Ida Mailler*	129	E. E. Mulliner	Var. Muller.

REGULAR LINE

N. L. McCready & Co., 7 Coenties Slip, New York agents. John W. McKee, 100 Spear's Wharf, Baltimore agent. Established June, 1844, to sail every Wednesday.

YEAR	VESSEL	TONS	MASTERS	REMARKS
1844	Sch. *Commodore Kearney*	147	J. Paine	
"	*Ovoca*	139	J. Squires	David Ireland master in 1853.

REGULAR LINE (*continued*)

YEAR	VESSEL	TONS	MASTERS	REMARKS
1844	Sch. *John W. Smith*	130	Asa Jarvis	David Tew master in 1845.
	" *Mirror*	109	William Nelson Avery	
1849	Sch. *Delaware Farmer*		Stockley	William J. McKee & Bros. became New
	" *George W. Corner*	102	George R. Graham	York agents.
1851	Sch. *William Tyson*	157	Benjamin Jones	Van Brunt & Slaght, 168 Maiden Lane, be-
	" *James W. McKee*	191	Jacob Wilse	came New York agents.
	" *Hurd*	99	Trott	
	" *Eldad*	137	Frederick Jarvis	
	" *Diamond*	115	Davis	
	" *Oregon*	114	J. Squires	
1852	Sch. *Asa Eldridge*	127	Amos N. Lowden	
	" *Hanover*	206	Lake	
	" *Aurora*	148	S. Carruthers	
	" *New Regulus*	120	George S. Walters	
	" *Ann Smith*	130	John A. Darling	

SECTION 12. NEW YORK—CHARLESTON

ESTABLISHED LINE. Later SHIP LINE.

Timothy Street & Co., Charleston agents. Anson G. Phelps, 179 Front St., New York, and Oroondates Mauran, Burling Slip, New York agents.

YEAR	VESSEL	TONS	MASTERS	REMARKS
1819	Sp. *Favorite*	274	D. Marshall	
1820	Sl. *Plato*	93	Bartlett	Phelps & Peck replaced A. G. Phelps.
	" *American Locust*	38	John Allen	Line called Established Line.
	Sch. *Thames*	135	Jacob Winant	
	Sp. *President*	243	John Allen	Thomas Fanning master in 1822.
	" *Franklin*	213	Shadrack Hoyt	J. S. Munro master in 1822.
	" *Empress*	266	George Sutton	William Sinclair master in 1824.
1822	Sp. *Saluda*	289	Joseph Tinkham	Abraham C. Jennings master in 1820. Sp. *Empress* added to Established Line to give weekly sailings. Line consisted of ships *Commodore Perry*, *President*, *Amelia*, *Franklin* and *Empress*. Barker & Hopkins, 80 South St., added as New York agents. Sailed Thurs. from New York and Mon. from Charleston.
1823	Bg. *Empress*	275	L. Banks	
	" *Tontine*	173	Elisha Mix	
	" *Charleston*	157	S. Disbrow	Altered to ship, 1824. E. L. Halsey master.
	Sch. *Agenoria*	114	J. Pike	
	Sp. *Amelia*	205	John R. Crane	
	" *Commodore Perry*	262	Thomas Fanning	Joel Thorp master in 1826.
1824	Sp. *Niagara*	253	John R. Crane	Sailed each Wed. and Sat. Eight ships.
	" *Calhoun*	285	Thomas Fanning	Joseph S. Munro master in 1826.
	" *Georgiana*	279	John Bailey	Dropped from line 1825.
	" *Othello*	264	S. Trowbridge	Lost, Rockaway, 1831.
	" *Lafayette*	342	Thomas Fanning	Hez. Allen master in 1830. T. & T. Street & Co. became Charleston agents, 1825. Capt. George Sutton became New York agent in fall. Sailings reduced to one every four days until further notice. Six ships in line in 1828, sailing every Mon. Street & Boinest, 6 Boyce & Co.'s Wharf, became Charleston agents, 1830.
1831	Sp. *William Drayton*	371	E. L. Halsey	
1832	Sp. *Anson*	324	William Sinclair	Joseph Galloway master in 1844.
	" *Sutton*	347	Michael Berry	
1833	Sp. *Henry Allen*	373	Henry Wilson	
1834	Sp. *Angelique*	420	Elisha L. Halsey	
1839	Sp. *Catherine*	478	Stephen Besher	Sutton moved to 88 South St., New York. Barkman & Sutton became Charleston agents, 1844. Street & Boinest again became
1845	Bg. *George*	208	J. P. Yates	Charleston agents in 1845, changing to T. Street in May.

ESTABLISHED LINE (*continued*)

YEAR		VESSEL	TONS	MASTERS	REMARKS
1845	Sp.	*South Carolina*	581	Joseph Hamilton	Thomas Wardle became New York agent in Jan., 1848, with R. H. Tucker, Jr., Charleston agent, with four ships—*South Carolina, Catherine, Anson,* and *Henry Allen*.
1849	Sp.	*Julia Howard*	590	William C. Bulkley	John H. Holmes, Central Wharf, became
	Bk.	*Walter*	257	John B. Thompson	Charleston agent.
	Sp.	*Columbia*	441	J. F. Setzer	Judson Sturges master in 1850.
	"	*Southport*	500	R. McCormack	
	"	*New York*	524	Burr Hull	
	"	*Sullivan*	437	William White	
	Bk.	*Carolina*	364	Mather Godfrey	
	Sp.	*Chace*	625	William White	
1850	Bk.	*Edward*	355	Knudson	
1851	Sp.	*Alliance*	525	Robinson	
	Bk.	*Petrea*	494	Judson Sturges	
1853	Sch.	*Charles Edmonston*	121	A. G. Johnson	
	Bg.	*Mary Hamilton*	292	A. B. Walker	
1854	Sch.	*Harriet P. Stoney*	227	Lewis P. Taylor	Holmes & Stoney became Charleston agents.
1855	Bg.	*Tybee*	329	John Ferguson	Line became relatively inactive in 1855 and
	Sp.	*Mary Lucretia*	412	J. C. Gibbs	was discontinued in 1856.
	Bg.	*Clinton*	379	George Thompson	

NEW LINE popularly called BRIG LINE

Drake Mills, Charleston agent. Saul Alley, 74 South St., and J. & O. Williams, 171 Water St., New York agents. Established Sept., 1822, as the New Line of Charleston Packets.

YEAR		VESSEL	TONS	MASTERS	REMARKS
1822	Bg.	*Tontine*	173	Elisha A. Mix	
	"	*Empress*	121	Lyman Banks	Cast away on Barnegat in snow storm,
	"	*Adams*	128	Elisha L. Halsey	Mar. 17, 1824. Capt. Moores.
	"	*Convoy*	138	Andrew Shaw	
	"	*Charleston*	166	Solomon Disbrow	
1825	Bg.	*Stranger*	124	Cartwright	Discontinued in 1826, Drake Mills taking
	"	*Panthea*	199	J. Bradley	Union Line of Schooners.

UNION LINE OF SCHOONERS

J. M. Catlin, 90 South St., New York agent. T. J. Wyman, Charleston agent. Established Oct., 1823, to leave New York and Charleston every Sat. William Cowing, 4 Fulton St., and William C. Barker, 80 South St., also New York agents. Sailed irregularly until 1825. Became Brig Line in 1832.

YEAR		VESSEL	TONS	MASTERS	REMARKS
1823	Sch.	*Ohio*	98	Abel Beers	
	"	*Erie*	93	Andrew Bulkley	
	"	*Gazelle*	143	William Bulkley	
	"	*Angenora*	96	Julius Pike	
1825	Sch.	*Harvest*	89	Jonathan Emery	
	"	*Orbit*	112	Calvin Babbidge	Wiggin Merrill master in 1826.
	"	*Hero*	97	Nathaniel Davis	
1826	Sl.	*Rapid*	80	Hawkin Wheeler	Dudley & Cowing became New York agents in Sept.; Drake Mills, Charleston agent.
1827	Sch.	*Spy*	99	Andrew Bulkley	Line sailed irregularly in 1827.
	"	*Eliza*	91	William Jocelin	
	"	*Coral*	127	William Bulkley	Later brig.
1828	Sch.	*Star*	124	John Hull Jr.	Dudley & Stuyvesant became New York
	"	*Juno*	140	William Pike	agents in Mar.; W. Jones, Charleston agent.
1829	Sch.	*Nile*	90	Judson Sturges	
1830	Bg.	*Courier*	148	Abel Beers	Daniel Brown master in 1832. P. W. Beers master in 1834.
1831	Sch.	*America*	115	Frederick Sherwood	
	Bg.	*York*	150	J. Brown	
	Sch.	*Defiance*	97	Salathiel Baker	
	"	*Frederick*	149	Frederick Sherwood	
1832	Bg.	*Edwina*	174	Judson Sturges	Capsized off Hatteras, June 3, 1832. Five passengers lost.

UNION LINE OF SCHOONERS (*continued*)

YEAR		VESSEL	TONS	MASTERS	REMARKS
1832	Bg.	*Lawrence*	170	Thomas Fanning	
	"	*Oregon*	108	Moses Bulkley	
	"	*Jones*	179	William Bulkley	
1833	Bg.	*Planter*	194	Judson Sturges	
1834	Bg.	*George*	208	Brown	George Bulkley became agent in July, 1834. Line consisted of brigs *York*, *George*, *Courier*, *Jones*, *Planter*, and *Lawrence*.
1835	Bg.	*Moses*	220	Daniel Brown	
1836	Bg.	*Sun*	353	George Brown	
1838	Sch.	*Thames*	99	Joseph Spencer	
	Bg.	*Tybee*	229	Thomas R. Herbest	
	"	*Clinton*	379	Thomas Lyon	
	Sp.	*Hero*	760	Charles R. Griffith	
1839	Bg.	*Moon*	278	Judson Sturges	Var. Sturgis
1840	Sp.	*Sullivan*	437	Daniel Brown	Lost, Fire Island, New York, Feb., 1855.
	Bg.	*Edward*	355	William C. Bulkley	W. Jones & Smith became Charleston agents
	Sp.	*Southport*	500	Thomas R. Herbest	in 1841.
1843	Sp.	*Charleston*	492	Daniel Brown	
1844	Sp.	*New York*	524	Burr Hull	
1846	Sp.	*Fairfield*	588	Samuel Loveland	
1850	Sp.	*E. Bulkley*	755	Daniel Brown	Line quite inactive 1851–3. Resumed in 1854
1854	Sch.	*Fanny* (Cl.)	363	Burr Hull	with schooner *Fanny*, brigs *Tybee*, *Moses* and
1856	Sp.	*Hero*	759	J. B. Stafford	*Clinton* and ships *New York* and *Fairfield*. Became relatively inactive in 1856 and ceased operations as a line late in 1858.

COMMERCIAL LINE

Dunham & Dimon and Allen & Paxon, 61 South St., New York agents. William A. Caldwell & Son, Charleston agents. Line began operation July, 1836.

YEAR		VESSEL	TONS	MASTERS	REMARKS
1836	Bg.	*Dimon*	199	Hampton Stuart	Sold New Bedford for whaler, 1845.
	"	*Cordelia*	200	Francis Sherwood	Asa Matthews master of *Dimon* in 1840.
	"	*Buenos Ayres* (*sic*)	192	L. Moore, Jr.	
	"	*Juno*	196	Calvin Babbidge	
1838	Bg.	*Homer*	185	Nabb	Allen & Paxon, 92 Wall St., became New
	"	*Emerald*	169	P. McKenzie	York agents starting Jan., 1828.
	"	*Calvin*	216	E. W. Gardner	
	"	*Fanny*		William W. Whittlesey	
	"	*Ashley*	285	Julius Pike	
1839	Bg.	*Moon*	279	Judson Sturges	Lost May 5, 1845, on Nag's Head.
	Bk.	*Gentleman*	227	George B. Woodworth	Dunham & Dimon replaced Allen & Paxon
	Sch.	*Wanderer*	142	Timothy G. Merwin	in Sept., 1839. (Thomas Dunham, Jr. &
	"	*Rosario*	155		Frederick Dimon).
	Sp.	*Nicholas Biddle*	784	Charles A. Hiern	
	Bg.	*Perry*	150	Joseph Hamilton	J. A. Knudson master in 1841.
	"	*Emily*	322	Frederick F. Sherwood	
1840	Bg.	*Carolina*	364	Franklin Sherwood	Altered to bark in 1842.
	Sch.	*Oneko*	111	Joseph W. Davis	Line composed of five brigs sailing each Mon. John W. Caldwell became Charleston agent in 1841.
1843	Bg.	*Acton*	184	F. M. Lambert	
	"	*Long Island*	174	Daniel Howell	
1844	Bk.	*Z. Ring*	324	Elbert Latham	
1845	Bg.	*Linden*	392	Gilbert A. Knudson	
	Sp.	*Duncan*	278	Philander Daggett	
	Bg.	*Harriet*	100	H. Baker	
	"	*Caroline E. Platt*	231	R. R. S. Pittman	
	Bk.	*Edward*	355	William C. Bulkley	
1846	Bg.	*Rufus Soule*	173	W. Jordan	Line sailed every Wed.
	"	*Detroit*	197	Porter	
	Bk.	*Texidor*	217	Hugo B. Major	
	Sch.	*Josephine*	213	David Latourette, Jr.	
	Sp.	*Marion*	450	Martin Thompson	
	"	*Columbia*	441	George Robinson	

COMMERCIAL LINE (*continued*)

YEAR		VESSEL	TONS	MASTERS	REMARKS
1847	Sp.	*Camden*	525	Francis Sherwood	
1848	Sp.	*Julia Howard*	590	William C. Bulkley	
1849	Bg.	*Jasper*	334	John D. Hasty	Lost overboard, June 19, 1852.
	Bg.	*Clement*	197	Seth Ryder, Jr.	
	"	*L. Baldwin*	270	Harrison Smith	
1850	Bg.	*American*		Ross	
1851	Sp.	*Dirigo*	497	Russell Doane	
1852	Bk.	*Dudley*	250	T. M. Morrison	
	"	*Gen. Greene*	242	G. W. Hammer	
	Bg.	*Empire*	220	David A. Nye	
	Sch.	*Patrick Henry*	211	Gilbert A. Knudson	
	Sp.	*Martha's Vineyard*	499	David A. Nye	
	Sch.	*Ellicott*	200	Mark Dissoway	
	"	*Ann Smith*	130	John A. Darling	
1853	Sch.	*George Luff*	198	Johnston	Popularly known in Charleston as Caldwell
	"	*Trader*	202	George Wheeler	Line.
	Sp.	*Gulnare*	324	Phillips	
	Bk.	*Harriet & Martha*	189	Ellems	
	Sch.	*James H. Chadbourne*	378	Edward Wainwright	
	Sp.	*Delia Maria*	584	Michaels	Lost at sea, Jan., 1855.
1854	Bk.	*Elizabeth*		Tufts	
	Sp.	*Hartford*	511	Diedrich Sannerman	
	Sch.	*Edward H. Rowley*	197	Wertley Rogers	
	Bk.	*Isabella*	356	J. Humphrey	B. G. Tufts master in 1854–5.
	Sch.	*Pocahontas*	217	H. Bulkley	
	Bg.	*Souther*	198	Hendricks	
	Sp.	*Richard Cobden*	710	G. Barrett	
	Bk.	*Jeddo*	242	John Payne	
	"	*Elizabeth Means*	243	Rasmussen	
	"	*Courier*	385	Edwin Sherwood	
1856	Bk.	*Joseph*		Bennett	
	"	*Martha*	470	J. H. Jenkins	
	Bg.	*Mary*	193	Jonathan Godfrey	
1857	Bk.	*Flight*	386	Asa H. Calhoun	
1858	Sch.	*George Davis*	336	Samuel F. Phillips	Sailings greatly reduced during 1858
	Sp.	*Quickstep*	857	Stephen Wade	
	Bk.	*Moneynick*	369	Ephraim Smith	
	Sp.	*Java*	715	L. C. Daggett	
1859	Sch.	*James H. Seguine*	267	Sebastian Ellis	Very little activity in 1859 and no sailings
	"	*Wm. L. Burroughs*	497	Hollis B. Jencks	noted thereafter.

TINKHAM & HART LINE

Tinkham & Hart, New York agents. Line began operation Mar., 1836. First credited with maintaining a schedule in Sept., 1836.

YEAR		VESSEL	TONS	MASTERS	REMARKS
1836	Bg.	*Montevideo*	243	Abraham Mulford	
	"	*Dimon*	199	Frederick Sherwood	
	"	*Buenos Ayres* (*sic*)	192	L. Moore, Jr.	
	"	*Juno*	196	Calvin Babbidge	
	Sp.	*Helen*	424	Benjamin Butman	Var. Butnam.
1837	Bg.	*Fanny*		William W. Whittlesey	Allen & Paxon became New York agents
	"	*William Jones*	196	W. P. Beecher	in May.
	"	*Perry*	269	Charles Perry	Line ceased operations early in 1838.
	"	*Ashley*	285	William W. Whittlesey	

A. B. COOLEY LINE

A. B. Cooley, New York agent. Line began operation, May, 1840.

YEAR		VESSEL	TONS	MASTERS	REMARKS
1840	Sch.	*Columbia*	112	John Townsend	
	"	*South Carolina*	91	William Goodwin	
	Bg.	*Cohansey*	193	David Moore	
	Sch.	*Michigan*	163	Robinson	

A. B. COOLEY LINE (*continued*)

YEAR		VESSEL	TONS	MASTERS	REMARKS
1840	Sch.	*Red Jacket*	156	William C. Rogers	Line began to maintain schedule with sailing
	Bg.	*Caspiam*	99	Alexander G. Swazey	of *Red Jacket* in Oct.
	Sch.	*Joseph Gorham*	146	Williams	
	"	*Antelope*	148	Thomas Gifford	
1841	Bg.	*J. Peterson*	194	James Green	No fixed schedule in 1841.
	Sch.	*States Rights*	102	Willett Mott	
	Sp.	*Henry Leeds*	379	Jones	
	"	*Congress*	401	Robert Marshall	
	Bk.	*Hobart*	204	James Collier	
	Sch.	*Increase*	135	Warren	
1842	Bk.	*Bevis*	214	George Briggs	Line inactive in 1842 and discontinued in 1843 after inactive season.

ELWELL LINE

J. Elwell & Co., New York agents. Line nominally established in 1842 but cleared very few ships before 1845.

YEAR		VESSEL	TONS	MASTERS	REMARKS
1845	Sp.	*Virginia*	649	James Eaton	
	"	*Ocean*	369	John Willard	
	"	*Diadem*	657	Henry W. Barstow	
	"	*Severn*	572	Charles Cheever	
	"	*Georgiana*	544	Charles F. W. Behm	
1847	Sch.	*Vandalier*	163	R. McIntyre	Inactive all through 1846.
	Sp.	*Europe*	557	Samuel Baker	After 1847 firm maintained only a token
	Bg.	*Susan Soule*	164	J. Bacon	service of at most three or four sailings a
	Sp.	*Albany*	469	Davis	year, which ended in 1854, the firm then
	Bg.	*Massachusetts*	164	S. S. Burgess	being J. W. Elwell & Co.
	Sch.	*Henry*	145	J. R. Fish	

STURGES & CLEARMAN LINE

Sturges & Clearman, New York agents.

YEAR		VESSEL	TONS	MASTERS	REMARKS
1847	Bg.	*Savannah*	396	Aaron Hawley	Vessels cleared every Sat. Line discontinued
	"	*Excel*	375	C. B. Smith	after 1848 although firm sent an occasional
	Bk.	*Exact*	431	J. Johnston	vessel for several years.
	Bg.	*Clinton*	379	Thomas Lyon	
	"	*Augusta*	399	Aaron M. Sherwood	
	"	*Madison*	314	Walter Bulkley	

MERCHANTS' LINE

N. L. McCready & Co., 36 South St., New York agents. Henry Missroon, Corner E. Bay & Adger's Wharf, Charleston agent. Notice of intention to establish given in Sept., 1846, but no activity of consequence until Jan., 1847.

YEAR		VESSEL	TONS	MASTERS	REMARKS
1847	Sch.	*Julia Eliza*	162	Richard Higbee	Popularly known as Schooner Line.
	"	*Louisa Reeves*	163	Cavilier	No regular schedule. Vessels in general ad-
	"	*S. Morris Waln*	148	John Somers	vertised to sail with dispatch and listed in
	"	*Cicero*	141	Baker	order of sailing without duplication of names.
	"	*William Burk*	136	D. Lawrence	
	"	*Jeroleman*	186	Robert W. Goslee	
	"	*Arietis*	131	R. W. Wheeler	Var. R. M. Wheeler.
	"	*Col. Simmons*		Hamblin	
1848	Bg.	*Radius*	194	Emerson	
	Sch.	*Richmond*	148	Alexander Seavey	
	"	*Renown*	129	T. M. Meldrum	Var. Melden.
	Bg.	*Magnolia*	135	Morris	
	Sch.	*Sea Mew*	150	Charles B. Hobart	
	"	*Leroy*	196	Copes	
	"	*Eugene*	162	A. Coleman	
	"	*Athos*	138	Theron B. Worth	
	"	*Julia*	167	Aaron Vangilder	
	"	*Samuel R. Jackson*	149	Corson	

MERCHANTS' LINE (*continued*)

YEAR	VESSEL	TONS	MASTERS	REMARKS
1848	Sch. *Charles D. Ellis*	128	Thomas Smith	
1849	Sch. *John Castner*	247	John Somers	
	" *J. W. Swain*	167	David T. Smith	
	" *Harp*	160	Andrew Gibbs	
	" *Sarah Elizabeth*	147	Somers	
	Bg. *Petersburg*	183	Edmund Cooper	
	Sch. *Lamartine*	180	Isaac C. Turner	
	Bg. *William T. Dugan*	144	Thomas Smith	Line began regular weekly schedule with sailing of *Dugan*, Feb. 28, 1849.
	Bk. *Leonesa*	195	William Monroe	
	Sch. *St. Mary*	187	Henry Lake	
	" *Kensington*	179	Charles P. Foster	
	" *Eliza Jane*	222	Daniel Townsend	
	Bg. *Mary Jane*	148	E. G. Lermond	
	Sch. *P. B. Savery*	127	Henry Wilden	
	" *Mary Jane Lonan*	189	Robinson	
	" *Cornelia A. Crooke*	189	Caleb Grant	
	" *Squire & Brothers*	163	Edward W. Lonan	Cleared for Darien, Isthmus of Panama.
	" *Louisine*	248	George W. Robinson	
	" *Robert W. Brown*	200	Lewis S. Davis	
	" *Col. Satterlee*	235	Lewis S. Davis	Var. *Col. Satterly.*
	" *James P. Lofland*	128	Leander Hallett	
	" *Helene*	244	B. F. Griffin	John C. Griffing master in 1849–50.
1850	Sch. *Alexander M.*	144	Mitchell	Regular line composed of schooners *Helene*,
	" *Abdel Kader*	152	Robert Pearce	*Charles D. Ellis, M. E. Wells, Col. Satterly* and
	" *M. E. Wells*	231	Benjamin T. Griffin	brig *Wm. T. Dugan*, sailing every Sat. Con-
	Bg. *John Dawson*	137	Rodick	tinued same through 1851. Vessels rated from
	Sch. *Jonas Smith*	236	James B. Nichols	1800 to 2500 barrels capacity.
	" *Fair*	217	James Post	
	" *William H. Smith*	191	George O. Smith	
1852	Sch. *Adele*	212	Albert S. Ackley	Schooner *Charles D. Ellis* dropped and
	" *Manhasset*	266	James Myers	schooners *Louisine*, Phineas Smith, master,
	" *Cataract*	319	Charles A. Rice	and *D. B. Warner*, Charles Mills, added. Now
	" *Julia M. Hallock*	280	Albert S. Ackley	sailed each Mon.
	Bk. *Escoriaza*	245	Pope	
	Sch. *D. B. Warner*	298	Charles Mills	
	" *N. W. Smith*	315	Edwin Smith	
	" *Francis Satterly*	310	Lewis S. Davis	Var. *Frances Satterly.*
1853	Sch. *E. L. B. Wales*	178	James S. Little	Firm became McCready, Mott & Co. in
	Bg. *Alfred Exall*	244	Joseph Golder	July, 1853; Nathaniel L. McCready and
	Bk. *Jeddo*	242	John Payne	John W. Mott.
	Sch. *Trader*	202	George Wheeler	
	" *Enchantress*	378	William I. Tyler	
	" *New Regulus*	120	Nathaniel Dickinson	
	" *Urania*	198	B. F. Henderson	
	Bg. *Clinton*	379	Walker	George Thompson master in 1856.
1854	Sch. *Jonas Smith*	236	Furman	
	" *B. N. Hawkins*	369	S. G. Griffing	
	" *J. Darling*	242	Robert W. Wheeler	
	Bg. *Martha Post*	195	R. H. Post	
	Sch. *W. A. Ellis*	255	Joseph B. Nichols	
	" *Edward Kidder* (Cl.)	318	William G. Tyler	George E. Horton master in 1856.
	" *Pocahontas* (Cl.)	217	Nathaniel Godfrey	
	Bg. *Charlotte*	330	J. T. Horton	
	Sch. *Wm. Smith*	314	George Smith	
	" *L. S. Davis*	319	Lewis S. Davis	
1855	Sch. *Myrover*	356	Francis Jackson	
	" *Lilly*	335	Barnabas Francis	
	" *C. B. Knudson*	234	W. H. Squires	
1856	Bg. *Black Swan*	200	J. W. Conner	F. J. Ogden became Charleston agent.
	Sch. *S. J. Waring*	372	Edwin Smith	
	" *N. W. Smith*	315	John P. Wyatt	
	Bk. *Peter Clinton*	502	M. S. Mandevill	
1857	Sch. *John Roe*	297	Edmund Hammond	Regular line consisted of six big schooners
	" *Robert Caldwell*	447	Charles S. Hudson	sailing each Mon. Henry Missroon became
	" *William H. Smith*	191	Goodspeed	Charleston agent again in Jan.

MERCHANTS' LINE (*continued*)

YEAR	VESSEL	TONS	MASTERS	REMARKS
1858	Sch. *Wm. C. Mershon*	390	Edward Cole	
	Bk. *Col. John McRae*	412	David P. Barry	Ex-schooner. Also called a barkentine.
	Sch. *George A. Tittle*	268	Reuben B. Adams	
	" *Smithsonian*	390	J. A. Van Brunt	
	" *Target*	388	G. L. Howe	
	" *Wide World*	274	J. H. Buckley	
1859	Sch. *D. C. Hulse*	243	R. C. Conklin	
	" *Fleetwing* (tern)	518	Lewis Davis, Jr.	
1860	Sch. *Margaret Y. Davis*	161	George W. Robinson	
	" *John A. Stanley*	238	Francis Jackson	
	" *Florence Rogers*	349	D. S. Rogers	
	" *Charles Dennis*	291	Isaac F. Horton	
	" *Loyal Scranton*	386	Amos N. Lowden	

ARMER PATTON & CO. LINE

Armer Patton & Co., New York agents. Notice of establishment of line given in Apr., 1848, but regular sailings did not start until fall season. Line discontinued latter part of 1848.

YEAR	VESSEL	TONS	MASTERS	REMARKS
1848	Sch. *Telegraph*	143	Hamilton Tooker	
	Sp. *Severn*	572	Charles Cheever	
	Sch. *Ira Bliss*	199	Samuel Dearborn	
	" *Pocahontas*	217	John H. Smack	
	" *Hume*	99	Darling	
	" *Athalia*	236	Lorenzo D. Purnell	
	" *Pauline*	156	Young	

EMPIRE LINE

Ladd & Church, 69 South St., New York agents. Line established Oct., 1851. No fixed schedule.

YEAR	VESSEL	TONS	MASTERS	REMARKS
1851	Sp. *May Flower*	721	J. Crooker	
	Bk. *Lucy Elioabeth*	335	Zenas Crosby	
1852	Sp. *Harrisburg*	493	Oliver Matthews	
	Sch. *Alexander M.*	144	Perry	Warren M. Christie master in 1855. Service discontinued during 1853. Resumed in fall of 1854. A. Ladd became New York agent.
1854	Sp. *Sonora*	707	T. Pritchard	Line discontinued latter part of 1854.
	Bk. *Hesper*	392	Hawes	
	Bk. *Massachusetts*	300	Knowles	

LANE & WEST LINE

Lane & West, 77 South St., New York agents. Line started operation, Oct., 1853. Line discontinued early in 1855.

YEAR	VESSEL	TONS	MASTERS	REMARKS
1853	Bk. *Julia Dean*	299	H. W. Mallory	H. T. Street master in 1854.
	Bg. *Tartar*	199	Sheer	
	Sch. *Echo*	197	Amos N. Lowden	
1854	Sch. *Stephen Hotchkiss*	291	A. H. Manson	
	" *St. Lawrence*	153	A. Hedlund	
	Sp. *Cotton Planter*	501	Hezekiah Ripley	

PALMETTO LINE

Dollner & Potter, 154 Front St., New York agents. Holmes & Stoney, Charleston agents. Sailings started Oct., 1854.

YEAR	VESSEL	TONS	MASTERS	REMARKS
1854	Bk. *Almena*	756	Bethuel E. Hallock	
	Sch. *William S. Cogswell*		Charles B. Elwood	
	" *George M. Smith*	178	Joseph B. Nichols	
	" *Franklin Nickerson*	258	James A. Wyatt	
	" *Harriet P. Stoney*	227	G. Erickson	
	" *Ann & Susan*	326	Samuel Myers	
	" *Albert Mason*	271	Samuel N. Smith	

PALMETTO LINE (*continued*)

YEAR		VESSEL	TONS	MASTERS	REMARKS
1855	Bg.	*Jehossee*	224	Samuel Myers	Dollner, Potter & Co. became New York
	"	*John H. Jones*	411	Charles Mills	agents in Jan., 1855.
	Sch.	*Lewis A. Edwards*	220	Joseph Hartick	The following sailed repeatedly in the line,
	"	*Laura Gertrude*	316	S. G. Fairchild	following their first appearance, and may be
	"	*Pocahontas*	217	Horatio Bulkley	regarded as of the established line, rather
	Bk.	*Julia Dean*	298	J. Gage	than transients, most of them continued to
	Sch.	*John A. Stanley*	239	John W. Simonson	1859–60. Schooners *Harriet P. Stoney, Ann &*
	"	*William A. Ellis*	255	Joseph B. Nichols	*Susan, William H. Gilliland, Albert Mason,*
					Sarah Bruen, Franklin Nickerson, T. B. Wagner,
					and brig *J. H. Jones*. Others continued to
					run regularly for shorter periods up to two
					or three years.
	"	*Vapor*	312	Horatio Wilson	Var. *Vapour*.
	"	*Alba*	394	Bradley Osborn	
	"	*William H. Gilliland*	348	D. B. Vincent	
	"	*Robert W. Brown*	200	Job Derrickson	
	"	*Americus*	262	Ezekiel S. Vanderbilt	
1856	Sch.	*Moonlight*	260	George W. Stutes	
	"	*E. W. Gardner*	212	Charles A. Browne	
	"	*Fleetwing* (tern)	518	Lewis Davis	
	"	*Sarah Bruen*	233	George T. Pearson	
	"	*James Miller* (tern)	471	Jesse N. Braddock	
	"	*T. B. Wagner*	390	Samuel N. Smith	Var. *T. D. Wagner*.
	Bk.	*Dudley*	249	Robinson	
1857	Sch.	*Tanner*	439	George T. Pearson	Var. Pierson.
	"	*Passport*	348	George Hawkins	
	Bk.	*Lexington*	394	Charles Thatcher	
	Sch.	*Sunny South*	228	Smith Weeks	
	"	*Mary J. Hoyt*	257	C. H. Hamilton	
	"	*Burdett Hart*	266	Albert Thomas	
1858	Sch.	*Samuel Eddy*	276	Wesley Patton	
	"	*Lydia B. Cowperthwaite*	367	Beatty	C. H. Hamilton master in Nov., 1858.
	"	*George Darby*	239	D. E. Mulliner	
	Bg.	*Daniel Maloney*	247	Absolom Steelman	
1859	Sch.	*D. W. Vaughan*	254	Samuel M. Gifford	
	"	*Mobile*	399	Allen Howes	
	Bk.	*Edisto*	358	N. Kendrick	Tonnage also reported 366.
	Sch.	*Surprise*	291	Winant J. Cole	
1860	Sch.	*John W. Rumsey* (tern)	368	Lewis P. Taylor	
	"	*Harry Maybee*	248	J. S. Maybee	

NEW REGULAR LINE

N. H. Brigham, New York agent. Established Feb., 1855. Discontinued after first season.

YEAR		VESSEL	TONS	MASTERS	REMARKS
1855	Sp.	*Alliance*	525	D. L. Tinkham	
	Bg.	*Daniel Webster*	194	G. W. Williams	

NEW REGULAR LINE

William B. Scranton and Henry H. Tallman, Scranton & Tallman, 19 Old Slip, New York agents. Henry Missroon, Charleston agent. Commenced operations Oct., 1855.

YEAR		VESSEL	TONS	MASTERS	REMARKS
1855	Sch.	*John Boston*	399	William B. Lingo	
	Bk.	*Columbia*			
	Sch.	*Pocahontas*	217	Horatio Bulkley	
	"	*T. C. Smyth*		Westerland	
	"	*John Castner*	247	R. Johnston	
	"	*William B. Scranton*	423	William Cathcart	
	"	*William Smith*	315	George Smith	
1856	Sch.	*Joseph W. Webster*	390	Roderick Bennett	
	"	*Henry Nutt*	236	John Garwood	
	"	*Eclipse*	305	Thomas Corwin	
	"	*Elizabeth C. Felter* (tern)	389	John Arnold	

NEW REGULAR LINE (*continued*)

YEAR	VESSEL	TONS	MASTERS	REMARKS
1856	Sch. *Manhasset*	267	Sweezy	
1857	Sch. *Joseph Grice*	247	A. T. Rogers	
	" *Margaret Y. Davis*	161	George W. Robinson	
	" *Thomas Holcombe*	392	Robert W. Goslee	
	" *Moonlight*	260	George W. Stutes	
	" *Kate Stewart*	388	Titus C. Mather	
1858	Bg. *Tavernier*	150	R. F. Whitty	
	Sch. *Ida*	258	J. Raymond	
1859	Sch. *Loyal Scranton*	386	Amos N. Lowden	William B. Scranton became sole New York
	Bg. *Eliza*	157	J. H. Steinmayer	agent in Oct.

Henry Missroon & Co., became Charleston agents, 1860. Line continued into 1861.

NEW LINE

Mailler, Lord & Quereau, 108 Wall St., New York agents. Henry P. Russell, Charleston agent. Established Nov., 1858. Became Murray's Line in Jan., 1859.

YEAR	VESSEL	TONS	MASTERS	REMARKS
1858	Sch. *Bennet Flanner*	321	Henry Applegit	
	" *Mary Emma*	247	George W. Hulse	
	" *Charles Colgate*	244	George B. Lowden	
	" *Southern Belle*	322	Thomas Smith	
1859	Sch. *Isaac Rich*		Horton	D. Colden Murray, 62 South St., became
	" *Virginia*	295	S. R. Davis	New York agent.
	" *John Roe*	297	Edmund Hammond	
	" *Charles T. Strong*	247	William Liscum	
	" *Sidney Price*	199	Godfrey	
	" *Emily*	279	Bradley Smith	
	" *Julia M. Hallock*	280	J. H. Nickerson	Also reported 238 tons.
	" *May*	283	D. B. Hobart	
	" *Lovett Peacock*	363	Lewis Mankin	
	" *Charles Smith*	397	James D. Swain	
	" *George Darby*	238	Blank	
	" *Edward Kidder*	319	Hans P. Harkssen	Var. Harkson.
	" *Helene*	243	Job Derrickson	
	" *Langdon Gilmore*	497	Jonathan Chase	
	" *Adele*	212	R. R. Baker	
	" *Charles Dennis*	291	Lewis S. Davis	
1860	Sch. *Edward Slade*	285	Joseph Bayles	
	" *D. A. Berry*	243	Peter H. Voorhees	
	" *Wide World*	274	Horatio Bulkley	
	" *Walter Raleigh*	472	Samuel Y. Phillips	
	" *W. Paxon*		Stevenson	
	" *John S. Lee*	266	Burrows Corson	
	" *Adeline Townsend*	284	Ebenezer M. Townsend	
	Bg. *John H. Jones*	411	Charles Mills	
	Sch. *D. C. Hulse*	242	Hamilton D. Conklin	
	" *Henry P. Russell*	111	Lewis Mankin	
	" *W. R. Beebe*		Riley Aumack	
	" *Harriet Brewster*	290	J. D. Hawkins	
	Bg. *Black Fish*	345	S. G. Fairchild	Continued to 1861.

SECTION 13. NEW YORK—SAVANNAH

ESTABLISHED LINE

James & Cornelius Seguine, 80 Custom House Slip, New York agents. Hall & Hoyt, Savannah agents.

YEAR	VESSEL	TONS	MASTERS	REMARKS
1819	Bg. *Jane*		Collier	
	" *Levant*	181	Denison Wood	
	Sch. *Gen. Scott*	144	Smith	
	" *Undaunted*	129	Thomas Wood	
	Sp. *Rubicon*	307	Nathan H. Holdredge	
1822	Sp. *Gen. Carrington*	198	Thomas Wood	

ESTABLISHED LINE (*continued*)

YEAR		VESSEL	TONS	MASTERS	REMARKS
1824	Sp.	*Emperor*	303	James H. Bennett	Whitlock Old Line and J. & C. Seguine com-
	"	*Louisa*	383	Denison Wood	bined Savannah operations in Jan., 1824;
					and continued as Established Line.
1825	Sp.	*Statira*	254	Thomas Wood	Cornelius Seguine master later in year.
					Hall, Shapter & Tupper became Savannah
					agents in 1826.
1827	Sp.	*Howard*	337	Denison Wood	Whitlock cleared most ships in 1826–7.
	"	*Eliza & Abby*	244	Denison Wood	J. & C. Seguine quite inactive. Hill & Stone,
					Mongin's Wharf, became Savannah agents.
					Whitlock retired as associate operator of line
					in Nov. 1828, J. & C. Seguine becoming sole
					New York agents. Sailed weekly on regular
					schedule.
1828	Sp.	*Macon*	360	Daniel L. Porter	
	"	*Florian*	335	Francis Harrison	T. J. Leavitt master in 1832.
	"	*Henry*	248	George Moore	
1829	Sp.	*Lafayette*	342	Thomas Fanning	Scott & Shapter added as New York agents.
	"	*Tybee*	299	Denison Wood	Line consisted of six ships sailing every six
	"	*Helen Mar*	308	Thomas Harrison	days.
	"	*Don Quixote*	260	Abner Tappan, Jr.	
	"	*Douglass*	248	Lemuel Bourne	
1830	Sp.	*Emperor*	302	J. R. Shapter	
	Bg.	*Georgia*	197	William H. Nichols	
1831	Sp.	*Othello*	264	Walter Bulkley	
	Sch.	*Agenoria*	114	Joseph G. Pearce	
	Bg.	*Atlantic*	215	William L. Nye	
1832	Sp.	*Queen Mab*	270	John Bailey	Regular line consisted of six ships sailing
	"	*Trenton*	428	Denison Wood	every Mon.
	Sch.	*Delight*	128	John Smith	
1833	Bg.	*Lela*	149	J. B. Fisk	Scott, Shapter & Morrell, 72 South St., be-
	Sp.	*Celia*	339	Daniel L. Porter	came New York agents in July, 1833, and
	"	*Belle*	341	John Bailey	George Hall and James S. and Frederick
	"	*Mogul*	395	P. Blake	Shapter became Savannah agents.
	Bg.	*Halcyon*	156	Daniel H. Truman	
1834	Sch.	*Rebecca*	130	G. Gay	
	Sp.	*John Taylor*	335	Thayer	
	"	*Tropic*	350	J. G. Russell	
	Bg.	*Augusta*	163	C. S. Curtis	
	"	*Sadi*	185	Russell Doane	
1835	Sp.	*Hilah*	395	Edmund Hammond	Tupper & Sistare became Savannah agents.
	"	*Franconia*	499	Eleazer Crabtree	
	"	*Ocmulgee*	461	Thomas J. Leavitt	
	Bg.	*Nelson*	195	Shaw	
	"	*New Hanover*	220	J. P. Levy	
1836	Sp.	*Macon*	360	D. Miner	Ladd, Tupper & Sistare became Savannah
	"	*Louisa*	496	D. H. Truman	agents. Name changed to Old Established
	"	*Angelique*	420	Samuel Nichols	Line.
	"	*Oconee*	461	J. D. Wilson	
	Bk.	*La Grange*	259	Russell Doane	
	Sp.	*Oconee*	461	Andrew Clark	
1837	Sch.	*New Union*	115	Benjamin F. Chase	Scott & Morrell became New York agents in
	Bg.	*Darien*	229	Charles P. Buckley	Feb., 1837. Cohen & Miller were Savannah
	Sp.	*Thomas Dickason*	454	W. L. Lyon	agents.
1838	Sp.	*Gaston*	456	Andrew T. Miller	Also William Whittlesey reported as master.
1839	Sp.	*Newark*	306	David G. Souillard	T. G. Merwin master in 1846.
	"	*Milledgeville*	389	Daniel L. Porter	
	"	*Orbit*	283	Elbert Latham	
	Bg.	*Mary Barnard*	160	J. S. H. Pitcher	
1840	Bg.	*L. Baldwin*	270	Theophilus Bassett	Horatio Bulkley master in 1846.
	"	*Wilson Fuller*	269	Charles Thatcher	Nathaniel Cobb master in 1846.
	"	*G. B. Lamar*	260	J. Johnston	D. Sannerman master in 1846.
	"	*Philura*	198	N. Merchant	Russell Doane master in 1846.
	"	*Sterling*	294	Risley	Joseph Hamilton master in 1846.

ESTABLISHED LINE (*continued*)

YEAR		VESSEL	TONS	MASTERS	REMARKS
1840	Sp.	*Southport*	500	Thomas R. Herbest	Continued through 1855, operating in close association with the Dunham & Dimon Georgia Line. For further activities see Georgia and Old Established Lines.

OLD LINE, combined in 1824 with Established Line and continued as Established Line. Popularly known as Ship Line.

William Whitlock, Jr., 70 South St., New York agent. George Hall and Charles Hoyt, as Hall & Hoyt, Savannah agents.

YEAR		VESSEL	TONS	MASTERS	REMARKS
1820	Bg.	*Levant*	181	Denison Wood	
1821	Sp.	*Augusta*	236	Thomas Wood	
1822	Sp.	*Niagara*	319	William Beebe	
	"	*Savannah*	248	Isaac Waite	Lost at Rio Grande, 1831.
1823	Sp.	*Louisa Matilda*	313	Daniel Van Dyke	Frederick Huntington master in 1826. Vessel
	"	*William Wallace*	229	Thomas Wood	lost, Aug. 25, 1827, on Boddy's Island.
	Bg.	*Native*	138	Cornelius Cole	

FIRST LINE

John Griswold, 68 South St., and John Green Pearson, New York agents. E. Williams and Charles C. Griswold, Savannah agents. Established Dec., 1823, "to sail punctually the 1st, 10th and 21st of each month from each port."

YEAR		VESSEL	TONS	MASTERS	REMARKS
1823	Sp.	*Corsair*	286	Daniel L. Porter	John Griswold and Samuel Coates, as Gris-
	"	*Clifford Wayne*	305	Isaac White	wold & Coates had been heavily engaged in
	"	*Garonne*	296	T. Stevens	the Savannah trade since 1820.
	"	*Cotton Plant*	301	Michael Fash	E. Wiley added as Savannah agent, 1824. Thaddeus Phelps & Co., 47 South St. added as New York agent.
1826	Bg.	*Pheasant*	170	John Bailey	Dispatched by Thaddeus Phelps. Line discontinued in latter part of year.

SCHOONER LINE

G. Allen & Co., 17 South St., and A. Cornwall, 167 Front St., New York agents. Cohen & Miller, Savannah agents. Established Mar., 1826. Not on fixed schedule at first.

YEAR		VESSEL	TONS	MASTERS	REMARKS
1826	Sch.	*Tobacco Plant*	93	Samuel Moorehouse, Jr.	
	"	*Trader*	86	Calvin Hayden	
	Sl.	*Harriet*	98	Holmes	
	Sch.	*Cheraw*	119	Samuel Nichols	
	"	*Erie*	92	John Osborne	
	"	*Magnolia*	98	P. S. Pitcher	
	"	*Glide*	131	Joseph Bartram	P. B. Macey master in 1829.
	"	*Frances*	99	William H. Nichols	William Whittlesey master in 1829.
	"	*Virginia*	75	E. Petty	
	"	*Ariel*	94	Bradford Williams	
	Bg.	*Amos Palmer*	167	E. Hilleker	Var. Heliker.
	Sch.	*Oregon*	148	Elisha Mix	Thomas Dunham, Jr., master in 1830.
	"	*Koret*	89	O. Buddington	
	"	*William & Thomas*	133	William Hyler	
1827	Sch.	*Othello*	136	Thomas Dunham, Jr.	Cornwall dropped out. G. Allen & Co. con-
	Sl.	*Eliza Allen*		Thomas Dunham, Jr.	tinued with schooners *Glide*, *Cheraw*, *Frances*,
	Bg.	*Louisiana*	216	Hamilton	*Oregon* and *Othello* as regular line.
1828	Sch.	*Ohio*	98	Arvin Baker	Line began regular schedule in fall of 1828.
	Sp.	*Henry*	258	George Barker	Var. Baker.
	"	*Chancellor*	276	John Bradley	
1829	Sch.	*Excel*	182	E. Hilleker	Line maintained regular schedule.
	Bg.	*Courier*	148	Abel Beers	
1830	Sch.	*Hycso*	83	Wheeler	G. Allen & Co. replaced in Jan., 1830, by

SCHOONER LINE (*continued*)

YEAR	VESSEL	TONS	MASTERS	REMARKS
1830	Sch. *Georgia*	197	William H. Nichols	Howland & Cornwall who continued with
	" *Exact*	178	Samuel Nichols	schooners *Exact*, *Glide*, *Excel*, *Oregon*, *Othello*,
	Bg. *Frances*	177	Nathaniel P. Durfey	*Frances* and *Virginia* and added two more.
				Line sailed from Pier 15, East River.
1832	Sp. *Andes*	364	Silvanus Briggs	Howland dropped out in Mar., 1832.
	" *John Taylor*	335	John McManus	A. Cornwall continued and in fall began
				running brigs and an occasional ship.
	Bg. *Madison*	314	Walter Bulkley	Moses S. Mandeuil master in 1836.
	" *William Taylor*	249	Joseph Bartram	
	" *Mary*	128	Thomas Dunham	
1833	Sch. *Edward Vincent*	187	Elbert Latham	Line consisted of four brigs and three schooners.
1835	Bg. *Camilla*	193	Lemuel Bourne	Padelford, Fay & Co. became Savannah agents in 1835.
1836	Sch. *Potomac*	147	Rufus Knapp	A. Cornwall & Fowler became New York
	" *Excel*	139	Watkins	agents in May, 1836. In Sept., Doane, Sturges
	Bg. *Tybee*	329	L. L. Lyon	& Co. replaced them as New York agents.
	" *Wm. Taylor*	249	Nicholas Hoey	Five brigs and four schooners in line.
	" *Georgia*	197	Samuel Nichols	
	" *Camilla*	193	William H. Nichols	
1837	Bg. *Savannah*	396	Joseph Livermore	Sturges & Clearman replaced Doane, Sturges & Co. as New York agents in Apr., 1837. Name changed to Regular Line but popularly called Brig Line.
1838	Bg. *Detroit*	211	Charles Baker	
	" *Clinton*	379	Thomas Lyon	
	" *Excel*	375	Edwin Sherwood	P. B. Macy master in 1845.
	" *Augusta*	399	Samuel Nichols	Aaron M. Sherwood master in 1844. C. D. Carter & Co. become Savannah agents in 1839. Replaced by Lewis & Wilder in Sept., 1840.
1841	Bg. *Exact*	431	J. Johnson	
1843	Bg. *Wetumpka*	267	John Fowler	Line called City Line. Line in 1844 consisted of seven brigs—*Exact*, *Excel*, *Savannah*, *Madison*, *Clinton*, *Augusta*, and *Camilla*.
1846	Bg. *Mobile*	328	Theodore Bulkley	Sturges, Clearman & Co., 110 Wall St., became New York agents.
	Sp. *Ashland*	631	Aaron Hawley	
1847	Bg. *Vernon*	467	Thomas Paxton	J. Washburn & Wilder become Savannah agents in 1847.
1848	Sch. *Senator*	249	Rufus Knapp	
	Bg. *Alabama*	272	Howard	
1849	Bg. *Exact*	431	S. G. Stevens	
	Sch. *Alex. Mitchell*	172	Elliot Honeywell	
	" *Columbia*	190	Rufus Knapp	
	Bk. *Georgia*	197	David Allen	
	Sp. *Southport*	500	R. McCormack	
	Sch. *Memento*	228	Terry	
1850	Bg. *Savannah*	493	Luther Martin	
	Sp. *Sandusky*	943	John Borland	
1852	Bk. *Harvest*	426	Hanford Nichols	
	Sp. *Dirigo*	497	Russell Doane	
1854	Bk. *Sarah Jane*	504	C. W. Saunders	
	Sch. *Montrose*	284	G. Winslow	
1855	Bg. *Empire*	218	William J. Axworthy	
	Sch. *Laura Gertrude*	316	S. G. Fairchild	
				Dana & Washburn became Savannah agents in 1856.
1857	Sch. *Haze*	321	Edward A. Langdon	
	" *Vapor*	312	William Powell	
	Bk. *Henry*	449	William Wilson	
1858	Sp. *Oswego*	647	S. G. Stevens	Sturges, Clearman & Co. associated with
	Sch. *Hartstein* (tern)	653	Joseph J. Graffam	Dunham & Dimon in all Savannah clearances from 1858 on.
	" *Mary E. Jones*	275	E. M. Jones	
	" *Eckford Webb*	495	William H. Tulledge	

BRIG LINE

Oroondates Mauran and Baldwin & Forbes, New York agents. John W. Long, Savannah agent. Established Apr., 1827, after Baldwin & Spooner had engaged heavily in the trade in 1826 and early 1827. Line very active in 1826, sending some of the vessels several times during season.

YEAR		VESSEL	TONS	MASTERS	REMARKS
1827	Bg.	*Panthea*	199	John Bradley	
	"	*Pheasant*	170	John Bailey	
	"	*Agenoria*	171	Nathaniel Webber	
	"	*Tobacco Plant*	177	John Robertson	Var. Robinson.
	Bg.	*Hercules*	193	Timothy Stevens	
	Sch.	*Excel*	182	Thomas Bell	
	"	*Caravan*	78	Richard Combs	Var. Coombs.
	Sl.	*Crawford*	77	Thomas West	
	"	*John Chevalier*		Sisson	
	Sp.	*Henry*	258	George Baker	
	"	*Chancellor*	276	John Bradley	
	Sch.	*Whale*	69	Trustum Dickens, Jr.	
	Bg.	*Eliza*		Burrows	
1828	Sch.	*Triton*	92	Seth Brooks	
	"	*Eagle*	75	Joseph S. Avery	
	"	*Exact*	178	Thomas Bell	
	"	*Manchester*	119	Thomas Dunham, Jr.	
	Sp.	*Queen Mab*	270	John Bailey	
	Bk.	*Armadillo*	256	John Robertson	
	Bg.	*Panthea*	199	John W. Fisher	
1829	Sch.	*Martha*		Hand	
	"	*Aspasia*	196	Norman Pease	
	Bg.	*Courier*	148	Elisha Mix	
	"	*America*	148	Edwin Sherwood	
	"	*Frances*	177	Palmer	Nathaniel F. Durfey master late in 1829.
	"	*Union*	172	Ephraim Jordan	
1830	Sch.	*Mary Ann*	98	Isaac Fithian	Line almost inactive in 1830.
	Sl.	*Express*		Curtis	
	"	*Mariner*		Sturdevant	John Cumming & Son became Savannah
	Bg.	*Charles Joseph*	314	Abraham B. Cary	agents with J. Stone & Co.
1831	Sch.	*Argo*		John Williams	Continued quite inactive.
1832	Bg.	*Dante*	218	Stephen Higgins	Baldwin & Co. became New York agents.
	"	*Sabattas*	273	Stephen Wheeler	Discontinued late in 1832.

ARNOLD LINE

I. Arnold, 80 South St., New York agent. Jeremy Stone, Savannah agent. Established Sept., 1829.

YEAR		VESSEL	TONS	MASTERS	REMARKS
1829	Sp.	*Eliza & Abby*	244	Cyrus B. Manchester	
	Bg.	*Lydia*	222	David Wood, Jr.	
	"	*Decatur*	164	Gustavus Williamson	
1830	Bg.	*Hercules*	193	Timothy Stevens	
	"	*Robert Cochran*	193	George W. Teel	Var. George W. Sell.
	"	*Armadillo*	256	Edward Hammond	Ex-bark.
					Baldwin & Forbes also agents. Very few sailings after 1830 and discontinued entirely in 1834.

HAZARD LINE

A. G. Hazard & Co., 158 Front St., New York agents. Jeremy Stone, Savannah agent. Established Apr., 1831.

YEAR		VESSEL	TONS	MASTERS	REMARKS
1831	Sp.	*Queen Mab*	270	John Bailey	
	Bg.	*Lydia*	222	David Wood, Jr.	
	"	*Emery*	285	J. M. Marshall	
	Sl.	*Wave*	65	Blankenship	
	Bg.	*Romulus*	250	Carlo Mauran	Oroondates Mauran also agent.
1832	Bg.	*Armadillo*	256	Edward Hammond	
	"	*Alto*	197	Tappan	C. & J. Barstow also agents.
	Sp.	*Citizen*	464	Newcomb	Line discontinued early in 1833.

OLD LINE

Cornelius Seguine, 86 Wall St., New York agent. J. Stone & Co., Savannah agents. Established Nov., 1833.

YEAR		VESSEL	TONS	MASTERS	REMARKS
1833	Sp.	*Atlantic*	290	Joseph G. Russell	Six ships in regular line plus extra sailings.
	"	*Agnes*	233	James S. Bennett	
	"	*Belle*	341	John Bailey	
	"	*Tropic*	350	Joseph G. Russell	
	"	*Eliza & Abby*	244	Robert W. Foster	
	Sch.	*Charles*	123	J. D. Brown	
1834	Sch.	*Edward Vincent*	187	E. Latham	
	Sp.	*Newark*	306	Robert W. Foster	Nathaniel P. Durfey master in 1836.
	Bg.	*Cornelia*	183	J. R. Shapter	
1835	Sp.	*Mason Barney*	249	I. Budd	Var. J. Budd.
	"	*Milledgeville*	389	Robert W. Foster	Stone, Washburn & Co. became Savannah agents in 1835.
1836	Sp.	*Republican*	351	Robert W. Foster	Johnson & Lowden, 86 Wall St., replaced
	"	*Thomas Dickason*	454	W. L. Lyon	Seguine as New York agent in Oct., 1836.
	"	*Lewis Cass*	318	William Whittlesey	
	Bg.	*Camilla*	193	Nichols	
	"	*Madison*	315	Walter Bulkley	
1837	Sp.	*Moctezuma*	436	N. S. Mauran	
	"	*Orbit*	283	W. H. Mead	
	"	*Trenton*	427	Denison Wood	
	"	*Auburn*	451	Nathaniel P. Durfey	
1838	Sch.	*Baltimore*	187	Abraham G. Woglom	Washburn & Lewis became Savannah agents.
	"	*Emma*	165	Isaac Cole	Line discontinued early in 1839.

GEORGIA LINE

T. Dunham, Jr., of Dunham & Dimon, 67 South St., New York agent. L. Baldwin, Esq., Savannah agent. Line established Sept., 1838. Operated in close association with the Old Established Line until 1855, sometimes having same agents.

YEAR		VESSEL	TONS	MASTERS	REMARKS
1838	Sch.	*Stuart F. Randolph*	130	James Champion	
	"	*Ann Elizabeth*	131	Summers	Var. Somers.
	"	*Victoria*	126	Anderson Melton	
	"	*William Hart*		Corsen	
	"	*Mogul*	129	Gavit	
	"	*Pennsylvania*	136	Smith	
	Bg.	*Tantivy*	139	J. Johnson	
	"	*Falcon*	165	A. Jones	
	"	*Paragon*		Carr	
1839	Bg.	*Philura*	197	W. Sherman	Dunham & Dimon became New York agents
	"	*Wilson Fuller*	269	Charles Thatcher	in Oct., 1839.
	"	*L. Baldwin*	270	Theophilus Bassett	
	"	*G. B. Lamar*	260	Risley Cobb	
	Sp.	*Newark*	306	David C. Soullard	Var. Souillard.
	Sch.	*Red Jacket*	156	William Albertson	
	"	*Empire*	180	Reuben Baker	
1840	Sch.	*Exchange*	94	Jared Pulsifer	
	"	*Messenger*	107	William T. White	
	"	*Wanderer*	142	West	
	"	*Franklin Snow*		Pressy	
	"	*Antelope*	148	Thomas Gifford	
	"	*Intrepid*	129	Ezra E. Wicks	
	Bg.	*Aldrich*	222	John Baker	
	"	*Morea*	261	William A. Chapman	
	Sp.	*Emily*	298	Miles H. Mead	John R. Crane master in 1841–3.
	"	*John Cumming*	721	George Thayer	
	Bk.	*La Grange*	259	Daniel L. Porter	
	Sch.	*Emma*	165	Isaac Cole	
	Sp.	*Lancashire*	661	John F. Marschalk	
1842	Bg.	*Acton*	184	Philander Daggett	Latter part of year firm began to dispatch vessels jointly with Sturges & Clearman or Scott & Morrell until early 1843. Dunham & Dimon sent brigs only during 1843 as listed above. L. Baldwin & Co. became Savannah agents in 1844. Old Established Line continued with Georgia Line.

GEORGIA LINE (*continued*)

YEAR		VESSEL	TONS	MASTERS	REMARKS
1844	Bg.	*Josephus*	142	Henry M. Allen	
	"	*Mary*	193	William W. Wakeman	
1845	Sp.	*Hartford*	511	D. Sanneman	L. Baldwin & Co. became Savannah agents.
	"	*Celia*	339	Charles Thatcher	
1846	Sch.	*St. Mary*	239	Anderson B. Lambkin	
1847	Bk.	*Beaver*	299	John Edmonds	Brigham & Kelly became Savannah agents.
	Bg.	*American*		James McNair	
1848	Bk.	*Texas*	408	James McNair	
1849	Sp.	*Marion*	449	M. Thompson	
	"	*Star Republic*	305	Rufus Jameson	Burned at sea, July 1, 1855. Rufus Cole, master.
	Bg.	*Lowell*	219	John P. Yates	
	Sch.	*Telegraph*	143	Hamilton Tooker	
1850	Sp.	*Martha's Vineyard*	499	D. A. Nye	Brigham, Kelly & Co. became Savannah agents.
	Bk.	*Savannah*	494	Luther Martin	
1852	Sp.	*Hudson*	335	Peter Nelson	
	Bk.	*Flight*	386	J. H. Luther	
1853	Bk.	*Milford*	427	T. J. Horton	H. H. Tallman, 16 Coenties Slip, became associated with Dunham & Dimon as New York agent.
	Bg.	*Empire*	218	Newman	
	Sch.	*Edna C.*	179	Elihu Kelly	
	Bg.	*Lucy*	196	A. P. Weeks	
	Sch.	*Kate Brigham* (tern)	470	John H. Luther	Richard Norton master in 1857.
	Bk.	*George Henry*	308	J. L. Pendleton	
	Sch.	*Edwin R. Bennett*	333	Abraham H. Wood	
	"	*Patrick Henry*	211	Gilbert A. Knudson	
	"	*Pocahontas*	217	Horatio Bulkley	
	Bg.	*Marshall*	197	Ryder	
1854	Bk.	*Robert Mills*	488	James McNair	
	Sp.	*New England*	573	Peter Protteau	
	Bk.	*Maria Morton*	426	William Bulkley	Edward M. Bulkley master in 1856.
	Bg.	*Delta*	198	Ozro F. Downes	
	"	*A. H. Wass*	170	T. Marshall	
	Sch.	*Manhassett*	267	Carman Smith	
	"	*Plandome*	266	Robert T. Brown	
	"	*Peter R. Burton*	174	William H. Lingo	
	Bg.	*Josephus*	142	John Wilson	
	Sp.	*Far West*	598	J. H. Bennett	Var. J. S. Bennett.
1855	Sch.	*Eckford Webb* (tern)	495	Joseph A. Graffam	
	"	*Wm. L. Burroughs* (tern)	497	Urban G. Griffin	Hollis B. Jencks master in 1856.
	"	*John Boston*	399	William H. Lingo	
	"	*Thomas Holcombe*	393	Robert W. Goslee	Scranton & Tallman replaced H. H. Tallman in 1855.
	"	*Loyal Scranton*	386	Amos N. Lowden	
	"	*Eclipse*	305	Robert W. Goslee	Cohen & Hertz became Savannah agents in 1855
	"	*John Castner*	348	R. Bennett	
	"	*Ephraim & Anna*	198	William Crawford	
	Sp.	*Julia Howard*	590	W. C. Bulkley	
1856	Sch.	*Hartstene* (tern)	653	Joseph A. Graffam	
	"	*Cordelia* (tern)	658	William C. Dunham	
	"	*Montrose*	284	George Winslow	
1857	Sp.	*Java*	715	E. Taylor	Line discontinued latter part of 1858.
	Sch.	*George Davis*	336	Samuel F. Phillips	Sturges, Clearman & Co. were joint agents for some of the vessels in that year. Brigham, Baldwin & Co. were Savannah agents.

NEW LINE

John Ogden, 169 South St., New York agent. Lippit & Wright, Savannah agents. Established June, 1842, sailing weekly.

YEAR		VESSEL	TONS	MASTERS	REMARKS
1842	Bg.	*Robert Bruce*	115	Thomas H. Fitzgerald	
	Bk.	*La Grange*	259	David L. Porter	
	Bg.	*Leonora*	195	George C. Collins	
	"	*Saratoga*	231	Jackson B. Bedell	
	"	*J. Peterson*	194	James Green	
	Sch.	*Adrian*	150	John Pitts	
	Bg.	*John A. Lancaster*	175	J. Loveland	

NEW LINE (*continued*)

YEAR		VESSEL	TONS	MASTERS	REMARKS
1842	Sch.	*Julia*	167	James Shoemaker	
	Bk.	*Weskeag*	248	H. Spaulding	
	Sp.	*Atalanta*	392	James Hart	
1843	Sch.	*Constitution*	168	Townsend	R. M. Demill added as New York agent in
	"	*Volusia*	98	Henry S. Clark	Sept., 1843.
	"	*Orator*	86	David P. Davis	
	"	*Bergen*	227	David Latourette	
	"	*Henry Chase*	130	Absolom Steelman	Var. *Chace*.
	"	*John W. Smith*	130	Asa Jarvis	
	"	*Margaret*	206	Abraham C. Woglom	
	"	*Planet*	197	Lucas B. Terry	
	Bg.	*Georgiana*	190	Washington Bedell	
	"	*New Jersey*	276	Robert T. Brown	
	"	*Macon*	223	Anson Bibbins	
	"	*Cayuga*	246	S. L. Jackson	
1844	Sp.	*Rhode Island*	381	Benedict Andros	Joseph L. Gardner master in 1845.
	Sch.	*Virginia*	134	George W. Hall	
	"	*Imperial*		Read	
	"	*Henry*	129	J. B. Look	
	Bg.	*Isaac Mead* (later Bk.)	385	Robert T. Brown	
	"	*Peter Demill*	294	Christopher Lewis	N. Hoey master in 1853–9.
					Ogden dropped out early in 1845 and R. M. Demill & Co. became New York agents.
1846	Bk.	*E. H. Chapin*	424	C. B. Smith	
	"	*Backus*	195	F. Fontaine	
	Bg.	*Alert*	141	Jameson	
	"	*John Enders*	195	John Johnson	
	Sch.	*George L. Jones*	164	J. B. Look	
					S. W. Wight & Son became Savannah agents, 1847; R. M. Demill, New York agent.
1848	Bg.	*Selma*	205	William Cullen	Crane & Rowland became Savannah agents.
	"	*Ohio*	214	Lockman	
1849	Sch.	*Athalia*	236	Lorenzo D. Purnell	
	Sp.	*Huguenot*	934	W. R. Gardner	
	Bg.	*Lowell*	219	D. B. Hobart	
	Sch.	*Virginia*	242	John Gould	J. Borland master in 1850.
1850	Sp.	*Columbia*	441	Grumley	Demill & Co., 186 Front St., became New
	Bg.	*Live Oak*	191	E. J. Sawyer	York agents.
	Sch.	*John K. Randall*	144	Dean	
	Bk.	*Maria Morton*	426	William Buckley	
1852	Bk.	*Rhodes*	480	James McNair	Rowland & Washburn became Savannah
	Sch.	*Plandome*	266	Robert T. Brown	agents.
	Sp.	*Catherine*	477	Henry Wilson	
1853	Sch.	*James House*	258	James Line	H. K. Washburn became Savannah agent.
	Sp.	*Chace*	625	William White	
	Bg.	*Wetumpka*	267	Jacob Johnson	
1854	Sch.	*Arlington*	249	William Murch	
	Sp.	*Florida*	1039	D. Sanneman	Var. *Sannerman*.
	Bk.	*R. H. Douglas*	260	Jacob Johnson	
1855	Sp.	*Southport*	500	William Wilson	
	Sch.	*Ann Maria*	133	Richard Conklin	
	"	*Wm. Cogswell*		Smith	
	"	*Richard M. Demill*	343	Hiram Look	C. Hendrickson master in 1858.
1856	Bg.	*Ben P. Dunning*	285	Ben P. Dunning	Rowland & Son became Savannah agents.
	Sch.	*Sea Foam*	264	John Wendell	Line called Demill's Line.
	"	*F. Merwin*	289	Albert Thomas	Also reported 209 tons.
1857	Sch.	*Adeline Townsend*	284	Ebenezer N. Townsend	Carleton & Parsons became Savannah agents.
	"	*Red Eagle*	249	N. L. Rodgers	Var. *Rogers*.
1858	Bk.	*R. A. Allen*	452	N. Robbins	Also reported 462 tons.
	"	*Lamartine*	386	Anderson	
					Charles Parsons became Savannah agent in 1859.
					Line called Regular Line.

UNION LINE

N. L. McCready & Co., 36 South St., New York agents. John O. Woodruff & Co., Savannah agents. Established Jan., 1847.

YEAR		VESSEL	TONS	MASTERS	REMARKS
1847	Sch.	*H. B. Bascom*	137	Robert Corson	
	"	*Frances Helen*	121	Taylor	
	"	*Lake*		Henry Lake	
	"	*Dart*	103	Somers	
	"	*Emeline*	128	John Garwood	
	"	*Julia Eliza*	162	Richard Higbee	
	"	*Jeremiah Leavins*	132	L. C. Townsend	
	"	*W. B. Peters*	124	Edwin Lord	
	"	*O. H. Perry*	111	Jeremiah Wooster	
	"	*Globe*		Tibbets	
	"	*Ruth Thomas*	134	J. O. Amsbury	Var. Amesbury.
	"	*Pauline*	149	Harris	
	"	*Sabine*	174	Alexander Robinson	
	"	*Sage*	151	William Joline	Willett Mott master in 1848.
	Bg.	*Selma*	205	William Cullen	
	"	*Alert*	141	Jones	
1848	Sch.	*Kensington*	179	Enoch Stevenson	
	"	*Abdel Kader*	152	Brown	Robert Pearce master in 1850–2.
	"	*Almira*	118	Carman Smith	Var. Cannon Smith.
	"	*Florio*	120	S. Thomas	
	Bg.	*Emma Prescott*	186	T. B. R. Lee	
	"	*Curacoa*	131	J. S. Higgins	
	Sch.	*Leroy*	196	Benjamin W. Bedell	
	Bg.	*E. Townsend*	139	Henry J. Koons	John D. Wanser master in 1849.
	"	*Petersburg*	183	William H. Oliver	
	"	*Hallowell*	203	Johnson	
1849	Sch.	*Charles C. Stratton*	162	John Vance	Joseph Westcott master in 1850.
	"	*Julia*	167	Frederick Vangilder	
	"	*Patmos*	148	William Childress	Nathan A. Conklin master in 1851.
	"	*Seguine*	200	Abraham R. Swain	
	Sp.	*Matilda*	689	W. Emmerson	
1850	Sch.	*Sarah & Elizabeth*	145	John Somers	
	"	*Ophir*	134	N. J. Boynton	
	"	*Cicero*	139	Baker	
	"	*Arietis*	131	Robert W. Wheeler	
	"	*S. Morris Waln*	148	John Erickson	
	"	*Jonas Smith*	236	Williams	
	"	*Louisine*	248	Nehemiah G. Smith	
	Bg.	*Gov. Carver*	180	Swift	Charles B. Hosmer master in 1850.
	"	*Buena Vista*	231	Ephraim Ackerman	Var. Atcherson.
	Bk.	*Harmony*	308	Jones	J. M. Texas master in Apr., 1850.
	Sp.	*Chaos*	771	Thomas Paxton	
	Bg.	*Gen. Taylor*	189	Horton	
	"	*Mary H. Chappell*	150	J. Hand	
	Sp.	*Emma Watts*	450	E. P. Watts	G. A. Dearborn master in 1851. Ship abandoned at sea, Mar. 13, 1854.
	"	*Georgia*	641	James G. Mills	
	Bg.	*William L. Jones*	220	William S. Tyler	
	"	*Sea Belle*	149	Royal Herriman, Jr.	
1852	Sch.	*Cataract*	319	C. A. Rice	Chas. A. Greiner became Savannah agent in Jan.; Willis & Brundage, Savannah agents in Sept.
	"	*Charles Mills*	240	Barnabas Francis	
	"	*Francis Satterly*	302	Lewis S. Davis	
	"	*North State*	431	Isaac F. Horton	Charles L. Horton master in 1855.
	"	*Enchantress*	378	William I. Tyler	
	"	*E. N. Smith*		Smith	
	"	*N. W. Smith*	315	D. C. Hulse	
	Bg.	*Alfred Exall*	244	Joseph Golder	Var. Golden
	"	*Kate Heath*	189	Theophilus C. Lee	
	Bk.	*J. J. Hathorn*	398	W. Brown	
1853	Bk.	*Prospect*	199	William F. Brown	McCready, Mott & Co. became New York agents. Ogden & Bunker, Savannah agents.
	Sch.	*Norfolk Packet*	350	James Bedell	
	"	*Alcyona*	148	J. Hand	

UNION LINE (*continued*)

YEAR	VESSEL	TONS	MASTERS	REMARKS
1853	Sch. *L. S. Davis*	319	Lewis S. Davis	
"	*Fanny*	363	Burr Hull	
Bk.	*Edward*	355	Patterson	Thomas Jones master in 1856.
Bg.	*Macon*	223	Edward Watkins	
1854	Sch. *S. J. Waring*	372	Barnabas Francis	Ogden, Starr & Co. became Savannah
"	*Cohasset*	176	E. Tobey	agents in Sept.
Bk.	*Culloma*	360	N. B. Grant	
"	*Golden Age*	311	W. H. Garrick	
Sch.	*Pocahontas*	217	Horatio Bulkley	
"	*John Castner*	247	R. Bennett	
1855	Sch. *William Smith*	314	George Smith	
Bg.	*Target*	389	Lewis S. Davis	
Sch.	*Envoy*	111	Collins	
1856	Sch. *Helene*	244	George W. Stutes	
"	*Mary Clinton*	279	Edward Cole	Also reported 229 tons.
"	*L. P. Smith*	195	West	
"	*Lilly*	335	Barnabas Francis	
"	*Theodore Raymond*	263	Paul Hulse	
"	*Wm. A. Ellis*	255	Joseph B. Nichols	
"	*John G. Heckscher*	392	Moses S. Manduel	
"	*Myrover*	355	Francis Jackson	
"	*W. W. Fulton*	190	Thatcher	
1857	Sch. *William Mason*	262	J. D. Gardner	
"	*Cerito*	257	W. H. Crowell	
"	*Sahwa*	175	Urban Huntley	
"	*Mary Stedman*	253	James H. Terry	
"	*D. C. Hulse*	242	W. Brown	
1858	Sch. *Smithsonian*	390	James A. Van Brunt	Starr & Hardee became Savannah agents.
"	*John Roe*	297	Edmund Hammond	
"	*Charles T. Strong*	247	William Liscomb	Var. Liscum.
"	*J. M. Holmes*		Brewster	
"	*Robert Caldwell*	447	Charles S. Hudson	
1859	Sch. *Hawkins*		Griffin	

GILMORE'S REGULAR LINE

J. R. Gilmore & Co., 74 South St., New York agents. Williams & Ratcliffe, Savannah agents. Established Nov., 1855.

YEAR	VESSEL	TONS	MASTERS	REMARKS
1855	Sch. *Edward Kidder*	318	William G. Tyler	
"	*Lovet Peacock*	363	Jetur F. Terry	
1856	Sch. *Bennett Flanner*	322	Henry Applegit	
"	*Alba*	394	Lewis P. Taylor	Joseph R. Merrihew master in 1857.
"	*Walter Raleigh*	472	Lewis Mankin	
"	*George Davis*	336	William G. Tyler	Samuel F. Phillips master in 1857.
"	*Langdon Gilmore*	497	William S. Tyler	Jonathan Chase master in 1859.
Bg.	*A. Dunbar*	200	F. N. Buck	
"	*Ocean Wave*	271	Silas M. Morton	
1857	Sch. *Lombard*	256	Nathaniel Harding	
1859	Sch. *Virginia*	242		Hunter & Gamwell became Savannah agents. Line ran very irregularly after 1856.

MURRAY'S LINE

D. Colden Murray, 62 South St., New York agent. Established Feb., 1857.

YEAR	VESSEL	TONS	MASTERS	REMARKS
1857	Sch. *Southern Belle*	322	William S. Tyler	
"	*Walter Raleigh*	472	Ephraim A. Nickerson	
"	*Bennett Flanner*	322	Henry Applegit	
"	*Kate Field*	291	Leonard W. Robbins	
"	*Emily*	279	David B. Hobart	
"	*George Davis*	336	Samuel F. Phillips	
"	*Mobile*	398	Allen Howes	
"	*Edward Kidder*	318	Hans P. Harkssen	Var. Harkson.
Bg.	*East*	297	Richard Hepburn	

MURRAY'S LINE (*continued*)

YEAR		VESSEL	TONS	MASTERS	REMARKS
1857	Bk.	*Greenfield*	560	Lucius C. Beattie	
1858	Sch.	*Helen*	272	T. Long	Mailler, Lord & Quereau added as New
	"	*Laura Gertrude*	316	Charles B. Elwood	York agents. Line continued through 1860.
	"	*Restless*	265	Bradley Smith	
	"	*Kate Merrill*	297	Benjamin Wicks	

SECTION 14. NEW YORK—MOBILE

REGULAR LINE

Peters & Herrick, 29 Coenties Slip, New York agents. Established 1819, running to Blakely and Mobile. No fixed schedule.

YEAR		VESSEL	TONS	MASTERS	REMARKS
1819	Sch.	*Nassau*	98	Lent M. Hitchcock	
	"	*Orleans Packet*	40	Abraham Heartt	
	Bg.	*Abeona*	176	Ebenezer Foster	
	"	*Alabama Packet*	168	Isaac Chapman	
1821	Bg.	*Catherine Rogers*	160	Isaac Dickenson	S. H. Herrick & Co. became New York agents.

DeFOREST LINE

DeForest & Son, New York agents. Established 1822, running to Blakely and Mobile. No fixed schedule.

YEAR		VESSEL	TONS	MASTERS	REMARKS
1822	Sp.	*Douglas*	248	E. DeForest	
	"	*Morning Star*	200	John Barstow	
	"	*Morgiana*	270	I. Dickenson	
1824	Bg.	*Concord*	190	George Thomas	
1826	Bg.	*William Tell*	207	M. Hinman	
	Sl.	*Intrepid*	74	Eustis	
1827	Bg.	*Ann Wayne*	190	George Thomas	Line ran very irregularly after 1827 and
	"	*Rook*	197	George Thomas	ceased operation after 1830, although W. W.
	"	*William Penn*		Hamor	DeForest & Co. purported to carry on the
1830	Bg.	*Mary*		Smith	line in 1838 for a brief time.

CENTER LINE

Ripley, Center & Co., 73 South St., New York agents. Center & Co., Mobile agents. Established Feb., 1824.

YEAR		VESSEL	TONS	MASTERS	REMARKS
1824	Sp.	*Eliza Jane*	207	Asahel Arnold	Var. Ashbel Arnold.
	"	*Robert Wilson*	299	Jacob Arnold	Asahel Arnold master in 1830.
1826	Sp.	*Comet*	304	William Follansbee	Sailed irregularly in early period. Only three sailings in 1826 and four in 1827.
1828	Bg.	*Jasper*	149	Oliver Colburn	
1829	Sch.	*John Ruggles*	125	Jonathan Emery	
1830	Bg.	*Asia*	208	Job Talman	
	Sp.	*Martha*	360	James D. Snow	
	"	*Catherine*	314	Josiah Thatcher	
1831	Bg.	*Agenoria*	171	Nathaniel Webber	
	"	*Concord*	146	John McKown	
	Sp.	*Montgomery*	399	John H. Size	
	"	*Mersey*	372	William Bowne	
	"	*Henry Kneeland*	304	Carleton White	
	"	*Pulaski*	468	Ezra D. Post	Lost on the Tortugas, Oct. 19, 1832.
1832	Sp.	*Marion*	355	Thomas Phillips	
	Bg.	*Tom*	240	Isaac Dickenson	
	"	*Pleiades*	261	Robert McCerren	
	"	*Thatcher*	145	Josiah Thatcher	
	"	*Victress*	268	John C. Graves	
	Sch.	*Corine*	84	Joseph Swiler	
1833	Bg.	*Ontario*	186	William Whittlesey	Center & Co. became New York agents in
	"	*Frances Ann*	182	B. Morley	Oct. Sailed on 10th and 20th of month.
	Sp.	*Agnes*	233	James S. Bennett	
	"	*Cahawba*	351	Asahel Arnold	W. D. Smith master in 1838. Var. Wm. W.

CENTER LINE (*continued*)

YEAR		VESSEL	TONS	MASTERS	REMARKS
1833	Sp.	Waverly	529	Thomas Phillips	
	"	Warsaw	332	Josiah Thatcher	W. P. Mendell master in 1838.
	"	Oceana	367	Henry Leslie	
	"	Paugus	321	Samuel Moody	
1834	Sp.	Lewis Cass	313	Samuel M. Whittlesey	
	"	Georgian	279	Antony H. Eldridge	
	"	Thames	414	James D. Snow	
	Bg.	Corinthian	250	Oliver Colburn	T. B. Haynes master in 1837.
	"	Daniel Kilby	108	Ferdinand Ilsley	
	"	Columbus	225	William Bowne	
	"	Rose	173	Robert Center	
1835	Bg.	Natchez	228	A. Tyler	
	"	Wellingsley	210	John Feare	
	"	Cornelia		Dunham	
	"	Iris	245	Harding	
	"	Susquehanna	207	J. Bright	
	"	Statira	166	A. H. Holmes	Calvin Babbidge master in 1838.
	Sp.	Glasgow	423	Robinson	
1836	Sp.	Cincinnati	457	Nathaniel Barstow	
1837	Sp.	Pactolus	494	Daniel Wise, Jr.	
	"	Mary & Susan	392	William F. Parrott	
	"	Neva	362	David M. Bunker	
	Bg.	Susan		Copeland	
	"	Lexington	197	Daniel Wise, Jr.	
1838	Sp.	Rob Roy	526	Asahel Arnold	Ezra D. Post master in 1840.
	"	Adeline	501	Israel L. Doane	J. S. Doane also master in 1838.
	Bg.	Mary Silsby	191	Samuel Pierson	Lost, Caicos Island, Sept. 3, 1842.
	Sp.	Cahawba	351	William D. Smith	Line sent very few vessels in 1839–40.
1842	Sch.	Staunch	91	Upton	James Spillings master in 1844.
1843	Sch.	Marion Gage	97	J. M. Reid	Var. Read.
1845	Bk.	Mallory	300	Benjamin R. Babbidge	Line virtually discontinued in 1845 although
	Sch.	Robert Bruce	81	Leander Merchant	the firm made a couple of trips in 1846 and an occasional trip thereafter.

HURLBUT LINE

E. D. Hurlbut & Co., 84 South St., New York agents. Dagget & Roberts and Stow, Ellis & Co., Mobile agents. Established Oct., 1825.

YEAR		VESSEL	TONS	MASTERS	REMARKS
1825	Sp.	Jane Blossom	298	Samuel Sanderson	Lost on Abaco Reef, 1827.
	"	Extio	278	Joseph Post	Russell Handy Post master in 1833.
	"	Indiana	306	Gideon Parker	Cornelius R. Doane master in 1828.
	"	Henry Hill	192	Alva Post	Ezra Denison Post master in 1826.
1826	Sp.	Amelia	244	W. H. Williams	Ezra Denison Post master in 1829.
	Bg.	Louisiana	217	Cornelius R. Doane	
1827	Bg.	Almira	158	Benjamin Miller	
	"	Admittance	202	Samuel Moody	
	Sp.	Elisha Denison	359	George West	
	Sch.	Dighton	68	William Dagget, III	
	"	Mobile	96	James Loomis	
	"	Harvest	89	Pitt	
	"	Leo	74	Josiah Spalding	
	"	Cannon	71	Houseworth	
1828	Bg.	Lewis	248	William Williams	Joseph E. Sheffield and T. M. English became Mobile agents.
	Sp.	St. John	398	Gideon Parker	
	Sch.	Magnolia	131	E. R. York	
1829	Bg.	Trent	249	Nicholas Barstow	
	Sch.	Atlas	100	Titus Tyler	
	Bg.	North	122	Samuel Moody	
1830	Sch.	Albion	107	Thomas Dickenson	Hurlbut was only New York firm sending
	Bg.	Chariot	131	Homer	vessels to Mobile in the summer at this
	Sp.	Tuskina	421	Joseph Post	period.
1831	Bg.	Sarah	187	Athearn	This was first year line was generally credited
	"	Empress	180	John C. Graves	with maintaining fixed schedule. Sent only
	"	Chipola	186	D. D. Churchill	brigs and schooners during summer months.

HURLBUT LINE (*continued*)

YEAR		VESSEL	TONS	MASTERS	REMARKS
1831	Bg.	*Lady Hope*	147	Sears Chase	
	"	*George*	206	Thomas Havens	
	"	*American*	238	William Matthews	
	Sp.	*Chancellor*	276	J. Bradley	
	"	*Splendid*	642	Alexander Britton	
	"	*Junior*	377	Gideon Parker	
	"	*Selma*	269	Thomas Longfield	
	Sch.	*Isabella*	129	Wilder	
1832	Sp.	*Alabamian*	384	Cornelius R. Doane	St. John & Leavens became Mobile agents.
	"	*Lorena*	527	John Urquehart	Joseph Conway master in 1848.
	Bg.	*Matilda*	263	Benjamin Ellison	
1833	Bg.	*Columbus*	224	Philo G. Knowles	
	"	*Pleiades*	261	Robert McCerren	
	"	*Panope*	142	S. Gay, Jr.	
	Sp.	*Russell Baldwin*	465	Francis West	
	"	*Hector*	557	W. H. Williams	
	"	*Cassander*	300	W. D. Robinson	
	"	*Matilda*	313	Ambrose H. Burrows	
1834	Sch.	*Fancy*	125	Horace Hayden	
	Sp.	*John Jay*	502	Russell E. Glover	Register surrendered Jan., 1864. Condemned abroad.
1835	Bg.	*Lion*		Sherman	
	Bk.	*C. P. Williams*	187	Henry Ashby	
	Bg.	*Tremont*	136	J. Sylvester	
	"	*Mary*		Collins	
	"	*Alto*	197	Jedediah Paine	
	"	*Stranger*	133	C. H. Soule	
	"	*Susan & Mary*	137	Robert Rogers	
	Sp.	*Washington Irving*	278	Francis West	Vessel lost, July, 1839.
1836	Sp.	*Georgia*	410	Enoch Talbot	
	Bg.	*Otranto*	149	Landon	
1837	Sp.	*Edwina*	538	Francis West	Gideon Parker & Co. became Mobile agents.
1838	Sp.	*Niantic*	452	Levi F. Doty	
	Bg.	*Mary Ann*	138	P. McFarland	
	Sch.	*Mary Louisa*		Owens	
	"	*Austin*	133	J. Sylvester	
	"	*Rosario*	155	Thomas Sears	
1839	Sp.	*John Baring*	529	Benjamin G. Palmer	J. N. Magna master in 1840.
	"	*Floridian*	400	William Pratt	
	"	*Southerner*	671	W. I. Tibbets	
	"	*Mary Frances*	311	John A. Westervelt	
	Bg.	*Citizen*	199	A. Thing	
	"	*Lawrence Copeland*	219	Thomas Sears	
	"	*Escambia*	217	Rufus Dunham	
	"	*Lucinda*	175	George P. Harkness	Lost, Jan., 1842.
	Sp.	*Cotton Planter*	501	Cornelius R. Doane	
	"	*Emblem*	610	Enoch Talbot	
1840	Bg.	*Jesse D. Noyes*	186	Simeon W. Ashby	B. L. Andrews & Co. became Mobile agents.
	"	*Chaires*	209	Israel Doane	
	"	*William H. Tallman*	158	David Hunt	
	"	*Morea*	261	Elbert Latham	George Edgar master in 1844.
	"	*Manhattan*	246	William A. Chapman	N. C. Johnson master in 1848.
	Sp.	*Elizabeth Denison*	645	Russell H. Post	
	"	*Lancashire*	661	T. Alexander	
	"	*Geneva*	458	Thomas Hale	
1841	Bg.	*Ann Eliza*	144	George Eldridge	Line consisted of eight ships in operation and two under construction to sail trimonthly when necessary.
	Sp.	*Peter Hattrick*	554	David R. Post	
1842	Bg.	*Republic*	139	Gurdon Gates	
	"	*Frances Ashby*	125	Charles L. Randall	
	"	*Sarah Brown*	348	Joseph M. Norton	
	Sp.	*Uncas*	523	Paul W. Latham	
	Bg.	*Handy*	94	Charles Post	
1843	Bg.	*Metamora*	196	Henry Ashby	
	"	*Croton*	311	D. V. Soullard	

HURLBUT LINE (*continued*)

YEAR		VESSEL	TONS	MASTERS	REMARKS
1843	Bk.	*Rose Standish*	427	Joseph W. Spencer	
"	"	*Ann Welsh*	382	Joseph N. Magna	
1844	Bg.	*Nicholas Brown*	196	Washington Read	Whitaker & Sampson became Mobile agents.
"	Sp.	*Martha Washington*	472	Justus S. Doane	J. Conway master in 1845. Foundered, Oct. 21, 1848, from New Orleans to Liverpool.
1845	Sp.	*Panthea*	642	William B. Lane	
"	Bk.	*Mayflower*	514	George H. Hitchcock	
"	"	*Z. Ring*	324	Elbert Latham	
"	"	*Rolla*	248	William T. Giberson	
"	Bg.	*Gen. Wilson*	185	J. W. Miner	
"	Sp.	*Manchester*	570	W. Tyler	
1846	Bk.	*Jane*	199	J. Matthews	Regular line consisted of eight ships, three
"	Bg.	*Caroline E. Platt*	231	R. R. S. Pittman	barks, and two brigs sailing every ten days.
1847	Bk.	*Weybosset*	322	Caleb Harris	
"	Bg.	*Virginia*		Hallock	
"	"	*Peconic*	239	William C. Park	
"	"	*Nathan Hale*	190	A. Crowell	
1848	Bk.	*Jane E. Williams*	397	Edward C. Williams	
"	"	*Pilgrim*	379	John E. Williams	
"	"	*Ocilla*	368	Henry S. Stark	
"	Bg.	*Almeda*	190	Pierre S. Rowland	
"	"	*Samson*	278	W. E. Wheeler	
"	Bk.	*Mousam*	321	Joseph Gerrish	
"	"	*Montauk*	338	Gurdon Gates	
"	Bg.	*Osceola*	195	Hiram Baker	
1849	Sp.	*Seine*	785	Edward C. Williams	Burned, Mobile Bay, Mar., 1852.
"	Bk.	*Fanny*	341	Elihu E. Spicer, Jr.	
"	"	*Elizabeth*	273	S. Young	
"	"	*Ophir*	225	H. W. Ramsdell	
"	Sch.	*Francisco*	114	N. S. Smith	
"	Bg.	*Linden*	392	Frederick W. Williams	
1850	Bk.	*Asa Fish*	320	Isaac D. Gates	Gurdon Gates master in 1851.
"	"	*Apphia Maria*	250	J. P. Trefethen	
"	"	*Loretto Fish*	247	Miles T. Gates	
"	Sch.	*Martha Post*	196	R. H. Post	
"	Sp.	*Elisha Denison*	360	William Morton	
1851	Bk.	*William H. Brodie*	386	George B. Crary	
"	Sp.	*Gertrude*	507	J. Weeks	
"	"	*Charles Mallory*	698	Francis B. Parker	Lost, coast of Brazil, June, 1853.
"	"	*Eliza Mallory*	649	John E. Williams	Lost, coast of Florida, Nov., 1859.
1852	Bg.	*Gen. Jones*	296	P. Harding	
"	Sch.	*Iram Smith*		Davis	
"	"	*Stephenson*	466	Ezra Denison Post	
"	"	*J. W. Miner*	386	John W. Miner	
"	"	*Echo*	197	William H. Lowden	
"	"	*Maria L. Davis*	195	William R. Davis	
1853	Sch.	*S. J. Moye*	320	Bethuel C. Hallock	
"	"	*Pocahontas*	217	Horatio Bulkley	Var. *Pocohontas.*
"	"	*Greyhound*		Monroe	
"	"	*Reindeer*	218	Isaac Cathcart	
"	"	*Amos Falkenberg*	181	Beatty	
"	"	*Ann & Susan*	326	Samuel Myers	
"	"	*John Elliott*	135	G. H. Wood	
"	Bg.	*B. M. Prescott*	138	J. Coombs	
"	"	*Gov. Brown*	299	Joseph W. Trim	
"	Bk.	*M. E. Trout*	253	E. Collamore	F. B. Ames master in 1858.
"	"	*Charlotte Wynns*	339	Jesse F. Hosmer	
"	"	*R. H. Gamble*	260	Frederick A. Hosmer	
1854	Bg.	*Handy King*	519	J. H. Starkey	In Aug., 1854, the New York agents were
"	Bk	*Milford*	437	George Barton	Post & Ryerson or Hurlbut & Co.
"	"	*Vernon*	467	Thomas Mayo	
"	"	*Petrea*	494	Osborne	David J. Sturges master in 1860.
"	"	*Col. Ledyard*	404	F. D. Beckwith	

HURLBUT LINE (*continued*)

YEAR		VESSEL	TONS	MASTERS	REMARKS
1854	Bg.	*John H. Jones*	411	Charles Mills	
	Sch.	*Orb*	253	Noah N. Tibbets	
1855	Sp.	*Advance*	1275	William Lecraw	Laytin, Hurlbut & Ryerson became New
	Sch.	*Minnie Schiffer*	193	John Wilson	York agents on Jan. 1, 1855.
	"	*R. R. Whitmore*		Brigham	Laytin & Hurlbut became New York agents
	"	*Queen of the South* (tern)	445	George Wheeler	latter part of 1855.
	"	*Meteor*	223	Henry L. Sturges	
	"	*Moonlight*	280	Burr Knapp	
	"	*Sarah Clark*	175	Adams	Joseph M. Griffing master in 1857.
1856	Sch.	*Franklin Bell*	206	O. S. Robinson	
	"	*Oliver H. Booth*	331	Oliver Burger	
	"	*Gardiner Pike* (tern)	305	Benjamin Whitaker	
	"	*Gulf Stream* (tern)	362	J. T. Godfrey	
	"	*Kate Stamler* (tern)	482	Ferdinand Andre	
	"	*Oliver M. Pettit*	269	Elijah Clark	
	Bk.	*Benjamin Hallett*	359	James I. Little	
	"	*Lexington*	395	Charles Thatcher	
	"	*Myrtle*	398	Charles T. Botsford	
	Sch.	*Emily Ward* (tern)	395	Henry S. Ward	
	"	*Indianola* (tern)	522	Joseph McMurray	
	"	*Laura Gertrude*	316	Samuel G. Fairchild	Charles B. Elwood master in 1857.
	"	*Argus Eye*	271	Alfred Sharp	
1857	Sch.	*Gulf Stream* (tern)	362	Jonathan T. Godfrey	
	Bk.	*Pacific*	274	Gardiner	
	"	*Angelina Brewer*	422	Bernard Ulmer	
	"	*James L. Davis*	441	Samuel G. Fairchild	
	"	*Mary & Louisa*	497	Benjamin Jones	
1858	Sch.	*Transit*	297	James Davis	
	"	*Mobile*	398	Allen Howes	
	"	*Emeline*	346	Francis W. Miner	
	"	*Julia Fox*	288	Humphrey Leaming	
	"	*Onrust*	222	James Thompson	
	Bg.	*Mary Hamilton*	292	W. B. Crowell	
	"	*Empire*	220	J. Miller	
	"	*Dirigo*	299	J. B. Brookings	
	"	*Georgia*		Pratt	
	"	*Pizarro*	275	A. L. Sturges	
	Bk.	*Trajan*	429	B. W. Conant	
	Bg.	*Jesse Rhynas*	309	Lorenzo Pendleton	
1859	Bk.	*David Nichols*	194	Z. B. Ellis	
	"	*Wave Crest*	409	J. C. Harmon	
	Bg.	*D. Maloney*	248	Absalom Steelman	
	"	*Zone*	286	M. T. Howland	
	"	*Ida McLeod*	348	D. P. Davis	
	"	*Circassian*	244	W. R. Hagan	Var. Heagan.
	"	*East*	297	Joseph A. Graffam	
	Sch.	*J. M. Holmes*		Brewster	
	"	*J. W. Lindsey*	199	D. Lewis	
	"	*Maryland*	288	W. W. Cathcart	
	"	*Village Queen*	220	William L. Hawkins	
	"	*Ralph Post*	426	Daniel Collum	Var. Collom.
	"	*Oklona*	683	William Wheeler	
	Bg.	*Mary Hamilton*	292	Bailey	
1860	Sch.	*Kate Merrill*	297	Benjamin Wicks	
	"	*A. K. McKenzie*	173	N. Bradford	
	"	*Emily W. Seyburn*	353	H. M. Nickels	
	"	*Orianna*	140	A. Thatcher	
	"	*Daniel S. Williams*	393	Daniel S. Williams	
	"	*James Miller* (tern)	471	Carbonnet	
	Bg.	*Energy*	292	A. H. DePass	Var. DuPass.
	Sch.	*Moses B. Bramhall*		Davy	
	"	*Cornelia Newkirk* (tern)	240	Eli Higbee	
	Bg.	*C. F. O'Brien*	283	D. G. Ames	
	Bk.	*Kate Stamler*	482	H. K. Manwaring	

CITY LINE

Sturges & Clearman, 92 Wall St., New York agents. O'Connor & Ryan, Mobile agents. Established July, 1837, to provide monthly sailings.

YEAR		VESSEL	TONS	MASTERS	REMARKS
1837	Bg.	Camilla	198	F. Nichols	
	"	Madison	315	Ashbel Hubbard	
	"	Victress	268	Josiah Thatcher	
	Sp.	Lewis Cass	318	Samuel W. Dickenson	Lost, west of Bermuda, Feb., 1842.
1838	Bg.	Warsaw	194	Pascal Sheffield	
	"	Detroit	211	Frederick W. Williams	
	"	Orion	159	L. B. Lee	
	"	Jones	179	Thomas R. Herbest	
	"	Mobile	329	James Livermore	
	Sch.	Splendid		Bates	
	Bg.	Georgia	197	F. Nichols	
	Sch.	Phebe Eliza	170	Jackson B. Bedell	
	Bk.	Nashua	301	George Pollard	
	Bg.	Alabama	272	Frederick W. Williams	
1839	Bg.	Franklin	198	John Paty	
	Sp.	Rienzi	327	Parker P. Norton	
	Bg.	Chieftain	196	Thomas Sears	
	"	Wetumpka	267	Joseph M. Norton	
	"	Selma	407	Martin Smith	
	"	Linden	392	Ashbel Hubbard	C. R. Griffith master in 1844.
1840	Bg.	Macon	223	Anson Bibbins	Sailed bimonthly in season.
	"	Otranto	149	John Fowler	
	Sp.	Mary Frances	311	Ichabod Sherman	
	Bg.	Will	156	Francis Griswold	
	"	Edward Vincent	187	William A. Judson	
	Bk.	Reform	322	Vincent Tilyou	
	Bg.	Rudolph Groning	190	D. Landon	
	"	Saratoga	232	Jackson B. Bedell	
	"	Sooy	197	C. R. Griffith	
1841	Bg.	Sarah Brown	348	Joseph M. Norton	
1842	Bg.	Savannah	396	Aaron Hawley	
1843	Bg.	Robert W. Brown	192	Walter Kelly	
	Bk.	Vernon	467	Walter Kelly	Christopher Faye master in 1852.
1844	Bk.	Z. Ring	324	Elbert Latham	J. Livermore master in 1846.
1846	Sch.	Statesman	197	Jonathan D. Cathell	John C. Ryan became Mobile agent.
1847	Bk.	Georgia	457	J. W. Huntington	Fosdick & Charlock, 86 Commerce St., became Mobile agents in 1848.
1849	Bg.	Selina	200	James Livermore	Sturges, Clearman & Co. became New York agents.
	Bk.	Edna	239	Israel Bibbins	
	Sch.	Ringgold	106	Daniel G. Loomis	
	"	Leroy	196	James P. Powell	
1850	Sch.	Arlington	249	Lewis	William Murch master in 1854.
	"	Patrick Henry	211	Seth Chester	
	"	Harriet Hallock	174	John J. Appleby	
1851	Bk.	Mara		Park	
	Sch.	Townsend Jones	197	S. A. Dayton	
	Sp.	Sandusky	943	John Borland	John D. Rice master in 1855.
	"	Seine	785	J. Pratt	Burned, Mobile Bay, Mar., 1852.
	"	Aberdeen	719	William Knott	
1852	Sch.	Montrose	284	Lewis	George Winslow master in 1853.
	"	Washington	240	William Murch	
	"	Norfolk Packet	350	James Bedell	
	"	Senator	249	Samuel Myers	Smith A. Dayton master in 1854.
	Bk.	Abeona	298	J. S. Arey	
	"	Sarah Jane	509	S. G. Stevens	R. Gray master in 1854.
	"	Goldfinch	317	C. Ryder	
1853	Sch.	Greenway	197	Henry Kirby	Samuel Wilson master in 1855.
	Bk.	Jane E. Williams	397	T. L. Masson	
	"	William H. Brodie	386	George Aldridge	George B. Crary master in 1855.
	Bg.	Jonathan Cilley	164	Tonneson	
	Sch.	Charles Carroll	131	Pratt	
1854	Sch.	Empire	250	Bradley Osborne	

CITY LINE (*continued*)

YEAR		VESSEL	TONS	MASTERS	REMARKS
1854	Sch.	*Virginia*	242	W. J. Axworthy	
	"	*Tempter*	219	Pardon W. Brown	Var. *Pardon T. Brown.*
	Bk.	*John Denham*	376	S. B. Davis	Hiram Gray master in 1858.
	Sch.	*Ringgold*	106	Daniel G. Loomis	
	Bk.	*T. B. Bartram*	547	Russell Gray	
	"	*Harvest*	426	Hanford Nichols	
1855	Sch.	*Pocahontas*	217	Horatio Bulkley	
	Bk.	*Ocilla*	368	Sidney Ashby	
	"	*E. Sherwood*	540	Samuel B. Hall	
1856	Bk.	*Courier*	386	Edwin Sherwood	
	Sch.	*Vapor*	312	William Burch	William Powell master in 1857.
	Bk.	*Goodspeed*	618	C. Faye	
	"	*Mary Coe*	563	Pardon W. Brown	
	"	*Asa Sawyer*	487	Isaac D. Gates	
1857	Bk.	*Ocilla*	368	Sidney Ashby	M. S. Charlock & Co. became Mobile agents.
	Bg.	*G. T. Ward*	444	Fish	
	"	*Emily*	322	David B. Hobart	
	Bk.	*Alice Provost*	497	William C. Dunham	
1858	Bk.	*Hiawatha*	574	D. H. Hall	
	Bk.	*Permelia Flood*	385	R. McCormack	
	Sch.	*Hannah Martin*	222	James Slaght	
1859	Sch.	*Kate Merrill*	297	Benjamin Wicks	This was the only Mobile line that observed a
	Bg.	*A. Hopkins*	493	Charles Murray	fixed schedule consistently during 1859–60.
	"	*Isabella Jewett*	198	G. M. Reed	
	Bk.	*Jacob Merrill*	343	W. C. Clark	
1860	Bk.	*Flight*	386	J. H. Hawks	
	Sch.	*Fanny*	363	H. Wicks	
	"	*Neptune's Bride*	263	Charles Z. Gillett	
	"	*B. Flanner*	392	Henry Applegit	
	"	*Energy*	292	A. H. DePass	
	"	*C. M. Nevins*	313	E. Hawkins	
	"	*Haze*	321	William H. Booth	
	Bk.	*Kate Stamler*	482	H. K. Manwaring	

MERCHANTS' LINE

John Elwell, 57 South St., New York agent. Fosdick & Charlock, Mobile agents. Established Jan., 1841, by John Elwell, who had been active in the Mobile and New Orleans trades for several years.

YEAR		VESSEL	TONS	MASTERS	REMARKS
1841	Sp.	*Merchant*	347	Joseph C. Jordan	
	"	*Sylvanus Jenkins*	547	Benjamin Seymour	Var. *Silvanus Jenkins.*
	"	*Cahawba*	351	William D. Smith	
	"	*Mary Kingsland*	797	Daniel Weare	
	"	*St. Lawrence*	462	Jesse Chase	
	"	*Isaac Newton*	600	Lyman D. Spaulding	
	"	*Carroll of Carrollton*	696	Thomas A. Bird	
	Bk.	*Iwanowna*	254	John Dyer	
1842	Bg.	*Alcenus*	188	Thomas Skolfield	J. Elwell & Co. became New York agents in
	Sp.	*Queen Victoria*	712	Wildes D. Thompson	Nov., 1842.
	Bg.	*Growler*	247	Barnard Ulmer	
	Sp.	*Brunswick*	604	Robert McManus	
	Sch.	*Robert Mills*	130	James Darling	
	Sp.	*Kensington*	494	J. W. Shumway	
1843	Bk.	*Teazer*	249	Jonathan Crockett, Jr.	Var. *Teaser.*
	Bg.	*David Duffell*	188	Israel S. Adams	
	Bk.	*Nicholas Brown*	196	Washington Read	
	Bg.	*Larkin Snow*	124	Pressey	George W. Brown master in Dec., 1843.
	"	*Susquehannah*	207	James Bancroft	
	"	*Confidence*	195	Samuel Bailey	
	Sp.	*Viola*	495	William Jameson	
1844	Bg.	*Northerner*	233	Lunt	James Witham master in 1847.
	Sch.	*Tasso*	146	Howe	
	Bg.	*Eliza & Susan*	241	Elisha Dyer	Wrecked, Feb., 1845.
	Bk.	*William & James*	264	Washington Read	Charles Mercier master in 1846.

MERCHANTS' LINE (*continued*)

YEAR		VESSEL	TONS	MASTERS	REMARKS
1844	Bk.	*Ranger*	246	Alexander Milliken	
	Bg.	*Lucy Ann*	240	Israel Snow	
	"	*Marsellois*	223	Albert Sleeper	George Thorndike master in 1847.
	"	*Damascus*	249	Enoch Chase	
1845	Sp.	*John P. Harward*	548	Washington Read	
	Bg.	*North America*	140	W. Bradbury	Var. M. Bradbury.
1846	Bg.	*Billow*	173	E. Lawrence	
	"	*Orlando*	134	Davis	
	"	*Overmann*	200	William Davis	
	Bk.	*Suwarrow*	292	Montgomery	Abandoned at sea, Feb., 1855.
	"	*Ariana*	266	James Maloney	
	"	*Alabama*	280	J. T. Sprague	
	"	*Loretta*	240	Wall	George Fogarty master in 1852.
	"	*Weskeag*	248	Bartlett	
	Bg.	*Oceana*	249	Ephraim Jordan	
1847	Bg.	*Sea*	249	Robert Norton	James W. Elwell & Co., 57 South St., became
	Sch.	*Commodore*	205	Powell	New York agents in Jan.
	"	*Metamora*	83	Stephen A. Hopkins	
	"	*Patrick Henry*	211	Seth Chester	
	Bk.	*Gipsey*	295	Smith	
	"	*Oberlin*	331	John J. Balch	
	Sp.	*Glasgow*	594	J. F. Manson	
	Bk.	*Edwin Augusta*	323	David Keazer	
	"	*St. Mary*	280	Alexander Milliken	
	Sp.	*Moslem*	450	J. E. Pettes	
	"	*Mortimer Livingston*	749	E. W. Barstow	Var. E. M. Barstow.
	Bk.	*Ocean Bird*	268	D. Cony	
1848	Bk.	*John Stroud*	269	George W. Brown	C. W. Savage became Mobile agent.
	"	*Desdemona*	298	Samuel S. Stinson	
1849	Bk.	*A. H. Kimball*	285	Jeremiah Sleeper	
	Bg.	*Amesbury*	168	William Rodbird	Var. W. Redbird.
	Bk.	*Thomas Prince*	293	R. Hallowell	J. H. Rivers & Co. became Mobile agents.
	Sch.	*Henrietta*	160	Bethuel C. Hallock	
	Bg.	*Azores*	274	J. O. Amsbury	
	Bk.	*Cloclia*	246	L. R. Bartlett	
	"	*Sarah Hand*	282	Nichols	
	"	*Eliza Barss*	246	D. P. Bramhall	
	Sp.	*Meteor*	494	David Lawrence	
	Sch.	*Pauline*	199	T. Stiles	Var. *Paulina.*
1850	Sch.	*Gwenemma*	141	J. Perry	
	Bg.	*Francis Lord*	198	Gladding	
	"	*J. L. Whipple*	169	James H. Kelleran	Var. Kellerman.
	"	*Germ*	171	Burke	
	"	*Wahsega*	248	Smith	
	"	*Denmark*	218	L. Keney	
	Bk.	*Catherine*	316	James Watts	
	"	*Mandarin*	275	James Colley	
	Bg.	*Pulaski*	249	J. Norris	Joseph Woods master in 1852.
	Sp.	*Robert Kelly*	1165	E. M. Barstow	Readmeasured 1131 tons.
1851	Bg.	*Sarah W. Cushing*	264	Wade	
	Bk.	*William Harris*		Hallett	
	"	*Wyandotte*	257	J. A. Heath	
	"	*Benjamin Adams*	245	George B. Cornish	
	Sp.	*South Carolina*	768	George A. Preble	
	Bg.	*Olivia*	176	Gaspall	
1852	Sp.	*Vanguard*	1196	Joseph M. Norton	
	"	*Champlain*	513	S. Woodward	
	Sch.	*Cohasset*	176	Robert T. Brown	
	Bk.	*N. Boynton*	438	W. W. Smalley	
1853	Bk.	*Lewellyn*	230	J. W. Sherman	Barnewall & Fitler became Mobile agents.
	"	*Isnardon*	247	Sparks	in Sept.
	Bg.	*B. R. Bingham*		Hoffman	Line sailed very irregularly for next few
	Sch.	*Charger*	161	Blakeman	years.
1854	Bk.	*Emma Lincoln*	299	C. Watts	
	"	*William Henry*	299	William H. Watts	

MERCHANTS' LINE (*continued*)

YEAR	VESSEL	TONS	MASTERS	REMARKS
1854	Sch. *A. R. Pharo*	239	Charles A. Falkenberg	
1860	Sch. *Joseph W. Allen*	285	W. H. Squires	McCready, Mott & Co. became New York
"	*John Roe*	297	Edmund Hammond	agents; H. O. Brewer & Co., Mobile agents.

COMMERCIAL LINE

Dunham & Dimon, 67 South St., New York agents. Fosdick & Charlock, Mobile agents. Line reported established Nov., 1841, but did not get under way until July, 1842.

YEAR	VESSEL	TONS	MASTERS	REMARKS
1841	Bg. *Georgia*	197	Frederick M. Lambert	Philander Daggett master in 1842.
1842	Bk. *Apthorp*	246	Philip Blake	
	Bg. *Acton*	184	Frederick M. Lambert	Lost at sea about Nov., 1847.
	" *Long Island*	174	Daniel Howell	
1843	Bg. *Frances Ann*	182	Green	Line consisted of eight vessels sailing every
	" *L. Baldwin*	270	Jesup Alvord	ten days.
	" *Wilson Fuller*	270	Samuel Cobb	William Crawford master in 1847.
	" *G. B. Lamar*	260	William W. Wakeman	
	" *Philura*	198	Russell Doane	Abram S. Williams master in 1853.
	Sp. *Newark*	306	Timothy G. Merwin	
	Sch. *Willis Putnam*		Cook	
	" *Two Marys*	116	Francis W. Miner	David W. Tyler master in 1844.
	" *Osceola*		Holmes	
	" *Mary Walker*	160	F. W. Thrane	
	Bg. *Mary*	194	Ephraim Richardson	
	" *William I. Watson*	152	John P. Levy	
	" *Isaac Mead*	384	Robert T. Brown	
	" *Peter Demill*	294	Christopher Lewis	Nicholas Hoey master in 1848–54.
	Sp. *Celia*	339	Charles Thatcher	George Thatcher master in 1843–4.
	Bk. *Weybosset*	322	George Collins, Jr.	
	" *H. W. Tyler*	300	James Tyler	
	Bg. *Virginia*	350	Josiah R. Talbot	Philander Daggett master in 1843–4.
1844	Bg. *Peconic*	239	Robert M. Wilbur	William C. Park master in 1844–5.
	" *Blakely*	234	Philander Daggett	
	Bk. *La Grange*	259	Daniel L. Porter	
	Sch. *Henry R. Roberts*	94	Henry R. Roberts	
1845	Bk. *Philena*	272	David Forbes	C. W. Swain master in 1849.
	" *John W. Cater*	217	Thomas Trott	
	Sp. *Manco*	350	George W. Nickels	
	Bk. *Julia*	318	James G. Allen	William H. Adams master in 1848.
	Sch. *John Roaless*	85	Lewis	
	" *Gen. Scott*	144	John Doughty	
1846	Bk. *Texidor*	216	Hugo B. Major	W. Snow master in 1848.
	" *Duc d'Orleans*	310	John Robinson	Very little activity in 1847 and line discon-
	Sch. *Energy*	135	Swift	tinued in 1848.

MUTUAL LINE

Mailler & Lord, 108 Wall St., New York agents. E. C. Center & Co., Mobile agents. Established Dec., 1846.

YEAR	VESSEL	TONS	MASTERS	REMARKS
1847	Bg. *Potomac*	167	Oliver Matthews	J. W. Smith master in 1848.
	" *Josephus*	144	R. Gray	
	" *Massachusetts*	164	S. S. Burgess	J. C. Nichols master in 1850.
	Sch. *Ganges*	74	W. Handy	
	Sp. *Rob Roy*	526	Asahel Arnold	
	" *Tallahassee*	489	W. B. Brodnax	
	Bg. *Gilbert Hatfield*	160	Eliphalet Kingsbury	
	" *Eliza Jane*	222	James Hart	
	" *Swiss Boy*	258	J. C. Maloney	Fosdick & Charlock became Mobile agents
	" *Emma Prescott*	186	T. B. R. Lee	in Nov.
	Bk. *Mary Broughton*	322	B. M. Melcher	
1848	Bg. *Union* (Cl.)	180	E. Hooper	
	" *John A. Lancaster*	175	J. Loveland	
	" *Puritan*	229	Sartelle	
	Sp. *Washington*	372	John H. Burleigh	

MUTUAL LINE (*continued*)

YEAR		VESSEL	TONS	MASTERS	REMARKS
1848	Bk.	Somerset	170	James M. Hood	
	"	Isnardon	247	B. F. Sanford	
1849	Bg.	Republic	139	W. T. Smith	
	"	Nathan Hale	190	A. Crowell	
	"	Virginia	168	Andros	
	Bk.	Ariana	266	James Maloney	R. B. Wade master in 1851.
	"	Tarquin	262	Moody	Line discontinued.

EAGLE LINE

Eagle & Hazard, 83 South St., New York agents. E. C. Center & Co., Mobile agents. Established Mar., 1848, by Horatio Eagle, succeeded in Aug. by Eagle & Hazard. Line regarded as a continuation of the Center Line. "Will sail as advertised, full or not full."

YEAR		VESSEL	TONS	MASTERS	REMARKS
1848	Bk.	Abeona	298	W. Reid.	Var. Reed. J. S. Arey master in 1849.
	"	Huma	380	Weeden	W. M. Henry master in 1849.
	Bg.	Ottawa	250	T. P. Lenox	
	"	George Shattuck	210	Daniel Bragdon	
	"	Martha	242	Ebenezer G. Adams	
	Bk.	Nahumkeag	266	J. Fisher	Henry Champlin master in 1849.
	Bg.	Peconic	239	William Park	
	Bk.	Autoleon	345	William C. Park	
	"	Nachoochee	252	T. Smith	
	Bg.	Gen. Wilson	183	Francis D. Beckwith	
	Sch.	Elizabeth	197	George B. Crary	
	Bk.	Alpha	518	Bennett	
	Bg.	E. L. Walton	195	C. Ryder	J. A. Granger master in 1850.
	"	Chenamus	201	J. Knowlton	J. L. Smith master in 1850.
	Bk.	Emily Miner	364	John W. Miner	
	"	Dudley	249	W. Purrington	
	Sch.	Harriet Hallock	174	John J. Appleby	
1849	Bg.	Virginia	350	Josiah R. Talbot	
	"	Metamora	196	Timothy B. Bunce	
	Bk.	Ophir	226	H. W. Ramsdell	
	Bg.	Grecian	230	Drew	
	Sp.	St. John	562	Samuel Skolfield	
	"	Rob Roy	526	Asahel Arnold	
	Bk.	Alexina	246	A. C. Burlingame	
	Bg.	J. B. Lunt	149	S. Hardy	J. P. Daggett master in 1851.
	Bk.	Jeddo	242	D. Eldridge	
	Sch.	Rebecca Frances	160	J. R. Nickerson	S. M. Ray master in 1854.
	"	Monterey	141	Downer	
1850	Sp.	Robert Center	829	Asahel Arnold	
	Bg.	Isabella	149	Oliver Matthews	James Nickerson, 2nd, master in 1850–4.
	Bk.	Gov. Briggs	198	J. H. Hallett	
	Bg.	Rolerson	196	Erastus Chase	R. H. Crowell master in 1851.
	Bk.	Byron	292	L. P. Upshur	James H. Titus master in 1853.
	"	Macedonia	242	Loring	
	"	Wahsega	248	Smith	
	"	Maine	272	P. H. Perkins	
	Bg.	Oliver	176	D. H. Sumner	
	Bk.	Asa Fish	320	Asa Sawyer	Isaac D. Gates master in 1852.
	Bg.	George L. Abbott	208	A. Stanley	
	"	Patrick Henry	148	John S. Ingraham	
	Sch.	Chester			
	"	Venice	127	Victor H. Appleby	
	Bg.	Annandale	160	J. M. Sherman	
	"	Catherine Rodgers	164	R. Colburn	S. S. Colburn master in 1853.
	Bk.	Jenny Lind	522	Timothy Bunce	
1851	Bg.	Versailles	199	Conant	
	Bk.	Gen. Jessup	189	William B. Fisher	
	Bg.	Francis P. Beck	257	J. E. Avery	Wrecked near Nassau, Apr., 1859.
	Sp.	Avalanche	396	Otis T. Baker	
	Bk.	Clyde	398	G. H. Kempton	Roswell B. Baldwin master in 1852.

EAGLE LINE (*continued*)

YEAR		VESSEL	TONS	MASTERS	REMARKS
1851	Sp.	*Lydia*	543	Francis B. Soule	
	Bk.	*Orion*	449	T. Jones	
	"	*Charlotte Wynns*	339	Jesse F. Hosmer	
1852	Sch.	*Marshall Post*		Post	Eagle & Hazard began running S. S. *Black*
	Sp.	*Chauncy Jerome, Jr.*	1154	J. Cone	*Warrior* to Mobile in Sept.
	Bk.	*Isnardon*	247	Adams	
	"	*William Henry*	299	William H. Watts	
	"	*Fanny*	341	Elihu Spicer, Jr.	
	Bg.	*Jonathan Cilley*	163	Daniel F. Mosman	
	Bk.	*Austin & Ellen*	413	N. Pendleton	
	"	*Francis Secor*	379	Jedidiah Paine	
	Bg.	*Thomas Potter*	153	Victor H. Appleby	
	"	*Reveille*	183	Conant	
1853	Bg.	*Julia Ford*	199	George Drinkwater	
	Bk.	*Girard*	199	O'Neill	
	Sch.	*Lewis*	195	Oren Crowell	
	Bg.	*Thomas B. Watson*	212	Blackburn	
	Sp.	*Marathon*	890	C. Tyler	
	Bg.	*Herald*	174	George L. Luce	
	"	*Samson*	277	W. E. Wheeler	
	Bk.	*Joseph Fish*	276	J. H. Seavy	
	Bg.	*Florence*	175	Samuel Gage	
	"	*Wappoo*	243	J. Coombs	
	Sch.	*Granite State*	199	W. Bearse	Gerry Bassett master in 1855.
1854	Bk.	*William H. Chandler*	350	Albert C. Bennett	Albert Gage master in 1856.
	Sch.	*Emma*	196	N. Hafford	
	Bk.	*Clara C. Bell*	282	Cole	Also reported 382 tons.
	Bg.	*John H. Jones*	411	Charles Mills	
	"	*Pilgrim*		Andros	
	Bk.	*Ocilla*	367	Henry S. Stark	
	Sch.	*Pocahontas*	217	Horatio Bulkley	
	"	*Minna Schiffer*	193	John Wilson	
	Bk.	*Edward*		Patterson	
	Bg.	*Cardenas*	208	Hutchinson	
	Bk.	*Jenny Lind*	523	Timothy D. Bunce	
	"	*Angela Brewer*	422	Bernard Ulmer	
	"	*Julia Chapin*		Howard	
	Sch.	*James Grierson*	149	Hallock	
	Bk.	*Charles Brewer*	318	C. Ellems	
	"	*Charles C. Fowler*	521	A. G. Palmer	W. C. Staples master in 1857.
	"	*Victorine*	540	Patterson	
1855	Sch.	*J. T. Grice*		Rogers	H. O. Brewer & Co. became Mobile agents.
	Bk.	*Fanny*	341	Jos. Warren Holmes	
	"	*West Wind*	427	Oliver P. Saunders	
	"	*Narramissic*	299	J. Lampher	
	Bg.	*Wacissa*	170	Whittey	
	"	*Mary Hamilton*	292	C. F. Botsford	
	Sch.	*Tempter*	219	Crawford	
	Bg.	*Baltic*	265	J. Josselyn	
1856	Sch.	*J. McAdam*		Willard	
	Bk.	*H. L. Rutgers*	405	Henry D. Delano	
	Bg.	*Jesse Rhynas*	310	Lorenzo Pendleton	
	Bk.	*Exchange*	564	W. P. Jones	
	Bg.	*Sheet Anchor*	276	T. Chesley	
	Bk.	*Samuel Moxley*	408	F. B. Parker	
	"	*Charles Keen*	683	Jones	
	Bg.	*J. G. Anderson*	267	J. E. Randall	
	Sch.	*Matron*	137	Taylor	
	Bk.	*Petrea*	494	Osborn	
	"	*Harvest*	426	Hanford Nichols	
1857	Sch.	*G. C. Waterbury*		W. W. Cook	
	Bk.	*Benjamin Hallett*	359	James S. Littell	
	Bg.	*Mystic*	271	Erastus Fish	
	Sch.	*Tanner*	439	George T. Pierson	
	Bk.	*W. H. Chandler*	350	Albert Gage	

EAGLE LINE (*continued*)

YEAR		VESSEL	TONS	MASTERS	REMARKS
1857	Bk.	*Jane A. Bishop*	415	Timothy D. Bunce	
	"	*Charles E. Fowler*	521	W. C. Staples	
1858	Bg.	*A. Hopkins*	493	Charles Murray	
	Sch.	*Julia Fox*	288	Humphrey Leaming	
	Bk.	*R. H. Gamble*	259	John Powell	
	"	*John Denham*	376	Hiram Gray	
1859	Sch.	*Sarah Mills*	216	Samuel H. Rowley	W. H. Hazard became New York agent in
	Bk.	*Mary Coe*	563	James A. Avery	Dec.
	"	*B. F. Shaw*	298	J. M. Conn	
	Sch.	*Eclipse*	269	William W. Cook	
	"	*A. J. Ingersoll*	280	A. J. Higbee	
	"	*David B. Bayles*	262	Benjamin F. Jayne	
	Bk.	*Hannah Secor*	589	S. Chase	
	"	*Old Dominion*	393	William Johnson	Also reported 420 tons.
	Bg.	*Eaglet*	293	W. M. Terry	
	Bk.	*James L. Davis*	441	Samuel Y. Fairchild	
	Bg.	*John R. Dow*	198	George Coggshall	
1860	Bg.	*Times*	175	D. Phinney	
	"	*Selma*	298	J. Stetson	
	Sch.	*B. C. Scribner*	327	Carlisle	
	"	*Maria Pike*	346	J. W. Crawford	
	"	*John Aumack*	281	Lewis E. Pearce	
	Bg.	*Galveston*	254	Whitfield	
	Bk.	*Robert B. Walker*	272	Raines	Var. Raynes.
	"	*Laura Russ*	284	J. A. Russ	
	Bg.	*Three Sisters*	299	Pinkham	
	"	*Centaur*	225	Holt	
	Sch.	*Cheviot*	127	A. Strout	

EMPIRE LINE

Alfred Ladd, 69 South St., New York agent. Savage & Calef, Mobile agents. Established Nov., 1849.

YEAR		VESSEL	TONS	MASTERS	REMARKS
1849	Bg.	*Monica*	179	A. Burke	
	"	*Herald*	174	Clark Delano	
	"	*Ellen Maria*	151	Hoyt	
	Sch.	*Minerva Wright*		Cox	
1850	Bg.	*Oriole*	185	W. H. Robinson	
	Sch.	*Isabella Thompson*	149	Corson	
	"	*Harp*	161	A. Gibbs	
	Bk.	*Nachoochee*	448	Thorp	
	"	*A. B. Sturges*	210	Scott	J. Rice master in 1853.
	Bg.	*Joseph*	178	Joshua A. Kellar	
	Bk.	*Thomas Prince*	293	P. Hallowell	G. L. Carney master in 1851.
	Sch.	*Brazos*	131	James E. Ward	
	"	*Glen Roy*	144	Ira Marcy	Var. Maxcy.
1851	Sch.	*May Ann*	99	J. Hopkins	Ladd & Stannard became New York agents.
	Bk.	*Louisa & Caroline*	323	Raven	Line now credited with maintaining a regu-
	Sp.	*Albert Gallatin*	849	John E. Salter	lar schedule.
	Bk.	*Baring Brothers*	291	William N. Colter	
	Sp.	*Catherine*	611	J. Edwards	
	"	*Shelter*	426	R. H. Lovitt	
	"	*Tam O'Shanter*	977	H. S. Soule	
	Bk.	*Isabella*	285	Preble	
	"	*Mary Varney*	199	M. P. Sturgis	Var. Sturges.
	"	*Joseph Bragdon*		Bartlett	
	"	*Montauk*	338	Cicero Brown	
	Sp.	*Gallia*	1191	Addison Richardson	Ladd & Church became New York agents in
	"	*Josephine*	947	Charles Lendholm	Oct.
	Bg.	*Bloomer*	234	J. Dyckman	Edward R. Rivers became Mobile agent.
	Bk.	*Norumbega*	323	Irvin B. Baxter	James Clark master in 1853.
	"	*Theoxana*	398	J. G. Borland	
1852	Bg.	*M. & J. C. Gilmore*	185	R. Eldridge	Alfred Eldridge master in 1856.

EMPIRE LINE (*continued*)

YEAR		VESSEL	TONS	MASTERS	REMARKS
1852	Bk.	*T. J. Southard*	296	J. Bishop	
	"	*John Denham*	376	Russell Gray	
	Sch.	*Frances*	161	Stotesbury	
	"	*Telegraph*	174	Fish	
	Bg.	*Eolian*	197	S. S. Jordan	W. M. Seaman master in 1853.
	"	*Caribbee*	219	Eleazer Crabtree	
	"	*Flora*	248	Voorhees	
	Bk.	*Margaret*	250	James D. Wood	
	Bg.	*Vernon*	199	E. D. Kent	Discontinued in 1853.

PELICAN LINE

E. H. Fosdick, 27 South St., New York agent. G. W. Bacchus, Mobile agent. Established Sept., 1852.

YEAR		VESSEL	TONS	MASTERS	REMARKS
1852	Sch.	*George C. Ackerly*	180	W. C. Baldwin	Savage & Calef became Mobile agents in
	Bk.	*Baring Brothers*	291	S. D. Gregg	Oct.
	"	*Hannah Spalding*	300	C. Spalding	
	Bg.	*Montgomery*	217	R. Montgomery	
1853	Sch.	*Caroline E. Hoppin*	103	Hoppin	
	Sp.	*Anna Tift*	745	James Ross	British-built ship late of Key West.
	Bg.	*Edward Lind*	196	J. Bucknam	Fosdick & Scammon became New York
	Bk.	*Yuba*	228	Robinson	agents in Sept., and Edward H. Rivers,
	Sp.	*William*	522	J. Berry	Mobile agent.
	Bg.	*Marine*	216	George W. Brown	
	Bk.	*G. W. Hall*	356	A. Carpenter	
1854	Sch.	*Echo*	197	Haff	
1855	Bg.	*Ann A. Tyng*	198	A. Pierce	Sailings greatly reduced during 1854 and
	Sp.	*Orphan*	682	G. H. Kempton	1855.
1856	Sp.	*Minnesota*	799	Charles A. Deshon	Edward H. Fosdick and John Q. Scammon
	Bg.	*Wetumpka*	267	H. Googins	dissolved partnership in Jan., 1855. Robson
	Sp.	*Roscius*	1031	Enoch Cook	& Fosdick continued line, but only scattered
1857	Sch.	*Walter Raleigh*	472	Lewis Mankin	sailings during 1856–7.
	Sp.	*Cerro Gordo*	577	David Keazer	Discontinued in fall of 1857, but firm continued New Orleans line.

NEW LINE

Lane & West, 76 South St., New York agents. J. G. Whitaker, Mobile agent. Established Oct., 1853. In Dec., consisted of six schooners "built expressly for the trade, sailing every 10 days."

YEAR		VESSEL	TONS	MASTERS	REMARKS
1853	Sch.	*John W. Miner*	386	D. P. Berry	
	"	*Kate Stewart*	388	Titus C. Mather	
	"	*Mary D. Lane*	398	John W. Miner	B. A. Gardner master in 1855.
	"	*Imogene*	397	J. Myers	A. G. Ruggles master in 1855.
	"	*Mobile*	398	M. C. Wimpenny	J. Couillard master in 1855.
	"	*Emeline*	345	Francis W. Miner	
1854	Sch.	*Stephen Hotchkiss*	291	A. H. Munson	Var. Manson.
	"	*Louise*	396	John W. Miner	Line consisted of eight schooners early in
	Sp.	*Connecticut*	1081	G. E. Welch	1854.
1855	Sch.	*James Miller* (tern)	471	Jesse N. Braddock	Lane, West & Co., 77 South St., became
	"	*Annie E. Coxe* (tern)	393	Littleton C. Wimpenny	New York agents.
	"	*Augusta C. Brewer*	399	Peleg Saunders	
	"	*Beulah E. Sharp*	140	Samuel H. Sharp	
1856	Bk.	*Ocean Eagle* (Cl.)	383	William Greenman	
	Sch.	*E. W. Farrington*	211	Britton	West & Walker became New York agents in
	"	*Kate Stamler* (tern)	482	Ferdinand Andre	Nov. Packets sailed weekly through season.
	"	*Amy Chase*	155	M. L. Chase	
1857	Sch.	*Nancy J. Brayton*	224	S. S. Rogers	
	"	*George & Emily*	190	Sturges	
	"	*B. S. Johnson*	170	Walters	
	"	*Republic*	250	Cahoon	
	"	*Southern Belle*	322	William S. Tyler	
1858	Bg.	*Times*	175	D. Phinney	Discontinued spring of 1858.

DISPATCH LINE
N. H. Brigham, 133 Water St., New York agent. Edward J. Rivers, Mobile agent. Established Nov., 1855.

YEAR	VESSEL	TONS	MASTERS	REMARKS
1855	Sch. *Vendoo*	157	Coombs	
	Bk. *Alabama*	280	L. L. Stockbridge	
1856	Bg. *Isabella Jewett*	195	J. Chipman	
	Bk. *H. B. Herriman*		Cooper	
	" *Theodore Curtis*	331	T. Edmonds	
	" *M. J. Colcord*	374	Josiah A. Colcord	
	Sch. *Mary Staples*	305	W. C. Staples	
	" *Mobile*	398	Allen Howes	
	Bg. *Adeline Sprague*	211	Smith	
1857	Sch. *Emma Furbish*	185	J. E. Kendall	
	Bg. *Flying Eagle*	275	W. Conant	
	Bk. *Edward*	355	Thomas Jones	
	Sch. *Americus*	262	Daniel Walters	
	Bk. *Thales*	234	Howland	
	Bg. *Pizarro*	275	A. L. Sturges	
	Sch. *Ann & Susan*	326	Samuel Myers	Ezekiel I. Vanderbilt master in 1858.
	Bk. *J. W. Andrews*	299	J. W. French	
	Sp. *Oregon*	649	T. N. Porter	
1858	Bg. *E. P. Sweet*	258	A. F. Jewett	Line ran on regular schedule throughout re-
	Bk. *George Leslie*	288	C. M. Hall	mainder of period.
	Bg. *Suwannee*	199	Osmer	
	Bk. *Charles Brewer*	318	S. Dean	
	Sch. *J. W. Maitland*		Speed	
	" *Cumberland*	283	W. Symmes	
	" *Black Monster*	293	F. A. Senter	
	Bk. *Asa Fish*	320	Thomas E. Wolfe	
	Bg. *Abruccabah*	220	Carlisle	
	Sch. *George C. Gibbs*	160	J. B. Gibbs	
	Bg. *A. C. Merryman*	230	Colburn	
	Bk. *Trovatora*	348	P. P. Carver	
	Bg. *Enoch Pratt*	211	Smith	
1859	Sch. *Zavalla*	153	F. J. Ward	
	Bg. *Gov. Brown*	299	William J. Axworthy	
	Sch. *Breeze*	262	S. J. Hulse	
	" *Narragansett*	248	S. Hall	
	" *John W. Miner*	386	D. P. Berry	
	Bg. *Martha Post*	195	S. Thompson	
	Bk. *Anna*	421	R. W. Wheeler	
	Sch. *Potomac*	242	F. Arnet	Var. Arnat.
	Bg. *Geranium*	433	H. M. Pierce	
	" *Amos M. Roberts*	219	S. Colson	
	Sp. *Oroondates*	768	Moses Pike	
	Sch. *William C. Mershon*	390	E. Cole	
	Bk. *Lone Star*	376	A. Spear	
	Sch. *Eclipse*	269	Lewis P. Cook	
	Bk. *Carolina*	364	J. S. Grindle	
	Sch. *George Maugham*	275	Crockett	Var. *George Mangham*.
	Bk. *Edwin*	449	R. McD. Nugent	
	" *Victorine*	540	J. Jones	
1860	Bk. *Magenta* (Cl.)	457	E. Hopkins	Trout, Fowler & Stannard became Mobile
	Bg. *Brothers*	196	R. B. Blaisdell	agents.
	Sch. *Billow*	90	Given	
	Bk. *St. Mary's*	279	Spavin	
	" *Eliza A. Cochrane*	325	A. Noyes	
	Sch. *Helen*	272	T. Long	
	Sp. *Bernard*	677	N. Hubbard	
	Bg. *Betsey Ames*	180	R. Bartlett	
	Sch. *J. W. Holmes*	123	Brewster	
	" *W. C. Atwater*		Allen	
	Bg. *New Era*	272	William Walker	
	Sch. *Cerito*	257	W. H. Crowell	
	" *Stephen Hotchkiss*	291	Elisha Doane	
	Bg. *Cygnet*	196	E. M. Jefferson	
	Sp. *Robert H. Dixey*	1252	Robt. H. Dixey	

DISPATCH LINE (*continued*)

YEAR	VESSEL	TONS	MASTERS	REMARKS
1860	Bg. *Lion*	180	Bradbury	
"	" *Wappoo*	243	H. N. Carver	
"	" *Manzoni*	227	J. Nichols	
"	Bk. *Heiress*	796	C. Clark	
"	Sch. *Nathaniel Doane*	247	C. Hall	
"	Bk. *Theoda*	440	P. P. Carroll	
"	Bg. *J. R. Nevins*	285	E. Tilley	
"	" *Benjamin Carver*	182	W. S. Carver	
"	Sch. *A. H. Manchester*	272	Asa W. Nickerson	
"	Bg. *A. Bradshaw*	270	A. Fish	

POST LINE

Post, Smith & Co., 85 South St., New York agents. Trout, Fowler & Stannard, Mobile agents. Established Jan., 1855.

YEAR	VESSEL	TONS	MASTERS	REMARKS
1855	Sch. *Southerner*	232	G. Bellows	
"	" *Martha Post*	195	Russell H. Post	
"	Bk. *H. A. Stephenson*	466	G. L. Smith	
"	Bg. *Rolerson*	196	R. H. Crowell	
"	Bk. *Clementine*		Wade	
"	" *Fanny Holmes*	700	G. H. Smith	
"	Sch. *Essex*	144	Albert Post	
1856	Bk. *Alice Tainter*	667	W. M. Post	
"	" *Mary Lucretia*	412	J. O. Gibbs	
"	" *Edwin*	449	Collamore	
"	Sp. *Chase*	381	J. Chase	
"	Sch. *Fanny Fern*	155	Isaac B. Briggs	
"	" *Presto*	278	Bethuel C. Hallock	
1857	Sp. *Elizabeth Denison*	644	E. Williams	Post, Smith & Co. became agents for S. S.
"	Sch. *E. W. Pratt*	218	E. B. Whelden	*Quaker City* in Feb.
"	Bk. *White Cloud*	285	Crowell	W. A. Sale master in 1858.
"	Sch. *Courier*	199	Loring	
"	" *Mobile*	398	Allen Howes	
"	Bk. *James M. Hicks*	721	William Greenman	
"	" *Wave Crest*	409	J. C. Harman	Var. Hermon.
"	Bg. *Altavela*	198	Gilkey	
"	" *Ida McLeod*	348	D. P. Davis	
"	Bk. *Ocean Home*	417	O. W. Hinckley	
1858	Sch. *W. S. Tisdale*	289	S. S. Hawkins	
"	Bk. *J. L. Davis*	441	Samuel Y. Fairchild	
"	Sch. *David B. Bayles*	262	Benjamin F. Jayne	
"	Bk. *Charles Keen*	683	John T. Chattin	
"	Sch. *Laura Gertrude*	316	Charles B. Elwood	
"	Bk. *Anna*	421	E. M. Tuthill	
"	Sch. *Kate Field*	291	Leonard W. Robbin	
"	" *Florence*	200	J. H. Mayo	
"	" *Helen*	272	T. Long	
"	" *Fanny*	363	H. Wicks	
"	Bk. *Goodspeed*	618	C. Faye	
"	Sch. *William C. Mershon*	390	E. Cole	
"	Bk. *Indian Belle*	318	J. P. Penny	
"	" *Mustang*	316	William Greenman	
"	Sch. *Jonathan May* (tern)	335	Josias M. Cobb	
1859	Sch. *Louisa*	152	William W. Hallock	
"	Bg. *Aurate*	298	Francis B. Davis	
"	Sch. *A. Bradshaw*	270	A. Fish	
"	" *Fleetwing* (tern)	518	Lewis Davis	
"	" *John A. Stanley*	239	Francis Jackson	
"	" *Edward H. Rowley*	197	White	
"	Bk. *William*	231	Williams	
"	" *Mary Coe*	563	James A. Avery	
"	" *James E. Ward*	349	S. R. Tibbets	
"	Sp. *Francis B. Cutting*	976	E. D. Post	J. B. Maloney master in 1860.
"	" *George Hurlbut*	1047	T. L. Masson	

POST LINE (*continued*)

YEAR	VESSEL	TONS	MASTERS	REMARKS
1859	Sch. *Republican*	334	Coville	
1860	Sch. *Eveline Bates*	321	J. Peterson	
	" *Sarah Hibbert*	242	J. Peterson	Var. *Hibberd.*
	Bk. *Addison Childs*	401	Joshua H. Smith	Discontinued after spring season, 1860.

OAKLEY & KEATING LINE

Oakley & Keating, New York agents. In Sept., 1859, became closely associated with McCready, Mott & Co., loading same vessels.

YEAR	VESSEL	TONS	MASTERS	REMARKS
1858	Bk. *Angeline Brewer*	422	Bernard Ulmer	
	Bg. *Maria White*	247	Elwell	
	Sch. *Essex*	144	Albert Post	
	" *Louisa A. Johnson*	296	Lewis D. Ellis	
	Bk. *Charles Brewer*	318	S. Dean	
	Sch. *D. W. Bagley*	121	Nathan F. Rogers	
	Bk. *Lamplighter*	365	John Payne	
	Bg. *Lavacca*	342	J. B. Greenman	
1859	Sch. *Mary Helen*	235	John P. Hutchinson	
	Bk. *Jane A. Bishop*	420	Timothy D. Bunce	
	" *James Andrews*	275	J. Small	
	Sch. *Julia Fox*	288	Humphrey Leaming	
	Bg. *Thomas W. Rowland*	395	H. L. Rowland	
	" *Zone*	286	H. T. Howland	
	Bk. *West Wind*	427	Oliver P. Saunders	
	Bg. *Daniel Maloney*	247	Absalom Steelman	
	Bk. *Permilia Flood*	385	Anderson	
	Bg. *Aurate*	299	Francis B. Davis	
	Bk. *Thomas G. Bunker*	497	E. Cooper	McCready, Mott & Co., joined in loading
	Sch. *North State*	431	Isaac F. Horton	the *Thomas G. Bunker* in Sept. and all vessels
	Bk. *Texana*	588	William Brand	listed below her name.
	Sch. *Fleetwing* (tern)	518	Benjamin F. Jayne	
	" *David B. Bayles*	262	Benjamin F. Jayne	
	" *Grandilla*	228	Johial Baker	
	Bk. *Wave Crest*	409	J. E. Harmon	
	Sch. *William C. Mershon*	390	E. Cole	
	Bk. *Charles Keen*	683	John T. Chattin	
	Sch. *Joseph W. Allen*	285	W. H. Squires	
	" *John N. Genin*	294	Samuel T. Phillips	
1860	Sch. *John Roe*	297	Edmund Hammond	
	Bg. *Yankee Blade*	320	J. A. Darling	
	Bk. *Christiana Keen*	213	Stacy	
	Sch. *Village Queen*	270	W. L. Hawkins	
	" *Thomas Holcombe*	392	Roderick Bennett	
	" *Eclipse*	269	Lewis P. Cook	
	" *Emeline*	345	Noyes R. Denison	
	" *Mobile* (tern)	398	Allen Howes	
	Bk. *Mary Sawyer*	306	W. N. Bartlett	
	" *James M. Hicks*	721	William Greenman	
	Bg. *Tanner*	439	Hodgkinson	
	Bk. *Edmund Dwight*	199	J. Nickerson	
	Sch. *Southern Belle*	322	Thomas Smith	C. Gillett also master in 1860.
	" *Lilly*	335	Barnabas Francis	

SECTION 15. NEW YORK—NEW ORLEANS

SMITH & BAILEY LINE

Phineas Smith and Benjamin Bailey, doing business as Smith & Bailey, New York agents. Talcott & Bowers, New Orleans agents. Line established Apr., 1817. No regular schedule. Discontinued in 1819.

YEAR	VESSEL	TONS	MASTERS	REMARKS
1817	Bg. *Superb*	213	James Meek	
	" *Day*	206	Alexander Don	
	Sp. *Caravan*	317	John Rathbun	Var. Rathbone.
	Bg. *Fredonia*	223	B. A. Muzzy	

RUSSELL LINE. Later known as OLD LINE.
John W. Russell, 93 Pine St., New York agent. Gilbert E. Russell & Co., New Orleans agents. Established 1818.

YEAR	VESSEL	TONS	MASTERS	REMARKS
1818	Sp. *Remittance*	406	Silas Holmes	
1819	Sp. *Maria Caroline*	271	Silas Holmes	
	Bg. *Nancy*	140	S. Packard	
	" *Casket*	235	Samuel G. Bailey	
	" *Sewell*	220	I. Stone	
	" *Monroe*	114	Edward B. Hallet	
1820	Bg. *Planter*	134	Robert Hart	
	" *Phoebe Ann*	244	Silas Holmes	
1821	Bg. *Edward*	255	Edward B. Hallet	
1822	Bg. *Hero*	239	Watson Crowell	
	" *Peruvian*	263	J. W. Russell	
	" *Levant*	219	William Beebe	
	Sp. *American*	340	Samuel Chew	
	" *William*	298	Richard Sears	
	" *Goree*	335	John Barstow	
1823	Sp. *Florian*	303	S. Packard	
	" *Virginia*	356	Edward B. Hallet	William Fosdick master in 1825.
	Bg. *Fanny*	254	Miles Lewis	
1824	Sp. *Frances*	368	Edward B. Hallet	James Rider master in 1828.
1825	Sp. *Russell*	385	Henry Packard	William Fosdick master in 1829.
	" *Azelia*	383	James Wibray	Charles Stoddard master in 1830.
	Bg. *Russell*	173	Samuel Thatcher	William Fosdick master in 1829.
1828	Sp. *DeWitt Clinton*	417	Henry Packard	Line sailed on fixed dates—consisted of five
	" *John Linton*	413	James Wibray	ships sailing 1st and 15th from New York, and 8th and 22nd from New Orleans. In Aug., C. & J. Barstow became New York agents and G. E. Russell & Barstow, New Orleans agents.
1830	Sp. *Ohio*	352	John J. Garvin	
1831	Sp. *John & Elizabeth*	296	Benjamin Barstow	Barstow & Adams became New Orleans
	Bg. *Marengo*	303	John M. Welsh	agents.
1832	Sp. *Warsaw*	332	N. Barstow	William P. Mendell master in 1838.
	" *Cincinnati*	457	Benjamin Barstow	
	" *Hanover*	329	Charles Mansfield	
	" *Saratoga*	542	A. C. Marshall	
1833	Sp. *Humphrey*	277	Crooker	Whitehall & Jaudon and C. Adams, Jr., became New Orleans agents.
	" *Garonne*	511	William Skiddy	
	" *New Jersey*	636	James Wibray	Six ships in line.
	" *Groton*	349	E. Baker	
1834	Sp. *Cyrus Butler*	360	J. Mauran	Adams & Andrews became New Orleans
	" *Louisa*	300	James Goodday	agents. Line did not adhere to schedule in fall
	" *Constitution*	275	S. G. Glidden	season and continued irregularly for several
	" *Mohawk*	344	J. Stevens	years following.
	" *Andes*	364	John Patten	
	" *Echo*	668	John Mallet	*Echo* sold Bremen, 1848.
	" *Citizen*	464	Merchant	
1835	Sp. *Howard*	399	B. Barstow	
	" *Congress*	401	John Holmes	
	" *St. Cloud*	471	Colburn	W. Emerson master in 1842.
	" *Henry Kneeland*	304	G. B. Emerson	
1836	Sp. *Superb*	296	Roswell P. Fish	Calvin Adams, Jr., became New Orleans
	" *Copia*	315	Lecraw	agent.
	" *Champion*	336	T. Torrey	
	" *Palestine*	469	A. N. Littlefield	
	" *Majestic*	297	Isaac Purington	
	" *Robert Bowne*	505	Charles Mansfield	
	" *Patriot*	437		
1837	Bk. *Condor*	237	David Hatch	
	" *Damariscotta*	283	Stetson	William F. Howes master in 1842.
	Sp. *New Orleans*	336	Stephen E. Cole	
	" *American*	339	William Martin	
	Bg. *Wellingsley*	212	Jabez Churchill	
1838	Bg. *Galen*	194	Brownell	C. Barstow & Pope became New York
	Sch. *Excel*	139	Orrin Sellew	agents in Sept.

RUSSELL LINE (*continued*)

YEAR	VESSEL	TONS	MASTERS	REMARKS
1838	Sp. *Osceola*	549	William Child	Var. Childs. Arthur Child master in 1842.
	" *Warsaw*	332	William R. Mendell	
1839	Sp. *St. Leon*	505	J. Wescott	
	" *Antioch*	395	J. Wescott	
1840	Bk. *Strafford*	314	Isaac B. Brewer	Sailings were greatly reduced in 1840 and ceased altogether in 1843.
1842	Bk. *Florence*	349	William Decker, Jr.	
	Sp. *Manchester*	570	Robert Bosworth	
	" *Ondiaka*	748	William Child	
	" *Oregon*	649	S. G. Glidden	
1843	Bk. *Kilby*	477	John Barstow	*Kilby* took part in the rescue of survivors of S.S. *San Francisco* in Dec., 1853, taking approximately 108.

NEW LINE

Collins Line in 1832. Stanton's Line in 1851. Foster & Hutton, 65 South St., New York agents. Foster & Hutton, Magazine St., New Orleans agents. Established 1823. Known in New Orleans as the Louisiana & New York Line.

YEAR	VESSEL	TONS	MASTERS	REMARKS
1823	Sp. *Venus*	283	Henry L. Champlin	
	" *Superior*	249	William Jocelin	William Tyler master in 1825.
1824	Sp. *Chancellor*	276	Gideon Parker	
	" *Crawford*	290	John Rathbone	
1825	Sp. *Resolution*	332	Edward Kennail	Var. Kennard.
	" *Lavinia*	310	Allen Miner	Richard Sears master in 1826.
	" *Louisiana*	354	Peter Price	Five ships in regular line in 1825, sailing 1st
	" *Niagara*	319	John R. Crane	and 15th from New York, and 8th and 22nd
	" *Talma*	391	John Rathbone	of month from New Orleans in season.
	" *Illinois*	415	Robert Waterman	
	Bg. *Edwin* (Temporary)	195	Seth Wheldon	Var. Wheldin
	" *Trent* (Temporary)	249	John Barstow	
1826	Sp. *Lafayette*	342	Thomas Fanning	
	" *Indiana*	306	Gideon Parker	
1827	Sp. *Kentucky*	416	John Rathbone	
	" *Tennessee*	415	Gilbert Fowler	
1831	Sp. *Louisville*	517	Peter Price	Thomas L. Servoss, 67 South St., became
	" *Nashville*	514	John Rathbone	New York agent. Line called Louisiana &
	" *Natchez*	524	Hartwell Reed	New York Line. George Wilbor, 23 Maga-
	" *Creole*	542	Ambrose S. Page	zine St., became New Orleans agent.
	" *Huntsville*	523	Charles Stoddard	N. B. Palmer master in 1835.
	" *American* (Temporary)	238	William Matthews	
	" *St. George* (Temporary)	408	John Taubman	T. J. Bond replaced Servoss as New York agent in June, 1832. In Oct., Edward Knight Collins became New York agent.
1833	Sp. *Congress*	376	John Collins	William G. Hewes, 9 Camp St., became New Orleans agent.
	" *Yazoo*	678	Henry Packard	James Wibray master in 1845.
	" *Mississippi*	648	Allen Miner	William Beebe master in 1839.
1835	Sp. *Vicksburg*	480	Philip Woodhouse	J. D. Bien and Aaron Cohen became New
	" *Shakespeare*	748	John Collins	Orleans agents.
1839	Sp. *St. John* (Temporary)	398	W. H. Hitchcock	
1841	Sp. *Gaston*	456	Elbert Latham	Oliver Eldridge master in 1842.
	" *Ocmulgee*	458	Thomas J. Leavitt	James E. Woodruff became New Orleans
	" *Memphis*	799	Samuel Nichols	agent. Line consisted of ten ships.
	" *Louisa*	496	Abraham Mulford	William Scott master in 1842.
1843	Sp. *Oswego*	647	David Wood	Hullin & Woodruff, 60 Camp St., became New Orleans agents. Ships sailed every five days, 5th, 10th, etc., in business season.
1844	Sp. *Java*	538	George S. Perry	James E. Woodruff became New Orleans
	Bk. *Vernon*	467	Walter Kelly	agent; eleven ships in line.
1845	Sp. *Arvum*	364	W. Smith	
	" *Angelo*	417	James A. Clarkson	
	" *Shanunga*	546	David Patton	

NEW LINE (*continued*)

YEAR	VESSEL	TONS	MASTERS	REMARKS
1845	Sp. *Clifton*	599	James B. Ingersoll	
	" *Genessee*	459	Thomas L. Miner	
	" *Damascus*	694	Eli C. Bliss	
	" *Sartelle*	416	Solomon Taylor	
	Bk. *Jane E. Williams*	397	Gideon Parker	
1846	Bk. *E. H. Chapin*	424	E. W. Welsh	
	Sp. *Geneva*	458	S. Goodhue	
	" *Wabash*	442	Edward Cornell	
1847	Bk. *Avola*	309	Swanton Whitmore	William Creevy became New Orleans agent
	" *Hebron*	384	Silas D. Gregg	in Nov.
	" *Croton*	311	David V. Soullard	
	Sp. *Samuel Hicks*	780	S. Goodhue	
	" *Richard Cobden*	710	G. Barrett	
1848	Sp. *Vandalia*	776	J. M. Norton	Johnson & Lowden became New York
	Bk. *Sherwood*	447	Isaac Bursley	agents; Fosdick & Bros. New Orleans agents.
	" *Thetis*	399	F. Crosby	Barks listed through this period represent
	" *Elizabeth*	273	Samuel Young	extra sailings for most part.
	" *California*	296	R. Robinson	
	" *Henry Harbeck*	398	T. G. Merwin	
	" *Huma*	380	Weeden	W. M. Henry master in 1849.
1849	Bk. *Delia Chapin*	400	B. McNear	Marcy & Shepherd became New Orleans agents.
	Sp. *Peter Marcy*	821	Daniel Marcy	A. Sampson master in 1849–50.
1850	Sp. *St. Charles*	798	Chester Hilliard	B. P. Bowers master in 1856.
	" *John G. Coster*	714	Nathaniel P. Durfey	
	" *Richard Alsop*	836	Jeremiah G. Smith	
	" *Christiana*	666	Edmund Hammond	
1851	Sp. *Hudson*	633	J. R. White	Thomas P. Stanton, 56 South St., became
	" *Hero*	750	E. K. Griffith	New York agent; J. W. Stanton & Co., New
	" *Bay State*	592	Lemuel B. Simmons	Orleans agents. Called Stanton's Line in
	" *Colombo*	577	N. O. Harris	New York and Louisiana Line in New
	" *Toronto*	631	Gideon Parker	Orleans.
	" *Quebec*	649	Nathaniel P. Durfey	Sunk in Mississippi in May, 1853.
	" *Southerner*	671	James Sullivan	
	" *Jersey*	849	John Day	
1852	Sp. *Island City*	526	Peleg Saunders	Abandoned at sea, Dec., 1853.
	" *Westminster*	631	Thomas R. Shapter	Stanton & Thompson, 114 South St., became New York agents.
1853	Sp. *Wellington*	726	J. E. Barstow	Chester Hilliard became New Orleans agent.
	" *Espindola*	742	J. Morse	
1854	Sp. *Toulon*	744	John L. Rich	L. D. Upshur master in 1856.
	" *Knickerbocker*	875	S. V. Peabody	Lost on Abaco, May 23, 1858.
	" *Garrick*	895	R. W. Foster	
	" *Sheridan*	895	S. Clark	
1855	Sp. *Louisiana*	747	James Sullivan	Lost at Liverpool in gale of Nov. 12, 1856.
	" *New Orleans*	924	John L. Rich	
	" *Liberty*	690	Benjamin Atkins	
	" *Wellington*	726	J. E. Barstow	
1856	Sp. *Westchester*	699	James T. Hiltz	
1857	Sp. *Lebanon*	697	Archibald G. Hamilton	Creevy & Farwell became New Orleans agents in 1859.
1860	Sp. *David Hoadley*	975	Joseph N. Magna	
	Bk. *Harriet A. Stephenson*	466	G. L. Smith	

HOLMES LINE

Silas Holmes, 62 South St., New York agent. Known as Nelson Line after 1838.

YEAR	VESSEL	TONS	MASTERS	REMARKS
1824	Sp. *Lavinia*	310	Sherburne Sears	Gilbert Fowler master in 1826.
1825	Sp. *Crawford*	290	John Rathbone	
	" *Chancellor*	277	Charles E. Coffin	George Barker master in 1826.

HOLMES LINE (*continued*)

YEAR	VESSEL	TONS	MASTERS	REMARKS
1825	Bg. *Edwin*	191	S. T. Wheldin	
1826	Sp. *Indiana*	360	Gideon Parker	Six ships in line in Oct., 1826; sailed on 1st
"	*Louisiana*	345	Robert Waterman	and 15th.
"	*Talma*	391	John Rathbone	
"	*Illinois*	413	Robert Waterman	
1828	Sp. *Kentucky*	418	John Rathbone	Lost on Florida Reef, Oct. 29, 1832.
"	*Tennessee*	415	Gilbert Fowler	Three lives lost. E. S. Dennis, master.
1830	Sp. *Alabama*	474	Peter Price	Charles C. Berry master in 1838.
				Wilbor & Hazard, 23 Magazine St., became
				New Orleans agents in 1831.
1832	Sp. *Saratoga*	542	William Hathaway	W. H. Russell master in 1841.
1833	Sp. *Arkansas*	629	Edward S. Dennis	Chester Hilliard master in 1850.
"	*Orleans*	599	Sherburne S. Sears	
"	*Missouri*			
1834	Sp. *Kentucky*	629	John Bunker	
"	*Nashville*	520	John Rathbone	A. A. Wood master in 1839.
				Bogert & Hawthorn became New Orleans
				agents in 1835.
1838	Sp. *Troy*	523	A. A. Wood	William Nelson became New York agent in
				Nov.
"	*Vicksburg*	480	John Bunker	W. C. Berry master in 1850.
				A. Cohen, 90 Common St., became New
				Orleans agent.
1839	Sp. *Panthea*	641	George W. Ashby	John P. Goodmanson master in 1841.
"	*Louisa*	496	Daniel H. Truman	
"	*Oconee*	461	W. S. Lyons	Lost on Stirrup Key, Mar., 1845.
"	*Ocmulgee*	458	Thomas J. Leavitt	
1841	Sp. *Annawan*		Edward S. Dennis	
1842	Sp. *United States*	651	Peter A. Decan	Reported foundered at sea, 1845.
1843	Sp. *Chester*	326	Christopher Van Dyke	
1844	Sp. *Rienzi*	327	Samuel Clark	
"	*Sultana*	664	Edward S. Dennis	Thomas A. Barrett master in 1848.
1845	Sp. *Silas Holmes*	645	Charles C. Berry	Foundered, Dec. 18, 1859. Master and 32
"	*Archelaous*	597	Charles Boutelle	passengers and crew lost.
1846	Sp. *Franconia*	499	J. P. Gannett	
"	*Memphis*	799	David S. Bunker	
"	*Galena*	881	Edward S. Dennis	T. J. Leavitt master in 1853.
1847	Sp. *Ashland*	631	J. D. Rice	
1848	Sp. *Maid of Orleans*	934	Edward S. Dennis	
1850	Sp. *Trumbull*	855	W. D. Smith	
"	*St. Louis*	939	David M. Bunker	
"	*Espindola*	741	George Barstow	
1851	Sp. *Forest Queen*	886	Alney Lovett	William Nelson & Sons became New York
"	*Greenwich*	787	A. C. Childs	agents.
1852	Sp. *Pacific*	531	Sherburne S. Sears	Horatio Nelson master in 1853.
"	*Isaac Allerton*	595	Sherburne S. Sears	
"	*Ravenswood*	666	Nathaniel C. Johnson	
1854	Sp. *Sartelle*	416	J. E. Cobb	Line consisted of ten ships sailing every Mon.
				during season.
1855	Sp. *Andover*	485	William C. Berry	Packets sailed every Wed. during season.
"	*Hampton*	443	C. R. Humphrey	
1856	Sp. *Glad Tidings*	899	Horatio Nelson	
	Bk. *Helicon*	414	C. R. Cole	
"	*Rover*	359	William T. Baker	E. Van Sice master in 1858.
1858	Sp. *Confidence*	649	Sherburne S. Sears	
	Sch. *Cordelia* (tern)	658	Francis Horn	
1859	Sp. *Missouri*	675	Thomas Hughes	
"	*J. P. Wheeler*	855	H. Gadd	
"	*Martha J. Ward*	745	Chase	Also reported 765 tons.
	Bk. *Dirigo*	499	James C. Young	Line continued in 1860 with ten regular
				packet ships. New masters included R. B.
				Benson of the *Sultana*, William Hull of the
				Pacific and C. E. Keeney of the *Andover*.

THIRD LINE

John Laidlaw, 78 South St., New York agent. Established Oct., 1826.

YEAR	VESSEL	TONS	MASTERS	REMARKS
1826	Sp. *Tuscaloosa*	284	Charles K. Lawrence	
	Bg. *Mexico*	273	Edward Killoran	
1827	Sp. *Margaret Scott*	307	Edward Kennard	Line began regular schedule in Oct., sailing
	" *Margaret*	375	Ebenezer McIntosh	12th and 27th of each month during season.
	" *Chelsea*	396	Acors Barnes	There were three regular scheduled lines be-
	" *Lavinia*	310	Allen Miner	tween New York and New Orleans, Holmes,
	" *Mobile*	285	Luke Perkins	Russell, and Third Lines.
	" *Florida*	350	Robert L. Taylor	Robert McCerren master in 1834.
	" *Cassander*	299	Smith	
	" *Georges*	318	Edward Robinson	
	Sch. *William & Henry*	130	Doan	
	Sp. *New Orleans*	336	Stephen E. Cole	
1829	Bk. *Armadillo*	256	John Robinson	
	" *William Smith*	273	Thomas McLellan	Samuel Blanchard master in 1832.
	Sp. *Lotus*	293	S. Watts	
	" *Martha*	360	James D. Snow	
	" *Hanover*	329	Edward Barstow	
	Bg. *Casket*	235	Josiah J. Tracy	
1830	Bg. *Venus*	182	Allen P. Holdredge	Line sailed irregularly. Only Barstow and
	Sp. *America*		Place	Holmes maintained regular packet service.
	" *Alabama*	474	Peter Price	
	" *Liverpool*	306	Thomas Phillips	
	" *Montpelier*	320	John M. Welsh	Var. Welch.
	Bg. *Eagle*		Chew	
	" *Lewis*	247	Shepherd	
1831	Bg. *Billow*		Sampson	Scott & Laidlaw became New York agents
	" *Carroll*	227	Joseph Richards	in Mar.
	Sp. *St. Louis*	354	W. W. Story	Line cleared very few ships in 1832.
	" *Oceana*	368	Henry Leslie	
	" *Florence*	449	Samuel Smith	
1833	Sp. *Newark*	323	Isaac Brewer	Firm began running packets to Natchez and
	Bk. *Silas E. Burrow*	250	E. C. Storm	Vicksburg. P. Laidlaw became New Orleans
	Bg. *Natchez*	228	A. Tyler	agent.
1834	Sp. *Creole*	542	A. S. Page	John Laidlaw became sole New York agent
	" *Robert Bowne*	505	C. Mansfield	in Feb.
1835	Sp. *Orient*	349	Lombard	John Laidlaw & Co. became New York
1837	Sp. *Amelia*	561	Wildes T. Thompson	agents. Firm sent most of its ships to Natchez
				and Vicksburg. Laidlaw, Lane & Co. became
				New York agents in Oct., and in 1838 John-
				son & Lowden took over as New York agents.
	" *Normandie*	500	William Tyson	Missing Dec., 1844.
1838	Bk. *Solomon Saltus*	317	Elbert Latham	Sailings continued, but with no attempt to
	Sp. *St. Mary*	444	Robert W. Foster	maintain a fixed schedule until fall of 1842.
	" *Kensington*	494	E. Curtis	
	" *Auburn*	451	Nathaniel P. Durfey	
	" *Southerner*	671	W. J. Tibbits	
	" *Republican*	521	James R. Russell	
1839	Bk. *Navarino*	249	Edwards	Peter Laidlaw, 86 Camp St., became New
	Sp. *Adirondack*	699	William G. Hackstaff	Orleans agent. Regular line consisted of
	" *Tarolinta*	549	Jeremiah G. Smith	ships *Auburn*, *St. Mary*, and *Republican* with
	" *Junior*	377	John Urquhart	two more building. Called New Line.
	" *Hilah*	395	Edmund Hammond	Foundered, Feb. 19, 1846.
	" *Powhattan*	521	Robert McCerren	
	" *Troy*	523	Wood	J. Follansbee master in 1842.
	" *Sea*	807	Reuben Fisher	
	" *Charlemagne*	442	David Jackson	
	" *Frankfort*	760	Joseph G. Russell	
	" *Fairfield*	685	William L. Lyon	Wrecked, Sept., 1844.
	" *Mary Kingsland*	797	Robert McCerren	
1840	Bk. *Falmouth*	278	John Davis	
	Sp. *Trenton*	429	James S. Bennett	Wrecked, Dec., 1842.
	" *Gov. Troup*	430	Benjamin B. Butman	
1841	Sp. *Isaac Allerton*	594	Thomas Torry	Sherburne Sears master in 1852.

THIRD LINE (*continued*)

YEAR	VESSEL	TONS	MASTERS	REMARKS
1841	Sp. *John Minturn*	399	Dudley Stark	Lost on Barnegat, Feb. 15, 1846, with all hands, including captain's wife and two children, about 45 in all.
1842	Sp. *American*	390	Holden	
	" *Union*	545	Joseph G. Russell	
1843	Sp. *Alfred*	453	L. C. Myers	
	" *Ohio*	737	Hezekiah Lyons	
	Bk. *Wakulla*	267	B. H. Johnston	
	" *Hercules*	382	Dawbien	
	" *Weybosset*	321	George Collins	George M. Peeling master in 1857.
1844	Bk. *Luzon*	300	J. F. Goodrich	Johnson & Lowden also had new S.S. *Republic*, John Crane, master, running to New Orleans.
	" *Clarissa*	224	J. Melcher	
	Bg. *Long Island*	174	Daniel Howell	
	" *Othello*	185	Albert F. Ryan	
	Bk. *Genessee*	337	Thomas S. Minott	
	Sp. *Empire*	1049	Joseph G. Russell	
	" *Persian*	492	Frederick Robbins	
	" *Splendid*		John E. Pettis	
	" *Parthenon*	560	Samuel T. Woodbury	
	" *Kalamazoo*	798	Robert McCerren	
	Bk. *Strafford*	314	William H. Robson	
1845	Bk. *John R. Gardner*	190	James Pedersen	Laidlaw & Ashbridge became New Orleans agents.
	" *Averon*	290	William Jordan	
	" *Epervier*	264	Nathan A. Farwell	
	Sp. *Hargrave*	484	James Bailey	
	" *Edgar*	420	Robert McManus	Vessel lost, Apr. 1846.
	" *Champlain*	624	James F. Miller	Vessel lost, 1850.
	" *Niagara*	459	Stephen E. Cole	
	" *James H. Shepherd*	635	St. Croix Redman	
1846	Sp. *American*		Lamson	
	" *Monongahela*	497	Theodore Julius	
	" *Grecian*	419	Thrane	
	" *Merchant*	389	S. Clark	
	" *Talleyrand*	549	Edmund Webb	
	" *John Holland*	529	William Henderson	
	Sch. *Mankin*	198	Lucas B. Terry	
1847	Bg. *Brothers*	220	Zebulon Mayhew	
	Bk. *Strafford*	314	William H. Robson	
	" *Gazelle*	269	S. Young	
	Sp. *Ianthe*	415	Christianson	Samuel Macoduck also master in 1847.
	" *Severn*	572	Charles Cheever	
	Bk. *Tarquin*	222	Stone	
	" *Gulnare*	273	Edward F. Byrne	
	Sp. *R. D. Shepherd*	794	Daniel Marcy	
	" *Louisiana*	747	H. W. Barstow	
	" *Niobe*	686	Briggs Thomas	
	" *Hargrave*	484	N. H. Duncan	
	" *Cato*	666	B. Oakes	John W. Robinson master in 1850.
	" *America*	1137	Edmund Dunn	
	" *Abby Pratt*	666	G. W. Shaw	
	Bk. *Elizabeth*	273	S. Young	
1848	Bk. *California*	296	R. Robinson	
	" *Henry Harbeck*	398	T. G. Merwin	
	Sp. *Lydia*	543	Henchman S. Soule	Francis B. Soule also master in 1848.
	" *Martha J. Ward*	745	T. Frost	
1849	Bk. *Delia Chapin*	400	B. McNear	Wrecked abroad prior to Mar., 1858.
	Sp. *Peter Marcy*	821	Daniel Marcy	A. Sampson also master in 1849.
	" *Judah Touro*	741	Joseph G. Nickerson	Also reported 716 tons. Daniel Marcy master in 1845.
1850	Sp. *Hindoo*	581	James F. Miller	J. H. Ashbridge & Co., 97 Camp St., became New Orleans agents. Line called Ashbridge's Line.
1851	Sp. *William Sprague*	716	Jesse Chase	
	" *Hemisphere*	1024	William Whittlesey	
	" *Helvetia*	972	S. F. Marsh	
1852	Bk. *Mary Broughton*	321	Pryor	

New York—New Orleans and Natchez

SCOTT & LAIDLAW LINE

Scott & Laidlaw, New York agents. Established July, 1833.

YEAR	VESSEL	TONS	MASTERS	REMARKS
1833	Sp. *St. Louis*	344	W. W. Story	
	" *Newark*	323	Isaac Brewer	Scott dropped out after the sailing of the
	" *Elisha Denison*	359	William B. Lane	*Denison.* J. Laidlaw continued and loaded the
	" *Indiana*	363	D. D. Churchill	*Denison* and *Indiana* in association with E. D.
	" *Florence*	449	Samuel Smith	Hurlbut & Co.
1834	Sp. *Florida*	330	Robert McCerren	J. Laidlaw & Co. became New York agents.
	" *Brooklyn*	450	Edward Richardson	
1836	Sp. *Lotus*	293	J. L. Watts	Line ran to Natchez and Vicksburg.
1839	Sp. *Ambassador*	452	Stacey Hall	

MERCHANTS' LINE

John Elwell, 57 South St., New York agent. Toby & Bogert, New Orleans agents. Established Aug., 1835.

YEAR	VESSEL	TONS	MASTERS	REMARKS
1835	Sp. *Boreas*	348	Winthrop S. Babbidge	Vessels listed represent approximately all
	" *Romulus*	366	J. Webster	sailings of line in early years, aside from repe-
	" *Brunette*	333	W. J. Fales	titions by a few ships, such as *Romulus,*
	" *William & John*	386	J. W. Robinson	*Edwin, Rienzi, Echo, Peruvian, Hilah,* and
	" *Madison*	445	Wood	*Chester.* No fixed schedule during early years.
	Bk. *John Brouwer*	310	Rose	
	" *Clement*	279	Clement Martin	George Jordan master in 1837.
1836	Sp. *Choctaw*	430	Roswell P. Fish	
	" *Hilah*	395	Edmund Hammond	Foundered, Feb. 19, 1846, from New Orleans
	" *Andrew Scott*	318	R. F. C. Hartley	for New York, lat. 32.40—long. 77.30.
	" *Hebrew*	399	John B. Carr	
	" *Rhode Island*	383	Schroeder	B. Andrews master in 1844.
	" *Peruvian*	476	John Spear, Jr.	
	" *Franklin*	421	O. Jordan	
	" *La Grange*	399	Patten	N. T. Thompson master in 1840.
1837	Bg. *Henry Tallman*	156	S. T. Lamont	
	" *Elcy*	180	A. S. Wall	
	" *Choctaw*	245	Cotts	
	" *Margaret Ann*	203	John Tompson	
	Bk. *Cuba*	240	D. Storer	
	Sp. *Edwin*	339	Life Wilson	
	" *Mary Maria*	409	S. Purington	
	" *Caravan*	329	Samuel Nichols	
	" *Mary Howland*	576	Samuel Weare	
	" *Rienzi*	327	Parker P. Norton	
	" *Echo*	668	J. Mallet	
	" *Congress*	401	W. Fox	
	Bg. *Mary Silsby*	191	Howard	David V. Soullard master in 1840. Vessel lost about Oct., 1842.
1838	Bg. *Baltimore*	167	Robt. C. Cheesebrough	
	" *Triumph*	204	McFarlane	James Ludlow master in 1841.
	" *Julia & Helen*	193	Joshua Thorndike	
	" *Patriot*	164	George Young	
	" *Ludwig*	244	Thomas McLellan	
	Bk. *Isaac Ellis*	222	J. H. Spring	
	Sp. *Star*	596	S. E. Glover	
	" *John Holland*	529	O. Jordan	William Henderson master in 1841–7.
	" *John Marshall*	449	John Curtis	Lost at sea early in 1840.
	" *Europe*	557	William Drummond	
	" *Chester*	326	Christian Van Dyke	
	" *Renown*	296	Sparrow Snow	
	Sch. *Reporter*	153	William Carney	
1839	Sp. *Oronoco*	656	R. Rogers	
	Bg. *Voltaire*	144	Jesse Sleeper	Henry Spalding master in 1840.
	" *Commaquid*	196	Snow Y. Sears	Caleb Sprague master in 1842.
	Sp. *Emporium*	309	Jotham Parsons	Henry W. Young, Jr., master in 1841.
	Bk. *Levant*	147	D. Herrick	
	Sp. *George Cabot*		Blackler	

MERCHANTS' LINE (*continued*)

YEAR	VESSEL	TONS	MASTERS	REMARKS
1839	Bg. *Northerner*	233	J. Stevens	William B. Hatch master in 1843.
	Bk. *Duc d'Orleans*	310	W. R. Hoodless	
	Sp. *Equator*	456	Jonathan Bisson	
	" *Ville de Paris*	537	Mitchell L. Trott	G. B. Sturges master in 1844. Vessel lost,
	" *Moslem*	450	John H. McLarren	1846.
	" *North America*	499	John O. Baker	
	Bk. *Sarah*	287	Bailey Foster	
1840	Bg. *Lime Rock*	174	A. Butler	Orris Fales master in 1842.
	" *Virginia*	188	Ephraim Jordan	
	" *Charles Hammond*	161	William C. Talbot	
	" *Confidence*	195	Cozens	Samuel C. Bailey master in 1840–5.
	Sp. *Emily*	298	Miles H. Mead	John R. Crane master in 1843.
	Bg. *Francis Ashby*	125	Charles L. Randall	
	Sp. *Isaac Hicks*	495	John E. Pettis	
	" *France*	441	John H. Marshall	
	" *St. Lawrence*	462	Jesse Chase	Register surrendered Mar. 18, 1850. Vessel lost.
	" *Queen Victoria*	712	Wildes D. Thompson	R. Collum master in 1854.
	" *Constellation*	276	Franklin Houdlette	
	" *Kutusoff*	415	Taylor	William H. Cox master in 1841.
	" *Globe*	479	W. C. Lowry	
1841	Bg. *Julia & Helen*	193	Joshua Bartlett	
	Sp. *Troy*	523	Alonzo Follansbee	Enoch Burnham master in 1845.
	" *Clifton*	599	James G. Ingersoll	
	Bk. *Lillius*	199	G. Gilchrist	
	Bg. *John H. Stephens*	186	William B. Hatch	
	" *Emily*	181	R. Hallowell	
	Sp. *Talbot*	629	John Storey	Vessel condemned, Aug., 1855.
	" *Lyons*	437	James Connor	
	" *Kalamazoo*	798	Robert McCerren	
	" *Hudson*	623	Pitkin Page	Joseph G. White master in 1853.
	" *North Carolina*	669	James Drummond	
	Bg. *Growler*	247	Barnard Ulmer	
	" *Lucy Ann*	240	Israel Snow	
	Bk. *Henry Newell*	257	Matthew Martin	Vessel lost, May, 1846.
1842	Bk. *Lucy Penniman*	270	Josiah P. Keller	J. Elwell & Co. became New York agents in
	" *Suwarrow*	292	Elias P. Sleeper	Aug.
	" *Mazeppa*	234	Kimball R. Smith	
	Bg. *Oneco*	197	A. Butler	Var. *Oneko*.
	" *Circassian*	161	J. O. Sprague	
	" *Vandalia*	197	A. S. Wall	
	" *Eliza*	199	M. Kinney	Var. Kenney.
	" *Laura*	198	William Dunham	
	" *Loretto*	244	James Henderson	
	Sp. *Jane Ross*	407	S. Merrill	
	" *Brunswick*	604	Robert McManus	
	" *Rajah*	531	Elkanah Bangs	
	" *Diadem*	657	Edwin W. Barstow	
	" *Metoka*	775	John H. McLaren	Var. McLellan.
	" *James Edward*	434	J. Webster	
	" *Mary Frances*		Albert A. Farnham	Edmund Crosby master in 1847.
1843	Bg. *Puritan*	229	Henry H. Ulmer	
	" *Carib*	149	R. Porterfield	
	Bk. *Nancy W. Stevens*	346	Waldo Stevens	
	Sp. *Spring*	283	Hamilton	
	Bk. *Albert Henry*	197	Andrew Barstow	
	" *Princeton*	296	Silas A. Houghton	J. W. Jewett master in 1853.
	Bg. *William*	128	George Bacon	
	Sp. *St. Louis*	344	James Marks	
	Bg. *Germ*	170	Joseph Lincoln	
	Bk. *Ionia*	186	James P. Wheeler	
	Bg. *Monaco*	199	Charles H. Wording	Var. Warding.
	" *Algonquin*	193	Andrew Williams	
	Bk. *Washington*	286	Dennis Pillsbury	
	" *Irad Ferry*	299	Stephen Chase	

MERCHANTS' LINE (*continued*)

YEAR	VESSEL	TONS	MASTERS	REMARKS
1843	Bg. *Peconic*	239	William Park	
	Sch. *Penjajawock*		Darling	
	Sp. *Damascus*	694	Tanner	
	" *Caspian*	529	O. Patten	
	" *Francis Depau*	600	Charles Sagory	
	" *Liverpool*	623	George Agry	
	" *Sharon*	554	N. T. Thompson	
	" *Berwick*	472	Samuel Harding, Jr.	
1844	Bk. *Strafford*	314	William H. Robson	
	Bg. *Washington*	260	Waldo Stevens	
	Bk. *Rammohun Roy*	359	William Cutts	
	" *Clarissa Perkins*	240	John H. Perkins	
	" *Mandarin*	275	James Colby	
	" *Henry Kelsey*	197	J. A. Gray	
	Bg. *St. George*	222	Robert Long	
	Sp. *South Carolina*	768	Moses Owen	
	" *Sabattis*	447	Smith C. Cox	
	" *Trenton*	429	Jesse B. Cotting	
	" *Martha*	534	Samuel Snow	
	Sch. *John Kendall*	169	D. Robinson	W. H. Dean master in 1852.
	Bg. *Oceana*	249	James A. Creighton	
	" *J. Peterson*	180	J. Best	
1845	Bg. *Virginia*	138	E. O. Cooper	
	Sch. *Oregon*	91	N. Wines	Var. Vines.
	Bk. *James Bayley*	207	George Bishop	
	Bg. *Helen McLeod*	268	David C. Landes	Var. Landis
	Sp. *William Engs*	310	Thomas L. Boss	
	Bk. *New England*	357	William Long	
	Bg. *Delia*	166	Fales	
	Sp. *Rockall*	644	Richard Evans	Thomas G. Hiler master in 1848.
	" *Genessee*	459	L. L. Watts	
	" *Monmouth*	728	D. S. Ryan	
	" *Glasgow*	594	G. F. Manson	
	Bg. *Sabine*	176	Bentley	
	Bk. *Iris*	329	John Merryman	
	Bk. *Baltic*	302	Henry H. Ulmer	W. L. Outerbridge master in 1850. Abandoned at sea, 1852.
	Bg. *Massachusetts*	164	R. Collins	
	Sp. *John P. Harward*	548	Washington Read	
	" *Hamburg*	289	William P. Larrabee	
	Bk. *Alabama*	280	G. T. Sprague	
	" *Claremont*	248	Moses Trussell	
1846	Sp. *Cherokee*		Cushing	
	" *Jessore*	437	D. Jackson	
	Bk. *Dana*	299	Oliver Smith	
	Bg. *Joseph*	178	Joshua A. Kellar	
	" *Ormus*	175	Eben R. Smith	Richard Smith also master in 1846.
	" *Jefferson*	197	B. Morgan	
	Bk. *Marcia*	342	Otis Harward	
	Sp. *Meteor*	494	E. Lawrence	
	" *Lyons*	437	John G. Franks	
	" *Devonshire*	778	M. T. Thompson	
	Bg. *Olivia*	176	Thomas McIntyre	
	" *Albertina*	204	J. Montgomery	
	" *James Marshall*	165	W. Carney	
	" *Velasco*	149	T. H. Bell	Var. Bill.
	Bk. *Bachelor*	277	Hiram Horton	
	Sp. *Queen Victoria*	712	Charles E. Ranlett	
	" *Leonidas*	690	Edwin S. Counce	
	Bg. *Long Island*	174	R. M. Thorp	
	" *Rowland*	230	A. Watts	
	" *Mary A. Jones*	191	A. Jones	William N. Wilkins master in 1846–7.
	Bk. *Empire*	284	David Keazer	
	Bg. *Puritan*	229	Armstrong	
	Bk. *John Stroud*	269	George W. Brown	

MERCHANTS' LINE (*continued*)

YEAR	VESSEL	TONS	MASTERS	REMARKS
1846	Sch. *Joseph Farwell*	98	S. V. Ames	
	Sp. *Granada*	594	Nathaniel Spooner	
	Bk. *Alvarado*	299	J. Ames	
1847	Bk. *Nautilus*	283	M. Martin	
	Bg. *Eolus*	148	Gerrish	
	Bk. *Louisa*	267	L. Lake	
	Bg. *Lightfoot*	149	Jeremiah Sleeper	
	" *Grecian*	230	C. Ryder	
	Bk. *James Smith*	236	C. Ballard	
	Sp. *Nicholas Biddle*	784	S. C. Knight	
	" *Arkansas*	627	Chester Hilliard	
	Bk. *Magdala*	298	J. Smith	A. R. Dodge master in 1849.
	Sp. *Franconia*	499	Eleazer Crabtree	
	Bk. *Lowell*	348	John A. Bradstreet	
	Sp. *Solon*	540	George Bucknam	
	" *Woodside*	634	Lewis Higgins	
	" *Emma Watts*	450	E. P. Watts	
	" *Elizabeth Ellen*	581	C. Tyler	D. H. Truman master in 1849.
	" *James Edward*	433	J. Webster	
	Bg. *Captain Tom*	225	William W. Smalley	
	Sp. *Christiana*	666	Edmund Hammond	
	" *Elisha Denison*	359	Thomas W. Sealy	
1848	Sp. *Columbiana*	631	T. J. Mallett	J. W. Elwell became sole New York agent
	Bk. *Claremont*	248	Edward Lermond	in May.
	Bg. *Susan Soule*	164	George Bacon	
	Bk. *Catherine*	316	J. Watts	
	" *Sarah Hand*	282	S. H. Whitney	
	" *Murillo*	309	Thomas S. Minott	
	Sp. *Forest King*	992	W. T. Thompson	
	" *Hindoo*	581	Brown	J. F. Miller master in 1850.
	Bk. *Pilah*	375	Edmond Burton	Var. Buxton.
	Sp. *Caledonia Brander*	549	Coulter	
	Bg. *Azores*	274	O. Amsbury	
1849	Bk. *Mandarin*	275	James Colby	
	" *Sarah Bridge*	483	J. Stout	Var. Strout.
	Bg. *Fornax*	249	J. Wilson	
	Sp. *Walter R. Jones*	400	J. Colley	Elliot Honeywell master in 1852.
	Bk. *Robert Walsh*	282	William Singer	
	Sp. *Realm*	548	J. J. Stevens	
	" *Florence*	298	Woodward	
	Bk. *Brilliant*	349	Peter Muller	
	" *N. D. Chase*	241	C. Dexter White	
	Sp. *Gondola*	409	R. Hutchinson	
	" *Camillus*	716	William Sylvester	
	Bg. *Marshall Ney*	250	A. Lillia	
	Bk. *Desdemona*	298	Samuel G. Stinson	
	Sp. *Lehigh*	565	Stewart	
	" *Rockaway*	815	R. Bosworth	Mark H. Lufkin master in 1856.
	" *Caroline Reid*	660	Washington Read	Var. *Read*.
	" *Edgar*	420	George H. Spall	Register surrendered Apr., 1846. Vessel lost.
	" *Affghan*	362	D. C. Copeland	
	" *Katahdin*	548	J. P. Morse	
	" *Margaret*	447	Joseph Webster	J. C. Merriman master in 1854.
	" *Champlain*	624	Robert R. Decan	
	Bk. *Roxana*	299	Sanders Curling	
1850	Bk. *Indiana*	608	William H. Watts	
	" *Miltiades*	447	E. A. Robinson	
	" *J. W. Dyer*	243	J. W. Dyer	
	Bg. *Emeline*	236	E. Watts	J. Packard master in 1854.
	Sch. *John Castner*	247	John Somers	
	Bg. *Machigonne*	185	W. N. Chamberlain	
	Sp. *Erie*	476	F. B. Lewis	
	Bk. *Patrick Henry*	442	William Hewes	
	" *Frances*		Ellis	
	Sp. *Talleyrand*	549	Williams	G. Young master in 1852.

MERCHANTS' LINE (*continued*)

YEAR		VESSEL	TONS	MASTERS	REMARKS
1850	Sp.	*Caroline C. Dow*	515	J. B. Blanchard	
	"	*John Hancock*	760	Caleb Levanseller	
	"	*Buena Vista*	661	George F. Mustard	
	Bk.	*Yankee Blade*	454	John A. Bradstreet	
1851	Bg.	*Denmark*	219	L. Kerrey	
	Sp.	*Hendrick Hudson*	823	S. C. Warner	
	"	*Manilla*	539	Horace A. Gray	S. V. Given, II, master in 1853.
	"	*Sharon*	554	R. Merryman	Var. Merriman.
	"	*Leodes*	445	Nathaniel B. Robbins	
	"	*Vandalia*	757	E. C. Smith	
	"	*Vaucluse*	699	Raymond J. Gilchrist	William Kearney master in 1857.
	"	*Charles Crooker*	960	C. C. Duncan	J. A. Morehead master in 1854.
	Bk.	*Clyde*	398	G. H. Kempton	
1852	Bg.	*Pulaski*	249	J. Morris	J. W. Elwell & Co. became New York agents
	Sp.	*Oxnard*	518	T. S. Minott	in Mar.
	"	*Humphrey Purington*	637	R. Given	
	Bk.	*A. H. Kimball*	285	Jeremiah Sleeper	
	"	*Mary Annah*	488	Billings	
	Sp.	*John Haven*	1038	M. D. Ricker	
	"	*Sea Nymph*	732	R. Patten	Adandoned at sea, Mar. 14, 1854.
	Bk.	*Theoxana*	398	John Borland	
	"	*George Henry*	308	J. L. Pendleton	
1853	Bg.	*G. W. Lawrence*	249	A. S. Wall	
	Bk.	*Byron*	291	W. A. Arthur	
	Bg.	*Versailles*	199	Conant	
	Sp.	*Elsinore*	597	Hodgdon	
	Bk.	*Warren*	271	Charles T. Haskell	
	"	*Loretto Fish*	247	Miles T. Gates	
	"	*Delia Chapin*	399	L. Howard	Wrecked abroad, Feb., 1858.
	"	*Kennebec*	297	J. P. Smith	
	"	*Gov. Briggs*	198	J. H. Hallett	
	"	*H. S. Bradley*	400	Benjamin W. Conant	
	"	*William Chase*	246	J. Downe	
	Sp.	*Marathon*	486	Christopher Van Dyke	
	"	*Louisiana*	747	Nathaniel Barstow	
1854	Bk.	*Undine*	532	R. Merryman	
	Bg.	*S. J. Peters*	171	M. Smith	
	Sp.	*Chimborazo*	937	Peter Vesper	R. G. Morse master in 1858.
	Bk.	*E. Sherwood*	540	Samuel B. Hall	
	Sp.	*Milwaukee*	736	H. S. Soule	
	"	*Shanghai*	649	H. A. Gray	
1855	Sp.	*Kate Swanton*	489	Reed	
	"	*Milton*	598	R. Mitchell	

TAYLOR & MERRILL LINE

Robert L. Taylor and Nathaniel W. Merrill doing business as Taylor & Merrill, 77 South St., New York agents. Established July, 1836.

YEAR		VESSEL	TONS	MASTERS	REMARKS
1836	Sp.	*Mary & Harriet*	396	H. J. Tibbits	
	"	*Crescent*	341	Nesbitt	D. B. Hammond master later in year.
	"	*Montgomery*	399	Grue	
	"	*Rockingham*	513	William L. Dwight	
	"	*Star*	686	Samuel E. Glover	Lost in 1837.
	"	*Echo*	668	John Mallett	
1837	Bk.	*Helen Mar*	269	Cook	Burned, Nov. 16, 1843, off Double Headed Shot Keys.
	Sp.	*Niagara*	458	Jacob Pike	
	"	*Sylvanus Jenkins*	547	George Barker	Var. *Silvanus Jenkins*.
	"	*Clarissa Andrews*	397	Samuel Crowell	Line sailed irregularly during 1837 and was
	"	*Star*	596	Samuel E. Glover	discontinued at end of year. Revived again in 1842; continued to 1846 but sailed very irregularly.

ORLEANS LINE

Scott & Morell, 72 South St., New York agents. Stetson & Avery, 88 Gravier St., New Orleans agents. Established Nov., 1837.

YEAR	VESSEL	TONS	MASTERS	REMARKS
1837	Sp. *Franconia*	499	E. Blake	Eleazer Crabtree master in 1839.
"	*Ocmulgee*	458	Thomas J. Leavitt	
1838	Sp. *Angelique*	420	E. G. Furber	
"	*Oconee*	461	W. S. Lyon	Ebenezer Knight master in 1839.
1839	Sp. *Warsaw*	332	William P. Mendell	Regular line in 1839 consisted of ships *Francis*
"	*Louisa*	496	Daniel S. Truman	*Depau, Louisa, Memphis, Oconee, Ocmulgee,* and
"	*Gaston*	456	William Whittlesey	*Franconia.*
"	*Francis Depau*	596	C. A. Forbes	
"	*Star*	596	Samuel E. Glover	
"	*Memphis*	799	Samuel Nichols	
1840	Sp. *Mary Kingsland*	796	Daniel Weare	Line cleared very few ships in 1841 and
	Bk. *Mazeppa*	234	Leonard Mallory	ceased operations at end of year.

STURGES & CLEARMAN LINE

Sturges & Clearman, 92 Wall St., New York agents. Established June, 1838.

YEAR	VESSEL	TONS	MASTERS	REMARKS
1838	Bg. *Georgia*	197	William H. Nichols	
"	*Rudolph Groning*	190	D. Landon	Vessel lost, Dec., 1847.
1841	Bg. *Mobile*	328	John A. Risley	Line operated very irregularly. No sailings in
"	*Savannah*	396	Thomas B. Shapter	1839 or 1840, and discontinued after spring of 1841.

COMMERCIAL LINE

Dunham & Dimon, 61 South St. and Nesmith & Leeds, New York agents. Fosdick & Bro., 57 Camp St., New Orleans agents. Established July, 1840.

YEAR	VESSEL	TONS	MASTERS	REMARKS
1840	Sp. *Newark*	323	David G. Soullard	
	Bg. *Georgia*	197	Diconson Lewis	
	Sp. *Britannia*	630	Enoch Cook	Lost at sea, summer of 1842.
	" *Charlemagne*	442	David Jackson	
	" *Levant*	382	S. W. Whittlesey	
1841	Bg. *Monroe*	199	Samuel Watts	
	Sp. *James Edward*	434	William Howard	
	" *Southport*	500	Thomas R. Herbest	
	Bg. *Monsoon*			
	" *Ludwig*	244	Edward Lermond	
	" *Powhattan*	237	Jeremiah Martin	
	Bk. *Eliza Thornton*	449	Acton P. Patterson	
	Sp. *Isaac Allerton*	594	Thomas Torry	Var. Torrey. Sherburne Sears master in 1852.
	" *Liverpool*	623	S. Davenport	
	" *Birmingham*	507	William J. Robinson	Lost, Bahamas, Nov. 16, 1843. Three lost.
	Bk. *Apthorp*	246	Philip Blake	Nesmith & Leeds dropped out early in year.
1842	Sp. *Alfred*	453	L. C. Meyers	J. Slater master in 1850.
	" *Mariposa*	317	Arthur W. Benson	Benjamin Haile master early in 1842.
	Bk. *Reform*	322	Vincent Tilyou	Joseph Livermore master in 1849.
	Sp. *Bowditch*	578	Samuel Crowell	
	Bk. *Iris*	330	John Merryman	
	Sch. *Merchant*			
1843	Bg. *Agnes*	206		
	" *Lime Rock*	174	Edward Auld	
	Bk. *Kilby*	477	Nathaniel Barstow	
	Sp. *Denmark*	512	George W. Frost	George Barton master in 1847.
	" *Niagara*	459	Stephen E. Cole	Foundered, Oct. 25, 1854, from New Orleans for Venice.
	" *Viola*	495	William Jamieson	
	" *Nicholas Biddle*	784	D. Henry Truman	
	" *Russell Glover*	795	Jabez Howes, Jr.	Wrecked early in 1852.
	" *Manchester*	570	Robert Bosworth	
	Bg. *Peconic*	239	Robert M. Wilbur	

COMMERCIAL LINE (*continued*)

YEAR	VESSEL	TONS	MASTERS	REMARKS
1844	Bg. *Peter Demill*	294	Christopher Lewis	Nicholas Hoey master in 1848.
	Bk. *Claremont*	248	Moses Trussell	
	Sp. *Queen Victoria*	712	Charles E. Ranlett	R. D. Brune master in 1847.
	" *Celia*	339	Charles Thatcher	
	" *Duncan*	278	Philander Daggett	
	Bk. *Strafford*	314	William H. Robson	J. Hammond also master in 1844.
	Sp. *Severn*	573	Charles Cheever	
	" *Arragon*	741	Daniel Knight	
	" *Jessore*	437	George W. Putnam	D. Jackson master in 1845.
1845	Bg. *Erato*	196	D. B. Swan	
	Sp. *American*	605	M. Hale	
	" *Rhode Island*	383	Joseph L. Gardner	
	" *Monticello*	392	T. D. Lambert	Vessel lost prior to Sept. 22, 1847.
	Bk. *John Brouwer*	310	David S. Sutton	
	" *Mersey*	372	J. T. Tucker	
	" *Loretto Fish*	247	John Bickmore	
	" *La Grange*	259	Daniel L. Porter	
	" *Tecumseh*	391	Hezekiah Ripley	Nathan Richmond master in 1849.
	Bg. *Martha Sanger*	188	W. H. Duncan	
	" *Josephus*	142	R. Gray	
	Sp. *Robert Parker*	599	J. D. Parsons	J. P. Trefethen master in 1852.
1846	Sp. *Panama*	508	E. Young	
	" *Birmingham*	507		
	" *Warsaw*	342	J. P. Schander	Condemned abroad, Nov., 1846.
	" *Chaos*	771	J. L. Wilson	
	Bk. *Weybosset*	322	C. Harris	
	" *Henry Harbeck*	398	T. G. Merwin	
1847	Sp. *Avalanche*	396	S. W. Whittlesey	Otis T. Baker master in 1851. George W. Pool master in 1854.
	" *Franconia*	499	Eleazer Crabtree	
	" *Alfred*	453	Pendleton	
	" *Margaret*	375	Robert R. Carr	
	" *Hargrave*	484	W. H. Duncan	Line discontinued at end of 1847.
	Bg. *Brothers*	217	T. N. Mayhew	

REGULAR or STAR LINE

Glover & McMurray, 100 Pine St., New York agents. Established 1840. No regular schedule. The firm acted primarily as passenger agents, but were principal owners of several of the vessels listed.

YEAR	VESSEL	TONS	MASTERS	REMARKS
1840	Sp. *Star*	596	John Mallett	
	" *Russell Glover*	795	Jabez Howes	Wrecked, 1852.
	" *Echo*	668	William Russell	Richard Sill master in 1841–2.
1841	Sp. *Trenton*	429	James S. Bennett	
	" *Elizabeth Denison*	645	Russell H. Post	
	" *Solon*	540	George Buckman	
	" *Windsor Castle*	621	George S. Glover	
	" *John G. Coster*	714	Tyler Parsons	

UNION LINE

Stanton & Frost, 134 Front St., New York agents. J. W. Stanton & Co., New Orleans agents. Established latter part of 1842. Known as Louisiana & New York Line in New Orleans.

YEAR	VESSEL	TONS	MASTERS	REMARKS
1842	Sp. *Union*	545	John B. Rathbone	Lost Gingerbread Shoals, Feb. 2, 1860.
1843	Sp. *Auburn*	451	Nathaniel P. Durfey	George C. Gardner master in 1844
	" *Emily*	298	John R. Crane	
	" *St. Mary*	444	Robert W. Foster	
	" *John Minturn*	399	Dudley Stark	
	" *Hilah*	395	Edmund Hammond	Foundered, Feb. 19, 1846.
	" *James Edward*	433	J. Webster	
	" *Cincinnati*	457	Samuel Rose	William Hathaway master in 1844.
	" *Wabash*	442	Charles T. Stanton	Lost, Barnegat, Sept. 1850.
	Bk. *Teazer*	249	Jonathan Crockett, Jr.	

UNION LINE (*continued*)

YEAR	VESSEL	TONS	MASTERS	REMARKS
1844	Sp. *Pacific*	551	J. Hall	Line was active with sailings every ten days
	" *Indiana*	607	James S. Bennett	during season.
	" *London*	637	John O. Baker	
	" *Corea*	366	George C. Gardner	
1845	Bk. *Z. Ring*	324	Elbert Latham	
	" *Albers*	359	A. Marwick	
	Sp. *Metoka*	775	J. H. McLaren	
	" *Thetis*	399	Peter Hanna	
	" *Clifton*	599	James G. Ingersoll	
1846	Sp. *Uncas*	423	Paul W. Latham	
	" *Charlemagne*	442	Henry Packard	
	" *Alabama*	697	George Wise	
	" *Edgar*	420	Thomas B. Shapter	
	" *New Hampshire*	593	C. H. Chase	
	" *Atlantic*	736	Samuel Rose	
	" *Palestine*	470	Oliver R. Mumford	B. H. Johnson master in 1847.
1847	Sp. *Marianna*	379	John W. Phillips	Stanton & Frost dissolved in Sept., 1847.
	Bk. *Newburyport*	341	Noyes	Thomas P. Stanton continued as Stanton's
	Sp. *Creole*	769	John B. Rathbone	Line during next year with J. W. Stanton &
	" *Southerner*	671	Alexander S. Palmer	Co. as New Orleans agents. William T.
	" *Charleston*	373	George S. Brewster	Frost formed firm of Frost & Hicks and con-
	" *Thomas Wright*	623	W. P. Gardner	tinued as Union Line (*q.v.*). Stanton's Line
	" *Quebec*	649	George S. Brewster	consisted of nine ships sailing every ten days.
	" *Robert Parker*	599	T. M. Weeks	
	" *Fairfield*	588	Samuel Loveland	
	" *E. Z.*	693	R. T. Hartshorne	
	" *John G. Coster*	714	Nathaniel P. Durfey	
	" *St. Charles*	798	Charles Sagory	
1848	Sp. *Hero*	750	E. K. Griffith	Thomas P. Stanton, 61 South St., was closely
	" *Manchester*	570	Smith	associated with Frost & Hicks as the Union
	" *Ashland*	631	J. D. Rice	Line but continued to clear separate ships.
	" *Oswego*	647	James G. Ingersoll	Accordingly, for clarity the activities of the
				two firms will continue to be listed as two
				separate Union Lines. See page 516.
1849	Bk. *Mary Smith*	324	Blanchard	Vessel lost, June, 1855.
	Sp. *Christiana*	666	Edmund Hammond	
	" *Toronto*	631	Gideon Parker	
	" *Richard Alsop*	836	Jeremiah G. Smith	B. Watlington master in 1857.
	" *Indian Queen*	411	Robert R. Drummond	
	" *Hudson*	633	J. G. White	
	" *Matilda*	690	Emerson	
	" *Mediator*	660	T. V. Bliffins	W. R. Bell master in 1855.
1851	Sp. *Minnesota*	799	William M. Allen	
	" *Antarctic*	1115	M. P. Ricker	
	" *William B. Travis*	569	John Bolles	
	" *William Rathbone*	917	Joseph W. Spencer	
	" *Princeton*	1131	William H. Russell	
1852	Bk. *Reindeer*	496	E. Lawrence	In Apr., 1852, Stanton began running steam-
	Sp. *Beatrice*	777	George L. Rogers	ers *William Penn* and *Benjamin Franklin* be-
	" *Ohio*	738	Conklin	tween New York and New Orleans, and con-
	" *Oxnard*	595	G. R. Minot	tinued through summer.
	" *John W. White*	549	B. McNear	
	" *Megunticook*	473	J. C. Fairbank	
1853	Sp. *Trumbull*	855	Jeremiah G. Smith	Frost & Hicks dissolved and William T.
	" *Mary Glover*	593	Josiah Chase	Frost, 68 South St., continued association
	" *Espindola*	741	G. Barstow	with Thomas P. Stanton. Stanton sent
	" *Cynthia*	375	J. C. Bartlett	steamer *Star of the South* to New Orleans twice
	" *Caroline C. Dow*	515	J. B. Blanchard	during summer and continued with several
	" *John H. Jarvis*	740	H. S. Rich	trips in 1854–5. Sailing service irregular in
	" *Mary E. Whittier*	495	Jones	1853.
1854	Sp. *Robert Carnley*	921	Nathaniel P. Durfey	
	" *Tempest*	862	L. Patten	
	" *Jersey*	849	John Day	
	" *Garrick*	895	R. W. Foster	
	" *Sheridan*	895	S. Clark	

UNION LINE (*continued*)

YEAR	VESSEL	TONS	MASTERS	REMARKS
1854	Sp. *Siddons*	895	J. S. Taylor	
1855	Sp. *Far West*	598	J. S. Bennett	George Page master in 1860.
"	*Diadem*	657	Noah Webber	Foundered, Aug., 1856.
				No sailings in 1856.
1857	Sp. *Annawan*	759	R. McNair	Packets sailed every ten days in 1857.
1858	Sp. *Silas Greenman*	733	Noah Webber	
"	*Augustus*	736	J. V. Kearney	
"	*New Orleans*	924	John L. Rich	
1860	Sch. *James Miller* (tern)	471	John W. Miner	

HURLBUT LINE or EXPRESS LINE

E. D. Hurlbut & Co., 84 South St., New York agents. William Proctor Scott, 62 Camp St., New Orleans agent.

YEAR	VESSEL	TONS	MASTERS	REMARKS
1843	Sp. *Emblem*	610	Lemuel Dyer	Hurlbut sailed irregularly from 1827, but ob-
"	*Tuskina*	421	F. W. Spencer	served no schedule until 1849.
"	*Commerce*	440	S. F. Ashton	
1844	Sp. *Bertrand*	397	A. M. Smith	
"	*Uncas*	423	J. Stewart	Paul W. Latham master in 1847.
"	*Lorena*	527	John Urquhart	
"	*Edwina*	538	George West	
1845	Sp. *Floridian*	400	William Pratt	
	Bk. *Rose Standish*	427	L. M. Spencer	Joseph W. Spencer master in 1849.
1846	Bg. *Ann Eliza*	144	John E. Williams	
"	*Peconic*	239	William Park	
1847	Sp. *Cotton Planter*	501	J. Pratt	
	Bg. *Metamora*	196	Jared Bunce	
1849	Bk. *Byron*	231	L. P. Upshur	
"	*May Flower*	515	S. Hurlbut	
	Sp. *Atlantic*	699	Joseph I. Lawrence	
"	*Elisha Denison*	359	W. L. Carpenter	
"	*Peter Hattrick*	554	J. E. Rockwell	
1850	Sp. *Carnatic*	602	J. Devereux	Regular line consisted of ships *Peter Hattrick*,
"	*Avalanche*	396	N. F. Hawkins	*Carnatic* and barks *Rose Standish*, *May Flower*,
"	*Rockaway*	815	Robert Bosworth	and *Jane E. Williams* "despatched every
"	*Caroline C. Dow*	515	J. B. Blanchard	other week or as often as business may de-
	Bk. *Jeddo*	242	Stetson	mand." Passage $40.
1851	Sp. *Excelsior*	1000	C. R. Crocker	Var. C. K. Crocker.
"	*Marathon*	486	C. Van Dyck	
"	*Elizabeth Denison*	644	W. L. Carpenter	
"	*Seine*	785	E. C. Williams	
"	*Edwina*	538	H. B. Parmalee	J. C. Broughton master later in year.
1852	Sp. *Isaac Bell*	1072	John Johnson	
	Bk. *Pilgrim*	379	J. M. Sawyer	
1853	Bk. *M. E. Trout*	253	E. Collamore	
	Sch. *Lewis*	195	Gorham Crowell	
"	*S. J. Moye*	320	Bethuel E. Hallock	
	Bk. *Charlotte Wynns*	339	Jesse F. Hosmer	
	Sp. *Unicorn*	397	George Pollard	
1854	Sp. *Catherine*	611	J. Edwards	In Aug., New York agents became Hurlbut
"	*White Falcon*	1372	D. F. Ryan	& Co. and Post, Ryerson & Co.
"	*Susan Hicks*	783	F. P. Claussen	
1855	Sp. *St. Bernard*	711	U. W. Mather	Laytin, Ryerson & Hurlbut became New
"	*Calcutta*	464	L. B. Wyman	York agents.
"	*Nicholas Biddle*	783	Garish	Var. Gerrish. William Evers master in 1858.
	Sch. *Mobile*	398	Joshua C. Couillard	
"	*Mary D. Lane*	380	Benjamin A. Gardner	
"	*Indianola*	522	Joseph McMurray	
"	*Fanny*	363	Marshall	B. Hull master in same year.
1856	Sch. *William C. Mershon*	390	William C. Mershon	Laytin & Hurlbut became New York agents
"	*Smithsonian*	390	Lewis S. Davis	in Feb., 1856.
	Bk. *Jane E. Williams*	397	John Urquhart	
	Sp. *Ambassador*	452	Olsen	
1857	Bk. *Lexington*	395	Charles Thatcher	

HURLBUT LINE OR EXPRESS LINE (*continued*)

YEAR	VESSEL	TONS	MASTERS	REMARKS
1857	Sp. *Sea Belle*	785	J. Lamphier	Var. Lamphear.
"	*Junius*	562	David M. Erskine	Line discontinued at end of year.

NEW LINE

I. B. Gager, 120 Wall St., New York agent. Andrews & Dewey, 91 Common St., New Orleans agents. Established Sept., 1844.

YEAR	VESSEL	TONS	MASTERS	REMARKS
1844	Sp. *Atalanta*	391	George B. Raymond	
"	*Portsmouth*	520	Charles G. Glover	
"	*May Flower*	507	Lemuel Weeks	
1845	Bk. *Epervier*	264	Nathan A. Farwell	Gager & Mailler became New York agents
	Bg. *Pensacola*	226	David Hallett	in Apr.
	Sp. *Hudson*	335	Samuel Bucknam, Jr.	
	Bk. *Tarquin*	222	William P. Paxton	
	Sp. *Jane Ross*	407	Eleazer Crabtree	
	" *Rose*	505	W. H. Harris	
	" *Cabot*	338	Burgess	
	" *Clyde*	398	Francis R. Theobald	Jacob G. Homer master in 1848.
	" *Robert Parker*	599	J. D. Parsons	
	" *London*	637	John O. Baker	
	" *Hindoo*	581	Joseph I. Lawrence	
	" *Warsaw*	342	J. H. Schander	
	Bk. *Tennessee*	224	N. Winslow	
	Bg. *Clarendon*	183	Chandler Clapp	
1846	Bk. *Lillius*	199	Alden Gilchrist	In Sept., I. B. Gager & Co. became New
	Bg. *Aldebaren*	156	William S. Leech	York agents and Mailler withdrew to form
	Bk. *Curtis*	250	C. D. Poole	firm of W. & C. Mailler, later Mailler &
	Sp. *Ohio*	738	Hezekiah Lyon	Lord.
	" *John Cumming*	721	William L. Dwight	
	Bg. *Newcastle*	226	Donnell	
	Bk. *Kilby*	477	John Carter	
	Bg. *Osceola*		Bacon	
	Sp. *Mary Pleasants*	680	John Wotten	Var. Wooten.
	Bk. *Magdala*	298	A. R. Dodge	
	" *Harriet T. Bartlett*	197	Elisha Baker	
	" *Louisa*	316	J. Galt	
	" *Gazelle*		Young	
	Sp. *Bowditch*	578	W. F. Pike	
	" *Adeline*	459	W. F. Pike	
	Bk. *Mary Broughton*	321		
	Sp. *Ann*	334	James M. Hill	
	" *France*	441	Pierce	John H. Marshall master in 1850.
	" *Vistula*	366	Gustavus Schneidau	David B. Moore master in 1848.
	Bk. *Pario*	300	Matthew Kinney	
	" *Mandarin*	275	James Colby	
	" *Tecumseh*	399	Hezekiah Ripley	
	" *Ohio*	373	J. Champion	
1847	Bk. *Ligonia*	286	John Hamilton	Gager & Latham became New York agents
	Sch. *Abner Hall*	158	Scolto B. Nickerson	in Mar. and in Apr. I. B. Gager was again
	" *Charlotte*		Studley	sole New York agent.
	Sp. *Flavius*	296	William Cook	
	Bk. *Undine*	253	William P. Paxton	
	Bg. *Georgiana*	249	Coffee	
	Bk. *Autoleon*	345	L. A. Cobb	
	" *Elliott*	249	Samuel Watts	
	Bg. *Ellis*	199	Harvey Mills	
	Bk. *George Henry*	308	Garcia	
	Sp. *Niantic*	452	Astrom	Henry Cleveland master in 1848.
	Bg. *Lowder*	149	J. H. Conklin	
	Sp. *La Grange*	400	William Hasty	
	Bk. *Bohemia*	281	W. B. Nason	
	" *Southerner*	277	H. L. Mayo	
	Sp. *Plato*	397	Bearse	William T. Becket master in 1848.

NEW LINE (*continued*)

YEAR	VESSEL	TONS	MASTERS	REMARKS
1847	Bk. *Ceres*	398	Henry Hodge	
	Sp. *May Flower*	507	Eleazer Crabtree	
	Bk. *Thetis*	396	F. Crosby	
	Sp. *Archelaus*	597	Charles Boutelle	
	Bk. *St. Andrew*	288	Edmund Doane	
	Sp. *Avalanche*	396	W. Whittlesey	
	Bk. *Hannah Thornton*	407	E. D. Choate	Peter Hanna master in 1849.
	Bg. *Essex*	272	J. Raynes	
	Sp. *Gardner*	346	William Hasty	Var. *Gardiner*.
	Bg. *Matamoros*	175	Josiah Wolten	
	" *Billow*	173	E. Lawrence	
	" *Ann Maria*	172	French	
	" *Florence*	197	Ames Hopkins	
1848	Sp. *Wiscasset*	380	W. J. Logan	
	" *Montreal*	542	Dixey	Thomas Curtis master in 1849.
	Bk. *Warsaw*	332	Swan	Line almost completely inactive for two
	" *Henry Harbeck*	398	T. G. Mervin	years, 1849 and 1850.
1851	Sp. *Revenue*	546	Seth Crowell, Jr.	
	Bk. *Laurens*	420	W. J. Logan	
	" *Catherine Augusta*	351	F. Bestman	
	" *Jennett*	196	N. M. Atwater	H. A. Bailey master in 1852–3.

NESMITH & WALSH LINE

Nesmith & Walsh, 27 South St., New York agents. Established 1844.

YEAR	VESSEL	TONS	MASTERS	REMARKS
1844	Bk. *Louisiana*	248	William S. Emery	Nesmith & Walsh succeeded Nesmith &
	" *Tarquin*	262	E. W. Hosmer	Leeds who had been very active in New
	Sp. *Wakona*	430	James Borlan	Orleans trade during 1841–2. Firm at no
1845	Sp. *Roland*	411	Paul G. Blanchard	time observed a fixed schedule.
	Bg. *Tom Paine*	198	Rasmus Anderson	
	" *Eriza*		Fountain	
	" *Vandalia*	197	A. S. Wall	A. W. Gore master in 1851.
	" *Alabama*	280	Charles E. Ranlett	
	Bk. *Mallory*	300	D. D. Brown	B. R. Babbidge master in 1845–6.
	Sch. *Civilian*	166	Thomas Nichols	
1846	Sch. *Mary Augusta*	143	William Hewes	
	" *Sarah Nash*	169	Herman Kopperholdt	
	Bg. *Fornax*	249	Joseph Wilson	
	Sp. *Oregon*	649	Samuel G. Glidden	
1848	Bk. *Brenda*	342	Young	Line discontinued after 1848 until Nesmith & Sons became active again in 1854–5 for a time with ships *City of Brooklyn*, *Dorcas Prince*, and others.

MUTUAL LINE

Mailler & Lord, 108 Wall St., New York agents. L. P. Sage, New Orleans agent.

YEAR	VESSEL	TONS	MASTERS	REMARKS
1846	Bk. *Curtis*	250	William A. Outerbridge	Line established in Oct. by W. & C. Mailler.
	Bg. *Lowder*	149	J. H. Conklin	Changed in Nov. to Mailler & Lord.
1847	Sp. *Rob Roy*	526	Asahel Arnold	
	" *Gardiner*	346	E. Young	
	" *Exchange*	425	S. Funck	Var. *Frinck*.
	" *Metoka*	775	Thomas McGuire	John H. McLellan master in 1847.
	" *York*	433	T. Milton, Jr.	
	" *Wataga*	415	W. Moore	
	Bk. *Texidore*	215	Hugo B. Major	
	" *Mallory*	300	Benjamin R. Babbidge	
	" *Mary Broughton*	320	George Melcher	
	" *Loretto Fish*	247	Dikeman	Miles T. Gates master in 1848.
	" *George Henry*	308	McCobb	O. T. Dillingham master in 1849.
	Sp. *Powhattan*	520	William L. Stone	
	" *Narragansett*	640	Peter Destebecho	

MUTUAL LINE (*continued*)

YEAR	VESSEL	TONS	MASTERS	REMARKS
1847	Sp. *Burlington*	535	Enoch Cook	
	" *Pacific*	531	J. Ludlam	
	Bg. *Seaman*	124	Andrew A. Blackman	
1848	Bg. *Fornax*	249	Joseph Wilson	
	Bk. *Hollander*	297	Beecher	
	" *John Potter*	166	J. Lane	W. L. Watts master in 1849.
	" *Touro*		Welch	
	Sp. *Tahmaroo*	372	William Sinclair	
	" *Callender*	428	B. N. Nason	Ivory Goodwin master in 1849.
	" *Washington*	372	John H. Burleigh	
1849	Bk. *Lunette*	227	H. Keen	Mailler & Lord became very active in California trade.
	Bg. *Times*	175	N. G. Groton	Var. *Time.*
	" *Detroit*	195	S. Gilchrist	
	Bk. *Sarah Hooper*	221	J. W. Hooper	
	Bg. *Emma Prescott*	186	T. B. Lee	
	Sch. *Midas*	186	J. C. Hagdon	Var. Hagedorn.
	Bg. *Rolerson*	196	Erastus Chase	R. H. Crowell master in 1850.
	Bk. *Wilhamet*	316	J. A. Cobb	
	Sp. *Orlando*	436	White	
	Bg. *Nathan Hale*	190	A. Crowell	
	Sp. *May Flower*	508	W. Crabtree	
	" *Ophir*	439	C. Silvester	Var. Sylvester.
	" *Corsica*	429	Godfrey	Firm inactive in New Orleans trade until 1851 when sailings were renewed briefly.
1851	Sp. *Adams*	592	J. H. Brooks	
	" *Saxony*	393	E. Crosby	B. B. Melcher also master in 1851.
	Bk. *Lady Knight*	399	A. H. Merryman	
1852	Bk. *Sarah Bridge*	483	Addison C. Sturdivant	Line discontinued.

McCREADY LINE

Nathaniel L. McCready, 9 Coenties Slip, New York agent. Established Apr., 1846. N. L. McCready & Co. became New York agents in Nov.

YEAR	VESSEL	TONS	MASTERS	REMARKS
1846	Sch. *C. D. Ellis*	128	Absalom Steelman	
	Bg. *Curacoa*	131	Elisha Higgins	
	" *William Davis*	173	Luther Handy	
	" *Fanny Coit*	208	Charles Baker	
	Sch. *F. J. Brognard*	159	Pennington	
1847	Sch. *Abdel Kader*	152	Jefferson	Robert Pearce master in 1850.
	" *Elliott*	199	Cook	Var. *Ellicott.*
	" *Gilbert Hatfield*	160	Eliphalet Kingsbury	
	" *New Globe*	147	James Tibbets, Jr.	
	Bg. *Billow*	123	E. Lawrence	
	Bk. *Pentucket*	295	E. C. Taylor	

UNION LINE

Frost & Hicks, 68 South St., New York agents. Established Sept., 1847. Line consisted of seven ships running twice monthly. Six regular lines ran between New York and New Orleans.

YEAR	VESSEL	TONS	MASTERS	REMARKS
1847	Sp. *Union*	545	R. M. Foster	
	" *Apollo*	413	Howe	
	" *Wisconsin*	942	Oliver R. Mumford	
	" *Atlantic*	736	Samuel Rose	William Williams master in 1860.
	" *Indiana*	607	James S. Bennett	H. F. Coffin master in 1860.
	" *Manchester*	570	W. Tyler	
	" *Wabash*	442	James Wibray	
1848	Sp. *Creole*	769	G. B. Rollins	Charles Pierce master in 1860.
	" *Niagara*	730	William H. Russell	
	" *Palestine*	470	B. H. Johnson	
	" *Chaos*	771	J. L. Wilson	
	" *Hector*	559	Alfred G. Spencer	
	" *Sarah & Eliza*	359	J. A. Cobb	

UNION LINE (*continued*)

YEAR	VESSEL	TONS	MASTERS	REMARKS
1848	Sp. *Mary Ann*	497	Horatio A. Patten	
	" *Toronto*	631	Gideon Parker	
	Bk. *Croton*	311	David V. Soullard	
1849	Sp. *Mediator*	660	T. V. Bliffins	
1850	Sp. *Christiana*	666	Edmund Hammond	
	" *Southerner*	671	J. Sullivan	
	" *Minnesota*	799	W. M. Allen	
	" *New England*		Manson	
	" *T. & P. Woodward*	390	T. Woodward	
1851	Sp. *Centurion*	745	Edward Coombs	
	" *Antarctic*	1115	M. P. Ricker	
	" *William B. Travis*	569	John Bolles	
	" *Leviathan*	1195	Rufus Knapp	
	" *William Rathbone*	917	Joseph W. Spencer	
1852	Sp. *Silas Greenman*	738	Alfred G. Spencer	N. Webber master in 1860.
	" *Brandywine*	730	P. G. Merryman	
	" *Annawan*	759	Setzer	
	" *Oswego*	647	William Williams	
	" *Hudson*	633	J. G. White	
1853	Sp. *Trumbull*	855	W. D. Smith	Frost & Hicks dissolved and William T. Frost
	" *Forest City*	492	D. A. Allen	continued as New York agent in Feb.; still
	" *Ashland*	631	Robert B. Benson	operated in close association with T. P. Stanton.
1854	Sp. *Ravenswood*	666	N. C. Johnston	Business extremely slow in fall "busy" season.
	" *Indiana*	607	H. F. Coffin	Ship *Atlantic* was 45 days loading in New York.
1855	Sp. *Diadem*	657	Nathaniel Webber	
	Bk. *Jonathan Godfrey*	487	Nathan B. Grant	
1856	Bk. *Hiawatha*	523	David H. Hall	
	Sp. *Marmion*	903	J. E. Hoadley	
1857	Sp. *Tarolinta*	549	James V. Kearney	
	" *Hartford*	511	Deidrick Sannerman	
	" *Clifton*	599	William Williams	
1858	Sp. *St. Charles*	798	Thomas Conway	
	" *Princeton*	1131	W. R. Bell	
1859	Sp. *Far West*	598	J. S. Bennett	George P. Sage master in 1860.
	" *Augustus*	736	J. V. Kearney	
	" *New Orleans*	923	John L. Rich	
1860	Sp. *West Point*	1046	Alfred G. Spencer	Regular line at close of 1860 consisted of ten ships: *Atlantic, Augustus, Creole, Far West, Indiana, New Orleans, Union, St. Charles, Silas Greenman, Wisconsin*, "To sail every Saturday during the season from Pier 16, foot of Wall St."

EAGLE LINE

Horatio Eagle, 83 South St., New York agent. Levi H. Gale, New Orleans agent. Established Oct., 1847.

YEAR	VESSEL	TONS	MASTERS	REMARKS
1847	Sp. *Niagara*	458	David A. Nye	
	" *Persian*	492	Frederick Robbins	
	" *Archelaus*	597	Charles Boutelle	
	Bg. *Mary Ann Jones*	191	J. Collins	
	Bk. *Warsaw*	332	Wood	
	" *Maria*	324	Judah P. Baker	
1848	Bk. *Daniel Webster*	264	Lot Clark	
	" *Grampus*	241	J. Dyer	
	" *Sherwood*	447	Isaac Bursley	
	Sp. *Monterey*	442	Tully Crosby	
	" *Rajah*	531	D. Jackson	
	" *Jessore*	437	Samuel Cobb	
	" *Edgar*	420	C. R. Smith	
	" *Pharsalia*	617	Allen	L. Dryer master in 1852.
	Bg. *Amulet*	179	J. T. Spofford	
	Sp. *Camera*	386	Albert Dunbar	

EAGLE LINE (*continued*)

YEAR		VESSEL	TONS	MASTERS	REMARKS
1848	Sp.	Sarah & Eliza	359	J. A. Cobb	
	"	Elizabeth Ellen	581	C. Tyler	
	"	Viola	495	William Jameson	
	Bk.	Juno	295	J. W. Dicks	
	Sp.	Talleyrand	549	Edmund Webb	
	"	Tennessee	457	A. Cook	F. D. Beckwith master in 1852.
	Bk.	Merlin	313	George C. Welsh	
	Sp.	Vandalia	775	J. M. Norton	
	Bk.	Genessee	337	O. T. Dillingham	T. L. Minot master in 1854.
	Sp.	Gen. Berry	469	B. Patterson	
1849	Sp.	Manchester	570	J. Coleman	Eagle & Hazard, 40 South St., became New
	Bk.	Autoleon	345	William C. Park	York agents in Aug.
	Sp.	Colombo	577	John S. Pray	Samuel Toby, New Orleans agent.
	Bk.	Ceres	398	H. Hodge	
	"	Wilhamet	317	J. A. Cobb	
	"	Hannah Thornton	407	Peter Hanna	
	Sp.	Sheffield	578	C. B. Smith	
	"	Inca	578	Isaac T. Goodrich	
	Bk.	J. A. Thompson	244	W. Freeman	R. Macy master in Aug., 1849.
	"	Eliza Barss	246	D. P. Bramhall	
	Sp.	Ashland	631	J. D. Rice	
	"	Humphrey Purington	637	R. Given	
	Bg.	J. B. Lunt	149	S. Hardy	
	Sp.	Jersey	849	John Day	F. Chesley master in 1854.
	"	Espindola	741	George Barstow	
	Bk.	Elijah Swift	391	David A. Nye	
	Sp.	Hindostan	495	William Cushing	
	"	John Hancock	746	A. Snow	
	"	Arkansas	627	Otis	P. S. Shepherd master in June, 1849
	"	Avalanche	396	N. F. Hawkins	
	Bk.	Rienzi	440	E. Bangs	
	Sp.	Jenny Lind	532	W. W. Robinson	
	"	Miasconomo		Knight	
1850	Sp.	Rappahannock	1133	William Cushing	
	"	Theoxena	398	J. G. Borland	
	"	Toronto	631	Gideon Parker	
	"	Caledonia Brander	549	H. S. Brown	
	"	Champlain	624	Peter A. Decan	
	Bk.	Rolla	227	N. Jarvis	
	Sp.	Rebecca	533	A. Sawyer	
	"	Devonshire	745	W. Strickland	
	"	Hungarian	1018	William Chase	Missing en route from Liverpool, Oct. 29,
	Bk.	J. J. Hathorn	399	J. Small	1856.
	Sp.	George Turner	518	S. B. McLellan	
1851	Sp.	Harrisburg	493	Oliver M. Matthews	
	"	Prince de Joinville	527	G. A. Adams	
	"	Juliet	524	Thomas G. Moulton	
	Bk.	Isnardon	247	Adams	
	Sp.	Columbiana	631	T. J. Mallett	
	"	Trumbull	855	W. D. Smith	
	"	Medora	400	J. Brown	
1852	Bk.	Laura Snow	293	Robbins	John Crockett master in 1857.
	Sp.	William Nelson	1039	Charles Cheever	
	"	Nathaniel Hooper	427	William Churchill	
	"	Kate Swanton	489	Evans	
	"	Sarah Purington	466	B. M. Melcher	
	Bk.	Albers	360	W. B. Purington	
	"	Emily Miner	364	J. L. Smith	
	Sp.	Pelican State	850	Otis T. Baker	
	"	Hemisphere	1024	John S. Pray	
	"	Delia Maria	584	J. H. Burleigh	
	Bk.	Lucy	396	Weeks	John H. Driver master in 1858.
	"	Pilah	373	T. G. Millet	Var. Philah. Var. Mallet.
1853	Bk.	Charles Wynns	339	Jesse F. Hosmer	
	"	Gov. Briggs	198	T. H. Hallett	

EAGLE LINE (*continued*)

YEAR		VESSEL	TONS	MASTERS	REMARKS
1853	Bk.	*Nevada*	280	Chase	
	Sp.	*Marathon*	890	H. S. Tyler	
	Bk.	*Pilgrim*	379	Benedict Andros	
	"	*Jenny Lind*	523	Timothy D. Bunce	
	Sp.	*Cornelia*	523	Joseph Blanchard	
	"	*Esther G. Barney*	520	C. S. Barney	
	Bk.	*Fanny*	341	Smith	Thomas Watts master in 1855.
	Sp.	*Hound*	714	Elihu Spicer, Jr.	
	"	*Eliza Mallory*	649	John E. Williams	
	Bk.	*Ocilla*	367	Henry Stark	
	Sp.	*Howadji*	695	George E. Balch	
1854	Bk.	*Rhone*	349	E. L. Moore	
	Sp.	*Heber*	434	Samuel Cobb	
	"	*Soldan*	648	Ebenezer A. Shaw	
	"	*Sagadahock*	575	J. Fisher	
	Bk.	*Maria Morton*	426	William Bulkley	Edward M. Bulkley master in 1856.
	"	*West Wind*	522	C. P. Saunders	
	"	*Laurens*	420	Olden	
	Sp.	*William*	522	J. Berry	
1855	Sp.	*Eagle*		Hazard	
	"	*Antoinette*	536	R. D. Smith	
	Bk.	*Ann*	641	Patterson	
	Sch.	*Minna Schiffer*	192	John Wilson	
	"	*Edmund S. Janes*	231	Townsend	
	Bk.	*Col. Ledyard*	404	Francis A. Beckwith	
	"	*Samuel Moxley, Jr.*	408	F. B. Parker	
	"	*N. P. Tallmadge*	370	J. T. Horton	
	"	*William & Jane*	502	J. Adam Cobb	
1856	Sp.	*Emma Jane*	1096	Springer	F. C. Jordan master in 1859.
	"	*Erie*	476	G. A. Knudson	
	"	*Sunshine*	1467	S. Pierce	
	Bk.	*Frances*	472	Thomas Watts	
	"	*Charles C. Fowler*	521	W. C. Staples	
	Sp.	*John & Albert*	567	H. Crowell	
	Bk.	*Hannah Secor*	588	J. Paine	
	Sp.	*Euphrasia*	487	W. Lanfall	
	Bk.	*Norewood*	390	J. L. Winchester	Var. *Norwood.*
	Sp.	*Charter Oak*	841	Phineas P. Carver	
1857	Bk.	*Hahneman*	417	Abbott	
	"	*N. H. Wolfe*	450	A. F. Holmes	
	Sch.	*Fleetwing* (tern)	518	Lewis Davis	
	Sp.	*Shepherd Knapp*	839	J. Jennings	
	"	*Sheridan*	895	B. Russell	
	"	*William D. Sewall*	672	Brown	
	Bk.	*J. M. Morales*	383	F. Burmeister	Vars. Biermeister, Baumaster.
	Sch.	*William C. Mershon*	390	Graham	Edward Cole master in 1858.
	Sp.	*Amelia*	623	Wallace	
	"	*Marquette*	1197	Watts	
	"	*Northampton*	969	Houghton	
	"	*B. D. Metcalf*	1189	J. Stetson	
	"	*John & Albert*	567	H. Crowell	
	"	*R. D. Shepherd*	794	James Gayle	Var. Gale.
	"	*Young Sam*	1012	J. C. Merryman	
	"	*Judah Touro*	741	J. G. Moses	
	"	*Sylvanus Blanchard*	1123	P. N. Blanchard	
1858	Bk.	*E. Schultz*	674	H. P. Carr	
	Sp.	*St. Peter*	438	A. F. Savin	
	Bk.	*H. L. Rutgers*	405	Henry C. Delano	
	Sp.	*Bennington*	513	Douglass	
	Sch.	*Ralph Post*	426	Hamilton D. Conklin	
	"	*Stephen Taber*	305	William W. Cook	
	Sp.	*Forest King*	992	H. M. Allen	
	"	*Clara Wheeler*	996	C. Delano	
	"	*Mary*	744	John H. Marshall	
	"	*Cultivator*	1448	W. H. Russell	

EAGLE LINE (*continued*)

YEAR	VESSEL	TONS	MASTERS	REMARKS
1858	Bk. *W. O. Alden*	274	McGill	
	Sch. *Eclipse*	269	William W. Cook	
1859	Sp. *Rachel*	818	S. Hamlin	
	Bk. *Isabella C. Jones*	588	C. H. Woodburn	Line discontinued at end of year.
	Sp. *John P. Harward*	548	Benedict Andros	Var. Andrews.
	Sch. *Emeline McLain*	208	E. Bucklin	

CRESCENT CITY LINE

Foster & Nickerson, 25 South St., New York agents. Fosdick & Co., 73 Magazine St., New Orleans agents. Established fall of 1849.

YEAR	VESSEL	TONS	MASTERS	REMARKS
1849	Sp. *Ellen Brooks*	465	Abram Hedge	
	" *Magnolia*	679	George Ulricks	B. H. Leckie master in 1852.
	Bk. *St. Andrew*	288	Edmund Doane	
	" *Alvarado*	299	E. C. Healey	
	" *N. H. Wolfe*	450	David Forbes	
	" *Gov. Hinckley*		W. Loring	R. Davis master in 1855.
	Sp. *Albania*	548	Ambrose Crowell	J. F. Schander master in 1850.
	" *Medomak*	632	Abraham Rich	
1850	Sp. *Charles Cooper*	678	William Cutts	
	" *Newton*	409	Eben Sears	
	" *Andover*	485	Allen H. Bearse	
	Bk. *Brothers*	493	Baxter	
	" *Adeline*	249	W. Gamage	
	" *Lota*		Bearse	
	" *Plymouth*	218	G. Perkins	
	" *Marmora*	388	Samuel Duncan	
	" *Kate & Alice*	305	Low	O. Thorp master in 1854.
	" *Cazone*		G. Porterfield	
	" *Nimrod*	449	G. W. Robinson	
	" *Archimedes*	291	S. T. Merrill	
	Sp. *Medomak*	632	E. Rich	
	" *May Flower*	507	Eleazer Crabtree	William Crabtree, Jr., master in same year.
	" *Moses Howes*	419	Allen H. Bearse	
	" *Elsinore*	597	John Riley	
	" *Oswego*	647	James B. Ingersoll	
1851	Sp. *Clifton*	599	James B. Ingersoll	Thomas Ingersoll master in 1855.
	" *Crescent*	753	David Forbes	
	" *Commonwealth*	636	J. Baxter	
	" *Muscongus*	669	James H. Kelleran	
	Bk. *Medora*	197	H. Roby	
	" *Hannah Brewer*	293	Bearse	Ebenezer Price master in Apr., 1851.
	" *Mary Annah*	488	R. Keating	
1852	Sp. *Martha J. Ward*	745	Thomas Trott	
	" *Java*	715	D. Jackson	
	" *Orlando*	437	E. B. White	
	" *Mary Crocker*	549	John Crocker	
	Bk. *Lady Knight*	399	E. D. Choate	
	" *Peter Pendleton*	368	Peter Pendleton	
	" *Petrel*	387	D. H. Norton	G. A. Avery master in 1854.
	Bg. *Metropolis*		Gillespie	
1853	Bk. *Vesta*	233	Percival	Fosdick & Co., 51 Camp St., became New
	" *Azof*	295	Chipman	Orleans agents.
	" *Saxony*	346	Allen Howes	Line discontinued in 1857.

LADD LINE

A. Ladd, 69 South St., New York agent. Established Nov., 1850.

YEAR	VESSEL	TONS	MASTERS	REMARKS
1850	Sp. *Unicorn*	597	George Pollard	Ladd was also active in the Florida and
	Bk. *Convoy*	261	J. Hupper	Mobile trades.
	" *Condor*	303	Wright	

LADD LINE (*continued*)

YEAR	VESSEL	TONS	MASTERS	REMARKS
1851	Bg. *Monterey*	422	Higgins Crowell	Ladd & Stannard became New York agents
	Sp. *Shelter*	426	McClintook	in Feb., changing to Ladd & Church in Oct.
	" *Caledonia Brander*	549	John Rowland	
	Bk. *Murillo*	309	J. Wait	Var. Waite.
	Sp. *Narragansett*	640	J. Edmonds	
	" *William Sprague*	716	Jesse Chase	T. E. Bower master in 1858.
	" *Hemisphere*	1024	W. Whittlesey	
	" *Helvetia*	972	S. F. Marsh	
	" *Meridian*	1300	John Manson	
	" *John & Lucy*	992	Sanders Curling	
	Bk. *John Caskie*	349	Edmund S. Raynes	
1852	Sp. *Marathon*	890	H. S. Tyler	C. Tyler master in 1852–3.
	" *Russell Glover*	795	B. W. Tucker	
	" *Comoro*	440	E. Scudder	
	Bk. *Mary Broughton*	322	Pryor	
	Sp. *Megunticook*	473	John C. Fairbanks	
	" *North Carolina*	669	William L. Flitner	J. V. Kearney master in 1853.
	Bk. *Susan Brewer*	399	J. Koopman	
	" *Nelson Place*	459	H. Gilchrist	A. Gilchrist master in 1855.
	Sp. *Levitt Storer*	879	Y. Gracie	Var. Gracia.
	" *Louisiana*	747	N. Barstow	
	" *Germania*	997	D. H. Wood	
	Bg. *Bloomer*	233	E. G. Adams	Discontinued at close of 1852.

STANTON & THOMPSON LINE

Stanton & Thompson, 141 Wall St., New York agents. Line established May, 1850.

YEAR	VESSEL	TONS	MASTERS	REMARKS
1850	Sp. *Quebec*	649	Thomas R. Shapter	James Thompson, Jr., master in 1850–1.
	" *Southerner*	671	James Sullivan	
	" *Toronto*	631	Gideon Parker	
	" *Francis P. Sage*	1146	W. H. Robson	
1851	Sp. *Colombo*	577	C. H. Gerrish	N. O. Harris master in 1851–2.
	" *Thomas Church*	741	Talbot	
	" *Westminster*	631	Thomas R. Shapter	J. C. Hagedorn master in 1853.
	" *Clifton*	599	James B. Ingersoll	
	" *Jersey*	849	John Day	
	Bk. *Fanny*	529	Robert Simonson	
	" *Arion*	425	Matthew B. Vennard	
1852	Sp. *Hudson*	623	Joseph G. White	
	" *Liberty*	690	Simon V. Peabody	John Atkins master in 1853–9.
1853	Sp. *Toulon*	744	John L. Rich	
	" *Wellington*	727	John E. Barstow	
	" *Island City*	526	Peleg Saunders	
	" *Houghton*	787	S. B. Doane	
	" *Silas Greenman*	738	S. C. Magna	
	Bk. *Linden*	440	Daniel Clark	
1854	Sp. *St. Charles*	798	P. B. Bowers	Thomas Conway master in 1855.
	" *Louisiana*	747	James Sullivan	
	" *Knickerbocker*	874	Simon V. Peabody	Lost on Abaco, June, 1858.
	Bk. *Hannah Thornton*	407	J. A. Congdon	
1855	Sp. *New Orleans*	924	John L. Rich	
	" *Lebanon*	697	A. G. Hamilton	
	Bk. *William Chase*	269	J. Dorry	Var. Davey.
1856	Bk. *Corilla*	496	J. Chase	O. L. Pettingill master in 1858.
	Sch. *Old Dominion* (tern)	393	L. Bunker	J. M. Vose master in 1858.
	Sp. *Richard Alsop*	836	B. Watlington	
1857	Bk. *John U. Brookman*	534	John U. Brookman	
1858	Sp. *William Rathbone*	917	J. C. Dowd	
	Bk. *Harvest*	426	Hanford Nichols	
	Sp. *Rome*	673	W. Lincoln	
	" *Cumberland*	1066	R. Merrill	
1859	Sp. *George Hurlbut*	1047	Thomas S. Masson	Line carried on by T. N. Stanton with Post,
	" *Arcole*	663	S. P. Crafts	Smith & Co. acting as joint agents of most of
	Bk. *Diana*	568	Paul R. Hazeltine	the vessels.

STANTON AND THOMPSON LINE (*continued*)

YEAR		VESSEL	TONS	MASTERS	REMARKS
1859	Bk.	*Alice Taintor*	637	W. M. Post	T. N. Stanton and Post, Smith & Co. became New York agents in ten clearances beginning Sept., 1859.
1860	Sp.	*David Hoadley*	975	Joseph N. Magna	J. & N. Smith & Co. replaced Post, Smith & Co. in July.
	"	*Catherine*	611	S. J. Foster	
	"	*Roger A. Hiern*	1089	J. S. Stewart	
	Bk.	*Harriet A. Stephenson*	466	Somes	
	Sp.	*South Carolina*	581	G. H. Kempton	
	"	*Francis B. Cutting*	975	J. B. Maloney	
	Sch.	*Mary D. Lane*	398	B. A. Gardner	

PELICAN. Later ORLEANS LINE.

E. H. Fosdick, 77 South St., New York agent. George A. Fosdick, 43 Natchez St., New Orleans agent. Established Sept., 1852.

YEAR		VESSEL	TONS	MASTERS	REMARKS
1852	Sp.	*Iowa*	479	C. H. Blake	
	"	*Vandalia*	775	E. C. Smith	
	"	*Manchester*	570	H. Tyler	
1853	Sp.	*Oregon*	649	Thomas Patterson	Charles A. Farwell, 57 Camp St., became
	Bg.	*Fairy*	166	Willeby	New Orleans agent.
	"	*Cleopatra*	195	W. S. Carver	
	"	*India*	195	Matthews	
	Bk.	*Morning Star*	299	Aaron Spear	
	Sp.	*Favorite*	777	G. E. Thomas	E. H. Fosdick & Co. became agents in July;
	Bk.	*Archimedes*	291	Mitchell	Fosdick & Scammon, agents in Oct.
	"	*Russian*	222	Gerry	
	"	*Tyringham*	608	C. Howes	
	"	*Abaellino*	620	Hall	
	Sch.	*Joseph Grice*	247	Andrew F. Rogers	
1854	Bk.	*S. Kirby*		Trecartin	
	"	*Ardennes*	231	Eugene Lambert	
	"	*P. R. Hazletine*	399	J. H. McCrillis	W. Gillis master in 1857–8.
	Sp.	*Trumbull*	855	W. D. Smith	
	"	*Bavaria*	1050	A. F. Bailey	
	"	*Rebecca*	533	A. Sawyer	
	"	*Alice Counce*	1156	W. J. Singer	
	Bk.	*Susan W. Lind*	263	H. L. Sweetzer	Var. Sweetser.
	"	*Sarah Bridge*	483	Addison C. Sturtevant	Loring Ballard master in 1856.
	Sch.	*Stephen Taber*	305	Minor Tuthill	William W. Cook master in 1859.
	"	*Morning Star*	172	Spear	
1855	Sp.	*Abby Langdon*	1035	J. B. Hall	Name changed to Orleans Line.
	"	*Fanny Fosdick*	730	William J. Crabtree	R. Olmsted master in 1860.
	"	*Ostervald*	902	F. H. Jarvis	
	"	*Orphan*	682	G. H. Kempton	Robson & Fosdick became New York agents
	"	*Heidelberg*	1053	S. G. Williams	in Aug.
	"	*Ophir*	439	E. T. Byrne	B. W. Ward master in 1856.
	"	*James Titcomb*	491	Redding	
	"	*Realm*	548	J. Burgess	
	"	*Genoa*	549	B. U. Wood	B. W. Ward master in 1856.
	"	*Chicora*	467	P. W. Sawyer	
	"	*Mary & Susan*	392	G. Gilderdale	
	Bk.	*L. D. Carver*	414	L. S. Carver	
1856	Sp.	*Cabinet*	302	Brown	
	"	*Wilbur Fisk*	949	Albert Burwell	
	"	*Fanny Forrester*	624	Enoch Cook	
	"	*St. Peter*	438	A. T. Savin	
	"	*Brandywine*	730	P. G. Merriman	
1857	Bk.	*Genessee*	674	J. Merryman	
	"	*Splendid*	642	J. O. Amsbury	
	Sp.	*Logan*	1541	E. C. Taylor	
	"	*William Rathbone*	1117	Jabez Pratt	
	Bk.	*Oregon*	401	C. Soule	
	Sp.	*Hannah Crooker*	499	H. M. Huntoon	
	"	*Pocahontas*	1088	Benjamin Delano	W. M. Cotter also master in 1857.

PELICAN LINE (*continued*)

YEAR		VESSEL	TONS	MASTERS	REMARKS
1857	Sp.	Martha J. Ward	748	Charles A. Storer	
	"	Globe	798	George Baker	
	"	S. Gildersleeve	847	W. L. Johnson	
	"	Ben Bolt	709	J. G. Loring	Register surrendered Oct. 10, 1860. Vessel wrecked.
	"	William Nelson	1039	Charles Cheever	
	"	Normandy	1491	H. Tyler	
1858	Bk.	Lone Star	376	S. Dizer	
	Sp.	Arcole	664	S. P. Crafts	
	"	Marathon	890	H. S. Tyler	
	"	Belle of the Ocean	966	Washington Read	
	"	Western Empire	1398	C. Soule	
	"	Bullion	553	A. Hodgdon	
	"	St. Peter	438	A. F. Savin	
	"	Escort	907	Bryant	
1859	Bk.	Nicholas Curwin	528	J. Montford	Var. Mumford.
	Sp.	J. R. Keeler	1292	H. M. Allen	
	Bg.	North	297	David Davidson	
	Bk.	E. Schultz	674	H. P. Carr	
	Sp.	Volant	896	Stephen P. Bray	
	"	Emerald	1080	William W. Cook	
	Bk.	Dorcas C. Yeaton	481	S. Pote	
	Sp.	Harriet	834	T. Bassett	
	Bg.	Selma	298	J. Stetson	
	Bk.	J. M. Hicks	541	William Greenman	
	Sp.	Juliet Trundy	899	T. R. Pillsbury	
	"	Independence	1278	Merritt	Register surrendered at New Orleans, May 16, 1860. Vessel burned.
	"	Nathaniel Thompson	546	Shannon	
	"	Chimborazo	957	Gilchrist	
	"	William S. Lindsay	1165	H. A. Gray	
	"	Vigilant	652	Peleg Curtis	
1860	Sp.	Artisan	923	George Pollard	A majority of vessels here listed made several trips in the line but the principal ships were the *Fanny Fosdick*, *Realm*, *Genoa*, *Hannah Crooker*, *Fanny Forrester*, and bark *Genessee*.
	Bk.	N. Boynton	438	W. W. Smalley	
	Sp.	Canova	581	A. P. Hutchins	
	"	Maverick	689	T. Ellis	
	"	Helvetia	971	A. G. Higgins	
	"	Delft Haven	941	A. G. Freese	
	"	Havre	871	S. Atkins	
	"	Carlyle	1181	Robert W. Simpson	
	"	Cerro Gordo	577	J. L. Randall	Lost, Nov., 1860.
	"	Georgiana	1100	John H. Salter	
	"	Ella	994	Goss	
	"	J. H. Jarvis	741	A. L. Rich	
	"	Scioto	864	Minot	
	Bk.	Lyman	369	Micah Humphreys	
	"	John Winthrop	346	Eldridge	
	"	Young America	375	Collins	
	"	Old Dominion	420	George W. Johnson	

LANE & WEST LINE

Lane & West, New York agents. Established June, 1853. Sailed irregularly throughout.

YEAR		VESSEL	TONS	MASTERS	REMARKS
1853	Sch.	John W. Miner	386	John W. Miner	D. P. Berry master in 1856.
	"	Mobile	398	Isaac P. Hodges	L. C. Wimpenny master in 1854.
	Bg.	Mary Hamilton	292	S. S. Jordan	A. B. Walker master in 1854.
1854	Bk.	Julia Dean	298	H. W. Mallory	Lane, West & Co. became agents in July.
	Sch.	Imogene	396	James Myers	
	Sp.	Globe	797	George Baker	
	Bk.	Velocity	247	G. Ryder	
1855	Sp.	St. Bernard	711	U. W. Mather	
	Sch.	Mary D. Lane	398	B. A. Gardner	
	"	Emeline	346	Francis W. Miner	

LANE & WEST LINE (*continued*)

YEAR		VESSEL	TONS	MASTERS	REMARKS
1855	Sch.	*Kate Stewart*	388	Titus C. Mather	
	Bk.	*Uncle Sam*	336	G. Cole	
1856	Sch.	*Fannie Curtis*	295	S. Dearborn	
	Sp.	*Crescent*	754	David Forbes	
	"	*Kitty Simpson*	697	Samuel L. Bragdon	
	"	*J. Emerson Smith*	1260	Henry M. Snow	
1857	Bg.	*New World*	221	Brown	Discontinued in summer of 1857.

BRIGHAM LINE

N. H. Brigham, New York agent. Established Jan., 1854.

YEAR		VESSEL	TONS	MASTERS	REMARKS
1854	Bk.	*Mary & Jane*	346	E. Richardson	J. A. Richardson master in 1855.
	Sp.	*Germania*	996	D. H. Wood	
	"	*Astrachan*	536	Edward K. Smith	
	"	*Robert L. Lane*	1080	Hugo B. Major	
	Bk.	*Edward*	182	Z. A. Tilton	
	Sp.	*Helvetia*	972	S. M. Marsh	
	"	*Orphan*	682	G. M. Kempton	
	"	*Heidelberg*	1053	S. G. Williams	Frederick G. Rodewald master in 1856–60.
	Bk.	*Julia Dean*	298	H. W. Mallory	
	Sch.	*Imogene*	396	James Myers	
	Sp.	*Celestial Empire*	1390	J. G. Pierce	
	"	*William Jarvis*	670	Calvin Ballard	
	"	*May Queen*	619	C. Skolfield	
	"	*Rome*	673	Moulton	
	"	*Tarquin*	462	W. Doughty	
	"	*Seth Sprague*	598	A. Wadsworth	Peter Protteau master in 1858.
	"	*Joshua Mauran*	546	George Barton	
	"	*Modern Times*	643	P. Howes	
	"	*Guttenberg*	1092	Townsend Weeks	
	"	*Katahdin*	548	Eustis	
	"	*Omar Pasha*	769	W. H. Barnes	
1855	Sp.	*John W. White*	549	Reuben Snow	
	Bk.	*Anna*	421	R. W. Wheeler	
	Sch.	*Mary Eddy*	199	Seth Cole	
	Bk.	*Delphos*	398	Soule	
	Sp.	*T. J. Rogers*	543	Maxwell	
	"	*Nathaniel Thompson*	550	McCulloch	
	"	*Charles Crocker*	960	J. A. Moorehead	
	"	*Ashland*	631	Fletcher	Edward Moore master in 1856.
	Bk.	*Rhone*	350	E. L. Moore	
	"	*Mount Vernon*	557	Numa Lesseps	
	Sp.	*Julia Howard*	590	Coles	Wrecked in West Indies, Nov., 1856.
	"	*John Cottle*	1744	R. Hallowell	
	Bk.	*Growler*	484	Dennis Pillsbury	
	Sp.	*Anna F. Schmidt*	785	M. J. Milliken	
	Bk.	*Leroy*	350	A. S. Smalley	
	Sp.	*Dictator*	1293	G. M. Shaw	
	"	*Narragansett*	640	Lemuel Hall	F. S. Brandt master in 1860.
	Bk.	*Warden*		Mosher	
	"	*Grand Turk*	282	S. B. Johnson	
	"	*Juniata*	299	Newman	
	Sch.	*Old Dominion* (tern)	393	L. Bunker	
	"	*Mary Staples* (tern)	305	W. C. Staples	
	"	*Richard W. Tull*	292	William R. Newcombe	
	Sp.	*Regulus*	599	J. Thompson	
	Bk.	*Morning Star*	299	Edward Close	
	Sp.	*William Nelson*	1039	Charles Cheever	
	"	*Henry H. Boody*	664	Hussey	
	Sch.	*Claremont* (tern)	341	Smith	
	Bk.	*Aura*	293	Philander Crosby	
	"	*Thales*	234	Howland	C. B. Jervey master in 1858.
1856	Sp.	*Harry of the West*	998	William H. Adams	

BRIGHAM LINE (*continued*)

YEAR		VESSEL	TONS	MASTERS	REMARKS
1856	Sp.	*Scotland*	821	D. Burt	
	"	*Marathon*	486	Christian Van Dyke	
	"	*Addie Snow*	990	Howes	
	"	*Epaminondas*	549	F. S. Brandt	
	"	*Volant*	900	Stephen P. Bray	
	Bk.	*Brilliant*	349	William P. Sigsbee	
	Sp.	*Rachel*	818	S. Hamblin	
	"	*Excelsior*	1000	J. Q. A. Swift	
	Bk.	*Philah*	373	W. Spofford	
	Sch.	*Narragansett*	248	Lemuel Hall	
	Sp.	*Pyramid*	740	J. Henderson	
	"	*Atmosphere*	1485	John S. Pray	
1857	Bk.	*Roman*	245	E. M. Laury	
	Sp.	*William V. Moses*	862	Daniel Jones	
	"	*John Sidney*	866	Wheeler	
	"	*Emily A. Hall*	1015	R. Merrill	A. Sawyer master in 1858.
	Bk.	*Mary R. Barney*	281	Daniel B. Luther	
	"	*Warwick*	337	L. P. Hall	
	Sp.	*Erie*	477	Gilbert A. Knudson	
	Bk.	*Abeona*	298	Oliver Page	
	"	*Marmion*	359	J. Crocker	
	Sch.	*Fleetwing* (tern)	518	Zadock A. Tilton	
	Bk.	*Rhone*	350	Draper	
	Sp.	*Hemisphere*	1024	Taylor	
	"	*Manchester*	570	White	
	"	*City of Brooklyn*	1514	Jacob A. Mitchell	
	"	*Aquila*	1119	Oliver	
	"	*Forest City*	492	Tyler	
	"	*Dorcas Prince*	699	P. N. Blanchard	
	"	*Shawmut*	950	Higgins	
	"	*William H. Prescott*	1390	Charles Batcheller	Var. Batchelder.
	"	*Byzantium*	1048	W. B. Hilton	
	"	*J. E. Humphrey*	853	W. H. Moore	
	"	*William Jarvis*	670	Calvin Ballard	
	"	*Independence*	1278	Joseph Eustis	Burned near New Orleans, May, 1860.
1858	Sp.	*Rockaway*	815	Mark H. Lufkin	
	Bk.	*Hebron*	386	Shephard	
	Sp.	*Gibraltar*	746	N. G. Clifford	
	Bk.	*Cephas Starrett*	424	G. Gregory	
	"	*Thales*	234	C. B. Jarvey	Var. Jervey.
	Sp.	*Troy*	712	Hagan	
	"	*Sheridan*	895	Joseph G. Russell	
	Sch.	*James Miller* (tern)	471	John W. Miner	
	"	*Benjamin C. Scribner*	327	Carlisle	
	"	*Potomac*	242	F. Arnott	
	Sp.	*Cynosure*	1258	N. C. Harris	
	"	*Caroline Nesmith*	832	Branscomb	
	"	*William F. Storer*	1473	Charles Conery	Var. Comery.
	"	*Northampton*	983	Cotter	
	"	*Tranquebar*	868	C. F. Goodwin	
	"	*Frank Flint*	1180	C. A. Robertson	Var. Robinson.
	"	*Abner Stetson*	1075	J. H. Stetson	
	"	*Belle Wood*	1399	John C. Bush	
	Bk.	*Undine*	532	J. Merryman	
	Sp.	*Adirondack*	699	T. Taylor	
	"	*Charlemagne*	742	Brown	
	Bg.	*Dunkirk*	293	J. W. Griffin	
	Bk.	*Linwood*	491	H. Martin	
	Sp.	*Columbia*	441	L. Sturges	
	Bk.	*Dorcas C. Yeaton*	480	S. Pote	
	"	*Harriet S. Fisk*	563	M. H. Fisk	
1859	Sp.	*Tropic*	882	George W. Norvell	Var. Nowell.
	Bk.	*Nineveh*	439	R. K. Robinson	
	"	*B. Fountain*	389	M. Keller	
	Sp.	*Thomas Jefferson*	989	Waldo Hill	

BRIGHAM LINE (*continued*)

YEAR	VESSEL	TONS	MASTERS	REMARKS
1859	Sch. *Atwater*		Jewashy	
	Sp. *Milan*	700	C. H. Badger	
	" *Success*	1183	Arthur Childs	Var. Child.
	" *Charles & Jane*	499	Bowker	
	" *America*	1137	J. W. Howe	
	Bk. *Atlas*	440	J. C. Bartlett	
	Sp. *Aramede Snow*	553	William A. Harnden	
	Bk. *Star*	298	James Smith	
	Sp. *Australia*	1448	Jeremiah G. Smith	
	Bk. *Old Dominion*	420	George W. Johnson	
	Sp. *Sebastapol*	498	E. S. Raynes	
	" *Advance*	1276	Arthur Childs	
	" *Fanny McHenry*	1237	Alfred F. Smith	
	" *Forest City*	492	Tyler	W. G. Axworthy master in 1860.
	Bk. *Nicholas Curvin*	528	J. W. Chace	
	Sch. *Republic*	250	Thomas Snow	
	Bk. *Comet*	469	D. Rodgers	
	Sch. *D. F. Keeler*	128	James Simpkins	
	" *James Miller* (tern)	471	Alfred O. Paine	
	Sp. *Mary Hammond*	1030	Dyer	
	" *J. S. Parsons*	1398	W. Crowell	
	" *B. S. Kimball*	1192	J. F. Hosmer	
	" *Ironsides*	1319	Fessenden Chase	
	" *Vandalia*	775	R. E. Patten	
	" *Trumbull*	855	Conklin	
	" *William Singer*	1142	Forby	Var. Farley.
	" *Antarctic*	1115	G. C. Stouffer	
	Sp. *Joseph Fish*	1191	Gideon Young	
	Bk. *Grace Hammond*	499	Harrison Mahoney	
	Sp. *Centurion*	775	D. Caulkins	
	" *Ophelia*	597	William B. Nason	
	" *R. Jacobs*	1122	J. Henderson	Register surrendered at Liverpool, July 5,
	" *Marquette*	1197	J. Watts	1861. Vessel lost.
	" *Vaucluse*	670	William Carney	
	Bk. *Isabella C. Jones*	588	A. Jones	
	Sp. *George Green*	866	J. E. Fairbanks	
	Bg. *Richmond*	174	Job Clark	
	Sp. *Hesperus*	1020	John Lewin	Burned at Woosung, Jan. 8, 1861.
	" *E. Z.*	673	L. B. Hodges	
	" *Aldanah*	1048	John Bunker	
	" *Southern Chief*	1199	A. G. Higgins	
	Bk. *Eliza A. Cochran*	325	E. A. Noyes	
	Sp. *Macauley*	1139	J. J. Rodgers	
	Bk. *Laura Russ*	284	J. A. Russ	
1860	Sp. *Arctic*	1115	Augustus Zerega	
	" *Mediator*	660	W. J. Flitner	
	" *Michael Angelo*	783	John W. Carleton	
	" *Ocean Belle*	1097	James H. Kelleran	Var. Kellar.
	Bk. *Windward*	529	Emerson	
	" *Susan W. Lind*	264	W. C. Faulkner	
	Sp. *Grotto*	511	S. W. Stewart	
	Bg. *Arcadian*	204	A. Wilson	
	Sp. *Planter*	1094	A. F. Derby	
	" *Charles Cooper*	977	J. V. Jordan	
	" *Donati*	899	William H. Adams	
	Bk. *William Woodside*	463	C. S. Pennell	
	Sp. *James Guthrie*	987	R. A. L. Pittman	
	" *Stephen Crowell*	937	E. Burgess	
	Bk. *Maria Morton*	425	Edward M. Bulkley	
	Sch. *J. W. Lindsey*	199	D. Lewis	
	Sp. *J. S. Parsons*	1398	W. Crowell	Follansbee substituted for Crowell.
	" *Golden Eagle*	1273	Horace A. Wilson	
	" *Mary*	1149	J. Bridges	
	" *Cordelia*	666	E. Bishop	

BRIGHAM LINE (*continued*)

YEAR		VESSEL	TONS	MASTERS	REMARKS
1860	Sp.	*Charles Davenport*	975	J. R. Kelly	
	Bg.	*Phoebe M. Tinker*	276	Carlisle	
	Bk.	*Indian Belle*	319	J. P. Penny	
	Sp.	*Amity*	799	Stinson	
	Bk.	*R. A. Allen*	462	W. B. Potter	
	"	*L. D. Carver*	414	S. Wylie	
	"	*Medora*	197	Webster	
	"	*Benjamin Hallett*	359	James S. Little	
	Sp.	*Rhine*	535	Stooker	Var. Starkey.
	Bk.	*Ocean Home*	417	Harriman	
	Sch.	*Pocahontas*	216	Edwin Nickerson	
	Bk.	*G. W. Hall*	356	J. K. Potter	
	Bg.	*John Freeman*	299	John Loring	
	"	*Col. Penniman*	247	T. Coffin	
	"	*Emily Fisher*	230	J. R. Staples	
	Bk.	*G. S. Hunt*	405	J. P. Woodbury	
	Sch.	*James Miller*	471	Carbourette	
	"	*Florence Rogers*	199	D. S. Rogers	
	"	*Louisa A. Johnson*	296	Lewis P. Ellis	
	Bk.	*George W. Horton*	299	W. Sleeper	

MARSH & BROWN LINE

Marsh & Brown, New York agents. Established Jan., 1855. Discontinued after four sailings in 1855. Marsh & Brown became joint agents with McCready, Mott & Co. in their New Orleans line.

YEAR		VESSEL	TONS	MASTERS	REMARKS
1855	Sp.	*Masonic*	439	Blair	
	Bg.	*Parthenon*	199	Simmons	

McCREADY, MOTT LINE

McCready, Mott & Co., 36 South St., New York agents. Established Jan., 1855. Discontinued in fall of 1855.

YEAR		VESSEL	TONS	MASTERS	REMARKS
1855	Sch.	*Lillie Saunders*	163	Ebenezer Corson	Var. *Lilla Saunders.*
	Bg.	*Mystic*	271	Erastus Fish	E. H. Fosdick became joint agent.
	Sch.	*Indianola* (tern)	522	Isaac Cathcart	Marsh & Brown became joint agents.
	"	*Narragansett*	248	S. Hale	
	Sp.	*Euphrasia*	487	Marshall	
	Bk.	*Brilliant*	349	William P. Sigsbee	

POST, SMITH LINE

Post, Smith & Co., New York agents. Announced establishment of line, Sept., 1855.

YEAR		VESSEL	TONS	MASTERS	REMARKS
1855	Bk.	*Rose Standish*	427	James Gale	Only two sailings in 1855. Participated in loading three ships, 1856. No activity in 1857.
1858	Sp.	*John Hancock*	760	Coffin	These ships ran as regular packets in fall of 1858.
	"	*South Carolina*	580	C. D. Smith	During 1859–60 firm acted as joint agents with T. N. Stanton in dispatching a number of ships.

OAKLEY & KEATING LINE

Oakley & Keating, New York agents. Established Aug., 1859. Discontinued after sailing of *Potomac* in Dec.

YEAR		VESSEL	TONS	MASTERS	REMARKS
1859	Sp.	*Eliza Mallory*	649	Charles H. Barrett	
	"	*N. Larrabee*	1036	Percy	
	"	*Horizon*	1666	W. Reed	
	"	*Linda*	1078	Robert McManus	
	Sch.	*Potomac*	242	F. Arnot	

SECTION 16. NEW YORK—MISCELLANEOUS EAST COAST AND GULF PORTS

New York—Wilmington, N. C.

NEW LINE

Hallet & Brown, 58 South St., New York agents in 1838. Brown & Potter, 93 Wall St., New York agents in 1840.

YEAR	VESSEL	TONS	MASTERS	REMARKS
1838	Sch. *Alfred F. Thorne*	198	John Gould	
"	*Regulus*	149	Charles Mills	
"	*Repeater*	135	D. H. Sanford	
"	*Tell*	129	R. Hawkins	
"	*Topic*	115	Jacob Smith	
1840	Bg. *Dispatch*	180	E. J. Lincoln	
	Sch. *Charles B. Thorne*	200	William J. Tyler	
"	*Intrepid*	128	Ezra Wicks	Called Regular Line in 1841. John Ogden became New York agent.
1843	Sch. *Alaric*	177	Lorenzo D. Purnell	Called Old Line.
1846	Sch. *Gen. Scott*	144	J. Doughty	N. L. McCready, 7 Coenties Slip, became New York agent.
"	*A. J. DeRosset*	198	Charles Mills	DeRosset & Brown, 159 Front St., became New York agents in Nov.
"	*J. D. Jones*	191	John C. Griffing	
"	*R. W. Brown*	153	Barnabas Francis	
"	*Jonas Smith*	185	J. T. Horton	Sailed every sixth day.
"	*L. P. Smith*	195	G. W. Brewster	
1848	Sch. *Charles Mills*	240	John C. Griffing	Dollner & Potter, 166 Front St. became New York agents. Called Smith's Line.
1851	Bg. *John Dawson*	137	A. Briggs	
1853	Sch. *Ann & Susan*	326	Samuel Myers	Dollner, Potter & Co., 154 Front St., became New York agents in 1856.

REGULAR DISPATCH LINE

Powell & Mills, New York agents. George W. Davis, Wilmington agent.

YEAR	VESSEL	TONS	MASTERS	REMARKS
1841	Sch. *Bergen*	227	David Latourette	
"	*William Hart*		P. Corson	
"	*Pizzaro*	133	Robert Taylor	
"	*Repeater*	135	Barnabas Francis	
"	*Regulus*	149	J. Marston	
	Bg. *Belle*	194	L. D. Purnell	
"	*Aeolus*	148	S. R. Davis	E. S. Powell, 69 Wall St., became New York agent in 1843.
1846	Bg. *David Duffell*	189	D. Williams	
	Sch. *Jonas Smith*	185	Robert Taylor	
"	*Charles E. Thorne*	200	Sidney L. Jackson	
1847	Sch. *George W. Davis*	170	William Murch	Sailed every Sat. throughout year, "full or not full."
"	*E. S. Powell*	193	James P. Powell	
"	*Ellen Sedgwick*			
1849	Sch. *Ira Brewster*	178	Ira T. Horton	
1851	Sch. *Lamartine*	180	Isaac E. Turner	Called Old Line or Regular Line.
1856	Sch. *John*	363	John C. Burton	E. S. Powell, 104 Wall St., became New York agent; George Harris, Wilmington agent.

OLD LINE

N. L. McCready & Co., New York agents.

YEAR	VESSEL	TONS	MASTERS	REMARKS
1848	Sch. *William B. Spafford*		Harvey	
"	*Olive*	173	William Smith	
1849	Sch. *Elouise*	162	Joseph B. Robinson	
1851	Sch. *Minerva Wright*		David Cox	
"	*Charles D. Ellis*	128	John B. Harmon	McCready, Mott & Co., 36 South St., became New York agents; T. C. Worth, Wilmington agent, in 1854.
1854	Sch. *William Smith*	314	William Smith	
1856	Sch. *D. C. Hulse*	242	Overton	R. E. Conklin master in 1858.
1857	Sch. *Myrover*	356	Francis Jackson	

New York—Apalachicola

POST LINE

Post & Phillips, 68 South St., New York agents.

YEAR		VESSEL	TONS	MASTERS	REMARKS
1841	Sp.	Harbinger	262	Charles H. Coffin	
1842	Bg.	Florida	209	Mendall Crocker	
	"	Mary Silsby	191	David V. Soullard	Lost, Oct., 1842.
	Sp.	Marianna	379	John T. Phillips	
	"	Rienzi	327	Samuel Clark	Lost on Carysfort Reef, May 15, 1845.
1843	Sp.	Mary Phillips	386	Daniel Pratt	Post & Phillips took over agency in 1848 for
	"	Martha Washington	473	Albert Tyler	E. D. Hurlbut's Apalachicola line, although
	"	Liverpool	428	Charles H. Coffin	Hurlbut continued to clear some vessels.

EAGLE LINE

Eagle & Hazard, 40 South St., New York agents. W. G. Porter & Co., Apalachicola agents.

YEAR		VESSEL	TONS	MASTERS	REMARKS
1851	Bg.	Gen. Wilson	183	Francis D. Beckwith	
	Bk.	J. Denham	376	H. Gray	
	"	Rhone	350	J. D. Carlisle	
1853	Sch.	J. Grierson		Northrup	
1854	Bk.	Edward	355	Patterson	
	"	Cuba	248	Robert McCormick	
	"	Col. Ledyard	404	Francis D. Beckwith	William H. Hazard—late Eagle & Hazard—
1855	Sch.	Tanner	439	Ranna O. Welton	192 Front St., became New York agent in
1856	Bk.	M. E. Trout	253	L. F. Dean	1860. Other New York firms active in Apa-
	"	J. Vail	165	H. Delano	lachicola trade included Sturges & Clear-
1857	Sch.	M. C. Attwater		Mears	man and Alfred Ladd, later Ladd & Church.
1858	Sch.	Norfolk Packet	350	James Bedell	Hurlbut was also active in the St. Marks,
	"	Ik Marvel	191	Isaac B. Eldridge	Florida, trade, as were Coe, Anderson & Co.,
1860	Sch.	James M. Holmes		Brewster	later Smallwood, Anderson & Co., 10 Beaver St., New York.

HURLBUT'S LINE

E. D. Hurlbut & Co., 84 South St., New York agents.

YEAR		VESSEL	TONS	MASTERS	REMARKS
1836	Sp.	Indiana	306	D. D. Churchill	The firm had been running vessels to Apa-
	"	Georgia	410	Enoch Talbot	lachicola for several years, but it was not
	Bk.	Washington Irving	278	Paul W. Latham	until 1836 that it began to maintain a regular
	"	Charles P. Williams	187	Henry Ashby	service.
1839	Bg.	Lucinda	175	George P. Harkness	
1841	Bg.	Republic	139	Gurdon Gates	
	Sp.	Floridian	400	William Pratt	Foundered, Feb. 28, 1849, with Capt. E. D. Whitmore, nearly 200 passengers and all but three of crew, bound from Antwerp for New York.
	"	Uncas	423	Paul W. Latham	
	"	Emblem	610	Enoch Talbot	
	Bg.	Manhattan	246	W. H. Doane	
	"	Ann Eliza	144	George Eldridge, Jr.	
	"	Charles		Justus S. Doane	Passage $50 without wines.
	"	Emeline	198	Nathan G. Fish	
1843	Bg.	Metamora	196	Henry Ashby	
1844	"	Croton	311	David V. Soullard	Var. Souillard.
	"	Almeda	190	Pierre V. Rowland	
1845	Sp.	Liberty	690	Parker P. Norton	
1846	Bk.	Wabash	299	Enoch Talbot	
	Sp.	Tuskina	421	R. T. Williams	Samuel O. Williams master, 1848.
1847	Bk.	Ocilla	368	Henry S. Stark	
1848	Sp.	Arthur		Enoch Talbot	Ralph Post and J. W. Phillips, as Post &
	"	Marianna	379	Ginn	Phillips, 68 South St., became New York
1849	Bg.	Moses	220	Moses Bulkley	agents.
	"	Herald	174	Russell Gray	
	"	E. L. Walton	195	C. Ryder	

HURLBUT'S LINE (*continued*)

YEAR		VESSEL	TONS	MASTERS	REMARKS
1851	Bk.	*Jane E. Williams*	397	Thomas L. Masson	
	"	*Abeona*	298	J. S. Arey	
	"	*Edward*	182	Pattison	
	Sp.	*Cotton Planter*	502	Hayden	E. J. Parker master in 1852.
1853	Bk.	*Mary R. Barney*	281	Daniel B. Luther	
1855	Sp.	*John H. Ryerson*	954	Paul W. Latham	Post, Smith & Co., 85 South St., became
	"	*Forest City*	492	D. Allen	New York agents.
1856	Sch.	*Sarah Mills*	216	S. H. Rowley	
	"	*Ralph Post*	426	Hamilton D. Conklin	
1857	Sch.	*Presto*	278	Bethuel E. Hallock	
1860	Sch.	*Tanner*	439	Kittridge	

New York—Galveston

STAR LINE

William J. McKee, Southern Packet Office, 71 Wall St., New York agent. James McKee, 17 Coenties Slip, New York agent in 1841. Line soon discontinued.

YEAR		VESSEL	TONS	MASTERS	REMARKS
1840	Sch.	*Colorado*	111	Hess	
	"	*Springfield*		Green	

REGULAR LINE

John Ogden, 92 Wall St., New York agent. Established in 1842 by Ogden, who had been running transient schooners to Galveston for a year or two. John H. Brower, 75 Wall St., became associated as New York agent in 1842.

YEAR		VESSEL	TONS	MASTERS	REMARKS
1842	Sch.	*Robert Mills*	148	Daniel N. Moss	
	Sp.	*Star Republic*	305	William Hendley	J. J. Hendley master in 1844.
1843	Sch.	*Charles Henry*	85	John Smith	Brower withdrew in 1845 to start the New Line to Galveston.

NEW LINE

Brower & Neilson, 91 Front St., New York agents. Wm. Hendley & Co., Galveston agents. Established in 1845, to sail 1st of each month from each port, starting Sept. 1.

YEAR		VESSEL	TONS	MASTERS	REMARKS
1845	Bg.	*Empire*	218	J. B. Baxter	
	"	*G. B. Lamar*	260	E. Richardson	Sold to Chile, 1848.
	"	*Mary*	194	Peter Norris	
	Sp.	*Star Republic*	305	Daniel N. Moss	Burned at sea, July 1, 1855, from New York for Galveston; Rufus Cole, master.
1846	Bg.	*American*	256	James McNair	
	"	*Herald*	174	Henry M. Allen	
	Sch.	*Eleanor Stephens*	148	David Cox	
1847	Sp.	*Stephen F. Austin*	448	Daniel N. Moss	Lost on the Abaco, Aug. 15, 1858.
	Bk.	*Glencoe*	215	W. A. Abbot	J. H. Brower & Co. became New York
1848	Sp.	*Benjamin F. Milan*		H. M. Allen	agents.
	Bk.	*Montauk*	338	Gurdon Gates	Cicero Brown master in 1852.
	Sp.	*William B. Travis*	569	Frederick B. Bolles	
1849	Bk.	*Norumbega*	324	William Buckingham	Thomas Neilson became Philadelphia agent.
1850	Bk.	*J. H. Fanning*		Peter Norris	
1851	Sp.	*William H. Wharton*	693	Gurdon Gates	
1854	Sch.	*Nebraska*	187	John Washington	
1856	Bk.	*Cavallo*	296	Isaac Washington	
1857	Sch.	*Mustang*	316	William Greenman	
1858	Sch.	*Anthem*	174	Brutus Burrows, Jr.	Galveston trade continued very active in 1860
	"	*Stampede*	326	William Brand	with all lines and transients heavily engaged.
	"	*A. H. Manchester*	272	J. R. Potter	
	"	*Thomas H. Hall*		Rice	
	Bk.	*Mustang*	316	William Greenman	Ex-schooner.

MURRAY'S LINE

D. Colden Murray, 62 South St., New York agent. Established Feb., 1853, but did not get in full operation until following year.

YEAR	VESSEL	TONS	MASTERS	REMARKS
1853	Sch. *Louisa*	152	George Bellows	
1854	Bg. *Geranium*	433	E. H. Pierce	
1855	Bg. *North*	297	David Davidson	
"	*South*	272	Ensign Baker	
1856	Bg. *East*	297	E. W. Bray	Francis K. Studley master in 1857.
"	*West*	297	Francis K. Studley	
1858	Bg. *Bell Flower*	319	Duell	

STAR LINE

Wakeman, Dimon & Co., 74 South St., New York agents. J. C. Kuhn, Galveston agent.

YEAR	VESSEL	TONS	MASTERS	REMARKS
1854	Bg. *Amonoosuck*	250	John N. Munson	
"	*Lucy*	196	A. P. Weeks	
	Bk. *Robert Mills*	488	James McNair	
1855	Bk. *Houston*	518	W. A. McGill	
"	*Golden Age*	311	W. H. Garrick	
"	*Alamo*	507	Frederick Sherwood	
"	*Texas*	554	R. Luce	
"	*Milton*	536	W. Bradford	
	Bg. *Sabine*	399	Abraham H. Trask	
	Sp. *Star Republic*	305	Rufus Cole	Burned at sea, July 1, 1855.

New York—Matagorda

MERCHANTS' LINE

N. L. McCready & Co., 36 South St., New York agents.

YEAR	VESSEL	TONS	MASTERS	REMARKS
1851	Sch. *Reindeer*	218	Isaac Cathcart	
"	*Desdemona*	160	J. S. Chattin	Var. J. L. Chattin.
1853	Sch. *Indianola* (tern)	523	Charles P. Leverich	
"	*Telegraph*	174	John Green	
"	*Anthem*	174	Benjamin Burrows, Jr.	Also reported 124 tons.
1854	Sch. *William H. Hazard*	325	Oliver P. Saunders	Stanton & Thompson also agents for *Anthem* and *William H. Hazard*.
1856	Bg. *Lavacca*	342	Silas B. Greenman	McCready, Mott & Co. also agents for *Lavacca*.
1857	Sch. *Mustang*	316	William Greenman	

STAR LINE

Stanton & Thompson, 114 Wall St., New York agents.

YEAR	VESSEL	TONS	MASTERS	REMARKS
1851	Sch. *Urbanna*	138	John T. Lawless	
"	*William H. Hazard*	195	Oliver P. Saunders	
"	*Clinton*	237	Thomas Smith	
	Bg. *Empire*		Avery	
	Bk. *Greenfield*	560	Hepburn	
	Sp. *Star Republic*	305	Rufus Jameson	

New York—Matagorda, Lavacca and Indianola

TEXAS & NEW YORK LINE

J. H. Brower & Co., 46 South St., New York agents.

YEAR	VESSEL	TONS	MASTERS	REMARKS
1856	Sch. *Stampede*	326	John Washington	
"	*Mustang*	316	William Greenman	
1857	Sp. *J. W. Fannin*	409	J. H. Briggs	Lost near Galveston, Nov. 7, 1857.
1860	Bk. *Lapwing*	590	Silas B. Greenman	Taken by Privateer *Florida*, Mar. 27, 1863.

SECTION 17. PHILADELPHIA—CHARLESTON

SHIP LINE

Samuel Brooks, Philadelphia agent. Benjamin R. Smith, Charleston agent.

YEAR	VESSEL	TONS	MASTERS	REMARKS
1820	Sp. *Georgia Packet*	233	Jared Bunce	
	" *Pennsylvania*	240	William Bunce	Var. Willard Bunce.
1821	Sp. *Gen. Wade Hampton*	240	Francis Harrison	Fleming & Ross added as Charleston agents. Vendue Range, Robert Fleming, and Smith & Stewardson, Girard's Wharf, became Philadelphia agents.
1824	Sp. *Langdon Cheeves*	238	John Baker	
	" *Carolinian*	238	Anthony W. Robinson	A. Hewes master in 1825–6.
1826	Sp. *Florian*	335	Francis Harrison	Tonnage also reported 302.91.
1828	Sp. *Helen Mar*	307	Thomas Harrison	Line discontinued in 1830, the frequent sailings of the Philadelphia-Liverpool packets to Charleston possibly making a ship line between the two ports unprofitable.

SMITH'S LINE

Eventually known as Regular Line. Morris Smith, Girard's Wharf, Philadelphia agent. Benjamin R. Smith, Charleston agent.

YEAR	VESSEL	TONS	MASTERS	REMARKS
1830	Bg. *Langdon Cheeves*	207	John Baker	
	Sch. *John C. Calhoun*	117	John Ireland	
	" *Transport*	125	George Doiles	Isaac Henry master in 1833.
	" *Fifield*	107	Aaron Crum	
	Bg. *Freedom*	131	Thomas Steelman	
1832	Sch. *Ann Eliza*	126	L. Doyles	Sloan, Morris & Amory, Girard's Wharf,
	" *Protection*	107	John Ireland	became Philadelphia agents.
1833	Bg. *Star*	129	John Ireland	Francis & Co., and Sloan & Morris, became Philadelphia agents; Smith Mowry & Co., Charleston agents. Called Regular Line.
1834	Bg. *Mary Pauline*	172	David L. Wilcox	E. Pollard master in 1835.
	" *Stranger*	124	Isaac Henry	
	" *Comet*	118	James M. Averill	
	" *Emolument*	140	H. D. Booth	
	Sch. *Randolph*	123	G. Doyle	
1839	Sch. *Ajax*	110		
	Bg. *Paul T. Jones*	174	John Ireland	
	" *Virginia*	188	Ephraim Jordan	Timothy Treadway master in 1847.
1841	Bg. *Aldrich*	222	P. C. Cope	Smith Mowry, Jr., became Charleston agent.
1845	Sch. *Constitution*	168	Leonard Milton	Henry F. Baker became Charleston agent.
	" *Buena Vista*	120	William Brock	Alexander Heron & Co., 35½ N. Wharves,
	" *M. B. Mahoney*	131	Melchior McLaughlin	became Philadelphia agents.
1846	Bk. *Palmetto*	282	Nathaniel Kendrick	
1847	Sch. *H. Westcott*	122	Erastus Lodge	
	" *Julia*	167	Aaron Vangilder	
	" *Charles C. Stratton*	127	John Vance	Lost, 1858.
	" *William Hart*		Scudder	
1848	Bg. *Thomas Walter*	149	Charles P. Marshman	Var. *Thomas Walker.*
1849	Bg. *Charles Kershaw*	123	J. O. Atkinson	Var. Aitchison.
	Sch. *David Smith*	186	David Smith	
	" *S. Morris Waln*	148	John Erickson	
	" *Charles H. Rodgers*	199	Absalom Steelman	Var. Abraham Steelman.
1850	Sch. *Louisa*		Gray	
1851	Bg. *Delaware*	170	Peter Harding	George Heron became Charleston agent.
1853	Sch. *Edward H. Rowley*	197	Wertley Rodgers	Henry Missroon became Charleston agent.
1854	Sch. *Mary & Louisa*	167	Reuben Adams	
	" *Virginia*	180	Dean	H. F. Baker & Co. became Charleston
	" *Leesburg*	174	James P. Godfrey	agents. Baker also had Baltimore Merchants'
1855	Bg. *Daniel Maloney*	247	Henry Wildin	Line.
	Sch. *Roxbury*	118	Daniel Brown	
	Bg. *May Queen*	257	John W. Jackson	
	Sch. *John W. Rumsey* (tern)	368	Lewis P. Taylor	

SMITH'S LINE (*continued*)

YEAR	VESSEL	TONS	MASTERS	REMARKS
1856	Sch. *Mary H. Banks*			
	" *George Harris*	182	Ebenezer Corson	
	" *H. W. Gandy*		Fargo	
	" *Benjamin Hallet* (tern)	359	James S. Little	
1858	Sch. *Joseph M. Houston*	250	William Russell	Pettit, Martin & Co. became Philadelphia
1859	Sch. *Richard Vaux*	293	B. Frink	agents. Called Eagle Line.

NEW LINE

Joseph Hand, Philadelphia agent. James Chapman, Exchange St., Charleston agent.

YEAR	VESSEL	TONS	MASTERS	REMARKS
1839	Sch. *John Stull*	106	David Teal	
	" *Emma*	152	Daniel Bancroft	
1841	Bg. *Packet*	100	Charles Ward	Andrew Clark master in 1843.
	" *William J. Watson*	152	John P. Levy	
	Sp. *Wales*	446	I. E. Watts	Lost, Mar., 1844.
1842	Bg. *Paul T. Jones*	174	John Ireland	
1843	Sch. *Driver*	138	James Taylor	
1844	Sch. *Squire & Brothers*	163	William Price	
1845	Sch. *Patmos*	148	Daniel Townsend	Levi Eldridge, 7 N. Wharves, became Phila-
	" *Leader*	117	H. King	delphia agent.
1849	Sch. *Boston*	111	Charles C. Hilliard	Thomas G. Budd became Charleston agent; Levi Eldridge & Co., Philadelphia agent.

NEW LINE

James Chapman, Charleston agent.

YEAR	VESSEL	TONS	MASTERS	REMARKS
1839	Bg. *Paul T. Jones*	174	John Ireland	
1845	Bg. *Washington*	185	Thomas G. Monroe	S. S. Bishop & Co. became Philadelphia
1847	Sch. *Maria Theresa*	149	R. Smalley	agents.

NEW LINE

Barclay & Bernabeu, 9 N. Wharves, Philadelphia agents. Eugene Huchet, Lamb's Wharf, Charleston agent. Missroon & Milliken, Boyce & Co.'s Wharf, Charleston agents.

YEAR	VESSEL	TONS	MASTERS	REMARKS
1839	Sch. *Mediterranean*	139	Isaac Henry	
	Bg. *Langdon Cheeves*	202	Jeremiah Norgrave	
	Sp. *Alleghany*	414	Anthony Michaels	
1842	Sch. *Holder Borden*	148	Baker	S. S. Bishop & Co. and C. B. Barclay became
	Bg. *Randolph*	123	Samuel Goldsmith	Philadelphia agents.
	" *Washington*	185	J. Johnson	Thomas G. Moore master in 1846.
	" *Oneko*	128	S. Tobey	
1843	Sch. *President*	165	J. W. Symmes	
	Bg. *Huntress*	186	Henry F. Baker	
1844	Bk. *J. Patton, Jr.*	168	J. W. Symmes	

PATTON'S LINE

Armer Patton, 50 S. Wharves, Philadelphia agent.

YEAR	VESSEL	TONS	MASTERS	REMARKS
1839	Sch. *America*		H. Somers	
	" *Seaman*	169	Somers Scull	
	" *White Oak*	97	Edward Hughes	
1845	Sch. *J. Townsend*		Strong	
	" *J. & W. Errickson*	173	David Smith	

DISPATCH LINE

A. J. Culin & Co., Packet Office, 9 N. Wharves, Philadelphia agents.

YEAR	VESSEL	TONS	MASTERS	REMARKS
1846	Sch. *Dart*	104	Lewis Somers	
	Bg. *Thomas & Edward*	200	Harvey Mills	

DISPATCH LINE (*continued*)

YEAR	VESSEL	TONS	MASTERS	REMARKS
1846	Sch. *Ellen*	166	Boon	Sylvester Bearse master in July, 1846.
1849	Sch. *Monterey*	177	Carlisle	
"	*Abby Morton*	79	Joseph Wright	Bolton & Culin became Philadelphia agents in 1850.
1851	Bg. *Narragaugus*	189	M. Hinckley	Toram & Culin became Philadelphia agents.
	Sch. *Ontario*	199	A. C. Johnson	
"	*Alcyone*	148	J. Whitaker	A. J. Culin became Philadelphia agent in 1852. Line continued as Culin's Line.

CULIN'S LINE

Culin, Stille & Co., Philadelphia agents. H. F. Baker, Charleston agent.

YEAR	VESSEL	TONS	MASTERS	REMARKS
1853	Sch. *Three Sons*	242	Albert DeGroot	
"	*T. J. Brognard*	160	John Adams	

INDEPENDENT LINE

John H. Linton, Philadelphia agent. Thomas G. Budd, Charleston agent.

YEAR	VESSEL	TONS	MASTERS	REMARKS
1851	Sch. *Alcyone*	197	J. Whitaker	
1855	Bg. *George Whitney*		Baker	T. S. & T. G. Buddy, 76 E. Bay, became
	Sch. *Humming Bird*	319	William W. Morris	Charleston agents.
"	*William C. Mershon* (tern)	390	William C. Mershon	

MERCHANTS' REGULAR LINE

Baker & Stetson, Philadelphia agents. Discontinued in 1859.

YEAR	VESSEL	TONS	MASTERS	REMARKS
1853	Bg. *David S. Brown*	309	Benjamin B. Naylor	
1856	Sch. *James H. Stroup*		Corson	
"	*Mary H. Banks*		Banks	
1859	Bg. *David G. Wilson*	348	Benjamin E. Peacock	D. S. Stetson became Philadelphia agent.
	Sch. *Lizzie Maul*	281	Henderson	
	Bk. *Tremont*	198	Baker	

SECTION 18. PHILADELPHIA—SAVANNAH

Although there are frequent references to the sailing of "line" ships between Philadelphia and Savannah from 1826 on, available sources of information have failed to disclose any firm or individual in either port who publicly undertook to maintain a regular line service between the ports until the appearance of the Hand Line in 1838. A similar situation is to be noted with reference to the service between Philadelphia and Savannah and Mobile and between Baltimore and other southern ports with the exception of New Orleans. Facts may yet come to light that will definitely establish the existence of organized lines between such ports at earlier dates than noted herein.

JAMES HAND'S SCHOONER LINE

James Hand, Philadelphia agent.

YEAR	VESSEL	TONS	MASTERS	REMARKS
1838	Sch. *Adelaide Janey*		Thomas Young	
"	*Sarah*	84	H. Green	
"	*Samaritan*	127	Corson	Thomas Lombard master in 1841.
1840	Sch. *Charles M. Thompson*	107	E. B. Lynmire	Var. Lynmaniere.
"	*Marie Etta Ryon*	129	Henry Wilden	James Hand & Co. became Philadelphia
"	*Charles Pittman*	149	Elijah Townsend	agents.
"	*Ann Elizabeth*	131	H. Somers	
1841	Sch. *Dexter*	71	John Mason	
1845	Sch. *Imperial*		J. H. Read	Levi Eldridge, 7 N. Wharves, became Philadelphia agent for all of Hand Lines.

NEW LINE

Barclay & Bernabeu, 9 N. Wharves, Philadelphia agents. White & Bartell, Savannah agents.

YEAR	VESSEL	TONS	MASTERS	REMARKS
1839	Sch. *Constellation*	161	Joseph G. Price	
	" *Antelope*	148	Thomas Gifford	
	" *Gen. Warren*		Colley	
	" *Extra*	111	Thomas H. Wilson	
	" *Otis*	85	Joshua B. Bangs	
1845	Sch. *American Eagle*	125	Thomas Lombard	S. S. Bishop & Co. became Philadelphia agents.
1853	Sch. *Central America*	208	M. L. Chase	Baker & Stetson became Philadelphia agents.
	Bk. *Casaba*		Haines	Called Savannah Merchants' Line.
1856	Sch. *Aid*	98	English	
	Bk. *Edmund Dwight*	199	J. Nickerson	
1859	Sch. *Lucy L. Sharp*	274	Compton	D. S. Stetson & Co. became Philadelphia agents. Called Keystone Line.

LOPER LINE

R. F. Loper and William Baird, Philadelphia agents.

YEAR	VESSEL	TONS	MASTERS	REMARKS
1842	Bg. *W. J. Watson*	152	John P. Levy	William M. Baird & Co. took Loper Lines in 1852.

NEW LINE

James Buker, Savannah agent.

YEAR	VESSEL	TONS	MASTERS	REMARKS
1845	Bg. *Lancet*	154	J. McIntire	
1846	Sch. *Ann*	74	R. S. Phinney	
1847	Sch. *Oscar*	140	Peter S. Hickman	

ELDRIDGE LINE

Levi Eldridge, Philadelphia agent. Cohen, Norris & Co., Savannah agents.

YEAR	VESSEL	TONS	MASTERS	REMARKS
1845	Sch. *Imperial*		J. H. Read	
	Bg. *Havana*	164	Benjamin Gilpatrick	
	Sch. *American Eagle*	125	James S. French	
	Bk. *Phoenix*	244	Nathaniel Boush	
1847	Sch. *Santee*	92	J. Carle	

DISPATCH LINE

A. J. Harper & Co., Packet Office, 9 N. Wharves, Philadelphia agent. Established Feb., 1846.

YEAR	VESSEL	TONS	MASTERS	REMARKS
1846	Sch. *North Carolina*	117	David Miller	
	" *Dart*	104	Lewis Somers	
	" *Shylock*	120	Robert Crocker	

HERON'S LINE

Alexander Heron, Philadelphia agent. Greiner & Beall, Savannah agents.

YEAR	VESSEL	TONS	MASTERS	REMARKS
1847	Sch. *Oscar*	108	John Adams	
	" *Julia*	167	Aaron Vangilder	Sailed every Sat. in 1848.
1849	Sch. *John H. Holmes*	123	Erastus Lodge	Also reported 153 tons.
	" *Julia Eliza*	162	Richard Higbee	
1850	Sch. *H. Westcott*	144	Zelepheard Hand	
	" *Sarah Elizabeth*	147	Blackman	
	" *George Harris*	182	John Somers	Ebenezer Corson master in 1854.
1851	Sch. *Dart*	104	Lewis Somers	Heron & Martin became Philadelphia agents; C. A. Greiner, Savannah agent.
1852	Sch. *David Smith*	186	David Smith	Brundage & Willis became Savannah agents in June; Ogden & Bunker, Savannah agent in Oct.
	" *Samuel N. Smith*	157	Samuel N. Smith	
	" *Monterey*	177		

HERON'S LINE (*Continued*)

YEAR	VESSEL	TONS	MASTERS	REMARKS
1852	Sch. *Joseph F. Tobias*	180	Zelepheard Hand	
1853	Sch. *George P. Mercer*	255	R. Higbee	
1854	Sch. *L. D. Scull*			
1855	Sch. *Christopher Loeser*	197	James Snow	
	Bg. *Alfred Exall*	244	Samuel Beaston	Abandoned at sea, May, 1860.
				C. A. Greiner became Savannah agent.
1856	Sch. *N. B. Tridall Thompson*	179	William Barnes	
1858	Sch. *Alice Lea*	282	Thompson	Pettit, Martin & Co. became Philadelphia
	" *Joseph H. Flanner*	194		agents; C. A. Greiner & Co., Savannah
	" *George Harris*	182	Ebenezer Corson	agents.
1859	Sch. *Julia Anna*	193	Joseph Harding	Called Eagle Line.
	Bk. *Edward Everett*	221	Joseph Harding	

SECTION 19. PHILADELPHIA—MOBILE

JOSEPH HAND'S LINE

Joseph Hand, Philadelphia agent. Gardner & Sager, Mobile agents.

YEAR	VESSEL	TONS	MASTERS	REMARKS
1835	Bg. *Virginia*	127	N. Long	
	" *Stranger*	124	Isaac Henry	
1836	Bg. *Treaty*	241	John L. Dunton	
	" *Comet*	118	John F. Trout	
	" *George Turner*	217	J. D. Blanchard	
	" *Syren*	239	J. L. Pendleton	
	" *William Henry*	249	Morrell	
	Sp. *Archer*	322	John Johnson	
	Bk. *Josephine*	325	John Johnson	
1838	Sp. *Franklin*		S. Goodhue	
	Sch. *White Oak*	97	Aquila Wells	
	Bg. *Aldrich*	222	Jeremiah Norgrave	
	Bk. *Coosa*	259	David B. Moore	
1839	Sch. *Pelican*	100	Fentress	
	Bg. *Huntress*	186	David Davidson, Jr.	
	Sp. *Spring*	283	John Fletcher	
1843	Sch. *Gilbert A. Hatfield*	186	Felix Smith	Levi Eldridge, 7 N Wharves, became Philadelphia agent in 1845.
1848	Bk. *Hermione*	259	John Somers	

JAMES HAND'S LINE

James Hand, Philadelphia agent.

YEAR	VESSEL	TONS	MASTERS	REMARKS
1838	Sch. *Holder Borden*	148	Julius Baker	
	" *Will*	156	E. Dyer	
	" *Albert M. Hale*	135	Sylvester M. Sage	
1840	Sch. *Pensacola*	120	Leonard Buck	
	Bg. *Junius*	121	Wilkins	
	Sch. *Gardner H. Wright*	135	Elkanan Burton	
1845	Sch. *Emma*	152	Daniel Bancroft	
	" *Orralloo*	122	Asa Lufkin	
1848	Bk. *Hermione*	259	E. Howard	Levi Eldridge & Co., 7 N. Wharves, became
	Sch. *John Castner*	247	John Somers	Philadelphia agents.
	Bg. *Eliza Jane*	222	Daniel Townsend	

PATTON'S LINE

Armer Patton, 48 S. Wharves, Philadelphia agent. Clement B. Barclay, New Orleans agent.

YEAR	VESSEL	TONS	MASTERS	REMARKS
1839	Sch. *Armer Patton*	167	Andrew Thompson	
1840	Sch. *Thomas Ewing*		John Ireland	
	Bg. *Indiana*	192	Aquilla Wells	
	Sch. *George Klotts*	140	Beal	
1841	Sch. *Columbia*	112	John Townsend	

PATTON'S LINE (*continued*)

YEAR	VESSEL	TONS	MASTERS	REMARKS
1841	Sch. *Gilbert A. Hatfield*	186	Felix Smith	
"	*Ninetta*	128	James Baymore	

NEW LINE

S. S. Bishop & Co., Philadelphia agents.

YEAR	VESSEL	TONS	MASTERS	REMARKS
1842	Bg. *Victor*	125	Francis Gorham	
	Sch. *Council*	99	William Baker	
	Bk. *Wakulla*	367	John B. Rathbone	
1843	Bg. *Acton*	184	B. B. Daggett	Lost at sea, Nov., 1847.
1844	Bg. *Freighter*	214	N. B. Knight	
1845	Bk. *J. Patton, Jr.*	168	Washington Symmes	
	Bg. *G. H. Wright*	135	W. Renton	Var. *Gardner H. Wright*.
	" *Margaret*		A. Brook	
	" *Yucatan*	177	S. Baker	
1847	Sch. *Segachet*	156	Artemas W. Watts	Beers & Smith became New Orleans agents.
	" *Arietas*	133	J. H. Sterling	Var. *Arietis*.
				Bishop & Boggs became Philadelphia agents in 1848.
1849	Bg. *Matinic*	192	W. H. Thorndike	Bishop & Watson became Philadelphia agents.
1853	Sch. *Theresa C.*	179	Sylvanus Carson	Baker & Stetson, 43 N. Wharves, became Philadelphia agents.
	Bg. *Osceola*	265	Joseph Farrell	
	Bk. *Roderick Dhu*	224	Smith	Called Alabama Merchants' Line.
1856	Sch. *Haze*	321	Edward A. Langdon	
	" *Adeline Townsend*	289	Ebenezer N. Townsend	Baker & Stetson dissolved in 1858, and D. S. Stetson & Co. started Keystone Line.
1859	Bg. *John Welsh*	273	John C. Fifield	Jairus Baker, 138 N. Wharves, became Philadelphia agent.
				Prout, Fowler & Stanard became Mobile agents.

CULIN & CO.'S REGULAR LINE

A. J. Culin & Co., Philadelphia agents. Fosdick & Charlock, Mobile agents.

YEAR	VESSEL	TONS	MASTERS	REMARKS
1848	Bk. *Alice Tarleton*	309	Archelaus F. Trefethen	
	Bg. *Monica*	179	A. Buck	
	Sch. *E. J. Brognard*	159	Pennington	
	" *Palestine*		Errickson	
	" *Maj. Eastland*	183	Wells	S. French master in 1850.
	" *Frances Esther*	147	Burr Nash	
1849	Bg. *Edinburg*	195	David W. Swett	
	" *Rockingham*	149	Batt Flowers	
1851	Sch. *Howard*		Wood	Bolton & Culin became Philadelphia agents; changed to Toram & Culin in Apr. A. J. Culin became Philadelphia agent in 1852.
	Bk. *Jane Gano*	256	Beaman	

HERON'S LINE

Alexander Heron, Jr., Philadelphia agent. N. O. Brewer, Mobile agent.

YEAR	VESSEL	TONS	MASTERS	REMARKS
1849	Sch. *H. Westcott*	144	Hand	Var. 122 tons.
1851	Sch. *Mary & Louisa*	167	Reuben Adams	Heron & Martin became Philadelphia agents; E. C. Center & Co., Mobile agents.
	" *H. F. Baker*	181	Melchior McGlauchlin	
	" *Leesburg*	174	B. B. Naylor	
1852	Bg. *Thomas B. Watson*	212	A. A. Blackmore	
1853	Sch. *John Potts Brown*	203	Henry Collet	H. O. Brewer & Co. became Mobile agents.
1854	Sch. *Virginia*	188	Dean	
1856	Sch. *Richard Vaux*	293	Frink	
	" *Edward H. Rowley*	197	J. P. Godfrey	
1858	Sch. *Dirigo*	343	Robert C. Cook	Pettit, Martin & Co. became Philadelphia agents.

HERON'S LINE (*continued*)

YEAR	VESSEL	TONS	MASTERS	REMARKS
1859	Sch. *Mary E. Smith*	246	David Smith	Called Eagle Line.
"	*George A. Tittle*	268	Reuben B. Adams	
"	*Joseph Crandall*	245	Anthony S. Megathlin	
"	*Harriet A. Rogers*	270	Rogers	

KEYSTONE LINE

D. S. Stetson & Co., Philadelphia agents.

YEAR	VESSEL	TONS	MASTERS	REMARKS
1858	Sch. *David Faust*	199	William Morlander	

SECTION 20. PHILADELPHIA—NEW ORLEANS

NEW ORLEANS PACKET LINE

C. Price & Morgan, Philadelphia agents. Morgan, Dorsey & Co., New Orleans agents.

YEAR	VESSEL	TONS	MASTERS	REMARKS
1818	Bg. *Feliciana*	294	Nathaniel Franklin	
	Sp. *Balize*	307	Hezekiah Harding	John Longcope master in 1819.
1819	Sp. *Orleans*	219	John Grover	
"	*Ohio*	284	Simeon Toby	
"	*Franklin*	391	John J. Garvin	
"	*Tennessee*	275	Solomon Maxwell	Thomas Barnes master in 1821.
1821	Sp. *Schuylkill*	229	Solomon Maxwell	
	Bg. *Hercules*	382	Hezekiah Harding	
"	*Swan*	352	Nathaniel Franklin	
1824	Sp. *Margaret*	291	John Grover	
1825	Sp. *Ohio*	352	John J. Garvin	
	Bg. *Alfred*	260	Paul A. Oliver	
1826	Sp. *Benjamin Morgan*	408	J. E. Mathieu	Samuel P. Morgan became New Orleans agent.
1828	Sp. *Chandler Price*	441	Lewis Paleskie	Samuel P. Morgan & Co. became New Orleans agents.
1832	Sp. *John Sergeant*	384	Christopher Van Dyke	Bevan & Humphreys, 35 S. Wharves, and J. G. and D. B. Stacey became Philadelphia agents. Called New Line; sailed every two weeks.
"	*Chester*	326	Samuel Storer	
"	*Edward Bonaffe*	325	John J. Garvin	
				Thomas A. Morgan added as Philadelphia agent in 1833.
1834	Bk. *Hercules*	382	James Marks	J. A. Brown replaced Bevan & Humphreys.
	Sp. *Walter*	475	G. Foulks	
	Bg. *Po*	145	Daniel Dean	
1836	Bk. *Delaware*	198	Horner	J. Reid & Co., 35 Royal St., became New Orleans agents.
	Sp. *North Star*	391		Isbon Benedict master in 1842.
1842	Bk. *Iris*	240	Thomas Merryman	S. S. Bishop, 38 N. Wharves, became Philadelphia agent.
"	*Renown*	296	William Watson	
	Bg. *Growler*	247	Bernard Ulmer	
"	*Joseph*	185	William Cammett	George Loring master in 1843.
1843	Sp. *St. Louis*	444	James Marks	
"	*Globe*	479	William C. Lowry	
"	*Berwick*	472	Sam Harding, Jr.	
1844	Sch. *J. T. Bertine*	150	Jesse E. Brown	Aaron Cohen, 90 Common St., became New Orleans agent.
1845	Bk. *Yarmouth*	326	Nathaniel Matthews	
	Bg. *Republic*	139	Gurdon Gates	S. S. Bishop & Co., 9 N. Wharves, became Philadelphia agents.
1846	Sp. *Alleghany*	414	William Shankland	
"	*Lady Arabella*	399	J. Simpson	Tristam Chesley master in 1848.
1847	Sch. *Holder Borden*	148	Elisha H. Rhodes	C. J. Meeker became New Orleans agent.
"	*Maria Theresa*	149	R. Smalley	
1848	Sp. *George Skolfield*	414	Thomas Skolfield	Bishop & Boggs became Philadelphia agents.
"	*Gen. Taylor*	597	St. Croix Redmond	Var. Redman.
"	*York*	341	Christopher Van Dyke	

NEW ORLEANS PACKET LINE (*continued*)

YEAR		VESSEL	TONS	MASTERS	REMARKS
1848	Bk.	*Warwick*	337	Wilcox	George W. Anthony master in 1849.
	"	*Saragossa*	349	William Watson	Albert Turley master in 1854.
	"	*Louisa Bliss*	395	Jordon	
1849	Sp.	*John & Albert*	567	Joseph Harwood	Bishop & Watson became Philadelphia
1850	Sp.	*France*	441	John H. Marshall	agents.
	"	*Cordova*	332	John H. Lowell	
	Bg.	*Thomas & Edward*	200	Levi Smalley	
1851	Sp.	*Nicholas Biddle*	784	David Caulkins	
	"	*Lone Star*	512	William Boutelle	
1852	Bk.	*Marmora*	388	Montgomery	Bishop, Simons & Co. became Philadelphia agents.
	Sp.	*Marathon*	486	Christian Van Dycke	Called Louisiana Line; sailed every ten days.
	"	*Lydia*	543	Francis B. Soule	
	"	*Mayflower*	721	J. Crooker	
	"	*Walter R. Jones*	400	Elliot Honeywell	
	"	*Lucas*	350	J. H. Smith	
1853	Sp.	*Naples*	508	W. H. Duncan	C. J. Meeker & Co. became New Orleans
	Bk.	*Golden Era*	443	Joseph Thorndike	agents.
	Sp.	*William*	522	R. M. Doane	
1854	Sp.	*Isaac Jeanes*	843	William Chipman	Bogart, Williams & Co. became New Orleans agents.
	"	*Horatio*	507	H. Hall	Var. Hale.
	Bk.	*Henry Warren*	360	B. Raerden	
					Commencing in 1855 operations interrupted for several years.
1859	Bk.	*Cochituate*	348	Crosby	Bishop, Simons & Co. resumed operations.
1860	Sp.	*American Union*	1147	S. Merchant	

HAND'S LINE

Joseph Hand, 7 N. Wharves, Philadelphia agent. Thomas Toby, New Orleans agent.

YEAR		VESSEL	TONS	MASTERS	REMARKS
1831	Bg.	*Ella*	235	Jeremiah Cole	Oliver Marston master in 1831–2.
1832	Sp.	*Archer*	322	Jeremiah Cole	
1834	Bg.	*John Burgin*	195	John Veazie	Thomas Toby & Co. became New Orleans
	Bk.	*Madeline*	293	John McManus	agents.
	Bg.	*J. L. Hudgins*		Naylor	
	"	*William Henry*	249	A. Morrell	
	"	*Virginia*	127	Oliver Marston	
1835	Bk.	*Josephine*	310	John Johnson	
	"	*Falmouth*	278	P. E. Merrill	Var. Merritt.
1836	Sp.	*Montezuma*	436	Barr	
	Bk.	*Gazelle*	260	A. H. Eldridge	Edward A. Merry master in 1839. James D. Denegre became New Orleans agent in 1837.
1838	Bg.	*Swan*		Ames	
	Bk.	*Ella Hand*	383	Daniel L. Kurtz	Lost on Stirrup Keys, Oct., 1838.
	Sch.	*Mexico*		James Baymore	
	Sp.	*Ohio*	352	John J. Garvin	
	"	*Georgian*	279	Antony H. Eldridge	
1839	Bk.	*Baptist Mezick*	360	John J. Garvin	
	Sp.	*Adelaide*	373	L. I. Yorke	
	Bk.	*Coosa*	259	David B. Moore	
1841	Bg.	*Corinthian*	250	John Stone	
	Bk.	*Renown*	296	William Watson	
1843	Bk.	*Sarah Hand*	282	Daniel Herrick	J. Y. Bailey master in 1845.
1844	Bk.	*Irad Ferry*	299	Stephen Chase	Levi Eldridge, 7 N. Wharves, became Phila-
	Sp.	*Ebro*	350	Crosby	delphia agent in place of Hand. T. Toby &
	Bk.	*Rammohun Roy*	359	William Cutts	Bogert became New Orleans agents.
1845	Bk.	*Baltic*	302	John Gregory, Jr.	Abandoned at sea, 1852.
1847	Bk.	*Lowell*	348	John A. Bradstreet	"To sail every 8 or 10 days." Also a weekly
	"	*Indiana*	255	William H. Watts	packet to Charleston and all four Chesapeake
	"	*Franklin*	300	George H. Gilchrist	ports, except a sailing every other day to
	Bg.	*Ormus*	174	Eben R. Smith	Baltimore. Packets to Boston, New York, Mobile and Savannah as freights offered.

HAND'S LINE (*continued*)

YEAR	VESSEL	TONS	MASTERS	REMARKS
1848	Sp. *Osceola*	549	Barstow	
	Bk. *Sultan*	339	Robert R. Decan	Levi Eldridge & Co. became Philadelphia
	" *Pario*	300	Samuel Watts	agents; R. M. Harrison & Co., New Orleans agents.
1850	Bk. *Roxanna*	299	Hall	Var. *Roxana.*
1851	Bg. *Emeline*	236	E. Watts	
	Bk. *Convoy*	261	Joel Hupper	
	" *J. W. Dyer*	243	J. W. Dyer	
	" *James Bayley*	207	George Bishop	

LOUISIANA & PHILADELPHIA LINE or REGULAR LINE

Samuel Comley and Robert Fleming, Philadelphia agents.

YEAR	VESSEL	TONS	MASTERS	REMARKS
1833	Sp. *Helen Mar*	307	Francis Harrison	
1834	Bg. *Alcyone*	197	Sparrow Snow	T. Julius master in 1835.
	" *Ann & Leah*	150	S. Goldsmith	
	" *Constitution*	199	Sylvester M. Sage	
	" *Criterion*	183	Hugh McQuillen	
	" *Arria*		Thorndike	
	Sp. *Eliza & Susan*	317	Hugh McQuillen	
1839	Sp. *Renown*	296	Sparrow Snow	Line called Pennsylvania & Louisiana Line;
1840	Bg. *Aldrich*	222	John Baker	M. S. Comly & Co., 97 Camp St., became
	" *Cecilia*	152	E. W. Watson	New Orleans agents.
	" *Langdon Cheeves*	207	John Gallagher	C. B. Barclay became Philadelphia agent.

JAMES HAND'S LINE

James Hand & Co., Philadelphia agents.

YEAR	VESSEL	TONS	MASTERS	REMARKS
1838	Bg. *Tappanooly*	218	Francis Davis	
	" *Mohegan*	161	Elkanah Stackpole	
	" *J. Palmer*	125	C. P. Marshman	
	" *Cazenove*	171	S. Cory	
	" *Sisters*		Coverdale	
1839	Sp. *Charles Lanahan*			
	" *Galen*	514	J. Snow	
	" *Columbia*	600	Thomas G. Clark	Var. Thomas B. Clark.
				During 1840 and later, both James and
1840	Sp. *Stephen Baldwin*	635	William T. Glidden	Joseph Hand sent packet ships up the river to
	Bk. *Lark*	287	William C. Lowry	Memphis, Vicksburg, and Natchez.
	Bg. *Coosa*	258	Michael Powers	James Hand & Co. became Philadelphia
1841	Bg. *Impulse*	135	James Gavet	agents.

PENNSYLVANIA & LOUISIANA LINE

Barclay & Bernabeu, 9 N. Wharves, Philadelphia agents. Moss & Harris, 45 Royal St., New Orleans agents.

YEAR	VESSEL	TONS	MASTERS	REMARKS
1839	Sp. *Manchester*	570	Robert Bosworth	
	" *Palmyra*	612	John Cushing	
	" *St. Louis*	340	William Watson	James Marks master in 1842.
	" *Ohio*	351	G. L. Kurtz	Daniel Rusk master in 1841.
	Bk. *Ronaldson*	319	J. E. Mathieu	William C. Stotesbury master in 1846.
1840	Bg. *Cecilia*	152	E. W. Watson	
1841	Sp. *Wakona*	430	James Borland	Levi H. Gale, 92 Common St., and Moss &
	" *Walter*	475		Harris, 24 Old Levee, became New Orleans agents.
	Bg. *Loretto*	245	James Henderson	C. B. Barclay became Philadelphia agent in 1842; Aaron Cohen, New Orleans agent

PATTON'S LINE

Armer Patton, Philadelphia agent.

YEAR	VESSEL	TONS	MASTERS	REMARKS
1839	Sp. *Constellation*	276	Franklin Houdlette	
	Bk. *Laurens*	420	Ben Merrill	
1841	Bg. *David Duffell*	188	S. Tilton	A. B. Cooley became Philadelphia agent.

PHILADELPHIA & NEW ORLEANS LINE

Penrose & Burton, 34 S. Delaware St., Philadelphia agents. J. H. Ashbridge, 97 Camp St., New Orleans agent.

YEAR		VESSEL	TONS	MASTERS	REMARKS
1843	Sp.	*Champlain*	624	James F. Miller	Vessel lost as per Havana certificate dated Apr. 15, 1850.
	Bk.	*Joshua Emlen*		D. L. Wilcox	
	Sp.	*United States*	449	James Maloney	
	"	*Caledonia Brander*	549	Peter A. Decan	Sold foreign, Nov., 1853.
	"	*Solon*	540	George Buchanan	
1844	Bk.	*Josephine*	325	James Maloney	
	Sp.	*Stephen Baldwin*	635	William T. Glidden	
	"	*Alleghany*	414	Henry S. Brown	
	"	*Hudson*	335	Samuel Buckman, Jr.	
	Bk.	*Nashua*	301	Rinier Skaats	
	"	*Robert Morris*	241	William S. Outerbridge	
1845	Bk.	*Mary & Jane*	346	S. O. Flitner	
	Sp.	*Wataga*	415	E. Moore	C. B. Ashbridge became New Orleans agent
1847	Bk.	*Delaware*	198	William B. Fisher	in 1846.
	Sp.	*Robert Burton*	398	Peter A. Decan	
	"	*Lehigh*	565	J. H. Young	
	Bk.	*Curtis*	250	William S. Outerbridge	
	Bg.	*Juniata*	184	Silas Martin	
	"	*Eliza Fountain*			
1848	Sp.	*Lucas*	350	William S. Outerbridge	Line consisted of seven ships and one bark.
	"	*Hindoo*	581	Henry S. Brown	
1850	Bk.	*Sultan*	339	Thomas J. Watson	
1852	Sp.	*Westmoreland*	999	Peter A. Decan	Robert R. Decan master in 1854.
1854	Sp.	*Howadji*	695	George E. Balch	J. H. Ashbridge & Co., 119 Common St., became New Orleans agent.
1855	Sp.	*Lancaster*	1566	Peter A. Decan	
1856	Bk.	*Old Hickory*	432	James Veacock	Burton & Clement became Philadelphia agents. Called Burton & Clement's Line. No record of line after 1858. Ashbridge & Co. went into Havre and Liverpool trade heavily.

DISPATCH LINE

A. J. Harper & Co., Packet Office, 9 N. Wharves, Philadelphia agent.

YEAR		VESSEL	TONS	MASTERS	REMARKS
1846	Bg.	*Thomas & Edward*	200	Levi Smalley	J. H. Bass became New Orleans agent in 1854. Line consisted of brigs. Jones, Mackinder & Co., 91 Gravier St., became New Orleans agents in 1856. Bass took Merchants' Line. Jones and Mackinder had Crescent Line to Boston.
	"	*St. George*	222	Levi Smalley	

HERON'S LINE

Alexander Heron, Jr., 35½ N. Wharves, Philadelphia agent. Samuel Churchman, New Orleans agent.

YEAR		VESSEL	TONS	MASTERS	REMARKS
1846	Bg.	*Oceana*	249	James A. Creighton	
	Bk.	*Rio Grande*	298	John H. Cousins	
1847	Sch.	*Charles D. Ellis*	128	Absalom Steelman	
	"	*Chester*		Walton	
1851	Bg.	*J. A. Taylor*	196	John Sleeper	O. Wickham became New Orleans agent
	"	*New World*	232	Anthony Castner	
	"	*Alfred Exall*	244	Joseph Golder	Samuel Beaston master in 1855.
	Sch.	*Fannie*	262	John Vance	
1852	Sp.	*Diana*	568	Francis Fred Claussen	Heron & Martin became Philadelphia agents.
	"	*Joseph Holmes*	614	Adams	
	Bg.	*May Queen*	257	Erastus Lodge	
	"	*Ann Elizabeth*	196	John Vance	
	Bk.	*Robert Walsh*	282	Josiah Kelloch	C. C. Wickham and R. M. Harrison & Co. became New Orleans agents.
1853	Bk.	*Loretto Fish*	247	Chase	

HERON'S LINE (*continued*)

YEAR		VESSEL	TONS	MASTERS	REMARKS
1853	Bk.	*Jacob B. Lancaster*	352	William Somers	
1855	Bk.	*Tammany*	330	Absalom Steelman	Heron & Martin advertised three barks, three
	Sch.	*Andrew Manderson* (tern)	360	B. F. Henderson	brigs, three schooners, for freight or charter.
	Bk.	*Frederick Lenning*	347	George V. White	Washington Symmes master in 1856.
1856	Bk.	*Washington Butcher*	345	Walter Collins	
	Sch.	*Henry Nutt*	235	Joseph Williams	
	"	*A. L. Crawford*	247	Andrew A. Blackman	
1858	Bk.	*Charles B. Truitt*	316	Somers Scull	Pettit, Martin & Co. became Philadelphia
1859	Sch.	*Margaret Reinhardt*	247	Jacob Peterson	agents.
	Bk.	*Brilliant*	349	William P. Sigsbee	George W. Hynson became New Orleans
	"	*Benjamin Hallet*	359	James S. Little	agent.
	"	*Isaac R. Davis*	348	Joseph Hand	Called Eagle Line.
1860	Sch.	*Edmund S. Jaynes*	231	J. P. Godfrey	

COMMERCIAL LINE

E. Lincoln & Co., Philadelphia agents. Andrews & Dorsey, 91 Common St., New Orleans agents.

YEAR		VESSEL	TONS	MASTERS	REMARKS
1846	Sp.	*Robert G. Shaw*	402	Richard Matthews	
	Bk.	*Jacob S. Waln*	264	Gorham Howland	Nathaniel Percival master in 1849.
	"	*Yarmouth*	327	Marks	
	"	*James Andrews*	275	Josiah French	
	"	*Adeline & Eliza*	249	Wiliam W. Baker	
1847	Bk.	*David Nichols*	194	David Nichols	
	"	*Cyrus*	247	Candage	Sailed twice a month during business season.
	"	*Curtis*	250	William A. Outerbridge	
	Bg.	*Julia Moulton*	198	J. S. Glidden	
1848	Bg.	*Hamlet*	219	Richard Robinson, Jr.	Andrews & Dewey became New Orleans
	Bk.	*Floyd*	224	Freeman Mayberry	agents.
1849	Sp.	*Alleghany*	414	William S. Shankland	
1850	Sp.	*Hindoo*	581	J. F. Miller	J. W. Andrews & Co. became New Orleans agents.

CULIN'S LINE

A. J. Culin & Co., Philadelphia agents.

YEAR		VESSEL	TONS	MASTERS	REMARKS
1848	Sp.	*Soldan*	648	Nathaniel Thomas	
1849	Bg.	*Josephine*	232	Timothy N. Porter	
	"	*Gov. Carver*	180	Nathaniel Coleman	
	"	*Maj. Eastland*	183	Wells	S. French master in 1850.
	"	*Albermarle*	220	Charles Comery	
1852	Sp.	*John Spear*	629	A. Spear	A. J. Culin became Philadelphia agent.
1853	Bg.	*Linden*	392	Benjamin Rowe	Cullin, Stille & Co. became Philadelphia
1854	Bg.	*Charlotte E. Fay*	199	William T. Clark	agents; R. M. Harrison & Co., New Orleans agents.

MERCHANTS' LINE

Baker & Stetson, 43 N. Wharves, Philadelphia agents. G. C. Bogert & Co., 70 Camp St., New Orleans agents.

YEAR		VESSEL	TONS	MASTERS	REMARKS
1852	Bk.	*Rainbow*	341	Lawrence	Atkins Hughes master in 1855.
	Bg.	*Cimbrus*	200	Herman Kopperholdt	
	Sp.	*Europe*	618	William S. Shankland	
1853	Bk.	*Emily Banning*	282	Horace B. Ray	Bogert & Williams became New Orleans
	"	*Jacob Prentiss*	393	J. G. Loring	agents.
	"	*St. Mary's*	280	Alexander Milliken	
	Bg.	*David S. Brown*	309	Benjamin Taylor	
	Sch.	*Edmund S. Janes*	231	Joseph Westcott	
1854	Sch.	*J. E. Roache*		Bateman	
	"	*George Maugham*	275	William C. Scudder	
	Bg.	*Osceola*	265	Joseph Farrell	Bogert, Williams & Co. became New Orleans
1855	Sp.	*Bosphorus*	1470	James G. Pendleton	agents.
	Bk.	*Charles W. Poultney*	399	Benjamin W. Conant	
	Sch.	*William C. Mershon* (tern)	390	William C. Mershon	

MERCHANTS' LINE (*continued*)

YEAR		VESSEL	TONS	MASTERS	REMARKS
1856	Bk.	*James C. Hand*	311	Joseph D. Westcott	William Marshman master in 1856–7.
"		*David G. Wilson*	348	Benjamin E. Peacock	J. H. Bass became New Orleans agent in 1857.
1859	Bk.	*David Kimball*	449	A. H. Linnell	Jairus Baker, 138 N. Wharves, became Philadelphia agent.
					Baker also had Merchants' Lines to Galveston, Mobile, and Wilmington, N. C.

SECTION 21. BALTIMORE—CHARLESTON

BRIG LINE

Charles Gwinn, 7 Spear's Wharf, Baltimore agent. James M. Stocker and Samuel Lord, Charleston agents. Established Jan., 1834, to sail 1st, 10th, and 20th of month.

YEAR		VESSEL	TONS	MASTERS	REMARKS
1834	Bg.	*Gen. Marion*	197	Henry D. Delano	
"		*Gen. Sumter*	187	William Bennett	George Hobbs master in 1841.
	Sch.	*Laura*	93	Harrod	
"		*Frances Jane*	169	Isaac Kirby	
1838	Bg.	*Gen. Pinckney*	195	Lewis Ford	Jonathan B. Sanner master in 1844.
1841	Bg.	*Wankingo*	98	Russell Howland	
1842	Bg.	*Northumberland*	167	William C. Nason	John K. Randall became Baltimore agent,
"		*Eleanor*	150	Alexander Jones	apparently a temporary arrangement.
	Sch.	*J. Cohen, Jr.*		Moore	
"		*Thames*	99	William J. Axworthy	
1843	Sch.	*Henrietta*	74	James T. Forrest	James A. Dubel master in 1850.
"		*Tom Wood*	135	Brown	
1844	Bg.	*Kirkwood*	211	H. Martin	
"		*Victorine*	238	Jonathan B. Sanner	G. F. Brown master in 1850.
					John K. Randall, 104 Smith's Wharf, became Baltimore agent in 1849.

REGULAR LINE

John K. Randall & Co., 104 Smith's Wharf, Baltimore agents. J. Lord & J. M. Stocker, Charleston agents.

YEAR		VESSEL	TONS	MASTERS	REMARKS
1837	Sch.	*New Jersey*	151	Richard L. West	
	Bg.	*Gen. Pinckney*	195	Lewis Ford	
"		*Gen. Marion*	196	Henry D. Delano	
"		*Gen. Sumter*	187	William Bennett	
1838	Bg.	*Solon*	155	James T. Forrest	Lord & Stocker became Baltimore agents.
"		*Edwin*	133	Jeremiah T. Speights	William Hubbard master in 1841.
1839	Sch.	*Lady Warrington*	98	Jeremiah T. Speights	William Hubbard master in 1841.
1841	Sch.	*Tom Wood*	135	Joseph Symonds	Thomas Whitridge and John K. Randall became Baltimore agents.
	Bg.	*Wankingo*	98	Russell Howland	
	Sch.	*T. R. Betton*	138	Samuel M. Travers	
1844	Bg.	*Kirkwood*	211	Hugh Marlin	Var. Martin.
1850	Bg.	*Emma*	166	S. Hughs	
	Sch.	*Mary Emeline*	142	J. Bonny	Var. Benney.
"		*Chief*	135	J. R. Gayle	

MERCHANTS' LINE

Charles Pendergast & Son, Smith's Wharf, Baltimore agents. Thomas J. Kerr, Charleston agent.

YEAR		VESSEL	TONS	MASTERS	REMARKS
1844	Sch.	*Kate Pendergast*	160	S. Barnum	G. W. Evans master in 1845–6.
"		*Lady Warrington*	97	J. Bonny	Solomon F. Tyler master in 1846.
"		*Mary Catherine*	96	Joseph R. Gayle	
"		*Iowa*	100	Lawson I. Applegate	
"		*Alice Ann Pendergast*	90	J. R. Stevens	
1849	Bg.	*Vandalia*	133	Washington Brown	
	Sch.	*Triton*	108	Washington Brown	
"		*Brilliant*	98	Henderson	John Washington master in 1856.
1850	Sch.	*Truth*	95	Samuel Phillips	Henry F. Baker became Charleston agent.

MERCHANTS' LINE (*continued*)

YEAR	VESSEL	TONS	MASTERS	REMARKS
1850	Sch. *Ellen Goldsborough*	98	J. R. Stevens	Line called Southern Line in Baltimore.
"	*Corinthian*	104	William E. Plummer	
"	*Havana*	85	W. Symmes	
1851	Sch. *Champion*		Osborn	James F. Pendergast became Baltimore agent.
"	*Edwin Farrar*	99	John W. Mitchell	
"	*Aurora*	148	Travis	
"	*Olivet*	112	George W. Foxwell	
"	*Iona*	154	James R. Stevens	
"	*Samuel Butler*	114	Joseph Booze	
Bg.	*Osprey*	99	James Robinson	
Sch.	*Henrietta*	74	Hammond	
1852	Sch. *Alice*	119	Samuel Phillips	
"	*Union*	88	Washington Brown	
1853	Sch. *D. H. Baldwin*	109	Levin H. Parker	
1854	Sch. *Emily Kerr*	161	John Linden	Thomas J. Kerr became Charleston agent.
"	*Susan Cannon*	145	Staples	H. C. Bunch master in 1855.
"	*B. B. Mahoney*		Nichols	H. F. Baker & Co. became Charleston agents.
"	*Yorktown* (Cl.)	145	Samuel Phillips	
"	*Virginia Griffiths*	177	William E. Plummer	
"	*Georgia*	133	William H. Mitchell	
1855	Sch. *Storm King*	220	W. Lanfere	
"	*Sussex*	153	William H. Knight	
1857	Bk. *Nashua* (Cl.)	196	Augustus A. Lewis	Charles Pendergast became Baltimore agent.
"	*Helen Maria*	194	Zenas Nickerson, Jr.	
Sch.	*Magnolia*		Josiah Richardson	
1859	Sch. *Somerset*	118	John Sterling	Henry P. Russell became Baltimore agent. Continued through 1861.

SOUTHERN LINE

Kelsey & Gray, Baltimore agents.

YEAR	VESSEL	TONS	MASTERS	REMARKS
1851	Sch. *Charles W. Bentley*	119	W. R. Davis	Benjamin S. Mills master July, 1851.
Bg.	*Rowland*	230	Alfred Watts	
"	*Paragon*	157	W. S. McNally	
Ketch	*Commerce*	174	B. Sowbriates	L. W. Kinkly master in 1855
Sch.	*Samuel R. Jackson*	149	Andrew A. Blackman	
"	*C. L. Bayles*	155	Hamilton Tooker	
"	*Eureka*	141	William B. Kirwan	
1852	Sch. *Naiad*	86	Richard C. Watts	
Bg.	*Empire*	197	Peter Crowell	
1853	Sch. *Gen. Taylor*	124	Daniel Abbott	

SECTION 22. BALTIMORE—SAVANNAH

SORRELL & ANDERSON LINE

Sorrell & Anderson, Savannah agents.

YEAR	VESSEL	TONS	MASTERS	REMARKS
1830	Sch. *Hannah Bartlett*	75	H. Swift, Jr.	
"	*Mirror*	98	Lodowick P. Babcock	
1837	Bg. *Gen. McIntosh*		Thomas Chapman	Francis Sorrell became Savannah agent;
"	*Eliza Ann*	161	Michael McDonald	James I. Fisher, Frederick St. Dock, Balti-
1838	Bg. *Opelousas*	161	Reuben Collins, Jr.	more agent.
1839	Bk. *R. H. Douglass*	261	Reuben Collins, Jr.	
1847	Sch. *Mary Catherine*	96	James Tyler	

GWINN'S LINE

Charles Gwinn, 7 Spear's Wharf, Baltimore agent. Francis Sorrell, Savannah agent.

YEAR	VESSEL	TONS	MASTERS	REMARKS
1834	Sch. *Hyperion*	125	J. Creighton	
Bg.	*Laura*	158	Harrod	

GWINN'S LINE (*continued*)

YEAR		VESSEL	TONS	MASTERS	REMARKS
1834	Sch.	*Richard Henry*	123	Sturdevant	
	"	*Aeriel*	123	Asbury McNamara	
1835	Sch.	*Eliza Caroline*	117	Meekins	
	"	*Marion*	112	Henry B. Parker	G. W. Parker also master in 1835.
	"	*Ajax*	94	S. Saunders	
	Bg.	*Oglethorpe*	131	Henry Fitzgerald	

REGULAR LINE

John K. Randall & Co., 105 Smith's Wharf, Baltimore agents. S. Philbrick & Co., Belton's Range, Savannah agents.

YEAR		VESSEL	TONS	MASTERS	REMARKS
1836	Bg.	*Oglethorpe*	131	Henry Fitzgerald	
	"	*Falcon*	166	F. Neal	Var. Neill.
1838	Sch.	*Wave*	118	Colin S. Baker	
1839	Bg.	*Eleanor*	150	Henry Fitzgerald	Alexander Jones master in 1839–40.
	"	*Gen. Sumter*	187	William Bennett	
	Sch.	*Nimrod*	98	Sewell	
	Bg.	*Edwin*	133	William C. Amos	Thomas H. Fitzgerald also master in 1839.
1840	Bg.	*Wankingo*	98	Russell Howland	
1841	Bg.	*Jane*		Henry Fitzgerald	
	"	*Robert Bruce*	115	Thomas H. Fitzgerald	
	Sch.	*Tom Wood*	135	Joseph Symonds	

REGULAR LINE

James Girvin, 93 Smith's Wharf, Baltimore agent. Brigham, Kelly & Co., Telfair's Wharf, Savannah agents.

YEAR		VESSEL	TONS	MASTERS	REMARKS
1850	Sch.	*Ocean*	97	Levin H. Parker	
	"	*H. N. Gambrill*	119	William Bradford	
	"	*Alvarado*	83	Marcellus Booze	
1851	Sch.	*D. H. Baldwin*	109	Levin H. Parker	
1852	Sch.	*Ann Maria*	142	John Wilson	
	"	*Woodward*		William Bradford	
1853	Bg.	*Chattanooga*	208	William Bradford	
	"	*Saltillo*	162		
1854	Sch.	*Woodbridge*	165	Samuel G. White	
	"	*Kate Brigham*	470	J. H. Luther	
	"	*Somerset*	118	John Sterling	
1855	Sch.	*Louisiana*	132	Albion L. Hathaway	
	"	*Frambes*		Frambes	
	"	*S. L. Levering*			
1856	Bg.	*John S. Cotton*	199	M. Allen	
	Sch.	*Zuleika*	235	E. R. Blair	
	Bg.	*Josephus*	142	Terral	
	Sch.	*E. L. B. Wales*	178	Hoffman	

SOUTHERN LINE

Kelsey & Gray, Gay & Pratt Sts., Baltimore agents. Ogden & Bunker, Savannah agents.

YEAR		VESSEL	TONS	MASTERS	REMARKS
1851	Sch.	*George M. Robertson*	133	George H. Lanfare	
	"	*Naiad*	86	John Linden	
	"	*Telegraph*	143	Nathaniel Dickinson	
	"	*Charles W. Bentley*	119	Benjamin S. Mills	Cosgrove also master in 1851.
	"	*Mary Mankin*	232	David Latourette	
	Bk.	*Sunny Eye*	252	D. Seabury	Var. *Sunny Age.*
	"	*Ellen Morrison*	213	James Gavet	
	Sch.	*Corinthian*	104	Wainwright	
1853	Sch.	*George J. Jones*	164	Hiram Look	
1854	Sch.	*Willow*	100	H. W. Miller	

SECTION 23. BALTIMORE—MOBILE

HOWELL LINE

William Howell & Son, 48 S. Gay St., Baltimore agents.

YEAR	VESSEL	TONS	MASTERS	REMARKS
1834	Sch. *Sophia*	110	H. Martin	
1835	Bg. *Rebecca Frances*	127	Borum	

BOYLE LINE

Hugh Boyle & Co., 75 Smith's Wharf, Baltimore agents.

YEAR	VESSEL	TONS	MASTERS	REMARKS
1835	Sch. *Galante Marie*			
	" *Hyperion*	125	J. Baker	

HANKEY'S LINE

J. Hankey, 2 Spear's Wharf, Baltimore agent.

YEAR	VESSEL	TONS	MASTERS	REMARKS
1836	Sch. *Vandalia*	93	Zebedee Kirwan	
1839	Sch. *Morning Star*	89	George H. York	

REGULAR LINE

Thomas Hooper, 5 Spear's Wharf, Baltimore agent. Henry A. Schroeder, Mobile agent.

YEAR	VESSEL	TONS	MASTERS	REMARKS
1841	Sch. *James Fisher*	99	W. Smith	Evan Hooper master in 1842.
	" *Columbia*	119	Zebedee Kirwan	
	" *Candid*	88	William W. Wilkins	
1842	Sch. *D. C. Wilson*		Merritt B. Benjamin	
	" *D. W. Hall*		Benjamin Atwell	
1843	Sch. *H. A. Schroeder*	96	John B. Stafford	
1844	Sch. *Mary M. Hooper*	161	Samuel M. Travers	Also reported brig
	" *T. R. Betton*	138	John Griffith	

SECTION 24. BALTIMORE—NEW ORLEANS

THOMPSON LINE

Henry Thompson, Baltimore agent. Smith & Dorsey, New Orleans agents.

YEAR	VESSEL	TONS	MASTERS	REMARKS
1815	Sp. *Walter*	294	Samuel C. Childs	
	" *Marmion*	291	Thomas Parker	

HAMMOND & NEWMAN LINE

Hammond & Newman, 82 Bowly's Wharf, Baltimore agents.

YEAR	VESSEL	TONS	MASTERS	REMARKS
1826	Bg. *Talent*	266	Isaac Winsor	
	" *Arctic*	231	Elijah Soule	
	" *Trafalgar*	160	Isaac Winsor	

PAYSON LINE

Henry Payson & Co., Baltimore agents.

YEAR	VESSEL	TONS	MASTERS	REMARKS
1828	Bg. *Arctic*	231	James Phillips	
	" *Sultana*	230	Robert D. Stansbury	

REGULAR LINE OF PACKETS

A. J. Dinnies & Co., Baltimore agents. C. J. Henshaw, New Orleans agent. Established Apr. 2, 1831. Consisted of four brigs to sail from Baltimore the 1st and from New Orleans the 15th.

REGULAR LINE

Clark & Kellogg, Baltimore agents. George Bedford, New Orleans agent.

YEAR	VESSEL	TONS	MASTERS	REMARKS
1834	Bg. *Pilgrim*	199	Jeremiah Stevens	
	" *Nancy*	154	S. Titcomb	
	" *Ranger*	164	Jonathan Twining	
1835	Bg. *Patriot*	174	Lewis A. Johnson	
	" *Hector*	198	John Farrow	
	" *Nelson Clark*	187	John A. Smith	
1836	Bg. *Harriet*	180	Lunt	
	Bk. *Poacher*	219	B. F. Fosdick	
1837	Sch. *John*	111	Warden	Line consisted normally of five vessels sailing
	" *Patapsco*	90	Brewster	approximately twice a month in season.
	Bg. *Damon*	183	Scott	
	" *Ralph*			
	Bk. *Tiberius*	299	George Sears	
	Bg. *Julia & Helen*	193	Joshua Thorndike	
	Bk. *Mary*	244	T. G. Wingate	T. S. Nickerson master in 1839.
1838	Bg. *Northerner*	233	J. Stevens	William B. Hatch master in 1843.
	" *Architect*	164	Adams Gray	
	Bk. *Lafayette*	260	D. C. Landis	
	Bg. *Choctaw*	245	H. Stevens	
	Sp. *Constellation*	276	Thomas B. Sampson	
	Bg. *Ligonia*	237	Eben Creighton	
1839	Sp. *Seaman*	241	Miner	Cabin fare $60.
	Bk. *Irad Ferry*	299	J. Ignatius Stevens	
	" *Solomon Saltus*	317	Elbert Latham	E. Peterson master in 1844.
	Bg. *Caucassian*	161	Burton Vose	
	Sp. *Herald*	248	Louis A. Casteau	Var. Chatham.
	Bg. *Georges*	192	Ambrose Snow	
	Bk. *Galileo*	268	George Lombard	
1841	Sp. *Tippecanoe*	450	Adams Gray	G. Bedford & Beck, 24 Custom House St., became New Orleans agents.
1843	Bg. *Radius*	195	John Plummer	Bailey & Baxter, 77 Common St., became
	" *Oceana*	249	James A. Creighton	New Orleans agents in 1844.

NEW REGULAR LINE

McCorkell & Moore, Smith's Wharf & Pratt St., Baltimore agents.

YEAR	VESSEL	TONS	MASTERS	REMARKS
1839	Sp. *Metamora*		Lowe	
	" *Gibraltar*			
	Bg. *Russell*	183	Samuel Matthews	
	" *Empress*	130	A. Littlefield	

NEW LINE

William Moore, Smith's Wharf, Baltimore agent.

YEAR	VESSEL	TONS	MASTERS	REMARKS
1841	Bg. *Raymond*	205	Caleb Levenseller	
	Bk. *Tennessee*	224	Samuel Schofield	
1842	Bg. *Gazelle*	146	Caleb Thomas	

ORLEANS LINE

John A. Merritt & C. J. Meeker, 34 Poydras St., New Orleans agents.

YEAR	VESSEL	TONS	MASTERS	REMARKS
1844	Bg. *Victorine*	239	Alex Jones	
	Bk. *Eleanor*	302	L. Slemmer	
	" *Henry Kelsey*	197	Adams Gray	A. Bornholm master in 1854.
1845	Bg. *Helen McLeod*	268	D. C. Landis	
1847	Bk. *Iwanona*	254	Robert Shinn	
	" *Abby Baker*	257	Pratt	
	Bg. *Virginia*	138	E. O. Cooper	
	" *Dracut*	213	J. G. Smith	

ORLEANS LINE (*continued*)

YEAR		VESSEL	TONS	MASTERS	REMARKS
1847	Bg.	*Gen. Pinckney*	195	G. B. Cole	
1851	Sp.	*Edward Everett*	623	F. A. Gunby	
"	"	*Helen A. Miller*	510	Washington Galt	
	Bk.	*Abbot Lord*	437	A. Ruark	
1852	Sch.	*Henry A. Barling*	161	Marshall	
1854	Sp.	*Pharsalia*	617	Dyer	
1855	Sch.	*White Swan* (Cl.)	273	J. Linden	George W. Hynson & Co. became New Orleans agents.
1857	Bk.	*Hebron*	386	Sheppard	Regular line consisted of four ships.

BALTIMORE & NEW ORLEANS LINE

John Henderson & Co., 77 Pratt St., Baltimore agents. J. H. Ashbridge, 97 Camp St., New Orleans agent.

YEAR		VESSEL	TONS	MASTERS	REMARKS
1847	Sch.	*Willow*	100	J. Roney	Var. Renny.
"	"	*Mary Augusta*	145	William Hewes	
	Bk.	*Louisa*	316	George Young	F. A. Gunby master in 1850.
1848	Bk.	*E. H. Chapin*	424	George W. Collier	
"	"	*Pioneer*	347	Washington Galt	
"	"	*Leda*	258	A. Ruark	
	Bg.	*Frances Amy*	161	F. A. Gunby	
1849	Sp.	*Charles*	387	George W. Collier	Joseph W. Ashbridge became New Orleans
1850	Sch.	*Henry A. Barling*	161	Washington Galt	agent.
	Sp.	*Elsinore*	597	John Riley	Called Henderson & Co.'s Dispatch Line.
	Bk.	*Abbot Lord*	437	A. Ruark	
	Sp.	*Jane Henderson*	638	William Wallace	W. Gault master in 1858.
	Sch.	*George C. Ackerly*	180	William C. Baldwin	
1851	Bk.	*Cora*	431	Hiram Horton	
"	"	*Sarah Bridges*	483	Jonathan Stout	Var. Strout.
"	"	*Herman*	419	T. B. Skinner	Vessel lost, 1854.
	Bg.	*Waverly*	192	G. Anderson	
	Sp.	*Edward Everett*	623	F. A. Gunby	
"	"	*Helen A. Miller*	510	W. Galt	
1854	Sp.	*Pharsalia*	617	L. Dyer	
1855	Sch.	*White Swan* (Cl.)	273	J. Linden	George W. Hynson & Co. became New Orleans agents. Regular line consisted of four
1857	Bk.	*Hebron*	386	Sheppard	ships.

HOOPER'S UNION LINE

James Hooper, E. Baltimore St., Baltimore agent.

YEAR		VESSEL	TONS	MASTERS	REMARKS
1849	Bg.	*Union*	180	J. H. Goodmanson	Hooper & Graff became Baltimore agents in
	Bk.	*Southerner*	338	E. Hooper	Nov.

APPENDIX III

Ownership of American Vessels of 400 to 1000 Tons From 1790 to 1800

T HE trend toward centralized ownership and operation of American vessels may be gathered from the following incomplete list of great ships ranging from 400 to 1000 tons built or acquired by American merchants in the 11 years from 1790 to 1800, inclusive. Before the Revolution very few vessels of 400 tons had been built in the colonies, and most of those were owned in part abroad, while ships of 500 tons were very rare. It will be noted that 16 of the 41 ships here listed were owned by single individuals, and most of the others by firms of two or three persons. Before the Revolution the great majority of vessels registered less than 100 tons and their ownership usually was divided between several persons.

Ship	Tonnage	Place & Date Built	Owner
America	561	New York, 1788	Isaac Gouverneur, *et al.*, New York
American	520	Philadelphia, 1793	John Hollingsworth, *et al.*, Philadelphia
Ann & Hope	550	Providence, 1798	Brown and Ives, Providence
Canton	483½	France, 1781	John Dewhurst, New York, 1791
Canton	518	New York, 1799	Thomas W. Francis, *et al.*, Philadelphia
China	1009	Philadelphia, 1799	James Josiah, Philadelphia
Commerce	443	Amesbury, Mass., 1790	Robert William, Boston
Confederacy	459	Glastonbury, Conn., 1794	Reuben Smith, *et al.*, New York
Connecticut	548	Connecticut, 1799	Jordan Wright, New York
Elizabeth	562	Not stated	Richard and Samuel Ward, New York, 1794
Ganges	504	Philadelphia, 1795	Thomas W. Francis, *et al.*, Philadelphia
George Washington	627	Providence, 1794	Lewis Clapier, *et al.*, Philadelphia
Governor Strong	439	A prize, 1800	William H. Bordman, Boston
Grand Turk	564	Salem, 1791	John Earl, New York
Hannibal	481	France, 1792	Stephen Dutilh, *et al.*, Philadelphia
Hercules	597	Amesbury, Mass., 1791	Edward Jones, Boston
Hercules	498	Exeter, Mass., 1793	Ebenezer Frothingham, *et al.*, Boston
Hindostan	562	Georgetown, Mass., 1800	William Cramond, Philadelphia
India	401	Philadelphia, 1793	John Miller, *et al.*, Philadelphia
Indian Chief	401	Philadelphia, 1793	Thomas Keown, Petersburg, Va.
John	490	Newbury, Mass., 1792	Benjamin Joy, Boston
John Jay	464	Providence, 1794	Brown and Ives, Providence
Kingston	409	Bath, 1796	Walter Sims, Philadelphia
Manhattan	667	New York, 1800	Philip and Frederick, Rhinelander, New York

Ship	Tonnage	Place & Date Built	Owner
Mary	429	Warren, R. I., 1792	Richard S. Hallett, New York
Mary Ann	460	Providence, 1800	Nicholas Brown, *et al.*, Providence
Massachusetts	791	Braintree, Mass., 1789	Samuel Shaw and Thomas Randall, Boston
Massachusetts	616	Newbury, Mass., 1799	James Perkins, *et al.*, Boston
Molly	401	Virginia, 1789	John Knox, New York
Monticello	455	Newbury, Mass., 1798	Nathaniel Fellowes, Boston
Mount Vernon	431	Philadelphia, 1796	Samuel and William P. Meeker, Philadelphia
New Jersey	401	Philadelphia, 1795	Robert E. Griffith, *et al.*, Philadelphia
Ocean	402	Guilford, Conn., 1794	Isaac Clason, New York
Ontario	611	New York, 1794	Abraham Franklin, *et al.*, New York
Patapsco	418	Baltimore, 1799	Charles Ross, *et al.*, Philadelphia
Penman	447	Chatham, Conn., 1800	Preserved Fish, *et al.*, New York
President Washington	858	Providence, 1791	John Brown, *et al.*, Providence
Resource	424	Hartford, Conn., 1795	Edward Dexter, Providence
Semiramis	459	Warren, R. I., 1796	Hezekiah B. Pierpont, *et al.*, Newport
Trumbull	536	Norwich, Conn., 1800	William H. Robinson, *et al.*, New York
Washington	540½	Maryland, 1788	Samuel Shaw & Thomas Randall, New York

Schooners of 300 Tons and Upwards
Built in the United States, 1850-60

Down to 1850 comparatively few schooners registered as much as 150 tons and the great majority registered less than 100 tons. A few large privateer schooners were laid down during the War of 1812, one of the fastest and best known of which was the *Comet* of Baltimore. She measured 246 tons and was very lofty, carrying a skysail and royal studding sails.

After the war the first large schooner noted was the *Exchange*, a two-decker built at Middletown, Connecticut, in 1821. She rated 314.41 tons and was owned by Horace Stocking and commanded by Jared Arnold.

The next one of comparable size was built in 1827 in Matthews County, Virginia. This was the *Pocahontas*, a tern measuring 380.45 tons, 122′ × 29.3′. She had two decks and a figurehead. She was owned by Henry Mankin, a prominent shipowner and merchant of Baltimore, and is of special importance as the first sailing vessel noted in the American records fitted with iron rigging. The *Boston Gazette* for Nov. 5, 1827, described her as "a schooner of three masts rigged fore and aft fashion. Her standing rigging is all iron served with rope yarn. The shrouds are continuous bars, and the cross pieces, usually termed ratlines, are strips of wood. The stays are composed of long links about a yard in length."

Baltimore produced the next large schooner noted. This was the *Engineer*—also reported *Eugenia*—launched in 1832. She was a tern of the following measurements: 310.20 tons, 120′ × 30.1′ × 9.5′. She was sold foreign shortly after launching and it is probable that the last two, if not all the above, were laid down with a view to the slave trade.

One or two other big schooners were built prior to 1850, and between 1815 and 1850 a number of small terns ranging around 150 tons were constructed—craft of the *Pan Matanzas, May,* and *Norfolk* description—but it was not until 1851 that construction of large schooners was begun on a substantial scale. Several factors contributed to bring this about, the principal one being the urge to meet steamship competition that was rapidly taking over the more remunerative areas of the coastal trade. The big schooners failed to attain that objective but proved so economical compared with the square-riggers that construction continued until the practical limitations were reached in the huge five- and six-masted craft of 40 years later.

Aside from a number of 300-tonners built on the Great Lakes and the Ohio River and its tributaries, which are omitted, the following list includes a substantial majority of American schooners of 300 tons and more, built 1850-60, inclusive. All are two-masters, except those described as terns. The enrollment numbers ran consecutively beginning with the first of each year in each port.

Tern *Addison Child.* Boston enrollment 217, Oct. 15, 1855. Built, 1855, at Essex, Conn. 401.13 tons, 130.6′ × 29.4′ × 11.6′. Henry Bell, master and managing owner.

Adeline D., of New York. New York enrollment 554, Aug. 10, 1853. Built, 1853, at Poughkeepsie, by Henry Finch. 354.50 tons, 123.3′ × 30′ × 10.8′. John Podger, master. Elzey S. Powell, Samuel S. and Isaac O. Thorp, Abraham Denike and builder, owners.

Alba, of New York. New York enrollment 840, Aug. 19, 1853. Built, 1853, at Poughkeepsie, by Henry Finch. 394.10 tons, 130.9′ × 32.7′ × 10.4′. David Haff, master. Elzey S. Powell, Stewart S. Haff, George Sweeney, Abraham Denike and builder, owners. Joseph R. Merrihew, master in 1857.

Tern *Andrew Manderson,* of Philadelphia. Philadelphia enrollment 440, Nov. 11, 1854. Built, 1854, at Petty's Island, Pa. 360.34 tons, 125′ × 28′ × 11.3′. Flush deck. B. F. Henderson, master, and part owner with Charles Miller, James Stuart, George Walters, *et al.,* of Philadelphia.

Ann & Eliza, of New York. New York enrollment 453, June 24, 1857. Built, 1852, at Norwalk, Conn. 325.67 tons, 120′ × 28.8′ × 10.6′. Samuel Myers, master, and part owner with Gilbert Potter, Jr., and Harold Dollner, copartners, and Samuel B. Ashby, of Brooklyn, James S. Truslow, of New York, and Joseph H. Flanner, of Wilmington, N.C.

Ann & Susan, of New York. New York enrollment 5, Jan. 4, 1853. Built, 1852, at Norwalk, Conn., by John Friend and Edward R. Vincent. 325.67 tons, 120′ × 28.8′ × 10.6′. John R. Crary, master. Owners same as in *Ann & Eliza,* above. Samuel Myers, master in 1853, and George T. Pearson, master in 1854.

Tern *Annie E. Coxe,* of New York. New York enrollment 351, May 1, 1855. Built, 1855, at Essex, Conn., by Francis West. 393.19 tons, 134.6′ × 29′ × 11′. Woman figurehead. Littleton C. Wimpenny, of Edgartown, Mass., master, and part owner with Robert H. Lane, Hugo B. Major, Charles M. and Nathaniel M. Terry and Joseph Della Torre, copartners; Elisha Baker, Henry Couillard, and Elbert Hoagland and William Van Pelt, copartners, of New York. H. W. Mallery, master in July, 1855.

Tern *Augusta C. Brewer,* of New York. New York enrollment 327, Apr. 24, 1855. Built, 1854, at Millbridge, Me. 399.45 tons, 131.6′ × 27.6′ × 12′. Peleg Saunders, of Westerly, R.I., master, and part owner with Robert H. Lane, Hugo B. Major, Francis West, and Charles M. and Nathaniel M. Terry and Joseph Della Torre, copartners; and William Brewer, of New York, Robert E. Coxe, of Montgomery, Ala., and Alonzo C. Small, of Cherryfield, Me. David P. Berry, master in 1855.

B. C. Scribner, of Milford, Del. Philadelphia temporary register 20, 1861. Built, 1856, at Milford. 327.26 tons, 121' × 28.6' × 10.6'. Joshua H. Irons, master. William A. Scribner, owner.

Tern *B. Watson,* of Philadelphia. Philadelphia register 69, Oct. 9, 1857. Built, 1855, at Milford, Del. (See Philadelphia Proof of Ownership 507, Oct. 31, 1855.) 298.26 tons, 118' × 28' × 10'. Burton Robinson, master, and part owner with W. N. W. Dorsey, William Sharp, Thomas Wallace, and Manlove R. Carlisle, all of Philadelphia.

Bay City, of New York. New York register 708, Nov. 29, 1853. Built, 1853, at New York. 406.79 tons. J. H. Wardle, master. William Lubbock, owner. Register surrendered at Rio de Janeiro, no date.

Ben, of New York. New York enrollment 806, Dec. 9, 1853. Built, 1853, at Belleville, N.J., by Cornelius C. Jerolemon. 362.3 tons, 124.6' × 30.4' × 10.3'. Christian Zoll, master. Elzey S. Powell, Samuel S. and Israel O. Thorp, Abraham Denike, and James W. Olson, all of New York, owners. Robert H. McCready, master in 1858.

Bennet Flanner, of New York. New York enrollment 315, Apr. 15, 1855. Built, 1855, at Newcastle, Del. 321.93 tons, 122' × 30.6' × 9.8'. Poop deck. Henry Applegit, master, and part owner with Charles F. Haywood, George S. Perry and Frederick Kidder, of New York, James R. Gilmore, *et al.,* of Brooklyn, and Bennet Flanner, of Wilmington, N.C. In 1858 D. Colden Murray, *et al.,* of New York, were part owners.

Cataract, of New York. New York enrollment 613, Oct. 3, 1851. Built, 1851, at New York, by Perine, Patterson & Stack. 318.81 tons, 117.3' × 28.4' × 10.8'. Charles A. Rice, master. Nathaniel L. McCready, Adrian B. Holmes, and Samuel S. and Isaac O. Thorp, all of New York, owners.

Tern *Champion,* of Boston. New York temporary register 328, July 1, 1859. Built, 1854, at Harpswell, Me. 563.78 tons, 133.55' × 30.6'. Two decks. James B. Nichols, master. William D. Sewall, of Bath, owner.

Charles G. Waterbury, of New York. Charleston, S.C., temporary register 39, Oct. 3, 1857. Built, 1854, at Hoboken, N.J. 307.82 tons, 117.6' × 30.6' × 9.8'. Figurehead. William W. Cook, master, and part owner with William Work, Willet S. Robins, George Klots, *et al.,* of New York. See also New York enrollment 482, July 3, 1857.

Tern *Charles Smith,* of Wilmington, N.C. New York temporary register 265, Apr. 24, 1857. Built, 1856, at Amesbury, Mass., by Charles R. Littlefield. 397 tons, 131' × 30.5' × 11'. Charles W. Bartlett, of Charleston, S.C., master and owner.

Tern *Claremont,* of New York. New York enrollment 141, Mar. 23, 1857. Built at Bulls Ferry by Henry Finch. 340.91 tons, 128' × 32.7' × 9.1'. Here reported as two-master but called a tern elsewhere. George W. Johnson, master. H. C. Jewel, John G. Wright, and Joshua Wood, of New York, and William Allen, of Claremont, Va., owners.

Colonel John McRae, of New York. New York register 247, Apr. 7, 1855. Built, 1855, at Hoboken, N.J. 411.71 tons. C. Bogart, master. D. Reid, owner.

Cordelia, of New York. New York register 300, May 16, 1856. Built, 1856, at Brooklyn. 658.50 tons, 145' × 31.6' × 20'. Two decks, two masts, and eagle head. Reported a tern in New York register 152, Mar. 24, 1859. William C. Dunham, master. Thomas Dunham, Philander Daggett, Merritt Trimble, Joseph Tuchermory, William L. Burroughs, and Peter Nugent, of New York, and Henry Brigham and Daniel H. Baldwin, of Savannah, Ga., owners.

Tern *Daniel S. Williams,* of New York. New York enrollment 600, Sept. 10, 1859. Built, 1858-9, at Forked River, N.J., by John Vaughn. 393.13 tons, 134' × 32' × 10'. Daniel S. Williams, of New York, master and managing owner.

Dirigo, of Philadelphia. Philadelphia enrollment 14, Jan. 21, 1858. Built, 1858, at Allowaystown, N.J. 343.13 tons, 117' × 30.6' × 10.8'. Robert C. Cook of Tom's River, N.J., master. John H. Allen and John Tracy, of Philadelphia, *et al.,* owners.

E. C. Howard, of Chatham, Conn. New York enrollment 33, Oct. 1, 1855. Built, 1854, at Essex, Conn. 308.61 tons, 108' × 29.5' × 10.7'. Caleb Nickerson, master, and part ownei with C. H. Pratt, *et al.*

Tern *Eckford Webb,* of New York. New York enrollment 321, Apr. 20, 1855. Built, 1855, at New York by Eckford Webb. 494.75 tons, 137' × 30' × 13.2'. Eagle head. Joseph A. Graffam, master. Thomas Dunham, *et al.,* of New York, and Henry Brigham, of Savannah, owners. Proved very fast, reporting 16 knots in her 21-day passage across the Atlantic. George B. Cottle, master in 1857.

Eclipse, of Suffolk, Va. New Orleans temporary register 60, May 22, 1854. Built, 1852, at New York. 305.25 tons, 120.4' × 29' × 9.7'. R. W. Goslee, master. William B. Whitehead, of Suffolk, owner.

Edward Kidder, of New York. New York enrollment 302, May 3, 1854. Built, 1854, at Belleville, N.J., by Cornelius C. Jerolemon. 318.55 tons, 119.8' × 30.4' × 9.1'. William S. Tyler, master. Abraham Denike, Samuel S. and Isaac O. Thorp, of New York, and Joseph H. Flanner, of Georgetown, N.C., owners.

Tern *Edwin R. Bennett,* of New York. New York enrollment 640, Sept. 30, 1853. Built, 1853, at Westfield, N.Y., by W. H. and J. M. Rutan. 332.85 tons, 129.9' × 29.9' × 9.6'. Abraham H. Wood, master. Henry S. Seguine, of Westfield, James S. Seguine, of Norfolk, Va., and the builders, owners.

Tern *Elizabeth C. Felter,* of New York. New York enrollment 312, Apr. 17, 1855. Built, 1855, at Hoboken, N.J., by Capes & Allison. 389.36 tons, 136.4' × 31.6' × 10'. John Arnold of Squan, N.J., master. Jonathan T. Johnson, Charles H. Thorn, William Work, Winant V. Pierce, *et al.,* of N.Y., owners.

Ellen, of Richmond, Va., New York temporary enrollment 420, Sept. 25, 1852. Built, 1852, at Belleville, N.J., by Tunis A. Brown. 305.51 tons, 95.1' × 27' × 13'. Two decks. Daniel Rogers, of Richmond, master. John Currie and Thomas McCance, of Richmond, owners.

Emeline, of New York. New York enrollment 99, Feb. 16, 1854. Built, 1853, at Millbridge, Me. 345.63 tons, 108.6' × 28.4' × 12.8'. Francis W. Miner, master. Robert L. Lane, Charles M. and Nathaniel M. Terry and Joseph Della Torre, Hugo B. Major, *et al.,* of New York, and Robert E. Coxe, of Montgomery, Ala., owners.

Tern *Emily Ward,* of New York. New York enrollment 936, Dec. 13, 1854. Built, 1854, at Elizabethport, N.J., by Crowell & Colon. 395.15 tons, 140.1' × 30' × 10.3'. Henry S. Ward, master, and part owner with Jonathan T. Johnson, Stephen Bogert, William Swain, *et al.,* of New York, and George Harris, of Wilmington, N.C.

Enchantress, of New York. New York enrollment 562, Sept. 9, 1852. Built, 1852, at Hoboken, N.J., by Isaac C. Smith. 378.11 tons, 125.8' × 30.6' × 11'. William I. Tyler, of Brookhaven, master. N. L. McCready and Cornelius and Richard Poillon, owners.

Fanny, of New York. New York enrollment 191, Mar. 16, 1855. Built, 1855, at New York. 363.28 tons, 112.3′ × 28.8′ × 12.1′. Burr Hull, of Fairfield, Conn., master, and part owner with William B. Smith and George W. Rice, of New York, and William Lloyd, of Charleston, S.C.

Tern *Far West,* of New York. Register 702, Nov. 10, 1855. Built, 1846, at Newbury, Mass. 595.40 tons, 154.4′ × 30′ × 15′. James S. Bennett, master. William T. Frost, owner.

Flash, of Newburyport. Register Apr. 9, 1852. Built, 1852, at Newburyport. 344 tons, 124′ × 25′ × 12′. Eagle head. Thomas W. Wilson, master. Peter and Louis Hargous, of New York, owners.

Tern *Fleetwing,* of Brookhaven. New York enrollment 698, Nov. 11, 1856. Built, 1855, at Brookhaven. 518.43 tons, 147.9′ × 31.11′ × 12′. Lewis Davis, Jr., master, of Brookhaven. Charles M. and Nathaniel M. Terry and Joseph Della Torre, *et al.,* of New York, owners.

Forest King, of Portland, Me. Register 36, Feb. 27, 1857. 366.10 tons. J. R. Fish, master and owner.

Frances Satterly, of New York. Enrollment 44, Feb. 6, 1852. Built, 1851-2, at Brookhaven, by Jonas Smith. 310.14 tons, 112.4′ × 26.7′ × 11.6′. Lewis S. Davis, master, Jonas Smith, owner. John C. Griffing, master in 1854.

Frank A. Hall, of Philadelphia. Philadelphia enrollment, Dec. 27, 1854. Built, 1854, at Wilmington, Del. 310.12 tons, 123.6′ × 30′ × 9.3′. Alexander H. Cain, master, and Barnabas Hammett, both of Philadelphia, and R. L. Fay, of Boston, and William and Albert Thacher, of Wilmington, owners.

G. M. Nevins, of New York. New York enrollment 337, June 18, 1860. Built, 1860. 313.62 tons. E. Hawkins, owner.

Tern *Gardner Pike,* of New York. Enrollment 414, June 25, 1853. Built, 1853, at Hoboken, N.J., by Isaac Smith. 305.13 tons, 121.9′ × 30.3′ × 9.3′. Abraham W. Cranmer, master, of Philadelphia. Henry L. Slaght and James A. Van Brunt, copartners, *et al.,* of New York, owners.

George Davis, of New York. Enrollment 1034, Dec. 21, 1855. Built, 1855, at Newcastle, Del. 335.70 tons, 122′ × 20.8′ × 10′. Counter stern. Poop deck. Daniel M. Smith, master. Frederick Kidder, Samuel S. and Isaac O. Thorp, *et al.,* of New York, and Bennett Flanner, of Wilmington, N.C., owners. In 1857 owned by Thomas Dunham, of New York, and Charles Dimon, of Norwalk, Conn., *et al.*

Tern *Gulf Stream,* of New York. Register 546, Sept. 11, 1857. Built, 1853, at Newburgh, N.Y. 362.26 tons, 130.6′ × 31.5′ × 9.1′. Dragon head. Jonathan T. Godfrey, of Hudson, N.Y., master. Henry L. Slaght, James A. Van Brunt, *et al.,* owners.

H. B. Emery, of Castine, Me. Enrollment 62, Dec. 29, 1856. 346.73 tons. M. Perkins, master. G. F. Tilden, owner.

Harriet A. Stephenson, of New York. Enrollment 635, Oct. 5, 1852. Built, 1852, at Saybrook, Conn., by Nehemiah Hayden. 465.77 tons, 116.7′ × 30′. Two decks. Ezra D. Post, master. James Smith, Albert Stow, Eben F. Stephenson, and James D. Fish, of New York, *et al.,* owners.

Tern *Hartstene,* of New York. Enrollment 161, Mar. 22, 1856. Built, 1856, at Green-point, N.Y., by Eckford Webb. 653.30 tons, 144′ ×31.6′ × 19.6′. Two decks. Eagle head. Joseph A. Graffam, master. Thomas Dunham, Mary Dunham, Stephen Crary, Philander Daggett, William Burroughs, C. A. Ten Eyck, *et al.,* of New York, owners.

Haze, of New York. Enrollment 920, Oct. 17, 1855. Built, 1855, at Madison, Conn., by Jonathan S. Hoyt. 320.77 tons, 115′ × 30.6′ × 10.4′. William Smith, master. Erastus C. Scranton and Jonathan S. Hoyt, of Madison, William Merriam, of Brooklyn, and John P. Britton and Caroline Knapp, of Fairfield, *et al.,* owners.

Tern *Heloise,* of New York. Register 516, Sept. 12, 1853. Built, 1853, at New York, by Perine, Patterson & Stack. 338.39 tons, 117′ × 26.6′ × 12′. Billet head. Edward McKeige, master. Gilbert Allen and Samuel Paxon, copartners, and Pennell Churchman and John S. Roberts, owners.

Henry P. Russell, of Saybrook, Conn. Middletown enrollment 64, June 30, 1860. Built, 1860, at Deep River, Conn., by Ely Denison. 396.20 tons, 130′ × 29′ × 10.1′ Round stern. Scroll head. Lewis Mankin, master, of Williamsburg. Atlantic Navigation Company and Ely Denison, owners.

Hero, of New York. Register 329, June 23, 1860. Built, 1855, at Madison, Conn. 328.77 tons. Also reported 320.77. 115′ × 30.6′ × 10.4′. William H. Booth, master. William Sturges, of New York, William Munson, of Brooklyn, Erastus C. Scranton, of New Haven, John Britton, William Knapp, *et al.,* of Fairfield, owners.

Hugh Barclay, of Chicago. Baltimore temporary register 112, Nov. 29, 1860. Built, 1857, at Cleveland, Ohio. 388 tons, 135′ × 26.06′ × 11.85′. Charles J. Chidwick, of Plymouth, Ohio, master. William T. Mather and Stephen Clary, of Chicago, owners.

Humming Bird, of New York. Enrollment 180, Mar. 15, 1854. Built, 1853, at Belleville, N.J., by T. A. and H. W. Brown. 318.65 tons, 121.5′ × 20.8′ × 9.7′. Caspar Bogart, master. C. W. and Benjamin Blossom, owners.

Imogene, of New York. Enrollment 838, Dec. 29, 1853. Built, 1853, at New York, by Abraham C. Bell. 396.69 tons, 119.4′ × 29′ × 12.9′. Eagle head. James Myers, master. Robert L. Lane, Francis West, and A. C. Bell, owners.

Tern *Indianola,* of New York. New Orleans temporary register 60, June 18, 1856. Built, 1852, at Perth Amboy, N.J., by Charles Keen. 522.52 tons, 139.4′ × 28.6′ × 16′. Two decks. Robert Donald, master. Charles P. Leverich and William Layton, of New York, *et al.,* owners. Isaac Cathcart, of New Brunswick, N.J., first master.

Island City, of New York. New York enrollment 902, Nov. 28, 1854. Built, 1854, at Poughkeepsie, by Henry Finch. 315.50 tons, 119′ × 30.1′ × 9.8′. Ephraim Atcherson, master. Garrett E. Winants, John G. Wright, *et al.,* owners.

Tern *James H. Chadbourne,* of Wilmington, N.C. New York temporary register 502, Sept. 1, 1853. Built, 1853, at Hoboken, by Capes & Ellison. 378.57 tons, 135.8′ × 30.8′ × 10′. Man bust. Edward Wainwright, of Hoboken, master. John D. Harris and John Saxton, of New York, and James H. Chadbourne, of Wilmington, N.C., owners.

Tern *James Miller,* of New York. Enrollment 717, Oct. 4, 1854. Built, 1854, at Essex, Conn., by Nehemiah Hayden. 471.32 tons, 130.6′ × 30.1′ × 13.4′. Scroll head. Jesse N. Braddock, master. Robert L. Lane, James D. Fish, Silas Fish, Uriah H. Dudley, and Charles M. and Nathaniel M. Terry and Joseph Della Torre, copartners, of New York, *et al.,* owners.

John, of New York. Enrollment 883, Sept. 29, 1855. Built, 1855, at Belleville, N.J., by Cornelius C. Jeroleman. 363.36 tons, 127.1′ × 30.2′ × 10.6′. John C. Burton, master. Elzey S. Powell, Abraham Denike, *et al.*, of New York, and George Harris, of Wilmington, N.C., owners.

John Boston, of New York. Enrollment 15, Jan. 11, 1855. Built, 1854, at New York, by Abraham C. Bell. 399.12 tons, 122′ × 29′ × 12.6′. William B. Lingo, master. William B. Scranton, *et al.*, of New York, owners.

John G. Hecksher, of New York. Register 670, Nov. 11, 1856. Built, 1853, at Milton, Del. 392.57 tons, 113.02′ × 27.8′ × 13.9′. Two decks. George L. Howe, master. Luther N. Fuller, owner.

John W. Miner, of New York. Enrollment 756, Dec. 7, 1852. Built, 1852, at East Haddam, Conn., by Matthew Hubbard. 386.45 tons, 120.8′ × 28.4′ × 12.6′. John W. Miner, of New London, master. Robert L. Lane and Horatio N. Stebbing, of New York, *et al.*, owners.

Tern *John W. Rumsey*, of New York. Enrollment 694, Sept. 27, 1854. Built, 1854, at Newburgh, N.Y., by Thomas S. Marvel. 368.32 tons, 135.1′ × 31.6′ × 9.6′. Lewis P. Taylor, master. Elijah R. Aumack, of New York, John W. Rumsey, of Sing Sing, *et al.*, owners.

Tern *Jonathan May*, of Philadelphia. Register, Apr. 23, 1857. Built, 1857, at Berlin, Md. 341.57 tons, 124.7′ × 30.5′ × 10′. Josias M. Cobb, master. Henry May, owner.

Joseph W. Webster, of New York. Enrollment 15, Jan. 19, 1856. Built, 1855, at New York, by Abraham C. Bell. 390.20 tons, 124.6′ × 29′ × 12′. Roderick Bennett, master. William B. Scranton, Henry B. Tallman, Abraham C. Bell, of New York, and Henry Missroon, of Charleston, S.C., owners.

Katahdin, of Camden, Me. Register 2, July 4, 1857. 349 tons. T. Amsbury, master and owner.

Tern *Kate Brigham*, of New York. Enrollment 17, Feb. 7, 1854. Built, 1853, at Greenpoint, N.Y., by John T. Williams. 470.55 tons, 131.1′ × 30.3′ × 13′. Eagle head. John H. Luther, master. Thomas Dunham, *et al.*, of New York, and Henry Brigham, John T. Kelly, and John T. Williams, of Savannah, owners.

Tern *Kate Stamler*, of New York. Enrollment 522, Aug. 23, 1856. Built, 1856, at Essex, Conn., by Francis West. 481.90 tons, 135′ × 32.4′ × 12.3′. Ferdinand Andre, master. Robert L. Lane, Jacob A. Stamler, *et al.*, of New York, owners.

Kate Stewart, of New York. Enrollment 782, Nov. 28, 1853. Built, 1853, at Old Saybrook, Conn., by Titus C. Mather. 387.92 tons, 117.1′ × 29′ × 12.9′. Titus C. Mather, master. Robert L. Lane and Jonathan B. Stewart, of Brooklyn, and William Van Pelt, *et al.*, of New York, owners.

L. S. Davis, of New York. Providence temporary enrollment, May 23, 1868. Built, 1853, at Brookhaven, N.Y., by Jonas Smith. 318.89 tons, 116′ × 29.4′ × 11′. Figurehead. E. F. Bishop, master. Lewis S. Davis, of New York, and Jonas Smith, of Brookhaven, owners.

Langdon Gilmore, of New York Enrollment 524, Aug. 25, 1856. Built, 1856, at Belleville, N.J., by Cornelius C. Jeroleman. 497.42 tons, 131′ × 31.1′ × 13′. William S. Tyler, master. Charles C. Backus, William G. Todd, Ira Bursley, *et al.,* of New York, and James R. Gilmore, of Orange, N.J., *et al.,* owners.

Laura Gertrude, of New York. Enrollment 568, Aug. 6, 1857. Built, 1855, in Carteret County, N.C. 315.92 tons, 117' × 27.1' × 10.9'. Charles B. Elwood, master. Gilbert Potter, Jr., Harold Dollner, of Brooklyn, and Thomas Duncan and William and Benjamin Lecraft, of Carteret County, owners.

Lilly, of New York. Enrollment 627, Aug. 24, 1854. Built, 1854, at Belleville, N.J., by Cornelius C. Jeroleman. 334.78 tons, 123.4' × 29.8' × 10'. Barnabas Francis, master in 1855. Nathaniel L. McCready, John Mott, Cornelius and Richard Poillon, *et al.,* of New York, and T. C. Worth, of Wilmington, N.C., owners.

Louise, of New York. Enrollment 762, Oct. 20, 1854. Built, 1854, at New York, by Abraham C. Bell. 396.21 tons, 120.6' × 29.3' × 12.6'. Woman figurehead. John W. Miner, of Groton, Conn., master. Robert L. Lane, Abraham C. Bell, *et al.,* of New York, owners.

Loyal Scranton, of New York. Enrollment 637, Aug. 31, 1854. Built, 1854, at New York, by Abraham C. Bell. 385.91 tons, 118.4' × 28.4' × 12.9'. Amos N. Lowden, master. William R. Scranton and Henry H. Tallman, copartners, *et al.,* of New York, Daniel T. and Henry N. Scranton and Joseph Johnson, copartners, of Savannah, owners.

Lucy T. Davis, of New York. New York enrollment 749, Nov. 10, 1853. 347.64 tons. G. W. Lynch, master. L. T. Davis, owner.

Tern *Lydia B. Copperthwaite.* Providence enrollment, June 17, 1870. Built, 1856, at Forked River, N.J., by John Vaughn. 367.03 tons, 120' × 31' × 6.6'. Thomas Gardner, master. George H. Newhall, *et al.,* owners.

Marcella Tilton, of Philadelphia. Enrollment 127, May 8, 1858. 319.30 tons. E. Tilton, master and owner.

Tern *Maria Pike,* of New York. New York enrollment 716, Oct. 29, 1853. Built, 1853, at Elizabethport, N.J., by Crowell & Colon. 346.51 tons, 130.2' × 30.9' × 9.7'. Riley Aumack, master. Albert A. Martin, *et al.,* owners.

Marine, of New York. Enrollment 537, Sept. 1, 1852. Built, 1852, at Poughkeepsie, by Henry Finch. 348.78 tons, 120.8' × 30.6' × 10.7'. James P. Powell, master. Elzey S. Powell and Samuel S. and Isaac O. Thorp, of New York, owners.

Mary D. Lane, of New York. Enrollment 819, Dec. 15, 1853. Built, 1853, at East Haddam, Conn., by Daniel B. Warner. 397.67 tons, 119.7' × 29' × 12.9'. John W. Miner, of Groton, Conn., master. Robert L. Lane, Elbert Hoagland, and James D. Fish, of New York, and Daniel B. Warner, of East Haddam, owners. Benjamin A. Gardner, master in 1854.

Tern *Mary Lucretia,* of New York. Enrollment 841, Nov. 9, 1854. Built, 1854, at Derby, Conn., by Zepheniah and S. Hallock. 412.28 tons, 134' × 29.6' × 11.9'. John C. Gibbs, master. John T. B. Gibbs and Calvin and Joshua Gibbs, *et al.,* owners.

Tern *Mobile,* of New York. Enrollment 51, Jan. 21, 1854. Built, 1853, at Old Saybrook, Conn. 398.53 tons, 115.11' × 28.5' × 13.3'. Littleton Wimpenny, of Edgartown, Mass., master. Robert L. Lane and Samuel W. Ashby, of New York, Francis West and Henry Hart, of Old Saybrook, and Samuel B. Stewart, of Brooklyn, owners.

Tern *Moses Taylor*, of New York. Philadelphia Proof 20, Mar. 25, 1852. Built, 1852, at Milton, Del. 355.27 tons, 118.8′ × 27′ × 13.5′. John G. Attridge, master. Peter Clinton, of New York, owner. M. T. Thorndike, master in 1853.

Myrover, of New York. New York enrollment 71, Feb. 23, 1857. Built, 1854, at Belleville, N.J., by Cornelius C. Jeroleman. 355.65 tons, 127′ × 31′ × 10.4′. Francis Jackson, master. Nathaniel L. McCready, John W. Mott, *et al.*, of New York, and Henry L. Myrover, of Fayetteville, N.C., owners.

N. W. Smith, of New York. Charleston temporary register 2, Jan. 11, 1859. Built, 1852, at Brookhaven, N.Y., by Jonas Smith. 315.40 tons, 114.9′ × 26.4′ × 11.6′. Edward N. Smith, master, and Jonas Smith, owners. John P. Wyatt, master in 1859.

Ned, of New York. New York enrollment 71, Feb. 13, 1858. Built, 1855, at Poughkeepsie, by Henry Finch. 365.44 tons, 124.6′ × 30.1′ × 10.6′. Full model. J. K. Henderson, master and managing owner.

Tern *New Light*, of Baltimore. Baltimore register 31, Feb. 23, 1855. Built, 1855, at Baltimore. 316.25 tons, 135.6′ × 30.1′ × 8.6′. Charles Brown, master. Thomas Pierce, Samuel Phillips, and Samuel Hurlbut, all of Baltimore, owners.

Norfolk Packet, of New York. Enrollment 552, Sept. 8, 1851. Built, 1851, at East Haddam, Conn., by George E. Goodspeed. 349.61 tons, 108.6′ × 27.1′ × 13′. James Bedell, of Brooklyn, master. Joseph and John C. Hunter, of New York, owners.

North State, of New York. Enrollment 87, Feb. 27, 1852. Built, 1851-2, at Southold, N.Y. 430.87 tons, 116.1′ × 28.8′. Two decks. Isaac F. Horton, master. Nathaniel L. McCready and John W. Mott, copartners, Samuel Willets, *et al.*, of New York, and Miles Costin, of Wilmington, N.C., owners.

Tern *Okolona*, of Bridgeport. Fairfield, Conn., register 1, Dec. 1, 1859. Built, 1859, at Bridgeport, by James H. Moore. 683.53 tons, 146.9′ × 32′ × 16′. Two decks. Scroll head. William Wheeler, of Long Island, master. Burr Knapp, James H. Moore, *et al.*, of Bridgeport, and James Whitaker, of Mobile, owners.

Tern *Old Dominion*, of New York. Enrollment 755, Nov. 14, 1853. Built, 1853, at Elizabethport, N.J., by Crowell & Colon. 392.92 tons, 133.7′ × 30.4′ × 10.8′. Alfred Weeks, master. James Anderson, Secretary of Cumberland Coal & Iron Co., Inc., of Maryland, owner.

Oliver H. Booth, of Poughkeepsie. New York enrollment 53, Feb. 20, 1856. Built, 1856, at Poughkeepsie, by Henry Finch. 331.59 tons, 124′ × 32.6′ × 9.6′. Eagle head. Oliver Burger, master. Oliver H. Booth and Henry Finch, owners.

Tern *Only Daughter*, of New York. American Lloyds, 1861. Built, 1854, at Forked River, N.J. 437 tons, 136.1′ × 27.2′ × 9.9′. Centerboard. Collins, master.

Onward. American Lloyds, 1861. Built, 1855, at Chelsea, Mass. 303 tons. Fuller, master.

Tern *Palma*. American Lloyds, 1861. Built, 1860, at Fairhaven, Mass., by G. Baldwin. 417 tons, 125′ × 27′ × 13.6′. Full model. Terry, master.

Passport, of New York. Register 794, Dec. 29, 1858. Built, 1856, at Greenport, N.Y. 348.39 tons, 125.6′ × 30.8′ × 10′. Also reported 345.39 tons. George Hawkins, of Jamesport, N.Y., master and owner.

Tern *Queen of the South,* of Fairfield, Conn. Fairfield register 3, Dec. 23, 1854. Built, 1854, at Bridgeport, by James H. Moore. 445 tons, 138' × 31.6' × 11.4'. Centerboard. George Wheeler, master. Burr Knapp, James H. Moore, *et al.,* owners.

Tern *Queen of the South,* of New York. Register 609, Oct. 14, 1856. Built, 1856, in Beaufort County, N.C. 335.56 tons, 133' × 29' × 9.6'. Seth R. Robins (Roberts), owner and master. William W. Neff, master in Oct., 1856.

Ralph Post, of New York. Enrollment 693, Sept. 26, 1854. Built, 1854, at Port Jefferson, N.Y. 426.4 tons, 132.4' × 32.4' × 11.6'. Hamilton D. Conklin, master. Charles M. and Nathaniel M. Terry, Joseph Della Torre, *et al.,* of New York, and Benjamin Ellison, of Apalachicola, owners.

Richard M. Demill, of New York. Enrollment 970, Nov. 15, 1855. Built, 1855, at Marion, Mass. 343.26 tons, 116.8' × 27.9' × 11.9'. Figurehead. Hiram Look, master. Richard M. Demill, of Brooklyn, Thomas A. Demill, Charles T. Goodwin and Simon P. Wyckoff, of New York, and Stephen Delano, of Marion, owners.

Robert Caldwell, of New York. Enrollment 665, Oct. 27, 1856. Built, 1856, at Belleville, N.J., by Cornelius C. Jeroleman. 446.70 tons, 127.8' × 31.8' × 12.4'. Charles S. Hudson, master. Nathaniel L. McCready, John Mott, George Thorburn, Henry Hubbell, *et al.,* of New York, and builder, and James Adger, of Charleston, S.C., owners.

S. J. Moye, of New York. Enrollment 668, Oct. 27, 1852. Built, 1852, at Greenpoint, N.Y., by Edward F. Williams. 319.94 tons, 118.4' × 28.1' × 10.8'. Bethuel E. Hallock, of Riverhead, master. Charles M. and Nathaniel M. Terry, of New York, *et al.,* owners.

S. J. Waring, of Brookhaven. New York temporary enrollment 647, Oct. 1, 1853. Built, 1853, at Brookhaven, by Jonas Smith. 372.16 tons, 119' × 29' × 12'. Barnabas Francis, master. Jonas Smith, owner.

Sally J. Aiken. American Lloyds, 1861. Built, 1860, at Wilmington, Del. 342 tons. H. Godfrey, master. Joseph C. Atkins, owner.

Tern *Santa Claus,* of Philadelphia. Wilmington temporary enrollment 15, May 17, 1850. Built, 1850, at Wilmington, Del. 300.75 tons, 142' × 25' × 9'. J. W. C. Perritt, master. George W. Aspinwall, *et al.,* owners.

Sarah Judkins, of Bath, Me. Bath register 34, July 2, 1856. Built, 1856, at Bath. 545.89 tons. T. Smith, master. S. D. Braley, owner. Destroyed by fire at Apalachicola prior to Apr. 19, 1858.

Smithsonian, of Brookhaven. New York enrollment 754, Dec. 6, 1856. Built, 1856, at Brookhaven, by Jonas Smith. 390.30 tons, 121' × 30' × 12'. Lewis S. Davis, master. Jonas Smith, owner.

Southern Belle, of New York. Enrollment 85, Feb. 16, 1855. Built, 1855, at Islip, N.Y., by Erastus Younge. 322.25 tons, 117' × 29.4' × 10.6'. Woman figurehead. William S. Tyler, master in 1857. D. Colden Murray and Benjamin C. Eaton, of New York, and Joseph H. Flanner, of Wilmington, N.C., *et al.,* owners.

Tern *Spray,* of Wilmington, Del. Temporary enrollment 37, Oct. 10, 1849. Built, 1849, at Wilmington. 320.3 tons, 122' × 26' × 11'. Isaac Cathcart, master. J. Bishop, owner. Sailed for San Francisco.

Stampede, of Mystic River, Conn. Stonington enrollment 26, July 28, 1854. Built, 1854, at Groton, Conn., by Maxson, Fish & Co. 325.81 tons, 125' × 32' × 9.6'. One and one-half decks, centerboard. John Washington, master. George B. Packer, Simeon and Nathan G. Fish, Benjamin F. Hoxie, *et al.,* owners.

Stephen Taber, of New York. Enrollment 561, Sept. 23, 1857. Built, 1852, at Brookhaven, by James N. and Charles L. Bayles. 304.81 tons, 112.6' × 26.1' × 11.5'. Miner Tuthill, master. Alonzo S. Tuthill and builders, owners.

Sylvanus Allen, of Dennis, Mass. New York temporary enrollment 97, Mar. 3, 1859. Built, 1855, at Dennis. 299.70 tons, 112' × 28.9' × 10.5'. American Lloyds, 1861, gives 307 tons, readmeasurement. Grafton Sears, master. Samuel Crowell, Sylvanus Sears, *et al.,* owners.

T. D. Wagner, of New York. Enrollment 569, Sept. 15, 1856. Built, 1856, at Patchogue, N.Y., by Oliver P. Smith. 390.30 tons, 129' × 30.6' × 11'. Eagle head. Samuel N. Smith, master. Gilbert Potter and Harold Dollner, of Brooklyn, copartners, and Abraham Denike and John W. Belden, of New York, owners.

Tanner, of Brookhaven. New York enrollment 84, Feb. 15, 1855. Built, 1854-55, at Smithtown, N.Y., by Samuel Carmen. 439.33 tons, 130' × 30.6' × 12.6'. Ranna O. Welton, master. Gilbert Potter and Harold Dollner, of New York, copartners, *et al.,* owners.

Target, of New York. Enrollment 867, Sept. 22, 1855. Built, 1855, at Brookhaven, by Jonas Smith. 388.55 tons, 125' × 30' × 11.6'. Lewis S. Davis, master. Jonas Smith, owner.

Thomas Holcombe, of New York. Enrollment 842, Sept. 11, 1855. Built, 1855, at New York, by Abraham C. Bell. 392.71 tons, 124.6' × 28.4' × 12.3'. Robert W. Goslee, master. William B. Scranton, Henry W. Tallman, William T. Hemingway, William H. Lingo, *et al.,* of New York, owners.

Vapor (Vapour), of New York. Enrollment 651, Sept. 7, 1854. Built, 1854, at Madison, Conn., by Jonathan S. Hoyt. 312.46 tons, 113.4' × 30.2' × 10.4'. Horatio Wilson, master. Erastus Scranton, of Madison, and William and Samuel Aymar and James A. Degrain, copartners, of New York, owners. Mark Dissoway, master and owner in 1860.

Vaquero, of San Francisco. Baltimore temporary register 42, Apr. 14, 1853. Built, 1853, at Baltimore. 370.36 tons, 126.7' × 28.1' × 11.5'. Figurehead. Round stern. Josiah D. Nason, of San Francisco, master and owner. Noted for her fast runs on the Pacific.

Wake, of New York. Enrollment 865, Sept. 20, 1855. Built, 1851, at Belleville, N.J., by Cornelius C. Jeroleman. 304.56 tons, 118.7' × 28.9' × 11'. James W. Taylor, master. Elzey S. Powell, George Sweeney, of New York, *et al.,* owners.

Walter Raleigh, of New York. Enrollment 275, May 15, 1856. Built, 1856, at Belleville, N.J., by Cornelius C. Jeroleman. 471.90 tons, 130.4' × 32.4' × 12.6'. Lewis Mankin, master. William Todd, Charles C. Backus, Ira Bursley, *et al.,* of New York, James R. Gilmore, of Orange, N.J., and Day O. Kellogg, of Brooklyn, owners.

Tern *Welcome R. Beebe.* American Lloyds, 1861. Built, 1860, at Belleville, N.J. Crawford, master. S. C. Nelson, *et al.,* owners.

Tern *William B. Scranton,* of New York. Enrollment 564, June 14, 1855. Built, 1855, at Elizabethport, N.J., by Crowell & Colon. 422.60 tons, 138' × 31.4' × 10.9'. William Cathcart, master. William B. Scranton and Henry H. Tallman, copartners, of New York, *et al.,* owners.

Tern *William C. Mershon,* of Lamberton, N.J. Built, 1851, at Bordentown, N.J. 390.17 tons, 135' × 28' × 11.2'. Full poop. Scroll head. William C. Mershon, master. Daniel S. and Jacob Mershon, owners. Owned in 1860 by N. L. McCready, *et al.;* E. Cole, master.

William H. Gilliland, of New York. Register 739, Nov. 22, 1855. Built, 1855, at Brooklyn. 347.80 tons. D. B. Vincent, master and owner.

William H. Hazard, of New York. Register 62, Feb. 4, 1860. Built, 1847, at Westerly, R.I. 325.21 tons, 100.6' × 27.1' × 19.05'. Two decks. Figurehead. Sylvanus A. Snow, master, and Charles Larson, both of New York, owners.

Tern *William L. Burroughs,* of New York. Enrollment 864, Sept. 20, 1855. Built, 1855, at Greenpoint, N.Y., by Eckford Webb. 496.80 tons, 136' × 30' × 13.4'. Urban G. Griffin, master. Thomas Dunham, Samuel T. Ferguson, Stephen W. Crary, Peter Rice, Peter Nugent, of New York, and William L. Burroughs, of Brooklyn, owners. Hollis B. Jencks, master in 1856.

William Smith, of New York. Enrollment 491, Aug. 31, 1858. Built, 1853, at Brookhaven. 314.7 tons, 102' × 26.4' × 15'. One deck. Thomas R. Fisher, of Accomac County, Va., master. William B. Scranton and Henry H. Tallman, copartners, *et al.,* of New York, and Henry Missroon and Henry Bischoff, of Charleston, S.C., owners.

Tern *Young America,* of New York. Enrollment 577, Aug. 29, 1853. Built, 1853, at Elizabethport, N.J., by Crowell & Colon. 370.50 tons, 126.8' × 30.2' × 10.9'. John Bearse, master. Newell Sturtevant, President of the Cumberland Coal & Iron Co., Inc., of Maryland, owner.

APPENDIX V

Fast Packet Passages

COMPARATIVELY few packet ship logs have survived and the abstracts of a majority of those available are fragmentary, rarely showing the precise times of departures and arrivals. Many begin only on the second day out and a still larger number end some distance from the intended port. Accordingly, it has been necessary to depend to a great extent on newspaper reports for critical information. For this reason most of the passages here reported cannot be depended upon completely as to accuracy. It is believed, however, that the majority are substantially correct, and some have been corroborated by private letters and journals. Except for several cited for purposes of comparison, passages of the clipper packets have been omitted.

TRANSATLANTIC—EASTBOUND

Boston to Cork. 2827 miles. Sp. *Plymouth Rock.* A. C. Caldwell, master. 12½ days. Sailed Feb. 5, 1851. Arrived off Cork, Feb. 19. *New York Herald,* Mar. 18, 1851.

Boston to Liverpool. 3058 miles. Sp. *Star of Empire* (medium clipper). Albert H. Brown, master. 14 days, 15 hrs., dock to dock. Sailed Jan. 13, 1854. Arrived Jan. 28. *New York Journal of Commerce,* Feb. 17, 1854.

Boston to Liverpool. Sp. *Staffordshire.* Albert H. Brown, master. 14 days, 18 hrs., dock to dock. Made Tuskar Light in 12 days. Sailed Aug. 5, 1851. Arrived Aug. 20. *Boston Daily Courier,* Aug. 6; *New York Herald,* Jan. 13, 1852.

New York to Cork. 2988 miles. Sp. *Orpheus.* David G. Bailey, master. 12½ days. Sailed Nov. 19, 1838. Arrived off Cork, Dec. 2, and arrived Liverpool, Dec. 5. *New York Herald,* Nov. 20, 1838, and Jan. 14, 1839.

New York to Liverpool. 3332 miles. Sp. *Dreadnought.* Samuel Samuels, master. 13 days, 8 hrs., Sandy Hook to Rock Light. Sailed Feb. 27, 1859. Arrived Liverpool Mar. 12. Abstract of log. Captain Clark's *Clipper Ship Era,* p. 246.

New York to Liverpool. Sp. *Dreadnought.* Same master. 13 days, 11 hrs., 15 min., Sandy Hook to Pt. Lynas (about 50 miles from Liverpool). Sailed Nov. 21, 1854, and arrived Dec. 4. Abstract of log. *Monthly Nautical Magazine,* Vol. 4, p. 464.

New York to Liverpool. Sp. *Washington.* Pitkin Page, master. 13 days, 14 hrs., Sandy Hook to Liverpool lightship. Sailed Jan. 20, 1852, at 7 P.M. Arrived off lightship Feb. 3, at 2 P.M. Log in National Archives, Vol. 86.

New York to Liverpool. Sp. *United States.* John Britton, master. 14 days. Sailed Feb. 15, 1842. Arrived Mar. 2. *New York Herald,* Feb. 15 and Mar. 30, 1842.

563

New York to Liverpool. Sp. *Yorkshire.* David G. Bailey, master. 14 days. Sailed Jan. 18, 1846. Arrived Feb. 2. Log in National Archives, Vol. 387.

>   It will be noted that the passages of the *Washington, United States,* and *Yorkshire,* which were from port to port, compare favorably with those of the *Dreadnought,* which are computed to a point some 40 to 50 miles short of port.

New York to Liverpool. Sp. *John Eliot Thayer.* Gaius Sampson, master. 14 days, land to land. Sailed Dec. 8, 1855. Arrived Dec. 24. *New York Tribune,* Dec. 10, 1855; *Boston Courier,* Jan. 15, 1856.

New York to Liverpool. Sp. *Independence.* Ezra Nye, master. 14½ days. Made in spring of 1836. *New York Evening Post,* June 15, 1836.

New York to Liverpool. Sp. *Garrick.* Nathaniel B. Palmer, master. 15 days, 4 hrs., pilot to pilot. Sailed June 26, 1841. Arrived July 12. *New York Commercial Advertiser,* Aug. 30, 1841.

New York to Liverpool. Sp. *New York.* David Bennett, master. 15 days, 16 hrs. Sailed Dec. 16, 1823. Arrived Jan. 1, 1824. *New York American,* Dec. 20, 1823. *New York Commercial Advertiser,* Feb. 14, 1824.

New York to Liverpool. Sp. *Virginian.* William B. Allen, master. 15 days. Sailed Dec. 15, 1842. Arrived Dec. 30. Log in National Archives, Vol. 385.

New York to Liverpool. Sp. *Liverpool.* John Eldridge, master. 15 days, 17 hrs. Sailed Dec. 21, 1844. Arrived Jan. 6, 1845. Log in National Archives, Vol. 18.

New York to Liverpool. Sp. *Pacific.* William Bowne, master. 16 days to Holyhead. Sailed Jan. 18, 1817. Arrived Feb. 6. *Liverpool Mercury,* Feb. 7, 1817.

>   The *New York Herald* for Jan. 11, 1839, reported that the following ships made their last passages to Liverpool in very fast time—*Siddons,* 15 days; *Independence,* 14 days, 12 hrs.; *Europe,* 14 days, 8 hrs.; *St. Andrew,* 14 days, 20 hrs.; *Orpheus,* 14 days, 6 hrs.; and *President,* 14 days, 12 hrs.

New York to Havre. 3293 miles. Sp. *New York.* David Lines, master. 14 days. Sailed Sept. 22, 1848. Arrived Oct. 8, having been hove to outside the port awaiting a high tide. Log in National Archives, Vol. 95.

New York to Havre. Sp. *St. Denis.* G. W. Howe, master. 14 days. Sailed Jan. 3, 1851. Arrived Jan. 17. *New York Herald,* Feb. 20, 1851.

New York to Havre. Sp. *Admiral.* James A. Wotten, master. 14 days, 2 hrs. Sailed Nov. 27, 1847. Arrived Dec. 11. Passed Scilly 12 days, 20 hrs. from New York. Log in National Archives, Vol. 74.

New York to Havre. Sp. *Duchesse d'Orleans.* Richardson, master. 15 days. Sailed Feb. 9, 1844. Arrived Feb. 26. *New York Herald,* Mar. 24, 1844.

New York to Havre. Sp. *Havre.* Allen C. Ainsworth, master. 15 days. Sailed Nov. 17, 1845. Arrived Dec. 2. Log in National Archives, Vol. 152.

New York to Havre. Sp. *New York.* David Lines, master. 15 days. Arrived Feb. 8, 1850. Log in National Archives, Vol. 146.

The *New York Herald* for Jan. 11, 1839, reported that the Havre packet *Louis Phillipe* made her last trip out in 13 days, 20 hrs., which, if confirmed, would stand as the record.

New York to Brest. 3072 miles. Sp. *St. Nicholas.* John Bragdon, master. 14 days. Sailed Feb. 2, 1856. Arrived Feb. 17. *New York Herald,* Mar. 20, 1856.

Philadelphia (Capes of the Delaware) to Liverpool. 3275 miles. Sp. *Pocahontas.* James West, master. 14 days, land to land. Sailed from Capes Nov. 20, 1833. Arrived Liverpool in 17 days. *National Gazette* (Philadelphia), Feb. 20, 1834.

This passage—the best found of a regular Philadelphia packet—is to be compared with the remarkable 13-day port-to-port passage of the very sharp clipper packet *Nonpareil,* Edmund Dunn, master, which arrived in Liverpool Apr. 11, 1855.

TRANSATLANTIC—WESTBOUND

Liverpool to Boston. 3010 miles. Sp. *Emerald.* Philip Fox, master. 15 days, 14 hrs. Sailed Feb. 20, 1824. Arrived Mar. 8. *Columbian Centinel,* Mar. 10, 1824.

Liverpool to New York. Sp. *Yorkshire.* David G. Bailey, master. 15½ days to Sandy Hook. Sailed Nov. 2, 1846. Arrived Sandy Hook, night of Nov. 17, and at New York noon, Nov. 18. Log in National Archives, Vol. 387.

The *New York Commercial Advertiser* for Apr. 22, 1830, lists the following series of near-record westbound passages:

"We have recorded below a succession of short arrivals at this port, which we believe to be unparalleled in navigation, at least from Europe to America. For the last three weeks, the wind, we believe, without intermission, has prevailed from the N.E. variable to E.S.E., but principally at N.E. The shortness of these trips will appear astonishing, when we consider that over thirty days is the yearly average of passages from Europe to New York.

Vessels names	Where from	Sailed	Arrived
DeRham	The English Channel (Havre)	March 25	April 9
Charlemagne	Havre	March 22	April 13
Hudson	The Lizard	March 26	April 13
Josephine	Belfast	March 27	April 12
William Thompson	Liverpool	March 25	April 15
George Canning	Liverpool	March 25	April 15
Concordia	Liverpool	March 25	April 15
Walter	Liverpool	March 26	April 15
Admittance	Rochelle	March 26	April 15
Jubilee	Liverpool	March 29	April 16
Charles Joseph	Liverpool	March 29	April 16
Columbia	Portsmouth	April 1	April 17
Caledonia	Liverpool	April 1	April 17

The ship *Josephine,* Capt. Britton, is most conspicuous having performed her passage in 15 days and 12 hours. Liverpool vessels in general have been only 13 days from land to land."

COASTAL PASSAGES

New York to Charleston. 627 miles. Sp. *H. Allen.* Henry Wilson, master. 67 hrs. Arrived Charleston Nov. 22, 1833. *Charleston Courier,* Nov. 23, 1833.

New York to Savannah. 700 miles. Sp. *Courier*. Green, master. 67 hrs. Sailed Feb. 6, 1830. *New York Commercial Advertiser,* Feb. 6, 1830. *Savannah Georgian,* Feb. 12, 1830.

New York to Savannah. Bk. *Greenfield*. Beattie, master. 63 hrs. Sailed Nov. 10, 1857. *New York Herald,* Nov. 22, 1857.

New York to Mobile. 1699 miles. Sp. *Aberdeen*. Asahel Hubbard, master. 8 days. Sailed Nov. 5, 1851. Arrived Nov. 13. *New York Herald,* Dec. 12, 1851.

New York to New Orleans (S.W. Pass). 1700 miles. Sp. *Nashville*. Chase, master. 8 days. Sailed Feb. 20, 1842. Arrived Mar. 1. *New York Herald,* Mar. 17, 1842.

New York to New Orleans. Sp. *Trenton*. James S. Bennett, master. 8 days, 3 hrs. Sailed Feb. 27, 1842. Arrived Mar. 4. *Shipping & Commercial List,* Mar. 19, 1842.

> Several other packets made this run in a few hours over 8 days, but for distance run on this course the passage of the Sp. *St. Mary,* Foster, master, of 7 days from off Navesink to the Balize in Mar., 1844, is the best found.

Galveston to New York. 1887 miles. Bk. *Montauk*. Gurdon Gates, master. 11 days. Sailed Nov. 23, 1848. Arrived Dec. 4. *New York Spectator,* Dec. 7, 1848.

Norfolk to New York. 290 miles. Sch. *Mary Jane*. Powell, master. 23 hrs. Sailed May 27, 1845. Arrived May 28. *New York Herald,* May 29, 1845.

> The record for the above course was the 18-hour run of the clipper ship *Harvey Birch* from Hampton Roads to New York, Dec. 25, 1857.

New York to Boston. Sch. *John Cooley & Co.* 30 hrs. Arrived July 10, 1844. "The quickest trip probably ever made by a sailing vessel between the two ports." *New York Herald,* July 17, 1844.

Ship and Sail Plans

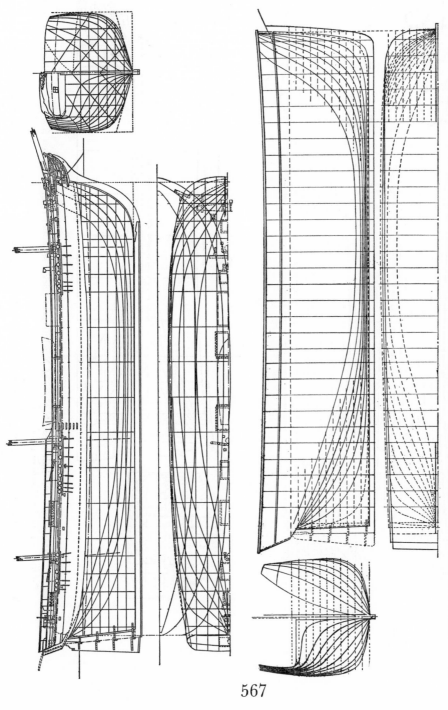

Upper: Philadelphia-New Orleans packet ship *Ohio*, built in Philadelphia in 1825, and regarded as the finest coastal packet of her year. Courtesy of the Smithsonian Institution.

Lower: Packet ship *Shenandoah* built in Philadelphia for the Cope Line of Philadelphia-Liverpool packets. An early example of the relatively flat-floored packets, she was a good carrier and a fast sailer. Courtesy of the Franklin Institute.

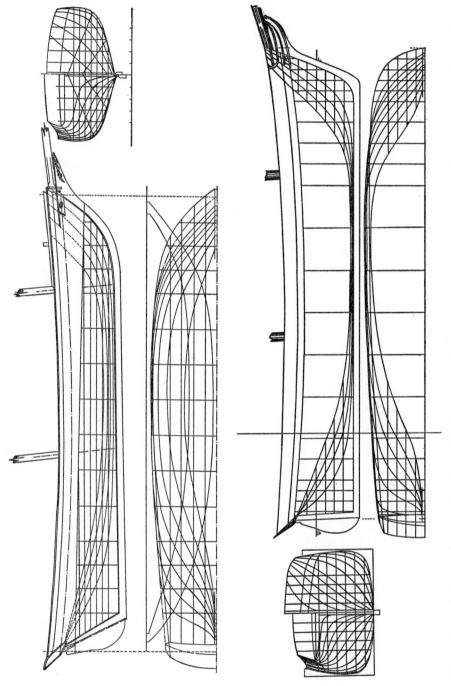

Upper: Sheer, body, and half-breadth plans of Newburyport packet schooner *Charmer*, taken from the Baltimore packet schooner *Iowa*. Courtesy of the Smithsonian Institution.

Lower: Coastal packet schooners *Plandome* and *Manhasset*, 250 tons. They were typical large schooner packets of the early eighteen-fifties.

568

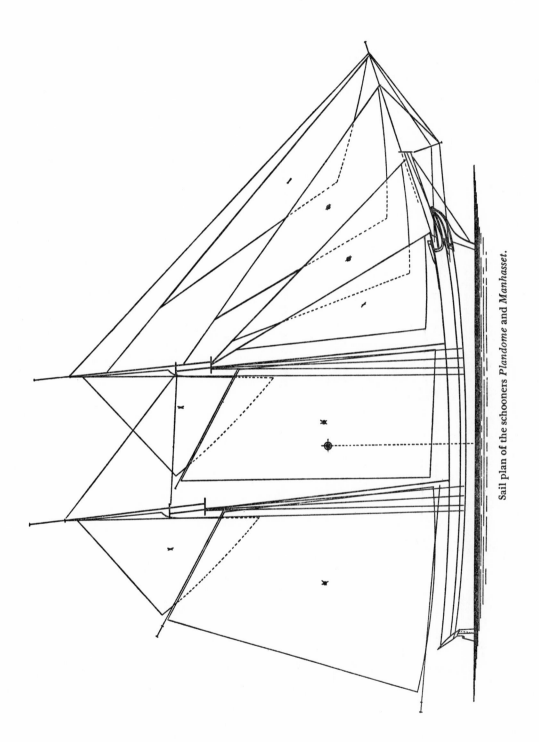

Sail plan of the schooners *Plandome* and *Manhasset*.

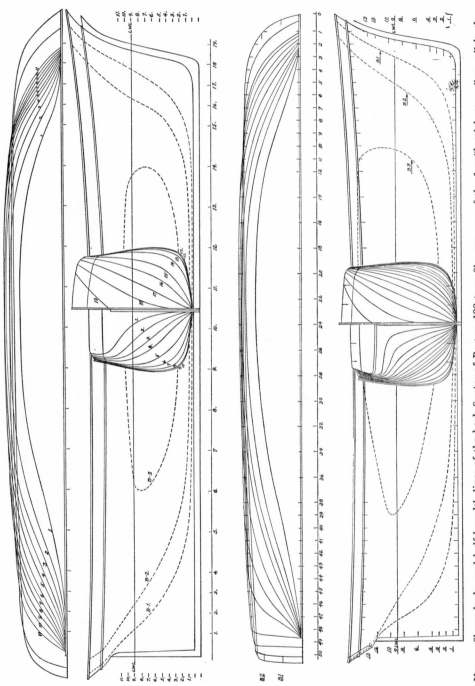

Upper: Sheer, body, and half-breadth lines of the bark *Santee* of Boston, 192 tons. She was one of the few "kettlebottoms" to sail in the coastal packet lines.

Lower: Sheer, body, and half-breadth lines of the ship *George Peabody* of Boston, 1402 tons.

570

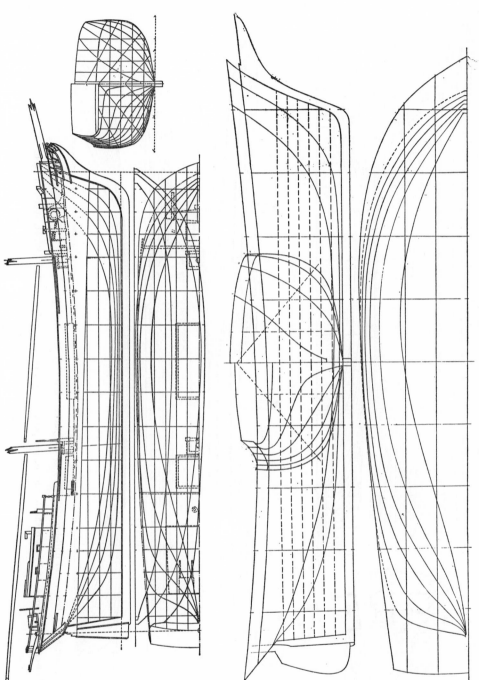

Upper: Sheer, body, and half-breadth lines of topsail schooners *Arroasic* and *Eagle*, built in 1847. The *Eagle* became a Boston-Bath packet. They were typical of the smaller packet schooners of their day. Courtesy of the Smithsonian Institution.

Lower: Sheer, body, and half-breadth lines of a Connecticut River packet sloop of the period from 1840 to 1850. This type differed from the Hudson River sloop by being relatively deeper and narrower. Courtesy of the Marine Historical Association, Inc.

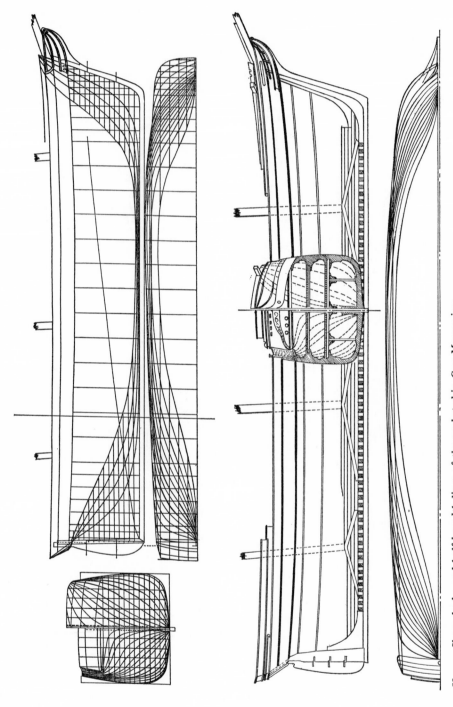

Upper: Sheer, body, and half-breadth lines of the packet ship *Guy Mannering.*

Lower: Sheer, body, and half-breadth lines of the packet ship *Ocean Monarch*, built by W. H. Webb in 1856.

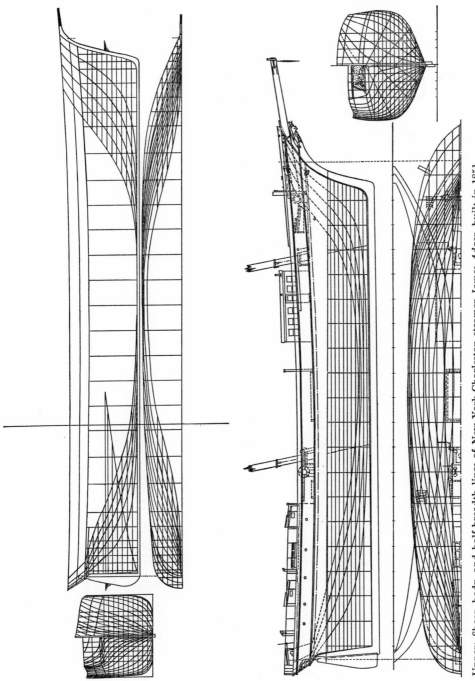

Upper: Sheer, body, and half-breadth lines of New York-Charleston steamer *James Adger*, built in 1851.

Lower: Baltimore topsail schooner *Vaquero*. Although built for the Pacific trade, she is a good example of the large clipper packet schooners of the eighteen-fifties. Courtesy of the Smithsonian Institution.

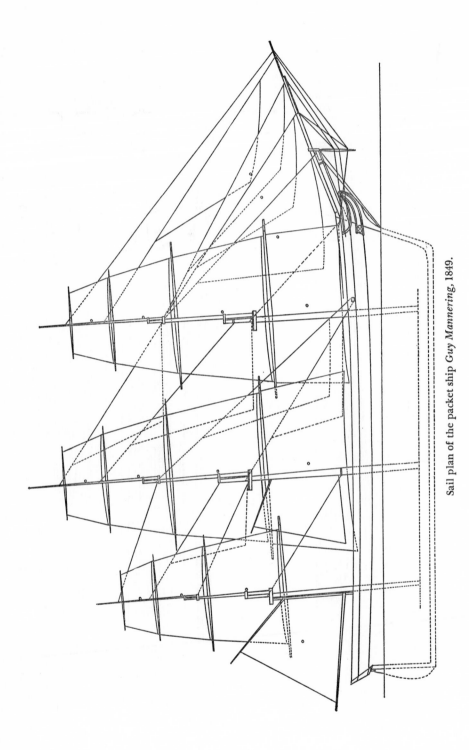

Sail plan of the packet ship *Guy Mannering*, 1849.

574

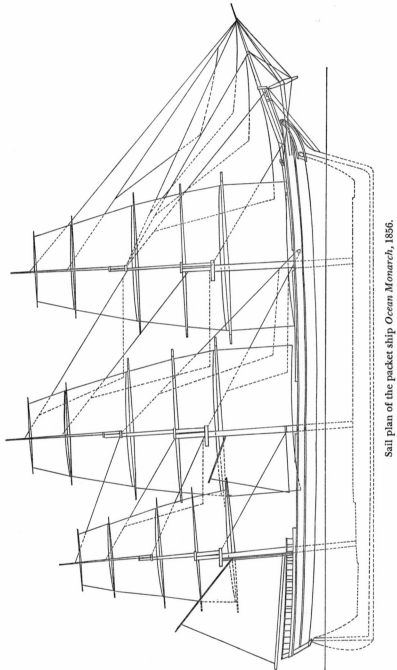

Sail plan of the packet ship *Ocean Monarch*, 1856.

Indexes

Notes to Indexes

WHEN the spelling of a ship's name varies in the records, an alternate spelling is given in parentheses: *Abaellino (Abaelino)*.

When there are more than two ships of the same name, the rigs of the vessels are given using the following abbreviations:

Sl.	Sloop
Sch.	Schooner
Bg.	Brig
Stm. Bg.	Steam Brig
Bk.	Bark
Sp.	Ship
Stbt.	Steamboat
SS	Steam Ship (paddle)
St. Prop.	Steam Propeller

As a further aid in distinguishing vessels of the same name, their tonnages are given in parentheses.

The letters (Cl.) after a vessel's name indicate that she was clipper-built. The expression (tern) after a schooner's name indicates that she was a three-masted vessel.

Index to Ships' Names

Alciope, 454
Alcyone (Alcyona), Sch. (148), 481, 534
Alcyone, Sch. (197), 534
Alcyone, Bg. (197), 540
Aldanah, 526
Aldebaren, 514
Aldrich, 478, 532, 536, 540
Alert, Sch. (91), 419
Alert, Bg. (141), 480, 481
Alexander, Sp., 163, 164
Alexander, Sp. (461), 403
Alexander, Sp. (591), 409, 410
Alexander M., 470, 471
Alexander Marshall, 344, 377
Alexander McNeill, 407
Alex. Mitchell, 476
Alexandria, Sch. (165), 463, 464
Alexandria, Bg. (206), 435
Alexandria, Sp. (492), 408
Alexina, 492
Alfred, Bg. (260), 538
Alfred, Sp. (453), 504, 510, 511
Alfred Barrett, 460
Alfred Exall, 470, 481, 536, 541
Alfred F. Thorne, 528
Algerine, 425
Algonquin, Bg. (193), 506
Algonquin, Sp. (482), 171, 403
Alhambra, 438
Alice, Sch. (119), 544
Alice, Sch. (184), 464
Alice Ann Pendergast, 543
Alice Counce, 373, 522
Alice Lea, 536
Alice Munroe, 373
Alice Provost, 489
Alice Tainter, 399, 412, 497, 522
Alice Tarleton, 440, 455, 537
Alida, 444
Alkmaar, 452
Allbree, 444
Alleghany, Sp. (414), 533, 538, 541, 542
Alleghany, St. Prop., 233
Alliance, 381, 395, 466, 472
Almeda, 486, 529
Almena, Bg. (175), 427, 429, 431
Almena, Bk. (756), 471
Almira, Sch. (119), 481
Almira, Bg. (158), 484
Almira, Bg. (194), 455
Almira, Bg. (229), 126, 434
Alpha, 492
Alphage, 443
Alpine, 433, 437
Alps, 292
Altavela, 497
Althera Cornelius, 459
Alto, 477, 485
Alvarado, Sch. (83), 545
Alvarado, Bk. (299), 508, 520
Alverton, 383
Amalia, 397

Amanda, Sch. (154), 463
Amanda, Sp. (222), 403
Amanda Frances Myrick, 464
Amanda Ophelia, 432
Amazon, Sch. (71), 459
Amazon, Sp. (570), 446
Amazon, Sp. (1771), 390
Ambassador, 444, 505, 513
Ambuscade, 118
Amelia, Sch. (126), 464
Amelia, Sp. (205), 227, 465
Amelia, Sp. (244), 484
Amelia, Sp. (561), 503
Amelia, Sp. (573), 375, 410, 433
Amelia, Sp. (623), 406, 454, 519
America, Sch., 533
America, Sch. (115), 466
America, Bg., 434
America, Bg. (129), 461
America, Bg. (148), 477
America, Bg. (172), 444
America, Sp., 503
America, Sp. (561), 549
America, Sp. (700+), 69
America, Sp. (1137), 259, 382, 504, 526
American, Bg. (238), 485
American, Bg. (256), 468, 479, 530
American, Sp., 73, 504
American, Sp. (238), 500
American, Sp. (340), 177, 499
American, Sp. (390), 408, 504
American, Sp. (520), 549
American, Sp. (605), 511
American Belle, 346, 414, 416
American Congress, 345, 391
American Eagle, Sch. (126), 460 535
American Eagle, Sp. (900), 390, 391
American Locust, 465
American Union, Sp. (999), 407, 412
American Union, Sp. (1147), 331, 379, 387, 539
Americus, 472, 496
Amesbury, 490
Amethyst, 165, 169, 196, 203, 212, 371
Amity, Sch. (98), 459
Amity, Sp. (382), 99, 103, 106, 150, 356, 376, 377
Amity, Sp. (799), 527
Amonoosuck, 531
Amos Falkenberc, 486
Amos M. Roberts, 496
Amos Palmer, 475
Amos Patten, 456
Amphibious, 459
Amulet, Bg. (179), 517
Amulet, Sp. (253), 390
Amy, 421, 422
Amy Chase, 495
Anaconda, 417

Anahuac, 401
Andalusia, 408
Andes, Sch. (114), 441
Andes, Sp. (364), 391, 476, 499
Andes, SS (British), 292
Andover, 502, 520
Andrew Brown, 415, 420
Andrew Foster, 318, 333, 383
Andrew Jackson, 178
Andrew Manderson, 337, 542, 552
Andrew Scott, 505
Angelina, 117
Angelina (Angela) Brewer, 487, 493, 498
Angelique, 392, 465, 474, 510
Angelo, 455, 500
Angenora, 466
Anglo-American, 372
Anglo-Saxon, Bg. (200), 450
Anglo-Saxon, Sp. (704), 272, 371
Angola, 431
Anita, 426
Ann, Sch. (74), 535
Ann, Sch. (80), 442
Ann, Sch. (116), 460
Ann, Bk. (641), 519
Ann, Sp. (299), 404
Ann, Sp. (334), 356, 446, 452, 514
Ann & Eliza, 552
Ann & Hope, 549
Ann & Leah, 540
Ann & Susan, 471, 472, 486, 496, 528, 552
Ann A. Tyng, 495
Ann E. Cattell, 425
Ann E. Hooper, 380, 406, 409
Ann Eliza, Sch. (126), 532
Ann Eliza, Bg. (144), 485, 513, 529
Ann Elizabeth, Sch. (131), 478, 534
Ann Elizabeth, Bg. (196), 541
Ann Harley, 393
Ann Louisa, 401
Ann Maria, Sch. (133), 480
Ann Maria, Sch. (142), 545
Ann Maria, Bg. (172), 515
Ann S. Cannon, 418
Ann Smith, 464, 465, 468
Ann T. Stipple (Sipple), 419
Ann Washburn, 412
Ann Wayne, 483
Ann Welch, 384, 486
Anna, 496, 497, 524
Anna Decatur, 373
Anna F. Schmidt, 398, 524
Anna Kimball, 389, 398
Anna Maria, 356
Anna Reynolds, 421
Anna Rich, 372
Anna Somers, 459
Anna Tift, 495

Fanny Fern, Sp. (594), 409
Fanny Forrester, 522, 523
Fanny Fosdick, 406, 522, 523
Fanny Giffney, 411
Fanny Holmes, 497
Fanny McHenry, 406, 526
Far West, Sch. (595), 555
Far West, Sp. (598), 383, 479, 513, 517
Fashion, 457
Favorite, Sp. (274), 465
Favorite, Sp. (777), 412, 522
Favourite, British sloop-of-war, 92
Favourite, Sl., 111
Faxon, 451
Fear Not, 375
Felicia, 412
Feliciana, 128, 538
Fellowship, 5
Fells Point, 76
Ferax, 451
Fernandia, 438
Fidelia, 375, 377
Fidelity, 145
Fides, 397
Fifield, 459, 532
Finland, 405
Firebrand, 63
Flash, 401, 555
Flavilla, 432
Flavio, 450
Flavius, 514
Fleetwing, Sch. (497-518), 336, 471, 472, 497, 498, 519, 525, 555
Fleetwing, Sp. (Cl., 896), 452
Flight, 468, 479, 489
Flora, Sl., 462 ..
Flora, Bg. (248), 495
Flora McDonald, 409
Florence, Sch., 425
Florence, Sch. (84), 419
Florence, Sch. (199-200), 497
Florence, Bg. (175), 493
Florence, Bg. (197), 515
Florence, Bk. (349), 400, 451, 500
Florence, Sp. (298), 508
Florence, Sp. (449), 503, 505
Florence Rogers, Sch. (199), 527
Florence Rogers, Sch. (349), 471
Florian, 177, 474, 499, 532
Florida, Sch. (157), 425
Florida, Bg. (209), 529
Florida, Sp. (330), 505
Florida, Sp. (350), 503
Florida, Sp. (523), 154, 164, 377, 391, 396, 404
Florida, Sp. (1039), 405, 480
Florida, SS (1161), 285
Florida, SS (privateer), 531
Floridan, 323
Floridian, 485, 513, 529

Florio, 481
Floyd, 542
Fly, 76
Flying Scud, 346
Flying Eagle, 496
Forest, Sch., 459
Forest, Bg. (158), 448
Forest City, 517, 525, 526, 530
Forest King, Sch. (99), 431, 433
Forest King, Sch. (366), 555
Forest King, Sp. (992), 383, 384, 508, 519
Forest Prince, 450
Forest Queen, 385, 387, 502
Forest State, 375, 405
Formosa, 394
Fornax, Sch. (111), 425, 426
Fornax, Bg. (249), 448, 508, 515, 516
Forrest, 456
Fortitude, 460
Forum, 448
Foster, 425, 426, 429, 430
Fountain, 424
Fox, Sl. (British), 256
Fox, Bg., 127
Frambes, 545
France, Sp. (411), 394, 506
France, Sp. (441), 196, 514, 539
Frances, Sch. (71), 436
Frances, Sch. (99), 475
Frances, Sch. (161), 423, 495
Frances, Bg. (177), 476, 477
Frances, Bg. (191), 445
Frances, Bk. (472), 508, 519
Frances, Sp. (368), 499
Frances, Sp. (595), 450
Frances Amy, 548
Frances Ann, Bg. (182), 483, 491
Frances Ann, Sp. (446), 433, 447, 454, 456
Frances Ashby, 485
Frances Burr, 446
Frances Esther, 537
Frances Hallet, 417, 442
Frances Helen, 481
Frances Henrietta, 157, 220, 392
Frances Jane, 543
Frances Satterly, 555
Francis A. Goodwin, 464
Francis A. Palmer, 388, 396
Francis Ashby, 506
Francis B. Cutting, 388, 397, 398, 497, 522
Francis Depau, 324, 394, 507, 510
Francis Elmore, 464
Francis Lord, 490
Francis P. Beck, 443, 492
Francis P. Sage, 385, 386, 388, 521
Francis Satterly, 470, 481
Francis Secor, 493
Francis Stanton, 451

Francis Travers, 323
Francisco, 486
Francois I, 394
Franconia, 404, 409, 436, 437, 451, 454, 474, 502, 508, 510, 511
Frank, 436, 443
Frank A. Hall, 555
Frank Flint, 525
Frank Haynie, 407
Frank Herbert, 424
Frank Pierce, 372, 376, 413
Frankfort, 503
Franklin, Sl. (100), 457
Franklin, Sch. (91), 422, 427
Franklin, Bg. (198), 125, 431, 432, 488
Franklin, Bk., 399
Franklin, Bk. (300), 539
Franklin, Sp., 536
Franklin, Sp. (213), 120, 465
Franklin, Sp. (301), 446
Franklin, Sp. (391), 538
Franklin, Sp. (421), 505
Franklin, SS (2183), 277, 297
Franklin Bell, 487
Franklin Haven, 344, 376
Franklin King, 411
Franklin Nickerson, 432, 471, 472
Franklin Snow, 478
Frazar, 442
Freak, 392
Frederick, Sch. (149), 466
Frederick, Bg. (147), 256
Frederick Gebhard, 388, 397
Frederick Lenning, 542
Fredonia, 121, 498
Freedom, Sch. (131), 463
Freedom, Bg. (131), 532
Freeman, 402
Freighter, 537
Friend, 416
Friends, Sp., 73
Friends, Sp. (403), 156, 392
Friendship, 63
Frontenac, 140
Fulton, Sl. (78), 414
Fulton, Stbt. (327), 214
Fulton, SS (2308), 277, 299, 301

G. B. Lamar, Bg. (260), 474, 478, 491, 530
G. B. Lamar, Sp. (933), 383, 392
G. C. Waterbury, 493
G. F. Chapman, 374
G. H. Wright, 537
G. L., 414
G. M. Nevins, 555
G. S. Hunt, 527
G. T. Ward, 489
G. W. Hall, 495, 527
G. W. Lawrence, 509
Galante Marie, 546
Galaxy, 442

Harry Maybee, 472
Harry of the West, 524
Hartford, Sp. (511), 468, 479, 517
Hartford, SS (251), 283, 299
Hartley, 411, 450
Hartstene (Hartstein), 476, 479, 556
Harvard, 449
Harvest, Sch. (89), 466, 484
Harvest, Sch. (96), 417, 435, 437
Harvest, Bk. (426), 476, 489, 493, 521
Harvest, Sp. (614), 409
Harvest, Sp. (646), 399
Harvest Queen, 377
Harvey Birch, 311, 344, 345, 380, 566
Havana, Sch. (85), 544
Havana, Bg. (164), 535
Havelock, 374
Havre, Bg. (291), 435
Havre, Sp. (481), 394
Havre, Sp. (871), 395, 523, 564
Hawkins, 482
Haze, 476, 489, 537, 556
Heber, 519
Hebrew, 443, 505
Hebron, 440, 449, 501, 525, 548
Hector, Sch. (99), 420
Hector, Bg. (198), 439, 547
Hector, Sp. (557-559), 356, 396, 485, 516
Heiress, 497
Heidelberg, 349, 413, 522, 524
Helen, Sl. (83), 416
Helen, Sch. (146-149), 425, 462
Helen, Sch. (272), 483, 496, 497
Helen, Bk. (315), 443
Helen, Sp. (424), 381, 390, 468
Helen, Sp. (976), 450
Helen A. Miller, 548
Helen Augusta, 398
Helen Frazar, 429
Helen McLeod, 507, 547
Helen McGaw, 385, 386, 404, 406
Helen Mar, Sch. (195), 424
Helen Mar, Bk. (269), 509
Helen Mar, Sp. (307-308), 444, 474, 532, 540
Helen Maria, 426, 427, 429, 544
Helen R. Cooper, 398
Helen Thompson, 407
Helena Sloman, 285, 309, 398
Helene, 470, 473, 482
Helicon, 502
Hellespont, Sp. (249), 402
Hellespont, Sp. (347), 400, 448
Heloise, 556
Helvetia, Sp. (972), 504, 521, 523, 524
Helvetia Sp. (Raised three decks, 1351), 395

Hemisphere, 385, 389, 504, 518, 521, 525
Hendrick Hudson, Sp. (824), 247, 390, 391, 509
Hendrick Hudson, Stbt (1185), 244
Henrietta, Sch. (74), 543, 544
Henrietta, Sch. (160), 490
Henrietta Marcy, 412
Henry, Sl. (95), 457
Henry, Sch. (92), 440
Henry, Sch. (121), 416, 417
Henry, Sch. (129), 480
Henry, Sch. (145), 469
Henry, Bg. (98), 463
Henry, Bk. (449), 476
Henry, Sp. (248-258), 161, 390, 394, 474, 475, 477
Henry, Sp. (396), 447
Henry A. Barling, 548
Henry Allen, 125, 392, 465, 466, 565
Henry Barger, 463
Henry Buck, 440
Henry Camerdon, 226
Henry Chase, 480
Henry Clay, Sch., 441
Henry Clay, Sch. (89), 427
Henry Clay, Sp. (436), 378, 447
Henry Clay, Sp. (1207), 258, 320, 378, 380, 389
Henry Curtis, 417, 418, 419
Henry Eubank, 431
Henry Franklin, 419, 422, 432
Henry Gibbs, 417
Henry G. King, 435
Henry Grinnell, 405
Henry H. Boody, 411, 524
Henry Harbeck, 501, 504, 511, 515
Henry Hill, 484
Henry Kelsey, 507, 547
Henry Kneeland, 220, 483, 499
Henry Leeds, 469
Henry Nesmith, 409
Henry Newell, 432, 448, 451, 506
Henry Nutt, 472, 542
Henry P. Russell, Sch. (111), 473
Henry P. Russell, Sch. (396), 556
Henry Payson, 425, 436
Henry Reed, 398
Henry R. Roberts, 491
Henry Tallman, 505
Henry Thompson, 400, 444
Henry W. Safford, 459
Henry Ware, 454
Henry Warren, 539
Henry IV, 212, 394
Heraclide, 445
Herald, Sch. (90), 458
Herald, Bg. (174), 493, 494, 529, 530

Herald, Sp. (248), 547
Herald, Sp. (359), 165, 371
Herbert, 452
Herculean, 436, 445, 451
Hercules, Bg. (193), 477
Hercules, Bg. (382), 538
Hercules, Bk. (382), 504, 538
Hercules, Sp. (335), 102, 149, 377, 378
Hercules, Sp. (371), 398, 431, 433, 434, 440
Hercules, Sp. (498), 356, 549
Hercules, Sp. (597), 549
Herman, 408, 548
Hermann, 277
Hermione, 536
Hero, Sl. (41), 256
Hero, Sl. (85), 414, 416
Hero, Sch. (97), 466
Hero, Sch. (329, 321), 556
Hero, Bg., 126
Hero, Bg. (239), 499
Hero, Sp. (750-760-765), 388, 398, 405, 467, 501, 512
Hero of the Nile, 390
Hersilia, 431, 435, 438, 450
Hesper, Bg. (157), 401
Hesper, Bk. (392), 471
Hesper, Bk. (640), 376
Hesperus, Sch. (85), 247
Hesperus, Sp. (1019), 373, 526
Hiawatha, Bk. (523), 517
Hiawatha, Bk. (574), 489
Hibernia, Sp. (551), 206, 324, 377, 380
Hibernia, Sp. (877), 384, 386, 387, 404
Highflyer, 321, 383
Highlander, 420, 429
Hilah, 474, 503, 505, 511
Hindoo, 504, 508, 514, 541, 542
Hindostan, Sp. (495), 518
Hindostan, Sp. (562-563), 74, 549
Hiram, 461
Hiram Gerard, 464
Hitty Tom, 436
Hobart, Bk. (204), 469
Hobart, Sp. (306), 444, 447
Hogan, 451
Hokomok, 441
Holder Borden, 533, 536, 538
Hollander, 516
Holyoke, 411
Home, Sch. (137), 421, 422, 423
Home, Bg. (137), 421, 424
Home, Stbt, (537), 218, 220, 221
Homer, Sch. (175), 414
Homer, Bg. (185), 467
Homer, Sp. (296), 444
Hope, Sch., 463
Hope, Bg. (260), 106
Hope, Sp., 87
Hope, Sp. (870), 451
Hope, Sp. (971), 372

Manzoni, 497
Mara, 488
Marathon, Sp. (382), 431, 435, 449
Marathon, Sp. (485), 454, 509, 513, 525, 539
Marathon, Sp. (890), 396, 493, 519, 521, 523
Marcella, 400
Marcella Tilton, 558
Marcellus, Sp. (385), 116
Marcellus, Sp. (660), 446, 456
March, 427, 428
Marcia, 449, 453, 507
Marcia Greenleaf, 412
Marco Bozzaris, 213
Marengo, 499
Margaret, Sch. (206), 480
Margaret, Bg., 440, 537
Margaret, Bg. (186), 444
Margaret, Bk. (250), 495
Margaret, Sp. (291), 538
Margaret, Sp. (375), 503, 511
Margaret, Sp. (447), 508
Margaret Ann, Sch. (108), 464
Margaret Ann, Bg. (203), 505
Margaret Evans, 390
Margaret Forbes, 444
Margaret Reinhardt, 542
Margaret Scott, 503
Margaret Tyson, 388
Margaret Y. Davis, 471, 473
Maria, Sch. (115), 463
Maria, Sch. (124), 458
Maria, Sch. (171), 461, 462
Maria, Bg. (129), 456
Maria, Bk. (324), 452, 517
Maria Ann, 457
Maria Caroline, 499
Maria L. Davis, 429, 486
Maria Louisa, 397
Maria M. Klots, 418
Maria Morton, 479, 480, 519, 526
Maria Pike, 494, 558
Maria Spear, 442
Maria Theresa, Sch. (148), 533, 538
Maria Theresa, Bg. (229), 445
Maria White, 498
Maria Wilhelmina, 24, 45
Marianna, 400, 512, 529
Marianne Nottebohm, 333, 380, 388, 397
Marie Etta Ryon, 534
Marietta, 416
Marine, Sch. (349), 558
Marine, Bg. (216), 495
Marine, Bk. (213), 441
Mariner, Sl., 477
Mariner, Sch. (117), 417
Mariner, Sp. (1282), 372, 447
Marion, Sch. (112), 432, 545
Marion, Sp. (355), 483
Marion, Sp. (450), 467, 479
Marion, SS (900), 288, 295

Marion Gage, 484
Mariposa, 510
Maritana, 375, 453, 457
Mark, 459
Mark Time, 457
Marmion, Bk. (359), 525
Marmion, Sp. (278-291), 159, 160, 394, 546
Marmion, Sp. (903), 381, 382, 384, 517
Marmora, 520, 539
Marquette, Sp. (1197), 519, 526
Marquette, Sp. (1363), 389
Mars, 376
Marsellois, 438, 443, 490
Marshall, 479
Marshall Ney, Bg. (193), 426
Marshall Ney, Bg. (250), 508
Marshall O. Roberts, 388
Marshall Post, 493
Marshfield, 412
Martha, Sch., 477
Martha, Sch. (104), 458
Martha, Sch. (119), 461
Martha, Sch. (126), 463
Martha, Bg. (169), 428
Martha, Bg. (242), 492
Martha, Bk. (242), 439
Martha, Bk. (470), 468
Martha, Sp. (260), 153, 154, 378
Martha, Sp. (360), 119, 356, 483, 503
Martha, Sp. (534), 449, 507
Martha, Sp. (1179), 374
Martha J. Ward, 502, 504, 520, 523
Martha Post, Sch. (196), 486, 497
Martha Post, Bg. (195), 470, 496
Martha Rideout, 389
Martha Sanger, 511
Martha's Vineyard, 393, 468, 479
Martha Washington, 384, 397, 486, 529
Mary, Sl. (96), 418, 420
Mary, Sch., 67, 126
Mary, Sch. (99), 424
Mary, Bg., 483, 485
Mary, Bg. (115), 429
Mary, Bg. (128), 476
Mary, Bg. (169), 430
Mary, Bg. (193), 468, 479, 491, 530
Mary, Bk. (195), 423, 425
Mary, Bk. (244), 547
Mary, Sp. (268), 449
Mary, Sp. (429), 72, 549
Mary, Sp. (744), 519
Mary, Sp. (1149), 526
Mary & Harriet, 509
Mary & Jane, 524, 541
Mary & Louisa, Sch. (167), 532, 537
Mary & Louisa, Bk. (497), 487

Mary & Susan, Sp. (392), 446, 484, 522
Mary & Susan, Sp. (550), 412
Mary A. Howland, 461
Mary A. Jones, 507
Mary A. Williams, 460
Mary Ann, Sch. (98), 477
Mary Ann, Sch. (103), 461
Mary Ann, Bg. (138), 400, 435, 485
Mary Ann, Sp. (339), 164
Mary Ann, Sp. (460), 549
Mary Ann, Sp. (497), 371, 431, 433, 446, 449, 517
Mary Ann Guest, 459, 460
Mary Ann Jones, 517
Mary Annah, Bk. (488), 409, 509, 520
Mary Annah, Sp. (500), 405
Mary Archer, 461
Mary Augusta, Sch. (143-145), 515, 548
Mary Augusta, Sp. (281), 119
Mary Augusta, Sp. (300), 120
Mary Ballard, 431
Mary Barnard, 474
Mary Bradford, 391
Mary Broughton, 491, 504, 514, 515, 521
Mary C. Ames, 417
Mary Carson, 405
Mary Catherine, 543, 544
Mary Clinton, 482
Mary Coe, 489, 494, 497
Mary Crocker, 520
Mary D. Lane, 495, 513, 522, 523, 558
Mary Dunham, 393
Mary E. Balch, 373
Mary Eddy, 524
Mary E. Jones, 476
Mary E. Whittier, 512
Mary Emeline, 543
Mary Emma, 473
Mary E. Smith, 538
Mary F. Lutterloch, 433
Mary F. Slade, 422, 424, 426
Mary Frances (Mary Francis), Sp. (311), 485, 488
Mary Frances, Sp. (326), 445, 455
Mary Francis, 506
Mary Glover, 372, 512
Mary H., 422, 424
Mary Hale, 409
Mary Hammond, 373, 526
Mary H. Banks, 533, 534
Mary Hamilton, 466, 487, 493, 523
Mary Helen, Sch. (235), 498
Mary Helen, Bg. (158), 431, 434
Mary Howland, 505
Mary J. Hoyt, 472
Mary Jane, Sch. (158), 566
Mary Jane, Bg. (148), 470
Mary Jane Lonan, 470

<remoj"

St. John, Sp. (398), 378, 484, 500
St. John, Sp. (562), 384, 492
St. Lawrence, Sch. (153), 471
St. Lawrence, Sp. (356), 449
St. Lawrence, Sp. (462), 489, 506
St. Leon, 500
St. Louis, Sp. (340-344-354), 401, 503, 505, 506, 540
St. Louis, Sp. (444), 538
St. Louis, Sp. (459), 445
St. Louis Sp. (533), 456
St. Louis, Sp. (630), 405
St. Louis, Sp. (939), 388, 502
St. Louis, SS (1621), 277, 295
St. Mary, Sch. (187), 470
St. Mary, Sch. (239), 479
St. Mary, Sp. (444), 503, 511, 566
St. Mary's (St. Mary), 490, 496, 542
St. Nicholas, 395, 396, 565
St. Patrick, Sp. (896-900), 324, 384
St. Patrick, Sp. (1049), 405
St. Paul, 396
St. Peter, 519, 522, 523
St. Petersburg, 371, 433, 445
St. Simon (Simonds), 437, 439, 443
Sabattas, 477
Sabattis, 507
Sabine, Sl. (76), 414
Sabine, Sch. (174), 481
Sabine, Bg. (176), 507
Sabine, Bg. (399), 531
Sadi, 474
Sagadahock, Sp. (385), 126
Sagadahock, Sp. (575), 331, 519
Sagamore, 374, 407
Sage, 459, 481
Saginaw, 419, 441
Sahwa, 482
Saladin, 435
Salem, 416, 437
Sally, Bg. (149), 126
Sally, Sp. (348-358), 77, 78
Sally J. Aiken, 560
Saltillo, 454, 545
Saluda, 465
Samaritan, 534
Samoset, 395
Sampson, 391
Samson, 486, 493
Samuel, 428
Samuel & Margaret, 73
Samuel Brown, 430, 441
Samuel Butler, 544
Samuel Castner, 460
Samuel Eddy, 472
Samuel Gilman, 415
Samuel H. Appleton, 414, 427, 429
Samuel Hicks, 379, 381, 383, 384, 501

Samuel Lawrence, 374, 411
Samuel M. Fox, 330, 388, 395
Samuel Moxley, 493
Samuel Moxley, Jr., 519
Samuel N. Smith, 535
Samuel P. Lord, 464
Samuel P. Paynter, 459
Samuel R. Jackson, 469, 544
Samuel Robertson, 212, 391
Samuel Willets, 388
San Francisco, 293, 294, 331, 386, 500
Sandusky, 385, 388, 476, 488
Santa Claus, Sch. (301), 560
Santa Claus, Sp. (1256), 373
Santee, Sch. (92), 439, 535
Santee, Bk. (192), 446, 452, 454
Saone, 447, 454
Sapphire, 165, 371
Saracen, 393
Saragossa, 447, 539
Sarah, Sch. (84), 534
Sarah, Sch. (94), 463
Sarah, Sch. (130), 463
Sarah, Bg. (136), 461
Sarah, Bg. (187), 484
Sarah, Bk. (British), 323
Sarah, Bk. (287), 506
Sarah, Sp. (327), 70
Sarah, Sp. (453), 446
Sarah, Sp. (536) (British), 393
Sarah & Arselia, 381, 400
Sarah & Elizabeth, 481
Sarah & Eliza, 516, 518
Sarah A. Hammond, 421, 422, 424
Sarah Abigail, 426
Sarah Ann, Sch. (146), 460
Sarah Ann, Bk. (431), 434
Sarah Ann Roe, 464
Sarah Bridges (Bridge), 409, 508, 516, 522, 548
Sarah Brown, 485, 488
Sarah Bruen, 472
Sarah Clark, 487
Sarah E. Merrill, 464
Sarah Elizabeth, Sch. (101), 417
Sarah Elizabeth, Sch. (147), 470, 535
Sarah E. Pettigrew, 408, 413
Sarah G. Hyde, 397
Sarah Hand, 490, 508, 539
Sarah Herrick, 249
Sarah Hibbert, 498
Sarah Hooper, 516
Sarah Jane, 476, 488
Sarah Judkins, 560
Sarah L. Stevens, 421
Sarah Louisa, 375
Sarah Mills, 494, 530
Sarah Nash, 515
Sarah Olney, 450
Sarah Purington, 518
Sarah Ralston, 404
Sarah Sands, 239, 241, 304, 379

Sarah Sheafe, 397
Sarah Vose, 423
Sarah W. Cushing, 490
Sarah Wales, 435
Saranac, 431
Saranak, 403
Saratoga, Sch. (95), 431
Saratoga, Bg. (231), 479, 488
Saratoga, Sp. (542), 324, 499, 502
Saratoga, Sp. (1200), 383
Sardinia, 377, 382
Sartelle, 452, 501, 502
Savannah, Sch. (88-97), 435, 437
Savannah, Bg. (396), 438, 469, 476, 488, 510
Savannah, Bg. (493), 476
Savannah, Bk. (493), 479
Savannah, Sp. (248), 401, 475
Savannah, Sp. (380 rebuilt 389), 106
Savannah, SS (319), 142, 145, 276
Savannah, Teamboat, 134
Savannah Packet, 119, 126
Saxon, Sp. (344-345), 432, 445
Saxon, Sp. (734), 411
Saxony, Bk. (346), 431, 432, 450, 520
Saxony, Sp. (393), 375, 516
Schuylkill, 538
Science, 463
Scio, 450
Scioto, 523
Scotia, 408
Scotland, Sch., 436
Scotland, Sp. (548), 452
Scotland, Sp. (627), 378
Scotland, Sp. (821), 412, 525
Scourge, 458
Sea, Bg. (249), 443, 490
Sea, Sp. (807), 381, 382, 384, 503
Sea Belle, Bg. (149), 437, 481
Sea Belle, Sp. (785), 450, 514
Sea Drift, 435
Sea Flower, Bg. (150), 425, 438
Sea Flower, Sp. (1024), 373, 411
Sea Foam, 480
Sea Island, Bg. (186), 119, 126
Sea Island, Bg. (213), 434
Sea King, 373
Sea Lark, 388, 398
Sea Lion, 400
Seafort, 14, 25
Seaman, Sch. (169), 533
Seaman, Bg. (124), 516
Seaman, Sp. (241), 431, 450, 547
Seaman's Bride, 389
Sea Mew, 469
Sea Nymph, 326, 409, 509
Sea Star, 392
Sea Witch, Sl. (95), 457
Sea Witch, Cl. (908), 284
Searsville, 430
Sebastapol, 526
Sebastian Cabot, 408

General Index

615

Brewton & Co., 49
Briard, Capt., 376
Briard, Capt. John A., 446
Briard, Capt. William A., 383, 446
Bridges, Capt. C. F., 400
Bridges, Capt. Henry G., 456
Bridges, Capt. J., 526
Briggs, Capt. A., 528
Briggs, Capt. Burton, 462, 463
Briggs, Capt. Caleb L., 460, 463
Briggs, Capt. Ethan C., 463
Briggs, Capt. George, 383, 469
Briggs, Capt. Isaac B., 497
Briggs, J., 459
Briggs, Capt. J. H., 531
Briggs, Capt. Jeremiah, 458, 463
Briggs, Capt. L. J., 382
Briggs, Capt. Nathan, 448
Briggs, Capt. Sylvanus, 476
Briggs, J. & N., Co-partners, 232, 460, 463
Brigham, Capt., 487
Brigham, Henry, 336, 553, 554, 557
Brigham, N. H., 472
Brigham, Stephen, 117
Brigham & Kelley, 436, 479
Brigham, Baldwin & Co., 479
Brigham, Kelly & Co., 313, 479, 545
Bright, Capt. J., 484
Brightman, Capt., 463
Briscoe & Partridge, 131
Bristol-New York, Great Western SS Co., 229, 237, 241, 248
British & American Steam Navigation Co. See Liverpool-New York B. & A.
British Navigation Acts, (Repeal of), 317
British Orders in Council, 84, 93
Brittingham, Capt. A. J., 458
Britton, Capt., 495, 565
Britton, Capt. Alexander, 392, 485
Britton, Capt. John, 378, 380, 390, 392, 556, 563
Britton, Capt. John P., 272, 463, 556
Britton, Thomas, 74
Britton, Capt. Thomas, 197, 272, 391
Broadfoot & McNeel, 125
Brock, Capt. William, 532
Brodnax, Capt. W. B., 491
Bromfield, Edward, 24
Brook, Capt. A., 537
Brookfield, Capt. J. S., 440
Brookings, Capt. J. B., 487
Brookman, Capt. John U., 521
Brooks, Capt. C. H., 413

Brooks, Capt. J. H., 413, 516
Brooks, Peter Chardon, 66
Brooks, Samuel, 122
Brooks, Capt. Seth, 477
Brooks, William, Jr., 86
Brooks & Potter, 125
Brooks, Davis & Co., 288
Broome, Sam & John, Co-partners, 37
Broughton, Capt. J. C., 513
Brower, John H., 268, 530
Brower, Theophilus, 72
Brower, Capt. William W., 109, 456
Brower & Neilson, 268, 530
Brower, J. H. & Co., 311, 530
Brown, Capt., 434, 439, 447, 467, 481, 508, 519, 522, 524, 525, 543
Brown, Acquila, Jr., 76, 77
Brown, Capt. Albert H., 371, 372, 431, 433, 446, 563
Brown, Alexander, 87, 88, 154
Brown, Capt. Charles, 559
Brown, Capt. Cicero, 406, 409, 494, 530
Brown, Capt. D., 415, 430
Brown, Capt. D. D., 515
Brown, Capt. Daniel, 387, 466, 467, 532
Brown, Capt. David, 122
Brown, Capt. David, Jr., 411
Brown, Capt. E., 437
Brown, Capt. Ezekiel, 424, 432
Brown, Capt. G. F., 543
Brown, George, 120, 226, 467
Brown, Capt. George W., 490, 495, 507
Brown, H. W., 556
Brown, Capt. Henry S., 518, 541
Brown, Capt. J., 466, 518
Brown, Capt. J. A., 397, 538
Brown, James, 296
Brown, Capt. James, 38, 443
Brown, James W., 313
Brown, Capt. Jesse E., 538
Brown, John, 74, 550
Brown, Capt. John, Jr., 443
Brown, John H., 87
Brown, Capt. John M., 455
Brown, John W., 176, 458, 463
Brown, Capt. Joseph H., 418
Brown, Capt. Joseph K. (R.), 384, 400
Brown, Capt. Joseph M., 400
Brown, Capt. Nelson, 436
Brown, Nicholas, 549
Brown, Noah, 150, 159
Brown, Capt. Pardon W. (T.), 489
Brown, Capt. Richard, 384, 395, 449
Brown, Capt. Richard S., 456

Brown, Capt. Robert T., 285, 479, 480, 490, 491
Brown, Tunis A., 554, 556
Brown, Capt. W., 459, 481, 482
Brown, Capt. W. B., 382
Brown, Capt. Washington, 543, 544
Brown, William, 87, 163, 297
Brown, Sir William, 154
Brown, Capt. William F., 481
Brown, William H., 228, 432
Brown & Bell, 150, 184, 218, 252, 253, 258
Brown & Harrison, 264, 375
Brown & Harrisons, 312, 405-406, 408, 409
Brown & Ives, 549
Brown & Potter, 528
Brown, Alexander & Sons, 124, 163, 403
Brown Brothers & Co., 296
Brown, George & Harrison, 264
Brown, John A. & Co., 403
Brown, Shipley & Co., 312, 400, 403, 408
Brown, William & James, Co-partners, 154
Brown, Wm. & James Brown & Co., 154, 211, 371, 380, 403, 404
Browne, Capt. Charles A., 472
Browne, James & Co., 264, 310, 312, 348, 375, 405, 408, 410
Brownell, Capt., 499
Bruce, Benjamin, 264, 433, 437, 442, 455
Bruce & Cheney, 442, 455
Brumley, Reuben, 87
Brundage & Willis, 535
Brundige, James, 426
Brundige, Vose & Co., 123, 425
Brune, Capt. R. D., 511
Brunel, Isambard Kingdom, 237
Bryant, Capt., 523
Bryant, Capt. James M., 377
Bryer, Capt. James M., 377
Buchanan, Dr., 184
Buchanan, Andrew, 77
Buchanan family, 69
Buchanan, Capt. George, 541
Buchanan, James A., 76, 303
Buchanan, Thomas, 69
Buchanan, Wood & Co., 125, 144
Buck, Capt. A., 537
Buck, Capt. Charles W., 408, 409
Buck, Capt. F. N., 482
Buck, Capt. Leonard, 536
Buck, B. & Sons, 313
Buckingham, Capt. William, 530
Buckley, Capt. Charles P., 474

Coffin, Capt. Hasadiah, 404
Coffin, Capt. Hector, 165, 371
Coffin, Admiral Sir Isaac, 170, 197
Coffin, Capt. Isaac S., 445, 448, 451
Coffin, Capt. J. W., 374
Coffin, Capt. Rowland T., 383
Coffin, Capt. T., 527
Coffin School, 170
Coggshall, Capt. George, 494
Cohen, Aaron, 208, 266, 500, 502, 538, 540
Cohen, Philip S., 220
Cohen & Hertz, 479
Cohen & Miller, 179, 474, 475
Cohen, Isaac & Co., 127
Cohen, Norris & Co., 535
Coit family, 69
Coit, Henry, 86, 121
Coit, John, 81
Coit, Capt. William, 126
Colburn, Capt., 496, 499
Colburn, Capt. Oliver, 483, 484
Colburn, Capt. R., 492
Colburn, Capt. Reuben, 398, 400
Colburn, Capt. S. S., 492
Colby, Capt. Edwin G., 405, 439
Colby, Capt. J., 443
Colby, Capt. James, 455, 507, 508, 514
Colcock & Gibbons, 78
Colcord, Capt. Josiah A., 496
Cole, Capt., 493
Cole, Capt. Abraham, 461, 462
Cole, Capt. Abraham, Jr., 461
Cole, Capt. C. R., 502
Cole, Capt. Cornelius, 475
Cole, Capt. E., 562
Cole, Capt. Edward, 471, 482, 496, 497, 498, 519
Cole, Capt. G., 524
Cole, Capt. G. B., 548
Cole, Capt. Isaac, 462, 478
Cole, Capt. J., 457
Cole, Capt. Jeremiah, 539
Cole, Capt. Rufus, 433, 479, 530, 531
Cole, Capt. Seth, 524
Cole, Capt. Stephen E., 379, 451, 499, 503, 504, 510
Cole, Capt. Winant J., 472
Cole, Capt. Winant S., 462
Coleman, Capt. Asa, 419, 420, 569
Coleman, Capt. J., 518
Coleman, Capt. Nathaniel, 542
Coleman, Capt. Perry S., 434
Coles, Capt., 524
Colhoun, Gustavus & Hugh, 122
Collamore, Capt., 497

Collamore, Capt. E., 486, 513
Collet, Capt. Henry, 537
Colley, Capt., 535
Colley, Capt. J. (W. J.), 406, 455, 508
Colley, Capt. James, 397, 412, 490
Colley, Capt. William S., 406
Collier, Capt., 473
Collier, Capt. George W., 412, 446, 548
Collier, Capt. James, 469
Collins, Capt., 407, 482, 485, 523, 559
Collins, Capt. Charles, 374
Collins, Capt. Edward Knight, 198, 208, 211, 242, 243, 296, 380, 401, 500
Collins, Capt. George, 491, 504
Collins, Capt. George, Jr., 491
Collins, Capt. George C., 479
Collins (Collings), Capt. George W., 418
Collins, Capt. J., 459, 517
Collins, Capt. James A., 444
Collins, Capt. John, 68, 380, 401, 500
Collins, Capt. Jonathan, 417
Collins, Capt. Mark, 65
Collins, Capt. R., 507
Collins, Capt. Reuben, Jr., 416, 437, 544
Collins, Capt. Walter, 542
Collins, Capt. William, 393
Collins, Israel G. & Son, 198, 241, 401
Collom (Collum), Capt. Daniel, 487
Collum, Capt. R., 506
Collyer, William, 285, 292
Colson (Coulson), Capt. George W., 373
Colson, Capt. S., 496
Colt, Henry, 128
Colt, Samuel T., 128
Colter, Capt. William N., 494
Comery (Conery), Capt. Charles, 373, 374, 542
Comley, Samuel, 202
Comly, M. S. & Co., 540
Commerce:
    Baltimore, 76, 163
    Charleston, 76, 77, 79-80
    Mobile, 129, 130
    New Orleans, 128, 219
    New York, 75, 76, 158, 167, 201
    of New Orleans in 1816, 363, note 26, Chap. V
    Philadelphia, 75, 76
    Savannah, 80, 81
    volume of arrivals and departures, 36, 38, 43, 47-48, 75-76, 79, 81, 116, 128
Compton, Capt., 535

Conant, Capt., 492, 493, 509
Conant, Benjamin, 207, 416
Conant, Capt. Benjamin W. (N.), 461, 487, 509, 542
Conant, Samuel S., 176, 415
Conant, Capt. W., 496
Conant & Codman, 415
Conant, Benjamin & Co., 428
Conditions on early steamships, 236
Cone, Capt. J., 493
Cone, Capt. Jun., 388, 493
Conery (Comery), Capt. Charles, 525
Congdon, Capt. J. A., 521
Conklin, Capt., 512, 526
Conklin, Capt. Hamilton D., 441, 473, 519, 530, 560
Conklin, Capt. J. H., 514, 515
Conklin, Capt. Nathan A., 424, 437, 481
Conklin, Capt. R. C., 471
Conklin, Capt. Richard, 480
Conklin, Capt. R. E., 528
Conkling, Capt. R. E. (C.), 471
Conn, Capt. George, 404
Conn (Cann), Capt. J. M., 494
Conn, Capt. Richard D., 351, 395
Conn & Tyson, 351
Connecticut Military Adventurers, 52
Conner, Capt. J. W., 470
Connor, Capt. J., 409
Connor, Capt. James, 506
Constable, Mr., 152
Constable, William & James, Co-partners, 72
Converse, Mr., 152
Conway, Capt. Chaplin, 461
Conway, Capt. Joseph, 379, 485-486
Conway, Capt. P., 392
Conway, Capt. Thomas, 412, 517, 521
Cony, Capt. D., 490
Cook, Capt., 491, 509, 516
Cook, Capt. A., 518
Cook, Capt. Benjamin, 445
Cook, Capt. David, 323
Cook, Capt. David R., 456
Cook, Capt. Enoch, 495, 510, 516, 522
Cook, Capt. Enoch, Jr., 393
Cook, Capt. Henry, 372, 407, 446, 454
Cook, Capt. J., 384
Cook, Capt. James, 82, 439
Cook, Capt. Lewis P., 496, 498
Cook, Capt. Richard H., 437
Cook, Capt. Robert C., 537, 554
Cook, Capt. W., 393
Cook, Capt. William, 373, 380, 514

Davis, Adolphus, 209, 414, 428, 430
Davis, Capt. C. M., 405
Davis, Capt. Charles, 443
Davis, Capt. Charles W., 456
Davis, Capt. David P., 480, 487, 497
Davis, Capt. Ebenezer, 445
Davis, Capt. Eli, 226
Davis, Capt. Elias, 449
Davis, Capt. Francis, 441, 540
Davis, Capt. Francis B., 497, 498
Davis, Capt. G., 442
Davis, Capt. George, 447, 455
Davis, George W., 528
Davis, Capt. George W., 378
Davis, Capt. George Washington, 153
Davis, H., 419
Davis, Capt. Henry, 401
Davis, Capt. Hezekiah, 416
Davis, Capt. J., 386, 443
Davis, Capt. J. L., 432
Davis, Capt. J. P., 462
Davis, Capt. J. W., 416
Davis, Capt. James, 487
Davis, Capt. James W., 415, 428
Davis, Capt. John, 373, 381, 398, 406, 454, 503
Davis, Capt. John J., 443
Davis, Capt. John T., 423
Davis, Capt. Joseph W., 414, 416, 467
Davis, L. T., 558
Davis, Capt. Lewis, 472, 497, 519
Davis, Capt. Lewis, Jr., 471, 555
Davis, Capt. Lewis S., 470, 473, 481, 482, 513, 555, 560, 561
Davis, N., 418
Davis, Capt. Nathaniel, 466
Davis, Capt. R., 520
Davis, Capt. S. B., 489
Davis, Capt. S. H., 435
Davis, Capt. S. R., 473, 528
Davis, Capt. Samuel, 426
Davis, T., 438
Davis, Capt. T. H., 432
Davis, Capt. T. J., 373
Davis, Capt. Vincent, 463
Davis, Capt. William, 443, 454, 490
Davis, Capt. William R., 486, 544
Davis & Blake, 414, 428
Davis & Brooks, 198, 291, 400
Davis & Center, 111, 174, 418
Davis, Samuel & Co., 114
Davis, Snow & Co., 419
Davy, Capt., 487
Dawbien, Capt., 504
Dawson, Capt. T., 388, 461

Dawson & Hancock, 312, 407
Day, Capt. Alden B., 411, 440, 452, 454
Day, Capt. John, 385, 387, 455, 501, 512, 518, 521
Dayton, Capt. Albert, 464
Dayton, Capt. S. A., 488
Dayton, Capt. Smith A., 488
Dayton & Sprague, 419
Dean, Capt., 480, 532, 537
Dean, Capt. Daniel, 538
Dean, Capt. George, 453
Dean, Joseph, 48
Dean, Capt. L. F., 529
Dean, Capt. S., 496, 498
Dean, Capt. W. H., 507
Deane, Richard, 45
Dearborn, Capt. George A., 398, 481
Dearborn, Capt. S., 524
Dearborn, Capt. Samuel, 417, 471
Death rate on emigrant ships, 331, 332
Deblois, Lewis, 44
Decan, Capt. Peter A., 404, 405, 406, 502, 518, 541
Decan, Capt. Robert (Richard) R., 403, 405, 406, 508, 540, 541
Decker, Capt. William, Jr., 451, 500
De Cost, Capt. Nash, 153, 350, 378
Deering, Capt. J. W., 412
DeForest, Capt. E., 483
DeForest family, 72
Deforest, W. W., 401
DeForest, Lockwood & W., Co-partners, 118
Deforest & Son, 176
DeForest, W. W. & Co., 483
Defraye, M., 78
Degrain, James A., 561
de Grasse, Count, 159
DeGroot, Capt. Albert, 534
DeGroot, Capt. James, 458
Delano, Amasa, 86
Delano, Capt. B. F., 383, 413
Delano, Capt. Benjamin, 374, 522
Delano, Capt. C., 390, 519
Delano, Capt. Clark, 372, 494
Delano, Capt. Ephraim, 68
Delano family, 250
Delano, Frank, 412, 457
Delano, Capt. H., 529
Delano, Capt. Henry C., 519
Delano, Capt. Henry D., 493, 543
Delano, Capt. James C., 400
Delano, Capt. John A., 378
Delano, Capt. John P., 413
Delano, Capt. Joseph C., 204, 356, 378

Delano, Capt. Joseph S., 197, 390
Delano, Stephen, 560
Delano, Warren, 270
Delauncy, Iselin & Clark, Co-partners, 333
Delaware & Raritan Canal, 207, 232, 233, 266
Delevan & Co., Henry W., 457
Della Torre, Joseph, 552, 554, 555, 556, 560
Demill, Richard M., 480, 560
Demill, Thomas A., 560
Demill & Co., 480
Demill, R. M. & Co., 480
Denegre, James D., 539
Denight, Capt., 417
Denike, Abraham, 552, 553, 554, 557, 561
Denison, Capt., 440
Denison, Ely, 556
Denison, Capt. J. C., 458, 461, 463
Denison, Capt. Noyes R., 498
Dennett, Capt. J. D., 447
Dennett, Capt. William, 461
Dennis, Capt. Edward S., 201, 502
Dennis, Richard, 80
Dennison, Capt. Zind, 461
Dennistoun, Hill, & Co., 129
Dennistoun, J. & A., Cross & Co., 333
DePass (DuPass), Capt. A. H., 487, 489
Depau family, 88
Depau, Francis & Co., 125, 159, 161, 162, 394
De Peyster family, 27
Depeyster, Capt. Frederick A., 247, 251, 380, 394
DePeyster, Capt. Pierre, 73, 87
Depredations, 361, note 10, Chap. 3
Depression (1816-1820), 110-111, 170-172
Derby, Capt. A. F., 526
Derby, "King," 49
DeRosset & Brown, 528
Derrickson, Capt., 459
Derrickson, Capt. A. L., 460
Derrickson, Capt. Job, 472, 473
Derrickson, Capt. William R., 460
Desbrosses, James, 37
Deshon, Capt. Charles A., 495
Deshon, Daniel, 210, 451
Deshon, Moses, 44
Deshon, Capt. N. H., 439
Destebecho, Capt. Peter, 451, 515
DeTocqueville, 31
Devereux, Capt. John, 412, 452, 513

Dunn, Capt. Edmund (Edward), 273, 327, 404, 504, 565
Dunning, Capt. Ben. P., 480
Dunning, Leman, 363, note 2, Chap. 5
Dunton, Capt. John L., 536
Dupont family, 49
Durfey, Capt. Nathaniel P., 377, 476, 477, 478, 501, 503, 511, 512
Duryee, Capt. Richard, 378
Dutilh, Stephen, 549
Dutilh, E. & Co., 74
Dwight, Capt. William L., 454, 509, 514
Dyckmar, Capt. J., 494
Dyer, Capt., 526, 548
Dyer, Capt. A. L., 397
Dyer, Capt. Benjamin, 395, 434
Dyer, Capt. E., 536
Dyer, Capt. Elisha, 412
Dyer, Capt. J., 444, 517
Dyer, Capt. J. W., 398, 508, 540
Dyer, Capt. John, 412, 413
Dyer (Dryer), Capt. L., 548
Dyer, Capt. Lemuel, 513

Eager, William, 455
Eagle, Horatio, 492, 517
Eagle & Hazard, 177, 311, 492, 493, 518, 529
Earl, John, 72, 549
East India Company, 22
Easterbrook, Capt. Benjamin, 35
Eastman, Capt. Enoch, 445
Eaton, Benjamin C., 560
Eaton, Capt. James, 386, 469
Eaton & Benson, 63
Eckford, Henry, 150, 209
Edes & Potter, 126
Edgar family, 48
Edgar, Capt. George, 485
Edgar, William, 69
Edge, Capt. George W., 412
Edison, 141
Edmonds, Capt. J., 521
Edmonds, Capt. John, 453, 479
Edmonds, Capt. T., 496
Edmonston, Charles, 88, 144
Edwards, Capt., 503
Edwards, Capt. J., 397, 494, 513
Edwards, Capt. John, 397
Edwards, Capt. William, 381, 382, 384
Egen, Capt., 213
Ehlers, Capt. P., 399
Elder, Gelston & Co., 429
Eldridge, Capt., 417, 428, 440, 523
Eldridge, Capt. A., 416
Eldridge, Capt. Alfred, 424, 425, 428, 437, 438, 494

Eldridge, Capt. Anthony (Antony) H., 484, 539
Eldridge, Capt. Asa, 288, 293, 301, 416, 434, 435, 445
Eldridge, Capt. Benjamin, 436
Eldridge, Capt. C. W., 431
Eldridge, Capt. Clarington W., 440
Eldridge, Capt. D., 439, 443, 492
Eldridge, Capt. David, 429, 430, 431, 450, 451
Eldridge, Capt. David, 2nd, 429
Eldridge, Capt. Ephraim, 424, 429
Eldridge family, 28
Eldridge, Capt. George, 485
Eldridge, Capt. George, Jr., 529
Eldridge, Capt. H., 421
Eldridge, Capt. Henry, 421
Eldridge, Capt. Isaac B., 529
Eldridge, Capt. John, 67, 254, 373, 379, 380, 422, 564
Eldridge, Capt. Jonathan, 149, 377, 421, 422
Eldridge, Capt. Joseph, 425
Eldridge, Capt. Kimball, 423
Eldridge, Capt. Kimball, Jr., 423, 428, 430
Eldridge, Levi, 265, 312, 533, 534, 535, 536, 539
Eldridge, Capt. Luther, 441
Eldridge, Capt. Oliver, 250, 378, 500
Eldridge, Capt. Oliver W., 430
Eldridge, Capt. R., 494
Eldridge, Capt. S., 447
Eldridge, Capt. Zepheniah, 427, 429, 432
Eldridge, Levi & Co., 533, 536, 540
Eliot, Samuel, 44, 68
Elizabeth, Queen, 34
Ellems, Capt., 468
Ellems, Capt. C., 493
Ellery, Capt., 423
Elliot, Capt., 453
Elliot, Capt. David, 454
Elliot, Capt. G. N., 372
Elliott, Capt. D., 374, 375, 411
Elliott, Capt. D., 2nd, 412
Elliott, Capt. David, 411, 453-54
Elliott, William, 418
Ellis, Capt., 376, 435, 450, 508
Ellis, Daniel C., 123
Ellis, Capt. David, 435
Ellis, Capt. J., 441
Ellis, Capt. Lewis D., 498
Ellis, Capt. Lewis P., 527
Ellis, Capt. R. H., 402
Ellis, Capt. Sebastian, 468
Ellis, Capt. Seth W., 434
Ellis, Capt. T., 523
Ellis, Capt., T. S., 409

Ellis, Capt. Thomas, 446, 448
Ellis, Capt. Z. B., 487
Ellison, Capt. Benjamin, 485, 560
Elwell, Capt., 498
Elwell, Capt. David, 447, 450
Elwell, Capt. J., 440
Elwell, Capt. J. B., 443
Elwell, James W., 311, 508
Elwell, John, 268, 489, 505
Elwell, Capt. Joseph S., 407
Elwell, Capt. Joshua, 427
Elwell, J. & Co., 469, 506
Elwell, J. W. & Co., 469, 509
Elwell, James W. & Co., 490
Elwood, Capt. Charles B., 471, 483, 487, 497, 558
Elwood, Capt. John B., 464
Ely, Richard S., 380
Embargo of 1808, 84-85
Emerson, Capt., 469, 512, 526
Emerson, Capt. G. B., 499
Emerson, Capt. Walter, 413, 448, 454
Emerson, Capt. William S., 443
Emery, Capt. Jonathan, 466, 483
Emery (Emory), Capt. Joseph, 423, 427
Emery, Capt. R. T., 409
Emery, Capt. Robert, 68
Emery, Capt. William S., 515
Emigrant lines, 155, 156-57, 164, 372, 375, 388, 389
Emigration, 362, note 2, Chapter 4
Emlen, George, 28, 88
Emlen, George, Jr., 48
Emlen, Joseph, 458
Emlen & Howell, 112, 363, note 2, Chap. 5
Emmerson (Emerson), Capt. W., 481, 499
Emory, Capt. William S., 456
Endicott, Capt. Joab, 417
English, Capt., 535
English, Capt. Samuel, 435, 437
English, T. M., 484
English & Brandon, 376, 407, 412
Erickson, Capt. J. (G.), 434, 471
Erickson, Capt. John, 481, 532
Ericsson, John, 194, 223, 231, 232, 238, 266, 276
Ericsson Propeller. See Propeller, Development of
Erie Canal, 166, 190
Errickson, Capt., 537
Erskine, Capt. David M., 374, 514
Eustis, Capt., 483, 524
Eustis, Capt. Joseph, 525
Eustis, Capt. Leonard, 452
Evans, Capt., 376, 518
Evans, Capt. A. S. D., 462

Evans, Capt. G. W., 543
Evans, Capt. J., 461
Evans, John R., 87
Evans, Capt. Luther, 461
Evans, Oliver, 83, 142
Evans, Capt. Richard, 37, 435, 507
Evelyn, John, 360, note 1.
Everett & Battelle, 401
Everhart, William, 152
Everitt (Everett), Silas K. See Everitt & Brown
Everitt, Childs & Co., 173, 414
Everleight, Capt. Nathaniel W., 400
Evers, Capt. William, 381, 513
Ewer, Capt. John, 436, 450
Ewer (Evers), Capt. William, 436
Ewing, William, 80
Exports, 7, 20, 22, 27, 29-30, 40, 47-48, 83, 101-103, 169, 182, 189-190, 192, 195, 205, 260
Eyre, Samuel, 74
Eyre & Massey, 163

Fairbank, Capt. J. C., 512
Fairbanks, Capt. J. E., 526
Fairbanks, Capt. John C., 521
Fairchild, Capt. John W., 411
Fairchild, Capt. S. G., 472, 473, 476
Fairchild, Capt. Samuel G., 487
Fairchild, Capt. Samuel Y., 494, 497
Fairfield, Capt. J. W., 372
Fairfield, John, 201, 210, 433, 439, 444
Fairfield, Capt. John W., 449, 455
Fairfield & Lincoln, 437, 439, 445
Fairfield, John & Co., 439, 445-446
Fairfield, Lincoln & Co., 435, 437, 439, 445-446
Falconer, Jackson & Co., 119
Fales, Capt., 507
Fales, Capt. Arthur M., 412
Fales, Capt. Orris, 506
Fales, Capt. Washburn W., 405
Fales, Capt. William J., 448, 505
Falkenberg, Capt. Charles A., 491
Fall River Line, 215, 294
Falls & Brown, 88
Famine, 259, 261
Faneuil, Andrew & Peter, Co-partners, 24, 34
Fanning, Capt. Thomas, 377, 465, 467, 474, 500
Fargo, Capt., 533
Farley, J. P., 438, 443

Farley, Capt. Joseph K., 435
Farnham, Capt. Albert A., 506
Farnham, Capt. O., 442
Farnsworth, Capt. 444
Farragut, Lt. David Glasgow, 161
Farrell, Capt. Joseph, 537, 542
Farren, Capt. John S., 385
Farrow, Capt. John, 547
Farwell, Charles A., 450, 522
Farwell, Capt. Nathan A., 398, 443, 446, 504, 514
Fash, Capt. Michael, 119, 126, 475
Faulk, Faulke (see Foulke)
Faulkin, Capt. George, 419
Faulkner, Capt. W. C., 526
Fay, Capt. Benjamin, 433, 437
Fay, Capt. J. H. (see Fry, Capt. J. H.)
Fay, Joseph S., 279
Fay, R. L., 555
Fay & Jones, 457
Faye, Capt. C., 489, 497
Faye, Capt. Charles, 409
Faye, Capt. Christopher, 488
Feare, Capt. John, 484
Fearing, Capt. 442
Fellowes, Nathaniel, 67, 549
Fentress, Capt., 536
Ferguson, Benjamin, 123, 131
Ferguson, James, 202, 225, 410
Ferguson, Capt. John, 131, 466
Ferguson, Samuel T., 562
Fernald, Capt., 448
Fernald & Pettigrew, 259
Ferrier, Capt. John, 69
Ferris, Capt. Watson G., 382
Ferry service. (Steam), 133-134
Fessenden, Capt. Isaac, 432, 440
Fessenden, Capt. John, 440
Fessenden, Capt. Sewell, 419
Fickett & Crockett, 149, 150
Fickett, Scott & Francis, 150
Fielden Brothers & Co., 380
Fifield, Capt. John C., 537
Filmore, Pres. Willard, 288
Finch, Henry, 552, 553, 556, 558, 559
First regularly scheduled packet line, 108-109
Fish, Capt., 489, 495
Fish, Capt. A., 497
Fish, Capt. Erastus, 493, 527
Fish, Capt. J. R., 469, 555
Fish, James D., 555, 556, 558
Fish, Capt. Nathan G., 529, 561
Fish, Capt. Preserved, 72, 391, 550
Fish, Capt. Roswell P., 499, 505
Fish, Silas, 556
Fish, Simeon, 561
Fish & Grinnell, 118, 153, 156, 177, 350-351, 355, 378, 389

Fish, Goldie & McFie, Co-partners, 388
Fish, Grinnell & Co., 154, 197, 203, 378, 389, 390
Fishbourne family, 28
Fishbourne, William, 37
Fisher, Prof. Alexander Metcalf, 153
Fisher family, 48
Fisher, Capt. J., 492, 519
Fisher, James I., 544
Fisher, Capt. John W., 477
Fisher, Capt. Reuben, 410, 503
Fisher, Thomas, 28
Fisher, Capt. Thomas R., 562
Fisher, Capt. William B., 420-421, 422, 492, 541
Fisher, Hughes & Edwards, Co-partners, 78
Fisk, Capt. J. B., 474
Fisk, Capt. M. H., 525
Fiske, Dr., 173
Fitch, Capt. E. M., 408
Fitch, John, 83
Fitch, Latham, 208
Fithian, Capt. Isaac, 477
Fitz, Capt. William, 443, 453
Fitz, William, Jr., 174
Fitzgerald, Capt. Henry, 545
Fitzgerald, Capt. Thomas H., 479, 545
Flack, John, 87, 155
Flanders, Capt. C., 446
Flanders, Capt. Charles, 452
Flanner, Bennet, 553, 555
Flanner, Joseph H., 552, 554, 560
Fleming, Robert, 122, 202, 532
Fleming & Ross, 181, 532
Flemming, Thomas, 88
Fletcher, Capt., 524
Fletcher, Capt. Artemas T. (Artemas F.), 326, 379, 391
Fletcher, Capt. John, 536
Flinn, Capt. Edmund, 422, 423, 428, 432, 436, 438, 458
Flinn, Capt. John, 423
Flinn, Capt. Josiah N., 421, 423, 433
Flinn, Capt. William W., 436
Flitner, Capt. J. O., 406
Flitner, Capt. S. A. (S. O.), 406, 409, 541
Flitner, Capt. W. J., 526
Flitner, Capt. William L., 521
Flitner, Capt. Z., 410
Flor, Capt. O. H., 399
Flowers, Capt. Batt, 537
Fluorescent lighting, 141, 364, note 17, Chap. 6
Fly, Capt., 35
Flynn, Capt. Edmund (see Capt. Edmund Flinn)
Foard & Rogers, 349, 409
Focke & Boult, 264, 375, 387

Godfrey, Capt. Christopher, 433
Godfrey, Capt. D. Jr., 414
Godfrey, Capt. H., 560
Godfrey, Capt., J. T., 487
Godfrey, Capt. James P., 453, 532, 537, 542
Godfrey, Capt. Jonathan, 468
Godfrey, Capt. Jonathan, Jr., 416
Godfrey, Capt., Jonathan T., 487, 555
Godfrey, Capt., Mather, 466
Godfrey, Capt. Nathan, 433
Godfrey, Capt. Nathaniel, 470
Goelet family, 37, 47
Goelet, Capt. James, 73
Gold: discovery, 279-280
Golden, Capt. Joseph (see Golder, Capt. Joseph)
Golder, Capt. Joseph, 470, 481, 541
Goldsmith, Capt. Daniel, 458
Goldsmith, Capt. Samuel, 540
Goodday, Capt. James, 499
Goodhue, Capt. J., 378
Goodhue, Capt. S., 536
Goodhue, Capt. Samuel, 382, 384, 501
Goodhue & Co., 206, 377
Goodhue & Ward, 118
Gooding, Capt., 410
Gooding, Capt. Mather R., 432
Goodmanson, Capt. J. H., 548
Goodmanson, Capt. John P., 502
Goodrich, Capt. Isaac F., 449, 453
Goodrich, Capt. Isaac T., 518
Goodrich, Capt. J. (I.) F., 449, 504
Goodsell, Capt. Curtis B., 419
Goodspeed, Capt., 470
Goodspeed, George E., 335, 559
Goodspeed, Capt. George M., 426
Goodwin, Capt. C. F., 525
Goodwin, Charles T., 560
Goodwin, Capt. Ivory, 516
Goodwin, Capt. S. R., 374, 406, 409, 411
Goodwin, Capt. William, 468
Googins, Capt. H., 495
Gordon, Capt. F. C., 406, 409
Gordon, George, 127
Gordon, Capt. Joseph R., 371
Gordon, Capt. R., 391
Gordon, Grant & Co., 129
Gore, Capt. A. W., 515
Gore, John, 44
Gorham, Capt., 432
Gorham, Capt. Ezekiel, 448
Gorham, Capt. Francis, 423, 427, 537
Gorham, Capt. Jabez, 35

Gorham, Capt. Josiah, 372, 373, 446, 448-49
Gorham, Capt. N., 439, 440
Gorham, Capt. Thacher, 372
Gorham, Capt. Willard, 418
Goslee, Capt. Robert W., 469, 473, 479, 554, 561
Goss, Capt., 523
Gough, Maj., 153
Gould brothers, 83
Gould, Capt. David, Jr., 430
Gould, Capt. J., 417
Gould, Capt. James, 461
Gould, Capt. John, 480, 528
Gould, Capt. Richard, 415
Gould, Capt. Richard, Jr., 415
Gouverneur family, 69
Gouverneur, Isaac, 549
Gracia, Capt. Y. (see Gracie, Capt. Y.)
Gracie, Archibald, 69, 70
Gracie, Capt. Y., 521
Gracie, Prime & Co., 206, 379
Graffam, Capt. Joseph A., 479, 487, 554, 556
Graffam, Capt. Joseph J., 476
Graffam, Capt. Oliver J., 393
Grafton, Capt. Joseph, Jr., 454
Graham, Capt., 519
Graham, Capt. George R., 465
Graham, Capt. Hugh, 324, 377, 392
Graham, Capt. John C., 406, 409
Gramsby, Capt. George, 458
Granger, Capt. J. A., 492
Grant, Capt. Amos, 464
Grant, Capt. Caleb, 470
Grant, Capt. Nathan B., 482, 517
Grant & Stone, 173
Grant & Twells, 421, 422
Grants & Stone, 420, 421
Graves, Capt. Alexander, 382
Graves, Capt. E., 455
Graves, Capt. John C., 483, 484
Gray, Capt., 407, 440, 532
Gray, Capt. Adams, 547
Gray, Edward, 36
Gray, Capt. Edward, 383, 449
Gray, Capt. H., 529
Gray, Capt. Hiram, 489, 494
Gray, Capt. Horace A., 411, 412, 509, 523
Gray, Capt. J. A., 507
Gray, Capt. R., 488, 491, 511
Gray, Capt. Robert, 65
Gray, Capt. Russell, 489, 495, 529
Gray, Samuel, 44
Gray, William, 67, 195, 397
Gray, William R., 86
Gray & Harden, 157
"Great Migration" (see population)

Great Western Steamship Co. (see Bristol-New York)
Greek frigate scandal, 172, 185
Greeley, Horace, 148, 234
Green, Capt., 463, 491, 530, 566
Green, Capt. B. G., 404
Green, Capt. F., 411
Green, George, 444
Green, Capt. H., 534
Green, Capt. H. W., 412
Green, Capt. Henry, 109, 457
Green, Hetty, 443
Green, Capt. James, 469, 479
Green, Capt. John, 64, 531
Greenman, Capt. J. B., 498
Greenman, Capt. Silas B., 531
Greenman, Capt. William, 495, 497-498, 523, 530, 531
Greenock-New York, A. Bell & Co.'s Line, 156-157
Gregerson, Capt. George, 431, 433, 434
Gregg, Capt. S. D., 461, 495
Gregg, Capt. Silas D., 449, 501
Gregory, Capt. G., 525
Gregory, Capt. John, Jr., 539
Gregory, Capt. M. B., 409
Greiner, Charles A., 481, 535-536
Greiner & Beall, 535
Greiner, C. A. & Co., 481, 536
Greve, Capt. H. W., 408
Griffin, Capt., 482
Griffin, Capt. B. F., 470
Griffin, Capt. Benjamin T., 470
Griffin, Capt. E. W., 447
Griffin, Capt. J. W., 525
Griffin, Capt. Urban G., 479, 562
Griffing, Capt. B. F., 464
Griffing, Capt. Daniel, 461-462
Griffing, Capt. John C., 470, 528, 555
Griffing, Capt. Joseph M., 487
Griffing, Capt. S. G., 470
Griffing, Capt. Samuel, 461
Griffith, Capt. C. R., 488
Griffith, Capt. E. K., 501, 512
Griffith, Capt. John, 546
Griffith, Robert E., 550
Griffiths (Griffith), Capt. Charles R., 388, 405, 467, 488
Griggs, David R., 419
Griggs, S., 415
Grim, D. & Peter, Co-pts., 118
Grim, David, 176, 458
Grim, Philip, 458
Grimshaw, Caleb, 389
Grimshaw, Caleb & Co., 262, 309, 381, 382, 383, 384, 389
Grimshaw, Fitzhugh & Caleb, 199
Grindle, Capt. J. S., 496
Grinnell, Cornelius, 379
Grinnell, Henry, 180

Hawes, Capt., 462, 471
Hawes, Isaac, 44
Hawes, Capt. Reuben C., 436
Hawkins, Capt., 14, 419
Hawkins, E., 489, 555
Hawkins, Capt. Elnathan, 159, 394
Hawkins, Capt. George, 472, 559
Hawkins, Capt. J. D., 473
Hawkins, Capt. N. F., 513, 518
Hawkins, Capt. Nathaniel T., 393
Hawkins, Capt. R., 528
Hawkins, Capt. S. S., 497
Hawkins, Capt. William L., 487, 498
Hawks, Capt. J. H., 489
Hawley, Capt. A., 383
Hawley, Capt. Aaron, 469, 476, 488
Haws, Capt., 433
Hawthorne, Capt. Jefferson, 407
Hay, Capt. J. T., 396
Hayden, Capt., 530
Hayden, Capt. Calvin, 475
Hayden, Capt. F. N., 388
Hayden, Capt. H. W., 397
Hayden, Capt. Horace, 485
Hayden, Nehemiah, 335, 555, 556
Hayden, Capt. W. F., 409
Haynes, Capt. J. F., 409
Haynes, Capt. T. B., 484
Hayward, Capt. Abraham, 445
Haywood, Charles F., 553
Hazard, Capt., 519
Hazard, William H., 494, 529
Hazard, A. G. & Co., 477
Hazeltine, Capt. Paul R., 521
Heagan, Capt. W. R., 487
Healey, Capt. Dodge, 375, 387, 451, 455
Healey, Capt. E. C., 520
Healey, Capt. W. P., 381
Heard, Capt. J. J., 446
Heartt, Capt. Abraham, 483
Heartt, C., 129
Heath, Capt. J. A., 490
Hebard, Capt. Frederick H., 378, 390, 391
Hedge, Capt. Abram, 449, 520
Hedlund, Capt. A., 471.
Heirn (Hiern), Capt. Charles A., 379, 467
Heliker, Capt. E. (see Hilleker, Capt. E.)
Hemingway, William T., 561
Hempstead, Joshua, 36
Henchman, Capt. George, 447
Henderson, Capt., 393, 424, 534, 543
Henderson, Capt. B. F., 470, 542, 552

Henderson, Capt. Dunbar, 408, 412, 443
Henderson, Capt. J., 525, 526
Henderson, Capt. J. K., 559
Henderson, Capt. James, 373, 408, 412, 506, 540
Henderson, Capt. R., 398
Henderson, Capt. William, 448, 451, 454, 455, 504, 505
Henderson, John & Co., 269, 548
Hendewell, Capt. (British), 392
Hendley, Capt. J. J., 530
Hendley, Capt. William, 530
Hendley & Co., William, 530
Hendricks, Capt., 468
Hendricks, Benjamin, 47
Hendrickson, Capt. C., 480
Henry, Capt. Isaac, 459, 532, 536
Henry, Capt. W. M., 492, 501
Henshaw, C. J., 546
Hepburn, Capt., 531
Hepburn, Capt. Richard, 482
Herbert (see Herbest)
Herbert, M. & Co., 126
Herbest (Herbert), Capt. Thomas R., 406, 410, 467, 475, 488, 510
Herdman, John, 259, 381
Herdman, J. & Co., 259, 262
Herdman, Keenan & Co., 249, 250, 259, 381
Hermon, Capt. J. C. (see Harman, Capt. J. C.)
Herndon, Capt. William L., 351
Heron, Alex, 535
Heron, Alex, Jr., 312, 537, 541
Heron, George, 532
Heron & Martin, 312, 535, 537, 541, 542
Heron, Alexander & Co., 268, 532
Herrick, Capt. D., 505
Herrick, Capt. Daniel, 539
Herrick, W. T., 414
Herrick, E. & J., 414
Herrick, E. & W., 414
Herrick, S. H. & Co., 414, 458, 462, 483
Herriman, Capt. Royal, Jr., 481
Hersey, Alfred C., 267, 414, 417-418, 423, 424, 432, 446, 452
"Hesperus: The Wreck of the," 247
Hess, Capt., 530
Heverin, Capt., 425
Hewes, Capt., 433
Hewes, Capt. A., 532
Hewes, Samuel, 44
Hewes, Capt. William, 508, 515, 548
Hewes, William G., 500

Hewes, R. & Co., 77
Hewitt, Frederick, 249
Hickman, Capt. J., 460
Hickman, Capt. Peter S., 535
Hicks, Dennis, 46
Hicks, Elias, 72
Hicks, Capt. Isaac, 378
Hicks, Samuel, 87
Hicks, Lawrence & Co., 155
Hicks, Samuel & Co., 378
Hicks, Trimble & Co., 378
Higbee, Capt. A. J., 494
Higbee, Capt. Eli, 487
Higbee, Capt. R., 536
Higbee, Capt. Richard, 469, 481, 535
Higgins, Capt., 447, 525
Higgins, Capt. A. G., 523, 526
Higgins, Capt. Aaron C., 454
Higgins, Capt. Elisha, 516
Higgins, Capt. Elkanah, 434
Higgins, Capt. J. C., 372, 374
Higgins, Capt. James S., 416, 423, 439, 440, 481
Higgins, Capt. John, 412
Higgins, Capt. Lewis, 508
Higgins, Capt. R. G., 406
Higgins, Capt. Samuel, 448
Higgins, Capt. Stephen, 451, 477
Higginson, Stephen, 67
High pressure engine, 141, 184
Higham & Fife, 125
Hiler, Capt. Thomas G., 372, 375, 411, 439, 454, 507
Hiler & Waterman, 445
Hill family, 28
Hill, Capt. George S., 389
Hill, Henry, 48
Hill, Capt. James M., 446, 452, 514
Hill, Capt. T., 412
Hill, Capt. W., 406
Hill, Capt. Waldo, 525
Hill & Mills, 117
Hill & Stone, 474
Hilleker, Capt. E., 475
Hilliard, Capt. Charles C., 533
Hilliard, Capt. Chester, 388, 501-502, 508
Hilliard, Capt. Nathaniel Green, 126
Hilton, Capt. W. R. (B.), 389, 392, 525
Hiltz, Capt. James T., 501
Hiltz, Capt. I. (J.) T., 392, 397
Hinckley, David, 86, 117
Hinckley, Capt. I., 419
Hinckley, Capt. J. N., 421-422
Hinckley, Capt. Leander, 417
Hinckley, Capt. Lot, 418, 419
Hinckley, Capt. M., 463, 534
Hinckley, Capt. O. W., 497
Hinckley, Capt. W., 419
Hinckley, Capt. William, 441

Hinckley, Capt. William B., 446, 448
Hines, Capt. W. F., 445
Hinman, Capt. M., 483
Hipkins, Capt. John, 401
Hiscock, Capt. Joseph, 456
Hiss, Stevenson, 462
Hiss & Corner, 462
Hitchcock, Capt. Augustus, 452
Hitchcock, Capt. George H., 397, 399, 486
Hitchcock, Capt. Lent M., 483
Hitchcock, Capt. W. H., 500
Hoadley, Capt. J. E., 517
Hoaglund, Elbert, 552, 558
Hobart, Capt. Charles B., 469
Hobart, Capt. D. B., 473, 480
Hobart, Capt. David B., 482, 489
Hobart, Capt. S. B., 434
Hobart, Capt. Samuel B., 444
Hobbs, Capt. George, 543
Hodgdon, Capt., 509
Hodgdon, Capt. A., 523
Hodgdon, Capt. David, 424
Hodge, Capt. H., 518
Hodge, Capt. Henry, 445, 515
Hodges, Capt. Isaac, 419-420
Hodges, Capt. Isaac P., 523
Hodges, Capt. J. B., 386
Hodges, Capt. L. B., 526
Hodgkinson, Capt., 498
Hodgkinson, Capt. Michael, 430
Hoey, Capt. Nicholas, 436, 438, 476, 480, 491, 511
Hoffman, Capt., 490, 545
Hoffman, Nicholas & Martin, 72
Hogg & Delameter, 232, 281
Holberton, Capt. Nicholas, 307, 383, 395, 434
Holbrook, Capt. W. A., 453
Holcombe & Peck, 232
Holden, Capt., 504
Holdredge, Capt. Allen P., 503
Holdredge, Capt. Henry, 378
Holdredge, Capt. N. H., 378, 379
Holdredge, Capt. Nathan, 160, 394, 473
Holdredge, Capt. Nathan H., 127
Holdridge, Capt. Nathan H., 378
Holland, John, 86
Holland, John W., 117
Holland, Stewart, 296-297
Hollingsworth brothers, 87
Hollingsworth, John, 74, 198, 392, 549
Hollingsworth, Levi, 28, 48
Hollingsworth, Richard, 12
Hollingsworth, Samuel, 76
Hollins, John, 76

Hollins & McBlair, 88
Hollister, Capt. Joseph, 433, 454, 455
Holmes, Capt., 128, 460, 475, 491
Holmes, Capt. A. F., 519
Holmes, Capt. A. H., 484
Holmes, Adrian B., 553
Holmes, Capt. Edward, 445
Holmes, Capt. G. M., 439
Holmes, Capt. Gorham P., 461
Holmes, Capt. John, 448, 454, 499
Holmes, John H., 466
Holmes, Capt. Joseph, 441
Holmes, Capt. Joseph Warren, 493
Holmes, Capt. Paraclete, 444, 451
Holmes, Capt. Samuel, 111, 457
Holmes, Capt. Silas, 121, 177, 499
Holmes & Storey (Stoney), 311, 434, 466, 471
Holt, Capt., 494
Homan (Homer), Capt. William, 196, 371, 383, 384, 441, 447
Homer, Capt., 484
Homer, Hartshorne, 444
Homer, Capt. Jacob G., 454, 514
Homer, Capt. James B., 454
Honeywell, Capt., 460
Honeywell, Capt. Elliott, 476, 508, 539
Hood, Capt. Daniel, 440
Hood, Capt. James M., 492
Hoodless, Capt. William R., 381, 384, 385, 386, 506
Hooper, David, 422
Hooper, Capt. E., 387, 491, 548
Hooper, Capt. Evan, 546
Hooper, Capt. J., 380
Hooper, Capt. J. W., 516
Hooper, James, 313, 548
Hooper, James A., 439
Hooper, Thomas, 269, 546
Hooper, Capt. W. B., 406
Hooper & Graff, 313, 548
Hoover, Capt. George, 460
Hopkins, Capt., 439
Hopkins, Capt. Ames, 515
Hopkins, Capt. E., 496
Hopkins, Capt. Farley, 442
Hopkins, Capt. J., 494
Hopkins, Capt. John B., Esq., 63
Hopkins, Capt. Reuben, 450
Hopkins, Capt. Stephen A., 490
Hoppin, Capt., 495
Horn, Capt. Francis, 502
Horner, Capt., 538
"Horse Jockey" trade, 66
Horton, Capt., 473, 481

Horton, Capt. Charles L., 481
Horton, Capt. George E., 470
Horton, Capt. Hiram, 507, 548
Horton, Capt. Ira T., 528
Horton, Capt. Isaac F. (T.), 434, 438, 471, 481, 498, 559
Horton, Capt. J. T., 470, 519, 528
Horton, Capt. Reuben, 420
Horton, Capt. T. J., 479
Hosman (see Hosmer)
Hosman, Capt. P. A. (see Hosmer, Capt. P. A.)
Hosmer, Capt. Charles B., 481
Hosmer, Capt. E. W., 515
Hosmer, Capt. Ephraim W., 432, 441
Hosmer, Capt. Frederick A., 486
Hosmer, Capt. Jesse F., 412, 486, 493, 513, 518, 526
Hosmer, Capt. P. A., 406
Houdlette, Capt. Franklin, 374, 396, 406, 451-452, 506, 540
Hough, Capt. Samuel W., 459
Houghton, Capt., 519
Houghton, Capt. Silas A., 506
House, Capt. Timothy, 420-21
Houseworth, Capt. 484
Hovey, Capt. Henry R., 285, 390
Hovey, John, 117
Howard, Capt. 476, 493, 505
Howard, Capt. E., 536
Howard, Capt. L., 509
Howard, Samuel & Charles, 126
Howard, Capt. Simeon S., 405
Howard, Capt. William, 510
Howard, Capt. William H., 372
Howard & Mercy, 494
Howard, J. & Son, 279, 284
Howe, Capt., 450, 516
Howe, Capt. George L., 471, 557
Howe, Capt. George W., 380, 395, 564
Howe, Capt. J. L., 447
Howe, Capt. J. W., 526
Howe, Lord, 70
Howe, Capt. Octavius, 372, 373, 391, 412, 446-447, 456
Howe, Capt. Zachariah, 434
Howell, Capt. Daniel, 467, 491, 504
Howell, Capt. John, 37
Howell, Sam & Walter, Co-partners, 72
Howell, Samuel, 74
Howell, William & Son, 401, 546
Howes, Capt., 416, 438, 440, 447, 451-452, 525
Howes, Capt. Abner, 411
Howes, Capt. Abraham, 421, 422

Maxwell, Capt. William K., 374

May, Capt. George E., 459

May, Capt. Henry, 459, 557

May & Payson, 77

Maybee, Capt. J. S., 472

Mayberry, Capt. Freeman, 542

Mayell, Capt. John C., 392, 404

Mayhew, Capt. Nathaniel, 448

Mayhew, Capt. P. N., 383, 392

Mayhew, Capt. T. N., 511

Mayhew, Capt. Zebulon, 504

Mayo, Capt., 429, 431

Mayo, Capt. Abijah B., 417

Mayo, Capt. Alpheus, 414

Mayo, Capt. David E., 431-432, 440, 443

Mayo family, 250

Mayo, H., 421

Mayo, Capt. H. D., 400

Mayo, Capt. H. L., 514

Mayo, Capt. Hezekiah, 421

Mayo, Capt. J. H., 497

Mayo, Capt. P., 433

Mayo, Capt. Shubael, 452

Mayo, Capt. Thomas, 486

Mayo, Capt. Timothy L., 424

Mazin, V. & Cie., 396

Meacom, Capt. George, 407

Mead, Capt. Miles H., 478, 506

Mead, Capt. W. H., 478

Meade, Capt. W. A., 409

Mears, Capt., 529

Mecke, Plate & Co., 262, 408

Meek, Capt. James, 121, 498

Meeker, C. J., 538, 547

Meeker, Capt. Darius, 416

Meeker, Samuel & William P., Co-partners, 74, 550

Meeker, C. J. & Co., 539

Meekins, Capt., 545

Megathlin, Capt. Anthony S., 538

Megrath & Jones, 91, 124

Meigs & Reid, 126

Meincke, Professor, 141

Melcher, Capt. B. B., 516

Melcher, Capt. B. M., 375, 491, 518

Melcher, Capt. George, 374, 412, 450, 515

Melcher, Capt. J., 504

Meldrum (Melden), Capt. T. M., 469

Melton, Capt. Anderson, 478

Mendell, Capt. William P. (R.), 484, 499, 500, 510

Mercantile Line of Wagons & Packets, 107, 111

Mercer & Schenck, 46

Merchant, Capt., 499

Merchant, Capt. Elihu, 434

Merchant, Capt. Leander, 484

Merchant, Capt. N., 474

Merchant, Capt. S., 539

Merchant Marine
Depredations upon, 89
Early growth, 12-14, 16, 24, 25, 30
1770-1774, 53, 54, 55, 89, 188, 193
1840's, 223, 243, 256

Merchants of Baltimore, 76-77, 88, 201

Merchants of Boston
Colonial period, 35, 43, 44
Federalist period, 68, 86, 116-118, 197

Merchants of Charleston
Colonial period, 49
Federalist period, 78, 88, 189, 192

Merchants of Mobile, 129-130

Merchants of New Orleans, 128-129

Merchants of New York
Colonial period, 36, 37
Federalist period, 69-73, 86-87, 191

Merchants of Philadelphia
Colonial period, 37, 48
Federalist period, 73-74, 87-88

Merchants of Savannah, 80-81

Mercier, Capt. Charles, 434

Meredith, Reese, 37

Merle & Co., John A., 444

Merriam, William, 556

Merrihew, Capt. Charles, 380

Merrihew, Capt. Joseph R., 482, 552

Merrill, Capt. Ben, 540

Merrill, Capt. H. M., 408, 409

Merrill, Capt. Leonard R., 457

Merrill, Capt. Leonard W., 438

Merrill, Nathaniel W., 268, 381, 509

Merrill (Merritt), Capt. P. E., 539

Merrill, Capt. R., 521, 525

Merrill, Capt. S., 506

Merrill, Capt. S. T., 520

Merrill, Capt. Wiggin, 466

Merriman, Capt. J. C., 508

Merriman, Capt. P. G., 522

Merriman, Capt. R. (see Merryman, Capt. R.)

Merrithew, Capt. J. C., 452

Merritt, Capt., 523

Merritt, Capt. Henry, 447

Merritt (Merrit), John A., 450, 453, 547

Merrow, Capt. L. T., 408, 453

Merry, Capt. Edward A., 539

Merry, Capt. Jonathan, 68

Merry, Capt. Thomas H., 356

Merryman, Capt. A. H., 374, 516

Merryman, Capt. J., 452, 525

Merryman, Capt. J. C., 519

Merryman, Capt. John, 507, 510, 522

Merryman, Capt. P. G., 517

Merryman (Merriman), Capt. R., 455, 509

Merryman, Capt. Richard, 412

Merryman, Capt. Thomas, 446, 538

Mershon, Daniel S., 562

Mershon, Jacob, 562

Mershon, Capt. William C., 450, 513, 534, 542, 562

Mervin, Capt. T. G. (see Merwin, Capt. T. G.)

Merwin, Capt. T. G., 474, 501, 504, 511, 515

Merwin, Capt. Timothy G., 467, 491

Messionier, Henry, 88

Meyer, David G., 176, 458

Meyer, Capt. Philip S., 402

Meyers, Capt. L. C., 510

Michael, Capt. Anthony, 404

Michaels, Capt. 468

Michaels, Capt. Anthony M., 405

Michaels, Capt. B., 410

Mickell, Capt. H., 402

Midwood, S., 78

Miercken, Capt. Henry F., 405

Miercken, Capt. Jonathan W., 403

Mifflin family, 28

Mifflin, George, 28

Mifflin, Capt. Sam, 48

Mifflin, Thomas, Jr., 74

Migration: Intercolonial and westward, 31, 82-83, 114, 208

Miller, Capt., 453

Miller, Capt. Andrew T., 474

Miller, Capt. Benjamin, 484

Miller, Charles, 552

Miller, Capt. David, 535

Miller family, 28

Miller, Capt. George K., 419

Miller, Capt. H. W., 545

Miller, Capt. J., 487

Miller, Capt. J. F., 508, 542

Miller, Capt. James, 376, 541

Miller, Capt. James F., 504

Miller, John, 71, 549

Miller, Capt. Peter, 374

Miller, William, 48

Miller & Bancker, 459

Millet, Capt. T. G. (see Mallet, Capt. T. G.)

Milliken, Capt. Alexander, 439, 446, 451, 490, 542

Milliken, Capt. M. J., 524

Milliken, Capt. M. T., 398

Mills, Capt. Benjamin S., 544, 545

Mills, Capt. Charles, 470, 472, 473, 487, 493, 528

Mulligan family, 88
Mulliner, Capt. D. E., 472
Mulliner (Muller), Capt. E. E., 464
Mulliner, Capt. W. R., 379
Mumford, Gurdon, 86
Mumford, Capt. J. (see Montford, Capt. J.)
Mumford, Capt. Oliver R., 385, 387, 391, 512, 516
Munro, Capt., 125
Munro, Capt. Joseph S., 465
Munro, Milne, H. & Co., 129
Munroe, Capt., 398
Munson, Capt. A. H., 471, 495
Munson, Capt. John N., 531
Munson, William, 556
Munson & Barnard, 117
Murch, Capt. William, 480, 488, 528
Murdoch (Murdock), Capt. James, 371, 372
Murdock, Capt., 443
Murdock, Capt. James, 453
Murphy, Capt. J., 411, 455
Murphy, Capt. T., 409
Murray, Capt. Charles, 489, 494
Murray, D. Colden, 348, 473, 482, 531, 553, 560
Murray family, 69, 70
Murray, John, 70
Murray, Lindley, 70
Murray, Robert, 37, 70
Mustard, Capt. George F., 409, 509
Muzzy, Capt. B. A., 121, 498
Myer, Capt. Frederick R., 391
Myers, Capt., 137, 460
Myers, Capt. James, 470, 495, 523, 524, 556
Myers, Capt. L. C., 504
Myers, Capt. Samuel, 471-472, 486, 488, 496, 528, 552
Myrick, Capt., 126, 400
Myrick, Capt. W., 416
Myrover, Henry L., 559

Nabb, Capt., 467
Naghel, Capt. Francis, 160, 394
Napier, A. & T., 88
Napier, Smith & Co., 88
Napier, Thomas & Co., 88
Napoleonic Decrees, 84, 93
Nash, Capt. Burr, 537
Nason, Capt., 453
Nason, Capt. Albert G., 445, 449
Nason, Capt. B. N., 516
Nason, Capt. Edward, 454
Nason, Capt. Joseph L., 447
Nason, Capt. Joseph T., 453
Nason, Capt. Josiah D., 561
Nason, Capt. T., 375

Nason, Capt. W. B., 411, 514
Nason, Capt. William B., 446, 450, 526
Nason, Capt. William C., 543
Navigation Acts, 22
Naylor, Capt., 539
Naylor, Capt. Benjamin B., 534, 537
Neal, Capt. F., 545
Neal, Capt. John, 459
Neef, Capt. Henry, 371, 440, 446
Neff, Capt. William W., 560
Neill, Capt. F., (see Neal, Capt. F.)
Neill, Capt. Thomas M., 412
Neilson, Capt. John, 37
Neilson, Thomas, 530
Neilson, William, 69
Nelson, Capt., 148, 433
Nelson, Capt. Horatio, 502
Nelson, Capt. J. W., 447
Nelson, Capt. P., 392
Nelson, Capt. Peter, 479
Nelson, S. C., 561
Nelson, William, 502
Nelson, Capt. William H., 380
Nelson, William & Sons, 502
Nesbitt, Capt., 509
Nesmith & Leeds, 268, 510, 515
Nesmith & Sons, 332, 386, 515
Nesmith & Walsh, 268, 515
New, Capt. Myrus, 440
New Bedford-Taunton Railroad, 352
New Orleans-Galveston, Morgan SS Line, 228
New Orleans-Hamburg, Sagory's Line, 413
New Orleans-Havana, Zacherie's Line, 175
New Orleans-Havre Line, 314
New Orleans-Liverpool, Crescent City Line, 313-314, 410-411
New Orleans-Texas SS service, 227
New York (early development), 25, 26
New York Marine Society, 46
New York & Havre Steam Navigation Co., 277-278, 285, 297, 299, 302
New York-Albany & Troy
    Line of Packets, 457
    New Line, 457
    Trotter & Douglass Thursday Line, 109, 457
New York-Alexandria. Line of Alexandria Packets, 130
New York-Antwerp
    Gerding & Kunkelman Line, 259
    Gerding's Regular Line, 397

Hurlbut Line, 309, 323, 397, 399
Layton & Co.'s Line, 333, 397
Post, Smith & Co.'s Line, 333, 348, 398-399
Schmidt & Balchen's S Line, 398
Zerega's Red Z Line, 398
New York-Apalachicola
    Eagle & Hazard's Eagle Line, 529
    Hurlbut Line, 208, 309, 529
    Post & Phillips' Line, 265, 529
New York-Baltimore
    Anderson's Dispatch Line, 207, 462
    Briggs' Union Line, 463
    Dispatch Line, 181, 207
    Gager's Line, 268
    Gager's New Line, 464
    Johnson & Lowden's Old Regular Line, 267
    Lowry's New Line, 462
    McCready & Co.'s Line, 268
    McCready's Regular Line, 464
    Mankin's Regular Line, 461
    Regular Line, 130-131, 461-462
New York-Belfast
    Belfast Line, 392
    Richardson & Watson's Line, 260
New York-Bremen, Ocean Steam Navigation Co., 240, 244, 277-278, 342
New York-Cartagena, Baldwin & Spooner Cartagena Line, 212, 401
New York-Chagres
    Law's SS Line, 279-282, 287-289, 298
    Independent SS Lines, 291, 292
New York-Charleston
    Brig Line, 198
    Brigham's New Regular Line, 472
    Bulkley's Union Line of Brigs, 198, 348, 467
    Caldwell Line, 209, 467-468
    Cooley's Line, 468
    Dunham & Dimon's Commercial Line, 209, 324, 348, 467
    Elwell's Line, 469
    Empire Line, 471
    Established or Ship Line, 124, 178, 465
    Lane & West's Line, 471
    Mailler's New Line, 473
    McCready's Merchants' Line, 469

Nichols, Capt. William H., 457, 474-476, 510
Nichols, Capt. William I., 111
Nichols & Whitney, 414, 420-421, 428
Nicholson, Capt. Dan, 38
Nicholson, Capt. J., 410
Nickels, Capt. Edward C., 439, 440
Nickels, Capt. George W., 439, 491
Nickels, Capt. H. M., 487
Nickerson, Capt., 417, 419, 425-426, 432
Nickerson, Capt. Asa W., 423, 497
Nickerson, Capt. B. T., 408
Nickerson, Capt. Caleb, 416, 554
Nickerson, Capt. Cyrus, 418
Nickerson, Capt. David B., 431
Nickerson, Capt. E., 414, 422
Nickerson, Ebenezer, 86
Nickerson, Capt. Edwin, 527
Nickerson, Capt. Eli, 426
Nickerson, Capt. Ephraim A., 482
Nickerson, Capt. F., 417
Nickerson family, 250
Nickerson, Capt. Francis, 431
Nickerson, Capt. Franklin, 414
Nickerson, Capt. Frederick, 427, 429
Nickerson, Capt. Freeman, 425-426
Nickerson, Capt. Freeman J., 423
Nickerson, Capt. Freeman S., 433
Nickerson, Capt. George R., 405, 412, 430
Nickerson, Capt. Isaiah, 419
Nickerson, Capt. J., 426, 498, 535
Nickerson, Capt. J. B., 417
Nickerson, Capt. J. G., 462
Nickerson, Capt. J. H., 473
Nickerson, Capt. J. R., 428, 430, 492
Nickerson, Capt. James, 419
Nickerson, Capt. James, 2nd, 435, 441, 492
Nickerson, Capt. John K., 417
Nickerson, Capt. Jonathan, 422, 439
Nickerson, Capt. Joseph, 414, 429, 432, 445
Nickerson, Capt. Joseph G., 504
Nickerson, Capt. Joseph J., 372, 449, 454
Nickerson, Capt. Joshua, 414
Nickerson, Capt. Josiah H., 429
Nickerson, Capt. L., 430

Nickerson, Capt. L. W., 417, 428
Nickerson, M., 421
Nickerson, Capt. Moses, 421
Nickerson, Capt. S., 420
Nickerson, Capt. Samuel, 418
Nickerson, Capt. Scolto B., 514
Nickerson, Capt. Seth, 417
Nickerson, Capt. T. S., 547
Nickerson, Capt. Thomas H., 460
Nickerson, Capt. Thomas J., 415
Nickerson, Capt. Tully, 427
Nickerson, Capt. V. R., 430
Nickerson, Capt. Zenas, 458
Nickerson, Capt. Zenas, Jr., 544
Nicklin, Philip, 74
Nicoll, Capt. Edward, 199, 399
Noble, Capt. D. P., 458
Nock, Capt. J. B., 463
Nolfe, 168
Norgrave, Capt. Jeremiah, 536
Norris, 244
Norris, Isaac, 28
Norris, Capt. J., 490
Norris, Capt. John, 37
Norris, Capt. Peter, 530
Norris, Richard, 28
Norris, Robert, 78
Norris, Capt. T. J., 419
North & Blake, 78
Northrup, Capt., 529
North River Steamboat Company, 183
Norton, Capt. D. H., 410, 520
Norton, Capt. J., 410
Norton, Capt. J. M., 385, 413, 501, 518
Norton, Capt. Joseph M., 485, 488, 490
Norton, Capt. Parker P., 381, 488, 505, 529
Norton, Capt. Richard, 479
Norton, Capt. Robert, 443, 490
Norvell, Capt. George W., 525
Norville, Capt. W., 409
Nowell (Norwall), Capt. A. P., 418
Nowell, Capt. George W., 411-412 (see Norvell, Capt. George W.)
Nowell, Capt. Robert T., 411
Noyes, Capt., 512
Noyes, Capt. A., 496
Noyes, Capt. E. A., 526
Nugent, Peter, 553, 562
Nugent, Capt. R. McD., 496
Nye, Capt. David A., 449, 468, 479, 517, 518
Nye, Capt. Ezra, 203, 204, 247, 258, 356, 378, 564
Nye, Capt. S. G., 391
Nye, Thomas W., 329
Nye, Capt. William L., 474

Oakley, Capt. Joseph, 461-462
Oakley & Keating, 498, 527
Oakman, Capt., 442
Oaks, Capt. B., 428, 430, 504
O'Connor & Ryan, 265, 488
Ogden, Charles L., 69
Ogden, David, 259, 307, 321, 371
Ogden, F. J., 434, 470
Ogden, John, 242, 267, 479, 528, 530
Ogden & Bunker, 313, 481, 535, 545
Ogden, Albert & Co., 119
Ogden, Starr & Co., 437-438, 482
O'Hara family, 88
Ohio Life Insurance & Trust Co., 333
Olden, Capt., 519
Oliver, Capt., 525
Oliver, Capt. F. (see Oliver, Capt. T.)
Oliver, Francis J., 86
Oliver, Capt. Paul A., 538
Oliver, R. & J., 88
Oliver, Capt. T., 406
Oliver, Capt. William H., 481
Olmsted, Capt. R., 522
Olsen, Capt., 513
Olson, James W., 553
O'Neale, John, 136
O'Neill, Capt., 493
Orders in Council, 84, 93
Oregon boundary, 260
Orne, Capt. William (B.), 394-395
Osborn, Capt., 493, 544
Osborn (Osborne), Capt. Bradley, 472, 488
Osborn, Capt. John, 458, 461, 475
Osborn, Capt. John, Jr., 415
Osborn, Capt. Morris, 463
Osborn, Capt. William, 417
Osborne, Capt., 486
Osborne, Capt. James W., 426
Osborne (Osborn), Capt. John, 458, 461, 475
Osborne & Whitridge, 426
Osmer, Capt. 496
Ostrander, Capt., 109
Otis, Capt., 518
Otis, Capt. Albert C., 407, 412
Otis, Capt. William M., 408, 455
Outerbridge, Capt. W. L., 507
Outerbridge, Capt. William A., 515, 542
Outerbridge, Capt. William S., 541
Overton, Capt., 528
Owen (Owens), Capt. Charles, 375, 452, 455
Owen, Capt. Moses, 507

Popham, Capt. C. W., 274, 379
Population, 15, 17-19, 23-26, 29-30, 33, 39, 49-51, 76-77, 79-80, 89-90, 113, 124, 129, 146, 224-25
Population: authorities, 360, note 5
Porter, Capt., 467
Porter, Capt. Daniel L., 120, 437, 474-475, 478, 491, 511
Porter, Capt. David B., 295
Porter, Capt. David L., 479
Porter, Capt. George S., 384, 398
Porter, Capt. James M., 377
Porter, T. N., 496
Porter, Capt. Timothy N., 443, 447, 542
Porter & Co., W. G., 529
Porterfield, Capt. G., 520
Porterfield, Capt. R., 506
Post, Capt., 493
Post, Capt. Albert, 497-498
Post, Capt. Alva, 484
Post, Capt. Charles, 485
Post, Capt. D., 457
Post, Capt. David R., 485
Post, Capt. Ezra Denison, 388, 397, 483-484, 486, 497, 555
Post, Henry, 87
Post, Capt. J. D., 382
Post, Capt. James, 464, 470
Post, Capt. Joseph, 484
Post, Capt. Ralph, 265, 529
Post, Capt. Russell Handy, 470, 484-486, 497, 511
Post, Capt. W. M., 412, 497, 522
Post & Phillips, 265, 529
Post & Russell, 80
Post & Ryerson, 396, 397, 486
Post, Ryerson & Co., 513
Post, Smith & Co., 309, 333, 397, 398, 399, 497, 521, 522, 530
Post Office Packets, 45, 158
Pote, Capt. S., 523, 525
Pott & McKinne, 119, 126
Potter, Gilbert, Jr., 552, 558, 561
Potter, Capt. J. K., 527
Potter, Capt. J. R., 530
Potter, Capt. James, 448
Potter, Capt. James R., 442
Potter, Capt. S., 440
Potter, Capt. W. B., 527
Potts, Capt. Thomas, 164, 403
Powell, Capt., 490, 566
Powell, E. S., 528
Powell, Elzey S., 552, 553, 557, 558, 561
Powell family, 28
Powell, Capt. James P., 488, 528, 558
Powell, Capt. John, 494

Powell, Capt. William, 476, 489
Powell & Mills, 528
Power, Tyrone, 237
Powers, Capt. Michael, 540
Pratt, Capt., 384, 487, 488, 547
Pratt, Capt. Asa, 447
Pratt, C. H., 554
Pratt, Capt. Daniel, 529
Pratt, Capt. E. D., 397
Pratt, Capt. George, 451
Pratt, Henry, 74
Pratt, Capt. Isaiah, 390
Pratt, Capt. J., 382, 513
Pratt, Capt. Jabez, 397, 522
Pratt, Capt. Levi, 448
Pratt, Capt. Peter, 444
Pratt, Thomas H. & Henry, Co-partners, 87
Pratt, Capt. William, 485, 513, 529
Pratt & Durant, 457
Pratt, John & Son, 117, 174, 444
Pray, Capt. John S., 389, 456, 518, 525
Pray, Capt. William F., 456
Preble, Capt., 494
Preble, Ebenezer, 67
Preble, Capt. George A., 490
Prentice, Capt. S. H. G. (Prestice, Capt. S. H. J.), 409
Prescott, Capt. Charles, 447
Pressy, Capt., 478
Price, Capt. Albert (see Price, Capt. Alfred)
Price, Capt. Alfred, 464
Price, Chandler, 90, 123, 181
Price, Capt. Ebenezer, 520
Price family, 28, 48
Price, Capt. John, 28, 37
Price, Capt. Joseph G., 535
Price, Capt. Peter, 500, 502-503
Price, Capt. William, 533
Price, C. & Morgan, 123, 128, 181, 538
Prime, Capt. George M., 435
Prime, Capt. George W., 432
Prime, Nathaniel, 73
Prince, Capt. George W., 437
Prince, Capt. James, 68
Prince, Capt. Job, 35
Prince, Capt. John, 448
Prindle, Capt. B., 438
Pringle, Mark, 77
Prioleau, Samuel, Jr., 49
Prior, Capt., 521
Prior, Capt. Henry, 442
Pritchard, Capt., 398
Pritchard, Capt. T., 471
Privateering, 34, 42, 59, 60, 92-93
Proal, Capt. Augustus, 384, 405
Procter, Capt. John, 432
Proctor, Joseph, Jr., 444
Proctor (Procter), Capt. N., 373

Propeller: development of, 230-233, 235, 237-239, 281
Protteau, Capt. Peter, 392, 393, 479, 524
Prout, Fowler & Stanard, 537
Providence-Baltimore-Merchant & Miner's SS Line, 346
Provost, Col., 153
Pryor, Capt., 504
Pugh, Capt., 391
Pulsifer, Capt. Jared, 478
Purington (Purrington), Capt. A., 371, 374, 407
Purington, Capt. Isaac, 499
Purington (Purrington), Capt. S., 505
Purington, Capt. W. B., 518
Puritan philosophy, 9, 21, 58, 96-97, 357
Purnell, Capt. L. D., 528
Purnell, Capt. Lorenzo D., 471, 480, 528
Purrington, Capt., 128
Purrington, Capt. W., 492
Putnam, Capt. B., 400
Putnam, Capt. George W., 372, 373, 511

Quakers, 96, 97, 100
Quincy, Josiah, 49

Race, Capt. J., 428, 430
Racing, 251
Radcliffe, Capt. E., 375
Raerden, Capt. B., 539
Raffles, Capt. J. D., 409
Railroads, 197, 216-17, 219, 295
Raines, Capt., 494
Rains, Capt. L., 409
Rains, Capt. T. S. (see Rains, Capt. L.)
Ramsdell, Capt. H. W., 486, 492
Randall, Capt. Charles L., 485, 506
Randall, Capt. J. E., 493
Randall, Capt. J. L., 406, 407, 523
Randall, John K., 543
Randall, John K. & Co., 210, 543, 545
Randall, Thomas, 46, 68, 549, 550
Randolph, John, 360, note 6
Range, Vendue, 532
Ranlett, Capt. Charles E. (A.), 210, 250, 384, 393, 395, 439, 445, 446, 448, 452, 455, 507, 511, 515
Rasmussen, Capt., 468
Rathbone family, 99
Rathbone, Capt. John, 121, 122, 177, 246, 263, 377, 498, 500, 501, 502, 511, 512

Silloway, Calef & Co., 307, 434, 437, 443, 444, 453
Silloway, Joseph & Co., 267, 347, 434, 443, 444, 455
Silsby, E., 117
Silsby, Capt. I. R., 399
Silvester (see Sylvester)
Simmons, Capt., 408, 527
Simmons, Capt. I. B., 375
Simmons, Capt. J., 387, 418, 422
Simmons, Capt. Lemuel B., 501
Simmons, Capt. Samuel B., 456
Simonson, 299
Simonson, Capt. John W., 472
Simonson, Capt. Robert, 521
Simpkins, Capt. James, 526
Simpson, Capt., 450
Simpson, Capt. J., 538
Simpson, Capt. James, 412, 451
Simpson, Capt. John, 435, 454
Simpson, Capt. Robert H. (W.), 374, 411, 412, 523
Sims, Andrew, 28
Sims, John & Richard, Co-partners, 37
Sims, Joseph, 74
Sims, Walter, 549
Sims, Woodrop, 74
Sinclair, Capt. William, 465, 516
Singer, Capt. W. J., 373, 522
Singer, Capt. William, 443, 455, 508
Sisson, Capt., 477
Size, Capt. C. F., 387, 406
Size, Capt. John H., 483
Skaats, Capt. Rinier, 400, 541
Sketchley, Capt. William, Jr., 105, 119, 153, 356, 377, 378
Skiddy, Capt. John R., 73, 87, 127, 159, 162, 394
Skiddy, Capt. William, 291, 371, 378, 379, 394, 499
Skidmore, Capt., 118
Skidmore, Capt. Hubbard, 73
Skinner, Capt. T. B., 409, 548
Skolfield, Capt. C., 524
Skolfield, Capt. J. (I.), 386
Skolfield, Capt. Samuel, 373, 384, 492
Skolfield, Capt. Thomas, 538
Skolfield, Capt. W. S., 406
Slaght, Henry L., 555
Slaght, Capt. James (see Sleicht, James)
Slate, Gardner & Co., 383
Slate, Gardner & Howell, 260, 383
Slater, Capt. J., 510
Slave trade, 6, 13, 14, 34, 85, 95, 122, 191, 228
Sleeboom, Capt. W. M., 399
Sleeper, Capt. Albert, 490

Sleeper, Capt. Elias P., 506
Sleeper, Capt. Jeremiah, 490, 508, 509
Sleeper, Capt. Jesse, 505
Sleeper, Capt. John, 541
Sleeper, Capt. W., 527
Sleicht, Capt. James, 464, 489
Slemmer, Capt. L., 547
Sloan & Morris, 202, 532
Sloan, Morris & Amory, 532
Sloman (Slowman), Capt. T., 437
Smack, Capt. John H., 471
Small, Capt., 389, 435
Small, Alonzo C., 552
Small, Capt. D. H., 424
Small, Capt. Elisha, 426, 427
Small, Capt. Henry C., 418
Small, Capt. Hiram, 427
Small, Capt. J., 422, 498, 518
Small, Capt. Joe, 441
Small, Capt. John, 443
Small, Capt. Samuel, 426
Smalley, Capt., 447
Smalley, Capt. A. S., 524
Smalley, Capt. James, Jr., 418
Smalley, Capt. Levi, 539, 541
Smalley, Capt. R., 533, 538
Smalley, Capt. Rowland, 429
Smalley, Capt. W. W., 379, 411, 490, 523
Smalley, Capt. William W., 508
Smallwood, Anderson & Co. (Joseph L. Smallwood, George Anderson & John H. Earl), 311, 529
Smart, Capt. C. C., 388
Smith, Capt., 93, 349, 375, 426, 432, 433, 436, 440, 461, 473, 478, 480, 481, 483, 490, 492, 496, 503, 512, 519, 524, 537
Smith, Capt. A. M., 513
Smith, Capt. Alfred F., 405, 406, 526
Smith, Capt. Ammi, 374
Smith, Capt. Benjamin, 380, 402
Smith, Capt. Benjamin, Jr., 452
Smith, Benjamin R., 181, 532
Smith, Capt. Bradley, 473, 483
Smith, Capt. C., 424
Smith, Capt. C. B., 469, 480, 518
Smith, Capt. C. D., 527
Smith, Capt. C. R., 517
Smith, Capt. Cannon (see Smith, Capt. Carman)
Smith, Capt. Carman, 479, 481
Smith, Charles, 457
Smith, Capt. D., 463
Smith, Capt. Daniel M., 555
Smith, Capt. David, 422, 424, 532, 533, 534, 538
Smith, Capt. David T., 470

Smith, Capt. Duncan, 393
Smith, Capt. E. C., 509, 522
Smith, Capt. Eben R., 507, 539
Smith, Capt. Ebenezer, 463
Smith, Capt. Edward K., 446, 524
Smith, Capt. Edward N., 464, 559
Smith, Capt. Edwin, 470
Smith, Capt. Elisha W., 421, 422, 424
Smith, Capt. Ephraim, 432, 468
Smith, Capt. Ezra C., 439
Smith, Capt. F., 459
Smith family, 27
Smith, Capt. Felix, 536, 537
Smith, Capt. Francis, 427
Smith, Capt. Frank, 433
Smith, Capt. G. H., 497
Smith, Capt. G. L., 398, 497, 501
Smith, Capt. George, 470, 472, 482
Smith, Capt. George O., 470
Smith, Capt. Harrison, 468
Smith, Capt. Heman, 415
Smith, Capt. Henry, 451, 454
Smith, Capt. Isaac, 442, 555
Smith, Isaac C., 554
Smith, Capt. J., 387, 459, 508
Smith, Capt. J. A., 404
Smith, Capt. J. G., 547
Smith, Capt. J. H., 539
Smith, Capt. J. L., 492, 518
Smith, Capt. J. P., 509
Smith, Capt. J. W., 491
Smith, Capt. Jacob, 400, 528
Smith, James, 555
Smith, Capt. James, 452, 526
Smith, Capt. Jarvis, 464
Smith, Capt. Jeremiah G., 379, 380, 381, 385, 398, 501, 503, 512, 526
Smith, Capt. John, 474, 530
Smith, Capt. John A., **409, 547**
Smith, John H., 176, 415
Smith, Capt. John P., 159, 204, 246, 378, 394
Smith, Capt. John W., 459, 460
Smith, Jonas, 555, 557, 559, 560, 561
Smith, Capt. Joseph, 427, 428, 434
Smith, Capt. Joshua H., 498
Smith, Junius, 217, 229, 230, 237, 240, 242, 391
Smith, Capt. Kimball R., 249, 463, 506
Smith, Capt. M., 509
Smith, Capt. Martin, 385, 387, 488
Smith, Morris, 532
Smith, Capt. N. S., 486
Smith, Capt. Nehemiah G., 481

The text of this book is set in Linotype Baskerville. It is eleven point with three points of leading. The chapter titles are twenty-four point Monotype Baskerville 353.

The book is printed on fifty-pound White Warren's Olde Style paper, with the illustrations on seventy-pound White Woodbine Folding Enamel. The cloth is White Lynnene, natural finish.

Typographic design is by John Robson. The book was composed, printed, and bound by George Banta Company, Incorporated, Menasha, Wisconsin.

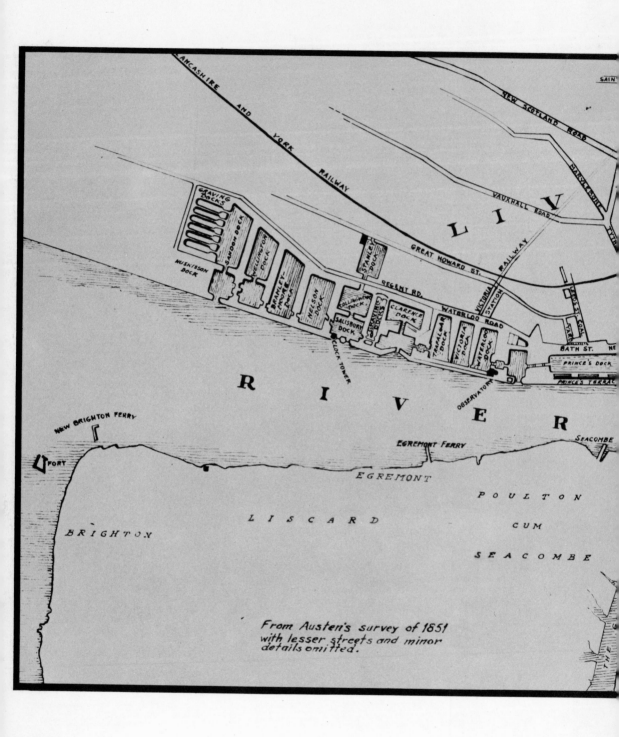

LIVERPOOL in 1851